W9-CHG-483

LAW, DIVERSITY, AND BUSINESS: MANAGERIAL IMPLICATIONS

LINKING BUSINESS LAW to . . .

(BackyardProduction/iStockphoto.com)

Business Law Today:
The Essentials
DIVERSE, ETHICAL, ONLINE, AND GLOBAL ENVIRONMENT

Tenth Edition

Roger LeRoy Miller
Institute for University Studies
Arlington, Texas

SOUTH-WESTERN
CENGAGE Learning

Australia • Brazil • Japan • Korea • Mexico • Singapore • Spain • United Kingdom • United States

SOUTH-WESTERN
CENGAGE Learning

Business Law Today:
The Essentials

Diverse, Ethical, Online, and Global Environment

TENTH EDITION

Roger LeRoy Miller

Editorial Director:
Erin Joyner

Editor-in-Chief:
Rob Dewey

Senior Acquisitions Editor:
Vicky True-Baker

Senior Developmental Editor:
Jan Lamar

Director, Market Development Manager:
Lisa Lysne

Senior Brand Manager:
Kristen Hurd

Senior Marketing Communications Manager:
Sarah Greber

Production Manager:
Bill Stryker

Senior Media Editor:
Kristen Meere

Manufacturing Planner:
Kevin Kluck

Editorial Assistant:
Tristann Jones

Compositor:
Parkwood Composition Service

Senior Art Director:
Michelle Kunkler

Cover and Internal Designer:
Stratton Design

Cover Image:
© Comstock Images/Getty Images, Inc.

For product information and technology assistance, contact us at
Cengage Learning Academic Resource Center
1-800-423-0563

For permission to use material from this text or product,
submit all requests online at
www.cengage.com/permissions.

Further permissions questions can be emailed to
permissionrequest@cengage.com.

Library of Congress Control Number: 2012952003

Instructor's Edition:
ISBN 13: 978-1-285-42421-7
ISBN 10: 1-285-42421-2

Student Edition:
ISBN 13: 978-1-133-19135-3
ISBN 10: 1-133-19135-5

South-Western Cengage Learning
5191 Natorp Blvd.
Mason, OH 45040
USA

Cengage Learning products are represented in Canada by Nelson Education, Ltd.

For your course and learning solutions, visit **www.cengage.com**.

Purchase any of our products at your local college store or at our preferred online store **www.cengagebrain.com**.

Printed in the United States
1 2 3 4 5 6 7 16 15 14 13 12

Contents in Brief

APPENDICES

Contents

Preface to the Instructor

Today's business and legal environment is changing at a pace never before experienced. In many instances, technology is both driving and facilitating this change. The expanded use of the Internet for both business and personal transactions has led to new ways of doing business in the twenty-first century. Other factors that have affected the legal environment include the recent economic recession and our nation's ongoing struggle to regain financial stability, combat joblessness, and reduce the national debt.

In the midst of this evolving environment, however, one thing remains certain: For those entering the business world, an awareness of business law and the legal environment is critical. *Business Law Today: The Essentials*, Tenth Edition, provides the information your students need in an interesting and contemporary way. The Tenth Edition of *Business Law Today: The Essentials* continues its established tradition of being the most up-to-date text on the market.

I have spent a great deal of effort incorporating the latest legal developments and giving this book a visual appeal that will encourage students to learn the law. The law presented in this text includes new statutes, regulations, and cases, as well as recent developments in cyberlaw.

What's New in the Tenth Edition

Instructors have come to rely on the coverage, accuracy, and applicability of *Business Law Today*. To make sure that the text engages your students' interest, solidifies their understanding of the legal concepts presented, and provides the best teaching tools available, the following items are now offered either in the text or in conjunction with the text.

New *Spotlight Cases* and *Spotlight Case Problems*

For the Tenth Edition of *Business Law Today: The Essentials*, certain cases and case problems have been carefully chosen to spotlight as good teaching cases. **Spotlight Cases** and **Spotlight Case Problems** are labeled either by the name of one of the parties or by the subject involved. Some examples include *Spotlight on Amazon, Spotlight on Apple, Spotlight on the Seattle Mariners, Spotlight on Commercial Speech,* and *Spotlight on Internet Porn.*

Instructors will find these *Spotlight Cases* useful to illustrate the legal concepts under discussion, and students will enjoy studying these cases because they involve interesting and memorable facts.

Suggested answers to all case-ending questions and case problems are included in both the *Instructor's Manual* and the *Answers Manual* for this text.

New Focus on Diversity

This Tenth Edition of *Business Law Today* recognizes the tremendous impact of diversity on the business world and legal environment today. Therefore, the text includes a special new feature entitled **Law, Diversity, and Business: Managerial Implications** that emphasizes diversity issues. These features address important topics such as marriage equality laws, appearance-discrimination legislation, and discriminatory mortgage lending. The new *Law, Diversity, and Business: Managerial Implications* features include the following:

- *Derogatory Trademarks* (Chapter 5)
- *Native Americans and Criminal Justice* (Chapter 6)

- *How Should Airlines Deal with "Customers of Size"?* (Chapter 12)
- *The Worldwide Lack of Women on Boards of Directors* (Chapter 21)

New *Appendix to Chapter 9* Focuses on Reading and Analyzing Contracts

Because reading and analyzing contracts is such a crucial skill for businesspersons, **a special new Appendix to Chapter 9** has been added. This appendix follows the last contracts chapter and explains how to read and analyze a contract. Then, it presents an example of an employee noncompetition and nondisclosure agreement. The sample contract is annotated so that students can quickly see what each contract provision means.

New *Debate This* Feature

To encourage student participation and motivate students to think critically about the rationale underlying the law on a particular topic, a new feature has been created for the Tenth Edition. Entitled *Debate This,* it consists of a brief statement or question concerning the chapter material that can be used to spur lively classroom or small group discussions. It can also be used as a written assignment. This feature follows the *Reviewing* feature (discussed shortly) at the end of each chapter. **Suggested pro and con responses to the *Debate This* features can be found in both the *Instructor's Manual* and the *Answers Manual* for this text.**

New Cases and Case Problems

The Tenth Edition of *Business Law Today: The Essentials* is filled with new cases and case problems. Nearly every chapter features at least one new case and new case problem from 2011 and 2012. Many chapters include two recent case summaries and problems. That means more than 75 percent of the cases are new to this edition.

The new cases have been carefully selected based on these criteria: (1) they illustrate important points of law, (2) they are of high interest to students and instructors, and (3) they are simple enough factually for business law students to understand. I have made it a point to find recent cases that enhance learning. I have also eliminated cases that are too difficult procedurally or factually.

New *Group Projects*

For instructors who want to have their classes perform group projects, each chapter of the Tenth Edition includes a **new *Business Law Critical Thinking Group Assignment.*** Each project begins by describing a business scenario and then requires each group of students to answer a specific question pertaining to the scenario based on the information that they learned in the chapter. These projects may be used in class to spur discussion or as homework assignments. **Suggested answers to the group assignments are included in both the *Instructor's Manual* and the *Answers Manual* for this text.**

A New Chapter on *Mortgages and Foreclosures after the Recession*

The Tenth Edition includes an entirely new chapter (Chapter 16) entitled ***Mortgages and Foreclosures after the Recession.*** This chapter examines some of the mortgage-lending practices that contributed to the Great Recession that began in 2008 and discusses the legal reforms enacted in response to it.

New Coverage of Current Significant Topics

To pique student interest from the outset, many chapters in the Tenth Edition open with the latest news related to important legal topics. For example:

- Chapter 1 covers the constitutional challenge to the Obama administration's Patient Protection and Affordable Care Act and the United States Supreme Court's 2012 decision in that matter.
- Chapter 5 discusses the patent infringement lawsuit that Apple, Inc., brought against Samsung for imitating the iPhone and iPad too closely.
- Chapter 18 mentions the United States Supreme Court's 2012 decision on the extent to which federal law preempts the states from enacting immigration legislation.

Coverage of the latest developments in the topics under discussion is a priority throughout the text.

Practical and Effective Learning Tools

Today's business leaders must often think "outside the box" when making business decisions. For this reason, I have included numerous critical-thinking elements in the Tenth Edition that are designed to challenge students' understanding of the materials beyond simple retention. I have also retained, improved, and streamlined the many practical features of this text to help students learn how the law applies to business.

Highlighted and Numbered *Case Examples*

One of the most appreciated features of *Business Law Today: The Essentials* has always been the highlighted numbered examples that appear throughout the book to illustrate the legal principles under discussion. Further, many instructors use cases to illustrate how the law applies to business. For this reason, the in-text numbered examples have been expanded to include **Case Examples.**

These *Case Examples* are integrated appropriately throughout the text and present the facts, issues, and rulings from actual court cases. These are especially useful to simplify difficult areas of law. Students can read through the case examples and quickly see how courts apply the legal principles under discussion in the real world.

Linking Business Law to . . . Feature

The Tenth Edition of *Business Law Today: The Essentials* also includes a **special feature entitled *Linking Business Law to . . .* [one of the six functional fields of business].** As will be discussed in Chapter 1, the six functional fields of business are *corporate management, production and transportation, marketing, research and development, accounting and finance,* and *human resources management.*

This feature appears in selected chapters to underscore how the law relates to other fields of business. Some of the new *Linking Business Law to . . .* features include:

- *Linking Business Law to Accounting and Finance*—Managing a Company's Reputation (Chapter 2)
- *Linking Business Law to Marketing*—Trademarks and Service Marks (Chapter 5)
- *Linking Business Law to Corporate Management*—What Can You Do to Prepare for a Chapter 11 Reorganization? (Chapter 15)
- *Linking Business Law to Accounting and Finance*—Sources of Funds (Chapter 20)

Business Application

Many chapters end with a ***Business Application* feature** that focuses on practical considerations related to the chapter's contents. This feature concludes with a **checklist** of tips for the businessperson. For example, these topics include the following:

• *Protecting Your Company against Hacking of Your Bank Accounts* (Chapter 6)
• *What Can You Do When a Contract Is Breached?* (Chapter 11)
• *How to Develop a Policy on Employee Use of the Internet and Social Media* (Chapter 18)
• *How to Choose and Use a Lawyer* (Chapter 25)

Preventing Legal Disputes

The Tenth Edition of *Business Law Today: The Essentials* continues the emphasis on providing practical information in every chapter through a special feature entitled ***Preventing Legal Disputes***. These brief, integrated sections offer sensible guidance on steps that businesspersons can take in their daily transactions to avoid legal disputes and litigation in a particular area.

Adapting the Law to the Online Environment

The Tenth Edition contains many new ***Adapting the Law to the Online Environment*** features, which examine cutting-edge cyberlaw issues coming before today's courts. Here are some examples of these features:

• *Vulgar Facebook Photos Receive First Amendment Protection* (Chapter 1)
• *The Validity of E-Signatures for Online Colleges and Universities* (Chapter 7)
• *The Supreme Court Takes a Stand on Warning Labels for Video Games* (Chapter 12)
• *Live Chatting with Your State's Bankruptcy Court* (Chapter 15)
• *Social Media in the Workplace Come of Age* (Chapter 18)
• *The New Era of Crowdfunding* (Chapter 20)
• *The Justice Department Goes after E-Book Pricing* (Chapter 22)

Each feature concludes with a *Critical Thinking* question that asks the student to analyze some facet of the issues discussed in the feature. **Suggested answers to these questions are included in both the** *Instructor's Manual* **and the** *Answers Manual* **for this text.**

Summarized Case Presentation

Each case is presented in a certain format, which begins with the case title and citation (including parallel citations). Whenever possible, a URL that can be used to access the case online appears just below the case citation (a footnote to the URL explains how to find the specific case at that Web site). I then briefly outline the facts of the dispute, the legal issue presented, and the court's decision.

To enhance student understanding, I paraphrase the reason for the court's decision and provide bracketed explanations for any unfamiliar terms. Each case concludes with a question, which may include a *Critical Thinking, What If the Facts Were Different?* or *Why Is This Case Important?* question. *Classic Cases* include a special section entitled *Impact of This Case on Today's Law* to clarify the relevance of the case to modern law. **Suggested answers to all case-ending questions are included in both the** *Instructor's Manual* **and the** *Answers Manual* **for this text.**

Critical Thinking and Legal Reasoning Elements

The chapter-ending materials include a separate section of questions that focus on critical thinking and writing. This section includes the *Business Law Critical Thinking Group Assignment* (discussed previously) and may also include one or more of the following:

• *Critical Legal Thinking* questions require students to think critically about some aspect of the law discussed in the chapter.
• *Business Law Writing* questions require students to compose a written response to a business-oriented critical-thinking question.

Reviewing . . . Features

Each chapter in this text ends with a **Reviewing . . . feature** that helps solidify students' understanding of the chapter materials. Each of these features presents a hypothetical scenario and then asks a series of questions that require students to identify the issues and apply the legal concepts discussed in the chapter. The questions are intended to help students review the chapter materials in a simple and interesting way.

An instructor can use this feature as the basis for a lively in-class discussion or can encourage students to use it for self-study and assessment prior to completing homework assignments.

ExamPrep Sections

Following the chapter summary in every chapter is an **ExamPrep** section that includes two **Issue Spotters related to the chapter's topics** that facilitate student learning and review of the chapter materials. For this edition, the answers to the *Issue Spotters* are provided in *Appendix E* at the end of this text.

Beyond Our Borders

The **Beyond Our Borders** feature gives students an awareness of the global legal environment by indicating how international laws or the laws of other nations deal with specific legal concepts or topics being discussed in the chapter. This feature always concludes with a *Critical Thinking* question. **Suggested answers to these questions are included in both the *Instructor's Manual* and the *Answers Manual* for this text.**

Landmark in the Law

The **Landmark in the Law** feature discusses a landmark case, statute, or other legal development that has had a significant effect on business law. Each of these features has a section titled **Application to Today's World,** which indicates how the law discussed in the feature affects the legal landscape of today's world.

Sample Answers

Each chapter includes a **Question with Sample Answer** that is answered in *Appendix G* and a **Case Problem with Sample Answer** that is based on an actual case and answered in *Appendix H.* Students can compare their own answers to the answers provided to determine whether they have applied the law correctly and to learn what needs to be included when answering the end-of-chapter *Business Scenarios and Case Problems*.

Ethical Issues

In addition to a full chapter on ethics, chapter-ending ethical questions, and the **Ethical Considerations** in many of the *Critical Thinking* questions in the cases, this text includes a feature called **Ethical Issues.** This feature, which is closely integrated with the text, opens with a question addressing an ethical dimension of the topic being discussed. The feature is designed to make sure that students understand that ethics is an integral part of a business law course.

Business Law Today:
The Essentials on the Web

The Web site for the Tenth Edition of *Business Law Today: The Essentials* can be found by going to **www.cengagebrain.com** and entering ISBN 9781133191353. The Web site offers a broad array of teaching/learning resources, including the following:

- *Practice quizzes* for every chapter in this text.
- *Appendix A: How to Brief Cases and Analyze Case Problems*
- *Legal reference materials* including a "Statutes" page that offers links to the full text of selected statutes referenced in the text, a Spanish glossary, and other important legal resources.
- *CourseMate* access can also be purchased by the students, where they will find additional study tools, such as an e-Book, additional quizzes, flashcards, key terms, and PowerPoint slides.

Other Pedagogical Devices within Each Chapter

- *Learning Objectives* (a series of brief questions at the beginning of each chapter provide a framework for the student as he or she reads through the chapter). *For this edition, to facilitate learning, I repeat the Learning Objective question in the margin adjacent to where the question is answered in the text.*
- *Chapter Outline* (an outline of the chapter's first-level headings).
- *Margin Definitions.*
- *Margin Quotations.*
- *Exhibits.*
- *Photographs (often with critical-thinking questions) and cartoons.*

Chapter-Ending Pedagogy

- *Reviewing . . .* **feature** (in every chapter).
- *Debate This* (in every chapter).
- *Key Terms* (with appropriate page references).
- *Chapter Summary* (in table format with page references).
- *ExamPrep* (including two *Issue Spotters* for each chapter that are answered in *Appendix E*).
- *For Review* (the questions set forth in the chapter-opening *Learning Objectives* section are presented again to aid students in reviewing the chapter. For this edition, answers to the even-numbered questions for each chapter are provided in *Appendix F.*).
- *Business Scenarios and Case Problems* (every chapter includes a *Question with Sample Answer* (answered in *Appendix G*), a *Case Problem with Sample Answer* (answered in *Appendix H*), *A Question of Ethics,* and a *Business Law Critical Thinking Group Assignment.* Selected chapters also include a *Spotlight Case Problem.*)

Supplemental Teaching Materials

This edition of *Business Law Today: The Essentials* is accompanied by an expansive number of teaching and learning supplements, which are available on the *Instructor's Resource CD-ROM,* or IRCD, as well as on the password-protected portion of the companion Web site. Individually and in conjunction with a number of colleagues, I have developed supplementary teaching materials that I believe are the best available today. The many components of the supplements package are listed below.

Instructor's Resource CD-ROM (IRCD)

The IRCD includes the following supplements:

- *Instructor's Manual* (includes at least one **additional case on point** per chapter, answers to all *Critical Thinking* questions, *Reviewing* features, *Business Law Critical Thinking Group Assignments,* and *Business Scenarios and Case Problems*).
- *Answers Manual* (includes answers to all the *Business Scenarios and Case Problems,* and *Critical Thinking* questions, and **Alternate Problem Sets with Answers**).
- A comprehensive **Test Bank.**
- **Case-Problem Cases.**
- **Case Printouts.**
- **ExamView.**
- **PowerPoint slides.**
- *Instructor's Manual* for the *Drama of the Law* video series.
- *Handbook of Landmark Cases and Statutes in Business Law and the Legal Environment.*
- *Handbook on Critical Thinking in Business Law and the Legal Environment.*
- *A Guide to Personal Law.*

Software, Video, and Multimedia Supplements

- *Business Law Digital Video Library*—Provides access to ninety videos that spark class discussion and clarify core legal concepts. Access is available as an optional package with each new text at no additional cost. You can access the *Business Law Digital Video Library,* along with corresponding *Video Questions,* at **login.cengage.com.**
- **Westlaw®**—Ten free hours on Westlaw are available to qualified adopters.
- *CengageNOW* for *Business Law Today* (at an additional cost)—Arguably the most comprehensive online learning and assessment tool for business law and the legal environment on the market today. For more information, contact your South-Western/Cengage Learning Sales Representative. For a demo of this complete online learning system, go to **www.cengage.com/now.**
- *CourseMate*—Brings business law concepts to life with interactive learning, study, and exam preparation tools that support this printed textbook. Built-in engagement tracking tools allow you to assess your students' study activities. Additionally, *CourseMate* includes an interactive e-Book, which contains the entire contents of this printed textbook enhanced by the many advantages of a digital environment.

For Users of the Ninth Edition

I thought that those of you who have been using *Business Law Today: The Essentials* would like to know some of the major changes that have been made for the Tenth Edition.

New Features and Special Pedagogy

I have added the following entirely new elements for the Tenth Edition:

- *Law, Diversity, and Business: Managerial Implications* feature in selected chapters.
- *Spotlight Cases* and *Spotlight Case Problems* in selected chapters.
- An *Appendix to Chapter 10* on reading and analyzing contracts.
- A *Debate This* feature in every chapter.
- A *Business Law Critical Thinking Group Assignment* in every chapter.
- *Appendix E* (Answers to the *Issue Spotters*), *Appendix F* (Answers to Even-Numbered *For Review* Questions), and *Appendix H* (Sample Answers for *Case Problems with Sample Answer*).

Significantly Revised Chapters

Every chapter of the Tenth Edition has been revised as necessary to incorporate new developments in the law, and to simplify or streamline the presentations. Other major changes and additions made for this edition include the following:

- **Chapter 1 (The Constitutional Foundations)**—This chapter has been thoroughly updated and revised. It opens with a discussion of the constitutional issue raised by the Obama administration's Patient Protection and Affordable Care Act and considers how the United States Supreme Court's decision in the matter will affect business. The privacy concerns raised by social networking Web sites are also discussed. A feature addresses First Amendment rights and postings on Facebook, and another feature examines the legal issues presented by same-sex marriage and marriage equality laws.

- **Chapter 5 (Intellectual Property and Internet Law)**—The materials on intellectual property rights have been thoroughly revised and updated. The chapter incorporates the major changes to patent law made by the America Invents Act, which make the first person to file for a patent application the holder. A new subsection addresses patent infringement lawsuits and high-tech companies, and the suit brought by Apple, Inc., against Samsung over iPhones, iPads, and Android software is discussed. Coverage of domain names and cybersquatting has been updated. Numerous updates and new examples have been added to illustrate how intellectual property laws apply in the digital world. A *Spotlight on Internet Porn* case covers trademark dilution by a porn site using a toymaker's domain name. There is also a discussion of the 2012 United States Supreme Court decision addressing Congress's authority to restore copyright protection to foreign works that were already in the public domain. A *Beyond Our Borders* feature outlines the provisions of a new international treaty to combat global counterfeiting and piracy.

- **Chapter 6 (Criminal Law and Cyber Crime)**—This chapter has been substantially revised to deal with the growing problem of cyber crime, including many types of Internet fraud, identity theft, phishing, and hacking. It also covers some of the difficulties involved in prosecuting cyber crime. The chapter incorporates recent United States Supreme Court decisions on whether police can attach a GPS tracking device to a suspect's vehicle and whether police officers can be held personally liable for performing an illegal search. New features examine whether a person can be prosecuted for posting fake photos on Facebook and provide guidance on how businesspersons can prevent their bank accounts from being hacked.

- **Chapters 7 through 9 (the contracts chapters)**—The discussion of online contracting and electronic signatures has been merged with the coverage of traditional contracts. More examples, case examples, updates throughout, and streamlined coverage have been added. *Spotlight Cases* have been added to each chapter, including *Spotlight on Amazon*, *Spotlight on the Improv,* and *Spotlight on Liquidated Damages.*

- **Chapter 12 (Consumer Law)**—The chapter has been thoroughly updated and incorporates recent changes to menu labeling requirements, the recent health-care reforms, and new federal credit-card rules. New features have been added on the United States Supreme Court's ruling on warning labels for violent video games, how airlines deal with "customers of size," and the proper way to use credit reporting services.

- **Chapter 16 (Mortgages and Foreclosures after the Recession)**—For this edition, we have included an entirely new chapter on Mortgages and Foreclosures after the Recession. Chapter 16 provides a timely look at the mortgage crisis, predatory lending practices, and the laws enacted to address some of the problems that became evident during the recession.

- **Chapter 18 (Employment Law)**—This chapter has been thoroughly revised and updated to include discussions of legal issues facing employers today. A feature covers the use of social media in the workplace, and another feature explains how to develop policies on social media and Internet use. The chapter includes a section on immigration law, a topic of increasing importance to employers, and discusses the United States Supreme Court's decision on whether federal law preempts state immigration laws. The chapter also includes an updated discussion of the Family and Medical Leave Act, employee privacy rights and electronic monitoring of employees—including social media communications. The materials covering employment discrimination have been significantly updated and now emphasize diversity. A feature was added on combating appearance-based discrimination.

- **Chapter 20 (Corporations)**—This chapter has been reworked to simplify and streamline the presentation of the materials. It includes a new feature on crowdfunding and a *new Landmark in the Law* feature on the *Citizens United* case.

- **Chapter 21 (Investor Protection, Insider Trading, and Corporate Governance)**—This chapter has been substantially reworked to simplify complex materials into basic concepts. The materials on insider trading, Ponzi schemes, and fraud have been updated, new examples have been added, and a new *Spotlight Case* focuses on securities fraud.

- **Chapter 22 (Antitrust Law and Promoting Competition)**—The materials in this chapter have been reworked to focus on overriding principles of antitrust law and provide concrete information. The chapter includes updated figures on interlocking directorates and an updated discussion of global antitrust law. Features cover the Justice Department's concern about pricing of e-books for Kindles and iPads, and whether cable and other TV programmers violate the Sherman Act by bundling services. A *Spotlight Case on the Weyerhaeuser Company* was added.

- **Chapters 23 through 24 (the property chapters)**—These two chapters have been updated to deal with issues surrounding virtual and digital property and how to manage risk in cyberspace. A *Spotlight on Haunted Houses* case appears in Chapter 24.

Acknowledgments

Numerous careful and conscientious users of *Business Law Today: The Essentials* were kind enough to help me revise the book. In addition, the staff at South-Western/Cengage Learning went out of their way to make sure that this edition came out early and in accurate form. In particular, I wish to thank Rob Dewey and Vicky True-Baker for their countless new ideas, many of which have been incorporated into the Tenth Edition. I also extend special thanks to Jan Lamar, my longtime developmental editor, for her many useful suggestions and for her efforts in coordinating reviews and ensuring the timely and accurate publication of all supplemental materials. I am particularly indebted to Lisa Lysne for her support and excellent marketing advice.

My production manager and designer, Bill Stryker, made sure that I came out with an error-free, visually attractive edition. I will always be in his debt. I thank my photo researcher, Anne Sheroff, for providing an amazingly varied number of choices of photographs for this edition. I am also indebted to the staff at Parkwood Composition, the compositor. Their ability to generate the pages for this text quickly and accurately made it possible for me to meet my ambitious printing schedule.

I must especially thank Katherine Marie Silsbee for her management of the project, as well as for the application of her superb research and editorial skills. I also wish to thank William Eric Hollowell, coauthor of the *Instructor's Manual, Study Guide,* and *Test Bank,* for his excellent research efforts. The copyediting services of Beverly Peavler were invaluable, and the proofreading by Jeanne Yost will not go unnoticed. I thank, too, Maggie Jarpey, for her indexing expertise. I also thank Vickie Reierson and Roxanna Lee for their proofreading and other assistance, which helped to ensure an error-free text. Finally, my appreciation goes to Suzanne Jasin for her many special efforts on the projects.

Acknowledgments for Previous Editions

John J. Balek
Morton College, Illinois

John Jay Ballantine
University of Colorado, Boulder

Lorraine K. Bannai
Western Washington University

Marlene E. Barken
Ithaca College, New York

Daryl Barton
Eastern Michigan University

Denise A. Bartles
Missouri Western State University

Merlin Bauer
Mid State Technical College, Wisconsin

Donna E. Becker
Frederick Community College, Maryland

Richard J. Bennet
Three Rivers Community College, Connecticut

Anne Berre
Schreiner University, Texas

Brad Botz
Garden City Community College, Kansas

Teresa Brady
Holy Family College, Philadelphia

Lee B. Burgunder
California Polytechnic University—San Luis Obispo

Bradley D. Childs
Belmont University, Tennessee

Dale Clark
Corning Community College, New York

Peter Clapp
St. Mary's College, Moraga, California

Tammy W. Cowart
University of Texas, Tyler

Stanley J. Dabrowski
Hudson County Community College, New Jersey

Sandra J. Defebaugh
Eastern Michigan University

Patricia L. DeFrain
Glendale College, California

Julia G. Derrick
Brevard Community College, Florida

Joe D. Dillsaver
Northeastern State University, Oklahoma

Claude W. Dotson
Northwest College, Wyoming

Larry R. Edwards
Tarrant County Junior College, South Campus, Texas

Jacolin Eichelberger
Hillsborough Community College, Florida

George E. Eigsti
Kansas City, Kansas, Community College

Florence E. Elliott-Howard
Stephen F. Austin State University, Texas

Tony Enerva
Lakeland Community College, Ohio

Benjamin C. Fassberg
Prince George's Community College, Maryland

Jerry Furniss
University of Montana

Elizabeth J. Guerriero
Northeast Louisiana University

Phil Harmeson
University of South Dakota

Nancy L. Hart
Midland College, Texas

Janine S. Hiller
*Virginia Polytechnic Institute &
State University*

Karen A. Holmes
Hudson Valley Community College, New York

Fred Ittner
College of Alameda, California

Susan S. Jarvis
University of Texas, Pan American

Jack E. Karns
East Carolina University, North Carolina

Sarah Weiner Keidan
Oakland Community College, Michigan

Richard N. Kleeberg
Solano Community College, California

Bradley T. Lutz
Hillsborough Community College, Florida

Darlene Mallick
*Anne Arundel Community College,
Maryland*

John D. Mallonee
Manatee Community College, Florida

Joseph D. Marcus
*Prince George's Community College,
Maryland*

Woodrow J. Maxwell
Hudson Valley Community College, New York

Beverly McCormick
Morehead State University, Kentucky

William J. McDevitt
Saint Joseph's University, Pennsylvania

John W. McGee
Aims Community College, Colorado

James K. Miersma
*Milwaukee Area Technical Institute,
Wisconsin*

Susan J. Mitchell
Des Moines Area Community College, Iowa

Jim Lee Morgan
West Los Angeles College, California

Jack K. Morton
University of Montana

Solange North
Fox Valley Technical Institute, Wisconsin

Jamie L. O'Brien
South Dakota State University

Ruth R. O'Keefe
Jacksonville University, Florida

Robert H. Orr
*Florida Community College
at Jacksonville*

George Otto
Truman College, Illinois

Thomas L. Palmer
Northern Arizona University

David W. Pan
University of Tulsa, Oklahoma

Victor C. Parker, Jr.
North Georgia College and State University

Donald L. Petote
Genessee Community College, New York

Francis D. Polk
Ocean County College, New Jersey

Gregory Rabb
Jamestown Community College, New York

Brad Reid
Abilene Christian University, Texas

Anne Montgomery Ricketts
University of Findlay, Ohio

Donald A. Roark
University of West Florida

Hugh Rode
Utah Valley State College

Dr. William J. Russell
Northwest Nazarene University, Idaho

William M. Rutledge
Macomb Community College, Michigan

Martha Wright Sartoris
*North Hennepin Community College,
Minnesota*

Anne W. Schacherl
Madison Area Technical College, Wisconsin

Edward F. Shafer
Rochester Community College, Minnesota

Lance Shoemaker
West Valley College, California

Lou Ann Simpson
Drake University, Iowa

xxiv

PREFACE to the Instructor

Denise Smith
Missouri Western State College

Hugh M. Spall
Central Washington University

Catherine A. Stevens
College of Southern Maryland

Maurice Tonissi
*Quinsigamond Community College,
Massachusetts*

James D. Van Tassel
Mission College, California

Russell A. Waldon
College of the Canyons, California

Frederick J. Walsh
Franklin Pierce College, New Hampshire

James E. Walsh, Jr.
*Tidewater Community College,
Virginia*

Randy Waterman
Richland College, Texas

Jerry Wegman
University of Idaho

Edward L. Welsh, Jr.
Phoenix College, Arizona

Clark W. Wheeler
Santa Fe Community College, Florida

Lori Whisenant
University of Houston, Texas

Kay O. Wilburn
The University of Alabama at Birmingham

John G. Williams
Northwestern State University, Louisiana

James L. Wittenbach
University of Notre Dame, Indiana

Joseph Zavaglia, Jr.
Brookdale Community College, New Jersey

I also wish to extend special thanks to the following individuals for their valuable input for the new Chapter 16 and for helping revise Chapter 24:

Robert C. Bird
University of Connecticut

Dean Bredeson
University of Texas at Austin

Corey Ciocchetti
University of Denver

Thomas D. Cavenagh
North Central College, Illinois

Joan Gabel
Florida State University

Eric D. Yordy
Northern Arizona University

Acknowledgments for the Tenth Edition

John Jay Ballantine
University of Colorado, Boulder

Laura Barnard
Lakeland Community College, Ohio

Bonnie S. Bolinger
*Ivy Tech Community College,
Wabash Valley Region, Indiana*

Sandra Defebaugh
Eastern Michigan University

Joseph L. Flack
Washtenaw Community College, Michigan

Mo Hassan
Cabrillo College, California

Andy E. Hendrick
Coastal Carolina University, South Carolina

Diane MacDonald
Pacific Lutheran University, Washington

Susan Mitchell
Des Moines Area Community College, Iowa

Annie Laurie I. Myers
*Northampton Community College,
Pennsylvania*

Jamie L. O'Brien
South Dakota State University

Gerald M. Rogers
Front Range Community College, Colorado

I know that I am not perfect. If you or your students find something you don't like or want me to change, use the "Contact Us" button on this text's Web site. In the alternative, pass along your thoughts to your South-Western/Cengage Learning sales representative. Your comments will help us make *Business Law Today: The Essentials* an even better book in the future.

Roger LeRoy Miller

Dedication

To Leslie,

I know that courage was
your middle name, but
I didn't know it was
your first name, too!

R.L.M.

CHAPTER 1

The Constitutional Foundations

(JustASC/Shutterstock.com)

CHAPTER OUTLINE

- Sources of American Law
- The Common Law Tradition
- Classifications of Law
- The Constitutional Powers of Government
- Business and the Bill of Rights
- Privacy Rights

LEARNING OBJECTIVES

The five learning objectives below are designed to help improve your understanding of the chapter. After reading this chapter, you should be able to answer the following questions:

1 What are four primary sources of law in the United States?

2 What is a precedent? When might a court depart from precedent?

3 What is the difference between remedies at law and remedies in equity?

4 What constitutional clause gives the federal government the power to regulate commercial activities among the various states?

5 What is the Bill of Rights? What freedoms do the First Amendment guarantee?

"Laws should be like clothes.
They should be made to fit the people they are meant to serve."
—Clarence Darrow, 1857–1938 (American lawyer)

In the chapter-opening quotation, Clarence Darrow asserts that law should be created to serve the public. As you are part of that public, the law is important to you. Those entering the world of business will find themselves subject to numerous laws and government regulations. A basic knowledge of these laws and regulations is beneficial—if not essential—to anyone contemplating a successful career in today's business environment.

Although the law has various definitions, they all are based on the general observation that **law** consists of *enforceable rules governing relationships among individuals and between individuals and their society.* In some societies, these enforceable rules consist of unwritten principles of behavior, while in other societies they are set forth in ancient or contemporary law codes. In the United States, our rules consist of written laws and court decisions created by modern legislative and judicial bodies. Regardless of how such rules are created, they all have one feature in common: *they establish rights, duties, and privileges that are consistent with the values and beliefs of a society or its ruling group.*

Law A body of enforceable rules governing relationships among individuals and between individuals and their society.

1

In this introductory chapter, we describe the basic sources of American law, the common law tradition, and some general classifications of law. We then turn to constitutional law and examine how certain fundamental freedoms guaranteed by the Constitution affect businesspersons and the workplace. In a feature on page 18, we look at whether the First Amendment applies to suggestive photos posted online by high school students at social networking sites.

We also consider the constitutional protection of privacy. In recent years, many users of online social networks have become concerned at the amount of their personal information that exists in cyberspace and the possibility that it might be misused. Such concerns led the Federal Trade Commission in 2012 to charge Facebook, Twitter, and Google with misleading users about the way their personal data were being used. All three companies agreed to revise their privacy policies as a result.

Sources of American Law

There are numerous sources of American law. **Primary sources of law,** or sources that establish the law, include the following:

- The U.S. Constitution and the constitutions of the various states.
- Statutes, or laws, passed by Congress and by state legislatures.
- Regulations created by administrative agencies, such as the federal Food and Drug Administration.
- Case law (court decisions).

We describe each of these important primary sources of law in the following pages. (See the appendix at the end of this chapter for a discussion of how to find statutes, regulations, and case law.)

Secondary sources of law are books and articles that summarize and clarify the primary sources of law. Legal encyclopedias, compilations (such as *Restatements of the Law,* which summarize court decisions on a particular topic), official comments to statutes, treatises, articles in law reviews published by law schools, and articles in other legal journals are examples of secondary sources of law. Courts often refer to secondary sources of law for guidance in interpreting and applying the primary sources of law discussed here.

Constitutional Law

The federal government and the states have separate written constitutions that set forth the general organization, powers, and limits of their respective governments. **Constitutional law** is the law as expressed in these constitutions.

The U.S. Constitution is the supreme law of the land. As such, it is the basis of all law in the United States. A law in violation of the U.S. Constitution, if challenged, will be declared unconstitutional and will not be enforced, no matter what its source. Because of its paramount importance in the American legal system, we present the complete text of the U.S. Constitution in Appendix B at the end of this text.

The Tenth Amendment to the U.S. Constitution reserves to the states all powers not granted to the federal government. Each state in the union has its own constitution. Unless it conflicts with the U.S. Constitution or a federal law, a state constitution is supreme within that state's borders.

Statutory Law

Laws enacted by legislative bodies at any level of government, such as the statutes passed by Congress or by state legislatures, make up the body of law generally referred to as **statutory law.** When a legislature passes a statute, that statute ultimately is included in

LEARNING OBJECTIVE 1
What are four primary sources of law in the United States?

Primary Source of Law A statement that establishes the law on a particular issue, such as a constitution, a statute, an administrative rule, or a court decision.

Secondary Source of Law A publication that summarizes or interprets the law, such as a legal encyclopedia, a legal treatise, or an article in a law review.

Constitutional Law The body of law derived from the U.S. Constitution and the constitutions of the various states.

Statutory Law The body of law enacted by legislative bodies (as opposed to constitutional law, administrative law, or case law).

Citation A reference to a publication in which a legal authority—such as a statute or a court decision—or other source can be found.

Ordinance A regulation enacted by a city or county legislative body that becomes part of that state's statutory law.

Uniform Law A model law developed by the National Conference of Commissioners on Uniform State Laws for the states to consider enacting into statute.

the federal code of laws or the relevant state code of laws. Whenever a particular statute is mentioned in this text, we usually provide a footnote showing its **citation** (the reference to a publication in which a legal authority can be found). In the appendix following this chapter, we explain how you can use these citations to find statutory law.

Statutory law also includes local **ordinances**—statutes (laws, rules, or orders) passed by municipal or county governing units to administer matters not covered by federal or state law. Ordinances commonly have to do with city or county land use (zoning ordinances), building and safety codes, and other matters affecting only the local governing unit.

A federal statute, of course, applies to all states. A state statute, in contrast, applies only within the state's borders. State laws thus may vary from state to state. No federal statute may violate the U.S. Constitution, and no state statute or local ordinance may violate the U.S. Constitution or the relevant state constitution.

Uniform Laws During the 1800s, the differences among state laws frequently created difficulties for businesspersons conducting trade and commerce among the states. To counter these problems, a group of legal scholars and lawyers formed the National Conference of Commissioners on Uniform State Laws (NCCUSL, online at **www.nccusl.org**) in 1892 to draft **uniform laws** ("model statutes") for the states to consider adopting. The NCCUSL still exists today and continues to issue uniform laws: it has issued more than two hundred uniform acts since its inception.

Each state has the option of adopting or rejecting a uniform law. *Only if a state legislature adopts a uniform law does that law become part of the statutory law of that state.* Furthermore, a state legislature may choose to adopt only part of a uniform law or to rewrite the sections that are adopted. Hence, even though many states may have adopted a uniform law, those laws may not be entirely "uniform."

The Uniform Commercial Code (UCC) One of the most important uniform acts is the Uniform Commercial Code (UCC), which was created through the joint efforts of the NCCUSL and the American Law Institute.[1] The UCC was first issued in 1952 and has been adopted in all fifty states,[2] the District of Columbia, and the Virgin Islands. As you will read in Chapters 10 and 11, the UCC facilitates commerce among the states by providing a uniform, yet flexible, set of rules governing commercial transactions. Because of its importance in the area of commercial law, we also present Articles 2 and 2A of the UCC in Appendix C. (For a discussion of the creation of the UCC, see the *Landmark in the Law* feature on page 293 in Chapter 10.)

Administrative Law

Administrative Law The body of law created by administrative agencies in order to carry out their duties and responsibilities.

Administrative Agency A federal, state, or local government agency created by the legislature to perform a specific function, such as to make and enforce rules pertaining to the environment.

Another important source of American law is **administrative law,** which consists of the rules, orders, and decisions of administrative agencies. An **administrative agency** is a federal, state, or local government agency established to perform a specific function. Rules issued by various administrative agencies now affect almost every aspect of a business's operations, including the firm's capital structure and financing, its hiring and firing procedures, its relations with employees and unions, and the way it manufactures and markets its products. (See this chapter's *Linking Business Law to Management* feature on pages 20–29.)

Federal Agencies At the national level, numerous *executive agencies* exist within the cabinet departments of the executive branch. For example, the Food and Drug Administration is within the U.S. Department of Health and Human Services. Executive

---

1. This institute was formed in the 1920s and consists of practicing attorneys, legal scholars, and judges.
2. Louisiana has adopted only Articles 1, 3, 4, 5, 7, 8, and 9.

agencies are subject to the authority of the president, who has the power to appoint and remove their officers.

There are also major *independent regulatory agencies* at the federal level, including the Federal Trade Commission, the Securities and Exchange Commission, and the Federal Communications Commission. The president's power is less pronounced in regard to independent agencies, whose officers serve for fixed terms and cannot be removed without just cause.

State and Local Agencies

There are administrative agencies at the state and local levels as well. Commonly, a state agency (such as a state pollution-control agency) is created as a parallel to a federal agency (such as the Environmental Protection Agency). Just as federal statutes take precedence over conflicting state statutes, so do federal agency regulations take precedence over conflicting state regulations. Because the rules of state and local agencies vary widely, we focus here exclusively on federal administrative law.

Agency Creation

Because Congress cannot possibly oversee the actual implementation of all the laws it enacts, it must delegate such tasks to others, especially when the legislation involves highly technical matters, such as air and water pollution. Congress creates an administrative agency by enacting **enabling legislation,** which specifies the name, composition, purpose, and powers of the agency being created.

EXAMPLE 1.1 The Federal Trade Commission (FTC) was created in 1914 by the Federal Trade Commission Act.[3] This act prohibits unfair and deceptive trade practices. It also describes the procedures the agency must follow to charge persons or organizations with violations of the act. Other portions of the act grant the FTC powers to make rules and regulations, conduct investigations of business practices, obtain reports from interstate corporations, investigate possible violations, publish findings of its investigations, and recommend new legislation. The act also empowers the FTC to hold trial-like hearings and to **adjudicate** (resolve judicially) certain kinds of disputes involving its regulations. ●

Note that the powers granted to the FTC incorporate functions associated with the legislative branch of government (rulemaking), the executive branch (investigation and enforcement), and the judicial branch (adjudication). Taken together, these functions constitute **administrative process,** which is the administration of law by administrative agencies.

Rulemaking

A major function of an administrative agency is **rulemaking**—formulating new regulations. When Congress enacts an agency's enabling legislation, it confers the power to make **legislative rules,** or substantive rules, which are legally binding on all businesses. The Administrative Procedure Act (APA)[4] imposes strict procedural requirements that agencies must follow in legislative rulemaking and other functions. Agencies must provide the public with notice of proposed rulemaking proceedings, allow for public comment on the proposed rules, and take these comments into consideration when issuing final rules.

EXAMPLE 1.2 The Occupational Safety and Health Act authorized the Occupational Safety and Health Administration (OSHA) to develop and issue rules governing safety in the workplace. When OSHA wants to formulate rules regarding safety in the steel industry, it has to follow specific procedures outlined by the APA. ● (See the appendix at the end of this chapter on page 35 for an explanation of how to find agency regulations.)

In addition to making *legislative rules,* which are subject to the procedural requirements of the APA, agencies also issue **interpretive rules**—rules that specify how the agency will interpret and apply its regulations. The APA does not apply to interpretive rulemaking and

---

3. 15 U.S.C. Sections 45–58.
4. 5 U.S.C. Sections 551–706.

Enabling Legislation A statute enacted by Congress that authorizes the creation of an administrative agency and specifies the name, composition, purpose, and powers of the agency being created.

Adjudicate To render a judicial decision. Adjudication is the trial-like proceeding in which an administrative law judge hears and resolves disputes involving an administrative agency's regulations.

Administrative Process The procedure used by administrative agencies in administering the law.

Rulemaking The process by which an administrative agency formally adopts a new regulation or amends an old one.

Legislative Rule An administrative agency's rule that carries the same weight as a congressionally enacted statute.

Interpretive Rule A nonbinding rule or policy statement issued by an administrative agency that explains how it interprets and intends to apply the statutes it enforces.

these rules are not legally binding. **EXAMPLE 1.3** The Equal Employment Opportunity Commission periodically issues interpretive rules indicating how it plans to interpret the provisions of certain statutes, such as the Americans with Disabilities Act. These informal rules provide enforcement guidelines for agency officials. •

Investigation and Enforcement

Agencies have both investigatory and prosecutorial powers. An agency can request that individuals or organizations hand over specified books, papers, electronic records, or other documents. In addition, agencies may conduct on-site inspections, although a search warrant is normally required for such inspections. Sometimes, a search of a home, an office, or a factory is the only means of obtaining evidence needed to prove a regulatory violation. Agencies investigate a wide range of activities, including coal mining, automobile manufacturing, and the industrial discharge of pollutants into the environment.

After investigating a suspected rule violation, an agency may decide to take action against an individual or a business. Most administrative actions are resolved through negotiated settlement at their initial stages without the need for formal adjudication. If a settlement cannot be reached, though, the agency may issue a formal complaint and proceed to adjudication.

Adjudication

Agency adjudication involves a trial-like hearing before an **administrative law judge (ALJ).** Hearing procedures vary widely from agency to agency. After the hearing, the ALJ renders a decision in the case. The ALJ can fine the charged party or prohibit the party from carrying on some specified activity. Either the agency or the charged party may appeal the ALJ's decision to the commission or board that governs the agency. If the party fails to get relief there, appeal can be made to a federal court. If neither side appeals the case, the ALJ's decision becomes final.

Case Law and Common Law Doctrines

The rules of law announced in court decisions constitute another basic source of American law. These rules of law include interpretations of constitutional provisions, of statutes enacted by legislatures, and of regulations created by administrative agencies. Today, this body of judge-made law is referred to as **case law.** Case law—the doctrines and principles announced in cases—governs all areas not covered by statutory law or administrative law and is part of our common law tradition. We look at the origins and characteristics of the common law tradition in some detail in the pages that follow.

The Common Law Tradition

Because of our colonial heritage, much of American law is based on the English legal system. A knowledge of this tradition is crucial to understanding our legal system today because judges in the United States still apply common law principles when deciding cases.

Early English Courts

After the Normans conquered England in 1066, William the Conqueror and his successors began the process of unifying the country under their rule. One of the means they used to do this was the establishment of the king's courts, or *curiae regis.* The king's courts sought to establish a uniform set of rules for the country as a whole. What evolved in these courts was the beginning of the **common law**—a body of general rules that applied throughout

---

Administrative Law Judge (ALJ) One who presides over an administrative agency hearing and has the power to administer oaths, take testimony, rule on questions of evidence, and make determinations of fact.

Case Law The rules of law announced in court decisions. Case law interprets statutes, regulations, constitutional provisions, and other case law.

Common Law The body of law developed from custom or judicial decisions in English and U.S. courts, not attributable to a legislature.

the entire English realm. Eventually, the common law tradition became part of the heritage of all nations that were once British colonies, including the United States.

Courts developed the common law rules from the principles underlying judges' decisions in actual legal controversies. Judges attempted to be consistent, and whenever possible, they based their decisions on the principles suggested by earlier cases. They sought to decide similar cases in a similar way and considered new cases with care because they knew that their decisions would make new law. Each interpretation became part of the law on the subject and served as a legal **precedent**—that is, a court decision that furnished an example or authority for deciding subsequent cases involving identical or similar legal principles or facts.

In the early years of the common law, there was no single place or publication where court opinions, or written decisions, could be found. Beginning in the late thirteenth and early fourteenth centuries, however, portions of significant decisions from each year were gathered together and recorded in *Year Books*. The *Year Books* were later discontinued, and other reports of cases became available. (See the appendix to this chapter starting on page 34 for a discussion of how cases are reported, or published, in the United States today.)

Stare Decisis

The practice of deciding new cases with reference to former decisions, or precedents, eventually became a cornerstone of the English and U.S. judicial systems. The practice forms a doctrine called **stare decisis**[5] ("to stand on decided cases"). Under the doctrine of *stare decisis,* once a court has set forth a principle of law as being applicable to a certain set of facts, that court and courts of lower rank must adhere to that principle and apply it in future cases involving similar fact patterns.

The doctrine of *stare decisis* helps the courts to be more efficient because if other courts have carefully reasoned through a similar case, their legal reasoning and opinions can serve as guides. *Stare decisis* also makes the law more stable and predictable. If the law on a given subject is well settled, someone bringing a case to court can usually rely on the court to make a decision based on what the law has been.

Controlling Precedent
Controlling precedents in a *jurisdiction* (an area in which a court or courts have the power to apply the law) are referred to as binding authorities. A **binding authority** is any source of law that a court must follow when deciding a case. Binding authorities include constitutions, statutes, and regulations that govern the issue being decided, as well as court decisions that are controlling precedents within the jurisdiction. United States Supreme Court case decisions, no matter how old, remain controlling until they are overruled by a subsequent decision of the Supreme Court, by a constitutional amendment, or by congressional legislation.

At times, a case may raise issues that have not been raised before in that jurisdiction, so the court has no precedents on which to base its decision. When deciding such cases, called "cases of first impression," courts often look at precedents established in other jurisdictions for guidance. Precedents from other jurisdictions, because they are not binding on the court, are referred to as **persuasive authorities.** A court may also consider other factors, including legal principles and policies underlying previous court decisions or existing statutes, fairness, social values and customs, public policy, and data and concepts drawn from the social sciences.

Departures from Precedent
Although courts are obligated to follow precedents, sometimes a court will depart from the rule of precedent. If a court decides that a precedent is simply incorrect or that technological or social changes have rendered the

---

LEARNING OBJECTIVE 2
What is a precedent? When might a court depart from precedent?

Precedent A court decision that furnishes an example or authority for deciding subsequent cases involving identical or similar facts.

Stare Decisis A common law doctrine under which judges are obligated to follow the precedents established in prior decisions.

→ KNOW THIS ←
Courts normally must follow the rules set forth by higher courts in deciding cases with similar fact patterns.

Binding Authority Any source of law that a court *must* follow when deciding a case.

Persuasive Authority Any legal authority or source of law that a court may look to for guidance but need not follow when making its decision.

---

5. Pronounced *stah-ree dih-si-sis.*

School integration occurred after *Brown v. Board of Education of Topeka.*

(Library of Congress)

Remedy The relief given to an innocent party to enforce a right or compensate for the violation of a right.

Plaintiff One who initiates a lawsuit.

Defendant One against whom a lawsuit is brought, or the accused person in a criminal proceeding.

precedent inapplicable, the court may rule contrary to the precedent. Cases that overturn precedent often receive a great deal of publicity.   **CASE EXAMPLE 1.4** In *Brown v. Board of Education of Topeka,*[6] the United States Supreme Court expressly overturned precedent when it concluded that separate educational facilities for whites and blacks, which had been upheld as constitutional in numerous previous cases,[7] were inherently unequal. The Supreme Court's departure from precedent in the *Brown* decision received a tremendous amount of publicity as people began to realize the ramifications of this change in the law. •

Equitable Remedies and Courts of Equity

A **remedy** is the means given to a party to enforce a right or to compensate for the violation of a right.   **EXAMPLE 1.5** Elena is injured because of Rowan's wrongdoing. If Elena files a lawsuit and is successful, a court can order Rowan to compensate Elena for the harm by paying her a certain amount. The compensation is Elena's remedy. •

The kinds of remedies available in the early king's courts of England were severely restricted. If one person wronged another, the king's courts could award as compensation either money or property, including land. These courts became known as *courts of law,* and the remedies were called *remedies at law.* When a person wanted a remedy other than economic compensation, the courts of law could do nothing.

Remedies in Equity *Equity* is a branch of law, founded on what might be described as notions of justice and fair dealing, that seeks to supply a remedy when no adequate remedy at law is available. When individuals could not obtain an adequate remedy in a court of law, they petitioned the king for relief. Most of these petitions were referred to the *chancellor,* an adviser to the king who had the power to grant new and unique remedies. Eventually, formal chancery courts, or *courts of equity,* were established. Thus, two distinct court systems were created, each having its own set of judges and its own set of remedies. The remedies granted by the chancery courts were called *remedies in equity.*

Plaintiffs (those bringing lawsuits) had to specify whether they were bringing an "action at law" or an "action in equity," and they chose their courts accordingly.   **EXAMPLE 1.6** A plaintiff might ask a court of equity to order the **defendant** (the person against whom a lawsuit is brought) to perform within the terms of a contract. A court of law could not issue such an order. A court of equity, however, could issue a decree for *specific performance*—an order to perform what was promised. A court of equity could also issue an *injunction,* directing a party to do or refrain from doing a particular act. In certain cases, a court of equity could allow for the *rescission* (cancellation) of the contract, thereby returning the parties to the positions that they held prior to the contract's formation. • Equitable remedies will be discussed in greater detail in Chapter 9.

The Merging of Law and Equity Today, in most states, the courts of law and equity have merged, and thus the distinction between the two courts has largely disappeared. A plaintiff may now request both legal and equitable remedies in the same action, and the trial court judge may grant either form—or both forms—of relief.

The distinction between legal and equitable remedies remains significant, however, because a court normally will grant an equitable remedy only when the remedy at law (monetary damages) is inadequate. To request the proper remedy, a businessperson (or her

---

6. 347 U.S. 483, 74 S.Ct. 686, 98 L.Ed. 873 (1954).
7. See *Plessy v. Ferguson,* 163 U.S. 537, 16 S.Ct. 1138, 41 L.Ed. 256 (1896).

Exhibit 1.1 Procedural Differences between an
Action at Law and an Action at Equity

PROCEDURE	ACTION AT LAW	ACTION IN EQUITY
Initiation of lawsuit	By filing a complaint.	By filing a petition.
Decision	By jury or judge.	By judge (no jury).
Result	Judgment.	Decree.
Remedy	Monetary damages.	Injunction, specific performance, or rescission.

or his attorney) must know what remedies are available for the specific kinds of harms suffered. Exhibit 1.1 above summarizes the procedural differences (applicable in most states) between an action at law and an action in equity.

Classifications of Law

Substantive Law Law that defines, describes, regulates, and creates legal rights and obligations.

Procedural Law Law that establishes the methods of enforcing the rights established by substantive law.

Cyberlaw An informal term used to refer to all laws governing electronic communications and transactions, particularly those conducted via the Internet.

Civil Law The branch of law dealing with the definition and enforcement of all private or public rights, as opposed to criminal matters.

Civil Law System A system of law derived from Roman law that is based on codified laws (rather than on case precedents).

Criminal Law The branch of law that defines and punishes wrongful actions committed against the public.

The law may be broken down according to several classification systems. For example, one classification system divides law into **substantive law** (all laws that define, describe, regulate, and create legal rights and obligations) and **procedural law** (all laws that establish the methods of enforcing the rights established by substantive law).
EXAMPLE 1.7 A state law that provides employees with the right to workers' compensation benefits for any on-the-job injuries they sustain is a substantive law because it creates legal rights (workers' compensation laws will be discussed in Chapter 18). Procedural laws, in contrast, establish the method by which an employee must notify the employer about an on-the-job injury, prove the injury, and periodically submit additional proof to continue receiving workers' compensation benefits. Note that a law concerning workers' compensation may contain both substantive and procedural provisions. •

Other classification systems divide law into federal law and state law or private law (dealing with relationships between persons) and public law (addressing the relationship between persons and their governments). Frequently, people use the term **cyberlaw** to refer to the body of law that governs transactions conducted via the Internet. Nonetheless, cyberlaw is not really a classification of law, nor is it a new *type* of law. Rather, it is an informal term used to describe how the law is evolving to govern specific legal issues that arise in the online context.

Civil Law and Criminal Law

A witness points out someone in the courtroom to the judge.

(Junial Enterprises/Shutterstock.com)

Civil law spells out the rights and duties that exist between persons and between persons and their governments, and the relief available when a person's rights are violated. **EXAMPLE 1.8** If a seller fails to perform a contract with a buyer, the buyer may bring a lawsuit against the seller. The purpose of the lawsuit will be either to compel the seller to perform as promised or, more commonly, to obtain monetary damages for the seller's failure to perform. •

Much of the law that we discuss in this text is civil law. Note that *civil law* is not the same as a *civil law system*. As you will read shortly, a **civil law system** is a legal system based on a written code of laws.

Criminal law has to do with wrongs committed against society for which society demands redress. Criminal acts are proscribed by local, state, or federal government statutes (see Chapter 6). Thus, criminal defendants are prosecuted by public officials, such as a district attorney (D.A.), on behalf of the state, not by their victims or other private parties. Whereas in a civil case the object is to obtain a remedy (such as monetary damages) to compensate the injured party, in a criminal case the object is to punish the wrongdoer in an attempt to deter others from similar actions. Penalties for violations of criminal statutes consist of fines and/or imprisonment—and, in some cases, death. We will discuss the differences between civil and criminal law in more detail in Chapter 6.

National and International Law

Although the focus of this book is U.S. business law, increasingly businesspersons in this country engage in transactions that extend beyond our national borders. In these situations, the laws of other nations or the laws governing relationships among nations may come into play. For this reason, those who pursue a career in business today should have an understanding of the global legal environment (discussed further in Chapter 25).

National Law Law that pertains to a particular nation (as opposed to international law).

National Law The law of a particular nation, such as the United States or Sweden, is **national law.** National law, of course, varies from country to country because each country's law reflects the interests, customs, activities, and values that are unique to that nation's culture. Even though the laws and legal systems of various countries differ substantially, broad similarities do exist, as discussed in this chapter's *Beyond Our Borders* feature on the following page.

International Law The law that governs relations among nations.

International Law In contrast to national law, international law applies to more than one nation. **International law** can be defined as a body of written and unwritten laws observed by independent nations and governing the acts of individuals as well as governments. It is a mixture of rules and constraints derived from a variety of sources, including the laws of individual nations, customs developed among nations, and international treaties and organizations. Each nation is motivated not only by the need to be the final authority over its own affairs, but also by the desire to benefit economically from trade and harmonious relations with other nations. In essence, international law is the result of centuries-old attempts to strike a balance between these competing needs.

The key difference between national law and international law is that government authorities can enforce national law. If a nation violates an international law, however, enforcement is up to other countries or international organizations, which may or may not choose to act. If persuasive tactics fail, the only option is to take coercive actions against the violating nation. Coercive actions range from the severance of diplomatic relations and boycotts to, as a last resort, war. We will examine the laws governing international business transactions in Chapter 25.

The Constitutional Powers of Government

Laws that govern business in the United States have their origin in the lawmaking authority granted by the U.S. Constitution, which is the supreme law in this country.[8] As mentioned earlier, neither Congress nor any state can enact a law that is in conflict with the Constitution. Constitutional disputes frequently come before the courts. For example, numerous states challenged the Obama administration's Affordable Care Act, claiming that the provisions that require most Americans to have health insurance by 2014 exceeded the constitutional authority of the federal government. In 2012, the United States Supreme Court rejected this argument and upheld the law.[9] The Court's decision significantly affects business because many individuals obtain insurance through their employers, and because businesses can face fines for failing to provide insurance to their employees.

---

8. See Appendix B for the full text of the U.S. Constitution.
9. *National Federation of Independent Business v. Sebelius,* ___ U.S. ___, 132 S.Ct. 2566, 183 L.Ed.2d 450 (2012).

BEYOND OUR BORDERS   National Law Systems

Despite their varying cultures and customs, almost all countries have laws governing torts, contracts, employment, and other areas. Two types of legal systems predominate around the globe today. One is the common law system of England and the United States, which we have discussed elsewhere. The other system is based on Roman civil law, or "code law," which relies on the legal principles enacted into law by a legislature or governing body.

Civil Law Systems

Although national law systems share many commonalities, they also have distinct differences. In a *civil law system*, the primary source of law is a statutory code, and case precedents are not judicially binding, as they normally are in a common law system. Although judges in a civil law system commonly refer to previous decisions as sources of legal guidance, those decisions are not binding precedents (*stare decisis* does not apply).

Exhibit 1.2 below lists some countries that today follow either the common law system or the civil law system. Generally, those countries that were once colonies of Great Britain have retained their English common law heritage. The civil law system, which is used in most continental European nations, has been retained in the countries that were once colonies of those nations. In the United States, the state of Louisiana, because of its historical ties to France, has in part a civil law system, as do Haiti, Québec, and Scotland.

Islamic Legal Systems

A third, less prevalent legal system is common in Islamic countries, where the law is often influenced by *sharia*, the religious law of Islam. Islam is both a religion and a way of life. *Sharia* is a comprehensive code of principles that governs the public and private lives of Islamic persons and directs many aspects of day-to-day life, including politics, economics, banking, business law, contract law, and social issues.

Although *sharia* affects the legal codes of many Muslim countries, the extent of its impact and its interpretation vary widely. In some Middle Eastern nations, aspects of *sharia* have been codified in modern legal codes and are enforced by national judicial systems.

Critical Thinking

Does the civil law system offer any advantages over the common law system, or vice versa? Explain.

Exhibit 1.2 The Legal Systems of Selected Nations

CIVIL LAW		COMMON LAW	
Argentina	Indonesia	Australia	Nigeria
Austria	Iran	Bangladesh	Singapore
Brazil	Italy	Canada	United Kingdom
Chile	Japan	Ghana	United States
China	Mexico	India	Zambia
Egypt	Poland	Israel	
Finland	South Korea	Jamaica	
France	Sweden	Kenya	
Germany	Tunisia	Malaysia	
Greece	Venezuela	New Zealand	

Federal Form of Government A system of government in which the states form a union and the sovereign power is divided between the central government and the member states.

The U.S. Constitution created a **federal form of government** in which the national government and the states *share* sovereign power. The Constitution sets forth specific powers that can be exercised by the national government and provides that the national government has the implied power to undertake actions necessary to carry out its expressly designated powers. All other powers are "reserved" to the states. The broad language of the Constitution, though, has left much room for debate over the specific nature and scope of these powers. Generally, it has been the task of the courts to determine where the boundary line between state and national powers should lie—and that line changes over time.

The Separation of Powers

To make it difficult for the national government to use its power arbitrarily, the Constitution divided the national government's powers among the three branches of government. The legislative branch makes the laws, the executive branch enforces the laws, and the judicial branch interprets the laws. Each branch performs a separate function, and no branch may exercise the authority of another branch.

Additionally, a system of **checks and balances** allows each branch to limit the actions of the other two branches, thus preventing any one branch from exercising too much power. The following are examples of these checks and balances:

1. The legislative branch (Congress) can enact a law, but the executive branch (the president) has the constitutional authority to veto that law.
2. The executive branch is responsible for foreign affairs, but treaties with foreign governments require the advice and consent of the Senate.
3. Congress determines the jurisdiction of the federal courts, and the president appoints federal judges (with the advice and consent of the Senate), but the judicial branch has the power to hold actions of the other two branches unconstitutional.[10]

Checks and Balances The principle under which the powers of the national government are divided among three separate branches — the executive, legislative, and judicial branches — each of which exercises a check on the actions of the others.

The Commerce Clause

LEARNING OBJECTIVE 4
What constitutional clause gives the federal government the power to regulate commercial activities among the various states?

To prevent states from establishing laws and regulations that would interfere with trade and commerce among the states, the Constitution expressly delegated to the national government the power to regulate interstate commerce. Article I, Section 8, of the U.S. Constitution expressly permits Congress "[t]o regulate Commerce with foreign Nations, and among the several States, and with the Indian Tribes." This clause, referred to as the **commerce clause**, has had a greater impact on business than any other provision in the Constitution.

Commerce Clause The provision in Article I, Section 8, of the U.S. Constitution that gives Congress the power to regulate interstate commerce.

Initially, the commerce power was interpreted as being limited to *interstate* commerce (commerce among the states) and not applicable to *intrastate* commerce (commerce within a state). In 1824, however, in the case of *Gibbons v. Ogden*,[11] the United States Supreme Court

---

10. See the *Landmark in the Law* feature on page 67 in Chapter 3 on the case of *Marbury v. Madison* (1803), in which the doctrine of judicial review was clearly enunciated by Chief Justice John Marshall.
11. 22 U.S. (9 Wheat.) 1, 6 L.Ed. 23 (1824).

The U.S. Constitution provides for a system of checks and balances. How does the president check the power of Congress? In what ways can Congress check the power of the president?

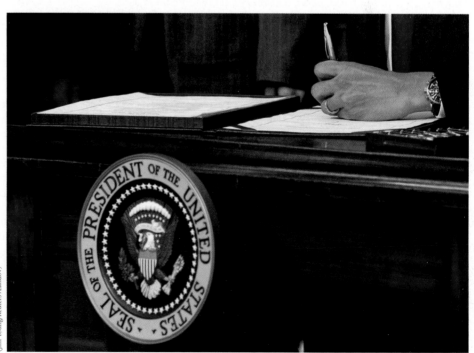

(Jim Young/Reuters/Landov)

held that commerce within a state could also be regulated by the national government as long as the commerce *substantially affected* commerce involving more than one state.

As the nation grew and faced new kinds of problems, the commerce clause became a vehicle for the additional expansion of the national government's regulatory powers. Even activities that seemed purely local came under the regulatory reach of the national government if those activities were deemed to substantially affect interstate commerce. **CASE EXAMPLE 1.9** In 1942, in *Wickard v. Filburn*,[12] the Supreme Court held that wheat production by an individual farmer intended wholly for consumption on his own farm was subject to federal regulation. The Court reasoned that the home consumption of wheat reduced the market demand for wheat and thus could have a substantial effect on interstate commerce. •

The following *Classic Case* involved a challenge to the scope of the national government's constitutional authority to regulate local activities.

---

12. 317 U.S. 111, 63 S.Ct. 82, 87 L.Ed. 122 (1942).

Classic Case 1.1

Heart of Atlanta Motel v. United States

Supreme Court of the United States,
379 U.S. 241, 85 S.Ct. 348, 13 L.Ed.2d 258 (1964).
www.law.cornell.edu/supct/cases/name.htm [a]

Morton Rolleston in front of his Heart of Atlanta Motel.

HISTORICAL AND SOCIAL SETTING *In the first half of the twentieth century, state governments sanctioned segregation on the basis of race. In 1954, the United States Supreme Court held that racially segregated school systems violated the Constitution. In the following decade, the Court ordered an end to racial segregation imposed by the states in other public facilities, such as beaches, golf courses, buses, parks, auditoriums, and courtroom seating. Privately owned facilities that excluded or segregated African Americans and others on the basis of race were not subject to the same constitutional restrictions, however. Congress passed the Civil Rights Act of 1964 to prohibit racial discrimination in "establishments affecting interstate commerce." These facilities included "places of public accommodation."*

FACTS The owner of the Heart of Atlanta Motel, in violation of the Civil Rights Act of 1964, refused to rent rooms to African Americans. The motel owner brought an action in a federal district court to have the Civil Rights Act declared unconstitutional on the ground that Congress had exceeded its constitutional authority to regulate commerce by enacting the statute. The owner argued that his motel was not engaged in interstate commerce but was "of a purely local character." The motel, however, was accessible to state and interstate highways. The owner advertised nationally, maintained billboards throughout the state, and accepted convention trade from outside the state (75 percent of the guests were residents of other states). The

district court ruled that the act did not violate the Constitution and enjoined (prohibited) the owner from discriminating on the basis of race. The owner appealed. The case ultimately went to the United States Supreme Court.

ISSUE Did Congress exceed its constitutional power to regulate interstate commerce by enacting the Civil Rights Act of 1964?

DECISION No. The United States Supreme Court upheld the constitutionality of the act.

REASON The Court noted that the act was passed to correct "the deprivation of personal dignity" accompanying the denial of equal access to "public establishments." Testimony before Congress leading to the passage of the act indicated that African Americans in particular experienced substantial discrimination in attempting to secure lodging while traveling. This discrimination impeded interstate travel and thus impeded interstate commerce.

As for the owner's argument that his motel was "of a purely local character," the Court said that even if this was true, the motel affected interstate commerce. According to the Court, "if it is interstate commerce that feels the pinch, it does not matter how local the operation that applies the squeeze." Therefore,

---

a. This URL will take you to the "Historic Supreme Court Decisions—by Party Name" page within the "Supreme Court" collection at the Web site of the Legal Information Institute. Click on the "H" link, or scroll down the list of cases to the entry for the *Heart of Atlanta* case. Click on the case name, and select the format in which you wish to view the case.

Classic Case 1.1—Continued

under the commerce clause, "the power of Congress to promote interstate commerce also includes the power to regulate the local incidents thereof, including local activities."

IMPACT OF THIS CASE ON TODAY'S LAW *If the United States Supreme Court had invalidated the Civil Rights Act of 1964, the legal landscape of the United States would be much different today. The act prohibits discrimination based* *on race, color, national origin, religion, or gender in all "public accommodations," including hotels and restaurants. The act also prohibits discrimination in employment based on these criteria. Although state laws now prohibit many of these forms of discrimination as well, the protections available vary from state to state—and it is not certain whether such laws would have been passed had the outcome in this case been different.*

The Commerce Clause Today

Today, at least theoretically, the power over commerce authorizes the national government to regulate almost every commercial enterprise in the United States. The breadth of the commerce clause permits the national government to legislate in areas in which Congress has not explicitly been granted power.

In the last twenty years, the Supreme Court has on occasion curbed the national government's regulatory authority under the commerce clause. In 1995, the Court held—for the first time in sixty years—that Congress had exceeded its regulatory authority under the commerce clause. The Court struck down an act that banned the possession of guns within one thousand feet of any school because the act attempted to regulate an area that had "nothing to do with commerce."[13] Subsequently, the Court invalidated key portions of two other federal acts on the ground that they exceeded Congress's commerce clause authority.[14]

In one notable case, however, the Supreme Court did allow the federal government to regulate noncommercial activities taking place wholly within a state's borders. **CASE EXAMPLE 1.10** About a dozen states, including California, have adopted laws that legalize marijuana for medical purposes. Marijuana possession, however, is illegal under the federal Controlled Substances Act (CSA).[15] After the federal government seized the marijuana that two seriously ill California women were using on the advice of their physicians, the women filed a lawsuit. They argued that it was unconstitutional for the federal statute to prohibit them from using marijuana for purposes that were legal within the state. The Supreme Court disagreed. It held that Congress can prohibit the *intra*state possession of marijuana as part of a larger regulatory scheme (the CSA).[16] In other words, state medical marijuana laws do not insulate the users from federal prosecution. •

The Regulatory Powers of the States

As part of their inherent sovereignty, state governments have the authority to regulate affairs within their borders. State regulatory powers are often referred to as **police powers.** The term encompasses not only the enforcement of criminal law but also the right of state governments to regulate private activities in order to protect or promote

Police Powers Powers possessed by the states to protect or promote the public order, health, safety, morals, and general welfare.

Because the Constitution reserves to the states all powers not delegated to the national government, the states can and do regulate many types of commercial activities within their borders. So, too, do municipalities. One example is the power to impose building codes. What is the general term that applies to such powers?

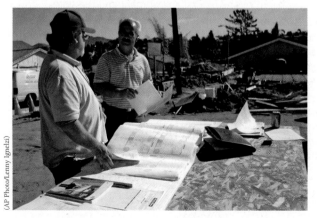

(AP Photo/Lenny Ignelzi)

13. The Court held the Gun-Free School Zones Act of 1990 to be unconstitutional in *United States v. Lopez,* 514 U.S. 549, 115 S.Ct. 1624, 131 L.Ed.2d 626 (1995).
14. See *Printz v. United States,* 521 U.S. 898, 117 S.Ct. 2365, 138 L.Ed.2d 914 (1997), involving the Brady Handgun Violence Prevention Act of 1993; and *United States v. Morrison,* 529 U.S. 598, 120 S.Ct. 1740, 146 L.Ed.2d 658 (2000), concerning the federal Violence Against Women Act of 1994.
15. 21 U.S.C. Sections 801 *et seq.*
16. *Gonzales v. Raich,* 545 U.S. 1, 125 S.Ct. 2195, 162 L.Ed.2d 1 (2005).

Can state and city governments regulate the ingredients in fast food?

the public order, health, safety, morals, and general welfare. Fire and building codes, anti-discrimination laws, parking regulations, zoning restrictions, licensing requirements, and thousands of other state statutes have been enacted pursuant to a state's police powers. Local governments, including cities, also exercise police powers. Although a state may not directly regulate interstate commerce, it may indirectly affect interstate commerce through the reasonable exercise of its police powers. Generally, state laws enacted pursuant to a state's police powers carry a strong presumption of validity.

The "Dormant" Commerce Clause

The United States Supreme Court has interpreted the commerce clause to mean that the national government has the *exclusive* authority to regulate commerce that substantially affects trade and commerce among the states. This express grant of authority to the national government, which is often referred to as the "positive" aspect of the commerce clause, implies a negative aspect—that the states do *not* have the authority to regulate interstate commerce. This negative aspect of the commerce clause is often referred to as the "dormant" (implied) commerce clause.

The dormant commerce clause comes into play when state regulations affect interstate commerce. In this situation, the courts normally weigh the state's interest in regulating a certain matter against the burden that the state's regulation places on interstate commerce. Because courts balance the interests involved, predicting the outcome in a particular case can be extremely difficult.

CASE EXAMPLE 1.11 Tri-M Group, LLC, a Pennsylvania electrical contractor, was hired to work on a veteran's home in Delaware that was partially state funded. Delaware's regulations allowed contractors on state-funded projects to pay a lower wage rate to apprentices if the contractors had registered their apprenticeship programs in the state. Out-of-state contractors, however, were not eligible to pay the lower rate unless they maintained a permanent office in Delaware. Tri-M filed a suit in federal court claiming that Delaware's regulations discriminated against out-of-state contractors in violation of the dormant commerce clause. The state argued that the regulations were justified as part of its program to regulate apprenticeships and thus protect the welfare of apprentices. The court, however, held that the state could have used other means to accomplish that goal. The regulations were discriminatory and thus violated the dormant commerce clause.[17] ●

The Supremacy Clause

Article VI of the Constitution provides that the Constitution, laws, and treaties of the United States are "the supreme Law of the Land." This article, commonly referred to as the **supremacy clause,** is important in the ordering of state and federal relationships. When there is a direct conflict between a federal law and a state law, the state law is rendered invalid. Because some powers are *concurrent* (shared by the federal government and the states), however, it is necessary to determine which law governs in a particular circumstance.

Preemption occurs when Congress chooses to act exclusively in a concurrent area. In this circumstance, a valid federal statute or regulation will take precedence over a conflicting state or local law or regulation on the same general subject. Often, it is not clear whether Congress, in passing a law, intended to preempt an entire subject area against state regulation. In these situations, the courts determine whether Congress intended to exercise exclusive power over a given area. No single factor is decisive as to whether a court will find preemption. Generally, congressional intent to preempt will be found if a federal law regulating an activity is so pervasive, comprehensive, or detailed that the states have little or no room to regulate in that area. Also, when a federal statute creates an agency—such as the National Labor Relations Board—to enforce the law, matters that may come within the agency's jurisdiction will likely preempt state laws.

Supremacy Clause The requirement in Article VI of the U.S. Constitution that provides that the Constitution, laws, and treaties of the United States are "the supreme Law of the Land."

Preemption A doctrine under which certain federal laws preempt, or take precedence over, conflicting state or local laws.

---

17. *Tri-M Group, LLC v. Sharp*, 638 F.3d 406 (3d Cir. 2011). Sharp was the name of the secretary of the Delaware Department of Labor.

CASE EXAMPLE 1.12   The United States Supreme Court ruled on a case involving a man who alleged that he had been injured by a faulty medical device (a balloon catheter that had been inserted into his artery following a heart attack). The Court noted that the Medical Device Amendments of 1976 had included a preemption provision. The medical device had passed the U.S. Food and Drug Administration's rigorous premarket approval process. Therefore, the Court ruled that the federal regulation of medical devices preempted the man's state law claims for negligence, strict liability, and implied warranty (see Chapters 4 and 12).[18] •

LEARNING OBJECTIVE 5
What is the Bill of Rights? What freedoms does the First Amendment guarantee?

Business and the Bill of Rights

The importance of having a written declaration of the rights of individuals caused the first Congress of the United States to enact twelve amendments to the Constitution and submit them to the states for approval. The first ten of these amendments, commonly known as the **Bill of Rights,** were adopted in 1791 and embody a series of protections for the individual against various types of interference by the federal government.

Bill of Rights The first ten amendments to the U.S. Constitution.

Some constitutional protections apply to business entities as well. For example, corporations exist as separate legal entities, or legal persons, and enjoy many of the same rights and privileges as natural persons do. Summarized here are the protections guaranteed by these ten amendments (see the Constitution in Appendix B for the complete text of each amendment):

1. The First Amendment guarantees the freedoms of religion, speech, and the press and the rights to assemble peaceably and to petition the government.
2. The Second Amendment guarantees the right to keep and bear arms.
3. The Third Amendment prohibits, in peacetime, the lodging of soldiers in any house without the owner's consent.
4. The Fourth Amendment prohibits unreasonable searches and seizures of persons or property.
5. The Fifth Amendment guarantees the rights to *indictment* (formal accusation) by a grand jury, to due process of law, and to fair payment when private property is taken for public use. The Fifth Amendment also prohibits compulsory self-incrimination and double jeopardy (trial for the same crime twice).
6. The Sixth Amendment guarantees the accused in a criminal case the right to a speedy and public trial by an impartial jury and with counsel. The accused has the right to cross-examine witnesses against him or her and to solicit testimony from witnesses in his or her favor.
7. The Seventh Amendment guarantees the right to a trial by jury in a civil (noncriminal) case involving at least twenty dollars.[19]
8. The Eighth Amendment prohibits excessive bail and fines, as well as cruel and unusual punishment.
9. The Ninth Amendment establishes that the people have rights in addition to those specified in the Constitution.
10. The Tenth Amendment establishes that those powers neither delegated to the federal government nor denied to the states are reserved for the states.

---

18. *Riegel v. Medtronic, Inc.,* 552 U.S. 312, 128 S.Ct. 999, 169 L.Ed.2d 892 (2008).
19. Twenty dollars was forty days' pay for the average person when the Bill of Rights was written.

As originally intended, the Bill of Rights limited only the powers of the national government. Over time, however, the United States Supreme Court "incorporated" most of these rights into the protections against state actions afforded by the Fourteenth Amendment to the Constitution. That amendment, passed in 1868 after the Civil War, provides, in part, that "[n]o State shall . . . deprive any person of life, liberty, or property, without due process of law." Starting in 1925, the Supreme Court began to define various rights and liberties guaranteed in the national Constitution as constituting "due process of law," which was required of state governments under the Fourteenth Amendment. Today, most of the rights and liberties set forth in the Bill of Rights apply to state governments as well as to the national government.

The rights secured by the Bill of Rights are not absolute. Many of the rights guaranteed by the first ten amendments are described in very general terms. For example, the Second Amendment states that people have a right to keep and bear arms, but it does not explain the extent of this right. As the Supreme Court noted in 2008, this does not mean that people can "keep and carry any weapon whatsoever in any manner whatsoever and for whatever purpose."[20] Legislatures can prohibit the carrying of concealed weapons or certain types of weapons, such as machine guns. Ultimately, it is the Supreme Court, as the final interpreter of the Constitution, that gives meaning to these rights and determines their boundaries.

The First Amendment—Freedom of Speech

A democratic form of government cannot survive unless people can freely voice their political opinions and criticize government actions or policies. Freedom of speech, particularly political speech, is thus a prized right, and traditionally the courts have protected this right to the fullest extent possible.

Symbolic Speech Nonverbal expressions of beliefs. Symbolic speech, which includes gestures, movements, and articles of clothing, is given substantial protection by the courts.

Symbolic speech—gestures, movements, articles of clothing, and other forms of expressive conduct—is also given substantial protection by the courts. The Supreme Court held that the burning of the American flag to protest government policies is a constitutionally protected form of expression.[21] Similarly, wearing a T-shirt with a photo of a presidential candidate would be a constitutionally protected form of expression. The test is whether a reasonable person would interpret the conduct as conveying some sort of message. **EXAMPLE 1.13** As a form of expression, Nam has gang signs tattooed on his torso, arms, neck, and legs. If a reasonable person would interpret this conduct as conveying a message, then it might be a protected form of symbolic speech. •

Reasonable Restrictions Expression—oral, written, or symbolized by conduct—is subject to reasonable restrictions. A balance must be struck between a government's obligation to protect its citizens and those citizens' exercise of their rights. Reasonableness is analyzed on a case-by-case basis.

Content-Neutral Laws Laws that regulate the time, manner, and place, but not the content, of speech receive less scrutiny by the courts than do laws that restrict the content of expression. If a restriction imposed by the government is content neutral, then a court may allow it. To be content neutral, the restriction must be aimed at combating some secondary societal problem, such as crime, and not be aimed at suppressing the expressive conduct or its message.

Courts have often protected nude dancing as a form of symbolic expression. Nevertheless, the courts typically allow content-neutral laws that ban *all* public nudity. **CASE EXAMPLE 1.14** Ria Ora was charged with dancing nude at an annual "anti-Christmas" protest in Harvard Square in Cambridge, Massachusetts. Ora argued that the statute was overbroad and unconstitutional, and a trial court agreed. On appeal, a state appellate court

---

20. *District of Columbia v. Heller,* 554 U.S. 570, 128 S.Ct. 2783, 171 L.Ed.2d 637 (2008).
21. See *Texas v. Johnson,* 491 U.S. 397, 109 S.Ct. 2533, 105 L.Ed.2d 342 (1989).

These policemen look on at the Occupy Portland encampment set up in a public place. When the mayor of Portland, Oregon, ordered the demonstrators to "pull up stakes," was he violating their right to free speech?

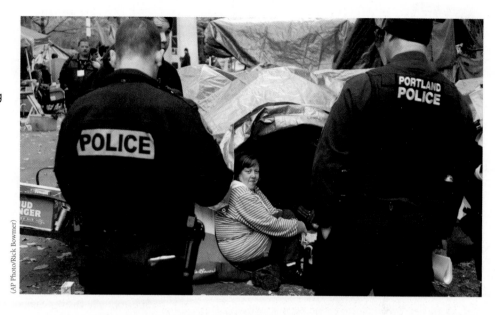

(AP Photo/Rick Bowmer)

reversed. The court found that the statute was constitutional because it banned any public displays of open and gross lewdness in situations in which there was an unsuspecting or unwilling audience.[22] ●

Laws That Restrict the Content of Speech   If a law regulates the content of expression, the law must meet the **compelling government interest** test. That is, it must serve a compelling state interest and must be narrowly written to achieve that interest.

Compelling Government Interest   A test of constitutionality that requires the government to have convincing reasons for passing any law that restricts fundamental rights, such as free speech, or distinguishes between people based on a suspect trait.

The United States Supreme Court has held that schools may restrict students' speech at school events. **CASE EXAMPLE 1.15**   Some high school students held up a banner saying "Bong Hits 4 Jesus" at an off-campus but school-sanctioned event. The majority of the Court ruled that school officials did not violate the students' free speech rights when they confiscated the banner and suspended the students for ten days. Because the banner could reasonably be interpreted as promoting drugs, the Court concluded that the school's actions were justified. Several justices disagreed, however, noting that the majority's holding creates a special exception that will allow schools to censor any student speech that mentions drugs.[23] ●

Can a high school suspend teenagers from extracurricular activities because they posted suggestive photos of themselves online at social networking sites? For a discussion of this issue, see this chapter's *Adapting the Law to the Online Environment* on the following page.

Corporate Political Speech   Political speech by corporations also falls within the protection of the First Amendment. Many years ago, the United States Supreme Court reviewed a Massachusetts statute that prohibited corporations from making political contributions that individuals were permitted to make and ruled the law unconstitutional.[24] Corporate political speech continues to be given significant protection under the First Amendment. In 2010, the Supreme Court overturned a twenty-year-old precedent when it ruled that corporations can spend freely to support or oppose candidates for president and Congress.[25] (See the *Landmark in the Law* feature in Chapter 20 for a discussion of this issue.)

► **KNOW THIS** ◄

The First Amendment guarantee of freedom of speech applies only to *government* restrictions on speech.

---

22. *Commonwealth v. Ora,* 451 Mass. 125, 883 N.E.2d 1217 (2008).
23. *Morse v. Frederick,* 551 U.S. 393, 127 S.Ct. 2618, 168 L.Ed.2d 290 (2007).
24. *First National Bank of Boston v. Bellotti,* 435 U.S. 765, 98 S.Ct. 1407, 55 L.Ed.2d 707 (1978).
25. *Citizens United v. Federal Election Commission,* 558 U.S. 310, 130 S.Ct. 876, 175 L.Ed.2d 753 (2010).

ADAPTING THE LAW TO THE ONLINE ENVIRONMENT

VULGAR FACEBOOK PHOTOS RECEIVE FIRST AMENDMENT PROTECTION

A federal judge in Indiana ruled that a high school did not have the right to punish students for posting raunchy photos of themselves on the Internet. According to the court, "the case poses timely questions about the limits school officials can place on out-of-school speech by students in the information age where Twitter, Facebook, MySpace, texts, and the like rule the day."[a]

High School Suspended the Teens from Extracurricular Activities

T.V. and M.K. were both entering the tenth grade at a public high school. During summer sleepovers, the girls took photos of each other pretending to suck penis-shaped rainbow-colored lollipops and holding them in various suggestive positions. They later posted the photos on Facebook, MySpace, and Photo Bucket to be seen by persons granted "friend" status or given a password. The images did not identify the school that the girls attended.

When a parent complained to the school about the provocative online display, school officials suspended both girls from extracurricular activities for a portion of the upcoming school year. Both T.V. and M.K. were members of the high school's volleyball team, and M.K. was also a member of the cheerleading squad and the show choir. Through their parents, the girls filed a lawsuit claiming that the school had violated their First Amendment rights.

Can Online Photos Qualify as Symbolic Speech?

Expressive conduct is entitled to First Amendment protection if it meets a two-part intent-plus-perception test. Conduct is symbolic speech if the "intent to convey a particularized message was present" and if "the likelihood was great that the message would be understood by those who viewed it."[b] Here, both girls testified that they were just trying to be funny when they took the photos and posted them online for their friends to see. Although the photos were suggestive, the girls were fully clothed, and the images were not pornographic or obscene. The court reasoned that the conduct depicted in the photos was intended to be humorous and would be understood as such by their teenage audience. Therefore, the photos were entitled to First Amendment protection as symbolic speech, even if they were "juvenile and silly."

Did the Off-Campus Speech Substantially Disrupt School Activities?

Although schools can restrict students' speech at times, this was not one of those times, according to the court. The conduct took place off campus and did not substantially disrupt the work and discipline of the high school. Schools generally can punish students only for off-campus speech that becomes an in-school problem, such as bullying, but here, the photos had only a minimal effect on the volleyball team. (Some of the other players and two parents had complained that the photos were inappropriate.) The court also struck down the provision in the student handbook banning out-of-school conduct that brings discredit or dishonor on the school, finding that it was impermissibly broad and vague.

Critical Thinking

How might the outcome of this case have been different if the girls had posted the photos on the high school's public Web site for all to see?

---

a. *T.V. ex rel. B.V. v. Smith-Green Community School Corp.*, 807 F.Supp.2d 767 (N.D.Ind. 2011).

b. See *Texas v. Johnson*, 491 U.S. 397, 109 S.Ct. 2533, 105 L.Ed.2d 342 (1989).

Commercial Speech   The courts also give substantial protection to *commercial speech*, which consists of communications—primarily advertising and marketing—made by business firms that involve only their commercial interests. The protection given to commercial speech under the First Amendment is not as extensive as that afforded to noncommercial speech, however. A state may restrict certain kinds of advertising, for instance, in the interest of protecting consumers from being misled.

States also have a legitimate interest in the beautification of roadsides, and this interest allows states to place restraints on billboard advertising.   **CASE EXAMPLE 1.16**   Café Erotica, a nude dancing establishment, sued the state after being denied a permit to erect a billboard along an interstate highway in Florida. The state appellate court decided that because the law directly advanced a substantial government interest in highway beautification and safety, it was not an unconstitutional restraint on commercial speech.[26] •

Generally, a restriction on commercial speech will be considered valid as long as it (1) seeks to implement a substantial government interest, (2) directly advances that interest, and (3) goes no further than necessary to accomplish its objective. A substantial government interest exists when the government has an important purpose in taking an action, as described in the preceding paragraph. This substantial-interest requirement limits the power of the government to regulate commercial speech.

At issue in the following *Spotlight Case* was whether a government agency had unconstitutionally restricted commercial speech when it prohibited the inclusion of a certain illustration on beer labels.

---

26. *Café Erotica v. Florida Department of Transportation,* 830 So.2d 181 (Fla.App. 2002); review denied, *Café Erotica/ We Dare to Bare v. Florida Department of Transportation,* 845 So.2d 888 (Fla. 2003).

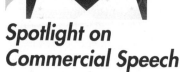

Spotlight on Commercial Speech

(Courtesy of Bad Frog Beer)

Can a state ban a label for being too offensive?

Case 1.2
Bad Frog Brewery, Inc. v. New York State Liquor Authority
United States Court of Appeals, Second Circuit, 134 F.3d 87 (1998).
www.findlaw.com/casecode/index.html[a]

FACTS Bad Frog Brewery, Inc., makes and sells alcoholic beverages. Some of the beverages feature labels with a drawing of a frog making the gesture generally known as "giving the finger." Bad Frog's authorized New York distributor, Renaissance Beer Company, applied to the New York State Liquor Authority (NYSLA) for brand label approval, as required by state law before the beer could be sold in New York. The NYSLA denied the application, in part, because "the label could appear in grocery and convenience stores, with obvious exposure on the shelf to children of tender age." Bad Frog filed a suit in a federal district court against the NYSLA, asking for, among other things, an injunction against the denial of the application. The court granted summary judgment in favor of the NYSLA. Bad Frog appealed to the U.S. Court of Appeals for the Second Circuit.

ISSUE Was the NYSLA's ban of Bad Frog's beer labels a reasonable restriction on commercial speech?

DECISION No. The U.S. Court of Appeals for the Second Circuit reversed the judgment of the district court and remanded the case for judgment to be entered in favor of Bad Frog.

REASON The appellate court held that the NYSLA's denial of Bad Frog's application violated the First Amendment. The ban on the use of the labels lacked a "reasonable fit" with the state's interest in shielding minors from vulgarity, and the NYSLA did not adequately consider alternatives to the ban. The court acknowledged that the NYSLA's interest "in protecting children from vulgar and profane advertising" was "substantial." The question was whether banning Bad Frog's labels "directly advanced" that interest. "In view of the wide currency of vulgar displays throughout contemporary society, including comic books targeted directly at children, barring such displays from labels for alcoholic beverages cannot realistically be expected to reduce children's exposure to such displays to any significant degree." The court concluded that a commercial speech limitation must be "part of a substantial effort to advance a valid state interest, not merely the removal of a few grains of offensive sand from a beach of vulgarity." Finally, as to whether the ban on the labels was more extensive than necessary to serve this interest, the court pointed out that there were "numerous less intrusive alternatives." For example, the NYSLA could have placed restrictions on the permissible locations where the appellant's products could be displayed in stores.

WHAT IF THE FACTS WERE DIFFERENT? *If Bad Frog had sought to use the label to market toys instead of beer, would the court's ruling likely have been the same? Explain your answer.*

---

a. Under the heading "US Court of Appeals," click on "2nd." Enter "Bad Frog Brewery" in the "Party name:" box, and click on "Search." On the resulting page, click on the case name to access the opinion.

Unprotected Speech   The United States Supreme Court has made it clear that certain types of speech will not be given any protection under the First Amendment. Speech that harms the good reputation of another, or defamatory speech (see Chapter 4), is not protected. Speech that violates criminal laws (such as threatening speech) is not constitutionally protected. Other unprotected speech includes "fighting words," or words that are likely to incite others to respond violently, and obscene speech. Establishing an objective definition of obscene speech has proved difficult, however, and the Court has grappled with this problem from time to time.

In 2000, Congress enacted the Children's Internet Protection Act (CIPA),[27] which requires public schools and libraries to block adult content from access by children by installing **filtering software.** Such software is designed to prevent persons from viewing certain Web sites by responding to a site's Internet address or its **meta tags,** or key words. CIPA was challenged on constitutional grounds, but in 2003 the Supreme Court held that the act did not violate the First Amendment. The Court concluded that because libraries can disable the filters for any patrons who ask, the system is reasonably flexible and does not burden free speech to an unconstitutional extent.[28]

In 2003, Congress enacted the Prosecutorial Remedies and Other Tools to End the Exploitation of Children Today Act (Protect Act).[29] The act makes it a crime to knowingly advertise, present, distribute, or solicit "any material or purported material in a manner that reflects the belief, or that is intended to cause another to believe, that the material or purported material" is illegal child pornography. Thus, it is a crime to intentionally distribute virtual child pornography, which uses computer-generated images, not actual people. The Supreme Court upheld that statute because it does not prohibit a substantial amount of protected speech and generally prohibits offers to provide, and requests to obtain, child pornography.[30]

The First Amendment—Freedom of Religion

The First Amendment states that the government may neither establish any religion nor prohibit the free exercise of religious practices. The first part of this constitutional provision is referred to as the *establishment clause,* and the second part is known as the *free exercise clause.* Government action, both federal and state, must be consistent with this constitutional mandate.

The Establishment Clause   The **establishment clause** prohibits the government from establishing a state-sponsored religion, as well as from passing laws that promote (aid or endorse) religion or show a preference for one religion over another. Although the establishment clause involves the separation of church and state, it does not require a complete separation.

Establishment clause cases often involve such issues as the legality of allowing or requiring school prayers, using state-issued vouchers to pay tuition at religious schools, and teaching creation theories versus evolution. Federal or state laws that do not promote or place a significant burden on religion are constitutional even if they have some impact on religion. For a government law or policy to be constitutional, it must not have the primary effect of promoting or inhibiting religion.

Religious displays on public property have often been challenged as violating the establishment clause, and the United States Supreme Court has ruled on a number of such cases. Generally, the Court has focused on the proximity of the religious display to nonreligious

Filtering Software A computer program that is designed to block access to certain Web sites, based on their content. The software blocks the retrieval of a site whose URL or key words are on a list within the program.

Meta Tag A key word in a document that can serve as an index reference to the document. On the Web, search engines return results based, in part, on the tags in Web documents.

Establishment Clause The provision in the First Amendment that prohibits the government from establishing any state-sponsored religion or enacting any law that promotes religion or favors one religion over another.

---

27. 17 U.S.C. Sections 1701–1741.

28. *United States v. American Library Association,* 539 U.S. 194, 123 S.Ct. 2297, 156 L.Ed.2d 221 (2003).

29. 18 U.S.C. Section 2252A(a)(5)(B).

30. *United States v. Williams,* 553 U.S. 285, 128 S.Ct. 1830, 170 L.Ed.2d 650 (2008).

This large cross on Mount Soledad can be viewed by freeway drivers in San Diego. Because the land on which it sits became public property, should it be removed as a violation of the establishment clause?

Free Exercise Clause The provision in the First Amendment that prohibits the government from interfering with people's religious practices or forms of worship.

symbols, such as reindeer and candy canes, or to symbols from different religions, such as a menorah (a nine-branched candelabrum used in celebrating Hanukkah). The Supreme Court eventually took a slightly different approach when it held that public displays having historical, as well as religious, significance do not necessarily violate the establishment clause.[31]

CASE EXAMPLE 1.17 Mount Soledad is a prominent hill near San Diego. There has been a forty-foot cross on top of Mount Soledad since 1913. In the 1990s, a war memorial was constructed next to the cross that included six walls listing the names of veterans. The site was privately owned until 2006, when Congress authorized the property's transfer to the federal government "to preserve a historically significant war memorial." Shortly after that, Steve Trunk and the Jewish War Veterans filed lawsuits claiming that the cross display violated the establishment clause because it endorsed the Christian religion. A federal appellate court agreed, finding that the primary effect of the memorial as a whole sent a strong message of endorsement and exclusion (of non-Christian veterans). The court noted that although not all cross displays at war memorials violate the establishment clause, the cross in this case physically dominated the site, was originally dedicated to religious purposes, had a long history of religious use, and was the only portion visible to drivers on the freeway below.[32] •

The Free Exercise Clause

The **free exercise clause** guarantees that a person can hold any religious belief that she or he wants, or a person can have no religious belief. The constitutional guarantee of personal religious freedom restricts only the actions of the government, however, and not those of individuals or private businesses.

When religious *practices* work against public policy and the public welfare, though, the government can act. For instance, the government can require a child to receive certain types of vaccinations or medical treatment when the child's life is in danger—regardless of the child's or parent's religious beliefs. When public safety is an issue, an individual's religious beliefs often have to give way to the government's interests in protecting the public. **EXAMPLE 1.18** According to the Muslim faith, a woman should not appear in public without a scarf, known as a *hijab,* over her head. Due to public safety concerns, many courts today do not allow the wearing of any headgear (hats or scarves) in courtrooms. In Douglasville, Georgia, a Muslim woman was prevented from entering a courthouse with her husband because she refused to remove her scarf. As she left, she uttered an expletive at the court official and was arrested and brought before the judge, who ordered her to serve ten days in jail. Similar incidents have occurred in other states. •

A large and heavy monument showing the Ten Commandments is being removed from a state government building. Why would a federal judge order that it be moved from public view?

The United States Supreme Court has ruled that the free exercise clause protects the use of a controlled substance in the practice of a sincerely held religious belief. **CASE EXAMPLE 1.19** A religious sect in New Mexico follows the practices of a Brazil-based church. Its members ingest hoasca tea as part of a ritual to connect with and better understand God. Hoasca tea, which is brewed from plants native to the Amazon rain forest, contains an illegal hallucinogenic drug that is regulated by the federal Controlled Substances Act. When federal drug agents confiscated the church's shipment of hoasca tea as it entered the country, the church members filed a lawsuit claiming that the confiscation violated their right to freely exercise their religion.

---

31. See *Van Orden v. Perry,* 545 U.S. 677, 125 S.Ct. 2854, 162 L.Ed.2d 607 (2005). The Court held that a six-foot-tall monument of the Ten Commandments on the Texas state capitol grounds did not violate the establishment clause because the Ten Commandments had historical significance.

32. *Trunk v. City of San Diego,* 629 F.3d 1099 (9th Cir. 2011).

Ultimately, the Supreme Court agreed, ruling that the government had failed to demonstrate a sufficiently compelling interest in barring the sect's sacramental use of hoasca.[33] ●

In the following case, the court had to decide whether a county ordinance that prohibited the use of steel cleats on tires was a violation of a church's right to freely exercise its religion.

33. *Gonzales v. O Centro Espirita Beneficente Uniao Do Vegetal*, 546 U.S. 418, 126 S.Ct. 1211, 163 L.Ed.2d 1017 (2006).

Case 1.3

Mitchell County v. Zimmerman

Supreme Court of Iowa,
810 N.W.2d 1 (2012).

(Lingbeek/iStockphoto.com)

Some Mennonites still use animal power.

FACTS Members of the Old Order Groffdale Conference Mennonite Church generally use horses and buggies for transportation. About forty years ago, they started using tractors, particularly for hauling their agricultural products to market. To ensure that the tractors are not used for pleasure purposes (thereby displacing the horse and buggy), their tires have to be fitted with steel cleats that slow down the tractors. Thus, it is a religious requirement of the Mennonites that any motorized tractor driven by a church member be equipped with steel cleats. To minimize road damage, over time the steel cleats have been made wider and are mounted on rubber belts to provide cushioning. Nevertheless, in 2009, finding that the Mennonites' steel cleats tended to damage newly resurfaced roads, Mitchell County adopted a road protection ordinance: "No tire on a vehicle moved on a highway is allowed to have any block, stud, flange, cleat, or spike, or any other protuberances of any material other than rubber." Eli Zimmerman, a Mennonite, received a citation for violating this ordinance. Zimmerman filed a motion to dismiss, which the trial court denied. Zimmerman appealed.

ISSUE Was Mitchell County's ordinance a violation of the free exercise clause of the First Amendment?

DECISION Yes. The reviewing court reversed the trial court's decision and remanded the case for entry of an order of dismissal.

REASON The First Amendment states, in part, that Congress shall make no law "prohibiting the free exercise" of religion.

The First Amendment was made applicable to the states by the Fourteenth Amendment. Consequently, "laws that are not neutral or of general applicability require heightened scrutiny. They must be justified by a compelling governmental interest and must be narrowly tailored to advance that interest." The court first observed that the ordinance's language on the use of steel cleats was nonreligious and therefore neutral. Nevertheless, the court found that the ordinance was not *operationally* neutral because it was adopted specifically to address the Mennonites' use of steel cleats despite their forty-year religious practice of using such cleats.

Finally, the ordinance was not *generally applicable* because it contained exceptions for tire chains for snowy weather and steel-studded snow tires. In other words, Mitchell County chose "to prohibit only a particular source of harm to the roads that had a religious origin." The ordinance was not clearly tailored to achieve the stated objective of road preservation. "The question here is whether the County's goal of road preservation can be accomplished less restrictively without banning the tractors' use by the Mennonites. On the record, we believe it can." The court therefore concluded that the application of the ordinance to Zimmerman violated his right to free exercise of religion.

WHAT IF THE FACTS WERE DIFFERENT? *Suppose that Mitchell County had passed an ordinance that allowed the Mennonites to continue to use steel cleats on the newly resurfaced roads provided that the drivers paid a $5 fee each time they were on the road. Would the court have ruled differently? Why or why not?*

Due Process and Equal Protection

Two other constitutional guarantees of great significance to Americans are mandated by the due process clauses of the Fifth and Fourteenth Amendments and the equal protection clause of the Fourteenth Amendment.

Due Process Clause The provisions in the Fifth and Fourteenth Amendments that guarantee that no person shall be deprived of life, liberty, or property without due process of law. State constitutions often include similar clauses.

Due Process Both the Fifth and the Fourteenth Amendments provide that no person shall be deprived "of life, liberty, or property, without due process of law." The **due process clause** of each of these constitutional amendments has two aspects—procedural and substantive. Note that the due process clause applies to "legal persons," such as corporations, as well as to individuals.

Procedural Due Process Procedural due process requires that any government decision to take life, liberty, or property must be made fairly. This means that the government must give a person proper notice and an opportunity to be heard, and that it must use fair procedures in determining whether a person will be subjected to punishment or have some burden imposed on him or her.

Fair procedure has been interpreted as requiring that the person have at least an opportunity to object to a proposed action before a fair, neutral decision maker (who need not be a judge). **EXAMPLE 1.20** In most states, a driver's license is construed as a property interest. Therefore, the state must provide some sort of opportunity for the driver to object before suspending or terminating the person's license. •

PREVENTING LEGAL DISPUTES

Many of the constitutional protections discussed in this chapter have become part of our culture in the United States. Due process, especially procedural due process, has become synonymous with what Americans consider "fair." For this reason, if you wish to avoid legal disputes, consider giving due process to anyone who might object to some of your business decisions or actions, whether that person is an employee, a partner, an affiliate, or a customer. For instance, provide ample notice of new policies to all affected persons, and give them at least an opportunity to express their opinions on the matter. Providing an opportunity for people to be heard is often the ideal way to make them feel that they are being treated fairly. People are less likely to sue a businessperson or firm that they believe is fair and listens to both sides of an issue.

"Our Constitution protects aliens [extraterrestrials], drunks, and U.S. senators."

Will Rogers, 1879–1935 (American humorist)

Substantive Due Process Substantive due process protects an individual's life, liberty, and property against certain government actions regardless of the fairness of the procedures used to implement them. Substantive due process limits what the government may do in its legislative and executive capacities. Legislation must be fair and reasonable in content and must further a legitimate governmental objective. Only when state conduct is arbitrary or shocks the conscience, however, will it rise to the level of violating substantive due process.

If a law or other governmental action limits a fundamental right, the courts will hold that it violates substantive due process unless it promotes a compelling or overriding state interest. Fundamental rights include interstate travel, privacy, voting, marriage and family, and all First Amendment rights. Thus, a state must have a substantial reason for taking any action that infringes on a person's free speech rights.

In situations not involving fundamental rights, a law or action does not violate substantive due process if it rationally relates to any legitimate governmental end. It is almost impossible for a law or action to fail the "rationality" test. Under this test, almost any government regulation of business will be upheld as reasonable.

Equal Protection Clause The provision in the Fourteenth Amendment that requires state governments to treat similarly situated individuals in a similar manner.

Equal Protection Under the Fourteenth Amendment, a state may not "deny to any person within its jurisdiction the equal protection of the laws." The United States Supreme Court has used the due process clause of the Fifth Amendment to make the **equal protection clause** applicable to the federal government as well. Equal protection means that the government must treat similarly situated individuals in a similar manner.

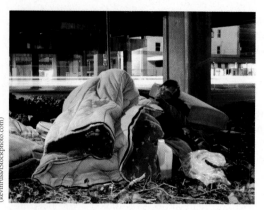

(kevinruss/iStockphoto.com)

Does the equal protection clause protect the homeless? If so, how?

Both substantive due process and equal protection require review of the substance of the law or other governmental action rather than review of the procedures used. When a law or action limits the liberty of all persons to do something, it may violate substantive due process. When a law or action limits the liberty of some persons but not others, it may violate the equal protection clause. **EXAMPLE 1.21** If a law prohibits all advertising on the sides of trucks, it raises a substantive due process question. If the law makes an exception to allow truck owners to advertise their own businesses, it raises an equal protection issue. •

In an equal protection inquiry, when a law or action distinguishes between or among individuals, the basis for the distinction—that is, the classification—is examined. Depending on the classification, the courts apply different levels of scrutiny, or "tests," to determine whether the law or action violates the equal protection clause. The courts use one of three standards: strict scrutiny, intermediate scrutiny, or the "rational basis" test.

Strict Scrutiny   If a law or action prohibits or inhibits some persons from exercising a fundamental right, the law or action will be subject to "strict scrutiny" by the courts. A classification based on a *suspect trait*—such as race, national origin, or citizenship status—will also be subject to strict scrutiny. Under this standard, the classification must be necessary to promote a *compelling government interest* (see page 17). Compelling state interests include remedying past unconstitutional or illegal discrimination, but do not include correcting the general effects of "society's discrimination."

EXAMPLE 1.22 For a city to give preference to minority applicants in awarding construction contracts, it normally must identify past unconstitutional or illegal discrimination against minority construction firms. Because the policy is based on suspect traits (race and national origin), it will violate the equal protection clause *unless* it is necessary to promote a compelling state interest. • Generally, few laws or actions survive strict-scrutiny analysis by the courts.

Intermediate Scrutiny   Another standard, that of "intermediate scrutiny," is applied in cases involving discrimination based on gender or legitimacy. Laws using these classifications must be *substantially related to important government objectives*. **EXAMPLE 1.23** An important government objective is preventing illegitimate teenage pregnancies. Because males and females are not similarly situated in this regard—only females can become pregnant—a law that punishes men but not women for statutory rape will be upheld even though it treats men and women unequally. •

The "Rational Basis" Test   In matters of economic and social welfare, a classification will be considered valid if there is any conceivable "rational basis" on which the classification might relate to a *legitimate government interest*. It is almost impossible for a law or action to fail the rational basis test. **EXAMPLE 1.24** A city ordinance that in effect prohibits all pushcart vendors, except a specific few, from operating in a particular area of the city will be upheld if the city offers a rational basis—such as reducing traffic in that area—for the ordinance. •

Privacy Rights

The U.S. Constitution does not explicitly mention a general right to privacy. It was not until the 1960s that a majority of the Supreme Court endorsed the view that the Constitution protects individual privacy rights. In a landmark 1965 case, *Griswold v. Connecticut*,[34] the

---

34. 381 U.S. 479, 85 S.Ct. 1678, 14 L.Ed.2d 510 (1965).

Supreme Court invalidated a Connecticut law that effectively prohibited the use of contraceptives on the ground that it violated the right to privacy. The Supreme Court held that a constitutional right to privacy was implied by the First, Third, Fourth, Fifth, and Ninth Amendments.

Today, privacy rights receive protection under various federal statutes as well the U.S. Constitution. State constitutions and statutes also secure individuals' privacy rights, often to a significant degree. Privacy rights are also protected to an extent under tort law (see Chapter 4), consumer law (see Chapter 12), and employment law (see Chapter 18). In this section, after a brief look at some of the most important federal statutes protecting the privacy of individuals, we examine some current topics related to privacy rights. One such topic, the debate over marriage equality laws, is discussed in this chapter's *Law, Diversity, and Business: Managerial Implications* feature below.

Federal Statutes Protecting Privacy Rights

In the last several decades, Congress has enacted a number of statues that protect the privacy of individuals in various areas of concern. Most of these statues deal with personal information collected by governments or private businesses. For example, the Freedom of

LAW, DIVERSITY, AND BUSINESS: MANAGERIAL IMPLICATIONS

MARRIAGE EQUALITY AND THE CONSTITUTION

The debate over whether to allow same-sex marriage has been raging across the country for many years. The legal issues raised by marriage equality involve both the privacy rights protected by state and federal constitutions and the full faith and credit clause of the U.S. Constitution, which requires states to enforce judicial decisions (and marriage decrees) issued in other states.

Although marriage equality may not appear at first glance to be business related, it is a pertinent legal issue for managers, as Target Corporation learned in 2010. The company contributed $150,000 to a political group backing the Republican candidate in the Minnesota gubernatorial race, who had taken a stand against same-sex marriage. Target insisted that it made its donation because of the candidate's probusiness stance. Nevertheless, boycotts of Target stores sprang up across the country.

State Laws   A few states have enacted laws that allow gay marriage, most of which have been challenged in court. For example, in 2011, just days after New York's same-sex marriage law took effect, a conservative group filed a lawsuit seeking to overturn all of the marriages performed under authority of that law. Numerous other states have passed statutes that define marriage solely as a union between a man and a woman.

In California, where same-sex couples had been able to obtain marriage certificates in the past, voters in 2008 enacted Proposition 8 to restrict marriage to one man and one woman. Then, in 2012, a federal appellate court struck down Proposition 8 as a violation of the equal protection clause, reasoning that it was not rationally related to California's interests. "Although the Constitution permits communities to enact most laws they believe to be desirable," the court stated, "it requires that there be at least a legitimate reason for the passage of a law that treats different classes of people differently." In the court's view, Prop 8 served no legitimate purpose other than to "lessen the status and human dignity of gay men and lesbians in California."[a]

Business Implications   *In this era of social networking, a company's policies can become public almost instantly—the boycotts of Target mentioned earlier were largely organized via Facebook. Consequently, businesspersons must carefully consider and address the rights and needs of their colleagues and employees who have different sexual orientations.*

At a minimum, managers should formulate policies that clearly specify how same-sex partners will be treated in terms of family and medical leave, health insurance coverage, pensions, and other benefits. Managers will need to evaluate their company's policies, taking into account such factors as the firm's size, location, composition, and client base.

a. *Perry v. Brown*, 671 F.3d 1052 (9th Cir. 2012).

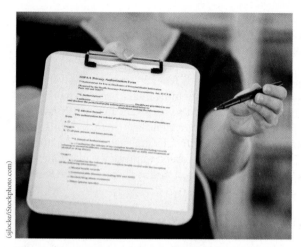

Hospital patients are always informed about privacy rights under HIPAA.

Information Act allows any person to request copies of any information about her or him contained in federal government files. In 1974, Congress passed the Privacy Act, which also gives persons the right to access such information. These and other major federal laws protecting privacy rights are listed and described in Exhibit 1.3 on the facing page.

In 1996, Congress passed the Health Insurance Portability and Accountability Act (HIPAA),[35] which protects the privacy of individuals' health records. This act defines and limits the circumstances in which an individual's "protected health information" may be used or disclosed.

HIPAA requires health-care providers and health-care plans, including certain employers who sponsor health plans, to inform patients of their privacy rights and of how their personal medical information may be used. The act also generally states that a person's medical records may not be used for purposes unrelated to health care—such as marketing—or disclosed to others without the individual's permission. In 2009, Congress expanded HIPAA's provisions to apply to *vendors* (those who maintain personal health records for health-care providers) and to electronic records shared by multiple medical providers. Congress also authorized the Federal Trade Commission to enforce HIPAA and pursue violators.

Technological Advances and Privacy Rights

Although advances in technology offer many benefits, they may also raise privacy issues. At the beginning of this chapter, we noted the concerns raised by the personal data collected by social networking sites. Here, we look briefly at two other areas in which technological developments are raising privacy issues today—the online dissemination of court records and the U.S. government's efforts to combat terrorism.

Court Records   The online dissemination of information concerning civil and criminal cases raises new privacy issues. Although court proceedings have always been a matter of public record, previously people had to go to a courthouse to examine the physical records. Now, technological improvements in information sharing allow civil and criminal justice records to be shared, synthesized, sold, and analyzed electronically. From anywhere in the world, private individuals, businesses, and other organizations can instantly access court records directly either in a state database or from a private data firm.

Moreover, states earn substantial revenues by selling certain records—such as residents' criminal history and tax records—to private data firms. These revenues make it unlikely that the states will refrain from selling such information in the future. Although most states have some privacy protections in place, once the information leaves the state's control, it can be given to anyone and used for any purpose. Additionally, if a state sells inaccurate or incomplete information to a company, there may be no way of correcting inaccuracies after the information has been sold.

The advent of electronically available court documents raises difficult questions about how to protect a person's privacy. Court records (and police reports) frequently disclose the names and addresses of witnesses and victims, and may also include their date of birth, ethnicity, Social Security number, credit information, and details about their children and family. Criminals might use this information to perpetrate identity theft (see Chapter 6) or to intimidate or harass a witness or victim. Employers and landlords may use the information

"The things most people want to know about are usually none of their business."

George Bernard Shaw, 1856–1950 (Irish dramatist and socialist)

35. 29 U.S.C.A. Sections 1181 *et seq.*

Exhibit 1.3 Federal Legislation Relating to Privacy

TITLE OF ACT	PROVISIONS CONCERNING PRIVACY
Freedom of Information Act (1966)	Provides that individuals have a right to obtain access to information about them collected in government files.
Family and Educational Rights and Privacy Act (1974)	Limits access to computer-stored records of education-related evaluations and grades in private and public colleges and universities.
Privacy Act (1974)	Protects the privacy of individuals about whom the federal government has information. Under this act, agencies that use or disclose personal information must make sure that the information is reliable and guard against its misuse. Individuals must be able to find out what data concerning them the agency is compiling and how the data will be used. In addition, the agency must give individuals a means to correct inaccurate data and must obtain their consent before using the data for any other purpose.
Tax Reform Act (1976)	Preserves the privacy of personal financial information.
Right to Financial Privacy Act (1978)	Prohibits financial institutions from providing the federal government with access to a customer's records unless the customer authorizes the disclosure.
Electronic Communications Privacy Act (1986)	Prohibits the interception of information communicated by electronic means.
Driver's Privacy Protection Act (1994)	Prevents states from disclosing or selling a driver's personal information without the driver's consent.
Health Insurance Portability and Accountability Act (1996)	Prohibits the use of a consumer's medical information for any purpose other than that for which such information was provided, unless the consumer expressly consents to the use.
Financial Services Modernization Act (Gramm-Leach-Bliley Act) (1999)	Prohibits the disclosure of nonpublic personal information about a consumer to an unaffiliated third party unless strict disclosure and opt-out requirements are met.

to screen potential applicants. An employer might decide not to hire a person who was involved in a civil or criminal case, and a landlord might not rent property to that person.

The USA Patriot Act   The USA Patriot Act was passed by Congress in the wake of the terrorist attacks of September 11, 2001, and then reauthorized in 2006.[36] The Patriot Act has given government officials increased authority to monitor Internet activities (such as e-mail and Web site visits) and to gain access to personal financial information and student information. Law enforcement officials may now track the telephone and e-mail communications of one party to find out the identity of the other party or parties. To gain access to these communications, the government must certify that the information likely to be obtained by such monitoring is relevant to an ongoing criminal investigation, but it does not need to provide proof of any wrongdoing. Privacy advocates argue that this law adversely affects the constitutional rights of all Americans, and it has been widely criticized in the media.

ETHICAL ISSUE

Does the threat of terrorism justify the U.S. government's use of body scanners at airports? The Transportation Security Administration (TSA) screens all persons seeking to board commercial airline flights for weapons, explosives, and other dangerous substances. In 2010, the TSA started using advanced imaging technology (AIT), or full-body scanners, as the primary screening device at many airports. Many travelers complained that they were being forced to undergo an electronic strip search because the scanners showed every part of one's body. Privacy advocates brought a lawsuit against the U.S. Department of Homeland Security, arguing that AIT was overly invasive and violated the Fourth Amendment's prohibition against unreasonable searches.

---

36. The Uniting and Strengthening America by Providing Appropriate Tools Required to Intercept and Obstruct Terrorism Act of 2001, also known as the USA Patriot Act, was enacted as Pub. L. No. 107-56 (2001) and reauthorized by Pub. L. No. 109-173 (2006).

In 2011, a federal appellate court held that the use of full-body scanners at airports was constitutional. The court balanced the intrusiveness of a full-body scan against a scan's ability to further a compelling governmental interest. Here, the government had a critical need to ensure airline safety, and the full-body scanners, which can detect liquids and powders in addition to traditional weapons, furthered that interest. The court also found, however, that the TSA had violated the Administrative Procedure Act by changing its regulations to require AIT without following formal rulemaking procedures (see page 4). Therefore, the court ordered the TSA to open itself up for public comments on the use of the scanners.[37]

---

37. *Electronic Privacy Information Center v. U.S. Department of Homeland Security,* 653 F.3d 1 (D.C.Cir. 2011).

Reviewing . . . The Constitutional Foundations

A state legislature enacted a statute that required any motorcycle operator or passenger on the state's highways to wear a protective helmet. Jim Alderman, a licensed motorcycle operator, sued the state to block enforcement of the law. Alderman asserted that the statute violated the equal protection clause because it placed requirements on motorcyclists that were not imposed on other motorists. Using the information presented in the chapter, answer the following questions.

1. Why does this statute raise equal protection issues instead of substantive due process concerns?
2. What are the three levels of scrutiny that the courts use in determining whether a law violates the equal protection clause?
3. Which level of scrutiny or test would apply to this situation? Why?
4. Applying this standard or test, is the helmet statute constitutional? Why or why not?

DEBATE THIS Legislation aimed at protecting people from themselves concerns the individual as well as the public in general. Protective helmet laws are just one example of such legislation. Should individuals be allowed to engage in unsafe activities if they choose to do so?

LINKING BUSINESS LAW to Management

Dealing with Administrative Law

Whether you work for a large corporation or own a small business, you will be dealing with multiple aspects of administrative law. Recall from page 3 that administrative law involves all of the rules, orders, and decisions of administrative agencies. All federal, state, and local government administrative agencies create rules that have the force of law. As a manager, you probably will need to pay more attention to administrative rules and regulations than to laws passed by local, state, and federal legislatures.

Federal versus State and Local Agency Regulations

The three levels of government create three levels of rules and regulations though their respective administrative agencies. At the federal level, these agencies include the Food and Drug Administration, the Equal Employment Opportunity Commission, and the Occupational Safety and Health Administration. At the state level, there are often agencies that govern business activities in a manner similar to federal agencies.

As a manager, you will have to learn about agency regulations that pertain to your business activities. It will be up to you, as a manager or small-business owner, to discern which of those regulations are most important and could potentially create the most liability if you violate them.

When Should You Participate in the Rulemaking Process?

All federal agencies and many state agencies invite public comments on proposed rules. Suppose that you manage a large construction company and your state occupational safety agency proposes a new rule requiring every employee on a construction site to wear hearing protection. You believe that the rule will lead to a *less* safe environment because your employees will not be able to communicate easily with one another.

Should you spend time offering comments to the agency? As an efficient manager, you make a trade-off calculation. First, you determine the value of the time that you would spend attempting to prevent or at least alter the proposed rule. Then you compare this implicit cost with your estimate of the potential benefits your company would receive if the rule is *not* put into place.

Be Prepared for Investigations

All administrative agencies have investigatory powers. Agencies' investigators usually have the power to search business premises, although normally they first have to obtain a search warrant. As a manager, you often have the choice of cooperating with agency investigators or providing just the minimum amount of assistance. If your business is routinely investigated, you will often opt for cooperation. In contrast, if your business is rarely investigated, you may decide that the on-site proposed inspection is overreaching. Then you must contact your company's attorney for advice on how to proceed.

If an administrative agency cites you for a regulatory violation, you will probably negotiate a settlement with the agency rather than take your case before an administrative law judge. Again, as a manager, you have to weigh the cost of the negotiated settlement with the potential cost of fighting the enforcement action.

Critical Thinking

Why are owner/operators of small businesses at a disadvantage relative to large corporations when they attempt to decipher complex regulations that apply to their businesses?

Key Terms

adjudicate 4	compelling government interest 17	international law 9	preemption 14
administrative agency 3	concurring opinion 41	interpretive rule 4	primary source of law 2
administrative law 3	constitutional law 2	law 1	procedural law 8
administrative law judge (ALJ) 5	criminal law 8	legislative rule 4	remedy 7
administrative process 4	cyberlaw 8	majority opinion 41	rulemaking 4
Bill of Rights 15	defendant 7	meta tag 20	secondary source of law 2
binding authority 6	dissenting opinion 41	national law 9	*stare decisis* 6
case law 5	due process clause 23	ordinance 3	statutory law 2
checks and balances 11	enabling legislation 4	*per curiam* opinion 41	substantive law 8
citation 3	equal protection clause 23	persuasive authority 6	supremacy clause 14
civil law 8	establishment clause 20	police powers 13	symbolic speech 16
civil law system 8	federal form of government 10	plaintiff 7	uniform law 3
commerce clause 11	filtering software 20	plurality opinion 41	
common law 5	free exercise clause 21	precedent 6	

Chapter Summary: The Constitutional Foundations

Sources of American Law (See pages 2–5.)	1. *Constitutional law*—The law as expressed in the U.S. Constitution and the various state constitutions. The U.S. Constitution is the supreme law of the land. State constitutions are supreme within state borders to the extent that they do not violate the U.S. Constitution or a federal law. 2. *Statutory law*—Laws or ordinances created by federal, state, and local legislatures and governing bodies. None of these laws can violate the U.S. Constitution or the relevant state constitutions. Uniform laws, when adopted by a state legislature, become statutory law in that state. 3. *Administrative law*—The rules, orders, and decisions of federal or state government administrative agencies. Federal administrative agencies are created by enabling legislation enacted by the U.S. Congress. Agency functions include rulemaking, investigation and enforcement, and adjudication. 4. *Case law and common law doctrines*—Judge-made law, including interpretations of constitutional provisions, of statutes enacted by legislatures, and of regulations created by administrative agencies. The common law—the doctrines and principles embodied in case law—governs all areas not covered by statutory law or administrative law.
The Common Law Tradition (See pages 5–8.)	1. *Common law*—Law that originated in medieval England with the creation of the king's courts, or *curiae regis,* and the development of a body of rules that were common to (or applied in) all regions of the country. 2. *Stare decisis*—A doctrine under which judges "stand on decided cases"—or follow the rule of precedent—in deciding cases. *Stare decisis* is the cornerstone of the common law tradition. 3. *Remedies*—A remedy is the means by which a court enforces a right or compensates for a violation of a right. Courts typically grant legal remedies (monetary damages) but may also grant equitable remedies (specific performance, injunction, or rescission) when the legal remedy is inadequate or unavailable.
Classifications of Law (See pages 8–9.)	The law may be broken down according to several classification systems, such as substantive or procedural law, federal or state law, and private or public law. Two broad classifications are civil and criminal law, and national and international law. Cyberlaw is not really a classification of law but a term that is used for the growing body of case and statutory law that applies to Internet transactions.

The Constitutional Powers of Government (See pages 9–15.)	The U.S. Constitution established a federal form of government, in which government powers are shared by the national government and the state governments. At the national level, government powers are divided among the legislative, executive, and judicial branches.
	1. *The commerce clause*—The commerce clause expressly permits Congress to regulate commerce. Over time, courts expansively interpreted this clause, thereby enabling the national government to wield extensive powers over the economic life of the nation.
	  a. Today, the commerce power authorizes the national government, at least theoretically, to regulate almost every commercial enterprise in the United States. In recent years, the Supreme Court has reined in somewhat the national government's regulatory powers under the commerce clause.
	  b. The Tenth Amendment reserves to the states all powers not expressly delegated to the national government. Under their police powers, state governments may regulate private activities in order to protect or promote the public order, health, safety, morals, and general welfare.
	  c. If state regulations substantially interfere with interstate commerce, they will be held to violate the "dormant commerce" clause of the U.S. Constitution. The positive aspect of the commerce clause, which gives the national government the exclusive authority to regulate interstate commerce, implies a "dormant" aspect—that the states do *not* have this power.
	2. *The supremacy clause*—The U.S. Constitution provides that the Constitution, laws, and treaties of the United States are "the supreme Law of the Land." Whenever a state law directly conflicts with a federal law, the state law is rendered invalid.

Business and the Bill of Rights (See pages 15–24.)	The Bill of Rights, which consists of the first ten amendments to the U.S. Constitution, was adopted in 1791 and embodies a series of protections for individuals—and, in some instances, business entities—against various types of interference by the federal government. Today, most of the protections apply against state governments as well. 1. *Freedom of speech*—Under the First Amendment, speech, including symbolic speech, is given the fullest possible protection by the courts. Corporate political speech and commercial speech also receive substantial protection under the First Amendment. Certain types of speech, such as defamatory speech and lewd or obscene speech, are not protected under the First Amendment. Government attempts to regulate unprotected forms of speech in the online environment have, to date, met with numerous challenges. 2. *Freedom of religion*—Under the First Amendment, the government may neither establish any religion (the establishment clause) nor prohibit the free exercise of religion (the free exercise clause). 3. *Due process*—Both the Fifth and the Fourteenth Amendments provide that no person shall be deprived of "life, liberty, or property, without due process of law." Procedural due process requires that any government decision to take life, liberty, or property must be made fairly, using fair procedures. Substantive due process focuses on the content of legislation. Generally, a law that limits a fundamental right violates substantive due process unless the law promotes a compelling state interest, such as public safety.

Chapter Summary: The Constitutional Foundations—Continued

Business and the Bill of Rights—Continued	4. *Equal protection*—Under the Fourteenth Amendment, a law or action that limits the liberty of some persons but not others may violate the equal protection clause. Such a law may be upheld, however, if there is a rational basis for the discriminatory treatment of a given group or if the law substantially relates to an important government objective.
Privacy Rights (See pages 24–28.)	Americans are increasingly becoming concerned about privacy issues raised by Internet-related technology. The Constitution does not contain a specific guarantee of a right to privacy, but such a right has been derived from guarantees found in several constitutional amendments. A number of federal statutes protect privacy rights. Privacy rights are also protected by many state constitutions and statutes, as well as under tort law.

ExamPrep

ISSUE SPOTTERS

1. Apples & Oranges Corporation learns that a federal administrative agency is considering a rule that will have a negative impact on the firm's ability to do business. Does the firm have any opportunity to express its opinion about the pending rule? Explain. **(See page 4.)**
2. Can a state, in the interest of energy conservation, ban all advertising by power utilities if conservation could be accomplished by less restrictive means? Why or why not? **(See pages 18–19.)**

—**Check your answers to the Issue Spotters against the answers provided in Appendix E at the end of this text.**

BEFORE THE TEST

Go to www.cengagebrain.com, enter the ISBN 9781133191353, and click on "Find" to locate this textbook's Web site. Then, click on "Access Now" under "Study Tools," and select Chapter 1 at the top. There, you will find a Practice Quiz that you can take to assess your mastery of the concepts in this chapter, as well as Flashcards, a Glossary of important terms, and Video Questions (when assigned).

For Review

Answers to the even-numbered questions in this For Review section can be found in Appendix F at the end of this text.

1. What are four primary sources of law in the United States?
2. What is a precedent? When might a court depart from precedent?
3. What is the difference between remedies at law and remedies in equity?
4. What constitutional clause gives the federal government the power to regulate commercial activities among the various states?
5. What is the Bill of Rights? What freedoms do the First Amendment guarantee?

Business Scenarios and Case Problems

1–1 Binding versus Persuasive Authority. A county court in Illinois is deciding a case involving an issue that has never been addressed before in that state's courts. The Iowa Supreme Court, however, recently decided a case involving a very similar fact pattern. Is the Illinois court obligated to follow the Iowa Supreme Court's decision on the issue? If the United States Supreme Court had decided a similar case, would that decision be binding on the Illinois court? Explain. (See page 6.)

1–2 Question with Sample Answer—Sources of Law. Under a Massachusetts state statute, large wineries could sell their products through wholesalers or to consumers directly, but not both. Small wineries could use both methods. Family Winemakers of California filed a suit against the state, arguing that this restriction gave small wineries a competitive advantage in violation of the U.S. Constitution. The court agreed that the statute was in conflict with the Constitution. Which source of law takes priority, and why? [*Family Winemakers of California v. Jenkins*, 592 F.3d 1 (1st Cir. 2010)] **(See page 2.)**

—For a sample answer to Question 1–2, go to Appendix G at the end of this text.

1–3 Due Process. The Russ College of Engineering and Technology of Ohio University announced in a press conference that it had found "rampant and flagrant plagiarism" in the theses of mechanical engineering graduate students. Faculty singled out for "ignoring their ethical responsibilities" included Jay Gunasekera, chair of the department. Gunasekera was prohibited from advising students. He filed a suit against Dennis Irwin, the dean of Russ College, for violating his due process rights. What does due process require in these circumstances? Why? [*Gunasekera v. Irwin*, 551 F.3d 461 (6th Cir. 2009)] **(See page 23.)**

1–4 The Commerce Clause. Under the federal Sex Offender Registration and Notification Act (SORNA), sex offenders must register and update their registration as sex offenders when they travel from one state to another. David Hall, a convicted sex offender in New York, moved to Virginia, where he did not update his registration. He was charged with violating SORNA. He claimed that the statute is unconstitutional, arguing that Congress cannot criminalize interstate travel if no commerce is involved. Is that reasonable? Why or why not? [*United States v. Guzman*, 591 F.3d 83 (2d Cir. 2010)] **(See pages 11–13.)**

1–5 **Case Problem with Sample Answer—Establishment Clause.** Judge James DeWeese hung a poster in his courtroom showing the Ten Commandments. The American Civil Liberties Union (ACLU) filed a suit, alleging that the poster violated the establishment clause. DeWeese responded that his purpose was not to promote religion but to express his view about "warring" legal philosophies—moral relativism and moral absolutism. "Our legal system is based on moral absolutes from divine law handed down by God through the Ten Commandments." Does this poster violate the establishment clause? Why or why not? [*American Civil Liberties Union of Ohio Foundation, Inc. v. DeWeese*, 633 F.3d 424 (6th Cir. 2011)] **(See page 20.)**

—For a sample answer to Problem 1–5, go to Appendix H at the end of this text.

1–6 **Spotlight on AOL—Common Law.** AOL, LLC, mistakenly made public the personal information of 650,000 of its members. The members filed a suit, alleging violations of California law. AOL asked the court to dismiss the suit on the basis of a "forum-selection" clause in its member agreement that designates Virginia courts as the place where member disputes will be tried. Under a decision of the United States Supreme Court, a forum-selection clause is unenforceable "if enforcement would contravene a strong public policy of the forum in which suit is brought." California has declared in other cases that the AOL clause contravenes a strong public policy. If the court applies the doctrine of *stare decisis*, will it dismiss the suit? Explain. [*Doe 1 v. AOL, LLC*, 552 F.3d 1077 (9th Cir. 2009)] **(See page 6.)**

1–7 The Dormant Commerce Clause. In 2001, Puerto Rico enacted a law that requires specific labels on cement sold in Puerto Rico and imposes fines for any violations of these requirements. The law prohibits the sale or distribution of cement manufactured outside Puerto Rico that does not carry a required label warning that the cement may not be used in government-financed construction projects. Antilles Cement Corp., a Puerto Rican firm that imports foreign cement, filed a complaint in federal court, claiming that this law violated the dormant commerce clause. (The dormant commerce clause doctrine applies not only to commerce among the states and U.S. territories, but also to international commerce.) Did the 2001 Puerto Rican law violate the dormant commerce clause? Why or why not? [*Antilles Cement Corp. v. Fortuno*, 670 F.3d 310 (1st Cir. 2012)] **(See page 14.)**

1–8 **A Question of Ethics—Free Speech.** Aric Toll owns and manages the Balboa Island Village Inn, a restaurant and bar in Newport Beach, California. Anne Lemen lives across from the Inn. Lemen complained to the authorities about the Inn's customers, whom she called "drunks" and "whores." Lemen told the Inn's bartender Ewa Cook that Cook "worked for Satan." She repeated her statements to potential customers, and the Inn's sales dropped more than 20 percent. The Inn filed a suit against Lemen. [*Balboa Island Village Inn, Inc. v. Lemen*, 40 Cal.4th 1141, 156 P.3d 339 (2007)] **(See page 17.)**

1. Are Lemen's statements about the Inn's owners and customers protected by the U.S. Constitution? In whose favor should the court rule? Why?
2. Did Lemen behave unethically in the circumstances of this case? Explain.

Critical Thinking and Writing Assignments

1–9 Business Law Writing. John's company is involved in a lawsuit with a customer, Beth. John argues that for fifty years higher courts in that state have decided cases involving circumstances similar to his case in a way that indicates he can expect a ruling in his company's favor. Write at least one paragraph discussing if this is a valid argument. Write another paragraph discussing whether the judge in this case must rule as those other judges did, and why. **(See pages 6–7.)**

1–10 **Business Law Critical Thinking Group Assignment.** For many years, New York City has had to deal with the vandalism and defacement of public property caused by unauthorized graffiti. In an effort to stop the damage, the city banned the sale of aerosol spray-paint cans and broad-tipped indelible markers to persons under twenty-one years of age. The new rules also prohibited people from possessing these items on property other than their own. Within a year, five people under age twenty-one were cited for violations of these regulations, and 871 individuals were arrested for actually making graffiti.

Lindsey Vincenty and other artists wished to create graffiti on legal surfaces, such as canvas, wood, and clothing but were unable to buy supplies in the city or to carry them in the city if they were bought elsewhere. Vincenty and others filed a lawsuit on behalf of themselves and other young artists against Michael Bloomberg, the city's mayor, and others. The plaintiffs claimed that, among other things, the new rules violated their right to freedom of speech.

1. One group will argue in favor of the plaintiffs and provide several reasons why the court should hold that the city's new rules violate the plaintiffs' freedom of speech.

2. Another group will develop a counterargument that outlines the reasons why the new rules do not violate free speech rights.

3. A third group will argue that the city's ban violates the equal protection clause because it applies only to persons under age twenty-one.

Appendix to Chapter 1:
Finding and Analyzing the Law

The statutes, agency regulations, and case law referred to in this text establish the rights and duties of businesspersons engaged in various types of activities. The cases presented in the following chapters provide you with concise, real-life illustrations of how the courts interpret and apply these laws. Because of the importance of knowing how to find statutory, administrative, and case law, this appendix offers a brief introduction to how these laws are published and to the legal "shorthand" employed in referencing these legal sources.

Finding Statutory and Administrative Law

When Congress passes laws, they are collected in a publication titled *United States Statutes at Large*. When state legislatures pass laws, they are collected in similar state publications. Most frequently, however, laws are referred to in their codified form—that is, the form in which they appear in the federal and state codes. In these codes, laws are compiled by subject.

United States Code

The *United States Code* (U.S.C.) arranges all existing federal laws of a public and permanent nature by subject. Each of the fifty subjects into which the U.S.C. arranges the laws is given a title and a title number. For example, laws relating to commerce and trade are collected in "Title 15, Commerce and Trade." Titles are subdivided by sections. A citation to the U.S.C. includes title and section numbers. Thus, a reference to "15 U.S.C. Section 1" means that the statute can be found in Section 1 of Title 15. ("Section" may be designated by the symbol §, and "Sections" by §§.) In addition to the print publication of the U.S.C., the federal government also provides a searchable online database of the *United States Code* at **www.gpo.gov** (click on "Libraries" and then "Core Documents of Our Democracy" to find the *United States Code*).

Commercial publications of these laws are available and are widely used. For example, West Group publishes the *United States Code Annotated* (U.S.C.A.). The U.S.C.A. contains the complete text of laws included in the U.S.C., notes of court decisions that interpret and apply specific sections of the statutes, and the text of presidential proclamations and executive orders. The U.S.C.A. also includes research aids, such as cross-references to related statutes, historical notes, and other references. A citation to the U.S.C.A. is similar to a citation to the U.S.C.: "15 U.S.C.A. Section 1."

State Codes

State codes follow the U.S.C. pattern of arranging laws by subject. The state codes may be called codes, revisions, compilations, consolidations, general statutes, or statutes, depending on the state. In some codes, subjects are designated by number. In others, they are designated by name. For example, "13 Pennsylvania Consolidated Statutes Section 1101" means that the statute can be found in Title 13, Section 1101, of the Pennsylvania code. "California Commercial Code Section 1101" means the statute can be found in Section 1101 under the subject heading "Commercial Code" of the California code. Abbreviations may be used. For example, "13 Pennsylvania Consolidated Statutes Section 1101" may be abbreviated

"13 Pa. C.S. § 1101," and "California Commercial Code Section 1101" may be abbreviated "Cal. Com. Code § 1101."

Administrative Rules

Rules and regulations adopted by federal administrative agencies are compiled in the *Code of Federal Regulations* (C.F.R.). Like the U.S.C., the C.F.R. is divided into fifty titles. Rules within each title are assigned section numbers. A full citation to the C.F.R. includes title and section numbers. For example, a reference to "17 C.F.R. Section 230.504" means that the rule can be found in Section 230.504 of Title 17.

Finding Case Law

Before discussing the case reporting system, we need to look briefly at the court system (which will be discussed in detail in Chapter 3). There are two types of courts in the United States: federal courts and state courts. Both the federal and the state court systems consist of several levels, or tiers, of courts. *Trial courts,* in which evidence is presented and testimony is given, are on the bottom tier (which also includes lower courts handling specialized issues). Decisions from a trial court can be appealed to a higher court, which commonly would be an intermediate *court of appeals,* or an *appellate court.* Decisions from these intermediate courts of appeals may be appealed to an even higher court, such as a state supreme court or the United States Supreme Court.

State Court Decisions

Most state trial court decisions are not published. Except in New York and a few other states that publish selected opinions of their trial courts, decisions from state trial courts are merely filed in the office of the clerk of the court, where the decisions are available for public inspection. (Increasingly, they can be found online as well.)

Written decisions of the appellate, or reviewing, courts, however, are published and distributed. As you will note, most of the state court cases presented in this book are from state appellate courts. The reported appellate decisions are published in volumes called *reports* or *reporters,* which are numbered consecutively. State appellate court decisions are found in the state reporters of that particular state.

Additionally, state court opinions appear in regional units of the *National Reporter System,* published by West Group. Most lawyers and libraries have the West reporters because they report cases more quickly and are distributed more widely than the state-published reports. In fact, many states have eliminated their own reporters in favor of West's National Reporter System. The National Reporter System divides the states into the following geographic areas: *Atlantic* (A. or A.2d), *North Eastern* (N.E. or N.E.2d), *North Western* (N.W. or N.W.2d), *Pacific* (P., P.2d, or P.3d), *South Eastern* (S.E. or S.E.2d), *South Western* (S.W., S.W.2d, or S.W.3d), and *Southern* (So., So.2d, or So.3d). (The *2d* and *3d* in the abbreviations refer to *Second Series* and *Third Series,* respectively.) The states included in each of these regional divisions are indicated in Exhibit 1A.1 on the following page, which illustrates West's National Reporter System.

After appellate decisions have been published, they are normally referred to (cited) by the name of the case; the volume, name, and page number of the state's official reporter (if different from West's National Reporter System); the volume, name, and page number of the *National Reporter;* and the volume, name, and page number of any other selected reporter. This information is included in the *citation.* (Citing a reporter by volume number, name, and page number, in that order, is common to all citations.) When more than one reporter is cited for the same case, each reference is called a *parallel citation.* Note that some states have adopted a "public domain citation system" that uses a somewhat different format for

Exhibit 1A.1 West's National Reporter System—Regional/Federal

Regional Reporters	Coverage Beginning	Coverage
Atlantic Reporter (A., A.2d, or A.3d)	1885	Connecticut, Delaware, District of Columbia, Maine, Maryland, New Hampshire, New Jersey, Pennsylvania, Rhode Island, and Vermont.
North Eastern Reporter (N.E. or N.E.2d)	1885	Illinois, Indiana, Massachusetts, New York, and Ohio.
North Western Reporter (N.W. or N.W.2d)	1879	Iowa, Michigan, Minnesota, Nebraska, North Dakota, South Dakota, and Wisconsin.
Pacific Reporter (P., P.2d, or P.3d)	1883	Alaska, Arizona, California, Colorado, Hawaii, Idaho, Kansas, Montana, Nevada, New Mexico, Oklahoma, Oregon, Utah, Washington, and Wyoming.
South Eastern Reporter (S.E. or S.E.2d)	1887	Georgia, North Carolina, South Carolina, Virginia, and West Virginia.
South Western Reporter (S.W., S.W.2d, or S.W.3d)	1886	Arkansas, Kentucky, Missouri, Tennessee, and Texas.
Southern Reporter (So., So.2d, or So.3d)	1887	Alabama, Florida, Louisiana, and Mississippi.

Federal Reporters		
Federal Reporter (F., F.2d, or F.3d)	1880	U.S. Circuit Courts from 1880 to 1912; U.S. Commerce Court from 1911 to 1913; U.S. District Courts from 1880 to 1932; U.S. Court of Claims (now called U.S. Court of Federal Claims) from 1929 to 1932 and since 1960; U.S. Courts of Appeals since 1891; U.S. Court of Customs and Patent Appeals since 1929; U.S. Emergency Court of Appeals since 1943.
Federal Supplement (F.Supp. or F.Supp.2d)	1932	U.S. Court of Claims from 1932 to 1960; U.S. District Courts since 1932; U.S. Customs Court since 1956.
Federal Rules Decisions (F.R.D.)	1939	U.S. District Courts involving the Federal Rules of Civil Procedure since 1939 and Federal Rules of Criminal Procedure since 1946.
Supreme Court Reporter (S.Ct.)	1882	United States Supreme Court since the October term of 1882.
Bankruptcy Reporter (Bankr.)	1980	Bankruptcy decisions of U.S. Bankruptcy Courts, U.S. District Courts, U.S. Courts of Appeals, and the United States Supreme Court.
Military Justice Reporter (M.J.)	1978	U.S. Court of Military Appeals and Courts of Military Review for the Army, Navy, Air Force, and Coast Guard.

NATIONAL REPORTER SYSTEM MAP

Legend:
- Pacific
- North Western
- South Western
- North Eastern
- Atlantic
- South Eastern
- Southern

the citation. For example, in Wisconsin, a Wisconsin Supreme Court decision might be designated "2012 WI 23," meaning that the decision was the twenty-third issued by the Wisconsin Supreme Court in the year 2012. Parallel citations to the *Wisconsin Reports* and West's *North Western Reporter* are still included after the public domain citation.

Consider the following citation: *Goldstein v. Lackard,* 81 Mass.App.Ct. 1112, 961 N.E.2d. 163 (2012). We see that the opinion in this case can be found in Volume 81 of the official *Massachusetts Appellate Court Reports,* on page 1112. The parallel citation is to Volume 961 of the *North Eastern Reporter, Second Series,* page 163. When we present opinions in this text, in addition to the reporter, we give the name of the court hearing the case and the year of the court's decision. Sample citations to state court decisions are listed and explained in Exhibit 1A.2 on pages 38–40.

Federal Court Decisions

Federal district (trial) court decisions are published unofficially in the *Federal Supplement* (F. Supp. or F.Supp.2d), and opinions from the circuit courts of appeals (federal reviewing courts) are reported unofficially in the *Federal Reporter* (F., F.2d, or F.3d). Cases concerning federal bankruptcy law are published unofficially in West's *Bankruptcy Reporter* (Bankr. or B.R.).

The official edition of United States Supreme Court decisions is the *United States Reports* (U.S.), which is published by the federal government. Unofficial editions of Supreme Court cases include West's *Supreme Court Reporter* (S.Ct.) and the *Lawyers' Edition of the Supreme Court Reports* (L.Ed. or L.Ed.2d). Sample citations for federal court decisions are also listed and explained in Exhibit 1A.2.

Unpublished Opinions

Many court opinions that are not yet published or that are not intended for publication can be accessed through Westlaw® (abbreviated in citations as "WL"), an online legal database. When no citation to a published reporter is available for cases cited in this text, we give the WL citation (such as 2012 WL 573109, which means it was case number 573109 decided in the year 2012). Sometimes, both in this text and in other legal sources, you will see blanks left in a citation. This occurs when the decision will be published, but the particular volume number or page number is not yet available.

Old Cases

On a few occasions, this text cites opinions from old, classic cases dating to the nineteenth century or earlier. Some of these cases are from the English courts. The citations to these cases may not conform to the descriptions given above because they were published in reporters that are no longer used today.

Reading and Understanding Case Law

The cases in this text have been condensed from the full text of the courts' opinions and paraphrased by the authors. For those wishing to review court cases for future research projects or to gain additional legal information, the following sections will provide useful insights into how to read and understand case law.

Case Titles and Terminology

The title of a case, such as *Adams v. Jones,* indicates the names of the parties to the lawsuit. The *v.* in the case title stands for *versus,* which means "against." In the trial court, Adams was the plaintiff—the person who filed the suit. Jones was the defendant. If the case is

Exhibit 1A.2 How to Read Citations

STATE COURTS

282 Neb. 990, 808 N.W.2d 48 (2012)ª

> *N.W.* is the abbreviation for West's publication of state court decisions rendered in the *North Western Reporter* of the National Reporter System. *2d* indicates that this case was included in the *Second Series* of that reporter. The number 808 refers to the volume number of the reporter; the number 48 refers to the page in that volume on which this case begins.

> *Neb.* is an abbreviation for *Nebraska Reports,* Nebraska's official reports of the decisions of its highest court, the Nebraska Supreme Court.

204 Cal.App.4th 112, 138 Cal.Rptr.3d 519 (2012)

> *Cal.Rptr.* is the abbreviation for West's unofficial reports—titled *California Reporter*—of the decisions of California courts.

93 A.D.3d 493, 940 N.Y.S.2d 75 (2012)

> *N.Y.S.* is the abbreviation for West's unofficial reports—titled *New York Supplement*—of the decisions of New York courts.

> *A.D.* is the abbreviation for *Appellate Division*, which hears appeals from the New York Supreme Court—the state's general trial court. The New York Court of Appeals is the state's highest court, analogous to other states' supreme courts.

313 Ga.App. 804, 723 S.E.2d 39 (2012)

> *Ga.App.* is the abbreviation for *Georgia Appeals Reports,* Georgia's official reports of the decisions of its court of appeals.

FEDERAL COURTS

___ U.S. ___, 132 S.Ct. 1201, 182 L.Ed.2d 42 (2012)

> *L.Ed.* is an abbreviation for *Lawyers' Edition of the Supreme Court Reports*, an unofficial edition of decisions of the United States Supreme Court.

> *S.Ct.* is the abbreviation for West's unofficial reports—titled *Supreme Court Reporter*—of decisions of the United States Supreme Court.

> *U.S.* is the abbreviation for *United States Reports*, the official edition of the decisions of the United States Supreme Court. The blank lines in this citation (or any other citation) indicate that the appropriate volume of the case reporter has not yet been published and no page number is available.

a. The case names have been deleted from these citations to emphasize the publications. It should be kept in mind, however, that the name of a case is as important as the specific page numbers in the volumes in which it is found. If a citation is incorrect, the correct citation may be found in a publication's index of case names. In addition to providing a check on errors in citations, the date of a case is important because the value of a recent case as an authority is likely to be greater than that of older cases from the same court.

Exhibit 1A.2 How to Read Citations—Continued

FEDERAL COURTS (Continued)

668 F.3d 1148 (9th Cir. 2012)

9th Cir. is an abbreviation denoting that this case was decided in the U.S. Court of Appeals for the Ninth Circuit.

___ F.Supp.2d ___ (S.D. Fla. 2012)

S.D. Fla. is an abbreviation indicating that the U.S. District Court for the Southern District of Florida decided this case.

ENGLISH COURTS

9 Exch. 341, 156 Eng.Rep. 145 (1854)

Eng.Rep. is an abbreviation for *English Reports, Full Reprint,* a series of reports containing selected decisions made in English courts between 1378 and 1865.

Exch. is an abbreviation for *English Exchequer Reports,* which includes the original reports of cases decided in England's Court of Exchequer.

STATUTORY AND OTHER CITATIONS

18 U.S.C. Section 1961(1)(A)

U.S.C. denotes *United States Code,* the codification of *United States Statutes at Large.* The number 18 refers to the statute's U.S.C. title number and 1961 to its section number within that title. The number 1 in parentheses refers to a subsection within the section, and the letter A in parentheses to a subsection within the subsection.

UCC 2–206(1)(b)

UCC is an abbreviation for *Uniform Commercial Code.* The first number 2 is a reference to an article of the UCC, and 206 to a section within that article. The number 1 in parentheses refers to a subsection within the section, and the letter b in parentheses to a subsection within the subsection.

Restatement (Third) of Torts, Section 6

Restatement (Third) of Torts refers to the third edition of the American Law Institute's *Restatement of the Law of Torts.* The number 6 refers to a specific section.

17 C.F.R. Section 230.505

C.F.R. is an abbreviation for *Code of Federal Regulations,* a compilation of federal administrative regulations. The number 17 designates the regulation's title number, and 230.505 designates a specific section within that title.

Continued

Exhibit 1A.2 How to Read Citations—Continued

WESTLAW® CITATIONS[b]

2012 WL 3235164

WL is an abbreviation for Westlaw. The number 2012 is the year of the document that can be found with this citation in the Westlaw database. The number 3235164 is a number assigned to a specific document. A higher number indicates that a document was added to the Westlaw database later in the year.

UNIFORM RESOURCE LOCATORS (URLs)

http://www.westlaw.com[c]

The suffix *com* is the top-level domain (TLD) for this Web site. The TLD *com* is an abbreviation for "commercial," which usually means that a for-profit entity hosts (maintains or supports) this Web site.

westlaw is the host name—the part of the domain name selected by the organization that registered the name. In this case, West Group registered the name. This Internet site is the Westlaw database on the Web.

www is an abbreviation for "World Wide Web." The Web is a system of Internet servers that support documents formatted in *HTML* (hypertext markup language) and other formats as well.

http://www.uscourts.gov

This is "The Federal Judiciary Home Page." The host is the Administrative Office of the U.S. Courts. The TLD *gov* is an abbreviation for "government." This Web site includes information and links from, and about, the federal courts.

http://www.law.cornell.edu/index.html

This part of a URL points to a Web page or file at a specific location within the host's domain. This page is a menu with links to documents within the domain and to other Internet resources.

This is the host name for a Web site that contains the Internet publications of the Legal Information Institute (LII), which is a part of Cornell Law School. The LII site includes a variety of legal materials and links to other legal resources on the Internet. The TLD *edu* is an abbreviation for "educational institution" (a school or a university).

http://www.ipl.org/div/news

This part of the Web site points to a static *news* page at this Web site, which provides links to online newspapers from around the world.

ipl is an abbreviation for "Internet Public Library," which is an online service that provides reference resources and links to other information services on the Web. The IPL is supported chiefly by the School of Information at the University of Michigan. The TLD *org* is an abbreviation for "organization" (normally nonprofit).

div is an abbreviation for "division," which is the way that the Internet Public Library tags the content on its Web site as relating to a specific topic.

b. Many court decisions that are not yet published or that are not intended for publication can be accessed through Westlaw, an online legal database.

c. The basic form for a URL is "service://hostname/path." The Internet service for all of the URLs in this text is *http* (hypertext transfer protocol). Because most Web browsers add this prefix automatically when a user enters a host name or a hostname/path, we have generally omitted the *http://* from the URLs listed in this text.

appealed, however, the appellate court will sometimes place the name of the party appealing the decision first, so the case may be called *Jones v. Adams*. Because some reviewing courts retain the trial court order of names, it is often impossible to distinguish the plaintiff from the defendant in the title of a reported appellate court decision. You must carefully read the facts of each case to identify the parties.

The following terms and phrases are frequently encountered in court opinions and legal publications. Because it is important to understand what these terms and phrases mean, we define and discuss them here.

Parties to Lawsuits

As mentioned in Chapter 1, the party initiating a lawsuit is referred to as the *plaintiff* or *petitioner,* depending on the nature of the action, and the party against whom a lawsuit is brought is the *defendant* or *respondent*. Lawsuits frequently involve more than one plaintiff and/or defendant. When a case is appealed, the party appealing the case is called the *appellant*. The *appellee* is the party against whom the appeal is taken. (In some appellate courts, the party appealing a case is referred to as the *petitioner,* and the party against whom the suit is brought or appealed is called the *respondent*.)

Judges and Justices

The terms *judge* and *justice* are usually synonymous. All members of the United States Supreme Court are referred to as justices. Appellate court judges are also usually called justices, although this is not always the case. In New York, a justice is a judge of the trial court (which is called the Supreme Court), and a member of the Court of Appeals (the state's highest court) is called a judge. The term *justice* is commonly abbreviated to J., and *justices* to JJ. A Supreme Court case might refer to Justice Sotomayor as Sotomayor, J., or to Chief Justice Roberts as Roberts, C.J.

Decisions and Opinions

Most decisions reached by reviewing, or appellate, courts are explained in written *opinions*. The opinion contains the court's reasons for its decision, the rules of law that apply, and the judgment. You may encounter several types of opinions as you read appellate cases, including the following:

- When all the judges (or justices) agree, a *unanimous opinion* is written for the entire court.
- When there is not unanimous agreement, a **majority opinion** is generally written. It outlines the views of the majority of the judges deciding the case.
- A judge who agrees (concurs) with the majority opinion as to the result but not as to the legal reasoning often writes a **concurring opinion.** In it, the judge explains the reasoning that he or she considers correct.
- A **dissenting opinion** presents the views of one or more judges who disagree with the majority view. The dissenting opinion is important because it may form the basis of arguments used years later in overturning the precedential majority opinion.
- Sometimes, no single position is fully supported by a majority of the judges deciding a case. In this situation, we may have a **plurality opinion.** This is the opinion that has the support of the largest number of judges, but the group in agreement is less than a majority.
- Finally, a court occasionally issues a ***per curiam* opinion** (*per curiam* is Latin for "of the court"), which does not indicate which judge wrote the opinion.

A Sample Court Case

Knowing how to read and analyze a court opinion is an essential step in undertaking accurate legal research. A further step involves "briefing" the case. Legal researchers routinely brief cases by summarizing and reducing the texts of the opinions to their essential elements. Briefing cases facilitates the development of critical thinking skills that are crucial

Majority Opinion A court opinion that represents the views of the majority (more than half) of the judges or justices deciding the case.

Concurring Opinion A court opinion by one or more judges or justices who agree with the majority but want to make or emphasize a point that was not made or emphasized in the majority's opinion.

Dissenting Opinion A court opinion that presents the views of one or more judges or justices who disagree with the majority's decision.

Plurality Opinion A court opinion that is supported by the largest number of the judges or justices hearing the case, but less than half of the total number.

***Per Curiam* Opinion** A court opinion that does not indicate which judge or justice authored the opinion.

for businesspersons when evaluating relevant business law. (For instructions on how to brief a case, go to Appendix A at the end of this text.)

The cases contained within the chapters of this text have already been analyzed and briefed by the authors, and the essential aspects of each case are presented in a convenient format consisting of four basic sections: *Facts, Issue, Decision,* and *Reason,* as shown in Exhibit 1A.3 below, which has also been annotated (see the next page) to illustrate the kind of information that is contained in each section.

Throughout this text, in addition to this basic format, we sometimes include a special introductory section entitled *Historical and Social [Economic, Technological, Political,* or *other] Setting.* In some instances, a *Company Profile* is included in place of the introductory setting. These profiles provide background on one of the parties to the lawsuit.

Each case is followed by a question or section that is designed to enhance your analysis. *Critical Thinking* sections, such as the one shown in Exhibit 1A.3, present a question about some issue raised by the case. *Why Is This Case Important?* sections explain the significance of the case. *What If the Facts Were Different?* questions alter the facts slightly and ask you to consider how this would change the outcome. A section entitled *Impact of This Case on Today's Law* concludes each of the *Classic Cases* that appear throughout the text to indicate the significance of the case for today's legal landscape.

Exhibit 1A.3 A Sample Court Case

Sample Case

United States v. Jones

1

FACTS Antoine Jones owned and operated a nightclub in the District of Columbia and was suspected of drug trafficking. As part of an investigation, the government installed a Global Positioning System (GPS) tracking device underneath a vehicle belonging to Jones's wife. Although it did not have a valid warrant, the government tracked the vehicle for four weeks, ultimately gathering enough evidence of drug trafficking to obtain an indictment. Before the trial, Jones filed a motion to suppress the evidence obtained with the device, arguing that the government had violated his Fourth Amendment rights by subjecting him to an unlawful "search." The district court held that most of the evidence was admissible, and Jones was convicted and sentenced to life in prison. A federal appellate court reversed the conviction, and the government appealed to the United States Supreme Court.

4

ISSUE Did the government engage in a "search" within the meaning of the Fourth Amendment by installing the GPS tracking device and then monitoring the vehicle's movements?

5

DECISION Yes. The United States Supreme Court affirmed the judgment of the federal appellate court. The government engaged in a Fourth Amendment "search" by installing and using the tracking device.

6

Supreme Court of the United States **2**
___ U.S.___, 132 S.Ct. 945, 181 L.Ed.2d 911 (2012). **3**
www.supremecourt.gov/opinions/11pdf/10-1259.pdf

(Radoslav Stoilov/Shutterstock.com)

Tracking device for automobiles.

REASON The Fourth Amendment prohibits "unreasonable searches and seizures" based on "the right of the people to be secure in their persons, houses, papers, and effects." A vehicle is an "effect," and the government's installation and use of the tracking device constituted a "search." Traditionally, the Supreme Court recognized the Fourth Amendment's close connection to property rights and found a "search" only if the government's conduct would have amounted to trespass under English common law. In 1967, however, the Supreme Court ruled that the Fourth Amendment also protects a person's "reasonable expectation of privacy."

7

Whether or not Jones had a reasonable expectation of privacy in either the vehicle's undercarriage or its movements on public streets was irrelevant in this situation. The Court reasoned that its precedent on privacy did not eliminate the traditional rule that a common law trespass may also establish a search. In this case, the government engaged in trespass, and therefore a search, by installing the tracking device without consent.

CRITICAL THINKING—Ethical Consideration *Was the government's conduct ethical? Why or why not?* **8**

Review of Sample Court Case

1 The name of the case is *United States v. Jones*. The government prosecuted Jones in federal court, and now the government is appealing, or challenging, a decision by the U.S. Court of Appeals for the District of Columbia (the federal appellate court).

2 The court deciding this case is the United States Supreme Court.

3 The case citation includes a citation to the *Supreme Court Reporter*, which contains only decisions of the United States Supreme Court. The case can be found in Volume 132 of the *Supreme Court Reporter*, beginning on page 945. The heading also provides a Web address at which you can view the opinion.

4 The *Facts* section identifies the parties, summarizes the relevant facts, and explains the procedural history leading up to the decision being summarized.

5 The *Issue* section presents the central issue(s) that the court must decide. In this case, for example, the United States Supreme Court must determine whether the government's conduct constituted a "search" for purposes of the Fourth Amendment. Most cases address more than one issue, but this textbook's authors have edited many cases to focus on just one issue.

6 The *Decision* section summarizes the court's decision about an issue. The decision reflects the opinion of the judge or, if a panel heard the case, the majority's opinion. For an appellate court case, the *Decision* section will frequently explain whether the appellate court "affirmed" or "reversed" a lower court's ruling. In either situation, the appellate court may remand the case, meaning it sends the case back for further proceedings consistent with its decision.

7 The *Reason* section explains how the court arrived at its decision, summarizing the key legal principles and authorities. In the *Jones* case, for example, the Supreme Court held that the government performed a Fourth Amendment search by installing and using a GPS tracking device. The Court found that a search may occur if the government violates either a reasonable expectation of privacy or a person's property rights.

8 The *Critical Thinking* section raises a question relating to the summarized case. Here, the question concerns an "ethical" consideration. Other cases in this text raise critical thinking questions that focus on diversity, e-commerce, economics, global, legal environment, political, social, or technological issues.

Ethics and Business Decision Making

LEARNING OBJECTIVES

The five learning objectives below are designed to help improve your understanding of the chapter. After reading this chapter, you should be able to answer the following questions:

1 What is business ethics, and why is it important?

2 How can business leaders encourage their companies to act ethically?

3 How do duty-based ethical standards differ from outcome-based ethical standards?

4 What are six guidelines that an employee can use to evaluate whether his or her actions are ethical?

5 What types of ethical issues might arise in the context of international business transactions?

(pixdeluxe/iStockphoto.com)

"New occasions teach new duties."
—James Russell Lowell, 1819–1891 (American editor, poet, and diplomat)

Ethics scandals erupted throughout corporate America during the first decade of the 2000s. Heads of major corporations were tried for fraud, conspiracy, grand larceny, and obstruction of justice. For example, Jeffrey Skilling, the head of Enron Corporation (a multibillion-dollar enterprise that ended in one of the largest bankruptcies in U.S. history), was convicted of securities fraud and insider trading for deceiving investors and covering up losses.

Ethical problems plagued many U.S. financial institutions and Wall Street firms as well. These ethical scandals contributed to the onset of the deepest recession since the Great Depression of the 1930s. In the economic crisis that began in 2008, not only did some $9 trillion in investment capital evaporate, but millions of workers lost their jobs. Many people lost their life savings in a Ponzi scheme (an illegal pyramid operation) perpetrated for decades by Bernard Madoff, who pleaded guilty in 2009 to bilking investors out of more than $65 billion.

In short, the scope and scale of corporate unethical behavior, especially in the financial sector, skyrocketed (with enormous repercussions worldwide). As the chapter-opening quotation states, "New occasions teach new duties." The ethics scandals of the last several years have taught everyone that business ethics cannot be taken lightly. How businesspersons should act and whose interests they should consider—those of the firm, its executives, its employees, its shareholders, and more—are the focus of this chapter on business ethics.

Business Ethics

Ethics Moral principles and values applied to social behavior.

As you might imagine, business ethics is derived from the concept of ethics. **Ethics** can be defined as the study of what constitutes right or wrong behavior. It is the branch of philosophy that focuses on morality and the way in which moral principles are derived and applied to one's conduct in daily life. Ethics has to do with questions relating to the fairness, justness, rightness, or wrongness of an action.

Business Ethics What constitutes right or wrong behavior and the application of moral principles in a business context.

Business ethics focuses on what constitutes right or wrong behavior in the business world and on how businesspersons apply moral and ethical principles to situations that arise in the workplace. Because business decision makers often address more complex ethical dilemmas than they face in their personal lives, business ethics is more complicated than personal ethics.

Why Is Business Ethics Important?

LEARNING OBJECTIVE 1
What is business ethics, and why is it important?

To see why business ethics is so important, think about the corporate executives who were sentenced to prison for the crimes that you read about in the first paragraphs of this chapter. They could have avoided this outcome had they engaged in ethical decision making during their careers. As a result of their crimes, all of their companies suffered losses, and some were forced to enter bankruptcy, causing thousands of workers to lose their jobs.

Moral Minimum The minimum degree of ethical behavior expected of a businessperson, which is usually defined as compliance with the law.

If the executives had acted ethically, the corporations, shareholders, and employees of those companies would not have paid such a high price. Thus, an in-depth understanding of business ethics is important to the long-run viability of a corporation. It is also important to the well-being of individual officers and directors and to the firm's employees. Finally, unethical corporate decision making can negatively affect suppliers, consumers, the community, and society as a whole.

The Moral Minimum

The minimum acceptable standard for ethical business behavior—known as the **moral minimum**—normally is considered to be compliance with the law. In many corporate scandals, had most of the businesspersons involved simply followed the law, they would not have gotten into trouble. Note, though, that in the interest of preserving personal freedom, as well as for practical reasons, the law does not—and cannot—codify all ethical requirements.

As they make business decisions, businesspersons must remember that just because an action is legal does not necessarily make it ethical. For instance, no law specifies the salaries that public corporations can pay their officers. Nevertheless, if a corporation pays its officers an excessive amount relative to other employees, or to what officers at other corporations are paid, the executives' compensation might be challenged by some as unethical. (Executive bonuses can also present ethical problems—see the discussion later in this chapter.)

"Have you noticed ethics creeping into some of these deals lately?"

In the following case, the court had to determine if a repair shop was entitled to receive full payment of an invoice or some lesser amount, given its conduct in the matter.

Case 2.1

Johnson Construction Co. v. Shaffer

Court of Appeal of Louisiana, Second Circuit, 87 So.3d 203 (2012).

Can an auto repair shop hold a truck "hostage" during a payment dispute with its owner?

FACTS A truck owned by Johnson Construction Company needed repairs. So John Robert Johnson, Jr., took the truck with its attached fifteen-ton trailer to Bubba Shaffer, doing business as Shaffer's Auto and Diesel Repair, LLC. The truck was supposedly fixed, and Johnson paid the bill. Thereafter, though, the truck continued to leak oil and water. Johnson returned the truck to Shaffer who again claimed to have fixed the problem. Johnson paid the second bill. The problems with the truck continued, however, so Johnson returned the truck and trailer to Shaffer a third time. Johnson was given a verbal estimate of $1,000 for the repairs, but Shaffer ultimately sent an invoice for $5,863. Johnson offered to settle for $2,480, the amount of the initial estimate ($1,000), plus the costs of parts and shipping. Shaffer refused the offer and would not return Johnson's truck or trailer until full payment was made. Shaffer retained possession for almost four years and also charged Johnson a storage fee of $50 a day and 18 percent interest on the $5,863.

Johnson Construction filed a suit against Shaffer alleging unfair trade practices. The trial court determined that Shaffer had acted deceptively and wrongfully in maintaining possession of Johnson Construction's trailer, on which it had performed no work. The trial court awarded Johnson $3,500 in general damages plus $750 in attorneys' fees. Shaffer was also awarded the initial estimate of $1,000. Shaffer appealed.

ISSUE Was Shaffer entitled to receive the full amount of his invoice ($5,863) and reasonable storage fees for the truck and trailer?

DECISION No. The reviewing court affirmed the trial court's decision and also assessed Shaffer all costs of the appeal.

REASON The reviewing court examined the testimony with respect to the verbal estimate of $1,000 for the repairs of the truck. In Louisiana, to enforce an oral agreement pertaining to something priced in excess of $500, the contract must be authenticated by at least one additional witness or other corroborating circumstances. Johnson testified that he had agreed to the initial $1,000 estimate but he had not authorized Shaffer to perform additional repairs or tear down the engine. A mechanic employed by Shaffer testified that Johnson had not authorized additional repairs to the truck. Thus, those repairs were not part of any agreement because they involved tearing down the engine. The trial court had not been in error when it viewed Shaffer's testimony on the issue as "disingenuous." The court noted, "As for the amount that Shaffer contends is due for storage, had it invoiced Mr. Johnson the amount of the original estimate in the first place, there would have been no need to store the truck or trailer." Therefore, the reviewing court rejected the request for storage fees.

Finally, that Shaffer kept the trailer for nearly four years even though no work had been done on it was viewed by the court as holding the trailer "hostage in an effort to force payment for unauthorized repairs." The award of $3,500 in general damages to Johnson Construction seemed appropriate for such lengthy unlawful conversion of the trailer.

WHAT IF THE FACTS WERE DIFFERENT? *Suppose that Shaffer had invoiced Johnson for only $1,500. Would the outcome have been different? Explain your answer.*

Short-Run Profit Maximization

Some people argue that a corporation's only goal should be profit maximization, which will be reflected in a higher market valuation. When all firms strictly adhere to the goal of profit maximization, resources tend to flow to where they are most highly valued by society. Thus, in theory, profit maximization ultimately leads to the most efficient allocation of scarce resources.

Corporate executives and employees have to distinguish, however, between *short-run* and *long-run* profit maximization. In the short run, a company may increase its profits by continuing to sell a product, even though it knows that the product is defective. In the long run, though, because of lawsuits, large settlements, and bad publicity, such unethical conduct will cause profits to suffer. Thus, business ethics is consistent only with long-run profit maximization. An overemphasis on short-term profit maximization is the most common reason that ethical problems occur in business.

CASE EXAMPLE 2.1 When the powerful narcotic painkiller OxyContin was first marketed, its manufacturer, Purdue Pharma, claimed that it was unlikely to lead to drug addiction or abuse. Internal company documents later showed, however, that the company's executives knew that OxyContin could be addictive, but they kept this risk a secret to boost sales and maximize short-term profits. Purdue Pharma and three former executives pleaded guilty to criminal charges that they misled regulators, patients, and physicians about OxyContin's risks. Purdue Pharma agreed to pay $600 million in fines and other payments. The three former executives agreed to pay $34.5 million in fines and were barred from federal health programs for a period of fifteen years. Thus, the company's focus on maximizing profits in the short run led to unethical conduct that hurt profits in the long run.[1] ●

"Gray Areas" in the Law

In many situations, business firms can predict with a fair amount of certainty whether a given action would be legal. For instance, firing an employee solely because of that person's race or gender would clearly violate federal laws prohibiting employment discrimination. In some situations, though, the legality of a particular action may be less clear. In part, this is because there are so many laws regulating business that it is increasingly possible to violate one of them without realizing it. The law also contains numerous "gray areas," making it difficult to predict with certainty how a court will apply a given law to a particular action.

In addition, many rules of law require a court to determine what is "foreseeable" or "reasonable" in a particular situation. Because a business has no way of predicting how a specific court will decide these issues, decision makers need to proceed with caution and evaluate an action and its consequences from an ethical perspective. The same problem often occurs in cases involving the Internet because it is often unclear how a court will apply existing laws in the context of cyberspace. Generally, if a company can demonstrate that it acted in good faith and responsibly in the circumstances, it has a better chance of successfully defending its action in court or before an administrative law judge.

The Importance of Ethical Leadership

Talking about ethical business decision making is meaningless if management does not set standards. Furthermore, managers must apply the same standards to themselves as they do to the employees of the company.

If a company discovers that a manager has behaved unethically or engaged in misconduct, the company should take prompt remedial action. The following case illustrates what can happen when a manager fails to follow the standards that apply to other employees.

"It's easy to make a buck. It's a lot tougher to make a difference."

Tom Brokaw, 1940–present (American television journalist)

← KNOW THIS →

When it is not entirely clear how a law applies, a company's best defense to allegations of misconduct is to show that the firm acted honestly and responsibly under the circumstances.

LEARNING OBJECTIVE 2
How can business leaders encourage their companies to act ethically?

---

1. *United States v. Purdue Frederick Co.*, 495 F. Supp.2d 569 (W.D.Va. 2007).

Case 2.2

Mathews v. B and K Foods, Inc.

Missouri Court of Appeals,
332 S.W.3d 275 (2011).

(Robyn Mackenzie/
Shutterstock.com)

FACTS Dianne Mathews was employed by B and K Foods, Inc., as a floral manager. In 2010, she was terminated for submitting falsified timesheets. She filed for unemployment compensation (see Chapter 24), but B and K objected, arguing that Mathews was not entitled to unemployment benefits because she had been discharged for misconduct in connection with work. At an employment commission hearing, the chief executive officer of B and K testified that it was company policy to pay employees who worked through their lunch breaks. To be paid, a person turned in a "no-lunch sheet." Mathews, however, turned in "no-lunch sheets" when she ran personal errands.

She admitted to knowing about the policy, but she contended that her conduct was warranted. She claimed that a former employee who was a higher-level manager at B and K had told her that it was unnecessary to adjust her timesheet when she spent a few minutes on a personal errand. The employment commission ruled that Mathews could not receive unemployment compensation benefits. Mathews appealed.

ISSUE Was it misconduct for Mathews to be paid for time spent running personal errands when this was against company policy?

DECISION Yes. A state intermediate appellate court affirmed the employment commission's decision that Mathews should not receive unemployment benefits.

Many employees fill out timesheets for payroll purposes.

REASON According to the court, " 'work-related misconduct' must involve a willful violation of the rules or standards of the employer." The employer met its burden of proving such misconduct. B and K presented substantial evidence that Mathews had falsified time cards by turning in "no-lunch" sheets for time she had spent running personal errands. Mathews admitted that she was familiar with the company's no-lunch policy. Furthermore, she was responsible for seeing that her subordinate employees followed the policy. The court accepted the B and K executive's statement that "they had no choice but to terminate [Mathews] because she was in a higher position and had a responsibility to enforce the lunch policy."

WHAT IF THE FACTS WERE DIFFERENT? *Suppose that Mathews had not admitted to knowing about the "no-lunch sheet" policy. Would the result in this case have been different? Why or why not?*

Attitude of Top Management

One of the most important ways to create and maintain an ethical workplace is for top management to demonstrate its commitment to ethical decision making. A manager who is not totally committed to an ethical workplace rarely succeeds in creating one. Management's behavior, more than anything else, sets the ethical tone of a firm. Employees take their cues from management. **EXAMPLE 2.2** Devon, a BioTek employee, observes his manager cheating on her expense account. Later, when Devon is promoted to a managerial position, he "pads" his expense account as well, knowing that he is unlikely to face sanctions for doing so. •

Managers who set unrealistic production or sales goals increase the probability that employees will act unethically. If a sales quota can be met only through high-pressure, unethical sales tactics, employees will try to act "in the best interest of the company" and will continue to behave unethically.

A manager who looks the other way when she or he knows about an employee's unethical behavior also sets an example—one indicating that ethical transgressions will be accepted. Managers have found that discharging even one employee for ethical reasons has a tremendous impact as a deterrent to unethical behavior in the workplace.

Behavior of Owners and Managers

Business owners and managers sometimes take more active roles in fostering unethical and illegal conduct. This may indicate

> ➤ **KNOW THIS** ◂
> One of the best ways to encourage good business ethics at a workplace is to take immediate corrective action in response to any unethical conduct.

to their co-owners, co-managers, employees, and others that unethical business behavior will be tolerated. **EXAMPLE 2.3** Lawyer Samir Zia Chowhan posted a help-wanted ad on Craigslist seeking an "energetic woman" for the position of legal secretary. The ad stated that the position included secretarial and paralegal work, as well as "additional duties" for two lawyers in the firm. Applicants were asked to send pictures and describe their physical features. When a woman applied for the job, Chowhan sent her an e-mail saying that "in addition to the legal work, you would be required to have sexual interaction with me and my partner, sometimes together sometimes separate." He also explained that she would need to perform sexual acts on them at the job interview so that he and his partner could determine whether she would be able to handle these duties. The woman filed a complaint with the Illinois Bar Association, which suspended Chowhan's law license for a year for making false statements about the ad. Because the bar association's ethics rules prohibited attorneys from having sex with their clients, but not with potential employees, Chowhan could only be disciplined for lying. ●

Creating Ethical Codes of Conduct

One of the most effective ways of setting a tone of ethical behavior within an organization is to create an ethical code of conduct. A well-written code of ethics explicitly states a company's ethical priorities and demonstrates the company's commitment to ethical behavior.

See this chapter's foldout exhibit showing the code of ethics of Costco Wholesale Corporation as an example. This code of conduct indicates Costco's commitment to legal compliance, as well as to the welfare of its members (those who purchase its goods), employees, and suppliers. The code also details some specific ways in which the interests and welfare of these different groups will be protected. You will also see that Costco acknowledges that by protecting these groups' interests, it will realize its "ultimate goal"—rewarding its shareholders with maximum shareholder value.

Providing Ethics Training to Employees
For an ethical code to be effective, its provisions must be clearly communicated to employees. Most large companies have implemented ethics training programs, in which managers discuss with employees on a face-to-face basis the firm's policies and the importance of ethical conduct. Smaller firms should also offer some form of ethics training to employees because if a firm is accused of an ethics violation, the court will consider the presence or absence of such training in evaluating the firm's conduct.

Some firms hold periodic ethics seminars during which employees can openly discuss any ethical problems that they may be experiencing and learn how the firm's ethical policies apply to those specific problems. Other companies require their managers to meet individually with employees and grade them on their ethical (or unethical) behavior.

Global companies are finding that they need to communicate their ethics policies to their foreign suppliers as well as their domestic employees. **EXAMPLE 2.4** Like other high-tech companies, Apple, Inc., relies heavily on foreign suppliers for components and assembly of many of its products. Following a number of high-profile labor problems with its foreign suppliers and manufacturers, Apple started to evaluate practices at companies in its supply chain and to communicate its ethics policies to them. After its audits revealed numerous violations, in 2012 Apple released a list of its suppliers for the first time. Apple's five-hundred-page "Supplier Responsibility Report" showed that sixty-seven facilities had docked worker pay as a disciplinary measure. Some had falsified pay records and forced workers to use machines without safeguards. Others had engaged in unsafe environmental practices, such as dumping wastewater on neighboring farms. Apple terminated its relationship with one supplier and turned over its findings to the Fair Labor Association for further inquiry. ●

"What you do speaks so loudly that I cannot hear what you say."

Ralph Waldo Emerson,
1803–1882
(American essayist and poet)

PREVENTING
LEGAL DISPUTES

To avoid disputes over ethical violations, you should first create a written ethical code that is expressed in clear and understandable language. The code should establish specific procedures that employees can follow if they have questions or complaints. It should assure employees that their jobs will be secure and that they will not face reprisals if they do file a complaint. A well-written code might also include examples to clarify what the company considers to be acceptable and unacceptable conduct. You should also hold periodic training meetings so that you can explain to employees face to face why ethics is important to the company. If your company does business internationally, you might also communicate the code to firms in your supply chain and make sure they follow your ethics policies.

The Sarbanes-Oxley Act and Web-Based Reporting Systems

Congress enacted the Sarbanes-Oxley Act[2] to help reduce corporate fraud and unethical management decisions. The act requires companies to set up confidential systems so that employees and others can "raise red flags" about suspected illegal or unethical auditing and accounting practices. (The Sarbanes-Oxley Act will be discussed in more detail in Chapter 21, and excerpts and explanatory comments on this important law appear in Appendix D of this text.)

Some companies have implemented online reporting systems to accomplish this goal. In one system, employees can click on an icon on their computers that anonymously links them with EthicsPoint, an organization based in Portland, Oregon. Through EthicsPoint, employees can report suspicious accounting practices, sexual harassment, and other possibly unethical behavior. EthicsPoint, in turn, alerts management personnel or the audit committee at the designated company to the possible problem. Those who have used the system say that it is less inhibiting than calling a company's toll-free number.

> "Never let your sense of morals prevent you from doing what is right."
>
> Isaac Asimov, 1920–1992
> (Russian-born writer and scientist)

Ethical Transgressions by Financial Institutions

One of the best ways to learn the ethical responsibilities inherent in operating a business is to look at the mistakes made by other companies. In the following subsections, we describe some of the most egregious ethical failures of financial institutions during the last decade. Many of these ethical wrongdoings received wide publicity and raised public awareness of the need for ethical leadership throughout all businesses.

Corporate Stock Buybacks

During the economic crisis that started in 2008, many of the greatest financial companies in the United States either went bankrupt, were taken over by the federal government, or had to be bailed out by U.S. taxpayers. What many people do not know is that those same corporations were using their own cash funds to prop up the value of their stock in the years just before the economic crisis.

Stock Buyback The purchase of shares of a company's own stock by that company on the open market.

The theory behind a **stock buyback** is simple—the management of a corporation believes that the market price of its shares is "below their fair value." Therefore, instead of issuing dividends to shareholders or reinvesting profits, management uses the company's funds to buy its shares in the open market, thereby boosting the price of the stock. From 2005 to 2007, stock buybacks for the top five hundred U.S. corporations added up to $1.4 *trillion*.

---

2. 15 U.S.C. Sections 7201 *et seq.*

Stock Option An agreement that grants the owner the option to buy a given number of shares of stock at a set price, usually within a specific time period.

Who benefits from stock buybacks? The main individual beneficiaries are corporate executives who have been given **stock options,** which enable them to buy shares of the corporation's stock at a set price. When the market price rises above that level, the executives can profit by selling their shares. Although stock buybacks are legal and can serve legitimate purposes, they can easily be abused if managers use them just to increase the stock price in the short term so that they can profit from their options without considering the long-term needs of the company.

In the investment banking business, which almost disappeared in the latter half of 2008, stock buybacks were particularly egregious. **EXAMPLE 2.5** Goldman Sachs, an investment bank, bought back $15 billion of its stock in 2007. Yet by 2009, U.S. taxpayers had provided $10 billion in bailout funds to that same company. Lehman Brothers Holdings had also bought back large amounts of stock before it filed for bankruptcy in 2008. •

Startling Executive Decisions at American International Group

American International Group (AIG) was once a respected, conservative worldwide insurance company based in New York. Then it decided to enter an area in which it had little expertise—the issuance of insurance contracts guaranteeing certain types of complicated financial contracts. When many of those insured contracts failed, AIG experienced multibillion-dollar losses. Finally, the company sought a federal bailout that eventually amounted to almost $200 billion of U.S. taxpayers' funds.

While some company executives were testifying before Congress after receiving the funds, other AIG executives spent almost $400,000 on a retreat at a resort in California. In essence, U.S. taxpayers were footing the bill.

Executive Bonuses

Until the economic crisis began in 2008, the bonuses paid in the financial industry did not make headlines. After all, times were good, and why shouldn't those responsible for record company earnings be rewarded? When investment banks and commercial banks began to fail, however, or had to be bailed out or taken over by the federal government, executive bonuses became an important issue.

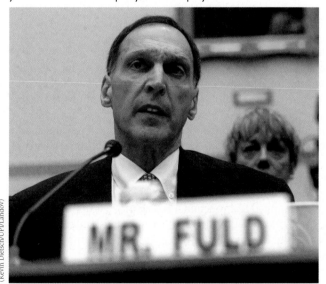

Richard Fuld, a former head of investment bank Lehman Brothers, earned nearly $500 million in bonuses during the years before the company's bankruptcy.

(Kevin Dietsch/UPI/Landov)

The industry had been profiting from the sale of risky assets to investors. Executives and others in the industry who had created and sold those risky assets suffered no liability—and even received bonuses. Of course, some of those firms that had enjoyed high short-run returns from their risky investments—and paid bonuses based on those profits—found themselves facing bankruptcy. **EXAMPLE 2.6** Lehman Brothers' chief executive officer earned almost $500 million between 2000 and the firm's demise in 2008. Even after Lehman Brothers entered bankruptcy, its new owners, Barclays and Nomura, legally owed $3.5 billion in bonuses to employees still on the payroll. In 2006, Goldman Sachs awarded its employees a total of $16.5 billion in bonuses, or an average of almost $750,000 for each employee. •

Public outrage at the bonuses paid by firms receiving taxpayer funds subsequently caused Congress to include a provision in the American Recovery and Reinvestment Tax Act of

2009 to change the compensation system in the financial industry. The provision did not cap executive salaries but did severely restrict the bonuses that could be paid by firms that had received bailout funds under the Troubled Asset Relief Program (TARP).[3] Although cash bonuses to Wall Street executives fell, the total compensation for financial service firms increased in 2010 to nearly $150 billion.

Approaches to Ethical Reasoning

Ethical Reasoning A reasoning process in which an individual links his or her moral convictions or ethical standards to the particular situation at hand.

Each individual, when faced with a particular ethical dilemma, engages in **ethical reasoning**—that is, a reasoning process in which the individual examines the situation at hand in light of his or her moral convictions or ethical standards. Businesspersons do likewise when making decisions with ethical implications.

How do business decision makers decide whether a given action is the "right" one for their firms? What ethical standards should be applied? Broadly speaking, ethical reasoning relating to business traditionally has been characterized by two fundamental approaches. One approach defines ethical behavior in terms of duty, which also implies certain rights. The other approach determines what is ethical in terms of the consequences, or outcome, of any given action. We examine each of these approaches here.

In addition to the two basic ethical approaches, several theories have been developed that specifically address the social responsibility of corporations. Because these theories also influence today's business decision makers, we conclude this section with a short discussion of the different views of corporate social responsibility.

Duty-Based Ethics

LEARNING OBJECTIVE 3
How do duty-based ethical standards differ from outcome-based ethical standards?

Duty-based ethical standards often are derived from revealed truths, such as religious precepts. They can also be derived through philosophical reasoning.

Religious Ethical Standards   In the Judeo-Christian tradition, the Ten Commandments of the Old Testament establish fundamental rules for moral action. Other religions have their own sources of revealed truth. Religious rules generally are absolute with respect to the behavior of their adherents. The commandment "Thou shalt not steal" is an absolute mandate for a person who believes that the Ten Commandments reflect revealed truth. Even a benevolent motive for stealing (such as Robin Hood's) cannot justify the act because the act itself is inherently immoral and thus wrong.

> "When I do good,
> I feel good. When
> I do bad, I feel bad.
> And that's my
> religion."
>
> Abraham Lincoln, 1809–1865
> (Sixteenth president of the
> United States, 1861–1865)

Kantian Ethics   Duty-based ethical standards may also be derived solely from philosophical reasoning. The German philosopher Immanuel Kant (1724–1804), for example, identified some general guiding principles for moral behavior based on what he believed to be the fundamental nature of human beings. Kant believed that human beings are qualitatively different from other physical objects and are endowed with moral integrity and the capacity to reason and conduct their affairs rationally. Therefore, a person's thoughts and actions should be respected. When human beings are treated merely as a means to an end, they are being treated as the equivalent of objects and are being denied their basic humanity.

Categorical Imperative An ethical guideline developed by Immanuel Kant under which an action is evaluated in terms of what would happen if everybody else in the same situation, or category, acted the same way.

A central theme in Kantian ethics is that individuals should evaluate their actions in light of the consequences that would follow if *everyone* in society acted in the same way. This **categorical imperative** can be applied to any action. **EXAMPLE 2.7** Suppose that you are deciding whether to cheat on an examination. If you have adopted Kant's categorical imperative, you will decide *not* to cheat because if everyone cheated, the examination (and the entire education system) would be meaningless. ●

---

3. 12 U.S.C. Section 5211.

The Principle of Rights   Because a duty cannot exist without a corresponding right, duty-based ethical standards imply that human beings have basic rights. The principle that human beings have certain fundamental rights (to life, liberty, and the pursuit of happiness, for example) is deeply embedded in Western culture. Our nation traditionally embraces the concept that certain actions (such as killing another person) are morally wrong because they are contrary to nature (the natural desire to continue living).

Principle of Rights The belief that human beings have certain fundamental rights. Whether a business action or decision is ethical depends on how it affects the rights of various groups, such as owners, employees, consumers, suppliers, the community, and society.

Those who adhere to this **principle of rights**, or "rights theory," believe that a key factor in determining whether a business decision is ethical is how that decision affects the rights of others. These others include the firm's owners, its employees, the consumers of its products or services, its suppliers, the community in which it does business, and society as a whole.

Conflicting Rights   A potential dilemma for those who support rights theory, however, is that there are often conflicting rights and people may disagree on which rights are most important. When considering all those affected by a business decision to downsize a firm, for example, how much weight should be given to employees relative to shareholders? Which employees should be laid off first, those with the highest salaries or those who have worked there for less time (and have less seniority)? How should the firm weigh the rights of customers relative to the community, or employees relative to society as a whole?

Resolving Conflicts   In general, rights theorists believe that whichever right is stronger in a particular circumstance takes precedence. **EXAMPLE 2.8**   A firm can either keep a manufacturing plant open, saving the jobs of twelve workers, or shut the plant down and avoid contaminating a river with pollutants that would endanger the health of tens of thousands of people. In this situation, a rights theorist can easily choose which group to favor. (Not all choices are so clear-cut, however.) ●

Outcome-Based Ethics: Utilitarianism

"The greatest good for the greatest number" is a paraphrase of the major premise of the utilitarian approach to ethics. **Utilitarianism** is a philosophical theory developed by Jeremy Bentham (1748–1832) and modified by John Stuart Mill (1806–1873)—both British philosophers. In contrast to duty-based ethics, utilitarianism is outcome oriented. It focuses on the consequences of an action, not on the nature of the action itself or on any set of preestablished moral values or religious beliefs.

Utilitarianism An approach to ethical reasoning in which an action is evaluated in terms of its consequences for those whom it will affect. A "good" action is one that results in the greatest good for the greatest number of people.

Under a utilitarian model of ethics, an action is morally correct, or "right," when, among the people it affects, it produces the greatest amount of good for the greatest number. When an action affects the majority adversely, it is morally wrong. Applying the utilitarian theory thus requires (1) a determination of which individuals will be affected by the action in question; (2) a **cost-benefit analysis**, which involves an assessment of the negative and positive effects of alternative actions on these individuals; and (3) a choice among alternative actions that will produce maximum societal utility (the greatest positive net benefits for the greatest number of individuals).

Cost-Benefit Analysis A decision-making technique that involves weighing the costs of a given action against the benefits of that action.

Corporate Social Responsibility

For many years, groups concerned with civil rights, employee safety and welfare, consumer protection, environmental preservation, and other causes have pressured U.S. corporations to behave in a responsible manner with respect to these causes. Thus was born the concept of **corporate social responsibility**—the idea that those who run corporations can and should act ethically and be accountable to society for their actions. Just what constitutes corporate social responsibility has been debated for some time, however, and there are a number of different theories today.

Corporate Social Responsibility The idea that corporations can and should act ethically and be accountable to society for their actions.

Stakeholder Approach   One view of corporate social responsibility stresses that corporations have a duty not just to shareholders, but also to other groups affected by corporate decisions ("stakeholders"). Under this approach, a corporation would consider the impact of its decision on the firm's employees, customers, creditors, suppliers, and the community in which the corporation operates. The reasoning behind this "stakeholder view" is that in some circumstances, one or more of these other groups may have a greater stake in company decisions than the shareholders do. Although this may be true, as mentioned earlier, it is often difficult to decide which group's interests should receive greater weight if the interests conflict.

During the last few years, layoffs numbered in the millions. Nonetheless, some corporations succeeded in reducing labor costs without layoffs. To avoid slashing their workforces, these employers turned to alternatives such as (1) four-day workweeks, (2) unpaid vacations and voluntary furloughs, (3) wage freezes, (4) pension cuts, and (5) flexible work schedules. Some companies asked their workers to accept wage cuts to prevent layoffs, and the workers agreed. Companies finding alternatives to layoffs included Dell (extended unpaid holidays), Cisco Systems (four-day end-of-year shutdowns), Motorola (salary cuts), and Honda (voluntary unpaid vacation time).

Corporate Citizenship   Another theory of social responsibility argues that corporations should be good citizens by promoting goals that society deems worthwhile and taking positive steps toward solving social problems. The idea is that because business controls so much of the wealth and power of this country, business, in turn, has a responsibility to society to use that wealth and power in socially beneficial ways.

Under a corporate citizenship view, companies are judged on how much they donate to social causes, as well as how they conduct their operations with respect to employment discrimination, human rights, environmental concerns, and similar issues. **EXAMPLE 2.9**   Google has teamed up with investment firm Kohlberg Kravis Roberts to develop four solar energy farms that will serve the Sacramento Municipal Utility District in California. The four solar farms reportedly cost $95 million and will provide enough power for more than 13,000 average U.S. homes. •

A Way of Doing Business   A survey of U.S. executives undertaken by the Boston College Center for Corporate Citizenship found that more than 70 percent of those polled agreed that corporate citizenship must be treated as a priority. More than 60 percent said that good corporate citizenship added to their companies' profits. Strategist Michelle Bernhart has argued that corporate social responsibility cannot attain its maximum effectiveness unless it is treated as a way of doing business rather than as a special program.

Not all socially responsible activities can benefit a corporation, however. Corporate responsibility is most successful when a company undertakes activities that are relevant and significant to its stakeholders and related to its business operations. **EXAMPLE 2.10**   A Brazilian mining firm invested more than $150 million in social projects, including health care, infrastructure, and education. At the same time, it invested

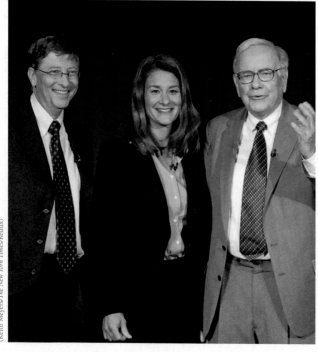

Microsoft founder Bill Gates and his wife, Melinda, are shown below with financier Warren Buffett (right) after Buffett gave $40 billion to the Bill and Melinda Gates Foundation.

(Keith Meyers/*The New York Times*/Redux)

"Next to doing the right thing, the most important thing is to let people know you are doing the right thing."

John D. Rockefeller, 1839–1897 (American industrialist and philanthropist)

more than $300 million in environmental protection. One of its projects involves the rehabilitation of native species in the Amazon Valley. To that end, it is planting almost 200 million trees in an attempt to restore 1,150 square miles of land where cattle breeding and farming have caused deforestation. ● (See the *Linking Business Law to Accounting and Finance* feature at the end of this chapter for more examples of corporate responsibility.)

Making Ethical Business Decisions

The George S. May International Company has provided six basic guidelines to help corporate employees judge their actions. Each employee—no matter what her or his level in the organization—should evaluate her or his actions using the following six guidelines:

1. *The law.* Is the action you are considering legal? If you do not know the laws governing the action, then find out. Ignorance of the law is no excuse.
2. *Rules and procedures.* Are you following the internal rules and procedures that have already been laid out by your company? They have been developed to avoid problems. Is what you are planning to do consistent with your company's policies and procedures? If not, stop.
3. *Values.* Laws and internal company policies reinforce society's values. You might wish to ask yourself whether you are attempting to find a loophole in the law or in your company's policies. Next, you have to ask yourself whether you are following the "spirit" of the law as well as the letter of the law or the internal policy.
4. *Conscience.* If you feel any guilt, let your conscience be your guide. Alternatively, ask yourself whether you would be happy to be interviewed by the national news media about the actions you are going to take.
5. *Promises.* Every business organization is based on trust. Your customers believe that your company will do what it is supposed to do. The same is true for your suppliers and employees. Will your actions live up to the commitments you have made to others, both inside the business and outside?
6. *Heroes.* We all have heroes who are role models for us. Is what you are planning on doing an action that your "hero" would take? If not, how would your hero act? That is how you should be acting.

LEARNING OBJECTIVE 4
What are six guidelines that an employee can use to evaluate whether his or her actions are ethical?

ETHICAL ISSUE

Should you do the right thing even when it puts your job at risk? Dean Krehmeyer, executive director of the Business Roundtable's Institute for Corporate Ethics, once said, "Evidence strongly suggests being ethical—doing the right thing—pays." Sometimes, however, being ethical in the business world costs an employee his or her job. For instance, Michael Woodford was chief executive officer for Olympus Corporation, a Tokyo-based camera maker. He had worked thirty years for Olympus when he discovered that the company had been engaging in questionable accounting practices. After confronting management in 2011 about excessive spending on certain acquisitions, Woodford was fired from the board of directors. He then resigned as chair and called for the other board members to resign and for a shareholders' meeting to be held to select a new board. Olympus initially denied any wrongdoing but later acknowledged a $687 million payment for financial advice and expensive acquisitions to cover up investment losses. Many speculate that the company falsified a large amount of information in its financial reports over the years. Olympus's bookkeeping is now under investigation in Japan, the United States, and Great Britain. But Woodford, who did the right thing by encouraging the company to come clean about the cover-up, no longer works for the company. He plans to sue Olympus, but because it is a Japanese company, he may never be compensated for losing his job.

Practical Solutions to Corporate Ethics Questions

Corporate ethics officers and ethics committees require a practical method to investigate and solve specific ethics problems. Ethics consultant Leonard H. Bucklin of Corporate-Ethics.US has devised a procedure that he calls Business Process Pragmatism.[4] It involves the following five steps:

1. *Inquiry.* Of course, an understanding of the facts must be the initial action. The parties involved might include the mass media, the public, employees, or customers. At this stage of the process, the ethical problem or problems are specified. A list of relevant ethical principles is created.
2. *Discussion.* Here, a list of action options is developed. Each option carries with it certain ethical principles. Finally, resolution goals should also be listed.
3. *Decision.* Working together, those participating in the process craft a consensus decision, or a consensus plan of action for the corporation.
4. *Justification.* Does the consensus solution withstand moral scrutiny? At this point in the process, reasons should be attached to each proposed action or series of actions. Will the stakeholders involved accept these reasons?
5. *Evaluation.* Do the solutions to the corporate ethics issue satisfy corporate values, community values, and individual values? Ultimately, can the consensus resolution to the corporate ethics problem withstand the moral scrutiny of the decisions taken and the process used to reach those decisions?

Business Ethics on a Global Level

Given the various cultures and religions throughout the world, it is not surprising that conflicts in ethics frequently arise between foreign and U.S. businesspersons. For instance, in certain countries, the consumption of alcohol and specific foods is forbidden for religious reasons. Under such circumstances, it would be thoughtless and imprudent for a U.S. businessperson to invite a local business contact out for a drink.

The role played by women in other countries may also present some difficult ethical problems for firms doing business internationally. Equal employment opportunity is a fundamental public policy in the United States, and Title VII of the Civil Rights Act of 1964 prohibits discrimination against women in the employment context (see Chapter 18). Some other countries, however, offer little protection for women against gender discrimination in the workplace, including sexual harassment. (See this chapter's *Law, Diversity, and Business: Managerial Implications* feature on the facing page for a discussion of the impact of cultural differences on global marketing strategies.)

We look here at how laws governing workers in other countries, particularly developing countries, have created some especially difficult ethical problems for U.S. sellers of goods manufactured in foreign countries. We also examine some of the ethical ramifications of laws prohibiting U.S. businesspersons from bribing foreign officials to obtain favorable business contracts.

Monitoring the Employment Practices of Foreign Suppliers

Many U.S. businesses now contract with companies in developing nations to produce goods, such as shoes and clothing, because the wage rates in those nations are significantly lower than wages in the United States. Yet what if a foreign company exploits its

"If you are uncertain about an issue, it's useful to ask yourself, 'Would I be absolutely comfortable for my actions to be disclosed on the front page of my hometown newspaper?'"

Warren E. Buffett, 1930–present (American businessperson and philanthropist)

LEARNING OBJECTIVE 5
What types of ethical issues might arise in the context of international business transactions?

---

4. Corporate-Ethics.US and Business Process Pragmatism are registered trademarks.

LAW, DIVERSITY, AND BUSINESS: MANAGERIAL IMPLICATIONS

RESPECTING CULTURAL DIFFERENCES IN FOREIGN MARKETS

Today, more businesses engage in global activities than ever before. Certainly, anyone developing marketing strategies for a foreign market needs to be aware of all aspects of culture, including religion, language, values, and customs.

Global Marketing and the Need to Consider Each Culture Separately No matter how "small" the world has become, countries still have different sets of shared values that affect their citizens' preferences. Samsonite, for example, made a major cultural blunder when it used an advertisement showing its luggage being carried on a "magic" flying carpet. Most Middle Eastern consumers thought that Samsonite was selling carpets. As another example, Green Giant learned to its dismay that it could not use its logo with a man in a green hat in certain parts of Asia. Why not? The reason was that in those areas a green hat signifies a man who has an unfaithful wife.

The Translation of Names and Slogans Can Be a Problem, Too In the same vein, the translation of slogans and names into other languages is fraught with pitfalls. Toyota had to drop the "2" from its model MR2 in France because the combination of sounds was very close to a French swear word. Mitsubishi Motors had to rename one of its models in Spanish-speaking

countries because the original name described a sexual activity.

Can Global Marketing Standardization Work in a Diverse World? Many multinationals have adopted global marketing standardization, meaning that they try to adapt product features, advertising, and packaging so that they are usable throughout the world. Those in favor of such standardization—a global vision, as it were—contend that advances in communications and technology have created a small, interconnected world. Consumers everywhere want the same items that they see in popular movies. Coca-Cola, Colgate-Palmolive, and McDonald's, for example, tend toward global marketing standardization.

Business Implications *Managers in any company wishing to do business abroad have to be aware that their marketing campaigns may offend potential consumers (and even governments). Given that almost 15 percent of U.S. production is sold abroad, this issue is an important one and will become more important as standards of living increase in poorer parts of the globe. Higher standards of living usually lead to more imports. Many of those imports will come from the United States and will have to be marketed carefully.*

workers—by hiring women and children at below-minimum-wage rates, for example, or by requiring its employees to work long hours in a workplace full of health hazards? What if the company's supervisors routinely engage in workplace conduct that is offensive to women? What if plants that are operated abroad routinely violate labor and environmental standards?

EXAMPLE 2.11 Apple, Inc., owns Pegatron Corporation, a subsidiary company based in China, that supplies parts for iPads and other Apple products. In December 2011, dozens of employees at the Pegatron factory in Shanghai were injured when aluminum dust created from polishing cases for iPads caught fire and exploded. Apple did not respond to allegations that conditions at the factory violated labor and environmental standards. •

Given today's global communications network, few companies can assume that their actions in other nations will go unnoticed by "corporate watch" groups that discover and publicize unethical corporate behavior. (For a discussion of how the Internet has increased the ability of critics to publicize a corporation's misdeeds, see this chapter's *Adapting the Law to the Online Environment* feature on the following page.) As a result, U.S. businesses today usually take steps to avoid such adverse publicity—either by refusing to deal with certain suppliers or by arranging to monitor their suppliers' workplaces to make sure that the employees are not being mistreated.

ADAPTING THE LAW TO THE ONLINE ENVIRONMENT

CORPORATE REPUTATIONS UNDER ATTACK

In the pre-Internet days, disgruntled employees and customers wrote letters of complaint to corporate management or to the editors of local newspapers. Occasionally, an investigative reporter would write an exposé of alleged corporate misdeeds. Today, those unhappy employees and customers have gone online. To locate them, just type in the name of any major corporation. You will find electronic links to blogs, wikis, message boards, and online communities—many of which post harsh criticisms of corporate giants. Some disgruntled employees and consumers have even created rogue Web sites that mimic the look of the target corporation's official Web site—except that the rogue sites feature chat rooms and postings of "horror stories" about the corporation.

Damage to Corporate Reputations

Clearly, by providing a forum for complaints, the Internet has increased the potential for damage to the reputation of any major (or minor) corporation. Now a relatively small number of unhappy employees, for example, may make the entire world aware of a single incident that is not at all representative of how the corporation ordinarily operates.

Special Interest Groups Go on the Attack

Special interest groups are also using the Internet to attack corporations they do not like. Rather than writing letters or giving speeches to a limited audience, a special interest group can now go online and mercilessly "expose" what it considers to be a corporation's "bad practices." Wal-Mart and Nike in particular have been frequent targets for advocacy groups that believe that those corporations exploit their workers.

Online Attacks: Often Inaccurate, but Probably Legal

Corporations often point out that many of the complaints and charges leveled against them are unfounded or exaggerated. Sometimes, management has tried to argue that the online attacks are libelous. The courts, however, disagree. To date, most courts have regarded online attacks as simply the expression of opinion and therefore a form of speech protected by the First Amendment.

In contrast, if employees breach company rules against the disclosure of internal financial information or trade secrets, the courts have been willing to side with the employers. Note, also, that companies that succeed in lawsuits against inappropriate employee online disclosures always have a clear set of written guidelines about what employees can do when they blog or generate other online content.

Critical Thinking

How might online attacks actually help corporations in the long run? (Hint: Some online criticisms might be accurate.)

The Foreign Corrupt Practices Act

> "Never doubt that a small group of committed citizens can change the world; indeed, it is the only thing that ever has."
>
> Margaret Mead, 1901–1978 (American anthropologist)

Another ethical problem in international business dealings has to do with the legitimacy of certain "side" payments to government officials. In the United States, most contracts are formed within the private sector. In many countries, however, government regulation and control over trade and industry are much more extensive than in the United States, so government officials make the decisions on most major construction and manufacturing contracts. Side payments to government officials in exchange for favorable business contracts are not unusual in such countries, where they are not considered to be unethical. In the past, U.S. corporations doing business in these countries largely followed the dictum "When in Rome, do as the Romans do."

In the 1970s, however, large side payments by U.S. corporations to foreign representatives for the purpose of securing advantageous international trade contracts led to a number of scandals. In response, in 1977 Congress passed the Foreign Corrupt Practices Act[5] (FCPA), which prohibits U.S. businesspersons from bribing foreign officials to secure advantageous contracts.

---

5. 15 US.C. Sections 78 dd-1 *et seq.*

Prohibition against the Bribery of Foreign Officials

The first part of the FCPA applies to all U.S. companies and their directors, officers, shareholders, employees, and agents. This part prohibits the bribery of officials of foreign governments if the purpose of the payment is to induce the officials to act in their official capacity to provide business opportunities.

The FCPA does not prohibit payment of substantial sums to minor officials whose duties are ministerial. These payments are often referred to as "grease," or facilitating payments. They are meant to accelerate the performance of administrative services that might otherwise be carried out at a slow pace. Thus, for example, if a firm makes a payment to a minor official to speed up an import licensing process, the firm has not violated the FCPA. Generally, the act, as amended, permits payments to foreign officials if such payments are lawful within the foreign country. The act also does not prohibit payments to private foreign companies or other third parties unless the U.S. firm knows that the payments will be passed on to a foreign government in violation of the FCPA. Business firms that violate the FCPA may be fined up to $2 million. Individual officers or directors who violate the act may be fined up to $100,000 (the fine cannot be paid by the company) and may be imprisoned for up to five years.

Accounting Requirements

In the past, bribes were often concealed in corporate financial records. Thus, the second part of the FCPA is directed toward accountants. All companies must keep detailed records that "accurately and fairly" reflect the company's financial activities. In addition, all companies must have an accounting system that provides "reasonable assurance" that all transactions entered into by the company are accounted for and legal. These requirements assist in detecting illegal bribes. The FCPA further prohibits any person from making false statements to accountants or false entries in any record or account.

Reviewing . . . Ethics and Business Decision Making

Isabel Arnett was promoted to be chief executive officer of Tamik, Inc., a pharmaceutical company that manufactures a vaccine called Kafluk, which supposedly provides some defense against bird flu. The company began marketing Kafluk throughout Asia. After numerous media reports that bird flu might soon become a worldwide epidemic, the demand for Kafluk increased, sales soared, and Tamik earned record profits. Arnett then began receiving disturbing reports from Southeast Asia that in some patients, Kafluk had caused psychiatric disturbances, including severe hallucinations, and heart and lung problems. She was also informed that six children in Japan had committed suicide by jumping out of windows after receiving the vaccine. To cover up the story and prevent negative publicity, Arnett instructed Tamik's partners in Asia to offer cash to the Japanese families whose children had died in exchange for their silence. Arnett also refused to authorize additional research within the company to study the potential side effects of Kafluk. Using the information presented in the chapter, answer the following questions.

1. This scenario illustrates one of the main reasons why ethical problems occur in business. What is that reason?
2. Would a person who adheres to the principle of rights consider it ethical for Arnett not to disclose potential safety concerns and to refuse to perform additional research on Kafluk? Why or why not?
3. If Kafluk prevented fifty Asian people who were exposed to bird flu from dying, would Arnett's conduct in this situation be ethical under a utilitarian cost-benefit analysis? Why or why not?
4. Did Tamik or Arnett violate the Foreign Corrupt Practices Act in this scenario? Why or why not?

DEBATE THIS Executives in large corporations are ultimately rewarded if their companies do well, particularly as evidenced by rising stock prices. Consequently, shouldn't we just let those who run corporations decide what level of negative side effects of their goods or services is "acceptable"?

LINKING BUSINESS LAW to Accounting and Finance

Managing a Company's Reputation

While in business school, all of you must take basic accounting courses. Accounting generally is associated with developing balance sheets and profit-and-loss statements, but it can also be used as a support system to provide information that can help managers do their jobs correctly. Enter managerial accounting, which involves the provision of accounting information for a company's internal use. Managerial accounting is used within a company for planning, controlling, and decision making.

Increasingly, managerial accounting is also being used to *manage corporate reputations*. To this end, more than 2,500 multinationals now release to the public large quantities of managerial accounting information.

Internal Reports Designed for External Scrutiny

Some large companies refer to the managerial accounting information that they release to the public as their corporate sustainability reports. Dow Chemical Company, for example, issues its Global Reporting Initiative Sustainability Report annually. So does Waste Management, Inc., which calls its report "The Color of Our World."

Other corporations call their published documents social responsibility reports. The antivirus software company Symantec Corporation issued its first corporate responsibility report in 2008. The report demonstrated the company's focus on critical environmental, social, and governance issues. Among other things, Symantec pointed out that it had adopted the Calvert Women's Principles, the first global code of corporate conduct designed to empower, advance, and invest in women worldwide.

A smaller number of multinationals provide what they call citizenship reports. For example, in 2011 General Electric (GE)

released its Seventh Annual Citizenship Report, which it calls "Sustainable Growth." GE's emphasis is on energy and climate change, demographics, growth markets, and financial markets. It even has a Web site that provides detailed performance metrics (www.ge.com/citizenship).

The Hitachi Group releases an Annual Corporate Social Responsibility Report, which outlines its environmental strategy, including its attempts to reduce carbon dioxide emissions (so-called greenhouse gases). It typically discusses human rights policy and its commitment to human rights awareness.

Why Use Managerial Accounting to Manage Reputations?

We live in an age of information. Any news, whether positive or negative, about a corporation will be known throughout the world almost immediately given the 24/7 cable and online news networks, social media, Internet bloggers, and smartphones. Consequently, corporations want to manage their reputations by preparing and releasing the news that the public, their shareholders, and government officials will receive. In a world in which corporations are often blamed for anything bad that happens, corporations are finding that managerial accounting information can provide a useful counterweight. To this end, some corporations have combined their social responsibility reports with their traditional financial accounting information. When a corporation's reputation is on the line, the future is at stake.

Critical Thinking

Valuable company resources are used to create and publish corporate social responsibility reports. Under what circumstances can a corporation justify such expenditures?

Key Terms

business ethics 45	cost-benefit analysis 53	moral minimum 45	stock option 57
categorical imperative 52	ethical reasoning 52	principle of rights 53	utilitarianism 53
corporate social responsibility 53	ethics 45	stock buyback 50	

Chapter Summary: Ethics and Business Decision Making

Business Ethics (See pages 45–50.)	1. *Ethics*—Business ethics focuses on how moral and ethical principles are applied in the business context. 2. *The moral minimum*—Lawful behavior is the moral minimum. The law has its limits, though, and some actions may be legal but not ethical. 3. *Short-term profit maximization*—One of the most pervasive reasons why ethical breaches occur is the focus on short-term profit maximization. Executives should distinguish between short-run and long-run profit goals and focus on maximizing profits over the long run because only long-run profit maximization is consistent with business ethics. 4. *Legal uncertainties*—It may be difficult to predict with certainty whether particular actions are legal, given the numerous and frequent changes in the laws regulating business and the "gray areas" in the law. 5. *The importance of ethical leadership*—Management's commitment and behavior are essential in creating an ethical workplace. Management's behavior, more than anything else, sets the ethical tone of a firm and influences the behavior of employees. 6. *Ethical codes*—Most large firms have ethical codes or policies and training programs to help employees determine whether specific actions are ethical. In addition, the Sarbanes-Oxley Act requires firms to set up confidential systems so that employees and others can report suspected illegal or unethical auditing or accounting practices.
Ethical Transgressions by Financial Institutions (See pages 50–52.)	During the first decade of the 2000s, corporate wrongdoing among U.S. financial institutions escalated. A number of investment banking firms, such as Goldman Sachs, were nearly bankrupted by their risky investments, and others, such as Lehman Brothers, were forced into bankruptcy. Earlier these same firms had engaged in the abusive use of stock buybacks and stock options. AIG, an insurance giant, was also on the brink of bankruptcy when the government stepped in with federal bailout funds. Exorbitant bonuses paid to Wall Street executives added to the financial industry's problems and fueled public outrage. U.S. taxpayers paid the price through the federal bailouts and a deepening nationwide recession.
Approaches to Ethical Reasoning (See pages 52–55.)	1. *Duty-based ethics*—Ethics based on religious beliefs; philosophical reasoning, such as that of Immanuel Kant; and the basic rights of human beings (the principle of rights). A potential problem for those who support this approach is deciding which rights are more important in a given situation. Management constantly faces ethical conflicts and trade-offs when considering all those affected by a business decision. 2. *Outcome-based ethics (utilitarianism)*—Ethics based on philosophical reasoning, such as that of Jeremy Bentham and John Stuart Mill. Applying this theory requires a cost-benefit analysis, weighing the negative effects against the positive and deciding which course of action produces the better outcome. 3. *Corporate social responsibility*—A number of theories based on the idea that corporations can and should act ethically and be accountable to society for their actions. These include the stakeholder approach and corporate citizenship.
Making Ethical Business Decisions (See page 55.)	Making ethical business decisions is crucial in today's legal environment. Doing the right thing pays off in the long run, both by increasing profits and by avoiding negative publicity and the potential for bankruptcy. We provide six guidelines for making ethical business decisions on page 201.
Practical Solutions to Corporate Ethics Questions (See page 56.)	Corporate ethics officers and ethics committees require a practical method to investigate and solve specific ethics problems. For a five-step pragmatic procedure to solve ethical problems recommended by one expert, see page 202.
Business Ethics on a Global Level (See pages 56–59.)	Businesses must take account of the many cultural, religious, and legal differences among nations. Notable differences relate to the role of women in society, employment laws governing workplace conditions, and the practice of giving side payments to foreign officials to secure favorable contracts.

ExamPrep

ISSUE SPOTTERS

1. Delta Tools, Inc., markets a product that under some circumstances is capable of seriously injuring consumers. Does Delta have an ethical duty to remove this product from the market, even if the injuries result only from misuse? Why or why not? **(See pages 46–47.)**

2. Acme Corporation decides to respond to what it sees as a moral obligation to correct for past discrimination by adjusting pay differences among its employees. Does this raise an ethical conflict between Acme and its employees? Between Acme and its shareholders? Explain your answers. **(See page 51.)**

—**Check your answers to the Issue Spotters against the answers provided in Appendix E at the end of this text.**

BEFORE THE TEST

Go to www.cengagebrain.com, enter the ISBN 9781133191353, and click on "Find" to locate this textbook's Web site. Then, click on "Access Now" under "Study Tools," and select Chapter 2 at the top. There, you will find an Interactive Quiz that you can take to assess your mastery of the concepts in this chapter, as well as Flashcards, a Glossary of important terms, and Video Questions (when assigned).

For Review

Answers to the even-numbered questions in this For Review section can be found in Appendix F at the end of this text.

1. What is business ethics, and why is it important?
2. How can business leaders encourage their companies to act ethically?
3. How do duty-based ethical standards differ from outcome-based ethical standards?
4. What are six guidelines that an employee can use to evaluate whether his or her actions are ethical?
5. What types of ethical issues might arise in the context of international business transactions?

Business Scenarios and Case Problems

2–1 Business Ethics. Jason Trevor owns a commercial bakery in Blakely, Georgia, that produces a variety of goods sold in grocery stores. Trevor is required by law to perform internal tests on food produced at his plant to check for contamination. Three times in 2011, the tests of food products that contained peanut butter were positive for salmonella contamination. Trevor was not required to report the results to U.S. Food and Drug Administration officials, however, so he did not. Instead, Trevor instructed his employees to simply repeat the tests until the outcome was negative. Therefore, the products that had originally tested positive for salmonella were eventually shipped out to retailers. Five people who ate Trevor's baked goods in 2011 became seriously ill, and one person died from salmonella. Even though Trevor's conduct was legal, was it unethical for him to sell goods that had once tested positive for salmonella? If Trevor had followed the six basic guidelines for making ethical business decisions, would he still have sold the contaminated goods? Why or why not? (**See page 55.**)

2–2 🔵 **Question with Sample Answer—Ethical Duties.** Shokun Steel Co. owns many steel plants. One of its plants is much older than the others. Equipment at that plant is outdated and inefficient, and the costs of production at that plant are now twice as high as at any of Shokun's other plants. The company cannot raise the price of steel because of competition, both domestic and international. The plant employs more than a thousand workers and is located in Twin Firs, Pennsylvania, which has a population of about 45,000. Shokun is contemplating whether to close the plant. What factors should the firm consider in making its decision? Will the firm violate any ethical duties if it closes the plant? Analyze these questions from the two basic perspectives on ethical reasoning discussed in this chapter. (**See pages 52–53.**)

—**For a sample answer to Question 2–2, go to Appendix G at the end of this text.**

2–3 📷 **Spotlight on Pfizer—Corporate Social Responsibility.** Methamphetamine (meth) is an addictive drug made chiefly in small toxic labs (STLs) in homes, tents, barns, or hotel rooms. The manufacturing process is dangerous, often resulting in explosions, burns, and toxic fumes. Government entities spend time and resources to find and destroy STLs, imprison meth dealers and users, treat addicts, and provide services for affected families. Meth cannot be made without ingredients that are also used in cold and allergy medications. Arkansas has one of the highest numbers of STLs in the United States. To recoup the costs of fighting the meth epidemic, twenty counties in Arkansas filed a suit against Pfizer, Inc., which makes cold and allergy medications. What is Pfizer's ethical responsibility here, and to whom is it owed? Why? [*Ashley County, Arkansas v. Pfizer, Inc.,* 552 F.3d 659 (8th Cir. 2009)] (**See page 54.**)

2–4 ⚖️ **Case Problem with Sample Answer—Ethics and the Law.** Prudential Insurance Co. of America has a company guideline not to change the amount of a salesperson's commission once a client has been quoted a price for insurance. Despite this principle, in order to reduce the quoted price for insurance offered to York International Corp., Prudential cut the fee that it paid to a broker. A competing broker, Havensure, LLC, filed a suit, arguing that the reduced quote caused it to lose York as a potential customer. Is a company's violation of its own policy unethical? Is it a basis for legal liability? Explain. [*Havensure, LLC v. Prudential Insurance Co. of America,* 595 F.3d 312 (6th Cir. 2010)] (**See page 49.**)

—**For a sample answer to Problem 2–4, go to Appendix H at the end of this text.**

2–5 Ethical Leadership. David Krasner, who worked for HSH Nordbank AG, complained that his supervisor, Roland Kiser, fostered an atmosphere of sexism that was demeaning to women. Among other things, Krasner claimed that career advancement was based on "sexual favoritism." He objected to Kiser's relationship with a female employee, Melissa Campfield, who was promoted before more qualified employees, including Krasner. How do a manager's attitudes and actions affect the workplace? [*Krasner v. HSH Nordbank AG,* 680 F.Supp.2d 502 (S.D.N.Y. 2010)] **(See pages 48–49.)**

2–6 Ethical Misconduct. Frank Pasquale used his father's Social Security number to obtain a credit card. Later, pretending to act on behalf of his father's firm, Pasquale borrowed $350,000. When he defaulted on the loan and his father confronted him, he produced forged documents that showed the loan had been paid. Adams Associates, LLC, which held the unpaid loan, filed a suit against both Pasquales. Should the court issue a judgment against the father and the son? Discuss. [*Adams Associates, LLC v. Frank Pasquale Limited Partnership,* __ A.3d __ (N.J.Super. A.D. 2011)] **(See pages 50–51.)**

2–7 ⬥ A Question of Ethics—Copyrights. Steven Soderbergh is the Academy Award–winning director of *Erin Brockovich, Traffic,* and many other films. CleanFlicks, LLC, filed a suit in a federal district court against Soderbergh, fifteen other directors, and the Directors Guild of America. The plaintiff asked the court to rule that it had the right to sell DVDs of the defendants' films altered without the defendants' consent to delete scenes of "sex, nudity, profanity and gory violence." CleanFlicks sold or rented the edited DVDs under the slogan "It's About Choice" to consumers, sometimes indirectly through retailers. It would not sell to retailers that made unauthorized copies of the edited films. The defendants, with DreamWorks LLC and seven other movie studios that own the copyrights to the films, filed a counterclaim against CleanFlicks and others engaged in the same business, alleging copyright infringement. Those filing the counterclaim asked the court to enjoin (prevent) CleanFlicks and the others from making and marketing altered versions of the films. [*CleanFlicks of Colorado, LLC v. Soderbergh,* 433 F.Supp.2d 1236 (D.Colo. 2006)] **(See page 55.)**

1. Movie studios often edit their films to conform to content and other standards and sell the edited versions to network television and other commercial buyers. In this case, however, the studios objected when CleanFlicks edited the films and sold the altered versions directly to consumers. Similarly, CleanFlicks made unauthorized copies of the studios' DVDs to edit the films, but objected when others made unauthorized copies of the altered versions. Is there anything unethical about these apparently contradictory positions? Why or why not?

2. CleanFlicks and its competitors asserted, in part, that they were making "fair use" of the studios' copyrighted works. They argued that by their actions "they are criticizing the objectionable content commonly found in current movies and that they are providing more socially acceptable alternatives to enable families to view the films together, without exposing children to the presumed harmful effects emanating from the objectionable content." If you were the judge, how would you view this argument? Is a court the appropriate forum for making determinations of public or social policy? Explain.

Critical Thinking and Writing Assignments

2–8 Critical Legal Thinking. Human rights groups, environmental activists, and other interest groups concerned with unethical business practices have often conducted publicity campaigns against various corporations that those groups feel have engaged in unethical practices. Can a small group of well-organized activists dictate how a major corporation conducts its affairs? Should a small group be able to do so? Discuss fully. **(See page 56.)**

2–9 Business Law Writing. Assume that you are a high-level manager for a shoe manufacturer. You know that your firm could increase its profit margin by producing shoes in Indonesia, where you could hire women for $100 a month to assemble them. You also know that human rights advocates recently accused a competing shoe manufacturer of engaging in exploitative labor practices because the manufacturer sold shoes made by Indonesian women for similarly low wages. You personally do not believe that paying $100 a month to Indonesian women is unethical because you know that in their country, $100 a month is a better-than-average wage rate. Write one page explaining whether you would have the shoes manufactured in Indonesia and make higher profits for the company or avoid the risk of negative publicity and its potential adverse consequences for the firm's reputation. Are there other alternatives? Discuss fully. **(See page 56.)**

2–10 ⬤ Business Law Critical Thinking Group Assignment. In the 1990s, Pfizer, Inc., developed a new antibiotic called Trovan (trovafloxacin mesylate). Tests showed that in animals Trovan had life-threatening side effects, including joint disease, abnormal cartilage growth, liver damage, and a degenerative bone condition. In 1996, an epidemic of bacterial meningitis swept across Nigeria. Pfizer sent three U.S. physicians to test Trovan on children who were patients in Nigeria's Infectious Disease Hospital. Pfizer did not obtain the patients' consent, alert them to the risks, or tell them that Médecins Sans Frontières (Doctors without Borders) was providing an effective conventional treatment at the same site. Eleven children died in the experiment, and others were left blind, deaf, paralyzed, or brain damaged. Rabi Abdullahi and other Nigerian children filed a suit in a U.S. federal court against Pfizer, alleging a violation of a customary international law norm prohibiting involuntary medical experimentation on humans. [*Abdullahi v. Pfizer, Inc.,* 562 F.3d 163 (2d Cir. 2009)]

1. One group should use the principles of ethical reasoning discussed in this chapter to develop three arguments on how Pfizer's conduct was a violation of ethical standards.

2. A second group should take a pro-Pfizer position and argue that the company did not violate any ethical standards (and counter the first group).

3. A third group should come up with proposals for what Pfizer might have done differently to avert the consequences.

Courts and Alternative Dispute Resolution

(Alina555/iStockphoto.com)

CHAPTER OUTLINE

- The Judiciary's Role in American Government
- Basic Judicial Requirements
- The State and Federal Court Systems
- Following a State Court Case
- The Courts Adapt to the Online World
- Alternative Dispute Resolution

LEARNING OBJECTIVES

The five learning objectives below are designed to help improve your understanding of the chapter. After reading this chapter, you should be able to answer the following questions:

1 What is judicial review? How and when was the power of judicial review established?

2 Before a court can hear a case, it must have jurisdiction. Over what must it have jurisdiction? How are the courts applying traditional jurisdictional concepts to cases involving Internet transactions?

3 What is the difference between a trial court and an appellate court?

4 What is discovery, and how does electronic discovery differ from traditional discovery?

5 What are three alternative methods of resolving disputes?

"An eye for an eye will make the whole world blind."
—Mahatma Gandhi, 1869–1948 (Indian political and spiritual leader)

Every society needs to have an established method for resolving disputes. Without one, as Mahatma Gandhi implied in the chapter-opening quotation, the biblical "eye for an eye" would lead to anarchy. This is particularly true in the business world—almost every businessperson will face a lawsuit at some time in his or her career. For this reason, anyone involved in business needs to have an understanding of court systems in the United States, as well as the various methods of dispute resolution that can be pursued outside the courts.

In this chapter, after examining the judiciary's overall role in the American governmental scheme, we discuss some basic requirements that must be met before a party may bring a lawsuit before a particular court. We then look at the court systems of the United States in some detail and, to clarify judicial procedures, follow a hypothetical case through a state court system. Because Islamic legal systems are prevalent in many parts of the world, some judges in this country have been asked to accept some Islamic law. You will read later in this chapter about this controversy.

Throughout this chapter, we indicate how court doctrines and procedures are being adapted to the needs of a cyber age. The chapter concludes with an overview of some alternative methods of settling disputes, including online dispute resolution.

The Judiciary's Role in American Government

As you learned in Chapter 1, the body of American law includes the federal and state constitutions, statutes passed by legislative bodies, administrative law, and the case decisions and legal principles that form the common law. These laws would be meaningless, however, without the courts to interpret and apply them. This is the essential role of the judiciary—the courts—in the American governmental system: to interpret and apply the law. (For a discussion of the impact of increased diversity on our nation's court system, see this chapter's *Law, Diversity, and Business: Managerial Implications* feature on the following page.)

Judicial Review

LEARNING OBJECTIVE 1
What is judicial review? How and when was the power of judicial review established?

Judicial Review The process by which a court decides on the constitutionality of legislative enactments and actions of the executive branch.

As the branch of government entrusted with interpreting the laws, the judiciary can decide, among other things, whether the laws or actions of the other two branches are constitutional. The process for making such a determination is known as **judicial review.** The power of judicial review enables the judicial branch to act as a check on the other two branches of government, in line with the checks-and-balances system established by the U.S. Constitution. (Today, nearly all nations with constitutional democracies, including Canada, France, and Germany, have some form of judicial review.)

The Origins of Judicial Review in the United States

The U.S. Constitution does not mention judicial review, but the concept was not new at the time the nation was founded. Indeed, before 1789 state courts had already overturned state legislative acts that conflicted with state constitutions. Additionally, many of the founders expected the United States Supreme Court to assume a similar role with respect to the federal Constitution. Alexander Hamilton and James Madison both emphasized the importance of judicial review in their essays urging the adoption of the new Constitution. How was the doctrine of judicial review established? See this chapter's *Landmark in the Law* feature on page 67 for the answer.

(Library of Congress)

James Madison (1751–1836) wrote in favor of the states' adopting the new Constitution. What did he think of judicial review?

Jurisdiction The authority of a court to hear and decide a specific case.

Basic Judicial Requirements

Before a court can hear a lawsuit, certain requirements must first be met. These requirements relate to jurisdiction, venue, and standing to sue. We examine each of these important concepts here.

Jurisdiction

In Latin, *juris* means "law," and *diction* means "to speak." Thus, "the power to speak the law" is the literal meaning of the term **jurisdiction.** Before any court can hear a case, it must have jurisdiction over the person (or company) against whom the suit is brought (the defendant) or over the property involved in the suit. The court must also have jurisdiction over the subject matter of the dispute.

LAW, DIVERSITY, AND BUSINESS: MANAGERIAL IMPLICATIONS

INCREASED DIVERSITY IN THE FEDERAL JUDICIARY

The United States Supreme Court first met in 1790, but the first female associate justice—Sandra Day O'Connor—was not appointed until 1981. In the Court's 220-year history, only three other women have been appointed—Ruth Bader Ginsburg in 1993; Sonia Sotomayor in 2009, who was also the first Hispanic on the Court; and Elena Kagan in 2010. When Kagan joined the Court, for the first time in its history, one-third of the justices were women.

Obama's Judicial Nominations Set a Record for Women and Minorities As president, Barack Obama moved at a historic pace to diversify the federal judiciary. Nearly three of every four individuals confirmed for the federal bench have been women or members of minority groups. Indeed, he is the first president who has not selected a majority of white males for lifetime judgeships. During the first three years of Obama's presidency, 21 percent of his nominees who were confirmed were African American, 11 percent were Hispanic, and 7 percent were Asian American. Almost half were women.

The Benefits of a More Diverse Judiciary According to the Alliance for Justice, the more diverse the courts, the more confidence people have in our judicial system. Having a diverse judiciary enriches the decision-making process.

Does having more women on the bench change the way the law is interpreted? Yes, according to Vanderbilt University law professor Tracey George. She cites research that suggests including a woman in a decision-making group influences the behavior of the rest of the group. In particular, some academic studies have found evidence that in gender discrimination lawsuits, if a three-judge panel of a federal appeals court includes a woman, the court is more likely to rule in favor of the person asserting discrimination.

Business Implications *A more diverse federal judiciary will mean that managers must be more conscientious about their employment decisions and make sure that they are not motivated by gender or racial discrimination. Business owners and managers should also establish internal decision-making and record-keeping procedures that are fair and neutral, to avoid any appearance of bias at the workplace. If allegations of discrimination arise, managers should promptly investigate and evaluate the company's conduct, and consider the possibility of settling the claim before trial.*

Jurisdiction over Persons or Property

Generally, a court can exercise personal jurisdiction (*in personam* jurisdiction) over any person or business that resides in a certain geographic area. A state trial court, for example, normally has jurisdictional authority over residents (including businesses) in a particular area of the state, such as a county or district. A state's highest court (often called the state supreme court)[1] has jurisdiction over all residents of that state.

A court can also exercise jurisdiction over property that is located within its boundaries. This kind of jurisdiction is known as *in rem* jurisdiction, or "jurisdiction over the thing." **EXAMPLE 3.1** A dispute arises over the ownership of a boat in dry dock in Fort Lauderdale, Florida. The boat is owned by an Ohio resident, over whom a Florida court normally cannot exercise personal jurisdiction. The other party to the dispute is a resident of Nebraska. In this situation, a lawsuit concerning the boat could be brought in a Florida state court on the basis of the court's *in rem* jurisdiction. ●

Long Arm Statute A state statute that permits a state to exercise jurisdiction over nonresident defendants.

Long Arm Statutes Under the authority of a state **long arm statute**, a court can exercise personal jurisdiction over certain out-of-state defendants based on activities that took place within the state. Before exercising long arm jurisdiction over a nonresident, however, the court must be convinced that the defendant had sufficient contacts, or *minimum*

---

1. As will be discussed shortly, a state's highest court is frequently referred to as the state supreme court, but there are exceptions. For example, in New York, the supreme court is a trial court.

LANDMARK IN THE LAW

Marbury v. Madison (1803)

The power of judicial review was established in the Supreme Court's decision in the case of *Marbury v. Madison*.[a] Though the decision is widely viewed as a cornerstone of constitutional law, the case had its origins in early U.S. politics.

When Thomas Jefferson defeated the incumbent president, John Adams, in the presidential elections of 1800, Adams feared the Jeffersonians' antipathy toward business and toward a strong national government. Adams thus rushed to "pack" the judiciary with loyal Federalists (those who believed in a strong national government) by appointing what came to be called "midnight judges" just before he left office. But Adams's secretary of state (John Marshall) was able to deliver only forty-two of the fifty-nine judicial appointment letters by the time Jefferson took over as president. Jefferson refused to order his secretary of state, James Madison, to deliver the remaining commissions.

Marshall's Dilemma William Marbury and three others to whom the commissions had not been delivered sought a writ of *mandamus* (an order directing a government official to fulfill a duty) from the United States Supreme Court, as authorized by the Judiciary Act of 1789. As fate would have it, John Marshall had just been appointed as chief justice of the Supreme Court. Marshall faced a dilemma: If he ordered the commissions delivered, the new secretary of state (Madison) could simply refuse to deliver them—and the Court had no way to compel him to act. At the same time, if Marshall simply allowed the new administration to do as it wished, the Court's power would be severely eroded.

---

a. 5 U.S. (1 Cranch) 137, 2 L.Ed. 60 (1803).

Marshall's Decision Marshall masterfully fashioned his decision to enlarge the power of the Supreme Court by affirming the Court's power of judicial review. He stated, "It is emphatically the province and duty of the Judicial Department to say what the law is. . . . If two laws conflict with each other, the Courts must decide on the operation of each. . . . [I]f both [a] law and the Constitution apply to a particular case, . . . the Court must determine which of these conflicting rules governs the case."

Marshall's decision did not require anyone to do anything. He concluded that the highest court did not have the power to issue a writ of *mandamus* in this particular case. Although the Judiciary Act of 1789 specified that the Supreme Court could issue writs of *mandamus* as part of its original jurisdiction, Article III of the Constitution, which spelled out the Court's original jurisdiction, did not mention writs of *mandamus*. Because Congress did not have the right to expand the Supreme Court's jurisdiction, this section of the Judiciary Act of 1789 was unconstitutional— and thus void. The *Marbury* decision stands to this day as a judicial and political masterpiece.

Application to Today's World *Since the* Marbury v. Madison *decision, the power of judicial review has remained unchallenged and today is exercised by both federal and state courts. If the courts did not have the power of judicial review, the constitutionality of Congress's acts could not be challenged in court—a congressional statute would remain law unless changed by Congress. The courts of other countries that have adopted a constitutional democracy often cite this decision as a justification for judicial review.*

---

contacts, with the state to justify the jurisdiction.[2] Generally, this means that the defendant must have enough of a connection to the state for the judge to conclude that it is fair for the state to exercise power over the defendant. If an out-of-state defendant caused an automobile accident or sold defective goods within the state, for instance, a court will usually find that minimum contacts exist to exercise jurisdiction over that defendant.

CASE EXAMPLE 3.2 After an Xbox game system caught fire in Bonnie Broquet's home in Texas and caused substantial personal injuries, Broquet filed a lawsuit in a Texas court against Ji-Haw Industrial Company, a nonresident company that made the Xbox components. Broquet alleged that Ji-Haw's components were defective and had caused the fire. Ji-Haw argued that the Texas court lacked jurisdiction over it, but a state appellate court held that the Texas long arm statute authorized the exercise of jurisdiction over the out-of-state defendant.[3] ●

---

2. The minimum-contacts standard was established in *International Shoe Co. v. State of Washington*, 326 U.S. 310, 66 S.Ct. 154, 90 L.Ed. 95 (1945).

3. *Ji-Haw Industrial Co. v. Broquet*, 2008 WL 441822 (Tex.App.—San Antonio 2008).

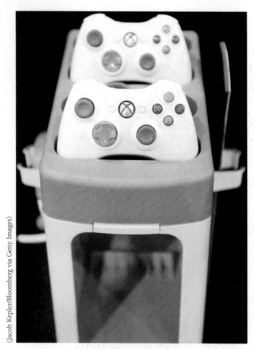

Suppose that a young gamer is injured because Microsoft's Xbox, shown above, released an electrical shock. Whom can the parents sue?

Similarly, a state may exercise personal jurisdiction over a nonresident defendant who is sued for breaching a contract that was formed within the state, even when that contract was negotiated over the phone or through correspondence. **EXAMPLE 3.3** Sharon Mills, a California resident, forms a corporation to distribute a documentary film on global climate change. Brad Cole, an environmentalist who lives in Ohio, loans the corporation funds that he borrows from an Ohio bank. A year later, the film is still not completed. Mills agrees to repay Cole's loan in a contract arranged through phone calls and correspondence between California and Ohio. When Mills does not repay the loan, Cole files a lawsuit in an Ohio court. In this situation, the Ohio court can likely exercise jurisdiction over Mills because her phone calls and letters have established sufficient contacts with the state of Ohio. ●

Corporate Contacts Because corporations are considered legal persons, courts use the same principles to determine whether it is fair to exercise jurisdiction over a corporation.[4] A corporation normally is subject to personal jurisdiction in the state in which it is incorporated, has its principal office, and is doing business. Courts apply the minimum-contacts test to determine if they can exercise jurisdiction over out-of-state corporations.

The minimum-contacts requirement is usually met if the corporation advertises or sells its products within the state, or places its goods into the "stream of commerce" with the intent that the goods be sold in the state. **EXAMPLE 3.4** A business is incorporated under the laws of Maine but has a branch office and manufacturing plant in Georgia. The corporation also advertises and sells its products in Georgia. These activities would likely constitute sufficient contacts with the state of Georgia to allow a Georgia court to exercise jurisdiction over the corporation. ●

Some corporations do not sell or advertise products or place any goods in the stream of commerce. Determining what constitutes minimum contacts in these situations can be more difficult. In the following case, the question before the court was whether a New Jersey firm had minimum contacts with a North Carolina firm.

---

4. In the eyes of the law, corporations are "legal persons"—entities that can sue and be sued. See Chapter 20.

Case 3.1

Southern Prestige Industries, Inc. v. Independence Plating Corp.

Court of Appeals of North Carolina, 690 S.E.2d 768 (2010). www.nccourts.org[a]

Many parts in these jets must be metal coated.

FACTS Independence Plating Corporation (the defendant) is a New Jersey corporation that provides metal-coating services. Its only office and all of its personnel are located in New Jersey. It does not advertise out of state, but it had a long-standing business relationship with Kidde Aerospace in North Carolina (filing under the name Southern Prestige Industries,

Inc.). For almost a year, Independence and Kidde engaged in frequent transactions. On November 18, 2008, Kidde initiated an action for breach of contract in a North Carolina state court, alleging defects in the metal-plating process carried out by Independence. Independence filed a motion to dismiss for lack of personal jurisdiction, which the trial court denied.

---

a. In the right-hand column of the page, click on "Court Opinions." When that page opens, select the year 2010 under the heading "Court of Appeals Opinions." Scroll down to February 2, 2010, and click on the case title under "Unpublished Opinions" to access the opinion. The North Carolina court system maintains this Web site.

Case 3.1—Continued

Independence appealed, arguing that it had insufficient contacts with North Carolina for the state to exercise jurisdiction.

ISSUE Did Independence Plating Corporation have sufficient minimum contacts with North Carolina for the state to exercise personal jurisdiction?

DECISION Yes. The North Carolina appellate court affirmed the trial court's decision. Independence had sufficient minimum contacts with North Carolina to satisfy the due process of law requirements necessary for the state to exercise jurisdiction.

REASON In determining whether minimum contacts existed, the court looked at several factors, including the number of contacts and their nature and quality, as well as the interests of North Carolina, the forum state. In this case, thirty-two separate purchase orders were exchanged between the two parties in a period of less than twelve months. Independence sent invoices totaling more than $21,000, and these invoices were paid from Southern's corporate bank account. "North Carolina has a single 'manifest interest' in providing the plaintiff with 'a convenient forum for redressing injuries inflicted by' [the] defendant, an out-of-state merchant."

CRITICAL THINKING—Ethical Consideration *Was it fair for the North Carolina courts to require a New Jersey company to litigate in North Carolina? Explain.*

Jurisdiction over Subject Matter

Jurisdiction over subject matter is a limitation on the types of cases a court can hear. In both the federal and the state court systems, there are courts of *general* (unlimited) *jurisdiction* and courts of *limited jurisdiction.* An example of a court of general jurisdiction is a state trial court or a federal district court. An example of a state court of limited jurisdiction is a probate court. **Probate courts** are state courts that handle only matters relating to the transfer of a person's assets and obligations after that person's death, including matters relating to the custody and guardianship of children. An example of a federal court of limited subject-matter jurisdiction is a bankruptcy court. **Bankruptcy courts** handle only bankruptcy proceedings, which are governed by federal bankruptcy law (discussed in Chapter 15).

A court's jurisdiction over subject matter is usually defined in the statute or constitution creating the court. In both the federal and the state court systems, a court's subject-matter jurisdiction can be limited not only by the subject of the lawsuit but also by the amount in controversy, by whether a case is a felony (a more serious type of crime) or a misdemeanor (a less serious type of crime), or by whether the proceeding is a trial or an appeal.

Probate Court A state court of limited jurisdiction that conducts proceedings relating to the settlement of a deceased person's estate.

Bankruptcy Court A federal court of limited jurisdiction that handles only bankruptcy proceedings, which are governed by federal bankruptcy law.

Original and Appellate Jurisdiction

The distinction between courts of original jurisdiction and courts of appellate jurisdiction normally lies in whether the case is being heard for the first time. Courts having original jurisdiction are courts of the first instance, or trial courts—that is, courts in which lawsuits begin, trials take place, and evidence is presented. In the federal court system, the *district courts* are trial courts. In the various state court systems, the trial courts are known by various names, as will be discussed shortly.

The key point here is that any court having original jurisdiction is normally known as a trial court. Courts having appellate jurisdiction act as reviewing courts, or appellate courts. In general, cases can be brought before appellate courts only on appeal from an order or a judgment of a trial court or other lower court.

Jurisdiction of the Federal Courts

Because the federal government is a government of limited powers, the jurisdiction of the federal courts is limited. Federal courts have subject-matter jurisdiction in two situations.

Federal Questions Article III of the U.S. Constitution establishes the boundaries of federal judicial power. Section 2 of Article III states that "[t]he judicial Power shall extend to

KNOW THIS Federal courts do not have the power to hear every case. They have jurisdiction to hear a dispute only when it raises a federal question or when the parties are residents of different states (or countries) and the amount involved in the controversy exceeds $75,000.

Federal Question A question that pertains to the U.S. Constitution, an act of Congress, or a treaty and provides a basis for federal jurisdiction in a case.

all Cases, in Law and Equity, arising under this Constitution, the Laws of the United States, and Treaties made, or which shall be made, under their Authority." This clause means that whenever a plaintiff's cause of action is based, at least in part, on the U.S. Constitution, a treaty, or a federal law, then a **federal question** arises, and the federal courts have jurisdiction. Any lawsuit involving a federal question, such as a person's rights under the U.S. Constitution, can originate in a federal court. Note that in a case based on a federal question, a federal court will apply federal law.

Diversity of Citizenship A basis for federal court jurisdiction over a lawsuit between citizens of different states and countries.

Diversity of Citizenship   Federal district courts can also exercise original jurisdiction over cases involving **diversity of citizenship.** The most common type of diversity jurisdiction has two requirements:[5] (1) the plaintiff and defendant must be residents of different states, and (2) the dollar amount in controversy must exceed $75,000. For purposes of diversity jurisdiction, a corporation is a citizen of both the state in which it is incorporated and the state in which its principal place of business is located. A case involving diversity of citizenship can be filed in the appropriate federal district court. If the case starts in a state court, it can sometimes be transferred, or "removed," to a federal court. A large percentage of the cases filed in federal courts each year are based on diversity of citizenship.

As noted, a federal court will apply federal law in cases involving federal questions. In a case based on diversity of citizenship, in contrast, a federal court will apply the relevant state law (which is often the law of the state in which the court sits).

Exclusive versus Concurrent Jurisdiction   When both federal and state courts have the power to hear a case, as is true in lawsuits involving diversity of citizenship, **concurrent jurisdiction** exists. When cases can be tried only in federal courts or only in state courts, **exclusive jurisdiction** exists. Federal courts have exclusive jurisdiction in cases involving federal crimes, bankruptcy, patents, and copyrights; in suits against the United States; and in some areas of admiralty law (law governing transportation on the seas and ocean waters). State courts also have exclusive jurisdiction over certain subject matter—for instance, divorce and adoption.

Concurrent Jurisdiction Jurisdiction that exists when two different courts have the power to hear a case.

Exclusive Jurisdiction Jurisdiction that exists when a case can be heard only in a particular court or type of court.

When concurrent jurisdiction exists, a party may bring a suit in either a federal court or a state court. A number of factors can affect the decision of whether to litigate in a federal or a state court, such as the availability of different remedies, the distance to the respective courthouses, or the experience or reputation of a particular judge. For instance, if the dispute involves a trade secret, a party might conclude that a federal court—which has exclusive jurisdiction over copyrights, patents, and trademarks—would have more expertise in the matter.

A resident of another state might also choose a federal court over a state court if he or she is concerned that a state court might be biased against an out-of-state plaintiff. In contrast, a plaintiff might choose to litigate in a state court if it has a reputation for awarding substantial amounts of damages or if the judge is perceived as being pro-plaintiff. The concepts of exclusive and concurrent jurisdiction are illustrated in Exhibit 3.1 on the facing page.

Jurisdiction in Cyberspace

The Internet's capacity to bypass political and geographic boundaries undercuts the traditional basis on which courts assert personal jurisdiction. As already discussed, for a court to compel a defendant to come before it, there must be at least minimum contacts—the

---

5. Diversity jurisdiction also exists in cases between (1) a foreign country and citizens of a state or of different states and (2) citizens of a state and citizens or subjects of a foreign country. These bases for diversity jurisdiction are less commonly used.

Exhibit 3.1 **Exclusive and Concurrent Jurisdiction**

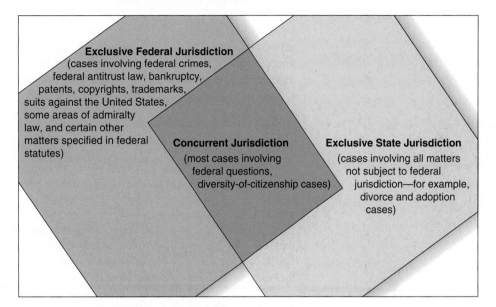

Exclusive Federal Jurisdiction
(cases involving federal crimes, federal antitrust law, bankruptcy, patents, copyrights, trademarks, suits against the United States, some areas of admiralty law, and certain other matters specified in federal statutes)

Concurrent Jurisdiction
(most cases involving federal questions, diversity-of-citizenship cases)

Exclusive State Jurisdiction
(cases involving all matters not subject to federal jurisdiction—for example, divorce and adoption cases)

presence of a salesperson within the state, for example. Are there sufficient minimum contacts if the defendant's only connection to a jurisdiction is an ad on a Web site originating from a remote location?

LEARNING OBJECTIVE 2
Before a court can hear a case, it must have jurisdiction. Over what must it have jurisdiction? How are the courts applying traditional jurisdictional concepts to cases involving Internet transactions?

The "Sliding-Scale" Standard The courts have developed a standard—called a "sliding-scale" standard—for determining when the exercise of jurisdiction over an out-of-state defendant is proper. In developing this standard, the courts have identified three types of Internet business contacts: (1) substantial business conducted over the Internet (with contracts and sales, for example), (2) some interactivity through a Web site, and (3) passive advertising. Jurisdiction is proper for the first category, improper for the third, and may or may not be appropriate for the second.[6] An Internet communication is typically considered passive if people have to voluntarily access it to read the message, and active if it is sent to specific individuals.

In certain situations, even a single contact can satisfy the minimum-contacts requirement. **CASE EXAMPLE 3.5** Daniel Crummey purchased a used recreational vehicle (RV) from sellers in Texas after viewing numerous photos of it on eBay. The sellers' statements on eBay claimed that "everything works great on this RV and will provide comfort and dependability for years to come. This RV will go to Alaska and back without problems!" Crummey picked up the RV in Texas, but on the drive home, the RV quit working. He filed a suit in Louisiana against the sellers alleging that the vehicle was defective, but the sellers claimed that the Louisiana court lacked jurisdiction. Because the sellers had used eBay to market and sell the RV to a Louisiana buyer—and had regularly used eBay to sell vehicles to remote parties in the past—the court found that jurisdiction was proper.[7] ●

---

6. For a leading case on this issue, see *Zippo Manufacturing Co. v. Zippo Dot Com, Inc.*, 952 F.Supp. 1119 (W.D.Pa. 1997).

7. *Crummey v. Morgan*, 965 So.2d 497 (La.App.1 Cir. 2007). But note that a single sale on eBay does not necessarily confer jurisdiction. Jurisdiction depends on whether the seller regularly uses eBay as a means for doing business with remote buyers. See *Boschetto v. Hansing*, 539 F.3d 1011 (9th Cir. 2008).

**PREVENTING
LEGAL DISPUTES**

Those of you with an entrepreneurial spirit may be eager to establish Web sites to promote products and solicit orders. Be aware, however, that you can be sued in states in which you have *never* been physically present if you have had sufficient contacts with residents of those states over the Internet. Before you create a Web site that is the least bit interactive, you need to consult an attorney to find out whether you will be subjecting yourself to jurisdiction in every state. Becoming informed about the extent of your potential exposure to lawsuits in various locations is an important part of preventing litigation.

International Jurisdictional Issues   Because the Internet is global in scope, it obviously raises international jurisdictional issues. The world's courts seem to be developing a standard that echoes the minimum-contacts requirement applied by U.S. courts. Most courts are indicating that minimum contacts—doing business within the jurisdiction, for example—are enough to compel a defendant to appear and that a physical presence is not necessary. The effect of this standard is that a business firm has to comply with the laws in any jurisdiction in which it targets customers for its products. This situation is complicated by the fact that many countries' laws on particular issues—free speech, for example—are very different from U.S. laws

The following case illustrates how federal courts apply a sliding-scale standard to determine if they can exercise jurisdiction over a foreign defendant whose only contact with the United States is through a Web site.

Spotlight on Gucci

Case 3.2
Gucci America, Inc. v. Wang Huoqing
United States District Court, Northern District of California, ____ F.Supp.3d ____ (2011).

(Alessia Pierdomenico/
Bloomberg via GettyImages)

Gucci luxury leather products are often counterfeited. Can Gucci sue an Asian company in the United States, nonetheless?

FACTS Gucci America, Inc., is a New York corporation headquartered in New York City. Gucci manufactures and distributes high-quality luxury goods, including footwear, belts, sunglasses, handbags, and wallets, which are sold worldwide. In connection with its products, Gucci uses twenty-one federally registered trademarks (trademark law will be discussed in Chapter 5). Gucci also operates a number of boutiques, some of which are located in California.

Wang Huoqing, a resident of the People's Republic of China, operates numerous Web sites. When Gucci discovered that Huoqing's Web sites were selling counterfeit goods—products with Gucci's trademarks but not genuine Gucci articles—it hired a private investigator in San Jose, California, to buy goods from the Web sites. The investigator purchased a wallet that was labeled Gucci but was counterfeit. Gucci filed a trademark infringement lawsuit against Huoqing in a federal district court in California seeking damages and an injunction to prevent further infringement. Huoqing was notified of the lawsuit via e-mail (see the discussion of *service of process* on page 80) but did not appear in court. Gucci asked the court to enter a default judgment—that is, a judgment entered when the defendant fails to appear—but the court first had to determine whether it had personal jurisdiction over Huoqing based on the Internet sales.

ISSUE Can a U.S. federal court exercise personal jurisdiction over a resident of China whose only contact with the United States was through an interactive Web site that advertised and sold counterfeit goods?

DECISION Yes. The U.S. District Court for the Northern District of California held that it had personal jurisdiction over the foreign defendant, Huoqing. The court entered a default judgment against Huoqing and granted Gucci an injunction.

REASON The court reasoned that the due process clause allows a federal court to exercise jurisdiction over a defendant who has had sufficient minimum contacts with the court's forum—the place where the court exercises jurisdiction.

Case 3.2—Continued

Specifically, jurisdiction exists when (1) the nonresident defendant engages in some act or transaction with the forum "by which he purposefully avails himself of the privilege of conducting activities in the forum, thereby invoking the benefits and protections of its laws; (2) the claim must be one which arises out of or results from the defendant's forum-related activities; and (3) exercise of jurisdiction must be reasonable."

To determine whether Huoqing had purposefully conducted business activities in Gucci's district, the court used a sliding-scale analysis. Under this analysis, passive Web sites do not create sufficient contacts for such a finding, but interactive sites may do so. Huoqing's Web sites were fully interactive. In addition, Gucci presented evidence that Huoqing had advertised and sold the counterfeited goods within the court's district, and that he had made one actual sale within the district—the sale to Gucci's private investigator.

WHAT IF THE FACTS WERE DIFFERENT? *Suppose that Gucci had not presented evidence that Huoqing had made one actual sale through his Web site to a resident (the private investigator) of the court's district. Would the court still have found that it had personal jurisdiction over Huoqing? Why or why not?*

Venue

Venue The geographic district in which a legal action is tried and from which the jury is selected.

Jurisdiction has to do with whether a court has authority to hear a case involving specific persons, property, or subject matter. **Venue**[8] is concerned with the most appropriate physical location for a trial. Two state courts (or two federal courts) may have the authority to exercise jurisdiction over a case, but it may be more appropriate or convenient to hear the case in one court than in the other.

Basically, the concept of venue reflects the policy that a court trying a suit should be in the geographic neighborhood (usually the county) where the incident leading to the lawsuit occurred or where the parties involved in the lawsuit reside. Venue in a civil case typically is where the defendant resides, whereas venue in a criminal case normally is where the crime occurred. Pretrial publicity or other factors, though, may require a change of venue to another community, especially in criminal cases when the defendant's right to a fair and impartial jury has been impaired.

EXAMPLE 3.6 Police raid a compound of religious polygamists in Texas and remove many children from the ranch. Authorities suspect that some of the girls were being sexually and physically abused. The raid receives a great deal of media attention, and the people living in the nearby towns are likely influenced by this publicity. In this situation, if the government files criminal charges against a member of the religious sect, that individual may request—and will probably receive—a change of venue to another location. ●

Standing to Sue

Standing to Sue The legal requirement that an individual must have a sufficient stake in a controversy before he or she can bring a lawsuit.

Justiciable Controversy A controversy that is not hypothetical or academic but real and substantial; a requirement that must be satisfied before a court will hear a case.

Before a person can bring a lawsuit before a court, the party must have **standing to sue,** or a sufficient "stake" in the matter to justify seeking relief through the court system. In other words, to have standing, a party must have a legally protected and tangible interest at stake in the litigation. The party bringing the lawsuit must have suffered a harm, or have been threatened by a harm, as a result of the action about which she or he has complained. Standing to sue also requires that the controversy at issue be a **justiciable**[9] **controversy**—a controversy that is real and substantial, as opposed to hypothetical or academic. As Chief Justice John Roberts recently noted in a United States Supreme Court decision, a lack of

---

8. Pronounced *ven*-yoo.
9. Pronounced jus-*tish*-uh-bul.

standing is like Bob Dylan's line in the song "Like a Rolling Stone": "When you got nothing, you got nothing to lose."[10]

CASE EXAMPLE 3.7 James Bush visited the office of the Federal Bureau of Investigation (FBI) in San Jose, California, on two occasions. He filled out forms indicating that he was seeking records under the Freedom of Information Act regarding a police brutality claim and the FBI's failure to investigate it. Bush later filed a suit against the U.S. Department of Justice in an attempt to compel the FBI to provide the requested records. The court dismissed the lawsuit on the ground that no justiciable controversy existed. Because Bush had not complied with the requirements of the FOIA, the FBI was not obligated to provide any records, and thus there was no actual controversy for the court to decide.[11] •

Note that in some situations a person may have standing to sue on behalf of another person, such as a minor or a mentally incompetent person. **EXAMPLE 3.8** Three-year-old Emma suffers serious injuries as a result of a defectively manufactured toy. Because Emma is a minor, her parent or legal guardian can bring a lawsuit on her behalf. •

The State and Federal Court Systems

As mentioned earlier in this chapter, each state has its own court system. Additionally, there is a system of federal courts. Even though there are fifty-two court systems—one for each of the fifty states, one for the District of Columbia, plus a federal system—similarities abound. Exhibit 3.2 on the facing page illustrates the basic organizational structure characteristic of the court systems in many states. The exhibit also shows how the federal court system is structured. Keep in mind that the federal courts are not superior to the state courts. They are simply an independent system of courts, which derives its authority from Article III, Sections 1 and 2, of the U.S. Constitution. We turn now to an examination of these court systems, beginning with the state courts.

The State Court Systems

Typically, a state court system will include several levels, or tiers, of courts. As indicated in Exhibit 3.2 on the facing page, state courts may include (1) trial courts of limited jurisdiction, (2) trial courts of general jurisdiction, (3) appellate courts, and (4) the state's highest court (often called the state supreme court). Generally, any person who is a party to a lawsuit has the opportunity to plead the case before a trial court and then, if he or she loses, before at least one level of appellate court. If the case involves a federal statute or a federal constitutional issue, the decision of a state supreme court on that issue may be further appealed to the United States Supreme Court.

The states use various methods to select judges for their courts. Generally, judges are elected, but in some states, they are appointed. Usually, states specify the number of years that a judge will serve. In contrast, as you will read shortly, judges in the federal court system are appointed by the president of the United States and, if confirmed by the Senate, hold office for life—unless they engage in blatantly illegal conduct.

LEARNING OBJECTIVE 3
What is the difference between a trial court and an appellate court?

Trial Courts   Trial courts are exactly what their name implies—courts in which trials are held and testimony taken. State trial courts have either general or limited jurisdiction.

---

10. The chief justice stated, "The absence of any substantive recovery means that respondents cannot benefit from the judgment they seek and thus lack Article III standing." He then quoted Bob Dylan's lyrics from "Like a Rolling Stone," on *Highway 61 Revisited* (Columbia Records 1965). This was the first time that a member of the Supreme Court cited rock lyrics in an opinion. See *Sprint Communications Co. v. APCC Services, Inc.*, 554 U.S. 269, 128 S.Ct. 2531, 171 L.Ed.2d 424 (2008).

11. *Bush v. Department of Justice*, 2008 WL 5245046 (N.D.Cal. 2008).

Exhibit 3.2 The State and Federal Court Systems

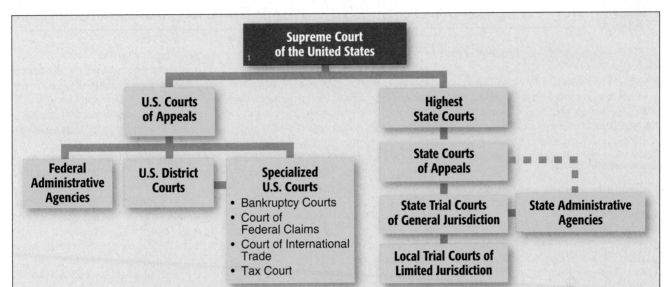

Trial courts that have general jurisdiction as to subject matter may be called county, district, superior, or circuit courts.[12] The jurisdiction of these courts is often determined by the size of the county in which the court sits. State trial courts of general jurisdiction have jurisdiction over a wide variety of subjects, including both civil disputes and criminal prosecutions. (In some states, trial courts of general jurisdiction may hear appeals from courts of limited jurisdiction.)

Some courts of limited jurisdiction are called special inferior trial courts or minor judiciary courts. **Small claims courts** are inferior trial courts that hear only civil cases involving claims of less than a certain amount, such as $5,000 (the amount varies from state to state). Suits brought in small claims courts are generally conducted informally, and lawyers are not required (in a few states, lawyers are not even allowed).

Another example of an inferior trial court is a local municipal court that hears mainly traffic cases. Decisions of small claims courts and municipal courts may sometimes be appealed to a state trial court of general jurisdiction. Other courts of limited jurisdiction as to subject matter include domestic relations or family courts, which handle primarily divorce actions and child-custody disputes, and probate courts, as mentioned earlier. A few states have even established Islamic law courts, which are courts of limited jurisdiction that serve the American Muslim community. (See this chapter's *Beyond Our Borders* feature on the following page for a discussion of the rise of Islamic law courts.)

Appellate, or Reviewing, Courts

Every state has at least one court of appeals (appellate court, or reviewing court), which may be an intermediate appellate court or the state's highest court. About three-fourths of the states have intermediate appellate courts.

Generally, courts of appeals do not conduct new trials, in which evidence is submitted to the court and witnesses are examined. Rather, an appellate court panel of three or more judges reviews the record of the case on appeal, which includes a transcript of the trial proceedings, and determines whether the trial court committed an error.

Small Claims Court A special court in which parties can litigate small claims without an attorney.

---

12. The name in Ohio is court of common pleas, and the name in New York is supreme court.

BEYOND OUR BORDERS   Islamic Law Courts Abroad and at Home

As discussed in Chapter 1, Islamic law is one of the world's three most common legal systems, along with civil law and common law systems. In most Islamic countries, the law is based on *sharia*, a system of law derived from the Qur'an and the sayings and doings of Muhammad and his followers. Today, many non-Islamic countries are establishing Islamic courts for their Muslim citizens.

Islamic Law in Britain, Canada, and Belgium

For several years, Great Britain has had councils that arbitrate disputes between British Muslims involving child custody, property, employment, and housing. These councils do not deal with criminal law or with any civil issues that would put *sharia* in direct conflict with British statutory law. Most Islamic law cases involve marriage or divorce. Starting in 2008, Britain officially sanctioned the authority of *sharia* judges to rule on divorce and financial disputes of Muslim couples. Britain now has eighty-five officially recognized *sharia* courts that have the full power of their equivalent courts within the traditional British judicial system.

In Ontario, Canada, a group of Canadian Muslims established a judicial tribunal using *sharia*. To date, this tribunal has resolved only marital disagreements and some other civil disputes. Under Ontario law, the regular judicial system must uphold such agreements as long as they are voluntary and negotiated through an arbitrator. Any agreements that violate Canada's Charter of Rights and Freedoms will not be upheld.

In 2011, Belgium established its first *sharia* court. This court also handles primarily family law disputes for Muslim immigrants in Belgium.

Islamic Law Courts in the United States

The use of Islamic courts in the United States has been somewhat controversial. The legality of arbitration clauses that require disputes to be settled in Islamic courts has been upheld by regular state courts in some states, including Minnesota and Texas.

In the Texas case, an American Muslim couple was married and was issued an Islamic marriage certificate. Years later, a dispute arose over marital property and the nonpayment of a "dowry for the

bride." The parties involved had signed an arbitration agreement stating that all claims and disputes were to be submitted to arbitration in front of the Texas Islamic Court. A Texas appeals court ruled that the arbitration agreement was valid and enforceable.[a]

In some other states, however, there has been a public backlash against the use of Islamic courts. For instance, in Detroit, Michigan, which has a large American Muslim population, a controversy over the community's attempt to establish Islamic courts erupted in 2008. In 2011, a law that would prohibit judges from enforcing foreign laws, including *sharia*, was proposed in the Michigan state legislature.

Critical Thinking

One of the arguments against allowing sharia courts in the United States is that we would no longer have a common legal framework within our society. Do you agree or disagree? Why?

---

a. *Jabri v. Qaddura,* 108 S.W.3d 404 (Tex.App.—Fort Worth 2003).

Question of Fact In a lawsuit, an issue that involves only disputed facts, and not what the law is on a given point.

Question of Law In a lawsuit, an issue involving the application or interpretation of a law.

Focus on Questions of Law Appellate courts generally focus on questions of law, not questions of fact. A **question of fact** deals with what really happened in regard to the dispute being tried—such as whether a party actually burned a flag. A **question of law** concerns the application or interpretation of the law—such as whether flag-burning is a form of speech protected by the First Amendment to the U.S. Constitution. Only a judge, not a jury, can rule on questions of law.

Defer to the Trial Court's Findings of Fact Appellate courts normally defer (or give weight) to a trial court's findings on questions of fact because the trial court judge and jury were in a better position to evaluate testimony by directly observing witnesses' gestures, demeanor, and nonverbal behavior during the trial. At the appellate level, the judges review the written transcript of the trial, which does not include these nonverbal elements.

An appellate court will challenge a trial court's finding of fact only when the finding is clearly erroneous (that is, when it is contrary to the evidence presented at trial) or when there is no evidence to support the finding. **EXAMPLE 3.9** A jury concludes that a manufacturer's product harmed the plaintiff, but no evidence was submitted to the court to support that conclusion. In this situation, the appellate court will hold that the trial court's decision was erroneous. ● The options exercised by appellate courts will be discussed further later in this chapter.

Highest State Courts   The highest appellate court in a state is usually called the supreme court but may be called by some other name. For example, in both New York and Maryland, the highest state court is called the court of appeals. The decisions of each state's highest court are final on all questions of state law. Only when issues of federal law are involved can a decision made by a state's highest court be overruled by the United States Supreme Court.

The Federal Court System

The federal court system is basically a three-tiered model consisting of (1) U.S. district courts (trial courts of general jurisdiction) and various courts of limited jurisdiction, (2) U.S. courts of appeals (intermediate courts of appeals), and (3) the United States Supreme Court.

Unlike state court judges, who are usually elected, federal court judges—including the justices of the Supreme Court—are appointed by the president of the United States and confirmed by the U.S. Senate. All federal judges receive lifetime appointments because under Article III they "hold their offices during Good Behavior."

ETHICAL ISSUE

Can justice be served when courts are underfunded? The economic downturn that started a few years ago has led to massive budget cuts for many of this nation's court systems. In California, for example, which is experiencing unsustainable state government budget deficits, court funding has been reduced by hundreds of millions of dollars. As a consequence, a typical civil lawsuit may take several years to be heard by a court. Nationwide, the American Bar Association found that in the last several years most states have cut court funding by almost 15 percent. Twenty-six states have stopped filling judicial vacancies. Some have even forced judges to take a leave of absence without pay. One municipal court in Ohio stopped accepting new cases because it could not buy paper.

The end result is that the courts are limiting access to the justice system. According to Rebecca Love Kourlis of the Institute for the Advancement of the American Legal System, our traditional idea that everyone has an equal right to justice is being threatened. The American Bar Association reports that its members fear that "the underfunding of our judicial system threatens the fundamental nature of our tripartite system of government." That brings to mind the words of Judge Learned Hand, who said in 1951: "If we are to keep our democracy, there must be one commandment: Thou shalt not ration justice."

U.S. District Courts   At the federal level, the equivalent of a state trial court of general jurisdiction is the district court. There is at least one federal district court in every state. The number of judicial districts can vary over time, primarily owing to population changes and corresponding caseloads. Today, there are ninety-four federal judicial districts. U.S. district courts have original jurisdiction in federal matters. Federal cases typically originate in district courts. Federal courts with original, but special (or limited), jurisdiction include the bankruptcy courts and others shown in Exhibit 3.2 on page 75.

U.S. Courts of Appeals   In the federal court system, there are thirteen U.S. courts of appeals—also referred to as U.S. circuit courts of appeals. The federal courts of appeals for twelve of the circuits, including the U.S. Court of Appeals for the District of Columbia Circuit, hear appeals from the federal district courts located within their respective judicial circuits. The Court of Appeals for the Thirteenth Circuit, called the Federal Circuit, has national appellate jurisdiction over certain types of cases, such as cases involving patent law and cases in which the U.S. government is a defendant.

The decisions of the circuit courts of appeals are final in most cases, but appeal to the United States Supreme Court is possible. Exhibit 3.3 below shows the geographic boundaries of the U.S. circuit courts of appeals and the boundaries of the U.S. district courts within each circuit.

The United States Supreme Court   The highest level of the three-tiered model of the federal court system is the United States Supreme Court. According to the language of Article III of the U.S. Constitution, there is only one national Supreme Court. All other courts in the federal system are considered "inferior." Congress is empowered to create other inferior courts as it deems necessary. The inferior courts that Congress has created include the second tier in our model—the U.S. courts of appeals—as well as the district courts and any other courts of limited, or specialized, jurisdiction.

The United States Supreme Court consists of nine justices. Although the Supreme Court has original, or trial, jurisdiction in rare instances (set forth in Article III, Section 2), most of its work is as an appeals court. The Supreme Court can review any case decided by any of the federal courts of appeals, and it also has appellate authority over some cases decided in the state courts.

Writ of *Certiorari* A writ from a higher court asking a lower court for the record of a case.

Appeals to the Supreme Court   To bring a case before the Supreme Court, a party requests that the Court issue a writ of *certiorari*. A **writ of *certiorari***[13] is an order issued

---

13. Pronounced sur-shee-uh-*rah*-ree.

Exhibit 3.3 Boundaries of the U.S. Courts of Appeals and U.S. District Courts

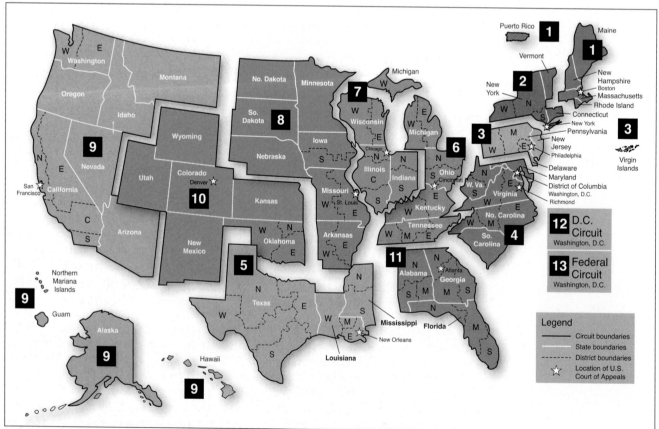

Source: Administrative Office of the United States Courts.

Rule of Four A rule of the United States Supreme Court under which the Court will not issue a writ of *certiorari* unless at least four justices approve of the decision to issue the writ.

by the Supreme Court to a lower court requiring that court to send the record of the case for review. Under the **rule of four,** the Court will not issue a writ unless at least four of the nine justices approve. Whether the Court will issue a writ of *certiorari* is entirely within its discretion. The Court is not required to issue one, and most petitions for writs are denied. (Although thousands of cases are filed with the Supreme Court each year, it hears, on average, fewer than one hundred of these cases.)[14] A denial is not a decision on the merits of a case, nor does it indicate agreement with the lower court's opinion. Furthermore, a denial of the writ has no value as a precedent.

Petitions Granted by the Court Typically, the Court grants petitions when cases raise important constitutional questions or when the lower courts are issuing conflicting decisions on a significant issue. The justices, however, never explain their reasons for hearing certain cases and not others, so it is difficult to predict which type of case the Court might select.

Following a State Court Case

"Lawsuit: A machine which you go into as a pig and come out of as a sausage."

Ambrose Bierce, 1842–1914 (American journalist)

Litigation The process of resolving a dispute through the court system.

To illustrate the procedures that would be followed in a civil lawsuit brought in a state court, we present a hypothetical case and follow it through the state court system. The case involves an automobile accident in which Kevin Anderson, driving a Lexus, struck Lisa Marconi, driving a Hyundai Genesis. The accident occurred at the intersection of Wilshire Boulevard and Rodeo Drive in Beverly Hills, California. Marconi suffered personal injuries and incurred medical and hospital expenses as a result, as well as lost wages for four months. Anderson and Marconi are unable to agree on a settlement, and Marconi sues Anderson. Marconi is the plaintiff, and Anderson is the defendant. Both are represented by lawyers.

During each phase of the **litigation** (the process of working a lawsuit through the court system), Marconi and Anderson will have to observe strict procedural requirements. A large body of law—procedural law—establishes the rules and standards for determining disputes in courts. Procedural rules are very complex, and they vary from court to court and from state to state. In addition to the various sets of rules for state courts, the federal courts have their own rules of procedure. Additionally, the applicable procedures will depend on whether the case is a civil or criminal proceeding. Generally, the Marconi-Anderson civil lawsuit will involve the procedures discussed in the following subsections. Keep in mind that attempts to settle the case may be ongoing throughout the trial.

The Pleadings

Pleadings Statements by the plaintiff and the defendant that detail the facts, charges, and defenses of a case.

The complaint and answer (and the counterclaim and reply)—all of which are discussed next—taken together are called the **pleadings.** The pleadings inform each party of the other's claims and specify the issues (disputed questions) involved in the case. The style and form of the pleadings may be quite different in different states.

Complaint The pleading made by a plaintiff alleging wrongdoing on the part of the defendant. When filed with a court, the complaint initiates a lawsuit.

The Plaintiff's Complaint
Marconi's suit against Anderson commences when her lawyer files a **complaint** with the appropriate court. The complaint contains a statement alleging (1) the facts necessary for the court to take jurisdiction, (2) a brief summary of the facts necessary to show that the plaintiff is entitled to relief (a remedy),[15] and

---

14. From the mid-1950s through the early 1990s, the United States Supreme Court reviewed more cases per year than it has in the last few years. In the Court's 1982–1983 term, for example, the Court issued opinions in 151 cases. In contrast, in its 2011–2012 term, the Court issued opinions in only 77 cases.

15. The factual allegations in a complaint must be enough to raise a right to relief above the speculative level. They must plausibly suggest that the plaintiff is entitled to a remedy. See *Bell Atlantic Corp. v. Twombly,* 550 U.S. 544, 127 S.Ct. 1955, 167 L.Ed.2d 929 (2007).

(3) a statement of the remedy the plaintiff is seeking. Complaints may be lengthy or brief, depending on the complexity of the case and the rules of the jurisdiction.

Service of Process   After the complaint has been filed, the sheriff, a county deputy, or another *process server*—that is, one who delivers a complaint and summons—serves a **summons** and a copy of the complaint on defendant Anderson. The summons notifies Anderson that he must file an answer to the complaint with both the court and the plaintiff's attorney within a specified time period (usually twenty to thirty days). The summons also informs Anderson that failure to answer may result in a **default judgment** for the plaintiff, meaning the plaintiff could be awarded the damages sought in her complaint. Service of process is essential in our legal system. No case can proceed to trial unless the plaintiff can prove that he or she has properly served the defendant.

The Defendant's Answer   The defendant's **answer** either admits the statements or allegations set forth in the complaint or denies them and outlines any defenses that the defendant may have. If Anderson admits to all of Marconi's allegations in his answer, the court will enter a judgment for Marconi. If Anderson denies any of Marconi's allegations, the litigation will go forward.

Anderson can deny Marconi's allegations and set forth his own claim that Marconi was negligent and therefore owes him compensation for the damage to his Lexus. This is appropriately called a **counterclaim.** If Anderson files a counterclaim, Marconi will have to answer it with a pleading, normally called a **reply,** which has the same characteristics as an answer.

Anderson can also admit the truth of Marconi's complaint but raise new facts that may result in dismissal of the action. This is called raising an *affirmative defense.* For example, Anderson could assert the expiration of the time period under the relevant *statute of limitations* (a state or federal statute that sets the maximum time period during which a certain action can be brought or rights enforced) as an affirmative defense.

Motion to Dismiss   A **motion to dismiss** requests the court to dismiss the case for stated reasons. Grounds for dismissal of a case include improper delivery of the complaint and summons, improper venue, and the plaintiff's failure to state a claim for which a court could grant relief. For instance, if Marconi had suffered no injuries or losses as a result of Anderson's negligence, Anderson could move to have the case dismissed because Marconi would not have stated a claim for which relief could be granted.

If the judge grants the motion to dismiss, the plaintiff generally is given time to file an amended complaint. If the judge denies the motion, the suit will go forward, and the defendant must then file an answer. Note that if Marconi wishes to discontinue the suit because, for example, an out-of-court settlement has been reached, she can likewise move for dismissal. The court can also dismiss the case on its own motion.

Pretrial Motions

Either party may attempt to get the case dismissed before trial through the use of various pretrial motions. We have already mentioned the motion to dismiss. Two other important pretrial motions are the motion for judgment on the pleadings and the motion for summary judgment.

At the close of the pleadings, either party may make a **motion for judgment on the pleadings,** or on the merits of the case. The judge will grant the motion only when there is no dispute over the facts of the case and the sole issue to be resolved is a question of law. In deciding on the motion, the judge may consider only the evidence contained in the pleadings.

Summons A document informing a defendant that a legal action has been commenced against her or him and that the defendant must appear in court on a certain date to answer the plaintiff's complaint.

Default Judgment A judgment entered by a court against a defendant who has failed to appear in court to answer or defend against the plaintiff's claim.

Answer Procedurally, a defendant's response to the plaintiff's complaint.

Counterclaim A claim made by a defendant in a civil lawsuit against the plaintiff. In effect, the defendant is suing the plaintiff.

Reply Procedurally, a plaintiff's response to a defendant's answer.

Motion to Dismiss A pleading in which a defendant admits the facts as alleged by the plaintiff but asserts that the plaintiff's claim to state a cause of action has no basis in law.

Motion for Judgment on the Pleadings A motion by either party to a lawsuit at the close of the pleadings requesting the court to decide the issue solely on the pleadings without proceeding to trial. The motion will be granted only if no facts are in dispute.

Motion for Summary Judgment A motion requesting the court to enter a judgment without proceeding to trial. The motion can be based on evidence outside the pleadings and will be granted only if no facts are in dispute.

In contrast, in a **motion for summary judgment,** the court may consider evidence outside the pleadings, such as sworn statements (affidavits) by parties or witnesses, or other documents relating to the case. Either party can make a motion for summary judgment. Like the motion for judgment on the pleadings, a motion for summary judgment will be granted only if there are no genuine questions of fact and the sole question is a question of law.

Discovery

LEARNING OBJECTIVE 4
What is discovery, and how does electronic discovery differ from traditional discovery?

Discovery A method by which the opposing parties obtain information from each other to prepare for trial.

Before a trial begins, each party can use a number of procedural devices to obtain information and gather evidence about the case from the other party or from third parties. The process of obtaining such information is known as **discovery.** Discovery includes gaining access to witnesses, documents, records, and other types of evidence.

The Federal Rules of Civil Procedure and similar rules in the states set forth the guidelines for discovery. Generally, discovery is allowed regarding any matter that is not privileged and is relevant to the claim or defense of any party. Discovery rules also attempt to protect witnesses and parties from undue harassment and to safeguard privileged or confidential material from being disclosed.

If a discovery request involves privileged or confidential business information, a court can deny the request and can limit the scope of discovery in a number of ways. For instance, a court can require the party to submit the materials to the judge in a sealed envelope so that the judge can decide if they should be disclosed to the opposing party.

Discovery prevents surprises at trial by giving parties access to evidence that might otherwise be hidden. This allows both parties to learn what to expect during a trial before they reach the courtroom. Discovery also serves to narrow the issues so that trial time is spent on the main questions in the case.

Deposition The testimony of a party to a lawsuit or a witness taken under oath before a trial.

Depositions and Interrogatories
Discovery can involve the use of depositions or interrogatories, or both. A **deposition** is sworn testimony by a party to the lawsuit or any witness. The person being deposed (the deponent) answers questions asked by the attorneys, and the questions and answers are recorded by an authorized court official and sworn to and signed by the deponent. (Occasionally, written depositions are taken when witnesses are unable to appear in person.)

The answers given to depositions will, of course, help the attorneys prepare for the trial. They can also be used in court to impeach (challenge the credibility of) a party or a witness who changes her or his testimony at the trial. In addition, a witness's deposition can be used as testimony if he or she is not available for the trial.

Interrogatories A series of written questions for which written answers are prepared by a party to a lawsuit, usually with the assistance of the party's attorney, and then signed under oath.

Interrogatories are written questions for which written answers are prepared and then signed under oath. The main difference between interrogatories and written depositions is that interrogatories are directed to a party to the lawsuit (the plaintiff or the defendant), not to a witness, and the party can prepare answers with the aid of an attorney. The scope of interrogatories is broader because parties are obligated to answer the questions, even if that means disclosing information from their records and files.

Requests for Other Information
A party can serve a written request on the other party for an admission of the truth on matters relating to the trial. Any matter admitted under such a request is conclusively established for the trial. For example, Marconi can ask Anderson to admit that he was driving at a speed of forty-five miles an hour. A request for admission saves time at trial because the parties will not have to spend time proving facts on which they already agree.

A party can also gain access to documents and other items not in her or his possession in order to inspect and examine them. Likewise, a party can gain "entry upon land" to inspect the premises. Anderson's attorney, for example, normally can gain permission to inspect and photocopy Marconi's car repair bills.

When the physical or mental condition of one party is in question, the opposing party can ask the court to order a physical or mental examination, but the court will do so only if the need for the information outweighs the right to privacy of the person to be examined. If the court issues the order, the opposing party can obtain the results of the examination.

Electronic Discovery

E-Evidence A type of evidence that consists of all computer-generated or electronically recorded information.

Any relevant material, including information stored electronically, can be the object of a discovery request. The federal rules and most state rules now specifically allow all parties to obtain electronic "data compilations." Electronic evidence, or **e-evidence**, includes all types of computer-generated or electronically recorded information, such as e-mail, voice mail, tweets, blogs, spreadsheets, as well as documents and other data stored on computers. E-evidence can reveal significant facts that are not discoverable by other means. For example, computers automatically record certain information about files—such as who created the file and when, and who accessed, modified, or transmitted it—on their hard drives. This information can be obtained only from the file in its electronic format—not from printed-out versions.

E-Discovery Procedures   Amendments to the Federal Rules of Civil Procedure that took effect in 2006 deal specifically with the preservation, retrieval, and production of electronic data. Although traditional means, such as interrogatories and depositions, are still used to find out about the e-evidence, a party must usually hire an expert to retrieve evidence in its electronic format. The expert uses software to reconstruct e-mail exchanges and establish who knew what and when they knew it. The expert can even recover files that the user thought had been deleted from a computer.

Advantages and Disadvantages   Electronic discovery has significant advantages over paper discovery. Back-up copies of documents and e-mail can provide useful—and often quite damaging—information about how a particular matter progressed over several weeks or months. E-discovery can uncover the proverbial smoking gun that will win the lawsuit, but it is also time consuming and expensive, especially when lawsuits involve large firms with multiple offices. Also, many firms are finding it difficult to fulfill their duty to preserve electronic evidence from a vast number of sources. For a discussion of some of the problems associated with preserving electronic evidence for discovery, see this chapter's *Adapting the Law to the Online Environment* feature on the facing page.

Pretrial Conference

Either party or the court can request a pretrial conference, or hearing. Usually, the hearing consists of an informal discussion between the judge and the opposing attorneys after discovery has taken place. The purpose of the hearing is to explore the possibility of a settlement without trial and, if this is not possible, to identify the matters that are in dispute and to plan the course of the trial.

Jury Selection

◄ KNOW THIS ►

Picking the "right" jury is often an important aspect of litigation strategy, and a number of firms now specialize in jury consulting services.

A trial can be held with or without a jury. The Seventh Amendment to the U.S. Constitution guarantees the right to a jury trial for cases in *federal* courts when the amount in controversy exceeds $20, but this guarantee does not apply to state courts. Most states have similar guarantees in their own constitutions (although the threshold dollar amount is higher than $20). The right to a trial by jury does not have to be exercised, and many cases are tried without a jury. In most states and in federal courts, one of the parties must request a jury in a civil case, or the judge presumes that the parties waive the right.

ADAPTING THE LAW TO THE ONLINE ENVIRONMENT

THE DUTY TO PRESERVE ELECTRONIC EVIDENCE FOR DISCOVERY

Today, less than 0.5 percent of new information is created on paper. Instead of sending letters and memos, people send e-mails and text messages, creating a massive amount of electronically stored information (ESI). The law requires parties to preserve ESI whenever there is a "reasonable anticipation of litigation."

Why Companies Fail to Preserve E-Evidence

Preserving e-evidence can be a challenge, though, particularly for large corporations that have electronic data scattered across multiple networks, servers, desktops, laptops, iPhones, iPads, and other smartphones and tablets. Although many companies have policies regarding back-up of office e-mail and computer systems, these may cover only a fraction of the e-evidence requested in a lawsuit.

Technological advances further complicate the situation. Users of BlackBerrys, for example, can configure them so that messages are transmitted with limited or no archiving rather than going through a company's servers and being recorded. How can a company preserve e-evidence that is never on its servers? In one case, the court held that a company had a duty to preserve transitory "server log data," which exist only temporarily on a computer's memory.[a]

Potential Sanctions and Malpractice Claims

A court may impose sanctions (such as fines) on a party that fails to preserve electronic evidence or to comply with e-evidence requests. A firm may be sanctioned if it provides e-mails without the attachments, does not produce all of the e-discovery requested, overwrites the contents of files, or fails to suspend its automatic e-mail deletion procedures.[b] Sanctions for e-discovery

violations have become increasingly common in recent years.[c] Attorneys who fail to properly advise their clients concerning the duty to preserve e-evidence or who fail to supervise vendors, contract attorneys, or subordinates who work for the clients also often face sanctions and malpractice claims.[d]

Lessons from Intel

A party that fails to preserve e-evidence may even find itself at such a disadvantage that it will settle a dispute rather than continue litigation. For instance, Advanced Micro Devices, Inc. (AMD), sued Intel Corporation, one of the world's largest microprocessor suppliers, for violating antitrust laws. Immediately after the lawsuit was filed, Intel began collecting and preserving the ESI on its servers. Although the company instructed its employees to retain documents and e-mails related to competition with AMD, many employees saved only copies of the e-mails that they had received and not e-mails that they had sent.

In addition, Intel did not stop its automatic e-mail deletion system, causing other information to be lost. In the end, although Intel produced data that were equivalent to "somewhere in the neighborhood of a pile 137 miles high" in paper, its failure to preserve e-discovery led it to settle the dispute.[e]

Critical Thinking

How might a large company protect itself from allegations that it intentionally failed to preserve electronic data?

---

a. See *Columbia Pictures v. Brunnell*, 2007 WL 2080419 (C.D.Cal. 2007).

b. See, for example, *Io Group, Inc. v. GLBT, Ltd*, 2011 WL 4974337 (N.D.Cal. 2011); *E. I. Du Pont de Nemours & Co. v. Kolon Industries, Inc.*, 803 F.Supp.2d 469 (E.D.Va. 2011); *Genger v. TR Investors, LLC*, 26 A.3d 180 (Del.Supr. 2011); *PIC Group, Inc. v. LandCoast Insulation, Inc.*, 2011 WL 2669144 (S.D.Miss. 2011).

c. Elizabeth E. McGinn and Karen M. Morgan, "New Ethical Issues and Challenges in E-Discovery," *New York Law Journal*, October 5, 2011.

d. See, for example, *Surowiec v. Capital Title Agency, Inc.*, 790 F.Supp.2d 997 (D.Ariz. 2011).

e. See *In re Intel Corp. Microprocessor Antitrust Litigation*, 2008 WL 2310288 (D.Del. 2008). See also *Net2Phone, Inc. v. eBay, Inc.*, 2008 WL 8183817 (D.N.J. 2008).

Voir Dire An important part of the jury selection process in which the attorneys question prospective jurors about their backgrounds, attitudes, and biases to ascertain whether they can be impartial jurors.

Before a jury trial commences, a jury must be selected. The jury selection process is known as **voir dire**.[16] During *voir dire* in most jurisdictions, attorneys for the plaintiff and the defendant ask prospective jurors oral questions to determine whether a potential jury member is biased or has any connection with a party to the action or with a prospective witness. In some jurisdictions, the judge may do all or part of the questioning based on written questions submitted by counsel for the parties.

During *voir dire*, a party may challenge a prospective juror *peremptorily*—that is, ask that an individual not be sworn in as a juror without providing any reason. Alternatively, a party

---

16. Pronounced vwahr *deehr.*

may challenge a prospective juror *for cause*—that is, provide a reason why an individual should not be sworn in as a juror. If the judge grants the challenge, the individual is asked to step down. A prospective juror may not be excluded from the jury by the use of discriminatory challenges, however, such as those based on racial criteria or gender.

At the Trial

At the beginning of the trial, the attorneys present their opening arguments, setting forth the facts that they expect to prove during the trial. Then the plaintiff's case is presented. In our hypothetical case, Marconi's lawyer would introduce evidence (relevant documents, exhibits, and the testimony of witnesses) to support Marconi's position. The defendant has the opportunity to challenge any evidence introduced and to cross-examine any of the plaintiff's witnesses.

Directed Verdicts   At the end of the plaintiff's case, the defendant's attorney has the opportunity to ask the judge to direct a verdict for the defendant on the ground that the plaintiff has presented no evidence that would justify the granting of the plaintiff's remedy. This is called a **motion for a directed verdict** (known in federal courts as a *motion for judgment as a matter of law*).

    If the motion is not granted (it seldom is granted), the defendant's attorney then presents the evidence and witnesses for the defendant's case. At the conclusion of the defendant's case, the defendant's attorney has another opportunity to make a motion for a directed verdict. The plaintiff's attorney can challenge any evidence introduced and cross-examine the defendant's witnesses.

Closing Arguments and Awards   After the defense concludes its presentation, the attorneys present their closing arguments, each urging a verdict in favor of her or his client. The judge instructs the jury in the law that applies to the case (these instructions are often called *charges*), and the jury retires to the jury room to deliberate a verdict. In the Marconi-Anderson case, the jury will not only decide for the plaintiff or for the defendant but, if it finds for the plaintiff, will also decide on the amount of the **award** (the compensation to be paid to her).

Posttrial Motions

After the jury has rendered its verdict, either party may make a posttrial motion. If Marconi wins and Anderson's attorney has previously moved for a directed verdict, Anderson's attorney may make a **motion for judgment n.o.v.** (from the Latin *non obstante veredicto*, which means "notwithstanding the verdict"—called a *motion for judgment as a matter of law* in the federal courts). Such a motion will be granted only if the jury's verdict was unreasonable and erroneous. If the judge grants the motion, the jury's verdict will be set aside, and a judgment will be entered in favor of the opposite party (Anderson).

    Alternatively, Anderson could make a **motion for a new trial**, asking the judge to set aside the adverse verdict and to hold a new trial. The motion will be granted if, after looking at all the evidence, the judge is convinced that the jury was in error but does not feel that it is appropriate to grant judgment for the other side. A judge can also grant a new trial on the basis of newly discovered evidence, misconduct by the participants or the jury during the trial, or error by the judge.

The Appeal

Assume here that any posttrial motion is denied and that Anderson appeals the case. (If Marconi wins but receives a smaller monetary award than she sought, she can appeal also.) Keep in mind, though, that a party cannot appeal a trial court's decision simply because he

---

Motion for a Directed Verdict   A motion for the judge to take the decision out of the hands of the jury and to direct a verdict for the party making the motion on the ground that the other party has not produced sufficient evidence to support her or his claim.

Award   The monetary compensation given to a party at the end of a trial or other proceeding.

Motion for Judgment N.O.V.   A motion requesting the court to grant judgment in favor of the party making the motion on the ground that the jury's verdict against him or her was unreasonable and erroneous.

Motion for a New Trial   A motion asserting that the trial was so fundamentally flawed (because of error, newly discovered evidence, prejudice, or another reason) that a new trial is necessary to prevent a miscarriage of justice.

The members of the California Supreme Court, that state's highest court, ready themselves for a hearing. Do all parties to legal disputes have a right to be heard by an appellate court?

(AP Photo/Paul Sakuma)

or she is dissatisfied with the outcome of the trial. A party must have legitimate grounds to file an appeal. In other words, he or she must be able to claim that the lower court committed an error. If Anderson has grounds to appeal the case, a notice of appeal must be filed with the clerk of the trial court within a prescribed time. Anderson now becomes the appellant, or petitioner, and Marconi becomes the appellee, or respondent.

Filing the Appeal

Anderson's attorney files the record on appeal with the appellate court. The record includes the pleadings, the trial transcript, the judge's rulings on motions made by the parties, and other trial-related documents. Anderson's attorney will also provide the reviewing court with a condensation of the record, known as an *abstract,* and a brief. The **brief** is a formal legal document outlining the facts and issues of the case, the judge's rulings or jury's findings that should be reversed or modified, the applicable law, and arguments on Anderson's behalf (citing applicable statutes and relevant cases as precedents).

Marconi's attorney will file an answering brief. Anderson's attorney can file a reply to Marconi's brief, although it is not required. The reviewing court then considers the case.

Brief A written summary or statement prepared by one side in a lawsuit to explain its case to the judge.

Appellate Review

As explained earlier, a court of appeals does not hear evidence. Instead, the court reviews the record for errors of law. Its decision concerning a case is based on the record on appeal, the abstracts, and the attorneys' briefs. The attorneys can present oral arguments, after which the case is taken under advisement.

After reviewing a case, an appellate court has the following options:

1. The court can *affirm* the trial court's decision.
2. The court can *reverse* the trial court's judgment if it concludes that the trial court erred or that the jury did not receive proper instructions.
3. The appellate court can *remand* (send back) the case to the trial court for further proceedings consistent with its opinion on the matter.
4. The court might also affirm or reverse a decision *in part.* For example, the court might affirm the jury's finding that Anderson was negligent but remand the case for further proceedings on another issue (such as the extent of Marconi's damages).

5. An appellate court can also *modify* a lower court's decision. If the appellate court decides that the jury awarded an excessive amount in damages, for example, the court might reduce the award to a more appropriate, or fairer, amount.

Appeal to a Higher Appellate Court   If the reviewing court is an intermediate appellate court, the losing party may decide to appeal to the state supreme court (the highest state court). Such a petition corresponds to a petition for a writ of *certiorari* from the United States Supreme Court. Although the losing party has a right to ask (petition) a higher court to review the case, the party does not have a right to have the case heard by the higher appellate court.

Appellate courts normally have discretionary power and can accept or reject an appeal. Like the United States Supreme Court, state supreme courts generally deny most appeals. If the appeal is granted, new briefs must be filed before the state supreme court, and the attorneys may be allowed or requested to present oral arguments. Like the intermediate appellate court, the supreme court may reverse or affirm the appellate court's decision or remand the case. At this point, the case typically has reached its end (unless a federal question is at issue and one of the parties has legitimate grounds to seek review by a federal appellate court).

Enforcing the Judgment

The uncertainties of the litigation process are compounded by the lack of guarantees that any judgment will be enforceable. Even if a plaintiff wins an award of damages in court, the defendant may not have sufficient assets or insurance to cover that amount. Usually, one of the factors considered before a lawsuit is initiated is whether the defendant has sufficient assets to pay the damages sought, should the plaintiff win the case. What other factors should be considered when deciding whether to bring a lawsuit? See this chapter's *Business Application* feature on page 94 for answers to this question.

The Courts Adapt to the Online World

We have already mentioned that the courts have attempted to adapt traditional jurisdictional concepts to the online world. Not surprisingly, the Internet has also brought about changes in court procedures and practices, including new methods for filing pleadings and other documents and issuing decisions and opinions. Some jurisdictions are exploring the possibility of cyber courts, in which legal proceedings could be conducted totally online.

Electronic Filing

The federal court system has now implemented its electronic filing system, Case Management/Electronic Case Files (CM/ECF), in nearly all of the federal courts. The system is available in federal district, appellate, and bankruptcy courts, as well as the U.S. Court of International Trade and the U.S. Court of Federal Claims. More than 33 million cases are on the CM/ECF system. Users can create a document using conventional document-creation software, save it as a PDF (portable digital file), then log on to a court's Web site and submit the PDF to the court via the Internet. Access to the electronic documents filed on CM/ECF is available through a system called PACER (Public Access to Court Electronic Records), which is a service of the U.S. Judiciary.

More than 60 percent of the states have some form of electronic filing. Some states, including Arizona, California, Colorado, Delaware, Mississippi, New Jersey, New York, and Nevada, offer statewide e-filing systems. Generally, when electronic filing is made available, it is optional. Nonetheless, some state courts have now made e-filing mandatory in certain types of disputes, such as complex civil litigation.

Courts Online

Most courts today have sites on the Web. Of course, each court decides what to make available at its site. Some courts display only the names of court personnel and office phone numbers. Others add court rules and forms. Many appellate court sites include judicial decisions, although the decisions may remain online for only a limited time. In addition, in some states, including California and Florida, court clerks offer **docket** (the court's schedule of cases to be heard) information and other searchable databases online.

Docket The list of cases entered on a court's calendar and thus scheduled to be heard by the court.

Appellate court decisions are often posted online immediately after they are rendered. Recent decisions of the U.S. courts of appeals, for example, are available online at their Web sites. The United States Supreme Court also has an official Web site and publishes its opinions there immediately after they are announced to the public. In fact, even decisions that are designated as "unpublished" opinions by the appellate courts are usually published online.

Cyber Courts and Proceedings

Someday, litigants may be able to use cyber courts, in which judicial proceedings take place only on the Internet. The parties to a case could meet online to make their arguments and present their evidence. This might be done with e-mail submissions, through video cameras, in designated chat rooms, at closed sites, or through the use of other Internet and social media facilities. These courtrooms could be efficient and economical. We might also see the use of virtual lawyers, judges, and juries—and possibly the replacement of court personnel with computer software.

Already the state of Michigan has passed legislation creating cyber courts that will hear cases involving technology issues and high-tech businesses. The state of Wisconsin has also enacted a rule authorizing the use of videoconferencing in both civil and criminal trials, at the discretion of the trial court.[17] In some situations, a Wisconsin judge can allow videoconferencing even if the parties object, provided that certain operational criteria are met.

The courts may also use the Internet in other ways. For instance, some bankruptcy courts in Arizona, New Mexico, and Nevada recently began offering online chatting at their Web sites, which you will read about in Chapter 15. The model for these online chats came from retailers in the private sector, and chatting may eventually be offered on all federal bankruptcy court Web sites. Other courts are ordering parties to use the Internet as part of their judgments. A Florida county court granted "virtual" visitation rights in a couple's divorce proceedings so that the child could visit with each parent online (through a videoconferencing system or Skype, for instance) during stays at the other parent's residence.

Alternative Dispute Resolution

Litigation is expensive. It is also time consuming. Because of the backlog of cases pending in many courts, several years may pass before a case is actually tried. For these and other reasons, more and more businesspersons are turning to **alternative dispute resolution (ADR)** as a means of settling their disputes.

Alternative Dispute Resolution (ADR) The resolution of disputes in ways other than those involved in the traditional judicial process, such as negotiation, mediation, and arbitration.

The great advantage of ADR is its flexibility. Methods of ADR range from the parties sitting down together and attempting to work out their differences to multinational corporations agreeing to resolve a dispute through a formal hearing before a panel of experts. Normally, the parties themselves can control how they will attempt to settle their dispute, what procedures will be used, whether a neutral third party will be present or make a decision, and whether that decision will be legally binding or nonbinding.

---

17. Wisconsin Statute Section 751.12.

Today, more than 90 percent of cases are settled before trial through some form of ADR. Indeed, most states either require or encourage parties to undertake ADR prior to trial. Many federal courts have instituted ADR programs as well. In the following pages, we examine the basic forms of ADR. Keep in mind, though, that new methods of ADR—and new combinations of existing methods—are constantly being devised and employed.

Negotiation

LEARNING OBJECTIVE 5
What are three alternative methods of resolving disputes?

Negotiation A process in which parties attempt to settle their dispute informally, with or without attorneys to represent them.

The simplest form of ADR is **negotiation,** in which the parties attempt to settle their dispute informally, with or without attorneys to represent them. Attorneys frequently advise their clients to negotiate a settlement voluntarily before they proceed to trial. Parties may even try to negotiate a settlement during a trial or after the trial but before an appeal. Negotiation traditionally involves just the parties themselves and (typically) their attorneys. The attorneys, though, are advocates—they are obligated to put their clients' interests first.

Mediation

Mediation A method of settling disputes outside the courts by using the services of a neutral third party, who acts as a communicating agent between the parties and assists them in negotiating a settlement.

In **mediation,** a neutral third party acts as a mediator and works with both sides in the dispute to facilitate a resolution. The mediator talks with the parties separately as well as jointly and emphasizes their points of agreement in an attempt to help the parties evaluate their options. Although the mediator may propose a solution (called a *mediator's proposal*), he or she does not make a decision resolving the matter. States that require parties to undergo ADR before trial often offer mediation as one of the ADR options or (as in Florida) the only option.

One of the biggest advantages of mediation is that it is not as adversarial as litigation. In a trial, the parties "do battle" with each other in the courtroom, trying to prove each other wrong, while the judge is usually a passive observer. In mediation, the mediator takes an active role and attempts to bring the parties together so that they can come to a mutually satisfactory resolution. The mediation process tends to reduce the hostility between the disputants, allowing them to resume their former relationship without bad feelings. For this reason, mediation is often the preferred form of ADR for disputes involving business partners, employers and employees, or other parties involved in long-term relationships.

EXAMPLE 3.10 Two business partners, Mark Shalen and Charles Rowe, have a dispute over how the profits of their firm should be distributed. If the dispute is litigated, Shalen and Rowe will be adversaries, and their respective attorneys will emphasize how the parties' positions differ, not what they have in common. In contrast, when the dispute is mediated, the mediator emphasizes the common ground shared by Shalen and Rowe and helps them work toward agreement. The two men can work out the distribution of profits without damaging their continuing relationship as partners. ●

Arbitration

Arbitration The settling of a dispute by submitting it to a disinterested third party (other than a court), who renders a decision.

In **arbitration,** a more formal method of ADR, an arbitrator (a neutral third party or a panel of experts) hears a dispute and imposes a resolution on the parties. Arbitration differs from other forms of ADR in that the third party hearing the dispute makes a decision for the parties. Exhibit 3.4 on the facing page outlines the basic differences among the three traditional forms of ADR. Usually, the parties in arbitration agree that the third party's decision will be *legally binding,* although the parties can also agree to *nonbinding* arbitration. (Arbitration that is mandated by the courts often is nonbinding.) In nonbinding arbitration, the parties can go forward with a lawsuit if they do not agree with the arbitrator's decision.

In some respects, formal arbitration resembles a trial, although usually the procedural rules are much less restrictive than those governing litigation. In a typical arbitration, the

Exhibit 3.4 Basic Differences in the Traditional Forms of Alternative Dispute Resolution

TYPE OF ADR	DESCRIPTION	NEUTRAL THIRD PARTY PRESENT	WHO DECIDES THE RESOLUTION
Negotiation	The parties meet informally with or without their attorneys and attempt to agree on a resolution.	No	The parties themselves reach a resolution.
Mediation	A neutral third party meets with the parties and emphasizes points of agreement to help them resolve their dispute.	Yes	The parties decide the resolution, but the mediator may suggest or propose a resolution.
Arbitration	The parties present their arguments and evidence before an arbitrator at a hearing, and the arbitrator renders a decision resolving the parties' dispute.	Yes	The arbitrator imposes a resolution on the parties that may be either binding or nonbinding.

parties present opening arguments and ask for specific remedies. Both sides present evidence and may call and examine witnesses. The arbitrator then renders a decision.

The Arbitrator's Decision   The arbitrator's decision is called an *award*. It is usually the final word on the matter. Although the parties may appeal an arbitrator's decision, a court's review of the decision will be much more restricted in scope than an appellate court's review of a trial court's decision. The general view is that because the parties were free to frame the issues and set the powers of the arbitrator at the outset, they cannot complain about the results. A court will set aside an award only in the event of one of the following:

1. The arbitrator's conduct or "bad faith" substantially prejudiced the rights of one of the parties.
2. The award violates an established public policy.
3. The arbitrator exceeded her or his powers—that is, arbitrated issues that the parties did not agree to submit to arbitration.

Arbitration Clause A clause in a contract that provides that, in the event of a dispute, the parties will submit the dispute to arbitration rather than litigate the dispute in court.

Arbitration Clauses   Just about any commercial matter can be submitted to arbitration. Frequently, parties include an **arbitration clause** in a contract. The clause provides that any dispute that arises under the contract will be resolved through arbitration rather than through the court system. Parties can also agree to arbitrate a dispute after a dispute arises.

Arbitration Statutes   Most states have statutes (often based in part on the Uniform Arbitration Act of 1955) under which arbitration clauses will be enforced, and some state statutes compel arbitration of certain types of disputes, such as those involving public employees. At the federal level, the Federal Arbitration Act (FAA), enacted in 1925, enforces arbitration clauses in contracts involving maritime activity and interstate commerce (though its applicability to employment contracts has been controversial, as discussed in a later subsection). Because of the breadth of the commerce clause (see Chapter 1), arbitration agreements involving transactions only slightly connected to the flow of interstate commerce may fall under the FAA.

CASE EXAMPLE 3.11   Buckeye Check Cashing, Inc., cashes personal checks for consumers in Florida. Buckeye would agree to delay submitting a consumer's check for payment if the consumer paid a "finance charge." For each transaction, the consumer signed an agreement that included an arbitration clause. A group of consumers filed a lawsuit claiming that Buckeye was charging an illegally high rate of interest in violation of state law. Buckeye filed a motion to compel arbitration, which the trial court denied, and the case was appealed. The plaintiffs argued that the entire contract—including the arbitration clause—was illegal and therefore arbitration was not required.

The United States Supreme Court found that the arbitration provision was *severable*, or capable of being separated, from the rest of the contract. The Court held that when the challenge is to the validity of a contract as a whole, and not specifically to an arbitration clause within the contract, an arbitrator must resolve the dispute. Even if the contract itself later proves to be unenforceable, arbitration will still be required because the FAA established a national policy favoring arbitration and that policy extends to both federal and state courts.[18] ●

In the following case, the parties had agreed to arbitrate disputes involving their contract, but a state law allowed one party to void a contractual provision that required arbitration outside the state. The court had to decide if the FAA preempted the state law.

---

18. *Buckeye Check Cashing, Inc. v. Cardegna,* 546 U.S. 440, 126 S.Ct. 1204, 163 L.Ed.2d 1038 (2006).

Case 3.3

Cleveland Construction, Inc. v. Levco Construction, Inc.

Court of Appeals of Texas, First District, 359 S.W.3d 843 (2012).
law.justia.com[a]

(Bertold Werkmann/Shutterstock.com)
An excavation machine.

FACTS   Cleveland Construction, Inc. (CCI), was the general contractor on a project to build a grocery store in Houston, Texas. CCI hired Levco Construction, Inc., as a subcontractor to perform excavation and grading. The contract included an arbitration provision stating that any disputes would be resolved by arbitration in Ohio. When a dispute arose between the parties, Levco filed a suit against CCI in a Texas state court. CCI sought to compel arbitration in Ohio under the Federal Arbitration Act (FAA), but a Texas statute allows a party to void a contractual provision that requires arbitration outside Texas. The Texas court granted an emergency motion preventing arbitration. CCI appealed.

ISSUE   Does the FAA preempt the Texas statute, which denies enforcement of arbitration clauses that require a party to submit to arbitration outside Texas?

DECISION   Yes. The Texas appellate court reversed the trial court, holding that the FAA preempts the Texas statute.

REASON   The FAA requires courts to enforce valid arbitration agreements, and it "preempts . . . inconsistent state laws . . . under the Supremacy Clause of the United States Constitution." (See page 15 in Chapter 1.) In this case, the Texas statute provided that an agreement to arbitrate was voidable if it required arbitration outside Texas. Thus, if the court applied the Texas statute, it would void the parties' agreement to arbitrate any disputes in Ohio. Voiding the agreement, however, the court found "would undermine the declared federal policy of rigorous enforcement of arbitration agreements." The court ruled that the parties had a valid arbitration agreement, so the FAA preempted the Texas statute.

CRITICAL THINKING—Legal Consideration   *How would business be affected if each state could pass a statute, like the one in Texas, allowing parties to void out-of-state arbitrations?*

---

a. In the search box, type "Cleveland Construction v. Levco Construction" and click on "Search Justia." On the page that opens, click on the link to access this case opinion. Justia Company maintains this Web site.

The Issue of Arbitrability

Notice that in the preceding *Case Example 3.11,* the issue before the United States Supreme Court was *not* the basic controversy (whether the interest rate charged was illegally high) but rather the issue of arbitrability—that is, whether the matter had to be resolved by arbitration under the arbitration clause. Actions over arbitrability often occur when a dispute arises over an agreement that contains an arbitration clause: one party files a motion to compel arbitration, while the other party wants to have the dispute settled by a court, not by arbitration.

If the court finds that the dispute is covered by the arbitration clause, it may compel the other party to submit to arbitration, even though his or her claim involves the violation of a statute, such as an employment statute. Usually, if the court finds that the legislature, in enacting the statute, did not intend to prohibit arbitration, the court will allow the claim to be arbitrated.

No party will be ordered to submit a particular dispute to arbitration, however, unless the court is convinced that the party consented to do so.[19] Additionally, the courts will not compel arbitration if it is clear that the prescribed arbitration rules and procedures are inherently unfair to one of the parties.

The terms of an arbitration agreement can limit the types of disputes that the parties agree to arbitrate. When the parties do not specify limits, however, disputes can arise as to whether a particular matter is covered by the arbitration agreement. Then it is up to the court to resolve the issue of arbitrability.

Mandatory Arbitration in the Employment Context

A significant question in the last several years has concerned mandatory arbitration clauses in employment contracts. Many claim that employees' rights are not sufficiently protected when workers are forced, as a condition of being hired, to agree to arbitrate all disputes and thus waive their rights under statutes specifically designed to protect employees. The United States Supreme Court, however, has generally held that mandatory arbitration clauses in employment contracts are enforceable.

> ▶ **KNOW THIS** ◀
>
> Litigation—even of a dispute over whether a particular matter should be submitted to arbitration—can be time consuming and expensive.

CASE EXAMPLE 3.12   In a landmark decision, *Gilmer v. Interstate Johnson Lane Corp.,*[20] the Supreme Court held that a claim brought under a federal statute prohibiting age discrimination (see Chapter 18) could be subject to arbitration. The Court concluded that the employee had waived his right to sue when he agreed, as part of a required registration application to be a securities representative with the New York Stock Exchange, to arbitrate "any dispute, claim, or controversy" relating to his employment. •

Since the *Gilmer* decision, some courts have refused to enforce one-sided arbitration clauses on the ground that they are unconscionable (see Chapter 8).[21] Thus, businesspersons considering using arbitration clauses in employment contracts should be careful that they are not too one sided—especially provisions on how the parties will split the costs of the arbitration procedure.

Private Arbitration Proceedings

In 2011, the Delaware Chancery Court established a new confidential arbitration process, which allows parties to arbitrate their disputes in private. Because many companies are headquartered in Delaware, the court's caseload is heavy, and its influence on the business environment is significant. Delaware's decision to authorize secret arbitration proceedings has been controversial.

---

19. See, for example, *Wright v. Universal Maritime Service Corp.,* 525 U.S. 70, 119 S.Ct. 391, 142 L.Ed.2d 361 (1998).

20. 500 U.S. 20, 111 S.Ct. 1647, 114 L.Ed.2d 26 (1991).

21. See, for example, *Macias v. Excel Building Services, LLC,* 767 F.Supp.2d 1002 (N.D.Cal. 2011), citing *Davis v. O'Melveny & Myers, LLC,* 485 F.3d 1066 (9th Cir. 2007), and *Nagrampa v. MailCoups, Inc.,* 469 F.3d 1257 (9th Cir. 2006).

EXAMPLE 3.13 Two smartphone makers were the first to use Delaware's confidential arbitration procedures to reach a settlement of their dispute. Skyworks Solutions, Inc., makes technology that transmits signals from smartphones, and Advanced Analogic Technologies, Inc. (AATI), makes power management devices for smartphones. Skyworks had agreed to a merger deal with AATI for $262.5 million, but then backed out, claiming that AATI had not properly accounted for revenue. Both parties filed lawsuits and ended up arbitrating using Delaware's new process. The two reached a settlement to complete the merger for $256 million, without disclosing the details of their agreement. •

Other Types of ADR

The three forms of ADR just discussed are the oldest and traditionally the most commonly used. In recent years, several new types of ADR have emerged. Some parties today are using *assisted negotiation*, in which a third party participates in the negotiation process. The third party may be an expert in the subject matter of the dispute.

In *early neutral case evaluation*, the parties explain the situation to an expert, and the expert assesses the strengths and weaknesses of each party's claims. Another form of assisted negotiation is the *mini-trial*, in which the parties present arguments before the third party (usually an expert), who renders an advisory opinion on how a court would likely decide the issue. This proceeding is designed to assist the parties in determining whether they should settle or take the dispute to court.

Other types of ADR combine characteristics of mediation and arbitration. In *binding mediation*, for example, the parties agree that if they cannot resolve the dispute, the mediator may make a legally binding decision on the issue. In *mediation-arbitration*, or "med-arb," the parties agree to attempt to settle their dispute through mediation. If no settlement is reached, the dispute will be arbitrated.

Today's courts are also experimenting with a variety of ADR alternatives to speed up (and reduce the cost of) justice. Numerous federal courts now hold **summary jury trials (SJTs)**, in which the parties present their arguments and evidence and the jury renders a verdict. The jury's verdict is not binding, but it does act as a guide to both sides in reaching an agreement during the mandatory negotiations that immediately follow the trial. Other alternatives being employed by the courts include summary procedures for commercial litigation and the appointment of special masters to assist judges in deciding complex issues.

Summary Jury Trial (SJT) A method of settling disputes by holding a trial in which the jury's verdict is not binding but instead guides the parties toward reaching an agreement during the mandatory negotiations that immediately follow.

Providers of ADR Services

ADR services are provided by both government agencies and private organizations. A major provider of ADR services is the American Arbitration Association (AAA), which was founded in 1926 and now handles more than 200,000 claims a year in its numerous offices worldwide. Most of the largest U.S. law firms are members of this nonprofit association. Cases brought before the AAA are heard by an expert or a panel of experts in the area relating to the dispute and are usually settled quickly. The AAA has a special team devoted to resolving large, complex disputes across a wide range of industries.

Hundreds of for-profit firms around the country also provide various forms of dispute-resolution services. Typically, these firms hire retired judges to conduct arbitration hearings or otherwise assist parties in settling their disputes. The judges follow procedures similar to those of the federal courts and use similar rules. Usually, each party to the dispute pays a filing fee and a designated fee for a hearing session or conference.

Online Dispute Resolution

Online Dispute Resolution (ODR) The resolution of disputes with the assistance of organizations that offer dispute-resolution services via the Internet.

An increasing number of companies and organizations offer dispute-resolution services using the Internet. The settlement of disputes in these online forums is known as **online dispute resolution (ODR)**. The disputes have most commonly involved disagreements over the rights to domain names or over the quality of goods sold via the Internet, including goods sold through Internet auction sites.

ODR may be best suited for resolving small- to medium-sized business liability claims, which may not be worth the expense of litigation or traditional ADR. Rules being developed in online forums may ultimately become a code of conduct for everyone who does business in cyberspace. Most online forums do not automatically apply the law of any specific jurisdiction. Instead, results are often based on general, universal legal principles. As with most offline methods of dispute resolution, any party may appeal to a court at any time.

Interestingly, some local governments are using ODR to resolve claims. **EXAMPLE 3.14** New York City has used Cybersettle.com to resolve auto accident, sidewalk, and other personal-injury claims made against the city. Parties with complaints submit their demands, and the city submits its offers confidentially online. If an offer exceeds a demand, the claimant keeps half the difference as a bonus. •

Reviewing . . . Courts and Alternative Dispute Resolution

Stan Garner resides in Illinois and promotes boxing matches for SuperSports, Inc., an Illinois corporation. Garner created the promotional concept of the "Ages" fights—a series of three boxing matches pitting an older fighter (George Foreman) against a younger fighter, such as John Ruiz or Riddick Bowe. The concept included titles for each of the three fights ("Challenge of the Ages," "Battle of the Ages," and "Fight of the Ages"), as well as promotional epithets to characterize the two fighters ("the Foreman Factor"). Garner contacted George Foreman and his manager, who both reside in Texas, to sell the idea, and they arranged a meeting at Caesar's Palace in Las Vegas, Nevada. At some point in the negotiations, Foreman's manager signed a nondisclosure agreement prohibiting him from disclosing Garner's promotional concepts unless they signed a contract. Nevertheless, after negotiations between Garner and Foreman fell through, Foreman used Garner's "Battle of the Ages" concept to promote a subsequent fight. Garner filed a lawsuit against Foreman and his manager in a federal district court in Illinois, alleging breach of contract. Using the information presented in the chapter, answer the following questions.

1. On what basis might the federal district court in Illinois exercise jurisdiction in this case?
2. Does the federal district court have original or appellate jurisdiction?
3. Suppose that Garner had filed his action in an Illinois state court. Could an Illinois state court exercise personal jurisdiction over Foreman or his manager? Why or why not?
4. Assume that Garner had filed his action in a Nevada state court. Would that court have personal jurisdiction over Foreman or his manager? Explain.

DEBATE THIS In this age of the Internet, when people communicate via e-mail, tweets, FaceBook, and Skype, is the concept of jurisdiction losing its meaning?

BUSINESS APPLICATION

To Sue or Not to Sue?*

Inadvertently or intentionally, wrongs are committed every day in the United States. Sometimes, businesspersons believe that wrongs have been committed against them by other businesspersons, by consumers, or by the government. If you are deciding whether to sue for a wrong committed against you or your business, you must consider many issues.

The Question of Cost

Competent legal advice is not inexpensive. Commercial business law attorneys charge $100 to $600 an hour, plus expenses. It is almost always worthwhile to make an initial visit to an attorney who has skills in the area in which you are going to sue to get an estimate of the expected costs of pursuing redress for your grievance. Note that less than 10 percent of all corporate lawsuits go to trial—the rest are settled beforehand. You may end up settling for far less than you think you are "owed" simply because of the length of time a lawsuit would take and the cost of going to court. And then you might not win anyway!

Basically, you must do a cost-benefit analysis to determine whether you should sue. Your attorney can give you an estimate of the dollar costs involved in litigating the dispute. Realize, though, that litigation also involves nondollar costs such as time away from your business, stress, inconvenience, and publicity. You can "guesstimate" the benefits by multiplying the probable size of the award by the probability of obtaining that award.

---

* This *Business Application* is not meant to substitute for the services of an attorney who is licensed to practice law in your state.

The Alternatives before You

Negotiation, mediation, arbitration, and other ADR forms are becoming increasingly attractive alternatives to court litigation because they usually yield quick results at a comparatively low cost. Most disputes relating to business can be mediated or arbitrated through the American Arbitration Association (AAA).

There are numerous other ADR providers as well. You can obtain information on ADR from the AAA, courthouses, chambers of commerce, law firms, state bar associations, and the American Bar Association. The Yellow Pages in large metropolitan areas usually list agencies and firms that can help you settle your dispute out of court. You can also locate providers on the Web by using a general search engine and searching for arbitration providers in a specific city.

Checklist for Deciding Whether to Sue

1. Are you prepared to pay for going to court? Make this decision only after you have consulted an attorney to get an estimate of the costs of litigating the dispute.
2. Do you have the patience to follow a court case through the judicial system, even if it takes several years?
3. Is there a way for you to settle your grievance without going to court? Even if the settlement is less than you think you are owed, you may be better off settling now for the smaller figure.
4. Can you use some form of ADR? Investigate these alternatives—they are usually cheaper and quicker to use than the courts.

Key Terms

Chapter Summary: Courts and Alternative Dispute Resolution

The Judiciary's Role in American Government (See page 65.)	The role of the judiciary—the courts—in the American governmental system is to interpret and apply the law. Through the process of judicial review—determining the constitutionality of laws—the judicial branch acts as a check on the executive and legislative branches of government.

Basic Judicial Requirements (See pages 65–74.)	1. *Jurisdiction*—Before a court can hear a case, it must have jurisdiction over the person against whom the suit is brought or the property involved in the suit, as well as jurisdiction over the subject matter.
	   a. Limited versus general jurisdiction—Limited jurisdiction exists when a court is limited to a specific subject matter, such as probate or divorce. General jurisdiction exists when a court can hear any kind of case.
	   b. Original versus appellate jurisdiction—Original jurisdiction exists when courts have authority to hear a case for the first time (trial courts). Appellate jurisdiction is exercised by courts of appeals, or reviewing courts, which generally do not have original jurisdiction.
	   c. Federal jurisdiction—Arises (1) when a federal question is involved (when the plaintiff's cause of action is based, at least in part, on the U.S. Constitution, a treaty, or a federal law) or (2) when a case involves diversity of citizenship (citizens of different states, for example) and the amount in controversy exceeds $75,000.
	   d. Concurrent versus exclusive jurisdiction—Concurrent jurisdiction exists when two different courts have authority to hear the same case. Exclusive jurisdiction exists when only state courts or only federal courts have authority to hear a case.
	2. *Jurisdiction in cyberspace*—Because the Internet does not have physical boundaries, traditional jurisdictional concepts have been difficult to apply in cases involving activities conducted via the Web. Gradually, the courts are developing standards to use in determining when jurisdiction over a Web site owner or operator located in another state is proper.
	3. *Venue*—Venue has to do with the most appropriate location for a trial, which is usually the geographic area where the event leading to the dispute took place or where the parties reside.
	4. *Standing to sue*—A requirement that a party must have a legally protected and tangible interest at stake sufficient to justify seeking relief through the court system. The controversy at issue must also be a justiciable controversy—one that is real and substantial, as opposed to hypothetical or academic.

The State and Federal Court Systems (See pages 74–79.)	1. *Trial courts*—Courts of original jurisdiction, in which legal actions are initiated.
	   a. State—Courts of general jurisdiction can hear any case. Courts of limited jurisdiction include domestic relations courts, probate courts, traffic courts, and small claims courts.
	   b. Federal—The federal district court is the equivalent of the state trial court. Federal courts of limited jurisdiction include the U.S. Tax Court, the U.S. Bankruptcy Court, and the U.S. Court of Federal Claims.
	2. *Intermediate appellate courts*—Courts of appeals, or reviewing courts, which generally do not have original jurisdiction. Many states have an intermediate appellate court. In the federal court system, the U.S. circuit courts of appeals are the intermediate appellate courts.
	3. *Supreme (highest) courts*—Each state has a supreme court, although it may be called by some other name. Appeal from the state supreme court to the United States Supreme Court is possible only if the case involves a federal question. The United States Supreme Court is the highest court in the federal court system and the final arbiter of the U.S. Constitution and federal law.

Following a State Court Case (See pages 79–86.)	Rules of procedure prescribe the way in which disputes are handled in the courts. Rules differ from court to court, and separate sets of rules exist for federal and state courts, as well as for criminal and civil cases. A civil court case in a state court would involve the following procedures:
	1. *The pleadings*—
	   a. Complaint—Filed by the plaintiff with the court to initiate the lawsuit. The complaint is served with a summons on the defendant.
	   b. Answer—A response to the complaint in which the defendant admits or denies the allegations made by the plaintiff. The answer may assert a counterclaim or an affirmative defense.
	   c. Motion to dismiss—A request to the court to dismiss the case for stated reasons, such as the plaintiff's failure to state a claim for which relief can be granted.
	2. *Pretrial motions (in addition to the motion to dismiss)*—
	   a. Motion for judgment on the pleadings—May be made by either party. It will be granted if the parties agree on the facts and the only question is how the law applies to the facts. The judge bases the decision solely on the pleadings.
	   b. Motion for summary judgment—May be made by either party. It will be granted if the parties agree on the facts and the sole question is a question of law. The judge can consider evidence outside the pleadings when evaluating the motion.

Continued

Chapter Summary: Courts and Alternative Dispute Resolution— Continued

Following a State Court Case — Continued	3. *Discovery*—The process of gathering evidence concerning the case. Discovery involves depositions (sworn testimony by a party to the lawsuit or any witness), interrogatories (written questions and answers to these questions made by parties to the action with the aid of their attorneys), and various requests (for admissions, documents, and medical examinations, for example). Discovery may also involve electronically recorded information, such as e-mail, voice mail, word-processing documents, and other data compilations. Although electronic discovery has significant advantages over paper discovery, it is also more time consuming and expensive and often requires the parties to hire experts.
	 4. *Pretrial conference*—Either party or the court can request a pretrial conference to identify the matters in dispute after discovery has taken place and to plan the course of the trial.
	 5. *Trial*—Following jury selection (*voir dire*), the trial begins with opening statements from both parties' attorneys. The following events then occur:
	    a. The plaintiff's introduction of evidence (including the testimony of witnesses) supporting the plaintiff's position. The defendant's attorney can challenge evidence and cross-examine witnesses.
	    b. The defendant's introduction of evidence (including the testimony of witnesses) supporting the defendant's position. The plaintiff's attorney can challenge evidence and cross-examine witnesses.
	    c. Closing arguments by the attorneys in favor of their respective clients, the judge's instructions to the jury, and the jury's verdict.
	 6. *Posttrial motions*—
	    a. Motion for judgment *n.o.v.* ("notwithstanding the verdict")—Will be granted if the judge is convinced that the jury was in error.
	    b. Motion for a new trial—Will be granted if the judge is convinced that the jury was in error. The motion can also be granted on the grounds of newly discovered evidence, misconduct by the participants during the trial, or error by the judge.
	 7. *Appeal*—Either party can appeal the trial court's judgment to an appropriate court of appeals. After reviewing the record on appeal, the abstracts, and the attorneys' briefs, the appellate court holds a hearing and renders its opinion.

The Courts Adapt to the Online World (See pages 86–89.)	A number of state and federal courts now allow parties to file litigation-related documents with the courts via the Internet or other electronic means. Nearly all of the federal appellate courts and bankruptcy courts and a majority of the federal district courts have implemented electronic filing systems. Almost every court now has a Web page offering information about the court and its procedures, and increasingly courts are publishing their opinions online. In the future, we may see cyber courts, in which all trial proceedings are conducted online.
Alternative Dispute Resolution (See pages 87–93.)	1. *Negotiation*—The parties come together, with or without attorneys to represent them, and try to reach a settlement without the involvement of a third party. 2. *Mediation*—The parties themselves reach an agreement with the help of a neutral third party, called a mediator. The mediator may propose a solution but does not make a decision resolving the matter. 3. *Arbitration*—A more formal method of ADR in which the parties submit their dispute to a neutral third party, the arbitrator, who renders a decision. The decision may or may not be legally binding, depending on the circumstances. 4. *Other types of ADR*—These include assisted negotiation, early neutral case evaluation, mini-trials, and summary jury trials (SJTs). 5. *Providers of ADR services*—The leading nonprofit provider of ADR services is the American Arbitration Association. Hundreds of for-profit firms also provide ADR services. 6. *Online dispute resolution*—A number of organizations and firms are now offering negotiation, mediation, and arbitration services through online forums. These forums have been a practical alternative for the resolution of domain name disputes and e-commerce disputes in which the amount in controversy is relatively small.

ExamPrep

ISSUE SPOTTERS

1. Sue contracts with Tom to deliver a quantity of computers to Sue's Computer Store. They disagree over the amount, the delivery date, the price, and the quality. Sue files a suit against Tom in a state court. Their state requires that their dispute be submitted to mediation or nonbinding arbitration. If the dispute is not resolved, or if either party disagrees with the decision of the mediator or arbitrator, will a court hear the case? Explain. **(See page 88.)**
2. At the trial, after Sue calls her witnesses, offers her evidence, and otherwise presents her side of the case, Tom has at least two choices between courses of action. Tom can call his first witness. What else might he do? **(See page 84.)**

—**Check your answers to the Issue Spotters against the answers provided in Appendix E at the end of this text.**

BEFORE THE TEST
Go to www.cengagebrain.com, enter the ISBN 9781133191353, and click on "Find" to locate this textbook's Web site. Then, click on "Access Now" under "Study Tools," and select Chapter 3 at the top. There, you will find a Practice Quiz that you can take to assess your mastery of the concepts in this chapter, as well as Flashcards, a Glossary of important terms, and Video Questions (when assigned).

For Review

Answers to the even-numbered questions in this For Review section can be found in Appendix F at the end of this text.

1. What is judicial review? How and when was the power of judicial review established?
2. Before a court can hear a case, it must have jurisdiction. Over what must it have jurisdiction? How are the courts applying traditional jurisdictional concepts to cases involving Internet transactions?
3. What is the difference between a trial court and an appellate court?
4. What is discovery, and how does electronic discovery differ from traditional discovery?
5. What are three alternative methods of resolving disputes?

Business Scenarios and Case Problems

3–1 Standing to Sue. Jack and Maggie Turton bought a house in Jefferson County, Idaho, located directly across the street from a gravel pit. A few years later, the county converted the pit to a landfill. The landfill accepted many kinds of trash that cause harm to the environment, including major appliances, animal carcasses, containers with hazardous content warnings, leaking car batteries, and waste oil. The Turtons complained to the county, but the county did nothing. The Turtons then filed a lawsuit against the county alleging violations of federal environmental laws pertaining to groundwater contamination and other pollution. Do the Turtons have standing to sue? Why or why not? **(See page 73.)**

3–2 Question with Sample Answer—Jurisdiction. Marya Callais, a citizen of Florida, was walking along a busy street in Tallahassee when a large crate flew off a passing truck and hit her. Callais sustained numerous injuries. She incurred a great deal of pain and suffering plus significant medical expenses, and she could not work for six months. She wishes to sue the trucking firm for $300,000 in damages. The firm's headquarters are in Georgia, although the company does business in Florida. In what court may Callais bring suit—a Florida state court, a Georgia state court, or a federal court? What factors might influence her decision? **(See pages 66–67.)**

—For a sample answer to Question 3–2, go to Appendix G at the end of this text.

3–3 Discovery. Advance Technology Consultants, Inc. (ATC), contracted with RoadTrac, LLC, to provide software and client software systems for the products of global positioning satellite (GPS) technology being developed by RoadTrac. RoadTrac agreed to provide ATC with hardware with which ATC's software would interface. Problems soon arose, however, and RoadTrac filed a lawsuit against ATC alleging breach of contract. During discovery, RoadTrac requested ATC's customer lists and marketing procedures. ATC objected to providing this information because RoadTrac and ATC had become competitors in the GPS industry. Should a party to a lawsuit have to hand over its confidential business secrets as part of a discovery request? Why or why not? What limitations might a court consider imposing before requiring ATC to produce this material? **(See pages 81–82.)**

3–4 Case Problem with Sample Answer—Arbitration. Kathleen Lowden sued cellular phone company T-Mobile USA, Inc., contending that its service agreements were not enforceable under Washington state law. Lowden moved to create a class-action lawsuit, in which her claims would extend to similarly affected customers. She contended that T-Mobile had improperly charged her fees beyond the advertised price of service and charged her for roaming calls that should not have been classified as roaming. T-Mobile moved to force arbitration in accordance with provisions that were clearly set forth in the service agreement. The agreement also specified that no class-action lawsuit could be brought, so T-Mobile asked the court to dismiss the class-action request. Was T-Mobile correct that Lowden's only course of action would be to file for arbitration personally? Explain. [*Lowden v. T-Mobile USA, Inc.,* 512 F.3d 1213 (9th Cir. 2008)] **(See page 90.)**

—For a sample answer to Problem 3–4, go to Appendix H at the end of this text.

3–5 Venue. Brandy Austin used powdered infant formula to feed her infant daughter shortly after her birth. Austin claimed that a can of Nestlé Good Start Supreme Powder Infant Formula was contaminated with *Enterobacter sakazakii* bacteria, which can cause infections of the bloodstream and central nervous system, in particular, meningitis (inflammation of the tissue surrounding the brain or spinal cord). Austin filed an action against Nestlé in Hennepin County District Court in Minnesota. Nestlé argued for a change of venue because the alleged tortious action on the part of Nestlé occurred in South Carolina. Austin is a South Carolina resident and gave birth to her daughter in that state. Should the case be transferred to a South Carolina venue? Why or why not? [*Austin v. Nestlé USA, Inc.*, 677 F.Supp.2d 1134 (D.Minn. 2009)] **(See page 73.)**

3–6 **Arbitration.** PRM Energy Systems owned patents licensed to Primenergy, LLC, to use in the United States. Their contract stated that "all disputes" would be settled by arbitration. Kobe Steel of Japan was interested in using the technology represented by PRM's patents. Primenergy agreed to let Kobe use the technology in Japan without telling PRM. When PRM learned about the secret deal, the firm filed a suit against Primenergy for fraud and theft. Does this dispute go to arbitration or to trial? Why? [*PRM Energy Systems v. Primenergy, LLC*, 592 F.3d 830 (8th Cir. 2010)] **(See page 89.)**

3–7 **Spotlight on National Football—Arbitration.** Bruce Matthews played football for the Tennessee Titans. As part of his contract, he agreed to submit any dispute to arbitration. He also agreed that Tennessee law would determine all matters related to workers' compensation. After Matthews retired, he filed a workers' compensation claim in California. The arbitrator ruled that Matthews could pursue his claim in California but only under Tennessee law. Should this award be set aside? Explain. [*National Football League Players Association v. National Football League Management Council*, 2011 WL 1137334 (S.D.Cal. 2011)] **(See pages 84–87.)**

3–8 **Minimum Contacts.** Seal Polymer Industries sold two freight containers of latex gloves to Med-Express, Inc., a company based in North Carolina. When Med-Express failed to pay the $104,000 owed for the gloves, Seal Polymer sued in an Illinois court and obtained a judgment against Med-Express. Med-Express argued that it did not have minimum contacts with Illinois and therefore the Illinois judgment based on personal jurisdiction was invalid. Med-Express stated that it was incorporated under North Carolina law, had its principal place of business in North Carolina, and therefore had no minimum contacts with Illinois. Was this statement alone sufficient to prevent the Illinois judgment from being collected against Med-Express in North Carolina? Why or why not? [*Seal Polymer Industries v. Med-Express, Inc.*, 725 S.E.2d 5 (N.C.App. 2012)] **(See pages 66–68.)**

3–9 **A Question of Ethics—Agreement to Arbitrate.** Nellie Lumpkin, who suffered from dementia, was admitted to the Picayune Convalescent Center, a nursing home. Because of her mental condition, her daughter, Beverly McDaniel, signed the admissions agreement. It included a clause requiring the parties to submit any dispute to arbitration. After Lumpkin left the center two years later, she filed a suit against Picayune to recover damages for mistreatment and malpractice. [*Covenant Health & Rehabilitation of Picayune, LP v. Lumpkin*, 23 So.2d 1092 (Miss. App. 2009)] **(See page 91.)**

1. Is it ethical for this dispute—involving negligent medical care, not a breach of a commercial contract—to be forced into arbitration? Why or why not? Discuss whether medical facilities should be able to impose arbitration when there is generally no bargaining over such terms.

2. Should a person with limited mental capacity be held to the arbitration clause agreed to by her next of kin who signed on her behalf? Why or why not?

Critical Thinking and Writing Assignments

3–10 **Business Law Critical Thinking Group Assignment.** Assume that a statute in your state requires that all civil lawsuits involving damages of less than $50,000 be arbitrated and allows such a case to be tried in court only if a party is dissatisfied with the arbitrator's decision. The statute also provides that if a trial does not result in an improvement of more than 10 percent in the position of the party who demanded the trial, that party must pay the entire costs of the arbitration proceeding.

1. One group will argue that the state statute violates litigants' rights of access to the courts and to trial by jury.

2. Another group will argue that the statute does not violate litigants' rights of access to the courts.

3. A third group will evaluate how the determination on rights of access would be changed if the statute was part of a pilot program and affected only a few judicial districts in the state.

Torts and Cyber Torts

(Oxford/iStockphoto.com)

LEARNING OBJECTIVES

The five learning objectives below are designed to help improve your understanding of the chapter. After reading this chapter, you should be able to answer the following questions:

1 What is the purpose of tort law? What types of damages are available in tort lawsuits?

2 What are two basic categories of torts?

3 What is defamation? Name two types of defamation.

4 Identify the four elements of negligence.

5 What is meant by strict liability? In what circumstances is strict liability applied?

"Two wrongs do not make a right."
—English Proverb

Tort A wrongful act (other than a breach of contract) that results in harm or injury to another and leads to civil liability.

Torts are wrongful actions (the word *tort* is French for "wrong"). Most of us agree with the chapter-opening quotation—two wrongs do not make a right. Through tort law, society tries to ensure that those who have suffered injuries as a result of the wrongful conduct of others receive compensation from the wrongdoers. Although some torts, such as assault and trespass, originated in the English common law, the field of tort law continues to expand. As technological advances such as the Internet provide opportunities to commit new types of wrongs, the courts are extending tort law to cover these wrongs. For instance, not too long ago, Google announced that it was starting a competing service similar to Facebook's. The unveiling of Google+ was met with praise and some very damning criticisms that turned out to have been initiated by a public relations firm that Facebook regularly used. Was a cyber tort committed? You'll decide later in this chapter.

As you will see in later chapters of this book, many of the lawsuits brought by or against business firms are based on the tort theories discussed in this chapter. Some of the torts examined here can occur in any context, including the business environment. Others, traditionally referred to as **business torts,** involve wrongful interference with the business

Business Tort Wrongful interference with another's business rights and relationships.

Cyber Tort A tort committed in cyberspace.

rights of others. Business torts include such vague concepts as *unfair competition* and *wrongfully interfering with the business relations of another.*

Torts committed via the Internet are sometimes referred to as **cyber torts.** We look at how the courts have applied traditional tort law to wrongful actions in the online environment in the concluding pages of this chapter.

The Basis of Tort Law

Two notions serve as the basis of all torts: wrongs and compensation. Tort law is designed to compensate those who have suffered a loss or injury due to another person's wrongful act. In a tort action, one person or group brings a personal suit against another person or group to obtain compensation (monetary **damages**) or other relief for the harm suffered.

Damages A monetary award sought as a remedy for a breach of contract or a tortious action.

The Purpose of Tort Law

LEARNING OBJECTIVE 1
What is the purpose of tort law? What types of damages are available in tort lawsuits?

Generally, the purpose of tort law is to provide remedies for the invasion of various *protected interests.* Society recognizes an interest in personal physical safety, and tort law provides remedies for acts that cause physical injury or interfere with physical security and freedom. Hence, society recognizes an interest in protecting real and personal property. Tort law provides remedies for acts that cause destruction or damage to property. Society also recognizes an interest in protecting certain intangible interests, such as personal privacy, family relations, reputation, and dignity. Consequently, tort law provides remedies for invasion of these interests.

Damages Available in Tort Actions

Because the purpose of tort law is to compensate the injured party for the damage suffered, it is important to have a basic understanding of the types of damages that plaintiffs seek in tort actions.

Compensatory Damages A monetary award equivalent to the actual value of injuries or damage sustained by the aggrieved party.

Compensatory Damages   **Compensatory damages** are intended to compensate or reimburse plaintiffs for actual losses—to make the plaintiffs whole and put them in the same position that they would have been in had the tort not occurred. Compensatory damages awards are often broken down into *special damages* and *general damages.*

Special damages compensate the plaintiff for quantifiable monetary losses, such as medical expenses, lost wages and benefits (now and in the future), extra costs, the loss of irreplaceable items, and the costs of repairing or replacing damaged property. **CASE EXAMPLE 4.1** Seaway Marine Transport operates the *Enterprise,* a large cargo ship with twenty-two hatches for storing coal. When the *Enterprise* moved into position to receive a load of coal on the shores of Lake Erie in Ohio, it struck a land-based coal-loading machine operated by Bessemer & Lake Erie Railroad Company. A federal court found Seaway liable for negligence and awarded $522,000 in special damages to compensate Bessemer for the cost of repairing the damage to the loading machine.[1] •

General damages compensate individuals (not companies) for the nonmonetary aspects of the harm suffered, such as pain and suffering. A court might award general damages for physical or emotional pain and suffering, loss of companionship, loss of consortium (losing the emotional and physical benefits of a spousal relationship), disfigurement, loss of reputation, or loss or impairment of mental or physical capacity.

Punitive Damages Monetary damages that may be awarded to a plaintiff to punish the defendant and deter similar conduct in the future.

Punitive Damages   Occasionally, **punitive damages** may also be awarded in tort cases to punish the wrongdoer and deter others from similar wrongdoing. Punitive damages are appropriate only when the defendant's conduct was particularly egregious (bad)

---

1. *Bessemer & Lake Erie Railroad Co. v. Seaway Marine Transport,* 596 F.3d 357 (6th Cir. 2010).

or reprehensible (unacceptable). Usually, this means that punitive damages are available mainly in intentional tort actions and only rarely in negligence lawsuits (*intentional torts* and *negligence* will be explained later in the chapter). They may be awarded, however, in suits involving *gross negligence,* which can be defined as an intentional failure to perform a manifest duty in reckless disregard of the consequences of such a failure for the life or property of another. (See this chapter's *Business Application* feature on page 126 for steps businesses can take to avoid tort liability and the large damages awards that may go with it.)

Courts exercise great restraint in granting punitive damages to plaintiffs in tort actions because punitive damages are subject to the limitations imposed by the due process clause of the U.S. Constitution (discussed in Chapter 1). The United States Supreme Court has held that a punitive damages award that is grossly excessive furthers no legitimate purpose and violates due process requirements.[2] Consequently, an appellate court will sometimes reduce the amount of punitive damages awarded to a plaintiff because the amount was excessive and thereby violates the due process clause.

Tort Reform

Although tort law performs a valuable function by enabling injured parties to obtain compensation, critics contend that certain aspects of today's tort law encourage too many trivial and unfounded lawsuits, which clog the courts and add unnecessary costs. They say that damages awards are often excessive and bear little relationship to the actual damage suffered, which inspires more plaintiffs to file lawsuits. The result, in the critics' view, is a system that disproportionately rewards a few plaintiffs while imposing a "tort tax" on business and society as a whole. Among other consequences, physicians and hospitals order more tests than necessary in an effort to avoid medical malpractice suits, thereby adding to the nation's health-care costs.

Measures to reduce the number of tort cases include (1) limiting the amount of both punitive damages and general damages that can be awarded, (2) capping the amount that attorneys can collect in contingency fees (attorneys' fees that are based on a percentage of the damages awarded to the client), and (3) requiring the losing party to pay both the plaintiff's and the defendant's expenses.

In 2005, the Class Action Fairness Act (CAFA)[3] shifted jurisdiction over large interstate tort and product liability class-action lawsuits (lawsuits filed by a large number of plaintiffs) from the state courts to the federal courts. The intent was to prevent plaintiffs' attorneys from *forum shopping*—looking for a state court known to be sympathetic to their clients' cause and predisposed to award large damages. At the state level, more than thirty states have limited damages, especially in medical malpractice suits.

Classifications of Torts

LEARNING OBJECTIVE 2
What are two basic categories of torts?

There are two broad classifications of torts: *intentional torts* and *unintentional torts* (torts involving negligence). The classification of a particular tort depends largely on how the tort occurs (intentionally or negligently) and the surrounding circumstances. In the following pages, you will read about these two classifications of torts.

Intentional Torts against Persons

Intentional Tort A wrongful act knowingly committed.

Tortfeasor One who commits a tort.

An **intentional tort,** as the term implies, requires *intent*. The **tortfeasor** (the one committing the tort) must intend to commit an act, the consequences of which interfere with the personal or business interests of another in a way not permitted by law. An evil or harmful

---

2. *State Farm Mutual Automobile Insurance Co. v. Campbell,* 538 U.S. 408, 123 S.Ct. 1513, 155 L.Ed.2d 585 (2003).
3. 28 U.S.C. Sections 1453, 1711–1715.

motive is not required—in fact, the person committing the action (the actor) may even have a beneficial motive for committing what turns out to be a tortious act.

In tort law, intent means only that the actor intended the consequences of his or her act or knew with substantial certainty that certain consequences would result from the act. The law generally assumes that individuals intend the *normal* consequences of their actions. Thus, forcefully pushing another—even if done in jest and without any evil motive—is an intentional tort if injury results, because the object of a strong push can ordinarily be expected to fall down.

We now discuss intentional torts against persons, which include assault and battery, false imprisonment, infliction of emotional distress, defamation, invasion of the right to privacy, appropriation, misrepresentation, abusive or frivolous litigation, and wrongful interference.

Assault and Battery

An **assault** is any intentional and unexcused threat of immediate harmful or offensive contact, including words or acts that create in another person a reasonable apprehension of harmful contact. An assault can be completed even if there is no actual contact with the plaintiff, provided the defendant's conduct causes the plaintiff to have a reasonable apprehension of imminent harm. Tort law aims to protect individuals from having to expect harmful or offensive contact.

If the act that created the apprehension is *completed* and results in harm to the plaintiff, it is a **battery,** which is defined as an unexcused and harmful or offensive physical contact *intentionally* performed. **EXAMPLE 4.2** Ivan threatens Jean with a gun and then shoots her. The pointing of the gun at Jean is an assault. The firing of the gun (if the bullet hits Jean) is a battery. • The contact can be harmful, or it can be merely offensive (such as an unwelcome kiss). Physical injury need not occur. The contact can involve any part of the body or anything attached to it—for example, a hat, a purse, or a wheelchair in which one is sitting. The contact can also occur as a result of some force set in motion by the defendant, such as throwing a rock. Whether the contact is offensive or not is determined by the *reasonable person standard.*[4]

If the plaintiff shows that there was contact, and the jury (or judge, if there is no jury) agrees that the contact was offensive, the plaintiff has a right to compensation. A plaintiff may be compensated for the emotional harm resulting from a battery, as well as for physical harm. The defendant may raise a number of legally recognized **defenses** (reasons why plaintiffs should not obtain what they are seeking) that justify his or her conduct, including self-defense and defense of others.

False Imprisonment

False imprisonment is the intentional confinement or restraint of another person's activities without justification. False imprisonment interferes with the freedom to move without restraint. The confinement can be accomplished through the use of physical barriers, physical restraint, or threats of physical force. Moral pressure or threats of future harm do not constitute false imprisonment. It is essential that the person under restraint does not wish to be restrained.

Businesspersons are often confronted with suits for false imprisonment after they have attempted to confine a suspected shoplifter for questioning. Under the "privilege to detain" granted to merchants in most states, a merchant can use *reasonable force* to detain or delay a person suspected of shoplifting the merchant's property. Although the details of the

---

KNOW THIS
In intentional tort actions, the defendant must intend to commit the act but need not have intended to cause harm to the plaintiff.

Assault Any word or action intended to make another person fearful of immediate physical harm—a reasonably believable threat.

Battery Unexcused, harmful or offensive, physical contact with another that is intentionally performed.

Defense A reason offered and alleged by a defendant in an action or lawsuit as to why the plaintiff should not recover or establish what she or he seeks.

---

4. The reasonable person standard is an objective test of how a reasonable person would have acted under the same circumstances. See "The Duty of Care and Its Breach" later in this chapter.

privilege vary from state to state, generally laws require that any detention be conducted in a *reasonable* manner and for only a *reasonable* length of time. Undue force or unreasonable detention can lead to liability for the business.

Cities and counties may also face lawsuits for false imprisonment if they detain individuals without reason. In the following case, a man sued the County of Los Angeles for false imprisonment.

Case 4.1

Shoyoye v. County of Los Angeles

Court of Appeal of California, Second District,
203 Cal.App.4th 947, 137 Cal.Rptr.3d 839 (2012).

Cities and counties can be sued for
false imprisonment.

FACTS Adetokunbo Shoyoye was lawfully arrested in 2007 when he was at a police station reporting an unrelated incident. The police discovered that he had two outstanding warrants: one for an unpaid subway ticket, and another for grand theft, which was actually issued because a former roommate had stolen his identity and been convicted of grand theft under Shoyoye's name. Shoyoye was incarcerated. Shortly thereafter, he appeared before a magistrate who ordered him released on the first warrant. A few days later, a different court released him on the second warrant.

A Los Angeles County employee mistakenly attached information related to another person—who was scheduled to be sent to state prison for violating his parole—to Shoyoye's paperwork. Subsequently, this erroneous information was entered into the computer system under Shoyoye's name. As a result, instead of being released as ordered, Shoyoye was held in jail for sixteen days, subjected to strip searches, required to wait naked in line to shower in close proximity to other inmates, and shackled. During this time, Shoyoye made numerous attempts to explain to various officials that he was being detained for no reason. He was housed in a large dormitory with hundreds of inmates, many of whom were gang members, and witnessed criminal activity and fights. He feared that he might be sent to prison, be put into "the hole" for discipline, or become a victim of violence. After his release, he sued the County of Los Angeles for, among other things, false imprisonment. A jury awarded him $22,700 in economic damages (for past and future lost earnings and property loss), and $180,000 in noneconomic

damages (for past and future pain and suffering). The County of Los Angeles appealed.

ISSUE Did the County of Los Angeles wrongfully detain Shoyoye because of its clerical errors?

DECISION Yes. The reviewing court found that Shoyoye had experienced false imprisonment and held that the jury award for economic damages and noneconomic damages was appropriate under the circumstances.

REASON "The elements of a tortious claim of false imprisonment are: (1) the non-consensual, intentional confinement of a person, (2) without lawful privilege, and (3) for an appreciable period of time, however brief." The court concluded that the evidence presented at trial "was clearly sufficient to establish these elements." Had any county employees simply looked at the paper file on Shoyoye rather than the computer records, they would have realized that the "hold" on Shoyoye did not pertain to him. The erroneous paperwork on Shoyoye resulted in sixteen days of undeserved detention in a less-than-desirable environment.

CRITICAL THINKING—Ethical Consideration *Shoyoye asked numerous county employees to verify that he had been wrongfully detained. What obligation did those employees have to attempt to discover "the truth"?*

Intentional Infliction of Emotional Distress

Actionable Capable of serving as the basis of a lawsuit. An actionable claim can be pursued in a lawsuit or other court action.

The tort of *intentional infliction of emotional distress* can be defined as an extreme and outrageous act, intentionally committed, that results in severe emotional distress to another. To be **actionable** (capable of serving as the ground for a lawsuit), the conduct must be so extreme and outrageous that it exceeds the bounds of decency accepted by society.

Outrageous Conduct   Courts in most jurisdictions are wary of emotional distress claims and confine them to truly outrageous behavior. Generally, repeated annoyances (such as those experienced by a person who is being stalked), coupled with threats, are sufficient to support a claim. Acts that cause indignity or annoyance alone usually are not enough.

EXAMPLE 4.3   A father attacks a man who has had consensual sexual relations with the father's nineteen-year-old daughter. The father handcuffs the man to a steel pole and threatens to kill him unless he leaves town immediately. The father's conduct may be sufficiently extreme and outrageous to be actionable as an intentional infliction of emotional distress. •

Limited by the First Amendment   Note that when the outrageous conduct consists of speech about a public figure, the First Amendment's guarantee of freedom of speech also limits emotional distress claims.   **CASE EXAMPLE 4.4**   *Hustler* magazine once printed a fake advertisement that showed a picture of the Reverend Jerry Falwell and described him as having lost his virginity to his mother in an outhouse while he was drunk. Falwell sued the magazine for intentional infliction of emotional distress and won, but the United States Supreme Court overturned the decision. The Court held that creators of parodies of public figures are protected under the First Amendment from claims of intentional infliction of emotional distress. (The Court applied the same standards that apply to public figures in defamation lawsuits, discussed next.)[5] •

Defamation

LEARNING OBJECTIVE 3
What is defamation? Name two types of defamation.

Defamation Anything published or publicly spoken that causes injury to another's good name, reputation, or character.

Libel Defamation in writing or another form having the quality of permanence (such as a digital recording).

Slander Defamation in oral form.

As discussed in Chapter 1, the freedom of speech guaranteed by the First Amendment to the U.S. Constitution is not absolute. In interpreting the First Amendment, the courts must balance free speech rights against other strong social interests, including society's interest in preventing and redressing attacks on reputation. (Nations with fewer free speech protections have seen an increase in defamation lawsuits targeting U.S. citizens and journalists as defendants. See this chapter's *Beyond Our Borders* feature on page 106 for a discussion of this trend.)

Defamation of character involves wrongfully hurting a person's good reputation. The law has imposed a general duty on all persons to refrain from making *false*, defamatory *statements of fact* about others. Breaching this duty in writing or some other permanent form (such as a digital recording) constitutes the tort of **libel**. Breaching this duty orally is the tort of **slander**. As you will read later in this chapter, the tort of defamation can also arise when a false statement of fact is made about a person's product, business, or legal ownership rights to property.

Statement of Fact Requirement   Often at issue in defamation lawsuits (including online defamation, discussed later in this chapter) is whether the defendant made a statement of fact or a *statement of opinion*.[6] Statements of opinion normally are not actionable because they are protected under the First Amendment. In other words, making a negative statement about another person is not defamation unless the statement is false and represents something as a fact (for example, "Lane cheats on his taxes") rather than a personal opinion (for example, "Lane is a jerk").

Whether an attorney's statement to a reporter about another attorney constituted fact or opinion was at issue in the following case.

---

5. *Hustler Magazine, Inc. v. Falwell*, 485 U.S. 46, 108 S.Ct. 876, 99 L.Ed.2d 41 (1988). For another example of how the courts protect parody, see *Busch v. Viacom International, Inc.*, 477 F.Supp.2d 764 (N.D.Tex. 2007), involving a fake endorsement of televangelist Pat Robertson's diet shake.

6. See, for example, *Lott v. Levitt*, 469 F.Supp.2d 575 (N.D.Ill. 2007).

Case 4.2

Orlando v. Cole

Appeals Court of Massachusetts,
76 Mass.App.Ct. 1112, 921 N.E.2d 566 (2010).

High school women's basketball remains popular.

(Jamie Roach/Shutterstock.com)

FACTS   Joseph Orlando, an attorney, was representing a high school student who had sued her basketball coach for sexual assault. The coach, Thomas Atwater, was apparently an acquaintance of Orlando. Before he had retained an attorney, Atwater approached Orlando and admitted that he had committed the assault. Atwater signed an affidavit to that effect and then made a full confession to the police. A few days later, Orlando spoke to two newspaper reporters, gave them a copy of Atwater's affidavit, and explained the circumstances under which Atwater gave the affidavit. The reporters then asked Garrick Cole, who was now representing Atwater, for comments. Cole responded that the affidavit was "inaccurate" and called Orlando's actions "deceitful" and "fraudulent." The newspaper published an article that quoted both Orlando and Cole, and also indicated that Cole would not say what he thought was inaccurate in the affidavit. Both Orlando's and Cole's comments were reported together in various publications. Orlando sued Cole for slander, alleging that Cole's comments were false, described conduct undertaken by Orlando in his profession and business, and imputed "an unfitness for or a misconduct in his office or employment." Orlando claimed that he had suffered harm to his reputation as an attorney as a result of Cole's comments. The trial court granted Cole's motion to dismiss the complaint, and Orlando appealed.

ISSUE   Did Cole's statements that another attorney filed an "inaccurate" affidavit and engaged in "fraudulent" and "deceptive" conduct with regard to a case constitute statements of fact that give rise to a defamation claim?

DECISION   Yes. The Appeals Court of Massachusetts reversed the trial court's judgment and held that Cole's statements were "reasonably susceptible of a defamatory connotation [implication]." The appellate court remanded the case to allow for a jury trial.

REASON   The reviewing court reasoned that the dismissal was premature because "a statement is defamatory in the circumstances if it discredits a person in the minds of any considerable and respectable class of the community." The terms that Cole had used—"inaccurate," "fraudulent," and "deceitful"—implied professional misconduct. Further, those statements are capable of being proved false in a trial. The comments were not offered simply as opinions, nor did any cautionary language accompany them. They appeared to be based on undisclosed defamatory facts. A jury should be allowed to decide whether defamation had occurred.

CRITICAL THINKING—Legal Consideration   *Orlando sued Cole for slander. Why didn't he sue Cole for libel, given that the comments were reported in various news publications?*

The Publication Requirement   The basis of the tort of defamation is the publication of a statement or statements that hold an individual up to contempt, ridicule, or hatred. *Publication* here means that the defamatory statements are communicated to persons other than the defamed party.   **EXAMPLE 4.5**   If Thompson writes Andrews a private letter falsely accusing him of embezzling funds, the action does not constitute libel. If Peters falsely states that Gordon is dishonest and incompetent when no one else is around, the action does not constitute slander. In neither instance was the message communicated to a third party. •

The courts have generally held that even dictating a letter to a secretary constitutes publication, although the publication may be privileged (privileged communications will be discussed shortly). Moreover, if a third party overhears defamatory statements by chance, the courts usually hold that this also constitutes publication. Defamatory statements made via the Internet are also actionable, as you will read later in this chapter. Note further that anyone who republishes or repeats defamatory statements is liable even if that person reveals the source of the statements.

BEYOND OUR BORDERS   "Libel Tourism"

As mentioned earlier, U.S. plaintiffs some-times engage in forum shopping by trying to have their complaints heard by a particular state court that is likely to be sympathetic to their claims. *Libel tourism* is essentially forum shopping on an international scale. Rather than filing a defamation lawsuit in the United States where the freedoms of speech and press are strongly protected, a plaintiff files it in a foreign jurisdiction where there is a greater chance of winning.

The Threat of Libel Tourism
Libel tourism can have a chilling effect on the speech of U.S. journalists and authors because the fear of liability in other nations may prevent them from freely discussing topics of profound public importance. Libel tourism could even increase the threat to our nation's security if it discourages authors from writing about persons who support or finance terrorism or other dangerous activities.

The threat of libel tourism captured media attention when Khalid bin Mahfouz, a Saudi Arabian businessman, sued U.S.

resident Dr. Rachel Ehrenfeld in London, England. Ehrenfeld had written a book on terrorist financing that claimed Mahfouz financed Islamic terrorist groups. Mahfouz filed the case in England because English law assumes that the offending speech is false (libelous), and the author must prove that the speech is true in order to prevail.

The English court took jurisdiction because twenty-three copies of the book had been sold online to residents of the United Kingdom. Ehrenfeld did not go to England to defend herself, and the court entered a judgment of $225,000 against her. She then countersued Mahfouz in a U.S. court in an attempt to show that she was protected under the First Amendment and had not committed libel, but that case was dismissed for lack of jurisdiction.[a]

The U.S. Response
In response to the *Ehrenfeld* case, the New York state legislature enacted the Libel

Terrorism Reform Act in 2008.[b] That act enables New York courts to assert jurisdiction over anyone who obtains a foreign libel judgment against a writer or publisher living in New York State. It also prevents courts from enforcing foreign libel judgments unless the foreign country provides equal or greater free speech protection than is available in the United States and New York. In 2010, the federal government passed similar legislation that makes foreign libel judgments unenforceable in U.S. courts unless they comply with the First Amendment.[c]

Critical Thinking
Why do we need special legislation designed to control foreign libel claims against U.S. citizens? Explain.

a. *Ehrenfeld v. Mahfouz*, 518 F.3d 102 (2d Cir. 2008).

b. McKinney's Consolidated Laws of New York, Sections 302 and 5304.

c. Securing the Protection of our Enduring and Established Constitutional Heritage Act, 28 U.S.C. Sections 4101–4105.

Damages for Libel   Once a defendant's liability for libel is established, general damages are presumed as a matter of law. As mentioned earlier, general damages are designed to compensate the plaintiff for nonspecific harms such as disgrace or dishonor in the eyes of the community, humiliation, injured reputation, and emotional distress—harms that are difficult to measure. In other words, to recover damages in a libel case, the plaintiff need not prove that she or he was actually harmed in any specific way as a result of the libelous statement.

Damages for Slander   In contrast to cases alleging libel, in a case alleging slander, the plaintiff must prove *special damages* to establish the defendant's liability. In other words, the plaintiff must show that the slanderous statement caused the plaintiff to suffer actual economic or monetary losses. Unless this initial hurdle of proving special damages is overcome, a plaintiff alleging slander normally cannot go forward with the suit and recover any damages. This requirement is imposed in cases involving slander because slanderous statements have a temporary quality. In contrast, a libelous (written) statement has the quality of permanence, can be circulated widely, especially through tweets and blogs, and usually results from some degree of deliberation on the part of the author.

Exceptions to the burden of proving special damages in cases alleging slander are made for certain types of slanderous statements. If a false statement constitutes "slander *per se*," no proof of special damages is required for it to be actionable. The following four types of false utterances are considered to be slander *per se:*

1. A statement that another has a loathsome disease (historically, leprosy and sexually transmitted diseases, but now also including allegations of mental illness).
2. A statement that another has committed improprieties while engaging in a business, profession, or trade.
3. A statement that another has committed or has been imprisoned for a serious crime.
4. A statement that a person (usually only unmarried persons and sometimes only women) is unchaste or has engaged in serious sexual misconduct.

Defenses against Defamation   Truth is normally an absolute defense against a defamation charge. In other words, if the defendant in a defamation suit can prove that his or her allegedly defamatory statements were true, normally no tort has been committed. Other defenses to defamation may exist if the statement is privileged or concerns a public figure. Note that the majority of defamation actions in the United States are filed in state courts, and the states may differ both in how they define defamation and in the particular defenses they allow, such as privilege (discussed next).

Privileged Communications   In some circumstances, a person will not be liable for defamatory statements because she or he enjoys a **privilege,** or immunity. Privileged communications are of two types: absolute and qualified.[7] Only in judicial proceedings and certain government proceedings is an absolute privilege granted. Thus, statements made in a courtroom by attorneys and judges during a trial are absolutely privileged, as are statements made by government officials during legislative debate.

In other situations, a person will not be liable for defamatory statements because he or she has a *qualified,* or conditional, privilege. An employer's statements in written evaluations of employees are an example of a qualified privilege. Generally, if the statements are made in good faith and the publication is limited to those who have a legitimate interest in the communication, the statements fall within the area of qualified privilege. **EXAMPLE 4.6**   Jorge worked at Facebook for five years and was being considered for a management position. His supervisor, Lydia, wrote a memo about Jorge's performance to those evaluating him for the management position. The memo contained certain negative statements. As long as Lydia honestly believed that what she wrote was true and limited her disclosure to company representatives, her statements would likely be protected by a qualified privilege. ●

Public Figures   Politicians, entertainers, professional athletes, and other persons who are in the public eye are considered *public figures.* In general, public figures are considered fair game, and false and defamatory statements about them that appear in the media will not constitute defamation unless the statements are made with **actual malice.**[8] To be made with actual malice, a statement must be made *with either knowledge of its falsity or a reckless disregard of the truth.*

Statements about public figures, especially when made via a public medium, are usually related to matters of general interest. They are made about people who substantially affect all of us. Furthermore, public figures generally have some access to a public medium for answering disparaging (belittling, discrediting) falsehoods about themselves, whereas

---

> "My initial response was to sue her for defamation of character, but then I realized that I had no character."
>
> Charles Barkley, 1963–present (National Basketball Association player, 1984–2000)

Privilege   In tort law, immunity from liability for an action that would otherwise be a tort.

Actual Malice   The deliberate intent to cause harm that exists when a person makes a statement with either knowledge of its falsity or reckless disregard of the truth. Actual malice is required to establish defamation against public figures.

---

7. Note that the term *privileged communication* in this context is not the same as privileged communication between a professional, such as an attorney, and his or her client.
8. *New York Times Co. v. Sullivan,* 376 U.S. 254, 84 S.Ct. 710, 11 L.Ed.2d 686 (1964).

Lynne Spears, mother of singer Britney Spears, wrote a "tell all" book entitled *Through the Storm: A Real Story of Fame and Family in a Tabloid World.*

private individuals do not. For these reasons, public figures have a greater burden of proof in defamation cases (they must prove actual malice) than do private individuals.

CASE EXAMPLE 4.7   Lynne Spears, the mother of pop star Britney Spears, wrote a book in which she claimed that Sam Lutfi, Britney's former business manager, contributed to a mental breakdown that Britney experienced in 2008. Among other things, the book stated that Lutfi added psychiatric drugs to Britney's food, disabled her cars and phones, and stole funds from her bank accounts. Lutfi filed a lawsuit for defamation and asserted that Lynne's statements were untrue, disparaging, and made with actual malice. A court found that Lutfi was a public figure but had presented enough evidence in his complaint for the case to go forward to trial. Lynne appealed, but the appellate court affirmed the ruling and refused to dismiss Lufti's complaint.[9] ●

Invasion of the Right to Privacy and Appropriation

A person has a right to solitude and freedom from prying public eyes—in other words, to privacy. As discussed in Chapter 1, the Supreme Court has held that a fundamental right to privacy is implied by various amendments to the U.S. Constitution. Some state constitutions also explicitly provide for privacy rights. In addition, a number of federal and state statutes have been enacted to protect individual rights in specific areas. Tort law also safeguards these rights through the torts of *invasion of privacy* and *appropriation*.

Invasion of Privacy   Four acts qualify as an invasion of privacy:

1. *Intrusion into an individual's affairs or seclusion.* Invading someone's home or illegally searching someone's briefcase is an invasion of privacy. The tort has been held to extend to eavesdropping by wiretap, the unauthorized scanning of a bank account, compulsory blood testing, and window peeping. **EXAMPLE 4.8**   A female sports reporter for ESPN was digitally videoed while naked through the peephole in the door of her hotel room. She subsequently won a lawsuit against the man who took the video and posted it on the Internet. ●

2. *False light.* Publication of information that places a person in a false light is also an invasion of privacy. For example, writing a story about a person that attributes ideas and opinions not held by that person is an invasion of privacy. (Publishing such a story could involve the tort of defamation as well.) **EXAMPLE 4.9**   An Arkansas newspaper printed an article with the headline "Special Delivery: World's oldest newspaper carrier, 101, quits because she's pregnant!" Next to the article was a picture of a ninety-six-year-old woman who was not the subject of the article (and not pregnant). She sued the paper for false light and won. ●

3. *Public disclosure of private facts.* This type of invasion of privacy occurs when a person publicly discloses private facts about an individual that an ordinary person would find objectionable or embarrassing. A newspaper account of a private citizen's sex life or financial affairs could be an actionable invasion of privacy, even if the information revealed is true, because it should not be a matter of public concern.

4. *Appropriation of identity.* Under the common law, using a person's name, picture, or other likeness for commercial purposes without permission is a tortious invasion of privacy. An individual's right to privacy normally includes the right to the exclusive use of her or his identity. **EXAMPLE 4.10**   An advertising agency asks a singer with a distinctive voice and stage presence to do a marketing campaign for a new automobile. The singer rejects the offer. If the agency then uses someone who imitates the singer's voice and dance moves in the ad, this would be actionable as an appropriation of identity. ●

9. *Lutfi v. Spears,* 2010 WL 4723437 (2010).

Appropriation In tort law, the use by one person of another person's name, likeness, or other identifying characteristic without permission and for the benefit of the user.

Appropriation

Most states today have codified the common law tort of appropriation of identity in statutes that establish the distinct tort of **appropriation** or right of publicity. **CASE EXAMPLE 4.11** Vanna White, the hostess of the popular television game show *Wheel of Fortune*, brought an appropriation action against Samsung Electronics America, Inc. Without White's permission, Samsung had included in one of its advertisements a depiction of a robot dressed in a wig, gown, and jewelry, posed in a scene that resembled the *Wheel of Fortune* set, in a stance for which White is famous. The court held in White's favor, reasoning that Samsung's robot ad left "little doubt" as to the identity of the celebrity whom the ad was meant to depict.[10] ●

States differ as to the degree of likeness that is required to impose liability for appropriation, however. Some courts have held that even when an animated character in a video or a video game is made to look like an actual person, there are not enough similarities to constitute appropriation. **CASE EXAMPLE 4.12** The Naked Cowboy, Robert Burck, has been a street entertainer in New York City's Times Square for years. He performs for tourists wearing only a white cowboy hat, white cowboy boots, and white underwear and carrying a guitar strategically placed to give the illusion of nudity. Burck has become a well-known persona, appearing in television shows, movies, and video games, and has licensed his name and likeness to various companies, including Chevrolet. When Mars, Inc., the maker of M&Ms candy, installed a video on billboards in Times Square that depicted a blue M&M dressed exactly like The Naked Cowboy, Burck sued for appropriation. A federal district court held that Mars's use of a cartoon character dressed in The Naked Cowboy's signature costume did not amount to appropriation by use of Burck's "portrait or picture." (Burck was allowed to continue his lawsuit against Mars for allegedly violating trademark law—to be discussed in Chapter 5.)[11] ●

Fraudulent Misrepresentation

A misrepresentation leads another to believe in a condition that is different from the condition that actually exists. This is often accomplished through a false or incorrect statement. Although persons sometimes make misrepresentations accidentally because they are unaware of the existing facts, the tort of **fraudulent misrepresentation**, or fraud, involves *intentional* deceit for personal gain. The tort includes several elements:

Fraudulent Misrepresentation Any misrepresentation, either by misstatement or by omission of a material fact, knowingly made with the intention of deceiving another and on which a reasonable person would and does rely to his or her detriment.

1. The misrepresentation of facts or conditions with knowledge that they are false or with reckless disregard for the truth.
2. An intent to induce another to rely on the misrepresentation.
3. Justifiable reliance by the deceived party.
4. Damage suffered as a result of the reliance.
5. A causal connection between the misrepresentation and the injury suffered.

Puffery A salesperson's often exaggerated claims concerning the quality of property offered for sale. Such claims involve opinions rather than facts and are not legally binding promises or warranties.

For fraud to occur, more than mere **puffery**, or *seller's talk,* must be involved. Fraud exists only when a person represents as a fact something she or he knows is untrue. For example, it is fraud to claim that a roof does not leak when one knows it does. Facts are objectively ascertainable, whereas seller's talk is not. "I am the best accountant in town" is seller's talk. The speaker is not trying to represent something as fact because the term *best* is a subjective, not an objective, term.[12]

---

10. *White v. Samsung Electronics America, Inc.,* 971 F.2d 1395 (9th Cir. 1992).

11. *Burck v. Mars, Inc.,* 571 F.Supp.2d 446 (S.D.N.Y. 2008). Also see *Kirby v. Sega of America, Inc.,* 144 Cal.App.4th 47, 50 Cal.Rptr.3d 607 (2006).

12. In contracts for the sale of goods, Article 2 of the Uniform Commercial Code distinguishes, for warranty purposes, between statements of opinion (puffery) and statements of fact. See Chapter 12 for a further discussion of this issue.

Statement of Fact versus Opinion   Normally, the tort of misrepresentation or fraud occurs only when there is reliance on a *statement of fact*. Sometimes, however, the tort may involve reliance on a *statement of opinion* if the individual making the statement has a superior knowledge of the subject matter. For instance, when a lawyer makes a statement of opinion about the law in a state in which the lawyer is licensed to practice, a court would construe reliance on that statement to be equivalent to reliance on a statement of fact. We will examine fraudulent misrepresentation in further detail in Chapter 8, in the context of contract law.

Negligent Misrepresentation   Sometimes, a tort action can arise from misrepresentations that are made negligently rather than intentionally. The key difference between intentional and negligent misrepresentation is whether the person making the misrepresentation had actual knowledge of its falsity. Negligent misrepresentation requires only that the person making the statement or omission did not have a reasonable basis for believing its truthfulness. Liability for negligent misrepresentation usually arises when the defendant who made the misrepresentation owed a duty of care to the particular plaintiff to supply correct information. Statements or omissions made by attorneys and accountants to their clients, for example, can lead to liability for negligent misrepresentation.

Abusive or Frivolous Litigation

Persons or businesses generally have a right to sue when they have been injured, but they do not have a right to file meritless lawsuits or use the legal system simply to harass others. Tort law recognizes that people have a right not to be sued without a legally just and proper reason, and therefore it protects individuals from the misuse of litigation. Torts related to abusive litigation include malicious prosecution and abuse of process.

If a person initiates a lawsuit out of malice and without probable cause (a legitimate legal reason) and ends up losing the suit, he or she can be sued for *malicious prosecution*. In some states, the plaintiff (who was the defendant in the first proceeding) must also prove injury beyond the normal costs of litigation, such as lost profits. *Abuse of process* can apply to any person using a legal process against another in an improper manner or to accomplish a purpose for which it was not designed. The key difference between the torts of abuse of process and malicious prosecution is the level of proof required to succeed.

Abuse of process does not require the plaintiff to prove malice or show that the defendant (who was previously the plaintiff) lost in a prior legal proceeding. In addition, an abuse of process claim is not limited to prior litigation. It can be based on the wrongful use of subpoenas, court orders to attach or seize real property, or other types of formal legal process.

Wrongful Interference

Business torts involving wrongful interference are generally divided into two categories: wrongful interference with a contractual relationship and wrongful interference with a business relationship.

Wrongful Interference with a Contractual Relationship   Three elements are necessary for wrongful interference with a contractual relationship to occur:

1. A valid, enforceable contract must exist between two parties.
2. A third party must know that this contract exists.
3. The third party must *intentionally* induce a party to breach the contract.

CASE EXAMPLE 4.13 A landmark case involved an opera singer, Joanna Wagner, who was under contract to sing for a man named Lumley for a specified period of years. A man named Gye, who knew of this contract, nonetheless "enticed" Wagner to refuse to carry out the agreement, and Wagner began to sing for Gye. Gye's action constituted a tort because it wrongfully interfered with the contractual relationship between Wagner and Lumley.[13] (Of course, Wagner's refusal to carry out the agreement also entitled Lumley to sue Wagner for breach of contract.) ●

The body of tort law relating to intentional interference with a contractual relationship has expanded greatly in recent years. In principle, any lawful contract can be the basis for an action of this type. The contract could be between a firm and its employees or a firm and its customers. Sometimes, a competitor draws away one of a firm's key employees. To recover damages from the competitor, the original employer must show that the competitor knew of the contract's existence and intentionally induced the breach.

Wrongful Interference with a Business Relationship
Business-persons devise countless schemes to attract customers, but they are prohibited from unreasonably interfering with another's business in their attempts to gain a share of the market. There is a difference between *competitive methods* and *predatory behavior*—actions undertaken with the intention of unlawfully driving competitors completely out of the market.

Attempting to attract customers in general is a legitimate business practice, whereas specifically targeting the customers of a competitor is more likely to be predatory. **EXAMPLE 4.14** A shopping mall contains two athletic shoe stores: Joe's and Ultimate Sport. Joe's cannot station an employee at the entrance of Ultimate Sport to divert customers by telling them that Joe's will beat Ultimate Sport's prices. This type of activity constitutes the tort of wrongful interference with a business relationship, which is commonly considered to be an unfair trade practice. If this activity were permitted, Joe's would reap the benefits of Ultimate Sport's advertising. ●

Defenses to Wrongful Interference
A person can avoid liability for the tort of wrongful interference with a contractual or business relationship by showing that the interference was justified or permissible.

Bona fide competitive behavior is a permissible interference even if it results in the breaking of a contract. **EXAMPLE 4.15** If Antonio's Meats advertises so effectively that it induces Sam's Restaurant to break its contract with Burke's Meat Company, Burke's will be unable to recover against Antonio's Meats on a wrongful interference theory. After all, the public policy that favors free competition in advertising outweighs any possible instability that such competitive activity might cause in contractual relations. ●

Although luring customers away from a competitor through aggressive marketing and advertising obviously interferes with the competitor's relationship with its customers, courts typically allow such activities in the spirit of competition. (For a discussion of Facebook's advertising campaign that alleged sweeping privacy violations by Google's social network, see this chapter's *Adapting the Law to the Online Environment* on the next page.)

Intentional Torts against Property

Intentional torts against property include trespass to land, trespass to personal property, conversion, and disparagement of property. These torts are wrongful actions that interfere with individuals' legally recognized rights with regard to their land or personal property.

---

13. *Lumley v. Gye*, 118 Eng.Rep. 749 (1853).

ADAPTING THE LAW TO THE ONLINE ENVIRONMENT

FACEBOOK USES PRIVACY CONCERNS TO "SMEAR" GOOGLE

With close to one billion users, Facebook is the largest social network in the world. Although Facebook has had various competitors, none has posed as much of a threat as Google. Several years ago, Google added a social-networking feature called Social Circles that eventually became part of Google+. Today, Google+ has more than 100 million users and is growing faster than Facebook.

Privacy Policies Matter

For many users of social networks, privacy is a major concern. Facebook has faced a number of complaints about its privacy policy and has changed its policy several times to satisfy its critics and to ward off potential government investigations. One of Google's main advertising points has been its social network's ability to keep "conversations" private and limited to as few individuals as users desire.

As the rivalry between Google and Facebook intensified, Facebook hired Burson-Marsteller, a public relations firm, to plant anonymous stories raising questions about Google's privacy policy. Although Facebook later claimed that Burson-Marsteller was only supposed to investigate how Social Circles collected and used data, several influential bloggers reported that they were approached by Burson-Marsteller and asked to publish negative stories about privacy concerns on Social Circles. In some instances, Burson-Marsteller even offered to supply the stories—one would have claimed that Social Circles "enables people to trace their contacts' connections and profile information by crawling and scraping the sites you and your contacts use, such as Twitter, YouTube, and Facebook."

The Campaign Backfires

If Facebook's goal was to discredit Google, the plan failed dramatically. Bloggers across the Web responded with a mixture of derision and amazement. Some pointed out that planting anonymous stories violated Facebook's privacy policy for its own site, while others said that Facebook's effort to attack Google showed that the social-networking giant was running scared. Writing in *Wired* magazine, Steven Levy concluded that "Facebook was running a smear campaign against itself."[a]

Critical Thinking

If you were part of Google's legal team, on what basis might you think that you could sue Facebook and its public relations firm?

---

a. Steven Levy, "Facebook's Stealth Attack on Google Exposes Its Own Privacy Problem," *Wired*, May 12, 2011. See also Sam Gustin, "Burson-Marsteller Deletes Critical Facebook Posts, Spares Google-Smear Flacks," *Wired*, May 13, 2011; David Sarno, "Sibling Rivalry? Facebook vs. Google," *Los Angeles Times*, May 13, 2011; and Barbara Ortutay, "Facebook-Google Rivalry Intensifies with PR Fiasco," *Huffington Post*, May 12, 2011.

The law distinguishes real property from personal property (see Chapters 23 and 24). *Real property* is land and things "permanently" attached to the land. *Personal property* consists of all other items, which are basically movable. Thus, a house and lot are real property, whereas the furniture inside the house is personal property. Cash and stocks and bonds are also personal property.

Trespass to Land

Trespass to Land Entry onto, above, or below the surface of land owned by another without the owner's permission or legal authorization.

A **trespass to land** occurs anytime a person, without permission, enters onto, above, or below the surface of land that is owned by another; causes anything to enter onto the land; or remains on the land or permits anything to remain on it. Actual harm to the land is not an essential element of this tort because the tort is designed to protect the right of an owner to exclusive possession of her or his property.

Common types of trespass to land include walking or driving on someone else's land, shooting a gun over the land, throwing rocks at a building that belongs to someone else, building a dam across a river and thereby causing water to back up on someone else's land, and constructing a building so that part of it is on an adjoining landowner's property.

Trespass Criteria, Rights, and Duties Before a person can be a trespasser, the real property owner (or other person in actual and exclusive possession of the property) must establish that person as a trespasser. For example, "posted" trespass signs expressly establish as a trespasser a person who ignores these signs and enters onto the property. A guest in your home is not a trespasser—unless she or he has been asked to leave but refuses. Any person who enters onto your property to commit an illegal act (such as a thief entering a lumberyard at night to steal lumber) is established impliedly as a trespasser, without posted signs.

At common law, a trespasser is liable for any damage caused to the property and generally cannot hold the owner liable for injuries sustained on the premises. This common law rule is being abandoned in many jurisdictions in favor of a *reasonable duty of care* rule that varies depending on the status of the parties. For instance, a landowner may have a duty to post a notice that guard dogs patrol the property. Also, under the *attractive nuisance* doctrine, children do not assume the risks of the premises if they are attracted to the property by some object, such as a swimming pool, an abandoned building, or a sand pile. Trespassers normally can be removed from the premises through the use of reasonable force without the owner being liable for assault, battery, or false imprisonment.

Defenses against Trespass to Land One defense to a claim of trespass to land is to show that the trespass was warranted—for instance, that the trespasser entered the property to assist someone in danger. Another defense is for the trespasser to show that he or she had a license to come onto the land. A *licensee* is one who is invited (or allowed to enter) onto the property of another for the licensee's benefit. A person who enters another's property to read an electric meter, for example, is a licensee. When you purchase a ticket to attend a movie or sporting event, you are licensed to go onto the property of another to view that movie or event.

Note that licenses to enter are *revocable* by the property owner. If a property owner asks a meter reader to leave and the meter reader refuses to do so, the meter reader at that point becomes a trespasser.

Trespass to Personal Property

Trespass to Personal Property
Wrongfully taking or harming the personal property of another or otherwise interfering with the lawful owner's possession of personal property.

Whenever an individual wrongfully takes or harms the personal property of another or otherwise interferes with the lawful owner's possession of personal property, **trespass to personal property** occurs (also called *trespass to chattels* or *trespass to personalty*[14]). In this context, harm means not only destruction of the property, but also anything that diminishes its value, condition, or quality.

Trespass to personal property involves intentional meddling with a possessory interest (the right to possess), including barring an owner's access to personal property. **EXAMPLE 4.16** Kelly takes Ryan's business law book as a practical joke and hides it so that Ryan is unable to find it for several days before the final examination. Here, Kelly has engaged in a trespass to personal property. (Kelly has also committed the tort of *conversion*—to be discussed next.) ●

A complete defense to a claim of trespass to personal property is to show that the trespass was warranted. Most states, for example, allow automobile repair shops to retain a customer's car (under what is called an *artisan's lien*—see Chapter 15) when the customer refuses to pay for repairs already completed.

---

14. Pronounced *per-sun-ul-tee*.

Conversion

Conversion Wrongfully taking or retaining possession of an individual's personal property and placing it in the service of another.

Whenever a person wrongfully possesses or uses the personal property of another without permission, the tort of **conversion** occurs. Any act that deprives an owner of personal property or the use of that property without that owner's permission and without just cause can be conversion. Even the taking of electronic records and data can be a form of conversion.[15]

Often, when conversion occurs, a trespass to personal property also occurs because the original taking of the personal property from the owner was a trespass, and wrongfully retaining it is conversion. Conversion is the civil side of crimes related to theft, but it is not limited to theft. Even if the rightful owner consented to the initial taking of the property, so there was no theft or trespass, a failure to return the personal property may still be conversion. **EXAMPLE 4.17** Chen borrows Mark's iPad to use while traveling home from school for the holidays. When Chen returns to school, Mark asks for his iPad back. Chen tells Mark that she gave it to her little brother for Christmas. In this situation, Mark can sue Chen for conversion, and Chen will have to either return the iPad or pay damages equal to its replacement value. ●

> **KNOW THIS**
>
> It is the *intent* to do an act that is important in tort law, not the motive behind the intent.

Even if a person mistakenly believed that she or he was entitled to the goods, the tort of conversion may occur. In other words, good intentions are not a defense against conversion. In fact, conversion can be an entirely innocent act. Someone who buys stolen goods, for example, can be liable for conversion even if he or she did not know that the goods were stolen. If the true owner brings a tort action against the buyer, the buyer must either return the property to the owner or pay the owner the full value of the property, despite having already paid the purchase price to the thief. A successful defense against the charge of conversion is that the purported owner does not, in fact, own the property or does not have a right to possess it that is superior to the right of the holder.

Disparagement of Property

Disparagement of Property An economically injurious falsehood about another's product or property.

Disparagement of property occurs when economically injurious falsehoods are made about another's product or property, not about another's reputation. Disparagement of property is a general term for torts specifically referred to as *slander of quality* or *slander of title*. Publication of false information about another's product, alleging that it is not what its seller claims, constitutes the tort of **slander of quality**, or **trade libel**. To establish trade libel, the plaintiff must prove that the improper publication caused a third party to refrain from dealing with the plaintiff and that the plaintiff sustained economic damages (such as lost profits) as a result.

Slander of Quality (Trade Libel) The publication of false information about another's product, alleging that it is not what its seller claims.

An improper publication may be both a slander of quality and defamation of character. For example, a statement that disparages the quality of a product may also, by implication, disparage the character of the person who would sell such a product.

Slander of Title The publication of a statement that denies or casts doubt on another's legal ownership of any property, causing financial loss to that property's owner.

When a publication denies or casts doubt on another's legal ownership of any property, and the property's owner suffers financial loss as a result, the tort of **slander of title** may exist. Usually, this is an intentional tort that occurs when someone knowingly publishes an untrue statement about property with the intent of discouraging a third party from dealing with the property's owner. For instance, a car dealer would have difficulty attracting customers after competitors published a notice that the dealer's stock consisted of stolen automobiles.

---

15. See, for example, *Thyroff v. Nationwide Mutual Insurance Co.*, 8 N.Y.3d 283, 864 N.E.2d 1272, 832 N.Y.S.2d 873 (2007).

Unintentional Torts (Negligence)

Negligence The failure to exercise the standard of care that a reasonable person would exercise in similar circumstances.

The tort of **negligence** occurs when someone suffers injury because of another's failure to live up to a required *duty of care*. In contrast to intentional torts, in torts involving negligence, the tortfeasor neither wishes to bring about the consequences of the act nor believes that they will occur. The actor's conduct merely creates a *risk* of such consequences. If no risk is created, there is no negligence. Moreover, the risk must be foreseeable—that is, it must be such that a reasonable person engaging in the same activity would anticipate the risk and guard against it. In determining what is reasonable conduct, courts consider the nature of the possible harm.

LEARNING OBJECTIVE 4
Identify the four elements of negligence.

Many of the actions discussed earlier in the chapter in the section on intentional torts constitute negligence if the element of intent is missing. **EXAMPLE 4.18** Juan walks up to Maya and intentionally shoves her. Maya falls and breaks an arm as a result. In this situation, Juan has committed an intentional tort (assault and battery). If Juan carelessly bumps into Maya, however, and she falls and breaks an arm as a result, Juan's action will constitute negligence. In either situation, Juan has committed a tort. •

To succeed in a negligence action, the plaintiff must prove each of the following:

1. *Duty.* That the defendant owed a duty of care to the plaintiff.
2. *Breach.* That the defendant breached that duty.
3. *Causation.* That the defendant's breach caused the plaintiff's injury.
4. *Damages.* That the plaintiff suffered a legally recognizable injury.

We discuss each of these four elements of negligence next.

The Duty of Care and Its Breach

Duty of Care The duty of all persons, as established by tort law, to exercise a reasonable amount of care in their dealings with others. Failure to exercise due care, which is normally determined by the reasonable person standard, constitutes the tort of negligence.

Central to the tort of negligence is the concept of a **duty of care.** The basic principle underlying the duty of care is that people in society are free to act as they please so long as their actions do not infringe on the interests of others.

When someone fails to comply with the duty to exercise reasonable care, a potentially tortious act may have been committed. Failure to live up to a standard of care may be an act (setting fire to a building) or an omission (neglecting to put out a campfire). It may be a careless act or a carefully performed but nevertheless dangerous act that results in injury.

Reasonable Person Standard The standard of behavior expected of a hypothetical "reasonable person." It is the standard against which negligence is measured and that must be observed to avoid liability for negligence.

Courts consider the nature of the act (whether it is outrageous or commonplace), the manner in which the act was performed (cautiously versus heedlessly), and the nature of the injury (whether it is serious or slight).

The Reasonable Person Standard Tort law measures duty by the **reasonable person standard.** In determining whether a duty of care has been breached, the courts ask how a reasonable person would have acted in the same circumstances. The reasonable person standard is said to be (though in an absolute sense it cannot be) objective. It is not necessarily how a particular person would act. It is society's judgment on how people *should* act. If the so-called reasonable person existed, he or she would be careful, conscientious, even tempered, and honest.

The courts frequently use this hypothetical reasonable person in decisions relating to other areas of law as well. That individuals are required to exercise a reasonable standard of care in

*"Do you have any picture books that could help
a child understand tort reform?"*

their activities is a pervasive concept in business law, and many of the issues discussed in subsequent chapters of this text have to do with this duty.

In negligence cases, the degree of care to be exercised varies, depending on the defendant's occupation or profession, her or his relationship with the plaintiff, and other factors. Generally, whether an action constitutes a breach of the duty of care is determined on a case-by-case basis. The outcome depends on how the judge (or jury, if it is a jury trial) decides a reasonable person in the position of the defendant would act in the particular circumstances of the case.

ETHICAL ISSUE

Does a pharmacist's duty of care include a duty to warn customers of certain adverse effects when filling prescriptions? Pharmacists typically discuss the potential side effects of prescription medications with the customer when they first fill a prescription. Under what is known as the "learned intermediary doctrine," pharmacists are generally *immune* from liability for any negative effects resulting from medications that were prescribed by the customer's physician (the intermediary). Nevertheless, according to the Nevada Supreme Court, pharmacists may have a duty to warn a customer in some situations, if they are aware of certain customer-specific risks, such as allergies. The case involved a pharmacist at a Walgreen drugstore who filled a prescription for a woman even though the pharmacy's computer indicated that she was allergic to the medication prescribed. The woman subsequently died when her condition worsened. The court concluded that the pharmacist should have either warned the customer or notified the prescribing physician. The court noted, however, that the duty to warn exists only when the pharmacist *knows* of a possible adverse effect for the specific customer.[16]

The Duty of Landowners
Landowners are expected to exercise reasonable care to protect persons coming onto their property from harm. As mentioned earlier, in some jurisdictions, landowners are held to owe a duty to protect even trespassers against certain risks. Landowners who rent or lease premises to tenants are expected to exercise reasonable care to ensure that the tenants and their guests are not harmed in common areas, such as stairways, entryways, and laundry rooms.

Duty to Warn Business Invitees of Risks   Retailers and other firms that explicitly or implicitly invite persons to come onto their premises are usually charged with a duty to exercise reasonable care to protect those persons, who are considered **business invitees**. **EXAMPLE 4.19**   Liz enters a supermarket, slips on a wet floor, and sustains injuries as a result. If there was no sign warning that the floor was wet when Liz slipped, the owner of the supermarket would be liable for damages. A court would hold that the business owner was negligent because the owner failed to exercise a reasonable degree of care in protecting the store's customers against foreseeable risks about which the owner knew or *should have known*. That a patron might slip on the wet floor and be injured was a foreseeable risk, and the owner should have taken care to avoid this risk or to warn the customer of it (by posting a sign or setting out orange cones, for example). •

The landowner also has a duty to discover and remove any hidden dangers that might injure a customer or other invitee. Store owners have a duty to protect customers from potentially slipping and injuring themselves on merchandise that has fallen off the shelves, for instance.

Obvious Risks Are an Exception   Some risks, of course, are so obvious that the owner need not warn of them. For instance, a business owner does not need to warn customers to open a door before attempting to walk through it. Other risks, however, may seem obvious to a business owner but may not be so to someone else, such as a child. In addition, even if a risk is obvious, that does not necessarily excuse a business owner from the duty to protect its customers from foreseeable harm.

Business Invitee A person, such as a customer or a client, who is invited onto business premises by the owner of those premises for business purposes.

---

16. *Klasch v. Walgreen Co.*, 264 P.3d 1155 (Nev. 2011).

CASE EXAMPLE 4.20 Giorgio's Grill in Hollywood, Florida, is a restaurant that becomes a nightclub after hours. At those times, traditionally, as the manager of Giorgio's knew, the staff and customers throw paper napkins into the air as the music plays. The napkins land on the floor, but no one picks them up. One night, Jane Izquierdo went to Giorgio's. Although she had been to the club on other occasions and knew about the napkin-throwing tradition, she slipped on a napkin and fell, breaking her leg. She sued Giorgio's for negligence but lost at trial because the jury found that the risk of slipping on the napkins was obvious. A state appellate court reversed, however, holding that the obviousness of a risk does not discharge a business owner's duty to its invitees to maintain the premises in a safe condition.[17] ●

PREVENTING LEGAL DISPUTES

It can be difficult to determine whether a risk is obvious. Because you can be held liable if you fail to discover hidden dangers on business premises that could cause injuries to customers, you should post warnings of any conceivable risks on the property. Be vigilant and frequently reassess potential hazards. Train your employees to be on the lookout for possibly dangerous conditions at all times and to notify a superior immediately if they notice something. Remember that a finding of liability in a single lawsuit can leave a small enterprise close to bankruptcy. To prevent potential negligence liability, make sure that your business premises are as safe as possible for all persons who might be there, including children, senior citizens, and individuals with disabilities.

The Duty of Professionals If an individual has knowledge, skill, or training superior to that of an ordinary person, the individual's conduct must be consistent with that status. Because professionals—such as physicians, dentists, architects, engineers, accountants, and lawyers—are required to have a certain level of knowledge and training, a higher standard of care applies. In determining whether professionals have exercised reasonable care, the law takes their training and expertise into account. Thus, an accountant's conduct is judged not by the reasonable person standard, but by the reasonable accountant standard.

Malpractice Professional misconduct or the lack of the requisite degree of skill as a professional (negligence).

If a professional violates her or his duty of care toward a client, the professional may be sued for **malpractice**, which is essentially professional negligence. For example, a patient might sue a physician for *medical malpractice*. A client might sue an attorney for *legal malpractice*.

Causation

Another necessary element in a negligence action is *causation*. If a person fails in a duty of care and someone suffers an injury, the wrongful act must have caused the harm for the act to be considered a tort.

Courts Ask Two Questions In deciding whether there is causation, the court must address two questions:

Causation in Fact An act or omission without which an event would not have occurred.

1. *Is there causation in fact?* Did the injury occur because of the defendant's act, or would it have occurred anyway? If an injury would not have occurred without the defendant's act, then there is causation in fact. **Causation in fact** can usually be determined by the use of the *but for* test: "but for" the wrongful act, the injury would not have occurred. Theoretically, causation in fact is limitless. One could claim, for example, that "but for"

---

17. *Izquierdo v. Gyroscope, Inc.,* 946 So.2d 115 (Fla.App. 2007).

Proximate Cause Legal cause. It exists when the connection between an act and an injury is strong enough to justify imposing liability.

the creation of the world, a particular injury would not have occurred. Thus, as a practical matter, the law has to establish limits, and it does so through the concept of proximate cause.

2. *Was the act the proximate cause of the injury?* **Proximate cause,** or legal cause, exists when the connection between an act and an injury is strong enough to justify imposing liability. Courts use proximate cause to limit the scope of the defendant's liability to a subset of the total number of potential plaintiffs that might have been harmed by the defendant's actions. **EXAMPLE 4.21** Ackerman carelessly leaves a campfire burning. The fire not only burns down the forest but also sets off an explosion in a nearby chemical plant that spills chemicals into a river, killing all the fish for a hundred miles downstream and ruining the economy of a tourist resort. Should Ackerman be liable to the resort owners? To the tourists whose vacations were ruined? These are questions of proximate cause that a court must decide. •

Both of these questions regarding causation in fact and proximate cause must be answered in the affirmative for liability in tort to arise. If a defendant's action constitutes causation in fact but a court decides that the action was not the proximate cause of the plaintiff's injury, the causation requirement has not been met—and the defendant normally will not be liable to the plaintiff.

Foreseeability   Questions of proximate cause are linked to the concept of foreseeability because it would be unfair to impose liability on a defendant unless the defendant's actions created a foreseeable risk of injury. Probably the most cited case on proximate cause is the *Palsgraf* case, which is discussed in this chapter's *Landmark in the Law* feature on the facing page. In determining the issue of proximate cause, the court addressed the following question: Does a defendant's duty of care extend only to those who may be injured as a result of a foreseeable risk, or does it also extend to a person whose injury could not reasonably be foreseen?

The Injury Requirement and Damages

For a tort to have been committed, the plaintiff must have suffered a *legally recognizable* injury. To recover damages (receive compensation), the plaintiff must have suffered some loss, harm, wrong, or invasion of a protected interest. Essentially, the purpose of tort law is to compensate for legally recognized injuries resulting from wrongful acts. If no harm or injury results from a given negligent action, there is nothing to compensate—and no tort exists. **EXAMPLE 4.22** If you carelessly bump into a passerby, who stumbles and falls as a result, you may be liable in tort if the passerby is injured in the fall. If the person is unharmed, however, there normally cannot be a suit for damages because no injury was suffered. •

Compensatory damages are the norm in negligence cases. As noted earlier, a court will award punitive damages only if the defendant's conduct was grossly negligent, reflecting an intentional failure to perform a duty with reckless disregard of the consequences to others.

Defenses to Negligence

Defendants often defend against negligence claims by asserting that the plaintiffs failed to prove the existence of one or more of the required elements for negligence. Additionally,

Injuries from car accidents can cause handicaps that last a lifetime. Do such injuries satisfy the injury requirement for a finding of a negligence tort?

(Joyce Marshall/Fort Worth Star-Telegram/MCT via Getty Images)

LANDMARK IN THE LAW
Palsgraf v. Long Island Railroad Co. (1928)

In 1928, the New York Court of Appeals (that state's highest court) issued its decision in *Palsgraf v. Long Island Railroad Co.*,[a] a case that has become a landmark in negligence law and proximate cause.

The Facts of the Case   The plaintiff, Helen Palsgraf, was waiting for a train on a station platform. A man carrying a small package wrapped in newspaper was rushing to catch a train that had begun to move away from the platform. As the man attempted to jump aboard the moving train, he seemed unsteady and about to fall. A railroad guard on the train car reached forward to grab him, and another guard on the platform pushed him from behind to help him board the train. In the process, the man's package fell on the railroad tracks and exploded, because it contained fireworks. The repercussions of the explosion caused scales at the other end of the train platform to fall on Palsgraf, who was injured as a result. She sued the railroad company for damages in a New York state court.

The Question of Proximate Cause   At the trial, the jury found that the railroad guards were negligent in their conduct. On appeal, the question before the New York Court of Appeals was whether the conduct of the railroad guards was the proximate cause of Palsgraf's injuries. In other words, did the guards' duty of care extend to Palsgraf, who was outside the zone of danger and whose injury could not reasonably have been foreseen?

The court stated that the question of whether the guards were negligent *with respect to Palsgraf* depended on whether her injury was *reasonably foreseeable* by the railroad guards. Although the guards may have acted negligently with respect to the man boarding the train, this had no bearing on the question of their negligence with respect to Palsgraf. This was not a situation in which a person committed an act so potentially harmful (for example, firing a gun at a building) that he or she would be held responsible for any harm that resulted. The court stated that here "there was nothing in the situation to suggest to the most cautious mind that the parcel wrapped in newspaper would spread wreckage through the station." The court thus concluded that the railroad guards were not negligent with respect to Palsgraf because her injury was not reasonably foreseeable.

Application to Today's World   *The* Palsgraf *case established foreseeability as the test for proximate cause. Today, the courts continue to apply this test in determining proximate cause—and thus tort liability for injuries. Generally, if the victim of a harm or the consequences of a harm done are unforeseeable, there is no proximate cause. Note, though, that in the online environment, distinctions based on physical proximity, such as the "zone of danger" cited by the court in this case, are largely inapplicable.*

a. 248 N.Y. 339, 162 N.E. 99 (1928).

---

there are three basic *affirmative* defenses in negligence cases (defenses that a defendant can use to avoid liability even if the facts are as the plaintiff states): (1) assumption of risk, (2) superseding cause, and (3) contributory and comparative negligence.

Assumption of Risk A defense to negligence. A plaintiff may not recover for injuries or damage suffered from risks he or she knows of and has voluntarily assumed.

Assumption of Risk   A plaintiff who voluntarily enters into a risky situation, knowing the risk involved, will not be allowed to recover. This is the defense of **assumption of risk.** The requirements of this defense are (1) knowledge of the risk and (2) voluntary assumption of the risk. This defense is frequently asserted when the plaintiff is injured during recreational activities that involve known risk, such as skiing and skydiving. Note that assumption of risk can apply not only to participants in sporting events, but also to spectators and bystanders who are injured while attending those events.

The risk can be assumed by express agreement, or the assumption of risk can be implied by the plaintiff's knowledge of the risk and subsequent conduct. Courts do not apply the assumption of risk doctrine in emergency situations, though.

In the following case, the issue was whether a spectator at a baseball game voluntarily assumed the risk of being hit by an errant ball thrown while the players were warming up before the game.

Spotlight on the Seattle Mariners

Case 4.3
Taylor v. Baseball Club of Seattle, L.P.
Court of Appeals of Washington, 132 Wash.App. 32, 130 P.3d 835 (2006).

Many fans arrive at baseball games early so that they can watch the players warm up.

(Otto Greule Jr./Allsport/Getty Images)

FACTS Delinda Middleton Taylor went to a Mariners baseball game at Safeco Field with her boyfriend and two minor sons. Their seats were four rows up from the field along the right field foul line. They arrived more than an hour before the game began so that they could see the players warm up and get their autographs. When she walked in, Taylor saw that Mariners pitcher Freddy Garcia was throwing a ball back and forth with José Mesa right in front of their seats. As Taylor stood in front of her seat, she looked away from the field, and a ball thrown by Mesa got past Garcia and struck her in the face, causing serious injuries. Taylor sued the Mariners for the allegedly negligent warm-up throw. The Mariners filed a motion for a summary judgment in which they argued that Taylor, a Mariners fan, was familiar with baseball and the inherent risk of balls entering the stands, and therefore assumed the risk of her injury. The trial court granted the motion and dismissed Taylor's case. Taylor appealed.

ISSUE Was the risk of injury from an errant baseball thrown during pregame warm-up foreseeable to a reasonable person with Taylor's familiarity with baseball?

DECISION Yes. The state intermediate appellate court affirmed the lower court's judgment. Taylor, as a spectator in an unprotected area of seats, voluntarily undertook the risk associated with being hit by an errant baseball thrown during warm-ups before the start of the game.

REASON The court observed that there was substantial evidence that Taylor was familiar with the game. She was a seasoned Mariners fan, and both of her sons had played baseball for at least six years. "She attended many of her sons' baseball games, she witnessed balls entering the stands, she had watched Mariners' games both at the Kingdome and on television, and she knew that there was no screen protecting her seats, which were close to the field. In fact, as she walked to her seat she saw the players warming up and was excited about being in an unscreened area where her party might get autographs from the players and catch balls." It was not legally relevant that the injury occurred during the pregame warm-up because "it is the normal, every-day practice at all levels of baseball for pitchers to warm up in the manner that led to this incident." The Mariners had satisfied their duty to protect spectators from balls entering the stands by providing a protective screen behind home plate. Taylor chose not to sit in the protected area and thus knowingly put herself at risk.

CRITICAL THINKING—Ethical Consideration *Would the result in this case have been different if Taylor's minor son, rather than Taylor herself, had been struck by the ball? Should courts apply the doctrine of assumption of risk to children? Discuss.*

Superseding Cause An unforeseeable intervening event may break the connection between a wrongful act and an injury to another. If so, the event acts as a *superseding cause*—that is, it relieves a defendant of liability for injuries caused by the intervening event. **EXAMPLE 4.23** While riding his bicycle, Derrick negligently hits Julie, who is walking on the sidewalk. As a result of the impact, Julie falls and fractures her hip. While she is waiting for help to arrive, a small plane crashes nearby and explodes, and some of the fiery debris hits her, causing her to sustain severe burns. Derrick will be liable for Julie's fractured hip because the risk of hitting her with his bicycle was foreseeable. Normally, Derrick will not be liable for the burns caused by the plane crash—because the risk of a plane's crashing nearby and injuring Julie was not foreseeable. ●

Contributory Negligence A rule in tort law, used in only a few states, that completely bars the plaintiff from recovering any damages if the damage suffered is partly the plaintiff's own fault.

Contributory and Comparative Negligence All individuals are expected to exercise a reasonable degree of care in looking out for themselves. In the past, under the common law doctrine of **contributory negligence,** a plaintiff who was also negligent (failed to exercise a reasonable degree of care) could not recover anything from

Comparative Negligence A rule in tort law, used in the majority of states, that reduces the plaintiff's recovery in proportion to the plaintiff's degree of fault, rather than barring recovery completely.

the defendant. Under this rule, no matter how insignificant the plaintiff's negligence was relative to the defendant's negligence, the plaintiff was precluded from recovering any damages. Today, only a few jurisdictions still hold to this doctrine.

In most states, the doctrine of contributory negligence has been replaced by a **comparative negligence** standard. Under this standard, both the plaintiff's and the defendant's negligence are computed, and the liability for damages is distributed accordingly. Some jurisdictions have adopted a "pure" form of comparative negligence that allows the plaintiff to recover, even if the extent of his or her fault is greater than that of the defendant. For example, if the plaintiff was 80 percent at fault and the defendant 20 percent at fault, the plaintiff may recover 20 percent of his or her damages. Many states' comparative negligence statutes, however, contain a "50 percent" rule that prevents the plaintiff from recovering any damages if she or he was more than 50 percent at fault. Under this rule, a plaintiff who is 35 percent at fault could recover 65 percent of his or her damages, but a plaintiff who is 65 percent (more than 50 percent) at fault could recover nothing.

Special Negligence Doctrines and Statutes

There are a number of special doctrines and statutes relating to negligence. We examine a few of them here.

Res Ipsa Loquitur A doctrine under which negligence may be inferred simply because an event occurred, if it is the type of event that would not occur in the absence of negligence. Literally, the term means "the facts speak for themselves."

Res Ipsa Loquitur   Generally, in lawsuits involving negligence, the plaintiff has the burden of proving that the defendant was negligent. In certain situations, however, under the doctrine of *res ipsa loquitur*[18] (meaning "the facts speak for themselves"), the courts may infer that negligence has occurred. Then the burden of proof rests on the defendant—to prove she or he was *not* negligent. This doctrine is applied only when the event creating the damage or injury is one that ordinarily would occur only as a result of negligence.

CASE EXAMPLE 4.24   Mary Gubbins undergoes abdominal surgery and following the surgery has nerve damage in her spine near the area of the operation. She is unable to walk or stand for months, and even after regaining some use of her legs through physical therapy, her mobility is impaired and she experiences pain. In her subsequent negligence lawsuit, Gubbins can assert *res ipsa loquitur,* because the injury would never have occurred in the absence of the surgeon's negligence.[19] ●

Negligence *Per Se* An action or failure to act in violation of a statutory requirement.

Negligence *Per Se*   Certain conduct, whether it consists of an action or a failure to act, may be treated as **negligence *per se*** (*per se* means "in or of itself"). Negligence *per se* may occur if an individual violates a statute or ordinance and thereby causes the kind of harm that the statute was intended to prevent. The statute must clearly set out what standard of conduct is expected, when and where it is expected, and of whom it is expected. The standard of conduct required by the statute is the duty that the defendant owes to the plaintiff, and a violation of the statute is the breach of that duty.

CASE EXAMPLE 4.25   A Delaware statute states that anyone "who operates a motor vehicle and who fails to give full time and attention to the operation of the vehicle" is guilty of inattentive driving. Michael Moore was cited for inattentive driving after he collided with Debra Wright's car when he backed a truck out of a parking space. Moore paid the ticket, which meant that he pleaded guilty to violating the statute. The day after the accident, Wright began having back pain, which eventually required surgery. She sued Moore for damages, alleging negligence *per se*. The Delaware Supreme Court ruled that the inattentive driving statute set forth a sufficiently specific standard of conduct to warrant application of negligence *per se*.[20] ●

---

18. Pronounced *rehz ihp-*suh *low-*kwuh-tuhr.
19. *Gubbins v. Hurson*, 885 A.2d 269 (D.C. 2005).
20. *Wright v. Moore*, 931 A.2d 405 (Del.Supr. 2007).

"Danger Invites Rescue" Doctrine   Sometimes, a person who is trying to avoid harm—such as an individual who swerves to avoid a head-on collision with a drunk driver—ends up causing harm to another (such as a cyclist riding in the bike lane) as a result. In those situations, the original wrongdoer (the drunk driver in this scenario) is liable to anyone who is injured, even if the injury actually resulted from another person's attempt to escape harm. The "danger invites rescue" doctrine extends the same protection to a person who is trying to rescue another from harm—the original wrongdoer is liable for injuries to an individual attempting a rescue. The idea is that the rescuer should not be held liable for any damages because he or she did not cause the danger and because danger invites rescue.

EXAMPLE 4.26   Ludley drives down a street but fails to see a stop sign because he is trying to quiet his squabbling children in the car's back seat. Salter, who is standing on the curb, realizes that Ludley is about to hit a pedestrian and runs into the street to push the pedestrian out of the way. If Ludley's vehicle hits Salter instead, Ludley will be liable for Salter's injury, as well as for any injuries the other pedestrian sustained. ● Whether rescuers injure themselves, the person rescued, or even a stranger, the original wrongdoer will still be liable.

Good Samaritan Statute A state statute stipulating that persons who provide emergency services to, or rescue, someone in peril cannot be sued for negligence unless they act recklessly, thereby causing further harm.

Good Samaritan Statutes   Most states have enacted what are called **Good Samaritan statutes**.[21] Under these statutes, someone who is aided voluntarily by another cannot turn around and sue the "Good Samaritan" for negligence. These laws were passed largely to protect physicians and medical personnel who voluntarily render medical services in emergency situations to those in need, such as individuals hurt in car accidents. Indeed, the California Supreme Court has interpreted the state's Good Samaritan statute to mean that only a person who renders medical aid is immune from liability.[22] Thus, only medical personnel and persons rendering medical aid in emergencies are protected in California.

Dram Shop Act A state statute that imposes liability on the owners of bars and taverns, as well as those who serve alcoholic drinks to the public, for injuries resulting from accidents caused by intoxicated persons when the sellers or servers of alcoholic drinks contributed to the intoxication.

Dram Shop Acts   Many states have also passed **dram shop acts**,[23] under which a tavern owner or bartender may be held liable for injuries caused by a person who became intoxicated while drinking at the bar or who was already intoxicated when served by the bartender. Some states' statutes also impose liability on *social hosts* (persons hosting parties) for injuries caused by guests who became intoxicated at the hosts' homes. Under these statutes, it is unnecessary to prove that the tavern owner, bartender, or social host was negligent. **EXAMPLE 4.27**   Selena hosts a Super Bowl party at which Raul, a minor, sneaks alcoholic drinks. Selena is potentially liable for damages resulting from Raul's drunk driving after the party. ●

Strict Liability Liability regardless of fault, which is imposed on those engaged in abnormally dangerous activities, on persons who keep dangerous animals, and on manufacturers or sellers that introduce into commerce defective and unreasonably dangerous goods.

Strict Liability

Another category of torts is called **strict liability**, or *liability without fault*. Intentional torts and torts of negligence involve acts that depart from a reasonable standard of care and cause injuries. Under the doctrine of strict liability, liability for injury is imposed for reasons other than fault.

---

21. These laws derive their name from the Good Samaritan story in the Bible. In the story, a traveler who had been robbed and beaten lay along the roadside, ignored by those passing by. Eventually, a man from the country of Samaria (the "Good Samaritan") stopped to render assistance to the injured person.

22. *Van Horn v. Watson*, 45 Cal.4th 322, 197 P.3d 164, 86 Cal.Rptr.3d 350 (2008).

23. Historically, a *dram* was a small unit of liquid, and spirits were sold in drams. Thus, a dram shop was a place where liquor was sold in drams.

LEARNING OBJECTIVE 5
What is meant by strict liability? In what circumstances is strict liability applied?

Abnormally Dangerous Activities

Strict liability for damages proximately caused by an abnormally dangerous or exceptional activity is one application of this doctrine. Courts apply the doctrine of strict liability in such cases because of the extreme risk of the activity. For instance, even if blasting with dynamite is performed with all reasonable care, there is still a risk of injury. Because of the potential for harm, the person who is engaged in an abnormally dangerous activity—and benefits from it—is responsible for paying for any injuries caused by that activity. Although there is no fault, there is still responsibility because of the dangerous nature of the undertaking.

Other Applications of Strict Liability

The strict liability principle is also applied in other situations. Persons who keep wild animals, for example, are strictly liable for any harm inflicted by the animals. In addition, an owner of domestic animals may be strictly liable for harm caused by those animals if the owner knew, or should have known, that the animals were dangerous or had a propensity to harm others.

A significant application of strict liability is in the area of *product liability*—liability of manufacturers and sellers for harmful or defective products. Liability here is a matter of social policy and is based on two factors: (1) the manufacturer or seller can better bear the cost of injury because it can spread the cost throughout society by increasing prices of goods and services, and (2) the manufacturer or seller is making a profit from its activities and therefore should bear the cost of injury as an operating expense. We will discuss product liability in greater detail in Chapter 12.

Cyber Torts

Torts can also be committed in the online environment. One of the most common types of *cyber torts* is online defamation, as we discuss next. We also discuss how the courts are attempting to address the problems associated with bulk, unsolicited junk e-mails, or spam.

Identifying the Author of Online Defamation

An initial issue raised by online defamation was simply discovering who was committing it. In the real world, identifying the author of a defamatory remark generally is an easy matter, but suppose that a business firm has discovered that defamatory statements about its policies and products are being posted in an online forum. Such forums allow anyone—customers, employees, or crackpots—to complain about a firm that they dislike while remaining anonymous.

Therefore, a threshold barrier to anyone who seeks to bring an action for online defamation is discovering the identity of the person who posted the defamatory message. An Internet service provider (ISP)—a company that provides connections to the Internet—can disclose personal information about its customers only when ordered to do so by a court. Consequently, businesses and individuals are increasingly bringing lawsuits against "John Does" (John Doe, Jane Doe, and the like are fictitious names used in lawsuits when the identity of a party is not known or when a party wishes to conceal his or her name for privacy reasons). Then, using the authority of the courts, the plaintiffs can obtain from the ISPs the identity of the persons responsible for the defamatory messages.

Woody Allen sued a clothing company for using his image on the Web. Can the Internet service provider through which the offending ads were directed be held liable?

"Speech is not free when it comes postage due."

Jim Nitchals, 1962–1998 (Spam fighter and computer programmer)

Liability of Internet Service Providers

Recall from the discussion of defamation earlier in this chapter that those who repeat or otherwise disseminate defamatory statements made by others can be held liable for defamation. Thus, newspapers, magazines, and radio and television stations can be subject to liability for defamatory content that they publish or broadcast, even though the content was prepared or created by others. Applying this rule to cyberspace, however, raises an important issue: Should ISPs be regarded as publishers and therefore be held liable for defamatory messages that are posted by their users in online forums or other arenas?

Before 1996, the courts grappled with this question. Then Congress passed the Communications Decency Act (CDA), which states that "[n]o provider or user of an interactive computer service shall be treated as the publisher or speaker of any information provided by another information content provider."[24] Thus, under the CDA, ISPs generally are treated differently from publishers in other media and are not liable for publishing defamatory statements that come from a third party.[25] Although the courts generally have construed the CDA as providing a broad shield to protect ISPs from liability for third-party content, some courts have started establishing some limits to CDA immunity.[26]

The Spread of Spam

Businesses and individuals alike are targets of *spam,* or unsolicited "junk e-mails" that flood virtual mailboxes with advertisements, solicitations, and other messages. Considered relatively harmless in the early days of the Internet, by 2012 spam accounted for roughly 75 percent of all e-mails.

State Regulation of Spam   In an attempt to combat spam, thirty-six states have enacted laws that prohibit or regulate its use. Many state laws that regulate spam require the senders of e-mail ads to instruct the recipients on how they can "opt out" of further e-mail ads from the same sources. For instance, in some states an unsolicited e-mail ad must include a toll-free phone number or return e-mail address that the recipient can use to contact the sender to request that no more ads be e-mailed.

The Federal CAN-SPAM Act   In 2003, Congress enacted the Controlling the Assault of Non-Solicited Pornography and Marketing (CAN-SPAM) Act, which took effect on January 1, 2004. The legislation applies to any "commercial electronic mail messages" that are sent to promote a commercial product or service. Significantly, the statute preempts state antispam laws except for those provisions in state laws that prohibit false and deceptive e-mailing practices.

Generally, the act permits unsolicited commercial e-mail but prohibits certain spamming activities, including the use of a false return address and the inclusion of false, misleading, or deceptive information in e-mail. The statute also prohibits "dictionary attacks"—sending messages to randomly generated e-mail addresses—and the "harvesting" of e-mail addresses from Web sites with specialized software.

CASE EXAMPLE 4.28   In 2007, federal officials arrested Robert Alan Soloway, considered one of the world's most prolific spammers. Soloway, known as the "Spam King," had been using botnets (automated spamming networks—see Chapter 6) to send out hundreds of millions of unwanted e-mails. In 2008, Soloway pleaded guilty to mail fraud and failure to pay taxes.[27] ●

24. 47 U.S.C. Section 230.

25. See, for example, *Fair Housing Council of San Fernando Valley v. Roommate.com, LLC,* 521 F.3d 1157 (9th Cir. 2008).

26. See, for example, *Chicago Lawyers' Committee for Civil Rights Under Law, Inc. v. Craigslist, Inc.,* 519 F.3d 666 (7th Cir. 2008); *Anthony v. Yahoo, Inc.,* 421 F.Supp.2d 1257 (N.D.Cal. 2006); and *Almeida v. Amazon.com, Inc.,* 456 F.3d 1316 (11th Cir. 2006).

27. See www.usdoj.gov/usao/waw/press/2008/mar/soloway.html.

The U.S. Safe Web Act   After the CAN-SPAM Act prohibited false and deceptive e-mails originating in the United States, spamming from servers located in other nations increased. These cross-border spammers generally were able to escape detection and legal sanctions because the Federal Trade Commission (FTC) lacked the authority to investigate foreign spamming.

Congress sought to rectify the situation by enacting the U.S. Safe Web Act of 2006 (also known as the Undertaking Spam, Spyware, and Fraud Enforcement with Enforcers Beyond Borders Act). The act allows the FTC to cooperate and share information with foreign agencies in investigating and prosecuting those involved in Internet fraud and deception, including spamming and spyware. It also provides ISPs with a "safe harbor" (immunity from liability) for supplying information to the FTC concerning possible unfair or deceptive conduct in foreign jurisdictions.

There is some evidence that the U.S. Safe Web Act—in conjunction with the increased efforts of federal law enforcement and security experts—has been effective. The number of spam messages sent appeared to have decreased somewhat between 2010 and 2011, although spam still flows at a rate of 70 billion messages per day. The Federal Bureau of Investigation has worked with dozens of ISPs to stop some of the automated spamming networks and has also been actively cooperating with other nations, leading to the arrest of several major spammers located in the Netherlands and Russia.

Reviewing . . . Torts and Cyber Torts

Two sisters, Darla and Irene, are partners in an import business located in a small town in Rhode Island. Irene is also campaigning to be the mayor of their town. Both sisters travel to other countries to purchase the goods they sell at their retail store. Irene buys Indonesian goods, and Darla buys goods from Africa. After a tsunami destroys many of the towns in Indonesia to which Irene usually travels, she phones one of her contacts there and asks him to procure some items and ship them to her. He informs her that it will be impossible to buy these items now because the townspeople are being evacuated due to a water shortage. Irene is angry and tells her contact that if he cannot purchase the goods, he should simply take them without paying for them after the town has been evacuated. Darla overhears her sister's instructions and is outraged. They have a falling-out, and Darla decides that she no longer wishes to be in business with her sister. Using the information presented in the chapter, answer the following questions.

1. Suppose that Darla tells several of her friends about Irene's instructing her contact to take goods without paying for them after the tsunami. If Irene files a tort action against Darla alleging slander, will her suit be successful? Why or why not?
2. Now suppose that Irene wins the election and becomes the city's mayor. Darla then writes a letter to the editor of the local newspaper disclosing Irene's misconduct. If Irene accuses Darla of committing libel, what defenses could Darla assert?
3. If Irene accepts goods shipped from Indonesia that were wrongfully obtained, has she committed an intentional tort against property? Explain.
4. Suppose now that Darla was in the store one day with an elderly customer, Betty Green, who was looking for a graduation gift for her granddaughter. When Darla went to the counter to answer the phone, Green continued to wander around the store and eventually went through an open door into the stockroom, where she fell over some boxes on the floor and fractured her hip. Green files a negligence action against the store. Did Darla breach her duty of care? Why or why not?

DEBATE THIS   Because of the often anonymous nature of the Internet, defamation has become an outdated legal concept. It's now too difficult to track down the person responsible for the defamatory statement.

BUSINESS APPLICATION

How Important Is Tort Liability to Business?*

Although there are more claims for breach of contract than for any other category of lawsuits, the dollar amount of damages awarded in tort actions is typically much higher than the awards in contract claims. Tort claims are also commonplace for businesses.

Because of the potential for large damages awards for intentional and unintentional acts, businesspersons should take preventive measures to avoid tort liability as much as possible. Remember that injured persons can bring most tort actions against a business as well as against another person. In fact, if given a choice, plaintiffs often sue a business rather than an individual because the business is more likely to have "deep pockets" (the ability to pay large damages awards). Moreover, sometimes businesses can be held liable for torts that individuals cannot.

The Extent of Business Negligence Liability

A business can be exposed to negligence liability in a wide variety of instances. Liability to business invitees is a clear example. A business that fails to warn invitees that its floor is slippery after a rainstorm, or that its parking lot is icy after snow, may be liable to an injured customer. Indeed, business owners can be liable for nearly any fall or other injury that occurs on business premises.

Even the hiring of employees can lead to negligence liability. For example, a business can be liable if it fails to do a criminal background check before hiring a person to supervise a child-care center when an investigation would have revealed that the person had previously been convicted of sexual assault. Failure to

*This *Business Application* is not meant to substitute for the services of an attorney who is licensed to practice law in your state.

properly supervise or instruct employees can also lead to liability for a business.

Liability for Torts of Employees and Agents

A business can also be held liable for the negligence or intentional torts of its employees and agents. As you will learn in Chapters 17 and 18, a business is liable for the torts committed by an employee who is acting within the scope of his or her employment or an agent who is acting with the authority of the business. Therefore, if a sales agent commits fraud while acting within the scope of her or his employment, the business will be held liable.

Checklist for Minimizing Business Tort Liability

1. Constantly inspect the premises and look for areas where customers or employees might trip, slide, or fall. Take corrective action whenever you find a problem.
2. Train employees on the importance of periodic safety inspections and the procedures for reporting unsafe conditions.
3. Routinely maintain all business equipment (including vehicles).
4. Check with your liability insurance company for suggestions on improving the safety of your premises and operations.
5. Make sure that your general liability policy will adequately cover the potential exposure of the business, and reassess your coverage annually.
6. Review the background and qualifications of individuals you are considering hiring as employees or agents.
7. Investigate and review all negligence claims promptly. Most claims can be settled at low cost before a lawsuit is filed.

Key Terms

actionable 103
actual malice 107
appropriation 109
assault 102
assumption of risk 119
battery 102
business invitee 116
business tort 99
causation in fact 117
comparative negligence 121
compensatory damages 100

contributory negligence 120
conversion 114
cyber tort 100
damages 100
defamation 104
defense 102
disparagement of property 114
dram shop act 122
duty of care 115
fraudulent misrepresentation 109
Good Samaritan statute 122

intentional tort 101
libel 104
malpractice 117
negligence 115
negligence *per se* 121
privilege 107
proximate cause 118
puffery 109
punitive damages 100
reasonable person standard 115
res ipsa loquitur 121

slander 104
slander of quality (trade libel) 114
slander of title 114
strict liability 122
tort 99
tortfeasor 101
trespass to land 112
trespass to personal property 113

Chapter Summary: Torts and Cyber Torts

Intentional Torts against Persons (See pages 101–111.)	1. *Assault and battery*—An assault is an unexcused and intentional act that causes another person to be apprehensive of immediate harm. A battery is an assault that results in physical contact. 2. *False imprisonment*—The intentional confinement or restraint of another person's movement without justification. 3. *Intentional infliction of emotional distress*—An extreme and outrageous act, intentionally committed, that results in severe emotional distress to another. 4. *Defamation (libel or slander)*—A false statement of fact, not made under privilege, that is communicated to a third person and that causes damage to a person's reputation. For public figures, the plaintiff must also prove actual malice. 5. *Invasion of the right to privacy*—Includes four acts: wrongful intrusion into a person's private activities; publication of information that places a person in a false light; disclosure of private facts that an ordinary person would find objectionable; and appropriation of identity, which involves the use of a person's name, likeness, or other identifying characteristic, without permission and for a commercial purpose. Most states have enacted statutes establishing appropriation of identity as the tort of *appropriation* or right of publicity. Courts differ on the degree of likeness required. 6. *Misrepresentation (fraud)*—A false representation made by one party, through misstatement of facts or through conduct, with the intention of deceiving another and on which the other reasonably relies to his or her detriment. Negligent misrepresentation occurs when a person supplies information without having a reasonable basis for believing its truthfulness. 7. *Abusive or frivolous litigation*—When a person initiates a lawsuit out of malice and without probable cause, and loses the suit, he or she can be sued for the tort of *malicious prosecution*. When a person uses a legal process against another improperly or to accomplish a purpose for which it was not designed, she or he can be sued for *abuse of process*. 8. *Wrongful interference*—The knowing, intentional interference by a third party with an enforceable contractual relationship or an established business relationship between other parties for the purpose of advancing the economic interests of the third party.
Intentional Torts against Property (See pages 111–114.)	1. *Trespass to land*—The invasion of another's real property without consent or privilege. 2. *Trespass to personal property*—Unlawfully damaging or interfering with the owner's right to use, possess, or enjoy her or his personal property. 3. *Conversion*—Wrongfully taking or using the personal property of another without permission. 4. *Disparagement of property*—Any economically injurious falsehood that is made about another's product or property. The term includes the torts of *slander of quality* and *slander of title*.

Unintentional Torts (Negligence)
(See pages 115–122.)
	1. *Negligence*—The careless performance of a legally required duty or the failure to perform a legally required act. Elements that must be proved are that a legal duty of care existed, that the defendant breached that duty, that the breach caused the plaintiff's injury, and that the plaintiff suffered a legally recognizable injury.
	2. *Defenses to negligence*—The basic affirmative defenses in negligence cases are assumption of risk, superseding cause, and contributory or comparative negligence.
	3. *Special negligence doctrines and statutes*—
	   a. *Res ipsa loquitur*—A doctrine under which a plaintiff need not prove negligence on the part of the defendant because "the facts speak for themselves."
	   b. Negligence *per se*—A type of negligence that may occur if a person violates a statute or an ordinance and the violation causes another to suffer the kind of injury that the statute or ordinance was intended to prevent.
	   c. Special negligence statutes—State statutes that prescribe duties and responsibilities in certain circumstances. Violation of these statutes will impose civil liability. Dram shop acts and Good Samaritan statutes are examples of special negligence statutes.

Strict Liability (See pages 122–123.)	Under the doctrine of strict liability, a person may be held liable, regardless of the degree of care exercised, for damages or injuries caused by her or his product or activity. Strict liability includes liability for harms caused by abnormally dangerous activities, by dangerous animals, and by defective products (product liability).
Cyber Torts (See pages 123–125.)	General tort principles are being extended to cover cyber torts, or torts that occur in cyberspace, such as online defamation. Federal and state statutes may also apply to certain forms of cyber torts. For example, under the federal Communications Decency Act of 1996, Internet service providers (ISPs) are not liable for defamatory messages posted by their subscribers.

ExamPrep

ISSUE SPOTTERS

1. Jana leaves her truck's motor running while she enters a Kwik-Pik Store. The truck's transmission engages, and the vehicle crashes into a gas pump, starting a fire that spreads to a warehouse on the next block. The warehouse collapses, causing its billboard to fall and injure Lou, a bystander. Can Lou recover from Jana? Why or why not? **(See pages 115–118.)**

2. A water pipe bursts, flooding a Metal Fabrication Company utility room and tripping the circuit breakers on a panel in the room. Metal Fabrication contacts Nouri, a licensed electrician with five years' experience, to check the damage and turn the breakers back on. Without testing for short circuits, which Nouri knows that he should do, he tries to switch on a breaker. He is electrocuted, and his wife sues Metal Fabrication for damages, alleging negligence. What might the firm successfully claim in defense? **(See pages 116, 119–121.)**

—Check your answers to the Issue Spotters against the answers provided in Appendix E at the end of this text.

BEFORE THE TEST

Go to www.cengagebrain.com, enter the ISBN 9781133191353, and click on "Find" to locate this textbook's Web site. Then, click on "Access Now" under "Study Tools," and select Chapter 4 at the top. There, you will find a Practice Quiz that you can take to assess your mastery of the concepts in this chapter, as well as Flashcards, a Glossary of important terms, and Video Questions (when assigned).

For Review

Answers to the even-numbered questions in this For Review section can be found in Appendix F at the end of this text.

1. What is the purpose of tort law? What types of damages are available in tort lawsuits?
2. What are two basic categories of torts?
3. What is defamation? Name two types of defamation.
4. Identify the four elements of negligence.
5. What is meant by strict liability? In what circumstances is strict liability applied?

Business Scenarios and Case Problems

4–1 Liability to Business Invitees. Kim went to Ling's Market to pick up a few items for dinner. It was a stormy day, and the wind had blown water through the market's door each time it opened. As Kim entered through the door, she slipped and fell in the rainwater that had accumulated on the floor. The manager knew of the weather conditions but had not posted any sign to warn customers of the water hazard. Kim injured her back as a result of the fall and sued Ling's for damages. Can Ling's be held liable for negligence? Discuss. **(See page 116.)**

4–2 ❓ **Question with Sample Answer—Negligence.** Shannon's physician gives her some pain medication and tells her not to drive after taking it because the medication induces drowsiness. In spite of the doctor's warning, Shannon decides to drive to the store while on the medication. Owing to her lack of alertness, she fails to stop at a traffic light and crashes into another vehicle, causing a passenger in that vehicle to be injured. Is Shannon liable for the tort of negligence? Explain. **(See pages 117–118.)**

—For a sample answer to Question 4–2, go to Appendix G at the end of this text.

4–3 🗄 **Spotlight on Intentional Torts—Defamation.** Sharon Yeagle was an assistant to the vice president of student affairs at Virginia Polytechnic Institute and State University (Virginia Tech). As part of her duties, Yeagle helped students participate in the Governor's Fellows Program. The *Collegiate Times*, Virginia Tech's student newspaper, published an article about the university's success in placing students in the program. The article's text surrounded a block quotation attributed to Yeagle with the phrase "Director of Butt Licking" under her name. Yeagle sued the *Collegiate Times* for defamation. She argued that the phrase implied the commission of sodomy and was therefore actionable. What is *Collegiate Times*'s defense to this claim? [*Yeagle v. Collegiate Times,* 497 S.E.2d 136 (Va. 1998)] **(See page 104.)**

4–4 ⚖ **Case Problem with Sample Answer—Libel and Invasion of Privacy.** The *Northwest Herald*, a newspaper, received regular e-mail reports from police departments about criminal arrests. When it received a report that Caroline Eubanks had been charged with theft, the *Herald* published the information. Later, the police sent an e-mail that retracted the report about Eubanks. The *Herald* published a correction.

Eubanks filed a suit against the paper for libel and invasion of privacy. Does Eubanks have a good case for either tort? Why or why not? [*Eubanks v. Northwest Herald Newspapers,* 397 Ill. App.3d 746, 922 N.E.2d 1196 (2010)] **(See pages 106–108.)**

—**For a sample answer to Problem 4–4, go to Appendix H at the end of this text.**

4–5 **Proximate Cause.** Galen Stoller was killed at a railroad crossing when an Amtrak train hit his car. The crossing was marked with a stop sign and a railroad-crossing symbol but there were no flashing lights. Galen's parents filed a suit against National Railroad Passenger Corporation (Amtrak) and Burlington Northern & Santa Fe Railroad Corp alleging negligence in the design and maintenance of the crossing. The defendants argued that Galen had not stopped at the stop sign. Was Amtrak negligent? What was the proximate cause of the accident? [*Henderson v. National Railroad Passenger Corp.,* ___ F.3d ___ (10th Cir. 2011)] **(See page 118.)**

4–6 **Business Torts.** Medtronic, Inc., is a medical technology company that competes for customers with St. Jude Medical S.C., Inc. James Hughes worked for Medtronic as a sales manager. His contract prohibited him from working for a competitor for one year after leaving Medtronic. Hughes sought a position as a sales director for St. Jude. St. Jude told Hughes that his contract with Medtronic was unenforceable and offered him a job. Hughes accepted. Medtronic filed a suit, alleging wrongful interference. Which type of interference was most likely the basis for this suit? Did it occur here? Explain. [*Medtronic, Inc. v. Hughes,* __ N.W.2d __ (Minn.App. 2011)] **(See pages 110–111.)**

4–7 **Intentional Infliction of Emotional Distress.** While living in her home country of Tanzania, Sophia Kiwanuka signed an employment contract with Anne Margareth Bakilana, a Tanzanian living in Washington, D.C. Kiwanuka traveled to the United States to work as a babysitter and maid in Bakilana's house. When Kiwanuka arrived, Bakilana confiscated her passport, held her in isolation, and forced her to work long hours under threat of having her deported. Kiwanuka worked seven days a week without breaks and was subjected to regular verbal and psychological abuse by Bakilana. Kiwanuka filed a complaint against Bakilana for intentional infliction of emotional distress, among other claims. Bakilana argued that Kiwanuka's complaint should be dismissed because the allegations were insufficient to show outrageous intentional conduct that resulted in severe emotional distress. If you were the judge, in whose favor would you rule? Why? [*Kiwanuka v. Bakilana,* 2012 WL 593065 (D.D.C. 2012)] **(See pages 103–104.)**

4–8 ⟷ **A Question of Ethics—Wrongful Interference.** White Plains Coat & Apron Co. and Cintas Corp. are competitors. White Plains had five-year exclusive contracts with some of its customers. As a result of Cintas's soliciting of business, dozens of White Plains' customers breached their contracts and entered into rental agreements with Cintas. White Plains filed a suit against Cintas, alleging wrongful interference. [*White Plains Coat & Apron Co. v. Cintas Corp.,* 8 N.Y.3d 422, 867 N.E.2d 381 (2007)] **(See pages 110–111.)**

1. What are the two policies at odds in wrongful interference cases? When there is an existing contract, which of these interests should be accorded priority? Why?

2. Is a general interest in soliciting business for profit a sufficient defense to a claim of wrongful interference with a contractual relationship? What do you think? Why?

Critical Thinking and Writing Assignments

4–9 💡 **Business Law Critical Thinking Group Assignment.** Assume that your business partner, Gayanne Zokhrabov, was at the train station when a train, traveling at more than 70 mph, hit eighteen-year-old Hiroyuki Joho, who was running across the tracks. The impact killed Joho and flung parts of his body about 100 feet into the air. Some of them landed on Gayanne and knocked her to the ground. As a result, she hurt her shoulder and broke her leg and wrist. She has not been able to work and has hired an attorney to file a negligence lawsuit against Joho's estate. (The attorney believes that Gayanne cannot successfully sue Amtrak because of a lack of proximate cause—it was not reasonably foreseeable that Joho would run across the tracks and his body parts would cause injuries to others.)

1. One group should analyze whether Joho had a *duty* to Gayanne and whether his decision to run in front of the train was a *breach* of that duty because she was in the zone of danger.

2. A second group should consider proximate cause: Was it reasonably foreseeable that a train accident could send Joho's body parts into crowds of waiting passengers?

3. A third group should discuss whether it is ethical to sue the dead man's estate over flying body parts. Further, what impact might the case and the publicity surrounding it have on you and your partner's business reputation?

Intellectual Property and Internet Law

LEARNING OBJECTIVES

The five learning objectives below are designed to help improve your understanding of the chapter. After reading this chapter, you should be able to answer the following questions:

1. What is intellectual property?
2. Why is the protection of trademarks important?
3. How does the law protect patents?
4. What laws protect authors' rights in the works they create?
5. What are trade secrets, and what laws offer protection for this form of intellectual property?

(Login/Shutterstock.com)

"The Internet is just a world passing around notes in a classroom."
—Jon Stewart, 1962–present (American comedian and host of *The Daily Show*)

Intellectual Property Property resulting from intellectual and creative processes.

LEARNING OBJECTIVE 1
What is intellectual property?

Intellectual property is any property resulting from intellectual, creative processes—the products of an individual's mind. Although it is an abstract term for an abstract concept, intellectual property is nonetheless familiar to almost everyone. The information contained in books and computer files is intellectual property. The apps for your iPhone and iPad, the movies you watch, and the music you listen to are all forms of intellectual property. Although the need to protect creative works was first recognized in Article I, Section 8, of the U.S. Constitution (see Appendix B), statutory protection of these rights began in the 1940s and continues to evolve to meet the needs of modern society.

Of significant concern to businesspersons is the need to protect their rights in intellectual property, which may be more valuable than their physical property, such as machines and buildings. Consider, for instance, the importance of intellectual property rights to technology companies, such as Apple, Inc., the maker of the iPhone and iPad. In today's world, intellectual property rights can be a company's most valuable assets, which is why

Apple sued rival Samsung Electronics Company in 2011. Apple claimed that Samsung's Galaxy line of mobile phones and tablets (those that run Google's Android software) copy the look, design, and user interface of Apple's iPhone and iPad. Although Apple is one of Samsung's biggest customers and buys many of its components from Samsung, Apple also needs to protect its iPhone and iPad revenues from competing Android products. You will read about the verdict in this case on pages 143 and 144.

In today's global economy, however, protecting intellectual property in one country is no longer sufficient, and the United States is participating in various international agreements to secure ownership rights in intellectual property in other countries. Because the Internet allows the world to "pass around notes" so quickly, as Jon Stewart joked in the chapter-opening quotation on the facing page, protecting these rights in today's online environment has proved particularly challenging.

Trademarks and Related Property

Trademark A distinctive word, symbol, or design that identifies the manufacturer as the source of particular goods and distinguishes its products from those made or sold by others.

A **trademark** is a distinctive word, symbol, sound, or design that identifies the manufacturer as the source of particular goods and distinguishes its products from those made or sold by others. At common law, the person who used a symbol or mark to identify a business or product was protected in the use of that trademark. Clearly, by using another's trademark, a business could lead consumers to believe that its goods were made by the other business. The law seeks to avoid this kind of confusion. (For information on how companies use trademarks and service marks, see this chapter's *Linking Business Law to Marketing* feature on page 155.)

LEARNING OBJECTIVE 2
Why is the protection of trademarks important?

In the following *Classic Case* concerning Coca-Cola, the defendants argued that the Coca-Cola trademark was not entitled to protection under the law because the term did not accurately represent the product.

✴ Classic Case 5.1

Coca-Cola Co. v. Koke Co. of America

Supreme Court of the United States,
254 U.S. 143, 41 S.Ct. 113, 65 L.Ed. 189 (1920).
www.findlaw.com/casecode/supreme.html[a]

How is Coca-Cola protected?

COMPANY PROFILE   *John Pemberton, an Atlanta pharmacist, invented a caramel-colored, carbonated soft drink in 1886. His bookkeeper, Frank Robinson, named the beverage Coca-Cola after two of the ingredients, coca leaves and kola nuts. Asa Candler bought the Coca-Cola Company in 1891 and, within seven years, had made the soft drink available throughout the United States and in parts of Canada and Mexico as well. Candler continued to sell Coke aggressively and to open up new markets, reaching Europe before 1910. In doing so, however, he attracted numerous competitors, some of whom tried to capitalize directly on the Coke name.*

FACTS The Coca-Cola Company brought an action in a federal district court to enjoin (prevent) other beverage companies from using the words *Koke* and *Dope* for their products. The defendants contended that the Coca-Cola trademark was a fraudulent representation and that Coca-Cola was therefore not entitled to any help from the courts. By using the Coca-Cola name, the defendants alleged, the Coca-Cola Company represented that the beverage contained cocaine (from coca leaves). The district court granted the injunction, but the federal appellate court reversed. The

---

a. This is the "US Supreme Court Opinions" page within the Web site of the "FindLaw Internet Legal Resources" database. This page provides several options for accessing an opinion. Because you know the citation for this case, you can go to the "Citation Search" box, type in the appropriate volume and page numbers for the *United States Reports* ("254" and "143," respectively, for the *Coca-Cola* case), and click on "Search."

Classic Case 5.1—Continues next page ➡

Classic Case 5.1—Continued

Coca-Cola Company appealed to the United States Supreme Court.

ISSUE Did the marketing of products called Koke and Dope by the Koke Company of America and other firms constitute an infringement on Coca-Cola's trademark?

DECISION Yes for Koke, but no for Dope. The United States Supreme Court enjoined the competing beverage companies from calling their products Koke but did not prevent them from calling their products Dope.

REASON The Court noted that before 1900 the Coca-Cola beverage had contained a small amount of cocaine. This ingredient had been deleted from the formula by 1906 at the latest, however, and the Coca-Cola Company had advertised to the public that no cocaine was present in its drink. Coca-Cola was a widely popular drink "to be had at almost any soda fountain." Because of the public's widespread familiarity with Coca-Cola, the retention of the name (referring to coca leaves and kola nuts) was not misleading: "Coca-Cola probably means to most persons the plaintiff's familiar product to be had everywhere rather than a compound of particular substances." The name *Coke* was found to be so common a term for the trademarked product Coca-Cola that the defendants' use of the similar-sounding *Koke* as a name for their beverages was disallowed. The Court could find no reason to restrain the defendants from using the name *Dope*, however.

WHAT IF THE FACTS WERE DIFFERENT? *Suppose that Coca-Cola had been trying to make the public believe that its product contained cocaine. Would the result in the case likely have been different? Explain your answer.*

IMPACT OF THIS CASE ON TODAY'S LAW *In this early case, the United States Supreme Court made it clear that trademarks and trade names (and nicknames for those marks and names, such as "Coke" for "Coca-Cola") that are in common use receive protection under the common law. This holding is significant historically because it is the predecessor to the federal statute later passed to protect trademark rights (the Lanham Act of 1946, discussed below).*

Statutory Protection of Trademarks

Statutory protection of trademarks and related property is provided at the federal level by the Lanham Act of 1946.[1] The Lanham Act was enacted in part to protect manufacturers from losing business to rival companies that used confusingly similar trademarks. The act incorporates the common law of trademarks and provides remedies for owners of trademarks who wish to enforce their claims in federal court. Many states also have trademark statutes.

Trademark Dilution

Before 1995, federal trademark law prohibited only the unauthorized use of the same mark on competing—or on noncompeting but "related"—goods or services. Protection was given only when the unauthorized use would likely confuse consumers as to the origin of those goods and services. In 1995, Congress amended the Lanham Act by passing the Federal Trademark Dilution Act,[2] which allowed trademark owners to bring a suit in federal court for trademark *dilution*.

Trademark dilution laws protect "distinctive" or "famous" trademarks (such as Rolls Royce, McDonald's, Dell, and Apple) from certain unauthorized uses even when the use is on noncompeting goods or is unlikely to confuse. More than half of the states have also enacted trademark dilution laws.

Use of a Similar Mark May Constitute Trademark Dilution

A famous mark may be diluted not only by the use of an *identical* mark but also by the use of

---

1. 15 U.S.C. Sections 1051–1128.
2. 15 U.S.C. Section 1125.

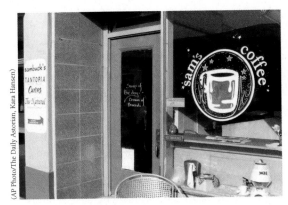

When an Oregon woman opened this store, its sign read "Sambuck's." On what ground did Starbuck's sue her so that she had to change the store's name?

a *similar* mark, provided that it reduces the value of the famous mark.[3]

CASE EXAMPLE 5.1 A woman opened a coffee shop under the name "Sambuck's Coffeehouse" in Astoria, Oregon, even though she knew that "Starbucks" was one of the largest coffee chains in the nation. When Starbucks Corporation filed a dilution lawsuit, the federal court ruled that use of the "Sambuck's" mark constituted trademark dilution because it created confusion for consumers. Not only was there a "high degree" of similarity between the marks, but also both companies provided coffee-related services through "stand-alone" retail stores. Therefore, the use of the similar mark (Sambuck's) reduced the value of the famous mark (Starbucks).[4] ●

Trademark Registration

Trademarks may be registered with the state or with the federal government. To register for protection under federal trademark law, a person must file an application with the U.S. Patent and Trademark Office in Washington, D.C. A mark can be registered (1) if it is currently in commerce or (2) if the applicant intends to put the mark into commerce within six months.

In special circumstances, the six-month period can be extended by thirty months, giving the applicant a total of three years from the date of notice of trademark approval to make use of the mark and to file the required use statement. Registration is postponed until the mark is actually used. Nonetheless, during this waiting period, the applicant's trademark is protected against any third party who has neither used the mark previously nor filed an application for it. Registration is renewable between the fifth and sixth years after the initial registration and every ten years thereafter (every twenty years for trademarks registered before 1990).

Trademark Infringement

Registration of a trademark with the U.S. Patent and Trademark Office gives notice on a nationwide basis that the trademark belongs exclusively to the registrant. The registrant is also allowed to use the symbol ® to indicate that the mark has been registered. Whenever someone else uses that trademark in its entirety or copies it to a substantial degree, intentionally or unintentionally, the trademark has been *infringed* (used without authorization).

When a trademark has been infringed, the owner has a cause of action against the infringer. To succeed in a lawsuit for trademark infringement, the owner must show that the defendant's use of the mark created a likelihood of confusion about the origin of the defendant's goods or services. The owner need not prove that the infringer acted intentionally or that the trademark was registered (although registration does provide proof of the date of inception of the trademark's use). See this chapter's *Adapting the Law to the Online Environment* feature on the following page for a discussion of how some companies are turning first to Internet forums, before they resort to costly trademark litigation.

The remedy most commonly granted for trademark infringement is an *injunction* to prevent further infringement. Under the Lanham Act, a trademark owner that successfully proves infringement can recover actual damages, plus the profits that the infringer wrongfully received from the unauthorized use of the mark. A court can also order the destruction of any goods bearing the unauthorized trademark. In some situations, the trademark owner may also be able to recover attorneys' fees.

---

3. See *Moseley v. V Secret Catalogue, Inc.*, 537 U.S. 418, 123 S.Ct. 1115, 155 L.Ed.2d 1 (2003).
4. *Starbucks Corp. v. Lundberg*, 2005 WL 3183858 (D.Or. 2005).

Distinctiveness of the Mark

A central objective of the Lanham Act is to reduce the likelihood that consumers will be confused by similar marks. For that reason, only those trademarks that are deemed sufficiently distinctive from all competing trademarks will be protected. (In addition, a trademark may not be derogatory, as the *Law, Diversity, and Business: Managerial Implications* feature on the facing page explains.)

Strong Marks   Fanciful, arbitrary, or suggestive trademarks are generally considered to be the most distinctive (strongest) trademarks. Because they are normally taken from outside the context of the particular product, strong marks provide the best means of distinguishing one product from another. Fanciful trademarks include invented words, such as *Xerox* for one manufacturer's copiers and *Google* for search engines. Arbitrary trademarks use common words that would not ordinarily be associated with the product, such as *Dutch Boy* as a name for paint.

A single letter used in a particular style can be an arbitrary trademark. **CASE EXAMPLE 5.2** Sports entertainment company ESPN, Inc., sued Quiksilver, Inc., a maker of youth-oriented clothing, alleging trademark infringement. ESPN claimed that

ADAPTING THE LAW TO THE ONLINE ENVIRONMENT

USING ONLINE SHAME IN TRADEMARK DISPUTES

Claims of trademark infringement have risen 5 percent each year for the past several years and will exceed four thousand in 2013. Trademark litigation is costly and can drag on for years. Small businesses, particularly start-ups, typically do not have the resources to engage in such lengthy litigation. Yet claims of infringement, even when they seem dubious, must be addressed. Some entrepreneurs are finding that online publicity and the shame it can bring are an effective alternative to going to federal court to resolve trademark disputes.

Can a Company Trademark the Letter "K"?

When Phil Michaelson created the Web site KeepRecipes.com to provide an Internet cookbook where people could collect and share recipes, he never thought the word "Keep" and the letter "K" could be someone's trademarks. On his site, users click on "K," short for "Keep," when they want to save the instructions for a recipe. Nevertheless, AdKeeper, a New York–based service company, immediately sent Michaelson a cease-and-desist letter. AdKeeper claimed that the use of "K" and "Keep," as well as the Web site name KeepRecipes.com, constituted "blatant trademark infringement."

Online Publicity Provides a Solution

Michaelson did not have the resources to engage in a prolonged legal battle with AdKeeper, even though he thought its claims had no merit. Instead, he turned to Chillingeffects.org, a Web site created by several universities to foster lawful online activity. Soon after he described his problem and posted the cease-and-desist letter, several lawyers who deal with Web site issues offered to represent him in his trademark dispute at no charge.

Using Social Media

Other small entrepreneurs facing lawsuits are turning to social media, especially Facebook and Twitter, where large companies' threats to sue small companies for trademark infringement are generally met with displeasure. When the restaurant company Chick-fil-A, Inc., threatened Vermont T-shirt manufacturer Bo Muller-Moore with a lawsuit, he created a Facebook page. Chick-fil-A claimed that Muller-Moore had infringed its trademarked slogan "Eat Mor Chikin" when he used the slogan "Eat More Kale" on his T-shirts—even though Muller-Moore used correct spelling and kale and chicken would seem to be rather different foods. Several thousand supporters regularly look at Muller-Moore's Facebook page and have donated $10,000 for his defense.

Critical Thinking

As social media becomes ever more pervasive in our lives, what do you expect to occur with respect to trademark disputes?

LAW, DIVERSITY, AND BUSINESS: MANAGERIAL IMPLICATIONS

DEROGATORY TRADEMARKS

When determining whether a trademark is sufficiently distinctive to warrant protection, the U.S. Patent and Trademark Office (USPTO) also considers whether the mark might be offensive to any of the diverse groups in our society. Under the Lanham Act, the USPTO must deny registration to trademarks that "may disparage or falsely suggest a connection with persons, living or dead, institutions, beliefs, or national symbols, or bring them into contempt, or derision."[a]

A Disparaging Mark Can Be Costly   Sometimes, the USPTO fails to recognize a potentially disparaging mark and approves its registration. Discovering too late that it has chosen the wrong trademark can be very expensive for a business. Biggby Coffee, one of the nation's fastest-growing coffee franchises, spent nearly $1 million to change its name from Beaner's Coffee to Biggby Coffee after it became aware that the word *beaners* is sometimes used as a disparaging term for Hispanic Americans.

Names of Sports Teams   One of the most controversial issues involving trademarks has to do with the use of American Indian names and mascots for sports teams. Many Native Americans find the use of these names highly offensive and demeaning. In 1992, seven Native Americans petitioned the Trademark Trial and Appeal Board, which hears appeals of USPTO decisions, and asked it to cancel six trademarks of the Washington Redskins football team

that had been registered since the late 1960s and 1970s. The board agreed that the use of the term *redskins* was offensive and canceled the marks. The team's owner appealed to a federal court, setting off a long-running legal battle that did not end until 2009 when a federal appellate court found that the Native Americans had waited too long to bring their suit. The United States Supreme Court subsequently declined to hear the case.[b]

Native Americans were more successful in their long struggle to end the use of the name *Fighting Sioux* for the University of North Dakota's teams. The National Collegiate Athletic Association (NCAA) had put the University of North Dakota (UND) on a list of schools with names and mascots that it found objectionable. All of the other schools on the list either changed their teams' names or obtained permission from Native Americans to keep them. After several months of debate and controversy, in June 2012, the citizens of North Dakota overwhelming voted to get rid of the UND's team name, and the state's board of higher education officially voted to remove it as well.

Business Implications   *As society becomes more sensitive to diversity issues, businesses can expect that their trademarks will be subject to increased scrutiny. When choosing a trademark, logo, or motto, a business must consider the diverse groups in our society.*

a. 15 U.S.C. Section 1052(a).

b. *Pro-Football Inc. v. Harjo,* 565 F.3d 880 (2009), *cert. denied; Harjo v. Pro-Football, Inc.,* 130 S. Ct. 631 (2009).

Quiksilver had used on its clothing the stylized "X" mark that ESPN uses in connection with the "X Games" (competitions in extreme action sports). Quiksilver filed counterclaims for trademark infringement and dilution, arguing that it had a long history of using the stylized X on its products. ESPN created the X Games in the mid-1990s, and Quiksilver has used the X mark since 1994. ESPN asked the court to dismiss Quiksilver's counterclaims, but the court refused, holding that the X on Quiksilver's clothing was clearly an arbitrary mark. The court found that the two Xs were "similar enough that a consumer might well confuse them."[5]

Suggestive Trademarks

Suggestive trademarks bring to mind something about a product without describing the product directly. For instance, "Dairy Queen" suggests an association between its products and milk, but it does not directly describe ice cream. "Blu-ray" is a suggestive mark that is associated with the high-quality, high-definition video contained on a particular optical data storage disc. Although blue-violet lasers are used to read blu-ray discs, the term *blu-ray* does not directly describe the disc.

---

5. *ESPN, Inc. v. Quiksilver, Inc.,* 586 F.Supp.2d 219 (S.D.N.Y. 2008).

Secondary Meaning   Descriptive terms, geographic terms, and personal names are not inherently distinctive and do not receive protection under the law *until* they acquire a secondary meaning. **CASE EXAMPLE 5.3**   Frosty Treats, Inc., sells frozen desserts out of ice cream trucks. The video game series Twisted Metal depicted an ice cream truck with a clown character on it that was similar to the clowns on Frosty Treats' trucks. In the last game of the series, the truck bears the label "Frosty Treats." Frosty Treats sued for trademark infringement, but the court held that "Frosty Treats" is a descriptive term that is not protected by trademark law unless it has acquired a secondary meaning. To establish secondary meaning, Frosty Treats would have to show that the public recognizes its trademark and associates it with a single source. Because Frosty Treats failed to do so, the court entered a judgment in favor of the video game producer.[6] •

A secondary meaning arises when customers begin to associate a specific term or phrase, such as "London Fog," with specific trademarked items (coats with "London Fog" labels) made by a particular company. Whether a secondary meaning becomes attached to a term or name usually depends on how extensively the product is advertised, the market for the product, the number of sales, and other factors. Once a secondary meaning is attached to a term or name, a trademark is considered distinctive and is protected. Even a color can qualify for trademark protection, such as the color schemes used by four state university sports teams, including Ohio State University and Louisiana State University.[7]

Generic Terms   Generic terms are terms that refer to an entire class of products, such as *bicycle* and *computer*. Generic terms receive no protection, even if they acquire secondary meanings. A particularly thorny problem for a business arises when its trademark acquires generic use. For instance, *aspirin* and *thermos* were originally trademarked products, but today the words are used generically. Other trademarks that have acquired generic use include *escalator, trampoline, raisin bran, dry ice, lanolin, linoleum, nylon,* and *cornflakes.*[8]

Service, Certification, and Collective Marks

A **service mark** is essentially a trademark that is used to distinguish the *services* (rather than the products) of one person or company from those of another. For instance, each airline has a particular mark or symbol associated with its name. Titles and character names used in radio and television are frequently registered as service marks.

Other marks protected by law include certification marks and collective marks. A **certification mark** is used by one or more persons, other than the owner, to certify the region, materials, mode of manufacture, quality, or other characteristic of specific goods or services. Certification marks include such marks as "Good Housekeeping Seal of Approval" and "UL Tested."

When used by members of a cooperative, association, labor union, or other organization, a certification mark is referred to as a **collective mark.** **EXAMPLE 5.4**   Collective marks appear at the end of a movie's credits to indicate the various associations and organizations that participated in making the movie. The labor union marks found on the tags of certain products are also collective marks. •

Trade Dress

The term **trade dress** refers to the image and overall appearance of a product. Trade dress is a broad concept that can include all or part of the total image or overall impression created by a product or its packaging. **EXAMPLE 5.5**   The distinctive decor, menu, and style of

Service Mark A trademark that is used to distinguish the services (rather than the products) of one person or company from those of another.

Certification Mark A mark used by one or more persons, other than the owner, to certify the region, materials, mode of manufacture, quality, or other characteristic of specific goods or services.

Collective Mark A mark used by members of a cooperative, association, union, or other organization to certify the region, materials, mode of manufacture, quality, or other characteristic of specific goods or services.

Trade Dress The image and overall appearance ("look and feel") of a product that is protected by trademark law.

---

6. *Frosty Treats, Inc. v. Sony Computer Entertainment America, Inc.,* 426 F.3d 1001 (8th Cir. 2005).

7. *Board of Supervisors of LA State University v. Smack Apparel Co.,* 438 F.Supp.2d 653 (2006). See also *Qualitex Co. v. Jacobson Products Co.,* 514 U.S. 159, 115 S.Ct. 1300, 131 L.Ed.2d 248 (1995).

8. See, for example, *Boston Duck Tours, LP v. Super Duck Tours, LLC,* 531 F.3d 1 (1st Cir. 2008).

service of a particular restaurant may be regarded as the restaurant's trade dress. Similarly, trade dress can include the layout and appearance of a mail-order catalogue, the use of a lighthouse as part of a golf hole, the fish shape of a cracker, or the G-shaped design of a Gucci watch. •

Basically, trade dress is subject to the same protection as trademarks. In cases involving trade dress infringement, as in trademark infringement cases, a major consideration is whether consumers are likely to be confused by the allegedly infringing use.

Counterfeit Goods

Counterfeit goods copy or otherwise imitate trademarked goods but are not genuine. The importation of goods bearing counterfeit (fake) trademarks poses a growing problem for U.S. businesses, consumers, and law enforcement. It is estimated that nearly 7 percent of the goods imported into the United States are counterfeit. In addition to having negative financial effects on legitimate businesses, sales of certain counterfeit goods, such as pharmaceuticals and nutritional supplements, can present serious public health risks.

Although Congress has enacted statutes against counterfeit goods (discussed next), the United States cannot prosecute foreign counterfeiters because our national laws do not apply to them. Instead, one effective tool that U.S. officials are using to combat online sales of counterfeit goods is to obtain a court order to close down the domain names of Web sites that sell such goods. **EXAMPLE 5.6** In 2011, U.S. agents shut down 150 domain names on the Monday after Thanksgiving ("Cyber Monday," the online version of "Black Friday," the day after Thanksgiving when the holiday shopping season begins). Although the criminal enterprises may continue selling counterfeit versions of brand-name products under different domain names, shutting down the Web sites, particularly on key shopping days, prevents some counterfeit goods from entering the United States. •

Stop Counterfeiting in Manufactured Goods Act
In 2006, Congress enacted the Stop Counterfeiting in Manufactured Goods Act[9] (SCMGA) to combat counterfeit goods. The act made it a crime to intentionally traffic in, or attempt to traffic in,

---

9. Pub. L. No. 109-181 (2006), which amended 18 U.S.C. Sections 2318–2320.

A federal customs officer displays about $4 million of counterfeit goods that were seized in the Los Angeles area. Is it possible to control the foreign sources of such merchandise?

(AP Photo/Nick Ut)

counterfeit goods or services, or to knowingly use a counterfeit mark on or in connection with goods or services. Before this act, the law did not prohibit the creation or shipment of counterfeit labels that were not attached to products.[10] Therefore, counterfeiters would make labels and packaging bearing a fake trademark, ship the labels to another location, and then affix them to inferior products to deceive buyers. The SCMGA closed this loophole by making it a crime to traffic in counterfeit labels, stickers, packaging, and the like, whether or not they are attached to goods.

Penalties for Counterfeiting   Persons found guilty of violating the SCMGA may be fined up to $2 million or imprisoned for up to ten years (or more if they are repeat offenders). If a court finds that the statute was violated, it must order the defendant to forfeit the counterfeit products (which are then destroyed), as well as any property used in the commission of the crime. The defendant must also pay restitution to the trademark holder or victim in an amount equal to the victim's actual loss.

CASE EXAMPLE 5.7   Wajdi Beydoun pleaded guilty to conspiring to import cigarette-rolling papers from Mexico that were falsely marked as "Zig-Zags" and sell them in the United States. The defendant was sentenced to prison and ordered to pay $566,267 in restitution. On appeal, the court affirmed the prison sentence but ordered the trial court to reduce the amount of restitution because it exceeded the actual loss suffered by the legitimate sellers of Zig-Zag rolling papers.[11] ●

Trade Names

Trade Name A name that a business uses to identify itself and its brand. A trade name is directly related to a business's reputation and goodwill and is protected under trademark law.

Trademarks apply to *products*. The term **trade name** is used to indicate part or all of a *business's name*, whether the business is a sole proprietorship, a partnership, or a corporation. Generally, a trade name is directly related to a business and its goodwill. Trade names may be protected as trademarks if the trade name is the same as the company's trademarked product—for example, Coca-Cola. Unless it is also used as a trademark or service mark, a trade name cannot be registered with the federal government.

Trade names are protected under the common law, however. As with trademarks, words must be unusual or fancifully used if they are to be protected as trade names. For instance, the courts held that the word *Safeway* was sufficiently fanciful to obtain protection as a trade name for a grocery chain.

Licensing

License An agreement by the owner of intellectual property to permit another to use a trademark, copyright, patent, or trade secret for certain limited purposes.

One way to make use of another's trademark or other form of intellectual property, while avoiding litigation, is to obtain a license to do so. A **license** in this context is an agreement permitting the use of a trademark, copyright, patent, or trade secret for certain limited purposes. The party that owns the intellectual property rights and issues the license is the *licensor,* and the party obtaining the license is the *licensee.*

A license grants only the rights expressly described in the license agreement. A licensor might, for example, allow the licensee to use the trademark as part of its company name, or as part of its domain name, but not otherwise use the mark on any products or services. Disputes frequently arise over licensing agreements, particularly when the license involves Internet uses.

Typically, license agreements are very detailed and should be carefully drafted. **CASE EXAMPLE 5.8**   George V Restauration S.A. and others owned and operated the Buddha Bar Paris, a restaurant with an Asian theme in Paris, France. In 2005, one of the owners

---

10. See, for example, *Commonwealth v. Crespo,* 884 A.2d 960 (Pa. 2005).
11. *United States v. Beydoun,* 469 F.3d 102 (5th Cir. 2006).

allowed Little Rest Twelve, Inc., to use the Buddha Bar trademark and its associated concept in New York City under the name *Buddha Bar NYC*. Little Rest paid royalties for its use of the Buddha Bar mark and advertised Buddha Bar NYC's affiliation with Buddha Bar Paris, a connection also noted on its Web site and in the media. When a dispute arose, the owners of Buddha Bar Paris withdrew their permission for Buddha Bar NYC's use of their mark, but Little Rest continued to use it. The owners of the mark filed a suit in a New York state court against Little Rest, and ultimately a state appellate court granted an injunction preventing Little Rest from using the mark.[12] ●

PREVENTING LEGAL DISPUTES

Consult with an attorney before signing any licensing contract to make sure that the wording of the contract is very clear as to what rights are or are not being conveyed. This can help to avoid litigation. Moreover, to prevent misunderstandings over the scope of the rights being acquired, determine whether any other parties hold licenses to use that particular intellectual property and the extent of those rights.

Cyber Marks

Cyber Mark A trademark in cyberspace.

In cyberspace, trademarks are sometimes referred to as **cyber marks.** We turn now to a discussion of how new laws and the courts are addressing trademark-related issues in cyberspace.

Domain Names

Domain Name Part of an Internet address, such as "cengage.com." The part to the right of the period is the top level domain and indicates the type of entity that operates the site, and the part to the left of the period, called the second level domain, is chosen by the entity.

As e-commerce expanded worldwide, one issue that emerged involved the rights of a trademark owner to use the mark as part of a domain name. A **domain name** is part of an Internet address, such as "cengage.com." Every domain name ends with a top level domain (TLD), which is the part to the right of the period that indicates the type of entity that operates the site (for example, "com" is an abbreviation for "commercial").

The second level domain (SLD)—the part of the name to the left of the period—is chosen by the business entity or individual registering the domain name. Competition for SLDs among firms with similar names and products has led to numerous disputes. By using the same, or a similar, domain name, parties have attempted to profit from a competitor's goodwill, sell pornography, offer for sale another party's domain name, or otherwise infringe on others' trademarks.

The Internet Corporation for Assigned Names and Numbers (ICANN), a nonprofit corporation, oversees the distribution of domain names and operates an online arbitration system. Due to numerous complaints, ICANN completely overhauled the domain name distribution system. In 2012, ICANN started selling new generic top level domain names (gTLDs) for an initial price of $185,000 plus an annual fee of $25,000. Whereas TLDs were limited to only a few terms (such as "com," "net," and "org"), gTLDs can take any form. ICANN anticipates that many companies and corporations will want gTLDs based on their brands. For example, Apple, Inc., might want to use "ipad or "imac" as a gTLD, and Coca-Cola might want "coke."

Cybersquatting The act of registering a domain name that is the same as, or confusingly similar to, the trademark of another and then offering to sell that domain name back to the trademark owner.

One of the goals of the new system is to alleviate the problem of *cybersquatting*. **Cybersquatting** occurs when a person registers a domain name that is the same as, or confusingly similar to, the trademark of another and then offers to sell the domain name back to the trademark owner.

---

12. *George V Restauration S.A. v. Little Rest Twelve, Inc.,* 58 A.D.3d 428, 871 N.Y.S.2d 65 (2009).

Anti-cybersquatting Legislation

During the 1990s, cybersquatting led to so much litigation that Congress passed the Anticybersquatting Consumer Protection Act (ACPA), which amended the Lanham Act—the federal law protecting trademarks discussed earlier. The ACPA makes it illegal to "register, traffic in, or use" a domain name (1) if the name is identical or confusingly similar to the trademark of another and (2) if the person registering, trafficking in, or using the domain name has a "bad faith intent" to profit from that trademark.

The Ongoing Problem of Cybersquatting   Despite the ACPA, cybersquatting continues to present a problem for businesses, largely because more TLDs are now available and many more companies are registering domain names. Indeed, domain name registrars have proliferated. Registrar companies charge a fee to businesses and individuals to register new names and to renew annual registrations (often through automated software). Many of these companies also buy and sell expired domain names.

Although all registrars are supposed to relay information about these transactions to ICANN and the other companies that keep a master list of domain names, this does not always occur. The speed at which domain names change hands and the difficulty in tracking mass automated registrations have created an environment in which cybersquatting can flourish.

Cybersquatters have also developed new tactics, such as *typosquatting* (registering a name that is a misspelling of a popular brand, for example, hotmial.com). Because many Internet users are not perfect typists, Web pages using these misspelled names can generate significant traffic. More traffic generally means increased profits (advertisers often pay Web sites based on the number of unique visits, or hits), which in turn provides incentive for more cybersquatters. Also, if the misspelling is significant, the trademark owner may have difficulty proving that the name is identical or confusingly similar to the owner's mark, as required by the ACPA.

Cybersquatting is costly for businesses, which must attempt to register all variations of a name to protect their domain name rights from would-be cybersquatters. Large corporations may have to register thousands of domain names across the globe just to protect their basic brands and trademarks.

Applicability of the ACPA and Sanctions under the Act   The ACPA applies to all domain name registrations of trademarks. Successful plaintiffs in suits brought under the act can collect actual damages and lost profits or elect to receive statutory damages that range from $1,000 to $100,000.

Although some companies have been successful suing under the ACPA, there are roadblocks to pursuing such lawsuits. Some domain name registrars offer privacy services that hide the true owners of Web sites, making it difficult for trademark owners to identify cybersquatters. Thus, before bringing a suit, a trademark owner has to ask the court for a subpoena to discover the identity of the owner of the infringing Web site. Because of the high costs of court proceedings, discovery, and even arbitration, many disputes over cybersquatting are settled out of court.

Meta Tags

Search engines compile their results by looking through a Web site's key-word field. *Meta tags,* or key words (see Chapter 1 on page 20), may be inserted into this field to increase the likelihood that a site will be included in search engine results, even though the site may have nothing to do with the inserted words. Using this same technique, one site may appropriate the key words of other sites with more frequent hits so that the appropriating site appears in the same search engine results as the more popular sites. Using another's trademark in a meta tag without the owner's permission, however, normally constitutes trademark infringement.

Some uses of another's trademark as a meta tag may be permissible if the use is reasonably necessary and does not suggest that the owner authorized or sponsored the use. **CASE EXAMPLE 5.9** Terri Welles, a former model who had been "Playmate of the Year" in *Playboy* magazine, established a Web site that used the terms *Playboy* and *Playmate* as meta tags. Playboy Enterprises, Inc., which publishes *Playboy,* filed a suit seeking to prevent Welles from using these meta tags. The court determined that Welles's use of Playboy's meta tags to direct users to her Web site was permissible because it did not suggest sponsorship and there were no descriptive substitutes for the terms *Playboy* and *Playmate.*[13] ●

Dilution in the Online World

As discussed earlier, trademark *dilution* occurs when a trademark is used, without authorization, in a way that diminishes the distinctive quality of the mark. Unlike trademark infringement, a claim of dilution does not require proof that consumers are likely to be confused by a connection between the unauthorized use and the mark. For this reason, the products involved do not have to be similar, as the following *Spotlight Case* illustrates.

---

13. *Playboy Enterprises, Inc. v. Welles,* 279 F.3d 796 (9th Cir. 2002). See also *Canfield v. Health Communications, Inc.,* 2008 WL 961318 (C.D.Cal. 2008).

Spotlight on Internet Porn

Case 5.2
Hasbro, Inc. v. Internet Entertainment Group, Ltd.
United States District Court, Western District of Washington, 1996 WL 84853 (1996).

Candy Land is a children's board game. Why did its parent company, Hasbro, Inc., sue a Web site?

FACTS Hasbro, Inc., the maker of Candyland, a children's board game, owns the Candyland trademark. The defendants, Brian Cartmell and the Internet Entertainment Group, Ltd., used *candyland.com* as a domain name for a sexually explicit Internet site. Any person who performed an online search for "candyland" was directed to this adult Web site. Hasbro filed a trademark dilution claim in a federal court, seeking a permanent injunction to prevent the defendants from using the Candyland trademark.

ISSUE Did the defendants' use of the word *candyland* in connection with a sexually explicit Web site violate Hasbro's trademark rights?

DECISION Yes. The district court granted Hasbro a permanent injunction and ordered the defendants to remove all content from the *candyland.com* Web site and to stop using the Candyland mark.

REASON The court reasoned that Hasbro had shown that the defendants' use of the Candyland mark and the domain name *candyland. com* in connection with their Internet site was causing irreparable injury to Hasbro. As required to obtain an injunction, Hasbro had demonstrated a likelihood of prevailing on its claims that the defendants' conduct violated both the federal and the Washington State statutes against trademark dilution. "The probable harm to Hasbro from defendants' conduct outweighs any inconvenience that defendants will experience if they are required to stop using the CANDYLAND name."

WHY IS THIS CASE IMPORTANT? *This was the first case alleging dilution on the Web. The court precluded the use of* candyland.com *as a URL for an adult site, even though consumers were not likely to confuse an adult Web site with a children's board game.*

Patents

Patent A property right granted by the federal government that gives an inventor an exclusive right to make, use, sell, or offer to sell an invention in the United States for a limited time.

LEARNING OBJECTIVE 3
How does the law protect patents?

A **patent** is a grant from the government that gives an inventor the exclusive right to make, use, and sell an invention for a period of twenty years. Patents for designs, as opposed to inventions, are given for a fourteen-year period.

Until recently, patent law in the United States differed from the laws of many other countries because the first person to invent a product or process obtained the patent rights rather than the first person to file for a patent. It was often difficult to prove who invented an item first, however, which prompted Congress to change the system in 2011 by passing the America Invents Act.[14] Now the first person to file an application for a patent on a product or process will receive patent protection. In addition, the new law established a nine-month limit for challenging a patent on any ground.

The period of patent protection begins on the date when the patent application is filed, rather than when the patent is issued, which can sometimes be years later. After the patent period ends (either fourteen or twenty years later), the product or process enters the public domain, and anyone can make, sell, or use the invention without paying the patent holder.

Searchable Patent Databases

(www.uspto.gov)

This is the home page of the U.S. Patent and Trademark Office. Is its database searchable?

A significant development relating to patents is the availability online of the world's patent databases. The Web site of the U.S. Patent and Trademark Office (www.uspto.gov) provides searchable databases covering U.S. patents granted since 1976. The Web site of the European Patent Office (www.epo.org) provides online access to 50 million patent documents in more than seventy nations through a searchable network of databases. Businesses use these searchable databases in many ways. Because patents are valuable assets, businesses may need to perform patent searches to list or inventory their assets.

What Is Patentable?

Under federal law, "[w]hoever invents or discovers any new and useful process, machine, manufacture, or composition of matter, or any new and useful improvement thereof, may obtain a patent therefor, subject to the conditions and requirements of this title."[15] Thus, to be patentable, an invention must be *novel, useful,* and *not obvious* in light of current technology.

Almost anything is patentable, except the laws of nature,[16] natural phenomena, and abstract ideas (including algorithms[17]). Even artistic methods and works of art, certain business processes, and the structures of storylines are patentable, provided that they are novel and not obvious.[18]

⟶ KNOW THIS ⟵

A patent is granted to inventions that are novel (new) and not obvious in light of prior discoveries.

Plants that are reproduced asexually (by means other than from seed), such as hybrid or genetically engineered plants, are patentable in the United States, as are genetically engineered (or cloned) microorganisms and animals. **CASE EXAMPLE 5.10** Monsanto, Inc., has been selling its patented genetically modified (GM) seeds to farmers as a way to achieve higher yields from crops using fewer pesticides. Monsanto requires farmers who buy GM seeds to sign licensing agreements promising to plant the seeds for only one crop and to

---

14. The full title of this law is the Leahy-Smith America Invents Act, Pub. L. No. 112-29 (2011), which amended 35 U.S.C. Sections 1, 41, and 321.

15. 35 U.S.C. 101.

16. *Laboratory Corporation of America Holdings v. Metabolite Laboratories, Inc.*, 548 U.S. 124, 126 S.Ct. 2921, 165 L.Ed.2d 399 (2006).

17. An *algorithm* is a step-by-step procedure, formula, or set of instructions for accomplishing a specific task—such as the set of rules used by a search engine to rank the listings contained within its index in response to a particular query.

18. For a United States Supreme Court case discussing the obviousness requirement, see *KSR International Co. v. Teleflex, Inc.*, 550 U.S. 398, 127 S.Ct. 1727, 167 L.Ed.2d 705 (2007). For a discussion of business process patents, see *In re Bilski*, 535 F.3d 943 (Fed.Cir. 2008).

pay a technology fee for each acre planted. To ensure compliance, Monsanto has assigned seventy-five employees whose job is to investigate and prosecute farmers who use the GM seeds illegally. Monsanto has filed more than ninety lawsuits against nearly 150 farmers in the United States and has been awarded more than $15 million in damages (not including out-of-court settlement amounts).[19]

Patent Infringement

If a firm makes, uses, or sells another's patented design, product, or process without the patent owner's permission, it commits the tort of patent infringement. Patent infringement may occur even though the patent owner has not put the patented product in commerce. Patent infringement may also occur even though not all features or parts of an invention are copied. (To infringe the patent on a process, however, all steps or their equivalent must be copied.)

Galaxy Tab 10.1 tablet computer at the company's Galaxy Zone showroom in Seoul.

(Seongjoon Cho/Bloomberg via Getty Images)

Patent Infringement Suits and High-Tech Companies

Obviously, companies that specialize in developing new technology stand to lose significant profits if someone "makes, uses, or sells" devices that incorporate their patented inventions. Because these firms are the holders of numerous patents, they are frequently involved in patent infringement lawsuits (as well as other types of intellectual property disputes). Many companies that make and sell electronics and computer software and hardware are based in foreign nations (for example, Samsung Electronics Company is a Korean firm). Foreign firms can apply for and obtain U.S. patent protection on items that they sell within the United States, just as U.S. firms can obtain protection in foreign nations where they sell goods.

Nevertheless, as a general rule, no patent infringement occurs under U.S. law when a patented product is made and sold in another country. The United States Supreme Court has narrowly construed patent infringement as it applies to exported software.

CASE EXAMPLE 5.11 AT&T Corporation holds a patent on a device used to digitally encode, compress, and process recorded speech. AT&T brought an infringement case against Microsoft Corporation, which admitted that its Windows operating system incorporated software code that infringed on AT&T's patent. The case reached the United States Supreme Court on the question of whether Microsoft's liability extended to computers made in another country. The Court held that it did not. Microsoft was liable only for infringement in the United States and not for the Windows-based computers produced in foreign locations. The Court reasoned that Microsoft had not "supplied" the software for the computers but had only electronically transmitted a master copy, which the foreign manufacturers then copied and loaded onto the computers.[20]

Apple, Inc. v. Samsung Electronics Company

As mentioned in the chapter introduction, Apple sued Samsung in federal court alleging that Samsung's Galaxy mobile phones and tablets infringe on Apple's patents. The complaint also included allegations of trade dress violations (that Samsung copied the "look and feel" of iPhones and iPads) and trademark infringement (that the icons used for many of the apps on Samsung's products are nearly identical to Apple's apps).

Apple claimed that its design patents cover the graphical user interface (the display of icons on the home screen), the device's shell, and the screen and button design. It also claimed that its patents cover the way information is displayed on iPhones and other

---

19. See, for example, *Monsanto Co. v. Scruggs*, 459 F.3d 1328 (2006); *Monsanto Co. v. McFarling*, 2005 WL 1490051 (E.D.Mo. 2005); and *Sample v. Monsanto Co.*, 283 F.Supp.2d 1088 (2003).
20. *Microsoft Corp. v. AT&T Corp.*, 550 U.S. 437, 127 S.Ct. 1746, 167 L.Ed.2d 737 (2007).

devices, the way windows pop open, and the way information is scaled and rotated, among other things. Apple argued that Samsung's phones and tablets that use Google's HTC Android operating system violate all of these patents.

In 2012, a jury issued a verdict in favor of Apple and awarded more than $1 billion in damages.[21] The jury found that Samsung had willfully infringed five of Apple's patents and had "diluted" Apple's registered iPhone trade dress. The jury's award was one of the largest ever in a patent case. The case also provides an important precedent for Apple in its legal attacks against Android devices made by other companies because for every iPhone sold worldwide, more than three Android-based smartphones are sold.

Remedies for Patent Infringement

If a patent is infringed, the patent holder may sue for relief in federal court. The patent holder can seek an injunction against the infringer and can also request damages for royalties and lost profits. In some cases, the court may grant the winning party reimbursement for attorneys' fees and costs. If the court determines that the infringement was willful, the court can triple the amount of damages awarded (treble damages).

In the past, permanent injunctions were routinely granted to prevent future infringement. In 2006, however, the United States Supreme Court ruled that patent holders are not automatically entitled to a permanent injunction against future infringing activities. According to the Supreme Court, a patent holder must prove that it has suffered irreparable injury and that the public interest would not be *disserved* by a permanent injunction.[22] This decision gives courts discretion to decide what is equitable in the circumstances and allows them to consider the public interest rather than just the interests of the parties.

CASE EXAMPLE 5.12   In the first case applying this rule, a court found that although Microsoft had infringed on the patent of a small software company, the latter was not entitled to an injunction. According to the court, the small company was not irreparably harmed and could be adequately compensated by monetary damages. Also, the public might suffer negative effects from an injunction because the infringement involved part of Microsoft's widely used Office suite software.[23] ●

Copyrights

A **copyright** is an intangible property right granted by federal statute to the author or originator of certain literary or artistic productions. The Copyright Act of 1976,[24] as amended, governs copyrights. Works created after January 1, 1978, are automatically given statutory copyright protection for the life of the author plus 70 years. For copyrights owned by publishing companies, the copyright expires 95 years from the date of publication or 120 years from the date of creation, whichever is first. For works by more than one author, the copyright expires 70 years after the death of the last surviving author.

Copyrights can be registered with the U.S. Copyright Office (www.copyright.gov) in Washington, D.C. A copyright owner no longer needs to place a © or *Copr.* or *Copyright* on the work, however, to have the work protected against infringement. Chances are that if somebody created it, somebody owns it.

21. *Apple, Inc. v. Samsung Electronics Co.*, Case Nos. CV 11-1846 and CV 12-0630 (N.D. Cal. August 24, 2012).
22. *eBay, Inc. v. MercExchange, LLC*, 547 U.S. 388, 126 S.Ct. 1837, 164 L.Ed.2d 641 (2006).
23. See *Z4 Technologies, Inc. v. Microsoft Corp.*, 434 F.Supp.2d 437 (2006).
24. 17 U.S.C. Sections 101 *et seq.*

What Is Protected Expression?

Works that are copyrightable include books, records, films, artworks, architectural plans, menus, music videos, product packaging, and computer software. To be protected, a work must be "fixed in a durable medium" from which it can be perceived, reproduced, or communicated. Protection is automatic. Registration is not required.

To obtain protection under the Copyright Act, a work must be original and fall into one of the following categories:

1. Literary works (including newspaper and magazine articles, computer and training manuals, catalogues, brochures, and print advertisements).
2. Musical works and accompanying words (including advertising jingles).
3. Dramatic works and accompanying music.
4. Pantomimes and choreographic works (including ballets and other forms of dance).
5. Pictorial, graphic, and sculptural works (including cartoons, maps, posters, statues, and even stuffed animals).
6. Motion pictures and other audiovisual works (including multimedia works).
7. Sound recordings.
8. Architectural works.

Artist Shepard Fairey created a poster portrait of Barack Obama. It was clearly based on an Associated Press file photo taken by Manny Garcia. Did Fairey violate copyright law?

(Jewel Samad/AFP/Getty Images)

Section 102 Exclusions It is not possible to copyright an idea. Section 102 of the Copyright Act specifically excludes copyright protection for any "idea, procedure, process, system, method of operation, concept, principle, or discovery, regardless of the form in which it is described, explained, illustrated, or embodied." Thus, others can freely use the underlying ideas or principles embodied in a work.

What is copyrightable is the particular way in which an idea is *expressed*. Whenever an idea and an expression are inseparable, the expression cannot be copyrighted. Generally, anything that is not an original expression will not qualify for copyright protection. Facts widely known to the public are not copyrightable. Page numbers are not copyrightable because they follow a sequence known to everyone. Mathematical calculations are not copyrightable.

ETHICAL ISSUE

Should the federal Copyright Act preempt plaintiffs from bringing "idea-submission" claims under state law? In the past, federal courts generally held that the Copyright Act preempted (or superseded—see Chapter 1 on page 14) claims in state courts alleging the theft of ideas. In 2011, however, a federal appellate court's decision in the case, *Montz v. Pilgrim Films,*[25] opened the door to such claims. The plaintiff, Larry Montz, had presented representatives from NBC Universal with a concept for a reality-style television program that would follow two paranormal investigators who search for evidence of ghosts. A number of meetings and discussions took place during which Montz provided scripts, videos, and other materials for the proposed show. Ultimately, the studio decided that it was not interested. Three years later, however, NBC partnered with Pilgrim Films to produce *Ghost Hunters*, a series on the Syfy channel that depicts a team of investigators who travel around the country looking for paranormal activity. Montz sued the producers for copyright infringement, breach of contract, and breach of confidence. He claimed that he had expressly conditioned the disclosure of his idea on an expectation that he would be a partner with NBC on the production and would receive a share of any profits.

The lower court dismissed his case, but the appellate court reversed, finding that the Copyright Act did not preempt Montz's two state law claims (breach of an implied contract and breach of confidence). The court reasoned that the state claims asserted rights that are qualitatively different from the rights protected by copyright. The contract claim survived preemption because it required proof of an extra element—the implied agreement of payment for use of a concept—which is

---

25. 649 F.3d 975 (9th Cir. 2011). See also *Gross v. Miramax Film Corp.*, 383 F.3d 965 (9th Cir. 2004), *cert.* denied, 546 U.S. 824, 126 S.Ct. 361, 163 L.Ed.2d 68 (2005).

a personal right that is different from copyright law. Similarly, the breach of confidence claim required the extra element of a confidential relationship between the parties.

Compilations of Facts   Unlike ideas, *compilations* of facts are copyrightable. Under Section 103 of the Copyright Act, a compilation is a work formed by the collection and assembling of preexisting materials or of data that are selected, coordinated, or arranged in such a way that the resulting work as a whole constitutes an original work of authorship.

The key requirement for the copyrightability of a compilation is originality. The White Pages of a telephone directory do not qualify for copyright protection because they simply list alphabetically names and telephone numbers. The Yellow Pages of a directory can be copyrightable, provided that the information is selected, coordinated, or arranged in an original way. Similarly, a court held that a compilation of information about yachts listed for sale may qualify for copyright protection.[26]

Copyright Infringement

Whenever the form or expression of an idea is copied, an infringement of copyright occurs. The reproduction does not have to be exactly the same as the original, nor does it have to reproduce the original in its entirety. If a substantial part of the original is reproduced, copyright infringement has occurred.

Remedies for Copyright Infringement   Those who infringe copyrights may be liable for damages or criminal penalties. These range from actual damages or statutory damages, imposed at the court's discretion, to criminal proceedings for willful violations. Actual damages are based on the harm caused to the copyright holder by the infringement, while statutory damages, not to exceed $150,000, are provided for under the Copyright Act. In addition, criminal proceedings may result in fines and/or imprisonment. In some instances, a court may grant an injunction against the infringer.

CASE EXAMPLE 5.13   Rusty Carroll operated an online term paper business, R2C2, Inc., that offered up to 300,000 research papers for sale on nine different Web sites. Individuals whose work was posted on these Web sites without their permission filed a lawsuit against Carroll for copyright infringement. A federal district court in Illinois ruled that an injunction was proper because the plaintiffs had shown that they had suffered irreparable harm and that monetary damages were inadequate to compensate them. Because Carroll had repeatedly failed to comply with court orders regarding discovery, the court found that the copyright infringement was likely to continue unless an injunction was issued. The court therefore issued a permanent injunction prohibiting Carroll and R2C2 from selling any term paper without sworn documentary evidence that the paper's author had given permission.[27] ●

The "Fair Use" Exception   An exception to liability for copyright infringement is made under the "fair use" doctrine. In certain circumstances, a person or organization can reproduce copyrighted material without paying royalties (fees paid to the copyright holder for the privilege of reproducing the copyrighted material). Section 107 of the Copyright Act provides as follows:

> [T]he fair use of a copyrighted work, including such use by reproduction in copies or phonorecords or by any other means specified by [Section 106 of the Copyright Act], for purposes such as criticism, comment, news reporting, teaching (including multiple copies for classroom use), scholarship, or research, is not an infringement of copyright. In determining whether the use

"Don't worry about people stealing an idea. If it's original and it's any good, you'll have to ram it down their throats."

Howard Aiken, 1900–1973
(Engineer and pioneer in computing)

---

26. *BUC International Corp. v. International Yacht Council, Ltd.*, 489 F.3d 1129 (11th Cir. 2007).
27. *Weidner v. Carroll*, No. 06-782-DRH, U.S. District Court for the Southern District of Illinois, January 21, 2010.

made of a work in any particular case is a fair use the factors to be considered shall include—

(1) the purpose and character of the use, including whether such use is of a commercial nature or is for nonprofit educational purposes;

(2) the nature of the copyrighted work;

(3) the amount and substantiality of the portion used in relation to the copyrighted work as a whole; and

(4) the effect of the use upon the potential market for or value of the copyrighted work.

What Is Fair Use?   Because these guidelines are very broad, the courts determine whether a particular use is fair on a case-by-case basis. Thus, anyone reproducing copyrighted material may be committing a violation. In determining whether a use is fair, courts have often considered the fourth factor to be the most important.

CASE EXAMPLE 5.14   The owner of copyrighted music, BMG Music Publishing, granted a license to Leadsinger, Inc., a manufacturer of karaoke devices. The license gave Leadsinger permission to reproduce the sound recordings, but not to reprint the song lyrics, which appeared at the bottom of a TV screen when the karaoke device was used. BMG demanded that Leadsinger pay a "lyric reprint" fee and a "synchronization" fee. Leadsinger refused to pay, claiming that its use of the lyrics was educational and thus did not constitute copyright infringement under the fair use exception. A federal appellate court disagreed. The court held that Leadsinger's display of the lyrics was not a fair use because it would have a negative effect on the value of the copyrighted work.[28] •

The First Sale Doctrine   Section 109(a) of the Copyright Act—also known as the first sale doctrine—provides that "the owner of a particular copy or phonorecord lawfully made under [the Copyright Act], or any person authorized by such owner, is entitled, without the authority of the copyright owner, to sell or otherwise dispose of the possession of that copy or phonorecord." In other words, once a copyright owner sells or gives away a particular copy of a work, the copyright owner no longer has the right to control the distribution of that copy. Thus, for example, a person who buys a copyrighted book can sell it to another person.

Until 2011, it was unclear whether the first sale doctrine applied to the promotional CDs that music companies often send to individuals in the music industry, such as music critics and radio programmers. **CASE EXAMPLE 5.15**   Universal Music Group (UMG) regularly ships promotional CDs to people in the music industry. The labels state that the CDs are "the property of the record company," "licensed to the intended recipient," and for "Promotional Use Only—Not for Sale." Troy Augusto obtained some of these promotional CDs from various sources and sold them through online auction sites. When UMG filed a copyright infringement lawsuit, Augusto argued that the music company had given up its right to control further distribution of the CDs under the first sale doctrine.

Ultimately, a federal appellate court held that UMG had conveyed title of the copyrighted promotional CDs to the recipients, rather than simply creating licenses. The court reasoned that the promotional CDs were dispatched to the recipients without any prior arrangement as to those particular copies. Furthermore, because the recipients had not agreed to a license, the written restriction placed on the CD labels was insufficient to create one. •

Copyright Protection for Software

In 1980, Congress passed the Computer Software Copyright Act, which amended the Copyright Act of 1976 to include computer programs in the list of creative works protected by federal copyright law.

---

28. *Leadsinger, Inc. v. BMG Music Publishing,* 512 F.3d 522 (9th Cir. 2008).

Generally, the courts have extended copyright protection not only to those parts of a computer program that can be read by humans, such as the high-level language of a source code, but also to the binary-language object code of a computer program, which is readable only by the computer. Additionally, such elements as the overall structure, sequence, and organization of a program have been deemed copyrightable. Not all aspects of software are protected, however. For the most part, though, courts have not extended copyright protection to the "look and feel"—the general appearance, command structure, video images, menus, windows, and other screen displays—of computer programs. (Note that copying the "look and feel" of another's product may be a violation of trade dress or trademark laws, as Apple, Inc., alleged in its iPhone lawsuit discussed on pages 143–144.)

Copyrights in Digital Information

Copyright law is probably the most important form of intellectual property protection on the Internet, largely because much of the material on the Web (software, for example) is copyrighted and, in order to be transferred online, it must be "copied." Technology has vastly increased the potential for copyright infringement. Generally, anytime a party downloads software or music into a device's random access memory, or RAM, without authorization, a copyright is infringed.

CASE EXAMPLE 5.16 In one case, a rap song that was included in the sound track of a movie had used only a few seconds from the guitar solo of another's copyrighted sound recording without permission. Nevertheless, a federal appellate court held that digitally sampling a copyrighted sound recording of any length constitutes copyright infringement.[29] ●

In 1998, Congress passed additional legislation to protect copyright holders—the Digital Millennium Copyright Act (DMCA). Because of its significance in protecting against the piracy of copyrighted materials in the online environment, this act is presented as this chapter's *Landmark in the Law* feature on the facing page. Despite the DMCA and other efforts to combat online piracy, it has continued unabated and even grown, as downloading e-books and movies has become more popular.

MP3 and File-Sharing Technology

Soon after the Internet became popular, a few enterprising programmers created software to compress large data files, particularly those associated with music, so that they could be more easily transmitted online. The best-known compression and decompression system is MP3, which enables music fans to download songs or entire CDs onto their computers or onto a portable listening device, such as an iPod. The MP3 system also made it possible for music fans to access other fans' files by engaging in file-sharing via the Internet.

Peer-to-Peer (P2P) Networking The sharing of resources (such as files, hard drives, and processing styles) among multiple computers.

Distributed Network A network used by persons located (distributed) in different places to share computer files.

File-Sharing File-sharing is accomplished through **peer-to-peer (P2P) networking.** The concept is simple. Rather than going through a central Web server, P2P involves numerous personal computers (PCs) that are connected to the Internet. Individuals on the same network can access files stored on a single PC through a **distributed network,** which has parts dispersed in many locations. Persons scattered throughout the country or the world can work together on the same project by using file-sharing programs. A popular method of sharing very large files over the Internet uses torrenting programs such as the technology first developed by BitTorrent.

---

29. *Bridgeport Music, Inc. v. Dimension Films*, 410 F.3d 792 (6th Cir. 2005).

LANDMARK IN THE LAW
The Digital Millennium Copyright Act of 1998

The United States leads the world in the production of creative products, including books, films, videos, recordings, and software. Exports of U.S. creative products surpass those of every other U.S. industry in value.

Given the importance of intellectual property to the U.S. economy, the United States has actively supported international efforts to protect ownership rights in intellectual property, including copyrights. In 1996, to curb unauthorized copying of copyrighted materials, the member nations of the World Intellectual Property Organization (WIPO) adopted a treaty to upgrade global standards of copyright protection, particularly for the Internet.

Implementing the WIPO Treaty Congress implemented the provisions of the WIPO treaty by enacting a new statute to update U.S. copyright law. The law—the Digital Millennium Copyright Act of 1998 (DCMA)—is a landmark step in the protection of copyright owners and, because of the leading position of the United States in the creative industries, serves as a model for other nations. Among other things, the DCMA established civil and criminal penalties for anyone who circumvents (bypasses) encryption software or other technological antipiracy protection. Also prohibited are the manufacture, import, sale, and distribution of devices or services for circumvention.

The act provides for exceptions to fit the needs of libraries, scientists, universities, and others. In general, the law does not restrict the "fair use" of circumvention methods for educational and other noncommercial purposes. For example, circumvention is allowed to test computer security, conduct encryption research, protect personal privacy, and enable parents to monitor their children's use of the Internet. The exceptions are to be reconsidered every three years.

Limiting the Liability of Internet Service Providers The DCMA also limited the liability of Internet service providers (ISPs). Under the act, an ISP is not liable for any copyright infringement by its customer *unless* the ISP is aware of the subscriber's violation. An ISP may be held liable only if it fails to take action to shut the subscriber down after learning of the violation. A copyright holder has to act promptly, however, by pursuing a claim in court, or the subscriber has the right to be restored to online access.

Application to Today's World *Without the DCMA, copyright owners would have a more difficult time obtaining legal redress against those who, without authorization, decrypt and/or copy copyrighted materials. Nevertheless, problems remain, particularly because of the global nature of the Internet.*

Cloud Computing A Web-based service that extends a computer's software or storage capabilities by allowing users to remotely access excess storage and computing capacity as needed.

A newer method of sharing files via the Internet is **cloud computing,** which is essentially a subscription-based or pay-per-use service that extends a computer's software or storage capabilities. Cloud computing can deliver a single application through a browser to multiple users, or it may be a utility program to pool resources and provide data storage and virtual servers that can be accessed on demand. Amazon, Apple, Facebook, Google, IBM, and Sun Microsystems are using and developing additional cloud computing services.

Sharing Stored Music Files When file-sharing is used to download others' stored music files, copyright issues arise. Recording artists and their labels are losing large amounts of royalties and revenues because few CDs are purchased and then made available on distributed networks, from which everyone can download them for free. **CASE EXAMPLE 5.17** The issue of file-sharing infringement has been the subject of an ongoing debate since highly publicized cases against two companies (Napster, Inc. and Grokster, Ltd.) that created software used for copyright infringement. In the first case, Napster operated a Web site with free software that enabled users to copy and transfer MP3 files via the Internet. Firms in the recording industry sued Napster. Ultimately, the court held that Napster was liable for contributory and vicarious[30] (indirect) copyright infringement. As technology evolved, Grokster, Ltd., and several other companies created and distributed new types of file-sharing software that did not maintain a central index of content, but allowed P2P network users to share stored music files. The court held that because the companies distributed file-sharing software "with the object of promoting its use to infringe the copyright," they were liable for the resulting acts of infringement by third-party users.[31] ●

Trade Secrets

The law of trade secrets protects some business processes and information that are not or cannot be protected under patent, copyright, or trademark law against appropriation by a competitor. A **trade secret** is basically information of commercial value. Trade secrets may include customer lists, plans, research and development, pricing information, marketing techniques, and production methods—anything that makes an individual company unique and that would have value to a competitor.

Unlike copyright and trademark protection, protection of trade secrets extends both to ideas and to their expression. (For this reason, and because there are no registration or filing requirements for trade secrets, trade secret protection may be well suited for software.) Of course, the secret formula, method, or other information must be disclosed to some persons, particularly to key employees. Businesses generally attempt to protect their trade secrets by having all employees who use the process or information agree in their contracts, or in confidentiality agreements, never to divulge it.[32]

State and Federal Law on Trade Secrets

Under Section 757 of the *Restatement of Torts,* those who disclose or use another's trade secret, without authorization, are liable to that other party if (1) they discovered the secret by improper means or (2) their disclosure or use constitutes a breach of a duty owed to the other party. The theft of confidential business data by industrial espionage, as when a business taps into a competitor's computer, is a theft of trade secrets without any contractual violation and is actionable in itself.

Although trade secrets have long been protected under the common law, today most states' laws are based on the Uniform Trade Secrets Act, which has been adopted in forty-seven states. Additionally, in 1996 Congress passed the Economic Espionage Act, which made the theft of trade secrets a federal crime. We will examine the provisions and significance of this act in Chapter 6, in the context of crimes related to business.

Trade Secrets in Cyberspace

Today's computer technology undercuts a business firm's ability to protect its confidential information, including trade secrets. For instance, a dishonest employee could e-mail trade secrets in a company's computer to a competitor or a future employer. If e-mail is not an option, the employee might walk out with the information on a flash pen drive.

---

30. *Vicarious (indirect) liability* exists when one person is subject to liability for another's actions. A common example occurs in the employment context, when an employer is held vicariously liable by third parties for torts committed by employees in the course of their employment.

31. *A&M Records, Inc. v. Napster, Inc.,* 239 F.3d 1004 (9th Cir. 2001); and *Metro-Goldwyn-Mayer Studios, Inc. v. Grokster, Ltd.,* 545 U.S. 913, 125 S.Ct. 2764, 162 L.Ed.2d 781 (2005). Grokster, Ltd., later settled this dispute out of court and stopped distributing its software.

32. See, for example, *Verigy US, Inc. v. Mayder,* 2008 WL 5063873 (N.D.Cal. 2008); and *Gleeson v. Preferred Sourcing, LLC,* 883 N.E.2d 164 (Ind.App. 2008).

A former employee's continued use of a Twitter account after leaving the company may be the grounds for a suit alleging misappropriation of trade secrets. **CASE EXAMPLE 5.18** Noah Kravitz worked for a company called PhoneDog for four years as a product reviewer and video blogger. PhoneDog provided him with the Twitter account "@PhoneDog_Noah." Kravitz's popularity grew, and he had approximately 17,000 followers by the time he quit in 2010. PhoneDog requested that Kravitz stop using the Twitter account. Although Kravitz changed his handle to "@noahkravitz," he continued to use the account. PhoneDog subsequently sued Kravitz for misappropriation of trade secrets, among other things. Kravitz moved for a dismissal, but the court found that the complaint adequately stated a cause of action for misappropriation of trade secrets and allowed the suit to continue.[33] ●

For a summary of trade secrets and other forms of intellectual property, see Exhibit 5.1 below.

International Protection for Intellectual Property

For many years, the United States has been a party to various international agreements relating to intellectual property rights. For example, the Paris Convention of 1883, to which about 173 countries are signatory, allows parties in one country to file for patent and trademark protection in any of the other member countries. Other international agreements

---

33. *PhoneDog v. Kravitz,* 2011 WL 5415612 (N.D.Cal. 2011).

Exhibit 5.1 Forms of Intellectual Property

	DEFINITION	HOW ACQUIRED	DURATION	REMEDY FOR INFRINGEMENT
Patent	A grant from the government that gives an inventor exclusive rights to an invention.	By filing a patent application with the U.S. Patent and Trademark Office and receiving its approval.	Twenty years from the date of the application; for design patents, fourteen years.	Monetary damages, including royalties and lost profits, *plus* attorneys' fees. Damages may be tripled for intentional infringements.
Copyright	The right of an author or originator of a literary or artistic work, or other production that falls within a specified category, to have the exclusive use of that work for a given period of time.	Automatic (once the work or creation is put in tangible form). Only the *expression* of an idea (and not the idea itself) can be protected by copyright.	For authors: the life of the author, plus 70 years. For publishers: 95 years after the date of publication or 120 years after creation.	Actual damages plus profits received by the party who infringed *or* statutory damages under the Copyright Act, *plus* costs and attorneys' fees in either situation.
Trademark (service mark and trade dress)	Any distinctive word, name, symbol, or device (image or appearance), or combination thereof, that an entity uses to distinguish its goods or services from those of others. The owner has the exclusive right to use that mark or trade dress.	1. At common law, ownership created by use of the mark. 2. Registration with the appropriate federal or state office gives notice and is permitted if the mark is currently in use or will be within the next six months.	Unlimited, as long as it is in use. To continue notice by registration, the owner must renew by filing between the fifth and sixth years, and thereafter, every ten years.	1. Injunction prohibiting the future use of the mark. 2. Actual damages plus profits received by the party who infringed (can be increased under the Lanham Act). 3. Destruction of articles that infringed. 4. *Plus* costs and attorneys' fees.
Trade Secret	Any information that a business possesses and that gives the business an advantage over competitors (including formulas, lists, patterns, plans, processes, and programs).	Through the originality and development of the information and processes that constitute the business secret and are unknown to others.	Unlimited, so long as not revealed to others. Once revealed to others, it is no longer a trade secret.	Monetary damages for misappropriation (the Uniform Trade Secrets Act also permits punitive damages if willful), *plus* costs and attorneys' fees.

include the Berne Convention, the Trade-Related Aspects of Intellectual Property Rights (known as the TRIPS agreement), and the Madrid Protocol.

To learn about a new international treaty that will affect international property rights, see this chapter's *Beyond Our Borders* feature on the facing page.

The Berne Convention

Under the Berne Convention of 1886, an international copyright agreement, if a U.S. citizen writes a book, every country that has signed the convention must recognize her or his copyright in the book. Also, if a citizen of a country that has not signed the convention first publishes a book in one of the 163 countries that have signed, all other countries that have signed the convention must recognize that author's copyright. Copyright notice is not needed to gain protection under the Berne Convention for works published after March 1, 1989.

This convention and other international agreements have given some protection to intellectual property on a worldwide level. None of them, however, has been as significant and far reaching in scope as the TRIPS agreement, discussed in the next subsection.

In 2011, the European Union agreed to extend the period of royalty protection for musicians from fifty years to seventy years. This decision aids major record labels as well as performers and musicians who previously faced losing royalties from sales of their older recordings. The profits of musicians and record companies have been shrinking in recent years because of the sharp decline in sales of compact discs and the rise in digital downloads (both legal and illegal).

In the following case, the United States Supreme Court had to decide if Congress had exceeded its authority under the U.S. Constitution when it enacted a law that restored copyright protection to many foreign works that were already in the public domain.

Case 5.3

Golan v. Holder

Supreme Court of the United States,
___ U.S. ___, 132 S.Ct. 873, 181 L.Ed.2d 835 (2012).
www.supremecourt.gov/opinions/11pdf/10-545.pdf

(Criben/Shutterstock.com)

Why do U.S. entertainers now have to pay royalties on older European compositions?

FACTS The United States joined the Berne Convention in 1989, but it failed to give foreign copyright holders the same protections enjoyed by U.S. authors. Contrary to the Berne Convention, the United States did not protect any foreign work that had already entered the public domain. In 1994, Congress enacted the Uruguay Round Agreements Act (URAA), which "restored" copyright protection for many foreign works that were already in the public domain. The URAA put foreign and domestic works on the same footing, allowing their copyrights to extend for the same terms.

Lawrence Golan, along with a group of musicians, conductors, and publishers, filed a suit against Eric Holder, in his capacity as the U.S. Attorney General, challenging the URAA and claiming that it violated the copyright clause of the U.S. Constitution. These individuals had enjoyed free access to foreign works in the public domain before the URAA's enactment and argued that Congress had exceeded its constitutional authority in passing the URAA. A federal appellate court held that Congress did not violate the copyright clause by passing the URAA. The petitioners appealed. The United States Supreme Court granted *certiorari* to resolve the matter.

ISSUE Does the URAA violate the copyright clause in the U.S. Constitution by restoring copyright protection for foreign works in the public domain?

DECISION No. The United States Supreme Court affirmed the judgment of the federal appellate court. Thus, Golan and the others could no longer use, without permission, any of the previous public domain foreign works, which are indeed protected by the URAA. By passing the URAA in the United States, Congress, in effect, took the foreign works that Golan and others had been using out of the public domain. Henceforth, U.S. copyright and patent laws cover all such foreign intellectual property.

REASON The copyright clause empowers Congress "to promote the Progress of Science . . . by securing for limited Times to Authors . . . the exclusive Right to their Writings." The Court concluded that Congress is not barred from protecting works in the public domain simply because a copyright must exist for only a "limited time." The Court relied heavily on the precedent set by its decision in an earlier case in which it held that Congress did

Case 5.3—Continued

not violate the copyright clause by extending existing copyrights by twenty years.[a] In that case, the Court declined to interpret the text of the copyright clause as requiring that a "time prescription, once set, becomes forever 'fixed' or 'inalterable.'" In passing the URAA, Congress did not create perpetual copyrights. Therefore, the URAA does not violate the copyright clause.

CRITICAL THINKING—Global Consideration *What does the Court's decision in this case mean for copyright holders in the United States who want copyright protection in other countries? Will other nations be more or less inclined to protect U.S. authors? Explain.*

a. See *Eldred v. Ashcroft,* 537 U.S. 186, 123 S.Ct. 769, 154 L.Ed.2d 683 (2003).

The TRIPS Agreement

Representatives from more than one hundred nations signed the TRIPS agreement in 1994. The agreement established, for the first time, standards for the international protection of intellectual property rights, including patents, trademarks, and copyrights for movies, computer programs, books, and music. The TRIPS agreement provides that each member country must include in its domestic laws broad intellectual property rights and effective remedies (including civil and criminal penalties) for violations of those rights.

Generally, the TRIPS agreement forbids member nations from discriminating against foreign owners of intellectual property rights (in the administration, regulation, or adjudication of such rights). In other words, a member nation cannot give its own nationals (citizens) favorable treatment without offering the same treatment to nationals of all member countries. **EXAMPLE 5.19** A U.S. software manufacturer brings a suit for the infringement of intellectual property rights under Germany's national laws. Because Germany is a member of the TRIPS agreement, the U.S. manufacturer is entitled to receive the same treatment as a German manufacturer. • Each member nation must also ensure that legal procedures

BEYOND OUR BORDERS   The Anti-Counterfeiting Trade Agreement

After several years of negotiations, in 2011 Australia, Canada, Japan, Korea, Morocco, New Zealand, Singapore, and the United States signed a new international treaty to combat global counterfeiting and piracy. The European Union, Mexico, Switzerland, and other nations that support the treaty are still developing domestic procedures to comply with its provisions. Once a nation has adopted appropriate procedures, it can ratify the treaty.

Provisions and Goals

The treaty, called the Anti-Counterfeiting Trade Agreement (ACTA), will have its own governing body. The goal of ACTA is to increase international cooperation, facilitate the best law enforcement practices,

and provide a legal framework to combat counterfeiting.

The treaty applies not only to counterfeit physical goods, such as medications, but also to pirated copyrighted works being distributed via the Internet. The idea is to create a new standard of enforcement for intellectual property rights that goes beyond the TRIPS agreement and encourages international cooperation and information sharing among signatory countries.

Border Searches

Under ACTA, member nations are required to establish border measures that allow officials, on their own initiative, to search commercial shipments of imports and exports for counterfeit goods. The treaty

neither requires nor prohibits random border searches of electronic devices, such as laptops and iPads, for infringing content. If border authorities reasonably believe that any goods in transit are counterfeit, the treaty allows them to keep the suspect goods unless the owner proves that the items are authentic and noninfringing.

The treaty allows member nations, in accordance with their own laws, to order online service providers to furnish information about (including the identity of) suspected trademark and copyright infringers.

Critical Thinking

Why will product counterfeiting always exist?

are available for parties who wish to bring actions for infringement of intellectual property rights. Additionally, a related document established a mechanism for settling disputes among member nations.

The Madrid Protocol

In the past, one of the difficulties in protecting U.S. trademarks internationally was that it was time consuming and expensive to apply for trademark registration in foreign countries. The filing fees and procedures for trademark registration vary significantly among individual countries. The Madrid Protocol, however, which was signed into law in 2003, may help to resolve these problems. The Madrid Protocol is an international treaty that has been signed by seventy-three countries. Under its provisions, a U.S. company wishing to register its trademark abroad can submit a single application and designate other member countries in which it would like to register the mark. The treaty was designed to reduce the costs of obtaining international trademark protection by more than 60 percent.

Although the Madrid Protocol may simplify and reduce the cost of trademark registration in foreign nations, it remains to be seen whether it will provide significant benefits to trademark owners. Even with an easier registration process, the question of whether member countries will enforce the law and protect the mark still remains.

Reviewing . . . Intellectual Property and Internet Law

Two computer science majors, Trent and Xavier, have an idea for a new video game, which they propose to call "Hallowed." They form a business and begin developing their idea. Several months later, Trent and Xavier run into a problem with their design and consult with a friend, Brad, who is an expert in creating computer source codes. After the software is completed but before Hallowed is marketed, a video game called Halo 2 is released for both the Xbox and Playstation 3 systems. Halo 2 uses source codes similar to those of Hallowed and imitates Hallowed's overall look and feel, although not all the features are alike. Using the information presented in the chapter, answer the following questions.

1. Would the name *Hallowed* receive protection as a trademark or as trade dress?
2. If Trent and Xavier had obtained a business process patent on Hallowed, would the release of Halo 2 infringe on their patent? Why or why not?
3. Based only on the facts presented above, could Trent and Xavier sue the makers of Halo 2 for copyright infringement? Why or why not?
4. Suppose that Trent and Xavier discover that Brad took the idea of Hallowed and sold it to the company that produced Halo 2. Which type of intellectual property issue does this raise?

DEBATE THIS Congress has amended the Copyright Act several times. Copyright holders now have protection for many decades. Was Congress justified in extending the copyright time periods? Why or why not?

LINKING BUSINESS LAW to Marketing

Trademarks and Service Marks

In your marketing courses, you have learned or will learn about the importance of trademarks. If you become a marketing manager, you will be involved in creating trademarks or service marks for your firm, protecting the firm's existing marks, and ensuring that you do not infringe on anyone else's marks.

The Broad Range of Trademarks and Service Marks

The courts have held that trademarks and service marks consist of much more than well-known brand names, such as Apple or Amazon. As a marketing manager, you will need to be aware that parts of a brand or other product identification often qualify for trademark protection.

- **Catchy Phrases**—Certain brands have established phrases that are associated with them, such as Nike's "Just Do It!" As a marketing manager for a competing product, you will have to avoid such catchy phrases in your own marketing program. Note, though, that not all phrases can become part of a trademark or service mark. When a phrase is extremely common, the courts normally will not grant trademark or service mark protection to it.

- **Abbreviations**—The public sometimes abbreviates a well-known trademark. For example Budweiser beer is known as Bud and Coca-Cola as Coke. As a marketing manager, you should avoid using any name for a product or service that closely resembles a well-known abbreviation, such as Koke for a cola drink.

- **Shapes**—The shape of a brand name, a service mark, or a container can take on exclusivity if the shape clearly aids in product or service identification. For example, just about everyone throughout the world recognizes the shape of a Coca-Cola bottle. As a marketing manager, you would do well to avoid using a similar shape for a new carbonated drink.

- **Ornamental Colors**—Sometimes color combinations can become part of a service mark or trademark. For example,

FedEx established its unique identity with the use of bright orange and purple. The courts have protected this color combination. The same holds for the black-and-copper color combination of Duracell batteries.

- **Ornamental Designs**—Symbols and designs associated with a particular mark are normally protected. Marketing managers should not attempt to copy them. Levi's places a small tag on the left side of the rear pocket of its jeans. Cross uses a cutoff black cone on the top of its pens.

- **Sounds**—Sounds can also be protected. For example, the familiar roar of the Metro-Goldwyn-Mayer (MGM) lion is protected.

When to Protect Your Trademarks and Service Marks

Every business should register its logo as a trademark, and perhaps also its business name and Web site address, to provide the company with the highest level of protection. A trademark will discourage counterfeiting and will give your firm the advantage in the event of future infringement.

Once your company has established a trademark or a service mark, as a manager, you will have to decide how aggressively you wish to protect those marks. If you fail to protect them, your company faces the possibility that they will become generic. Remember that *aspirin, cellophane, thermos, dry ice, shredded wheat,* and many other familiar terms were once legally protected trademarks. Protecting exclusive rights to a mark can be expensive, however, so you will have to determine how much it is worth to your company to protect your rights. If you work in a small company, making major expenditures to protect your trademarks and service marks might not be cost-effective.

Critical Thinking

The U.S. Patent and Trademark Office requires that a registered trademark or service mark be put into commercial use within three years after the application has been approved. Why do you think the federal government established this requirement?

Key Terms

Chapter Summary: Intellectual Property and Internet Law

Trademarks and Related Property (See pages 131–139.)	1. A *trademark* is a distinctive word, symbol, or design that identifies the manufacturer as the source of the goods and distinguishes its products from those made or sold by others. 2. The major federal statutes protecting trademarks and related property are the Lanham Act of 1946 and the Federal Trademark Dilution Act of 1995. Generally, to be protected, a trademark must be sufficiently distinctive from all competing trademarks. 3. *Trademark infringement* occurs when one uses a mark that is the same as, or confusingly similar to, the protected trademark, service mark, trade name, or trade dress of another without permission when marketing goods or services.
Cyber Marks (See pages 139–141.)	A *cyber mark* is a trademark in cyberspace. Trademark infringement in cyberspace occurs when one person uses, in a domain name or in meta tags, a name that is the same as, or confusingly similar to, the protected mark of another.
Patents (See pages 142–144.)	1. A *patent* is a grant from the government that gives an inventor the exclusive right to make, use, and sell an invention for a period of twenty years (fourteen years for a design patent) from the date when the application for a patent is filed. To be patentable, an invention (or a discovery, process, or design) must be genuine, novel, useful, and not obvious in light of current technology. Computer software may be patented. 2. Almost anything is patentable, except the laws of nature, natural phenomena, and abstract ideas (including algorithms). Even business processes or methods are patentable if they relate to a machine or transformation. 3. *Patent infringement* occurs when one uses or sells another's patented design, product, or process without the patent owner's permission. The patent holder can sue the infringer in federal court and request an injunction, but must prove irreparable injury to obtain a permanent injunction against the infringer. The patent holder can also request damages and attorneys' fees. If the infringement was willful, the court can grant treble damages.
Copyrights (See pages 144–150.)	1. A *copyright* is an intangible property right granted by federal statute to the author or originator of certain literary or artistic productions. The Copyright Act of 1976, as amended, governs copyrights. Computer software may be copyrighted. 2. *Copyright infringement* occurs whenever the form or expression of an idea is copied without the permission of the copyright holder. An exception applies if the copying is deemed a "fair use." 3. To protect copyrights in digital information, Congress passed the Digital Millennium Copyright Act of 1998. 4. Technology that allows users to share files via the Internet on distributed networks often raises copyright infringement issues. 5. The courts have ruled that companies that provide file-sharing software to users can be held liable for contributory and vicarious copyright liability.
Trade Secrets (See pages 150–151.)	*Trade secrets* include customer lists, plans, research and development, and pricing information. Trade secrets are protected under the common law and, in some states, under statutory law against misappropriation by competitors. The Economic Espionage Act of 1996 made the theft of trade secrets a federal crime (see Chapter 6).
International Protection for Intellectual Property (See pages 151–154.)	Various international agreements provide international protection for intellectual property. A landmark agreement is the 1994 agreement on Trade-Related Aspects of Intellectual Property Rights (TRIPS), which provides for enforcement procedures in all countries signatory to the agreement.

ExamPrep

ISSUE SPOTTERS

1. Global Products develops, patents, and markets software. World Copies, Inc., sells Global's software without the maker's permission. Is this patent infringement? If so, how might Global save the cost of suing World for infringement and at the same time profit from World's sales? **(See pages 139 and 143.)**
2. Eagle Corporation began marketing software in 2001 under the mark "Eagle." In 2012, Eagle.com, Inc., a different company selling different products, begins to use *eagle* as part of its URL and registers it as a domain name. Can Eagle Corporation stop this use of *eagle*? If so, what must the company show? **(See page 141.)**

—Check your answers to the Issue Spotters against the answers provided in Appendix E at the end of this text.

For Review

Answers to the even-numbered questions in this For Review section can be found in Appendix F at the end of this text.

1. What is intellectual property?
2. Why is the protection of trademarks important?
3. How does the law protect patents?
4. What laws protect authors' rights in the works they create?
5. What are trade secrets, and what laws offer protection for this form of intellectual property?

Business Scenarios and Case Problems

5–1 Patent Infringement. John and Andrew Doney invented a hard-bearing device for balancing rotors. Although they obtained a patent for their invention from the U.S. Patent and Trademark Office, it was never used as an automobile wheel balancer. Some time later, Exetron Corp. produced an automobile wheel balancer that used a hard-bearing device with a support plate similar to that of the Doneys' device. Given that the Doneys had not used their device for automobile wheel balancing, does Exetron's use of a similar device infringe on the Doneys' patent? **(See page 143.)**

5–2 Question with Sample Answer—Copyright Infringement. In which of the following situations would a court likely hold Maruta liable for copyright infringement? Why? **(See pages 146–147.)**

1. At the library, Maruta photocopies ten pages from a scholarly journal relating to a topic on which she is writing a term paper.
2. Maruta makes leather handbags and sells them in her small shop. She advertises her handbags as "Vutton handbags," hoping that customers will mistakenly assume that they were made by Vuitton, the well-known maker of high-quality luggage and handbags.
3. Maruta teaches Latin American history at a small university. She has a digital video recorder and frequently records television programs relating to Latin America and puts them on DVDs. She then takes the DVDs to her classroom so that her students can watch them.

—For a sample answer to Question 5–2, go to Appendix G at the end of this text.

5–3 Trade Secrets. Briefing.com offers Internet-based analyses of investment opportunities to investors. Richard Green is the company's president. One of Briefing.com's competitors is StreetAccount, LLC (limited liability company), whose owners include Gregory Jones and Cynthia Dietzmann. Jones worked for Briefing.com for six years until he quit in March 2003, and he was a member of its board of directors until April 2003. Dietzmann worked for Briefing.com for seven years until she quit in March 2003. As Briefing.com employees, Jones and Dietzmann had access to confidential business data. For instance, Dietzmann developed a list of contacts through which Briefing.com obtained market information to display online. When Dietzmann quit, however, she did not return all of the contact information to the company. Briefing.com and Green filed a suit in a federal district court against Jones, Dietzmann, and StreetAccount, alleging that they appropriated these data and other "trade secrets" to form a competing business. What are trade secrets? Why are they protected? Under what circumstances is a party liable at common law for their appropriation? How should these principles apply in this case? [*Briefing.com v. Jones*, 2006 WY 16, 126 P.3d 928 (2006)] **(See pages 150–151.)**

5–4 Licensing. Redwin Wilchcombe composed, performed, and recorded a song called *Tha Weedman* at the request of Lil Jon, a member of Lil Jon & the East Side Boyz (LJESB), for LJESB's album *Kings of Crunk*. Wilchcombe was not paid, but was given credit on the album as a producer. After the album had sold two million copies, Wilchcombe filed a suit against LJESB, alleging copyright infringement. The defendants claimed that they had a license to use the song. Do the facts support this claim? Explain. [*Wilchcombe v. TeeVee Toons, Inc.*, 555 F.3d 949 (11th Cir. 2009)] **(See page 138.)**

5–5 Case Problem with Sample Answer—Trade Secrets. Jesse Edwards, an employee of Carbon Processing and Reclamation, LLC (CPR), put unmarked boxes of company records in his car. Edwards's wife, Channon, who suspected him of hiding financial information from her, gained access to the documents. William Jones, the owner of CPR, filed a suit, contending that Channon's unauthorized access to the files was a theft of trade secrets. Could the information in the documents be trade secrets? Should liability be imposed?

Why or why not? [*Jones v. Hamilton*, 59 So.3d 134 (Ala.Civ. App. 2010)] **(See page 150.)**

—For a sample answer to Problem 5–5, go to Appendix H at the end of this text.

5–6 Spotlight on Macy's—Copyright Infringement. United Fabrics International, Inc., bought a fabric design from an Italian designer and registered a copyright to it with the U.S. Copyright Office. When Macy's, Inc., began selling garments with a similar design, United filed a copyright infringement suit against Macy's. Macy's argued that United did not own a valid copyright to the design and so could not claim infringement. Does United have to prove that the copyright is valid to establish infringement? Explain. [*United Fabrics International, Inc. v. C & J Wear, Inc.*, 630 F.3d 1255 (9th Cir. 2011)] **(See page 146.)**

5–7 Theft of Trade Secrets. Hanjuan Jin, a citizen of the People's Republic of China, began working at Motorola in 1998. He worked as a software engineer in a division that created proprietary standards for cellular communications. In 2004 and 2005, in contradiction to Motorola's policies, Jin also began working as a consultant for Lemko Corp. Lemko introduced Jin to Sun Kaisens, a Chinese software company. During 2005, Jin returned to Beijing on several occasions and began working with Sun Kaisens and with the Chinese military. The following year, she started corresponding with Sun Kaisens's management about a possible full-time job in China. During this period, she took several medical leaves of absence from Motorola. In

February 2007, after one of these medical leaves, she returned to Motorola. During the next several days at Motorola, she accessed and downloaded thousands of documents on her personal laptop as well as on pen drives. On the following day, she attempted to board a flight to China but was randomly searched by U.S. Customs and Border Protection officials at Chicago's O'Hare International Airport. Ultimately, U.S. officials discovered the thousands of downloaded Motorola documents. Are there any circumstances under which Jin could avoid being prosecuted for theft of trade secrets? If so, what are these circumstances? Discuss fully. [*United States v. Hanjuan Jin*, 833 F.Supp.2d 977 (N.D.Ill. 2012)] **(See pages 150–151.)**

5–8 A Question of Ethics—Copyright Infringement. Custom Copies, Inc., prepares and sells coursepacks, which contain compilations of readings for college courses. A teacher selects the readings and delivers a syllabus to the copy shop, which obtains the materials from a library, copies them, and binds the copies. Blackwell Publishing, Inc., which owns the copyright to some of the materials, filed a suit, alleging copyright infringement. [*Blackwell Publishing, Inc. v. Custom Copies, Inc.*, 2006 WL 152950 (N.D.Fla. 2006)] **(See pages 146–147.)**

1. Custom Copies argued, in part, that it did not "distribute" the coursepacks. Does a copy shop violate copyright law if it only copies materials for coursepacks? Does the fair use doctrine apply in these circumstances? Discuss.

2. What is the potential impact if copies of a book or journal are created and sold without the permission of, and the payment of royalties or a fee to, the copyright owner? Explain.

Critical Thinking and Writing Assignments

5–9 Business Law Writing. Sync Computers, Inc., makes computer-related products under the brand name "Sync," which the company registers as a trademark. Without Sync's permission, E-Product Corp. embeds the Sync mark in E-Product's Web site, in black type on a blue background. This tag causes the E-Product site to be returned at the top of the list of results on a search engine query for "Sync." Write three paragraphs explaining why E-Product's use of the Sync mark as a meta tag without Sync's permission constitutes trademark infringement. **(See pages 140–141.)**

5–10 Business Law Critical Thinking Group Assignment. After years of research, your company develops a product that might revolutionize the green (environmentally conscious) building industry. The product is made from relatively inex-

pensive and widely available materials combined in a unique way that can substantially lower the heating and cooling costs of residential and commercial buildings. The company has registered the trademark it intends to use on the product, and has filed a patent application with the U.S. Patent and Trademark Office.

1. One group should provide three reasons why this product does or does not qualify for patent protection.

2. Another group should develop a four-step procedure for how your company can best protect its intellectual property rights (trademark, trade secret, and patent) and prevent domestic and foreign competitors from producing counterfeit goods or cheap knockoffs.

3. Another group should list and explain three ways your company can utilize licensing.

CHAPTER 6

Criminal Law and Cyber Crime

(AlexKosev/iStockphoto.com)

CHAPTER OUTLINE

- Civil Law and Criminal Law
- Criminal Liability
- Types of Crimes
- Defenses to Criminal Liability
- Constitutional Safeguards and Criminal Procedures
- Criminal Process
- Cyber Crime

LEARNING OBJECTIVES

The five learning objectives below are designed to help improve your understanding of the chapter. After reading this chapter, you should be able to answer the following questions:

1 What two elements normally must exist before a person can be held liable for a crime?

2 What are five broad categories of crimes? What is white-collar crime?

3 What defenses can be raised to avoid liability for criminal acts?

4 What constitutional safeguards exist to protect persons accused of crimes?

5 How has the Internet expanded opportunities for identity theft?

> "The crime problem is getting really serious.
> The other day, the Statue of Liberty had both hands up."
> —Jay Leno, 1950–present (American comedian and television host)

Criminal law is an important part of the legal environment of business. Various sanctions are used to bring about a society in which businesses can compete and flourish. These sanctions include damages for various types of tortious conduct (see Chapter 4), damages for breach of contract (see Chapter 9), and various equitable remedies (see Chapter 1). Additional sanctions are imposed under criminal law. Many statutes regulating business provide for criminal as well as civil sanctions.

In this chapter, after a brief summary of the major differences between criminal and civil law, we look at the elements that must be present for criminal liability to exist. We then examine various categories of crimes, the defenses that can be raised to avoid liability for criminal actions, and the rules of criminal procedure. Advances in technology allow authorities to trace phone calls and track vehicle movements with greater ease and precision. One such technique is attaching tracking devices to a suspect's vehicle. Is such an action a violation of the constitutional rights of those suspects who are being tracked? You will discover what the courts have to say on this question later in this chapter.

Civil Law and Criminal Law

Remember from Chapter 1 that *civil law* spells out the duties that exist between persons or between persons and their governments, excluding the duty not to commit crimes. Contract law, for example, is part of civil law. The whole body of tort law, which deals with the infringement by one person on the legally recognized rights of another, is also an area of civil law.

Criminal law, in contrast, has to do with crime. A **crime** can be defined as a wrong against society proclaimed in a statute and, if committed, punishable by society through fines and/or imprisonment—and, in some cases, death. As mentioned in Chapter 1, because crimes are *offenses against society as a whole*, criminals are prosecuted by a public official, such as a district attorney (D.A.), rather than by the crime victims. Victims often report the crime to the police, but ultimately it is the D.A.'s office that decides whether to file criminal charges and to what extent to pursue the prosecution or carry out additional investigation.

Key Differences between Civil Law and Criminal Law

Because the state has extensive resources at its disposal when prosecuting criminal cases, and because the sanctions can be so severe, there are numerous procedural safeguards to protect the rights of defendants. We look here at one of these safeguards—the higher burden of proof that applies in a criminal case—and at the sanctions imposed for criminal acts. Exhibit 6.1 below summarizes these and other key differences between civil law and criminal law.

Burden of Proof   In a civil case, the plaintiff usually must prove his or her case by a *preponderance of the evidence*. Under this standard, the plaintiff must convince the court that, based on the evidence presented by both parties, it is more likely than not that the plaintiff's allegation is true.

In a criminal case, in contrast, the state must prove its case **beyond a reasonable doubt.** If the jury views the evidence in the case as reasonably permitting either a guilty or a not guilty verdict, then the jury's verdict must be *not* guilty. In other words, the government (prosecutor) must prove beyond a reasonable doubt that the defendant has committed every essential element of the offense with which she or he is charged. If the jurors are not convinced of the defendant's guilt beyond a reasonable doubt, they must find the defendant not guilty.

Note also that in a criminal case, the jury's verdict normally must be unanimous—agreed to by all members of the jury—to convict the defendant.[1] (In a civil trial by jury, in contrast, typically only three-fourths of the jurors need to agree.)

---

1. Note that there are exceptions—a few states allow jury verdicts that are not unanimous. Arizona, for example, allows six of eight jurors to reach a verdict in criminal cases. Louisiana and Oregon have also relaxed the requirement of unanimous jury verdicts.

Exhibit 6.1 Key Differences between Civil Law and Criminal Law

ISSUE	CIVIL LAW	CRIMINAL LAW
Party who brings suit	The person who suffered harm.	The state.
Wrongful act	Causing harm to a person or to a person's property.	Violating a statute that prohibits some type of activity.
Burden of proof	Preponderance of the evidence.	Beyond a reasonable doubt.
Verdict	Three-fourths majority (typically).	Unanimous (almost always).
Remedy	Damages to compensate for the harm or a decree to achieve an equitable result.	Punishment (fine, imprisonment, or death).

Crime A wrong against society proclaimed in a statute and, if committed, punishable by society through fines, imprisonment, or death.

Beyond a Reasonable Doubt The standard of proof used in criminal cases.

Criminal Sanctions The sanctions imposed on criminal wrongdoers are also harsher than those applied in civil cases. Remember from Chapter 4 that the purpose of tort law is to allow persons harmed by the wrongful acts of others to obtain compensation from the wrongdoer rather than to punish the wrongdoer.

In contrast, criminal sanctions are designed to punish those who commit crimes and to deter others from committing similar acts in the future. Criminal sanctions include fines as well as the much harsher penalty of the loss of one's liberty by incarceration in a jail or prison. The harshest criminal sanction is, of course, the death penalty.

Civil Liability for Criminal Acts

Some torts, such as assault and battery, provide a basis for a criminal prosecution as well as a tort action. **EXAMPLE 6.1** Carlos is walking down the street, minding his own business, when suddenly a person attacks him. In the ensuing struggle, the attacker (assailant) stabs Carlos several times, seriously injuring him. A police officer restrains and arrests the wrongdoer. In this situation, the attacker may be subject both to criminal prosecution by the state and to a tort lawsuit brought by Carlos. •

Exhibit 6.2 below illustrates how the same act can result in both a tort action and a criminal action against the wrongdoer.

Exhibit 6.2 Tort Lawsuit and Criminal Prosecution for the Same Act

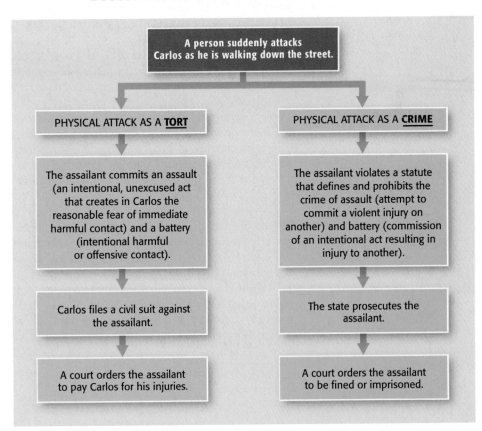

Criminal Liability

LEARNING OBJECTIVE 1
What two elements normally must exist before a person can be held liable for a crime?

Two elements normally must exist simultaneously for a person to be convicted of a crime: (1) the performance of a prohibited act and (2) a specified state of mind or intent on the part of the actor. Note that to establish criminal liability, there must be a *concurrence* between the act and the intent. In other words, these two elements must occur together.

The Criminal Act

Actus reus A guilty (prohibited) act. The commission of a prohibited act is one of the two essential elements required for criminal liability, the other element being the intent to commit a crime.

Every criminal statute prohibits certain behavior. Most crimes require an act of *commission.* That is, a person must *do* something in order to be accused of a crime. In criminal law, a prohibited act is referred to as the **actus reus**,[2] or guilty act. In some situations, an act of *omission* can be a crime, but only when a person has a legal duty to perform the omitted act, such as failing to file a tax return.

The *guilty act* requirement is based on one of the premises of criminal law—that a person is punished for harm done to society. For a crime to exist, the guilty act must cause some harm to a person or to property. Thinking about killing someone or about stealing a car may be wrong, but the thoughts do no harm until they are translated into action. Of course, a person can be punished for attempting murder or robbery, but normally only if he or she took substantial steps toward the criminal objective.

State of Mind

Mens rea The wrongful mental state ("guilty mind"), or intent, that is one of the key requirements to establish criminal liability for an act.

A wrongful mental state (**mens rea**)[3] is generally required to establish criminal liability. What constitutes such a mental state varies according to the wrongful action. For murder, the act is the taking of a life, and the mental state is the intent to take life. For theft, the guilty act is the taking of another person's property, and the mental state involves both the knowledge that the property belongs to another and the intent to deprive the owner of it.

Recklessness and Criminal Negligence

A court can also find that the required mental state is present when a defendant's acts are reckless or criminally negligent. A defendant is *criminally reckless* if he or she consciously disregards a substantial and unjustifiable risk. **EXAMPLE 6.2** A fourteen-year-old New Jersey girl posted a Facebook message saying that she was going to launch a terrorist attack on her high school and asking if anyone wanted to help. The police arrested the girl for the crime of making a terrorist threat, which requires the intent to commit an act of violence with "the intent to terrorize" or "in reckless disregard of the risk of causing" terror or inconvenience. Although the girl claimed that she did not intend to cause harm, she was prosecuted under the "reckless disregard" part of the statute. •

Criminal negligence occurs when the defendant takes an unjustified, substantial, and foreseeable risk that results in harm. A defendant can be negligent even if she or he was not actually aware of the risk but *should have been aware* of it.[4] A homicide is classified as *involuntary manslaughter* when it results from an act of criminal negligence and there is no intent to kill. **EXAMPLE 6.3** Dr. Conrad Murray, the personal physician of pop star Michael Jackson, was convicted of involuntary manslaughter in 2011 for prescribing the drug that led to Jackson's sudden death in 2009. Murray had given Jackson propofol, a powerful anesthetic normally used in surgery, as a sleep aid on the night of his death, even though Murray knew that Jackson had already taken other sedatives. •

---

2. Pronounced *ak*-tuhs *ray*-uhs.
3. Pronounced *mehns ray*-uh.
4. Model Penal Code Section 2.02(2)(d).

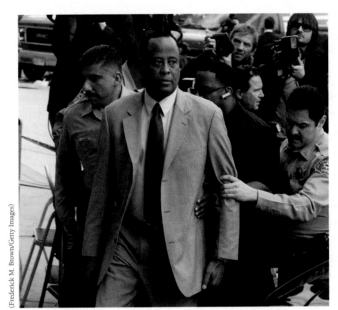

Why was Dr. Conrad Murray convicted of involuntary manslaughter in the death of pop star Michael Jackson?

Strict Liability and Overcriminalization In recent years, an increasing number of laws and regulations have imposed criminal sanctions for strict liability crimes—that is, offenses that do not require a wrongful mental state, or malice, to establish criminal liability.

Federal Crimes The federal criminal code now lists more than four thousand criminal offenses, many of which do not require a specific mental state. There are also at least ten thousand federal rules that can be enforced through criminal sanctions, and many of these rules do not require intent. **EXAMPLE 6.4** Eddie Leroy Anderson, a retired logger and former science teacher, and his son went digging for arrowheads near a campground in Idaho. They did not realize that they were on federal land and that it is a crime to take artifacts off federal land without a permit. Although the penalty could be as much as two years in prison, father and son pleaded guilty and were sentenced to probation and a $1,500 fine each. ●

Strict liability crimes are particularly common in environmental laws, laws aimed at combating illegal drugs, and other laws related to public health, safety, and welfare. Under federal law, for instance, tenants can be evicted from public housing if one of their relatives or guests used illegal drugs—regardless of whether the tenant knew or should have known about the drug activity.

State Crimes Many states have also enacted laws that punish behavior as criminal without the need to show criminal intent. **EXAMPLE 6.5** Under Arizona law, a hunter who shoots an elk outside the area specified by his or her permit has committed a crime. Criminal liability is imposed regardless of the hunter's intent or knowledge of the law.[5] ●

Overcriminalization Proponents of laws that establish strict liability crimes argue that they are necessary to protect the public and the environment. Critics say that the laws have led to *overcriminalization,* or the use of criminal law to attempt to solve social problems, such as illegal drug use. They argue that when the requirement of intent is removed from criminal offenses, people are more likely to commit crimes unknowingly—and perhaps even innocently. When an honest mistake can lead to a criminal conviction, the role of criminal law as a deterrent to future wrongful conduct is undermined.

Corporate Criminal Liability

As will be discussed in Chapter 19, a *corporation* is a legal entity created under the laws of a state. At one time, it was thought that a corporation could not incur criminal liability because, although a corporation is a legal person, it can act only through its agents (corporate directors, officers, and employees). Therefore, the corporate entity itself could not "intend" to commit a crime. Over time, this view has changed. Obviously, corporations cannot be imprisoned, but they can be fined or denied certain legal privileges (such as necessary licenses).

Liability of the Corporate Entity
Today, corporations are normally liable for the crimes committed by their agents and employees within the course and scope

---

5. See, for example, *State v. Slayton,* 214 Ariz. 511, 154 P.3d 1057 (2007).

of their employment.[6] For such criminal liability to be imposed, the prosecutor typically must show that the corporation could have prevented the act or that a supervisor within the corporation authorized or had knowledge of the act. In addition, corporations can be criminally liable for failing to perform specific duties imposed by law (such as duties under environmental laws or securities laws).

CASE EXAMPLE 6.6   A prostitution ring, the Gold Club, was operating out of motels in West Virginia. A motel manager, who was also an officer in the corporation that owned the motels, gave discounted rates to Gold Club prostitutes, and they paid him in cash. The corporation received a portion of the funds generated by the Gold Club's illegal operations. At trial, the jury found that the corporation was criminally liable because a supervisor within the corporation—the motel manager—had knowledge of the prostitution and the corporation had allowed it to continue.[7] ●

Liability of Corporate Officers and Directors   Corporate directors and officers are personally liable for the crimes they commit, regardless of whether the crimes were committed for their personal benefit or on the corporation's behalf. Additionally, corporate directors and officers may be held liable for the actions of employees under their supervision. Under the *responsible corporate officer doctrine*, a court may impose criminal liability on a corporate officer regardless of whether she or he participated in, directed, or even knew about a given criminal violation.[8]

CASE EXAMPLE 6.7   The Roscoe family owned the Customer Company, which operated an underground storage tank that leaked gasoline. After the leak occurred, an employee, John Johnson, notified the state environmental agency, and the Roscoes hired an environmental services firm to clean up the spill. The clean-up did not occur immediately, however, and the state sent many notices to John Roscoe, a corporate officer, warning him that the company was violating federal and state environmental laws. Roscoe gave the letters to Johnson, who passed them on to the environmental services firm, but the spill was not cleaned up. The state eventually filed criminal charges against the corporation and the Roscoes individually, and they were convicted. On appeal, the court affirmed the Roscoes' convictions under the responsible corporate officer doctrine. The Roscoes were in positions of responsibility, they had influence over the corporation's actions, and their failure to act constituted a violation of environmental laws.[9] ●

(AP Photo/Seth Wenig)

Gary Foster, formerly a Citigroup vice president, embezzled $22 million from his employer. Are corporate officers liable for their crimes?

PREVENTING LEGAL DISPUTES

If you become a corporate officer or director at some point in your career, you need to be aware that you can be held liable for the crimes of your subordinates. You should always be familiar with any criminal statutes relevant to the corporation's particular industry or trade. Also, make sure that corporate employees are trained in how to comply with the multitude of applicable laws, particularly environmental laws and health and safety regulations, which frequently involve criminal sanctions.

---

6. See Model Penal Code Section 2.07.

7. As a result of the convictions, the motel manager was sentenced to fifteen months in prison, and the corporation was ordered to forfeit the motel property. *United States v. Singh*, 518 F.3d 236 (4th Cir. 2008).

8. For a landmark case in this area, see *United States v. Park*, 421 U.S. 658, 95 S.Ct. 1903, 44 L.Ed.2d 489 (1975).

9. The Roscoes and the corporation were sentenced to pay penalties of $2,493,250. *People v. Roscoe*, 169 Cal.App.4th 829, 87 Cal.Rptr.3d 187 (3 Dist. 2008).

Types of Crimes

LEARNING OBJECTIVE 2
What are five broad categories of crimes? What is white-collar crime?

Federal, state, and local laws provide for the classification and punishment of hundreds of thousands of different criminal acts. Traditionally, though, crimes have been grouped into five broad categories: violent crime (crimes against persons), property crime, public order crime, white-collar crime, and organized crime. Within each of these categories, crimes may also be separated into more than one classification. Note also that many crimes may be committed in cyberspace, as well as the physical world. When they occur in the virtual world, we refer to them as cyber crimes, as discussed later in the chapter.

Violent Crime

Robbery The act of forcefully and unlawfully taking personal property of any value from another.

Crimes against persons, because they cause others to suffer harm or death, are referred to as *violent crimes*. Murder is a violent crime. So, too, is sexual assault, or rape. **Robbery**—defined as the taking of cash, personal property, or any other article of value from a person by means of force or fear—is another violent crime. Typically, states have more severe penalties for *aggravated robbery*—robbery with the use of a deadly weapon.

Assault and battery, which were discussed in Chapter 4 in the context of tort law, are also classified as violent crimes. Recall that assault can involve an object or force put into motion by a person. **EXAMPLE 6.8** On the anniversary of a landmark abortion rights decision, Paul drives his sport utility vehicle into a local abortion clinic. The police arrest him for aggravated assault even though no one is injured by his act. •

Each of these violent crimes is further classified by degree, depending on the circumstances surrounding the criminal act. These circumstances include the intent of the person committing the crime, whether a weapon was used, and (in cases other than murder) the level of pain and suffering experienced by the victim. (For a discussion of why some violent crimes committed on Indian reservations are not being prosecuted, see this chapter's *Law, Diversity, and Business: Managerial Implications* feature on the following page.)

Property Crime

The most common type of criminal activity is property crime—crimes in which the goal of the offender is some form of economic gain or the damaging of property. Robbery is a form of property crime, as well as a violent crime, because the offender seeks to gain the property of another. We look here at a number of other crimes that fall within the general category of property crime. (Note also that many types of cyber crime, discussed later in this chapter, are forms of property crime as well.)

Burglary The unlawful entry or breaking into a building with the intent to commit a felony.

Burglary Traditionally, **burglary** was defined under the common law as breaking and entering the dwelling of another at night with the intent to commit a felony. Originally, the definition was aimed at protecting an individual's home and its occupants. Most state statutes have eliminated some of the requirements found in the common law definition. The time of day at which the breaking and entering occurs, for example, is usually immaterial. State statutes frequently omit the element of breaking, and some states do not require that the building be a dwelling. When a deadly weapon is used in a burglary, the person can be charged with *aggravated burglary* and punished more severely.

Larceny The wrongful taking and carrying away of another person's personal property with the intent to permanently deprive the owner of the property.

Larceny Under the common law, the crime of **larceny** involved the unlawful taking and carrying away of someone else's personal property with the intent to permanently deprive the owner of possession. Put simply, larceny is stealing, or theft. Whereas robbery involves force or fear, larceny does not. Therefore, picking pockets is larceny, not robbery.

LAW, DIVERSITY, AND BUSINESS: MANAGERIAL IMPLICATIONS

NATIVE AMERICANS AND CRIMINAL JUSTICE

Thanks to freedom from state antigambling laws and "sin" taxes on alcohol and cigarettes, Native American reservations are often considered to be somewhat outside the law. Indeed, Vernon Roanhorse, a Navajo tribal official, calls his reservation a "lawless land." The problems, however, go much deeper than casinos and cheap cigarettes.

In its earliest days, the U.S. government treated the various Native American tribes as individual sovereign nations. Ever since, the government has allowed Native Americans a considerable amount of self-rule. Nevertheless, tribal leaders do not have complete jurisdiction over all events that occur on tribal lands, including crimes.

Problems with Criminal Jurisdiction   As far as criminal law is concerned, the 275 tribes operate in a jurisdictional void. They run their own court systems, but federal law denies tribal courts criminal jurisdiction over defendants who are not Indians or are Indians from a different tribe.

Furthermore, Native American courts *cannot prosecute felonies* (the most serious crimes) under any circumstances. For these crimes, they must rely on the Federal Bureau of Investigation (FBI) to act as their police force and U.S. attorneys to act as their prosecutors.

Lack of Federal Enforcement   The federal government's record in this area is dismal. About two hundred criminal charges involving Native Americans are dismissed each year because FBI agents fail to file arrest reports. For their part, U.S. attorneys decline to prosecute about two-thirds of all Indian country cases.

According to a 2011 report by the National Organization for Women, Native American women experience the highest rate of violence of any group in the United States. Domestic violence, sexual abuse, and stalking crimes are common. More than 80 percent of Native American rape victims identify their assailant as non-Indian, which means that these suspects are out of the reach of Native American jurisdiction and can be apprehended only by the often unresponsive federal criminal justice system.

Business Implications   *In today's legal environment, many crimes do not involve violence, but rather are violations of corporate, consumer, environmental, and intellectual property laws. Those who do business with Native Americans should be aware of the jurisdictional problems that affect criminal prosecutions, particularly with felony offenses. In contracts with Native Americans, businesspersons should consider using arbitration or forum-selection clauses that specify how and where any disputes will be resolved.*

Similarly, an employee who takes company products and supplies home for personal use without authorization commits larceny. (Note that a person who commits larceny generally can also be sued under tort law because the act of taking possession of another's property involves a trespass to personal property.)

Most states have expanded the definition of property that is subject to larceny statutes. Stealing computer programs may constitute larceny even though the "property" is not physical (see the discussion of computer crime later in this chapter). So, too, can the theft of natural gas or Internet and television cable service.

Obtaining Goods by False Pretenses

Obtaining goods by means of false pretenses is a form of theft that involves trickery or fraud, such as paying for an iPad with a stolen credit-card number. Statutes dealing with such illegal activities vary widely from state to state. They often apply not only to acquiring property, but also to obtaining services or funds by false pretenses—for example, selling an iPad that you claim is yours when you actually do not own it.

Receiving Stolen Goods

It is a crime to receive goods that a person knows or should have known were stolen or illegally obtained. To be convicted, the recipient of such goods need not know the true identity of the owner or the thief, and need not have paid for the goods. All that is necessary is that the recipient knows or should have known that the goods were stolen, and intended to deprive the true owner of those goods.

Arson The intentional burning of a building.

Arson   The willful and malicious burning of a building (and, in some states, vehicles and other items of personal property) is the crime of **arson.** At common law, arson traditionally applied only to burning down another person's house. The law was designed to protect human life. Today, arson statutes have been extended to cover the destruction of any building, regardless of ownership, by fire or explosion.

Every state has a special statute that covers the act of burning a building for the purpose of collecting insurance. **EXAMPLE 6.9** Benton owns an insured apartment building that is falling apart. If he sets fire to it or pays someone else to do so, he is guilty not only of arson but also of defrauding the insurer, which is attempted larceny. ● Of course, the insurer need not pay the claim when insurance fraud is proved.

Forgery The fraudulent making or altering of any writing in a way that changes the legal rights and liabilities of another.

Forgery   The fraudulent making or altering of any writing (including electronic records) in a way that changes the legal rights and liabilities of another is **forgery.** **EXAMPLE 6.10** Without authorization, Severson signs Bennett's name to the back of a check made out to Bennett and attempts to cash it. Severson has committed the crime of forgery. ● Forgery also includes changing trademarks, falsifying public records, counterfeiting, and altering a legal document.

Public Order Crime

Historically, societies have always outlawed activities that are considered to be contrary to public values and morals. Today, the most common public order crimes include public drunkenness, prostitution, gambling, and illegal drug use. These crimes are sometimes referred to as victimless crimes because they normally harm only the offender. From a

This West Hollywood, California, carport fire was one of twelve such fires that were set by an individual during a short time period. What type of crime was that person guilty of committing?

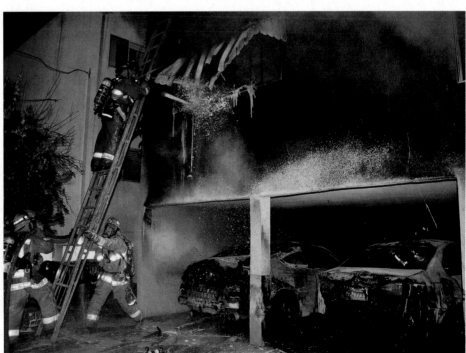

(Gene Blevins/Reuters /Landov)

broader perspective, however, they are deemed detrimental to society as a whole because they may create an environment that gives rise to property and violent crimes.

EXAMPLE 6.11   A man flying from Texas to California on a commercial airliner becomes angry and yells obscenities at a flight attendant when a beverage cart strikes his knee. After the pilot diverts the plane and makes an unscheduled landing at a nearby airport, police remove the passenger and arrest him. If the man is later found guilty of the public order crime of interfering with a flight crew, he may be sentenced to more than two years in prison. ●

White-Collar Crime

White-Collar Crime Nonviolent crime committed by individuals or corporations to obtain a personal or business advantage.

Crimes that typically occur only in the business context are popularly referred to as **white-collar crimes.** Although there is no official definition of white-collar crime, the term is commonly used to mean an illegal act or series of acts committed by an individual or business entity using some nonviolent means. Usually, this kind of crime is committed in the course of a legitimate occupation. Corporate crimes fall into this category. In addition, certain property crimes, such as larceny and forgery, may also be white-collar crimes if they occur within the business context.

Embezzlement The fraudulent appropriation of funds or other property by a person who was entrusted with the funds or property.

Embezzlement   When a person who is entrusted with another person's funds or property fraudulently appropriates it, **embezzlement** occurs. Typically, embezzlement is carried out by an employee who steals funds. Banks are particularly prone to this problem, but embezzlement can occur in any firm. In a number of businesses, corporate officers or accountants have fraudulently converted funds for their own benefit and then "fixed" the books to cover up their crime. Embezzlement is not larceny, because the wrongdoer does not physically take the property from another's possession, and it is not robbery, because force or fear is not used.

Embezzlement occurs whether the embezzler takes the funds directly from the victim or from a third person. If the financial officer of a corporation pockets checks from third parties that were given to her to deposit into the corporate account, she is embezzling. Frequently, an embezzler takes a relatively small amount at one time but does so repeatedly over a long period. The embezzler might underreport income or deposits and keep the remaining amount, for example, or create fictitious persons or accounts and write checks to them from the corporate account. An employer's failure to remit state withholding taxes that were collected from employee wages can also constitute embezzlement.

The intent to return embezzled property—or its actual return—is not a defense to the crime of embezzlement, as the following *Spotlight Case* illustrates.

Spotlight on White-Collar Crime

Case 6.1
People v. Sisuphan
Court of Appeal of California, First District,
181 Cal.App.4th 800, 104 Cal.Rptr.3d 654 (2010).

(Joe Raedle/Getty Images)

A Toyota dealership employee committed embezzlement but returned the funds. Is this a defense?

FACTS Lou Sisuphan was the director of finance at a Toyota dealership. Sisuphan complained repeatedly to management about another employee, Ian McClelland. The general manager, Michael Christian, would not terminate McClelland "because he brought a lot of money into the dealership." To jeopardize McClelland's employment, Sisuphan took and kept an envelope containing a payment of nearly $30,000 from one of McClelland's customers that McClelland had tried to deposit in the company's safe. Later, Sisuphan told the dealership what he had done, adding that he had "no intention of stealing the money"

Spotlight Case 6.1—Continued

and returned it. Christian fired Sisuphan the next day, and the district attorney later charged Sisuphan with embezzlement. After a jury trial, Sisuphan was found guilty. Sisuphan appealed.

ISSUE   Did Sisuphan take the funds with the intent to defraud his employer?

DECISION   Yes. The appellate court affirmed Sisphan's conviction for embezzlement. Sisuphan had the required intent at the time he took the funds, and the evidence that he repaid the dealership was properly excluded.

REASON   The court reasoned that evidence of repayment is admissible only if it shows that a defendant's intent at the

time of the taking was not fraudulent. In determining whether Sisuphan's intent was fraudulent at the time of the taking, the main issue was not whether he intended to spend the funds that he had taken, but whether he intended to use the payment "for a purpose other than that for which the dealership entrusted it to him." Sisuphan's stated purpose was to get McClelland fired. Because this purpose was beyond the scope of his responsibility, it was "outside the trust afforded him by the dealership" and indicated that he had fraudulent intent.

CRITICAL THINKING—Legal Consideration   *Why was Sisuphan convicted of embezzlement instead of larceny? What is the difference between these two crimes?*

> "It was beautiful and simple as all truly great swindles are."
>
> O. Henry, 1862–1910
> (American writer)

Mail and Wire Fraud   One of the most potent weapons against white-collar criminals are the federal laws that prohibit mail fraud[10] and wire fraud.[11] These laws make it a federal crime to devise any scheme that uses the U.S. mail, commercial carriers—such as FedEx or UPS—or wire, including telegraph, telephone, television, e-mail, and online social media, with the intent to defraud the public. These laws are often applied when persons send out advertisements or e-mails with the intent to obtain cash or property by false pretenses.

CASE EXAMPLE 6.12   Cisco Systems, Inc., offers a warranty program to authorized resellers of Cisco parts. Iheanyi Frank Chinasa and Robert Kendrick Chambliss formulated a scheme to use this program to defraud Cisco by obtaining replacement parts to which they were not entitled. The two men sent numerous e-mails and Internet service requests to Cisco to convince the company to ship them new parts via commercial carriers. Ultimately, Chinasa and Chambliss were convicted of mail and wire fraud, and conspiracy to commit mail and wire fraud.[12] •

The maximum penalty under these statutes is substantial. Persons convicted of mail, wire, and Internet fraud may be imprisoned for up to twenty years and/or fined. If the violation affects a financial institution or involves fraud in connection with emergency disaster-relief funds, the violator may be fined up to $1 million, imprisoned for up to thirty years, or both.

Bribery   The crime of bribery involves offering something of value to someone in an attempt to influence that person, who is usually, but not always, a public official, to act in a way that serves a private interest. Three types of bribery are considered crimes: bribery of public officials, commercial bribery, and bribery of foreign officials. As an element of the crime of bribery, intent must be present and proved. The bribe itself can be anything the recipient considers to be valuable. Realize that the *crime of bribery occurs when the bribe is offered*—it is not required that the bribe be accepted. *Accepting a bribe* is a separate crime.

Commercial bribery involves corrupt dealings between private persons or businesses. Typically, people make commercial bribes to obtain proprietary information, cover up an

---

10. The Mail Fraud Act of 1990, 18 U.S.C. Sections 1341–1342.
11. 18 U.S.C. Section 1343.
12. *United States v. Chinasa*, 789 F.Supp.2d 691 (E.D.Va. 2011).

inferior product, or secure new business. Industrial espionage sometimes involves commercial bribes.   **EXAMPLE 6.13**   Kent works at the firm of Jacoby & Meyers. He offers to pay Laurel, an employee in a competing firm, if she will give him her firm's trade secrets and pricing schedules. Kent has committed commercial bribery. ● So-called kickbacks, or payoffs for special favors or services, are a form of commercial bribery in some situations.

Bankruptcy Fraud   Federal bankruptcy law (see Chapter 15) allows individuals and businesses to be relieved of oppressive debt through bankruptcy proceedings. Numerous white-collar crimes may be committed during the many phases of a bankruptcy proceeding. A creditor may file a false claim against the debtor. Also, a debtor may attempt to protect assets from creditors by fraudulently transferring property to favored parties. For instance, a company-owned automobile may be "sold" at a bargain price to a trusted friend or relative. Closely related to the crime of fraudulent transfer of property is the crime of fraudulent concealment of property, such as hiding gold coins.

Theft of Trade Secrets   As discussed in Chapter 5 on page 150, trade secrets constitute a form of intellectual property that can be extremely valuable for many businesses. The Economic Espionage Act of 1996[13] made the theft of trade secrets a federal crime. The act also made it a federal crime to buy or possess trade secrets of another person, knowing that the trade secrets were stolen or otherwise acquired without the owner's authorization.

   Violations of the act can result in steep penalties. An individual who violates the act can be imprisoned for up to ten years and fined up to $500,000. If a corporation or other organization violates the act, it can be fined up to $5 million. Additionally, the law provides that any property acquired as a result of the violation, such as airplanes and automobiles, and any property used in the commission of the violation, such as servers and other electronic devices, are subject to criminal *forfeiture*—meaning that the government can take the property. A theft of trade secrets conducted via the Internet, for example, could result in the forfeiture of every computer or other device used to commit or facilitate the crime.

Insider Trading   An individual who obtains "inside information" about the plans of a publicly listed corporation can often make stock-trading profits by purchasing or selling corporate securities based on the information. **Insider trading** is a violation of securities law and will be considered more fully in Chapter 21. Generally, the rule is that a person who possesses inside information and has a duty not to disclose it to outsiders may not profit from the purchase or sale of securities based on that information until the information is made available to the public.

Insider Trading The purchase or sale of securities on the basis of *inside information* (information that has not been made available to the public).

Organized Crime

As mentioned, white-collar crime takes place within the confines of the legitimate business world. *Organized crime,* in contrast, operates *illegitimately* by, among other things, providing illegal goods and services. For organized crime, the traditional preferred markets are gambling, prostitution, illegal narcotics, and loan sharking (lending at higher than legal interest rates), along with counterfeiting and credit-card scams.

Money Laundering   Organized crime and other illegal activities generate many billions of dollars in profits each year from illegal drug transactions and, to a lesser extent, from racketeering, prostitution, and gambling. Under federal law, banks and other financial institutions are required to report currency transactions involving more than $10,000. Consequently, those who engage in illegal activities face difficulties when they try to deposit their cash profits from illegal transactions.

---

13. 18 U.S.C. Sections 1831–1839.

Money Laundering Engaging in financial transactions to conceal the identity, source, or destination of illegally gained funds.

As an alternative to simply storing cash from illegal transactions in a safe-deposit box, wrongdoers and racketeers launder their "dirty" money to make it "clean" by passing it through a legitimate business. **Money laundering** is engaging in financial transactions to conceal the identity, source, or destination of illegally gained funds.

EXAMPLE 6.14 Harris, a successful drug dealer, becomes a partner with a restaurateur. Little by little, the restaurant shows increasing profits. As a partner in the restaurant, Harris is able to report the "profits" of the restaurant as legitimate income on which he pays federal and state taxes. He can then spend those funds without worrying that his lifestyle may exceed the level possible with his reported income. •

The Racketeer Influenced and Corrupt Organizations Act To curb the entry of organized crime into the legitimate business world, Congress enacted the Racketeer Influenced and Corrupt Organizations Act (RICO).[14] The statute, which was enacted as part of the Organized Crime Control Act, makes it a federal crime to (1) use income obtained from racketeering activity to purchase any interest in an enterprise, (2) acquire or maintain an interest in an enterprise through racketeering activity, (3) conduct or participate in the affairs of an enterprise through racketeering activity, or (4) conspire to do any of the preceding activities.

(Debbie Egan-Chin/NY Daily News via Getty Images)

Vincent Gotti (center) is one of sixty alleged mobsters—members of organized crime—in New York and Sicily, Italy. What types of crimes are the most commonly committed by such individuals?

Broad Application of RICO The broad language of RICO has allowed it to be applied in cases that have little or nothing to do with organized crime. RICO incorporates by reference twenty-six separate types of federal crimes and nine types of state felonies[15] and declares that if a person commits two of these offenses, he or she is guilty of "racketeering activity." Under the criminal provisions of RICO, any individual found guilty is subject to a fine of up to $25,000 per violation, imprisonment for up to twenty years, or both. Additionally, the statute provides that those who violate RICO may be required to forfeit (give up) any assets, in the form of property or cash, that were acquired as a result of the illegal activity or that were "involved in" or an "instrumentality of" the activity.

Penalties In the event of a RICO violation, the government can seek civil penalties, such as the divestiture of a defendant's interest in a business (called forfeiture) or the dissolution of the business. Moreover, in some cases, the statute allows private individuals to sue violators and potentially to recover three times their actual losses (treble damages), plus attorneys' fees, for business injuries caused by a violation of the statute. This is perhaps the most controversial aspect of RICO and one that continues to cause debate in the nation's federal courts. The prospect of receiving treble damages in civil RICO lawsuits has given plaintiffs a financial incentive to pursue businesses and employers for violations.

Classification of Crimes

Felony A crime—such as arson, murder, rape, or robbery—that carries the most severe sanctions, ranging from more than one year in a state or federal prison to the death penalty.

In addition to being grouped into the five categories just discussed, crimes are also classified as felonies or misdemeanors depending on their degree of seriousness. **Felonies** are serious crimes punishable by death or by imprisonment for more than a year. Many states

---

14. 18 U.S.C. Sections 1961–1968.
15. See 18 U.S.C. Section 1961(1)(A).

Misdemeanor A lesser crime than a felony, punishable by a fine or incarceration in jail for up to one year.

Petty Offense The least serious kind of criminal offense, such as a traffic or building-code violation.

LEARNING OBJECTIVE 3
What defenses can be raised to avoid liability for criminal acts?

Self-Defense The legally recognized privilege to do what is reasonably necessary to protect oneself, one's property, or someone else against injury by another.

also define different degrees of felony offenses and vary the punishment according to the degree. **Misdemeanors** are less serious crimes, punishable by a fine or by confinement for up to a year. In most jurisdictions, **petty offenses** are considered to be a subset of misdemeanors. Petty offenses are minor violations, such as jaywalking or violations of building codes. Even for petty offenses, however, a guilty party can be put in jail for a few days, fined, or both, depending on state or local law.

Defenses to Criminal Liability

Persons charged with crimes may be relieved of criminal liability if they can show that their criminal actions were justified under the circumstances. In certain circumstances, the law may also allow a person to be excused from criminal liability because she or he lacks the required mental state. We look at several of the defenses to criminal liability here.

Note that procedural violations, such as obtaining evidence without a valid search warrant, may also operate as defenses. As you will read later in this chapter, evidence obtained in violation of a defendant's constitutional rights normally may not be admitted in court. If the evidence is suppressed, then there may be no basis for prosecuting the defendant.

Justifiable Use of Force

Probably the best-known defense to criminal liability is **self-defense.** Other situations, however, also justify the use of force: the defense of one's dwelling, the defense of other property, and the prevention of a crime. In all of these situations, it is important to distinguish between deadly and nondeadly force. *Deadly force* is likely to result in death or serious bodily harm. *Nondeadly force* is force that reasonably appears necessary to prevent the imminent use of criminal force.

Generally speaking, people can use the amount of nondeadly force that seems necessary to protect themselves, their dwellings, or other property or to prevent the commission of a crime. Deadly force can be used in self-defense if the defender *reasonably believes* that imminent death or grievous bodily harm will otherwise result. In addition, normally the attacker must be using unlawful force, and the defender must not have initiated or provoked the attack.

Traditionally, deadly force could be used to defend a dwelling only when the unlawful entry was violent and the person believed deadly force was necessary to prevent imminent death or great bodily harm. Today, however, in some jurisdictions, deadly force can also be used if the person believes it is necessary to prevent the commission of a felony in the dwelling. Many states are expanding the situations in which the use of deadly force can be justified. Florida, for example, allows the use of deadly force to prevent the commission of a "forcible felony," including robbery, carjacking, and sexual battery. Similar laws have been passed in at least seventeen other states.

Necessity

Sometimes, criminal defendants are relieved of liability if they can show that a criminal act was necessary to prevent an even greater harm. **EXAMPLE 6.15** Trevor is a convicted felon and, as such, is legally prohibited from possessing a firearm. While he and his wife are in a convenience store, a man draws a gun, points it at the cashier, and demands all the cash. Afraid that the man will start shooting, Trevor grabs the gun and holds on to it until police arrive. In this situation, if Trevor is charged with possession of a firearm, he can assert the defense of necessity. ●

Amy Bishop, shown with her attorney, killed three of her fellow college professors and wounded three more. She pleaded not guilty by reason of insanity. What does she have to prove to prevail at trial?

Insanity

A person who suffers from a mental illness may be incapable of the state of mind required to commit a crime. Thus, insanity can be a defense to a criminal charge. Note that an insanity defense does not allow a person to avoid prison. It simply means that if the defendant successfully proves insanity, she or he will be placed in a mental institution.

The courts have had difficulty deciding what the test for legal insanity should be, however, and psychiatrists as well as lawyers are critical of the tests used. Almost all federal courts and some states use the relatively liberal substantial-capacity test set forth in the Model Penal Code:

> A person is not responsible for criminal conduct if at the time of such conduct as a result of mental disease or defect he [or she] lacks substantial capacity either to appreciate the wrongfulness of his [or her] conduct or to conform his [or her] conduct to the requirements of the law.

Some states use the *M'Naghten* test,[16] under which a criminal defendant is not responsible if, at the time of the offense, he or she did not know the nature and quality of the act or did not know that the act was wrong. Other states use the irresistible-impulse test. A person operating under an irresistible impulse may know an act is wrong but cannot refrain from doing it. Under any of these tests, proving insanity is extremely difficult. For this reason, the insanity defense is rarely used and usually is not successful.

Mistake

Everyone has heard the saying "Ignorance of the law is no excuse." Ordinarily, ignorance of the law or a mistaken idea about what the law requires is not a valid defense. A *mistake of fact*, as opposed to a *mistake of law*, can excuse criminal responsibility if it negates the mental state necessary to commit a crime.

EXAMPLE 6.16 If Oliver Wheaton mistakenly walks off with Julie Tyson's briefcase because he thinks it is his, there is no crime. Theft requires knowledge that the property belongs to another. (If Wheaton's act causes Tyson to incur damages, however, she may sue him in a civil action for trespass to personal property or conversion—torts that were discussed in Chapter 4.) •

Duress

Duress exists when the *wrongful threat* of one person induces another person to perform an act that she or he would not otherwise perform. In such a situation, duress is said to negate the mental state necessary to commit a crime because the defendant was forced or compelled to commit the act.

Duress can be used as a defense to most crimes except murder. The states vary in how duress is defined and what types of crimes it can excuse, however. Generally, to successfully assert duress as a defense, the defendant must reasonably believe in the immediate danger, and the jury (or judge) must conclude that the defendant's belief was reasonable.

> ◆ **KNOW THIS** ◆
>
> "Ignorance" is a lack of information. "Mistake" is a confusion of information, which can sometimes negate criminal intent.

Duress Unlawful pressure brought to bear on a person, causing the person to perform an act that she or he would not otherwise perform.

---

16. A rule derived from *M'Naghten's* Case, 8 Eng.Rep. 718 (1843).

(AP Photo/*The Huntsville Times*, Glenn Baeske)

Entrapment

Entrapment is a defense designed to prevent police officers or other government agents from enticing persons to commit crimes so that they can later be prosecuted for criminal acts. In the typical entrapment case, an undercover agent *suggests* that a crime be committed and pressures or induces an individual to commit it. The agent then arrests the individual for the crime.

For entrapment to succeed as a defense, both the suggestion and the inducement must take place. The defense is not intended to prevent law enforcement agents from ever setting a trap for an unwary criminal. Rather, its purpose is to prevent them from pushing the individual into a criminal act. The crucial issue is whether the person who committed a crime was predisposed to commit the illegal act or did so only because the agent induced it.

Statute of Limitations

With some exceptions, such as for the crime of murder, statutes of limitations apply to crimes just as they do to civil wrongs. In other words, the state must initiate criminal prosecution within a certain number of years. If a criminal action is brought after the statutory time period has expired, the accused person can raise the statute of limitations as a defense.

Immunity

Accused persons are understandably reluctant to give information if it will be used to prosecute them, and they cannot be forced to do so. The privilege against **self-incrimination** is granted by the Fifth Amendment to the U.S. Constitution, which reads, in part, "nor shall [any person] be compelled in any criminal case to be a witness against himself." When the state wishes to obtain information from a person accused of a crime, the state can grant *immunity* from prosecution or agree to prosecute for a less serious offense in exchange for the information. Once immunity is given, the person can no longer refuse to testify on Fifth Amendment grounds because he or she now has an absolute privilege against self-incrimination.

Often, a grant of immunity from prosecution for a serious crime is part of the **plea bargaining** between the defendant and the prosecuting attorney. The defendant may be convicted of a lesser offense, while the state uses the defendant's testimony to prosecute accomplices for serious crimes carrying heavy penalties.

Constitutional Safeguards and Criminal Procedures

Criminal law brings the power of the state, with all its resources, to bear against the individual. Criminal procedures are designed to protect the constitutional rights of individuals and to prevent the arbitrary use of power by the government.

The U.S. Constitution provides specific safeguards for those accused of crimes, as mentioned in Chapter 1. Most of these safeguards protect individuals against state government actions, as well as federal government actions, by virtue of the due process clause of the Fourteenth Amendment. These protections are set forth in the Fourth, Fifth, Sixth, and Eighth Amendments.

Fourth Amendment Protections

Search Warrant An order granted by a public authority, such as a judge, that authorizes law enforcement personnel to search particular premises or property.

The Fourth Amendment protects the "right of the people to be secure in their persons, houses, papers, and effects." Before searching or seizing private property, law enforcement officers must obtain a **search warrant**—an order from a judge or other public official authorizing the search or seizure.

ETHICAL ISSUE

Should the police be able to use high-tech tracking devices without a search warrant? Police increasingly are using new technologies for surveillance. In particular, a Global Positioning System (GPS) tracker can easily be attached to a suspect's car while it is parked on a public street. If police do this without obtaining a search warrant, have they conducted an unreasonable search in violation of the Fourth Amendment? According to the United States Supreme Court, they have. In *United States v. Jones,*[17] a unanimous Court said that the government "physically occupied private property [the car] for the purpose of obtaining information. We have no doubt that such physical intrusion would have been considered a 'search' within the meaning of the Fourth Amendment when it was adopted." In other words, attaching a GPS tracker to a car is analogous to entering a person's home to make a search. Both require search warrants.

Undoubtedly, there will be continued debate about how technology can legally be used to track people's movements. How much surveillance should society accept? Should the Supreme Court's decision be extended to cell phones and other digital devices? For instance, federal and local law enforcement agents routinely engage in secret cell phone tracking by using devices called Stingrays. Does such tracking violate the Fourth Amendment? It may, given that the Supreme Court expressed concern about the invasion of privacy represented by the GPS tracker in the *Jones* case.

---

17. ___ U.S. ___, 132 S.Ct. 945, 181 L.Ed.2d 911 (2012). This case was presented in Exhibit 1A.3 on page 42.

Federal Bureau of Investigation (FBI) agents remove numerous boxes of documents from Solyndra, a bankrupt solar energy company in Fremont, California. U.S. taxpayers lost $535 million in loan guarantees because of the bankruptcy. Because of the Fourth Amendment, did the FBI have to first obtain a search warrant to enter the company's offices?

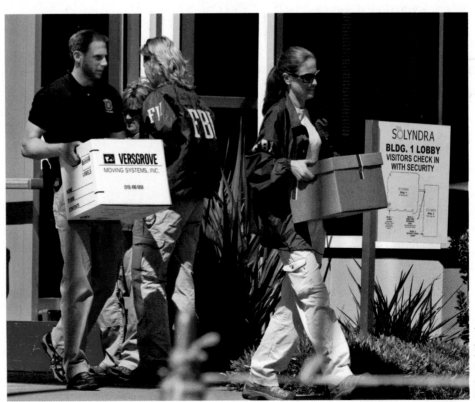

(AP Photo/Paul Sakuma)

Search Warrants and Probable Cause   To obtain a search warrant, law enforcement officers must convince a judge that they have reasonable grounds, or **probable cause,** to believe a search will reveal a specific illegality. Probable cause requires the officers to have trustworthy evidence that would convince a reasonable person that the proposed search or seizure is more likely justified than not.

Furthermore, the Fourth Amendment prohibits general warrants. It requires a particular description of what is to be searched or seized. General searches through a person's belongings are impermissible. The search cannot extend beyond what is described in the warrant. Although search warrants require specificity, if a search warrant is issued for a person's residence, items in that residence may be searched even if they do not belong to that individual.

CASE EXAMPLE 6.17   Paycom Billing Services, Inc., an online payment service, stores vast amounts of customer credit-card information in its computers. Christopher Adjani, a former employee, threatened to sell Paycom's confidential client information if the company did not pay him $3 million. The FBI obtained a search warrant to search Adjani's person, automobile, and residence, including computer equipment. When the FBI agents served the warrant, they discovered evidence of the criminal scheme on a computer in Adjani's residence. The computer belonged to Adjani's live-in girlfriend. Adjani filed a motion to suppress this evidence, claiming that because he did not own the computer, it was beyond the scope of the warrant. A federal appellate court disagreed, however, and held that the search of the computer was proper, given the alleged involvement of computers in the crime.[18] ●

In the following case, police officers obtained a search warrant and conducted a search of a gang member's foster mother's home for weapons. A judge later ruled that the warrant was not supported by probable cause, and the homeowners sued individual police officers for executing an illegal search warrant.

---

18. *United States v. Adjani,* 452 F.3d 1140 (9th Cir. 2006).

Case 6.2

Messerschmidt v. Millender

Supreme Court of the United States,
___ U.S. ___, 132 S.Ct. 1235,
182 L.Ed.2d 47 (2012).

(Mario Villafuerte/Getty Images)

Police officers conduct a search.

The United States Supreme Court granted *certiorari* to determine whether the police officers were immune from personal liability.

FACTS The Los Angeles County Sheriff's Department was protecting a woman from Jerry Ray Bowen when he tried to kill her with a sawed-off shotgun. The woman told the police that she and Bowen used to date, that Bowen was a gang member, and that she thought Bowen was staying at the home of Augusta Millender, his foster mother. After investigating the incident further, the police prepared a warrant to search the foster mother's home for all guns and gang-related material, and a judge approved it. When police officers, including Curt Messerschmidt, served the search warrant, they discovered that Bowen was not at the home but searched it anyway. Millender sued individual police officers in federal court for subjecting her to an illegal search. A federal appellate court held that the police lacked probable cause for such a broad search and that the police officers could be held personally liable. The police officers appealed.

ISSUE Assuming that the search violated the Fourth Amendment to the U.S. Constitution, are the police officers immune from liability?

DECISION Yes. The United States Supreme Court reversed the decision of the federal appellate court, granting the officers immunity from liability.

REASON The doctrine of qualified immunity "gives government officials breathing room to make reasonable but

Case 6.2—Continued

mistaken judgments." The Court explained that immunity depends on whether an official "acted in an objectively reasonable manner." Here, the police officers acted reasonably, in part, because a neutral judge approved the search warrant. Moreover, a reasonable police officer could have believed that the warrant was proper. For example, even if the warrant was too broad because it authorized a search for all guns rather than just the one Bowen fired, a reasonable police officer could conclude that Bowen had other guns. After all, the Court reasoned, he owned a sawed-off shotgun, he was a known gang member, and he had just tried to kill a woman

for calling the police. Similarly, one could reasonably conclude that there was probable cause to search for gang-related material because it would be helpful in prosecuting Bowen for attacking his ex-girlfriend. Finally, the officers conducted a detailed investigation and had the warrant application reviewed three times before submitting it to the judge.

CRITICAL THINKING—Legal Consideration *How would police officers behave if they could always be held personally liable for executing unconstitutional warrants? Would they be more or less inclined to apply for and execute search warrants? Explain.*

Searches and Seizures in the Business Context Because of the strong governmental interest in protecting the public, a warrant normally is not required for seizures of spoiled or contaminated food. Nor are warrants required for searches of businesses in such highly regulated industries as liquor, guns, and strip mining.

Generally, however, government inspectors do not have the right to search business premises without a warrant, although the standard of probable cause is not the same as in nonbusiness contexts. The existence of a general and neutral plan of enforcement will justify the issuance of a warrant. Lawyers and accountants frequently possess the business records of their clients, and inspecting these documents while they are out of the hands of their true owners also requires a warrant. Inspecting a physician's medical records also generally requires a warrant, although an exception may be made if the physician agrees to allow the search.[19]

Fifth Amendment Protections

The Fifth Amendment offers significant protections for accused persons. One is the guarantee that no one can be deprived of "life, liberty, or property without due process of law." Two other important Fifth Amendment provisions protect persons against double jeopardy and self-incrimination.

Due Process of Law   Remember from Chapter 1 on page 23 that *due process of law* has both procedural and substantive aspects. Procedural due process requirements underlie criminal procedures. The law must be carried out in a fair and orderly way. In criminal cases, due process means that defendants should have an opportunity to object to the charges against them before a fair, neutral decision maker, such as a judge. Defendants must also be given the opportunity to confront and cross-examine witnesses and accusers and to present their own witnesses.

Double Jeopardy The Fifth Amendment requirement that prohibits a person from being tried twice for the same criminal offense.

Double Jeopardy   The Fifth Amendment also protects persons from **double jeopardy** (being tried twice for the same criminal offense). The prohibition against double jeopardy means that once a criminal defendant is acquitted (found "not guilty") of a particular crime, the government may not retry him or her for the same crime.

---

19. See, for example, *United States v. Moon*, 513 F.3d 527 (2008).

The prohibition against double jeopardy does not preclude the crime victim from bringing a civil suit against that same defendant to recover damages, however. In other words, a person found "not guilty" of assault and battery in a state criminal case can be sued for damages by the victim in a civil tort case.

Additionally, a state's prosecution of a crime will not prevent a separate federal prosecution relating to the same activity (and vice versa), provided the activity can be classified as a different crime. **CASE EXAMPLE 6.18** Professional football player Michael Vick was convicted in federal court for operating a dogfighting ring and sentenced to serve twenty-three months in federal prison. A year later, the state where the crime took place, Virginia, filed its own charges against Vick for dogfighting. He pleaded guilty to those charges and received a *suspended sentence* (meaning that the judge reserved the option of imposing a sentence later if circumstances, such as future violations, warranted it).[20] •

Self-Incrimination   As explained earlier, the Fifth Amendment grants a privilege against self-incrimination. Thus, in any criminal proceeding, an accused person cannot be compelled to give testimony that might subject her or him to any criminal prosecution.

The Fifth Amendment's guarantee against self-incrimination extends only to natural persons. Because a corporation is a legal entity and not a natural person, the privilege against self-incrimination does not apply to it. Similarly, the business records of a partnership do not receive Fifth Amendment protection. When a partnership is required to produce these records, it must do so even if the information incriminates the persons who constitute the business entity. Sole proprietors and sole practitioners (those who fully own their businesses) who have not incorporated normally cannot be compelled to produce their business records. These individuals have full protection against self-incrimination because they function in only one capacity—there is no separate business entity (see Chapter 19).

Protections under the Sixth and Eighth Amendments

The Sixth Amendment guarantees several important rights for criminal defendants: the right to a speedy trial, the right to a jury trial, the right to a public trial, the right to confront witnesses, and the right to counsel. The Sixth Amendment right to counsel is one of the rights of which a suspect must be advised when he or she is arrested. In many cases, a statement that a criminal suspect makes in the absence of counsel is not admissible at trial unless the suspect has knowingly and voluntarily waived this right.

The Eighth Amendment prohibits excessive bail and fines, as well as cruel and unusual punishment. Under this amendment, prison officials are required to provide humane conditions of confinement, including adequate food, clothing, shelter, and medical care. If a prisoner has a serious medical problem, for instance, and a correctional officer is deliberately indifferent to it, a court could find that the prisoner's Eighth Amendment rights were violated. Critics of the death penalty claim that it constitutes cruel and unusual punishment.[21]

The Exclusionary Rule and the *Miranda* Rule

Two other procedural protections for criminal defendants are the exclusionary rule and the *Miranda* rule.

The Exclusionary Rule   Under what is known as the **exclusionary rule**, all evidence obtained in violation of the constitutional rights spelled out in the Fourth, Fifth,

Exclusionary Rule A rule that prevents evidence that is obtained illegally or without a proper search warrant—and any evidence derived from illegally obtained evidence—from being admissible in court.

---

20. See *United States v. Kizeart*, 2010 WL 3768023 (S.D.Ill. 2010), for a discussion of the Michael Vick dogfighting case.

21. For an example of a case challenging the constitutionality of the death penalty, see *Baze v. Rees*, 552 U.S. 597, 128 S.Ct. 1520, 170 L.Ed.2d 420 (2008).

and Sixth Amendments, as well as all evidence derived from illegally obtained evidence, normally must be excluded from the trial. Evidence derived from illegally obtained evidence is known as the "fruit of the poisonous tree." For example, if a confession is obtained after an illegal arrest, the arrest is "the poisonous tree," and the confession, if "tainted" by the arrest, is the "fruit."

The purpose of the exclusionary rule is to deter police from conducting warrantless searches and engaging in other misconduct. The rule is sometimes criticized because it can lead to injustice. Many a defendant has "gotten off on a technicality" because law enforcement personnel failed to observe procedural requirements. Even though a defendant may be obviously guilty, if the evidence of that guilt was obtained improperly (without a valid search warrant, for example), it normally cannot be used against the defendant in court.

The *Miranda* Rule In *Miranda v. Arizona,* a case decided in 1966, the United States Supreme Court established the rule that individuals who are arrested must be informed of certain constitutional rights, including their Fifth Amendment right to remain silent and their Sixth Amendment right to counsel. If the arresting officers fail to inform a criminal suspect of these constitutional rights, any statements the suspect makes normally will not be admissible in court. Although the Supreme Court's *Miranda* ruling was controversial, the decision has survived attempts by Congress to overrule it.[22] Because of its importance in criminal procedure, the *Miranda* case is presented as this chapter's *Landmark in the Law* feature on the following page.

Exceptions to the *Miranda* Rule Over time, as part of a continuing attempt to balance the rights of accused persons against the rights of society, the United States Supreme Court has carved out numerous exceptions to the *Miranda* rule. For example, the Court has recognized a "public safety" exception, holding that certain statements—such as statements concerning the location of a weapon—are admissible even if the defendant was not given *Miranda* warnings. Additionally, to stop police questioning, a suspect must unequivocally and assertively request to exercise his or her right to counsel. Saying "Maybe I should talk to a lawyer" during an interrogation after being taken into custody is not enough. Police officers are not required to decipher the suspect's intentions in such situations.

Criminal Process

As mentioned, as a result of the effort to safeguard the rights of the individual against the state, a criminal prosecution differs from a civil case in several respects. Exhibit 6.3 on page 181 summarizes the major procedural steps in processing a criminal case. Here, we discuss three phases of the criminal process—arrest, indictment or information, and trial—in more detail.

Arrest

Before a warrant for arrest can be issued, there must be probable cause to believe that the individual in question has committed a crime. As discussed earlier, *probable cause* can be defined as a substantial likelihood that the person has committed or is about to commit a crime. Note that probable cause involves a likelihood, not just a possibility. An arrest can be made without a warrant if there is no time to get one, but the action of the arresting officer is still judged by the standard of probable cause.

---

22. *Dickerson v. United States,* 530 U.S. 428, 120 S.Ct. 2326, 147 L.Ed.2d 405 (2000).

> ➤ **KNOW THIS** ➤
> Once a suspect has been informed of his or her rights, anything that person says can be used as evidence in a trial.

LANDMARK IN THE LAW
Miranda v. Arizona (1966)

The United States Supreme Court's decision in *Miranda v. Arizona*[a] has been cited in more court decisions than any other case in the history of U.S law. Through television shows and other media, the case has also become familiar to most of the adult population in the United States.

The case arose after Ernesto Miranda was arrested in his home on March 13, 1963, for the kidnapping and rape of an eighteen-year-old woman. Miranda was taken to a police station in Phoenix, Arizona, and questioned by two police officers. Two hours later, the officers emerged from the interrogation room with a written confession signed by Miranda.

Rulings by the Lower Courts　The confession was admitted into evidence at the trial, and Miranda was convicted and sentenced to prison for twenty to thirty years. Miranda appealed his conviction, claiming that he had not been informed of his constitutional rights. He did not assert that he was innocent of the crime or that his confession was false or made under duress. He claimed only that he would not have confessed if he had been advised of his right to remain silent and to have an attorney. The Supreme Court of Arizona held that Miranda's constitutional rights had not been violated and affirmed his conviction. In its decision, the court emphasized that Miranda had not specifically requested an attorney.

a. 384 U.S. 436, 86 S.Ct. 1602, 16 L.Ed.2d 694 (1966).

The Supreme Court's Decision　The *Miranda* case was subsequently consolidated with three other cases involving similar issues and reviewed by the United States Supreme Court. In its decision, the Court stated that whenever an individual is taken into custody, "the following measures are required: He must be warned prior to any questioning that he has the right to remain silent, that anything he says can be used against him in a court of law, that he has the right to the presence of an attorney, and that if he cannot afford an attorney one will be appointed for him prior to any questioning if he so desires." If the accused waives his or her rights to remain silent and to have counsel present, the government must be able to demonstrate that the waiver was made knowingly, intelligently, and voluntarily.

Application to Today's World　*Today, both on television and in the real world, police officers routinely advise suspects of their "Miranda rights" on arrest. When Ernesto Miranda himself was later murdered, the suspected murderer was "read his Miranda rights." Interestingly, this decision has also had ramifications for criminal procedure in Great Britain. British police officers are required, when making arrests, to inform suspects, "You do not have to say anything. But if you do not mention now something which you later use in your defense, the court may decide that your failure to mention it now strengthens the case against you. A record will be made of everything you say, and it may be given in evidence if you are brought to trial."*

Indictment　A formal charge by a grand jury that there is probable cause to believe that a named person has committed a crime.

Grand Jury　A group of citizens who decide, after hearing the state's evidence, whether a reasonable basis (probable cause) exists for believing that a crime has been committed and that a trial ought to be held.

Information　A formal accusation or complaint (without an indictment) issued in certain types of actions (usually criminal actions involving lesser crimes) by a government prosecutor.

Indictment or Information

Individuals must be formally charged with having committed specific crimes before they can be brought to trial. If issued by a grand jury, this charge is called an **indictment**.[23] A **grand jury** usually consists of more jurors than the ordinary trial jury. A grand jury does not determine the guilt or innocence of an accused party. Rather, its function is to hear the state's evidence and to determine whether a reasonable basis (probable cause) exists for believing that a crime has been committed and that a trial ought to be held.

Usually, grand juries are used in cases involving serious crimes, such as murder. For lesser crimes, an individual may be formally charged with a crime by what is called an **information,** or criminal complaint. An information will be issued by a government prosecutor if the prosecutor determines that there is sufficient evidence to justify bringing the individual to trial.

---

23. Pronounced in-*dyte*-ment.

Exhibit 6.3 Major Procedural Steps in a Criminal Case

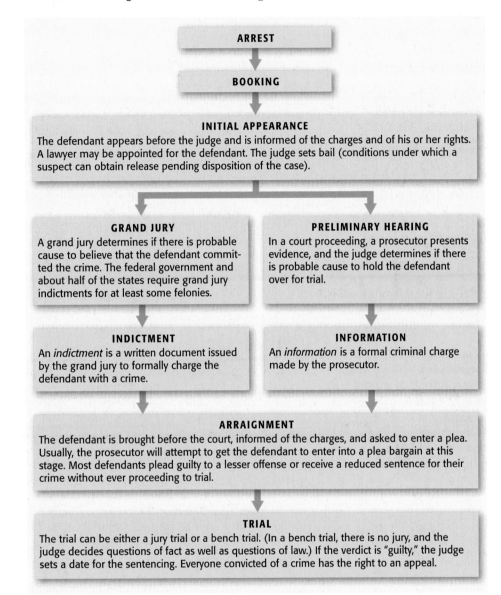

Trial

At a criminal trial, the accused person does not have to prove anything—the entire burden of proof is on the prosecutor (the state). As mentioned earlier, the prosecution must show that, based on all the evidence presented, the defendant's guilt is established *beyond a reasonable doubt*. If there is a reasonable doubt as to whether a criminal defendant committed the crime with which she or he has been charged, then the verdict must be "not guilty." Note that giving a verdict of "not guilty" is not the same as stating that the defendant is innocent. It merely means that not enough evidence was properly presented to the court to prove guilt beyond a reasonable doubt.

Courts have complex rules about what types of evidence may be presented and how the evidence may be brought out in criminal cases. These rules are designed to ensure that evidence in trials is relevant, reliable, and not prejudicial toward the defendant.

Sentencing Guidelines

The U.S. Sentencing Commission has developed standardized sentences for federal crimes. The commission's guidelines establish a range of possible penalties for each federal crime and require the judge to select a sentence from within that range. The guidelines originally established a mandatory system because judges were not allowed to deviate from the specified sentencing range, but in 2005, the Supreme Court held that certain provisions of the federal sentencing guidelines were unconstitutional.[24] Essentially, the Court's ruling changed the federal sentencing guidelines from mandatory to advisory. Depending on the circumstances of the case, a federal trial judge may now depart from the guidelines if he or she believes that it is reasonable to do so.

The sentencing judge must take into account the various sentencing factors that apply to an individual defendant before concluding that a particular sentence is reasonable. When the defendant is a business firm, these factors include the company's history of past violations, management's cooperation with federal investigators, and the extent to which the firm has undertaken specific programs and procedures to prevent criminal activities by its employees.

Cyber Crime

The U.S. Department of Justice broadly defines **computer crime** as any violation of criminal law that involves knowledge of computer technology for its perpetration, investigation, or prosecution. A number of the white-collar crimes discussed earlier in this chapter, such as fraud, embezzlement, and the theft of intellectual property, are now often committed with the aid of computers and are thus considered computer crimes.

Many computer crimes fall under the broad label of **cyber crime,** which describes any criminal activity occurring via a computer in the virtual community of the Internet. Most cyber crimes are not "new" crimes. Rather, they are existing crimes in which the Internet is the instrument of wrongdoing. Here, we look at several types of activity that constitute cyber crimes against persons or property. Other cyber crimes will be discussed in later chapters as they relate to particular topics, such as consumer law or investor protection.

Cyber Fraud

As mentioned in Chapter 4, fraud is any misrepresentation knowingly made with the intention of deceiving another and on which a reasonable person would and does rely to her or his detriment. **Cyber fraud** is fraud committed over the Internet. Frauds that were once conducted solely by mail or phone can now be found online, and new technology has led to increasingly creative ways to commit fraud.

EXAMPLE 6.19 The "Nigerian letter fraud scam" is perhaps the longest-running Internet fraud. Swindlers send e-mails asking recipients if they will send funds to help fictitious officials from Nigeria transfer millions of nonexistent dollars to Western banks. The e-mails promise that the recipients will be reimbursed and will also receive compensation (a fee or percentage) for transferring the funds. Variations of the scam reflect current events. For instance, the e-mails may ask for financial help in retrieving the fortune of a loved one or

> "In school, every period ends with a bell. Every sentence ends with a period. Every crime ends with a sentence."
>
> Steven Wright, 1955–present (American comedian)

KNOW THIS When determining the appropriate sentence for a business firm, courts focus on three things: previous violations, cooperation with authorities, and good faith efforts to avoid violations.

Computer Crime The unlawful use of a computer or network to take or alter data, or to gain the use of computers or services without authorization.

Cyber Crime A crime that occurs in the online environment rather than in the physical world.

Cyber Fraud Any misrepresentation knowingly made over the Internet with the intention of deceiving another for the purpose of obtaining property or funds.

---

24. *United States v. Booker,* 543 U.S. 220, 125 S.Ct. 738, 160 L.Ed.2d 621 (2005).

an associate who perished in the conflict in Iraq or Afghanistan or during the earthquake and tsunami in Japan. ●

Online Auction Fraud Online auction fraud, in its most basic form, is a simple process. A person puts up an expensive item for auction, on either a legitimate or a fake auction site, and then refuses to send the product after receiving payment. Or, as a variation, the wrongdoer may send the purchaser an item that is worth less than the one offered in the auction.

The larger online auction sites, such as eBay, try to protect consumers against such schemes by providing warnings about deceptive sellers or offering various forms of insurance. The nature of the Internet, however, makes it nearly impossible to completely block fraudulent auction activity. Because users can assume multiple identities, it is very difficult to pinpoint fraudulent sellers—they will simply change their screen names with each auction.

Online Retail Fraud Somewhat similar to online auction fraud is online retail fraud, in which consumers pay directly (without bidding) for items that are never delivered. As with other forms of online fraud, it is difficult to determine the actual extent of online sales fraud, but anecdotal evidence suggests that it is a substantial problem. **CASE EXAMPLE 6.20** Jeremy Jaynes grossed more than $750,000 per week selling nonexistent or worthless products such as "penny stock pickers" and "Internet history erasers." By the time he was arrested, he had amassed an estimated $24 million from his various fraudulent schemes.[25] ●

Cyber Theft

In cyberspace, thieves are not subject to the physical limitations of the "real" world. A thief can steal data stored in a networked computer with Internet access from anywhere on the globe. Only the speed of the connection and the thief's computer equipment limit the quantity of data that can be stolen.

Identity Theft Not surprisingly, there has been a marked increase in identity theft in recent years. **Identity theft** occurs when the wrongdoer steals a form of identification—such as a name, date of birth, or Social Security number—and uses the information to access the victim's financial resources. This crime existed to a certain extent before the widespread use of the Internet. Thieves would rifle through garbage to find credit-card or bank account numbers and then use those numbers to purchase goods or to withdraw funds from the victims' accounts.

The Internet has provided even easier access to private data. Frequent Web surfers surrender a wealth of information about themselves without knowing it. Many Web sites use "cookies" to collect data on those who visit their sites. The data may include the areas of the site the user visits and the links on which the user clicks.

Furthermore, Web browsers often store information such as the consumer's name and e-mail address. Finally, every time a purchase is made online, the item is linked to the purchaser's name, allowing Web retailers to amass a database of who is buying what. Of course, the database also includes purchasers' credit-card numbers. Cyber criminals who steal people's identities normally do not use the identifying information themselves. Instead, they sell the credit-card numbers and other information on the Internet.

In the following case, the court had to decide whether to suppress evidence of an identity theft crime that officers found at a defendant's girlfriend's house.

A state government official examines counterfeit jewelry, much of which would have been sold online.

(AP Photo/Paul Sakuma)

Identity Theft The illegal use of someone else's personal information to access the victim's financial resources.

LEARNING OBJECTIVE 5
How has the Internet expanded opportunities for identity theft?

---
25. *Jaynes v. Commonwealth of Virginia,* 276 Va.App. 443, 666 S.E.2d 303 (2008).

Case 6.3

United States v. Oliver

United States Court of Appeals, Fifth Circuit, 630 F.3d 397 (2011).

Identity theft often leads to various types of fraud.

FACTS Lonnie Oliver, Jr., was arrested by officers investigating a scheme to file fraudulent claims for unemployment benefits. Oliver and others were suspected of gaining access to people's names and Social Security numbers and using this information to receive unemployment benefits. After he was read his *Miranda* rights, Oliver confessed to his role in the scheme. Oliver also consented to a search of his car, but he refused to consent to a search of his home. Oliver's co-defendant then told the police that Oliver had stored a laptop computer and a cardboard box containing items related to the scheme at the apartment of Erica Armstrong, Oliver's girlfriend. Acting on this information, agents went to Armstrong's apartment, and she gave them the box and the laptop computer. Inside the box, officers found hundreds of personal identifiers of victims, along with credit and debit cards. They also found a notebook labeled "business ideas" with Oliver's notes for the scheme.

After the laptop was seized, officers obtained a warrant to search its contents and found evidence that Oliver had used it to submit fraudulent unemployment claims. Oliver filed a motion to suppress the evidence in the cardboard box on the ground that it had been obtained unconstitutionally because he had not consented to the search. Further, he claimed that the evidence found on the laptop should also be excluded as "fruit of the poisonous tree" (see page 179) because the warrant to search the laptop was issued on the basis of an affidavit that relied, in part, on the evidence in the box. The district court denied the motion. Oliver appealed.

ISSUE Were the searches of Oliver's laptop and box lawful under the Fourth Amendment?

DECISION Yes. A federal appellate court affirmed the lower court's decision that the search was legal and that the evidence in the box and on the laptop computer was admissible.

REASON The court explained that the private search doctrine legitimized the search of the box and that the independent source doctrine applied to the computer. Under the private search doctrine, when a private individual examines the contents of a closed container, a subsequent search of the container by government officials does not constitute an unlawful search for purposes of the Fourth Amendment. In this case, Armstrong testified that she had looked through the contents of the box before the police came to her apartment. Even though the officers were unaware of her actions at that time, the private search doctrine applied to and legitimized the officers' search.

As for the laptop, under the independent source doctrine, evidence obtained through a legal, independent source need not be suppressed. Both Oliver and his co-defendant had admitted to using a laptop computer to submit fraudulent unemployment claims. Therefore, police had an independent source for obtaining a warrant to search the laptop, whether or not its original seizure was legal.

WHAT IF THE FACTS WERE DIFFERENT? *Suppose that Armstrong had not looked through the cardboard box before the police searched it. Would the box's contents have been admissible? Why or why not?*

Phishing An e-mail fraud scam in which the messages purport to be from legitimate businesses to induce individuals into revealing their personal financial data, passwords, or other information.

Phishing

A distinct form of identity theft known as **phishing** has added a different wrinkle to the practice. In a phishing attack, the perpetrators "fish" for financial data and passwords from consumers by posing as a legitimate business such as a bank or credit-card company. The "phisher" sends an e-mail asking the recipient to "update" or "confirm" vital information, often with the threat that an account or some other service will be discontinued if the information is not provided. Once the unsuspecting individual enters the information, the phisher can use it to masquerade as that person or to drain his or her bank or credit account.

EXAMPLE 6.21 Customers of Wells Fargo Bank receive official-looking e-mails telling them to input personal information on an online form to complete a mandatory installation of a new Internet security certificate. But the Web site is bogus. When the customers complete the forms, their computers are infected and funnel their data to a computer server. The cyber criminals then sell the data. •

Employment Fraud Cyber criminals also look for victims at online job-posting sites. Claiming to be an employment officer in a well-known company, the criminal sends bogus e-mails to job seekers. The message asks the unsuspecting job seeker to reveal enough information to allow for identity theft. **EXAMPLE 6.22** The job site Monster.com had to ask all of its users to change their passwords after cyber thieves broke into its databases and stole user identities, passwords, and other data. The theft of 4.5 million users' personal information from Monster.com was one of Britain's largest cyber theft cases. •

Credit-Card Theft As mentioned, identity theft often includes credit-card theft. An important point to note, however, is that stolen credit-card numbers are much more likely to hurt merchants and credit-card issuers (such as banks) than consumers. In most situations, the legitimate holders of credit cards are not held responsible for the costs of purchases made with a stolen number (see Chapter 12). That means the financial burden must be borne either by the merchant or by the credit-card company. Most credit-card issuers require merchants to cover the costs—especially if the address to which the goods are sent does not match the billing address of the credit card.

Additionally, companies take risks by storing their online customers' credit-card numbers. By doing so, companies can provide quicker service because a consumer can make a purchase by providing a code or clicking on a particular icon without entering a lengthy card number. These electronic warehouses are quite tempting to cyber thieves, however. **EXAMPLE 6.23** A cyber thief was able to gain access to computerized records at CardSystems Solutions, a company in Tucson, Arizona, that processes credit-card transactions for small Internet businesses. The breach exposed 40 million credit-card numbers. •

Hacking

Hacker A person who uses computers to gain unauthorized access to data.

Botnet A network of compromised computers connected to the Internet that can be used to generate spam, relay viruses, or cause servers to fail.

A **hacker** is someone who uses one computer to break into another. (Smartphones can be hacked, too.) The danger posed by hackers has increased significantly because of **botnets,** or networks of computers that have been appropriated by hackers without the knowledge of their owners. A hacker will secretly install a program on thousands, if not millions, of personal computer "robots," or "bots," that allows him or her to forward transmissions to an even larger number of systems. To read about a group of well-known hackers in Russia, see this chapter's *Beyond Our Borders* feature on the next page.

EXAMPLE 6.24 In 2011, a hacker broke into Sony Corporation's PlayStation 3 video gaming and entertainment networks. The incident forced the company to temporarily shut down its online gaming services and affected more than 100 million online accounts that provide gaming, chat, and music streaming services. •

Malware Malicious software programs, such as viruses and worms, that are designed to cause harm to a computer, network, or other device.

Worm A software program that automatically replicates itself over a network but does not alter files and is usually invisible to the user until it has consumed system resources.

Virus A software program that can replicate itself over a network and spread from one device to another, altering files and interfering with normal operations.

Malware Botnets are one of the latest forms of **malware,** a term that refers to any program that is harmful to a computer or, by extension, its user. A **worm,** for example, is a software program that is capable of reproducing itself as it spreads from one computer to the next. **EXAMPLE 6.25** Within three weeks, the computer worm called "Conflicker" spread to more than 1 million personal computers around the world in 2009. It was transmitted to some computers through the use of Facebook and Twitter. This worm also infected servers and devices plugged into infected computers via USB ports, such as iPods, iPhones, iPads, and USB flash drives. •

A **virus,** another form of malware, is also able to reproduce itself but must be attached to an "infested" host file to travel from one computer network to another. For example,

BEYOND OUR BORDERS   Hackers Hide in Plain Sight in Russia

According to the security software maker Symantec, few Internet users and businesses have completely avoided computer crime. Consumers alone lose about $120 billion a year worldwide because of hackers and e-fraudsters.

The KoobFace Gang

A group of at least five men who live comfortably in St. Petersburg, Russia, started hacking four years ago—and they are still at it. Calling themselves KoobFace, they created a system of illegal botnets that includes 800,000 infected personal computers. Via this system, they have succeeded in using the KoobFace worm to infiltrate Facebook accounts. The KoobFace gang continues to make $2 million to $5 million a year from this venture. KoobFace is considered a pioneer in the criminal exploitation of social networks.

Knowing the Perpetuators Does Not Lead to Convictions

Authorities worldwide know the identities of the members of KoobFace, yet so far none of them has been charged with a crime. No law enforcement agencies have even confirmed that the group is under investigation. Because Western law officials do not have the resources to tackle even well-known hackers, the Russians hackers are free to continue their activities. It is not surprising that Russia has gained a reputation as a "hacker haven."

Critical Thinking

Why might it be difficult for U.S. authorities to ever investigate the KoobFace gang?

---

hackers are now capable of corrupting banner ads that use Adobe's Flash Player. When an Internet user clicks on the banner ad, a virus is installed. Worms and viruses can be programmed to perform a number of functions, such as prompting host computers to continually "crash" and reboot, or otherwise infect the system.

Service-Based Hacking   A recent trend in business computer applications is the use of "software as a service." Instead of buying software to install on a computer, the user connects to Web-based software. The user can write e-mails, edit spreadsheets, and the like using his or her Web browser. Cyber criminals have adapted this method and now offer "crimeware as a service."

A would-be thief no longer has to be a computer hacker to create a botnet or steal banking information and credit-card numbers. He or she can rent the online services of cyber criminals to do the work on such sites as NeoSploit. The thief can even target individual groups, such as U.S. physicians or British attorneys. The cost of renting a Web site to do the work is only a few cents per target computer. (For some tips on protecting a company against hackers, see the *Business Application* on page 189.)

Cyberterrorism

Cyberterrorists, as well as hackers, may target businesses. Whereas the goals of a hacker might include theft of data, such as a merchant's customer files, or monitoring a server to discover a business firm's plans and transactions, a cyberterrorist would aim to do more immediate damage. For instance, by inserting false codes or data, a cyberterrorist might change the processing control system of a food manufacturer to alter the levels of ingredients so that consumers of the food would become ill.

A cyberterrorist attack on a major financial institution, such as the New York Stock Exchange or a large bank, could leave securities or money markets in flux and seriously affect the daily lives of millions of citizens. Similarly, any prolonged disruption of computer, cable, satellite, or telecommunications systems due to the actions of expert hackers

> "A hacker does for love what others would not do for money."
>
> Laura Creighton
> (Computer programmer and entrepreneur)

would have serious repercussions on business operations—and national security—on a global level.

Prosecution of Cyber Crime

Cyber crime has raised new issues in the investigation of crimes and the prosecution of offenders. Determining the "location" of a cyber crime and identifying a criminal in cyberspace are two significant challenges for law enforcement.

Jurisdiction and Identification Challenges A threshold issue is, of course, jurisdiction. Jurisdiction is normally based on physical geography, as discussed in Chapter 3 on pages 65–68, and each state and nation has jurisdiction over crimes committed within its boundaries. But geographic boundaries simply do not apply in cyberspace. A person who commits an act against a business in California, where the act is a cyber crime, might never have set foot in California but might instead reside in New York, or even in Canada, where the act may not be a crime.

Identifying the wrongdoer can also be difficult. Cyber criminals do not leave physical traces, such as fingerprints or DNA samples, as evidence of their crimes. Even electronic "footprints" (digital evidence) can be hard to find and follow. For example, e-mail may be sent through a remailer, an online service that guarantees that a message cannot be traced to its source.

For these reasons, laws written to protect physical property are often difficult to apply in cyberspace. Nonetheless, governments at both the state and the federal level have taken significant steps toward controlling cyber crime, both by applying existing criminal statutes and by enacting new laws that specifically address wrongs committed in cyberspace. California, for instance, which has the highest identity theft rate in the nation, established a new eCrime unit in 2011 to investigate and prosecute cyber crimes. Other states, including Florida, Louisiana, and Texas, also have special law enforcement units that focus solely on Internet crimes.

" THE PRISONS ARE FILLED WITH CYBER- CRIMINALS, SO I'M SENTENCING YOU TO FOUR YEARS OF WAITING FOR INTERNET ACCESS."

The Computer Fraud and Abuse Act Perhaps the most significant federal statute specifically addressing cyber crime is the Counterfeit Access Device and Computer Fraud and Abuse Act.[26] This act is commonly known as the Computer Fraud and Abuse Act, or CFAA.

Among other things, the CFAA provides that a person who accesses a computer online, without authority, to obtain classified, restricted, or protected data (or attempts to do so) is subject to criminal prosecution. Such data could include financial and credit records, medical records, legal files, military and national security files, and other confidential information in government or private computers. The crime has two elements: accessing a computer without authority and taking the data.

This theft is a felony if it is committed for a commercial purpose or for private financial gain, or if the value of the stolen information exceeds $5,000. Penalties include fines and imprisonment for up to twenty years. For a discussion of whether it should be a violation of the CFAA to post fake pictures on the Internet's social media sites, see this chapter's *Adapting the Law to the Online Environment* feature on the following page.

---

26. 18 U.S.C. Section 1030.

ADAPTING THE LAW TO THE ONLINE ENVIRONMENT

PROSECUTING THOSE WHO POST FALSE INFORMATION ON THE INTERNET

As discussed in the text, the Computer Fraud and Abuse Act (CFAA) was enacted nearly thirty years ago. At that time, the new law was aimed at computer hacking. Since then, Congress has greatly expanded the act's reach. Today, the CFAA criminalizes any computer use that "exceeds authorized access" to any computer.

Posting Fake Photos Can Be a Crime

Just a few years ago, the Justice Department prosecuted a woman for supposedly violating the "terms of service" of MySpace.com. The woman had set up a MySpace account pretending to be a sixteen-year-old boy and had used the account to harass a thirteen-year-old girl (who subsequently committed suicide). Because the woman's profile did not use her actual photo, she was charged with conspiracy to violate the CFAA because MySpace's terms of service require that all profile information be truthful.[a] Another defendant was prosecuted for posing as someone else and posting sexually inappropriate messages on Facebook that purported to be from her.[b] In both instances, many suggested that the prosecutors were attempting to criminalize actions that, however blameworthy they may have been, were hardly crimes under the law.

a. *United States v. Drew*, 259 F.R.D. 449 (C.D.Cal. 2009).
b. *In re Rolando S.*, 197 Cal.App.4th 936, 129 Cal.Rptr.3d 49 (2011).

Civil Suits Filed by Private Parties

In addition to potential criminal penalties, the CFAA also allows private parties to bring civil suits against other private parties. An employer can sue a former employee for excessive Internet usage while at work. In other words, if the employer can prove (through keystroke monitoring, for example) that the employee visited Facebook and sent too many personal e-mails from work, the employer has grounds to sue. In one case, the terms of service on a company's Web site stated that no competitors could visit it. When one of them did, the company sued that competitor.

Have We Gone Too Far?

Agreements are breached every day. Employees routinely ignore their bosses' instructions. If such actions involve a computer or the Internet, however, they become federal crimes. In other words, the law today gives computer owners the power to criminalize any computer use with which they disagree.

Critical Thinking

Is the expansion of the 1984 Computer Fraud and Abuse Act part of the overcriminalization trend in this country? Why or why not?

Reviewing . . . Criminal Law and Cyber Crime

Edward Hanousek worked for Pacific & Arctic Railway and Navigation Company (P&A) as a roadmaster of the White Pass & Yukon Railroad in Alaska. As an officer of the corporation, Hanousek was responsible "for every detail of the safe and efficient maintenance and construction of track, structures, and marine facilities of the entire railroad," including special projects. One project was a rock quarry, known as "6-mile," above the Skagway River. Next to the quarry, and just beneath the surface, ran a high-pressure oil pipeline owned by Pacific & Arctic Pipeline, Inc., P&A's sister company. When the quarry's backhoe operator punctured the pipeline, an estimated 1,000 to 5,000 gallons of oil were discharged into the river. Hanousek was charged with negligently discharging a harmful quantity of oil into a navigable water of the United States in violation of the criminal provisions of the Clean Water Act (CWA). Using the information presented in the chapter, answer the following questions.

1. Did Hanousek have the required mental state (*mens rea*) to be convicted of a crime? Why or why not?
2. Which theory discussed in the chapter would enable a court to hold Hanousek criminally liable for violating the statute regardless of whether he participated in, directed, or even knew about the specific violation?
3. Could the quarry's backhoe operator who punctured the pipeline also be charged with a crime in this situation? Explain.
4. Suppose that, at trial, Hanousek argued that he could not be convicted because he was not aware of the requirements of the CWA. Would this defense be successful? Why or why not?

DEBATE THIS Because of overcriminalization, particularly by the federal government, Americans may be breaking the law regularly without knowing it. Should Congress rescind many of the more than four thousand federal crimes now on the books?

BUSINESS APPLICATION

Protecting Your Company against Hacking of Your Bank Accounts*

Each year, conventional, old-fashioned crooks rob banks to the tune of about $50 million. In contrast, every year cybercrooks steal billions of dollars from the bank accounts of small and mid-size companies in Europe and the United States. Why? The reason is that small businesses tend to be lax in protecting themselves from hackers. They keep their accounts in community or regional banks, have only rudimentary security measures, and usually fail to hire an on-site cyber security expert.

You May Not Receive Compensation for Your Losses

Many small-business owners believe that if their bank accounts are hacked and disappear, their banks will reimburse them. That is not always the case, however. Just ask Mark Patterson, the owner of Patco Construction in Stanford, Maryland. He lost more than $350,000 to cyberthieves. When People's United Bank would not agree to a settlement, Patterson sued, claiming that the bank should have monitored his account. So far, federal judges have agreed with the bank—that its protections were "commercially reasonable," which is the only standard that banks have to follow.

---

*This *Business Application* is not meant to substitute for the services of an attorney who is licensed to practice law in your state.

Insurance May Not Be the Answer

Similarly, small-business owners often think that their regular insurance policy will cover cyber losses at their local banks. In reality, unless there is a specific "rider" to a business's insurance policy, its bank accounts are not covered. So, just because your business will be reimbursed if thieves break in and steal your machines and network servers, that does not mean you will be covered if cybercrooks break into your bank account.

Checklist for Preventing Cyberthefts of Your Bank Accounts

1. Meet with your bank managers and discuss what you can do to protect your company's bank accounts.
2. Have your company sign up for identity-theft services. Many large banks provide these.
3. Change your company's passwords frequently. Always use long, complicated passwords.
4. Instruct your employees never to reply to unknown e-mail requests, particularly if they ask for any information about the company.
5. Have a computer expert test the firewalls safeguarding your internal computer network.

Key Terms

Chapter Summary: Criminal Law and Cyber Crime

Civil Law and Criminal Law (See pages 160–161.)	1. *Civil law*—Spells out the duties that exist between persons or between persons and their governments, excluding the duty not to commit crimes.
	2. *Criminal law*—Has to do with crimes, which are wrongs against society proclaimed in statutes and, if committed, punishable by society through fines and/or imprisonment—and, in some cases, death. Because crimes are *offenses against society as a whole*, they are prosecuted by a public official, not by the victims.
	3. *Key differences*—An important difference between civil and criminal law is that the standard of proof is higher in criminal cases (see Exhibit 6.1 on page 160 for other differences between civil and criminal law).
	4. *Civil liability for criminal acts*—A criminal act may give rise to both criminal liability and tort liability (see Exhibit 6.2 on page 161 for an example of criminal and tort liability for the same act).

Continued

Chapter Summary: Criminal Law and Cyber Crime—Continued

Criminal Liability (See pages 162–164.)	1. *Guilty act*—In general, some form of harmful act must be committed for a crime to exist. 2. *Intent*—An intent to commit a crime, or a wrongful mental state, is generally required for a crime to exist.

Types of Crimes
(See pages 165–172.)
	1. Crimes fall into five general categories: violent crime, property crime, public order crime, white-collar crime, and organized crime.
	   a. Violent crimes are those that cause others to suffer harm or death, including murder, assault and battery, sexual assault (rape), and robbery.
	   b. Property crimes are the most common form of crime. The offender's goal is to obtain some economic gain or to damage property. This category includes burglary, larceny, obtaining goods by false pretenses, receiving stolen property, arson, and forgery.
	   c. Public order crimes are acts, such as public drunkenness, prostitution, gambling, and illegal drug use, that a statute has established are contrary to public values and morals.
	   d. White-collar crimes are illegal acts committed by a person or business using nonviolent means to obtain a personal or business advantage. Usually, such crimes are committed in the course of a legitimate occupation. Examples include embezzlement, mail and wire fraud, bribery, bankruptcy fraud, theft of trade secrets, and insider trading.
	   e. Organized crime is a form of crime conducted by groups operating illegitimately to satisfy the public's demand for illegal goods and services (such as gambling or illegal narcotics). This category of crime also includes money laundering and racketeering (RICO) violations.
	2. Crimes may also be classified according to their degree of seriousness. Felonies are serious crimes punishable by death or by imprisonment for more than one year. Misdemeanors are less serious crimes punishable by fines or by confinement for up to one year.

Defenses to Criminal Liability (See pages 172–174.)	Defenses to criminal liability include justifiable use of force, necessity, insanity, mistake, duress, entrapment, and the statute of limitations. Also, in some cases defendants may be relieved of criminal liability, at least in part, if they are given immunity.
Constitutional Safeguards and Criminal Procedures (See pages 174–179.)	1. *Fourth Amendment*—Provides protection against unreasonable searches and seizures and requires that probable cause exist before a warrant for a search or an arrest can be issued. 2. *Fifth Amendment*—Requires due process of law, prohibits double jeopardy, and protects against self-incrimination. 3. *Sixth Amendment*—Guarantees a speedy trial, a trial by jury, a public trial, the right to confront witnesses, and the right to counsel. 4. *Eighth Amendment*—Prohibits excessive bail and fines, and cruel and unusual punishment. 5. *Exclusionary rule*—A criminal procedural rule that prohibits the introduction at trial of all evidence obtained in violation of constitutional rights, as well as any evidence derived from the illegally obtained evidence. 6. *Miranda rule*—A rule set forth by the Supreme Court in *Miranda v. Arizona* holding that individuals who are arrested must be informed of certain constitutional rights, including their right to counsel.
Criminal Process (See pages 179–182.)	1. *Arrest, indictment, and trial*—Procedures governing arrest, indictment, and trial for a crime are designed to safeguard the rights of the individual against the state. See Exhibit 6.3 on page 181 for a summary of the procedural steps involved in prosecuting a criminal case. 2. *Sentencing guidelines*—The federal government has established sentencing laws or guidelines, which are no longer mandatory but provide a range of penalties for each federal crime.
Cyber Crime (See pages 182–188.)	1. *Cyber fraud*—Occurs when misrepresentations are knowingly made over the Internet to deceive another. Two widely reported forms are online auction fraud and online retail fraud. 2. *Cyber theft*—In cyberspace, thieves can steal data from anywhere in the world. Identity theft is made easier by the fact that many e-businesses store information such as the consumer's name, e-mail address, and credit-card numbers. Phishing and employment fraud are variations of identity theft. The financial burden of stolen credit-card numbers falls more on merchants and credit-card issuers than on consumers. 3. *Hacking*—A hacker is a person who uses one computer to break into another. Malware is any program that is harmful to a computer or, by extension, a computer user. Worms, viruses, and botnets are examples. 4. *Cyberterrorism*—Cyberterrorists aim to cause serious problems for computer systems. A cyberterrorist attack on a major U.S. financial institution or telecommunications system could have serious repercussions, including jeopardizing national security. 5. *Prosecution of cyber crime*—Prosecuting cyber crime is more difficult than prosecuting traditional crime. Identifying the wrongdoer through electronic footprints left on the Internet is complicated, and jurisdictional issues may arise when the suspect lives in another jurisdiction or nation. A significant federal statute addressing cyber crime is the Computer Fraud and Abuse Act.

ExamPrep

ISSUE SPOTTERS

1. Daisy takes her roommate's credit card, intending to charge expenses that she incurs on a vacation. Her first stop is a gas station, where she uses the card to pay for gas. With respect to the gas station, has she committed a crime? If so, what is it? **(See page 166.)**

2. Without permission, Ben downloads consumer credit files from a computer belonging to Consumer Credit Agency. He then sells the data to Dawn. Has Ben committed a crime? If so, what is it? **(See page 168.)**

—**Check your answers to the Issue Spotters against the answers provided in Appendix E at the end of this text.**

BEFORE THE TEST

Go to www.cengagebrain.com, enter the ISBN 9781133191353, and click on "Find" to locate this textbook's Web site. Then, click on "Access Now" under "Study Tools," and select Chapter 6 at the top. There, you will find a Practice Quiz that you can take to assess your mastery of the concepts in this chapter, as well as Flashcards, a Glossary of important terms, and Video Questions (when assigned).

For Review

Answers to the even-numbered questions in this *For Review* section can be found in Appendix F at the end of this text.

1. What two elements normally must exist before a person can be held liable for a crime?
2. What are five broad categories of crimes? What is white-collar crime?
3. What defenses can be raised to avoid liability for criminal acts?
4. What constitutional safeguards exist to protect persons accused of crimes?
5. How has the Internet expanded opportunities for identity theft?

Business Scenarios and Case Problems

6–1 **Double Jeopardy.** Armington, while robbing a drugstore, shot and seriously injured Jennings, a drugstore clerk. Armington was subsequently convicted of armed robbery and assault and battery in a criminal trial. Jennings later brought a civil tort suit against Armington for damages. Armington contended that he could not be tried again for the same crime, as that would constitute double jeopardy, which is prohibited by the Fifth Amendment to the U.S. Constitution. Is Armington correct? Explain. **(See pages 177–178.)**

6–2 **Question with Sample Answer—Cyber Fraud.** Kayla, a student at Learnwell University, owes $20,000 in unpaid tuition. If Kayla does not pay the tuition, Learnwell will not allow her to graduate. To obtain the funds to pay the debt, she sends e-mails to people that she does not know asking them for financial help to send her child, who has a disability, to a special school. In reality, Kayla has no children. Is this a crime? If so, which one? **(See pages 169 and 182.)**

—**For a sample answer to Question 6–2, go to Appendix G at the end of this text.**

6–3 **White-Collar Crime.** Helm Instruction Co. hired Patrick Walsh to work as its comptroller. Walsh convinced Helm's president, Richard Wilhelm, to hire Shari Price as Walsh's assistant. Wilhelm was not aware that Walsh and Price were engaged in an extramarital affair. Over the next five years, Walsh and Price spent more than $200,000 of Helm's funds on themselves. Among other things, Walsh drew unauthorized checks on Helm's accounts to pay his personal credit-card bills. Walsh also issued unauthorized salary increases, overtime payments, and tuition reimbursement payments to Price and himself, altering Helm's records to hide the payments. After an investigation, Helm officials confronted Walsh. He denied the affair with Price and argued that his unauthorized use of Helm's funds was an "interest-free loan." Walsh claimed that it was less of a burden on the company to pay his credit-card bills than to give him the salary increases to which he felt he was entitled. Did Walsh commit a crime? If so, what crime did he commit? Discuss. [*State v. Walsh*, 113 Ohio St.3d 1515, 866 N.E.2d 513 (6 Dist. 2007)] **(See page 168.)**

6–4 Cyber Crime. Jiri Klimecek was a member of a group that overrode copyright protection in movies and music to make them available for download online. Klimecek bought and installed a server and paid to connect it to the Internet. He knew that users could access the server to upload and download copyrighted works. He obtained access to movies and music to make them available. When charged with copyright infringement, he claimed that he had not understood the full scope of the operation. Did Klimecek commit a crime? Explain. [*United States v. Klimecek,* __ F.3d __ (7th Cir. 2009)] **(See pages 182–183.)**

6–5 Case Problem with Sample Answer—Search and Seizure. Three police officers, including Maria Trevizo, pulled over a car with suspended registration. One of the occupants, Lemon Johnson, wore clothing consistent with membership in the Crips gang. Trevizo searched him "for officer safety" and found a gun. Johnson was charged with illegal possession of a weapon. What standard should apply to an officer's search of a passenger during a traffic stop? Should a warrant be required? Could a search proceed solely on the basis of probable cause? Would a reasonable suspicion short of probable cause be enough? Discuss. [*Arizona v. Johnson,* 555 U.S. 323, 129 S.Ct. 781, 172 L.Ed.2d 694 (2009)] **(See page 176.)**

—For a sample answer to Problem 6–5, go to Appendix H at the end of this text.

6–6 Search. Charles Byrd was in a minimum-security county jail awaiting trial. A team of sheriff's deputies wearing T-shirts and jeans took Byrd and several other inmates into a room for a strip search without any apparent justification. Byrd was ordered to remove all his clothing except his boxer shorts. A female deputy searched Byrd while several male deputies watched. One of the male deputies videotaped the search. Byrd filed a suit against the sheriff's department. Did the search violate Byrd's rights? Discuss. [*Byrd v. Maricopa County Sheriff's Department,* 629 F.3d. 1135 (9th Cir. 2011)] **(See page 176.)**

6–7 Credit- and Debit-Card Theft. Jacqueline Barden was shopping for school clothes with her children when her purse and automobile were taken. In Barden's purse were her car keys, credit and debit cards for herself and her children, as well

as the children's Social Security cards and birth certificates needed for enrollment at school. Immediately after the purse and car were stolen, Rebecca Mary Turner attempted to use Barden's credit card at a local Exxon gas station, but the card was declined. The gas station attendant recognized Turner because she had previously written bad checks and used credit cards that did not belong to her. Turner was later arrested while attempting to use one of Barden's checks to pay for merchandise at a Walmart—where the clerk also recognized Turner from prior criminal activity. Turner claimed that she had not stolen Barden's purse or car, and that a friend had told her he had some checks and credit cards and asked her to try using them at Walmart. Turner was convicted at trial. She appealed, claiming that there was insufficient evidence that she committed credit- and debit-card theft. Was the evidence sufficient to uphold her conviction? Why or why not? [*Turner v. State of Arkansas,* 2012 Ark.App. 150 (2012)] **(See page 166.)**

6–8 A Question of Ethics—Identity Theft. Twenty-year-old Davis Omole had earned good grades in high school and played on the football and chess team. He then went on to college. Omole worked at a cell phone store where he stole customers' personal information. He used the stolen identities to create a hundred different accounts on eBay and held more than three hundred auctions listing for sale items that he did not own (including cell phones, plasma televisions, and stereos). From these auctions, he collected $90,000. To avoid getting caught, he continuously closed and opened the eBay accounts, activated and deactivated cell phone and e-mail accounts, and changed mailing addresses and post office boxes. Omole, who had previously been convicted in a state court for Internet fraud, was convicted in a federal district court of identity theft and wire fraud. [*United States v. Omole,* 523 F.3d 691 (7th Cir. 2008)] **(See page 183.)**

1. Omole displayed contempt for the court and ridiculed his victims, calling them stupid for having been cheated. What does this behavior suggest about Omole's ethics?

2. Under federal sentencing guidelines, Omole could have been imprisoned for more than eight years, but he received only three years, two of which were the mandatory sentence for identity theft. Was this sentence too lenient? Explain.

Critical Thinking and Writing Assignments

6–9 Critical Legal Thinking. Ray steals a purse from an unattended car at a gas station. Because the purse contains money and a handgun, Ray is convicted of grand theft of property (cash) and grand theft of a firearm. On appeal, Ray claims that he is not guilty of grand theft of a firearm because he did not know that the purse contained a gun. Can Ray be convicted of grand theft of a firearm even though he did not know that the gun was in the purse? Explain. **(See page 165.)**

6–10 Business Law Critical Thinking Group Assignment. Cyber crime costs consumers millions of dollars every year, and it costs businesses, including banks and other credit-card issuers, even more. Nonetheless, when cyber criminals are caught and convicted, they are rarely ordered to pay restitution or sentenced to long prison terms.

1. One group should argue that stiffer sentences would reduce the amount of cyber crime.

2. A second group should determine how businesspersons can best protect themselves from cyber crime and avoid the associated costs.

CHAPTER 7

Agreement and Consideration in Contracts

(nuno/iStockphoto.com)

CHAPTER OUTLINE

- An Overview of Contract Law
- Types of Contracts
- Agreement
- E-Contracts
- Consideration

LEARNING OBJECTIVES

The five learning objectives below are designed to help improve your understanding of the chapter. After reading this chapter, you should be able to answer the following questions:

1. What is a contract? What is the objective theory of contracts?

2. What are the four basic elements necessary to the formation of a valid contract?

3. What elements are necessary for an effective offer? What are some examples of nonoffers?

4. How do shrink-wrap and click-on agreements differ from other contracts? How have traditional laws been applied to these agreements?

5. What is consideration? What is required for consideration to be legally sufficient?

"All sensible people are selfish,
and nature is tugging at every contract to make the terms of it fair."

—Ralph Waldo Emerson, 1803–1882 (American poet)

Promise A declaration that binds the person who makes it (the promisor) to do or not to do a certain act.

Promisor A person who makes a promise.

Promisee A person to whom a promise is made.

As Ralph Waldo Emerson observed in the chapter-opening quotation, people tend to act in their own self-interest, and this influences the terms they seek in their contracts. Contract law must therefore provide rules to determine which contract terms will be enforced and which promises must be kept. A **promise** is a declaration by a person (the **promisor**) to do or not to do a certain act. As a result, the person to whom the promise is made (the **promisee**) has a right to expect or demand that something either will or will not happen in the future.

Like other types of law, contract law reflects our social values, interests, and expectations at a given point in time. It shows, for example, what kinds of promises our society thinks should be legally binding. It distinguishes between promises that create only *moral* obligations (such as a promise to take a friend to lunch) and promises that are legally binding (such as a promise to pay a monthly service fee for a smartphone). Can a series of e-mails bind Amazon.com to a contract? You will see what the court had to say when you read the *Spotlight Case* on page 205.

In this chapter, we discuss the basic requirements for a valid and enforceable contract and examine some general principles of contract law. We look closely at two requirements—*agreement* and *consideration*. Because many contracts are formed online, we also examine online offers and acceptances that apply to electronic contracts, or *e-contracts*.

An Overview of Contract Law

Before we look at the numerous rules that courts use to determine whether a particular promise will be enforced, it is necessary to understand some fundamental concepts of contract law. In this section, we describe the sources and general function of contract law and introduce the objective theory of contracts.

Sources of Contract Law

The common law governs all contracts except when it has been modified or replaced by statutory law, such as the Uniform Commercial Code (UCC),[1] or by administrative agency regulations. Contracts relating to services, real estate, employment, and insurance, for example, generally are governed by the common law of contracts. (See the appendix at the end of Chapter 9 for an example of a common law contract used in employment.)

Contracts for the sale and lease of goods, however, are governed by the UCC to the extent that the UCC has modified general contract law. The relationship between general contract law and the law governing sales and leases of goods will be explored in detail in Chapter 10. In Chapters 7 through 9, we indicate briefly in footnotes the areas in which the UCC has significantly altered common law contract principles.

The Function of Contracts

No aspect of modern life is entirely free of contractual relationships. You acquire rights and obligations, for example, when you borrow funds, buy or lease a house, obtain insurance, form a business, and purchase goods or services. Contract law is designed to provide stability and predictability for both buyers and sellers in the marketplace.

Contract law assures the parties to private agreements that the promises they make will be enforceable. Clearly, many promises are kept because the parties involved feel a moral obligation to keep their promises, because keeping a promise is in their mutual self-interest, or for some other reason. Nevertheless, the rules of contract law are often followed in business agreements to avoid potential problems.

By supplying procedures for enforcing private agreements, contract law provides an essential condition for the existence of a market economy. Without a legal framework of reasonably assured expectations within which to plan and venture, businesspersons would be able to rely only on the good faith of others. Duty and good faith are usually sufficient, but when dramatic price changes or adverse economic conditions make it costly to comply with a promise, these elements may not be enough. Contract law is necessary to ensure compliance with a promise or to entitle the innocent party to some form of relief.

Definition of a Contract

Contract A set of promises constituting an agreement between parties, giving each a legal duty to the other and also the right to seek a remedy for the breach of the promises or duties.

A **contract** is an agreement that can be enforced in court. It is formed by two or more parties who agree to perform or to refrain from performing some act now or in the future. Generally, contract disputes arise when there is a promise of future performance. If the

---

1. See Chapter 1 on page 3 and Chapter 10 for further discussions of the significance and coverage of the Uniform Commercial Code. Articles 2 and 2A from the UCC are presented in Appendix C at the end of this book.

LEARNING OBJECTIVE 1
What is a contract? What is the objective theory of contracts?

contractual promise is not fulfilled, the party who made it is subject to the sanctions of a court (see Chapter 9). That party may be required to pay monetary damages for failing to perform the contractual promise and, in certain limited instances, may be required to perform the promised act.

The Objective Theory of Contracts

In determining whether a contract has been formed, the element of intent is of prime importance. In contract law, intent is determined by what is referred to as the **objective theory of contracts,** not by the personal or subjective intent, or belief, of a party. The theory is that a party's intention to enter into a contract is judged by outward, objective facts as interpreted by a *reasonable person,* rather than by the party's secret, subjective intentions.

Objective Theory of Contracts The view that contracting parties are bound only by terms that can be objectively inferred from promises made.

Objective facts include (1) what the party said when entering into the contract, (2) how the party acted or appeared, and (3) the circumstances surrounding the transaction. As will be discussed later in this chapter, in the discussion of express versus implied contracts, intent to form a contract may be manifested by conduct, as well as by words, oral or written.

Freedom of Contract and Freedom from Contract

As a general rule, the law recognizes everyone's ability to enter freely into contractual arrangements. This recognition is called *freedom of contract,* a freedom protected in Article I, Section 10, of the U.S. Constitution. Because freedom of contract is a fundamental public policy of the United States, courts rarely interfere with contracts that have been voluntarily made.

Of course, as in other areas of the law, there are many exceptions to the general rule that contracts voluntarily negotiated will be enforced. For example, illegal bargains, agreements that unreasonably restrain trade, and certain unfair contracts made between one party with a great amount of bargaining power and another with little power are generally not enforced. In addition, as you will read in Chapter 8, certain contracts and clauses may not be enforceable if they are contrary to public policy, fairness, or justice. These exceptions provide *freedom from contract* for persons who may have been pressured into making contracts unfavorable to their interests.

Requirements of a Valid Contract

The following list briefly describes the four requirements that must be met for a valid contract to exist. If any of these elements is lacking, no contract will have been formed. (We discuss the first two requirements in more detail later in this chapter, and we discuss the third and fourth in Chapter 8.)

LEARNING OBJECTIVE 2
What are the four basic elements necessary to the formation of a valid contract?

1. *Agreement.* An agreement to form a contract includes an *offer* and an *acceptance.* One party must offer to enter into a legal agreement, and another party must accept the terms of the offer.
2. *Consideration.* Any promises made by the parties must be supported by legally sufficient and bargained-for consideration (something of value received or promised to convince a person to make a deal).
3. *Contractual capacity.* Both parties entering into the contract must have the contractual capacity to do so, meaning that the law must recognize them as possessing characteristics that qualify them as competent parties.
4. *Legality.* The contract's purpose must be to accomplish some goal that is legal and not against public policy.

Defenses to the Enforceability of a Contract

Even if all of the elements of a valid contract are present, a contract may be unenforceable if the following requirements are not met.

1. *Voluntary consent.* The apparent consent of both parties must be voluntary. For instance, if a contract was formed as a result of fraud, mistake, or duress (coercion), the contract may not be enforceable.
2. *Form.* The contract must be in whatever form the law requires. Some contracts must be in writing to be enforceable.

The failure to fulfill either requirement may be raised as a defense to the enforceability of an otherwise valid contract. Both requirements will be explained in more detail in Chapter 8.

Types of Contracts

Contracts are categorized based on legal distinctions as to their *formation, performance,* and *enforceability.*

Contract Formation

Contracts are classified based on how and when they are formed. Exhibit 7.1 below illustrates three classifications of contracts based on their mode of formation. The best way to explain each type of contract is to compare one type with another, as we do in the following pages.

Bilateral versus Unilateral Contracts

Offeror A person who makes an offer.

Offeree A person to whom an offer is made.

Every contract involves at least two parties. The **offeror** is the party making the offer. The **offeree** is the party to whom the offer is made. The offeror always promises to do or not to do something and thus is also a promisor. Whether the contract is classified as *bilateral* or *unilateral* depends on what the offeree must do to accept the offer and bind the offeror to a contract.

Bilateral Contract A type of contract that arises when a promise is given in exchange for a return promise.

Bilateral Contracts   If the offeree can accept simply by promising to perform, the contract is a **bilateral contract.** Hence, a bilateral contract is a "promise for a promise." No performance, such as the payment of funds or delivery of goods, need take place for a bilateral

Exhibit 7.1 Classifications Based on Contract Formation

contract to be formed. The contract comes into existence at the moment the promises are exchanged. (The appendix to Chapter 9 includes an example of a bilateral contract.)

EXAMPLE 7.1 Javier offers to buy Ann's Android-based smartphone for $200. Javier tells Ann that he will give her the cash for the phone on the following Friday, when he gets paid. Ann accepts Javier's offer and promises to give him the phone when he pays her on Friday. Javier and Ann have formed a bilateral contract. •

Unilateral Contracts If the offer is phrased so that the offeree can accept only by completing the contract performance, the contract is a **unilateral contract.** Hence, a unilateral contract is a "promise for an act." In other words, the contract is formed not at the moment when promises are exchanged but rather when the contract is *performed*.

EXAMPLE 7.2 Reese says to Kata, "If you drive my car from New York to Los Angeles, I'll give you $1,000." Only on Kata's completion of the act—bringing the car to Los Angeles—does she fully accept Reese's offer to pay $1,000. If she chooses not to accept the offer to drive the car to Los Angeles, there are no legal consequences. •

Contests, lotteries, and other competitions offering prizes are also examples of offers for unilateral contracts. If a person complies with the rules of the contest—such as by submitting the right lottery number at the right place and time—a unilateral contract is formed, binding the organization offering the prize to perform as promised in the offer.

Unilateral Contract A contract that results when an offer can be accepted only by the offeree's performance.

ETHICAL ISSUE

Can a company that sponsors a contest change the prize from what it originally advertised? Courts have historically treated contests as unilateral contracts, which typically cannot be modified by the offeror after the offeree has begun to perform. But this principle may not always apply to contest terms or advertisements.

For instance, Little Poker League, LLC (LPL), conducted a poker tournament in which players competed for a spot in the World Series of Poker Main Event (WSOP) in Las Vegas. LPL would pay the $10,000 WSOP entry fee for the winner and would provide $2,500 for travel-related expenses. John Rogalski won the tournament and accepted $2,500 for travel expenses from LPL but did not attend the WSOP. Rogalski then sued LPL for $10,000. He claimed that in its initial advertisements for the tournament, LPL had offered two options: it would pay the winner's entry fee and expenses, or the winner could choose to receive the cash value of the prizes ($12,500). Rogalski argued that through its advertisements, LPL had made a unilateral offer, which he had accepted by participating in the tournament.

LPL, however, countered that during the later stages of the tournament, Rogalski and other contestants had signed a "World Series of Poker (WSOP) Agreement." The agreement stated that if the winner did not attend the WSOP, he or she would give up his seat in the event and return the $2,500 expense money to LPL. Based on this agreement, LPL filed a counterclaim to recover $2,500 from Rogalski. The court ruled in favor of LPL, finding that the contract was formed when Rogalski signed the WSOP agreement and not when he began participating in the tournament. Thus, Rogalski had to return the $2,500 to LPL.[2]

Revocation of Offers for Unilateral Contracts A problem arises in unilateral contracts when the promisor attempts to *revoke* (cancel) the offer after the promisee has begun performance but before the act has been completed. Suppose that Seiko offers to buy Jin's sailboat, moored in San Francisco, on delivery of the boat to Seiko's dock in Newport Beach, three hundred miles south of San Francisco. Seiko has offered to form a unilateral contract, and only Jin's delivery of the sailboat at her dock is an acceptance. Jin rigs the boat and sets sail. Shortly before his arrival at Newport Beach, Jin receives a message from Seiko withdrawing her offer. Has the offer been terminated?

In contract law, offers are normally *revocable* (capable of being canceled) until accepted. Under the traditional view of unilateral contracts, Seiko's revocation would terminate the

---

2. *Rogalski v. Little Poker League, LLC,* 2011 WL 589636 (Minn.App. 2011).

offer. Because of the harsh effect on the offeree of the revocation of an offer to form a unilateral contract, the modern-day view is that once performance has been *substantially* undertaken, the offeror cannot revoke the offer. Thus, in our example, even though Jin has not yet accepted the offer by complete performance, Seiko is prohibited from revoking it. Jin can deliver the boat and bind Seiko to the contract.

Formal versus Informal Contracts

Formal Contract An agreement that by law requires a specific form for its validity.

Another classification system divides contracts into formal contracts and informal contracts. **Formal contracts** are contracts that require a special form or method of creation (formation) to be enforceable.[3] For example, *negotiable instruments,* which include checks, drafts, promissory notes, and certificates of deposit (as will be discussed in Chapter 13), are formal contracts because, under the Uniform Commercial Code, a special form and language are required to create them. Letters of credit, which are frequently used in international sales contracts (as discussed in Chapter 25), are another type of formal contract.

Informal Contract A contract that does not require a specific form or method of creation to be valid.

Informal contracts (also called *simple contracts*) include all other contracts. No special form is required (except for certain types of contracts that must be in writing), as the contracts are usually based on their substance rather than their form. Typically, businesspersons put their contracts in writing to ensure that there is some proof of a contract's existence should problems arise.

Express versus Implied Contracts

Express Contract A contract in which the terms of the agreement are stated in words, oral or written.

Contracts may also be categorized as express or implied by the conduct of the parties. In an **express contract,** the terms of the agreement are fully and explicitly stated in words, oral or written. A signed lease for an apartment or a house is an express written contract. If a classmate accepts your offer to sell your textbooks from last semester for $75, an express oral contract has been made.

Implied Contract A contract formed in whole or in part from the conduct of the parties.

A contract that is implied from the conduct of the parties is called an **implied contract.** This type of contract differs from an express contract in that the *conduct* of the parties, rather than their words, creates and defines at least some of the terms of the contract. For an implied contract to arise, certain requirements must be met.

Requirements for Implied Contracts   Normally, if the following conditions exist, a court will hold that an implied contract was formed:

1. The plaintiff furnished some service or property.
2. The plaintiff expected to be paid for that service or property, and the defendant knew or should have known that payment was expected (based on the objective theory of contracts discussed on page 195).
3. The defendant had a chance to reject the services or property and did not.

EXAMPLE 7.3   Oleg, a small-business owner, needs an accountant to complete his tax return. He drops by a local accountant's office, explains his situation to the accountant, and learns what fees she charges. The next day, he returns and gives the receptionist all of the necessary documents to complete his return. Then he walks out without saying anything further to the accountant. In this situation, Oleg has entered into an implied contract to pay the accountant the usual fees for her services. The contract is implied because of Oleg's conduct and hers. She expects to be paid for completing the tax return, and by bringing in the records she will need to do the job, Oleg has implied an intent to pay her. ●

---

3. See *Restatement (Second) of Contracts,* Section 6, which explains that formal contracts include (1) contracts under seal, (2) recognizances, (3) negotiable instruments, and (4) letters of credit. As mentioned in Chapter 1, *Restatements of the Law* are books that summarize court decisions on a particular topic and that courts often refer to for guidance.

Danica Patrick signs a contract to drive full-time in the NASCAR Nationwide Series circuit and select Sprint Cup.

(AP Photo/Paul Connors)

Mixed Contracts with Express and Implied Terms   Note that a contract can be a mixture of an express contract and an implied contract. In other words, a contract may contain some express terms, while others are implied. During the construction of a home, for instance, the homeowner often asks the builder to make changes in the original specifications.

CASE EXAMPLE 7.4   Lamar Hopkins hired Uhrhahn Construction & Design, Inc., for several projects during the construction of his home. For each project, there was a signed contract that required modifications to be in writing. When work was in progress, however, Hopkins made several requests for changes. There was no written record of these changes, but Uhrhahn performed the work and Hopkins paid for it. A dispute arose after Hopkins requested that Uhrhahn use Durisol blocks rather than cinder blocks. Uhrhahn orally agreed to the modification, but then demanded extra payment because the Durisol blocks were more costly to install. Hopkins refused to pay. Uhrhahn sued and won. The court found that that there was an implied contract for the Durisol blocks. The builder did the work, and the buyer accepted the work. Such oral modification of the original contract creates an enforceable contract, and payment is due for the extra work.[4] ●

Contract Performance

Contracts are also classified according to their state of performance. A contract that has been fully performed on both sides is called an **executed contract.** A contract that has not been fully performed on either side is called an **executory contract.** If one party has fully performed but the other has not, the contract is said to be executed on the one side and executory on the other, but the contract is still classified as executory.

EXAMPLE 7.5   You agreed to buy ten tons of coal from Western Coal Company. Western has delivered the coal to your steel mill, where it is now being burned. At this point, the contract is an executory contract—it is executed on the part of Western and executory on your part. After you pay Western for the coal, the contract will be executed on both sides. ●

Contract Enforceability

Yet another way to classify contracts concerns their enforceability. A **valid contract** has the four elements necessary for contract formation: (1) an agreement (offer and acceptance) (2) supported by legally sufficient consideration (3) for a legal purpose and (4) made by parties who have the legal capacity to enter into the contract. As you can see in Exhibit 7.2 on the following page, valid contracts may be enforceable, voidable, or unenforceable. Additionally, a contract may be *void.* We look next at the meaning of the terms *voidable, unenforceable,* and *void* in relation to contract enforceability.

Voidable Contracts   A **voidable contract** is a *valid* contract but one that can be avoided at the option of one or both of the parties. The party having the option can elect either to avoid any duty to perform or to *ratify* (make valid) the contract. If the contract is avoided, both parties are released from it. If it is ratified, both parties must fully perform their respective legal obligations.

As a general rule, contracts made by minors are voidable at the option of the minor (as will be discussed in Chapter 8). Additionally, contracts entered into under fraudulent conditions are voidable at the option of the defrauded party. Contracts entered into under legally defined duress or undue influence are also voidable (see Chapter 8).

Executed Contract   A contract that has been fully performed by both parties.

Executory Contract   A contract that has not yet been fully performed.

Valid Contract   A contract that results when the elements necessary for contract formation (agreement, consideration, legal purpose, and contractual capacity) are present.

Voidable Contract   A contract that may be legally avoided at the option of one or both of the parties.

---

4. *Uhrhahn Construction & Design, Inc. v. Hopkins,* 179 P.3d 808 (Utah App. 2008).

Exhibit 7.2 Enforceable, Voidable, Unenforceable, and Void Contracts

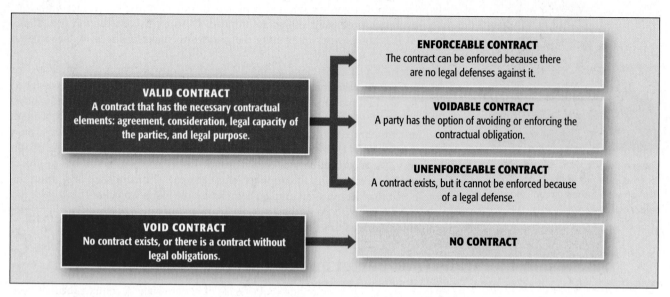

Unenforceable Contract A valid contract rendered unenforceable by some statute or law.

Unenforceable Contracts

An **unenforceable contract** is one that cannot be enforced because of certain legal defenses against it. It is not unenforceable because a party failed to satisfy a legal requirement of the contract. Rather, it is a valid contract rendered unenforceable by some statute or law. For example, some contracts must be in writing (see Chapter 8), and if they are not, they will not be enforceable except in certain exceptional circumstances.

Void Contract A contract having no legal force or binding effect.

Void Contracts

A **void contract** is no contract at all. The terms *void* and *contract* are contradictory. None of the parties has any legal obligations if a contract is void. A contract can be void because, for example, one of the parties was previously determined by a court to be legally insane and thus lacked the legal capacity to enter into a contract.

Quasi Contracts

Quasi Contract An obligation or contract imposed by law (a court), in the absence of an agreement, to prevent the unjust enrichment of one party.

Quasi contracts, or contracts *implied in law,* are wholly different from the actual contracts discussed up to now. The word *quasi* is Latin for "as if." Quasi contracts are not true contracts because they do not arise from any agreement, express or implied, between the parties themselves. Rather, quasi contracts are fictional contracts that courts can impose on the parties "as if" the parties had entered into an actual contract. They are equitable rather than legal contracts.

When the court imposes a quasi contract, a plaintiff may recover in *quantum meruit,*[5] a Latin phrase meaning "as much as he or she deserves." *Quantum meruit* essentially describes the extent of compensation owed under a quasi contract.

Usually, quasi contracts are imposed to avoid the *unjust enrichment* of one party at the expense of another. The doctrine of unjust enrichment is based on the theory that individuals should not be allowed to profit or enrich themselves inequitably at the expense of others. In the following case, the parties did not have an express contract, but one party enjoyed the benefits of the other party's services. The court had to decide if the parties had a quasi contract.

---

5. Pronounced *kwahn*-tuhm *mehr*-oo-wit.

Case 7.1

Seawest Services Association v. Copenhaver

Court of Appeals of Washington,
2012 WL 255857 (2012).
www.courts.wa.gov[a]

What purpose does a water meter serve?

(LordRunar/iStockphoto.com)

FACTS Seawest Services Association owned and operated a water-distribution system that served homes both inside and outside a housing development. Seawest had two classes of members. Full members owned property in the housing development, and limited members received water services for homes outside the development. Both full and limited members paid water bills and, as necessary, assessments for work performed on the water system. In 2001, the Copenhavers purchased a home outside the housing development. They did not have an express contract with Seawest, but they paid water bills for eight years and paid one $3,950 assessment for water system upgrades. In 2009, a dispute arose between the parties, and the Copenhavers began refusing to pay their water bills and assessments. Seawest sued the Copenhavers in a Washington state court. The trial court found that the Copenhavers were limited members of Seawest and thus were liable for the unpaid water bills and assessments. The Copenhavers appealed.

ISSUE Did the Copenhavers have a quasi contract with Seawest?

DECISION Yes. The Washington appellate court affirmed the decision of the trial court, holding that the Copenhavers were liable to Seawest for breach of a quasi contract.

REASON The court explained that a quasi contract exists when a person knowingly receives a benefit from another party and it would be "inequitable for the [person] to retain the benefit without the payment of its value." The Copenhavers enjoyed the benefits of Seawest's water services and even paid for them before their dispute arose. The court found that "the Copenhavers would be unjustly enriched if they could retain benefits provided by Seawest without paying for them." After all, the court reasoned, they purchased a home that received water services, and they knew that they could not receive water without being a limited member of Seawest.

CRITICAL THINKING—Ethical Consideration *In recognizing quasi contracts, does the law try to correct for unethical behavior? Discuss.*

a. In the left-hand column, click on "Court Opinions." In the page that opens, type "Seawest Services" in the "Search Opinions" box and click on "Search." In the result, click on the link to access the case. The Administrative Office of the Washington Courts administers this Web site.

Limitations on Quasi-Contractual Recovery   Although quasi contracts exist to prevent unjust enrichment, in some situations the party who obtains a benefit is not liable for its fair value. Basically, a party who has conferred a benefit on someone else unnecessarily or as a result of misconduct or negligence cannot invoke the doctrine of quasi contract. The enrichment in those situations will not be considered "unjust."

CASE EXAMPLE 7.6   Qwest Wireless, LLC, provides wireless phone services in Arizona and thirteen other states. Qwest marketed and sold handset insurance to its wireless customers, although it did not have a license to sell insurance in Arizona or in any other state. Patrick and Vicki Van Zanen sued Qwest in a federal court for unjust enrichment based on its receipt of sales commissions for the insurance. The court agreed that Qwest had violated the insurance-licensing statute, but found that the sales commissions did not constitute unjust enrichment because the customers had, in fact, received the handset insurance. Also, Qwest had not retained a benefit (the commissions) without paying for it (providing insurance). Therefore, the Van Zanens and other customers did not suffer unfair detriment.[6] ●

When an Actual Contract Exists   The doctrine of quasi contract generally cannot be used when an actual contract covers the area in controversy. In this situation, a

6. *Van Zanen v. Qwest Wireless, LLC*, 522 F.3d 1127 (10th Cir. 2008).

remedy already exists if a party is unjustly enriched because the other fails to perform—the nonbreaching party can sue the breaching party for breach of contract.

EXAMPLE 7.7 Fung contracts with Cameron to deliver a furnace to a building owned by Bateman. Fung delivers the furnace, but Cameron never pays Fung. Bateman has been unjustly enriched in this situation, to be sure. Nevertheless, Fung cannot recover from Bateman in quasi contract because Fung had an actual contract with Cameron. Fung already has a remedy—he can sue for breach of contract to recover the price of the furnace from Cameron. In this situation, the court does not need to impose a quasi contract to achieve justice. ●

Agreement

Agreement A mutual understanding or meeting of the minds between two or more individuals regarding the terms of a contract.

The first essential element for contract formation is **agreement**—the parties must agree on the terms of the contract. Ordinarily, agreement is evidenced by two events: an *offer* and an *acceptance*. One party offers a certain bargain to another party, who then accepts that bargain.

Because words often fail to convey the precise meaning intended, the law of contracts generally adheres to the *objective theory of contracts,* as discussed earlier. Under this theory, a party's words and conduct are held to mean whatever a reasonable person in the offeree's position would think they meant.

Requirements of the Offer

Offer A promise or commitment to perform or refrain from performing some specified act in the future.

An **offer** is a promise or commitment to perform or refrain from performing some specified act in the future. Three elements are necessary for an offer to be effective:

1. There must be a serious, objective intention by the offeror.
2. The terms of the offer must be reasonably certain, or definite, so that the parties and the court can ascertain the terms of the contract.
3. The offer must be communicated to the offeree.

Once an effective offer has been made, the offeree's acceptance of that offer creates a legally binding contract (providing the other essential elements for a valid and enforceable contract are present).

LEARNING OBJECTIVE 3
What elements are necessary for an effective offer? What are some examples of nonoffers?

Intention   The first requirement for an effective offer is a serious, objective intention on the part of the offeror. Intent is not determined by the *subjective* intentions, beliefs, or assumptions of the offeror. Rather, it is determined by what a reasonable person in the offeree's position would conclude the offeror's words and actions meant. Offers made in obvious anger, jest, or undue excitement do not meet the requirement of a serious, objective intent. Because these offers are not effective, an offeree's acceptance does not create an agreement.

EXAMPLE 7.8 You ride to school each day with Julio in his new automobile, which has a market value of $20,000. One cold morning, the car will not start. Julio yells in anger, "I'll sell this car to anyone for $500!" You drop $500 in his lap. A reasonable person, taking into consideration Julio's frustration and the obvious difference in value between the car's market price and the purchase price, would declare that Julio's offer was not made with serious and objective intent and that you do not have an agreement. ●

The concept of intention can be further clarified through an examination of the types of statements that are *not* offers. We look at these expressions and statements in the subsections that follow.

(alexskopje/Shutterstock.com)

When a contractor submits a bid proposal, is that proposal binding on the entity to whom the bid was addressed?

Expressions of Opinion   An expression of opinion is not an offer. It does not demonstrate an intention to enter into a binding agreement. **CASE EXAMPLE 7.9**   Hawkins took his son to McGee, a physician, and asked McGee to operate on the son's hand. McGee said that the boy would be in the hospital three or four days and that the hand would *probably* heal a few days later. The son's hand did not heal for a month, but nonetheless the father did not win a suit for breach of contract. The court held that McGee did not make an offer to heal the son's hand in three or four days. He merely expressed an opinion as to when the hand would heal.[7] ●

Statements of Future Intent   A statement of an *intention* to do something in the future is not an offer. **EXAMPLE 7.10**   If Samir says, "I *plan* to sell my stock in Novation, Inc., for $150 per share," no contract is created if John "accepts" and gives Samir $150 per share for the stock. Samir has merely expressed his intention to enter into a future contract for the sale of the stock. If John accepts and hands over the $150 per share, no contract is formed, because a reasonable person would conclude that Samir was only *thinking about* selling his stock, not *promising* to sell it. ●

Preliminary Negotiations   A request or invitation to negotiate is not an offer. It only expresses a willingness to discuss the possibility of entering into a contract. Examples are statements such as "Will you sell Forest Acres?" and "I wouldn't sell my car for less than $8,000." A reasonable person in the offeree's position would not conclude that such statements indicated an intention to enter into binding obligations.

Likewise, when governmental units and private firms need to have construction work done, they invite contractors to submit bids. The *invitation* to submit bids is not an offer, and a contractor does not bind the other party by submitting a bid. (The bid that the contractor submits is an offer, however, and the other party can bind the contractor by accepting the bid.) For a discussion of some problems with programs designed to promote equal opportunity in government contracting, see this chapter's *Law, Diversity, and Business: Managerial Implications* feature on the following page.

Advertisements, Catalogues, and Circulars   In general, advertisements, catalogues, price lists, and circular letters (meant for the general public) are treated as invitations to negotiate, not as offers to form a contract.[8] This applies whether the materials appear in traditional media or online. **CASE EXAMPLE 7.11**   An ad on *Science*NOW's Web site asked for "news tips." Erik Trell, a professor and physician, submitted a manuscript in which he claimed to have solved a famous mathematical problem. When *Science*NOW did not publish his solution, Trell filed a lawsuit for breach of contract. He claimed that *Science*NOW's ad was an offer, which he had accepted by submitting his manuscript. The court dismissed Trell's suit, holding that an ad is only an invitation for offers, and not an offer itself. Hence, responses to an ad are not acceptances—instead, the responses are the offers. Thus, Trell's submission of the manuscript for publication was the offer, which *Science*NOW did not accept.[9] ●

Price lists are another form of invitation to negotiate or trade. A seller's price list is not an offer to sell at that price. It merely invites the buyer to offer to buy at that price. In fact, the seller usually puts "prices subject to change" on the price list. Only in rare circumstances will a price quotation be construed as an offer.

Although most advertisements and the like are treated as invitations to negotiate, this does not mean that an advertisement can never be an offer. On some occasions, courts have

---

7. *Hawkins v. McGee*, 84 N.H. 114, 146 A. 641 (1929).
8. *Restatement (Second) of Contracts*, Section 26, Comment b.
9. *Trell v. American Association for the Advancement of Science*, 2007 WL 1500497 (W.D.N.Y. 2007).

LAW, DIVERSITY, AND BUSINESS: MANAGERIAL IMPLICATIONS

EQUAL OPPORTUNITY IN PUBLIC CONTRACTING

Cities and states often put projects out for bids. Undoubtedly, there has been discrimination against minorities and female contractors in such bidding processes in the past. The city of San Francisco, California, along with other cities, such as Seattle, Washington, and Madison, Wisconsin, created a system to "make up" for past discrimination.

San Francisco's Public Contracting Policy San Francisco allowed its city government officials to treat bids from businesses owned by women or members of minority groups as though the bids were as much as 10 percent lower than bids of the same amount from other businesses. Hence, if a bid from a minority-owned construction company was $1 million, city officials could consider it to be only $900,000 when comparing it with bids from nonminority-owned businesses.

Proposition 209 Changes the Policy In 1996, the voters of California approved Proposition 209, known as the California Civil Rights Initiative. The proposition amended the state constitution to prohibit state government institutions from considering

ethnicity, race, and gender in the areas of public contracting, public employment, and public education. San Francisco's preferential treatment of minority- and female-owned companies in public contracting was viewed as a violation of Proposition 209. When the California Supreme Court reviewed San Francisco's preferential bidding procedure, it ruled that the process was indeed a violation of the state constitution, as amended.[a]

Seattle, perhaps not wishing to be challenged in court, changed its preferential bidding system by replacing race and gender preferences with geographic preferences for "small" and "disadvantaged" businesses.

Business Implications *Without using preferential bidding, how might managers ensure that their bidding procedure is fair to all businesses, including those that may be suffering the effects of past discrimination?*

---

a. *Coral Construction, Inc. v. San Francisco*, 50 Cal.4th 315, 235 P.3d 947 (2010).

---

construed advertisements to be offers because the ads contained definite terms that invited acceptance (such as an ad offering a reward for the return of a lost dog).

Agreements to Agree In the past, agreements to agree—that is, agreements to agree to the material terms of a contract at some future date—were not considered to be binding contracts. The modern view, however, is that agreements to agree may be enforceable agreements (contracts) if it is clear that the parties intended to be bound by the agreements. In other words, today the emphasis is on the parties' intent rather than on form.

CASE EXAMPLE 7.12 After a customer nearly drowned on a water ride at one of its amusement parks, Six Flags, Inc., filed a lawsuit against the manufacturer that had designed the ride. The manufacturer claimed that the parties did not have a binding contract but had only engaged in preliminary negotiations that were never formalized into a contract to construct the ride. The court, however, held that a faxed document specifying the details of the ride, along with the parties' subsequent actions (beginning construction and handwriting notes on the fax), was sufficient to show an intent to be bound. Because of the court's finding, the manufacturer was required to provide insurance for the water ride at Six Flags, and its insurer was required to defend Six Flags in the personal-injury lawsuit that arose out of the incident.[10] •

Preliminary Agreements Increasingly, the courts are holding that a preliminary agreement constitutes a binding contract if the parties have agreed on all essential terms and

---

10. *Six Flags, Inc. v. Steadfast Insurance Co.*, 474 F.Supp.2d 201 (D.Mass. 2007).

no disputed issues remain to be resolved. In contrast, if the parties agree on certain major terms but leave other terms open for further negotiation, a preliminary agreement is binding only in the sense that the parties have committed themselves to negotiate the undecided terms in good faith in an effort to reach a final agreement.

In the following *Spotlight Case*, one party claimed that an agreement formed via e-mail was binding, and the other party claimed that it was merely an agreement to agree or to work out the terms of a settlement in the future.

Spotlight on Amazon.com

Case 7.2
Basis Technology Corp. v. Amazon.com, Inc.
Appeals Court of Massachusetts, 71 Mass.App.Ct. 29, 878 N.E.2d 952 (2008).

Jeff Bezos, the founder and CEO of Amazon.com, with a Japanese manager.

FACTS Basis Technology Corporation created software and provided technical services for a Japanese-language Web site operated by Amazon.com, Inc. The agreement between the two companies allowed for separately negotiated contracts for additional services that Basis might provide to Amazon. At the end of 1999, Basis and Amazon entered into stock-purchase agreements. Later, Amazon objected to certain actions related to the securities that Basis sold. Basis sued Amazon for various claims involving these securities and for failing to pay for services performed by Basis that were not included in the original agreement. During the trial, the two parties appeared to reach an agreement to settle out of court via a series of e-mail exchanges outlining the settlement. When Amazon reneged, Basis requested that a court enforce the proposed settlement. The trial judge entered a judgment against Amazon, which appealed.

ISSUE Did the agreement that Amazon entered into with Basis via e-mail constitute a binding settlement contract?

DECISION Yes. The Appeals Court of Massachusetts affirmed the trial court's finding that Amazon intended to be bound by the terms of the e-mail exchanges.

REASON The court examined the evidence consisting of e-mails between the two parties. It pointed out that in open court and on the record, counsel "reported the result of the settlement without specification of the terms." Amazon claimed that the e-mail terms were incomplete and were not definite enough to form an agreement. The court noted, however, that "provisions are not ambiguous simply because the parties have developed different interpretations of them." In the exchange of e-mails, the essential business terms were indeed resolved. Afterward, the parties were simply proceeding to record the settlement terms, not to create them. The e-mails constituted a complete and unambiguous statement of the parties' desire to be bound by the settlement terms.

WHAT IF THE FACTS WERE DIFFERENT? *Assume that, instead of exchanging e-mails, the attorneys for both sides had a phone conversation that included all of the terms to which they actually agreed in their e-mail exchanges. Would the court have ruled differently? Why or why not?*

PREVENTING LEGAL DISPUTES

To avoid potential legal disputes, be cautious when drafting a memorandum that outlines a preliminary agreement or understanding with another party. If all the major terms are included, a court might hold that the agreement is binding even though you intended it to be only a tentative agreement. One way to avoid being bound is to include in the writing the points of disagreement, as well as the points on which you and the other party agree. Alternatively, you could add a disclaimer to the memorandum stating that, although you anticipate entering a contract in the future, neither party intends to be legally bound to the terms that were discussed. That way, the other party cannot claim that you have already reached an agreement on all essential terms.

Definiteness   The second requirement for an effective offer involves the definiteness of its terms. An offer must have reasonably definite terms so that a court can determine if a breach has occurred and give an appropriate remedy.[11] The specific terms required depend, of course, on the type of contract. Generally, a contract must include the following terms, either expressed in the contract or capable of being reasonably inferred from it:

1. The identification of the parties.
2. The identification of the object or subject matter of the contract (also the quantity, when appropriate), including the work to be performed, with specific identification of such items as goods, services, and land.
3. The consideration to be paid.
4. The time of payment, delivery, or performance.

An offer may invite an acceptance to be worded in such specific terms that the contract is made definite. **EXAMPLE 7.13**   Nintendo of America, Inc., contacts your Play 2 Win Games store and offers to sell "from one to twenty-five Nintendo 3DS gaming systems for $75 each. State number desired in acceptance." You agree to buy twenty systems. Because the quantity is specified in the acceptance, the terms are definite, and the contract is enforceable. ●

Communication   A third requirement for an effective offer is communication—the offer must be communicated to the offeree. **EXAMPLE 7.14**   Tolson advertises a reward for the return of her lost cat. Dirk, not knowing of the reward, finds the cat and returns it to Tolson. Ordinarily, Dirk cannot recover the reward, because an essential element of a reward contract is that the one who claims the reward must have known it was offered. A few states would allow recovery of the reward, but not on contract principles—Dirk would be allowed to recover on the basis that it would be unfair to deny him the reward just because he did not know about it. ●

Termination of the Offer

The communication of an effective offer to an offeree gives the offeree the power to transform the offer into a binding, legal obligation (a contract) by an acceptance. This power of acceptance does not continue forever, though. It can be terminated either by the *action of the parties* or by *operation of law*. Termination by the action of the parties can involve a revocation by the offeror or a rejection or counteroffer by the offeree.

Termination by Action of the Offeror   The offeror's act of withdrawing an offer is referred to as **revocation**. Unless an offer is irrevocable, the offeror usually can revoke the offer (even if he or she has promised to keep it open), as long as the revocation is communicated to the offeree before the offeree accepts. Revocation may be accomplished by an express repudiation of the offer (such as "I withdraw my previous offer of October 17") or by the performance of acts that are inconsistent with the existence of the offer and that are made known to the offeree.

EXAMPLE 7.15   Misha offers to sell some land to Gary. A month passes, and Gary, who has not accepted the offer, learns that Misha has sold the property to Liam. Because Misha's sale of the land to Liam is inconsistent with the continued existence of the offer to Gary, the offer to Gary is effectively revoked. ●

The general rule followed by most states is that a revocation becomes effective when the offeree or the offeree's *agent* (a person who acts on behalf of another—see Chapter 23) actually receives it. Therefore, a statement of revocation sent via FedEx on April 1 and delivered at the offeree's residence or place of business on April 2 becomes effective on April 2.

> "I fear explanations explanatory of things explained."
>
> Abraham Lincoln, 1809–1865 (Sixteenth president of the United States, 1861–1865)

Revocation The withdrawal of a contract offer by the offeror. Unless an offer is irrevocable, it can be revoked at any time prior to acceptance without liability.

---

11. *Restatement (Second) of Contracts,* Section 33. The UCC has relaxed the requirements regarding the definiteness of terms in contracts for the sale of goods. See UCC 2–204(3).

Termination by Action of the Offeree
If the offeree rejects the offer—by words or by conduct—the offer is terminated. Any subsequent attempt by the offeree to accept will be construed as a new offer, giving the original offeror (now the offeree) the power of acceptance.

Like a revocation, a rejection of an offer is effective only when it is actually received by the offeror or the offeror's agent. **EXAMPLE 7.16** Goldfinch Farms offers to sell specialty Maitake mushrooms to a Japanese buyer, Kinoko Foods. If Kinoko rejects the offer by sending a letter via U.S. mail, the rejection will not be effective (and the offer will not be terminated) until Goldfinch receives the letter. •

Inquiries about an Offer   Merely inquiring about an offer does not constitute rejection. **EXAMPLE 7.17** Your friend offers to buy your Inkling digital pen—which automatically remembers whatever is drawn with it on any kind of paper—for $100. You respond, "Is that your best offer?" A reasonable person would conclude that you have not rejected the offer but have merely made an inquiry. You could still accept and bind your friend to the $100 price. •

Counteroffer An offeree's response to an offer in which the offeree rejects the original offer and at the same time makes a new offer.

Counteroffers   A **counteroffer** is a rejection of the original offer and the simultaneous making of a new offer. **EXAMPLE 7.18** Burke offers to sell his home to Lang for $270,000. Lang responds, "Your price is too high. I'll offer to purchase your house for $250,000." Lang's response is called a counteroffer because it rejects Burke's offer to sell at $270,000 and creates a new offer by Lang to purchase the home at a price of $250,000. •

At common law, the **mirror image rule** requires that the offeree's acceptance match the offeror's offer exactly. In other words, the terms of the acceptance must "mirror" those of the offer. If the acceptance materially changes or adds to the terms of the original offer, it will be considered not an acceptance but a counteroffer—which, of course, need not be accepted. The original offeror can, however, accept the terms of the counteroffer and create a valid contract.[12]

Mirror Image Rule A common law rule that requires that the terms of the offeree's acceptance adhere exactly to the terms of the offeror's offer for a valid contract to be formed.

Termination by Operation of Law
The power of the offeree to transform the offer into a binding legal obligation can be terminated by operation of law through the occurrence of any of the following events:

1. Lapse of time.
2. Destruction of the specific subject matter of the offer.
3. Death or incompetence of the offeror or the offeree.
4. Supervening illegality of the proposed contract. (A statute or court decision that makes an offer illegal automatically terminates the offer.)

Lapse of Time   An offer terminates automatically by law when the period of time *specified in the offer* has passed. If the offer states that it will be left open until a particular date, then the offer will terminate at midnight on that day. If the offer states that it will be left open for a number of days, this time period normally begins to run when the offer is actually *received* by the offeree, not when it is formed or sent.

If the offer does not specify a time for acceptance, the offer terminates at the end of a *reasonable* period of time. A reasonable period of time is determined by the subject matter of the contract, business and market conditions, and other relevant circumstances. An offer to sell farm produce, for instance, will terminate sooner than an offer to sell farm equipment because produce is perishable and subject to greater fluctuations in market value.

---

12. The mirror image rule has been greatly modified in regard to sales contracts. Section 2–207 of the UCC provides that a contract is formed if the offeree makes a definite expression of acceptance (such as signing the form in the appropriate location), even though the terms of the acceptance modify or add to the terms of the original offer (see Chapter 10).

Destruction or Death   An offer is automatically terminated if the specific subject matter of the offer (such as an iPad or a house) is destroyed before the offer is accepted. An offeree's power of acceptance is also terminated when the offeror or offeree dies or becomes legally incapacitated (capacity will be discussed in Chapter 8), *unless the offer is irrevocable.*

Irrevocable Offers

Although most offers are revocable, some can be made irrevocable. One form of irrevocable offer is an option contract. An **option contract** is created when an offeror promises to hold an offer open for a specified period of time in return for a payment (consideration) given by the offeree. An option contract takes away the offeror's power to revoke an offer for the period of time specified in the option. If no time is specified, then a reasonable period of time is implied. Option contracts are frequently used in conjunction with the sale of real estate.

Acceptance

An **acceptance** is a voluntary act by the offeree that shows assent, or agreement, to the terms of an offer. The offeree's act may consist of words or conduct. The acceptance must be unequivocal and must be communicated to the offeror. Generally, only the person to whom the offer is made or that person's agent can accept the offer and create a binding contract.

Unequivocal Acceptance

To exercise the power of acceptance effectively, the offeree must accept unequivocally. This is the *mirror image rule* previously discussed. If the acceptance is subject to new conditions or if the terms of the acceptance materially change the original offer, the acceptance may be deemed a counteroffer that implicitly rejects the original offer.

Certain terms included in an acceptance will not change the offer sufficiently to constitute rejection. **EXAMPLE 7.19** In response to an art dealer's offer to sell a painting, the offeree, Ashton Gibbs, replies, "I accept. Please send a written contract." Gibbs is requesting a written contract but is not making it a condition for acceptance. Therefore, the acceptance is effective without the written contract. In contrast, if Gibbs replies, "I accept *if* you send a written contract," the acceptance is expressly conditioned on the request for a writing, and the statement is not an acceptance but a counteroffer. (Notice how important each word is!)[13] ●

Silence as Acceptance

Ordinarily, silence cannot constitute acceptance, even if the offeror states, "By your silence and inaction, you will be deemed to have accepted this offer." This general rule applies because an offeree should not be put under a burden of liability to act affirmatively in order to reject an offer. No consideration—that is, nothing of value (see page 216)—has passed to the offeree to impose such a liability.

In some instances, however, the offeree does have a duty to speak. If so, his or her silence or inaction will operate as an acceptance. Silence may be an acceptance when an offeree takes the benefit of offered services even though he or she had an opportunity to reject them and knew that they were offered with the expectation of compensation. **EXAMPLE 7.20** Juan earns extra income by washing store windows. Juan taps on the window of a store, catches the attention of the store's manager, and points to the window and raises his cleaner, signaling that he will be washing the window. The manager does nothing to stop him. The store manager's silence constitutes an acceptance, and an implied contract is created. The store is bound to pay a reasonable value for Juan's work. ●

---

13. As noted in footnote 12, in regard to sales contracts, the UCC provides that an acceptance may still be effective even if some terms are added. The new terms are simply treated as proposals for additions to the contract, unless both parties are merchants. If the parties are merchants, the additional terms (with some exceptions) become part of the contract [UCC 2–207(2)].

Option Contract A contract under which the offeror cannot revoke the offer for a stipulated time period (because the offeree has given consideration for the offer to remain open).

Acceptance The act of voluntarily agreeing, through words or conduct, to the terms of an offer, thereby creating a contract.

 KNOW THIS

When an offer is rejected, it is terminated.

Silence can also operate as an acceptance when the offeree has had prior dealings with the offeror. If a merchant, for instance, routinely receives shipments from a supplier and in the past has always notified the supplier when defective goods are rejected, then silence constitutes acceptance. Also, if a buyer solicits an offer specifying that certain terms and conditions are acceptable, and the seller makes the offer in response to the solicitation, the buyer has a duty to reject—that is, a duty to tell the seller that the offer is not acceptable. Failure to reject (silence) will operate as an acceptance.

Communication of Acceptance   In a bilateral contract, communication of acceptance is necessary because acceptance is in the form of a promise (not performance), and the contract is formed when the promise is made (rather than when the act is performed). Communication of acceptance is not necessary if the offer dispenses with the requirement, however, or if the offer can be accepted by silence.

Because a unilateral contract calls for the full performance of some act, acceptance is usually evident, and notification is unnecessary. Nevertheless, exceptions do exist, such as when the offeror requests notice of acceptance or has no way of determining whether the requested act has been performed.

In the following case, the court had to decide whether a party's failure to respond to a settlement offer constituted acceptance.

Case 7.3

Powerhouse Custom Homes, Inc. v. 84 Lumber Co.

Court of Appeals of Georgia,
307 Ga.App. 605, 705 S.E.2d 704 (2011).

(grmnicholas/iStockphoto.com)
A custom home being built.

FACTS   Powerhouse Custom Homes, Inc., owed $95,260.42 to 84 Lumber Company under a credit agreement. When Powerhouse failed to pay, 84 Lumber filed a suit to collect. During mediation, the parties agreed to a deadline for objections to whatever agreement they might reach. If there was no objection, the agreement would be binding. Powerhouse then offered to pay less than the amount owed, and 84 Lumber did not respond. Powerhouse argued that 84 Lumber had accepted the offer by not objecting to it within the deadline.

ISSUE   Did 84 Lumber, by failing to object to Powerhouse's proposal to settle the debt for less than was owed, unequivocally accept the offer?

DECISION   No. The court held that for a contract to be formed, an offer must be accepted unequivocally. Without such an acceptance, there is no enforceable contract.

REASON   Powerhouse made an offer of a proposed settlement, but 84 Lumber did not communicate its acceptance. Thus, the court reasoned that the parties had not reached an agreement. Because 84 Lumber had not agreed to Powerhouse's proposal, the ten-day deadline did not apply. Powerhouse was liable for the entire debt, plus interest, attorneys' fees, and costs.

CRITICAL THINKING—Economic Consideration   *Why do judgments often include awards of interest, attorneys' fees, and costs?*

Mode and Timeliness of Acceptance   Acceptance in bilateral contracts must be timely. The general rule is that acceptance in a bilateral contract is timely if it is made before the offer is terminated. Problems may arise, though, when the parties involved are not dealing face to face. In such situations, the offeree should use an authorized mode of communication.

Mailbox Rule A common law rule that acceptance takes effect, and thus completes formation of the contract, at the time the offeree sends or delivers the acceptance via the communication mode expressly or impliedly authorized by the offeror.

The Mailbox Rule   Acceptance takes effect, and thus completes formation of the contract, at the time the offeree sends or delivers the acceptance via the mode of communication expressly or impliedly authorized by the offeror. This is the so-called **mailbox rule,** also called the *deposited acceptance rule,* which the majority of courts follow. Under this rule, if the authorized mode of communication is the mail, then an acceptance becomes valid when it is dispatched (placed in the control of the U.S. Postal Service)—not when it is received by the offeror.

The mailbox rule does not apply to instantaneous forms of communication, such as when the parties are dealing face to face, by phone, or by fax. In addition, a separate rule applies to e-mail. Under the Uniform Electronic Transactions Act (see page 215 later in this chapter) e-mail may be considered sent when it either leaves the sender's control or is received by the recipient. This rule, which takes the place of the mailbox rule if the parties have agreed to conduct transactions electronically, allows an e-mail acceptance to become effective when sent.

Authorized Means of Communication   A means of communicating acceptance can be expressly authorized by the offeror or impliedly authorized by the facts and circumstances of the situation. An acceptance sent by means not expressly or impliedly authorized normally is not effective until it is received by the offeror.

When an offeror specifies how acceptance should be made, such as by overnight delivery, the contract is not formed unless the offeree uses that mode of acceptance. Both the offeror and the offeree are bound in contract the moment the specified means of acceptance is employed. **EXAMPLE 7.21**   Motorola Mobility, Inc., offers to sell 144 Atrix 4G smartphones and 72 Lapdocks to Call Me Plus phone stores. The offer states that Call Me Plus must accept the offer via FedEx overnight delivery. The acceptance is effective (and a binding contract is formed) the moment that Call Me Plus gives the overnight envelope containing the acceptance to the FedEx driver. •

If the offeror does not expressly authorize a certain mode of acceptance, then acceptance can be made by *any reasonable means.*[14] Courts look at the prevailing business usages and the surrounding circumstances to determine whether the mode of acceptance used was reasonable. Usually, the offeror's choice of a particular means in making the offer implies that the offeree can use the *same or a faster* means for acceptance.

Substitute Method of Acceptance   If the offeror authorizes a particular method of acceptance, but the offeree accepts by a different means, the acceptance may still be effective if the substituted method serves the same purpose as the authorized means.

The use of a substitute method of acceptance is not effective on dispatch, though, and no contract will be formed until the acceptance is received by the offeror. Thus, if an offer specifies FedEx overnight delivery but the offeree accepts by UPS overnight delivery, the acceptance will still be effective, but not until the offeror receives it.

E-Contracts

E-Contract A contract that is formed electronically.

Many contracts are formed online. Electronic contracts, or **e-contracts,** must meet the same basic requirements (agreement, consideration, contractual capacity, and legality) as paper contracts. Disputes concerning e-contracts, however, tend to center on contract terms and whether the parties voluntarily agreed to those terms.

Online contracts may be formed not only for the sale of goods and services but also for *licensing.* The "sale" of software generally involves a license, or a right to use the software,

---

14. Note that UCC 2–206(1)(a) states specifically that an acceptance of an offer for the sale of goods can be made by any medium that is *reasonable* under the circumstances.

rather than the passage of title (ownership rights) from the seller to the buyer. As you read through the following subsections, keep in mind that although we typically refer to the offeror and the offeree as a *seller* and a *buyer,* in many online transactions these parties would be more accurately described as a *licensor* and a *licensee.*

Online Offers

Sellers doing business via the Internet can protect themselves against contract disputes and legal liability by creating offers that clearly spell out the terms that will govern their transactions if the offers are accepted. All important terms should be conspicuous and easy to view.

Displaying the Offer   The seller's Web site should include a hypertext link to a page containing the full contract so that potential buyers are made aware of the terms to which they are assenting. The contract generally must be displayed online in a readable format such as in a twelve-point typeface.

All provisions should be reasonably clear. **EXAMPLE 7.22** Netquip sells a variety of heavy equipment, such as trucks and trailers, online at its Web site. Because Netquip's pricing schedule is very complex, the schedule must be fully provided and explained on the Web site. In addition, the terms of the sale (such as any warranties and the refund policy) must be fully disclosed. •

Provisions to Include   An important rule to keep in mind is that the offeror (seller) controls the offer and thus the resulting contract. The seller should therefore anticipate the terms she or he wants to include in a contract and provide for them in the offer. In some instances, a standardized contract form may suffice. At a minimum, an online offer should include the following provisions:

1. *Acceptance of terms.* A clause that clearly indicates what constitutes the buyer's agreement to the terms of the offer, such as a box containing the words "I accept" that the buyer can click on to indicate acceptance. (Mechanisms for accepting online offers will be discussed in detail later in this chapter.)
2. *Payment.* A provision specifying how payment for the goods (including any applicable taxes) must be made.
3. *Return policy.* A statement of the seller's refund and return policies.
4. *Disclaimer.* Disclaimers of liability for certain uses of the goods. For example, an online seller of business forms may add a disclaimer that the seller does not accept responsibility for the buyer's reliance on the forms rather than on an attorney's advice.
5. *Limitation on remedies.* A provision specifying the remedies available to the buyer if the goods are found to be defective or if the contract is otherwise breached. Any limitation of remedies should be clearly spelled out.
6. *Privacy policy.* A statement indicating how the seller will use the information gathered about the buyer. (See the *Linking Business Law to Marketing* feature on pages 221–222 for a discussion of how the information may be used.)
7. *Dispute resolution.* Provisions relating to dispute settlement, such as an arbitration clause or a *forum-selection clause* (discussed next).

Dispute-Settlement Provisions   Online offers frequently include provisions relating to dispute settlement. For example, the offer might include an arbitration clause specifying that any dispute arising under the contract will be arbitrated in a designated forum. (For a discussion of how students enrolling in online education courses may agree to arbitration of future disputes, see this chapter's *Adapting the Law to the Online Environment* on the following page.)

> "If two men agree on everything, you can be sure one of them is doing the thinking."
>
> Lyndon Baines Johnson, 1908–1973
> (Thirty-sixth president of the United States, 1963–1969)

ADAPTING THE LAW TO THE ONLINE ENVIRONMENT

THE VALIDITY OF E-SIGNATURES ON AGREEMENTS WITH ONLINE COLLEGES AND UNIVERSITIES

The number of online institutions offering bachelor's, master's, and even doctoral degrees has grown dramatically over the past decade. Enrollment for these online colleges and universities is conducted online. Most, if not all, of the schools ask enrolling students to agree that any disputes will be solved by arbitration. How valid are these enrollment agreements when the students simply indicate their assent via what the online universities call e-signatures?

At Least Two Online Students Claimed That Their E-Signatures Were Invalid

Scott Rosendahl alleged that online Ashford University's enrollment adviser had claimed that Ashford offered one of the cheapest undergraduate degree programs in the country. In fact, it did not.

Veronica Clarke enrolled in the doctor of psychology program at the online University of the Rockies. She alleged that its enrollment adviser had told her that the doctor of psychology program would qualify her to become a clinical psychologist in the U.S. military, but that statement was false.

Rosendahl and Clarke sued their respective universities for violation of unfair competition laws and false advertising laws, fraud, and negligent misrepresentation.

The Online Universities Argued for Arbitration

The universities pointed out that each student had electronically consented to the enrollment agreement, which clearly required that all disputes be arbitrated. Each agreement stated, "Such arbitration shall be the sole remedy for the resolution of any dispute or controversy between the parties to this agreement."

One issue was whether the e-signatures on the agreement were valid. Each application form had an "acknowledgment and signature" paragraph that stated, "My signature on this application certifies that I have read, understood, and agreed to my rights and responsibilities as set forth in this application."

Both students had to click on an electronic box acknowledging that they had read the agreement and consented to it. When they clicked on the box, the phrase "Signed by E-Signature" appeared on the signature line.

The Court Ruled in Favor of the Online Universities

The universities submitted copies of Rosendahl's and Clarke's online application forms to the court. Both forms contained the arbitration agreement and were signed with e-signatures. Rosendahl and Clarke provided no proof that they had not consented to the enrollment agreements. Thus, the court held that the online universities had proved the existence of valid arbitration agreements.[a]

Critical Thinking

Did the fact that the arbitration agreements were valid prevent Rosendahl and Clarke from pursuing their claims for negligent misrepresentation and fraud? Why or why not?

a. *Rosendahl v. Bridgepoint Education, Inc.,* 2012 WL 667049 (S.D.Cal. 2012).

Forum-Selection Clause A provision in a contract designating the court, jurisdiction, or tribunal that will decide any disputes arising under the contract.

Many online contracts also contain a **forum-selection clause** indicating the forum, or location (such as a court or jurisdiction), for the resolution of any dispute arising under the contract. As discussed in Chapter 3 on pages 70–72, significant jurisdictional issues may occur when parties are separated by a great distance, as they often are when they form contracts via the Internet. A forum-selection clause will help to avert future jurisdictional problems and also help to ensure that the seller will not be required to appear in court in a distant state.

Some online contracts may also include a *choice-of-law clause* specifying that any dispute arising out of the contract will be settled in accordance with the law of a particular jurisdiction, such as a state or country. Choice-of-law clauses are particularly common in international contracts, but they may also appear in e-contracts to specify which state's laws will govern in the United States.

Exhibit 7.3 A Click-On Agreement

This exhibit illustrates an online offer to form a contract. To accept the offer, the user simply clicks on the "I Accept" button.

Click-On Agreement An agreement that arises when an online buyer clicks on "I agree" or otherwise indicates her or his assent to be bound by the terms of an offer.

LEARNING OBJECTIVE 4
How do shrink-wrap and click-on agreements differ from other contracts? How have traditional laws been applied to these agreements?

Shrink-Wrap Agreement An agreement whose terms are expressed in a document located inside a box in which goods (usually software) are packaged.

Online Acceptances

The *Restatement (Second) of Contracts*—a compilation of common law contract principles—states that parties may agree to a contract "by written or spoken words or by other action or by failure to act."[15] The Uniform Commercial Code (UCC), which governs sales contracts, has a similar provision. Section 2–204 of the UCC states that any contract for the sale of goods "may be made in any manner sufficient to show agreement, including conduct by both parties which recognizes the existence of such a contract."

Click-On Agreements   The courts have used these provisions to conclude that a binding contract can be created by conduct, including the act of clicking on a box indicating "I accept" or "I agree" to accept an online offer. The agreement resulting from such an acceptance is often called a **click-on agreement** (sometimes, *click-on license* or *click-wrap agreement*). Exhibit 7.3 to the left on this page shows a portion of a click-on agreement that accompanies a software package.

Generally, the law does not require that the parties have read all of the terms in a contract for it to be effective. Therefore, clicking on a box that states "I agree" to certain terms can be enough. The terms may be contained on a Web site through which the buyer is obtaining goods or services, or they may appear on a computer screen when software is loaded from a CD-ROM or DVD or downloaded from the Internet.

CASE EXAMPLE 7.23   Facebook, Inc., is headquartered in California. The "Terms of Use" that govern Facebook users' accounts include a forum-selection clause that provides for the resolution of all disputes in a court in Santa Clara County. Potential Facebook users cannot become actual users unless they click on an acknowledgment that they have agreed to this term. Mustafa Fteja was an active user of facebook.com when his account was disabled. He sued Facebook in a federal court in New York, claiming that it had disabled his Facebook page without justification and for discriminatory reasons. Facebook filed a motion to transfer the case to California under the forum-selection clause. The court found that the forum-selection clause in Facebook's online contract was binding and transferred the case. Fteja had been informed of the consequences of his click—he would be bound to the forum-selection clause. When he clicked on the button and became a Facebook user, he agreed to resolve all disputes with Facebook in Santa Clara County, California.[16] ●

Shrink-Wrap Agreements   A **shrink-wrap agreement** (or *shrink-wrap license*) is an agreement whose terms are expressed inside a box in which goods are packaged. (The term *shrink-wrap* refers to the plastic that covers the box.) Usually, the party who opens the box is told that she or he agrees to the terms by keeping whatever is in the box. Similarly, when the purchaser opens a software package, he or she agrees to abide by the terms of the limited license agreement.

EXAMPLE 7.24   Arial orders a new iMac from Big Dog Electronics, which ships it to her. Along with the iMac, the shipping box contains an agreement setting forth the terms of the sale, including what remedies are available. The document also states that Arial's retention of the iMac for longer than thirty days will be construed as an acceptance of the terms. ●

---

15. *Restatement (Second) of Contracts*, Section 19.
16. *Fteja v. Facebook, Inc.*, 841 F.Supp.2d 829 (S.D.N.Y. 2012).

In most instances, a shrink-wrap agreement is not between a retailer and a buyer, but between the manufacturer of the hardware or software and the ultimate buyer-user of the product. The terms generally concern warranties, remedies, and other issues associated with the use of the product.

Shrink-Wrap Agreements and Enforceable Contract Terms

In some cases, the courts have enforced the terms of shrink-wrap agreements in the same way as the terms of other contracts. These courts have reasoned that by including the terms with the product, the seller proposed a contract that the buyer could accept by using the product after having an opportunity to read the terms. Thus, a buyer's failure to object to terms contained within a shrink-wrapped software package may constitute an acceptance of the terms by conduct.

Shrink-Wrap Terms That May Not Be Enforced

Sometimes, however, courts have refused to enforce certain terms included in shrink-wrap agreements because the buyer did not expressly consent to them. An important factor is when the parties form their contract.

Suppose that a buyer orders a product over the telephone. If the contract is formed at that time and the seller does not mention terms such as an arbitration clause or forum-selection clause, clearly the buyer has not expressly agreed to these terms. If the clauses are then included in the shrink-wrap agreement, a court may conclude that those terms were only proposals for additional terms and not part of the original contract. After all, the buyer did not discover them until *after* the contract had been formed.

Browse-Wrap Term A term or condition of use that is presented when an online buyer downloads a product but that the buyer does not have to agree to before installing or using the product.

Browse-Wrap Terms   Like the terms of a click-on agreement, **browse-wrap terms** can occur in a transaction conducted over the Internet. Unlike a click-on agreement, however, browse-wrap terms do not require the buyer or user to assent to the terms before, say, downloading or using certain software. In other words, a person can install the software without clicking "I agree" to the terms of a license. Browse-wrap terms are often unenforceable because they do not satisfy the agreement requirement of contract formation.

Federal Law on E-Signatures and E-Documents

E-Signature An electronic sound, symbol, or process attached to or logically associated with a record and adopted by a person with the intent to sign the record.

Today, numerous technologies allow electronic documents to be signed. An **e-signature** has been defined as "an electronic sound, symbol, or process attached to or logically associated with a record and executed or adopted by a person with the intent to sign the record."[17] Thus, e-signatures include encrypted digital signatures, names (intended as signatures) at the ends of e-mail messages, and "clicks" on a Web page if the click includes the identification of the person.

In 2000, Congress enacted the Electronic Signatures in Global and National Commerce Act (E-SIGN Act),[18] which provides that no contract, record, or signature may be "denied legal effect" solely because it is in electronic form. In other words, under this law, an electronic signature is as valid as a signature on paper, and an e-document can be as enforceable as a paper one.

For an e-signature to be enforceable, the contracting parties must have agreed to use electronic signatures. For an electronic document to be valid, it must be in a form that can be retained and accurately reproduced.

The E-SIGN Act does not apply to all types of documents. Contracts and documents that are exempt include court papers, divorce decrees, evictions, foreclosures, health-insurance terminations, prenuptial agreements, and wills. Also, the only agreements governed by the

(Terry Davis/Shutterstock.com)

Many e-signatures are legally binding.

---

17. This definition is from the Uniform Electronic Transactions Act, discussed next.
18. 15 U.S.C. Sections 7001 *et seq.*

UCC that fall under this law are those covered by Articles 2 and 2A and UCC 1–107 and 1–206. Despite these limitations, the E-SIGN Act significantly expanded the possibilities for contracting online.

The Uniform Electronic Transactions Act

In 1999, the National Conference of Commissioners on Uniform State Laws and the American Law Institute promulgated the Uniform Electronic Transactions Act (UETA). The UETA has been adopted, at least in part, by forty-eight states.

The primary purpose of the UETA is to remove barriers to e-commerce by giving the same legal effect to electronic records and signatures as is given to paper documents and signatures. As mentioned earlier, the UETA broadly defines an *e-signature* as "an electronic sound, symbol, or process attached to or logically associated with a record and executed or adopted by a person with the intent to sign the record."[19] A **record** is "information that is inscribed on a tangible medium or that is stored in an electronic or other medium and is retrievable in perceivable [visual] form."[20]

Record Information that is either inscribed on a tangible medium or stored in an electronic or other medium and is retrievable.

The Scope and Applicability of the UETA
The UETA does not create new rules for electronic contracts but rather establishes that records, signatures, and contracts may not be denied enforceability solely due to their electronic form. The UETA does not apply to all writings and signatures. It covers only electronic records and electronic signatures *relating to a transaction*. A *transaction* is defined as an interaction between two or more parties relating to business, commercial, or governmental activities.[21] Furthermore, the act specifically does not apply to wills or testamentary trusts or to transactions governed by the UCC (other than those covered by Articles 2 and 2A).

The UETA will not apply to a transaction unless each of the parties has previously agreed to conduct transactions by electronic means. The agreement need not be explicit. It may be implied by the conduct of the parties and the surrounding circumstances. For instance, the party's agreement may be inferred from an e-mail or some verbal communication.

The Federal E-SIGN Act and the UETA
When Congress passed the E-SIGN Act in 2000, a year after the UETA was presented to the states for adoption, a significant issue was to what extent the federal E-SIGN Act preempted the UETA as adopted by the states. The E-SIGN Act[22] refers explicitly to the UETA and provides that if a state has enacted the uniform version of the UETA, it is not preempted by the E-SIGN Act. In other words, if the state has enacted the UETA without modification, state law will govern.

The problem is that many states have enacted nonuniform (modified) versions of the UETA. The E-SIGN Act specifies that those exclusions will be preempted to the extent that they are inconsistent with the E-SIGN Act's provisions.

The E-SIGN Act, however, explicitly allows the states to enact alternative requirements for the use of electronic records or electronic signatures. Generally, however, the requirements must be consistent with the provisions of the E-SIGN Act, and the state must not give greater legal status or effect to one specific type of technology. Additionally, if a state enacts alternative requirements *after* the E-SIGN Act was adopted, the state law must specifically refer to the E-SIGN Act.

---

19. UETA 102(8).
20. UETA 102(15).
21. UETA 2(12) and 3.
22. 15 U.S.C. Section 7002(2)(A)(i).

Consideration

Earlier in this chapter, we discussed the first requirement for a valid contract—agreement. We then explained some issues affecting agreement in e-contracts. Next, we turn to the second requirement for a valid contract—consideration.

In every legal system, some promises will be enforced, and other promises will not be enforced. The simple fact that a party has made a promise does not necessarily mean that the promise is enforceable. Under the common law, a primary basis for the enforcement of promises is consideration. **Consideration** usually is defined as the value given in return for a promise.

Often, consideration is broken down into two parts: (1) something of *legally sufficient value* must be given in exchange for the promise, and (2) there must be a *bargained-for exchange*.

Legally Sufficient Value

To be legally sufficient, consideration must be something of value in the eyes of the law. The "something of legally sufficient value" may consist of any of the following:

1. A promise to do something that one has no prior legal duty to do (to pay on receipt of certain goods, for example).
2. The performance of an action that one is otherwise not obligated to undertake (such as providing accounting services).
3. The refraining from an action that one has a legal right to undertake (called a **forbearance**).

Consideration in bilateral contracts normally consists of a promise in return for a promise, as explained earlier. In a contract for the sale of goods, for instance, the seller promises to ship specific goods to the buyer, and the buyer promises to pay for those goods when they are received. Each of these promises constitutes consideration for the contract.

In contrast, unilateral contracts involve a promise in return for a performance. **EXAMPLE 7.25** Anita says to her neighbor, "If you paint my garage, I will pay you $800." Anita's neighbor paints the garage. The act of painting the garage is the consideration that creates Anita's contractual obligation to pay her neighbor $800. ●

What if, in return for a promise to pay, a person refrains from pursuing harmful habits, such as the use of tobacco and alcohol? Does such forbearance create consideration for the contract? That was the issue in the 1891 case *Hamer v. Sidway,* which we present as this chapter's *Landmark in the Law* feature on the facing page.

Bargained-for Exchange

The second element of consideration is that it must provide the basis for the bargain struck between the contracting parties. The item of value must be given or promised by the promisor (offeror) in return for the promisee's promise, performance, or promise of performance. This element of bargained-for exchange distinguishes contracts from gifts.

EXAMPLE 7.26 Sheng-Li says to his son, "In consideration of the fact that you are not as wealthy as your brothers, I will pay you $5,000." The fact that the word *consideration* is used does not, by itself, mean that consideration has been given. Indeed, Sheng-Li's promise is not enforceable. Because the son does not need to give Sheng-Li something of legal value in return for his promise, there is no bargained-for exchange. Rather, Sheng-Li has simply stated his motive for giving his son a gift. ●

Adequacy of Consideration

Adequacy of consideration involves how much consideration is given. Essentially, adequacy of consideration concerns the fairness of the bargain. On the surface, fairness would appear to be an issue when the items exchanged are of unequal value. In general, however,

Consideration The value given in return for a promise or performance in a contractual agreement.

LEARNING OBJECTIVE 5
What is consideration? What is required for consideration to be legally sufficient?

Forbearance The act of refraining from an action that one has a legal right to undertake.

LANDMARK IN THE LAW
Hamer v. Sidway (1891)

In *Hamer v. Sidway,*[a] the issue before the court arose from a contract created in 1869 between William Story, Sr., and his nephew, William Story II. The uncle promised his nephew that if the nephew refrained from drinking alcohol, using tobacco, and playing billiards and cards for money until he reached the age of twenty-one, the uncle would pay him $5,000 (about $75,000 in today's dollars). The nephew, who indulged occasionally in all of these "vices," agreed to refrain from them and did so for the next six years. Following his twenty-first birthday in 1875, the nephew wrote to his uncle that he had performed his part of the bargain and was thus entitled to the promised $5,000 (plus interest). A few days later, the uncle wrote the nephew a letter stating, "[Y]ou shall have the five thousand dollars, as I promised you." The uncle said that the money was in the bank and that the nephew could "consider this money on interest."

The Issue of Consideration The nephew left the money in the care of his uncle, who held it for the next twelve years. When the uncle died in 1887, however, the executor of the uncle's estate refused to pay the $5,000 (plus interest) claim brought by Hamer, a third party to whom the promise had been *assigned*. (The law allows parties to assign, or transfer, rights in contracts to

third parties—see Chapter 9.) The executor, Sidway, contended that the contract was invalid because there was insufficient consideration to support it. The uncle had received nothing, and the nephew had actually benefited from fulfilling the uncle's wishes. Therefore, no contract existed.

The Court's Conclusion Although a lower court upheld Sidway's position, the New York Court of Appeals reversed and ruled in favor of the plaintiff, Hamer. "The promisee used tobacco, occasionally drank liquor, and he had a legal right to do so," the court stated. "That right he abandoned for a period of years upon the strength of the promise of the testator [one who makes a will] that for such forbearance he would give him $5,000. We need not speculate on the effort which may have been required to give up the use of those stimulants. It is sufficient that he restricted his lawful freedom of action within certain prescribed limits upon the faith of his uncle's agreement."

Application to Today's World *Although this case was decided more than a century ago, the principles enunciated by the court remain applicable to contracts formed today, including online contracts. For a contract to be valid and binding, consideration must be given, and that consideration must be something of legally sufficient value.*

a. 124 N.Y. 538, 27 N.E. 256 (1891).

a court will not question the adequacy of consideration if the consideration is legally sufficient. If people could sue merely because they had entered into an unwise contract, the courts would be overloaded with frivolous suits.

Nevertheless, a large disparity in the amount or value of the consideration exchanged may raise a red flag, causing a court to look more closely at the bargain. Shockingly inadequate consideration can indicate that fraud, duress, or undue influence was involved. (Defenses to enforceability will be discussed in Chapter 8.) Judges are uneasy about enforcing unequal bargains, and it is their task to make certain that there was not some defect in the contract's formation that negated voluntary consent.

Agreements That Lack Consideration

Sometimes, one or both of the parties to a contract may think that they have exchanged consideration when in fact they have not. Here, we look at some situations in which the parties' promises or actions do not qualify as contractual consideration.

Preexisting Duty
Under most circumstances, a promise to do what one already has a legal duty to do does not constitute legally sufficient consideration. A sheriff, for example, cannot collect a reward for information leading to the capture of a criminal if the sheriff already has a legal duty to capture the criminal.

(TFoxFoto/Shutterstock.com)

Are there circumstances under which a contractor who has performed cement work can legally demand a payment larger than what was stated in the contract?

Rescission A remedy whereby a contract is canceled and the parties are returned to the positions they occupied before the contract was made.

Past Consideration An act that took place in the past and that ordinarily, by itself, cannot be consideration for a later promise to pay for the act.

Likewise, if a party is already bound by contract to perform a certain duty, that duty cannot serve as consideration for a second contract. **EXAMPLE 7.27** Bauman-Bache, Inc., begins construction on a seven-story office building and after three months demands an extra $75,000 on its contract. If the extra $75,000 is not paid, the firm will stop working. The owner of the land, having no one else to complete construction, agrees to pay the extra $75,000. The agreement is not enforceable because it is not supported by legally sufficient consideration—Bauman-Bache had a preexisting contractual duty to complete the building. •

Unforeseen Difficulties   The preexisting duty rule is intended to prevent extortion and the so-called holdup game. Nonetheless, if, during performance of a contract, extraordinary difficulties arise that were totally unforeseen at the time the contract was formed, a court may allow an exception to the rule. Suppose that in *Example* 7.27 above, Bauman-Bache had encountered a rock formation that no one knew existed and the landowner had agreed to pay the firm the extra $75,000 to excavate the rock. In this situation, the court may refrain from applying the preexisting duty rule and enforce the agreement to pay the extra $75,000.

Note, however, that for the rule to be waived, the difficulties must be truly unforeseen and not be the types of risks ordinarily assumed in business. In *Example* 7.27, if the construction was taking place in an area where rock formations were common, a court would likely enforce the preexisting duty rule on the basis that Bauman-Bache had assumed the risk that it would encounter rock.

Rescission and New Contract   The law recognizes that two parties can mutually agree to rescind, or cancel, their contract, at least to the extent that it is *executory*—that is, not yet performed by both parties. **Rescission**[23] is the unmaking of a contract so as to return the parties to the positions they occupied before the contract was made.

Sometimes, parties rescind a contract and make a new contract at the same time. When this occurs, it is often difficult to determine whether there was consideration for the new contract or whether the parties had a preexisting duty under the previous contract. If a court finds there was a preexisting duty, then the new contract will be invalid because there was no consideration.

Past Consideration
Promises made in return for actions or events that have already taken place are unenforceable. These promises lack consideration in that the element of bargained-for exchange is missing. In short, you can bargain for something to take place now or in the future but not for something that has already taken place. Therefore, **past consideration** is no consideration.

CASE EXAMPLE 7.28 Jamil Blackmon became friends with Allen Iverson when Iverson was a high school student who showed tremendous promise as an athlete. Blackmon suggested that Iverson use "The Answer" as a nickname in the league tournaments, meaning that Iverson would be "The Answer" to the National Basketball Association's declining attendance. Later, Iverson said that he would give Blackmon 25 percent of any proceeds from the merchandising of products that used "The Answer" as a logo or a slogan. Because Iverson's promise was made in return for past consideration (Blackmon's earlier suggestion), it was unenforceable. In effect, Iverson stated his intention to give Blackmon a gift.[24] •

Illusory Promises
If the terms of the contract express such uncertainty of performance that the promisor has not definitely promised to do anything, the promise is said to be *illusory*—without consideration and unenforceable. **EXAMPLE 7.29** The president of Tuscan Corporation says to his employees, "All of you have worked hard, and if profits

---

23. Pronounced reh-*sih*-zhen.
24. *Blackmon v. Iverson,* 324 F.Supp.2d 602 (E.D.Pa. 2003).

remain high, a 10 percent bonus will be given at the end of the year if management thinks it is warranted." This is an *illusory promise,* or no promise at all, because performance depends solely on the discretion of the president (the management). There is no bargained-for consideration. The statement declares merely that management may or may not do something in the future. •

Settlement of Claims

Businesspersons and others often enter into contracts to settle legal claims. It is important to understand the nature of the consideration given in these settlement agreements, or contracts. Claims are commonly settled through an *accord and satisfaction,* in which a debtor offers to pay a lesser amount than the creditor says is owed. Claims may also be settled by the signing of a *release* or a *covenant not to sue.*

Accord and Satisfaction

In an **accord and satisfaction,** a debtor offers to pay, and a creditor accepts, a lesser amount than the creditor originally claimed was owed. The *accord* is the agreement under which one of the parties promises to give or perform, and the other to accept, in satisfaction of a claim, something other than that on which the parties originally agreed. *Satisfaction* is the performance (usually payment) of the accord. A basic rule is that there can be no satisfaction unless there is first an accord.

For accord and satisfaction to occur, the amount of the debt *must be in dispute.* If a debt is *liquidated,* accord and satisfaction cannot take place. A **liquidated debt** is one whose amount has been ascertained, fixed, agreed on, settled, or exactly determined. **EXAMPLE 7.30** Barbara Kwan signs an installment loan contract with her banker. In the contract, Kwan agrees to pay a specified rate of interest on a specified amount of borrowed funds at monthly intervals for two years. Because both parties know the precise amount of the total obligation, it is a liquidated debt. •

In the majority of states, acceptance of a lesser sum than the entire amount of a liquidated debt is not satisfaction, and the balance of the debt is still legally owed. The reason for this rule is that the debtor has given no consideration to satisfy the obligation of paying the balance to the creditor because the debtor has a preexisting legal obligation to pay the entire debt.

Release

A **release** is a contract in which one party forfeits the right to pursue a legal claim against the other party. It bars any further recovery beyond the terms stated in the release. Releases will generally be binding if they are (1) given in good faith, (2) stated in a signed writing (required by many states), and (3) accompanied by consideration.[25] Clearly, parties are better off if they know the extent of their injuries or damages before signing releases.

EXAMPLE 7.31 Kara's car is damaged in an accident caused by Raoul's negligence. Raoul offers to give Kara $3,000 if she will release him from further liability resulting from the accident. Kara believes that this amount will cover her repairs, so she agrees and signs the release. Later, Kara discovers that the repairs will cost $4,200. Can she collect the balance from Raoul? Normally, the answer is no. The release is a valid contract. •

Covenant Not to Sue

Unlike a release, a **covenant not to sue** does not always prevent further recovery. The parties simply substitute a contractual obligation for some other type of legal action based on a valid claim. Suppose that in the example above, Kara agrees not to sue Raoul for damages in a tort action if he will pay for the damage to her car. If Raoul fails to pay, Kara can bring an action for breach of contract.

Accord and Satisfaction A common means of settling a disputed claim, whereby a debtor offers to pay a lesser amount than the creditor purports to be owed.

Liquidated Debt A debt whose amount has been ascertained, fixed, agreed on, settled, or exactly determined.

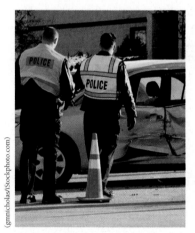

(grnnicholas/iStockphoto.com)

Is it possible to limit one's liability after a car accident?

Release An agreement in which one party gives up the right to pursue a legal claim against another party.

Covenant Not to Sue An agreement to substitute a contractual obligation for some other type of legal action based on a valid claim.

---

25. Under the Uniform Commercial Code (UCC), a written, signed waiver or renunciation by an aggrieved party discharges any further liability for a breach, even without consideration [UCC 1–107].

Promissory Estoppel

Promissory Estoppel A doctrine that can be used to enforce a promise when the promisee has justifiably relied on it and when justice will be better served by enforcing the promise.

Sometimes, individuals rely on promises, and their reliance may form a basis for a court to infer contract rights and duties. Under the doctrine of **promissory estoppel** (also called *detrimental reliance*), a person who has reasonably and substantially relied on the promise of another can obtain some measure of recovery. Promissory estoppel allows a party to recover on a promise even though it was made *without consideration*. Under this doctrine, a court may enforce an otherwise unenforceable promise to avoid an injustice that would otherwise result.

For the doctrine of promissory estoppel to be applied, the following elements are required:

1. There must be a clear and definite promise.
2. The promisor should have expected that the promisee would rely on the promise.
3. The promisee reasonably relied on the promise by acting or refraining from some act.
4. The promisee's reliance was definite and resulted in substantial detriment.
5. Enforcement of the promise is necessary to avoid injustice.

Estopped Barred, impeded, or precluded.

If these requirements are met, a promise may be enforced even though it is not supported by consideration. In essence, the promisor (the offeror) will be **estopped** (barred or prevented) from asserting lack of consideration as a defense.

EXAMPLE 7.32 An employer, Jay Bailey, orally promises to pay each of his five employees $2,000 a month for the remainder of their lives after they retire. When Sal Hernandez retires, he receives the monthly amount for two years, but then Bailey stops paying. Under the doctrine of promissory estoppel, Hernandez can sue Bailey in an attempt to enforce his promise. •

Promissory estoppel is similar in some ways to the doctrine of quasi contract that was discussed on page 200. In both situations, a court is acting in the interests of equity and imposes contract obligations on the parties to prevent unfairness even though no actual contract exists. In quasi contracts, however, no promise at all was made, whereas with promissory estoppel, a promise was made and relied on, but it was unenforceable.

Reviewing . . . Agreement and Consideration in Contracts

Ted and Betty Hyatt live in California, a state that has extensive statutory protection for consumers. The Hyatts decided to buy a computer so that they could use e-mail to stay in touch with their grandchildren, who live in another state. Over the phone, they ordered a computer from CompuEdge, Inc. When the box arrived, it was sealed with a brightly colored sticker warning that the terms enclosed within the box would govern the sale unless the customer returned the computer within thirty days. Among those terms was a clause that required any disputes to be resolved in Tennessee state courts. The Hyatts then signed up for Internet service through CyberTool, an Internet service provider. They downloaded CyberTool's software and clicked on the "quick install" box, which allowed them to bypass CyberTool's "Terms of Service" page. It was possible to read this page by scrolling to the next screen, but the Hyatts did not realize this. The terms included a clause stating that all disputes were to be submitted to a Virginia state court. As soon as the Hyatts attempted to e-mail their grandchildren, they experienced problems using CyberTool's e-mail service, which continually stated that the network was busy. They also were unable to receive the photos sent by their grandchildren. Using the information presented in the chapter, answer the following questions.

1. Did the Hyatts accept the list of contract terms included in the computer box? Why or why not? What is this type of e-contract called?
2. What type of agreement did the Hyatts form with CyberTool?

3. Suppose that the Hyatts experienced trouble with the computer's components after they had used the computer for two months. What factors will a court consider in deciding whether to enforce the forum-selection clause? Would a court be likely to enforce the clause in this contract? Why or why not?

4. Are the Hyatts bound by the contract terms specified on CyberTool's "Terms of Service" page, which they did not read? Which of the required elements for contract formation might the Hyatts claim were lacking? How might a court rule on this issue?

DEBATE THIS The terms and conditions in click-on agreements are so long and detailed that no one ever reads the agreements. Therefore, the act of clicking on "Yes, I agree" is not really an acceptance.

LINKING BUSINESS LAW to Marketing

Customer Relationship Management

Increasingly, the contracting process is moving online. Large and small e-commerce Web sites offer to sell millions of goods and services. The vast amount of data collected from online shoppers has pushed *customer relationship management* (CRM) to the fore. CRM is a marketing strategy that allows companies to acquire information about customers' wants, needs, and behaviors. The companies can then use that information to build customer relationships and loyalty. The focus of CRM is understanding customers as individuals rather than simply as a group. As Exhibit 7.4 shows, CRM is a closed system that uses feedback from customers to build relationships with those customers.

Two Examples—Netflix and Amazon

If you are a customer of Netflix.com, you choose Blu-ray discs and DVDs that are sent to you by mail or streamed online based on your individual tastes and preferences. Netflix asks you to rate movies you have rented (or even seen in theaters) on a scale of one to five stars. Using a computer algorithm, Netflix then creates an individualized rating system that predicts how you will rate thousands of different movies. As you rate more movies, the predictive reliability becomes more accurate. By applying your individual rating system to movies you have not seen, Netflix is able to suggest movies that you might like.

Amazon.com uses similar technology to recommend books and music that you might wish to buy. Amazon sends out numerous "personalized" e-mails to its customers with suggestions based on those customers' individual buying habits.

Thus, CRM allows both Netflix and Amazon to use a focused marketing effort, rather than the typical shotgun approach used by spam advertising on the Internet.

Exhibit 7.4 A Customer Relationship Management Cycle

CRM in Online versus Traditional Companies

For online companies such as Amazon and Netflix, the cost of obtaining, analyzing, and utilizing customer information is small. In contrast, traditional companies often must use a

Continued

process that is much more costly to obtain data to be used for CRM. An automobile company, for example, obtains customer information from a variety of sources, including dealers, customer surveys, online inquiries, and the like. Integrating, storing, and managing such information generally makes CRM much more expensive for traditional companies than for online companies.

Critical Thinking

Online companies such as Amazon not only target individual customers but also utilize each customer's buying habits to create generalized marketing campaigns. Might any privacy issues arise as an online company creates a database to be used for generalized marketing campaigns?

Key Terms

acceptance 208
accord and satisfaction 219
agreement 202
bilateral contract 196
browse-wrap term 214
click-on agreement 213
consideration 216
contract 194
counteroffer 207
covenant not to sue 219
e-contract 210
estopped 220

e-signature 214
executed contract 199
executory contract 199
express contract 198
forbearance 216
formal contract 198
forum-selection clause 212
implied contract 198
informal contract 198
liquidated debt 219
mailbox rule 210
mirror image rule 207

objective theory of contracts 195
offer 202
offeree 196
offeror 196
option contract 208
past consideration 218
promise 193
promisee 193
promisor 193
promissory estoppel 220
quasi contract 200
record 215

release 219
rescission 218
revocation 206
shrink-wrap agreement 213
unenforceable contract 200
unilateral contract 197
valid contract 199
void contract 200
voidable contract 199

Chapter Summary: Agreement and Consideration in Contracts

An Overview of Contract Law (See pages 194–195.)	1. *Sources of contract law*—The common law governs all contracts except when it has been modified or replaced by statutory law, such as the Uniform Commercial Code (UCC), or by administrative agency regulations. The UCC governs contracts for the sale or lease of goods (see Chapter 10). 2. *The function of contracts*—Contract law establishes what kinds of promises will be legally binding and supplies procedures for enforcing legally binding promises, or agreements. 3. *Definition of a contract*—A contract is an agreement that can be enforced in court. It is formed by two or more competent parties who agree to perform or to refrain from performing some act now or in the future. 4. *Objective theory of contracts*—In contract law, intent is determined by objective facts, not by the personal or subjective intent, or belief, of a party.
Requirements of a Valid Contract (See pages 195–196.)	The four requirements of a valid contract are agreement, consideration, contractual capacity, and legality. Even if the four requirements of a valid contract are met, a contract may be unenforceable if it lacks voluntary consent or is not in the required form.
Types of Contracts (See pages 196–202.)	1. *Bilateral*—A promise for a promise. 2. *Unilateral*—A promise for an act (acceptance is the completed—or substantial—performance of the contract by the offeree). 3. *Formal*—Requires a special form for contract formation. 4. *Informal*—Requires no special form for contract formation. 5. *Express*—Formed by words (oral, written, or a combination). 6. *Implied*—Formed at least in part by the conduct of the parties. 7. *Executed*—A fully performed contract. 8. *Executory*—A contract not yet fully performed. 9. *Valid*—A contract that has the four necessary contractual elements of agreement, consideration, capacity, and legality. 10. *Voidable*—A contract in which a party has the option of avoiding or enforcing the contractual obligation.

Chapter Summary: Agreement and Consideration in Contracts— Continued

Types of Contracts—Continued	11. *Unenforceable*—A valid contract that cannot be enforced because of a legal defense. 12. *Void*—No contract exists, or there is a contract without legal obligations. 13. *Quasi contract*—No contract exists, but a court imposes a contract on the parties to prevent unjust enrichment.
Requirements of the Offer (See pages 202–206.)	1. *Intent*—There must be a serious, objective intention by the offeror to become bound by the offer. Nonoffer situations include (a) expressions of opinion; (b) statements of future intent; (c) preliminary negotiations; (d) generally, advertisements, catalogues, price lists, and circulars; and (e) traditionally, agreements to agree in the future. 2. *Definiteness*—The terms of the offer must be sufficiently definite to be ascertainable by the parties or by a court. 3. *Communication*—The offer must be communicated to the offeree.

Termination of the Offer
(See pages 206–208.)
	1. *By action of the parties*—
	   a. Revocation—Unless the offer is irrevocable, it can be revoked at any time before acceptance without liability. Revocation is not effective until received by the offeree or the offeree's agent. Some offers, such as a merchant's firm offer and option contracts, are irrevocable.
	   b. Rejection—Accomplished by words or actions that demonstrate a clear intent not to accept the offer. A rejection is not effective until it is received by the offeror or the offeror's agent.
	   c. Counteroffer—A rejection of the original offer and the making of a new offer.
	2. *By operation of law*—
	   a. Lapse of time—The offer terminates (1) at the end of the time period specified in the offer or (2) if no time period is stated in the offer, at the end of a reasonable time period.
	   b. Destruction of the specific subject matter of the offer—Automatically terminates the offer.
	   c. Death or incompetence of the offeror or offeree—Terminates the offer unless the offer is irrevocable.
	   d. Illegality—Supervening illegality terminates the offer.

Acceptance (See pages 208–210.)	1. Can be made only by the offeree or the offeree's agent. 2. Must be unequivocal. Under the common law (mirror image rule), if new terms or conditions are added to the acceptance, it will be considered a counteroffer. 3. Acceptance of a unilateral offer is effective on full performance of the requested act. Generally, no communication is necessary. 4. Except in a few situations, an offeree's silence does not constitute an acceptance. 5. Acceptance of a bilateral offer can be communicated by the offeree by any authorized mode of communication and is effective on dispatch. If the offeror does not specify the mode of communication, acceptance can be made by any reasonable means. Usually, the same means used by the offeror or a faster means can be used.
E-Contracts (See pages 210–215.)	1. *Online offers*—The terms of contract offers presented via the Internet should be as inclusive as the terms in an offer made in a written (paper) document. The offer should be displayed in an easily readable format and should include some mechanism, such as an "I agree" or "I accept" box, by which the customer may accept the offer. Because jurisdictional issues frequently arise with online transactions, the offer should include dispute-settlement provisions, as well as a forum-selection clause. 2. *Click-on agreement*—An agreement created when a buyer, completing a transaction on a computer, is required to indicate her or his assent to be bound by the terms of an offer by clicking on a box that says, for example, "I agree." The courts have enforced click-on agreements, holding that by clicking on "I agree," the offeree has indicated acceptance by conduct. In contrast, browse-wrap terms may not be enforced, because the buyer or user is not required to express assent to the terms. 3. *Shrink-wrap agreement*—An agreement whose terms are expressed inside a box in which goods are packaged. The party who opens the box is informed that, by keeping the goods, he or she agrees to the terms of the shrink-wrap agreement. The courts have often enforced shrink-wrap agreements, even if the purchaser-user of the goods did not read the terms of the agreement. A court may deem a shrink-wrap agreement unenforceable, however, if the buyer learns of the shrink-wrap terms after the parties entered into the agreement. 4. *Federal law on e-signatures and e-documents*—The Electronic Signatures in Global and National Commerce Act (E-SIGN Act) of 2000 gave validity to e-signatures by providing that no contract, record, or signature may be "denied legal effect" solely because it is in an electronic form. The Uniform Electronic Transactions Act (UETA) defines an e-signature as "an electronic sound, symbol, or process attached to or logically associated with a record and executed or adopted by a person with the intent to sign the record." 5. *The Uniform Electronic Transactions Act (UETA)*—This uniform act has been adopted, at least in part, by most states, to create rules to support the enforcement of e-contracts. Under the UETA, contracts entered into online, as well as other documents, are presumed to be valid. The UETA does not apply to certain transactions governed by the UCC or to wills or testamentary trusts.

Continued

Chapter Summary: Agreement and Consideration in Contracts—Continued

Consideration (See pages 216–220.)	1. *Elements of consideration*—
	a. Something of *legally sufficient value* must be given in exchange for a promise.
	b. There must be a bargained-for exchange.
	2. *Legal sufficiency and adequacy of consideration*—Legal sufficiency means that something of legal value must be given in exchange for a promise. Adequacy relates to how much consideration is given and whether a fair bargain was reached. Courts will inquire into the adequacy of consideration only when fraud, undue influence, duress, or unconscionability may be involved.
	3. *Contracts that lack consideration*—Consideration is lacking in the following situations:
	a. Preexisting duty—A promise to do what one already has a legal duty to do is not legally sufficient consideration for a new contract.
	b. Past consideration—Actions or events that have already taken place do not constitute legally sufficient consideration.
	c. Illusory promises—When the nature or extent of performance is too uncertain, the promise is rendered illusory (without consideration and unenforceable).
	4. *Settlement of claims*—Disputes may be settled by the following, which are enforceable provided there is consideration:
	a. Accord and satisfaction—An *accord* is an agreement in which a debtor offers to pay a lesser amount than the creditor claims is owed. *Satisfaction* takes place when the accord is executed.
	b. Release—An agreement in which, for consideration, a party forfeits the right to seek further recovery beyond the terms specified in the release.
	c. Covenant not to sue—An agreement not to sue on a present, valid claim.
	5. *Promissory estoppel*—The equitable doctrine of promissory estoppel applies when a promisor should have expected a promise to induce definite and substantial action or forbearance by the promisee, and the promisee does act in reliance on the promise. Such a promise is binding, even though there is no consideration, if injustice can be avoided only by enforcement of the promise. Also known as the doctrine of *detrimental reliance*.

ExamPrep

ISSUE SPOTTERS

1. Fidelity Corporation offers to hire Ron to replace Monica, who has given Fidelity a month's notice of intent to quit. Fidelity gives Ron a week to decide whether to accept. Two days later, Monica decides not to quit and signs an employment contract with Fidelity for another year. The next day, Monica tells Ron of the new contract. Ron immediately faxes a formal letter of acceptance to Fidelity. Do Fidelity and Ron have a contract? Why or why not? **(See pages 206–207.)**
2. In September, Sharyn agrees to work for Totem Productions, Inc., at $500 a week for a year beginning January 1. In October, Sharyn is offered $600 a week for the same work by Umber Shows, Ltd. When Sharyn tells Totem about the other offer, they tear up their contract and agree that Sharyn will be paid $575. Is the new contract binding? Explain. **(See page 218.)**

—Check your answers to the Issue Spotters against the answers provided in Appendix E at the end of this text.

BEFORE THE TEST

Go to www.cengagebrain.com, enter the ISBN 9781133191353, and click on "Find" to locate this textbook's Web site. Then, click on "Access Now" under "Study Tools," and select Chapter 7 at the top. There, you will find a Practice Quiz that you can take to assess your mastery of the concepts in this chapter, as well as Flashcards, a Glossary of important terms, and Video Questions (when assigned).

For Review

Answers to the even-numbered questions in this For Review section can be found in Appendix F at the end of this text.

1. What is a contract? What is the objective theory of contracts?
2. What are the four basic elements necessary to the formation of a valid contract?

3. What elements are necessary for an effective offer? What are some examples of nonoffers?
4. How do shrink-wrap and click-on agreements differ from other contracts? How have traditional laws been applied to these agreements?
5. What is consideration? What is required for consideration to be legally sufficient?

Business Scenarios and Case Problems

7–1 Unilateral Contract. Rocky Mountain Races, Inc., sponsors the "Pioneer Trail Ultramarathon," with an advertised first prize of $10,000. The rules require the competitors to run 100 miles from the floor of Blackwater Canyon to the top of Pinnacle Mountain. The rules also provide that Rocky reserves the right to change the terms of the race at any time. Monica enters the race and is declared the winner. Rocky offers her a prize of $1,000 instead of $10,000. Did Rocky and Monica have a contract? Explain. **(See page 197.)**

7–2 Question with Sample Answer—Consideration. Daniel, a recent college graduate, is on his way home for the Christmas holidays from his new job. He gets caught in a snowstorm and is taken in by an elderly couple who provide him with food and shelter. After the snowplows have cleared the road, Daniel proceeds home. Daniel's father, Fred, is most appreciative of the elderly couple's action and in a letter promises to pay them $500. The elderly couple, in need of funds, accept Fred's offer. Then, because of a dispute with Daniel, Fred refuses to pay the elderly couple the $500. Discuss whether the couple can hold Fred liable in contract for the services rendered to Daniel. **(See page 218.)**

—For a sample answer to Question 7–2, go to Appendix G at the end of this text.

7–3 Contract Classification. For employment with the Firestorm Smokejumpers—a crew of elite paratroopers who parachute into dangerous situations to fight fires—applicants must complete a series of tests. The crew chief sends the most qualified applicants a letter stating that they will be admitted to Firestorm's training sessions if they pass a medical exam. Jake Kurzyniec receives the letter and passes the exam, but a new crew chief changes the selection process and rejects him. Is there a contract between Kurzyniec and Firestorm? If there is a contract, what type of contract is it? **(See pages 196–197.)**

7–4 Spotlight on Taco Bell—Implied Contract. Thomas Rinks and Joseph Shields developed Psycho Chihuahua, a caricature of a Chihuahua dog with a "do-not-back-down" attitude. They promoted and marketed the character through their company, Wrench, LLC. Ed Alfaro and Rudy Pollak, representatives of Taco Bell Corp., learned of Psycho Chihuahua and met with Rinks and Shields to talk about using the character as a Taco Bell "icon." Wrench sent artwork, merchandise, and marketing ideas to Alfaro, who promoted the character within Taco Bell. Alfaro asked Wrench to propose terms for Taco Bell's use of Psycho Chihuahua. Taco Bell did not accept Wrench's terms, but Alfaro continued to promote the character within the company. Meanwhile, Taco Bell hired a new advertising agency, which proposed an advertising campaign involving a Chihuahua. When Alfaro learned of this proposal, he sent the Psycho Chihuahua materials to the agency. Taco Bell made a Chihuahua the focus of its marketing but paid nothing to Wrench. Wrench filed a suit against Taco Bell in a federal court claiming that it had an implied contract with Taco Bell and that Taco Bell breached that contract. Do these facts satisfy the requirements for an implied contract? Why or why not? [*Wrench, LLC. v. Taco Bell Corp.,* 256 F.3d 446 (6th Cir. 2001), *cert.* denied, 534 U.S. 1114, 122 S.Ct. 921, 151 L.Ed.2d 805 (2002)] **(See page 198.)**

7–5 Acceptance. Troy Blackford smashed a slot machine while he was gambling at Prairie Meadows Casino. He was banned from the premises. Despite the ban, he later gambled at the casino and won $9,387. When he tried to collect his winnings, the casino refused to pay. He filed a suit for breach of contract, arguing that he and the casino had a contract because he had accepted its offer to gamble. Is there a contract between the casino and Blackford? Discuss. [*Blackford v. Prairie Meadows Racetrack and Casino,* 778 N.W.2d 184 (Iowa 2010)] **(See pages 208–210.)**

7–6 Case Problem with Sample Answer—Quasi Contract. Robert Gutkowski, a sports marketing expert, met with George Steinbrenner, the owner of the New York Yankees, many times to discuss the Yankees Entertainment and Sports Network (YES). Gutkowski was paid as a consultant. Later, he filed a suit, seeking an ownership share in YES. There was no written contract for the share, but he claimed that the matter had been discussed. Does Gutkowski have a valid claim for payment? Discuss. [*Gutkowski v. Steinbrenner,* 680 F.Supp.2d 602 (S.D.N.Y. 2010)] **(See pages 200–201.)**

—For a sample answer to Problem 7–6, go to Appendix H at the end of this text.

7–7 Quasi Contract. Kim Panenka asked to borrow $4,750 from her sister, Kris, to make a mortgage payment. Kris deposited a check for that amount into Kim's bank account. Hours later, Kim asked to borrow another $1,100. Kris took a cash advance on her credit card and deposited this amount into Kim's account. When Kim did not repay Kris, the sister filed a suit, arguing that she had "loaned" Kim the money. Can the court impose a contract between the sisters? Explain. [*Panenka v. Panenka,* 331 Wis.2d 731, 795 N.W.2d 493 (2011)] **(See pages 200–201.)**

7–8 Online Acceptances. Heather Reasonover opted to try Internet service from Clearwire Corp. Clearwire sent her a confirmation e-mail that included a link to its Web site. Clearwire also sent her a modem. In the accompanying written materials, at the bottom of a page, in small type was the Web site URL. When Reasonover plugged in the modem, an "I accept terms" box appeared. Without clicking on the box, Reasonover quit the page. A clause in Clearwire's "Terms of Service," accessible only through its Web site, required its subscribers to submit any dispute to arbitration. Is Reasonover bound to this clause? Why or why not? [*Kwan v. Clearwire Corp.*, 2012 WL 32380 (W.D.Wash. 2012)] **(See pages 213–214.)**

7–9 ⬌ A Question of Ethics—Promissory Estoppel. Claudia Aceves borrowed $845,000 from U.S. Bank to buy a home. Less than two years into the loan, she could no longer afford the monthly payments. The bank notified her that it planned to foreclose on her home. (Foreclosure is a process that allows a lender to repossess and sell the property that secures a loan—see Chapter 16.) The bank offered to modify Aceves's mortgage if she would forgo bankruptcy. In reliance on the bank's promise, she agreed. Once she withdrew the filing, however, the bank foreclosed and began eviction proceedings. Aceves filed a suit against the bank for promissory estoppel. [*Aceves v. U.S. Bank, N.A.*, 192 Cal.App.4th 218, 120 Cal.Rptr.3d 507 (2 Dist. 2011)] **(See page 220.)**

1. Could Aceves succeed in her claim of promissory estoppel? Why or why not?
2. Did Aceves or U.S. Bank behave unethically? Discuss.

Critical Thinking and Writing Assignments

7–10 Business Law Critical Thinking Group Assignment. To download a specific app to your smartphone or tablet device, you usually have to check a box indicating that you agree to the company's terms and conditions. Most individuals do so without ever reading those terms and conditions. Print out a set of terms and conditions from a downloaded app to use in this assignment. Everyone in the group must use the same set of terms and conditions.

1. One group will determine which of these terms and conditions are favorable to the company.
2. Another group will determine which of the terms and conditions could conceivably be favorable to the individual.
3. A third group will determine which terms and conditions, on balance, favor the company too much.

CHAPTER 8

Capacity, Legality, and Enforceability

(pixdeluxe/iStockphoto.com)

CHAPTER OUTLINE

- Contractual Capacity
- Legality
- Voluntary Consent
- The Writing Requirement

LEARNING OBJECTIVES

The five learning objectives below are designed to help improve your understanding of the chapter. After reading this chapter, you should be able to answer the following questions:

1 Does a minor have the capacity to enter into an enforceable contract? What does it mean to disaffirm a contract?

2 Under what circumstances will a covenant not to compete be enforced? When will such covenants not be enforced?

3 What is an exculpatory clause? In what circumstances might exculpatory clauses be enforced? When will they not be enforced?

4 What is the difference between a mistake of value or quality and a mistake of fact?

5 What are the elements of fraudulent misrepresentation?

"Liberty of contract is not an absolute concept.
It is relative to many conditions of time and place and circumstance."
—Benjamin Cardozo, 1870–1938 (Associate justice of the United States Supreme Court, 1932–1938)

Courts generally want contracts to be enforceable, and much of the law is devoted to aiding the enforceability of contracts. As indicated in the chapter-opening quotation, however, "liberty of contract" is not absolute. In other words, not all people can make legally binding contracts at all times. Contracts entered into by persons lacking the capacity to do so may be voidable. Similarly, contracts calling for the performance of an illegal act are illegal and thus void. In this chapter, we first examine the requirement of contractual capacity and then look at legality and enforceability.

As more commerce is done on the Internet, these issues arise more often in disputes over online business dealings. Should people be able to exchange organs for transplants on Craigslist? Should online gambling be allowed? These are some current topics you will learn about in this chapter.

Contractual Capacity

Contractual Capacity *The capacity required by the law for a party who enters into a contract to be bound by that contract.*

Contractual capacity is the legal ability to enter into a contractual relationship. Courts generally presume the existence of contractual capacity. In some situations, though, capacity is lacking or may be questionable. In other situations, a party has the capacity to enter into a valid contract but may also have the right to avoid liability under it. In this section, we look at the effect of youth, intoxication, and mental incompetence on contractual capacity.

Minors

Today, in almost all states, the *age of majority* (when a person is no longer a minor) for contractual purposes is eighteen years—the so-called coming of age.[1] In addition, some states provide for the termination of minority on marriage.

Emancipation *In regard to minors, the act of being freed from parental control.*

Minority status may also be terminated by a minor's **emancipation**, which occurs when a child's parent or legal guardian relinquishes the legal right to exercise control over the child. Normally, minors who leave home to support themselves are considered emancipated. Several jurisdictions permit minors to petition a court for emancipation. For business purposes, a minor may petition a court to be treated as an adult.

The general rule is that a minor can enter into any contract an adult can, provided that the contract is not one prohibited by law for minors (for example, the purchase of alcoholic beverages or tobacco products). A contract entered into by a minor, however, is voidable at the option of that minor, subject to certain exceptions (to be discussed shortly). To exercise the option to avoid a contract, a minor need only manifest (clearly show) an intention not to be bound by it. The minor "avoids" the contract by disaffirming it.

LEARNING OBJECTIVE 1
Does a minor have the capacity to enter into an enforceable contract? What does it mean to disaffirm a contract?

Disaffirmance *The legal avoidance, or setting aside, of a contractual obligation.*

Disaffirmance
The legal avoidance, or setting aside, of a contractual obligation is referred to as **disaffirmance**. To disaffirm, a minor must express, through words or conduct, his or her intent not to be bound to the contract. The minor must disaffirm the entire contract, not merely a portion of it. For instance, a minor cannot decide to keep part of the goods purchased under a contract and return the remaining goods. When a minor disaffirms a contract, the minor can recover any property that she or he transferred to the adult as consideration for the contract, even if it is then in the possession of a third party.[2]

A contract can ordinarily be disaffirmed at any time during minority[3] or for a reasonable time after the minor comes of age. What constitutes a "reasonable" time may vary. If an individual fails to disaffirm an executed contract within a reasonable time after reaching the age of majority, a court will likely hold that the contract has been ratified (*ratification* will be discussed shortly).

Note that an adult who enters into a contract with a minor cannot avoid his or her contractual duties on the ground that the minor can do so. Unless the minor exercises the option to disaffirm the contract, the adult party normally is bound by it.

A Minor's Obligations on Disaffirmance
Although all states' laws permit minors to disaffirm contracts (with certain exceptions), including executed contracts, state laws differ on the extent of a minor's obligations on disaffirmance. Courts in most states hold that the minor need only return the goods (or other consideration) subject to the contract, provided the goods are in the minor's possession or control. Even if the minor returns damaged goods, the minor often is entitled to disaffirm the contract and obtain a refund of the purchase price.

---

1. The age of majority may still be twenty-one for other purposes, such as the purchase and consumption of alcohol.
2. Section 2–403(1) of the UCC allows an exception if the third party is a "good faith purchaser for value." See Chapter 10.
3. In some states, a minor who enters into a contract for the sale of land cannot disaffirm the contract until she or he reaches the age of majority.

A growing number of states place an additional duty on the minor to restore the adult party to the position she or he held before the contract was made. These courts may hold a minor responsible for damage, ordinary wear and tear, and depreciation of goods that the minor used prior to disaffirmance.

CASE EXAMPLE 8.1 Sixteen-year-old Joseph Dodson bought a truck for $4,900 from a used-car dealer. Although the truck developed mechanical problems nine months later, Dodson continued to drive it until the engine blew up and the truck stopped running. Dodson then disaffirmed the contract and attempted to return the truck to the dealer for a refund of the full purchase price. The dealer refused to accept the truck or to provide a refund. Dodson filed a suit. Ultimately, the Tennessee Supreme Court allowed Dodson to disaffirm the contract but required him to compensate the seller for the depreciated value—not the purchase price—of the truck.[4] •

Exceptions to a Minor's Right to Disaffirm

State courts and legislatures have carved out several exceptions to the minor's right to disaffirm, including the following:

- Some contracts, such as marriage contracts and contracts to enlist in the armed services, cannot be avoided as a matter of law, on the ground of public policy.
- Although minors can ordinarily disaffirm contracts even when they have misrepresented their age, a growing number of states have enacted laws to prohibit disaffirmance in such situations. Some state laws also prohibit minors from disaffirming contracts entered into by a minor who is engaged in business as an adult.
- A minor who enters into a contract for necessaries may disaffirm the contract but remains liable for the reasonable value of the goods. **Necessaries** are basic needs, such as food, clothing, shelter, and medical services. What is a necessary for one minor, however, may be a luxury for another, depending on the minors' customary living standard.

Ratification

In contract law, **ratification** is the acceptance or confirmation of an act or agreement that gives legal force to an obligation that previously was not enforceable. A minor who has reached the age of majority can ratify a contract expressly or impliedly. *Express* ratification occurs when the individual, on reaching the age of majority, states orally or in writing that she or he intends to be bound by the contract. *Implied* ratification takes place when the minor, on reaching the age of majority, behaves in a manner inconsistent with disaffirmance.

EXAMPLE 8.2 Lin enters into a contract to sell her laptop to Andrew, a minor. Andrew does not disaffirm the contract. If, on reaching the age of majority, he writes a letter to Lin stating that he still agrees to buy the laptop, he has expressly ratified the contract. If, instead, Andrew takes possession of the laptop as a minor and continues to use it well after reaching the age of majority, he has impliedly ratified the contract. •

If a minor fails to disaffirm a contract within a reasonable time after reaching the age of majority, then a court must determine whether the conduct constitutes implied ratification or disaffirmance. Generally, courts presume that a contract that is *executed* (fully performed by both parties) was ratified. A contract that is still executory is normally considered to be disaffirmed.

Parents' Liability

As a general rule, parents are not liable for the contracts made by minor children acting on their own, except contracts for necessaries, which the parents are legally required to provide. This is why businesses ordinarily require parents to cosign any contract made with a minor. The parents then become personally obligated to perform the conditions of the contract, even if their child avoids liability. (See the *Business Application* feature on page 249 for additional tips on dealing with minors.)

Necessaries Necessities required for life, such as food, shelter, clothing, and medical attention.

Ratification The acceptance or confirmation of an act or agreement that gives legal force to an obligation that previously was not enforceable.

➤ **KNOW THIS** ◄

A minor's station in life (including financial position, social status, and lifestyle) is important in determining whether an item is a necessary or a luxury. For instance, clothing is a necessary, but if a minor from a low-income family contracts for the purchase of a $2,000 leather coat, a court may deem the coat a luxury. In this situation, the contract would not be for "necessaries."

---

4. *Dodson by Dodson v. Shrader*, 824 S.W.2d 545 (Tenn. 1992).

Intoxicated Persons

Intoxication is a condition in which a person's normal capacity to act or think is inhibited by alcohol or some other drug. A contract entered into by an intoxicated person can be either voidable or valid (and thus enforceable).

If the person was sufficiently intoxicated to lack mental capacity, then the transaction may be voidable at the option of the intoxicated person even if the intoxication was purely voluntary. If, despite intoxication, the person understood the legal consequences of the agreement, the contract is enforceable. Courts look at objective indications of the situation to determine if the intoxicated person possessed or lacked the required capacity.

For the contract to be voidable, the person must prove that the intoxication impaired her or his reason and judgment so severely that she or he did not comprehend the legal consequences of entering into the contract. In addition, the person claiming intoxication must be able to return all consideration received.

Mentally Incompetent Persons

Contracts made by mentally incompetent persons can be void, voidable, or valid. If a court has previously determined that a person is mentally incompetent and has appointed a guardian to represent the person, any contract made by that person is *void*—no contract exists. Only the guardian can enter into a binding contract on behalf of the mentally incompetent person.

If a court has not previously judged a person to be mentally incompetent, a contract entered into by that person may be *voidable*. The contract is voidable if the person did not know that he or she was entering into the contract or lacked the mental capacity to comprehend its nature, purpose, and consequences. In such situations, the contract is voidable or can be ratified at the option of the mentally incompetent person but not at the option of the other party.

A contract entered into by a mentally incompetent person who has not been declared incompetent may also be *valid* if the person had capacity *at the time the contract was formed.* Some people who are incompetent due to age or illness have *lucid intervals*—temporary periods of sufficient intelligence, judgment, and will—during which they will be considered to have legal capacity to enter into contracts.

Legality

For a contract to be valid and enforceable, it must be formed for a legal purpose. Legality is the fourth requirement for a valid contract to exist. A contract to do something that is prohibited by federal or state statutory law is illegal and, as such, is void from the outset and thus unenforceable. Additionally, a contract to commit a tortious act (see Chapter 4) or to commit an action that is contrary to public policy is illegal and unenforceable.

ETHICAL ISSUE

Should advertisements to buy or sell human organs be made legal on Web sites such as Craigslist? According to the United Network for Organ Sharing, between 4,500 and 5,000 people die each year in the United States while waiting on organ transplant lists. Increasingly, though, patients who need an organ transplant are sidestepping these traditional lists and advertising for organs on Web sites, such as Craigslist.com. The organ most requested is a kidney because most individuals have two but can survive with just one.

For example, Salina Hodge posted a plea for help on Craigslist asking for someone to donate a kidney. She received more than eight hundred responses from all over the world. One came from a young woman who lived just a few miles away. The transplant was successful, and both donor and donee are leading normal lives.

Federal law prohibits the sale or purchase of any organ for a payment that exceeds the donor's travel and hospital expenses. Nonetheless, individuals facing death will often try desperate means, and some ads posted on Craigslist clearly violate the law—for example, an offer to buy a kidney in exchange for $250,000 worth of paintings. Because the purchase or sale of an organ is illegal, such a contract would not be enforceable.

Some commentators argue that the law should be changed to allow an open market in human organs. They point out that dying patients and their families and friends will continue to offer side payments to obtain organs, even though the payments are technically illegal. Furthermore, some individuals in desperate need of money will always be willing to provide a kidney for, say, $100,000. Proponents of a legal market in organs claim that such a market would be preferable to a black market where there is nothing to prevent those living in poverty from being exploited.

Contracts Contrary to Statute

Statutes often specify which terms and clauses may be included in contracts and which are prohibited. Thus, a contract to sell illegal drugs in violation of criminal laws is unenforceable, as is a contract to hide a corporation's violation of the Sarbanes-Oxley Act (see Chapter 21). Similarly, a contract to smuggle undocumented workers from another country into the United States for an employer is illegal (see Chapter 18). So is a contract to dump hazardous waste in violation of environmental laws (see Chapter 24).

If the object or performance of a contract is rendered illegal by statute *after* the contract has been formed, the contract is considered to be discharged by law. (See the discussion in Chapter 9.)

Usury Charging an illegal rate of interest.

Usury
Almost every state has a statute that sets the maximum rate of interest that can be charged for various types of transactions, including ordinary loans. A lender who makes a loan at an interest rate above the lawful maximum commits **usury.** Although usurious contracts are illegal, most states simply limit the interest that the lender may collect on the contract to the lawful maximum interest rate in that state. In a few states, the lender can recover the principal amount of the loan but no interest.

Although usury statutes place a ceiling on allowable rates of interest, exceptions are made to facilitate business transactions. For example, many states exempt corporate loans from the usury laws. In addition, almost all states have special statutes allowing much higher interest rates on small loans to help those borrowers who need funds and could not otherwise obtain loans.

In 2009, the federal government placed some restrictions on the interest rates and fees that banks and credit-card companies can legally charge consumers, particularly for late payments. These rules are discussed in Chapter 12.

Gambling
Gambling is the creation of risk for the purpose of assuming it. Any scheme that involves the distribution of property by chance among persons who have paid valuable consideration for the opportunity (chance) to receive the property is gambling. Traditionally, the states have deemed gambling contracts illegal and thus void. It is sometimes difficult, however, to distinguish a gambling contract from the risk sharing inherent in almost all contracts. (For a discussion of how the federal government has changed its interpretation of the laws pertaining to online gambling, see the *Adapting the Law to the Online Environment* feature on page 233.)

All states have statutes that regulate gambling, and many states allow certain forms of gambling, such as horse racing, video poker machines, and charity-sponsored bingo. In addition, nearly all states allow state-operated lotteries and gambling on Native American reservations. Nevertheless, even in states that permit certain types of gambling, courts often find that gambling contracts are illegal. **CASE EXAMPLE 8.3** Video poker machines are legal in Louisiana, but their use requires the approval of the state video gaming commission. Gaming Venture, Inc., did not obtain this approval before agreeing with Tastee Restaurant Corporation to install poker machines in some of its restaurants. For this reason, when Tastee allegedly reneged on the deal by refusing to install poker machines, a state court held that the agreement was an illegal gambling contract and therefore void.[5] ●

Licensing Statutes

All states require members of certain professions—including physicians, lawyers, real estate brokers, accountants, architects, electricians, and stockbrokers—to have licenses. Some licenses are obtained only after extensive schooling and examinations, which indicate to the public that a special skill has been acquired. Others require only that the particular person be of good moral character and pay a fee.

Whether a contract with an unlicensed person is legal and enforceable depends on the purpose of the licensing statute. If the statute's purpose is to protect the public from unauthorized practitioners, then a contract involving an unlicensed practitioner generally is illegal and unenforceable. If the purpose is merely to raise government revenues, however, a contract with an unlicensed person may be enforced (and the unlicensed practitioner fined).

EXAMPLE 8.4   A state requires a stockbroker to be licensed and to file a bond with the state to protect the public from fraudulent transactions in stocks. Because the purpose of the statute is to protect the public, a court will deem a contract with an unlicensed stockbroker in that state to be illegal and unenforceable. ●

Can a member of a profession licensed in one jurisdiction recover on a contract to perform professional services in another jurisdiction? What if the contract was the result of a winning entry in an international competition? The court in the following case was asked these questions.

5. *Gaming Venture, Inc. v. Tastee Restaurant Corp.*, 996 So.2d 515 (La.App. 5 Cir. 2008).

Case 8.1

Sturdza v. United Arab Emirates

District of Columbia Court of Appeals,
11 A.3d 251 (2011).

(.shock/Shutterstock.com)

A team of architects checking its plans.

FACTS The United Arab Emirates (UAE) held a competition for the design of a new embassy in Washington, D.C. Elena Sturdza—an architect licensed in Maryland but not in the District of Columbia—won. Sturdza and the UAE exchanged proposals, but the UAE stopped communicating with her before the parties had signed a contract. Two years later, Sturdza learned that the UAE had contracted with a District of Columbia architect to use another design. Sturdza filed a suit against the UAE, alleging breach of contract.

ISSUE Can an architect who is not licensed in the District of Columbia sue to enforce a contract under which she was to perform architectural services in the District of Columbia?

DECISION No. According to the licensing statute, an architect cannot recover on a contract to perform architectural services in the District of Columbia if she or he lacks a District of Columbia license.

REASON Sturdza argued that the licensing statute should not apply to architects who submit plans in international architectural design competitions. The court held, however, that licensing requirements are necessary to ensure the safety of those who work in and visit buildings in the District of Columbia, as well as the safety of neighboring buildings. Besides, the statute contains no exception for international design competitions or any other type of client or service. "We must apply the statute as it is written and not create *ad hoc* [impromptu] exceptions by judicial decree based on nebulous [unclear] policy considerations."

CRITICAL THINKING—Global Consideration *The architectural services at the center of this case were to be performed for a foreign embassy. Should the court have made an exception for such a circumstance? Why or why not?*

ADAPTING THE LAW TO THE ONLINE ENVIRONMENT

AN INCREASING AMOUNT OF ONLINE GAMBLING IS IN OUR FUTURE

Until very recently, the federal government interpreted the Wire Act of 1961[a] as prohibiting all forms of interstate transmission of gambling-related communications. Presumably, that law meant that all online gambling was effectively illegal when it became a reality more than three decades later. In 2006, Congress passed the Unlawful Internet Gambling Enforcement Act[b] to further reduce the amount of online gambling. That act essentially prohibited credit-card companies from collecting online bets for online gambling companies.

The Justice Department Releases a Game Changer

In 2011, Illinois and New York asked the Office of Legal Counsel of the U.S. Justice Department to clarify the interpretation of the Wire Act of 1961. In response, the department declared that the Wire Act applies only to bets or wagers on sporting events or contests and that it does not cover purely *intra*state communications. In short, under the Obama administration's interpretation of the Wire Act, almost all federal antigambling legislation no longer applies to gaming that is legal under state laws. The decision will pave the way for all states to legalize Internet poker and certain other types of online betting.

a. 18 U.S.C. Section 1084.
b. 31 U.S.C. Section 5361–5367.

The District of Columbia and Nevada Are Just Starting Points

As of 2012, only two jurisdictions had legalized online gambling—the District of Columbia and Nevada. Therefore, start-up online gambling businesses can be expected to increase dramatically in the next few years in those jurisdictions.

Other jurisdictions are also seeking additional revenues to reduce their budget deficits. Several states, including California, are already considering changing their laws to allow legal in-state Internet gambling. The lure of taxing billions of online gambling profits each year is very tempting.

Expect More Mobile Gambling Apps

For the last two years, the residents of Nevada have been able to utilize a mobile gambling app. Even bettors who do not live in Nevada can use an app that allows them to place sports bets via their phones. The first mobile app was created by America Wagering, Inc., for BlackBerry mobile phone devices.

Today, a number of casinos in Nevada offer mobile gambling apps that work on iPhones and Android-based smartphones. More apps will follow as more states legalize online gaming.

Critical Thinking

Why do you think that the Justice Department still believes that the Wire Act of 1961 applies to betting on sporting events or contests?

Contracts Contrary to Public Policy

Although contracts involve private parties, some are not enforceable because of the negative impact they would have on society. These contracts are said to be *contrary to public policy.* Examples include a contract to commit an immoral act, such as selling a child, and a contract that prohibits marriage. Business contracts that may be contrary to public policy include contracts in restraint of trade and unconscionable contracts or clauses.

LEARNING OBJECTIVE 2
Under what circumstances will a covenant not to compete be enforced? When will such covenants not be enforced?

Covenant Not to Compete A contractual promise of one party to refrain from conducting business similar to that of another party for a certain period of time and within a specified geographical area.

Contracts in Restraint of Trade The United States has a strong public policy favoring competition in the economy. Thus, contracts in restraint of trade (anticompetitive agreements) generally are unenforceable because they are contrary to public policy. Typically, such contracts also violate one or more federal or state antitrust laws (these laws will be discussed in Chapter 22). An exception is recognized when the restraint is reasonable and is an ancillary (secondary, or subordinate) part of the contract. Such restraints often are included in contracts for the sale of an ongoing business and employment contracts.

Covenants Not to Compete and the Sale of an Ongoing Business Many contracts involve a type of restraint called a **covenant not to compete,** or a restrictive covenant.

A covenant not to compete may be created when a seller agrees not to open a new store in a certain geographic area surrounding the old store. Such an agreement enables the seller to sell, and the purchaser to buy, the goodwill and reputation of an ongoing business without having to worry that the seller will open a competing business a block away. Provided the restrictive covenant is reasonable and is an ancillary part of the sale of an ongoing business, it is enforceable.

Employment Contract A contract between an employer and an employee in which the terms and conditions of employment are stated.

Covenants Not to Compete in Employment Contracts   Agreements not to compete can also be included in **employment contracts.** (See the annotated contract at the end of Chapter 9 for an example of an employment contract containing a noncompete clause.) People in middle-level and upper-level management positions commonly agree not to work for competitors or start a competing business for a specified period of time after terminating employment. Such agreements are generally legal in most states so long as the specified period of time is not excessive in duration and the geographic restriction is reasonable. What constitutes a reasonable time period may be shorter in the online environment than in conventional employment contracts because the restrictions would apply worldwide.

To be reasonable, a restriction on competition must protect a legitimate business interest and must not be any greater than necessary to protect that interest.   **CASE EXAMPLE 8.5**   Safety and Compliance Management, Inc. (SCMI), provides drug-testing services. When SCMI hired Angela to pick up test specimens, she signed a covenant not to compete "in any area of SCMI business." Angela later quit SCMI's employ to work in a hospital where she sometimes collected patient specimens. SCMI claimed this was a breach of their noncompete agreement. A court ruled that the covenant was unreasonable because it imposed a greater restriction on Angela than was necessary to protect SCMI.[6] ●

The contract in the following *Spotlight Case* provided an exclusive license to open and operate comedy clubs under a certain famous trademark. It also included a covenant not to compete. The question was whether the restraint was reasonable.

6. *Stultz v. Safety and Compliance Management, Inc.,* 285 Ga.App. 799, 648 S.E.2d 129 (2007).

Spotlight on the Improv

Case 8.2
Comedy Club, Inc. v. Improv West Associates
United States Court of Appeals, Ninth Circuit, 553 F.3d 1277 (2009).
www.ca9.uscourts.gov[a]

How much control over the name Improv Comedy Club does its owner have?

FACTS   Improv West Associates is the founder of the Improv Comedy Club and owner of the "Improv" trademark. Comedy Club, Inc. (CCI), owns and operates restaurants and comedy clubs. Improv West granted CCI an exclusive license to open four Improv clubs per year in 2001, 2002, and 2003. Their agreement prohibited CCI from opening any non-Improv comedy clubs "in the contiguous United States" until 2019. When CCI failed to open eight clubs by the end of 2002, Improv West commenced arbitration. The arbitrator's award in 2005 stated that CCI had forfeited its right to open Improv clubs, but that the parties' agreement had not terminated and the covenant not to compete was enforceable—CCI could not open any new comedy clubs for its duration. A federal district court confirmed the award, and CCI appealed.

ISSUE   Is a covenant not to compete in the comedy club business for fourteen years in forty-eight states too broad to be enforced?

DECISION   Yes. The U.S. Court of Appeals for the Ninth Circuit reversed part of the lower court's confirmation of the award and remanded the case.

a. In the left-hand column, in the "Opinions" pull-down menu, click on "Published." On that page, click on "Advanced Search." Then, in the "by Case No.:" box, type "05-55739," and click on "Search." In the result, click on the "01/29/2009" link to access the opinion.

Case 8.2—Continued

REASON The court said that terminating CCI's exclusive right to open Improv clubs due to its inadequate performance of the parties' contract "makes sense" and that Improv West should be protected from "improper" competition. But the covenant not to compete in this case has "dramatic geographic and temporal [relating to time] scope. . . . For more than fourteen years the entire contiguous United States comedy club market, except for CCI's current Improv clubs, is off limits to CCI." The effect would be to foreclose competition in a substantial share of the comedy club business. This restraint is "too broad to be countenanced." The covenant should be tailored to cover only the areas in which CCI is operating Improv clubs under the parties' agreement. It should allow CCI to open non-Improv clubs in "all those counties" where it does not operate an Improv club.

WHY IS THIS CASE IMPORTANT? *Competition is a paramount principle of our capitalist economic system. But it requires the support of our laws if it is to be a reality. This case shows the multifaceted role that the law can play to encourage competition by removing unfair restraints and by enforcing proper limits to prevent abuse.*

Enforcement Problems The laws governing the enforceability of covenants not to compete vary significantly from state to state. California prohibits the enforcement of all covenants not to compete. In some states, such as Texas, such a covenant will not be enforced unless the employee has received some benefit in return for signing the noncompete agreement. This is true even if the covenant is reasonable as to time and area.

Occasionally, depending on the jurisdiction, courts will *reform* covenants not to compete. If a covenant is found to be unreasonable in time or geographic area, the court may convert the terms into reasonable ones and then enforce the reformed covenant. This presents a problem, however, in that the judge has implicitly become a party to the contract. Consequently, courts usually resort to contract **reformation** only when necessary to prevent undue burdens or hardships.

Reformation A court-ordered correction of a written contract so that it reflects the true intentions of the parties.

PREVENTING LEGAL DISPUTES

A business clearly has a legitimate interest in having employees sign covenants not to compete and in preventing them from using the valuable skills and training provided by the business for the benefit of a competitor. The problem is that these covenants frequently lead to litigation. Moreover, it is difficult to predict what a court will consider reasonable in a given situation. Therefore, you need to be aware of the difficulties in enforcing noncompete agreements. Seek the advice of counsel in the relevant jurisdiction when drafting covenants not to compete. Avoid overreaching in terms of time and geographic restrictions, particularly if you are the manager of a high-tech or Web-based company. Consider using noncompete clauses only for key employees. If necessary, offer them some compensation (consideration) for signing the agreement. If an employee signed a noncompete clause when he or she was hired, be sure to discuss the meaning of that clause and your expectations with the employee at the time of termination.

Unconscionable Contracts or Clauses
Ordinarily, a court does not look at the fairness or equity of a contract. Nor, as discussed earlier, does it inquire into the adequacy of consideration. Persons are assumed to be reasonably intelligent, and the courts will not come to their aid just because they have made unwise or foolish bargains. In certain circumstances, however, bargains are so oppressive that the courts relieve innocent parties of part or all of their duties. Such bargains are deemed **unconscionable**[7] because they are so unscrupulous or grossly unfair as to be "void of conscience."[8] A contract can

Unconscionable Unscrupulous or grossly unfair.

---

7. Pronounced un-*kon*-shun-uh-bul.

8. The Uniform Commercial Code (UCC) incorporates the concept of unconscionability in its provisions with regard to the sale and lease of goods. See UCC 2–302 and 2–719.

be unconscionable on either procedural or substantive grounds, as shown in Exhibit 8.1 below.

Procedural Unconscionability   Procedural unconscionability often involves inconspicuous print, unintelligible language ("legalese"), or the lack of an opportunity to read the contract or ask questions about its meaning. This type of unconscionability typically arises when a party's lack of knowledge or understanding of the contract terms deprived him or her of any meaningful choice.

Procedural unconscionability can also occur when there is such a disparity in bargaining power between the two parties that the weaker party's consent is not voluntary. This type of situation often involves an **adhesion contract,** which is a standard-form contract written exclusively by one party (the dominant party, usually the seller or creditor) and presented to the other (the adhering party, usually the buyer or borrower) on a take-it-or-leave-it basis. In other words, the adhering party has no opportunity to negotiate the terms of the contract. Not all adhesion contracts are unconscionable, only those that unreasonably favor the drafter.

Substantive Unconscionability   Substantive unconscionability occurs when contracts, or portions of contracts, are oppressive or overly harsh. Courts generally focus on provisions that deprive one party of the benefits of the agreement or leave that party without remedy for nonperformance by the other.

Substantive unconscionability can arise in a wide variety of business contexts. For example, a contract clause that gives the business entity unrestricted access to the courts but requires the other party to arbitrate any dispute with the firm may be unconscionable. Similarly, contracts drafted by cell phone providers and insurance companies have been struck down as substantively unconscionable when they included provisions that were overly harsh or one sided.[9]

Adhesion Contract A standard-form contract in which the stronger party dictates the terms.

---

9. See, for example, *Gatton v. T-Mobile USA, Inc.,* 152 Cal.App.4th 571, 61 Cal.Rptr.3d 344 (2007); and *Aul v. Golden Rule Insurance Co.,* 2007 WL 1695243 (Wis.App. 2007).

Exhibit 8.1 **Unconscionability**

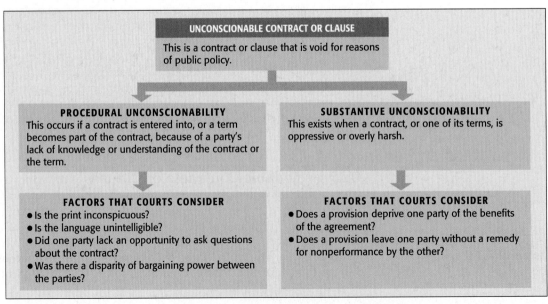

Exculpatory Clause A clause that releases a contractual party from liability in the event of monetary or physical injury, no matter who is at fault.

What is an exculpatory clause? In what circumstances might exculpatory clauses be enforced? When will they not be enforced?

(dwphotos/iStockphoto.com)

If a carnival swing is defective and causes an injury, can the swing's owner avoid liability if it has made each participant sign an exculpatory clause?

Exculpatory Clauses Often closely related to the concept of unconscionability are **exculpatory clauses,** which release a party from liability in the event of monetary or physical injury, *no matter who is at fault.* Indeed, courts sometimes refuse to enforce such clauses because they deem them to be unconscionable. Exculpatory clauses found in rental agreements for commercial property are frequently held to be contrary to public policy, and such clauses are almost always unenforceable in residential property leases. Exculpatory clauses in the employment context may be deemed unconscionable when they attempt to remove the employer's potential liability for injuries to employees.

Although courts view exculpatory clauses with disfavor, they do enforce such clauses when they do not contravene public policy, are not ambiguous, and do not claim to protect parties from liability for intentional misconduct. Businesses such as health clubs, racetracks, amusement parks, skiing facilities, horse-rental operations, golf-cart concessions, and skydiving organizations frequently use exculpatory clauses to limit their liability for patrons' injuries. Because these services are not essential, the firms offering them are sometimes considered to have no relative advantage in bargaining strength, and anyone contracting for their services is considered to do so voluntarily.

The Effect of Illegality

In general, an illegal contract is void: the contract is deemed never to have existed, and the courts will not aid either party. In most illegal contracts, both parties are considered to be equally at fault—*in pari delicto.* If the contract is executory (not yet fulfilled), neither party can enforce it. If it has been executed, neither party can recover damages. The courts usually are not concerned if one party is unjustly enriched at the expense of the other. Neither party can recover—except under the following circumstances:

1. *Justifiable ignorance of the facts.* When one of the parties to a contract has no reason to know that the contract is illegal, the courts will not enforce the contract, but will allow the parties to return to their original positions.
2. *Members of a protected class.* When a statute protects a certain class of people (such as flight attendants or certain other types of employees), a member of that class can enforce an illegal contract even though the other party cannot.
3. *Withdrawal from an illegal agreement.* If the illegal part of a bargain has not yet been performed, a party can withdraw from the contract and recover the performance or its value. **EXAMPLE 8.6** Marta and Ande decide to wager (illegally) on the outcome of a boxing match. Each deposits $1,000 with a stakeholder, who agrees to pay the winner of the bet. At this point, each party has performed part of the agreement, but the illegal part of the agreement will not occur until the winner is paid. Before payment occurs, either party is entitled to withdraw from the agreement by giving notice of withdrawal to the stakeholder and is entitled to a return of the $1,000. ●
4. *Severable, or divisible, contracts.* A contract that is *severable,* or divisible, consists of distinct parts that can be performed separately, with separate consideration provided for each part. If a contract is divisible into legal and illegal portions, a court may enforce the legal portion but not the illegal one, so long as the illegal portion does not affect the essence of the bargain. (Some contracts include a clause indicating that the parties intend the contract terms to be enforced to the "fullest extent permissible." See the *Appendix to Chapter 9: An Annotated Employment Contract* on page 289, paragraph 13, for an example.)
5. *Fraud, duress, or undue influence.* Sometimes, one party has been induced to enter into an illegal bargain through the other party's fraud, duress, or undue influence. In that situation, the first party will be allowed to recover for the performance or its value.

> "Understanding is
> a two-way street."
>
> —Eleanor Roosevelt, 1884–1962
> (First Lady of the United States,
> 1933–1945)

Voluntary Consent

An otherwise valid contract may still be unenforceable if the parties have not genuinely agreed to its terms. Voluntary consent (assent) may be lacking because of mistake, fraudulent misrepresentation, undue influence, or duress. Generally, a party who demonstrates that he or she did not genuinely agree to the terms of a contract can choose either to carry out the contract or to rescind (cancel) it and thus avoid the entire transaction. This is one reason why many contracts include definitions of important terms (see the *Appendix to Chapter 9: An Annotated Employment Contract* for an example).

Mistakes

We all make mistakes, so it is not surprising that mistakes are made when contracts are created. In certain circumstances, contract law allows a contract to be avoided on the basis of mistake. It is important to distinguish between *mistakes of fact* and *mistakes of value or quality*. Only a mistake of fact may allow a contract to be avoided.

LEARNING OBJECTIVE 4
What is the difference between a mistake of value or quality and a mistake of fact?

EXAMPLE 8.7 Paco buys a violin from Beverly for $250. Although the violin is very old, neither party believes that it is valuable. Later, however, an antiques dealer informs the parties that the violin is rare and worth thousands of dollars. Here, both parties were mistaken, but the mistake is a mistake of *value* rather than a mistake of *fact*. Therefore, Beverly cannot rescind the contract. •

Mistakes of fact occur in two forms—*unilateral* and *bilateral (mutual)*. A unilateral mistake is made by only one of the contracting parties, whereas a mutual mistake is made by both. We look next at these two types of mistakes and illustrate them graphically in Exhibit 8.2 on the facing page.

Unilateral Mistakes   A unilateral mistake occurs when only one party is mistaken as to a *material fact*—that is, a fact important to the subject matter of the contract. Generally, a unilateral mistake does not give the mistaken party any right to relief from the contract. In other words, the contract normally is enforceable against the mistaken party.

EXAMPLE 8.8 Elena intends to sell her motor home for $17,500. When she learns that Chin is interested in buying a used motor home, she sends him an e-mail offering to sell the vehicle to him. When typing the e-mail, however, she mistakenly keys in the price of $15,700. Chin immediately sends an e-mail to Elena, accepting her offer. Even though Elena intended to sell her motor home for $17,500, she has made a unilateral mistake and is bound by the contract to sell the vehicle to Chin for $15,700. •

This rule has at least two exceptions, however.

KNOW THIS
What a party to a contract knows or should know can determine whether the contract is enforceable.

1. If the *other* party to the contract knows or should have known that a mistake of fact was made, the contract may not be enforceable. In *Example 8.8*, if Chin had reason to know that Elena intended to sell her motor home for $17,500, then Elena's unilateral mistake (stating a price of $15,700 in her offer) may render the resulting contract unenforceable.
2. When a unilateral mistake of fact was due to a mathematical mistake that was made inadvertently and without gross (extreme) negligence, the contract may not be enforceable. Thus, if a contractor's bid was significantly low because he or she made a mistake in addition when totaling the estimated costs, any contract resulting from the bid normally can be rescinded.

Of course, in both situations, the mistake must involve a *material fact*.

Bilateral (Mutual) Mistakes   A bilateral mistake is a "mutual misunderstanding concerning a basic assumption on which the contract was made."[10] When both parties are mistaken about the same fact, the contract can be rescinded by either party. Note that,

---

10. *Restatement (Second) of Contracts*, Section 152.

Exhibit 8.2 Mistakes of Fact

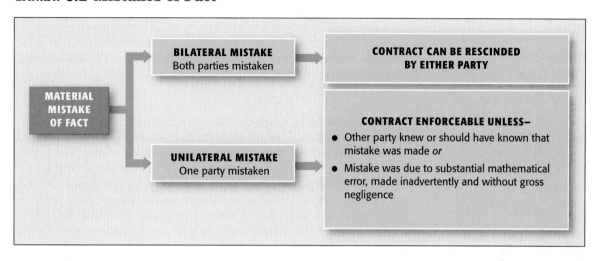

as with unilateral mistakes, the mistake must be about a material fact. When a bilateral mistake occurs, normally the contract is voidable by the adversely affected party and can be rescinded.

A word or term in a contract may be subject to more than one reasonable interpretation. If the parties to the contract attach materially different meanings to the term, their mutual misunderstanding may allow the contract to be rescinded.

CASE EXAMPLE 8.9   In a classic case, Wichelhaus purchased a shipment of cotton from Raffles to arrive on a ship called the *Peerless* sailing from Bombay, India. Wichelhaus meant a ship called *Peerless* leaving Bombay in October, but Raffles meant a different ship also named *Peerless* leaving Bombay in December. When the goods arrived on the December *Peerless* and Raffles tried to deliver them, Wichelhaus refused to accept them. The British court held for Wichelhaus, concluding that a mutual mistake had been made because the parties had attached materially different meanings to an essential term of the contract (which ship *Peerless* was to transport the goods).[11] •

Fraudulent Misrepresentation

Although fraud is a tort (see Chapter 4), the presence of fraud also affects the authenticity of the innocent party's consent to a contract. When an innocent party is fraudulently induced to enter into a contract, the contract usually can be avoided because she or he has not *voluntarily* consented to the terms.[12] Normally, the innocent party can either rescind (cancel) the contract and be restored to her or his original position or enforce the contract and seek damages for any harms resulting from the fraud.

Generally, fraudulent misrepresentation refers only to misrepresentation that is consciously false and is intended to mislead another. Typically, fraud involves three elements:

1. A misrepresentation of a material fact must occur.
2. There must be an intent to deceive.
3. The innocent party must justifiably rely on the misrepresentation.

Additionally, to collect damages, a party must have been harmed as a result of the misrepresentation.

"Mistakes are the inevitable lot of mankind."

Sir George Jessel, 1824–1883 (English jurist)

LEARNING OBJECTIVE 5
What are the elements of fraudulent misrepresentation?

➤ KNOW THIS ◄
To collect damages in almost any lawsuit, there must be some sort of injury.

---

11. *Raffles v. Wichelhaus,* 159 Eng.Rep. 375 (1864).
12. *Restatement (Second) of Contracts,* Sections 163 and 164.

Misrepresentation Has Occurred
The first element of proving fraud is to show that misrepresentation of a material fact has occurred. This misrepresentation can occur by words or actions. For instance, an art gallery owner's statement "This painting is a Picasso" is a misrepresentation of fact if the painting was done by another artist. Similarly, if a customer asks to see only Jasper Johns paintings and the owner immediately leads the customer over to paintings that were not done by Johns, the owner's actions may be a misrepresentation.

Misrepresentation by Conduct   Misrepresentation by conduct often occurs when a party takes specific action to conceal a fact that is material to the contract. For instance, if a seller, by her or his actions, prevents a buyer from learning of some fact that is material to the contract, the seller's behavior constitutes misrepresentation by conduct.

CASE EXAMPLE 8.10   Actor Tom Selleck contracted to purchase a horse named Zorro for his daughter from Dolores Cuenca. Cuenca acted as though Zorro was fit to ride in competitions, when in reality the horse suffered from a medical condition. Selleck filed a lawsuit against Cuenca for wrongfully concealing the horse's condition, and a jury awarded Selleck more than $187,000 for Cuenca's misrepresentation by conduct.[13] •

Statements of Opinion   Statements of opinion and representations of future facts (predictions) are generally not subject to claims of fraud. Every person is expected to exercise care and judgment when entering into contracts, and the law will not come to the aid of one who simply makes an unwise bargain. Statements such as "This land will be worth twice as much next year" and "This car will last for years and years" are statements of opinion, not fact. Contracting parties should recognize them as opinions and not rely on them. Therefore, a seller is allowed to use *puffery* to sell her or his goods without being liable for fraud.

Nevertheless, in certain situations, such as when a naïve purchaser relies on an opinion from an expert, the innocent party may be entitled to rescission or reformation. (Reformation, as mentioned earlier, is an equitable remedy by which a court alters the terms of a contract to reflect the true intentions of the parties.)

CASE EXAMPLE 8.11   In a classic case, an instructor at an Arthur Murray dance school told Audrey Vokes, a widow without family, that she had the potential to become an accomplished dancer. The instructor sold her 2,302 hours of dancing lessons for a total of $31,090.45 (equivalent to $142,000 in 2013). When it became clear to Vokes that she did not, in fact, have the potential to be an excellent dancer, she sued the school for fraudulent misrepresentation. The court held that because the dance school had superior knowledge about a person's dance potential, the instructor's statements could be considered statements of fact rather than opinion.[14] •

Misrepresentation of Law   Misrepresentation of law *ordinarily* does not entitle a party to be relieved of a contract.   **EXAMPLE 8.12**   Tanya has a parcel of property that she is trying to sell to Lev. Tanya knows that a local ordinance prohibits building anything higher than three stories on the property. Nonetheless, she tells Lev, "You can build a condominium one hundred stories high if you want to." Lev buys the land and later discovers that Tanya's statement is false. Lev generally cannot avoid the contract, because under the common law, people are assumed to know state and local laws. •

Exceptions to this rule occur when the misrepresenting party is in a profession known to require greater knowledge of the law than the average citizen possesses. For example, if Tanya, in *Example 8.12*, had been a lawyer or a real-estate broker, her misrepresentation could have constituted fraud.

---

13. *Selleck v. Cuenca*, Case No. GIN056909, North County of San Diego, California, decided September 9, 2009.
14. *Vokes v. Arthur Murray, Inc.*, 212 So.2d 906 (Fla.App. 1968).

> "If a man smiles all the time, he's probably selling something that doesn't work."
>
> George Carlin, 1937–2008
> (American comedian)

Should an architect have greater knowledge about building codes than the person paying for the project?

(shotbydave/iStockphoto.com)

Misrepresentation by Silence   Ordinarily, neither party to a contract has a duty to come forward and disclose facts, and a contract normally will not be set aside because certain pertinent information has not been volunteered. **EXAMPLE 8.13**   Jude is selling a car that has been in an accident and has been repaired. He does not need to volunteer this information to a potential buyer. If, however, the buyer asks him if the car has had extensive bodywork and he lies, Jude has committed fraudulent misrepresentation. •

In general, if the seller knows of a serious defect or a serious potential problem that the buyer cannot reasonably be expected to discover, the seller may have a duty to speak. Normally, the seller must disclose only *latent defects*—that is, defects that could not readily be ascertained. Because a buyer of a house could easily discover the presence of termites through an inspection, for instance, termites may not qualify as a latent defect Also, when the parties are in a *fiduciary relationship*—one of trust, such as partners, physician and patient, or attorney and client—there is a duty to disclose material facts. Failure to do so may constitute fraud.

In the following case, the issue of misrepresentation by silence was at the heart of the dispute. A real estate investor sued for fraud after a seller failed to disclose material facts about the property's value.

Case 8.3

Fazio v. Cypress/GR Houston I, LP

Court of Appeals of Texas, First District, 2012 WL 5324842 (2012).

(jnatkin/iStockphoto.com)

FACTS   Peter Fazio began talks with Cypress/GR Houston I, LP, to buy retail property. The property's main tenant was a Garden Ridge store. In performing a background investigation, Fazio and his agents became concerned about Garden Ridge's financial health. Nevertheless, after being assured that Garden Ridge had a positive financial outlook, Fazio sent Cypress a letter of intent to buy the property for $7.67 million "[b]ased on the currently reported absolute net income of $805,040.00." Cypress then agreed to provide all information in its possession, but it failed to disclose that (1) a consultant for Garden Ridge had recently requested a $240,000 reduction in the annual rent as part of a restructuring of the company's real estate leases and (2) Cypress's bank was so concerned about Garden Ridge's financial health that it had required a personal guaranty of the property's loan. The parties entered into a purchase agreement, but Garden Ridge went into bankruptcy shortly after the deal closed. Fazio sued Cypress for fraud after he was forced to sell the property for only $3.75 million. A jury found in Fazio's favor, but the trial court awarded judgment *n.o.v.* (see Chapter 3 page 84) to Cypress. Fazio appealed.

ISSUE   Was Fazio fraudulently induced to enter into the purchase agreement?

DECISION   Yes. The Texas appellate court reversed the trial court and held that Cypress was liable to Fazio for fraud.

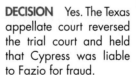
What does a rent-reduction request from a shopping mall's main tenant indicate?

REASON   The court found that Cypress had engaged in fraud as a matter of law. Before the parties entered into the purchase agreement, Cypress had agreed to provide all information in its possession. Cypress knew that Fazio had been concerned about Garden Ridge's financial health and that he had based the purchase price on the anticipated income from the property. Nevertheless, it withheld information about Garden Ridge's request for a rent reduction and about the fact that Cypress had been required to provide a personal guaranty of the property's loan—information to which a reasonable person in Fazio's position would have attached importance. Finally, in the purchase agreement, Fazio did not disclaim his reliance on Cypress's misrepresentations or waive possible claims for fraud.

CRITICAL THINKING—Ethical Consideration   *Was Cypress's conduct unethical? Why or why not?*

Scienter Knowledge by a misrepresenting party that material facts have been falsely represented or omitted with an intent to deceive.

Intent to Deceive   The second element of fraud is knowledge on the part of the misrepresenting party that facts have been misrepresented. This element, usually called *scienter*,[15] or "guilty knowledge," generally signifies that there was an intent to deceive. *Scienter* clearly exists if a party knows that a fact is not as stated. *Scienter* also exists if a party makes a statement that he or she believes not to be true or makes a statement recklessly, without regard to whether it is true or false. Finally, this element is met if a party says or implies that a statement is made on some basis, such as personal knowledge or personal investigation, when it is not.

CASE EXAMPLE 8.14   Robert Sarvis applied for a position as a business law professor two weeks after his release from prison. On his résumé, he said that he had been a corporate president for fourteen years and had taught business law at another college. After he was hired, his probation officer alerted the school to Sarvis's criminal history. The school immediately fired him, and Sarvis sued for breach of his employment contract. The court concluded that by not disclosing his history, Sarvis clearly exhibited an intent to deceive and that the school had justifiably relied on his misrepresentations. Therefore, the school could rescind Sarvis's employment contract.[16] ●

Justifiable Reliance on the Misrepresentation   The third element of fraud is *justifiable reliance* on the misrepresentation of fact. The deceived party must have a justifiable reason for relying on the misrepresentation, and the misrepresentation must be an important factor (but not necessarily the sole factor) in inducing the party to enter into the contract.

Reliance is not justified if the innocent party knows the true facts or relies on obviously extravagant statements. For instance, if a used-car dealer tells you, "This old Cadillac will get over sixty miles to the gallon," you normally will not be justified in relying on this statement.

➤ KNOW THIS ➤

An opinion is neither a contract offer, nor a contract term, nor fraud.

Injury to the Innocent Party   Most courts do not require a showing of harm when the action is to rescind (cancel) the contract. These courts hold that because rescission returns the parties to the positions they held before the contract was made, a showing of injury to the innocent party is unnecessary.

To recover damages caused by fraud, however, proof of an injury is universally required. The measure of damages is ordinarily equal to the property's value had it been delivered as represented, less the actual price paid for the property. Courts may also award *punitive,* or *exemplary, damages,* which compensate a plaintiff over and above the amount of the actual loss. As discussed on pages 100 and 101 of Chapter 4, the public-policy consideration underlying punitive damages is to punish the defendant and thereby set an example that will deter similar wrongdoing by others.

Undue Influence

Undue influence arises from relationships in which one party can greatly influence another party, thus overcoming that party's free will. A contract entered into under excessive or undue influence lacks voluntary consent and is therefore voidable.

In various types of relationships, one party may have an opportunity to dominate and unfairly influence another party. Minors and elderly people, for instance, are often under the influence of guardians (persons who are legally responsible for others). If a guardian induces a young or elderly ward (a person whom the guardian looks after) to enter into a contract that benefits the guardian, the guardian may have exerted undue influence.

---

15. Pronounced sy-*en*-ter.
16. *Sarvis v. Vermont State Colleges,* 172 Vt. 76, 772 A.2d 494 (2001).

Undue influence can arise from a number of confidential or fiduciary relationships, including attorney-client, physician-patient, guardian-ward, parent-child, husband-wife, and trustee-beneficiary.

The essential feature of undue influence is that the party being taken advantage of does not, in reality, exercise free will in entering into a contract. It is not enough that a person is elderly or suffers from some mental or physical impairment. There must be clear and convincing evidence that the person did not act out of her or his free will.

Duress

Agreement to the terms of a contract is not voluntary if one of the parties is forced into the agreement. The use of threats, blackmail, or extortion to force a party to enter into a contract constitutes *duress*. Duress is both a defense to the enforcement of a contract and a ground for rescission of a contract.

To establish duress, there must be proof of a threat. The threatened act must be wrongful or illegal and must render the person incapable of exercising free will. A threat to exercise a legal right, such as the right to sue someone, ordinarily does not constitute duress.

The Writing Requirement

Statute of Frauds A state statute that requires certain types of contracts to be in writing to be enforceable.

A contract that is otherwise valid may be unenforceable if it is not in the proper form. Every state has a statute that stipulates that certain types of contracts must be in writing or be evidenced by a written memorandum or electronic record that is signed by the party against whom enforcement is sought, unless certain exceptions apply. Although the statutes vary slightly from state to state, their primary purpose is to ensure that, for certain types of contracts, there is reliable evidence of the contracts and their terms. In this text, we refer to these statutes collectively as the **Statute of Frauds.**

The following types of contracts are said to fall "within" or "under" the Statute of Frauds and therefore require a writing:

1. Contracts involving interests in land.
2. Contracts that cannot by their terms be performed within one year from the day after the date of formation.
3. Collateral contracts, such as promises to answer for the debt or duty of another.
4. Promises made in consideration of marriage.
5. Under the Uniform Commercial Code (UCC—see Chapter 10), contracts for the sale of goods priced at $500 or more.

The actual name of the Statute of Frauds is misleading because it does not apply to fraud. Rather, in an effort to prevent fraud, the statute denies enforceability to certain contracts that do not comply with its requirements. The name derives from an English act passed in 1677 that was titled "An Act for the Prevention of Frauds and Perjuries."

Contracts Involving Interests in Land

Under the Statute of Frauds, a contract involving an interest in land must be evidenced by a writing to be enforceable.[17] **EXAMPLE 8.15**   If Carol contracts orally to sell Seaside Shelter to Axel but later decides not to sell, Axel cannot enforce the contract. Similarly, if Axel refuses to close the deal, Carol cannot force Axel to pay for the land by bringing a lawsuit. The Statute of Frauds is a defense to the enforcement of this type of oral contract. •

---

17. In some states, the contract will be enforced if each party admits to the existence of the oral contract in court or admits to its existence during discovery before trial (see Chapter 3).

A contract for the sale of land ordinarily involves the entire interest in the real property (discussed in Chapter 24), including buildings, growing crops, vegetation, minerals, timber, and anything else permanently attached to the land. Therefore, a *fixture* (personal property so affixed or so used as to become a part of the realty) is treated as real property.

The Statute of Frauds requires written contracts not just for the sale of land but also for the transfer of other interests in land, such as mortgages, easements, and leases. We describe these other interests in Chapters 16 and 24.

The One-Year Rule

> "A verbal contract isn't worth the paper it's written on."
>
> Samuel Goldwyn, 1879–1974
> (Hollywood motion picture producer)

A contract that cannot, *by its own terms,* be performed within one year *from the day after it is formed* must be in writing to be enforceable. Because disputes over such contracts are unlikely to occur until some time after the contracts are made, resolution of these disputes is difficult unless the contract terms have been put in writing. Exhibit 8.3 below graphically illustrates the one-year rule.

EXAMPLE 8.16   Superior University forms a contract with Kimi San stating that San will teach three courses in history during the coming academic year (September 15 through June 15). If the contract is formed in March, it must be in writing to be enforceable—because it cannot be performed within one year. If the contract is not formed until July, however, it will not have to be in writing to be enforceable—because it can be performed within one year. ●

Normally, the test for determining whether an oral contract is enforceable under the one-year rule is whether performance is *possible* within one year from the day after the date of contract formation—not whether the agreement is *likely* to be performed within one year. When performance of a contract is objectively impossible during the one-year period, the oral contract will be unenforceable.

EXAMPLE 8.17   Bankers Life orally contracts to lend $40,000 to Janet Lawrence "as long as Lawrence & Associates operates its financial consulting firm in Omaha, Nebraska." The contract does not fall within the Statute of Frauds—no writing is required—because Lawrence & Associates could go out of business in one year or less. In this event, the contract would be fully performed within one year. Similarly, an oral contract for lifetime employment does not fall within the Statute of Frauds. Because an employee who is hired "for life" can die within a year, the courts reason that the contract can be performed within one year. ●

Exhibit 8.3 The One-Year Rule

Under the Statute of Frauds, contracts that by their terms are impossible to perform within one year from the day after the date of contract formation must be in writing to be enforceable. Put another way, if it is at all possible to perform an oral contract within one year from the day after the contract is made, the contract will fall outside the Statute of Frauds and be enforceable.

Collateral Promises

Collateral Promise A secondary promise to a primary transaction, such as a promise made by one person to pay the debts of another if the latter fails to perform. A collateral promise normally must be in writing to be enforceable.

A **collateral promise,** or secondary promise, is one that is ancillary (subsidiary) to a principal transaction or primary contractual relationship. In other words, a collateral promise is one made by a third party to assume the debts or obligations of a primary party to a contract if that party does not perform. Any collateral promise of this nature falls under the Statute of Frauds and therefore must be in writing to be enforceable. To understand this concept, it is important to distinguish between primary and secondary promises and obligations.

Primary versus Secondary Obligations

A contract in which a party assumes a primary obligation—such as by agreeing to pay a bill when it is received—normally does not need to be in writing to be enforceable. In contrast, a contract in which a party assumes a secondary obligation does have to be in writing to be enforceable. **EXAMPLE 8.18** Kareem's mother borrows $10,000 from the Medford Trust Company on a promissory note payable in six months. Kareem promises the bank officer handling the loan that he will pay the $10,000 *if his mother does not pay the loan on time.* Kareem, in this situation, becomes what is known as a *guarantor* on the loan. He is guaranteeing to the bank (the creditor) that he will pay the loan if his mother fails to do so. This kind of collateral promise must be in writing to be enforceable. ● We will return to the concept of guaranty and the distinction between primary and secondary obligations in Chapter 15 in the context of creditors' rights.

An Exception—The "Main Purpose" Rule

An oral promise to answer for the debt of another is covered by the Statute of Frauds *unless* the guarantor's purpose in accepting secondary liability is to secure a personal benefit. Under the "main purpose" rule, this type of contract need not be in writing.[18] The assumption is that a court can infer from the circumstances of a case whether a "leading objective" of the promisor was to secure a personal benefit.

Prenuptial Agreement An agreement made before marriage that defines each partner's ownership rights in the other partner's property. Prenuptial agreements must be in writing to be enforceable.

EXAMPLE 8.19 Carrie Braswell contracts with Custom Manufacturing Company to have some machines custom made for her factory. She promises Newform Supply, Custom's supplier, that if Newform continues to deliver the materials to Custom for the production of the custom-made machines, she will guarantee payment. This promise need not be in writing, even though the effect may be to pay the debt of another, because Braswell's main purpose is to secure a benefit for herself. ●

Another typical application of the main purpose doctrine occurs when one creditor guarantees the debtor's debt to another creditor to forestall litigation. This allows the debtor to remain in business long enough to generate profits sufficient to pay *both* creditors. In this situation, the guaranty does not need to be in writing to be enforceable.

Promises Made in Consideration of Marriage

A unilateral promise to make a monetary payment or to give property in consideration of marriage must be in writing. The same rule applies to **prenuptial agreements**—agreements made before marriage (also called *antenuptial agreements*) that define each partner's ownership rights in the other partner's property. Prenuptial agreements must be in writing to be enforceable. Generally, courts tend to give more credence to prenuptial agreements that are accompanied by consideration.

(The New Yorker Collection © Henry Martin from CartoonBank.com. All Rights Reserved.)

"Wallace, have you forgotten our prenuptial contract? No whistling!"

---

18. *Restatement (Second) of Contracts,* Section 116.

EXAMPLE 8.20   After a divorce from actor Tom Cruise, actress Nicole Kidman entered into a prenuptial agreement with her fiancé, country singer Keith Urban. Kidman agreed that in the event of a divorce, she would pay Urban $640,000 for every year they were married, unless Urban relapsed and used drugs again. (Then he would receive nothing.) •

Contracts for the Sale of Goods

The Uniform Commercial Code (UCC—see Chapter 10) includes Statute of Frauds provisions that require written evidence or an electronic record of a contract for the sale of goods priced at $500 or more. (This low threshold amount may be increased in the future.) To satisfy the UCC requirement, a writing need only state the quantity term. Other terms agreed on can be omitted or stated imprecisely in the writing, as long as they adequately reflect both parties' intentions.

The contract will not be enforceable for any quantity greater than that set forth in the writing. In addition, the writing must have been signed by the person to be charged—that is, by the person who refuses to perform or the one being sued. Beyond these two requirements, the writing normally need not designate the buyer or the seller, the terms of payment, or the price. (See this chapter's *Beyond Our Borders* feature below to learn whether other countries have requirements similar to those in the Statute of Frauds.)

Exceptions to the Statute of Frauds

Exceptions to the applicability of the Statute of Frauds are made in certain situations. We describe those situations here.

Partial Performance

When a contract has been partially performed and the parties cannot be returned to the positions they held before the contract was formed, a court may grant *specific performance* (an equitable remedy that requires a contract to be performed according to its precise terms—see Chapter 9).

In cases involving oral contracts for the transfer of interests in land, courts usually look at whether justice is better served by enforcing the oral contract when partial performance has taken place. For instance, if the purchaser has paid part of the price, taken possession, and made valuable improvements to the property, a court may grant specific performance. The parties still have to prove that an oral contract existed, however.

 BEYOND OUR BORDERS   ### The Statute of Frauds and International Sales Contracts

As you will read in Chapter 10, the Convention on Contracts for the International Sale of Goods (CISG) governs international sales contracts between citizens of countries that have ratified the convention (agreement). The CISG does not incorporate any Statute of Frauds provisions. Rather, it states, in Article 11, that a "contract for sale need not be concluded in or evidenced by writing and is not subject to any other requirements as to form."

Article 11 accords with the legal customs of most nations, which no longer require contracts to meet certain formal or writing requirements to be enforceable. Ironically, even England, the nation that enacted the original Statute of Frauds in 1677, has repealed all of it except the provisions relating to collateral promises and to transfers of interests in land. Many other countries that once had such statutes have also repealed all or parts of them.

Civil law countries, such as France, have never required any types of contracts to be in writing. Obviously, without a writing requirement, contracts can take on any form.

Critical Thinking
If a country does not have a Statute of Frauds and a dispute arises over an oral agreement, how can the parties substantiate their positions?

In some states, mere reliance on certain types of oral contracts is enough to remove them from the Statute of Frauds. Under the UCC, an oral contract for goods priced at $500 or more is enforceable to the extent that a seller accepts payment or a buyer accepts delivery of the goods.[19]

Admissions   In some states, if a party against whom enforcement of an oral contract is sought admits in pleadings, testimony, or otherwise in court proceedings that a contract for sale was made, the contract will be enforceable. A contract subject to the UCC will be enforceable, but only to the extent of the quantity admitted.[20]

EXAMPLE 8.21   The president of Ashley Corporation admits under oath that an oral agreement was made with Com Best to pay $10,000 for certain business equipment. In this situation, a court will enforce the agreement only to the extent admitted (the $10,000), even if Com Best claims that the agreement involved $20,000 of equipment. •

Promissory Estoppel   In some states, an oral contract that would otherwise be unenforceable under the Statute of Frauds may be enforced under the doctrine of promissory estoppel (see page 220 in Chapter 7). Section 139 of the *Restatement (Second) of Contracts* provides that an oral promise can be enforceable, notwithstanding the Statute of Frauds, if the promisee has justifiably relied on it to her or his detriment. For the contract to be enforceable, the reliance must have been foreseeable to the person making the promise, and enforcing the promise must be the only way to avoid injustice.

Special Exceptions under the UCC   Special exceptions to the applicability of the Statute of Frauds exist for sales contracts. Oral contracts for customized goods may be enforced in certain circumstances. Another exception has to do with oral contracts *between merchants* that have been confirmed in writing. We will examine these exceptions in Chapter 10.

Exhibit 8.4 below graphically summarizes the types of contracts that fall under the Statute of Frauds and the various exceptions that apply.

---

19. UCC 2–201(3)(c). See Chapter 10.
20. UCC 2–201(3)(b). See Chapter 10.

Exhibit 8.4 Contracts Subject to the Statute of Frauds

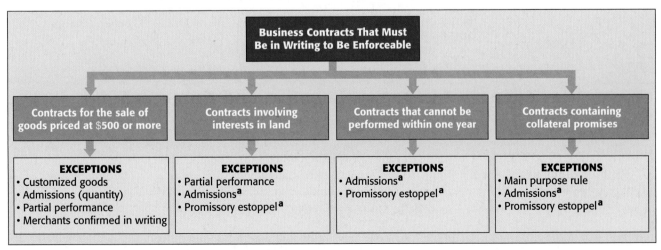

a. Some states follow Section 133 (on admissions) and Section 139 (on promissory estoppel) of the *Restatement (Second) of Contracts*.

Sufficiency of the Writing

A written contract will, of course, satisfy the writing requirement of the Statute of Frauds. (See the *Appendix to Chapter 9* for an example of a written contract and descriptions of the meaning of its terms.) A *written memorandum* (written or electronic evidence of the oral contract) signed by the party against whom enforcement is sought will also satisfy the writing requirement. The signature need not be placed at the end of the document but can be anywhere in the writing. It can even be initials rather than the full name. As mentioned in Chapter 7, in today's business world, there are many ways to create signatures electronically, and electronic signatures generally satisfy the Statute of Frauds.

What Constitutes a Writing?   A writing can consist of any confirmation, invoice, sales slip, check, fax, or e-mail—or such items in combination. The written contract need not consist of a single document to constitute an enforceable contract. One document may incorporate another document by expressly referring to it. Several documents may form a single contract if they are physically attached—such as by staple, paper clip, or glue—or even if they are only placed in the same envelope.

What Must Be Contained in the Writing?   A memorandum or note evidencing the oral contract need only contain the essential terms of the contract, not every term. There must also be some indication that the parties voluntarily agreed to the terms. A faxed or e-mailed memo of the terms of an agreement could be sufficient if it showed that there was a meeting of the minds and that the terms were not just part of the preliminary negotiations.[21] Under the UCC, in regard to the sale of goods, the writing need only state the quantity and be signed by the party against whom enforcement is sought.

Because only the party against whom enforcement is sought must have signed the writing, a contract may be enforceable by one of its parties but not by the other. **CASE EXAMPLE 8.22**   Beneficial Homeowner Service Corporation filed a suit against Stephen and Susan Steele to foreclose on a mortgage (a loan securing real property—see Chapter 16) and repossess their home in East Hampton, New York. Beneficial's copy of the mortgage loan agreement identified Stephen Steele as the sole party owing the debt, but the agreement had not been signed. The court concluded that the agreement was unenforceable. Because a mortgage involves the transfer of an interest in real property, the mortgage agreement and its underlying obligation must be in writing to satisfy the Statute of Frauds.[22] In this case, the writing was missing at least one necessary element—the signature of the party against whom enforcement was sought. •

> "The pen is mightier than the sword, and considerably easier to write with."
>
> Marty Feldman, 1934–1982 (English actor and comedian)

---

21. See, for example, *Coca-Cola Co. v. Babyback's International, Inc.*, 841 N.E.2d 557 (Ind.App. 2006).
22. *Beneficial Homeowner Service Corp. v. Steele*, 2011 WL 61728 (N.Y.Sup.Ct. 2011).

Reviewing . . . Capacity, Legality, and Enforceability

Renee Beaver started racing go-karts competitively in 2009, when she was fourteen. Many of the races required participants to sign an exculpatory clause, which she or her parents regularly signed. In 2012, right before her birthday, Beaver participated in the annual Elkhart Grand Prix, a series of races in Elkhart, Indiana. During the event, a piece of foam padding used as a course barrier was torn from its base and ended up on the track. A portion of the padding struck Beaver in the head, and another portion was thrown into oncoming traffic, causing a multikart collision during which she sustained severe injuries. Beaver filed an action against the race organizers for negligence. The organizers could not locate the exculpatory clause that Beaver was supposed to have signed. Race organizers argued that she must have signed one to enter the race, but even if she had not signed one, her actions showed her intent to be bound by its terms. Using the information presented in the chapter, answer the following questions.

1. Did Beaver have the contractual capacity to enter a contract with an exculpatory clause? Why or why not?
2. Assuming that Beaver did, in fact, sign the exculpatory clause, did she later disaffirm or ratify the contract? Explain.
3. Now assume that Beaver had stated that she was eighteen years old at the time that she signed the exculpatory clause. How might this affect Beaver's ability to disaffirm or ratify the contract?

DEBATE THIS After agreeing to an exculpatory clause or purchasing some item, such as an iPad, minors often seek to avoid the contract. Today's minors are far from naïve and should not be allowed to avoid their contractual obligations.

BUSINESS APPLICATION

Should Retailers Enter into Contracts with Minors and Intoxicated Persons?*

Sales personnel, particularly those who are paid on a commission basis, are often eager to make contracts. Sometimes, however, these salespersons must deal with minors and intoxicated persons, both of whom have limited contractual capacity. Therefore, if you are a retailer, you should make sure that your employees are acquainted with the law governing contracts with minors and intoxicated persons.

Contracts with Minors

If your business involves selling consumer durables, such as cell phones, electronics, gaming equipment, appliances, furniture, or automobiles, your sales personnel must be careful in forming contracts with minors and should heed the adage, "When in doubt, check." Remember that a contract signed by a minor (unless it is for necessaries) normally is voidable, and the minor may exercise the option to disaffirm the contract. Employees should demand proof of legal age when they have any doubt about whether a customer is a minor. If the customer is a minor, the employees should insist that an adult (such as a parent) be the purchaser or at least cosign any sales contract.

In addition, because the law governing minors' rights varies substantially from state to state, you should check with your attorney concerning the laws governing disaffirmance in your state. You and

those you hire to sell your products should know, for example, what the consequences will be if a minor disaffirms the sale or has misrepresented his or her age when forming a sales contract. Similarly, you need to find out whether and in what circumstances a minor, on disaffirming a contract, can be required to pay for damage to goods sold under the contract.

Dealing with Intoxicated Persons

Little need be said about a salesperson's dealings with obviously intoxicated persons. If the customer, despite intoxication, understands the legal consequences of signing the contract, the contract is enforceable. Nonetheless, it may be extremely difficult to establish that the intoxicated customer understood the consequences of entering into the contract if the customer claims that she or he did not understand. Therefore, the best advice is, "When in doubt, don't." In other words, if you suspect a customer may be intoxicated, do not sign a contract with that customer.

Checklist for the Retailer

1. *When in doubt about the age of a customer to whom you are about to sell major consumer durable goods or anything other than necessaries, require proof of legal age.*
2. *If such proof is not forthcoming, require that a parent or guardian sign the contract.*

*This *Business Application* is not meant to substitute for the services of an attorney who is licensed to practice law in your state.

Key Terms

Chapter Summary: Capacity, Legality, and Enforceability

CONTRACTUAL CAPACITY	

Minors
(See pages 228–229.)
	1. *General rule*—Contracts with minors are voidable at the option of the minor.
	2. *Disaffirmance*—The legal avoidance of a contractual obligation.
	   a. Disaffirmance can take place (in most states) at any time during minority and within a reasonable time after the minor has reached the age of majority.
	   b. The minor must disaffirm the entire contract, not just part of it.
	   c. When disaffirming executed contracts, the minor has a duty to return the received goods if they are still in the minor's control or (in some states) to pay their reasonable value.
	   d. A minor who has committed an act of fraud (such as misrepresenting her or his age) will be denied the right to disaffirm by some courts.
	   e. A minor may disaffirm a contract for necessaries but remains liable for the reasonable value of the goods.
	3. *Ratification*—The acceptance, or affirmation, of a legal obligation.
	   a. Express ratification—Occurs when the minor, in writing or orally, explicitly assumes the obligations imposed by the contract.
	   b. Implied ratification—Occurs when the conduct of the minor is inconsistent with disaffirmance or when the minor fails to disaffirm an executed contract within a reasonable time after reaching the age of majority.
	4. *Parents' liability*—Generally, except for contracts for necessaries, parents are not liable for the contracts made by minor children acting on their own.

Intoxicated Persons (See page 230.)	1. A contract entered into by an intoxicated person is voidable at the option of the intoxicated person if the person was sufficiently intoxicated to lack mental capacity, even if the intoxication was voluntary. 2. A contract with an intoxicated person is enforceable if, despite being intoxicated, the person understood the legal consequences of entering into the contract.
Mentally Incompetent Persons (See page 230.)	1. A contract made by a person previously judged by a court to be mentally incompetent is void. 2. A contract made by a person who is mentally incompetent, but has not been previously declared incompetent by a court, is voidable at the option of that person.
LEGALITY	
Contracts Contrary to Statute (See pages 231–232.)	1. *Usury*—Usury occurs when a lender makes a loan at an interest rate above the lawful maximum, which varies from state to state. 2. *Gambling*—Gambling contracts that contravene (go against) state statutes are deemed illegal and thus void. 3. *Licensing statutes*—Contracts entered into by persons who do not have a license, when one is required by statute, will not be enforceable unless the underlying purpose of the statute is to raise government revenues (and not to protect the public from unauthorized practitioners).
Contracts Contrary to Public Policy (See pages 233–237.)	1. *Contracts in restraint of trade*—Contracts to reduce or restrain free competition are illegal and prohibited by statutes. An exception is a *covenant not to compete*. Such covenants usually are enforced by the courts if the terms are secondary to a contract (such as a contract for the sale of a business or an employment contract) and are reasonable as to time and area of restraint. 2. *Unconscionable contracts and clauses*—When a contract or contract clause is so unfair that it is oppressive to one party, it may be deemed unconscionable. As such, it is illegal and cannot be enforced. 3. *Exculpatory clauses*—An exculpatory clause is a clause that releases a party from liability in the event of monetary or physical injury, no matter who is at fault. In certain situations, exculpatory clauses may be contrary to public policy and thus unenforceable.

Chapter Summary: Capacity, Legality, and Enforceability— Continued

Effect of Illegality (See page 237.)	In general, an illegal contract is void, and the courts will not aid either party when both parties are considered to be equally at fault *(in pari delicto)*. If the contract is executory, neither party can enforce it. If the contract is executed, neither party can recover damages. Exceptions to this general rule are listed on page 237.
VOLUNTARY CONSENT	
Mistakes (See pages 238–239.)	1. *Unilateral*—Generally, the mistaken party is bound by the contract *unless* (a) the other party knows or should have known of the mistake or (b) the mistake is an inadvertent mathematical error committed without gross negligence. 2. *Bilateral (mutual)*—When both parties are mistaken about the same material fact, such as identity, either party can avoid the contract.
Fraudulent Misrepresentation (See pages 239–241.)	When fraud occurs, usually the innocent party can enforce or avoid the contract. The following elements are necessary to establish fraud: 1. A misrepresentation of a material fact must occur. 2. There must be an intent to deceive. 3. The innocent party must justifiably rely on the misrepresentation.
Undue Influence (See pages 242–243.)	Undue influence arises from special relationships, such as fiduciary or confidential relationships, in which one party's free will has been overcome by the undue influence exerted by the other party. Usually, the contract is voidable.
Duress (See page 243.)	Duress is the tactic of forcing a party to enter a contract under the fear of a threat—for example, the threat of violence or serious economic loss. The party forced to enter the contract can rescind the contract.
THE WRITING REQUIREMENT	

The Statute of Frauds
(See pages 243–248.)
	1. *Applicability*—The following types of contracts fall under the Statute of Frauds and must be in writing to be enforceable:
	   a. Contracts involving interests in land, such as sales, leases, or mortgages.
	   b. Contracts that cannot by their terms be fully performed within one year from the day after the contract's formation.
	   c. Collateral promises, such as contracts made between a guarantor and a creditor whose terms make the guarantor secondarily liable. *Exception:* the "main purpose" rule.
	   d. Promises made in consideration of marriage, including promises to make a monetary payment or give property in consideration of a promise to marry and prenuptial agreements made in consideration of marriage.
	   e. Contracts for the sale of goods priced at $500 or more under the Statute of Frauds provision in Section 2–201 of the Uniform Commercial Code.
	2. *Exceptions*—Partial performance, admissions, and promissory estoppel.
	3. *Sufficiency of the Writing*—To constitute an enforceable contract under the Statute of Frauds, a writing must be signed by the party against whom enforcement is sought, name the parties, identify the subject matter, and state with reasonable certainty the essential terms of the contract. Under the UCC, a contract for a sale of goods is not enforceable beyond the quantity of goods shown in the contract.

ExamPrep

ISSUE SPOTTERS

1. Sun Airlines, Inc., prints on its tickets that it is not liable for any injury to a passenger caused by the airline's negligence. If the cause of an accident is found to be the airline's negligence, can it use the clause as a defense to liability? Why or why not? **(See page 237.)**
2. My-T Quality Goods, Inc., and Nu! Sales Corporation orally agree to a deal. My-T's president has the essential terms written up on company letterhead stationery, and the memo is filed in My-T's office. If Nu! Sales later refuses to complete the transaction, is this memo a sufficient writing to enforce the contract against it? Explain your answer. **(See page 248.)**

—Check your answers to the Issue Spotters against the answers provided in Appendix E at the end of this text.

BEFORE THE TEST

Go to www.cengagebrain.com, enter the ISBN 9781133191353 and click on "Find" to locate this textbook's Web site. Then, click on "Access Now" under "Study Tools," and select Chapter 8 at the top. There, you will find a Practice Quiz that you can take to assess your mastery of the concepts in this chapter, as well as Flashcards, a Glossary of important terms, and Video Questions (when assigned).

For Review

Answers to the even-numbered questions in this For Review section can be found in Appendix F at the end of this text.

1. Does a minor have the capacity to enter into an enforceable contract? What does it mean to disaffirm a contract?
2. Under what circumstances will a covenant not to compete be enforced? When will such covenants not be enforced?
3. What is an exculpatory clause? In what circumstances might exculpatory clauses be enforced? When will they not be enforced?
4. What is the difference between a mistake of value or quality and a mistake of fact?
5. What are the elements of fraudulent misrepresentation?

Business Scenarios and Case Problems

8–1   Contracts by Minors. Kalen is a seventeen-year-old minor who has just graduated from high school. He is attending a university two hundred miles from home and has contracted to rent an apartment near the university for one year at $500 per month. He is working at a convenience store to earn enough income to be self-supporting. After living in the apartment and paying monthly rent for four months, he becomes involved in a dispute with his landlord. Kalen, still a minor, moves out and returns the key to the landlord. The landlord wants to hold Kalen liable for the balance of the payments due under the lease. Discuss fully Kalen's liability in this situation. **(See pages 228–229.)**

8–2   ❓ Question with Sample Answer—Statute of Frauds. Gemma promises a local hardware store that she will pay for a lawn mower that her brother is purchasing on credit if the brother fails to pay the debt. Must this promise be in writing to be enforceable? Why or why not? **(See page 245.)**

—For a sample answer to Question 8–2, go to Appendix G at the end of this text.

8–3   Voluntary Consent. Jerome is an elderly man who lives with his nephew, Philip. Jerome is totally dependent on Philip's support. Philip tells Jerome that unless Jerome transfers a tract of land he owns to Philip for a price 30 percent below market value, Philip will no longer support and take care of him. Jerome enters into the contract. Discuss fully whether Jerome can set aside this contract. **(See pages 242–243.)**

8–4   📖 Spotlight on Arbitration Clauses—Unconscionable Contracts or Clauses. Roberto Basulto and Raquel Gonzalez, who did not speak English, responded to an ad on Spanish-language television sponsored by Hialeah Automotive, LLC, which does business as Potamkin Dodge. Potamkin's

staff understood that Basulto and Gonzalez did not speak or read English and conducted the entire transaction in Spanish. They explained the English-language contract, but did not explain an accompanying arbitration agreement. This agreement limited the amount of damages that the buyers could seek in court to less than $5,000, but did not limit Potamkin's right to pursue greater damages. Basulto and Gonzalez bought a Dodge Caravan and signed the contract in blank—that is, leaving some terms to be filled in later. Potamkin later filled in a lower trade-in allowance than agreed and refused to change it. The buyers returned the van—having driven it a total of seven miles—and asked for a return of their trade-in vehicle, but it had been sold. The buyers filed a suit in a Florida state court against Potamkin. The dealer sought arbitration. Was the arbitration agreement unconscionable? Why or why not? [*Hialeah Automotive, LLC v. Basulto*, 22 So.3d 586 (Fla.App. 3 Dist. 2009)] **(See pages 235–236.)**

8–5   ⚖ Case Problem with Sample Answer—Unconscionable Contracts or Clauses. Geographic Expeditions, Inc. (GeoEx), which guided climbs up Mount Kilimanjaro, required climbers to sign a release to participate in an expedition. The form required any disputes to be submitted to arbitration in San Francisco and limited damages to the cost of the trip. GeoEx told climbers that the terms were nonnegotiable and that other travel firms imposed the same terms. Jason Lhotka died on a GeoEx climb. His mother filed a suit against GeoEx. GeoEx sought arbitration. Was the arbitration clause unconscionable? Why or why not? [*Lhotka v. Geographic Expeditions, Inc.*, 181 Cal.App.4th 816, 104 Cal. Rptr.3d 844 (1 Dist. 2010)] **(See page 236.)**

—For a sample answer to Problem 8–5, go to Appendix H at the end of this text.

8–6 **Statute of Frauds.** Newmark & Co. Real Estate, Inc., contacted 2615 East 17 Street Realty, LLC, to lease certain real property on behalf of a client. Newmark e-mailed the landlord a separate agreement for the payment of Newmark's commission. The landlord e-mailed it back with a separate demand to pay the commission in installments. Newmark revised the agreement and e-mailed a final copy to the landlord. Do the parties have an agreement that qualifies as a writing under the Statute of Frauds? Explain. [*Newmark & Co. Real Estate, Inc. v. 2615 East 17 Street Realty, LLC,* 80 A.D.3d 476, 914 N.Y.S.2d 162 (1 Dept. 2011)] **(See page 243.)**

8–7 **Mental Incompetence.** Dorothy Drury suffered from dementia and chronic confusion. When she became unable to manage her own affairs, including decisions about medical and financial matters, her son Eddie arranged for her to move to an assisted living facility. During admission, she signed a residency agreement, which included an arbitration clause. After she sustained injuries in a fall at the facility, a suit was filed to recover damages. The facility asked the court to compel arbitration. Was Dorothy bound to the residency agreement? Discuss. [*Drury v. Assisted Living Concepts, Inc.,* 245 Or.App. 217, 262 P.3d 1162 (2011)] **(See page 230.)**

8–8 **Licensing Statutes.** PEMS Co. International, Inc., agreed to find a buyer for Rupp Industries, Inc., for a commission of 2 percent of the purchase price, which was to be paid by the buyer. Using PEMS's services, an investment group bought Rupp for $20 million and changed its name to Temp-Air, Inc. PEMS asked Temp-Air to pay a commission on the sale. Temp-Air refused, arguing that PEMS had acted as a broker in the deal without a license. The applicable statute defines a broker as any person who deals with the sale of a business. If this statute was intended to protect the public, can PEMS collect its commission? Explain. [*PEMS Co. International,*

Inc. v. Temp-Air, Inc., __ N.W.2d __ (Minn.App. 2011)] **(See page 232.)**

8–9 ↔ **A Question of Ethics—Bilateral Mistake.** On behalf of BRJM, LLC, Nicolas Kepple offered Howard Engelsen $210,000 for a parcel of land known as lot five on the north side of Barnes Road in Stonington, Connecticut. Engelsen's company, Output Systems, Inc., owned the land. Engelsen had the lot surveyed and obtained an appraisal. The appraiser valued the property at $277,000, after determining that it was 3 acres in size and thus could not be subdivided because it did not meet the town's minimum legal requirement of 3.7 acres for subdivision. Engelsen responded to Kepple's offer with a counteroffer of $230,000, which Kepple accepted. The parties signed a contract. When Engelsen refused to go through with the deal, BRJM filed a suit against Output, seeking specific performance and other relief. Output asserted the defense of mutual mistake on at least two grounds. [*BRJM, LLC v. Output Systems, Inc.,* 100 Conn.App. 143, 917 A.2d 605 (2007)] **(See pages 238–239.)**

1. In the counteroffer, Engelsen asked Kepple to remove from their contract a clause requiring written confirmation of the availability of a "free split," which meant that the property could be subdivided without the town's prior approval. Kepple agreed. After signing the contract, Kepple learned that the property was *not* entitled to a free split. Would this circumstance qualify as a mistake on which the *defendant* could avoid the contract? Why or why not?

2. After signing the contract, Engelsen obtained a second appraisal that established the size of lot five as 3.71 acres, which meant that it could be subdivided, and valued the property at $490,000. Can the defendant avoid the contract on the basis of a mistake in the first appraisal? Explain.

Critical Thinking and Writing Assignments

8–10 💡 **Business Law Critical Thinking Group Assignment.** Jason Novell, doing business as Novell Associates, hired Barbara Meade as an independent contractor. The parties orally agreed on the terms of employment, including payment of a share of the company's income to Meade, but they did not put anything in writing. Two years later, Meade quit. Novell then told Meade that she was entitled to $9,602—25 percent of the difference between the accounts receivable and the accounts payable as of Meade's last day of work. Meade disagreed and demanded more than $63,500—25 percent of the revenue from all invoices, less the cost of materials and outside processing, for each of the

years that she had worked for Novell. Meade filed a lawsuit against Novell for breach of contract.

1. The first group should evaluate whether the parties had an enforceable contract.

2. The second group should decide whether the parties' oral agreement falls within any exception to the Statute of Frauds.

3. The third group should discuss how the lawsuit would be affected if Novell admitted that the parties had an oral contract under which Meade was entitled to 25 percent of the difference between accounts receivable and payable as of the day Meade quit.

9 CHAPTER

Contract Performance, Breach, and Remedies

LEARNING OBJECTIVES

The five learning objectives below are designed to help improve your understanding of the chapter. After reading this chapter, you should be able to answer the following questions:

1 What is an assignment? What is the difference between an assignment and a delegation?

2 How are most contracts discharged?

3 What is the standard measure of compensatory damages when a contract is breached? How are damages computed differently in construction contracts?

4 Under what circumstances is the remedy of rescission and restitution available?

5 What is a limitation-of-liability clause, and when will courts enforce it?

(Muellek Josef/Shutterstock.com)

"The laws of a state change with the changing times."
—Aeschylus, 525–456 B.C.E. (Greek dramatist)

Privity of Contract The relationship that exists between the promisor and the promisee of a contract.

Because a contract is a private agreement between the parties who have entered into that contract, it is fitting that these parties alone should have rights and liabilities under the contract. This concept is referred to as **privity of contract,** and it establishes the basic principle that third parties have no rights in contracts to which they are not parties.

You may be convinced by now that for every rule of contract law, there is an exception. As times change, so must the laws, as indicated in the chapter-opening quotation. When justice cannot be served by adherence to a rule of law, exceptions to the rule must be made.

In this chapter, we first look at some exceptions to the rule of privity of contract. These exceptions include *assignments, delegations,* and *third party beneficiary contracts.* We then examine how contractual obligations can be *discharged.* Normally, contract discharge is accomplished by both parties performing the acts promised in the contract. We also consider the degree of *performance* required and some other ways in which discharge can occur.

Breach of Contract Failure, without legal excuse, of a promisor to perform the obligations of a contract.

When it is no longer advantageous for a party to fulfill his or her contractual obligations, breach of contract may result. A **breach of contract** occurs when a party fails to perform part or all of the required duties under a contract. Once this occurs, the other party—the nonbreaching party—can choose one or more of several remedies. These remedies are discussed in the last part of this chapter.

Assignment and Delegation

When third parties acquire rights or assume duties arising from contracts, the rights are transferred to them by *assignment,* and the duties are transferred by *delegation.*

Assignment

LEARNING OBJECTIVE 1
What is an assignment? What is the difference between an assignment and a delegation?

Assignment The transfer to another of all or part of one's rights under a contract.

In a bilateral contract, the two parties have corresponding rights and duties. One party has a *right* to require the other to perform some task, and the other has a *duty* to perform it. Sometimes, though, a party will transfer her or his rights under the contract to someone else. The transfer of contract *rights* to a third person is known as an **assignment.**

Assignments are important because they are often used in business financing. Lending institutions, such as banks, frequently assign the rights to receive payments under their loan contracts to other firms, which pay for those rights. If you obtain a loan from your local bank to purchase a car, you may later receive a notice stating that your bank has transferred (assigned) its rights to receive payments on the loan to another firm and that you should make your payments to that other firm. Billions of dollars change hands daily in the business world in the form of assignments of rights in contracts.

Assignor A party who transfers (assigns) his or her rights under a contract to another party.

Assignee A party to whom the rights under a contract are transferred, or assigned.

Obligee One to whom an obligation is owed.

Obligor One who owes an obligation to another.

Effect of an Assignment   In an assignment, the party assigning the rights to a third party is known as the **assignor,** and the party receiving the rights is the **assignee.** Other terms traditionally used to describe the parties in assignment relationships are the **obligee** (the person to whom a duty, or obligation, is owed) and the **obligor** (the person who is obligated to perform the duty).

When rights under a contract are assigned unconditionally, the rights of the *assignor* are extinguished.[1] The third party (the *assignee*) has a right to demand performance from the other original party to the contract (the *obligor*). **EXAMPLE 9.1**   Brent (the obligor) owes Alex $1,000, and Alex (the obligee) assigns to Carmen the right to receive the $1,000. Thus, Alex is now the assignor. Here, a valid assignment exists. Carmen, the assignee, can enforce the contract against Brent if Brent fails to perform (pay the $1,000). • Exhibit 9.1 on the following page illustrates assignment relationships.

Note that the assignee obtains only those rights that the assignor originally had. Also, the assignee's rights are subject to the defenses that the obligor has against the assignor. **EXAMPLE 9.2**   Brent agrees to buy Alex's MacBook Pro for $1,000, relying on Alex's fraudulent misrepresentation that the device has 8 gigabytes of memory. When Brent learns that the device has only 4 gigabytes of memory, he tells Alex he is going to cancel their contract. Meanwhile, Alex has assigned his right to the $1,000 payment to Carmen. Brent need not pay Carmen, however. He can raise the defense of Alex's fraudulent misrepresentation to avoid payment. •

In the following case, a lender assigned its rights to loan payments from a borrower. The court had to decide whether the borrower owed the payments to the assignee.

---

1. *Restatement (Second) of Contracts,* Section 317.

Case 9.1

Hosch v. Colonial Pacific Leasing Corp.

Court of Appeals of Georgia,
313 Ga.App. 873, 722 S.E.2d 778, (2012).
www.findlaw.com/casecode/index.html[a]

Can a loan for equipment be assigned without notice?

FACTS Edward Hosch entered into four loan agreements with Citicapital Commercial Corporation to finance the purchase of heavy construction equipment. A few months later, Citicapital merged into Citicorp Leasing, Inc., which was then renamed GE Capital Commercial, Inc. One year later, GE Capital assigned the loans to Colonial Pacific Leasing Corporation. When Hosch defaulted on the loans, Colonial Pacific served him with a notice of default and demanded payment. Hosch failed to repay the loans, so Colonial Pacific sued to collect. The trial court granted summary judgment to Colonial Pacific and entered final judgment against Hosch. On appeal, Hosch argued that there was insufficient evidence that the loans had been assigned to Colonial Pacific.

ISSUE Is Hosch liable to Colonial Pacific?

DECISION Yes. The Georgia appellate court affirmed the trial court's judgment in favor of the assignee, Colonial Pacific.

REASON The court stated that "a party may assign a contractual right to collect payment, including the right to sue to enforce the right." To be enforceable, the assignment must be in writing. In this case, there was sufficient evidence that GE Capital had assigned Hosch's loans to Colonial Pacific. Significantly, the record included a written assignment, other documents showing that the loans had been assigned, and affidavits of a GE litigation specialist. Against that evidence, Hosch merely asserted that he had not been notified of the assignment. Under the loan agreements, however, GE Capital could assign its rights without Hosch's knowledge or consent.

CRITICAL THINKING—Legal Consideration *Do borrowers benefit when lenders may freely assign their rights under loan agreements? If so, how?*

---

a. Under "State Resources," click on "Georgia." On the next page, under "State Court Opinions," click on "Georgia Court of Appeals Opinions." In the "Party name:" box, enter "Hosch," and click on "Search." In the result, click on the case name to access the opinion.

Exhibit 9.1 Assignment Relationships

In the assignment relationship illustrated here, Alex assigns his *rights* under a contract with Brent to a third party, Carmen. Alex thus becomes the *assignor* and Carmen the *assignee* of the contractual rights. Brent, the *obligor*, now owes performance to Carmen instead of to Alex. Alex's original contract rights are extinguished after the assignment.

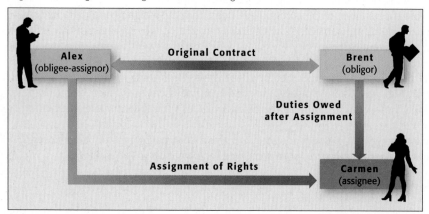

Rights That Cannot Be Assigned

As a general rule, all rights can be assigned. Exceptions are made, however, in the following special circumstances.

When a Statute Expressly Prohibits Assignment If a statute expressly prohibits assignment, the particular right in question cannot be assigned. **EXAMPLE 9.3** Marn is an employee of CompuFuture, Inc. CompuFuture is governed by workers' compensation statutes (see Chapter 18) in this state, so Marn is a covered employee. In need of a loan, Marn borrows from Stark, assigning to Stark all workers' compensation benefits due her should she be injured on the job. A state statute prohibits the assignment of *future* workers' compensation benefits, and thus such rights cannot be assigned. ●

When a Contract Is Personal in Nature   When a contract is for personal services, the rights under the contract normally cannot be assigned unless all that remains is a monetary payment.[2] **EXAMPLE 9.4**   Brent signs a contract to be a tutor for Alex's children. Alex then attempts to assign to Carmen his right to Brent's services. Carmen cannot enforce the contract against Brent. Brent may not like Carmen's children or for some other reason may not want to tutor them. Because personal services are unique to the person rendering them, rights to receive personal services cannot be assigned. ●

When an Assignment Will Significantly Change the Risk or Duties of the Obligor   A right cannot be assigned if assignment will significantly increase or alter the risks or the duties of the obligor.[3] **EXAMPLE 9.5**   Alex has a hotel, and to insure it, he takes out a policy with Northwest Insurance Company. The policy insures against fire, theft, floods, and vandalism. Alex attempts to assign the insurance policy to Carmen, who also owns a hotel. The assignment is ineffective. An insurance company evaluates the particular risk of insuring a certain party and tailors its policy to fit that risk. If the policy is assigned to a third party, the insurance risk is materially altered. ●

When the Contract Prohibits Assignment   If a contract stipulates that the right cannot be assigned, then *ordinarily* it cannot be assigned. (For an example of a contract that prohibits assignment by one party, see page 289, Paragraph 12, of *An Annotated Employment Contract,* which follows this chapter.) **EXAMPLE 9.6**   Brent agrees to build a house for Alex. The contract between Brent and Alex states, "This contract cannot be assigned by Alex without Brent's consent. Any assignment without such consent renders this contract void, and all rights hereunder will thereupon terminate." Alex then assigns his rights to Carmen without first obtaining Brent's consent. Carmen cannot enforce the contract against Brent. ●   This rule has several exceptions:

1. A contract cannot prevent an assignment of the right to receive funds. This exception exists to encourage the free flow of funds and credit in modern business settings.
2. The assignment of ownership rights in real estate often cannot be prohibited because such a prohibition is contrary to public policy in most states. Prohibitions of this kind are called restraints against **alienation** (the voluntary transfer of land ownership).
3. The assignment of negotiable instruments (see Chapter 13) cannot be prohibited.
4. In a contract for the sale of goods, the right to receive damages for breach of contract or for payment of an account owed may be assigned even though the sales contract prohibits such an assignment.[4]

Notice of Assignment
Once a valid assignment of rights has been made to a third party, that party should notify the obligor of the assignment. Giving notice is not legally necessary, because an assignment is effective immediately, whether or not notice is given. Two major problems arise, however, when notice is not given:

1. If the assignor assigns the same right to two different persons, a question arises as to which party has the right to receive performance from the obligor.
2. Until the obligor has notice of the assignment, the obligor can discharge his or her obligation by rendering performance to the assignor. Once the obligor receives proper notice, only performance rendered to the assignee can discharge the obligation.

This piano teacher has signed a contract to give weekly piano lessons. Can the teacher then assign this contract to another piano teacher?

"Man, an animal that makes bargains."

Adam Smith, 1723–1790
(Scottish economist and author)

Alienation   The voluntary transfer of land out of one's possession (thus "alienating" the land from oneself).

---

2. *Restatement (Second) of Contracts,* Sections 317 and 318.
3. See Section 2–210(2) of the Uniform Commercial Code (UCC).
4. UCC 2–210(2).

Delegation

Just as a party can transfer rights to a third party through an assignment, a party can also transfer duties. Duties are not assigned, however. They are *delegated*. Normally, a **delegation of duties** does not relieve the party making the delegation (the **delegator**) of the obligation to perform in the event that the party to whom the duty has been delegated (the **delegatee**) fails to perform. No special form is required to create a valid delegation of duties. As long as the delegator expresses an intention to make the delegation, it is effective. The delegator need not even use the word *delegate*. Exhibit 9.2 below graphically illustrates delegation relationships.

Duties That Cannot Be Delegated

As a general rule, any duty can be delegated. This rule has some exceptions, however. Delegation is prohibited in the following circumstances.

When the Duties Are Personal in Nature When special trust has been placed in the obligor or when performance depends on the obligor's personal skill or talents, contractual duties cannot be delegated. **EXAMPLE 9.7** Horton, who is impressed with Brower's ability to perform veterinary surgery, contracts with Brower to have her perform surgery on Horton's prize-winning stallion in July. Brower later decides that she would rather spend the summer at the beach, so she delegates her duties under the contract to Kuhn, who is also a competent veterinary surgeon. The delegation is not effective without Horton's consent, no matter how competent Kuhn is, because the contract is for *personal* performance. ●

In contrast, nonpersonal duties may be delegated. Assume that Brower contracts with Horton to pick up and deliver heavy construction machinery to Horton's property. Brower delegates this duty to Kuhn, who is in the

Delegation of Duties The transfer to another of all or part of one's duties under a contract.

Delegator A party who transfers (delegates) her or his obligations under a contract to another party.

Delegatee A party to whom contractual obligations are transferred, or delegated.

Exhibit 9.2 Delegation Relationships

In the delegation relationship illustrated here, Brent delegates his *duties* under a contract with Alex to a third party, Carmen. Brent thus becomes the *delegator* and Carmen the *delegatee* of the contractual duties. Carmen now owes performance of the contractual duties to Alex. Note that a delegation of duties normally does not relieve the delegator (Brent) of liability if the delegatee (Carmen) fails to perform the contractual duties.

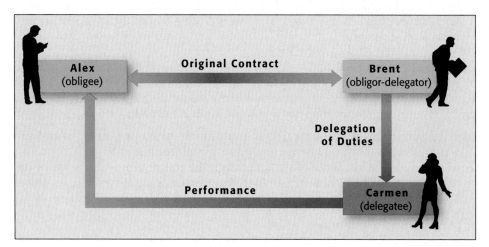

business of delivering heavy machinery. This delegation is effective because the performance required is of a *routine* and *nonpersonal* nature.

When Performance by a Third Party Will Vary Materially from That Expected by the Obligee When performance by a third party will vary materially from that expected by the obligee under the contract, contractual duties cannot be delegated. **EXAMPLE 9.8** Jared, a wealthy investor, established the company Heaven Sent to provide grants of capital to struggling but potentially successful businesses. Jared contracted with Merilyn, whose judgment Jared trusted, to select the recipients of the grants. Later, Merilyn delegated this duty to Donald. Jared did not trust Donald's ability to select worthy recipients. This delegation is not effective because it materially alters Jared's expectations under the contract with Merilyn. •

When the Contract Prohibits Delegation When the contract expressly prohibits delegation by including an *antidelegation clause,* the duties cannot be delegated. **EXAMPLE 9.9** Dakota Company contracted with Belisario, a certified public accountant, to perform its audits. Because the contract prohibited delegation, Belisario could not delegate the duty to perform the audits to another accountant—not even an accountant at the same firm. •

Effect of a Delegation
If a delegation of duties is enforceable, the obligee must accept performance from the delegatee. **EXAMPLE 9.10** Brent has a duty to pick up and deliver heavy construction machinery to Alex's property. Brent delegates his duty to Carmen. In this situation, Alex (the obligee) must accept performance from Carmen (the delegatee) because the delegation is effective. The obligee can legally refuse performance from the delegatee only if the duty is one that cannot be delegated. •

A valid delegation of duties does not relieve the delegator of obligations under the contract.[5] Although there are many exceptions, the general rule today is that the obligee can sue both the delegatee and the delegator if the delegatee fails to perform. Thus, in the situation in *Example 9.10*, if Carmen (the delegatee) fails to perform, Brent (the delegator) is still liable to Alex (the obligee).

The obligee can also hold the delegatee liable if the delegatee made a promise of performance that will directly benefit the obligee. In this situation, there is an "assumption of duty" on the part of the delegatee, and breach of this duty makes the delegatee liable to the obligee. For instance, if Carmen (the delegatee) promised Brent (the delegator), in a contract, to pick up and deliver the construction equipment to Alex's property but fails to do so, Alex (the obligee) can sue Brent, Carmen, or both.

"Assignment of All Rights"
Sometimes, a contract provides for an "assignment of all rights." The traditional view was that under this type of assignment, the assignee did not assume any duties. This view was based on the theory that the assignee's agreement to accept the benefits of the contract was not sufficient to imply a promise to assume the duties of the contract.

Modern courts, however, take the view that the probable intent in using such general words is to create both an assignment of rights and an assumption of duties.[6] Therefore, when general words are used (for example, "I assign the contract" or "I assign all my rights under the contract"), the contract is construed as implying both an assignment of rights and an assumption of duties.

> **➤ KNOW THIS ◄**
>
> In an assignment, the assignor's original contract rights are extinguished after the assignment. In a delegation, the delegator remains liable for performance under the contract if the delegatee fails to perform.

---

5. For a classic case on this issue, see *Crane Ice Cream Co. v. Terminal Freezing & Heating Co.,* 147 Md. 588, 128 A. 280 (1925).

6. See UCC 2–210(1), (4); and *Restatement (Second) of Contracts,* Section 328.

Third Party Beneficiaries

As mentioned earlier in this chapter, to have contractual rights, a person normally must be a party to the contract. In other words, privity of contract must exist. An exception to the doctrine of privity exists when the original parties to the contract intend, *at the time of contracting,* that the contract performance directly benefit a third person. In this situation, the third person becomes a **third party beneficiary** of the contract. As an **intended beneficiary** of the contract, the third party has legal rights and can sue the promisor directly for breach of the contract.

Who, though, is the promisor? In bilateral contracts, both parties to the contract are promisors because both make promises that can be enforced. In third party beneficiary contracts, courts determine the identity of the promisor by asking which party made the promise that benefits the third party—that person is the promisor. In effect, allowing the third party to sue the promisor directly circumvents the "middle person" (the promisee) and thus reduces the burden on the courts. Otherwise, the third party would sue the promisee, who would then sue the promisor.

Intended Beneficiaries

Two of the most common types of intended beneficiaries are creditor beneficiaries and donee beneficiaries. A *creditor beneficiary* benefits from a contract in which one party (the promisor) promises another party (the promisee) to pay a debt that the promisee owes to a third party (the creditor beneficiary). As an intended beneficiary, the creditor beneficiary can sue the promisor directly to enforce the contract.

CASE EXAMPLE 9.11   Autumn Allan owned a condominium unit in a Texas complex located directly beneath a condo unit owned by Aslan Koraev. Over the course of two years, Allan's unit suffered eight incidents of water and sewage incursion as a result of plumbing problems and misuse of appliances in Koraev's unit. Allan sued Koraev for breach of contract and won. Koraev appealed, arguing that he had no contractual duty to Allan. The court found that Allan was an intended third party beneficiary of the contract between Koraev and the condominium owners' association. Because the governing documents stated that each owner had to comply strictly with their provisions, failure to comply created grounds for an action by the condominium association or an aggrieved (wronged) owner. Here, Allan was clearly an aggrieved owner and could sue Koraev directly for his failure to perform his contract duties to the condominium association.[7] ●

Another type of intended beneficiary is a *donee beneficiary.* When a contract is made for the express purpose of giving a *gift* to a third party, the third party (the donee beneficiary) can sue the promisor directly to enforce the promise. The most common donee beneficiary contract is a life insurance contract. A life insurance company (the promisor) promises to pay a certain amount on the policyholder's death to anyone that person designates as a beneficiary. The designated beneficiary is a donee beneficiary under the life insurance policy and can enforce the promise.

Vesting

An intended third party beneficiary cannot enforce a contract against the original parties until the third party's rights have *vested*, meaning that the rights have taken effect and cannot be taken away. Until that time, the original parties to the contract can modify or rescind the contract without the consent of the third party.

When do the rights of third parties vest? Generally, the rights vest when one of the following occurs:

---

7. *Allan v. Nersesova*, 307 S.W.3d 564 (Tx.App—Dallas 2010).

Third Party Beneficiary One for whose benefit a promise is made in a contract but who is not a party to the contract.

Intended Beneficiary A third party for whose benefit a contract is formed. An intended beneficiary can sue the promisor if the contract is breached.

1. When the third party demonstrates express consent to the agreement, such as by sending a letter or note acknowledging awareness of, and consent to, a contract formed for her or his benefit.
2. When the third party materially alters his or her position in detrimental reliance on the contract, such as when a donee beneficiary contracts to have a home built in reliance on the receipt of funds promised to him or her in a donee beneficiary contract.
3. When the conditions for vesting are satisfied. For instance, the rights of a beneficiary under a life insurance policy vest when the insured person dies.

Incidental Beneficiaries

Incidental Beneficiary A third party who benefits from a contract even though the contract was not formed for that purpose. An incidental beneficiary has no rights in the contract and cannot sue to have it enforced.

Sometimes, a third person receives a benefit from a contract even though that person's benefit is not the reason the contract was made. Such a person is known as an **incidental beneficiary.** Because the benefit is unintentional, an incidental beneficiary cannot sue to enforce the contract.

    CASE EXAMPLE 9.12 Spectators at the infamous boxing match in which Mike Tyson was disqualified for biting his opponent's ear sued Tyson and the fight's promoters for a refund on the basis of breach of contract. The spectators claimed that they were third party beneficiaries of the contract between Tyson and the fight's promoters. The court, however, held that the spectators could not sue because they were not in contractual privity with the defendants. Any benefits they received from the contract were incidental to the contract. According to the court, the spectators got what they paid for: "the right to view whatever event transpired."[8] ●

    In determining whether a party is an incidental or an intended beneficiary, the courts focus on the parties' intent, as expressed in the contract language and implied by the surrounding circumstances. Any beneficiary who is not deemed an intended beneficiary is considered incidental. Exhibit 9.3 below graphically illustrates the distinction between intended and incidental beneficiaries.

---

8. *Castillo v. Tyson,* 268 A.D.2d 336, 701 N.Y.S.2d 423 (Sup.Ct.App.Div. 2000).

Exhibit 9.3 Third Party Beneficiaries

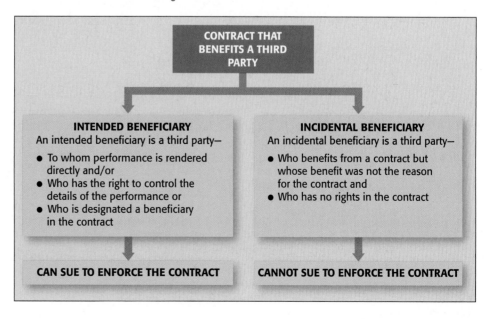

CONTRACT THAT BENEFITS A THIRD PARTY

INTENDED BENEFICIARY
An intended beneficiary is a third party—
● To whom performance is rendered directly and/or
● Who has the right to control the details of the performance or
● Who is designated a beneficiary in the contract

INCIDENTAL BENEFICIARY
An incidental beneficiary is a third party—
● Who benefits from a contract but whose benefit was not the reason for the contract and
● Who has no rights in the contract

CAN SUE TO ENFORCE THE CONTRACT

CANNOT SUE TO ENFORCE THE CONTRACT

Contract Discharge

The most common way to **discharge**, or terminate, contractual duties is by the **performance** of those duties. The duty to perform under a contract may be *conditioned* on the occurrence or nonoccurrence of a certain event, or the duty may be *absolute*. As shown in Exhibit 9.4 below, in addition to performance, a contract can be discharged in numerous other ways, including discharge by agreement of the parties and discharge by operation of law.

Conditions of Performance

In most contracts, promises of performance are not expressly conditioned or qualified. Instead, they are *absolute promises*. They must be performed, or the party promising the act will be in breach of contract. **EXAMPLE 9.13** JoAnne contracts to sell Alfonso a painting for $10,000. The parties' promises are unconditional: JoAnne will transfer the painting to Alfonso, and Alfonso will pay $10,000 to JoAnne. The payment does not have to be made if the painting is not transferred. ●

In some situations, however, contractual promises are conditioned. A **condition** is a qualification in a contract based on a possible future event, the occurrence or nonoccurrence of which will trigger the performance of a legal obligation or terminate an existing obligation under a contract. If the condition is not satisfied, the obligations of the parties are discharged.

EXAMPLE 9.14 Alfonso, in *Example 9.13*, offers to purchase JoAnne's painting only if an independent appraisal indicates that it is worth at least $10,000. JoAnne accepts Alfonso's offer. Their obligations (promises) are conditioned on the outcome of the appraisal. Should this condition not be satisfied (for example, if the appraiser deems the value of the painting to be only $5,000), their obligations to each other are discharged and cannot be enforced. ●

Discharge The termination of an obligation, such as occurs when the parties to a contract have fully performed their contractual obligations.

Performance The fulfillment of one's duties under a contract—the normal way of discharging one's contractual obligations.

LEARNING OBJECTIVE 2
How are most contracts discharged?

Condition A qualification, provision, or clause in a contractual agreement, the occurrence or nonoccurrence of which creates, suspends, or terminates the obligations of the contracting parties.

Exhibit 9.4 Contract Discharge

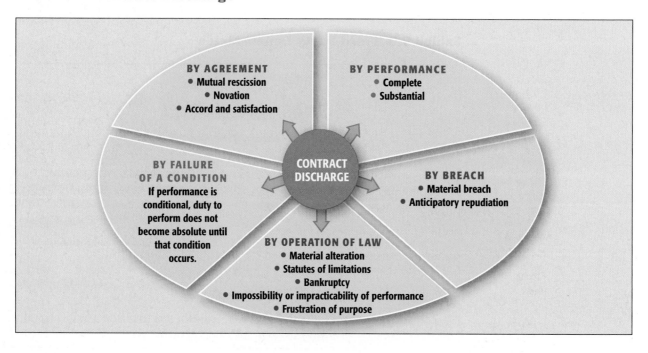

Condition Precedent A condition in a contract that must be met before a party's promise becomes absolute.

Conditions Precedent

A condition that must be fulfilled before a party's promise becomes absolute is called a **condition precedent.** The condition precedes the absolute duty to perform, as in the JoAnne-Alfonso example just given. For instance, insurance contracts frequently specify that certain conditions, such as passing a physical examination, must be met before the insurance company will be obligated to perform under the contract.

Condition Subsequent A condition in a contract that, if it occurs, operates to terminate a party's absolute promise to perform.

Conditions Subsequent

When a condition operates to terminate a party's absolute promise to perform, it is called a **condition subsequent.** The condition follows, or is subsequent to, the absolute duty to perform. If the condition occurs, the party need not perform any further. **EXAMPLE 9.15** A law firm hires Julia Darby, a recent law school graduate and a newly licensed attorney. Their contract provides that the firm's obligation to continue employing Darby is discharged if she fails to maintain her license to practice law. This is a condition subsequent because a failure to maintain the license will discharge a duty that has already arisen. •

Generally, conditions precedent are common, and conditions subsequent are rare. The *Restatement (Second) of Contracts* omits the terms *condition subsequent* and *condition precedent* and refers to both simply as "conditions."[9]

Concurrent Conditions Conditions that must occur or be performed at the same time—they are mutually dependent. No obligations arise until these conditions are simultaneously performed.

Concurrent Conditions

When each party's absolute duty to perform is conditioned on the other party's absolute duty to perform, **concurrent conditions** are present. These conditions exist only when the parties expressly or impliedly are to perform their respective duties *simultaneously.*

EXAMPLE 9.16 If a buyer promises to pay for goods when they are delivered by the seller, each party's absolute duty to perform is conditioned on the other party's absolute duty to perform. The buyer's duty to pay for the goods does not become absolute until the seller either delivers or attempts to deliver the goods. Likewise, the seller's duty to deliver the goods does not become absolute until the buyer pays or attempts to pay for the goods. Therefore, neither can recover from the other for breach without first tendering performance. •

Discharge by Performance

The contract comes to an end when both parties fulfill their respective duties by performing the acts they have promised. Performance can also be accomplished by tender. **Tender** is an unconditional offer to perform by a person who is ready, willing, and able to do so. Therefore, a seller who places goods at the disposal of a buyer has tendered delivery and can demand payment according to the terms of the agreement. A buyer who offers to pay for goods has tendered payment and can demand delivery of the goods.

Tender An unconditional offer to perform an obligation by a person who is ready, willing, and able to do so.

Once performance has been tendered, the party making the tender has done everything possible to carry out the terms of the contract. If the other party then refuses to perform, the party making the tender can consider the duty discharged and sue for breach of contract.

Complete Performance

When a party performs exactly as agreed, there is no question as to whether the contract has been performed. When a party's performance is perfect, it is said to be complete.

---

9. *Restatement (Second) of Contracts,* Section 224. Note that the difference between conditions precedent and conditions subsequent can be important procedurally, because a plaintiff must prove a condition precedent whereas the defendant normally proves a condition subsequent.

When is a deal to sell a new car completed?

Normally, conditions expressly stated in the contract must fully occur in all aspects for complete performance (strict performance) of the contract to take place. Any deviation breaches the contract and discharges the other party's obligations to perform.

For instance, most construction contracts require the builder to meet certain specifications. If the specifications are conditions, complete performance is required to avoid material breach. (*Material breach* will be discussed shortly.) If the conditions are met, the other party to the contract must then fulfill her or his obligation to pay the builder.

For some construction contracts, specifications are not explicitly stated as conditions. In such situations, sometimes the builder fails to meet the specifications, and that means the performance is not complete. What effect does that failure have on the other party's obligation to pay? The answer is part of the doctrine of *substantial performance.*

Substantial Performance   A party who in good faith performs substantially all of the terms of a contract can enforce the contract against the other party under the doctrine of substantial performance. Note that good faith is required. Intentionally failing to comply with the terms is a breach of the contract.

To qualify as *substantial performance,* the performance must not vary greatly from the performance promised in the contract, and it must create substantially the same benefits as those promised in the contract. If the omission, variance, or defect in performance is unimportant and can easily be compensated by awarding damages, a court is likely to hold that the contract has been substantially performed. Courts decide whether the performance was substantial on a case-by-case basis, examining all of the facts of the particular situation. If performance is substantial, the other party's duty to perform remains absolute. (The party can sue for damages due to the minor deviations, however.)

CASE EXAMPLE 9.17   Wisconsin Electric Power Company (WEPCO) contracted with Union Pacific Railroad to transport coal to WEPCO from mines in Colorado. The contract required WEPCO to notify Union Pacific monthly of how many tons of coal it wanted to have shipped the next month. Union Pacific was to make "good faith reasonable efforts" to meet the schedule. The contract also required WEPCO to supply the railcars. When WEPCO did not supply the railcars, Union Pacific used its own railcars and delivered 84 percent of the requested coal. In this situation, a federal court held that the delivery of 84 percent of the contracted amount constituted substantial performance.[10] ●

Performance to the Satisfaction of Another   Contracts often state that completed work must personally satisfy one of the parties or a third person. The question is whether this satisfaction becomes a condition precedent, requiring actual personal satisfaction or approval for discharge, or whether the test of satisfaction is performance that would satisfy a *reasonable person* (substantial performance).

When the subject matter of the contract is *personal,* a contract to be performed to the satisfaction of one of the parties is conditioned, and performance must actually satisfy that party. For instance, contracts for portraits and works of art are considered personal. Therefore, only the personal satisfaction of the party fulfills the condition—unless a court finds that the party is expressing dissatisfaction to avoid payment or otherwise is not acting in good faith.

Most other contracts need to be performed only to the satisfaction of a reasonable person unless they *expressly state otherwise.* When such contracts require performance to the

---

10. *Wisconsin Electric Power Co. v. Union Pacific Railroad Co.,* 557 F.3d 504 (7th Cir. 2009).

satisfaction of a third party (such as, "to the satisfaction of Robert Ames, the supervising engineer"), the courts are divided. A majority of courts require the work to be satisfactory to a reasonable person, but some courts hold that the personal satisfaction of the third party designated in the contract (here, Robert Ames) must be met. Again, the personal judgment must be made honestly, or the condition will be excused.

Material Breach of Contract

A breach of contract is the nonperformance of a contractual duty. A breach is *material* when performance is not at least substantial.[11] If there is a material breach, the nonbreaching party is excused from the performance of contractual duties and can sue for damages caused by the breach. If the breach is *minor* (not material), the nonbreaching party's duty to perform may sometimes be suspended until the breach is remedied, but the duty is not entirely excused. Once the minor breach is cured (corrected), the nonbreaching party must resume performance of the contractual obligations.

Any breach entitles the nonbreaching party to sue for damages, but only a material breach discharges the nonbreaching party from the contract. The policy underlying these rules is that contracts should go forward when only minor problems occur, but that contracts should be terminated if major problems arise.[12]

CASE EXAMPLE 9.18 Su Yong Kim sold an apartment building in Portland, Oregon. At the time of the sale, the building's plumbing violated the city's housing code. The contract therefore provided that Kim would correct the violations within eight months after signing the contract. A year later, Kim still had not made the necessary repairs, and the buyers were being fined by the city for the code violations. The buyers stopped making payments under the contract, and the dispute ended up in court. The court found that Kim's failure to make the repairs was a material breach of the contract because it defeated the purpose of the contract. The buyers had purchased the building to lease it out to tenants, but instead they were losing tenants and paying fines to the city. Because Kim's breach was material, the buyers were not obligated to continue to perform their obligation to make payments under the contract.[13] •

Anticipatory Repudiation of a Contract

Before either party to a contract has a duty to perform, one of the parties may refuse to perform her or his contractual obligations. This is called **anticipatory repudiation.** Quite often, an anticipatory repudiation occurs when a sharp fluctuation in market prices creates a situation in which performance of the contract would be extremely unfavorable to one of the parties.

When anticipatory repudiation occurs, it is treated as a material breach of the contract, and the nonbreaching party is permitted to bring an action for damages immediately, even though the scheduled time for performance under the contract may still be in the future. Until the nonbreaching party treats this early repudiation as a breach, however, the breaching party can retract the anticipatory repudiation by proper notice and restore the parties to their original obligations.

An anticipatory repudiation is treated as a present, material breach for two reasons. First, the nonbreaching party should not be required to remain ready and willing to perform when the other party has already repudiated the contract. Second, the nonbreaching party should have the opportunity to seek a similar contract elsewhere and may have the duty to do so to minimize his or her loss.

(AP Photo/Chris Pizzello)

If Paris Hilton agrees to attend a large party in exchange for $3,000, is she in breach of contract if she leaves after ten minutes?

Anticipatory Repudiation An assertion or action by a party indicating that he or she will not perform a contractual obligation.

➤ KNOW THIS ◄

The risks that prices will fluctuate and values will change are ordinary business risks for which the law does not provide relief.

---

11. *Restatement (Second) of Contracts,* Section 241.

12. See UCC 2–612, which deals with installment contracts for the sale of goods.

13. *Kim v. Park,* 192 Or.App. 365, 86 P.3d 63 (2004).

Discharge by Agreement

Any contract can be discharged by agreement of the parties. The agreement can be contained in the original contract, or the parties can form a new contract for the express purpose of discharging the original contract.

Discharge by Mutual Rescission
As mentioned in Chapter 7 on page 218, rescission occurs when the parties cancel their contract and are returned to the positions they occupied prior to the contract's formation. For *mutual rescission* to take place, the parties must make another agreement that also satisfies the legal requirements for a contract—there must be an *offer*, an *acceptance*, and *consideration*. Ordinarily, if the parties agree to rescind the original contract, their promises not to perform those acts promised in the original contract will be legal consideration for the second contract.

Oral agreements to rescind executory contracts that neither party has performed are enforceable even if the original agreement was in writing. Under the Uniform Commercial Code, however, an agreement rescinding a contract for the sale of goods, regardless of price, must be in writing when the contract requires a written rescission. Also, agreements to rescind contracts involving transfers of realty must be evidenced by a writing.

When one party has fully performed, an agreement to rescind the original contract usually is not enforceable unless additional consideration or restitution is made. Because the performing party has received no consideration for the promise to call off the original bargain, additional consideration is necessary.

Novation The substitution, by agreement, of a new contract for an old one, with the rights under the old one being terminated.

Discharge by Novation
The process of **novation** substitutes a third party for one of the original parties. Essentially, the parties to the original contract and one or more new parties get together and agree to the substitution. The requirements of a novation are as follows:

1. The existence of a previous, valid obligation.
2. Agreement by all of the parties to a new contract.
3. The extinguishing of the old obligation (discharge of the prior party).
4. A new, valid contract.

EXAMPLE 9.19 Union Corporation contracts to sell its pharmaceutical division to British Pharmaceuticals, Ltd. Before the transfer is completed, Union, British Pharmaceuticals, and a third company, Otis Chemicals, execute a new agreement to transfer all of British Pharmaceuticals' rights and duties in the transaction to Otis Chemicals. As long as the new contract is supported by consideration, the novation will discharge the original contract (between Union and British Pharmaceuticals) and replace it with the new contract (between Union and Otis Chemicals). •

A novation expressly or impliedly revokes and discharges a prior contract. The parties involved may expressly state in the new contract that the old contract is now discharged. If the parties do not expressly discharge the old contract, it will be impliedly discharged if the new contract's terms are inconsistent with the old contract's terms.

Discharge by Accord and Satisfaction
As Chapter 7 explained, in an *accord and satisfaction,* the parties agree to accept performance different from the performance originally promised. An *accord* is an executory contract to perform some act to satisfy an existing contractual duty that is not yet discharged.[14] A *satisfaction* is the performance of the accord agreement. An *accord* and its *satisfaction* discharge the original contractual obligation.

---

14. *Restatement (Second) of Contracts,* Section 281.

Once the accord has been made, the original obligation is merely suspended until the accord agreement is fully performed. If it is not performed, the party to whom performance is owed can bring an action on the original obligation or for breach of the accord.

EXAMPLE 9.20 Shea obtains a judgment of $8,000 against Marla. Later, both parties agree that the judgment can be satisfied by Marla's transfer of her automobile to Shea. This agreement to accept the auto in lieu of $8,000 in cash is the accord. If Marla transfers her automobile to Shea, the accord agreement is fully performed, and the $8,000 debt is discharged. If Marla refuses to transfer her car, the accord is breached. Because the original obligation is merely suspended, Shea can sue to enforce the judgment for $8,000 in cash or bring an action for breach of the accord. •

Discharge by Operation of Law

Under some circumstances, contractual duties may be discharged by operation of law. These circumstances include material alteration of the contract, the running of the relevant statute of limitations, bankruptcy, and impossibility of performance.

Material Alteration   To discourage parties from altering written contracts, the law allows an innocent party to be discharged when one party has materially altered a written contract without the knowledge or consent of the other party. If a party alters a material term of the contract—such as the quantity term or the price term—without the knowledge or consent of the other party, the party who was unaware of the alteration can treat the contract as discharged or terminated.

Statutes of Limitations   Statutes of limitations limit the period during which a party can sue on a particular cause of action. After the applicable limitations period has passed, a suit can no longer be brought. The period for bringing lawsuits for breach of oral contracts is usually two to three years, and for written contracts, four to five years. Lawsuits for breach of a contract for the sale of goods must be brought within four years after the cause of action has accrued. In their original contract, the parties can agree to reduce this four-year period to not less than one year. They cannot, however, agree to extend it beyond four years.

Bankruptcy   A proceeding in bankruptcy attempts to allocate a debtor's assets to creditors in a fair and equitable fashion. Once the assets have been allocated, the debtor receives a *discharge in bankruptcy* (see Chapter 15). A discharge in bankruptcy ordinarily bars creditors from enforcing most of the debtor's contracts.

Impossibility of Performance A doctrine under which a party to a contract is relieved of his or her duty to perform when performance becomes objectively impossible.

Impossibility of Performance   After a contract has been made, performance may become impossible in an objective sense. This is known as **impossibility of performance** and may discharge the contract.[15] The doctrine of impossibility of performance is applied only when the parties could not have reasonably foreseen, at the time the contract was formed, the event or events that rendered performance impossible.

Objective impossibility ("It cannot be done") must be distinguished from subjective impossibility ("I'm sorry, I cannot do it"). An example of subjective impossibility occurs when a party cannot make payment on time because the bank is closed. In effect, the nonperforming party is saying, "It is impossible for *me* to perform," rather than "It is impossible for *anyone* to perform." Accordingly, such excuses do not discharge a contract, and the nonperforming party is normally held in breach of contract.

---

15. *Restatement (Second) of Contracts*, Section 261. See also UCC 2–615.

Assume that this star dancer has a contract to appear in five ballets during the winter season. If he breaks his leg before the season starts, is he still bound by the contract?

When Performance Is Impossible   Three basic types of situations generally qualify as grounds for the discharge of contractual obligations based on impossibility of performance:

1. *When a party whose personal performance is essential to the completion of the contract dies or becomes incapacitated prior to performance.* **EXAMPLE 9.21** Fred, a famous dancer, contracts with Ethereal Dancing Guild to play a leading role in its new ballet. Before the ballet can be performed, Fred becomes ill and dies. His personal performance was essential to the completion of the contract. Thus, his death discharges the contract and his estate's liability for his nonperformance. •

2. *When the specific subject matter of the contract is destroyed.* **EXAMPLE 9.22** A-1 Farm Equipment agrees to sell Gudgel the green tractor on its lot and promises to have the tractor ready for Gudgel to pick up on Saturday. On Friday night, a truck veers off the nearby highway and smashes into the tractor, destroying it beyond repair. Because the contract identified this specific tractor, A-1's performance is rendered impossible. •

3. *When a change in the law renders performance illegal.* **EXAMPLE 9.23** Russo contracts with Playlist, Inc., to create a Web site through which users can post and share movies, music, and other forms of digital entertainment. Russo goes to work. Before the site is operational, however, Congress passes the No Online Piracy in Entertainment (NOPE) Act. The NOPE Act makes it illegal to operate a Web site on which copyrighted works are posted without the copyright owners' consent. In this situation, the contract is discharged by operation of law. The purpose of the contract has been rendered illegal, and contract performance is objectively impossible. •

Temporary Impossibility   An occurrence or event that makes performance temporarily impossible operates to suspend performance until the impossibility ceases. Ordinarily, the parties must then perform the contract as originally planned. Only if the lapse of time and the change in circumstances surrounding the contract make it substantially more burdensome for the parties to perform the promised acts will the contract be discharged.

     CASE EXAMPLE 9.24 On August 22, Keefe Hurwitz contracted to sell his home in Louisiana to Wesley and Gwendolyn Payne for $241,500. On August 26—just four days after the parties signed the contract—Hurricane Katrina made landfall and caused extensive damage to the house. The cost of repairs was estimated at $60,000, and Hurwitz would have to make the repairs before the closing date. Hurwitz refused, and the Paynes sued to enforce the contract. Hurwitz claimed that Hurricane Katrina had made it impossible for him to perform and had discharged his duties under the contract. The court ruled that Hurricane Katrina had caused only a temporary impossibility. Therefore, Hurwitz had to pay for the necessary repairs and to perform the contract as written. He could not obtain a higher purchase price to offset the cost of the repairs.[16] •

Commercial Impracticability   Courts may excuse parties from their performance obligations when the performance becomes much more difficult or expensive than the parties originally contemplated at the time the contract was formed. For someone to invoke the doctrine of **commercial impracticability** successfully, however, the anticipated performance must become *extremely* difficult or costly.

     The added burden of performing not only must be extreme but also *must not have been anticipated by the parties when the contract was made.* For instance, in one classic case, a court held that a contract could be discharged because a party would have had to pay ten times more than the original estimate to excavate a certain amount of gravel.[17] In another case, a power failure during a wedding reception relieved the owner of a banquet hall from

---

> **KNOW THIS**
>
> The doctrine of commercial impracticability does not provide relief from such events as ordinary price increases or easily predictable changes in the weather.

Commercial Impracticability A doctrine that may excuse the duty to perform a contract when performance becomes much more difficult or costly due to forces that neither party could have controlled or contemplated at the time the contract was formed.

---

16. *Payne v. Hurwitz,* 978 So.2d 1000 (La.App. 1st Cir. 2008).
17. *Mineral Park Land Co. v. Howard,* 172 Cal. 289, 156 P. 458 (1916).

BEYOND OUR BORDERS

Impossibility or Impracticability of Performance in Germany

In the United States, when a party alleges that contract performance is impossible or impracticable because of circumstances unforeseen at the time the contract was formed, a court will either discharge the party's contractual obligations or hold the party to the contract. In other words, if a court agrees that the contract is impossible or impracticable to perform, the remedy is to rescind (cancel) the contract. Under German law, however, a court may adjust the terms of (reform) a contract in light of economic developments. If an unforeseen event affects the foundation of the agreement, the court can alter the contract's terms to align with the parties' original expectations, thus making the contract fair to the parties.

Critical Thinking

When a contract becomes impossible or impracticable to perform, which remedy would a businessperson prefer—rescission or reformation? Why? Explain your answer.

---

the duty to perform a contract.[18] (See this chapter's *Beyond Our Borders* feature above for a discussion of Germany's approach to impracticability and impossibility of performance.)

Frustration of Purpose Closely allied with the doctrine of commercial impracticability is the doctrine of **frustration of purpose.** In principle, a contract will be discharged if supervening circumstances make it impossible to attain the purpose both parties had in mind when they made the contract. As with commercial impracticability, the supervening event must not have been foreseeable at the time of the contracting.

Frustration of Purpose A court-created doctrine under which a party to a contract will be relieved of her or his duty to perform when the objective purpose for performance no longer exists (due to reasons beyond that party's control).

Damages

A breach of contract entitles the nonbreaching party to sue for monetary damages. As you read in Chapter 4, tort law damages are designed to compensate a party for harm suffered as a result of another's wrongful act. In the context of contract law, damages are designed to compensate the nonbreaching party for the loss of the bargain. Often, courts say that innocent parties are to be placed in the position they would have occupied had the contract been fully performed.

Types of Damages

There are basically four broad categories of damages:

1. Compensatory (to cover direct losses and costs).
2. Consequential (to cover indirect and foreseeable losses).
3. Punitive (to punish and deter wrongdoing).
4. Nominal (to recognize wrongdoing when no monetary loss is shown).

Compensatory and punitive damages were discussed in Chapter 4 in the context of tort law. Here, we look at these types of damages, as well as consequential and nominal damages, in the context of contract law. (See this chapter's *Adapting the Law to the Online Environment* feature on the following page for a discussion of the effect of breaching the terms of use in an online service contract.)

Compensatory Damages Damages that compensate the nonbreaching party for the *loss of the bargain* are known as *compensatory damages.* These damages compensate

> **KNOW THIS**
>
> The terms of a contract must be sufficiently definite for a court to determine the amount of damages to award.

---

18. *Facto v. Panagis,* 390 N.J.Super. 227, 915 A.2d 59 (2007).

ADAPTING THE LAW TO THE ONLINE ENVIRONMENT

THE EFFECT OF BREACHING AN ONLINE TESTING SERVICE'S TERMS OF USE

Increasingly, online testing services are available for almost any use. Employers, for example, use online behavioral testing to evaluate the employability of applicants. Schools and counseling services can administer an online test to assess the probability that an adolescent is chemically dependent. California uses an online test to establish a driver impairment index for those who have been arrested for drunk driving.

Typical Terms and Conditions of Use

Most online testing services have a relatively short list of terms and conditions for using their tests. For example, most testing services require that fees be paid. Also, the school, employer, or other entity that is using the online test usually must agree that the persons who administer the test will be qualified. In addition, the test user must agree that no decision or diagnosis will be made solely on the basis of the online test results.

Violation of the Online Terms

If the test user violates any of the terms and conditions, the implied contract with the testing service has been breached.

The following is a typical provision from an online testing service:

> When You Breach This Agreement: Each time you administer a test, the agreement granted herein will automatically terminate once the scoring has been provided to you. The Company has the right to terminate the authorization granted to you if you breach the terms and conditions of use for any test or if you violate the terms and conditions and obligations under this agreement. Once you breach your duties under this agreement, the Company will suffer immediate and irreparable damages. You therefore acknowledge that injunctive relief will be appropriate.

Critical Thinking

What possible "immediate and irreparable" damages might an online testing service experience if the test user breaches the contract?

LEARNING OBJECTIVE 3
What is the standard measure of compensatory damages when a contract is breached? How are damages computed differently in construction contracts?

the injured party only for damages actually sustained and proved to have arisen directly from the loss of the bargain caused by the breach of contract. They simply replace what was lost because of the wrong or damage.

In general, the standard measure of compensatory damages is the difference between the value of the breaching party's promised performance under the contract and the value of her or his actual performance. This amount is reduced by any loss that the injured party has avoided.

EXAMPLE 9.25 You contract with Marinot Industries to perform certain personal services exclusively for Marinot during August for a payment of $4,000. Marinot cancels the contract and is in breach. You are able to find another job during August but can earn only $3,000. You normally can sue Marinot for breach and recover $1,000 as compensatory damages. You may also recover from Marinot the amount that you spent to find the other job. ● Expenses that are directly incurred because of a breach of contract—such as those incurred to obtain performance from another source—are called **incidental damages**.

The measurement of compensatory damages varies by type of contract. Certain types of contracts deserve special mention—contracts for the sale of goods, contracts for the sale of land, and construction contracts.

Incidental Damages Damages that compensate for expenses directly incurred because of a breach of contract, such as those incurred to obtain performance from another source.

Sale of Goods In a contract for the sale of goods, the usual measure of compensatory damages is the difference between the contract price and the market price at the time of delivery.[19]

---

19. This is the difference between the contract price and the market price at the time and place at which the goods were to be delivered or tendered. See Sections 2–708, 2–713, and 2–715(1) of the Uniform Commercial Code (UCC).

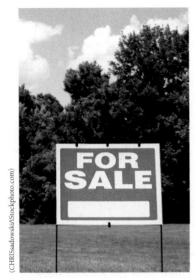

(CHRISsadowski/iStockphoto.com)

Under what circumstances will a court award monetary damages for a breached sale-of-land contract?

"A long dispute means that both parties are wrong."

Voltaire, 1694–1778
(French author)

Consequential Damages Foreseeable damages that result from a party's breach of contract but are caused by special circumstances beyond the contract itself.

EXAMPLE 9.26 Medik Laboratories contracts to buy ten model UTS 400 network servers from Cal Industries for $4,000 each, but Cal Industries fails to deliver the servers. The market price of the servers at the time Medik learns of the breach is $4,500. Therefore, Medik's measure of damages is $5,000 (10 × $500), plus any incidental damages (expenses) caused by the breach. ●

When the buyer breaches and the seller has not yet produced the goods, compensatory damages normally equal the seller's lost profits on the sale, rather than the difference between the contract price and the market price.

Sale of Land Ordinarily, because each parcel of land is unique, the remedy for a seller's breach of a contract for a sale of real estate is specific performance—that is, the buyer is awarded the property for which he or she bargained (*specific performance* will be discussed more fully later in the chapter). When this remedy is unavailable (because the property has been sold, for example) or when the buyer is the party in breach, the measure of damages is typically the difference between the contract price and the market price of the land. The majority of states follow this rule.

Construction Contracts The measure of damages in a building or construction contract depends on which party breaches and when the breach occurs. If the owner breaches *before performance has begun,* the contractor can recover only the profits that would have been made on the contract—that is, the total contract price less the cost of materials and labor. If the owner breaches *during performance,* the contractor can recover the profits plus the costs incurred in partially constructing the building. If the owner breaches *after the construction has been completed,* the contractor can recover the entire contract price plus interest.

When the contractor breaches the construction contract—either by failing to begin construction or by stopping work partway through the project—the measure of damages is the cost of completion, which includes reasonable compensation for any delay in performance. If the contractor finishes late, the measure of damages is the loss of use. Exhibit 9.5 below summarizes the rules for the measure of damages in breached construction contracts. (The *Business Application* feature on pages 279–280 offers some suggestions on what to do if you cannot perform.)

Consequential Damages Foreseeable damages that result from a party's breach of contract are called **consequential damages,** or *special damages.* They differ from compensatory damages in that they are caused by special circumstances beyond the contract itself and flow from the consequences, or results, of a breach.

When a seller fails to deliver goods, knowing that the buyer is planning to use or resell those goods immediately, a court may award consequential damages (in addition to compensatory damages) for the loss of profits from the planned use or resale. For the nonbreaching

Exhibit 9.5 Measurement of Damages— Breach of Construction Contracts

PARTY IN BREACH	TIME OF BREACH	MEASUREMENT OF DAMAGES
Owner	Before construction has begun.	Profits (contract price less cost of materials and labor).
Owner	During construction.	Profits plus costs incurred up to time of breach.
Owner	After construction is completed.	Full contract price, plus interest.
Contractor	Before construction has begun.	Cost in excess of contract price to complete work.
Contractor	Before construction is completed.	Generally, all costs incurred by owner to complete.

party to recover, the breaching party must know (or have reason to know) that special circumstances will cause the nonbreaching party to suffer an additional loss.[20]

EXAMPLE 9.27 Gilmore contracts to have a specific machine part shipped to her—one that she desperately needs to repair her printing press. In her contract with the shipper, Gilmore states that she must receive the part by Monday, or she will not be able to print her paper and will lose $3,000. If the shipper is late, Gilmore normally can recover the consequential damages caused by the delay (that is, the $3,000 in losses). ●

Punitive Damages   Punitive, or exemplary, damages, are almost never awarded in an action for breach of contract (unless a tort is involved). Such damages have no legitimate place in contract law because they are, in essence, penalties, and a breach of contract is not unlawful in a criminal sense. The law may compensate one party for the loss of the bargain—no more and no less.

Nominal Damages   When no actual damage or financial loss results from a breach of contract and only a technical injury is involved, the court may award **nominal damages** to the innocent party. Nominal damages awards are often small, such as one dollar, but they do establish that the defendant acted wrongfully. Most lawsuits for nominal damages are brought as a matter of principle under the theory that a breach has occurred and some damages must be imposed regardless of actual loss.

Mitigation of Damages

In most situations, when a breach of contract occurs, the injured party is held to a duty to mitigate, or reduce, the damages that he or she suffers. Under this doctrine of **mitigation of damages,** the required action depends on the nature of the situation.

One example of the application of this doctrine involves employment contracts. In the majority of states, a person whose employment has been wrongfully terminated has a duty to mitigate damages incurred because of the employer's breach of the employment contract. In other words, a wrongfully terminated employee has a duty to take a similar job if one is available. If the person fails to do this, the damages received will be equivalent to the person's former salary less the income he or she would have received in a similar job obtained by reasonable means. Normally, a terminated employee is under no duty to take a job that is not of the same type and rank.

CASE EXAMPLE 9.28   Harry De La Concha was employed by Fordham University. He claimed that he was injured in an fight with Fordham's director of human resources and filed for workers' compensation benefits (which are available for on-the-job injuries regardless of fault—see Chapter 18). Fordham then fired De La Concha, who argued that he had been terminated in retaliation for filing a workers' compensation claim. The New York state workers' compensation board held that De La Concha had failed to mitigate his damages because he had not even looked for another job, and a state court affirmed the decision. Because De La Concha had failed to mitigate his damages, any compensation he received for wrongful termination would be reduced by the amount he *could have obtained* from other employment.[21] ●

Liquidated Damages versus Penalties

A **liquidated damages** provision in a contract specifies that a certain dollar amount is to be paid in the event of a future default or breach of contract. (*Liquidated* means determined, settled, or fixed.) Liquidated damages provisions are frequently used in construction contracts.

---

20. UCC 2–715(2). See Chapter 11.
21. *De la Concha v. Fordham University,* 814 N.Y.S.2d 320, 28 A.3d 963 (2006).

▶ KNOW THIS ◀

To avoid the risk of consequential damages, a seller can limit the buyer's remedies via contract.

Nominal Damages A small monetary award (often one dollar) granted to a plaintiff when no actual damage was suffered.

Mitigation of Damages The requirement that a plaintiff do whatever is reasonable to minimize the damages caused by the defendant.

Liquidated Damages An amount, stipulated in a contract, that the parties to the contract believe to be a reasonable estimation of the damages that will occur in the event of a breach.

Penalty A contract clause that specifies a certain amount to be paid in the event of a default or breach of contract but that is designed to punish the breaching party rather than to provide a reasonable estimate of damages.

Liquidated damages differ from penalties. A **penalty** also specifies a certain amount to be paid in the event of a default or breach of contract, but it is designed to penalize the breaching party. Liquidated damages provisions normally are enforceable. In contrast, if a court finds that a provision calls for a penalty, the provision will not be enforced, and recovery will be limited to actual damages.[22]

Determining Enforceability

To determine whether a particular provision is for liquidated damages or a penalty, the court must answer two questions:

1. At the time the contract was formed, was it apparent that damages would be difficult to estimate in the event of a breach?
2. Was the amount set as damages a reasonable estimate and not excessive?[23]

If the answers to both questions are yes, the provision normally will be enforced. If either answer is no, the provision usually will not be enforced.

In the following *Spotlight Case*, the court had to decide whether a clause in a contract was an enforceable liquidated damages provision or an unenforceable penalty.

---

22. This is also the rule under the UCC. See UCC 2–718(1).
23. *Restatement (Second) of Contracts,* Section 356(1).

Spotlight on Liquidated Damages

Case 9.2
B-Sharp Musical Productions, Inc. v. Haber
New York Supreme Court, 27 Misc.3d 41, 899 N.Y.S.2d 792 (2010).

(oleg66/iStockphoto.com)

Bands contract their performance dates months in advance.

FACTS B-Sharp Musical Productions, Inc., and James Haber entered into a contract under which B-Sharp was to provide a band on a specified date to perform at Haber's son's bar mitzvah. Haber was to pay approximately $30,000 for the band's services. The contract contained a liquidated damages clause stating, "If [the contract] is terminated in writing by [Haber] for any reason within ninety (90) days prior to the engagement, the remaining balance of the contract will be immediately due and payable. If [the contract] is terminated in writing by [Haber] for any reason before the ninety (90) days period, 50% of the balance will be immediately due and payable."

Within ninety days before the date of the bar mitzvah, Haber sent a letter to B-Sharp stating that he was canceling the contract. When Haber refused to pay the remaining amount due under the contract—approximately $25,000—B-Sharp sued Haber and his wife in a New York state court to recover the damages. The court granted B-Sharp's motion for summary judgment, enforcing the liquidated damages clause, and the defendants appealed.

ISSUE Was the liquidated damages clause, which specified the amount to be paid in the event that the performance was canceled, enforceable?

DECISION Yes. The appellate court upheld the trial court's judgment. The clause in question was "not an unenforceable penalty." It was a reasonable estimate of damages, given that B-Sharp would be unlikely to book another engagement that close to the performance date.

REASON The clause used an estimate of B-Sharp's probable loss in the event of a cancellation as the measure of loss. This estimate reflected an understanding that "although the expense and possibility of rebooking a cancelled [performance] could not be ascertained with certainty, as a practical matter, the expense would become greater, and the possibility would be less, the closer to the [performance] the cancellation was made, until a point was reached, [ninety] days before the [performance], that any effort to rebook could not be reasonably expected."

CRITICAL THINKING—Ethical Consideration *Were there ethical reasons for the court to enforce the liquidated damages clause in this case? Explain.*

LEARNING OBJECTIVE 4

Under what circumstances is the remedy of rescission and restitution available?

> ➤ **KNOW THIS** ◀
>
> Restitution offers several advantages over traditional damages. First, restitution may be available in situations when damages cannot be proved or are difficult to prove. Second, restitution can be used to recover specific property. Third, restitution sometimes results in a greater overall award.

Restitution An equitable remedy under which a person is restored to his or her original position prior to loss or injury, or placed in the position he or she would have been in had the breach not occurred.

Former Detroit mayor Kwame Kilpatrick (below) at his restitution hearing.

(AP Photo/Paul Sancya, File)

Specific Performance An equitable remedy in which a court orders the parties to perform as promised in the contract. This remedy normally is granted only when the legal remedy (monetary damages) is inadequate.

Equitable Remedies

Sometimes, damages are an inadequate remedy for a breach of contract. In these situations, the nonbreaching party may ask the court for an equitable remedy. Equitable remedies include rescission and restitution, specific performance, and reformation.

Rescission and Restitution

As discussed on page 218 of Chapter 7, *rescission* is essentially an action to undo, or cancel, a contract—to return nonbreaching parties to the positions that they occupied prior to the transaction.[24] When fraud, mistake, duress, undue influence, lack of capacity, or failure of consideration is present, rescission is available. Rescission may also be available by statute. The failure of one party to perform under a contract entitles the other party to rescind the contract. The rescinding party must give prompt notice to the breaching party.

Restitution   To rescind a contract, both parties generally must make **restitution** by returning goods, property, or funds previously conveyed. If the property or goods can be returned, they must be. If the property or goods have been consumed, restitution must be made in an equivalent dollar amount.

Essentially, restitution involves the recapture of a benefit conferred on the defendant that has unjustly enriched her or him. **EXAMPLE 9.29**   Andrea pays $32,000 to Miles in return for his promise to design a house for her. The next day, Miles calls Andrea and tells her that he has taken a position with a large architectural firm in another state and cannot design the house. Andrea decides to hire another architect that afternoon. Andrea can require restitution of $32,000 because Miles has received an unjust benefit of $32,000. ●

Restitution Is Not Limited to Rescission Cases   Restitution may be required when a contract is rescinded, but the right to restitution is not limited to rescission cases. Because an award of restitution basically gives back, or returns, something to its rightful owner, a party can seek restitution in actions for breach of contract, tort actions, and other types of actions.

Restitution can be obtained when funds or property has been transferred by mistake or because of fraud or incapacity. Similarly, restitution might be available when there has been misconduct by a party with a special relationship with the other party. Even in criminal cases (see Chapter 6), a court can order restitution of funds or property obtained through embezzlement, conversion, theft, or copyright infringement.

Specific Performance

The equitable remedy of **specific performance** calls for the performance of the act promised in the contract. This remedy is attractive to a nonbreaching party because it provides the exact bargain promised in the contract. It also avoids some of the problems inherent in a suit for monetary damages, such as collecting a judgment and arranging another contract. Moreover, the actual performance may be more valuable (to the promisee) than the monetary damages.

Normally, however, specific performance will not be granted unless the party's legal remedy (monetary damages) is inadequate.[25] For this reason, contracts for the sale of goods rarely qualify for specific performance. Monetary damages ordinarily are adequate in sales contracts because substantially identical goods can be bought or sold in the market.

---

24. The rescission discussed here refers to *unilateral* rescission, in which only one party wants to undo the contract. In *mutual* rescission, which we discussed on page 266, both parties agree to undo the contract. Mutual rescission discharges the contract, whereas unilateral rescission is generally available as a remedy for breach of contract.

25. *Restatement (Second) of Contracts*, Section 359.

(dimdimich/Stockphoto.com)

Why would specific performance be preferred when antiques are the item in dispute?

Only if the goods are unique will a court grant specific performance. For instance, paintings, sculptures, and rare books and coins are often unique, and monetary damages will not enable a buyer to obtain substantially identical substitutes in the market.

Sale of Land A court may grant specific performance to a buyer in an action for a breach of contract involving the sale of land. In this situation, the legal remedy of monetary damages will not compensate the buyer adequately because every parcel of land is unique, as was discussed on page 271. The same land in the same location obviously cannot be obtained elsewhere. Only when specific performance is unavailable (for example, when the seller has sold the property to someone else) will damages be awarded instead.

CASE EXAMPLE 9.30 Howard Stainbrook entered into a contract to sell Trent Low forty acres of mostly timbered land for $45,000. Low agreed to pay for a survey of the property and other costs in addition to the price. He gave Stainbrook a check for $1,000 to show his intent to fulfill the contract. One month later, Stainbrook died. His son David became the executor of the estate. After he discovered that the timber on the property was worth more than $100,000, David asked Low to withdraw his offer to buy the forty acres. Low refused and filed a suit against David seeking specific performance of the contract. The court found that because Low had substantially performed his obligations under the contract and offered to perform the rest, he was entitled to specific performance.[26] ●

Contracts for Personal Services Personal-service contracts require one party to work personally for another party. Courts normally refuse to grant specific performance of contracts for personal services. This is because ordering a party to perform personal services against his or her will amounts to a type of involuntary servitude, which is contrary to the public policy expressed in the Thirteenth Amendment to the U.S. Constitution (see Appendix B). Moreover, the courts do not want to monitor the performance of contracts for personal services, which usually require the exercise of personal judgment or talent.

If a contract is not deemed personal, the remedy at law of monetary damages may be adequate if substantially identical service (for instance, lawn mowing) is available from other persons.

Reformation

Reformation is an equitable remedy used when the parties have *imperfectly* expressed their agreement in writing. Reformation allows a court to rewrite the contract to reflect the parties' true intentions. Exhibit 9.6 on the following page graphically presents the remedies, including reformation, that are available to the nonbreaching party.

Courts order reformation most often when fraud or mutual mistake is present. **EXAMPLE 9.31** If Carson contracts to buy a forklift from Yoshie but the written contract refers to a crane, a mutual mistake has occurred. Accordingly, a court could reform the contract so that the writing conforms to the parties' original intention as to which piece of equipment is being sold. ●

A court will also reform a contract when two parties enter into a binding oral contract but later make an error when they attempt to put the terms into writing. Usually, the court will allow into evidence the correct terms of the oral contract, thereby reforming the written contract.

Courts also may reform a written covenant not to compete (see page 233 of Chapter 8). If the covenant not to compete is for a valid and legitimate purpose (such as the sale of

> "Controversy equalizes fools and wise men—and the fools know it."
>
> Oliver Wendell Holmes, 1809–1894 (American author)

---

26. *Stainbrook v. Low*, 842 N.E.2d 386 (Ind.App. 2006).

Exhibit 9.6 Remedies for Breach of Contract

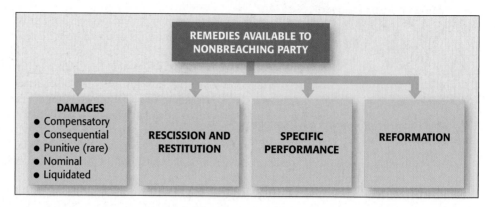

REMEDIES AVAILABLE TO
NONBREACHING PARTY

DAMAGES
- Compensatory
- Consequential
- Punitive (rare)
- Nominal
- Liquidated

RESCISSION AND RESTITUTION

SPECIFIC PERFORMANCE

REFORMATION

a business) but the area or time restraints are unreasonable, some courts will reform the restraints by making them reasonable and will enforce the entire contract as reformed. Other courts, however, will throw out the entire restrictive covenant as illegal.

In the following case, a physician claimed that the covenant not to compete that he signed was unreasonable and should therefore be declared illegal.

Case 9.3

Emerick v. Cardiac Study Center, Inc.

Court of Appeals of Washington, Division 2,
166 Wash.App. 1039 (2012).

Can a covenant not to compete apply to physician-shareholders in a medical group?

FACTS Cardiac Study Center, Inc., is a medical practice group of approximately fifteen cardiologists. In 2002, Cardiac hired Dr. Robert Emerick as an employee. In 2004, Emerick became a shareholder of Cardiac. He signed a shareholder employment agreement that included a covenant not to compete. The covenant stated that a physician who left the group promised not to practice competitively in the surrounding area for a period of five years. In 2005, patients and other medical providers began to complain to Cardiac about Emerick's conduct. Some physicians stopped referring patients to Cardiac as a result. Finally, Cardiac terminated Emerick's employment in 2009. Emerick sued Cardiac, seeking a declaration that the covenant not to compete was unenforceable. He prevailed at trial, and Cardiac appealed.

ISSUE Was the Cardiac Study Center's covenant not to compete unenforceable?

DECISION No. The state appellate court held that the covenant not to compete was reasonable.

REASON The reviewing court examined the reasonableness of the covenant not to compete in terms of how it protected the

employer's business or goodwill. The court pointed out that "an employee who joins an established business gains access to his employer's customers and acquires valuable information as to the nature and character of the business." Further, an employer has a "legitimate interest in protecting its existing client base and prohibiting the employee from taking its clients." Cardiac had provided Emerick with an immediate client base and established referral sources when he moved to the area. Emerick had access to Cardiac's business model and goodwill. The reviewing court explained that "restrictive covenants are common among professionals because they allow a new professional to step into an already established practice while protecting the employer from future competition."

WHY IS THIS CASE IMPORTANT? *If businesspersons create restrictive covenants that are reasonable, do not extend to a very large geographic area, and do not last for decades, courts will often hold them enforceable. Without the protection of restrictive covenants, businesses would be less willing to hire employees and give them access to client lists and unique business models.*

Recovery Based on Quasi Contract

In some situations, when no actual contract exists, a court may step in to prevent one party from being unjustly enriched at the expense of another party. As discussed in Chapter 7, *quasi contract* is a legal theory under which an obligation is imposed in the absence of an agreement. A quasi contract is not a true contract but rather a fictional contract that is imposed on the parties to prevent unjust enrichment.

KNOW THIS
The function of a quasi contract is to impose a legal obligation on a party who made no actual promise.

When Quasi Contract Is Used
Quasi contract allows a court to act as if a contract exists when there is no actual contract or agreement between the parties. Therefore, if the parties have entered into a contract concerning the matter in controversy, a court normally will not impose a quasi contract. A court can also use the doctrine when the parties entered into a contract, but it is unenforceable for some reason.

Quasi-contractual recovery is often granted when one party has partially performed under a contract that is unenforceable. Quasi contracts provide an alternative to suing for damages and allow the party to recover the reasonable value of the partial performance.

EXAMPLE 9.32   Ericson contracts to build two oil derricks for Petro Industries. The derricks are to be built over a period of three years, but the parties do not create a written contract. Therefore, the Statute of Frauds will bar the enforcement of the contract.[27] After Ericson completes one derrick, Petro Industries informs him that it will not pay for the derrick. Ericson can sue Petro Industries under the theory of quasi contract. •

The Requirements of Quasi Contract
To recover on a quasi contract theory, the party seeking recovery must show the following:

1. The party conferred a benefit on the other party.
2. The party conferred the benefit with the reasonable expectation of being paid.
3. The party did not act as a volunteer in conferring the benefit.
4. The party receiving the benefit would be unjustly enriched if allowed to retain the benefit without paying for it.

Applying these requirements to *Example 9.32* above, Ericson can sue in quasi contract because all of the conditions for quasi-contractual recovery have been fulfilled. Ericson conferred a benefit on Petro Industries by building the oil derrick. Ericson build the derrick with the reasonable expectation of being paid. He did not intend to act as a volunteer. Petro Industries would be unjustly enriched if it was allowed to keep the derrick without paying Ericson for the work. Therefore, Ericson should be able to recover the reasonable value of the oil derrick that was built (under the theory of *quantum meruit*[28]—"as much as he or she deserves"). The reasonable value is ordinarily equal to the fair market value.

Contract Provisions Limiting Remedies

KNOW THIS
Exculpatory clauses may be held unconscionable, depending on the relative bargaining positions of the parties and the importance to the public interest of the business seeking to enforce the clause.

A contract may include provisions stating that no damages can be recovered for certain types of breaches or that damages will be limited to a maximum amount. The contract may also provide that the only remedy for breach is replacement, repair, or refund of the purchase price. The contract can also provide that one party can seek injunctive relief if the other party breaches the contract (see Paragraph 11 on page 289 in *An Annotated Employment Contract,* which follows this chapter). Provisions stating that no damages can be recovered are called *exculpatory clauses* (see page 237 in Chapter 8). Provisions that affect the availability of certain remedies are called *limitation-of-liability clauses.*

---

27. Contracts that by their terms cannot be performed within one year from the day after the date of contract formation must be in writing to be enforceable (see Chapter 8).

28. Pronounced *kwahn*-tuhm *mehr*-oo-wuht.

The UCC Allows Sales Contracts to Limit Remedies

The Uniform Commercial Code (UCC) provides that remedies can be limited in a contract for the sale of goods. We will examine the UCC provisions on limitation-of-liability clauses in Chapter 11, in the context of the remedies available on the breach of a contract for the sale or lease of goods.

Enforceability of Limitation-of-Liability Clauses

LEARNING OBJECTIVE 5
What is a limitation-of-liability clause, and when will courts enforce it?

Whether a limitation-of-liability clause in a contract will be enforced depends on the type of breach that is excused by the provision. Normally, a provision excluding liability for fraudulent or intentional injury will not be enforced. Likewise, a clause excluding liability for illegal acts or violations of law will not be enforced.

A clause excluding liability for negligence may be enforced in certain situations, however. When an exculpatory clause for negligence is contained in a contract made between parties who have roughly equal bargaining positions, the clause usually will be enforced.

CASE EXAMPLE 9.33 Engineering Consulting Services, Ltd. (ECS), contracted with RSN Properties, Inc., a real estate developer, to render an opinion on the use of septic systems in a residential subdivision being developed. A clause in the contract limited ECS's liability to RSN to the value of the engineering services or the sum of $50,000, whichever was greater. ECS concluded that most of the lots were suitable for septic systems, so RSN proceeded with development.

Ultimately, ECS's conclusions turned out to be incorrect. The county refused to approve further development of the lots because they were unsuitable for septic systems. RSN sued ECS for breach of contract and argued that the limitation-of-liability clause was against public policy and unenforceable. The court, however, held that the "contract represented a reasonable allocation of risks in an arm's-length business transaction, and did not violate public policy for professional engineering practice." The court therefore enforced the limitation-of-liability clause.[29] •

**ETHICAL
ISSUE**

Should courts enforce a limitation-of-liability clause in a contract that cruise ship passengers are required to sign? In 2012, a cruise ship carrying 4,200 passengers and crew members capsized off the coast of Italy, killing more than thirty people. Captain Francesco Schettino, the captain of the ship *Costa Concordia*, was blamed for causing the accident because he brought the ship too close to shore, where it struck a rock that punctured its hull. Passengers have attempted to sue the corporate owner of the ship, Carnival Cruise Lines, over the incident. But Carnival included a carefully drafted limitation-of-liability clause in its contract, which each passenger is required to sign when purchasing a ticket. The clause limits the kinds of suits that can be brought, where they can be filed, and how much passengers can ultimately recover from Carnival.

U.S. courts have upheld similar limitations of liability in other cruise ship cases. Because no U.S. port was involved with the Italian cruise ship's accident, however, the contract specifies that litigation must take place in Italy. Thus, no U.S. court will be involved. Under international law, limitations on liability can be set aside only if the ship's owner engaged in egregious (obviously unacceptable) acts. The captain's acts were arguably egregious. For instance, he increased the *Costa Concordia*'s speed in shallow waters, in the dark, despite the proximity of obstacles, to make up for time he had spent having dinner with a woman. Then he abandoned the ship while passengers were stranded aboard. Nevertheless, the ship's owner, Carnival Cruise Lines, claims that it was unaware of the captain's reckless conduct until after the accident. Unless the passengers can persuade a court that Carnival is responsible for the acts of its captain, their recovery from the cruise line is likely to be limited.

---

29. *RSN Properties, Inc. v. Engineering Consulting Services, Ltd.*, 301 Ga.App. 52, 686 S.E.2d 853 (2009).

Reviewing . . . Contract Performance, Breach, and Remedies

Kyle Bruno enters into a contract with X Entertainment to be a stuntman in a movie. Bruno is widely known as the best motorcycle stuntman in the business, and the movie, *Xtreme Riders*, has numerous scenes involving high-speed freestyle street-bike stunts. Filming is set to begin August 1 and end by December 1 so that the film can be released the following summer. Both parties to the contract have stipulated that the filming must end on time in order to capture the profits from the summer movie market. The contract states that Bruno will be paid 10 percent of the net proceeds from the movie for his stunts. The contract also includes a liquidated damages provision, which specifies that if Bruno breaches the contract, he will owe X Entertainment $1 million. In addition, the contract includes a limitation-of-liability clause stating that if Bruno is injured during filming, X Entertainment's liability is limited to nominal damages. Using the information presented in the chapter, answer the following questions.

1. One day, while Bruno is preparing for a difficult stunt, he gets into an argument with the director and refuses to perform any stunts. Can X Entertainment seek specific performance of the contract? Why or why not?
2. Suppose that while performing a high-speed wheelie on a motorcycle, Bruno is injured by an intentionally reckless act of an X Entertainment employee. Will a court be likely to enforce the limitation-of-liability clause? Why or why not?
3. What factors would a court consider to determine if the $1 million liquidated damages clause is valid or is a penalty?
4. Suppose that there is no liquidated damages clause and X Entertainment breaches the contract. The breach causes the release of the film to be delayed until after summer. Could Bruno seek consequential (special) damages for lost profits from the summer movie market in that situation? Explain.

DEBATE THIS Courts should always uphold limitation-of-liability clauses, whether or not the two parties to the contract had equal bargaining power.

BUSINESS APPLICATION

What Do You Do When You Cannot Perform?*

Not every contract can be performed. If you are a contractor, you may take on a job that, for one reason or another, you cannot or do not wish to perform. Simply walking away from the job and hoping for the best normally is not the most effective way to avoid litigation—which can be costly, time consuming, and emotionally draining. Instead, you should consider various options that may reduce the likelihood of litigation.

For example, suppose that you are a building contractor and you sign a contract to build a home for the Andersons according to a set of plans that they have provided. Performance is to begin on June 15. On June 1, Central Enterprises offers you a position that will pay you two and a half times as much as you can earn

as an independent builder. To take the job, you have to start on June 15. You cannot be in two places at the same time, so if you accept the new position, you must breach the contract with the Andersons.

Consider Your Options

What can you do in this situation? One option is to subcontract the work to another builder and oversee the work yourself to make sure it conforms to the contract. Another option is to negotiate with the Andersons for a release. You can offer to find another qualified builder who will build a house of the same quality at the same price. Alternatively, you can offer to pay any additional costs if another builder takes the job and is more expensive. In any event, this additional cost would be one measure of damages that a court would impose on you if the Andersons prevailed in a suit for breach

*This *Business Application* is not meant to substitute for the services of an attorney who is licensed to practice law in your state.

Continued

of contract (in addition to any costs the Andersons suffer as a result of the breach, such as costs due to the delay in construction). Thus, by making the offer, you might be able to avoid the expense of litigation—if the Andersons accept your offer.

Settlement Offers

Often, parties are reluctant to propose compromise settlements because they fear that what they say will be used against them in court if litigation ensues. Generally, however, offers for settlement will not be admitted in court to prove that you are liable for a breach of contract (though they are at times admissible to prove that a party breached the duty of good faith).

Checklist for When You Cannot Perform

1. *Consider a compromise.*
2. *Subcontract out the work and oversee it.*
3. *Offer to find an alternative contractor to fulfill your obligation.*
4. *Make a cash offer to "buy" a release from your contract. Work with an attorney in making the offer unless the amount involved is insignificant.*

Key Terms

alienation 257
anticipatory repudiation 265
assignee 255
assignment 255
assignor 255
breach of contract 255
commercial impracticability 268
concurrent conditions 263
condition 262
condition precedent 263
condition subsequent 263
consequential damages 271
delegatee 258
delegation of duties 258
delegator 258
discharge 262
frustration of purpose 269
impossibility of performance 267
incidental beneficiary 261
incidental damages 270
intended beneficiary 260
liquidated damages 272
mitigation of damages 272
nominal damages 272
novation 266
obligee 255
obligor 255
penalty 273
performance 262
privity of contract 254
restitution 274
specific performance 274
tender 263
third party beneficiary 260

Chapter Summary: Contract Performance, Breach, and Remedies

THIRD PARTY RIGHTS	
Assignments (See pages 255–258.)	1. An assignment is the transfer of rights under a contract to a third party. The person assigning the rights is the *assignor,* and the party to whom the rights are assigned is the *assignee.* The assignee has a right to demand performance from the other original party to the contract. 2. Generally, all rights can be assigned *unless:* a. A statute expressly prohibits assignment. b. The contract is for personal services. c. The assignment will materially alter the obligor's risk or duties. d. The contract prohibits assignment.
Delegations (See pages 258–259.)	1. A delegation is the transfer of duties under a contract to a third party (the *delegatee*), who then assumes the obligation of performing the contractual duties previously held by the one making the delegation (the *delegator*). 2. As a general rule, any duty can be delegated *unless:* a. Performance depends on the obligor's personal skills or talents, or special trust has been placed in the obligor. b. Performance by a third party will vary materially from that expected by the obligee. c. The contract prohibits delegation. 3. A valid delegation of duties does not relieve the delegator of obligations under the contract. If the delegatee fails to perform, the delegator is still liable to the obligee. 4. An "assignment of all rights" or an "assignment of the contract" is often construed to mean that both the rights and the duties arising under the contract are transferred to a third party.
Third Party Beneficiaries (See pages 260–261.)	A third party beneficiary contract is one made for the purpose of benefiting a third party. 1. *Intended beneficiary*—One for whose benefit a contract is created. When the promisor (the one making the contractual promise that benefits a third party) fails to perform as promised, the third party can sue the promisor directly. Examples of third party beneficiaries are creditor and donee beneficiaries. 2. *Incidental beneficiary*—A third party who indirectly (incidentally) benefits from a contract but for whose benefit the contract was not specifically intended. Incidental beneficiaries have no rights to the benefits received and cannot sue to have the contract enforced.

Chapter Summary: Contract Performance, Breach, and Remedies—Continued

	CONTRACT DISCHARGE
Conditions of Performance (See pages 262–263.)	Contract obligations may be subject to the following types of conditions: 1. *Condition precedent*—A condition that must be fulfilled before a party's promise becomes absolute. 2. *Condition subsequent*—A condition that, if it occurs, operates to terminate a party's absolute promise to perform. 3. *Concurrent conditions*—Conditions that must be performed simultaneously. Each party's absolute duty to perform is conditioned on the other party's absolute duty to perform.
Discharge by Performance (See pages 263–265.)	A contract may be discharged by complete (strict) performance or by substantial performance. In some instances, performance must be to the satisfaction of another. Totally inadequate performance constitutes a material breach of the contract. An anticipatory repudiation of a contract allows the other party to sue immediately for breach of contract.
Discharge by Agreement (See pages 266–267.)	Parties may agree to discharge their contractual obligations in several ways: 1. *By rescission*—The parties mutually agree to rescind (cancel) the contract. 2. *By novation*—A new party is substituted for one of the primary parties to a contract, and a new contract is formed. 3. *By accord and satisfaction*—The parties agree to render and accept performance different from that on which they originally agreed.
Discharge by Operation of Law (See pages 267–269.)	Parties' obligations under contracts may be discharged by operation of law owing to one of the following: 1. Material alteration. 2. Statutes of limitations. 3. Bankruptcy. 4. Impossibility of performance. 5. Impracticability of performance. 6. Frustration of purpose.
	COMMON REMEDIES AVAILABLE TO NONBREACHING PARTY
Damages (See pages 269–273.)	The legal remedy designed to compensate the nonbreaching party for the loss of the bargain. By awarding monetary damages, the court tries to place the parties in the positions that they would have occupied had the contract been fully performed. The nonbreaching party frequently has a duty to *mitigate* (lessen or reduce) the damages incurred as a result of the contract's breach. There are four broad categories of damages. In addition, a contract may contain a provision for liquidated damages. 1. *Compensatory damages*—Damages that compensate the nonbreaching party for injuries actually sustained and proved to have arisen directly from the loss of the bargain resulting from the breach of contract. a. In breached contracts for the sale of goods, the usual measure of compensatory damages is the difference between the contract price and the market price. b. In breached contracts for the sale of land, the measure of damages is ordinarily the same as in contracts for the sale of goods. c. In breached construction contracts, the measure of damages depends on which party breaches and at what stage of construction the breach occurs. 2. *Consequential damages*—Damages that result from special circumstances beyond the contract itself. The damages flow from the consequences of a breach. For a party to recover consequential damages, the damages must be the foreseeable result of a breach of contract, and the breaching party must have known at the time the contract was formed that special circumstances existed that would cause the nonbreaching party to incur additional loss on breach of the contract. Also called *special damages*. 3. *Punitive damages*—Damages awarded to punish the breaching party. Usually not awarded in an action for breach of contract unless a tort is involved. 4. *Nominal damages*—Damages small in amount (such as one dollar) that are awarded when a breach has occurred but no actual injury has been suffered. Awarded only to establish that the defendant acted wrongfully. 5. *Liquidated damages*—Damages that may be specified in a contract as the amount to be paid to the nonbreaching party in the event the contract is breached. Clauses providing for liquidated damages are enforced if the damages were difficult to estimate at the time the contract was formed and if the amount stipulated is reasonable. If the amount is construed to be a penalty, the clause will not be enforced.
Rescission and Restitution (See page 274.)	1. *Rescission*—A remedy whereby a contract is canceled and the parties are restored to the original positions that they occupied prior to the transaction. Available when fraud, a mistake, duress, or failure of consideration is present. The rescinding party must give prompt notice of the rescission to the breaching party. 2. *Restitution*—When a contract is rescinded, both parties must make restitution to each other by returning the goods, property, or funds previously conveyed. Restitution prevents the unjust enrichment of the parties.

Continued

Chapter Summary: Contract Performance, Breach, and Remedies—Continued

Specific Performance (See pages 274–275.)	An equitable remedy calling for the performance of the act promised in the contract. This remedy is available only in special situations—such as those involving contracts for the sale of unique goods or land—when monetary damages would be an inadequate remedy. Specific performance is not available as a remedy for breached contracts for personal services.
Reformation (See pages 275–276.)	An equitable remedy allowing a contract to be "reformed," or rewritten, to reflect the parties' true intentions. Available when an agreement is imperfectly expressed in writing.
Recovery Based on Quasi Contract (See page 277.)	An equitable theory imposed by the courts to obtain justice and prevent unjust enrichment in a situation in which no enforceable contract exists. The party seeking recovery must show the following: 1. A benefit was conferred on the other party. 2. The party conferring the benefit did so with the expectation of being paid. 3. The benefit was not volunteered. 4. The party receiving the benefit would be unjustly enriched if allowed to retain the benefit without paying for it.
CONTRACT DOCTRINES RELATING TO REMEDIES	
Contract Provisions Limiting Remedies (See pages 277–278.)	A contract may provide that no damages (or only a limited amount of damages) can be recovered in the event the contract is breached. Under the Uniform Commercial Code, remedies may be limited in contracts for the sale of goods. Clauses excluding liability for fraudulent or intentional injury or for illegal acts cannot be enforced. Clauses excluding liability for negligence may be enforced if both parties hold roughly equal bargaining power.

ExamPrep

ISSUE SPOTTERS

1. Eagle Company contracts to build a house for Frank. The contract states that "any assignment of this contract renders the contract void." After Eagle builds the house, but before Frank pays, Eagle assigns its right to payment to Good Credit Company. Can Good Credit enforce the contract against Frank? Why or why not? **(See pages 256–257.)**
2. Greg contracts to build a storage shed for Haney, who pays Greg in advance. Greg completes only half the work. Haney pays Ipswich $500 to finish the shed. If Haney sues Greg, what will be the measure of recovery? **(See page 271.)**

—Check your answers to the Issue Spotters against the answers provided in Appendix E at the end of this text.

BEFORE THE TEST

Go to www.cengagebrain.com, enter the ISBN 9781133191353, and click on "Find" to locate this textbook's Web site. Then, click on "Access Now" under "Study Tools," and select Chapter 9 at the top. There, you will find a Practice Quiz that you can take to assess your mastery of the concepts in this chapter, as well as Flashcards, a Glossary of important terms, and Video Questions (when assigned).

For Review

Answers to the even-numbered questions in this For Review section can be found in Appendix F at the end of this text.

1. What is an assignment? What is the difference between an assignment and a delegation?
2. How are most contracts discharged?
3. What is the standard measure of compensatory damages when a contract is breached? How are damages computed differently in construction contracts?
4. Under what circumstances is the remedy of rescission and restitution available?
5. What is a limitation-of-liability clause, and when will courts enforce it?

Business Scenarios and Case Problems

9–1 Assignment. Aron, a college student, signs a one-year lease agreement that runs from September 1 to August 31. The lease agreement specifies that the lease cannot be assigned without the landlord's consent. In late May, Aron decides not to go to summer school and assigns the balance of the lease (three months) to a close friend, Erica. The landlord objects to the assignment and denies Erica access to the apartment. Aron claims that Erica is financially sound and should be allowed the full rights and privileges of an assignee. Discuss fully whether the landlord or Aron is correct. **(See pages 256–257.)**

9–2 ❓ Question with Sample Answer—Mitigation of Damages. Lauren Barton, a single mother with three children, lived in Portland, Oregon. Cynthia VanHorn also lived in Oregon until she moved to New York City to open and operate an art gallery. VanHorn asked Barton to manage the gallery under a one-year contract for an annual salary of $72,000. To begin work, Barton relocated to New York. As part of the move, Barton transferred custody of her children to her husband, who lived in London, England. In accepting the job, Barton also forfeited her husband's alimony and child-support payments, including unpaid amounts of nearly $30,000. Before Barton started work, VanHorn repudiated the contract. Unable to find employment for more than an annual salary of $25,000, Barton moved to London to be near her children. Barton filed a suit in an Oregon state court against VanHorn, seeking damages for breach of contract. Should the court hold, as VanHorn argued, that Barton did not take reasonable steps to mitigate her damages? Why or why not? **(See page 272.)**

—For a sample answer to Question 9–2, go to Appendix G at the end of this text.

9–3 🔦 Spotlight on Drug Testing—Third Party Beneficiaries. Bath Iron Works (BIW) offered a job to Thomas Devine, contingent on Devine's passing a drug test. The testing was conducted by NorDx, a subcontractor of Roche Biomedical Laboratories. When NorDx found that Devine's urinalysis showed the presence of opiates, a result confirmed by Roche, BIW refused to offer Devine permanent employment. Devine sued Roche, claiming that the ingestion of poppy seeds can lead to a positive result and that he tested positive for opiates only because of his daily consumption of poppy seed muffins. Devine argued that he was a third party beneficiary of the contract between his employer (BIW) and NorDx (Roche). Is Devine an intended third party beneficiary of the BIW–NorDx contract? Why or why not? Do drug-testing labs have a duty to the employees to exercise reasonable care in conducting the tests? Explain. [*Devine v. Roche Biomedical Laboratories*, 659 A.2d 868 (Me. 1995)] **(See page 260.)**

9–4 Liquidated Damages. Planned Pethood Plus, Inc. (PPP), a veterinary clinic, borrowed $389,000 from KeyBank. The term of the loan was ten years. A "prepayment penalty" clause provided a formula to add an amount to the balance due if PPP offered to repay its loan early. The additional amount depended on the time of the prepayment. Such clauses are common in loan agreements. After one year, PPP offered to pay its loan. KeyBank applied the formula to add $40,525.92 to the balance due. Is this a penalty or liquidated damages? Explain. [*Planned Pethood Plus, Inc. v. KeyCorp, Inc.*, 228 P.3d 262 (Colo.App. 2010)] **(See pages 272–273.)**

9–5 Conditions of Performance. James Maciel leased an apartment in Regent Village, a university-owned housing facility for Regent University (RU) students in Virginia Beach, Virginia. The lease ran until the end of the fall semester. Maciel had an option to renew the lease semester by semester as long as he maintained his status as an RU student. When Maciel completed his coursework for the spring semester, he told RU that he intended to withdraw. The university told him that he could stay in the apartment until May 31, the final day of the spring semester. Maciel asked for two additional weeks, but the university denied the request. On June 1, RU changed the locks on the apartment. Maciel entered through a window and e-mailed the university that he planned to stay "for another one or two weeks." When he was charged with trespassing, Maciel argued that he had "legal authority" to occupy the apartment. Was Maciel correct? Explain. [*Maciel v. Commonwealth*, __ S.E.2d __ (Va.App. 2011)] **(See pages 262–263.)**

9–6 Damages. Before buying a house, Dean and Donna Testa hired Ground Systems, Inc. (GSI), to inspect the sewage and water disposal system. GSI reported a split system with a watertight septic tank, a wastewater tank, a distribution box, and a leach field. The Testas bought the house. Later, Dean saw that the system was not as GSI described—there was no distribution box or leach field, and there was only one tank, which was not watertight. The Testas arranged for the installation of a new system and sold the house. Assuming that GSI is liable for breach of contract, what is the measure of damages? [*Testa v. Ground Systems, Inc.*, 206 N.J. 330, 20 A.3d 435 (App.Div. 2011)] **(See pages 269–271.)**

9–7 ⚖ Case Problem with Sample Answer—Consequential Damages. After submitting the high bid at a foreclosure sale, David Simard entered into a contract to purchase real property in Maryland for $192,000. Simard defaulted (failed to pay) on the contract, so a state court ordered the property to be resold at Simard's expense, as required by state law. The property was then resold for $163,000, but the second purchaser also defaulted on his contract. The court then ordered a second resale, resulting in a final price of $130,000. Assuming that Simard is liable for consequential damages, what is the extent of his liability? Is he liable for losses and expenses related to the first resale? If so, is he also liable for losses and expenses related to the second resale? Why or why not? [*Burson v. Simard*, 35 A.3d 1154 (Md. 2012)] **(See pages 271–272.)**

—For a sample answer to Problem 9–7, go to Appendix H at the end of this text.

9–8   ⬌ **A Question of Ethics—Assignment and Delegation.** Premier Building & Development, Inc., entered a listing agreement giving Sunset Gold Realty, LLC, the exclusive right to find a tenant for some commercial property. The terms of the listing agreement stated that it was binding on both parties and "their . . . assigns." Premier Building did not own the property at the time, but had an option to purchase it. To secure financing for the project, Premier Building established a new company called Cobblestone Associates. Premier Building then bought the property and conveyed it to Cobblestone. Meanwhile, Sunset Gold found a tenant for the property, and Cobblestone became the landlord. Cobblestone acknowledged its obligation to pay Sunset Gold for finding a tenant, but it later refused to pay Sunset Gold's commission. Sunset Gold then sued Premier Building and Cobblestone for breach of the listing agreement. [*Sunset Gold Realty, LLC v. Premier Building & Development, Inc.,* 133 Conn.App. 445, 36 A.3d 243 (2012)] **(See pages 255–259.)**

1. Is Premier Building relieved of its contractual duties if it assigned the contract to Cobblestone? Why or why not?
2. Given that Sunset Gold performed its obligations under the listing agreement, did Cobblestone behave unethically in refusing to pay Sunset Gold's commission? Why or why not?

Critical Thinking and Writing Assignments

9–9   **Critical Legal Thinking.** The concept of substantial performance permits a party to be discharged from a contract even though the party has not fully performed her or his obligations according to the contract's terms. Is this fair? Why or why not? What policy interests are at issue here? **(See page 264.)**

9–10   💡 **Business Law Critical Thinking Group Assignment.** ABC Clothiers, Inc., has a contract with John Taylor, owner of Taylor & Sons, a retailer, to deliver one thousand summer suits to Taylor's place of business on or before May 1. On April 1, John receives a letter from ABC informing him that ABC will not be able to make the delivery as scheduled. John is very upset, as he had planned a big ad campaign.

1. The first group will discuss whether John Taylor can immediately sue ABC for breach of contract (on April 2).
2. Now suppose that John Taylor's son, Tom, tells his father that they cannot file a lawsuit until ABC actually fails to deliver the suits on May 1. The second group will decide who is correct, John or Tom.
3. Assume that Taylor & Sons can either file immediately or wait until ABC fails to deliver the goods. The third group will evaluate which course of action is better, given the circumstances.

Appendix to Chapter 9:

An Annotated Employment Contract

As the text and cases in Chapters 7 through 9 have indicated, businesses use contracts to make their transactions more predictable. Contracts allow parties to clarify their obligations in great detail. Businesses also use contracts to resolve anticipated problems or conflicts and to clarify responsibility in the event of a breach. An understanding of what is in a typical contract is crucial to using contracts effectively.

Being able to read and understand a contract takes some practice, however. Contract terms often are highly technical and complex, and sometimes the vocabulary and phrasing can be unfamiliar. Nevertheless, businesspersons need to be able to understand the meaning of various contract provisions so that they will know what their business's obligations and rights are under the contract.

Reading a Contract

A contract is generally intended to serve two purposes:

1. To achieve some commercial purpose—such as a sale of goods, a lease of property, or an employment agreement.
2. To prevent future conflict by clarifying the obligations and rights of the parties.

Parties should address the details of the business agreement and also should think strategically about how a conflict should be resolved if something goes awry.

Different types of contracts will have different provisions. Sales contracts should contain information on the products being sold, the quantity, the price, and delivery terms. Employment contracts may contain information on the term of employment, employment duties, confidentiality and nondisclosure of the employer's documents and information, and restrictions on competing with the employer after leaving the position.

Although standard forms exist for many types of contracts, the parties to a particular contract may have specific requirements and thus may need to tailor the contract to fit their transaction. A larger transaction or more specialized goods or real estate will require a more specific and probably longer contract. For example, a sales contract between Airbus and American Airlines for the sale of an Airbus S.A.S. plane had more than 109 pages, not counting the eleven exhibits that followed the main contract.[1]

Regardless of the specificity of the contract provisions, it is important for a businessperson to read and evaluate the responsibilities or commitments of both parties to the contract. Sometimes, a single word or phrase can make an enormous difference. For example, a rental contract for a house may state that the owner is responsible for any plumbing issues, or it may specify that the renter is the responsible party. If a plumber has to be called to deal with clogged pipes on a holiday, that single phrase in the contract will determine who has to pay the plumber's very high holiday rates.

---

1. "Sample Business Contracts," *www.onecle.com*, July 14, 2012.

Usually, a person signs a contract after having reviewed it in detail (or after having an attorney review it).

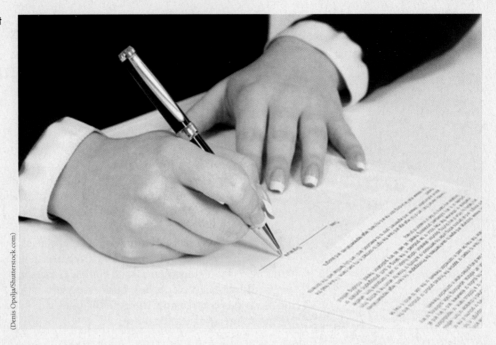

(Denis Opolja/Shutterstock.com)

Contract Analysis Exercise

The sample contract on pages 287–290 is based on an actual employment-related contract between a company and its chief financial officer (CFO). As you read the contract, think about the following questions:

1. Which party seems to have had the stronger bargaining position, and why?
2. Which specific provisions favor the employer?
3. Which specific provisions favor the employee?
4. The parties' main intentions in signing this contract were to protect the firm's confidential information and to explain how the CFO could use that information. Which provisions are related to those two purposes?
5. Which provisions seem entirely unrelated to the main purposes? Why are these other provisions included in the contract? What do they do for the parties?
6. What terms in the contract do you find difficult to understand?
7. As a potential employee being asked to sign this agreement, what concerns might you have?
8. Suppose that after one year the employee resigns from the company. Certain provisions of this contract will affect the employee's future, and the employee should review them before resigning. What are these provisions? When leaving the company, what actions should the employee take to ensure that he or she is in compliance with all obligations?

SEE SAMPLE CONTRACT ON THE FOLLOWING PAGES.

EMPLOYEE NONCOMPETITION
AND NONDISCLOSURE AGREEMENT

In consideration of my employment or continued employment, with Boulder Dry (the "Company"), and the compensation received from the Company, I hereby agree as follows:

1. *Proprietary Information and Inventions:* I understand and acknowledge that:

   A. The Company is engaged in research, development, production, marketing, and servicing. I am expected to make new contributions and inventions of value to the Company as part of my employment.

   B. My employment creates a relationship of trust between the Company and me with respect to information that may be made known to me or learned by me during my employment.

   C. The Company possesses information that has been discovered or developed by the Company that has commercial value to the Company and is treated by the Company as confidential. All such information is hereinafter called "Proprietary Information," which term shall include, but shall not be limited to, systems, processes, data, computer programs, discoveries, marketing plans, strategies, forecasts, new products, unpublished financial statements, licenses, and customer and supplier lists. The term "Proprietary Information" shall not include any of the foregoing that is in the public domain.

   D. All existing confidential lists of customers of the Company, and all confidential lists of customers developed during my employment, are the sole and exclusive property of the Company and I shall not have any right, title, or interest therein.

2. *Ownership of Proprietary Information:* All Proprietary Information shall be the sole property of the Company, including patents, copyrights, and trademarks. I hereby assign to the Company any rights I may have or acquire in such Proprietary Information. Both during and after my employment, I will keep in strictest confidence and trust all Proprietary Information. I will not use or disclose any Proprietary Information without the written consent of the Company, except as may be necessary in performing my duties as a Company employee.

3. *Commitment to Company and Other Employment:* During my employment, I will devote substantially all of my time to the Company, and I will not, without the Company's prior written consent, engage in any employment or business other than for the Company.

4. *Documentation:* Upon the termination of my employment, I will deliver to the Company all documents, computer programs, data, and other materials of any nature pertaining to my work with the Company. I will not take any originals or reproductions of the foregoing that are embodied in a tangible medium of expression.

5. *Disclosure of Inventions:* I will promptly disclose to the Company all discoveries, designs, inventions, blueprints, computer programs, and data ("Inventions") made by me, either alone or jointly with others, during my employment. Inventions include by definition those things that are related to the business of the Company or that result from the use of property owned, leased, or contracted for by the Company.

6. *Ownership of Inventions:* All Inventions shall be the sole property of the Company, and the Company shall be the sole owner of all patents, copyrights, trademarks, and other rights. I assign to the Company any rights I may have or acquire in such Inventions. I shall assist the Company to obtain and enforce patents, copyrights, trademarks, and other rights and protections relating to Inventions. This obligation shall continue beyond the termination of my employment, but the Company shall compensate me at a reasonable rate after my termination.

7. *Other Agreements:* I represent and warrant that this Agreement and the performance of it do not breach any other agreement to which I am a party. I have not entered into and shall not enter into any agreement in conflict with this Agreement.

8. *Use of Confidential Information of Other Persons:* I have not brought and will not bring with me to the Company any materials or documents of an employer or a former employer that are not generally available to the public. If I desire or need to use any materials from a prior employer, I will obtain express written authorization from such employer.

9. *Restrictive Covenant:* I hereby acknowledge my possession of Proprietary Information and the highly competitive nature of the business of the Company. I will not, during my employment and for three (3) years following my termination, directly or indirectly engage in any competitive business or assist others in engaging in any competitive business. I understand that this Section is not meant to prevent me from earning a living. It does intend to prevent any competitive business from gaining any unfair advantage from my knowledge of Proprietary Information. I understand that by making my new employer aware of the provisions of this Section 9, that employer can take such action as to avoid my breaching the provisions hereof and to indemnify me in the event of a breach.

COMMENTS TO CONTRACT PARAGRAPHS

Paragraph 1A. This is essentially a broad description of the employee's role at the company and explains why this agreement is necessary. Often, a clause like this precedes a statement indicating that the employer gets to keep any value that the employee adds to the firm.

Paragraph 1B. This paragraph establishes that a relationship of trust and confidence exists between employer and employee. Through this clause, both parties are agreeing they owe duties to each other related to information that benefits the company. The clause implies that that there will be negative consequences for the employee if he or she breaks that relationship.

Paragraph 1C. This paragraph establishes what the term "Proprietary Information" means. In contracts, terms that are capitalized and placed in quotation marks (sometimes in parentheses as well) are called "defined terms." Whenever the term "Proprietary Information" appears throughout the rest of the contract, it will have the definition set out in this paragraph. The definition is extremely broad and captures almost any intellectual property, data, and similar items. The contract asserts that this information is important to the business and gives the company some strategic advantage.

Paragraph 1D. This clause clarifies that customer lists belong to the employer even if the employee develops or expands the lists in some way. This may become important if the employee leaves the company because the clause clarifies that the employee may not recruit or "steal" customers.

Paragraph 2. Here, we see the defined term "Proprietary Information" again. This paragraph documents that the employer owns all Proprietary Information, as defined, even if it was created by the employee. Further, the employee agrees to give the employer any legal rights that the employee may obtain to any Proprietary Information.

Paragraph 3. In this clause, the employee promises that he or she will work full-time for the employer and will not take any additional employment without the employer's permission.

Paragraph 4. This clause further asserts that the company takes the confidential nature of the Proprietary Information seriously. Here, the employee promises that if he or she leaves the company's employment, he or she will turn over any work-related material to the company.

Paragraph 5. If the employee creates something of any kind at work, he or she must tell the employer about it, and the employer will receive any disclosures confidentially. The contract goes out of its way to ensure that almost anything the employee invents at work or that is related to work fits under this paragraph. Such items are given a new term called "Inventions." Note that the definition of inventions includes the same items that are in the definition of Proprietary Information as well as some additional ones. The paragraphs discussing Proprietary Information deal with information that the company already possesses and will continue to possess and that the employee will access or need. This paragraph expands the obligations of the employee to what could be called new proprietary information, defined as "Inventions."

Paragraph 6. Just as the employee agreed to give any right in already existing information (such as a modified customer list) to the employer, here the employee promises to give all legal rights to inventions to the employer. In addition, because the rights may originally belong to the employee, the employee promises to help the employer secure any rights or protections necessary to increase the value of the invention. This obligation to help the employer continues to exist after the employee leaves the firm, and the employer agrees to pay for the work required in that situation. The employer is making sure that it can keep anything the employee invents during work time or with company resources.

Paragraph 7. The employer wants to ensure that this contract does not conflict with any others the employee may have already signed. Here, the employee affirms that he or she has made no conflicting agreements. The clause implies that the employee will be responsible for any consequences that arise from such conflicts.

Paragraph 8. The employer does not want to become involved in a dispute with another company by hiring this employee. In this clause, the employee states that he or she is not bringing the employer any confidential information belonging to someone else.

Paragraph 9. This paragraph is a covenant not to compete, one of the most important provisions from the perspective of the employee. Employers worry that former employees will join a rival company and take their information and expertise with them. A covenant not to compete helps prevent that from happening. In short, a covenant not to compete prohibits an employee from working for a competing business for a specified time. This covenant applies regardless of whether the employee leaves the company or is terminated. Covenants not to compete have to be carefully drafted. A court will not enforce a covenant that is too broad in its coverage or that lasts for too long. Three years, the length of this covenant not to compete, is not unduly long. If the covenant is challenged, however, the employer will have to show that this length of time was necessary to protect its business interests. Employees do not appreciate covenants not to compete, but find that they are an inevitable part of employment in information-sensitive industries.

10. *Agreement Not to Solicit Customers:* During the course of my employment and for a period of three (3) years following my termination, I will not attempt to solicit any person, firm, or corporation that has been a customer account of the Company.

11. *Remedies:* I acknowledge that a remedy at law for any breach or threatened breach of the provisions of this Agreement would be inadequate. I therefore agree that the Company shall be entitled to injunctive relief in addition to any other available rights and remedies in case of any such breach or threatened breach. Nothing contained herein shall be construed as prohibiting the Company from pursuing any other remedies available for any such breach or threatened breach.

12. *Assignment:* This Agreement and the rights and obligations of the parties hereto shall bind and inure to the benefit of any successor(s) of the Company, whether by reorganization, merger, consolidation, sale of assets, or otherwise. Neither this Agreement nor any rights or benefits hereunder may be assigned by me.

13. *Interpretation:* It is the desire and intent of the parties hereto that the provisions of this Agreement shall be enforced to the fullest extent permissible. Accordingly, if any provision of this Agreement shall be adjudicated to be invalid or unenforceable, such provision shall be deemed deleted. Such deletion will apply only to the deleted provision in the particular jurisdiction in which such adjudication is made. If any provision contained herein shall be held to be excessively broad as to duration, geographical scope, activity, or subject, it shall be construed by limiting and reducing it so as to be enforceable.

14. *Notices:* All notices pursuant to this Agreement shall be given by personal delivery or by certified mail, return receipt requested. Notices to the Employee shall be addressed to the Employee at the address of record with the Company. Notices to the Company shall be addressed to its principal office. The date of personal delivery or the date of mailing any such notice shall be deemed to be the date of delivery thereof.

15. *Waivers:* Any waiver of breach of any provision of this Agreement shall not thereby be deemed a waiver of any preceding or succeeding breach of the same or any other provision of this Agreement.

16. *Headings:* The headings of the sections hereof are inserted for convenience only and shall not be deemed to constitute a part hereof nor to affect the meaning hereof.

17. *Governing Law:* This Agreement shall be governed by and construed and enforced in accordance with the laws of the State of New Hampshire.

18. *No Employment Agreement:* I acknowledge that this Agreement does not constitute an employment agreement. This Agreement shall be binding upon me regardless of whether my employment shall continue for any length of time and whether my employment is terminated for any reason whatsoever. This is true whether my employment is terminated by the Company or by me.

19. *Complete Agreement, Amendments, and Prior Agreements:* The foregoing is the entire agreement of the parties with respect to the subject matter hereof and may not be amended, supplemented, canceled, or discharged except by written instrument executed by both parties hereto. This Agreement supersedes any and all prior agreements between the parties hereto with respect to the matters covered hereby.

Date: _____   Employee: _____

Accepted and agreed to as of this date by Company:

Date: _____   By: _____

Name: _____

Title: _____

Paragraph 10.   Similar to a covenant not to compete, this clause prohibits an employee from soliciting the company's customers during his or her employment or for up to three years afterward. Without such protection, an employer would be vulnerable to any former employee taking customer lists and using them to solicit customers at a new employer or at his or her own business.

Paragraph 11.   This paragraph allows the employer to seek injunctive relief against the employee, should it be necessary. The employee agrees that the employer not only may seek monetary damages from the employee in the event that this agreement is breached but also may prohibit him or her from engaging in whatever behavior violates the contract. Recall that typically the first line of remedies is damages to compensate for injury. Here, the parties are acknowledging in advance (for the benefit of any court that later is involved) that the harm caused by a breach of the contract cannot be compensated or corrected with monetary damages.

Paragraph 12.   Companies change, and so do their owners. This paragraph states that the contract will survive even if ownership of the company changes due to a merger, reorganization, or other reason. The employee cannot avoid this contract simply because the owner that signed the agreement later sells the company to someone else. This paragraph and many of the subsequent paragraphs are often referred to as "boilerplate language," meaning provisions that appear in some form in many contracts. They are included because conflicts have arisen over these points in the past and courts have interpreted contracts without this language in a way that the parties want to avoid. Boilerplate language can be very dangerous because parties may see the headings and not read further because the language is similar from contract to contract. But boilerplate language can make a difference in which party later wins a dispute (because the language spells out the law that will be used to interpret the contract, where a case must be brought, the proper way to give notice of changes, and the like).

Paragraph 13.   Employers know that even the most carefully drafted agreements can sometimes be rendered unenforceable by a reviewing court. Laws change over time, and so do attitudes toward contract terms. This paragraph states that if part of this contract is rendered unenforceable for some reason, the rest of the contract will survive intact (that is, the unenforceable part of the contract is severable). The paragraph specifically references the covenant not to compete and the prohibition against solicitation. If a court rejects those terms as too broad in scope or too lengthy, the parties agree that the court should adjust the clause in order to make it enforceable under the law.

Paragraph 14.   This paragraph deals with notices. If the employer or the employee wants to communicate about the contract, the communication must be sent by personal delivery or registered/certified mail. Note that this means that an e-mail is not sufficient notice under this agreeement.

Paragraph 15.   This paragraph says "any party," but it is really meant to protect the employer. Sometimes, through generosity or neglect, employers fail to enforce every clause of a contract. For example, an employer may allow a former employee to start a competing business earlier than the contract states or permit an employee to take a second job. This paragraph ensures that if the employer allows some action that is prohibited in the contract, that does not mean that the contract term is waived forever. Just because the employer does not fully enforce the contract every time does not necessarily mean the employer is barred from doing so in the future.

Paragraph 16.   This clause is meant to clarify that the headings are just headings and do not change the interpretation of the language in the paragraphs or the overall meaning of the contract.

Paragraph 17.   This contract will be interpreted using the law of the state of New Hampshire. It is likely that the employer selected New Hampshire for some particular reason. Typically, an employer chooses a state where the law provides the most benefits for the employer. For example, employers typically choose the law of a particular state because it is their geographic home state and the employer's lawyers are familiar with its law. Employers may also choose a legal jurisdiction because its laws create a climate that is more favorable to the employer than the employee.

Paragraph 18.   In this paragraph, the employee acknowledges that this contract is about nondisclosure of information and does not constitute an employment agreement that promises any length of service or any promise of continued employment.

Paragraph 19.   This paragraph states that this contract is the complete agreement between the employer and the employee. Any other side agreements, e-mails, conversations, or other communications are irrelevant. The employee cannot rely on a manager's promise of a particular salary or terms of a covenant not to compete. This agreement is the final statement of the relationship between the employer and the employee.

CHAPTER 10

Sales and Lease Contracts

(Matthew Staver/Landov)

CHAPTER OUTLINE

- The Scope of the UCC and Articles 2 (Sales) and 2A (Leases)
- The Formation of Sales and Lease Contracts
- Title and Risk of Loss
- Contracts for the International Sale of Goods

LEARNING OBJECTIVES

The five learning objectives below are designed to help improve your understanding of the chapter. After reading this chapter, you should be able to answer the following questions:

1 How do Article 2 and Article 2A of the UCC differ? What types of transactions does each article cover?

2 In a sales contract, if an offeree includes additional or different terms in an acceptance, will a contract result? If so, what happens to these terms?

3 What exceptions to the writing requirements of the Statute of Frauds are provided in Article 2 and Article 2A of the UCC?

4 Risk of loss does not necessarily pass with title. If the parties to a contract do not expressly agree when risk passes and the goods are to be delivered without movement by the seller, when does risk pass?

5 What law governs contracts for the international sale of goods?

"I am for free commerce with all nations."
—George Washington, 1732–1799 (First president of the United States, 1789–1797)

The chapter-opening quotation echoes a sentiment that most Americans believe— free commerce will benefit our nation. This is particularly true with respect to the Uniform Commercial Code (UCC). The UCC facilitates commercial transactions by making the laws governing sales and lease contracts uniform and, as far as possible, clear, simple, and readily applicable to the numerous difficulties that can arise during such transactions.

Recall from Chapter 1 that the UCC is one of many uniform (model) acts drafted by the National Conference of Commissioners on Uniform State Laws and submitted to the states for adoption. Once a state legislature has adopted a uniform act, the act becomes statutory law in that state. Thus, when we turn to sales and lease contracts, we move away from common law principles and into the area of statutory law.

The Scope of the UCC and Articles 2 (Sales) and 2A (Leases)

The UCC attempts to provide a consistent, integrated framework of rules to deal with all phases ordinarily arising in a commercial sales or lease transaction. For example, consider the following events, all of which may occur during a single transaction:

1. *A contract for the sale or lease of goods is formed and executed.* Article 2 and Article 2A of the UCC provide rules governing all aspects of this transaction.
2. *The transaction may involve a payment—by check, electronic fund transfer, or other means.* Article 3 (on negotiable instruments), Article 4 (on bank deposits and collections), Article 4A (on fund transfers), and Article 5 (on letters of credit) cover this part of the transaction.
3. *The transaction may involve a bill of lading or a warehouse receipt that covers goods when they are shipped or stored.* Article 7 (on documents of title) deals with this subject.
4. *The transaction may involve a demand by the seller or lender for some form of security for the remaining balance owed.* Article 9 (on secured transactions) covers this part of the transaction.

The UCC has been adopted in whole or in part by all of the states.[1] Because of its importance in the area of commercial transactions, we present the UCC as this chapter's *Landmark in the Law* feature on the facing page.

Article 2—Sales

Sales Contract A contract for the sale of goods.

Article 2 of the UCC governs **sales contracts,** or contracts for the sale of goods. To facilitate commercial transactions, Article 2 modifies some of the common law contract requirements that were discussed in Chapters 7 through 9. To the extent that it has not been modified by the UCC, however, the common law of contracts also applies to sales contracts.

In general, the rule is that when a UCC provision addresses a certain issue, the UCC governs, but when the UCC is silent, the common law governs. The relationship between general contract law and the law governing sales of goods is illustrated in Exhibit 10.1 on the facing page. (For a discussion of an issue involving state taxation of sales that take place over the Internet, see this chapter's *Adapting the Law to the Online Environment* feature on page 294.)

Keep in mind that Article 2 deals with the sale of *goods*—it does not deal with real property (real estate), services, or intangible property such as stocks and bonds. Thus, if a dispute involves real estate or services, the common law applies. Also note that in some situations, the rules under the UCC can vary quite a bit depending on whether the buyer or the seller is a merchant. We look now at how the UCC defines a *sale, goods,* and *merchant status.*

Sale The passing of title to property from the seller to the buyer for a price.

What Is a Sale?   The UCC defines a **sale** as "the passing of title [evidence of ownership] from the seller to the buyer for a price" [UCC 2–106(1)]. The price may be payable in cash (or its equivalent) or in other goods or services.

Tangible Property Property that has physical existence and can be distinguished by the senses of touch and sight.

What Are Goods?   To be characterized as a *good,* the item of property must be *tangible,* and it must be *movable.*

Intangible Property Property that cannot be seen or touched but exists only conceptually, such as corporate stocks. Such property is not governed by Article 2 of the UCC.

Tangible and Movable Property   **Tangible property** has physical existence—it can be touched or seen. **Intangible property**—such as corporate stocks and bonds, patents and

---

1. Louisiana has not adopted Articles 2 and 2A, however.

LANDMARK IN THE LAW
The Uniform Commercial Code

Of all the attempts to produce a uniform body of laws relating to commercial transactions in the United States, none has been as comprehensive or successful as the Uniform Commercial Code (UCC).

The Origins of the UCC The UCC was the brainchild of William A. Schnader, president of the National Conference of Commissioners on Uniform State Laws (NCCUSL). The drafting of the UCC began in 1945. The most significant individual involved in the project was its chief editor, Karl N. Llewellyn of the Columbia University Law School. Llewellyn's intellect, continuous efforts, and ability to compromise made the first version of the UCC—completed in 1949—a legal landmark. Over the next several years, the UCC was substantially accepted by almost every state in the nation.

Periodic Changes and Updates Various articles and sections of the UCC are periodically changed or supplemented to clarify certain rules or to establish new rules when changes in

business customs render the existing UCC provisions inapplicable. For example, because of the increasing importance of leases of goods in the commercial context, Article 2A governing leases was added to the UCC. To clarify the rights of parties to commercial fund transfers, particularly electronic fund transfers, Article 4A was issued. Articles 3 and 4, on negotiable instruments and banking relationships, underwent significant revision in the 1990s. Because of other changes in business and in the law, the NCCUSL has recommended the repeal of Article 6 (on bulk transfers) and has offered a revised Article 6 to those states that prefer not to repeal it. The NCCUSL has also revised Article 9, covering secured transactions. The revised Article 9 has been adopted by all of the states.

Application to Today's World *By periodically revising the UCC's articles, the NCCUSL has been able to adapt its provisions to changing business customs and practices. UCC provisions governing sales and lease contracts have also been extended to contracts formed in the online environment.*

Exhibit 10.1 The Law Governing Contracts

This exhibit graphically illustrates the relationship between general contract law and statutory law (UCC Articles 2 and 2A) governing contracts for the sale and lease of goods. Sales contracts are not governed exclusively by Article 2 of the UCC but are also governed by general contract law whenever it is relevant and has not been modified by the UCC.

ADAPTING THE LAW TO THE ONLINE ENVIRONMENT

LOCAL GOVERNMENTS ATTEMPT TO TAX ONLINE TRAVEL COMPANIES

A battle is raging across the United States between state and local governments and online retailers. The online retailers claim that because they do not have a physical presence in a state, they should not have to collect state and local taxes for the goods and services they sell. Although most states have laws that require their residents to report online purchases and pay taxes on them (so-called use taxes), few U.S. consumers comply with these laws.

Local Governments Sue Online Travel Companies

Travelocity, Priceline.com, Hotels.com, and Orbitz.com are online travel companies (OTCs) that offer, among other things, hotel booking services. By 2013, more than twenty cities, including Atlanta, Charleston, Philadelphia, and San Antonio, had filed suits claiming that the OTCs owed taxes on hotel reservations that they had booked. All of the cities involved in the suits impose a hotel occupancy tax, which is essentially a sales tax.

The issue is not whether the OTCs should pay the tax but rather how it should be assessed and collected. OTCs typically purchase blocks of hotel rooms at a wholesale rate and then resell the rooms to customers at a marked-up resale rate, keeping the difference as profit. The OTCs forward to the hotels an amount intended to cover the hotel occupancy tax (sales tax) based on the wholesale prices of the rooms sold. The hotels then remit to the city taxing authority the tax on the rooms sold by the OTCs.

The cities claim, however, that the OTCs should assess the occupancy tax rates on the retail prices that they charge, rather than on the wholesale prices of the rooms. Of course, the retail prices are higher, so the cities would collect more tax if the retail price is used as the base. The cities also want the OTCs to register with the local jurisdictions and to collect and remit the required taxes directly.

The Cities Are Losing in Court

When these lawsuits were first brought a few years ago, city governments generally obtained favorable rulings, both in federal district courts[a] and in state courts.[b] In contrast, when some of these suits were retried or reviewed by higher courts, the OTCs prevailed. In 2012, for example, the city of Goodlettsville, Tennessee, lost its continuing case against Priceline.com and nine other OTCs. In siding with the OTCs, the court said, "If the Tennessee legislature intends to permit its political subdivisions to tax the retail rate paid by the consumers to the OTCs for hotel bookings, the legislature may do so through appropriate statutory language."[c]

In contrast, when the South Carolina Department of Revenue sued Travelscape, LLC, the Supreme Court of South Carolina held that the OTC had to remit taxes based on the retail price of the hotel rooms sold.[d] The South Carolina decision reflected a minority opinion, however. As of early 2012, the OTCs had prevailed in fifteen of nineteen cases nationwide.

Critical Thinking

What are possible benefits if cities and states do not impose a sales tax on the difference between the wholesale price of rooms and the retail price of rooms sold by OTCs?

---

a. See, for example, *City of Goodlettsville v. Priceline.com, Inc.,* 605 F.Supp.2d 982 (M.D.Tenn. 2009).

b. See *City of Atlanta v. Hotels.com, L.P.,* 285 Ga. 231, 674 S.E.2d 898 (2009).

c. *City of Goodlettsville v. Priceline.com, Inc.,* 2012 WL 573681 (M.D.Tenn. 2012).

d. *Travelscape, LLC v. South Carolina Department of Revenue,* 391 S.C. 89, 705 S.E.2d 28 (2011).

---

copyrights, and ordinary contract rights—has only conceptual existence and thus does not come under Article 2. A movable item can be carried from place to place (real estate is therefore excluded from Article 2).

Goods *associated* with real estate often fall within the scope of Article 2, however [UCC 2–107]. For instance, a contract for the sale of minerals, oil, or natural gas is a contract for the sale of goods if *severance, or separation, is to be made by the seller.* Similarly, a contract for the sale of growing crops or timber to be cut is a contract for the sale of goods *regardless of who severs them from the land.*

Predominant-Factor Test A test courts use to determine whether a contract is primarily for the sale of goods or for the sale of services.

Goods and Services Combined   In cases involving contracts in which goods and services are combined, courts generally use the **predominant-factor test** to determine whether a

If a couple buys a concessions business that includes a truck, trailer, and tables and chairs, would this purchase be a sale of goods or of services?

contract is primarily for the sale of goods or for the sale of services.[2] This determination is important because the UCC will apply to services provided under a mixed contract that is predominantly for goods, even though the majority of courts treat services as being excluded by the UCC.

If Contract Is Primarily for Goods, UCC Applies to All Disputes If a court decides that a mixed contract is primarily a goods contract, *any* dispute, even a dispute over the services portion, will be decided under the UCC. **CASE EXAMPLE 10.1** Gene and Martha Jannusch agreed to sell Festival Foods, a concessions business, to Lindsey and Louann Naffziger for a price of $150,000. The deal included a truck, a trailer, freezers, roasters, chairs, tables, a fountain service, signs, and lighting. The Naffzigers paid $10,000 down with the balance to come from a bank loan. They took possession of the equipment and began to use it immediately in Festival Foods operations at various events.

After six events, the Naffzigers returned the truck and all the equipment and wanted out of the deal because the business did not generate as much income as they expected. The Jannusches sued the Naffzigers for the balance due on the purchase price, claiming that the Naffzigers could no longer reject the goods under the UCC. The Naffzigers claimed that the UCC did not apply because the deal primarily involved the sale of a business rather than the sale of goods. The court found that the UCC governed under the predominant-factor test. The primary value of the contract was in the goods, not the value of the business. The parties had agreed on the essential terms of the contract (such as the price). Thus, a contract had been formed, and the Naffzigers had breached it. The Naffzigers took possession of the business and had no right to return it.[3] •

Who Is a Merchant?

Article 2 governs the sale of goods in general. It applies to sales transactions between all buyers and sellers. In a limited number of instances, however, the UCC presumes that certain special business standards ought to be imposed on merchants because they possess a relatively high degree of commercial expertise.[4] Such standards do not apply to the casual or inexperienced seller or buyer (a "consumer"). Section 2–104 sets out three ways in which merchant status can arise:

1. A merchant is a person who *deals in goods of the kind* involved in the sales contract. Thus, a retailer, a wholesaler, or a manufacturer is a merchant of those goods sold in the business. A merchant for one type of goods is not necessarily a merchant for another type. For instance, a sporting equipment retailer is a merchant when selling tennis rackets but not when selling a used iPad.
2. A merchant is a person who, by occupation, *holds himself or herself out as having special knowledge and skill* related to the practices or goods involved in the transaction. Note that this broad definition may include banks or universities as merchants.
3. A person who *employs a merchant as a broker, agent, or other intermediary* has the status of merchant in that transaction. Hence, if an art collector hires a broker to purchase or sell art for her, the collector is considered a merchant in the transaction.

Merchant Under the UCC, a person who deals in goods of the kind involved in the sales contract or who holds herself or himself out as having skill or knowledge peculiar to the practices or goods being purchased or sold.

In summary, a person is a **merchant** when she or he, acting in a mercantile (commercial) capacity, possesses or uses an expertise specifically related to the goods being sold. This basic distinction is not always clear-cut. For instance, state courts appear to be split on whether farmers should be considered merchants.

---

2. UCC 2–314(1) does stipulate that serving food or drinks is a "sale of goods" for purposes of the implied warranty of merchantability, as will be discussed in Chapter 12. The UCC also specifies that selling unborn animals and rare coins qualifies as a "sale of goods."
3. *Jannusch v. Naffziger,* 379 Ill.App.3d 381, 883 N.E.2d 711 (2008).
4. The provisions that apply only to merchants deal principally with the Statute of Frauds, firm offers, confirmatory memorandums, warranties, and contract modifications. These special rules reflect expedient business practices commonly known to merchants in the commercial setting. They will be discussed later in this chapter.

ETHICAL ISSUE

Should merchants be allowed to use buying patterns to learn personal information about their customers, such as whether they are pregnant? Whether you shop on the Internet or in stores, most major retailers compile information about you based on what, when, and how you buy. Sometimes, based on your purchases, you will instantly be given printed coupons at the cash register. These customized coupons reflect your preferences based on past behavior. If you regularly use Amazon.com, for instance, you receive customized offers every time you visit that site.

Target Brands, Inc., uses a very sophisticated data collection process that assigns each shopper a unique guest identification code. Over time, a shopper's habits become the source of predictions for future consumer behavior. For example, Target can accurately predict which female shoppers are pregnant based on their recent purchases of vitamin and mineral supplements. When Target's system detects a buying pattern suggesting that a customer is pregnant, it starts offering coupons for baby-related products and services.

A father in Minneapolis, Minnesota, complained to a Target manager that his daughter was receiving such coupons for no reason. In reality, Target's system had accurately discovered his daughter's pregnancy. The father was even more furious that his daughter had lied to him. Was Target's action legal? Probably, it was. Target had complied with the relevant federal and state privacy laws. Current laws even allow retailers to share their customer data with affiliate companies.

The Scope of Article 2A—Leases

Leases of personal property (goods) have become increasingly common. In this context, a **lease** is a transfer of the right to possess and use goods for a period of time in exchange for payment. Article 2A of the UCC was created to fill the need for uniform guidelines in this area.

Article 2A covers any transaction that creates a lease of goods, as well as subleases of goods [UCC 2A–102, 2A–103(1)(k)]. Except that it applies to leases, rather than sales, of goods, Article 2A is essentially a repetition of Article 2 and varies only to reflect differences between sales and lease transactions. (Note that Article 2A is not concerned with leases of real property, such as land or buildings. The laws governing leases of real property will be discussed in Chapter 24.)

Definition of a Lease Agreement
Article 2A defines a **lease agreement** as the bargain between a lessor and a lessee with respect to the lease of goods, as found in their language and as implied by other circumstances, including course of dealing and usage of trade or course of performance [UCC 2A–103(1)(k)]. A **lessor** is one who transfers the right to the possession and use of goods under a lease [UCC 2A–103(1)(p)]. A **lessee** is one who acquires the right to the temporary possession and use of goods under a lease [UCC 2A–103(1)(o)].

In other words, the lessee is the party who is leasing the goods from the lessor. Article 2A applies to all types of leases of goods, including commercial leases and consumer leases. Special rules apply to certain types of leases, however, including consumer leases.

Consumer Leases
Under UCC 2A–103(1)(e), *a consumer lease* involves three elements:

1. A lessor who regularly engages in the business of leasing or selling.
2. A lessee (except an organization) who leases the goods "primarily for a personal, family, or household purpose."
3. Total lease payments that are less than a dollar amount set by state statute.

To ensure special protection for consumers, certain provisions of Article 2A apply only to consumer leases. For instance, one provision states that a consumer may recover attorneys' fees if a court finds that a term in a consumer lease contract is unconscionable [UCC 2A–108(4)(a)].

LEARNING OBJECTIVE 1
How do Article 2 and Article 2A of the UCC differ? What types of transactions does each article cover?

Lease Under Article 2A of the UCC, a transfer of the right to possess and use goods for a period of time in exchange for payment.

Lease Agreement An agreement in which one person (the lessor) agrees to transfer the right to the possession and use of property to another person (the lessee) in exchange for rental payments.

Lessor A person who transfers the right to the possession and use of goods to another in exchange for rental payments.

Lessee A person who acquires the right to the possession and use of another's goods in exchange for rental payments.

The Formation of Sales and Lease Contracts

In regard to the formation of sales and lease contracts, Article 2 and Article 2A of the UCC modify common law contract rules in several ways. Remember, though, that parties to sales contracts are normally free to establish whatever terms they wish.

The UCC comes into play only when the parties have failed to provide in their contract for a contingency that later gives rise to a dispute. The UCC makes this clear time and again by using such phrases as "unless the parties otherwise agree" or "absent a contrary agreement by the parties."

Offer

In general contract law, the moment a definite offer is met by an unqualified acceptance, a binding contract is formed. In commercial sales transactions, the verbal exchanges, correspondence, and actions of the parties may not reveal exactly when a binding contractual obligation arises. The UCC states that an agreement sufficient to constitute a contract can exist even if the moment of its making is undetermined [UCC 2–204(2), 2A–204(2)].

Open Terms   Remember from page 206 of Chapter 7 that under the common law of contracts, an offer must be definite enough for the parties (and the courts) to ascertain its essential terms when it is accepted. In contrast, the UCC states that a sales or lease contract will not fail for indefiniteness even if one or more terms are left open as long as (1) the parties intended to make a contract and (2) there is a reasonably certain basis for the court to grant an appropriate remedy [UCC 2–204(3), 2A–204(3)].

The UCC provides numerous *open-term* provisions (discussed next) that can be used to fill the gaps in a contract. Thus, if a dispute occurs, all that is necessary to prove the existence of a contract is an indication (such as a purchase order) that there is a contract. Missing terms can be proved by evidence, or a court can presume that the parties intended whatever is reasonable under the circumstances.

The *quantity* of goods involved must be expressly stated in the contract, however. If the quantity term is left open, the courts will have no basis for determining a remedy.

► KNOW THIS ◄

Under the UCC, it is the actions of the parties that determine whether they intended to form a contract.

Open Price Term   If the parties have not agreed on a price, the court will determine a "reasonable price at the time for delivery" [UCC 2–305(1)]. If either the buyer or the seller is to determine the price, the price is to be fixed (set) in good faith [UCC 2–305(2)]. Under the UCC, *good faith* means honesty in fact and the observance of reasonable commercial standards of fair dealing in the trade [UCC 2–103(1)(b)]. The concepts of *good faith* and *commercial reasonableness* permeate the UCC.

Sometimes, the price fails to be fixed (specified) through the fault of one of the parties. In that situation, the other party can treat the contract as canceled or specify a reasonable price. **EXAMPLE 10.2**   Perez and Merrick enter into a contract for the sale of unfinished doors and agree that Perez will determine the price. Perez refuses to specify the price. Merrick can either treat the contract as canceled or set a reasonable price [UCC 2–305(3)]. ●

Open Payment Term   When parties do not specify payment terms, payment is due at the time and place at which the buyer is to receive the goods [UCC 2–310(a)]. The buyer can tender payment using any commercially normal or acceptable means, such as a check or credit card. If the seller demands payment in cash, however, the buyer must be given a reasonable time to obtain it [UCC 2–511(2)].

CASE EXAMPLE 10.3 Max Alexander agreed to purchase hay from Wagner's farm. Alexander left his truck and trailer at the farm for the seller to load the hay. Nothing was said about when payment was due, and the parties were unaware of the UCC's rules. When Alexander came back to get the hay, a dispute broke out. Alexander claimed that he had been given less hay than he had ordered and argued that he did not have to pay at that time. Wagner refused to release the hay (or the vehicles on which the hay was loaded) until Alexander paid for it. Eventually, Alexander jumped into his truck and drove off without paying for the hay—for which he was later prosecuted for the crime of theft (see Chapter 6). Because the parties had failed to specify when payment was due, UCC 2–310(a) controlled, and payment was due at the time Alexander picked up the hay.[5] ●

Open Delivery Term   When no delivery terms are specified, the buyer normally takes delivery at the seller's place of business [UCC 2–308(a)]. If the seller has no place of business, the seller's residence is used. When goods are located in some other place and both parties know it, delivery is made there. If the time for shipment or delivery is not clearly specified in the sales contract, the court will infer a "reasonable" time for performance [UCC 2–309(1)].

Duration of an Ongoing Contract   A single contract might specify successive performances but not indicate how long the parties are required to deal with each other. In this situation, either party may terminate the ongoing contractual relationship. Principles of good faith and sound commercial practice call for reasonable notification before termination, however, to give the other party time to make substitute arrangements [UCC 2–309(2), (3)].

Options and Cooperation Regarding Performance   When the contract contemplates shipment of the goods but does not specify the shipping arrangements, the *seller* has the right to make these arrangements in good faith, using commercial reasonableness in the situation [UCC 2–311].

When a sales contract omits terms relating to the assortment of goods, the *buyer* can specify the assortment. **EXAMPLE 10.4** Petry Drugs, Inc., agrees to purchase one thousand toothbrushes from Marconi's Dental Supply. The toothbrushes come in a variety of colors, but the contract does not specify color. Petry, the buyer, has the right to take six hundred blue toothbrushes and four hundred green ones if it wishes. Petry, however, must exercise good faith and commercial reasonableness in making its selection [UCC 2–311]. ●

Requirements and Output Contracts

Normally, if the parties do not specify a quantity, a court will have no basis for determining a remedy. No contract is formed because there is almost no way to determine objectively what is a reasonable quantity of goods for someone to buy (whereas a court can objectively determine a reasonable price for particular goods by looking at the market). Nevertheless, the UCC recognizes two exceptions involving requirements and output contracts [UCC 2–306(1)].

Requirements Contracts   In a **requirements contract,** the buyer agrees to purchase and the seller agrees to sell all or up to a stated amount of what the buyer *needs* or *requires.* **EXAMPLE 10.5** Umpqua Cannery forms a contract with Al Garcia. The cannery agrees to purchase from Garcia, and Garcia agrees to sell to the cannery, all of the green beans that the cannery needs or requires during the following summer. ●

There is implicit consideration in a requirements contract because the buyer (the cannery, in this situation) gives up the right to buy goods (green beans, in this example) from any other seller, and this forfeited right creates a legal detriment (that is, consideration).

Requirements contracts are common in the business world and normally are enforceable. In contrast, if the buyer promises to purchase only if the buyer *wishes* to do so, or

---

5. *State v. Alexander,* 186 Or.App. 600, 64 P.3d 1148 (2003).

if the buyer reserves the right to buy the goods from someone other than the seller, the promise is illusory (without consideration) and unenforceable by either party.

Output Contract An agreement in which a seller agrees to sell and a buyer agrees to buy all or up to a stated amount of what the seller produces.

Output Contracts In an **output contract,** the seller agrees to sell and the buyer agrees to buy all or up to a stated amount of what the seller *produces.* **EXAMPLE 10.6** Al Garcia forms a contract with Umpqua Cannery. Garcia agrees to sell to the cannery, and the cannery agrees to purchase from Garcia, all of the beans that Garcia produces on his farm during the following summer. ● Again, because the seller essentially forfeits the right to sell goods to another buyer, there is implicit consideration in an output contract.

The UCC imposes a *good faith limitation* on requirements and output contracts. The quantity under such contracts is the amount of requirements or the amount of output that occurs during a *normal* production year. The actual quantity purchased or sold cannot be unreasonably disproportionate to normal or comparable prior requirements or output [UCC 2–306(1)].

PREVENTING LEGAL DISPUTES

If a business owner leaves certain terms of a sales or lease contract open, the UCC allows a court to supply the missing terms. Although this rule can sometimes be advantageous (to establish that a contract existed, for instance), it can also be a major disadvantage. If a party fails to state a price in the contract offer, for example, a court will impose a reasonable price by looking at the market price of similar goods *at the time of delivery.* Thus, instead of receiving the usual price for the goods, a business will receive what a court considers a reasonable price when the goods are delivered. Therefore, when drafting contracts for the sale or lease of goods, make sure that the contract clearly states any terms that are essential to the bargain, particularly the price. It is generally better to establish the terms of a contract than to leave it up to a court to determine what terms are reasonable after a dispute has arisen.

Merchant's Firm Offer Under regular contract principles, an offer can be revoked at any time before acceptance. The major common law exception is an *option contract* (discussed in Chapter 7), in which the offeree pays consideration for the offeror's irrevocable promise to keep the offer open for a stated period. The UCC creates a second exception for firm offers made by a merchant to sell, buy, or lease goods.

Firm Offer An offer (by a merchant) that is irrevocable without the necessity of consideration for a stated period of time or, if no definite period is stated, for a reasonable time (neither period to exceed three months).

A **firm offer** arises when a merchant-offeror gives *assurances* in a *signed writing* that the offer will remain open. The offer must be both *written* and *signed* by the offeror.[6] When a firm offer is contained in a form contract prepared by the offeree, the offeror must also sign a separate assurance of the firm offer. A merchant's firm offer is irrevocable without the necessity of consideration[7] for the stated period or, if no definite period is stated, a reasonable period (neither period to exceed three months) [UCC 2–205, 2A–205].

EXAMPLE 10.7 Osaka, a used-car dealer, e-mails Saucedo on January 1 stating, "I have a 2013 Kia Sportage on the lot that I'll sell you for $18,000 any time between now and January 31." This e-mail creates a firm offer, and Osaka will be liable for breach if he sells that Kia Sportage to someone other than Saucedo before January 31. ●

Acceptance

KNOW THIS
The UCC provides that acceptance can be made by any means that is reasonable under the circumstances—including prompt shipment of the goods.

Acceptance of an offer to buy, sell, or lease goods generally may be made in any reasonable manner and by any reasonable means. The UCC permits acceptance of an offer to buy goods "either by a prompt *promise* to ship or by the prompt or current shipment of

---

6. *Signed* includes any symbol executed or adopted by a party with a present intention to authenticate a writing [UCC 1–201(39)]. A complete signature is not required. Therefore, initials, a thumbprint, a trade name, or any mark used in lieu of a written signature will suffice, regardless of its location on the document.

7. If the offeree pays consideration, then an option contract (not a merchant's firm offer) is formed.

conforming or nonconforming goods" [UCC 2–206(1)(b)]. *Conforming goods* accord with the contract's terms, whereas *nonconforming goods* do not.

The prompt shipment of nonconforming goods constitutes both an acceptance, which creates a contract, and a breach of that contract. This rule does not apply if the seller **seasonably** (within a reasonable amount of time) notifies the buyer that the nonconforming shipment is offered only as an *accommodation,* or a favor. The notice of accommodation must clearly indicate to the buyer that the shipment does not constitute an acceptance and that, therefore, no contract has been formed.

Seasonably Within a specified time period or, if no period is specified, within a reasonable time.

EXAMPLE 10.8 McFarrell Pharmacy orders five cases of Johnson & Johnson 3-by-5-inch gauze pads from H.T. Medical Supply, Inc. If H.T. ships five cases of Xeroform 3-by-5-inch gauze pads instead, the shipment acts as both an acceptance of McFarrell's offer and a *breach* of the resulting contract. McFarrell may sue H.T. for any appropriate damages. If, however, H.T. notifies McFarrell that the Xeroform gauze pads are being shipped *as an accommodation*—because H.T. has only Xeroform pads in stock—the shipment will constitute a counteroffer, not an acceptance. A contract will be formed only if McFarrell accepts the Xeroform gauze pads. ●

Notice of Acceptance Required   Under the common law, because a unilateral offer invites acceptance by a performance, the offeree need not notify the offeror of performance unless the offeror would not otherwise know about it. In other words, a unilateral offer can be accepted by beginning performance.

The UCC is more stringent than the common law in this regard because it requires notification. Under the UCC, if the offeror is not notified within a reasonable time that the offeree has accepted the contract by beginning performance, then the offeror can treat the offer as having lapsed before acceptance [UCC 2–206(2), 2A–206(2)].

LEARNING OBJECTIVE 2
In a sales contract, if an offeree includes additional or different terms in an acceptance, will a contract result? If so, what happens to these terms?

Additional Terms   Recall from page 207 of Chapter 7 that under the common law, the *mirror image rule* requires that the terms of the acceptance exactly match those of the offer. Thus, if Alderman makes an offer to Beale, and Beale accepts but in the acceptance makes some slight modification to the terms of the offer, there is no contract.

To avoid these problems, the UCC dispenses with the mirror image rule. Generally, the UCC takes the position that if the offeree's response indicates a *definite* acceptance of the offer, a contract is formed even if the acceptance includes additional or different terms from those contained in the offer [UCC 2–207(1)]. Whether the additional terms become part of the contract depends, in part, on whether the parties are nonmerchants or merchants.

In the following case, a party conditioned its acceptance of an offer on the other parties' agreement to additional terms by a specific date. When the parties agreed to the most important terms after the deadline, the court had to decide if there was an enforceable contract.

Case 10.1

WPS, Inc. v. Expro Americas, LLC

Court of Appeals of Texas, First District, 2012 WL 310937 (2012).
www.findlaw.com/casecode[a]

FACTS In April 2006, WPS, Inc., submitted a formal proposal to manufacture equipment for Expro Americas, LLC, and Surface Production Systems, Inc. (SPS). Expro and SPS then submitted two purchase orders. WPS accepted the first purchase order in part and the second order conditionally. Among other things, WPS required that, by April 28, 2006, Expro and SPS give their "full release to proceed" and agree "to pay all valid costs associated with any order cancellation." The parties' negotiations continued, and Expro and SPS eventually submitted a third purchase order on May 9,

---

a. Under "Popular State Resources," click on "Texas Caselaw." Under "Browse Texas Courts," click on "Court of Appeals of Texas." In the result, enter "WPS, Inc." in the "Party name:" box and click on "Search." When that page opens, click on the case name to access the opinion.

Case 10.1—Continued

2006. The third purchase order did not comply with all of WPS's requirements, but it did give WPS full permission to proceed and agreed that Expro and SPS would pay all cancellation costs. With Expro and SPS's knowledge, WPS then began work under the third purchase order. Expro and SPS soon canceled the order, however, so WPS sent them an invoice for the cancellation costs. At trial, the jury and court concluded that there was a contract and found in WPS's favor. Expro and SPS appealed.

ISSUE Did the parties have a contract even though Expro and SPS did not comply with all the requirements of WPS's conditional acceptance?

DECISION Yes. The Texas appellate court affirmed the judgment for WPS.

REASON The court found that the parties had a contract based on WPS's conditional acceptance and Expro and SPS's third purchase order. It did not matter that Expro and SPS submitted the third purchase order after WPS's deadline of April 28, 2006. Regardless of what WPS originally required, the parties continued their negotiations and "operated as if they had additional time to resolve the outstanding differences." Moreover, Expro and SPS agreed to nearly everything that WPS requested. Most important, they gave WPS "full release to proceed" and agreed "to pay all valid costs associated with any order cancellation." Those terms had been holding up the contract, and SPS's vice president conceded that the release to proceed "basically means that one party is in agreement." A jury could have reasonably concluded that, since the parties were in agreement, WPS was contractually obligated to move forward with its work.

CRITICAL THINKING—Legal Consideration *By allowing a party to condition its acceptance on additional terms, does contract law make negotiations more or less efficient? Explain.*

Rules When One Party or Both Parties Are Nonmerchants If one (or both) of the parties is a *nonmerchant,* the contract is formed according to the terms of the original offer submitted by the original offeror and not according to the additional terms of the acceptance [UCC 2–207(2)].

EXAMPLE 10.9 Tolsen offers in writing to sell his laptop and printer to Valdez for $1,500. Valdez replies to Tolsen stating, "I accept your offer to purchase your laptop and printer for $1,500. I *would like* a box of laser printer paper and two extra toner cartridges to be included in the purchase price." Valdez has given Tolsen a definite expression of acceptance (creating a contract), even though the acceptance also *suggests* an added term for the offer. Because Tolsen is not a merchant, the additional term is merely a proposal (suggestion), and Tolsen is not legally obligated to comply with that term. •

Rules When Both Parties Are Merchants The drafters of the UCC created a special rule for merchants to avoid the "battle of the forms," which occurs when two merchants exchange separate standard forms containing different contract terms.

Under UCC 2–207(2), in contracts *between merchants,* the additional terms *automatically* become part of the contract unless one of the following conditions exists:

1. The original offer expressly limited acceptance to its terms.
2. The new or changed terms materially alter the contract.
3. The offeror objects to the new or changed terms within a reasonable period of time.

Generally, if the modification does not involve any unreasonable element of surprise or hardship for the offeror, the court will hold that the modification did not materially alter the contract. Courts also consider the parties' prior dealings and course of performance when determining whether the alteration is material.

Conditioned on Offeror's Assent Regardless of merchant status, the UCC provides that the offeree's expression cannot be construed as an acceptance if it contains additional or different terms that are explicitly conditioned on the offeror's assent to those terms

[UCC 2–207(1)]. **EXAMPLE 10.10** Philips offers to sell Hundert 650 pounds of turkey thighs at a specified price and with specified delivery terms. Hundert responds, "I accept your offer for 650 pounds of turkey thighs *on the condition that you give me ninety days to pay for them.*" Hundert's response will be construed not as an acceptance but as a counteroffer, which Philips may or may not accept. ●

Additional Terms May Be Stricken   The UCC provides yet another option for dealing with conflicting terms in the parties' writings. Section 2–207(3) states that conduct by both parties that recognizes the existence of a contract is sufficient to establish a contract for the sale of goods even though the writings of the parties do not otherwise establish a contract. In this situation, "the terms of the particular contract will consist of those terms on which the writings of the parties agree, together with any supplementary terms incorporated under any other provisions of this Act."

In a dispute over contract terms, this provision allows a court simply to strike from the contract those terms on which the parties do not agree. **EXAMPLE 10.11** SMT Marketing orders goods over the phone from Brigg Sales, Inc., which ships the goods with an acknowledgment form (confirming the order) to SMT. SMT accepts and pays for the goods. The parties' writings do not establish a contract, but there is no question that a contract exists. If a dispute arises over the terms, such as the extent of any warranties, UCC 2–207(3) provides the governing rule. ●

Consideration

The common law rule that a contract requires consideration also applies to sales and lease contracts. Unlike the common law, however, the UCC does not require a contract modification to be supported by new consideration. An agreement modifying a contract for the sale or lease of goods "needs no consideration to be binding" [UCC 2–209(1), 2A–208(1)]. Of course, a contract modification must be sought in good faith [UCC 1–304].

In some situations, an agreement to modify a sales or lease contract without consideration must be in writing to be enforceable. If the contract itself prohibits any changes to the contract unless they are in a signed writing, for instance, then only those changes agreed to in a signed writing are enforceable.

If a consumer (nonmerchant buyer) is dealing with a merchant and the merchant supplies the form that contains a prohibition against oral modification, the consumer must sign a separate acknowledgment of such a clause [UCC 2–209(2), 2A–208(2)]. Also, any modification that brings a sales contract under Article 2's Statute of Frauds provision (discussed next) usually must be in writing to be enforceable.

The Statute of Frauds

> **► KNOW THIS ◄**
> It has been proposed that the UCC be revised to eliminate the Statute of Frauds.

The UCC contains Statute of Frauds provisions covering sales and lease contracts. Under these provisions, sales contracts for goods priced at $500 or more and lease contracts requiring payments of $1,000 or more must be in writing to be enforceable [UCC 2–201(1), 2A–201(1)]. (These low threshold amounts may eventually be raised.)

Sufficiency of the Writing   The UCC has greatly relaxed the requirements for the sufficiency of a writing to satisfy the Statute of Frauds. A writing or a memorandum will be sufficient as long as it indicates that the parties intended to form a contract and as long as it is signed by the party (or agent of the party—see Chapter 17) against whom enforcement is sought. The contract normally will not be enforceable beyond the quantity of goods shown in the writing, however. All other terms can be proved in court by oral testimony. For leases, the writing must reasonably identify and describe the goods leased and the lease term.

Special Rules for Contracts between Merchants

Once again, the UCC provides a special rule for merchants in sales transactions (there is no corresponding rule that applies to leases under Article 2A). Merchants can satisfy the Statute of Frauds if, after the parties have agreed orally, one of the merchants sends a signed written confirmation to the other merchant within a reasonable time. The communication must indicate the terms of the agreement, and the merchant receiving the confirmation must have reason to know of its contents. Unless the merchant who receives the confirmation gives written notice of objection to its contents within ten days after receipt, the writing is sufficient against the receiving merchant, even though she or he has not signed anything [UCC 2–201(2)]. Generally, courts even hold that it is sufficient if a merchant sends an e-mail confirmation of the agreement.[8]

EXAMPLE 10.12 Alfonso is a merchant-buyer in Cleveland. He contracts over the telephone to purchase $4,000 worth of spare aircraft parts from Goldstein, a merchant-seller in New York City. Two days later, Goldstein sends a written and signed confirmation detailing the terms of the oral contract, and Alfonso subsequently receives it. If Alfonso does not notify Goldstein in writing of his objection to the contents of the confirmation within ten days of receipt, Alfonso cannot raise the Statute of Frauds as a defense against the enforcement of the oral contract. ●

(Csaba Vanyi/Shutterstock.com)

The buyer and the seller of aircraft parts are both merchants.

LEARNING OBJECTIVE 3
What exceptions to the writing requirements of the Statute of Frauds are provided in Article 2 and Article 2A of the UCC?

Exceptions

In addition to the special rules for merchants, the UCC defines three exceptions to the writing requirements of the Statute of Frauds. An oral contract for the sale of goods priced at $500 or more or the lease of goods involving total payments of $1,000 or more will be enforceable despite the absence of a writing in the circumstances discussed in the following subsections [UCC 2–201(3), 2A–201(4)].

These exceptions and other ways in which sales law differs from general contract law are summarized in Exhibit 10.2 on the following page.

Specially Manufactured Goods An oral contract is enforceable if (1) it is for goods that are specially manufactured for a particular buyer or specially manufactured or obtained for a particular lessee, (2) these goods are not suitable for resale or lease to others in the ordinary course of the seller's or lessor's business, and (3) the seller or lessor has substantially started to manufacture the goods or has made commitments for their manufacture or procurement. In this situation, once the seller or lessor has taken action, the buyer or lessee cannot repudiate the agreement claiming the Statute of Frauds as a defense.

EXAMPLE 10.13 Womach orders custom-made draperies for her new boutique. The price is $6,000, and the contract is oral. When the merchant-seller manufactures the draperies and tenders delivery to Womach, she refuses to pay for them even though the job has been completed on time. Womach claims that she is not liable because the contract was oral. Clearly, if the unique style and color of the draperies make it improbable that the seller can find another buyer, Womach is liable to the seller. Note that the seller must have made a substantial beginning in manufacturing the specialized item prior to the buyer's repudiation. (Here, the manufacture was completed.) Of course, the court must still be convinced by evidence of the terms of the oral contract. ●

Admissions An oral contract for the sale or lease of goods is enforceable if the party against whom enforcement of the contract is sought admits in pleadings, testimony, or

---

8. See, for example, *Bazak International Corp. v. Tarrant Apparel Group,* 378 F.Supp.2d 377 (S.D.N.Y. 2005); and *Great White Bear, LLC v. Mervyns, LLC,* 2007 WL 1295747 (S.D.N.Y. 2007).

Exhibit 10.2 **Major Differences between Contract Law and Sales Law**

	CONTRACT LAW	SALES LAW
Contract Terms	Contract must contain all material terms.	Open terms are acceptable, if parties intended to form a contract, but the contract is not enforceable beyond quantity term.
Acceptance	Mirror image rule applies. If additional terms are added in acceptance, counteroffer is created.	Additional terms will not negate acceptance unless acceptance is made expressly conditional on assent to the additional terms.
Contract Modification	Modification requires consideration.	Modification does not require consideration.
Irrevocable Offers	Option contracts (with consideration).	Merchants' firm offers (without consideration).
Statute of Frauds Requirements	All material terms must be included in the writing.	Writing is required only for the sale of goods of $500 or more, but contract is not enforceable beyond quantity specified. Merchants can satisfy the requirement by a confirmatory memorandum evidencing their agreement. *Exceptions:* 1. Specially manufactured goods. 2. Admissions by party against whom enforcement is sought. 3. Partial performance.

other court proceedings that a contract for sale or lease was made. In this situation, the contract will be enforceable even though it was oral, but enforceability will be limited to the quantity of goods admitted.

CASE EXAMPLE 10.14 Gerald Lindgren, a farmer, agreed by phone to sell his crops to Glacial Plains Cooperative. The parties reached four oral agreements: two for the delivery of soybeans and two for the delivery of corn. Lindgren made the soybean deliveries and part of the first corn delivery, but he sold the rest of his corn to another dealer. Glacial Plains bought corn elsewhere, paying a higher price, and then sued Lindgren for breach of contract. In papers filed with the court, Lindgren acknowledged his oral agreements with Glacial Plains and admitted that he did not fully perform. The court applied the admissions exception and held that the four agreements were enforceable.[9] •

Partial Performance An oral contract for the sale or lease of goods is enforceable if payment has been made and accepted or goods have been received and accepted. This is the "partial performance" exception. The oral contract will be enforced at least to the extent that performance *actually* took place.

EXAMPLE 10.15 Jamal orally contracts to lease to Opus Enterprises a thousand chairs at $2 each to be used during a one-day concert. Before delivery, Opus sends Jamal a check for $1,000, which Jamal cashes. Later, when Jamal attempts to deliver the chairs, Opus refuses delivery, claiming the Statute of Frauds as a defense, and demands the return of its $1,000. Under the UCC's partial performance rule, Jamal can enforce the oral contract by tender of delivery of five hundred chairs for the $1,000 accepted. Similarly, if Opus had made no payment but had accepted the delivery of five hundred chairs from Jamal, the oral contract would have been enforceable against Opus for $1,000, the lease payment due for the five hundred chairs delivered. •

Parol Evidence

Parol evidence is testimony or other evidence of the parties' prior negotiations, prior agreements, or contemporaneous oral agreements. When the parties to a sales contract set forth its terms in a confirmatory memorandum or in other writing that is intended as a complete

> "Whatever is not nailed down is mine. Whatever I can pry loose is not nailed down."
>
> Collis P. Huntington, 1821–1900
> (U.S. railroad builder and owner)

---

9. *Glacial Plains Cooperative v. Lindgren*, 759 N.W.2d 661 (Minn.App. 2009).

Parol Evidence Rule A rule of contracts under which a court will not receive into evidence oral statements that contradict a written agreement.

and final statement of their agreement, the contract is considered *fully integrated,* and the **parol evidence rule** applies. The terms of a fully integrated contract cannot be contradicted by evidence of any prior agreements or contemporaneous oral agreements.

If, however, the writing contains some of the terms the parties agreed on but not others, the contract is not fully integrated. When a court finds that the terms of a sales contract are *not fully integrated* or are ambiguous, the court may allow evidence of *consistent additional terms* to explain or supplement the terms stated in the contract. The court may also allow the parties to submit evidence of *course of dealing, usage of trade,* or *course of performance* [UCC 2–202, 2A–202]. A court will not under any circumstances allow the parties to submit evidence that contradicts the stated terms (this is also the rule under the common law).

Course of Dealing and Usage of Trade

Under the UCC, the meaning of any agreement, evidenced by the language of the parties and by their actions, must be interpreted in light of commercial practices and other surrounding circumstances. In interpreting a commercial agreement, the court will assume that the course of prior dealing between the parties and the usage of trade were taken into account when the agreement was phrased.

Course of Dealing Prior conduct between the parties to a contract that establishes a common basis for their understanding.

Course of Dealing A **course of dealing** is a sequence of previous actions and communications between the parties to a particular transaction that establishes a common basis for their understanding [UCC 1–303(b)]. A course of dealing is restricted to that previous sequence of actions and communications. Under the UCC, a course of dealing between the parties is relevant in ascertaining the meaning of the parties' agreement. It may give particular meaning to specific terms of the agreement, and may supplement or qualify the terms of its agreement [UCC 1–303(d)]. (Usage of trade and course of performance may be relevant for the same purposes, as will be discussed next.)

Usage of Trade Any practice or method of dealing that is so regularly observed in a place, vocation, or trade that parties justifiably expect it will be observed in their transaction.

Usage of Trade Any practice or method of dealing that is so regularly observed in a place, vocation, or trade that the parties justifiably expect (or should expect) it to be observed in their transaction is a **usage of trade** [UCC 1–303(c)].

EXAMPLE 10.16 Phat Khat Loans, Inc., hires Title Review, LLC, to search the public records for prior claims on potential borrrowers' assets. Title's invoice states, "Liability limited to amount of fee." In the search industry, liability limits are common. After conducting many searches for Phat Khat, Title reports that there are no claims with respect to Main St. Autos. Phat Khat loans $100,000 to Main, with payment guaranteed by Main's assets. When Main defaults on the loan, Phat Khat learns that another lender has priority to Main's assets under a previous claim. In Phat Khat's suit against Title for breach of contract, Title's liability is limited to the amount of its fee. The statement in the invoice was part of the contract between Phat Khat and Title, according to the usage of trade in the industry and the parties' course of dealing. ●

Course of Performance The conduct that occurs under the terms of a particular agreement, which indicates what the parties to that agreement intended it to mean.

Course of Performance

A **course of performance** is the conduct that occurs under the terms of a particular agreement [UCC 1–303(a)]. Presumably, the parties themselves know best what they meant by their words, and the course of performance actually undertaken under their agreement is the best indication of what they meant [UCC 2–208(1), 2A–207(1)].

EXAMPLE 10.17 Janson's Lumber Company contracts with Barrymore to sell Barrymore a specified number of "two-by-fours." The lumber does not in fact measure 2 inches by 4 inches but rather 1⅞ inches by 3¾ inches. Janson's agrees to deliver the lumber in five deliveries, and Barrymore, without objection, accepts the lumber in the first three deliveries. On the fourth delivery, however, Barrymore objects that the two-by-fours do not measure 2 inches by 4 inches.

The course of performance in this transaction—that is, Barrymore's acceptance of three deliveries without objection under the agreement—is relevant in determining that here the term *two-by-four* actually means "1⅞ by 3¾." Janson's can also prove that two-by-fours need not be exactly 2 inches by 4 inches by applying course of prior dealing, usage of trade, or both. Janson's can, for example, show that in previous transactions, Barrymore took 1⅞-by-3¾-inch lumber without objection. In addition, Janson's can show that in the lumber trade, two-by-fours are commonly 1⅞ inches by 3¾ inches. •

Rules of Construction The UCC provides *rules of construction* for interpreting contracts. Express terms, course of performance, course of dealing, and usage of trade are to be construed together when they do not contradict one another. When such a construction is unreasonable, however, the following order of priority controls: (1) express terms, (2) course of performance, (3) course of dealing, and (4) usage of trade [UCC 1–303(e), 2–208(2), 2A–207(2)].

Unconscionability

As discussed on pages 235 and 236 in Chapter 8, an unconscionable contract is one that is so unfair and one sided that it would be unreasonable to enforce it. The UCC allows the court to evaluate a contract or any clause in a contract, and if the court deems it to have been unconscionable at the time it was made, the court can (1) refuse to enforce the contract, (2) enforce the remainder of the contract without the unconscionable clause, or (3) limit the application of any unconscionable clauses to avoid an unconscionable result [UCC 2–302, 2A–108].

The following *Classic Case* illustrates an early application of the UCC's unconscionability provisions.

Classic Case 10.2

Jones v. Star Credit Corp.

Supreme Court of New York, Nassau County, 59 Misc.2d 189, 298 N.Y.S.2d 264 (1969).

HISTORICAL AND ECONOMIC SETTING *In the sixth century* C.E., *Roman civil law allowed the courts to rescind a contract if the goods that were the subject of the contract had a market value that was less than half the contract price. This same ratio has appeared over the last decade in many cases in which courts have found contract clauses to be unconscionable under UCC 2–302 on the ground that the price was excessive. Most of the litigants who have used UCC 2–302 successfully have been consumers who were poor or otherwise at a disadvantage. In a Connecticut case, for example, the court held that a contract requiring a person who was poor to make payments totaling $1,248 for a television set that ordinarily sold for $499 was unconscionable.*[a] *The seller had not told the buyer the full purchase price. In a New York case, the court held that a contract*

requiring a Spanish-speaking consumer to make payments totaling nearly $1,150 for a freezer that had a wholesale price of less than $350 was unconscionable.[b] *The contract was in English, and the salesperson did not translate or explain it.*

Can a retailer sell a freezer at four times its wholesale price?

FACTS The Joneses, the plaintiffs, agreed to purchase a freezer for $900 as the result of a salesperson's visit to their home. Tax and financing charges raised the total price to $1,234.80. At trial, the freezer was found to have a maximum retail value of approximately $300. The plaintiffs, who had made payments totaling $619.88, brought a suit in a New York state court

---

a. *Murphy v. McNamara*, 36 Conn.Supp. 183, 416 A.2d 170 (1979).
b. *Frostifresh Corp. v. Reynoso*, 52 Misc.2d 26, 274 N.Y.S.2d 757 (1966), reversed on issue of damages, 54 Misc.2d 119, 281 N.Y.S.2d 946 (1967).

Case 10.2—Continued

to have the purchase contract declared unconscionable under the UCC.

ISSUE Can this contract be denied enforcement on the ground of unconscionability?

DECISION Yes. The court held that the contract was not enforceable as it stood, and the contract was reformed so that no further payments were required.

REASON The court relied on UCC 2–302(1), which states that if "the court as a matter of law finds the contract or any clause of the contract to have been unconscionable at the time it was made, the court may . . . so limit the application of any

unconscionable clause as to avoid any unconscionable result." The court then considered the disparity between the $900 purchase price and the $300 retail value, as well as the fact that the credit charges alone exceeded the retail value. These excessive charges were exacted despite the seller's knowledge of the plaintiffs' limited resources. The court reformed the contract so that the plaintiffs' payments, amounting to more than $600, were regarded as payment in full.

IMPACT OF THIS CASE ON TODAY'S LAW *This early case illustrates the approach that many courts today take when deciding whether a sales contract is unconscionable—an approach that focuses on "excessive" price and unequal bargaining power.*

Title and Risk of Loss

"To win, you have to risk loss."

Jean-Claude Killy, 1943–present
(French Alpine skier)

Before the creation of the UCC, *title*—the right of ownership—was the central concept in sales law and controlled all issues of rights and remedies of the parties to a sales contract. In some situations, title is still relevant under the UCC, and the UCC has special rules for determining who has title. (These rules do not apply to leased goods, obviously, because title remains with the lessor, or owner, of the goods.) In most situations, however, the UCC has replaced the concept of title with three other concepts: (1) identification, (2) risk of loss, and (3) insurable interest.

Identification

Identification In a sale of goods, the express designation of the goods provided for in the contract.

Before any interest in specific goods can pass from the seller or lessor to the buyer or lessee, the goods must exist and be identified as the specific goods designated in the contract. **Identification** takes place when specific goods are designated as the subject matter of a sales or lease contract.

Title and risk of loss cannot pass from seller to buyer unless the goods are identified to the contract. (Remember that title to leased goods does not pass to the lessee.) Identification is important because it gives the buyer or lessee the right to insure the goods and the right to recover from third parties who damage the goods.

The parties can agree in their contract on when identification will take place (although it will not effectively pass title and risk of loss to the buyer on future goods, such as unborn cattle). If the parties do not so specify, however, the UCC provisions discussed here determine when identification takes place [UCC 2–501(1), 2A–217].

Existing Goods If the contract calls for the sale or lease of specific goods that are already in existence, identification takes place at the time the contract is made. **EXAMPLE 10.18** You contract to purchase or lease a fleet of five cars designated by their vehicle identification numbers (VINs). Because the cars are identified by their VINs, identification has taken place, and you acquire an insurable interest in them at the time of contracting. ●

Future Goods Goods that are not both existing and identified to the contract are called *future goods*. For instance, if a sale involves unborn animals to be born within twelve months after contracting, identification takes place when the animals are conceived. If a lease involves any unborn animals, identification also occurs when the animals are conceived. If a sale involves crops that are to be harvested within twelve months (or the next harvest season occurring after contracting, whichever is longer), identification takes place when the crops are planted. Otherwise, identification takes place when the crops begin to grow.

In a sale or lease of any other future goods, identification occurs when the goods are shipped, marked, or otherwise designated by the seller or lessor as the goods to which the contract refers.

Goods That Are Part of a Larger Mass   As a general rule, goods that are part of a larger mass are identified when the goods are marked, shipped, or somehow designated by the seller or lessor as the particular goods that are the subject of the contract. **EXAMPLE 10.19**   A buyer orders 1,000 cases of beans from a 10,000-case lot. Until the seller separates the 1,000 cases of beans from the 10,000-case lot, title and risk of loss remain with the seller. •

Fungible Goods Goods that are alike by physical nature, agreement, or trade usage.

A common exception to this rule involves fungible goods. **Fungible goods** are goods that are alike by physical nature, by agreement, or by trade usage. They are usually stored in large containers—for example, specific grades or types of wheat, oil, and inexpensive wine. If two or more persons own an interest in fungible goods as *tenants in common* (see Chapter 23), one of those persons can pass title and risk of loss to a buyer without an actual separation of the goods. The buyer replaces the seller as an owner in common [UCC 2–105(4)].

Passage of Title

Once goods exist and are identified, the provisions of UCC 2–401 apply to the passage of title. In nearly all subsections of UCC 2–401, the words "unless otherwise explicitly agreed" appear, meaning that any explicit understanding between the buyer and the seller determines when title passes. Without an explicit agreement to the contrary, *title passes to the buyer at the time and the place the seller performs by delivering the goods* [UCC 2–401(2)]. For instance, if a person buys cattle at a livestock auction, title will pass to the buyer when the cattle are physically delivered to him or her (unless, of course, the parties agree otherwise).

If a seller gives up possession or control of goods, but keeps a "Certificate of Origin" supposedly showing ownership, has there been a delivery sufficient to pass title? That was the question in the following case.

Case 10.3

United States v. 2007 Custom Motorcycle

United States District Court, District of Arizona, ___ F.Supp.2d ___ (2011).

(Margo Harrison/Shutterstock.com)

When does passage of title occur?

FACTS   Timothy Allen commissioned a custom motorcycle from Indy Route 66 Cycles, Inc. Indy built the motorcycle and issued a "Certificate of Origin." Two years later, federal law enforcement officers arrested Allen on drug charges and seized his home and other property. The officers also seized the Indy-made motorcycle from the garage of the home of Allen's sister, Tena. The government alleged that the motorcycle was subject to forfeiture as the proceeds of drug trafficking. Indy filed a claim against the government, arguing that it owned the motorcycle, as evidenced by the "Certificate of Origin," which the company still possessed. Indy claimed that it had been keeping the motorcycle in storage. The government filed a motion to strike the claim, asserting that title to the motorcycle had passed when it was delivered to Allen.

ISSUE   Did ownership to the motorcycle pass at the time that Indy gave Allen possession and control over it?

Case 10.3—Continued

DECISION Yes. The district court issued a ruling in the government's favor and granted the motion to strike Indy's claim.

REASON Under UCC 2–401(2), "unless otherwise explicitly agreed, title passes to the buyer at the time and place at which the seller completes his performance with reference to the physical delivery of the goods." In the sales transaction in this case, the parties did not "otherwise explicitly agree" to different terms. Thus, the critical question was whether Indy had delivered the cycle to Allen. Testimony by Indy's former vice president, Vince Ballard, was "inconclusive" but implied

that Indy had delivered the motorcycle to Allen. The cycle was found in Tena's garage, which also indicated that Indy had delivered it to Allen. Thus, Indy had given up possession of the cycle to Allen. This was sufficient to pass title even though Indy had kept a "Certificate of Origin." As a consequence, the motorcycle was subject to forfeiture as the proceeds of drug trafficking.

WHAT IF THE FACTS WERE DIFFERENT? *Suppose that Indy had given the "Certificate of Origin" to Allen and had kept the motorcycle. Would the result have been different? Explain.*

Shipment Contract A contract for the sale of goods in which the seller is required or authorized to ship the goods by carrier. The seller assumes liability for any losses or damage to the goods until they are delivered to the carrier.

Destination Contract A contract for the sale of goods in which the seller is required or authorized to ship the goods by carrier and tender delivery of the goods at a particular destination. The seller assumes liability for any losses or damage to the goods until they are tendered at the destination specified in the contract.

Document of Title A paper exchanged in the regular course of business that evidences the right to possession of goods (for example, a bill of lading or a warehouse receipt).

LEARNING OBJECTIVE 4
Risk of loss does not necessarily pass with title. If the parties to a contract do not expressly agree when risk passes and the goods are to be delivered without movement by the seller, when does risk pass?

Shipment and Destination Contracts Unless otherwise agreed, delivery arrangements can determine when title passes from the seller to the buyer. In a **shipment contract,** the seller is required or authorized to ship goods by carrier, such as a trucking company. Under a shipment contract, the seller is required only to deliver conforming goods into the hands of a carrier, and title passes to the buyer at the time and place of shipment [UCC 2–401(2)(a)]. Generally, *all contracts are assumed to be shipment contracts if nothing to the contrary is stated in the contract.*

In a **destination contract,** the seller is required to deliver the goods to a particular destination, usually directly to the buyer, but sometimes to another party designated by the buyer. Title passes to the buyer when the goods are *tendered* at that destination [UCC 2–401(2)(b)]. As you will read in Chapter 11, *tender of delivery* occurs when the seller places or holds conforming goods at the buyer's disposal (with any necessary notice), enabling the buyer to take possession [UCC 2–503(1)].

Delivery without Movement of the Goods When the sales contract does not call for the seller to ship or deliver the goods (when the buyer is to pick up the goods), the passage of title depends on whether the seller must deliver a **document of title,** such as a bill of lading or a warehouse receipt, to the buyer. A *bill of lading* is a receipt for goods that is signed by a carrier and serves as a contract for the transport of the goods. A *warehouse receipt* is a receipt issued by a warehouser for goods stored in a warehouse.

When a document of title is required, title passes to the buyer *when and where the document is delivered.* Thus, if the goods are stored in a warehouse, title passes to the buyer when the appropriate documents are delivered to the buyer. The goods never move. In fact, the buyer can choose to leave the goods at the same warehouse for a period of time, and the buyer's title to those goods will be unaffected.

When no documents of title are required and delivery is made without moving the goods, title passes at the time and place the sales contract is made, if the goods have already been identified. If the goods have not been identified, title does not pass until identification occurs [UCC 2–401(3)]. **EXAMPLE 10.20** Juarez sells lumber to Bodan. They agree that Bodan will pick up the lumber at the lumberyard. If the lumber has been identified (segregated, marked, or in any other way distinguished from all other lumber), title passes to Bodan when the contract is signed. If the lumber is still in large storage bins at the lumberyard, title does not pass to Bodan until the particular pieces of lumber to be sold under this contract are identified. •

Sales or Leases by Nonowners

Problems occur when a person who acquires goods with *imperfect* title attempts to sell or lease them. Sections 2–402 and 2–403 of the UCC deal with the rights of two parties who lay claim to the same goods, sold with imperfect title. Generally, a buyer acquires at least whatever title the seller has to the goods sold.

Void Title   A buyer may unknowingly purchase goods from a seller who is not the owner of the goods. If the seller is a thief, the seller's title is *void*—legally, no title exists. Thus, the buyer acquires no title, and the real owner can reclaim the goods from the buyer. If the goods were leased, the same result would occur because the lessor has no leasehold interest to transfer.

EXAMPLE 10.21   If Saki steals diamonds owned by Maren, Saki has a *void title* to those diamonds. If Saki sells the diamonds to Shannon, Maren can reclaim them from Shannon even though Shannon acted in good faith and honestly was not aware that the goods were stolen. • (Article 2A contains similar provisions for leases.)

Voidable Title   A seller has *voidable title* if the goods that she or he is selling were obtained by fraud, paid for with a check that is later *dishonored*—that is, returned for insufficient funds—purchased from a minor, or purchased on credit when the seller was insolvent. Under the UCC, a person is **insolvent** when that person ceases to pay his or her debts in the ordinary course of business, cannot pay his or her debts as they come due, or is insolvent within the meaning of federal bankruptcy law [UCC 1–201(23)].

In contrast to a seller with *void title,* a seller with *voidable title* has the power to transfer good title to a good faith purchaser for value. A **good faith purchaser** is one who buys without knowledge of circumstances that would make a person of ordinary prudence inquire about the validity of the seller's title to the goods. One who purchases *for value* gives legally sufficient consideration (value) for the goods purchased. The real, or original, owner cannot recover goods from a good faith purchaser for value [UCC 2–403(1)].[10] If the buyer of the goods is not a good faith purchaser for value, then the actual owner of the goods can reclaim them from the buyer (or from the seller, if the goods are still in the seller's possession). Exhibit 10.3 on the facing page illustrates these concepts.

The Entrustment Rule

According to Section 2–403(2), when goods are entrusted to a merchant *who deals in goods of that kind,* the merchant has the power to transfer all rights to *a buyer in the ordinary course of business.* This is known as the **entrustment rule.** Entrusted goods include both goods that are turned over to the merchant and purchased goods left with the merchant for later delivery or pickup [UCC 2–403(3)]. Article 2A provides a similar rule for leased goods [UCC 2A–305(2)].

A buyer in the ordinary course of business is a person who, in good faith and without knowledge that the sale violates the ownership rights or security interest of a third party, buys in ordinary course from a person (other than a pawnbroker) in the business of selling goods of that kind [UCC 1–201(9)]. (A *security interest* is any interest in personal property that secures the payment of or the performance of an obligation.)

EXAMPLE 10.22   Jan leaves her watch with a jeweler to be repaired. The jeweler sells new and used watches. The jeweler sells Jan's watch to Kim, a customer, who is unaware that the jeweler has no right to sell it. Kim, as a good faith buyer, gets good title against Jan's claim of ownership.[11] Kim, however, obtains only those rights held by the person entrusting the goods (here, Jan). Suppose that Jan had stolen the watch from Greg and then left it with the jeweler to be repaired. The jeweler then sells it to Kim. In this situation, Kim gets good title against Jan, who entrusted the watch to the jeweler, but not against Greg (the real owner), who neither entrusted the watch to Jan nor authorized Jan to entrust it. •

Insolvent A condition in which a person cannot pay his or her debts as they become due or ceases to pay debts in the ordinary course of business.

Good Faith Purchaser A purchaser who buys without notice of any circumstance that would cause a person of ordinary prudence to inquire as to whether the seller has valid title to the goods being sold.

Entrustment Rule The rule that entrusting goods to a merchant who deals in goods of that kind gives that merchant the power to transfer those goods and all rights to them to a buyer in the ordinary course of business.

➤ **KNOW THIS** ◄
The purpose of holding most goods in inventory is to turn those goods into revenues by selling them. That is one of the reasons for the entrustment rule.

---

10. The real owner could, of course, sue the person who initially obtained voidable title to the goods.
11. Jan, of course, can sue the jeweler for the tort of trespass to personalty or conversion (see Chapter 4) for the equivalent cash value of the watch.

Exhibit 10.3 Void and Voidable Titles

If goods are transferred from their owner to another by theft, the thief acquires no ownership rights. Because the thief's title is *void*, a later buyer can acquire no title, and the owner can recover the goods. If the transfer occurs by fraud, the transferee acquires a *voidable* title. A later good faith purchaser for value can acquire good title, and the original owner cannot recover the goods.

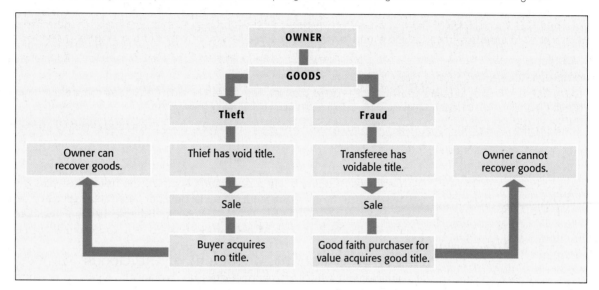

Risk of Loss

Under the UCC, risk of loss does not necessarily pass with title. When risk of loss passes from a seller or lessor to a buyer or lessee is generally determined by the contract between the parties. Sometimes, the contract states expressly when the risk of loss passes. At other times, it does not, and a court must interpret the performance and delivery terms of the contract to determine whether the risk has passed.

Delivery with Movement of the Goods—Carrier Cases
When the contract involves movement of the goods through a common carrier but does not specify when risk of loss passes, the courts first look for specific delivery terms in the contract.

The terms that have traditionally been used in contracts within the United States are listed and defined in Exhibit 10.4 on the following page. These terms determine which party will pay the costs of delivering the goods and who bears the risk of loss. If the contract does not include these terms, then the courts must decide whether the contract is a shipment or a destination contract.

Shipment Contracts In a shipment contract, the seller or lessor is required or authorized to ship goods by carrier, but is not required to deliver them to a particular final destination. The risk of loss in a shipment contract passes to the buyer or lessee when the goods are delivered to the carrier [UCC 2–319(1)(a), 2–509(1)(a), 2A–219(2)(a)].

EXAMPLE 10.23 A seller in Texas sells five hundred cases of grapefruit to a buyer in New York, F.O.B. Houston (free on board in Houston—that is, the buyer pays the transportation charges from Houston). The contract authorizes shipment by carrier. It does not require that the seller tender the grapefruit in New York. Risk passes to the buyer when conforming goods are properly placed in the possession of the carrier. If the goods are damaged in transit, the loss is the buyer's. (Actually, buyers have recourse against carriers, subject to certain limitations, and buyers usually insure the goods from the time the goods leave the seller.) ●

Exhibit 10.4 Contract Terms—Definitions

The contract terms listed and defined in this exhibit help to determine which party will bear the costs of delivery and when risk of loss will pass from the seller to the buyer.

F.O.B. (free on board) — Indicates that the selling price of goods includes transportation costs to the specific F.O.B. place named in the contract. The seller pays the expenses and carries the risk of loss to the F.O.B. place named [UCC 2–319(1)]. If the named place is the place from which the goods are shipped (for example, the seller's city or place of business), the contract is a shipment contract. If the named place is the place to which the goods are to be shipped (for example, the buyer's city or place of business), the contract is a destination contract.

F.A.S. (free alongside ship) — Requires that the seller, at his or her own expense and risk, deliver the goods alongside the vessel in the manner usual in that port or on a dock designated and provided by the buyer [UCC 2–319(2)]. An F.A.S. contract is essentially an F.O.B. contract for ships.

C.I.F. or **C.&F.** (cost, insurance, and freight or just cost and freight) — Requires, among other things, that the seller "put the goods in the possession of a carrier" before risk passes to the buyer [UCC 2–320(2)]. (These are basically pricing terms, and the contracts remain shipment contracts, not destination contracts.)

Delivery ex-ship (delivery from the carrying vessel) — Means that risk of loss does not pass to the buyer until the goods are properly unloaded from the ship or other carrier [UCC 2–322].

Destination Contracts   In a destination contract, the risk of loss passes to the buyer or lessee when the goods are tendered to the buyer or lessee at the specified destination [UCC 2–319(1)(b), 2–509(1)(b), 2A–219(2)(b)]. In *Example 10.23,* if the contract had been F.O.B. New York, the risk of loss during transit to New York would have been the seller's.

Delivery without Movement of the Goods
The UCC also addresses situations in which the contract does not require the goods to be shipped or moved. Frequently, the buyer or lessee is to pick up the goods from the seller or lessor, or the goods are held by a bailee.

Bailee Under the UCC, a party who, by a bill of lading, warehouse receipt, or other document of title, acknowledges possession of goods and/or contracts to deliver them.

Under the UCC, a **bailee** is a party who, by a bill of lading, warehouse receipt, or other document of title, acknowledges possession of goods and/or contracts to deliver them. A warehousing company, for example, or a trucking company that normally issues documents of title for the goods it receives is a bailee.[12]

Goods Held by the Seller   When the seller keeps the goods for pickup, a document of title usually is not used. If the seller is a merchant, risk of loss to goods held by the seller passes to the buyer when the buyer *actually takes physical possession of the goods* [UCC 2–509(3)]. In other words, the merchant bears the risk of loss between the time the contract is formed and the time the buyer picks up the goods.

If the seller is not a merchant, the risk of loss to goods held by the seller passes to the buyer on *tender of delivery* [UCC 2–509(3)]. This means that the seller bears the risk of loss until he or she makes the goods available to the buyer and notifies the buyer that the goods are ready to be picked up. With respect to leases, the risk of loss passes to the lessee on the lessee's receipt of the goods if the lessor is a merchant. Otherwise, the risk passes to the lessee on tender of delivery [UCC 2A–219(2)(c)].

Goods Held by a Bailee   When a bailee is holding goods for a person who has contracted to sell them and the goods are to be delivered without being moved, the goods are usually represented by a document of title, such as a bill of lading or a warehouse receipt.

Risk of loss passes to the buyer when (1) the buyer receives a negotiable document of title for the goods, (2) the bailee acknowledges the buyer's right to possess the goods, or (3) the buyer receives a nonnegotiable document of title or a writing (record) directing the bailee to deliver the goods *and* has had a *reasonable time* to present the document to the bailee and demand the goods. Obviously, if the bailee refuses to honor the document, the risk of loss remains with the seller [UCC 2–503(4)(b), 2–509(2)].

---

12. Bailments will be discussed in Chapter 23.

With respect to leases, if goods held by a bailee are to be delivered without being moved, the risk of loss passes to the lessee on acknowledgment by the bailee of the lessee's right to possession of the goods [UCC 2A–219(2)(b)].

Risk of Loss When the Contract Is Breached

When a sales or lease contract is breached, the transfer of risk operates differently depending on which party breaches. Generally, the party in breach bears the risk of loss.

When the Seller or Lessor Breaches   If the goods are so nonconforming that the buyer has the right to reject them, the risk of loss does not pass to the buyer until (1) the defects are **cured**—that is, until the goods are repaired, replaced, or discounted in price by the seller or (2) the buyer accepts the goods in spite of their defects (thus waiving the right to reject).

EXAMPLE 10.24   A buyer orders ten stainless steel refrigerators from a seller, F.O.B. the seller's plant. The seller ships white refrigerators instead. The white refrigerators (nonconforming goods) are damaged in transit. The risk of loss falls on the seller. Had the seller shipped stainless steel refrigerators (conforming goods) instead, the risk would have fallen on the buyer [UCC 2–510(1)]. •

If a buyer accepts a shipment of goods and later discovers a defect, acceptance can be revoked. Revocation allows the buyer to pass the risk of loss back to the seller, at least to the extent that the buyer's insurance does not cover the loss [UCC 2–510(2)].

When the Buyer or Lessee Breaches   The general rule is that when a buyer or lessee breaches a contract, the risk of loss immediately shifts to the buyer or lessee. This rule has three important limitations:

1. The seller or lessor must already have identified the contract goods.
2. The buyer or lessee bears the risk for only a commercially reasonable time after the seller or lessor has learned of the breach.
3. The buyer or lessee is liable only to the extent of any deficiency in the seller's insurance coverage [UCC 2–510(3), 2A–220(2)].

Insurable Interest

Parties to sales and lease contracts often obtain insurance coverage to protect against damage, loss, or destruction of goods. Any party purchasing insurance, however, must have a sufficient interest in the insured item to obtain a valid policy. Insurance laws—not the UCC—determine sufficiency (see Chapter 23). The UCC is helpful, however, because it contains certain rules regarding insurable interests in goods.

Insurable Interest of the Buyer or Lessee

A buyer or lessee has an **insurable interest** in identified goods. The moment the contract goods are identified by the seller or lessor, the buyer or lessee has a special property interest that allows the buyer or lessee to obtain necessary insurance coverage for those goods even before the risk of loss has passed [UCC 2–501(1), 2A–218(1)]. Buyers obtain an insurable interest in crops at the time of identification. **EXAMPLE 10.25**   In March, a farmer sells a cotton crop that he hopes to harvest in October. When the crop is planted, the buyer acquires an insurable interest in it because those goods (the cotton crop) are identified to the sales contract between the seller and the buyer. •

Insurable Interest of the Seller or Lessor

A seller has an insurable interest in goods if she or he retains title to the goods. Even after title passes to the buyer, a seller who has a security interest in the goods (a right to secure payment) still has an insurable interest and can insure the goods [UCC 2–501(2)]. Hence, both a buyer and a seller can

Cure The rights of a party who tenders nonconforming performance to correct his or her performance within the contract period.

Insurable Interest A property interest in goods being sold or leased that is sufficiently substantial to permit a party to insure against damage to the goods.

have an insurable interest in the same goods at the same time. Of course, the buyer or seller must sustain an actual loss to have the right to recover from an insurance company. In regard to leases, the lessor retains an insurable interest in leased goods until the lessee exercises an option to buy and the risk of loss has passed to the lessee [UCC 2A–218(3)]. (See the *Business Application* feature on page 316 for a discussion of insurance coverage and other measures that buyers and sellers can take to protect against losses.)

Contracts for the International Sale of Goods

LEARNING OBJECTIVE 5
What law governs contracts for the international sale of goods?

International sales contracts between firms or individuals located in different countries are governed by the 1980 United Nations Convention on Contracts for the International Sale of Goods (CISG). The CISG governs international contracts only if the countries of the parties to the contract have ratified the CISG and if the parties have not agreed that some other law will govern their contract. As of 2012, the CISG had been adopted by seventy-eight countries, including the United States, Canada, Mexico, some Central and South American countries, and most European nations.

Applicability of the CISG

Essentially, the CISG is to international sales contracts what Article 2 of the UCC is to domestic sales contracts. As discussed earlier, in domestic transactions the UCC applies when the parties to a contract for a sale of goods have failed to specify in writing some important term concerning price, delivery, or the like. Similarly, whenever the parties subject to the CISG have failed to specify in writing the precise terms of a contract for the international sale of goods, the CISG will be applied.

Unlike the UCC, *the CISG does not apply to consumer sales.* Neither the UCC nor the CISG applies to contracts for services.

Businesspersons must take special care when drafting international sales contracts to avoid problems caused by distance, including language differences and varying national laws. The fold-out exhibit for this chapter, which shows an actual international sales contract used by Starbucks Coffee Company, illustrates many of the special terms and clauses that are typically contained in international contracts for the sale of goods. Annotations in the exhibit explain the meaning and significance of specific clauses in the contract. (Other laws that frame global business transactions will be discussed in Chapter 25.)

A Comparison of CISG and UCC Provisions

The provisions of the CISG, although similar for the most part to those of the UCC, differ from them in certain respects. We have already mentioned some of these differences. In the *Beyond Our Borders* feature in Chapter 8 on page 246, for example, we pointed out that the CISG does not include any Statute of Frauds provisions. Under Article 11 of the CISG, an international sales contract does not need to be evidenced by a writing or to be in any particular form. We look here at some differences between the UCC and the CISG with respect to contract formation.

Offers   Some differences between the UCC and the CISG have to do with offers. For instance, the UCC provides that a merchant's firm offer is irrevocable, even without consideration, if the merchant gives assurances in a signed writing.

In contrast, under the CISG, an offer can become irrevocable without a signed writing. Article 16(2) of the CISG provides that an offer will be irrevocable if the merchant-offeror simply states orally that the offer is irrevocable or if the offeree reasonably relies on the offer as being irrevocable. In both of these situations, the offer will be irrevocable even without a writing and without consideration.

Another difference is that, under the UCC, if the price term is left open, the court will determine "a reasonable price at the time for delivery" [UCC 2–305(1)]. Under the CISG, however, the price term must be specified, or at least provisions for its specification must be included in the agreement. Otherwise, normally no contract will exist.

Acceptances   Like UCC 2–207, the CISG provides that a contract can be formed even though the acceptance contains additional terms, unless the additional terms materially alter the contract. Under the CISG, however, the definition of a "material alteration" includes virtually any change in the terms. If an additional term relates to payment, quality, quantity, price, time and place of delivery, extent of one party's liability to the other, or the settlement of disputes, the CISG considers the added term a "material alteration." In effect, then, the CISG requires that the terms of the acceptance mirror those of the offer.

Additionally, under the UCC, an acceptance is effective on dispatch. Under the CISG, however, a contract is not created until the offeror receives the acceptance. (The offer becomes irrevocable, however, when the acceptance is sent.) Also, in contrast to the UCC, the CISG provides that acceptance by performance does not require that the offeror be notified of the performance.

Reviewing . . . Sales and Lease Contracts

Guy Holcomb owns and operates Oasis Goodtime Emporium, an adult entertainment establishment. Holcomb wanted to create an adult Internet system for Oasis that would offer customers adult theme videos and "live" chat room programs using performers at the club. On May 10, Holcomb signed a work order authorizing Crossroads Consulting Group (CCG) "to deliver a working prototype of a customer chat system, demonstrating the integration of live video and chatting in a Web browser." In exchange for creating the prototype, Holcomb agreed to pay CCG $64,697. On May 20, Holcomb signed an additional work order in the amount of $12,943 for CCG to install a customized firewall system. The work orders stated that Holcomb would make monthly installment payments to CCG, and both parties expected the work would be finished by September. Due to unforeseen problems largely attributable to system configuration and software incompatibility, the project required more time than anticipated. By the end of the summer, the Web site was still not ready, and Holcomb had fallen behind in the payments to CCG. CCG was threatening to cease work and file suit for breach of contract unless the bill was paid. Rather than make further payments, Holcomb wanted to abandon the Web site project. Using the information presented in the chapter, answer the following questions.

1. Would a court be likely to decide that the transaction between Holcomb and CCG was covered by the Uniform Commercial Code (UCC)? Why or why not?
2. Would a court be likely to consider Holcomb a merchant under the UCC? Why or why not?
3. Did the parties have a valid contract under the UCC? Explain.
4. Suppose that Holcomb and CCG meet in October in an attempt to resolve their problems. At that time, the parties reach an oral agreement that CCG will continue to work without demanding full payment of the past-due amounts and Holcomb will pay CCG $5,000 per week. Assuming that the contract falls under the UCC, is the oral agreement enforceable? Why or why not?

DEBATE THIS   The UCC should require the same degree of definiteness of terms, especially with respect to price and quantity, as general contract law does.

BUSINESS APPLICATION

Who Bears the Risk of Loss—the Seller or the Buyer?*

The shipment of goods is a major aspect of commercial transactions. Many issues arise when an unforeseen event, such as fire or theft, causes damage to goods in transit. At the time of contract negotiation, both the seller and the buyer should determine the importance of the risk of loss. In some circumstances, risk is relatively unimportant (such as when ten boxes of copier paper are being sold), and the delivery terms should simply reflect costs and price. In other circumstances, risk is extremely important (such as when a fragile piece of pharmaceutical testing equipment is being sold), and the parties will need an express agreement as to the moment risk is to pass so that they can insure the goods accordingly. Risk should always be considered before a loss occurs, not after.

A major consideration relating to risk is when to insure goods against possible losses. Buyers and sellers should determine the point at which risk passes so that they can obtain insurance coverage to protect themselves against loss when they have an insurable interest in the goods.

Checklist to Determine Risk of Loss

The UCC uses a three-part checklist to determine risk of loss:

1. If the contract includes terms allocating the risk of loss, those terms are binding and must be applied.
2. If the contract is silent as to risk and either party breaches the contract, the breaching party is liable for the risk of loss.
3. If the contract makes no reference to risk and the goods are to be shipped or delivered, the risk of loss is borne by the party having control over the goods (delivery terms) if neither party breaches.

---

*This *Business Application* is not meant to substitute for the services of an attorney who is licensed to practice law in your state.

If You Are the Seller

If you are a seller of goods to be shipped, realize that as long as you have control over the goods, you are liable for any loss unless the buyer is in breach or the contract contains an explicit agreement to the contrary. When there is no explicit agreement, the delivery terms in your contract can serve as a basis for determining control. Thus, if goods are shipped "F.O.B. buyer's business," risk of loss does not pass to the buyer until there is a tender of delivery at the destination—the buyer's business. Any loss or damage in transit falls on the seller because the seller has control until proper tender has been made.

If You Are the Buyer

If you are a buyer of goods, it is important to remember that most sellers prefer "F.O.B. seller's business" as a delivery term. Under this term, once the goods are delivered to the carrier, the buyer bears the risk of loss. Thus, if conforming goods are completely destroyed or lost in transit, the buyer not only suffers the loss but is obligated to pay the seller the contract price.

Checklist for the Seller or the Buyer

1. Before entering into a contract, determine the importance of the risk of loss for a given sale.
2. If risk is extremely important, the contract should expressly state the moment the risk of loss will pass from the seller to the buyer. This clause could even provide that risk will not pass until the goods are "delivered, installed, inspected, and tested (or in running order for a period of time)."
3. If an express clause is not included, delivery terms determine the passage of risk of loss.
4. When appropriate, either party or both parties should consider procuring insurance.

Key Terms

Chapter Summary: Sales and Lease Contracts

The Scope of the UCC and Articles 2 (Sales) and 2A (Leases) (See pages 292–296.)	1. *The UCC*—The UCC attempts to provide a consistent, uniform, and integrated framework of rules to deal with all phases *ordinarily arising* in a commercial sales or lease transaction, including contract formation, passage of title and risk of loss, performance, remedies, payment for goods, warehoused goods, and secured transactions. 2. *Article 2 (sales)*—Article 2 governs contracts for the sale of goods (tangible, movable personal property). The common law of contracts also applies to sales contracts to the extent that the common law has not been modified by the UCC. If there is a conflict between a common law rule and the UCC, the UCC controls. 3. *Article 2A (leases)*—Article 2A governs contracts for the lease of goods. Except that it applies to leases, instead of sales, of goods, Article 2A is essentially a repetition of Article 2 and varies only to reflect differences between sales and lease transactions.

The Formation of Sales and Lease Contracts (See pages 297–307.)	1. *Offer*—
	  a. Not all terms have to be included for a contract to be formed (only the subject matter and quantity term must be specified).
	  b. The price does not have to be included for a contract to be formed.
	  c. Particulars of performance can be left open.
	  d. A written and signed offer by a *merchant*, covering a period of three months or less, is irrevocable without payment of consideration.
	2. *Acceptance*—
	  a. Acceptance may be made by any reasonable means of communication. It is effective when dispatched.
	  b. An offer can be accepted by a promise to ship or by prompt shipment of conforming goods, or by prompt shipment of nonconforming goods if not accompanied by a notice of accommodation.
	  c. Acceptance by performance requires notice within a reasonable time. Otherwise, the offer can be treated as lapsed.
	  d. A definite expression of acceptance creates a contract even if the terms of the acceptance differ from those of the offer, unless the additional or different terms in the acceptance are expressly conditioned on the offeror's assent to those terms.
	3. *Consideration*—A modification of a contract for the sale of goods does not require consideration.
	4. *The Statute of Frauds*—
	  a. All contracts for the sale of goods priced at $500 or more must be in writing. A writing is sufficient as long as it indicates a contract between the parties and is signed by the party against whom enforcement is sought. A contract is not enforceable beyond the quantity shown in the writing.
	  b. When written confirmation of an oral contract *between merchants* is not objected to in writing by the receiver within ten days, the contract is enforceable.
	  c. For exceptions to the Statute of Frauds, see Exhibit 10.2 on page 304.
	5. *Parol evidence rule*—
	  a. The terms of a clear and complete written contract cannot be contradicted by evidence of prior agreements or contemporaneous oral agreements.
	  b. Evidence is admissible to clarify the terms of a writing if the contract terms are ambiguous or if evidence of course of dealing, usage of trade, or course of performance is necessary to learn or to clarify the parties' intentions.
	6. *Unconscionability*—An unconscionable contract is one that is so unfair and one sided that it would be unreasonable to enforce it. If the court deems a sales contract to have been unconscionable at the time it was made, the court can (a) refuse to enforce the contract, (b) refuse to enforce the unconscionable clause, or (c) limit the application of any unconscionable clauses to avoid an unconscionable result.

Title and Risk of Loss (See pages 307–314.)	1. *Shipment contract*—In the absence of an agreement, title and risk pass on the seller's or lessor's delivery of conforming goods to the carrier [UCC 2–319(1)(a), 2–401(2)(a), 2–509(1)(a), 2A–219(2)(a)].
	2. *Destination contract*—In the absence of an agreement, title and risk pass on the seller's or lessor's *tender* of delivery of conforming goods to the buyer or lessee at the point of destination [UCC 2–319(1)(b), 2–401(2)(b), 2–509(1)(b), 2A–219(2)(b)].
	3. *Delivery without movement of the goods*—In the absence of an agreement, if the goods are not represented by a document of title, title passes on the formation of the contract, and risk passes on the buyer's or lessee's receipt of the goods if the seller or lessor is a merchant or on the tender of delivery if the seller or lessor is a nonmerchant.
	4. *Sales and leases by nonowners*—Between the owner and a good faith purchaser or between the lessee and a sublessee:
	  a. Void title—Owner prevails [UCC 2–403(1)].
	  b. Voidable title—Buyer prevails [UCC 2–403(1)].
	  c. Entrusted to a merchant—Buyer or sublessee prevails [UCC 2–403(2), (3); 2A–305(2)].

Continued

Chapter Summary: Sales and Lease Contracts—Continued

Title and Risk of Loss—Continued	5. *Risk of loss when the contract is breached—*
	  a. If the seller or lessor breaches by tendering nonconforming goods that are rejected by the buyer or lessee, the risk of loss does not pass to the buyer or lessee until the defects are cured (unless the buyer or lessee accepts the goods in spite of their defects, thus waiving the right to reject) [UCC 2–510(1), 2A–220(1)].
	  b. If the buyer or lessee breaches the contract, the risk of loss immediately shifts to the buyer or lessee for goods that are identified to the contract. The buyer or lessee bears the risk for only a commercially reasonable time after the seller or lessor has learned of the breach [UCC 2–510(3), 2A–220(2)].

Contracts for the International Sale of Goods (See pages 314–315.)	International sales contracts are governed by the United Nations Convention on Contracts for the International Sale of Goods (CISG)—if the countries of the parties to the contract have ratified the CISG (and if the parties have not agreed that some other law will govern their contract). Essentially, the CISG is to international sales contracts what Article 2 of the UCC is to domestic sales contracts. Whenever parties who are subject to the CISG have failed to specify in writing the precise terms of a contract for the international sale of goods, the CISG will be applied.

ExamPrep

ISSUE SPOTTERS

1. E-Design, Inc., orders 150 computer desks. Fav-O-Rite Supplies, Inc., ships 150 printer stands. Is this an acceptance of the offer or a counteroffer? If it is an acceptance, is it a breach of the contract? What if Fav-O-Rite told E-Design it was sending the printer stands as "an accommodation"? **(See pages 299–302.)**
2. Truck Parts, Inc. (TPI), often sells supplies to United Fix-It Company (UFC), which services trucks. Over the phone, they negotiate for the sale of eighty-four sets of tires. TPI sends a letter to UFC detailing the terms and two weeks later ships the tires. Is there an enforceable contract between them? Why or why not? **(See pages 297–299.)**

—Check your answers to the Issue Spotters against the answers provided in Appendix E at the end of this text.

BEFORE THE TEST

Go to www.cengagebrain.com, enter the ISBN 9781133191353, and click on "Find" to locate this textbook's Web site. Then, click on "Access Now" under "Study Tools," and select Chapter 10 at the top. There, you will find a Practice Quiz that you can take to assess your mastery of the concepts in this chapter, as well as Flashcards, a Glossary of important terms, and Video Questions (when assigned).

For Review

Answers to the even-numbered questions in this For Review section can be found in Appendix F at the end of this text.

1. How do Article 2 and Article 2A of the UCC differ? What types of transactions does each article cover?
2. In a sales contract, if an offeree includes additional or different terms in an acceptance, will a contract result? If so, what happens to these terms?
3. What exceptions to the writing requirements of the Statute of Frauds are provided in Article 2 and Article 2A of the UCC?
4. Risk of loss does not necessarily pass with title. If the parties to a contract do not expressly agree when risk passes and the goods are to be delivered without movement by the seller, when does risk pass?
5. What law governs contracts for the international sale of goods?

Business Scenarios and Case Problems

10–1 Statute of Frauds. Fresher Foods, Inc., orally agreed to purchase one thousand bushels of corn for $1.25 per bushel from Dale Vernon, a farmer. Fresher Foods paid $125 down and agreed to pay the remainder of the purchase price on delivery, which was scheduled for one week later. When Fresher Foods tendered the balance of $1,125 on the scheduled day of delivery and requested the corn, Vernon refused to deliver it. Fresher Foods sued Vernon for damages, claiming that Vernon had breached their oral contract. Can Fresher Foods recover? If so, to what extent? **(See pages 302–304.)**

10–2 **Question with Sample Answer—Merchant's Firm Offer.** On September 1, Jennings, a used-car dealer, wrote a letter to Wheeler, stating, "I have a 1955 Thunderbird convertible in mint condition that I will sell you for $13,500 at any time before October 9. [signed] Peter Jennings." By September 15, having heard nothing from Wheeler, Jennings sold the Thunderbird to another party. On September 29, Wheeler accepted Jennings's offer and tendered the $13,500. When Jennings told Wheeler he had sold the car to another party, Wheeler claimed Jennings had breached their contract. Is Jennings in breach? Explain. **(See page 299.)**

—**For a sample answer to Question 10–2, go to Appendix G at the end of this text.**

10–3 **Spotlight on Goods and Services—The Statute of Frauds.** Fallsview Glatt Kosher Caterers ran a business that provided travel packages, including food, entertainment, and lectures on religious subjects, to customers during the Passover holiday at a New York resort. Willie Rosenfeld verbally agreed to pay Fallsview $24,050 for the Passover package for himself and his family. Rosenfeld did not appear at the resort and never paid the money owed. Fallsview sued Rosenfeld for breach of contract. Rosenfeld claimed that the contract was unenforceable because it was not in writing and violated the UCC's Statute of Frauds. Is the contract valid? Explain. [*Fallsview Glatt Kosher Caterers, Inc. v. Rosenfeld,* 794 N.Y.S.2d 790 (N.Y. Super. 2005)] **(See pages 302–304.)**

10–4 **Case Problem with Sample Answer—Passage of Title.** Kenzie Godfrey was a passenger in a taxi when it collided with a car driven by Dawn Altieri. Altieri had originally leased the car from G.E. Capital Auto Lease, Inc. By the time of the accident, she had bought it, but she had not fully paid for it or completed the transfer-of-title paperwork. Godfrey suffered a brain injury and sought to recover damages from the owner of the car that Altieri was driving. Who had title to the car at the time of the accident? Explain. [*Godfrey v. G.E. Capital Auto Lease, Inc.,* 89 A.D.3d 471, 933 N.Y.S.2d 208 (1 Dept. 2011)] **(See page 308.)**

—**For a sample answer to Problem 10–4, go to Appendix H at the end of this text.**

10–5 **Additional Terms.** B.S. International, Ltd. (BSI), makes costume jewelry. JMAM, LLC, is a wholesaler of costume jewelry. JMAM sent BSI a letter with the terms for orders, including the necessary procedure for obtaining credit for items that customers rejected. The letter stated, "By signing below, you agree to the terms." Steven Baracsi, BSI's owner, signed the letter and returned it. For six years, BSI made jewelry for JMAM, which resold it. Items rejected by customers were sent back to JMAM, but were never returned to BSI. BSI filed a suit against JMAM, claiming $41,294.21 for the unreturned items. BSI showed the court a copy of JMAM's terms. Across the bottom had been typed a "PS" requiring the return of rejected merchandise. Was this "PS" part of the contract? Discuss. [*B.S. International, Ltd. v. JMAM, LLC,* 13 A.3d 1057 (R.I. 2011)] **(See page 300.)**

10–6 **Delivery without Movement of the Goods.** Aleris International, Inc., signed a contract to buy a John Deere loader from Holt Equipment Co. The agreement provided that "despite physical delivery of the equipment, title shall remain in the seller until" Aleris paid the full price. The next month, Aleris filed for bankruptcy. Holt asserted that it was the owner of the loader and filed a claim with the court to repossess it. Who is entitled to the loader, and why? [*In re Aleris International, Ltd.,* __ Bankr. __ (D.Del. 2011)] **(See page 309.)**

10–7 **Goods Held by the Seller or Lessor.** Douglas Singletary bought a manufactured home from Andy's Mobile Home and Land Sales. The contract stated that the buyer accepted the home "as is where is." Singletary paid the full price, and his crew began to ready the home to relocate it to his property. The night before the home was to be moved, however, it was destroyed by fire. Who suffered the loss? Explain. [*Singletary, III v. P&A Investments, Inc.,* 712 S.E.2d 681 (N.C.App. 2011)] **(See page 312.)**

10–8 **Partial Performance and the Statute of Frauds.** After a series of e-mails, Jorge Bonilla, the sole proprietor of a printing company in Uruguay, agreed to buy a used printer from Crystal Graphics Equipment, Inc., in New York. Crystal Graphics, through its agent, told Bonilla that the printing press was fully operational, contained all of its parts, and was in excellent condition except for some damage to one of the printing towers. Bonilla paid $95,000. Crystal Graphics sent him a signed, stamped invoice reflecting this payment. The invoice was dated six days after Bonilla's conversation with the agent. When the printing press arrived, Bonilla discovered that it was missing parts and was damaged. Crystal Graphics sent replacement parts, but they did not work. Ultimately, Crystal Graphics was never able to make the printer operational. Bonilla sued, alleging breach of contract, breach of the implied covenant of good faith and fair dealing, breach of express warranty, and breach of implied warranty. Crystal Graphics claimed that the contract was not enforceable because it did not satisfy the Statute of Frauds. Can Crystal Graphics prevail on this basis? Why or why not? [*Bonilla v. Crystal Graphics Equipment, Inc.,* 2012 WL 360145 (S.D.Fla. 2012)] **(See page 304.)**

10–9 **A Question of Ethics—Statute of Frauds.** Daniel Fox owned Fox & Lamberth Enterprises, Inc., a kitchen remodeling business. Fox leased a building from Carl Hussong. When Fox planned to close his business, Craftsmen Home Improvement, Inc., expressed an interest in buying his assets. Fox set a price of $50,000. Craftsmen's owners agreed and gave Fox a list of the desired items and a "Bill of Sale" that set the terms for payment. Craftsmen expected to negotiate a new lease with Hussong and modified the premises, including removal of some of the displays. When Hussong and Craftsmen could not agree on new terms, Craftsmen told Fox that the deal was off. [*Fox & Lamberth Enterprises, Inc. v. Craftsmen Home Improvement, Inc.*, __ N.E.2d __ (2 Dist. 2006)]

1. In Fox's suit for breach of contract, Craftsmen raised the Statute of Frauds as a defense. What are the requirements of the Statute of Frauds? Did the deal between Fox and Craftsmen meet these requirements? Did it fall under one of the exceptions? Explain. (**See pages 302–304.**)

2. Craftsmen also claimed that the "predominant factor" of its agreement with Fox was a lease for Hussong's building. What is the predominant-factor test? Does it apply here? In any event, is it fair to hold a party to a contract to buy a business's assets when the buyer is unable to negotiate a favorable lease of the premises on which the assets are located? Discuss. (**See pages 294–295.**)

Critical Thinking and Writing Assignments

10–10 **Business Law Critical Thinking Group Assignment.** Mountain Stream Trout Co. agreed to buy "market size" trout from trout grower Lake Farms, LLC. Their five-year contract did not define *market size*. At the time, in the trade, *market size* referred to fish of one-pound live weight. After three years, Mountain Stream began taking fewer, smaller deliveries of larger fish, claiming that *market size* varied according to whatever its customers demanded and that its customers now demanded larger fish. Lake Farms filed a suit for breach of contract.

1. The first group will decide whether parol (outside) evidence is admissible to explain the terms of this contract. Are there any exceptions that could apply?

2. A second group will determine the impact of course of dealing and usage of trade on the interpretation of contract terms.

3. A third group will discuss how parties to a commercial contract can avoid the possibility that a court will interpret the contract terms in accordance with trade usage.

CHAPTER 11

Performance and Breach in Sales and Lease Contracts

(Bobby Yip/Reuters/Landov)

CHAPTER OUTLINE

- Obligations of the Seller or Lessor
- Obligations of the Buyer or Lessee
- Anticipatory Repudiation
- Remedies of the Seller or Lessor
- Remedies of the Buyer or Lessee
- Limitation of Remedies

LEARNING OBJECTIVES

The five learning objectives below are designed to help improve your understanding of the chapter. After reading this chapter, you should be able to answer the following questions:

1 What are the respective obligations of the parties under a contract for the sale or lease of goods?

2 What is the perfect tender rule? What are some important exceptions to this rule that apply to sales and lease contracts?

3 What options are available to the nonbreaching party when the other party to a sales or lease contract repudiates the contract prior to the time for performance?

4 What remedies are available to a seller or lessor when the buyer or lessee breaches the contract? What remedies are available to a buyer or lessee if the seller or lessor breaches the contract?

5 In contracts subject to the UCC, are parties free to limit the remedies available to the nonbreaching party on a breach of contract? If so, in what ways?

"Gratitude is as the good faith of merchants: it holds commerce together."
—François de la Rochefoucauld, 1613–1680 (French author)

The performance required of the parties under a sales or lease contract consists of the duties and obligations each party has under the terms of the contract. Keep in mind that a party's "duties and obligations" include those specified by the agreement, by custom, and by the Uniform Commercial Code (UCC). Because, as the chapter-opening quotation indicates, good faith "holds commerce together," the UCC also imposes a duty of good faith on the parties involved in commercial contracts. This duty basically requires honesty and fair dealing. If a sales contract leaves open some particulars of performance, for instance, the parties must exercise good faith and commercial reasonableness when later specifying the details.

In the performance of a sales or lease contract, the basic obligation of the seller or lessor is to *transfer and deliver conforming goods*. The basic obligation of the buyer or lessee is *to accept and to pay for conforming goods* in accordance with the contract [UCC 2–301,

2A–516(1)]. Overall performance of a sales or lease contract is controlled by the agreement between the parties. When the contract is unclear and disputes arise, the courts look to the UCC and impose standards of good faith and commercial reasonableness.

Sometimes, circumstances make it difficult for a person to carry out the promised performance, and the contract is breached. When breach occurs, the aggrieved party looks for remedies—which we discuss in the second half of the chapter.

Obligations of the Seller or Lessor

Conforming Goods Goods that conform to contract specifications.

Tender of Delivery A seller's or lessor's act of placing conforming goods at the disposal of the buyer or lessee and providing whatever notification is reasonably necessary to enable the buyer or lessee to take delivery.

LEARNING OBJECTIVE 1
What are the respective obligations of the parties under a contract for the sale or lease of goods?

The major obligation of the seller or lessor under a sales or lease contract is to tender conforming goods to the buyer or lessee. Goods that conform to the contract description in every way are called **conforming goods**. To fulfill the contract, the seller or lessor must either deliver or tender delivery of conforming goods to the buyer or lessee. **Tender of delivery** occurs when the seller or lessor makes conforming goods available to the buyer or lessee and provides whatever notification is reasonably necessary to enable the buyer or lessee to take delivery [UCC 2–503(1), 2A–508(1)].

Tender must occur at a *reasonable hour* and in a *reasonable manner*. In other words, a seller cannot call the buyer at 2:00 A.M. and say, "The goods are ready. I'll give you twenty minutes to get them." Unless the parties have agreed otherwise, the goods must be tendered for delivery at a reasonable hour and kept available for a reasonable period of time to enable the buyer to take possession of them [UCC 2–503(1)(a)].

Normally, all goods called for by a contract must be tendered in a single delivery, unless the parties have agreed that the goods may be delivered in several lots or *installments* [UCC 2–307, 2–612, 2A–510]. Hence, an order for 1,000 shirts cannot be delivered 2 shirts at a time. If, however, the parties agree that the shirts will be delivered in four lots of 250 each as they are produced (for summer, fall, winter, and spring stock), then delivery may occur in this manner.

Place of Delivery

Fresh produce is loaded for delivery. Under what circumstances can the buyer reject this produce?

(AP Photo/Mike Groll)

As noted in Chapter 10, the UCC provides for the place of delivery pursuant to a contract only if the contract does not. The buyer and seller (or lessor and lessee) may agree that the goods will be delivered to a particular destination where the buyer or lessee will take possession. If the contract does not designate the place of delivery, then the goods must be made available to the buyer at the *seller's place of business* or, if the seller has none, at the seller's residence [UCC 2–308(a)]. If, at the time of contracting, the parties know that the goods identified to the contract are located somewhere other than the seller's business, then the *location of the goods* is the place for their delivery [UCC 2–308(b)].

EXAMPLE 11.1 Li Wan and Jo Boyd both live in San Francisco. In San Francisco, Wan contracts to sell Boyd five used trucks, which both parties know are located in a Chicago warehouse. If nothing more is specified in the contract, the place of delivery for the trucks is Chicago. Wan may tender delivery either by giving Boyd a negotiable or nonnegotiable document of title or by obtaining the bailee's (warehouser's) acknowledgment that the buyer is entitled to possession.[1] ●

Delivery via Carrier

In many instances, it is clear from the surrounding circumstances or delivery terms in the contract (such as F.O.B. or F.A.S. terms, shown in Exhibit 10.4 on page 312) that the parties intended the goods to be moved by a carrier. In carrier contracts, the seller fulfills the obligation to deliver the goods through either a shipment contract or a destination contract.

Shipment Contracts
Recall from Chapter 10 that a *shipment contract* requires or authorizes the seller to ship goods by a carrier, rather than to deliver them at a particular destination [UCC 2–319, 2–509(1)(a)]. Under a shipment contract, unless otherwise agreed, the seller must do the following:

1. Put the goods into the hands of the carrier.
2. Make a contract for their transportation that is reasonable according to the nature of the goods and their value. (For example, certain types of goods require refrigeration in transit.)
3. Obtain and promptly deliver or tender to the buyer any documents necessary to enable the buyer to obtain possession of the goods from the carrier.
4. Promptly notify the buyer that shipment has been made [UCC 2–504].

If the seller fails to notify the buyer that shipment has been made or fails to make a proper contract for transportation, the buyer can treat the contract as breached and reject the goods, but only if a *material loss* of the goods or a *significant delay* results. Of course, the parties can agree that a lesser amount of loss or that any delay will be grounds for rejection.

Destination Contracts
In a *destination contract,* the seller agrees to deliver conforming goods to the buyer at a particular destination. The seller must provide the buyer with any documents of title necessary to enable the buyer to obtain delivery from the carrier [UCC 2–503].

The Perfect Tender Rule

As previously noted, the seller or lessor has an obligation to ship or tender *conforming goods,* and the buyer or lessee is required to accept and pay for the goods according to the terms of the contract. Under the common law, the seller was obligated to deliver goods that conformed to the terms of the contract in every detail. This was called the *perfect tender* doctrine.

The UCC preserves the perfect tender doctrine by stating that if the goods or tender of delivery fail *in any respect* to conform to the contract, the buyer or lessee has the right to accept the goods, reject the entire shipment, or accept part and reject part [UCC 2–601, 2A–509].

The corollary to this rule is that if the goods conform in every respect, the buyer or lessee does not have a right to reject the goods, as the following case illustrates.

---

1. If the seller delivers a nonnegotiable document of title or merely instructs the bailee in a writing (or electronic record) to release the goods to the buyer without the bailee's *acknowledgment* of the buyer's rights, this is also a sufficient tender, unless the buyer objects [UCC 2–503(4)]. Risk of loss, however, does not pass until the buyer has a reasonable amount of time in which to present the document or to give the bailee instructions for delivery, as discussed in Chapter 10.

Case 11.1

Wilson Sporting Goods Co. v. U.S. Golf & Tennis Centers, Inc.

Court of Appeals of Tennessee, 2012 WL 601804 (2012).

FACTS U.S. Golf & Tennis Centers, Inc., operates two retail sporting goods stores that specialize in golf and tennis equipment. U.S. Golf agreed to buy 96,000 golf balls from Wilson Sporting Goods Company for a total price of $20,000. The parties negotiated the agreement via fax, and Wilson affirmed that U.S. Golf was receiving the lowest price ($5 per two-dozen unit) "that Wilson offered to any one in the market." Wilson shipped golf balls to U.S. Golf that conformed to the contract in quantity and quality, but it did not receive payment. U.S. Golf claimed that it had learned that Wilson had sold the product for $2 a unit to another buyer and asked Wilson to reduce the contract price of the balls to $4 per unit (for a total of $16,000). Wilson refused and filed a suit to collect the $20,000. The trial court entered judgment in favor of Wilson for $33,099.28, which included the contract price, interest, attorneys' fees, and certain allowable expenses. U.S. Golf appealed.

ISSUE When a seller has tendered conforming goods, can the buyer reject the goods and cancel the contract?

DECISION No. The state appellate court affirmed the lower court's judgment in favor of Wilson. When a seller tenders conforming goods, the buyer is obligated to accept and pay for the goods.

REASON Because it was undisputed that the shipment of golf balls conformed in quantity and quality to the contract specifications, U.S. Golf was obligated to accept the goods and pay the agreed-on price. U.S. Golf argued that Wilson had breached the contract by misrepresenting the price of the golf balls as its lowest price, but the court was not convinced. Evidence showed that the parties had agreed on a price of $20,000. U.S. Golf did not present any evidence to contradict the price term in the parties' agreement or to establish that Wilson had engaged in misrepresentation. Therefore, the perfect tender rule applied, and U.S. Golf was not entitled to reject the goods or cancel the contract.

WHAT IF THE FACTS WERE DIFFERENT? *Suppose that U.S. Golf had presented as evidence a contract between Wilson and another buyer a month after this shipment was delivered to U.S. Golf. In that contract, Wilson agreed to sell the same golf balls for $4 per unit to a different buyer. Would the court have ruled differently in this dispute? Why or why not?*

Exceptions to the Perfect Tender Rule

Because of the rigidity of the perfect tender rule, several exceptions to the rule have been created, some of which are discussed here.

Agreement of the Parties
Exceptions to the perfect tender rule may be established by agreement. If the parties have agreed, for example, that defective goods or parts will not be rejected if the seller or lessor is able to repair or replace them within a reasonable period of time, the perfect tender rule does not apply.

Cure
The UCC does not specifically define the term *cure,* but it refers to the right of the seller or lessor to repair, adjust, or replace defective or nonconforming goods [UCC 2–508, 2A–513].

Timing and Reasonable Grounds When any tender of delivery is rejected because of nonconforming goods and the time for performance has not yet expired, the seller or lessor can notify the buyer or lessee promptly of the intention to cure and can then do so *within the contract time for performance* [UCC 2–508(1), 2A–513(1)]. Once the time for

If a buyer has accepted these blue pens in the past when she ordered black pens, is the seller justified in shipping blue pens again?

(Sadovnikova Olga/Shutterstock.com)

Installment Contract A contract that requires or authorizes delivery in two or more separate lots to be accepted and paid for separately.

performance has expired, the seller or lessor still has a reasonable time in which to cure if, at the time of delivery, he or she had *reasonable grounds to believe that the nonconforming goods would be acceptable to the buyer or lessee* [UCC 2–508(2), 2A–513(2)].

EXAMPLE 11.2   In the past, EZ Office Supply frequently accepted blue pens when the seller, Baxter's Wholesale, did not have black pens in stock. In this context, Baxter's has reasonable grounds to believe that EZ will again accept such a substitute. Even if EZ rejects the substituted goods on a particular occasion, because Baxter's had reasonable grounds to believe that the substitution would be acceptable, it will have a reasonable time to cure by tendering black pens. •

A seller or lessor may sometimes tender nonconforming goods with a price allowance (discount), which can also serve as "reasonable grounds" to believe the buyer or lessee will accept the nonconforming tender.

Nature of Defect Must Be Disclosed   The right to cure means that, to reject goods, the buyer or lessee must inform the seller or lessor of a particular defect. For instance, if a lessee refuses a tender of goods as nonconforming but does not disclose the nature of the defect to the lessor, the lessee cannot later assert the defect as a defense if the defect is one that the lessor could have cured. Generally, buyers and lessees must act in good faith and state specific reasons for refusing to accept goods [UCC 2–605, 2A–514].

Substitution of Carriers

When an agreed-on manner of delivery (such as the carrier to be used to transport the goods) becomes impracticable or unavailable through no fault of either party, but a commercially reasonable substitute is available, the seller must use this substitute performance, which is sufficient tender to the buyer [UCC 2–614(1)].

EXAMPLE 11.3   A sales contract calls for a large generator to be delivered via Roadway Trucking Corporation on or before June 1. The contract terms clearly state the importance of the delivery date. The employees of Roadway Trucking go on strike. The seller is required to make a reasonable substitute tender, perhaps by rail if that is available. Note that the seller normally will be responsible for any additional shipping costs, unless other arrangements have been made in the sales contract. •

Installment Contracts

An **installment contract** is a single contract that requires or authorizes delivery in two or more separate lots to be accepted and paid for separately. With an installment contract, a buyer or lessee can reject an installment *only if the nonconformity substantially impairs the value* of the installment and cannot be cured [UCC 2–307, 2–612(2), 2A–510(1)]. If the buyer or lessee subsequently accepts a nonconforming installment and fails to notify the seller or lessor of cancellation, however, the contract is reinstated [UCC 2–612(3), 2A–510(2)].

Unless the contract provides otherwise, the entire installment contract is breached only when one or more nonconforming installments *substantially* impair the value of the *whole contract.* **EXAMPLE 11.4** A contract calls for the parts of a machine to be delivered in installments. The first part is necessary for the operation of the machine, but when it is delivered, it is irreparably defective. The failure of this first installment will be a breach of the whole contract because the machine will not operate without the first part. The situation would likely be different, however, if the contract had called for twenty carloads of plywood and only 6 percent of one carload had deviated from the thickness specifications in the contract. It is unlikely that a court would find that a defect in 6 percent of one installment substantially impaired the value of the whole contract. •

The point to remember is that the UCC significantly alters the right of the buyer or lessee to reject the entire contract if the contract requires delivery to be made in several installments. The UCC strictly limits rejection to cases of *substantial* nonconformity.

> "Obstacles are those frightful things you see when you take your eyes off your goal."
>
> Henry Ford, 1863–1947
> (Founder of Ford Motor Company)

Commercial Impracticability   As mentioned on page 268 in Chapter 9, occurrences unforeseen by either party when a contract was made may make performance commercially impracticable. When this occurs, the rule of perfect tender no longer holds. According to UCC 2–615(a) and 2A–405(a), a delay in delivery or nondelivery in whole or in part is not a breach when performance has been made impracticable "by the occurrence of a contingency the nonoccurrence of which was a basic assumption on which the contract was made." The seller or lessor must, however, notify the buyer or lessee as soon as practicable that there will be a delay or nondelivery.

Foreseeable versus Unforeseeable Contingencies   The doctrine of commercial impracticability extends only to problems that could not have been foreseen. **EXAMPLE 11.5**   A major oil company that receives its supplies from the Middle East has a contract to supply a buyer with 100,000 barrels of oil. Because of an oil embargo by the Organization of Petroleum Exporting Countries, the seller is unable to secure oil supplies to meet the terms of the contract. Because of the same embargo, the seller cannot secure oil from any other source. This situation comes under the commercial impracticability exception to the perfect tender doctrine. •

Can unanticipated increases in a seller's costs, which make performance "impracticable," constitute a valid defense to performance on the basis of commercial impracticability? The court dealt with this question in the following *Classic Case.*

Classic Case 11.2

Maple Farms, Inc. v. City School District of Elmira

Supreme Court of New York,
76 Misc.2d 1080, 352 N.Y.S.2d 784 (1974).

(princessdia/iStockphoto.com)

School districts often make long-term contracts for milk deliveries.

FACTS   On June 15, 1973, Maple Farms, Inc., formed an agreement with the city school district of Elmira, New York, to supply the school district with milk for the 1973–1974 school year. The agreement was in the form of a requirements contract, under which Maple Farms would sell to the school district all the milk the district required at a fixed price—which was the June market price of milk. By December 1973, the price of raw milk had increased by 23 percent over the price specified in the contract. This meant that if the terms of the contract were fulfilled, Maple Farms would lose $7,350. Because it had similar contracts with other school districts, Maple Farms stood to lose a great deal if it was held to the price stated in the contracts. When the school district would not agree to release Maple Farms from its contract, Maple Farms brought an action in a New York state court for a declaratory judgment (a determination of the parties' rights under a contract). Maple Farms contended that the substantial increase in the price of raw milk was an event not contemplated by the parties when the contract was formed and that, given the increased price, performance of the contract was commercially impracticable.

ISSUE   Could Maple Farms be released from the contract on the ground of commercial impracticability?

DECISION   No. the court ruled that performance in this case was not impracticable.

REASON   The court reasoned that commercial impracticability arises when an event occurs that is totally unexpected and unforeseeable by the parties. The increased price of raw milk was not totally unexpected, given that in the previous year the price of milk had risen 10 percent and that the price of milk had traditionally varied. Additionally, the general inflation of prices in the United States should have been anticipated. Maple Farms had reason to know these facts and could have included a clause in its contract with the school district to protect itself from its present situation. The court also noted that, for the school district, the primary purpose of the contract was to protect itself (for budgeting purposes) against price fluctuations.

WHAT IF THE FACTS WERE DIFFERENT?   *Suppose that the court had ruled in the plaintiff's favor. How might that ruling have affected the plaintiff's contracts with other parties?*

IMPACT OF THIS CASE ON TODAY'S LAW   *This case is a classic illustration of the UCC's commercial impracticability*

Classic Case 11.2—Continued

doctrine. Under this doctrine, parties who freely enter into contracts normally will not be excused from their contractual obligations simply because changed circumstances make performance difficult or unprofitable. Rather, to be excused from performance, a party must show that the changed circumstances were unforeseeable by both parties at the time the contract was formed. This principle continues to be applied today.

Partial Performance Sometimes, an unforeseen event only *partially* affects the capacity of the seller or lessor to perform, and the seller or lessor is thus able to fulfill the contract *partially* but cannot tender total performance. In this situation, the seller or lessor is required to allocate in a fair and reasonable manner any remaining production and deliveries among those to whom it is contractually obligated to deliver the goods, and this allocation may take into account its regular customers [UCC 2–615(b), 2A–405(b)]. The buyer or lessee must receive notice of the allocation and has the right to accept or reject it [UCC 2–615(c), 2A–405(c)].

EXAMPLE 11.6 A Florida orange grower, Best Citrus, Inc., contracts to sell this season's crop to a number of customers, including Martin's grocery chain. Martin's contracts to purchase two thousand crates of oranges. Best Citrus has sprayed some of its orange groves with a chemical called Karmoxin. When studies show that persons who eat products sprayed with Karmoxin may develop cancer, the Department of Agriculture issues an order prohibiting the sale of these products. Best Citrus picks only those oranges not sprayed with Karmoxin, but there are not enough to meet all the contracted-for deliveries. In this situation, Best Citrus is required to allocate its production. It notifies Martin's that it cannot deliver the full quantity specified in the contract and indicates the amount it will be able to deliver. Martin's can either accept or reject the allocation, but Best Citrus has no further contractual liability. •

ETHICAL ISSUE

Is it appropriate to use the latest global economic crisis as a reason to escape contractual obligations? Starting as early as 2007 and lasting through at least 2012, many companies were hit hard by the global economic crisis. When economic conditions make it difficult (or even impossible) for parties to perform, should the courts void agreements because of commercial impracticability? Many companies have argued that the latest economic crisis was the equivalent of a natural disaster (an act of God), but in general, financial difficulties do not excuse a defaulting party's breach. Sometimes, however, the courts make exceptions. One exception involved the automaker Chrysler.

In 1999, Chrysler entered into an agreement with the city of Twinsburg, Ohio, and the county in which it is located. Chrysler received a 50 percent tax exemption on certain property for a ten-year period. In exchange, the company was to invest about $125 million in a stamping plant in Twinsburg and maintain about three hundred full-time employment positions there. When the auto industry crashed during the financial crisis, Chrysler filed for bankruptcy in 2009. As part of its restructuring, Chrysler planned to close the Twinsburg plant. Under its agreement with the city, Chrysler could do so if its changed circumstances were due to changed economic conditions beyond its reasonable control. When the city challenged the plant's closing, the bankruptcy court determined that the closing was in fact caused by a change in economic conditions that were beyond Chrysler's control.[2] Thus, the global economic slowdown was equivalent to an act of God, at least in terms of commercial impracticability.

---

2. *In re Old Carco, LLC,* 452 Bankr. 100 (2011). The court used the name *Old Carco* to designate the prebankrupt Chrysler Company.

(AP Photo/Joseph Kaczmarek)

What happens to a contract for the sale of goods when those goods identified to the contract are completely destroyed by fire?

Destruction of Identified Goods

Sometimes, an unexpected event, such as a fire, totally destroys goods through no fault of either party and before risk passes to the buyer or lessee. In such a situation, *if the goods were identified at the time the contract was formed,* the parties are excused from performance [UCC 2–613, 2A–221]. If the goods are only partially destroyed, however, the buyer or lessee can inspect them and either treat the contract as void or accept the goods with a reduction of the contract price.

EXAMPLE 11.7 Atlas Sporting Equipment agrees to lease to River Bicycles sixty bicycles of a particular model that has been discontinued. No other bicycles of that model are available. River specifies that it needs the bicycles to rent to tourists. Before Atlas can deliver the bicycles, they are destroyed by a fire. In this situation, Atlas is not liable to River for failing to deliver the bicycles. The goods were destroyed through no fault of either party, before the risk of loss passed to the lessee. The loss was total, so the contract is avoided. Clearly, Atlas has no obligation to tender the bicycles, and River has no obligation to make the lease payments for them. •

Assurance and Cooperation

Two other exceptions to the perfect tender doctrine apply equally to parties to sales and lease contracts: the right of assurance and the duty of cooperation.

The Right of Assurance The UCC provides that if one party to a contract has "reasonable grounds" to believe that the other party will not perform as contracted, he or she may *in writing* "demand adequate assurance of due performance" from the other party. Until such assurance is received, he or she may "suspend" further performance (such as payments due under the contract) without liability. What constitutes "reasonable grounds" is determined by commercial standards. If such assurances are not forthcoming within a reasonable time (not to exceed thirty days), the failure to respond may be treated as a *repudiation* of the contract [UCC 2–609, 2A–401].

CASE EXAMPLE 11.8 Two companies that make road-surfacing materials, Koch Materials Company and Shore Slurry Seal, Inc., enter into a contract. Koch obtains a license to use Novachip, a special material made by Shore, and Shore agrees to buy all of its asphalt from Koch for the next seven years. A few years into the contract term, Shore notifies Koch that it is planning to sell its assets to Asphalt Paving Systems, Inc. Koch demands assurances that Asphalt Paving will continue the deal, but Shore refuses to provide assurances. In this situation, Koch can treat Shore's failure to give assurances as a repudiation and file a suit against Shore for breach of contract.[3] •

PREVENTING LEGAL DISPUTES

Whenever you have doubts about the other party's ability or willingness to perform a sales contract, you should demand adequate assurances. Rather than requiring a party to "wait and see" (and possibly incur significant losses as a result), the UCC allows a party with reasonable suspicions to seek adequate assurance of performance from the other party. If the other party fails to give assurance, you can treat it as an anticipatory repudiation (a breach, as will be discussed shortly) and pursue damages.

Perhaps more important, the other party's failure to give assurance allows you to suspend further performance, which can save your business from sustaining substantial losses that could be recovered only through costly and lengthy litigation. Ultimately, it may be better simply to withdraw from a deal when the other party will not provide assurances of performance than to continue performing under a contract that is likely to be breached anyway.

The Duty of Cooperation Sometimes, the performance of one party depends on the cooperation of the other. The UCC provides that when such cooperation is not forthcoming,

---

3. *Koch Materials Co. v. Shore Slurry Seal, Inc.,* 205 F.Supp.2d 324 (D.N.J. 2002).

the other party can suspend her or his own performance without liability and hold the uncooperative party in breach or proceed to perform the contract in any reasonable manner [UCC 2–311(3)].

EXAMPLE 11.9 Aman is required by contract to deliver 1,200 Samsung washing machines to various locations in California on or before October 1. Farrell, the buyer, is to specify the locations so that the deliveries can be made on time. Aman repeatedly requests the delivery locations, but Farrell does not respond. On October 1, the washing machines are ready to be shipped, but Farrell still refuses to give Aman the locations. Aman does not ship on October 1. Can Aman be held liable? The answer is no. Aman is excused for any resulting delay of performance because of Farrell's failure to cooperate. •

Obligations of the Buyer or Lessee

The main obligation of the buyer or lessee under a sales or lease contract is to pay for the goods tendered in accordance with the contract. Once the seller or lessor has adequately tendered delivery, the buyer or lessee is obligated to accept the goods and pay for them according to the terms of the contract.

Payment

"Death, they say, acquits us of all obligations."

Michel de Montaigne, 1533–1592 (French writer and philosopher)

In the absence of any specific agreements, the buyer or lessee must make payment at the time and place the goods are *received* [UCC 2–310(a), 2A–516(1)]. When a sale is made on credit, the buyer is obligated to pay according to the specified credit terms (for instance, 60, 90, or 120 days), not when the goods are received. The credit period usually begins on the *date of shipment* [UCC 2–310(d)]. Under a lease contract, a lessee must make the lease payment that was specified in the contract [UCC 2A–516(1)].

Payment can be made by any means agreed on by the parties—cash or any other method generally acceptable in the commercial world. If the seller demands cash when the buyer offers a check, credit card, or the like, the seller must permit the buyer reasonable time to obtain legal tender [UCC 2–511].

Right of Inspection

Unless the parties otherwise agree, or for C.O.D. (collect on delivery) transactions, the buyer or lessee has an absolute right to inspect the goods before making payment. This right allows the buyer or lessee to verify, before making payment, that the goods tendered or delivered are what were contracted for or ordered. If the goods are not what were ordered, the buyer or lessee has no duty to pay. *An opportunity for inspection is therefore a condition precedent to the right of the seller or lessor to enforce payment* [UCC 2–513(1), 2A–515(1)].

Inspection can take place at any reasonable place and time and in any reasonable manner. Generally, what is reasonable is determined by custom of the trade, past practices of the parties, and the like. The buyer bears the costs of inspecting the goods (unless otherwise agreed), but if the goods are rejected because they are not conforming, the buyer can recover the costs of inspection from the seller [UCC 2–513(2)].

Acceptance

A buyer or lessee demonstrates acceptance of the delivered goods by doing any of the following:

1. If, after having had a reasonable opportunity to inspect the goods, the buyer or lessee signifies to the seller or lessor that the goods either are conforming or are acceptable in spite of their nonconformity [UCC 2–606(1)(a), 2A–515(1)(a)].

2. If the buyer or lessee has had a reasonable opportunity to inspect the goods and has *failed to reject* them within a reasonable period of time, then acceptance is presumed [UCC 2–602(1), 2–606(1)(b), 2A–515(1)(b)].

3. In sales contracts, if the buyer *performs any act inconsistent with the seller's ownership,* then the buyer will be deemed to have accepted the goods. For example, any use or resale of the goods—except for the limited purpose of testing or inspecting the goods—generally constitutes an acceptance [UCC 2–606(1)(c)].

Partial Acceptance

If some of the goods delivered do not conform to the contract and the seller or lessor has failed to cure, the buyer or lessee can make a *partial* acceptance [UCC 2–601(c), 2A–509(1)]. The same is true if the nonconformity was not reasonably discoverable before acceptance. (In the latter situation, the buyer or lessee may be able to revoke the acceptance, as will be discussed later in this chapter.)

A buyer or lessee cannot accept less than a single commercial unit, however. The UCC defines a *commercial unit* as a unit of goods that, by commercial usage, is viewed as a "single whole" for purposes of sale, and its division would materially impair the character of the unit, its market value, or its use [UCC 2–105(6), 2A–103(1)(c)]. A commercial unit can be a single article (such as a machine), a set of articles (such as a suite of furniture or an assortment of sizes), a quantity (such as a bale, a gross, or a carload), or any other unit treated in the trade as a single whole.

Anticipatory Repudiation

LEARNING OBJECTIVE 3
What options are available to the nonbreaching party when the other party to a sales or lease contract repudiates the contract prior to the time for performance?

What if, before the time for contract performance, one party clearly communicates to the other the intention not to perform? As discussed in Chapter 9 on page 265, such an action is a breach of the contract by anticipatory repudiation.

Suspension of Performance Obligations

When anticipatory repudiation occurs, the nonbreaching party has a choice of two responses: (1) treat the repudiation as a final breach by pursuing a remedy or (2) wait to see if the repudiating party will decide to honor the contract despite the admitted intention to renege [UCC 2–610, 2A–402]. In either situation, the nonbreaching party may suspend performance.

A Repudiation May Be Retracted

The UCC permits the breaching party to "retract" his or her repudiation (subject to some limitations). This retraction can be done by any method that clearly indicates the party's intent to perform. Once retraction is made, the rights of the repudiating party under the contract are reinstated. There can be no retraction, however, if since the time of the repudiation the other party has canceled or materially changed position or otherwise indicated that the repudiation is final [UCC 2–611, 2A–403].

EXAMPLE 11.10 On April 1, Cora VanMeter, who owns a small inn, purchases a suite of furniture from Robert Horton, who owns Horton's Furniture Warehouse. The contract states, "Delivery must be made on or before May 1." On April 10, Horton informs VanMeter that he cannot make delivery until May 10 and asks her to consent to the modified delivery date. In this situation, VanMeter has the option of either treating Horton's notice of late delivery as a final breach of contract and pursuing a remedy or agreeing to the changed delivery date. Suppose that VanMeter does neither for two weeks. On April 24, Horton informs VanMeter that he will be able to deliver the furniture by May 1 after all. In effect, Horton has retracted his repudiation, reinstating the rights and obligations of the parties under the original contract. Note that if VanMeter had indicated after Horton's repudiation that she was canceling the contract, Horton would not have been able to retract his repudiation. •

Remedies of the Seller or Lessor

LEARNING OBJECTIVE 4
What remedies are available to a seller or lessor when the buyer or lessee breaches the contract? What remedies are available to a buyer or lessee if the seller or lessor breaches the contract?

When the buyer or lessee is in breach, the seller or lessor has numerous remedies available under the UCC. Generally, the remedies available to the seller or lessor depend on the circumstances at the time of the breach, such as which party has possession of the goods, whether the goods are in transit, and whether the buyer or lessee has rejected or accepted the goods.

When the Goods Are in the Possession of the Seller or Lessor

Under the UCC, if the buyer or lessee breaches the contract before the goods have been delivered to her or him, the seller or lessor has the right to pursue the following remedies:

1. Cancel (rescind) the contract.
2. Resell the goods and sue to recover damages.
3. Sue to recover the purchase price or lease payments due.
4. Sue to recover damages for the buyer's nonacceptance.

The Right to Cancel the Contract If the buyer or lessee breaches the contract, the seller or lessor can choose to cancel (rescind) the contract [UCC 2–703(f), 2A–523(1)(a)]. The seller must notify the buyer or lessee of the cancellation, and at that point all remaining obligations of the seller or lessor are discharged. The buyer or lessee is not discharged from all remaining obligations, however. She or he is in breach, and the seller or lessor can pursue remedies available under the UCC for breach.

The Right to Withhold Delivery In general, sellers and lessors can withhold or discontinue performance of their obligations under sales or lease contracts when the buyers or lessees are in breach. This is true whether a buyer or lessee has wrongfully rejected or revoked acceptance of contract goods (rejection and revocation of acceptance will be discussed later), failed to make a payment, or repudiated the contract [UCC 2–703(a), 2A–523(1)(c)]. The seller or lessor can also refuse to deliver the goods to a buyer or lessee who is insolvent (unable to pay debts as they become due), unless the buyer or lessee pays in cash [UCC 2–702(1), 2A–525(1)].

▸ KNOW THIS ◂
A buyer or lessee breaches a contract by wrongfully rejecting the goods, wrongfully revoking acceptance, refusing to pay, or repudiating the contract.

The Right to Resell or Dispose of the Goods When a buyer or lessee breaches or repudiates a sales contract while the seller or lessor is still in possession of the goods, the seller or lessor can resell or dispose of the goods. The seller can retain any profits made as a result of the sale and can hold the buyer or lessee liable for any loss [UCC 2–703(d), 2–706(1), 2A–523(1)(e), 2A–527(1)]. The seller must give the original buyer reasonable notice of the resale, unless the goods are perishable or will rapidly decline in value [UCC 2–706(2), (3)].

When the Goods Are Unfinished When the goods contracted for are unfinished at the time of breach, the seller or lessor can either (1) cease manufacturing the goods and resell them for scrap or salvage value or (2) complete the manufacture and resell or dispose of them, holding the buyer or lessee liable for any deficiency (amount less than the contract price).

In choosing between these two alternatives, the seller or lessor must exercise reasonable commercial judgment to mitigate the loss and obtain maximum value from the unfinished goods [UCC 2–704(2), 2A–524(2)]. Any resale of the goods must be made in good faith and in a commercially reasonable manner.

Incidental Damages All costs resulting from a breach of contract, including all reasonable expenses incurred because of the breach.

When the Resale Price Is Insufficient In sales transactions, the seller can recover any deficiency between the resale price and the contract price, along with **incidental damages**, defined as the costs resulting from the breach [UCC 2–706(1), 2–710]. In lease transactions, the lessor may lease the goods to another party and recover from the original lessee, as damages, any unpaid lease payments up to the beginning date of the lease term under the new lease. The lessor can also recover any deficiency between the lease payments due under the original lease contract and those due under the new lease contract, along with incidental damages [UCC 2A–527(2)].

The Right to Recover the Purchase Price or the Lease Payments Due

Under the UCC, an unpaid seller or lessor can bring an action to recover the purchase price or payments due under the lease contract, plus incidental damages [UCC 2–709(1), 2A–529(1)]. If a seller or lessor is unable to resell or dispose of goods and sues for the contract price or lease payments due, the goods must be held for the buyer or lessee. The seller or lessor can resell or dispose of the goods at any time before collection (of the judgment) from the buyer or lessee, but must credit the net proceeds from the sale to the buyer or lessee.

EXAMPLE 11.11 Southern Realty contracts to purchase one thousand pens with its name inscribed on them from Gem Point. When Gem Point tenders delivery of the pens, Southern Realty wrongfully refuses to accept them. In this situation, Gem Point can bring an action for the purchase price because it delivered conforming goods, but Southern Realty refused to accept or pay for the goods. Gem Point obviously cannot resell the pens inscribed with the buyer's business name, so this situation falls under UCC 2–709. Gem Point is required to make the pens available for Southern Realty, but can resell them (in the event that it can find a buyer) at any time prior to collecting the judgment from Southern Realty. ●

The Right to Recover Damages

If a buyer or lessee repudiates a contract or wrongfully refuses to accept the goods, a seller or lessor can maintain an action to recover the damages that were sustained. Ordinarily, the amount of damages equals the difference between the contract price or lease payments and the market price or lease payments at the time and place of tender of the goods, plus incidental damages [UCC 2–708(1), 2A–528(1)]. When the ordinary measure of damages is insufficient to put the seller or lessor in the same position as the buyer's or lessee's performance would have, the UCC provides an alternative. In that situation, the proper measure of damages is the lost profits of the seller or lessor, including a reasonable allowance for overhead and other expenses [UCC 2–708(2), 2A–528(2)].

When the Goods Are in Transit

If the seller or lessor has delivered the goods to a carrier or a bailee but the buyer or lessee has not yet received them, the goods are said to be *in transit*. If, while the goods are in transit, the seller or lessor learns that the buyer or lessee is insolvent, the seller or lessor can stop the carrier or bailee from delivering the goods. The seller or lessor can stop the delivery of goods in transit to an insolvent party regardless of the quantity of goods shipped, but this is not true if the buyer or lessee is only in breach. When the buyer or lessee is not insolvent, the seller or lessor can stop delivery of goods in transit only if the quantity shipped is at least a carload, a truckload, a planeload, or a larger shipment [UCC 2–705(1), 2A–526(1)].

EXAMPLE 11.12 Arturo Ortega orders a truckload of lumber from Timber Products, Inc., to be shipped to Ortega six weeks later. Ortega, who owes Timber Products for a past shipment, promises to pay the debt immediately and to pay for the current shipment as soon as it is received. After the lumber has been shipped, a bankruptcy court judge notifies Timber Products that Ortega has filed a petition in bankruptcy and listed Timber Products as one of his creditors (see Chapter 15). If the goods are still in transit, Timber Products can stop the carrier from delivering the lumber to Ortega. •

Requirements for Stopping Delivery To stop delivery, the seller or lessor must *timely notify* the carrier or other bailee that the goods are to be returned or held for the seller or lessor. If the carrier has sufficient time to stop delivery, it must hold and deliver the goods according to the instructions of the seller or lessor, who is liable to the carrier for any additional costs incurred [UCC 2–705(3), 2A–526(3)].

The seller or lessor has the right to stop delivery of the goods under UCC 2–705(2) and 2A–526(2) until the time when the following occurs:

1. The buyer or lessee obtains possession of the goods.
2. The carrier or the bailee acknowledges the rights of the buyer or lessee in the goods (by reshipping or holding the goods for the buyer or lessee, for example).
3. A negotiable document of title covering the goods has been properly transferred to the buyer (in sales transactions only), giving the buyer ownership rights in the goods [UCC 2–702].

Remedies Once the Goods Are Reclaimed Once the seller or lessor reclaims the goods in transit, she or he can pursue the remedies allowed to sellers and lessors when the goods are in their possession.

When the Goods Are in the Possession of the Buyer or Lessee

Suppose that the buyer or lessee breaches a sales or lease contract at a time when the goods are in the buyer's or lessee's possession. In that event, the seller or lessor can sue to recover the purchase price of the goods or the lease payments due, plus incidental damages [UCC 2–709(1), 2A–529(1)].

In some situations, a seller may also have a right to reclaim the goods from the buyer. For instance, in a sales contract, if the buyer has received the goods on credit and the seller discovers that the buyer is insolvent, the seller can demand return of the goods [UCC 2–702(2)]. Ordinarily, the demand must be made within ten days of the buyer's receipt of the goods.[4] The seller's right to reclaim the goods is subject to the rights of a good faith purchaser or other subsequent buyer in the ordinary course of business who purchases the goods from the buyer before the seller reclaims them.

In regard to lease contracts, if the lessee is in default (fails to make payments that are due, for example), the lessor may reclaim the leased goods that are in the lessee's possession [UCC 2A–525(2)].

KNOW THIS

Incidental damages include all reasonable expenses incurred because of a breach of contract.

---

4. The seller can demand and reclaim the goods at any time, though, if the buyer misrepresented his or her solvency in writing within three months prior to the delivery of the goods.

Remedies of the Buyer or Lessee

When the seller or lessor breaches the contract, the buyer or lessee has numerous remedies available under the UCC. Like the remedies available to sellers and lessors, the remedies of buyers and lessees depend on the circumstances existing at the time of the breach. (See the *Business Application* feature on pages 340 and 341 for some suggestions on what to do when a contract is breached.)

When the Seller or Lessor Refuses to Deliver the Goods

If the seller or lessor refuses to deliver the goods, or the buyer or lessee has rightfully rejected the goods, the remedies available to the buyer or lessee include the right to:

1. Cancel (rescind) the contract.
2. Obtain goods that have been paid for if the seller or lessor is insolvent.
3. Sue to obtain specific performance if the goods are unique or damages are an inadequate remedy.
4. Buy other goods (obtain *cover*—defined on page 335), and obtain damages from the seller.
5. Sue to obtain identified goods held by a third party (*replevy* goods—see page 335).
6. Sue to obtain damages.

The Right to Cancel the Contract
When a seller or lessor fails to make proper delivery or repudiates the contract, the buyer or lessee can cancel, or rescind, the contract. On notice of cancellation, the buyer or lessee is relieved of any further obligations under the contract but retains all rights to other remedies against the seller [UCC 2–711(1), 2A–508(1)(a)]. (The right to cancel the contract is also available to a buyer or lessee who has rightfully rejected goods or revoked acceptance, as will be discussed shortly.)

The Right to Obtain the Goods on Insolvency
If a buyer or lessee has made a partial or full payment for goods that are in the possession of a seller or lessor who is or becomes insolvent, the buyer or lessee has a right to obtain the goods. For this right to be exercised, the goods must be identified to the contract and the buyer or lessee must pay any remaining balance of the price to the seller or lessor [UCC 2–502, 2A–522].

The Right to Obtain Specific Performance
A buyer or lessee can obtain specific performance when the goods are unique and the remedy at law is inadequate [UCC 2–716(1), 2A–521(1)]. Ordinarily, a successful suit for monetary damages is sufficient to place a buyer or lessee in the position he or she would have occupied if the seller or lessor had fully performed.

When the contract is for the purchase of a particular work of art or a similarly unique item, however, monetary damages may not be sufficient. Under these circumstances, equity will require that the seller or lessor perform exactly by delivering the particular goods identified to the contract (a remedy of specific performance).

CASE EXAMPLE 11.13 Doreen Houseman and Eric Dare together bought a house and a pedigreed dog. When the couple separated, they agreed that Dare would keep the house (and pay Houseman for her interest in it), and Houseman would keep the dog. Houseman allowed Dare to take the dog for visits, but after one visit, Dare kept the dog. Houseman filed a lawsuit seeking specific performance of their agreement. The court found that because pets have special subjective value to their owners, a dog can be considered a unique good. Thus, an award of specific performance was appropriate.[5] ●

---

5. *Houseman v. Dare*, 405 N.J.Super. 538, 966 A.2d 24 (2009).

> ➤ **KNOW THIS** ◄
>
> A seller or lessor breaches a contract by wrongfully failing to deliver the goods, delivering nonconforming goods, making an improper tender of the goods, or repudiating the contract.

Cover A remedy that allows the buyer or lessee, on the seller's or lessor's breach, to obtain substitute goods from another seller or lessor.

The Right of Cover   In certain situations, buyers and lessees can protect themselves by obtaining **cover**—that is, by purchasing or leasing other goods to substitute for those due under the contract. This option is available when the seller or lessor repudiates the contract or fails to deliver the goods, or when a buyer or lessee has rightfully rejected goods or revoked acceptance.

In obtaining cover, the buyer or lessee must act in good faith and without unreasonable delay [UCC 2–712, 2A–518]. After purchasing or leasing substitute goods, the buyer or lessee can recover damages from the seller or lessor. The measure of damages is the difference between the cost of cover and the contract price (or lease payments), plus incidental and consequential damages. Any expenses (such as delivery costs) that were saved as a result of the breach are subtracted [UCC 2–712, 2–715, 2A–518]. Consequential damages are any losses suffered by the buyer or lessee that the seller or lessor could have foreseen (had reason to know about) at the time of contract formation. In addition, consequential damages may include any injury to the buyer's or lessee's person or property proximately resulting from the contract's breach [UCC 2–715(2), 2A–520(2)].

Buyers and lessees are not required to cover, and failure to do so will not bar them from using any other remedies available under the UCC. A buyer or lessee who fails to cover, however, may *not* be able to collect consequential damages that could have been avoided by purchasing or leasing substitute goods.

Replevin An action that can be used by a buyer or lessee to recover identified goods from a third party, such as a bailee, who is wrongfully withholding them.

The Right to Replevy Goods   Buyers and lessees also have the right to replevy goods. **Replevin**[6] is an action that a buyer or lessee can use to recover specific goods from a third party, such as a bailee, who is wrongfully withholding them. Under the UCC, the buyer or lessee can replevy goods subject to the contract if the seller or lessor has repudiated or breached the contract. To maintain an action to replevy goods, usually buyers and lessees must show that they are unable to cover for the goods after a reasonable effort [UCC 2–716(3), 2A–521(3)].

The Right to Recover Damages   If a seller or lessor repudiates the sales contract or fails to deliver the goods, the buyer or lessee can sue for damages. The measure of recovery is the difference between the contract price (or lease payments) and the market price of (or lease payments that could be obtained for) the goods at the time the buyer (or lessee) *learned* of the breach. The market price or market lease payments are determined at the place where the seller or lessor was supposed to deliver the goods.

> **KNOW THIS**
>
> Consequential damages compensate for a loss (such as lost profits) that is not direct but was reasonably foreseeable at the time of the breach.

The buyer or lessee can also recover incidental and consequential damages, less the expenses that were saved as a result of the breach [UCC 2–713, 2A–519]. **CASE EXAMPLE 11.14**   Les Entreprises Jacques Defour & Fils, Inc., contracted to buy a 30,000-gallon industrial tank from Dinsick Equipment Corporation for $70,000. Les Entreprises hired Xaak Transport, Inc., to pick up the tank, but when Xaak arrived at the pickup location, there was no tank. Les Entreprises paid Xaak $7,459 for its services and filed a suit against Dinsick. Here, the buyer can recover the contract price, plus the shipping costs. The court awarded compensatory damages of $70,000 for the tank and incidental damages of $7,459 for the transport. To establish a breach of contract requires an enforceable contract, substantial performance by the nonbreaching party, a breach by the other party, and damage to the nonbreaching party. Les Entreprises agreed to buy a tank and paid the price. Dinsick failed to tender or deliver the tank, or to refund the price. The shipping costs were a necessary part of performance, so this was a reasonable expense.[7] •

---

6. Pronounced ruh-*pleh*-vun. Note that outside the UCC, the term *replevin* refers to a process that takes place prior to a court's judgment that permits the seizure of specific personal property in which a party claims a right or an interest.
7. *Les Entreprises Jacques Defour & Fils, Inc. v. Dinsick Equipment Corp.*, 2011 WL 307501 (N.D.Ill. 2011).

When the Seller or Lessor Delivers Nonconforming Goods

When the seller or lessor delivers nonconforming goods, the buyer or lessee has several remedies available under the UCC.

The Right to Reject the Goods

If either the goods or the tender of the goods by the seller or lessor fails to conform to the contract *in any respect,* the buyer or lessee can reject the goods in whole or in part [UCC 2–601, 2A–509]. If the buyer or lessee rejects the goods, she or he may then obtain cover, cancel the contract, or sue for damages for breach of contract, just as if the seller or lessor had refused to deliver the goods (see the earlier discussion of these remedies).

CASE EXAMPLE 11.15   Jorge Jauregui contracted to buy a Kawai RX5 piano from Bobb's Piano Sales. Bobb's represented that the piano was in new condition and qualified for the manufacturer's warranty. Jauregui paid the contract price, but the piano was delivered with "unacceptable damage," according to Jauregui, who videotaped its condition. Jauregui rejected the piano and filed a lawsuit for breach of contract. The court ruled that Bobb's had breached the contract by delivering nonconforming goods. Jauregui was entitled to damages equal to the contract price, plus interest, the sales tax, delivery charge, and attorneys' fees.[8] ●

Timeliness and Reason for Rejection Required   The buyer or lessee must reject the goods within a reasonable amount of time after delivery and must *seasonably* (timely) notify the seller or lessor [UCC 2–602(1), 2A–509(2)]. If the buyer or lessee fails to reject the goods within a reasonable amount of time, acceptance will be presumed.

When rejecting goods, the buyer or lessee must also designate defects that would have been apparent to the seller or lessor on reasonable inspection. Failure to do so precludes the buyer or lessee from using such defects to justify rejection or to establish breach when the seller could have cured the defects if they had been disclosed in a timely fashion [UCC 2–605, 2A–514].

A worker inspects returned goods that will be sold at Overstock.com. Is such a resale of these goods commercially acceptable?

(AP Photo/Jim Urquhart)

Duties of Merchant Buyers and Lessees When Goods Are Rejected   What happens if a *merchant buyer* or *lessee* rightfully rejects goods and the seller or lessor has no agent or business at the place of rejection? In that situation, the merchant buyer or lessee has a good faith obligation to follow any reasonable instructions received from the seller or lessor with respect to the goods [UCC 2–603, 2A–511]. The buyer or lessee is entitled to be reimbursed for the care and cost entailed in following the instructions. The same requirements hold if the buyer or lessee rightfully revokes his or her acceptance of the goods at some later time [UCC 2–608(3), 2A–517(5)]. (Revocation of acceptance will be discussed shortly.)

If no instructions are forthcoming and the goods are perishable or threaten to decline in value quickly, the buyer can resell the goods in good faith. The buyer can then take the appropriate reimbursement from the proceeds and a selling commission (not to exceed

---

8. *Jauregui v. Bobb's Piano Sales & Service, Inc.,* 922 So.2d 303 (Fla.App. 2006).

10 percent of the gross proceeds) [UCC 2–603(1), (2); 2A–511(1), (2)]. If the goods are not perishable, the buyer or lessee may store them for the seller or lessor or reship them to the seller or lessor [UCC 2–604, 2A–512].

Revocation of Acceptance   Acceptance of the goods precludes the buyer or lessee from exercising the right of rejection, but it does not necessarily prevent the buyer or lessee from pursuing other remedies. In certain circumstances, a buyer or lessee is permitted to *revoke* her or his acceptance of the goods. Acceptance of a lot or a commercial unit can be revoked if the nonconformity *substantially* impairs the value of the lot or unit and if one of the following factors is present:

1. Acceptance was predicated on the reasonable assumption that the nonconformity would be cured, and it has not been cured within a reasonable time [UCC 2–608(1)(a), 2A–517(1)(a)].
2. The buyer or lessee did not discover the nonconformity before acceptance, either because it was difficult to discover before acceptance or because assurances made by the seller or lessor that the goods were conforming kept the buyer or lessee from inspecting the goods [UCC 2–608(1)(b), 2A–517(1)(b)].

Revocation of acceptance is not effective until the seller or lessor is notified, which must occur within a reasonable time after the buyer or lessee either discovers or *should have discovered* the grounds for revocation. Additionally, revocation must occur before the goods have undergone any substantial change (such as spoilage) not caused by their own defects [UCC 2–608(2), 2A–517(4)]. Once acceptance is revoked, the buyer or lessee can pursue remedies, just as if the goods had been rejected. (See this chapter's *Beyond Our Borders* feature below for a glimpse at how international sales law deals with revocation of acceptance.)

The Right to Recover Damages for Accepted Goods   A buyer or lessee who has accepted nonconforming goods may also keep the goods and recover damages caused by the breach. To do so, the buyer or lessee must notify the seller or lessor of the breach within a reasonable time after the defect was or should have been discovered. Failure to give notice of the defects (breach) to the seller or lessor bars the buyer or lessee from pursuing any remedy [UCC 2–607(3), 2A–516(3)]. In addition, the parties to a sales or lease contract can insert a provision requiring the buyer or lessee to give notice of any defects in the goods within a set period.

 BEYOND OUR BORDERS

The CISG's Approach to Revocation of Acceptance

Under the UCC, a buyer or lessee who has accepted goods may be able to revoke acceptance under the circumstances mentioned in the text above. The United Nations Convention on Contracts for the International Sale of Goods (CISG) also allows buyers to rescind their contracts after they have accepted the goods.

The CISG, however, takes a somewhat different—and more direct—approach to the problem than the UCC does. In the same circumstances that permit a buyer to revoke acceptance under the UCC, under the CISG the buyer can simply declare that the seller has *fundamentally* breached the contract and proceed to sue the seller for the breach. Article 25 of the CISG states that a "breach of contract committed by one of the parties is fundamental if it results in such detriment to the other party as substantially to deprive him [or her] of what he [or she] is entitled to expect under the contract." For example,

to revoke acceptance of a shipment under the CISG, a buyer need not prove that the nonconformity of one shipment substantially impaired the value of the whole lot. The buyer can simply file a lawsuit alleging that the seller is in breach.

Critical Thinking
What is the essential difference between revoking acceptance and bringing a suit for breach of contract?

When the goods delivered are not as promised, the measure of damages equals the difference between the value of the goods as accepted and their value if they had been delivered as warranted [UCC 2–714(2), 2A–519(4)]. The buyer or lessee is also entitled to incidental and consequential damages when appropriate [UCC 2–714(3), 2A–519(3)]. The UCC also permits the buyer or lessee, with proper notice to the seller or lessor, to deduct all or any part of the damages from the price or lease payments still due under the contract [UCC 2–717, 2A–516(1)].

Is two years after a sale of goods a reasonable time period in which to discover a defect in those goods and notify the seller or lessor of a breach? That was the question in the following *Spotlight Case.*

Spotlight on Baseball Cards

Case 11.3
Fitl v. Strek
Supreme Court of Nebraska, 269 Neb. 51, 690 N.W.2d 605 (2005).
caselaw.findlaw.com/courts/Nebraska[a]

(Terren in Virginia/Creative Commons)

A 1952 Mickey Mantle Topps baseball card.

FACTS Over the Labor Day weekend in 1995, James Fitl attended a sports-card show in San Francisco, California, where he met Mark Strek, doing business as Star Cards of San Francisco, an exhibitor at the show. Later, on Strek's representation that a certain 1952 Mickey Mantle Topps baseball card was in near-mint condition, Fitl bought the card from Strek for $17,750. Strek delivered the card to Fitl in Omaha, Nebraska, and Fitl placed it in a safe-deposit box. In May 1997, Fitl sent the card to Professional Sports Authenticators (PSA), a sports-card grading service. PSA told Fitl that the card was ungradable because it had been discolored and doctored. Fitl complained to Strek, who replied that Fitl should have returned the card within "a typical grace period for the unconditional return of a card, . . . 7 days to 1 month" of its receipt. In August, Fitl sent the card to ASA Accugrade, Inc. (ASA), another grading service, for a second opinion of the value. ASA also concluded that the card had been refinished and trimmed. Fitl filed a suit in a Nebraska state court against Strek, seeking damages. The court awarded Fitl $17,750, plus his court costs. Strek appealed to the Nebraska Supreme Court.

ISSUE Was two years after the sale of the baseball card a reasonable time to discover a defect and notify the seller of a breach?

DECISION Yes. The state supreme court affirmed the decision of the lower court.

REASON Section 2–607(3)(a) of the UCC states, "Where a tender has been accepted . . . the buyer must within a

reasonable time after he discovers or should have discovered any breach notify the seller of breach or be barred from any remedy." "What is a reasonable time for taking any action depends on the nature, purpose and circumstances of such action" [UCC 1–205(a)]. The state supreme court concluded that the buyer (Fitl) had reasonably relied on the seller's (Strek's) representation that the goods were "authentic," which they were not, and when their defects were discovered, Fitl had given timely notice. The court reasoned that "the policies behind the notice requirement, to allow the seller to correct a defect, to prepare for negotiation and litigation, and to protect against stale claims at a time beyond which an investigation can be completed, were not unfairly prejudiced by the lack of an earlier notice to Strek. Any problem Strek may have had with the party from whom he obtained the baseball card was a separate matter from his transaction with Fitl, and an investigation into the source of the altered card would not have minimized Fitl's damages."

WHAT IF THE FACTS WERE DIFFERENT? *Suppose that Fitl and Strek had included in their deal a written clause requiring Fitl to give notice of any defect in the card within "7 days to 1 month" of its receipt. Would the result have been different? Why or why not?*

---

a. Under "Browse Nebraska Courts," click on "Supreme Court of Nebraska." In the "Party name:" box, type "Fitl" and click on "Search." In the result, click on the name of the case to access the opinion.

Limitation of Remedies

LEARNING OBJECTIVE 5
In contracts subject to the UCC, are parties free to limit the remedies available to the nonbreaching party on a breach of contract? If so, in what ways?

The parties to a sales or lease contract can vary their respective rights and obligations by contractual agreement. For example, a seller and buyer can expressly provide for remedies in addition to those provided in the UCC. They can also provide remedies in lieu of those provided in the UCC, or they can change the measure of damages. The seller can provide that the buyer's only remedy on breach of warranty will be repair or replacement of the item, or the seller can limit the buyer's remedy to return of the goods and refund of the purchase price.

In sales and lease contracts, an agreed-on remedy is in addition to those provided in the UCC unless the parties expressly agree that the remedy is exclusive of all others [UCC 2–719(1), 2A–503(1), (2)].

Exclusive Remedies

(Andrey Snegirev/Shutterstock.com)

If this pipe-cutting machine has defective parts, can the buyer insist on replacement of the entire machine?

If the parties state that a remedy is exclusive, then it is the sole, or exclusive, remedy.
EXAMPLE 11.16 Standard Tool Company agrees to sell a pipe-cutting machine to United Pipe & Tubing Corporation. The contract limits United's remedy exclusively to repair or replacement of any defective parts. Thus, repair or replacement of defective parts is the buyer's exclusive remedy under this contract. •

When circumstances cause an exclusive remedy to fail in its essential purpose, however, it is no longer exclusive, and the buyer or lessee may pursue other remedies available under the UCC [UCC 2–719(2), 2A–503(2)]. **EXAMPLE 11.17** In *Example 11.16*, suppose that Standard Tool Company is unable to repair a defective part, and no replacement parts are available. In this situation, because the exclusive remedy failed in its essential purpose, the buyer normally will be entitled to seek other remedies provided to a buyer by the UCC. •

Limitations on Consequential Damages

As discussed in Chapter 9 on page 000, *consequential damages* are special damages that compensate for indirect losses (such as lost profits) resulting from a breach of contract that were reasonably foreseeable. Under the UCC, parties to a contract can limit or exclude consequential damages, provided the limitation is not unconscionable.

When the buyer or lessee is a consumer, any limitation of consequential damages for personal injuries resulting from consumer goods is *prima facie* (presumptively, or on its face) unconscionable. The limitation of consequential damages is not necessarily unconscionable when the loss is commercial in nature—for example, lost profits and property damage [UCC 2–719(3), 2A–503(3)].

Statute of Limitations

An action for breach of contract under the UCC must be commenced *within four years after the cause of action accrues*—that is, a buyer or lessee must file the lawsuit within four years after the breach occurs [UCC 2–725(1)]. In addition, a buyer or lessee who has accepted nonconforming goods usually must notify the breaching party of the breach within a reasonable time, or the aggrieved party is barred from pursuing any remedy [UCC 2–607(3 (a), 2A–516(3)].

The parties can agree in their contract to reduce this period to not less than one year, but cannot extend it beyond four years [UCC 2–725(1), 2A–506(1)]. A cause of action accrues for breach of warranty (to be discussed in Chapter 12) when the seller or lessor tenders delivery. This is the rule even if the aggrieved party is unaware that the cause of action has accrued [UCC 2–725(2), 2A–506(2)].

Reviewing . . . Performance and Breach in Sales and Lease Contracts

GFI, Inc., a Hong Kong company, makes audio decoder chips, one of the essential components used in the manufacture of MP3 players. Egan Electronics contracts with GFI to buy 10,000 chips on an installment contract, with 2,500 chips to be shipped every three months, F.O.B. Hong Kong via Air Express. At the time for the first delivery, GFI delivers only 2,400 chips but explains to Egan that even though the shipment is less than 5 percent short, the chips are of a higher quality than those specified in the contract and are worth 5 percent more than the contract price. Egan accepts the shipment and pays GFI the contract price. At the time for the second shipment, GFI makes a shipment identical to the first. Egan again accepts and pays for the chips. At the time for the third shipment, GFI ships 2,400 of the same chips, but this time GFI sends them via Hong Kong Air instead of Air Express. While in transit, the chips are destroyed. When it is time for the fourth shipment, GFI again sends 2,400 chips, but this time Egan rejects the chips without explanation. Using the information presented in the chapter, answer the following questions.

1. Did GFI have a legitimate reason to expect that Egan would accept the fourth shipment? Why or why not?
2. Does the substitution of carriers for the third shipment constitute a breach of the contract by GFI? Explain.
3. Suppose that the silicon used for the chips becomes unavailable for a period of time and that GFI cannot manufacture enough chips to fulfill the contract but does ship as many as it can to Egan. Under what doctrine might a court release GFI from further performance of the contract?
4. Under the UCC, does Egan have a right to reject the fourth shipment? Why or why not?

DEBATE THIS If a contract specifies a particular carrier, then the shipper must use that carrier or be in breach of the contract—no exceptions should ever be allowed.

BUSINESS APPLICATION

What Can You Do When a Contract Is Breached?*

A contract for the sale of goods has been breached. Can the dispute be settled without a trip to court? The answer depends on the willingness of the parties to agree on an appropriate remedy.

Contractual Clauses on Applicable Remedies

Often, the parties to sales and lease contracts agree in advance, in their contracts, on what remedies will be applicable in the event of a breach. This may take the form of a contract provision restricting

or expanding remedies available under the Uniform Commercial Code [UCC 2–719]. Such clauses help to reduce uncertainty and the necessity for costly litigation.

When the Contract Is Silent on Applicable Remedies

If your agreement does not cover a breach and you are the nonbreaching party, the UCC gives you a variety of alternatives. You need to determine the available remedies, analyze them and rank them in order of priority, then predict how successful you might be in pursuing each remedy if you decide to go to court. Next, look at the position of the breaching party to determine the basis for negotiating a settlement.

*This *Business Application* is not meant to substitute for the services of an attorney who is licensed to practice law in your state.

For example, when defective goods are delivered and accepted, usually it is preferable for the buyer and seller to reach an agreement on a reduced purchase price. Practically speaking, though, the buyer may be unable to obtain a partial refund from the seller. In this situation, UCC 2–717 allows the buyer to give notice of the intention to deduct the damages from any part of the purchase price not yet paid. If you are a buyer who has accepted defective goods and has not yet paid in full, you may wish to exercise your rights under UCC 2–717 and deduct appropriate damages from your final payment. Remember that most breaches of contract do not end up in court—they are settled beforehand.

Checklist for the Nonbreaching Party to a Contract

1. Ascertain if a remedy is explicitly written into your contract. Use that remedy, if possible, to avoid litigation.
2. If no specific remedy is available, look to the UCC.
3. Assess how successful you might be in pursuing a remedy if you go to court.
4. Analyze the position of the breaching party.
5. Determine whether a negotiated settlement is preferable to a lawsuit, which is best done by consulting your attorney.

Key Terms

conforming goods 322	incidental damages 332	replevin 335	tender of delivery 322
cover 335	installment contract 325		

Chapter Summary: Performance and Breach in Sales and Lease Contracts

REQUIREMENTS OF PERFORMANCE	
Obligations of the Seller or Lessor (See pages 322–329.)	1. The seller or lessor must tender *conforming* goods to the buyer or lessee. Tender must take place at a *reasonable hour* and in a *reasonable manner*. Under the perfect tender doctrine, the seller or lessor must tender goods that conform exactly to the terms of the contract [UCC 2–503(1), 2A–508(1)]. 2. If the seller or lessor tenders nonconforming goods prior to the performance date and the buyer or lessee rejects them, the seller or lessor may *cure* (repair or replace the goods) within the contract time for performance [UCC 2–508(1), 2A–513(1)]. If the seller or lessor had reasonable grounds to believe that the buyer or lessee would accept the tendered goods, on the buyer's or lessee's rejection the seller or lessor has a reasonable time to substitute conforming goods without liability [UCC 2–508(2), 2A–513(2)]. 3. If the agreed-on means of delivery becomes impracticable or unavailable, the seller must substitute an alternative means (such as a different carrier) if one is available [UCC 2–614(1)]. 4. If a seller or lessor tenders nonconforming goods in any one installment under an installment contract, the buyer or lessee may reject the installment only if its value is substantially impaired and cannot be cured. The entire installment contract is breached only when one or more nonconforming installments *substantially* impair the value of the *whole* contract [UCC 2–612, 2A–510]. 5. When performance becomes commercially impracticable owing to circumstances that were not foreseeable when the contract was formed, the perfect tender rule no longer holds [UCC 2–615, 2A–405].
Obligations of the Buyer or Lessee (See pages 329–330.)	1. On tender of delivery by the seller or lessor, the buyer or lessee must pay for the goods at the time and place the goods are *received*, unless the sale is made on credit. Payment may be made by any method generally acceptable in the commercial world unless the seller demands cash [UCC 2–310, 2–511]. In lease contracts, the lessee must make lease payments in accordance with the contract [UCC 2A–516(1)]. 2. Unless otherwise agreed, the buyer or lessee has an absolute right to inspect the goods before acceptance [UCC 2–513(1), 2A–515(1)]. 3. The buyer or lessee can manifest acceptance of delivered goods expressly in words or by conduct or by failing to reject the goods after a reasonable period of time following inspection or after having had a reasonable opportunity to inspect them [UCC 2–606(1), 2A–515(1)]. A buyer will be deemed to have accepted goods if he or she performs any act inconsistent with the seller's ownership [UCC 2–606(1)(c)]. 4. The buyer or lessee can make a partial acceptance if some of the goods do not conform to the contract and the seller or lessor failed to cure [2–601(c), 2A–509(1)].

Continued

Chapter Summary: Performance and Breach
in Sales and Lease Contracts—Continued

Anticipatory Repudiation (See pages 330–331.)	If, before the time for performance, one party clearly indicates to the other an intention not to perform, under UCC 2–610 and 2A–402, the aggrieved party may do the following: 1. Await performance by the repudiating party for a commercially reasonable time. 2. Resort to any remedy for breach. 3. In either situation, suspend performance.
REMEDIES FOR BREACH OF CONTRACT	

Remedies of the Seller or Lessor (See pages 331–333.)	1. *When the goods are in the possession of the seller or lessor*—The seller or lessor may do the following:
	   a. Cancel the contract [UCC 2–703(f), 2A–523(1)(a)].
	   b. Withhold delivery [UCC 2–703(a), 2A–523(1)(c)].
	   c. Resell or dispose of the goods [UCC 2–703(d), 2–706(1), 2A–523(1)(e), 2A–527(1)].
	   d. Sue to recover the purchase price or lease payments due [UCC 2–709(1), 2A–529(1)].
	   e. Sue to recover damages [UCC 2–708, 2A–528].
	2. *When the goods are in transit*—The seller or lessor may stop the carrier or bailee from delivering the goods under certain conditions [UCC 2–705, 2A–526].
	3. *When the goods are in the possession of the buyer or lessee*—The seller or lessor may do the following:
	   a. Sue to recover the purchase price or lease payments due [UCC 2–709(1), 2A–529(1)].
	   b. Reclaim the goods. A seller may reclaim goods received by an insolvent buyer if the demand is made within ten days of receipt (reclaiming goods excludes all other remedies) [UCC 2–702(2)]. A lessor may repossess goods if the lessee is in default [UCC 2A–525(2)].

Remedies of the Buyer or Lessee (See pages 334–338.)	1. *When the seller or lessor refuses to deliver the goods*—The buyer or lessee may do the following:
	   a. Cancel the contract [UCC 2–711(1), 2A–508(1)(a)].
	   b. Recover the goods if the seller or lessor becomes insolvent within ten days after receiving the first payment and the goods are identified to the contract [UCC 2–502, 2A–522].
	   c. Obtain specific performance (when the goods are unique and the remedy at law is inadequate) [UCC 2–716(1), 2A–521(1)].
	   d. Obtain cover [UCC 2–712, 2A–518].
	   e. Replevy the goods (if cover is unavailable) [UCC 2–716(3), 2A–521(3)].
	   f. Sue to recover damages [UCC 2–713, 2A–519].
	2. *When the seller or lessor delivers or tenders delivery of nonconforming goods*—The buyer or lessee may do the following:
	   a. Reject the goods [UCC 2–601, 2A–509].
	   b. Revoke acceptance if the nonconformity *substantially* impairs the value of the unit or lot and if one of the following factors is present:
	      (1) Acceptance was predicated on the reasonable assumption that the nonconformity would be cured, and it was not cured within a reasonable time [UCC 2–608(1)(a), 2A–517(1)(a)].
	      (2) The buyer or lessee did not discover the nonconformity before acceptance, either because it was difficult to discover before acceptance or because the seller's or lessor's assurance that the goods were conforming kept the buyer or lessee from inspecting the goods [UCC 2–608(1)(b), 2A–517(1)(b)].
	   c. Accept the goods and recover damages [UCC 2–607, 2–714, 2–717, 2A–519].

Limitation of Remedies (See page 339.)	1. Remedies may be limited in sales or lease contracts by agreement of the parties. If the contract states that a remedy is exclusive, then that is the sole remedy unless the remedy fails in its essential purpose. Sellers and lessors can also limit the rights of buyers and lessees to consequential damages unless the limitation is unconscionable [UCC 2–719, 2A–503]. 2. The UCC has a four-year statute of limitations for actions involving breach of contract. By agreement, the parties to a sales or lease contract can reduce this period to not less than one year, but they cannot extend it beyond four years [UCC 2–725(1), 2A–506(1)].

ExamPrep

ISSUE SPOTTERS

1. Country Fruit Stand orders eighty cases of peaches from Down Home Farms. Without stating a reason, Down Home untimely delivers thirty cases instead of eighty. Does Country have the right to reject the shipment? Explain. **(See page 323.)**

2. Brite Images, Inc. (BI), agrees to sell Catalog Corporation (CC) five thousand posters of celebrities, to be delivered on May 1. On April 1, BI repudiates the contract. CC informs BI that it expects delivery. Can CC sue BI without waiting until May 1? Why or why not? (**See pages 330–331.**)

—Check your answers to the Issue Spotters against the answers provided in Appendix E at the end of this text.

BEFORE THE TEST

Go to www.cengagebrain.com, enter the ISBN 9781133191353, and click on "Find" to locate this textbook's Web site. Then, click on "Access Now" under "Study Tools," and select Chapter 11 at the top. There, you will find a Practice Quiz that you can take to assess your mastery of the concepts in this chapter, as well as Flashcards, a Glossary of important terms, and Video Questions (when assigned).

For Review

Answers to the even-numbered questions in this For Review section can be found in Appendix F at the end of this text.

1. What are the respective obligations of the parties under a contract for the sale or lease of goods?
2. What is the perfect tender rule? What are some important exceptions to this rule that apply to sales and lease contracts?
3. What options are available to the nonbreaching party when the other party to a sales or lease contract repudiates the contract prior to the time for performance?
4. What remedies are available to a seller or lessor when the buyer or lessee breaches the contract? What remedies are available to a buyer or lessee if the seller or lessor breaches the contract?
5. In contracts subject to the UCC, are parties free to limit the remedies available to the nonbreaching party on a breach of contract? If so, in what ways?

Business Scenarios and Case Problems

11–1 Remedies. Genix, Inc., has contracted to sell Larson five hundred washing machines of a certain model at list price. Genix is to ship the goods on or before December 1. Genix produces one thousand washing machines of this model but has not yet prepared Larson's shipment. On November 1, Larson repudiates the contract. Discuss the remedies available to Genix in this situation. (**See page 331.**)

11–2 ❓ **Question with Sample Answer—Anticipatory Repudiation.** Moore contracted in writing to sell her 2010 Hyundai Santa Fe to Hammer for $16,500. Moore agreed to deliver the car on Wednesday, and Hammer promised to pay the $16,500 on the following Friday. On Tuesday, Hammer informed Moore that he would not be buying the car after all. By Friday, Hammer had changed his mind again and tendered $16,500 to Moore. Moore, although she had not sold the car to another party, refused the tender and refused to deliver. Hammer claimed that Moore had breached their contract. Moore contended that Hammer's repudiation released her from her duty to perform under the contract. Who is correct, and why? (**See page 330.**)

—**For a sample answer to Question 11–2, go to Appendix G at the end of this text.**

11–3 🔦 **Spotlight on Revocation of Acceptance—Remedies of the Buyer.** L.V.R.V., Inc., sells recreational vehicles (RVs) in Las Vegas, Nevada, as Wheeler's Las Vegas RV. In September 1997, Wheeler's sold a Santara RV made by Coachmen Recreational Vehicle Co. to Arthur and Roswitha Waddell. The Waddells hoped to spend two or three years driving around the country, but almost immediately—and repeatedly—they experienced problems with the RV. Its entry door popped open. Its cooling and heating systems did not work properly. Its batteries did not maintain a charge. Most significantly, its engine overheated when ascending a moderate grade. The Waddells brought it to Wheeler's service department for repairs. Over the next year and a half, the RV spent more than seven months at Wheeler's. In March 1999, the Waddells filed a complaint in a Nevada state court against the dealer to revoke their acceptance of the RV. What are the requirements for a buyer's revocation of acceptance? Were the requirements met in this case? In whose favor should the court rule? Why? [*Waddell v. L.V.R.V., Inc.*, 122 Nev. 15, 125 P.3d 1160 (2006)] (**See page 337.**)

11–4 Breach and Damages. Utility Systems of America, Inc., was doing roadwork when Chad DeRosier, a nearby landowner, asked Utility to dump 1,500 cubic yards of fill onto his property. Utility agreed but exceeded DeRosier's request by dumping 6,500 cubic yards. Utility offered to remove the extra fill for $9,500. DeRosier paid a different contractor $46,629 to remove the fill and do certain other work. He then filed a suit against Utility. Because Utility charged nothing for the fill, was there a breach of contract? If so, would the damages be greater than $9,500? Could consequential damages be justified? Discuss. [*DeRosier v. Utility Systems of America, Inc.,* 780 N.W.2d 1 (Minn.App. 2010)] **(See page 337.)**

11–5   Right of Inspection. Jessie Romero offered to deliver two trade-in vehicles—a 2003 Mitsubishi Montero and a 2002 Chevrolet Silverado pickup—to Scoggin-Dickey Chevrolet Buick, Inc., in exchange for a 2006 Silverado pickup. Scoggin-Dickey agreed. The parties negotiated a price, including a value for the trade-in vehicles, plus cash. Romero paid the cash and took the Silverado. On inspecting the trade-in vehicles, however, Scoggin-Dickey found that they had little value. The dealer repossessed the 2006 Silverado. Did the dealership have the right to inspect the goods and reject them when it did? Why or why not? [*Romero v. Scoggin-Dickey Chevrolet Buick, Inc.,* __ S.W.3d __ (Tex.Civ.App.—Amarillo 2010)] **(See page 329.)**

11–6   Right to Recover Damages. Woodridge USA Properties, L.P., bought eighty-seven commercial truck trailers from Southeast Trailer Mart, Inc. (STM). Gerald McCarty, an independent sales agent who arranged the deal, showed Woodridge the documents of title. They did not indicate that Woodridge was the buyer. Woodridge asked McCarty to sell the trailers, and within three months, they were sold. McCarty did not give the proceeds to Woodridge, however. Woodridge—without mentioning the title documents—asked STM to refund the contract price. STM refused. Does Woodridge have a right to recover damages from STM? Explain. [*Woodridge USA Properties, L.P. v. Southeast Trailer Mart, Inc.,* 2011 WL 303204 (11th Cir. 2011)] **(See page 332.)**

11–7   Case Problem with Sample Answer—Nonconforming Goods. Padma Paper Mills, Ltd., converts waste paper into usable paper. In 2007, Padma entered into a contract with Universal Exports, Inc., under which Universal Exports certified that it would ship white envelope cuttings, and Padma paid $131,000 for the paper. When the shipment arrived, however, Padma discovered that Universal Exports had sent multicolored paper plates and other brightly colored paper products. Padma accepted the goods but notified Universal Exports that they did not conform to the contract. Can Padma recover even though it accepted the goods knowing that they were nonconforming? If so, how? [*Padma Paper Mills, Ltd. v. Universal Exports, Inc.,* 34 Misc.3d 1236(A) (N.Y.Sup. 2012)] **(See pages 336–339.)**

—For a sample answer to Problem 11–7, go to Appendix H at the end of this text.

11–8   ⬌ A Question of Ethics—Revocation of Acceptance. Scotwood Industries, Inc., sells calcium chloride flake for use in ice melt products. Between July and September 2004, Scotwood delivered thirty-seven shipments of flake to Frank Miller & Sons, Inc. After each delivery, Scotwood billed Miller, which paid thirty-five of the invoices and processed 30 to 50 percent of the flake. In August, Miller began complaining about the quality. Scotwood assured Miller that it would remedy the situation. Finally, in October, Miller told Scotwood, "This is totally unacceptable. We are willing to discuss Scotwood picking up the material." Miller claimed that the flake was substantially defective because it was chunked. Calcium chloride maintains its purity for up to five years, but if it is exposed to and absorbs moisture, it chunks, making it unusable. In response to Scotwood's suit to collect payment on the unpaid invoices, Miller filed a counterclaim in a federal district court for breach of contract, seeking to recover based on revocation of acceptance, among other things. [*Scotwood Industries, Inc. v. Frank Miller & Sons, Inc.,* 435 F.Supp.2d 1160 (D.Kan. 2006)] **(See page 337.)**

1. What is revocation of acceptance? How does a buyer effectively exercise this option? Do the facts in this case support this theory as a ground for Miller to recover damages? Why or why not?

2. Is there an ethical basis for allowing a buyer to revoke acceptance of goods and recover damages? If so, is there an ethical limit to this right? Discuss.

Critical Thinking and Writing Assignments

11–9   Business Law Writing. Suppose that you are a collector of antique cars and you need to purchase spare parts for a 1938 engine. These parts are not made anymore and are scarce. You discover that Beem has the spare parts that you need. To get the contract with Beem, you agree to pay 50 percent of the purchase price in advance. You send the payment on May 1, and Beem receives it on May 2. On May 3, Beem, having found another buyer willing to pay substantially more for the parts, informs you that he will not deliver as contracted. That same day, you learn that Beem is insolvent. Write three paragraphs fully discussing any possible remedies that would enable you to take possession of the parts.

11–10   Business Law Critical Thinking Group Assignment. Kodiak agrees to sell 1,000 espresso machines to Lin to be delivered on May 1. Due to a strike during the last week of April, there is a temporary shortage of delivery vehicles. Kodiak can deliver the espresso makers 200 at a time over a period of ten days, with the first delivery on May 1.

1. The first group will determine if Kodiak has the right to deliver the goods in five lots. What happens if Lin objects to delivery in lots?

2. A second group will analyze whether the doctrine of commercial impracticability applies to this scenario, and if it does, what the result will be.

CHAPTER 12

Warranties, Product Liability, and Consumer Law

(Lisa/Shutterstock.com)

LEARNING OBJECTIVES

The five learning objectives below are designed to help improve your understanding of the chapter. After reading this chapter, you should be able to answer the following questions:

1 What implied warranties arise under the UCC?

2 Can a manufacturer be held liable to any person who suffers an injury proximately caused by the manufacturer's negligently made product?

3 What are the elements of a cause of action in strict product liability?

4 What defenses to liability can be raised in a product liability lawsuit?

5 When will advertising be deemed deceptive?

"I'll warrant him heart-whole."
—William Shakespeare, 1564–1616 (English dramatist and poet)

Warranty is an age-old concept. In sales and lease law, a warranty is an assurance by the seller or lessor of certain facts concerning the goods being sold or leased. In the chapter-opening quotation, a character in William Shakespeare's play *As You Like It* warranted his friend "heart-whole." Likewise, in commercial law, sellers and lessors warrant to those who purchase or lease their goods that the goods are as represented or will be as promised.

The Uniform Commercial Code (UCC) has many rules governing product warranties in sales and lease contracts, and we examine these rules in the first part of this chapter. A natural addition to the discussion is *product liability:* Who is liable to consumers, users, and bystanders for physical harm and property damage caused by a particular good or its use? In today's social environment of consumerism, businesspersons need to be keenly aware of how the sale or lease of defective products can lead to substantial liability.

Warranty law is part of the broad body of consumer protection law discussed in the last part of this chapter. The financial crisis that started in 2008 created a renewed interest in protecting consumers from credit-card companies, financial institutions, and insurance companies. Congress enacted new credit card regulations, as well as certain financial reforms to regulate the nation's largest banks. Congress also enacted health-care reforms, including a law that requires chain restaurants to post the caloric content of foods on their menus.

Warranties

Most goods are covered by some type of warranty designed to protect consumers. Article 2 (on sales) and Article 2A (on leases) of the UCC designate several types of warranties that can arise in a sales or lease contract, including warranties of title, express warranties, and implied warranties.

Warranties of Title

Under the UCC, three types of title warranties—*good title, no liens,* and *no infringements*—can automatically arise in sales and lease contracts.

Good Title
In most sales, sellers warrant that they have good and valid title to the goods sold and that transfer of the title is rightful [UCC 2–312(1)(a)]. If the buyer subsequently learns that the seller did not have good title to goods that were purchased, the buyer can sue the seller for breach of this warranty.

EXAMPLE 12.1 Alexis steals a diamond ring from Calvin and sells it to Emma, who does not know that the ring is stolen. If Calvin discovers that Emma has the ring, then he has the right to reclaim it from Emma. When Alexis sold Emma the ring, Alexis automatically warranted to Emma that the title conveyed was valid and that its transfer was rightful. Because a thief has no title to stolen goods, Alexis breached the warranty of title imposed by the UCC and became liable to Emma for appropriate damages. ● (There is no warranty of good title in lease contracts because, as noted on page 307 of Chapter 10, title to leased goods does not pass to the lessee.)

No Liens
A seller warrants that the goods sold are free of any encumbrances, or **liens** (claims, charges, or liabilities—see Chapter 15) against the goods [UCC 2–312(1)(b), 2A–211(1)]. A lessor warrants that the lessee will not be disturbed in her or his possession of the goods by the claims of a third party.

This warranty shields only buyers and lessees who are *unaware* of any liens against the goods at the time the contract is made. For instance, it protects buyers who unknowingly purchase goods that are subject to a creditor's *security interest* (an interest in the goods that secures payment or performance). If a creditor legally repossesses the goods from a buyer *who had no actual knowledge of the security interest,* the buyer can recover from the seller for breach of warranty.

No Infringements
A third type of title warranty is a warranty against infringement of any patent, trademark, or copyright. When the seller or lessor is a merchant, he or she automatically warrants that the buyer or lessee takes the goods *free of infringements.* In other words, a merchant promises that the goods delivered are free from any copyright, trademark, or patent claims of a third person [UCC 2–312(3), 2A–211(2)].

Express Warranties

A seller or lessor can create an **express warranty** by making representations concerning the quality, condition, description, or performance potential of the goods. Under UCC

Lien An encumbrance on a property to satisfy a debt or protect a claim for payment of a debt.

Express Warranty A contractual promise concerning the quality, condition, description, or performance of the goods being sold or leased.

Is this logo an express warranty?

2–313 and 2A–210, express warranties arise when a seller or lessor indicates any of the following:

1. That the goods conform to any *affirmation* (declaration that something is true) or *promise* of fact that the seller or lessor makes to the buyer or lessee about the goods. Such affirmations or promises are usually made during the bargaining process. Statements such as "these drill bits will penetrate stainless steel—and without dulling" are express warranties.
2. That the goods conform to any *description* of them. For example, a label that reads "Crate contains one 150-horsepower diesel engine" or a contract that calls for the delivery of a "camel's hair coat" creates an express warranty.
3. That the goods conform to any *sample* or *model* of the goods shown to the buyer or lessee.

Basis of the Bargain
To create an express warranty, a seller or lessor does not have to use words such as *warrant* or *guarantee* [UCC 2–313(2), 2A–210(2)]. It is only necessary that a reasonable buyer or lessee would regard the representation of fact as part of the basis of the bargain [UCC 2–313(1), 2A–210(1)]. The UCC does not define the "basis of the bargain," however, and it is a question of fact in each case whether a representation was made at such a time and in such a way that it induced the buyer or lessee to enter into the contract.

Statements of Opinion and Value
Only statements of fact create express warranties. If the seller or lessor makes a statement about the supposed value or worth of the goods, or offers an opinion or recommendation about the goods, the seller or lessor is not creating an express warranty [UCC 2–313(2), 2A–210(2)].

EXAMPLE 12.2 A car salesperson claims that "this is the best used car to come along in years. It has four new tires and a 250-horsepower engine just rebuilt this year." The seller has made several *affirmations of fact* that can create a warranty: the automobile has an engine, the engine has 250 horsepower and was rebuilt this year, there are four tires on the automobile, and the tires are new. The seller's *opinion* that the vehicle is "the best used car to come along in years," however, is known as "puffery" and creates no warranty. (*Puffery* is an expression of opinion by a seller or lessor that is not made as a representation of fact.) •

A statement about the value of the goods, such as "this is worth a fortune" or "anywhere else you'd pay $10,000 for it," usually does not create a warranty. If the seller or lessor is an expert and gives an opinion as an expert to a layperson, though, then a warranty may be created.

It is not always easy to determine whether a statement constitutes an express warranty or puffery. Often, the reasonableness of the buyer's or lessee's reliance is the controlling criterion. For instance, a salesperson's statements that a ladder "will never break" and will "last a lifetime" are so clearly improbable that no reasonable buyer should rely on them. Courts also look at the context in which a statement is made to determine the reasonableness of the buyer's or lessee's reliance. For instance, a reasonable person is more likely to rely on a written statement made in an advertisement than on a statement made orally by a salesperson.

PREVENTING LEGAL DISPUTES

If you are in the business of selling or leasing goods, be careful about the words you use with customers, in writing and orally. If you do not intend to make an express warranty, do not make a promise or an affirmation of fact concerning the performance or quality of a product that you sell. Examine your firm's advertisements, brochures, and promotional materials, as well as any standard order forms and contracts, for statements that could be considered express warranties. To avoid unintended warranties, instruct all employees on how the promises they make to buyers during a sale can create warranties.

Implied Warranties

Implied Warranty A warranty that arises by law because of the circumstances of a sale rather than by the seller's express promise.

An **implied warranty** is one that *the law derives* by implication or inference because of the circumstances of a sale. In an action based on breach of implied warranty, it is necessary to show that an implied warranty existed and that the breach of the warranty proximately caused[1] the damage sustained. We look here at some of the implied warranties that arise under the UCC.

Implied Warranty of Merchantability A warranty that goods being sold or leased are reasonably fit for the general purpose for which they are sold or leased, are properly packaged and labeled, and are of proper quality.

Implied Warranty of Merchantability   Every sale or lease of goods made *by a merchant who deals in goods of the kind sold or leased* automatically gives rise to an **implied warranty of merchantability** [UCC 2–314, 2A–212]. **EXAMPLE 12.3**   A merchant who is in the business of selling ski equipment makes an implied warranty of merchantability every time she sells a pair of skis. A neighbor selling his skis at a garage sale does not (because he is not in the business of selling goods of this type). •

Merchantable Goods   Goods that are *merchantable* are "reasonably fit for the ordinary purposes for which such goods are used." They must be of at least average, fair, or medium-grade quality. The quality must be comparable to a level that will pass without objection in the trade or market for goods of the same description. To be merchantable, the goods must also be adequately packaged and labeled, and they must conform to the promises or affirmations of fact made on the container or label, if any.

The warranty of merchantability may be breached even though the merchant did not know or could not have discovered that a product was defective (not merchantable). Of course, merchants are not absolute insurers against all accidents occurring in connection with their goods. For instance, a bar of soap is not unmerchantable merely because stepping on it could cause a user to slip and fall.

CASE EXAMPLE 12.4   Darrell Shoop bought a Dodge Dakota truck that had been manufactured by DaimlerChrysler Corporation. Almost immediately, he had problems with the truck. During the first eighteen months, the truck's engine, suspension, steering, transmission, and other components required repairs twelve times, including at least five times for the same defect, which remained uncorrected. Shoop eventually traded in the truck and filed a lawsuit against DaimlerChrysler for breach of the implied warranty of merchantability. The court held that Shoop could maintain an action against DaimlerChrysler and use the fact that the truck had required a significant number of repairs as evidence that it was unmerchantable.[2] •

LEARNING OBJECTIVE 1
What implied warranties arise under the UCC?

Merchantable Food   The UCC recognizes the serving of food or drink to be consumed on or off the premises as a sale of goods subject to the implied warranty of merchantability [UCC 2–314(1)]. "Merchantable" food means food that is fit to eat.

Courts generally determine whether food is fit to eat on the basis of consumer expectations. The courts assume that consumers should reasonably expect on occasion to find bones in fish fillets, cherry pits in cherry pie, or a nutshell in a package of shelled nuts, for example. In contrast, consumers would not reasonably expect to find moth larvae in a can of peas or a piece of glass in a soft drink.

In the following *Classic Case,* the court had to determine whether a diner should reasonably expect to find a fish bone in fish chowder.

---

1. Proximate, or legal, cause exists when the connection between an act and an injury is strong enough to justify imposing liability—see Chapter 4 on page 118.
2. *Shoop v. DaimlerChrysler Corp.,* 371 Ill.App.3d 1058, 864 N.E.2d 785 (2007).

Classic Case 12.1

Webster v. Blue Ship Tea Room, Inc.

Supreme Judicial Court of Massachusetts, 347 Mass. 421, 198 N.E.2d 309 (1964).

(hipokrat/iStockphoto.com)

Who is liable for fish bones in seafood chowder?

HISTORICAL AND CULTURAL SETTING *Chowder, a soup or stew made with fresh fish, may have originated in the fishing villages of Brittany (a French province to the west of Paris) and was probably carried to Canada and New England by Breton immigrants. Through the first half of the twentieth century, chowder recipes did not call for the removal of the fish bones—sometimes, for example, specifying that the fish head, tail, and backbone were to be broken in pieces and boiled, with the "liquor thus produced . . . added to the balance of the chowder."*[a] *By the middle of the twentieth century, there was a considerable body of case law concerning implied warranties and foreign and natural substances in food. It was perhaps inevitable that sooner or later, a consumer injured by a fish bone in chowder would challenge the merchantability of chowder containing fish bones.*

FACTS Blue Ship Tea Room, Inc., was located in Boston in an old building overlooking the ocean. Priscilla Webster, who had been born and raised in New England, went to the restaurant and ordered fish chowder. The chowder was milky in color. After three or four spoonfuls, she felt something lodged in her throat. As a result, she underwent two esophagoscopies; in the second esophagoscopy, a fish bone was found and removed. Webster filed a lawsuit against the restaurant in a Massachusetts state court for breach of the implied warranty of merchantability. The jury rendered a verdict for Webster, and the restaurant appealed to the state's highest court.

ISSUE Does serving fish chowder that contains a bone constitute a breach of an implied warranty of merchantability by the restaurant?

DECISION No. The Supreme Judicial Court of Massachusetts held that Webster could not recover against Blue Ship Tea Room because no breach of warranty had occurred.

REASON The court, citing UCC Section 2–314, stated that "a warranty that goods shall be merchantable is implied in a contract for their sale if the seller is a merchant with respect to goods of that kind. Under this section the serving for value of food or drink to be consumed either on the premises or elsewhere is a sale. . . . Goods to be merchantable must at least be . . . fit for the ordinary purposes for which such goods are used." The question here was whether a fish bone made the chowder unfit for eating. In the judge's opinion, "the joys of life in New England include the ready availability of fresh fish chowder. We should be prepared to cope with the hazards of fish bones, the occasional presence of which in chowders is, it seems to us, to be anticipated, and which, in the light of a hallowed tradition, do not impair their fitness or merchantability."

IMPACT OF THIS CASE ON TODAY'S LAW *This classic case, phrased in memorable language, was an early application of the UCC's implied warranty of merchantability to food products. The case established the rule that consumers should expect to occasionally find elements of food products that are natural to the product (such as fish bones in fish chowder). Courts today still apply this rule.*

a. Fannie Farmer, *The Boston Cooking School Cook Book* (Boston: Little, Brown, 1937), p. 166.

Implied Warranty of Fitness for a Particular Purpose A warranty that goods sold or leased are fit for the particular purpose for which the buyer or lessee will use the goods.

Implied Warranty of Fitness for a Particular Purpose

The **implied warranty of fitness for a particular purpose** arises when any seller or lessor (merchant or nonmerchant) knows the particular purpose for which a buyer or lessee will use the goods *and* knows that the buyer or lessee is relying on the skill and judgment of the seller or lessor to select suitable goods [UCC 2–315, 2A–213].

A "particular purpose" of the buyer or lessee differs from the "ordinary purpose for which goods are used" (merchantability). Goods can be merchantable but unfit for a particular purpose. **EXAMPLE 12.5** Cheryl needs a gallon of paint to match the color of her living room walls—a light shade between coral and peach. She takes a sample to the local hardware store and requests a gallon of paint of that color. Instead, she is given a gallon of bright blue paint. Here, the salesperson has not breached any warranty of implied merchantability—the bright blue paint is of high quality and suitable for interior walls—but he has breached an implied warranty of fitness for a particular purpose. •

A seller or lessor is not required to have actual knowledge of the buyer's or lessee's particular purpose, so long as the seller or lessor "has reason to know" the purpose. For an implied warranty to be created, however, the buyer or lessee must have *relied* on the skill or judgment of the seller or lessor in selecting or furnishing suitable goods.

Warranties Implied from Prior Dealings or Trade Custom

Implied warranties can also arise (or be excluded or modified) as a result of course of dealing or usage of trade [UCC 2–314(3), 2A–212(3)]. In the absence of evidence to the contrary, when both parties to a sales or lease contract have knowledge of a well-recognized trade custom, the courts will infer that both parties intended that trade custom to apply to their contract.

EXAMPLE 12.6   Suppose that it is an industry-wide custom to lubricate new cars before they are delivered to buyers. Latoya buys a new car from Bender Chevrolet. After the purchase, Latoya discovers that Bender failed to lubricate the car before delivering it to her. In this situation, Latoya can hold the dealer liable for damages resulting from the breach of an implied warranty. (This, of course, would also be negligence on the part of the dealer.) •

Overlapping Warranties

Sometimes, two or more warranties are made in a single transaction. An implied warranty of merchantability, an implied warranty of fitness for a particular purpose, or both can exist in addition to an express warranty. For instance, when a sales contract for a new car states that "this car engine is warranted to be free from defects for 36,000 miles or thirty-six months, whichever occurs first," the seller has made an express warranty against all defects and an implied warranty that the car will be fit for normal use.

The rule under the UCC is that express and implied warranties are construed as *cumulative* if they are consistent with one another [UCC 2–317, 2A–215]. In other words, courts interpret two or more warranties as being in agreement with each other unless this construction is unreasonable. If it is unreasonable, then a court will hold that the warranties are inconsistent and apply the following rules to interpret which warranty is most important:

1. *Express* warranties displace inconsistent *implied* warranties, except for implied warranties of fitness for a particular purpose.
2. Samples take precedence over inconsistent general descriptions.
3. Exact or technical specifications displace inconsistent samples or general descriptions.

Warranty Disclaimers

The UCC generally permits warranties to be disclaimed or limited by specific and unambiguous language, provided that the buyer or lessee is protected from surprise. The manner in which a seller or lessor can disclaim warranties varies depending on the type of warranty.

Express Warranties   A seller or lessor can disclaim all oral express warranties by including in the contract a written (or an electronically recorded) disclaimer that is expressed in clear language, conspicuous, and called to the buyer's or lessee's attention [UCC 2–316(1), 2A–214(1)]. This allows the seller or lessor to avoid false allegations that oral warranties were made, and it ensures that only representations made by properly authorized individuals are included in the bargain. Note, however, that a buyer or lessee must be made aware of any warranty disclaimers or modifications *at the time the contract is formed.*

Implied Warranties   Generally, unless circumstances indicate otherwise, the implied warranties of merchantability and fitness are disclaimed by the expressions "as is," "with all faults," and similar phrases. The phrase must be one that in common understanding calls the buyer's or lessee's attention to the fact that there are no implied warranties [UCC 2–316(3)(a), 2A–214(3)(a)]. (Note, however, that some states have laws that forbid "as is" sales. Other states do not allow disclaimers of warranties of merchantability for consumer goods.)

CASE EXAMPLE 12.7 Mandy Morningstar advertised a "lovely, eleven-year-old mare" with extensive jumping ability for sale. After examining the mare twice, Sue Hallett contracted to buy the horse. The contract she signed described the horse as an eleven-year-old mare, but indicated that the horse was being sold "as is." Shortly after the purchase, a veterinarian determined that the horse was actually sixteen years old and in no condition for jumping. Hallett stopped payment and tried to return the horse and cancel the contract. Morningstar sued for breach of contract. The court held that the statement in the contract describing the horse as eleven years old constituted an express warranty, which Morningstar had breached. Although the "as is" clause effectively disclaimed any implied warranties (of merchantability and fitness for a particular purpose, such as jumping), the court ruled that it did not disclaim the express warranty concerning the horse's age.[3] •

Disclaimer of the Implied Warranty of Merchantability To specifically disclaim an implied warranty of merchantability, a seller or lessor must mention the word *merchantability* [UCC 2–316(2), 2A–214(2)]. The disclaimer need not be written, but if it is, the writing (or record) must be conspicuous [UCC 2–316(2), 2A–214(4)].

Under the UCC, a term or clause is conspicuous when it is written or displayed in such a way that a reasonable person would notice it. Words are conspicuous when they are in capital letters, in a larger font size, or in a different color than the surrounding text.

Disclaimer of the Implied Warranty of Fitness To specifically disclaim an implied warranty of fitness for a particular purpose, the disclaimer *must* be in a writing (or record) and must be conspicuous. The word *fitness* does not have to be mentioned. It is sufficient if, for example, the disclaimer states, "THERE ARE NO WARRANTIES THAT EXTEND BEYOND THE DESCRIPTION ON THE FACE HEREOF."

Buyer's or Lessee's Examination or Refusal to Inspect If a buyer or lessee actually examines the goods (or a sample or model) as fully as desired before entering into a contract, or if the buyer or lessee refuses to examine the goods on the seller's or lessor's request, *there is no implied warranty with respect to defects that a reasonable examination would reveal or defects that are actually found* [UCC 2–316(3)(b), 2A–214(2)(b)].

EXAMPLE 12.8 Azumi buys a lamp at Gershwin's Store. No express warranties are made. Gershwin asks Azumi to inspect the lamp before buying it, but she refuses. Had Azumi inspected the lamp, she would have noticed that the base was obviously cracked and the electrical cord was loose. If the lamp later cracks or starts a fire in Azumi's home and she is injured, she normally will not be able to hold Gershwin's liable for breach of the warranty of merchantability. Because Azumi refused to examine the lamp when asked by Gershwin, Azumi will be deemed to have assumed the risk that it was defective. •

Warranty Disclaimers and Unconscionability The UCC sections dealing with warranty disclaimers do not refer specifically to unconscionability as a factor. Ultimately, however, the courts will test warranty disclaimers with reference to the UCC's unconscionability standards [UCC 2–302, 2A–108]. Such factors as lack of bargaining position, take-it-or-leave-it choices, and a buyer's or lessee's failure to understand or know of a warranty disclaimer will be relevant to the issue of unconscionability.

> **KNOW THIS**
> Courts generally view warranty disclaimers unfavorably, especially when consumers are involved.

---

3. *Morningstar v. Hallett,* 858 A.2d 125 (Pa.Super.Ct. 2004).

Magnuson-Moss Warranty Act

The Magnuson-Moss Warranty Act[4] was designed to prevent deception in warranties by making them easier to understand. The act modifies UCC warranty rules to some extent when *consumer* transactions are involved. The UCC, however, remains the primary codification of warranty rules for commercial transactions.

Under the Magnuson-Moss Act, a seller is not required to give an express written warranty for consumer goods sold. If a seller chooses to make an express written warranty, however, and the goods are priced at more than $25, the warranty must be labeled as "full" or "limited."

A *full warranty* requires free repair or replacement of any defective part. If the product cannot be repaired within a reasonable time, the consumer has the choice of a refund or a replacement without charge. A full warranty can be for an unlimited or limited time period, such as a "full twelve-month warranty." With a *limited warranty,* the buyer's recourse is limited in some fashion, such as to replacement of the item. The fact that only a limited warranty is being given must be conspicuously stated. The act further requires the warrantor to make certain disclosures concerning the warranty fully and conspicuously in a single document in "readily understood language."

> **KNOW THIS**
>
> When a buyer or lessee is a consumer, a limitation on consequential damages for personal injuries resulting from nonconforming goods is *prima facie* unconscionable.

Lemon Laws

Some purchasers of defective automobiles—called "lemons"—found that the remedies provided by the UCC were inadequate due to limitations imposed by the seller. In response to the frustrations of these buyers, all of the states have enacted *lemon laws.*

Basically, state lemon laws provide remedies to consumers who buy automobiles that repeatedly fail to meet standards of quality and performance. Although lemon laws vary by state, typically they apply to automobiles under warranty that are defective in a way that significantly affects their value or use. Lemon laws do not necessarily cover used-car purchases (unless the car is covered by a manufacturer's extended warranty) or vehicles that are leased.

Generally, the seller or manufacturer is given a number of opportunities to remedy the defect (usually four). If the seller fails to cure the problem despite a reasonable number of attempts (as specified by state law), the buyer is entitled to a new car, replacement of defective parts, or return of all consideration paid. If the seller fails to solve the problem, the owner must submit complaints to the arbitration program specified in the manufacturer's warranty before taking the case to court. Buyers who prevail in a lemon-law dispute may also be entitled to reimbursement of their attorneys' fees.

When do lemon laws apply?

(Monkey Business Images/Shutterstock)

Product Liability

Those who make, sell, or lease goods can be held liable for physical harm or property damage caused by those goods to a consumer, user, or bystander. This is called **product liability.** Product liability claims may be based on the warranty theories just discussed, as well as on the theories of negligence, misrepresentation, and strict liability. We look here at product liability based on negligence and misrepresentation.

Product Liability The legal liability of manufacturers, sellers, and lessors of goods for injuries or damage caused by the goods to consumers, users, or bystanders.

Negligence

Chapter 4 defined *negligence* as the failure to exercise the degree of care that a reasonable, prudent person would have exercised under the circumstances. If a manufacturer fails to exercise "due care" to make a product safe, a person who is injured by the product may sue the manufacturer for negligence.

---

4. 15 U.S.C. Sections 2301–2312.

The manufacturer must exercise due care in designing the product, selecting the materials, using the appropriate production process, assembling the product, and placing adequate warnings on the label informing the user of dangers of which an ordinary person might not be aware. The duty of care also extends to the inspection and testing of any purchased components that are used in the final product sold by the manufacturer.

As discussed in Chapter 9, *privity of contract* refers to the relationship that exists between the promisor and the promisee of a contract. Privity is the reason that normally only the parties to a contract can enforce that contract. In the context of product liability law, privity is not required. A person who is injured by a defective product can bring a negligence suit against the product's manufacturer or seller, even though that person is not the one who actually purchased the product—and thus is not in privity. A manufacturer is liable for its failure to exercise due care to *any person* who sustains an injury proximately caused by a negligently made (defective) product. For a leading case on this exception to the privity requirement, see this chapter's *Landmark in the Law* feature below.

LEARNING OBJECTIVE 2
Can a manufacturer be held liable to any person who suffers an injury proximately caused by the manufacturer's negligently made product?

Misrepresentation

When a user or consumer is injured as a result of a manufacturer's or seller's fraudulent misrepresentation, the basis of liability may be the tort of fraud. The intentional mislabeling of packaged cosmetics, for instance, or the intentional concealment of a product's defects constitutes fraudulent misrepresentation.

LANDMARK IN THE LAW
MacPherson v. Buick Motor Co. (1916)

In the landmark case of *MacPherson v. Buick Motor Co.*,[a] the New York Court of Appeals—New York's highest court—considered the liability of a manufacturer that failed to exercise reasonable care in manufacturing a finished product.

Case Background Donald MacPherson suffered injuries while riding in a Buick automobile that suddenly collapsed because one of the wheels was made of defective wood. The spokes crumbled into fragments, throwing MacPherson out of the vehicle and injuring him.

MacPherson had purchased the car from a Buick dealer, but he brought a lawsuit against the manufacturer, Buick Motor Company. Buick itself had not made the wheel but had bought it from another manufacturer. There was evidence, though, that the defects could have been discovered by a reasonable inspection by Buick and that no such inspection had taken place. MacPherson charged Buick with negligence for putting a human life in imminent danger.

The Issue before the Court and the Court's Ruling The primary issue was whether Buick owed a duty of care to anyone except the immediate purchaser of the car—that is, the Buick

dealer. In deciding the issue, Justice Benjamin Cardozo stated that "if the nature of a thing is such that it is reasonably certain to place life and limb in peril when negligently made, it is then a thing of danger. . . . If to the element of danger there is added knowledge that the thing will be used by persons other than the purchaser, and used without new tests, then, irrespective of contract, the manufacturer of this thing of danger is under a duty to make it carefully."

The court concluded that "beyond all question, the nature of an automobile gives warning of probable danger if its construction is defective. This automobile was designed to go 50 miles an hour. Unless its wheels were sound and strong, injury was almost certain." Although Buick itself had not manufactured the wheel, the court held that Buick had a duty to inspect the wheels and that Buick "was responsible for the finished product." Therefore, Buick was liable to MacPherson for the injuries he sustained when he was thrown from the car.

Application to Today's World *This landmark decision was a significant step in creating the legal environment of the modern world. As often happens, technological developments necessitated changes in the law. Today, automobile manufacturers are commonly held liable when their negligence causes automobile users to be injured.*

a. 217 N.Y. 382, 111 N.E. 1050 (1916).

The misrepresentation must be of a material fact, and the seller must have intended to induce the buyer to rely on the misrepresentation. Misrepresentation on a label or advertisement is enough to show an intent to induce reliance. Of course, to bring a lawsuit on this ground, the buyer must have relied on the misrepresentation.

Strict Product Liability

Under the doctrine of strict liability (discussed in Chapter 4), people may be liable for the results of their acts regardless of their intentions or their exercise of reasonable care. In addition, liability does not depend on privity of contract. The injured party does not have to be the buyer or a *third party beneficiary* (see page 260 in Chapter 9), as required under contract warranty theory. In the 1960s, courts applied the doctrine of strict liability in several landmark cases involving manufactured goods, and this doctrine has since become a common method of holding manufacturers liable.

The law imposes strict product liability as a matter of public policy. This public policy rests on the threefold assumption that:

1. Consumers should be protected against unsafe products.
2. Manufacturers and distributors should not escape liability for faulty products simply because they are not in privity of contract with the ultimate user of those products.
3. Manufacturers, sellers, and lessors of products are generally in a better position than consumers to bear the costs associated with injuries caused by their products—costs that they can ultimately pass on to all consumers in the form of higher prices.

California was the first state to impose strict product liability in tort on manufacturers. In a landmark decision, *Greenman v. Yuba Power Products, Inc.,*[5] the California Supreme Court set out the reason for applying tort law rather than contract law in cases involving consumers injured by defective products. According to the court, the "purpose of such liability is to [e]nsure that the costs of injuries resulting from defective products are borne by the manufacturers . . . rather than by the injured persons who are powerless to protect themselves."

Requirements for Strict Liability

After the *Restatement (Second) of Torts* was issued in 1964, Section 402A became a widely accepted statement of how the doctrine of strict liability should be applied to sellers of goods (including manufacturers, processors, assemblers, packagers, bottlers, wholesalers, distributors, retailers, and lessors).

LEARNING OBJECTIVE 3
What are the elements of a cause of action in strict product liability?

The bases for an action in strict liability that are set forth in Section 402A can be summarized as the following six requirements. Depending on the jurisdiction, if these requirements are met, a manufacturer's liability to an injured party can be almost unlimited.

1. The product must have been in a *defective condition* when the defendant sold it.
2. The defendant must normally be engaged in the *business of selling* (or otherwise distributing) that product.
3. The product must be *unreasonably dangerous* to the user or consumer because of its defective condition (in most states).
4. The plaintiff must incur *physical harm* to self or property by use or consumption of the product.
5. The defective condition must be the *proximate cause* of the injury or damage.
6. The *goods must not have been substantially changed* from the time the product was sold to the time the injury was sustained.

Proving a Defective Condition
Under these requirements, in any action against a manufacturer, seller, or lessor, the plaintiff does not have to show why or how

5. *59 Cal.2d 57, 377 P.2d 897, 27 Cal.Rptr. 697 (1963).*

Under what circumstances can a consumer prove that tires were sold in a defective condition?

Unreasonably Dangerous Product
A product that is so defective that it is dangerous beyond the expectation of an ordinary consumer or a product for which a less dangerous alternative was feasible but the manufacturer failed to produce it.

the product became defective. The plaintiff does, however, have to prove that the product was defective at the time it left the seller or lessor and that this defective condition made it "unreasonably dangerous" to the user or consumer. (See this chapter's *Beyond Our Borders* feature below for a discussion of how foreign suppliers were held liable for defective goods sold in the United States.)

Unless evidence can be presented that will support the conclusion that the product was defective when it was sold or leased, the plaintiff normally will not succeed. If the product was delivered in a safe condition and subsequent mishandling made it harmful to the user, the seller or lessor usually is not strictly liable.

Unreasonably Dangerous Products The *Restatement* recognizes that many products cannot possibly be made entirely safe for all uses. Thus, sellers or lessors are held liable only for products that are *unreasonably* dangerous. A court may consider a product so defective as to be an **unreasonably dangerous product** in either of the following situations.

1. The product is dangerous beyond the expectation of the ordinary consumer.
2. A less dangerous alternative was economically feasible for the manufacturer, but the manufacturer failed to produce it.

Product Defects

To clarify what makes a product unreasonably dangerous, the *Restatement (Third) of Torts: Products Liability* defines the three types of product defects that have traditionally been recognized in product liability law—manufacturing defects, design defects, and inadequate warnings.

Manufacturing Defects According to Section 2(a) of the *Restatement (Third) of Torts: Products Liability*, a product "contains a manufacturing defect when the product departs from its intended design even though all possible care was exercised in the preparation and marketing of the product." Basically, a manufacturing defect is a departure from a product unit's design specifications that results in products that are physically flawed, damaged, or incorrectly assembled. A glass bottle that is made too thin, causing it to explode in a consumer's face, is an example of a product with a manufacturing defect.

Usually, such defects occur when a manufacturer fails to assemble, test, or adequately check the quality of a product. Liability is imposed on the manufacturer (and on the

BEYOND OUR BORDERS

Imposing Product Liability as Far Away as China

Chinese drywall started being used in the construction of houses in the United States in 2003. By 2007, thousands of homes had been constructed with this product in Alabama, Florida, Louisiana, Mississippi, and a few other states. There was a problem, though—use of the Chinese drywall caused blackening and pitting of electrical wires. Homeowners began to notice an odor similar to that of rotten eggs.

Air-conditioning units started failing, as did ceiling fans, alarm systems, refrigerators, and other appliances.

Numerous lawsuits were filed against the Chinese drywall manufacturers, which initially fought the claims. When the number of lawsuits ran into the thousands, however, the Chinese companies decided to settle.

The estimated value of the settlement is between $800 million and $1 billion.

It includes an uncapped fund to pay for repairs for about 4,500 homes and a separate fund capped at $30 million that will be used to pay for health problems stemming from the defective Chinese drywall.

Critical Thinking
Could U.S. companies that sold Chinese drywall to consumers also be held liable for damages? Why or why not?

wholesaler and retailer) regardless of whether the manufacturer's quality control efforts were "reasonable." The idea behind holding defendants strictly liable for manufacturing defects is to encourage greater investment in product safety and stringent quality control standards.

CASE EXAMPLE 12.9 Kevin Schmude purchased an eight-foot stepladder and used it to install radio-frequency shielding in a hospital room. While Schmude was standing on the ladder, it collapsed, and he was seriously injured. He filed a lawsuit against the ladder's maker, Tricam Industries, Inc., based on a manufacturing defect. Experts testified that when the ladder was assembled, the preexisting holes in the top cap did not properly line up with the holes in the rear right rail and backing plate. As a result of the misalignment, the rivet at the rear legs of the ladder was more likely to fail. A jury concluded that this manufacturing defect made the ladder unreasonably dangerous and awarded Schmude more than $677,000 in damages.[6] ●

(antos777/iStockphoto.com)

If a ladder collapses, who is liable?

Design Defects Unlike a product with a manufacturing defect, a product with a design defect is made in conformity with the manufacturer's design specifications, but it nevertheless results in injury to the user because the design itself is flawed. The product's design creates an unreasonable risk to the user.

To successfully assert a design defect, a plaintiff has to show that a reasonable alternative design was available and that the defendant's failure to adopt the alternative design rendered the product unreasonably dangerous. In other words, a manufacturer or other defendant is liable only when the harm was reasonably preventable.

According to the Official Comments accompanying the *Restatement (Third) of Torts*, a court can consider a broad range of factors in deciding claims of design defects. These factors include the magnitude and probability of the foreseeable risks, as well as the relative advantages and disadvantages of the product as designed and as it alternatively could have been designed. Basically, most courts engage in a risk-utility analysis, determining whether the risk of harm from the product as designed outweighs its utility to the user and to the public.

CASE EXAMPLE 12.10 Jodie Bullock smoked cigarettes manufactured by Philip Morris for forty-five years. When she was diagnosed with lung cancer, Bullock brought a product liability suit against Philip Morris. She presented evidence that by the late 1950s, scientists had proved that smoking caused lung cancer. Nonetheless, Philip Morris had issued full-page announcements stating that there was no proof that smoking caused cancer and that "numerous scientists" questioned "the validity of the statistics." At trial, the judge instructed the jury to consider the gravity of the danger posed by the design, as well as the likelihood that the danger would cause injury.

The jury found that there was a defect in the design of the cigarettes and that they had been negligently designed. It awarded Bullock $850,000 in compensatory damages and $28 million in punitive damages. Philip Morris appealed, claiming that no evidence had been offered to show that there was a safer design for cigarettes. The reviewing court affirmed the jury's verdict but remanded the case for a reconsideration of the proper amount of punitive damages.[7] ●

Inadequate Warnings A product may also be deemed defective because of inadequate instructions or warnings. A product will be considered defective "when the foreseeable risks of harm posed by the product could have been reduced or avoided by the provision of reasonable instructions or warnings by the seller or other distributor, or a predecessor in the commercial chain of distribution, and the omission of the instructions

6. *Schmude v. Tricam Industries, Inc.*, 550 F.Supp.2d 846 (E.D.Wis. 2008).
7. *Bullock v. Philip Morris USA, Inc.*, 159 Cal.App.4th 655, 71 Cal.Rptr.3d 775 (2008). The California Court of Appeal subsequently upheld a punitive damages award of $13.8 million. See *Bullock v. Philip Morris USA, Inc.*, 198 Cal.App.4th 543, 131 Cal.Rptr.3d 382 (2011).

or warnings renders the product not reasonably safe."[8] Generally, a seller must also warn consumers of the harm that can result from the *foreseeable misuse* of its product.

Content of Warnings Important factors for a court to consider include the risks of a product, the "content and comprehensibility" and "intensity of expression" of warnings and instructions, and the "characteristics of expected user groups."[9] Courts apply a "reasonableness" test to determine if the warnings adequately alert consumers to the product's risks. For example, children will likely respond more readily to bright, bold, simple warning labels, while educated adults might need more detailed information.

In the following case, a patient filed a product liability suit alleging that a product had a design defect and that the manufacturer had provided inadequate warnings. The court had to decide whether the plaintiff could pursue either theory of recovery.

8. *Restatement (Third) of Torts: Products Liability,* Section 2(c).
9. *Restatement (Third) of Torts: Products Liability,* Section 2, Comment h.

Case 12.2

Johnson v. Medtronic, Inc.

Missouri Court of Appeals,
365 S.W.3d 226 (2012).
www.courts.mo.gov[a]

(Munshi Ahmed/Bloomberg via Getty Images)

Medtronic manufactures medical devices, including defibrillators.

FACTS In 2005, Jeffrey Johnson experienced an episode of atrial fibrillation, a heart rhythm disorder, and was taken to an emergency room. Dr. David Hahn used a defibrillator manufactured by Medtronic, Inc., to deliver electric shocks to Johnson's heart. The defibrillator had synchronous and asynchronous modes, and it reverted to the asynchronous mode after each use. Hahn intended to deliver synchronized shocks, which would have required him to select the synchronous mode for each shock. Hahn had not read the device's instructions, which Medtronic provided both in a manual and on the device itself. As a result, he delivered a synchronized shock followed by twelve asynchronous shocks, which endangered Johnson's life. Johnson and his wife filed a product liability suit against Medtronic, asserting that Medtronic had provided inadequate warnings about the defibrillator and that the device had a design defect. The trial court found for Medtronic under both product liability theories, and the Johnsons appealed.

ISSUE Could Johnson pursue a product liability claim alleging either that Medtronic's warnings were inadequate or that the device had a design defect?

DECISION No and yes, respectively. The Missouri appellate court held that Johnson could not pursue a claim based on the inadequacy of Medtronic's warnings, but that he could pursue a claim alleging a design defect. Thus, the trial court's decision was affirmed in part and reversed in part.

REASON The court first held that Johnson could not pursue a claim alleging that Medtronic provided inadequate warnings. Johnson offered no evidence that he was harmed because the defibrillator was sold without an adequate warning. Instead, the record showed that Medtronic's instructions would have prevented Johnson's injuries if Dr. Hahn had followed or even read them. Nevertheless, the court held that Johnson could pursue his design defect claim. Johnson provided evidence that Hahn's misuse was reasonably foreseeable. Importantly, Medtronic knew that other users had inadvertently delivered asynchronous shocks after failing to reset the device. The court concluded that Johnson was not precluded from bringing a claim for design defect simply because he could not pursue a claim of inadequate warnings. In some cases, "a manufacturer may be held liable where it chooses to warn of the danger . . . rather than preclude the danger by design."

CRITICAL THINKING—Legal Consideration *What could Medtronic do to avoid possible liability to plaintiffs like the Johnsons? Was there a reasonable alternative design for the defibrillator?*

---

a. In the right-hand column, click on "Opinions & Minutes." In the middle of the next page, after "Missouri Court of Appeals, Western District," click on "opinions." In the "Search Opinions . . ." box, type "Johnson v. Medtronic," and click on "Search." In the result, click on the case name to access the opinion.

Obvious Risks   There is no duty to warn about risks that are obvious or commonly known. Warnings about such risks do not add to the safety of a product and could even detract from it by making other warnings seem less significant. The obviousness of a risk and a user's decision to proceed in the face of that risk may be a defense in a product liability suit based on a warning defect. (This defense and other defenses in product liability suits will be discussed later in this chapter.)

An action alleging that a product is defective due to an inadequate label can be based on state law. For a discussion of a decision by the United States Supreme Court involving a state law that required warning labels on violent video games, see this chapter's *Adapting the Law to the Online Environment* feature on the facing page.

Other Applications of Strict Liability

Almost all courts extend the strict liability of manufacturers and other sellers to injured bystanders.   **EXAMPLE 12.11**   A forklift that Trent is operating will not go into reverse, and as a result, it runs into a bystander. In this situation, the bystander can sue the manufacturer of the defective forklift under strict liability (and possibly bring a negligence action against the forklift operator as well). ●

Strict liability also applies to suppliers of component parts.   **EXAMPLE 12.12**   Toyota buys brake pads from a subcontractor and puts them in Corollas without changing their composition. If those pads are defective, both the supplier of the brake pads and Toyota will be held strictly liable for the injuries caused by the defects. ●

Defenses to Product Liability

LEARNING OBJECTIVE 4
What defenses to liability can be raised in a product liability lawsuit?

Defendants in product liability suits can raise a number of defenses. One defense, of course, is to show that there is no basis for the plaintiff's claim. For instance, in a product liability case based on negligence, if a defendant can show that the plaintiff has *not* met the requirements for an action in negligence (such as causation), generally the defendant will not be liable.

Similarly, in a case involving strict product liability, a defendant can claim that the plaintiff failed to meet one of the requirements. If the defendant establishes that the goods were altered after they were sold, for instance, the defendant normally will not be held liable. A defendant may also assert that the *statute of limitations* (see page 80 in Chapter 3) for a product liability claim has lapsed.[10] Several other defenses may also be available to defendants, as discussed next.

Preemption

Today, some defendants are raising the defense of preemption—that government regulations preempt claims for product liability. In the past, a person who was injured by a product could assert a product liability claim regardless of whether the product was subject to government regulations. But that changed in 2008 when the United States Supreme Court held that an injured party may not be able to sue the manufacturer of defective products that are subject to federal regulatory schemes.

CASE EXAMPLE 12.13   In *Riegel v. Medtronic, Inc.,*[11] the United States Supreme Court held that a man who was injured by an approved medical device (in this case, a balloon catheter) could not sue its maker for negligence or strict product liability, or claim that the device was defectively designed. The Court observed that the Medical Device Amendments

---

10. Similar state statutes, called *statutes of repose*, place outer time limits on product liability actions.
11. 552 U.S. 312, 128 S.Ct. 999, 169 L.Ed.2d 892 (2008).

ADAPTING THE LAW TO THE ONLINE ENVIRONMENT

THE SUPREME COURT TAKES A STAND ON WARNING LABELS FOR VIDEO GAMES

Almost every product that you purchase in the physical world has one or more warning labels. Indeed, some critics argue that these labels have become so common that consumers ignore them. In other words, putting warnings on just about everything defeats their original purpose. In the online environment, warning labels are not so extensively used—at least not yet.

Until now, video games have largely escaped mandated warning labels, although the video game industry has instituted a voluntary rating system to provide information about a video game's content. Each video game is assigned one of six age-specific ratings, ranging from "Early Childhood" to "Adults Only."

Should video games, whether downloaded or bought on a CD-ROM or DVD, have additional warnings to advise potential users (or their parents) that the games might be overly violent? When the California legislature enacted a law imposing restrictions and a labeling requirement on the sale or rental of "violent video games" to minors, this issue became paramount.[a]

Video Software Dealers Sue the State

The Video Software Dealers Association, along with the Entertainment Software Association, immediately brought a suit in federal district court seeking to invalidate the law. The court granted summary judgment in favor of the plaintiffs.

The act defined a violent video game as one in which "the range of options available to a player includes killing, maiming, dismembering, or sexually assaulting an image of a human being." While agreeing that some video games are unquestionably violent by everyday standards, the trial court pointed out that many video games are based on popular novels or motion pictures and have extensive plot lines.

Accordingly, the court found that the definition of a violent video game was unconstitutionally vague and thus violated the First Amendment's guarantee of freedom of speech. The court also noted the existence of the voluntary rating system. The U.S. Court of Appeals for the Ninth Circuit affirmed the district court's decision.[b]

The United States Supreme Court's Decision

The state of California appealed to the United States Supreme Court, but in 2011 the Court affirmed the decision in favor of the video game and software industries. The Court noted that video games are entitled to First Amendment protection. Because California had failed to show that the statute was justified by a compelling government interest and that the law was narrowly tailored to serve that interest, the Court ruled that the statute was unconstitutional.[c]

Critical Thinking

Why do you think that some legislators believe that the six-part, age-specific voluntary labeling system for video games is not sufficient to protect minors?

---

a. California Civil Code Sections 1746–1746.5.

b. *Video Software Dealers Association v. Schwarzenegger,* 556 F.3d 950 (9th Cir. 2009).

c. *Brown v. Entertainment Merchants Association,* ___ U.S. ___, 131 S.Ct. 2729, 180 L.Ed.2d 708 (2011).

---

of 1976 (MDA) created a comprehensive scheme of federal safety oversight for medical devices. The MDA requires the U.S. Food and Drug Administration to review the design, labeling, and manufacturing of these devices before they are marketed to make sure that they are safe and effective. The Court reasoned that because premarket approval is a "rigorous process," it preempts all common law claims challenging the safety or effectiveness of a medical device that has been approved.

Since the *Medtronic* decision, some courts have extended the preemption defense to other product liability actions. Other courts have been unwilling to deny an injured party relief simply because the federal government was supposed to ensure the product's safety. Even the United States Supreme Court refused to extend the preemption defense to preclude a drug maker's liability in one subsequent case.[12]

---

12. *Wyeth v. Levine,* 555 U.S. 555, 129 S.Ct. 1187, 173 L.Ed.2d 51 (2009).

Assumption of Risk

Assumption of risk can sometimes be used as a defense in a product liability action. To establish such a defense, the defendant must show that (1) the plaintiff knew and appreciated the risk created by the product defect and (2) the plaintiff voluntarily assumed the risk, even though it was unreasonable to do so. (See Chapter 4 for a more detailed discussion of assumption of risk.)

Although assumption of risk is a defense in product liability actions, some courts do not allow it to be used as a defense to strict product liability claims. **CASE EXAMPLE 12.14** Executive Tans operated an upright tanning booth that had been manufactured by Sun Ergoline, Inc. Before using the booth, Savannah Boles signed a release form that contained an *exculpatory clause* (see page 237 in Chapter 8). The clause stated that she was using the booth at her own risk and that she released the manufacturer, among others, from any liability for injuries.

After Boles entered the booth, several of her fingers came in contact with an exhaust fan located at the top of the booth, partially amputating them. Boles sued Sun Ergoline, alleging strict product liability. Sun Ergoline argued that Boles's claims were barred by the release that she had signed. The lower courts agreed that Boles's claims were barred, but the Supreme Court of Colorado reversed. It concluded that, as a matter of public policy, assumption of risk (via the exculpatory clause) was not appropriate in a strict liability context. Therefore, Boles could sue Sun Ergoline to recover for her injuries.[13] •

Product Misuse

Similar to the defense of voluntary assumption of risk is that of product misuse, which occurs when a product is used for a purpose for which it was not intended. The courts have severely limited this defense, however, and it is now recognized as a defense only when the particular use was not reasonably foreseeable. If the misuse is foreseeable, the seller must take measures to guard against it.

Comparative Negligence (Fault)

Developments in the area of comparative negligence, or fault (discussed in Chapter 4), have also affected the doctrine of strict liability. Today, courts in many jurisdictions consider the negligent or intentional actions of both the plaintiff and the defendant when apportioning liability and awarding damages. A defendant may be able to limit at least some of its liability for injuries caused by its defective product if it can show that the plaintiff's misuse of the product contributed to the injuries. Although comparative negligence does not completely absolve the defendant of liability, it can reduce the amount of damages that will be awarded to the plaintiff.

CASE EXAMPLE 12.15 Dan Smith, a mechanic in Alaska, was not wearing a hard hat at work when he was asked to start the engine of an air compressor. Because the compressor was an older model, he had to prop open a door to start it. When Smith got the engine started, the door fell from its position and hit his head. The injury caused him to suffer from seizures and epilepsy. Smith sued the manufacturer, claiming that the engine was defectively designed. The manufacturer argued that Smith had been negligent by failing to wear his hard hat and by propping the door open in an unsafe manner. Smith's attorney claimed that the plaintiff's ordinary negligence could not be used as a defense in product liability cases, but the Alaska Supreme Court disagreed. Alaska, like many other states, allows comparative negligence to be raised as a defense in product liability lawsuits.[14] •

---

13. *Boles v. Sun Ergoline, Inc.*, 222 P.3d 724 (Co.Sup.Ct. 2010).
14. *Smith v. Ingersoll-Rand Co.*, 14 P.3d 990 (Alaska 2000). See also *Winschel v. Brown*, 171 P.3d 142 (Alaska 2007).

Commonly Known Dangers

The dangers associated with certain products (such as sharp knives and guns) are so commonly known that manufacturers need not warn users of those dangers. If a defendant succeeds in convincing the court that a plaintiff's injury resulted from a *commonly known danger,* the defendant normally will not be liable.

Knowledgeable User

A related defense is the *knowledgeable user* defense. If a particular danger (such as electrical shock) is or should be commonly known by particular users of a product (such as electricians), the manufacturer of the product need not warn these users of the danger.

CASE EXAMPLE 12.16 The parents of a group of overweight teenagers with health problems filed a product liability lawsuit against McDonald's. The teenagers claimed that the fast-food chain should be held liable for failing to warn customers of the adverse health effects of eating its food products. The court rejected this claim based on the knowledgeable user defense. The court found that it is well known that the food at McDonald's contains high levels of cholesterol, fat, salt, and sugar and is therefore unhealthful. The court's opinion, which thwarted numerous future lawsuits against fast-food restaurants, stated: "If consumers know (or reasonably should know) the potential ill health effects of eating at McDonald's, they cannot blame McDonald's if they, nonetheless, choose to satiate [satisfy] their appetite with a surfeit [excess] of supersized McDonald's products."[15] ●

Consumer Law

Warranties and product liability laws protect consumers, but consumer protection extends far beyond those areas. Sources of consumer protection exist at all levels of government. At the federal level, a number of laws have been passed to define the duties of sellers and the rights of consumers. Exhibit 12.1 below indicates many of the areas of consumer law that are regulated by statutes. Federal administrative agencies, such as the Federal Trade

---

15. *Pelman v. McDonald's Corp.,* 237 F.Supp.2d 512 (S.D.N.Y. 2003).

Exhibit 12.1 **Selected Areas of Consumer Law**
                       Regulated by Statutes

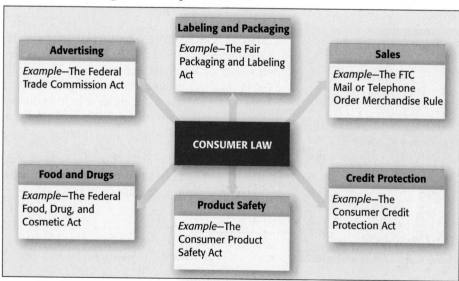

Advertising
Example—The Federal Trade Commission Act

Labeling and Packaging
Example—The Fair Packaging and Labeling Act

Sales
Example—The FTC Mail or Telephone Order Merchandise Rule

CONSUMER LAW

Food and Drugs
Example—The Federal Food, Drug, and Cosmetic Act

Product Safety
Example—The Consumer Product Safety Act

Credit Protection
Example—The Consumer Credit Protection Act

> "Ads are the cave art of the twentieth century."
>
> Marshall McLuhan, 1911–1980 (Canadian academic and commentator)

Deceptive Advertising Advertising that misleads consumers, either by making unjustified claims about a product's performance or by omitting a material fact concerning the product's composition or performance.

LEARNING OBJECTIVE 5
When will advertising be deemed deceptive?

Bait-and-Switch Advertising Advertising a product at an attractive price and then telling the consumer that the advertised product is not available or is of poor quality and encouraging her or him to purchase a more expensive item.

Were Campbell's health claims truthful?

(Lauri Patterson/iStockphoto.com)

Commission (FTC), also provide an important source of consumer protection. Nearly every agency and department of the federal government has an office of consumer affairs, and most states have one or more such offices, including the offices of state attorneys general, to assist consumers.

Deceptive Advertising

One of the earliest—and still one of the most important—federal consumer protection laws is the Federal Trade Commission Act. The act created the FTC to carry out the broadly stated goal of preventing unfair and deceptive trade practices, including deceptive advertising.

Generally, **deceptive advertising** occurs if a reasonable consumer would be misled by the advertising claim. Vague generalities and obvious exaggerations (that a reasonable person would not believe to be true) are permissible. As mentioned earlier in this chapter, these claims are known as puffery. When a claim has the appearance of authenticity, however, it may create problems. Advertising that *appears* to be based on factual evidence but that in fact cannot be scientifically supported will be deemed deceptive.

Some advertisements contain "half-truths," meaning that the information is true but incomplete and, therefore, leads consumers to a false conclusion. **EXAMPLE 12.17** The maker of Campbell's soups advertised that "most" Campbell's soups were low in fat and cholesterol and thus were helpful in fighting heart disease. What the ad did not say was that Campbell's soups were also high in sodium and that high-sodium diets may increase the risk of heart disease. Hence, the FTC ruled that the company's claims were deceptive. • Advertising featuring an endorsement by a celebrity may be deemed deceptive if the celebrity does not actually use the product.

Bait-and-Switch Advertising   The FTC has issued rules that govern specific advertising techniques. One of the more important rules is contained in the FTC's "Guides Against Bait Advertising."[16] The rule is designed to prevent **bait-and-switch advertising**—that is, advertising a very low price for a particular item and then encouraging the consumer to purchase a more expensive item. The low price is the "bait" to lure the consumer into the store. The salesperson is instructed to "switch" the consumer to a different, more expensive item. According to the FTC guidelines, bait-and-switch advertising occurs if the seller refuses to show the advertised item, fails to have reasonable quantities of it available, fails to promise to deliver the advertised item within a reasonable time, or discourages employees from selling the item.

Online Deceptive Advertising   Deceptive advertising can occur in the online environment as well. The FTC actively monitors online advertising and has identified numerous Web sites that have made false or deceptive claims for products ranging from medical treatments for various diseases to exercise equipment and weight-loss aids.

The FTC has issued guidelines to help online businesses comply with the laws prohibiting deceptive advertising.[17] These guidelines include the following three basic requirements:

1. All ads—both online and offline—must be truthful and not misleading.
2. The claims made in an ad must be substantiated—that is, advertisers must have evidence to back up their claims.

---

16. 16 C.F.R. Section 288.
17. "Advertising and Marketing on the Internet: Rules of the Road," Federal Trade Commission, _www.ftc.gov_, Sept. 2000, Web.

3. Ads cannot be unfair, which the FTC defines as "likely to cause substantial consumer injury that consumers could not reasonably avoid and that is not outweighed by the benefit to consumers or competition."

The guidelines also call for "clear and conspicuous" disclosure of any qualifying or limiting information. Because consumers may not read an entire Web page, the disclosure should be placed as close as possible to the claim being qualified. The next-best location is on a section of the page to which a consumer can easily scroll. Generally, hyperlinks to a disclosure are recommended only for lengthy disclosures.

Many states have also passed consumer protection laws that regulate deceptive online advertising. In the following case, an e-mail service provider claimed that an online marketing company had violated a California statute that prohibited deceptive content in e-mail advertising. As discussed on page 124 in Chapter 4, however, Congress had passed the federal CAN-SPAM Act to combat the problems associated with unsolicited commercial e-mails, or spam. The court had to decide whether the CAN-SPAM Act preempted the state statute (preemption was discussed in Chapter 1 on page 14).

Case 12.3

Hypertouch, Inc. v. ValueClick, Inc.

California Court of Appeal, Second District,
192 Cal.App.4th 805, 123 Cal.Rptr.3d 8 (2011).

FACTS Hypertouch, Inc., provides e-mail service to customers located inside and outside California. ValueClick, Inc., and its subsidiaries provide online marketing services to third party advertisers that promote retail products. ValueClick contracts with these advertisers to place offers on its Web sites. ValueClick also contracts with affiliates that send out commercial e-mail advertisements. The advertisements include links redirecting consumers to promotions on ValueClick's Web sites. If a consumer clicks through an e-mail advertisement and participates in a promotional offer, the affiliate that sent the initial e-mail is compensated for generating a customer "lead." The affiliate, rather than ValueClick, controls the content and headers of the e-mails. Hypertouch filed a complaint against ValueClick, its subsidiaries, and others for violating a California state statute that prohibits e-mail advertising that contains deceptive content and headings. The trial court held that the federal CAN-SPAM Act preempts the California statute and granted a summary judgment in favor of ValueClick. Hypertouch appealed.

ISSUE Does the federal CAN-SPAM Act preempt California's statute on deceptive e-mail advertising (spam)?

DECISION No. California's anti-spam statute is not preempted by the federal CAN-SPAM Act.

REASON The CAN-SPAM Act expressly exempts from preemption state laws that prohibit "falsity or deception" in commercial e-mail. The trial court had interpreted this exemption to apply only to state statutes that require a plaintiff to establish the elements of common law fraud. But the appellate court disagreed, finding that "sections of the CAN-SPAM Act indicate that the phrase 'falsity and deception' was not intended to apply only to common law fraud." According to the court, the states are "free to regulate the use of deceptive practices in commercial e-mails in whatever manner they [choose]."

The California statute imposes strict liability on anyone who advertises in a commercial e-mail that contains false, deceptive, or misleading information, whether or not the advertiser has knowledge of the violation. Evidence showed that ValueClick had advertised in more than 45,000 e-mails received by Hypertouch customers that contained deceptive "header information" in violation of the statute. Therefore, the court reversed the lower court's decision and remanded the case for trial.

CRITICAL THINKING—Social Consideration *How might the heading of an e-mail advertisement be deceptive? Describe several ways.*

Federal Trade Commission Actions   If the FTC concludes that a given advertisement is unfair or deceptive, it sends a formal complaint to the alleged offender. The company may agree to settle the complaint without further proceedings. If not, the FTC can conduct a hearing before an *administrative law judge* (see page 5 in Chapter 1) in which the company can present its defense.

If the FTC succeeds in proving that an advertisement is unfair or deceptive, it usually issues a **cease-and-desist order** requiring the company to stop the challenged advertising. In some circumstances, the FTC may also require **counteradvertising** in which the company advertises anew—in print, on the Internet, on radio, and on television—to inform the public about the earlier misinformation.

When a company's deceptive ad involves wrongful charges to consumers, the FTC may seek other remedies, including restitution.   **CASE EXAMPLE 12.18**   Verity International, Ltd., billed phone-line subscribers who accessed certain online pornography sites at the rate for international calls to Madagascar. When consumers complained about the charges, Verity employees told them that the charges were valid and had to be paid, or the consumers would face further collection action. A court later held that this representation of "uncontestability" was deceptive and ordered Verity to pay nearly $18 million in restitution to consumers.[18] ●

The Telemarketing Sales Rule

The FTC's Telemarketing Sales Rule (TSR)[19] requires a telemarketer to identify the seller, describe the product being sold, and disclose all material facts related to the sale. The rule makes it illegal for telemarketers to misrepresent information (including facts about their goods or services and earnings potential, for example).

A telemarketer must also remove a consumer's name from its list of potential contacts if the consumer so requests. An amendment to the Telemarketing Sales Rule established the national Do Not Call Registry. Telemarketers may not call consumers who have placed their names on the list.

Labeling and Packaging

In general, labels must be accurate, and they must use words that are understood by the ordinary consumer. In some instances, labels must specify the raw materials used in the product, such as the percentage of cotton, nylon, or other fibers used in a garment. In other instances, the product must carry a warning, such as those required on cigarette packages and advertising.

Fuel Economy Labels on Automobiles   The Energy Policy and Conservation Act (EPCA)[20] requires automakers to attach an information label to every new car. This label must include the Environmental Protection Agency's fuel economy estimate for the vehicle.   **CASE EXAMPLE 12.19**   Gaetano Paduano bought a new Honda Civic Hybrid in California. The information label on the car included the fuel economy estimate from the Environmental Protection Agency (EPA). Honda's sales brochure added, "Just drive the Hybrid like you would a conventional car and save on fuel bills."

---

18. *FTC v. Verity International, Ltd.*, 443 F.3d 48 (2d Cir. 2006).
19. 16 C.F.R. Sections 310.1–310.8.
20. 49 U.S.C. Section 32908(b)(1).

Cease-and-Desist Order   An administrative or judicial order prohibiting a person or business firm from conducting activities that an agency or court has deemed illegal.

Counteradvertising   New advertising that is undertaken to correct earlier false claims made about a product.

▶ KNOW THIS ◀

Changes in technology often require changes in the law.

Does federal law preempt state deceptive advertising laws with respect to published fuel economy estimates?

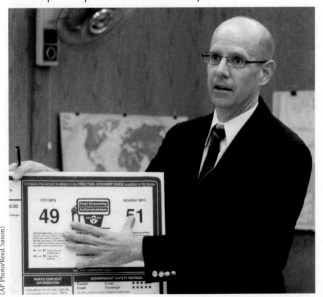

(AP Photo/Reed Saxon)

"A consumer is a
shopper who is sore
about something."

Harold Coffin, 1905–1981
(American humorist)

When Paduano discovered that the car's fuel economy was less than half of the EPA's estimate, he sued Honda for deceptive advertising. The automaker claimed that the federal law (the EPCA) preempted the state's deceptive advertising law, but the court held in Paduano's favor, finding that the federal statute did not preempt a claim for deceptive advertising made under state law.[21] ●

Food Labeling   Several statutes deal specifically with food labeling. The Fair Packaging and Labeling Act requires that food product labels identify (1) the product, (2) the net quantity of the contents, (3) the manufacturer, and (4) the packager or distributor.[22] The Nutrition Labeling and Education Act requires food labels to provide standard nutrition facts and regulates the use of such terms as *fresh* and *low fat*. The U.S. Food and Drug Administration (FDA) and the U.S. Department of Agriculture (USDA) are the primary agencies that issue regulations on food labeling. These rules are updated annually and now require the labels on fresh meats, vegetables, and fruits to indicate where the food originated.

Menu Labeling   The health-care reform bill enacted in 2010 (discussed later in this chapter) included a provision aimed at combating the problem of obesity in the United States. The provision requires all restaurant chains with twenty or more locations to post the caloric content of the foods on their menus so that customers will know how many calories they are eating.[23] In addition, restaurants are required to post guidelines on the number of calories that an average person requires daily. The new federal law supersedes all state and local laws already in existence.

Sales

A number of statutes protect consumers by requiring the disclosure of certain terms in sales transactions and providing rules governing specific types of sales and unsolicited merchandise. Many states and the FTC, for example, have **"cooling-off" laws** that permit the buyers of goods sold door to door to cancel their contracts within three business days. The FTC rule further requires that consumers be notified in Spanish of this right if the oral negotiations for the sale were in that language.

The FTC's Mail or Telephone Order Merchandise Rule[24] protects consumers who purchase goods over the phone, through the mail or a fax machine, or via the Internet. Merchants are required to ship orders within the time promised in their advertisements and to notify consumers when orders cannot be shipped on time. Merchants must also issue a refund within a specified period of time when a consumer cancels an order.

"Cooling-Off" Laws Laws that allow buyers to cancel door-to-door sales contracts within a certain period of time, such as three business days.

Protection of Health and Safety

Although labeling and packaging laws (discussed earlier) promote consumer health and safety, there is a significant distinction between regulating the information dispensed about a product and regulating the actual content of the product. The classic example is tobacco products. Producers of tobacco products are required to warn consumers about the hazards associated with the use of their products, but the sale of tobacco products has not been subjected to significant restrictions or banned outright despite the obvious dangers to health. (See this chapter's *Law, Diversity, and Business: Managerial Implications* feature on

---

21. *Paduano v. American Honda Motor Co.,* 169 Cal.App. 4th 1453, 88 Cal.Rptr.3d 90 (2009).
22. 15 U.S.C. Sections 4401–4408.
23. See Section 4205 of the Patient Protection and Affordable Care Act, Pub. L. No.111-148, March 23, 2010, 124 Stat. 119.
24. 16 C.F.R. Sections 435.1–435.2.

this page for a discussion of a safety issue facing airlines.) We now examine various laws that regulate the actual products made available to consumers.

Food and Drugs

The most important legislation regulating food and drugs is the Federal Food, Drug, and Cosmetic Act (FDCA).[25] To protect consumers against adulterated (contaminated) and misbranded foods and drugs, the FDCA establishes food standards, specifies safe levels of potentially hazardous food additives, and sets classifications of food and food advertising. Most of these statutory requirements are enforced by the U.S. Food and Drug Administration (FDA).

Under the FDCA, the FDA is also responsible for ensuring that drugs are safe, as well as effective, before they are marketed to the public. The FDA has established extensive procedures that drug manufacturers must follow to show that their drugs are safe.

CASE EXAMPLE 12.20 A group of terminally ill patients claimed that they were entitled, under the U.S. Constitution, to better access to experimental drugs before the FDA completed its clinical tests. The court, however, found that the FDA's policy of limiting access to drugs that were undergoing tests was rationally related to protecting patients from potentially unsafe drugs. Therefore, the court held that terminally ill patients do not have

> ### ► KNOW THIS ◄
> The U.S. Food and Drug Administration is authorized to obtain, among other things, orders for the recall and seizure of certain products.

---

25. 21 U.S.C. Section 301.

LAW, DIVERSITY, AND BUSINESS: MANAGERIAL IMPLICATIONS

HOW SHOULD AIRLINES DEAL WITH "CUSTOMERS OF SIZE"?

Anyone who travels by airline is aware that planes are crowded and seats are narrow. For some, they are too narrow. Airlines face a particular problem with "customers of size" because they may impinge on the comfort of those seated next to them. The issue involves more than comfort, however—it can also be a matter of safety.

Challenging Southwest Airlines Southwest Airlines has a policy for "customers of size." When an agent believes that a passenger will reduce the comfort of anyone seated next to her or him, the agent can ask the passenger to purchase a second seat. Kenlie Tiggeman, an overweight passenger, was not asked by an agent to do that. When she arrived at the gate, however, a gate attendant told her, in the presence of other passengers, that she would have to purchase a second seat. Tiggeman refused and has filed a lawsuit against Southwest, asserting that the airline's employees "did not follow their company policy and chose to discriminate, humiliate, and harass."

Further, she argued that Southwest takes "discriminatory action . . . toward obese customers." Tiggeman did not ask for damages. Rather, she wanted a court to order Southwest to clarify its policy with respect to larger passengers.

The Airlines Also Face a Safety Issue In 2010, to adjust for Americans' increasing weight, the Federal Aviation Administration (FAA) revised the passenger weights that it uses to calculate a flight's total weight and balance. The FAA now requires the airlines to use an average weight of 200 pounds for men and 179 pounds for women.

Yet the government's regulations for the strength of airline seats and seatbelts have not been revised since they were written about seventy years ago. They are based on a passenger weight of 170 pounds, even though today the average U.S. man weighs 194 pounds. Engineers and scientists claim that airline seats are unsafe for today's heavier passengers.

The safety implications are obvious. Airlines have a unique challenge in protecting larger passengers. Dr. Dietrich Jehle, a professor of emergency medicine at the State University of New York at Buffalo, says, "Since a third of the population is obese, we need to be doing some of our crash testing with obese dummies."

Business Implications *Government experts predict that by the year 2030, 44 percent of adult Americans will be obese—a development that businesses will have to take into consideration. Persons of size represent a significant segment of Americans, and businesses must adapt.*

(AP Photo/Office of Public Affairs, FDA)

Is there a way that the FDA can prevent fake drugs from being sold to consumers?

a fundamental constitutional right of access to experimental drugs.[26] ● The FDA also has the authority to regulate medical devices, such as pacemakers, and to withdraw from the market any such device that is mislabeled.

Consumer Product Safety In 1972, the Consumer Product Safety Act[27] created the first comprehensive scheme of regulation over matters concerning consumer safety. The act also established the Consumer Product Safety Commission (CPSC).

The CPSC conducts research on the safety of individual products and maintains a clearinghouse on the risks associated with various products. The Consumer Product Safety Act authorizes the CPSC to do the following:

1. Set safety standards for consumer products.
2. Ban the manufacture and sale of any product that the commission believes poses an "unreasonable risk" to consumers. (Products banned by the CPSC have included various types of fireworks, cribs, and toys, as well as many products containing asbestos or vinyl chloride.)
3. Remove from the market any products it believes to be imminently hazardous. The CPSC frequently works with manufacturers to voluntarily recall defective products from stores.
4. Require manufacturers to report any products already sold or intended for sale that have proved to be hazardous.
5. Administer other product-safety legislation, including the Child Protection and Toy Safety Act[28] and the Federal Hazardous Substances Act.[29]

The Consumer Product Safety Act also imposes notification requirements on distributors of consumer products. Distributors must immediately notify the CPSC when they receive information that a product "contains a defect which . . . creates a substantial risk to the public" or "an unreasonable risk of serious injury or death."

Health-Care Reforms

In 2010, Congress enacted health-care reforms that will give Americans new rights and benefits with regard to health care.[30] By 2014, these laws will have prohibited certain insurance company practices, such as denying coverage for preexisting conditions.

Expanded Coverage for Children and Seniors The reforms expanded access to health care by enabling more children to obtain health-insurance coverage and allowing young adults (under age twenty-six) to stay on their parents' health-insurance policies. The act also ended lifetime and most annual limits on care and gave patients access to recommended preventive services (such as cancer screening, vaccinations, and well-baby checks) without cost. Medicare recipients now receive a 50 percent discount on name-brand drugs, and the gap in Medicare's prescription drug coverage will be eliminated by 2020.

Controlling Costs of Health Insurance In an attempt to control the rising costs of health insurance, the law requires insurance companies to spend at least 85 percent of all premium dollars collected from large employers (80 percent of the premiums

26. *Abigail Alliance for Better Access to Developmental Drugs v. von Eschenbach,* 495 F.3d 695 (D.C.Cir. 2007).
27. 15 U.S.C. Section 2051.
28. 15 U.S.C. Section 1262(e).
29. 15 U.S.C. Sections 1261–1273.
30. Patient Protection and Affordable Health Care Act of 2010, Pub. L. No.111-148, March 23, 2010, 124 Stat. 119; and the Health Care and Education Reconciliation Act of 2010, Pub. L. No. 111-152, March 30, 2010, 124 Stat. 1029.

collected from individuals and small employers) on benefits and quality improvement. If insurance companies do not meet these goals, they must provide rebates to consumers. Additionally, states can require insurance companies to justify their premium increases to be eligible to participate in the new health-insurance exchanges created by the act.

Credit Protection

Credit protection is one of the most important aspects of consumer protection legislation. Nearly 80 percent of U.S. consumers have credit cards, and most carry a balance on these cards, which amounts to about $2.5 trillion of debt nationwide. In 2010, Congress established a new agency, the Consumer Financial Protection Bureau, to oversee the practices of banks, mortgage lenders, and credit-card companies.

Truth-in-Lending Act A key statute regulating the credit and credit-card industries is the Truth-in-Lending Act (TILA), the name commonly given to Title 1 of the Consumer Credit Protection Act (CCPA), as amended.[31] The TILA is basically a *disclosure law*. It is administered by the Federal Reserve Board and requires sellers and lenders to disclose credit terms or loan terms (such as the annual percentage rate, or APR, and any finance charges) so that individuals can shop around for the best financing arrangements.

TILA requirements apply only to those who, in the ordinary course of business, lend funds, sell on credit, or arrange for the extension of credit. Thus, sales or loans made between two consumers do not come under the act. Additionally, this law protects only debtors who are *natural* persons (as opposed to the artificial "person" of a corporation) and does not extend to other legal entities.

Regulation Z A set of rules issued by the Federal Reserve Board of Governors to implement the provisions of the Truth-in-Lending Act.

Disclosure The disclosure requirements are found in **Regulation Z,** issued by the Federal Reserve Board of Governors. If the contracting parties are subject to the TILA, the requirements of Regulation Z apply to any transaction involving an installment sales contract that calls for payment to be made in more than four installments. Transactions subject to Regulation Z typically include installment loans, retail and installment sales, car loans, home-improvement loans, and certain real estate loans if the amount of financing is less than $25,000.

Equal Credit Opportunity The Equal Credit Opportunity Act (ECOA) amended the TILA in 1974. The ECOA prohibits the denial of credit solely on the basis of race, religion, national origin, color, gender, marital status, or age. The act also prohibits credit discrimination based on whether an individual receives certain forms of income, such as public-assistance benefits.

Which federal law prohibits discrimination for credit-card applications?

(teekid/iStockphoto.com)

Under the ECOA, a creditor may not require the signature of an applicant's spouse, or a cosigner, on a credit instrument if the applicant qualifies under the creditor's standards of creditworthiness for the amount requested. **CASE EXAMPLE 12.21** Tonja, an African American, applied for financing with a used-car dealer. The dealer reviewed Tonja's credit report and, without submitting the application to the lender, decided that she would not qualify. Instead of informing Tonja that she did not qualify, the dealer told her that she needed a cosigner on the loan to purchase the car. According to a federal appellate court, the dealership qualified as a creditor in this situation because it unilaterally denied credit. Thus, the dealer could be held liable under the ECOA.[32] ●

31. 15 U.S.C. Sections 1601–1693r. The TILA was amended in 1980 by the Truth-in-Lending Simplification and Reform Act and again in 2009 by the Credit Card Accountability Responsibility and Disclosure Act of 2009.
32. *Treadway v. Gateway Chevrolet Oldsmobile, Inc.,* 362 F.3d 971 (7th Cir. 2004).

Credit-Card Rules   The TILA also contains provisions regarding credit cards. One provision limits the liability of a cardholder to $50 per card for unauthorized charges made before the creditor is notified that the card has been lost. If a consumer received an *unsolicited* credit card in the mail that is later stolen, the company that issued the card cannot charge the consumer for any unauthorized charges.

Another provision requires credit-card companies to disclose the computation method that is used to determine the outstanding balance and to state when finance charges begin to accrue. Other provisions set forth procedures for resolving billing disputes between a cardholder and the credit-card company.

Amendments to TILA's credit-card rules that became effective in 2010 have the following effects:

1. Protect consumers from retroactive increases in interest rates on existing card balances unless the account is sixty days delinquent.
2. Require companies to provide forty-five days' advance notice to consumers before changing credit-card terms, such as the annual percentage rate.
3. Require companies to send monthly bills to cardholders twenty-one days before the due date.
4. Prevent companies from increasing the interest rate charged on a customer's credit-card balance except in specific situations, such as when a promotional rate ends.
5. Prevent companies from charging over-limit fees except in specified situations.
6. Require companies to apply payments in excess of the minimum amount due to the customer's higher-interest balances first when the borrower has balances with different rates (such as the higher interest rates commonly charged for cash advances).
7. Prevent companies from computing finance charges based on the previous billing cycle (known as double-cycle billing, which hurts consumers because they are charged interest for the previous cycle even though they have paid the bill in full).

How does the Fair Credit Reporting Act protect consumers?

Fair Credit Reporting Act   The Fair Credit Reporting Act (FCRA)[33] protects consumers against inaccurate credit reporting and requires that lenders and other creditors report correct, relevant, and up-to-date information. The act provides that consumer credit reporting agencies may issue credit reports only for specified purposes, including the extension of credit, the issuance of insurance policies, and compliance with a court order, as well as in response to a consumer's request for a copy of her or his own credit report. (See the *Business Application* feature on page 372 for tips on how businesspersons can use credit reporting services.)

Any time a consumer is denied credit or insurance on the basis of his or her credit report, the consumer must be notified of that fact and of the name and address of the credit reporting agency that issued the report. The same notice must be sent to consumers who are charged more than others ordinarily would be for credit or insurance because of their credit reports.

Under the FCRA, consumers can request the source of any information used by the credit agency, as well as the identity of anyone who has received an agency's report. Consumers are also permitted to have access to the information about them contained in a credit reporting agency's files. If a consumer discovers that the agency's files contain inaccurate information, the agency, on the consumer's written request, must investigate the disputed information. Any unverifiable or erroneous information must be deleted within a reasonable period of time.

---

33. 15 U.S.C. Sections 1681 *et seq.*

Remedies for Violations   An agency that fails to comply with the act is liable for actual damages, plus additional damages not to exceed $1,000 and attorneys' fees. Creditors and other companies that use information from credit reporting agencies may also be liable for violations of the FCRA. The United States Supreme Court has held that an insurance company's failure to notify new customers that they were paying higher insurance rates as a result of their credit scores was a *willful* violation of the FCRA.[34]

CASE EXAMPLE 12.22   Branch Banking & Trust Company of Virginia (BB&T) gave Rex Saunders an auto loan but failed to give him a payment coupon book and rebuffed his attempts to make payments on the loan. Eventually, BB&T discovered its mistake and demanded full payment, plus interest and penalties. When payment was not immediately forthcoming, BB&T declared that Saunders was in default. It then repossessed the car and forwarded adverse credit information about Saunders to credit reporting agencies without noting that Saunders disputed the information. Saunders filed a lawsuit alleging violations of the FCRA and was awarded $80,000 in punitive damages. An appellate court found that the damages award was reasonable, given BB&T's willful violation.[35] •

Fair and Accurate Credit Transactions Act

Congress passed the Fair and Accurate Credit Transactions (FACT) Act to combat identity theft.[36] The act established a national fraud alert system so that consumers who suspect that they have been or may be victimized by identity theft can place an alert in their credit files. The act also requires the major credit reporting agencies to provide consumers with free copies of their credit reports every twelve months.

Another provision requires account numbers on credit-card receipts to be truncated (shortened) so that merchants, employees, and others who have access to the receipts cannot obtain a consumer's name and full credit-card number. The act also mandates that financial institutions work with the FTC to identify "red flag" indicators of identity theft and to develop rules for disposing of sensitive credit information.

Fair Debt Collection Practices Act

The Fair Debt Collection Practices Act (FDCPA)[37] attempts to curb abuses by collection agencies. The act applies only to specialized debt-collection agencies and attorneys who regularly attempt to collect debts on behalf of someone else, usually for a percentage of the amount owed. Creditors attempting to collect debts are not covered by the act unless, by misrepresenting themselves, they cause the debtors to believe that they are collection agencies. A debt collector who fails to comply with the act is liable for actual damages, plus additional damages not to exceed $1,000 and attorneys' fees.

Under the FDCPA, a collection agency may not do any of the following:

1. Contact the debtor at the debtor's place of employment if the debtor's employer objects.
2. Contact the debtor at inconvenient or unusual times (such as three o'clock in the morning), or at any time if the debtor is being represented by an attorney.
3. Contact third parties other than the debtor's parents, spouse, or financial adviser about payment of a debt unless a court authorizes such action.
4. Harass or intimidate the debtor (by using abusive language or threatening violence, for instance) or make false or misleading statements (such as posing as a police officer).
5. Communicate with the debtor at any time after receiving notice that the debtor is refusing to pay the debt, except to advise the debtor of further action to be taken by the collection agency.

> "Credit is a system whereby a person who can't pay gets another person who can't pay to guarantee that he can pay."
>
> Charles Dickens, 1812–1870
> (English novelist)

---

34. *Safeco Insurance Co. of America v. Burr,* 551 U.S. 47, 127 S.Ct. 2201, 167 L.Ed.2d 1045 (2007).
35. *Saunders v. Branch Banking & Trust Co. of Virginia,* 526 F.3d 142 (4th Cir. 2008).
36. Pub. L. No. 108-159, 117 Stat. 1952 (December 4, 2003).
37. 15 U.S.C. Section 1692.

The FDCPA also requires a collection agency to include a *validation notice* whenever it initially contacts a debtor for payment of a debt or within five days of that initial contact. The notice must state that the debtor has thirty days in which to dispute the debt and to request a written verification of the debt from the collection agency. The debtor's request for debt validation must be in writing.

ETHICAL ISSUE

Does leaving voice mail messages for a debtor violate the Fair Debt Collection Practices Act? Debt-collection practices have often raised privacy concerns. There have been many lawsuits against collection agencies over voice messages or voice mails left by debt collectors. The FDCPA prohibits disclosures about a debt to third parties. Does leaving a voice message regarding a debt on an answering machine constitute such a disclosure? That depends on the jurisdiction and the situation.

In one example, a Florida court ruled in favor of the debtor. It stated that if a collection agency leaves a voice message for a consumer on an answering machine—even at home—other people (third parties) could hear the message.[38] In contrast, a federal court in Minnesota held that leaving voice messages on a debtor's cell phone did not violate the FDCPA, even though the debtor's children listened to them. Because the messages did not identify the debtor or the debt, the court reasoned that "they conveyed no more information than would have been obvious in caller ID" and dismissed the suit against the debt collector.[39]

---

38. *Berg v. Merchants Association Collection Division, Inc.*, 586 F.Supp.2d 1336 (S.D.Fla. 2008).
39. *Zortman v. J.C. Christensen & Associates, Inc.*, 2012 WL 1563918 (D.Minn. 2012).

Reviewing . . . Warranties, Product Liability, and Consumer Law

Shalene Kolchek bought a Great Lakes Spa from Val Porter, a dealer who was selling spas at the state fair. Porter told Kolchek that Great Lakes spas are "top of the line" and "the Cadillac of spas" and indicated that the spa she was buying was "fully warranted for three years." After Kolchek signed an installment sale contract, Porter gave her the manufacturer's paperwork and arranged for the spa to be delivered and installed for her. Three months later, Kolchek noticed that one corner of the spa was leaking onto her new deck and causing damage. She complained to Porter, but he did nothing about the problem. Kolchek's family continued to use the spa. Using the information presented in the chapter, answer the following questions.

1. Did Porter's statement that the spa was "top of the line" and "the Cadillac of spas" create any type of warranty? Why or why not?
2. Did Porter breach the implied warranty of merchantability? Why or why not?
3. One night, Kolchek's six-year-old daughter, Litisha, was in the spa with her mother. Litisha's hair became entangled in the spa's drain, and she was sucked down and held under water for a prolonged period, causing her to suffer brain damage. Under which theory or theories of product liability can Kolchek sue Porter to recover for Litisha's injuries?
4. If Kolchek had negligently left Litisha alone in the spa before the incident described in the previous question, what defense to liability might Porter assert?

DEBATE THIS No express warranties should be created by the oral statements made by salespersons about a product.

BUSINESS APPLICATION

The Proper Way to Use Credit Reporting Services*

As explained in the chapter, the Fair Credit Reporting Act (FCRA) protects consumers against inaccurate credit reporting. Many credit reporting agencies provide much more than just credit reports, however. Increasingly, they are providing employers with employment histories, information on educational attainment, and criminal records for current employees and job applicants.

Disclosure Issues When Making Background Checks

If a company uses credit reporting agencies, it must disclose this fact to current employees and to applicants. If a company does not conform to the requirements of advance notice, disclosure, and consent, it can become involved in litigation.

For example, Vitran Express used credit reporting agencies to determine whether prospective employees had criminal records without disclosing this practice to applicants as required by the FCRA. One applicant lost a job offer because a credit reporting agency told the company that he had a criminal history when he did not. He and other job applicants brought a class-action lawsuit against Vitran Express, and the company ultimately agreed to pay millions of dollars to settle the case.

Steps That Employers Should Take to Avoid Litigation

All companies must make sure that they comply with federal law when they do background checks. Employers must give advance

*This *Business Application* is not meant to substitute for the services of an attorney who is licensed to practice law in your state.

notice and obtain each employee's or applicant's consent to any background check that exceeds a simple credit check.

To ensure that there are no legal problems, an employer should certify in writing to each credit reporting agency that it will follow federal rules concerning notice, authorization, disclosure, and adverse action notices (letters rejecting applicants).

Each prospective employee should be given a clear disclosure—in a separate document—stating that a background report may be requested from a consumer reporting service. At that time, the company should obtain the person's written consent.

Whenever a consumer report influences the company's decision not to hire someone, the company should provide the following documents to the individual *before* rejecting him or her:

- The Federal Trade Commission document called "A Summary of Your Rights under the Fair Credit Reporting Act."
- A copy of the consumer report on which the company based its negative decision.

Checklist for the Businessperson

1. *You or your in-house counsel should carefully review federal law in this matter.*
2. *Always let prospective employees know that you're going to use a consumer reporting service's report as part of the process of evaluating their application.*
3. *Create a separate document indicating that you are going to use a consumer reporting service.*

Key Terms

bait-and-switch advertising 362
cease-and-desist order 364
"cooling-off" laws 365
counteradvertising 364
deceptive advertising 362

express warranty 346
implied warranty 348
implied warranty of fitness
   for a particular purpose 346

implied warranty of
   merchantability 348
lien 346
product liability 352

Regulation Z 368
unreasonably dangerous product 355

Chapter Summary: Warranties, Product Liability, and Consumer Law

WARRANTIES	
Warranties of Title (See page 346.)	The UCC provides for the following warranties of title [UCC 2–312, 2A–211]: 1. *Good title*—A seller warrants that he or she has the right to pass good and rightful title to the goods. 2. *No liens*—A seller warrants that the goods sold are free of any liens, and a lessor warrants that the lessee will not be disturbed in her or his possession of the goods by the claims of a third party.

Chapter Summary: Warranties, Product Liability, and Consumer Law—Continued

Warranties of Title—Continued	3. *No infringements*—A merchant-seller warrants that the goods are free of claims that a patent, trademark, or copyright has been infringed.

Express Warranties
(See pages 346–347.)
	1. *Under the UCC*—An express warranty arises under the UCC when a seller or lessor indicates, as part of the basis of the bargain, any of the following [UCC 2–313, 2A–210]:
	   a. An affirmation or promise of fact.
	   b. A description of the goods.
	   c. A sample shown as conforming to the contract goods.
	2. *Under the Magnuson-Moss Warranty Act*—Express written warranties covering consumer goods priced at more than $25, *if made*, must be labeled as one of the following:
	   a. Full warranty—Free repair or replacement of defective parts. Or, if the goods cannot be repaired in a reasonable time, refund or replacement is available.
	   b. Limited warranty—When less than a full warranty is being offered.

Implied Warranty of Merchantability (See pages 348–349.)	When a seller or lessor is a merchant who deals in goods of the kind sold or leased, the seller or lessor warrants that the goods sold or leased are properly packaged and labeled, are of proper quality, and are reasonably fit for the ordinary purposes for which such goods are used [UCC 2–314, 2A–212].
Implied Warranty of Fitness for a Particular Purpose (See pages 349–350.)	Arises when the buyer's or lessee's purpose or use is expressly or impliedly known by the seller or lessor, and the buyer or lessee purchases or leases the goods in reliance on the seller's or lessor's selection [UCC 2–315, 2A–213]. Other implied warranties can arise as a result of course of dealing or usage of trade [UCC 2–314(3), 2A–212(3)].
Overlapping Warranties (See page 350.)	The UCC construes warranties as cumulative if they are consistent with each other. If warranties are inconsistent, then express warranties take precedence over implied warranties, except for the implied warranty of fitness for a particular purpose. Also, samples take precedence over general descriptions, and exact or technical specifications displace inconsistent samples or general descriptions.
Warranty Disclaimers (See pages 352–353.)	An oral express warranty can be disclaimed in writing if the disclaimer is clear, conspicuous, and called to the buyer's or lessee's attention at the time the contract is formed. A disclaimer of the implied warranty of merchantability must specifically mention the word *merchantability*. The disclaimer need not be in writing, but if it is written, it must be conspicuous. A disclaimer of the implied warranty of fitness *must* be in writing and be conspicuous, though it need not mention the word *fitness*.
PRODUCT LIABILITY	
Liability Based on Negligence (See pages 352–353.)	1. The manufacturer must use due care in designing the product, selecting materials, using the appropriate production process, assembling and testing the product, and placing adequate warnings on the label or product. 2. Privity of contract is not required. A manufacturer is liable for failure to exercise due care to any person who sustains an injury proximately caused by a negligently made (defective) product. 3. Fraudulent misrepresentation of a product may result in product liability based on the tort of fraud.
Strict Liability—Requirements (See pages 354–355.)	1. The defendant must have sold the product in a defective condition. 2. The defendant must normally be engaged in the business of selling that product. 3. The product must be unreasonably dangerous to the user or consumer because of its defective condition (in most states). 4. The plaintiff must incur physical harm to self or property by use or consumption of the product. 5. The defective condition must be the proximate cause of the injury or damage. 6. The goods must not have been substantially changed from the time the product was sold to the time the injury was sustained.
Strict Liability—Product Defects (See pages 355–358.)	A product may be defective in three basic ways: 1. In its manufacture. 2. In its design. 3. In the instructions or warnings that come with it.

Continued

Chapter Summary: Warranties, Product Liability, and Consumer Law—Continued

Other Applications of Strict Liability (See page 358.)	1. Manufacturers and other sellers are liable for harms suffered by bystanders as a result of defective products. 2. Suppliers of component parts are strictly liable for defective parts that, when incorporated into a product, cause injuries to users.
Defenses to Product Liability (See pages 358–361.)	1. *Preemption*—An injured party may not be able to sue the manufacturer of a product that is subject to comprehensive federal safety regulations, such as medical devices. 2. *Assumption of risk*—The user or consumer knew of the risk of harm and voluntarily assumed it. 3. *Product misuse*—The user or consumer misused the product in a way unforeseeable by the manufacturer. 4. *Comparative negligence*—Liability may be distributed between the plaintiff and the defendant under the doctrine of comparative negligence if the plaintiff's misuse of the product contributed to the risk of injury. 5. *Commonly known dangers*—If a defendant succeeds in convincing the court that a plaintiff's injury resulted from a commonly known danger, such as the danger associated with using a sharp knife, the defendant will not be liable. 6. *Knowledgeable user*—If a particular danger is or should be commonly known by particular users of the product, the manufacturer of the product need not warn these users of the danger.
CONSUMER LAW	

Deceptive Advertising (See pages 362–364.)	1. *Definition of deceptive advertising*—Generally, an advertising claim will be deemed deceptive if it would mislead a reasonable consumer.
	2. *Bait-and-switch advertising*—Advertising a lower-priced product (the bait) to lure consumers into the store and then telling them the product is unavailable or of poor quality and urging them to buy a higher-priced product (the switch) is prohibited by the FTC.
	3. *Online deceptive advertising*—The FTC has issued guidelines to help online businesses comply with the laws prohibiting deceptive advertising.
	4. *FTC actions against deceptive advertising*—
	  a. Cease-and-desist orders—Requiring the advertiser to stop the challenged advertising.
	  b. Counteradvertising—Requiring the advertiser to advertise to correct the earlier misinformation.

Labeling and Packaging (See pages 364–365.)	Manufacturers must comply with the labeling or packaging requirements for their specific products. In general, all labels must be accurate and not misleading.
Sales (See page 365.)	Federal and state statutes and regulations govern certain practices of sellers who solicit over the telephone or through the mails and protect consumers to some extent against fraudulent and deceptive online sales practices.
Health and Safety (See pages 365–368.)	1. *Food and drugs*—The Federal Food, Drug, and Cosmetic Act protects consumers against adulterated and misbranded foods and drugs. The act establishes food standards, specifies safe levels of potentially hazardous food additives, and sets classifications of food and food advertising. 2. *Consumer product safety*—The Consumer Product Safety Act seeks to protect consumers from injury from hazardous products. The Consumer Product Safety Commission has the power to remove products that are deemed imminently hazardous from the market and to ban the manufacture and sale of hazardous products.

Credit Protection (See pages 368–371.)	1. *Consumer Credit Protection Act, Title I (Truth-in-Lending Act, or TILA)*—A disclosure law that requires sellers and lenders to disclose credit terms or loan terms in certain transactions, including retail and installment sales and loans, car loans, home-improvement loans, and certain real estate loans. Additionally, the TILA provides for the following:
	  a. Equal credit opportunity—Creditors are prohibited from discriminating on the basis of race, religion, marital status, gender, national origin, color, or age.
	  b. Credit-card protection—Liability of cardholders for unauthorized charges is limited to $50, providing notice requirements are met. Consumers are not liable for unauthorized charges made on unsolicited credit cards. The act also sets out procedures to be used in settling disputes between credit-card companies and their cardholders.
	2. *Fair Credit Reporting Act*—Entitles consumers to request verification of the accuracy of a credit report and to have unverified or false information removed from their files.
	3. *Fair and Accurate Credit Transaction Act*—Combats identity theft by establishing a national fraud alert system. Requires account numbers to be truncated and credit reporting agencies to provide one free credit report per year to consumers.
	4. *Fair Debt Collection Practices Act*—Prohibits debt collectors from using unfair debt-collection practices, such as contacting the debtor at his or her place of employment if the employer objects or at unreasonable times, contacting third parties about the debt, and harassing the debtor.

ExamPrep

ISSUE SPOTTERS

1. Rim Corporation makes tire rims that it sells to Superior Vehicles, Inc., which installs them on cars. One set of rims is defective, which an inspection would reveal. Superior does not inspect the rims. The car with the defective rims is sold to Town Auto Sales, which sells the car to Uri. Soon, the car is in an accident caused by the defective rims, and Uri is injured. Is Superior Vehicles liable? Explain your answer. **(See pages 352–353.)**
2. Real Chocolate Company makes a box of candy and sells it to Sweet Things, Inc., a distributor. Sweet sells the box to a Tasty Candy store, where Jill buys it. Jill gives it to Ken. In the box is a stone the same size and color as a piece of the candy, and Ken breaks his tooth on it. If Real, Sweet, and Tasty were not negligent, can they be liable for the injury? Why or why not? **(See pages 352–353.)**

—Check your answers to the Issue Spotters against the answers provided in Appendix E at the end of this text.

BEFORE THE TEST

Go to www.cengagebrain.com, enter the ISBN 9781133191353, and click on "Find" to locate this textbook's Web site. Then, click on "Access Now" under "Study Tools," and select Chapter 12 at the top. There, you will find a Practice Quiz that you can take to assess your mastery of the concepts in this chapter, as well as Flashcards, a Glossary of important terms, and Video Questions (when assigned).

For Review

Answers to the even-numbered questions in this For Review section can be found in Appendix F at the end of this text.

1. What implied warranties arise under the UCC?
2. Can a manufacturer be held liable to any person who suffers an injury proximately caused by the manufacturer's negligently made product?
3. What are the elements of a cause of action in strict product liability?
4. What defenses to liability can be raised in a product liability lawsuit?
5. When will advertising be deemed deceptive?

Business Scenarios and Case Problems

12–1 Product Liability. Jason Clark, an experienced hunter, bought a paintball gun. Clark practiced with the gun and knew how to use it. Although Clark was aware that he could purchase protective eyewear, he chose not to. Clark had also taken gun safety courses and understood that it was "common sense" not to shoot anyone in the face. Clark's friend, Chris Wright, also owned a paintball gun and was similarly familiar with the gun's use and its risks. Clark, Wright, and their friends played a game that involved shooting paintballs at cars whose occupants also had the guns. One night, while Clark and Wright were cruising with their guns, Wright shot at Clark's car, but hit Clark in the eye. Clark filed a product liability lawsuit against the manufacturer of Wright's paintball gun to recover for the injury. Clark claimed that the gun was defectively designed. During the trial, Wright testified that his gun "never malfunctioned." In whose favor should the court rule? Why? **(See pages 354–358.)**

12–2 **Question with Sample Answer—Implied Warranties.** Tandy purchased a washing machine from Marshall Appliances. The sales contract included a provision explicitly disclaiming all express and implied warranties, including the implied warranty of merchantability. The disclaimer was printed in the same size and color as the rest of the contract. The machine turned out to be a "lemon" and never functioned properly. Tandy sought a refund of the purchase price, claiming that Marshall had breached the implied warranty of merchantability. Can Tandy recover her payment, notwithstanding the warranty disclaimer in the contract? Explain. **(See page 348.)**

—For a sample answer to Question 12–2, go to Appendix G at the end of this text.

12–3 Defenses to Product Liability. Brandon Stroud was driving a golf car made by Textron, Inc. The golf car did not have lights, but Textron did not warn against using it on public roads at night. When Stroud attempted to cross a road at 8:30 P.M., his golf car was struck by a vehicle driven by Joseph Thornley. Stroud was killed. His estate filed a suit against Textron, alleging strict product liability and product liability based on negligence. The charge was that the golf car was defective and unreasonably dangerous. What defense might Textron assert? Explain. [*Moore v. Barony House Restaurant, LLC*, 382 S.C. 35, 674 S.E.2d 500 (S.C.App. 2009)] **(See pages 360–361.)**

12–4 Deceptive Advertising. Brian Cleary and Rita Burke filed a suit against cigarette maker Philip Morris USA, Inc., seeking class-action status for a claim of deceptive advertising. They claimed that "light" cigarettes, such as Marlboro Lights, were advertised as safer than regular cigarettes, even though the health effects are the same. They contended that the tobacco companies concealed the true nature of light cigarettes. Philip Morris correctly claimed that it was authorized by the government to advertise cigarettes, including light cigarettes. Assuming that is true, should Cleary and Burke still be able to bring a deceptive advertising claim against the tobacco company? Why or why not? [*Cleary v. Philip Morris USA, Inc.*, 683 F.Supp.2d 730 (N.D.Ill. 2010)] **(See pages 362–364.)**

12–5 Product Liability. Yun Tung Chow tried to unclog a floor drain in the kitchen of the restaurant where he worked. He used a drain cleaner called Lewis Red Devil Lye that contained crystalline sodium hydroxide. The product label said to wear eye protection, to put one tablespoon of lye directly into the drain, and to keep one's face away from the drain because there could be dangerous backsplash. Not wearing eye protection, Chow mixed three spoonfuls of lye in a can and poured that mixture down the drain while bending over it. Liquid splashed back into his face, causing injury. He sued for product liability based on inadequate warnings and a design defect. The trial court granted summary judgment to the manufacturer. Chow appealed. An expert for Chow stated that the product was defective because it had a tendency to backsplash. Is that a convincing argument? Why or why not? [*Yun Tung Chow v. Reckitt & Coleman, Inc.*, 69 A.D.3d 413, 891 N.Y.S.2d 402 (N.Y.A.D. 1 Dept. 2010)] **(See pages 355–358.)**

12–6 Case Problem with Sample Answer—Product Liability. David Dobrovolny bought a new Ford F-350 pickup truck. A year later, the truck spontaneously caught fire in Dobrovolny's driveway. The truck was destroyed, but no other property was damaged, and no one was injured. Dobrovolny filed a suit in a Nebraska state court against Ford Motor Co. on a theory of strict product liability to recover the cost of the truck. Nebraska limits the application of strict product liability to situations involving personal injuries. Is Dobrovolny's claim likely to succeed? Why or why not? Is there another basis for liability on which he might recover? Explain. [*Dobrovolny v. Ford Motor Co.*, 281 Neb. 86, 793 N.W.2d 445 (2011)] **(See pages 352–358.)**

—For a sample answer to Problem 12–6, go to Appendix H at the end of this text.

12–7 Spotlight on Apple—Implied Warranties. Alan Vitt purchased an iBook G4 laptop computer from Apple, Inc. Shortly after the one-year warranty expired, the laptop stopped working. Vitt sued Apple, arguing that the laptop should have lasted "at least a couple of years," which Vitt believed was a reasonable consumer expectation for a laptop. Vitt claimed that Apple's descriptions of the laptop as "durable," "rugged," "reliable," and "high performance" were affirmative statements concerning the quality and performance of the laptop, which Apple did not meet. How should the court rule? Why? [*Vitt v. Apple Computer, Inc.*, 2012 WL 627702 (9th Cir. 2011)] **(See pages 348–351.)**

12–8 Fair Debt-Collection Practices. Bank of America hired Atlantic Resource Management, LLC, to collect a debt from Michael E. Engler. Atlantic called Engler's employer and asked his supervisor about the company's policy concerning the execution of warrants. It then told the supervisor that, to stop the process, Engler needed to call Atlantic about "Case Number 37291 NY0969" during the first three hours of his next shift. When Engler's supervisor told him about the call, Engler feared that he might be arrested, and he experienced discomfort, embarrassment, and emotional distress at work. Can Engler recover under the Fair Debt Collection Practices Act? Why or why not? [*Engler v. Atlantic Resource Management, LLC*, 2012 WL 464728 (W.D.N.Y. 2012)] **(See pages 370–371.)**

12–9 A Question of Ethics—Strict Product Liability. Susan Calles lived with her four daughters, Amanda, age 11, Victoria, age 5, and Jenna and Jillian, age 3. In March 1998, Calles bought an Aim N Flame utility lighter, which she stored on the top shelf of her kitchen cabinet. A trigger can ignite the Aim N Flame after an "ON/OFF" switch is slid to the "on" position. On the night of March 31, Calles and Victoria left to get videos. Jenna and Jillian were in bed, and Amanda was watching television. Calles returned to find fire trucks and emergency vehicles around her home. Robert Finn, a fire investigator, determined that Jenna had started a fire using the lighter. Jillian suffered smoke inhalation, was hospitalized, and died on April 21. Calles filed a suit in an Illinois state court against Scripto-Tokai Corp., which distributed the Aim N Flame, and others. In her suit, which was grounded, in part, in strict liability claims, Calles alleged that the lighter was an "unreasonably dangerous product." Scripto filed a motion for summary judgment. [*Calles v. Scripto-Tokai Corp.*, 224 Ill.2d 247, 864 N.E.2d 249, 309 Ill.Dec. 383 (2007)] **(See pages 354–355.)**

1. A product is "unreasonably dangerous" when it is dangerous beyond the expectation of the ordinary consumer. Whose expectation—Calles's or Jenna's—applies here? Why? Does the lighter pass this test? Explain.

2. A product is also "unreasonably dangerous" when its maker failed to use an alternative design that was economically feasible and less dangerous. Scripto contended that because its product was "simple" and the danger was

"obvious," it should not be liable under this test. Do you agree? Why or why not?

3. Calles presented evidence as to the likelihood and seriousness of injury from lighters that do not have child-safety devices. Scripto argued that the Aim N Flame is a useful, inexpensive, alternative source of fire and is safer than a match. Calles admitted that she was aware of the dangers presented by lighters in the hands of children. Scripto admitted that it had been a defendant in at least twenty-five suits for injuries that occurred under similar circumstances. With these factors in mind, how should the court rule? Why?

Critical Thinking and Writing Assignments

12–10 **Business Law Critical Thinking Group Assignment.** Many states have enacted laws that go even further than federal law to protect consumers. These laws vary tremendously from state to state.

1. The first group will decide whether having different laws is fair to sellers, who may be prohibited from engaging in a practice in one state that is legal in another.

2. The second group will consider how these different laws might affect a business.

3. A third group will determine whether it is fair that residents of one state have more protection than residents of another.

Negotiable Instruments

LEARNING OBJECTIVES

The five learning objectives below are designed to help improve your understanding of the chapter. After reading this chapter, you should be able to answer the following questions:

1 What requirements must an instrument meet to be negotiable?

2 What are the requirements for attaining the status of a holder in due course (HDC)?

3 What is the difference between signature liability and warranty liability?

4 Certain defenses are valid against all holders, including HDCs. What are these defenses called? Name four defenses that fall within this category.

5 Certain defenses can be used against an ordinary holder but are not effective against an HDC. What are these defenses called? Name four defenses that fall within this category.

(DNY59/iStockphoto.com)

"It took many generations for people
to feel comfortable accepting paper in lieu of gold or silver."
—Alan Greenspan, 1926–present
(Chair of the Board of Governors of the Federal Reserve System, 1987–2006)

Negotiable Instrument A signed writing (record) that contains an unconditional promise or order to pay an exact sum on demand or at a specified future time to a specific person or order, or to bearer.

Most commercial transactions would be inconceivable without negotiable instruments. A **negotiable instrument** is a signed writing (record) that contains an unconditional promise or order to pay an exact sum on demand or at a specified future time to a specific person or order, or to bearer. Most negotiable instruments are paper documents, which is why they are sometimes referred to as *commercial paper*. The checks you write are negotiable instruments.

A negotiable instrument can function as a substitute for cash or as an extension of credit. As indicated in the chapter-opening quotation, "many generations" passed before paper became an acceptable substitute for gold or silver in commerce. For a negotiable instrument to operate *practically* as either a substitute for cash or a credit device, or both, it is essential that the instrument be *easily transferable without danger of being uncollectible*. Each rule described in the following pages can be examined in light of this essential function of negotiable instruments.

Types of Instruments

Section 3–104(b) of the Uniform Commercial Code (UCC) defines *instrument* as a "negotiable instrument."[1] For that reason, whenever the term *instrument* is used in this book, it refers to a negotiable instrument. The UCC specifies four types of negotiable instruments: *drafts, checks, promissory notes,* and *certificates of deposit* (CDs).

These instruments, which are summarized briefly in Exhibit 13.1 below, are frequently divided into the two classifications that we will discuss in the following subsections: *orders to pay* (drafts and checks) and *promises to pay* (promissory notes and CDs).

Negotiable instruments may also be classified as either demand instruments or time instruments. A *demand instrument* is payable on demand. In other words, it is payable immediately after it is issued and thereafter for a reasonable period of time. All checks are demand instruments because, by definition, they must be payable on demand. A *time instrument* is payable at a future date.

Drafts and Checks (Orders to Pay)

A **draft** is an unconditional written order to pay rather than a promise to pay. Drafts involve three parties. The party creating the draft (the **drawer**) orders another party (the **drawee**) to pay funds, usually to a third party (the **payee**). The most common type of draft is a check, but drafts other than checks may be used in commercial transactions.

Time Drafts and Sight Drafts   A *time draft* is payable at a definite future time. A *sight draft* (or demand draft) is payable on sight—that is, when it is presented to the drawee (usually a bank or financial institution) for payment. A sight draft may be payable on acceptance. **Acceptance** is the drawee's written promise to pay the draft when it

Draft Any instrument drawn on a drawee that orders the drawee to pay a certain amount of funds, usually to a third party (the payee), on demand or at a definite future time.

Drawer The party that initiates a draft (such as a check), thereby ordering the drawee to pay.

Drawee The party that is ordered to pay a draft or check. With a check, a bank or a financial institution is always the drawee.

Payee The party to whom an instrument is made payable.

Acceptance In negotiable instruments law, a drawee's signed agreement to pay a draft when it is presented.

---

1. Note that all of the references to Article 3 of the UCC in this chapter are to the 1990 version of Article 3, which has been adopted by nearly every state.

Exhibit 13.1 Basic Types of Negotiable Instruments

INSTRUMENTS	CHARACTERISTICS	PARTIES
ORDERS TO PAY:		
Draft	An order by one person to another person or to bearer [UCC 3–104(e)].	Drawer—The person who signs or makes the order to pay [UCC 3–103(a)(3)].
Check	A draft drawn on a bank and payable on demand [UCC 3–104(f)].[a] (With certain types of checks, such as cashier's checks, the bank is both the drawer and the drawee—see Chapter 14 for details.)	Drawee—The person to whom the order to pay is made [UCC 3–103(a)(2)]. Payee—The person to whom payment is ordered.
PROMISES TO PAY:		
Promissory note	A promise by one party to pay funds to another party or to bearer [UCC 3–104(e)].	Maker—The person who promises to pay [UCC 3–103(a)(5)]. Payee—The person to whom the promise is made.
Certificate of deposit	A note issued by a bank acknowledging a deposit of funds and made payable to the holder of the note [UCC 3–104(j)].	

a. Under UCC 4–105(1), banks include savings banks, savings and loan associations, credit unions, and trust companies. (Trust companies are organizations that perform the fiduciary functions of trusts and agencies.)

comes due. Usually, an instrument is accepted by writing the word *accepted* across its face, followed by the date of acceptance and the signature of the drawee. A draft can be both a time and a sight draft. Such a draft is payable at a stated time after sight (a draft that states it is payable ninety days after sight, for instance).

Exhibit 13.2 below shows a typical time draft. For the drawee to be obligated to honor (pay) the order, the drawee must be obligated to the drawer either by agreement or through a debtor-creditor relationship. **EXAMPLE 13.1** On January 16, OurTown Real Estate orders $1,000 worth of office supplies from Eastman Supply Company, with payment due in ninety days. Also on January 16, OurTown sends Eastman a draft drawn on its account with the First National Bank of Whiteacre as payment. In this scenario, the drawer is OurTown, the drawee is OurTown's bank (First National Bank of Whiteacre), and the payee is Eastman Supply Company. •

> "The two most beautiful words in the English language are 'check enclosed.'"
>
> Dorothy Parker, 1893–1967
> (American author and poet)

Check A draft drawn by a drawer ordering the drawee bank or financial institution to pay a certain amount of funds to the payee on demand.

Trade Acceptances A *trade acceptance* is a type of draft that is commonly used in the sale of goods. In this draft, the seller is both the drawer and the payee. The buyer to whom credit is extended is the drawee. **EXAMPLE 13.2** Jackson Street Bistro buys its restaurant supplies from Osaka Industries. When Jackson requests supplies, Osaka creates a draft ordering Jackson to pay Osaka for the supplies within ninety days. Jackson accepts the draft by signing its face and is then obligated to make the payment. This is a trade acceptance and can be sold to a third party if Osaka is in need of cash before the payment is due. • (If the draft orders the buyer's bank to pay, it is called a *banker's acceptance.*)

Checks As mentioned, the most commonly used type of draft is a **check.** The writer of the check is the drawer, the bank on which the check is drawn is the drawee, and the person to whom the check is payable is the payee. Checks are demand instruments because they are payable on demand.

Checks will be discussed more fully in Chapter 14, but it should be noted here that with certain types of checks, such as *cashier's checks,* the bank is both the drawer and the drawee. The bank customer purchases a cashier's check from the bank—that is, pays the bank the amount of the check—and indicates to whom the check should be made payable. The bank, not the customer, is the drawer of the check, as well as the drawee.

Exhibit 13.2 A Typical Time Draft

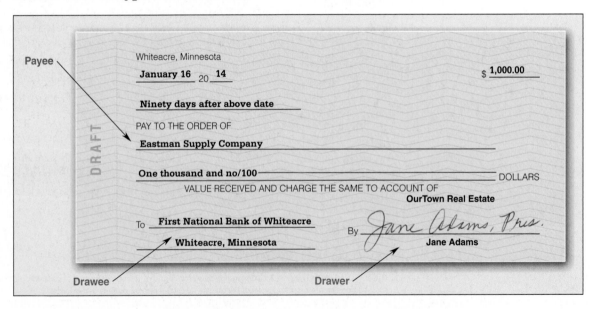

A cashier's check functions the same as cash because the bank has committed itself to paying the stated amount on demand.

Promissory Notes (Promises to Pay)

Promissory Note A written promise made by one person (the maker) to pay a fixed amount of funds to another person (the payee or a subsequent holder) on demand or on a specified date.

Maker One who promises to pay a fixed amount of funds to the holder of a promissory note or a certificate of deposit (CD).

A **promissory note** is a written promise made by one person (the **maker** of the promise to pay) to another (usually a payee). A promissory note, which is often referred to simply as a *note,* can be made payable at a definite time or on demand. It can name a specific payee or merely be payable to bearer (bearer instruments will be discussed later in this chapter).

EXAMPLE 13.3 On April 30, Laurence and Margaret Roberts sign a writing unconditionally promising to pay "to the order of" the First National Bank of Whiteacre $3,000 (with 8 percent interest) on or before June 29. This writing is a promissory note. •

A typical promissory note is shown in Exhibit 13.3 below.

CASE EXAMPLE 13.4 Joseph Cotton borrowed funds from a bank for his education and signed a promissory note for their repayment. The bank assigned the note to the U.S. Department of Education, and Cotton failed to pay the debt. The government then obtained a court order allowing it to garnish (take a percentage of) Cotton's wages and his federal income tax refund. Cotton filed a lawsuit seeking to avoid payment and claiming that the debt was invalid because he had not signed any document promising to pay the government. The court found that the signature on Cotton's employment records matched the one on the bank's note, which had been validly assigned to the government. Thus, the government was entitled to enforce the note.[2] •

Certificates of Deposit (Promises to Pay)

Certificate of Deposit (CD) A note issued by a bank in which the bank acknowledges the receipt of funds from a party and promises to repay that amount, with interest, to the party on a certain date.

A **certificate of deposit (CD)** is a type of note. A CD is issued when a party deposits funds with a bank that the bank promises to repay, with interest, on a certain date [UCC 3–104(j)]. The bank is the maker of the note, and the depositor is the payee. **EXAMPLE 13.5** On February 15, Sara Levin deposits $5,000 with the First National Bank of Whiteacre. The bank issues a CD, in which it promises to repay the $5,000, plus 3.25 percent annual interest, on August 15. •

---

2. *Cotton v. U.S. Department of Education,* 2006 WL 3313753 (M.D.Fla. 2006).

Exhibit 13.3 A Typical Promissory Note

Before Washington Mutual's demise in 2008, it was offering 4.25 percent certificates of deposit.

Certificates of deposit in small denominations (for amounts up to $100,000) are often sold by savings and loan associations, savings banks, commercial banks, and credit unions. Certificates of deposit for amounts over $100,000 are called large or jumbo CDs.

Because CDs are time deposits, the purchaser-payee typically is not allowed to withdraw the funds before the date of maturity (except in limited circumstances, such as disability or death). If a payee wants to access the funds prior to the maturity date, he or she can sell (negotiate) the CD to a third party.

Exhibit 13.4 below shows a typical small CD.

Requirements for Negotiability

For an instrument to be negotiable, it must meet the following requirements:

1. Be in writing.
2. Be signed by the maker or the drawer.
3. Be an unconditional promise or order to pay.
4. State a fixed amount of money.
5. Be payable on demand or at a definite time.
6. Be payable to order or to bearer, unless the instrument is a check.

LEARNING OBJECTIVE 1
What requirements must an instrument meet to be negotiable?

Written Form

Negotiable instruments must be in written form [UCC 3–103(a)(6), (9)]. This is because negotiable instruments must possess the quality of certainty that only formal, written expression can give. The writing must have the following qualities:

1. The writing must be on material that lends itself to *permanence*. Instruments carved in blocks of ice or recorded on other impermanent surfaces would not qualify as negotiable instruments. **EXAMPLE 13.6** Suzanne writes in the sand, "I promise to pay $500 to the order of Jack." This cannot be a negotiable instrument because, although it is in writing, it lacks permanence. ●

Exhibit 13.4 A Typical Small Certificate of Deposit

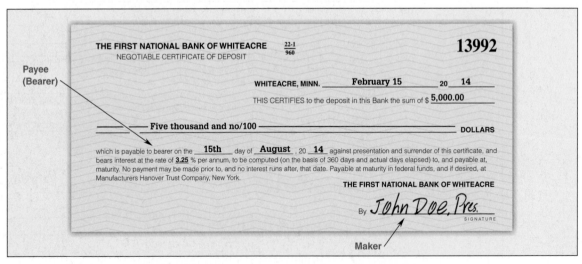

2. The writing must also have *portability*. Although the UCC does not explicitly state this requirement, if an instrument is not movable, it obviously cannot meet the requirement that it be freely transferable. **EXAMPLE 13.7** Charles writes on the side of a cow, "I promise to pay $500 to the order of Jason." Technically, this would meet the requirements of a negotiable instrument—except for portability. A cow cannot easily be transferred in the ordinary course of business. Thus, the "instrument" is nonnegotiable. •

The UCC nevertheless gives considerable leeway as to what can be a negotiable instrument. Courts have found checks and notes written on napkins, menus, tablecloths, shirts, and a variety of other materials to be negotiable instruments.

Signatures

"I'm a writer. I write checks. They're not very good."

Wendy Liebman, 1961–present (American comedian)

For an instrument to be negotiable, it must be signed by (1) the maker, if it is a note or a certificate of deposit, or (2) the drawer, if it is a draft or a check [UCC 3–103(a)(3)]. If a person signs an instrument as an authorized agent of the maker or drawer, the maker or drawer has effectively signed the instrument. (Agents' signatures will be discussed in Chapter 17.)

The UCC is quite lenient with regard to what constitutes a signature. Nearly any symbol executed or adopted by a person with the intent to authenticate a written document can be a signature. A signature can be made manually or by some device, such as a rubber stamp or thumbprint, and can consist of any name, including a trade or assumed name, or a word, mark, or symbol [UCC 3–401(b)]. If necessary, *parol evidence* (see pages 304–305 in Chapter 10) is admissible to identify the signer. When the signer is identified, the signature becomes effective.

The location of the signature on the document is unimportant, although the usual place is the lower right-hand corner. A *handwritten* statement on the body of the instrument, such as "I, Jerome Garcia, promise to pay Elena Greer," is sufficient to act as a signature.

PREVENTING LEGAL DISPUTES

Although there are almost no limitations on the manner in which a signature can be made, be careful about receiving an instrument that has been signed in an unusual way. Oddities on a negotiable instrument can open the door to disputes and lead to litigation. Furthermore, an unusual signature clearly decreases the *marketability* of an instrument because it creates uncertainty.

Unconditional Promise or Order to Pay

The terms of the promise or order must be included in the writing on the face of a negotiable instrument. The terms must also be *unconditional*—that is, they cannot be conditioned on the occurrence or nonoccurrence of some other event or agreement [UCC 3–104(a)].

➤ **KNOW THIS** ➤
Negotiable instruments are classified as promises to pay or orders to pay.

Promise or Order   For an instrument to be negotiable, it must contain an express order or promise to pay. If a buyer executes a promissory note using the words "I promise to pay Jonas $1,000 on demand for the purchase of these goods," then this requirement for a negotiable instrument is satisfied. A mere acknowledgment of the debt, such as an I.O.U. ("I owe you"), might logically *imply* a promise, but it is not sufficient under the UCC because the promise must be an affirmative (express) undertaking [UCC 3–103(a)(9)]. If such words as "to be paid on demand" or "due on demand" are added to an I.O.U., however, the need for an express promise to pay is satisfied.[3]

---

3. A certificate of deposit (CD) is an exception in this respect. A CD does not have to contain an express promise because the bank's acknowledgment of the deposit and the other terms of the instrument clearly indicate a promise by the bank to repay the funds [UCC 3–104(j)].

An *order* is associated with three-party instruments, such as checks, drafts, and trade acceptances. An order directs a third party to pay the instrument as drawn. In the typical check, for example, the word "pay" (to the order of a payee) is a command to the drawee bank to pay the check when presented—thus, it is an order. A command, such as "pay," is mandatory even if it is accompanied by courteous words as in "Please pay" or "Kindly pay." Stating "I wish you would pay" does not fulfill this requirement. An order may be addressed to one party or to more than one party, either jointly ("to A *and* B") or alternatively ("to A *or* B") [UCC 3–103(a)(6)].

Unconditionality of Promise or Order   Only unconditional promises or orders can be negotiable. A promise or order is conditional (and therefore *not* negotiable) if it states (1) an express condition to payment, (2) that the promise or order is subject to or governed by another writing, or (3) that the rights or obligations with respect to the promise or order are stated in another writing.

A mere reference to another writing, however, does not make the promise or order conditional [UCC 3–106(a)]. For example, the words "As per contract" or "This debt arises from the sale of goods X and Y" do not render an instrument nonnegotiable. Similarly, a statement in the instrument that payment can be made only out of a particular fund or source will not render the instrument nonnegotiable [UCC 3–106(b)(ii)].

EXAMPLE 13.8   The terms of Biggs's note state that payment will be made out of the proceeds of next year's cotton crop. This does not make the note nonnegotiable—although the payee of such a note may find the note commercially unacceptable and refuse to take it. ●

A Fixed Amount of Money

Negotiable instruments must state with certainty a fixed amount of money to be paid at any time the instrument is payable [UCC 3–104(a)]. The term *fixed amount* means an amount that is ascertainable from the face of the instrument. A demand note payable with 8 percent interest meets the requirement of a fixed amount because its amount can be determined at the time it is payable or at any time thereafter [UCC 3–104(a)].

The rate of interest may also be determined from information that is not contained in the instrument if that information is readily ascertainable by use of a formula or a source described in the instrument [UCC 3–112(b)]. For instance, an instrument that is payable at the *legal rate of interest* (a rate of interest fixed by statute) is negotiable. Mortgage notes tied to a variable rate of interest (a rate that fluctuates as a result of market conditions) are also negotiable.

Some instruments pay interest rates that are tied to the federal funds rate, shown below.

(AP Photo/Seth Wenig)

UCC 3–104(a) provides that a fixed amount is to be *payable in money.* The UCC defines money as "a medium of exchange authorized or adopted by a domestic or foreign government as a part of its currency" [UCC 1–201(24)]. Thus, a note that promises "to pay on demand $1,000 in gold" is not negotiable because gold is not a medium of exchange adopted by the U.S. government. An instrument payable in the United States with a face amount stated in a foreign currency is negotiable, however, and can be paid in the foreign currency or in the equivalent amount of U.S. dollars [UCC 3–107].

Payable on Demand or at a Definite Time

Acceptor A drawee that accepts, or promises to pay, an instrument when it is presented later for payment.

To determine the value of a negotiable instrument, it is necessary to know when the maker, drawee, or acceptor (an **acceptor** is a drawee that promises to pay an instrument when it is presented later for payment) is required to pay the instrument. A negotiable instrument must therefore "be payable on demand or at a definite time" [UCC 3–104(a)(2)].

Presentment The act of presenting an instrument to the party liable on the instrument in order to collect payment. Presentment also occurs when a person presents an instrument to a drawee for a required acceptance.

Payable on Demand   Instruments that are payable on demand include those that contain the words "Payable at sight" or "Payable upon presentment." **Presentment** means a demand made by or on behalf of a person entitled to enforce an instrument to either pay or accept the instrument [UCC 3–501]. Thus, presentment occurs when a person brings the instrument to the appropriate party for payment or acceptance.

The very nature of the instrument may indicate that it is payable on demand. For example, a check, by definition, is payable on demand [UCC 3–104(f)]. If no time for payment is specified and the person responsible for payment must pay on the instrument's presentment, the instrument is payable on demand [UCC 3–108(a)].

In the following case, the issue before the court was whether a promissory note was a demand note.

Case 13.1

Reger Development, LLC v. National City Bank

United States Court of Appeals, Seventh Circuit, 592 F.3d 759 (2010).
www.ca7.uscourts.gov[a]

Many promissory notes are payable on demand.

FACTS   Kevin Reger is the principal and sole member of Reger Development, LLC. Reger Development borrowed funds from National City Bank for several projects. National City then offered the company a line of credit to finance potential development opportunities, and Reger Development signed a promissory note requiring it to "pay this loan in full immediately upon Lender's demand."

About a year later, the bank asked Reger Development to pay down some of the loan and stated that it would be reducing the amount of cash available through the line of credit. Kevin Reger "expressed surprise" at these developments and asked if the bank would call in the line of credit if Reger Development did not agree to the requests. The bank said that there was a possibility that it would demand payment of the credit line. Reger Development then sued National City, alleging that the bank had breached the terms of the note. A federal district court granted the bank's motion to dismiss, and Reger Development appealed. The main question before the court was whether the note entitled National City to demand payment from Reger Development at will.

ISSUE   Was a note for a line of credit that stated it was a promissory note, but required the borrower (Reger Development) to pay the loan on the lender's demand, a demand instrument?

DECISION   Yes. The federal appellate court affirmed the district court's dismissal of Reger Development's complaint. The promissory note was a demand instrument, and thus National City had the right to collect payment from Reger Development at any time on demand.

REASON   The appellate court reasoned that although a covenant of fair dealing and good faith is implied in every contract, "the duty to act in good faith does not apply to lenders seeking payment on demand notes." Reger alleged that National City had arbitrarily and capriciously demanded payment, even though Reger was not in default, and that National City had unilaterally changed the fundamental terms of the contract. The appellate court, however, pointed out that explicit contract language set forth the lender's right to demand payment at any time. National City had the "right to collect scheduled monthly interest payments and [did] not deviate from the structure of a demand note."

CRITICAL THINKING—Ethical Consideration   In its opinion, the court pointed out "the duty to act in good faith does not apply to lenders seeking payment on demand notes." Why is this so?

a. Select "Opinions" under the "Case Information" heading. When the page opens, enter "09" and "2821" in the "Case Number" boxes, respectively, and click on "List Case(s)." On the page that appears next, click on the link to the case number to access the opinion (filed 01/20/2010). The U.S. Court of Appeals for the Seventh Circuit maintains this Web site.

Payable at a Definite Time

If an instrument is not payable on demand, to be negotiable it must be payable at a definite time. An instrument is payable at a definite time if it states that it is payable (1) on a specified date, (2) within a definite period of time (such as thirty days) after being presented for payment, or (3) on a date or time readily ascertainable at the time the promise or order is issued [UCC 3–108(b)]. The maker or drawee in a time draft, for example, is under no obligation to pay until the specified time.

When an instrument is payable by the maker or drawer on or before a stated date, it is clearly payable at a definite time. The maker or drawer has the *option* of paying before the stated maturity date, but the payee can still rely on payment being made by the maturity date. The option to pay early does not violate the definite-time requirement.

In contrast, an instrument that is undated and made payable "one month after date" is clearly nonnegotiable. There is no way to determine the maturity date from the face of the instrument.

Acceleration Clause A clause that allows a payee or other holder of a time instrument to demand payment of the entire amount due, with interest, if a certain event occurs, such as a default in the payment of an installment when due.

Holder Any person in possession of an instrument drawn, issued, or indorsed to him or her, to his or her order, to bearer, or in blank.

Acceleration Clause

An **acceleration clause** allows a payee or other holder of a time instrument to demand payment of the entire amount due, with interest, if a certain event occurs, such as a default in the payment of an installment when due. (A **holder** is any person in possession of an instrument drawn, issued, or indorsed to him or her, to his or her order, to bearer, or in blank [UCC 1–201(20)].)

Under the UCC, instruments that include acceleration clauses are negotiable because (1) the exact value of the instrument can be ascertained and (2) the instrument will be payable on a specified date if the event allowing acceleration does not occur [UCC 3–108(b)(ii)]. Thus, the specified date is the outside limit used to determine the value and negotiability of the instrument.

Extension Clause A clause in a time instrument that allows the instrument's date of maturity to be extended into the future.

Extension Clause

The reverse of an acceleration clause is an **extension clause,** which allows the date of maturity to be extended into the future [UCC 3–108(b)(iii), (iv)]. To keep the instrument negotiable, the interval of the extension must be specified if the right to extend the time of payment is given to the maker or drawer of the instrument. If, however, the holder of the instrument can extend the time of payment, the extended maturity date does not have to be specified.

Payable to Order or to Bearer

Because one of the functions of a negotiable instrument is to serve as a substitute for cash, freedom to transfer is essential. To ensure a proper transfer, the instrument must be "payable to order or to bearer" at the time it is issued or first comes into the possession of the holder [UCC 3–104(a)(1)]. An instrument is not negotiable unless it meets this requirement.

Order Instrument A negotiable instrument that is payable "to the order of an identified person" or "to an identified person or order."

Order Instruments

An **order instrument** is an instrument that is payable (1) "to the order of an identified person" or (2) "to an identified person or order" [UCC 3–109(b)]. An identified person is the person "to whom the instrument is initially payable" as determined by the intent of the maker or drawer [UCC 3–110(a)]. The identified person, in turn, may transfer the instrument to whomever he or she wishes. Thus, the maker or drawer is agreeing to pay either the person specified on the instrument or whomever that person might designate. In this way, the instrument retains its transferability.

Note that in order instruments, the person specified must be identified with *certainty* because the transfer of an order instrument requires the *indorsement*, or signature, of the payee (*indorsements* will be discussed at length later in this chapter). An order instrument made "Payable to the order of my nicest cousin," for instance, is not negotiable because it does not clearly specify the payee.

Bearer Instrument Any instrument that is not payable to a specific person, including instruments payable to the bearer or to "cash."

Bearer A person in possession of an instrument payable to bearer or indorsed in blank.

Bearer Instruments

A **bearer instrument** is an instrument that does not designate a specific payee [UCC 3–109(a)]. The term **bearer** refers to a person in possession of an instrument that is payable to bearer or indorsed in blank (with a signature only, as will be discussed shortly) [UCC 1–201(5), 3–109(a), 3–109(c)]. This means that the maker or drawer agrees to pay anyone who presents the instrument for payment.

Any instrument containing terms such as "Payable to Kathy Esposito or bearer" or "Pay to the order of cash" is a bearer instrument. In addition, an instrument that "indicates that it is not payable to an identified person" is a bearer instrument [UCC 3–109(a)(3)]. Thus, an instrument "payable to X" or "payable to Batman" can be negotiated as a bearer instrument, just as though it were payable to cash. An instrument made payable to a *nonexistent organization* or company is not a negotiable bearer instrument, however [UCC 3–109, Comment 2].

The bearer instrument at the center of the following *Spotlight Case* was a *gambling marker*—that is, a credit instrument that allows a gambler to receive tokens or chips from a casino based on a prior credit application. The court had to decide whether the gambling marker was negotiable.

Spotlight on Casino Markers

Case 13.2
Las Vegas Sands, LLC v. Nehme

United States Court of Appeals, Ninth Circuit, 632 F.3d 526 (2011).
www.ca9.uscourts.gov[a]

(nito/Shutterstock.com)

The Venetian Resort Hotel and Casino in Las Vegas.

FACTS Amine Nehme, a California resident, applied for credit at the Venetian Resort Hotel Casino in Las Vegas, Nevada. Nehme was granted $500,000 in credit. He soon accrued more than $1.2 million in gambling debts to the Venetian, which he paid. About a year later, Nehme deposited $1,000 with the Venetian and signed a gambling marker for $500,000. Generally, a gambling marker is an instrument that is dated, bears the gambler's name—and the name and account number of the gambler's bank—and states the instruction "Pay to the Order of" the casino. In this case, though, the line following "Pay to the Order of" was apparently left blank, which made the marker a bearer instrument. Nehme quickly lost $500,000 gambling and left the casino. The Venetian presented the marker for payment to Bank of America, Nehme's bank, which returned it for insufficient funds. The casino's owner, Las Vegas Sands, LLC, applied Nehme's deposit against the marker and filed a suit against him to recover the remainder—$499,000—plus interest, claiming that he had failed to pay a negotiable instrument. A federal district court issued a summary judgment in the Venetian's favor. Nehme appealed.

ISSUE Was the gambling marker under which Nehme borrowed funds from a casino a negotiable instrument?

DECISION Yes. The U.S. Court of Appeals for the Ninth Circuit agreed with the lower court that the marker was a negotiable instrument. To determine whether Nehme could establish a defense to liability, the appellate court reversed the lower court's judgment and remanded the case for a trial.

REASON In Nevada, a negotiable instrument is defined as an unconditional order to pay a fixed amount of money, payable on demand or at a definite time, and stating no "undertaking" in addition to the payment of money [Nevada Revised Statutes Section 104.3104, Nevada's version of UCC 3–104]. A check is defined as a draft "payable on demand and drawn on a bank." The court reasoned that the gambling marker fit these definitions. It specified a fixed amount of money, $500,000. It did not state a time for payment and thus was payable on demand. It was unconditional and stated no "undertaking" by Nehme in addition to the payment of a fixed sum. Thus, the Venetian could enforce the marker against Nehme unless he could establish a defense to liability.

WHAT IF THE FACTS WERE DIFFERENT? *Suppose that the marker had stated "Payable to the Order of the Venetian." Could the casino have transferred it for collection? If so, how?*

a. In the left column, in the "Opinions" pull-out menu, click on "Published." On the next page, click on "Advanced Search." In the "by Case No.:" box, type "09-16740," and click on "Search." In the result, click on the name of the case to access the opinion. The U.S. Court of Appeals for the Ninth Circuit maintains this Web site.

Factors That Do Not Affect Negotiability

Certain ambiguities or omissions will not affect the negotiability of an instrument. The UCC provides the following rules for clearing up ambiguous terms:

1. Unless the date of an instrument is necessary to determine a definite time for payment, the fact that an instrument is *undated* does not affect its negotiability. A typical example is an undated check, which is still negotiable. If a check is not dated, its date is the date of its issue, meaning the date the maker first delivers the check to another person to give that person rights in the check [UCC 3–113(b)].
2. Antedating or postdating an instrument does not affect the instrument's negotiability [UCC 3–113(a)]. *Antedating* occurs when a party puts a date on the instrument that is before the actual date, and *postdating* occurs when a party puts a date on an instrument that is after the actual date.

   EXAMPLE 13.9 On May 1, Avery draws a check on her account with First State Bank made payable to Consumer Credit Corporation. Avery postdates the check "May 15." Consumer Credit can negotiate the check, and, unless Avery tells First State otherwise, the bank can charge the amount of the check to Avery's account before May 15 [UCC 4–401(c)]. •
3. Handwritten terms outweigh typewritten and printed terms (preprinted terms on forms, for example), and typewritten terms outweigh printed terms [UCC 3–114].

   EXAMPLE 13.10 Like most checks, your check is printed "Pay to the order of" followed by a blank line. In handwriting, you insert in the blank, "Anita Delgado or bearer." The handwritten terms will outweigh the printed form (an order instrument), and the check will be a bearer instrument. •
4. Words outweigh figures unless the words are ambiguous [UCC 3–114]. This rule is important when the numerical amount and the written amount on a check differ.

   EXAMPLE 13.11 Rob issues a check payable to Standard Appliance Company. For the amount, he fills in the numbers "$100" but writes in the words "One thousand and 00/100" dollars. The check is payable in the amount of $1,000. •
5. When an instrument does not specify a particular interest rate but simply states "with interest," the interest rate is the *judgment rate of interest* (a rate of interest fixed by statute that is applied to a monetary judgment awarded by a court until the judgment is paid or terminated) [UCC 3–112(b)].
6. A check is negotiable even if there is a notation on it stating that it is "nonnegotiable" or "not governed by Article 3." Any other instrument, in contrast, can be made nonnegotiable if the maker or drawer conspicuously notes on it that it is "nonnegotiable" or "not governed by Article 3" [UCC 3–104(d)].

Transfer of Instruments

Once issued, a negotiable instrument can be transferred by *assignment* or by *negotiation*. The party receiving the instrument obtains the rights of a holder only if the transfer is by negotiation.

Transfer by Assignment

Recall from page 255 of Chapter 9 that an assignment is a transfer of rights under a contract. Under general contract principles, a transfer by assignment to an assignee gives the assignee only those rights that the assignor possessed. Any defenses that can be raised against an assignor can normally be raised against the assignee. This same principle applies when a negotiable instrument, such as a promissory note, is transferred by assignment. The transferee is then an *assignee* rather than a *holder*.

Sometimes, a transfer fails to qualify as a negotiation because it fails to meet one or more of the requirements of a negotiable instrument, just discussed. When this occurs, the transfer becomes an assignment.

Transfer by Negotiation

Negotiation The transfer of an instrument in such form that the transferee (the person to whom the instrument is transferred) becomes a holder.

Negotiation is the transfer of an instrument in such form that the transferee (the person to whom the instrument is transferred) becomes a holder [UCC 3–201(a)]. Under UCC principles, a transfer by negotiation creates a holder who, at the very least, receives the rights of the previous possessor [UCC 3–203(b)].

Unlike an assignment, a transfer by negotiation can make it possible for a holder to receive more rights in the instrument than the prior possessor had [UCC 3–202(b), 3–305, 3–306]. A holder who receives greater rights is known as a *holder in due course,* a concept we will discuss later in this chapter.

There are two methods of negotiating an instrument so that the receiver becomes a holder. The method used depends on whether the instrument is an order instrument or a bearer instrument.

Negotiating Order Instruments
An order instrument contains the name of a payee capable of indorsing it, as in "Pay to the order of Lloyd Sorenson." If the instrument is an order instrument, it is negotiated by delivery with any necessary indorsements.

EXAMPLE 13.12 National Express Corporation issues a payroll check "to the order of Lloyd Sorenson." Sorenson takes the check to the bank, signs his name on the back (an indorsement), gives it to the teller (a delivery), and receives cash. Sorenson has *negotiated* the check to the bank [UCC 3–201(b)]. •

Negotiating order instruments requires both delivery and indorsement (indorsements will be discussed shortly). If Sorenson had taken the check to the bank and delivered it to the teller without signing it, the transfer would not qualify as a negotiation. In that situation, the transfer would be treated as an assignment, and the bank would become an assignee rather than a holder.

Negotiating Bearer Instruments
If an instrument is payable to bearer, it is negotiated by delivery—that is, by transfer into another person's possession. Indorsement is not necessary [UCC 3–201(b)]. The use of bearer instruments thus involves more risk through loss or theft than the use of order instruments.

EXAMPLE 13.13 Richard Kray writes a check "payable to cash" and hands it to Jessie Arnold (a delivery). Kray has issued the check (a bearer instrument) to Arnold. Arnold places the check in her wallet, which is subsequently stolen. The thief has possession of the check. At this point, the thief has no rights to the check. If the thief "delivers" the check to an innocent third person, however, negotiation will be complete. All rights to the check will be passed absolutely to that third person, and Arnold will lose all rights to recover the proceeds of the check from that person [UCC 3–306]. Of course, Arnold could attempt to recover the amount from the thief if the thief can be found. •

Indorsements

Indorsement A signature placed on an instrument for the purpose of transferring one's ownership rights in the instrument.

Indorsements are required whenever the instrument being negotiated is classified as an order instrument. An **indorsement** is a signature with or without additional words or statements. It is most often written on the back of the instrument itself. If there is no room on the instrument, the indorsement can be on a separate piece of paper that is firmly affixed to the instrument, such as with staples [UCC 3–204(a)]. (See this chapter's *Beyond Our Borders* feature on the following page for a discussion of the approach to indorsements in France.)

BEYOND OUR BORDERS

Severe Restrictions on Check Indorsements in France

If you were reading a business law text-book in France, you would find very little on check indorsements. The reason is that checks rarely, if ever, can be indorsed. That means that almost all checks must be deposited in a bank account, rather than transferred to another individual or entity.

On the back of every French check are two parallel lines printed by the bank. These lines mean that the check can be transferred only to a bank employee or the head of a postal bank. In other words, you cannot indorse and transfer checks the way we do in the United States. The French government says that these restrictions on indorsements reduce the risk of loss and theft.

Critical Thinking
What would be the cost to individuals and businesses that use checks if a similar law were passed in this country?

A person who transfers an instrument by signing (indorsing) it and delivering it to another person is an *indorser.* The person to whom the check is indorsed and delivered is the *indorsee.*

We examine here the four categories of indorsements: blank, special, qualified, and restrictive. Note that a single indorsement may have characteristics of more than one category. In other words, these categories are not mutually exclusive.

Blank Indorsement An indorsement that specifies no particular indorsee and can consist of a mere signature. An order instrument that is indorsed in blank becomes a bearer instrument.

Blank Indorsements   A **blank indorsement** does not specify a particular indorsee and can consist of a mere signature [UCC 3–205(b)]. Hence, a check payable "to the order of Alan Luberda" is indorsed in blank if Luberda simply writes his signature on the back of the check, as shown in Exhibit 13.5 at left. An order instrument indorsed in blank becomes a bearer instrument and can be negotiated by delivery alone, as already discussed. In other words, a blank indorsement converts an order instrument to a bearer instrument, which anybody can cash.

Exhibit 13.5 A Blank Indorsement

Alan Luberda

Special Indorsement An indorsement on an instrument that identifies the specific person to whom the indorser intends to make the instrument payable. Thus, it names the indorsee.

Special Indorsements   A **special indorsement** contains the signature of the indorser and identifies the person to whom the instrument is made payable—that is, it names the indorsee [UCC 3–205(a)]. For instance, words such as "Pay to the order of Clay" or "Pay to Clay," followed by the signature of the indorser, create a special indorsement. When an instrument is indorsed in this way, it is an order instrument.

To avoid the risk of loss from theft, a holder may convert a blank indorsement to a special indorsement by writing, above the signature of the indorser, words identifying the indorsee [UCC 3–205(c)]. This changes the bearer instrument back to an order instrument.

EXAMPLE 13.14   A check is made payable to Peter Rabe. He indorses the check in blank by simply signing his name on the back and delivers the check to Anthony Bartomo. Anthony is unable to cash the check immediately and wants to avoid any risk should he lose the check. He therefore prints "Pay to Anthony Bartomo" above Peter's blank indorsement (see Exhibit 13.6 on the left). By doing this, Anthony has converted Peter's blank indorsement into a special indorsement. Further negotiation now requires Anthony Bartomo's indorsement plus delivery. •

Exhibit 13.6 A Special Indorsement

Pay to Anthony Bartomo
Peter Rabe

Qualified Indorsements   Generally, an indorser, *merely by indorsing,* impliedly promises to pay the holder or any subsequent indorser, the amount of the instrument in the event that the drawer or maker defaults on the payment [UCC 3–415(a)]. Usually, then, indorsements are *unqualified indorsements,* which means that the indorser is guaranteeing payment of the instrument in addition to transferring title to it.

Qualified Indorsement An indorsement on a negotiable instrument in which the indorser disclaims any contract liability on the instrument. The notation "without recourse" is commonly used to create a qualified indorsement.

An indorser who does not wish to be liable on an instrument can use a **qualified indorsement** to disclaim this liability [UCC 3–415(b)]. The notation "without recourse" is commonly used to create a qualified indorsement, such as the one shown in Exhibit 13.7 below and to the left.

The Effect of Qualified Indorsements

Qualified indorsements are often used by persons (agents) acting in a representative capacity, such as insurance agents who receive checks payable to them that are really intended as payment to the insurance company. The "without recourse" indorsement relieves the agent from any liability on a check. If the instrument is dishonored, the holder cannot recover from the agent who indorsed "without recourse" unless the indorser has breached one of the transfer warranties (relating to title, signature, and material alteration) that will be discussed later in this chapter.

Exhibit 13.7 A Qualified Indorsement

Pay to Elvie Ling, without recourse.
Bridgett Cage

Special versus Blank Qualified Indorsements

A qualified indorsement can be accompanied by either a special indorsement or a blank indorsement. A special qualified indorsement includes the name of the indorsee as well as the words *without recourse*. The special indorsement makes the instrument an order instrument, and it requires an indorsement, plus delivery, for negotiation. A blank qualified indorsement makes the instrument a bearer instrument, and only delivery is required for negotiation. In either situation, the instrument can be further negotiated.

The case that follows illustrates the effect of a blank qualified indorsement.

Case 13.3

Hammett v. Deutsche Bank National Co.

United States District Court, Eastern District of Virginia, 2010 WL 1225849 (2010).

FACTS Vernon Hammett and others (the plaintiffs) purchased a residential property in Alexandria, Virginia. As part of that transaction, the plaintiffs executed a promissory note in favor of Encore Credit Corporation in the amount of $475,000. The note was secured by the property being purchased. Subsequently, the note was negotiated by delivery to Deutsche Bank National Company. The note had an attached allonge,[a] which contained a blank indorsement reading as follows: "Pay to The Order of ____ without Recourse Encore Credit Corp. A California Corporation."

At some point after executing the note, the plaintiffs refused to continue making the payments due under the note. As the holder of the note, Deutsche Bank initiated foreclosure proceedings on the property and subsequently purchased the property at the foreclosure sale. The plaintiffs brought an action against Deutsche Bank, alleging that the bank had no rights in the note. Deutsche Bank filed a motion to dismiss the case.

ISSUE If a borrower executes a note with a blank indorsement to purchase a home, can the current holder of the note enforce it by foreclosing on the homeowner?

(Imaginechina via AP Images)

Deutsche Bank National Company received delivery of a promissory note.

DECISION Yes. The court granted the motion to dismiss the case. Deutsche Bank, as holder of the note, was entitled to enforce the instrument.

REASON The court reasoned that the note had included a blank qualified indorsement and thus only delivery of the instrument was required for negotiation. "If an instrument has a blank [i]ndorsement, it is considered 'payable to bearer' and it may be negotiated by transfer of possession alone." Because the face of the note showed that it had a blank indorsement, it was indeed negotiable by a simple change in possession. Thus, it

---

a. An *allonge* (pronounced uh-lonj) is a piece of paper firmly attached to a negotiable instrument on which indorsements can be made if there is no room on the instrument.

Case 13.3—Continues next page ➡

Case 13.3—Continued

was enforceable by its current possessor, Deutsche Bank. The court further stated that "by their own allegations, Plaintiffs admit that they 'refused to pay' on the Note. To permit parties to the [instrument] to object to its payment, on any of the grounds stated, would greatly impair the negotiability of bills and notes, their most distinguishing, most useful, and most valued feature."

WHAT IF THE FACTS WERE DIFFERENT? *Suppose that the indorsement at issue in this case had been written on a separate document that was not firmly affixed to the note. Would this document have constituted an allonge? Would Deutsche Bank have been entitled to enforce the note? Explain.*

Restrictive Indorsement Any indorsement on a negotiable instrument that requires the indorsee to comply with certain instructions regarding the funds involved. A restrictive indorsement does not prohibit the further negotiation of the instrument.

Restrictive Indorsements

A **restrictive indorsement** requires the indorsee to comply with certain instructions regarding the funds involved, but it does not prohibit further negotiation of the instrument [UCC 3–206(a)]. Although most indorsements are nonrestrictive because there are no instructions or conditions attached to the payment of funds, many forms of restrictive indorsements do exist, including those discussed here.

Conditional Indorsements When payment depends on the occurrence of some event specified in the indorsement, the instrument has a conditional indorsement. **EXAMPLE 13.15** Ken Barton indorses a check, "Pay to Lars Johansen if he completes the renovation of my kitchen by June 1, 2014. [Signed] Ken Barton." Barton has created a conditional indorsement. • A conditional indorsement (on the back of the instrument) does not prevent further negotiation of the instrument.

Indorsements for Deposit or Collection A common type of restrictive indorsement is one that makes the indorsee (almost always a bank) a collecting agent of the indorser [UCC 3–206(c)]. **EXAMPLE 13.16** Stephanie Mallak has received a check and wants to deposit it into her checking account at the bank. She can indorse the check "For deposit [or collection] only. [Signed] Stephanie Mallak" (see Exhibit 13.8 below). She may also wish to write her bank account number on the check. A "For deposit" or "For Collection" indorsement locks the instrument into the bank-collection process and thus prohibits further negotiation except by the bank. Following this indorsement, only the bank can acquire the rights of a holder. •

Exhibit 13.8 "For Deposit" and "For Collection" Indorsements

Trust (Agency) Indorsements An indorsement to a person who is to hold or use the funds for the benefit of the indorser or a third party is called a **trust indorsement** (also known as an *agency indorsement*) [UCC 3–206(d), (e)]. **EXAMPLE 13.17** Robert Emerson asks his accountant, Ada Johnson, to pay some bills for his invalid wife, Sarah, while he is out of the country. He indorses a check as follows: "Pay to Ada Johnson as Agent for Sarah Emerson." This agency indorsement obligates Johnson to use the funds only for the benefit of Sarah Emerson. •

Exhibit 13.9 on the facing page shows sample trust (agency) indorsements.

Trust Indorsement An indorsement to a person who is to hold or use funds for the benefit of the indorser or a third person. It is also known as an *agency indorsement*.

Misspelled Names

An indorsement should be identical to the name that appears on the instrument. A payee or indorsee whose name is misspelled can indorse with the

Exhibit 13.9 Trust (Agency) Indorsements

| Pay to Ada Johnson in trust for Sarah Emerson *Robert Emerson* | or | Pay to Ada Johnson as Agent for Sarah Emerson *Robert Emerson* |

misspelled name, the correct name, or both [UCC 3–204(d)]. For example, if Sheryl Kruger receives a check payable to the order of Sherrill Krooger, she can indorse the check either "Sheryl Kruger" or "Sherrill Krooger," or both.

The usual practice is to indorse with the name as it appears on the instrument, followed by the correct name. (See the *Business Application* feature on pages 404 and 405 for suggestions to help businesspersons avoid problems with indorsements.)

Alternative or Joint Payees

An instrument payable to two or more persons *in the alternative* (for example, "Pay to the order of Tuan or Johnson") requires the indorsement of only one of the payees. In contrast, if an instrument is made payable to two or more persons *jointly* (for example, "Pay to the order of Sharrie and Bob Covington"), all of the payees' indorsements are necessary for negotiation.

If an instrument payable to two or more persons does not clearly indicate whether it is payable in the alternative or jointly (for example, "Pay to the order of John and/or Sara Fitzgerald"), then the instrument is payable to the persons alternatively [UCC 3–110(d)]. The same principles apply to special indorsements that indicate more than one identified person to whom the indorser intends to make the instrument payable [UCC 3–205(a)].

CASE EXAMPLE 13.18 Hyatt Corporation hired Skyscraper Building Maintenance, LLC, to perform maintenance services at some of its Florida hotels. Under an agreement with Skyscraper, J & D Financial Corporation asked Hyatt to make checks for the services payable to Skyscraper and J & D. Hyatt issued many checks to the two payees, but two of the checks were made payable to "J & D Financial Corp. Skyscraper Building Maint." Parties listed in this manner—without including an "and" or "or" between them—are referred to as *stacked payees*. A bank negotiated the two checks, which were indorsed only by Skyscraper.

J & D and Hyatt filed a lawsuit against the bank, claiming that the checks were payable *jointly* and thus required indorsement by both payees. The bank argued that the checks were payable to J & D and Skyscraper *alternatively*. A state court found that the bank was not liable because a check payable to stacked payees is ambiguous (unclear) and thus is payable alternatively under UCC 3–110(d). Consequently, the bank could negotiate the checks even though they were indorsed by only one of the two payees.[4] ●

Holder in Due Course (HDC)

Often, whether a holder is entitled to obtain payment will depend on whether the holder is a *holder in due course*. An ordinary holder obtains only those rights that the transferor had in the instrument, as mentioned previously. In this respect, a holder has the same status as an assignee (see Chapter 9). Like an assignee, a holder normally is subject to the same defenses that could be asserted against the transferor.

---

4. *Hyatt Corp. v. Palm Beach National Bank*, 840 So.2d 300 (Fla.App. 2003).

Holder in Due Course (HDC) A holder who acquires a negotiable instrument for value, in good faith, and without notice that the instrument is defective (such as that it is overdue, has been dishonored, is subject to a defense against it or a claim to it, contains unauthorized signatures, has been altered, or is so irregular or incomplete as to call its authenticity into question).

In contrast, a **holder in due course** is a holder who, by meeting certain acquisition requirements (to be discussed shortly), takes an instrument *free* of most of the defenses and claims that could be asserted against the transferor.

EXAMPLE 13.19 Marcia Cambry signs a $1,000 note payable to Alex Jerrod in payment for some ancient Roman coins. Jerrod negotiates the note to Alicia Larson, who promises to pay Jerrod for it in thirty days. During the next month, Larson learns that Jerrod has breached his contract with Cambry by delivering coins that were not from the Roman era, as promised, and that for this reason Cambry will not honor the $1,000 note. Whether Larson can hold Cambry liable on the note depends on whether Larson has met the requirements for HDC status. If Larson has met these requirements and thus has HDC status, Larson is entitled to payment on the note. If Larson has not met these requirements, she has the status of an ordinary holder, and Cambry's defense of breach of contract against payment to Jerrod will also be effective against Larson. ●

Requirements for HDC Status

LEARNING OBJECTIVE 2

What are the requirements for attaining the status of a holder in due course (HDC)?

The basic requirements for attaining HDC status are set forth in UCC 3–302. A holder of a negotiable instrument is an HDC if she or he takes the instrument (1) for value, (2) in good faith, and (3) without notice that it is defective (such as when the instrument is overdue, dishonored, irregular, or incomplete). We now examine each of these requirements.

Taking for Value An HDC must have given *value* for the instrument [UCC 3–302(a)(2)(i)]. A person who receives an instrument as a gift or inherits it has not met the requirement of value. In these situations, the person becomes an ordinary holder and does not possess the rights of an HDC.

Under UCC 3–303(a), a holder takes an instrument for value if the holder has done any of the following:

1. Performed the promise for which the instrument was issued or transferred.
2. Acquired a security interest or other lien in the instrument, excluding a lien obtained by a judicial proceeding (which you will learn about in Chapter 15).
3. Taken the instrument in payment of, or as security for, a preexisting claim. **EXAMPLE 13.20** Zon owes Dwyer $2,000 on a past-due account. If Zon negotiates a $2,000 note signed by Gordon to Dwyer and Dwyer accepts it to discharge the overdue account balance, Dwyer has given value for the instrument. ●
4. Given a negotiable instrument as payment for the instrument. **EXAMPLE 13.21** Justin issued a $500 negotiable promissory note to Paulene. The note is due six months from the date issued. Paulene needs cash and does not want to wait for the maturity date to collect. She negotiates the note to her friend Kristen, who pays her $200 in cash and writes her a check—a negotiable instrument—for the balance of $300. Kristen has given full value for the note by paying $200 in cash and issuing Paulene the check for $300. ●
5. Given an irrevocable commitment (such as a letter of credit) as payment for the instrument.

If a person promises to perform or give value in the future, that person is not an HDC. A holder takes an instrument for value *only to the extent that the promise has been performed* [UCC 3–303(a)(1)]. Therefore, in the Larson-Cambry scenario, which was presented earlier as *Example 13.19*, Larson is not an HDC because she did not take the instrument (Cambry's note) for value—she has not yet paid Jerrod for the note. Thus, Cambry's defense of breach of contract is valid against Larson as well as Jerrod.

Exhibit 13.10 on the facing page illustrates these concepts.

Taking in Good Faith To qualify as an HDC, a holder must take the instrument in *good faith* [UCC 3–302(a)(2)(ii)]. This means that the holder must have acted honestly in

Exhibit 13.10 Taking for Value

By exchanging defective goods for the note, Jerrod breached his contract with Cambry. Cambry could assert this defense if Jerrod presented the note to her for payment. Jerrod exchanged the note for Larson's promise to pay in thirty days, however. Because Larson did not take the note for value, she is not a holder in due course. Thus, Cambry can assert against Larson the defense of Jerrod's breach when Larson submits the note to Cambry for payment. In contrast, if Larson had taken the note for value, Cambry could not assert that defense and would be liable to pay the note.

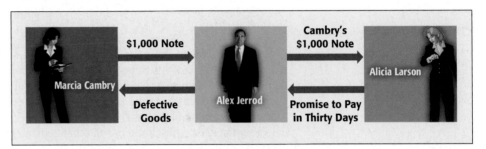

the process of acquiring the instrument. UCC 3–103(a)(4) defines *good faith* as "honesty in fact and the observance of reasonable commercial standards of fair dealing."

The good faith requirement applies only to the *holder*. It is immaterial whether the transferor acted in good faith. Thus, even a person who takes a negotiable instrument from a thief may become an HDC if the person acquired the instrument in good faith and had no reason to be suspicious of the transaction.

Because of the good faith requirement, courts must examine whether the purchaser, when acquiring the instrument, honestly believed that the instrument was not defective. **CASE EXAMPLE 13.22** Cassandra Demery worked as a bookkeeper at Clinton Georg's business, Freestyle, until she embezzled more than $200,000. Georg fired Demery and demanded repayment. Demery went to work for her parents' firm, Metro Fixtures, where she had some authority to write checks. Without specific authorization, however, she wrote a check to Freestyle for $189,000 on Metro's account and deposited it into Freestyle's account. She told Georg that the check was a loan to her from her family.

When Metro discovered Demery's theft, it filed a suit against Georg and Freestyle. Freestyle argued that it had taken the check in good faith and was an HDC. The Colorado Supreme Court agreed. Demery was the wrongdoer. Even though Metro did not authorize Demery to issue the check for $189,000, she had the authority to issue checks for Metro. Georg had no reason to know that Demery had lied about this check. Therefore, Metro would bear the loss.[5] ●

Taking without Notice
The final requirement for HDC status involves *notice* [UCC 3–302]. A person will not qualify for HDC protection if he or she is *on notice* (knows or has reason to know) that the instrument being acquired is defective in any one of the following ways [UCC 3–302(a)]:

1. It is overdue.
2. It has been dishonored.
3. It is part of a series of which at least one instrument has an uncured (uncorrected) default.
4. It contains an unauthorized signature or has been altered.
5. There is a defense against the instrument or a claim to it.
6. The instrument is so irregular or incomplete as to call its authenticity into question.

---

5. *Georg v. Metro Fixtures Contractors, Inc.*, 178 P.3d 1209 (Colo.Sup.Ct. 2008).

What Constitutes Notice?   A holder will be deemed to have notice if she or he (1) has actual knowledge of the defect, (2) has received written notice (such as a letter listing the serial numbers of stolen bearer instruments), or (3) has reason to know that a defect exists, given all the facts and circumstances known at the time in question [UCC 1–201(25)].

The holder must also have received the notice "at a time and in a manner that gives a reasonable opportunity to act on it" [UCC 3–302(f)]. Facts that a purchaser might know but that do not necessarily make the instrument defective, such as bankruptcy proceedings against the maker or drawer, do not constitute notice that the instrument is defective [UCC 3–302(b)].

Overdue Instruments   What constitutes notice that an instrument is overdue depends on whether it is a demand instrument (payable on demand) or a time instrument (payable at a definite time). A purchaser has notice that a *demand instrument* is overdue if she or he either takes the instrument knowing that demand has been made or takes the instrument an unreasonable length of time after its issue. For a check, a "reasonable time" is within ninety days after the date of the check. For all other demand instruments, what will be considered a reasonable time depends on the circumstances [UCC 3–304(a)].

Normally, a *time instrument* is overdue the day after its due date. Therefore, anyone who takes a time instrument after the due date is on notice that it is overdue [UCC 3–304(b)(2)]. Thus, if a promissory note due on May 15 is purchased on May 16, the purchaser will be an ordinary holder, not an HDC. If an instrument states that it is "Payable in thirty days," counting begins the day after the instrument is dated. Thus, a note dated December 1 that is payable in thirty days is due by midnight on December 31. If the payment date falls on a Sunday or holiday, the instrument is payable on the next business day.

Dishonor To refuse to pay or accept a negotiable instrument, whichever is required, even though the instrument is presented in a timely and proper manner.

Dishonored Instruments   An instrument is **dishonored** when it is presented in a timely manner for payment or acceptance, whichever is required, and payment or acceptance is refused. The holder is on notice if he or she (1) has actual knowledge of the dishonor or (2) has knowledge of facts that would lead him or her to suspect that an instrument has been dishonored [UCC 3–302(a)(2)]. Conversely, if a person purchasing an instrument does not know and has no reason to know that it has been dishonored, the person is not put on notice and therefore can become an HDC.

Notice of Claims or Defenses   A holder cannot become an HDC if she or he has notice of any claim to the instrument or any defense against it [UCC 3–302(a)(2)]. Any obvious irregularity on the face of an instrument that calls into question its validity or terms of ownership, or that creates an ambiguity as to the party to pay, will bar HDC status.

For instance, if an instrument is so incomplete on its face that an element of negotiability is lacking (for example, the amount is not filled in), the purchaser cannot become an HDC. A good forgery of a signature or the careful alteration of an instrument, however, can go undetected by reasonable examination. In that situation, the purchaser can qualify as an HDC.

Holder through an HDC

A person who does not qualify as an HDC but who derives his or her title through an HDC can acquire the rights and privileges of an HDC. This rule, which is sometimes called the **shelter principle**, is set out in UCC 3–203(b).

The shelter principle extends the benefits of HDC status and is designed to aid the HDC in readily disposing of the instrument. Under this rule, anyone—no matter how far removed from an HDC—who can ultimately trace his or her title back to an HDC may acquire the rights of an HDC. By extending the benefits of HDC status, the shelter principle promotes the marketability and free transferability of negotiable instruments.

► KNOW THIS ◄

A difference between the handwriting in the body of a check and the handwriting in the signature does not affect the validity of the check.

Shelter Principle The principle that the holder of a negotiable instrument who cannot qualify as a holder in due course (HDC), but who derives his or her title through an HDC, acquires the rights of an HDC.

There are some limitations on the shelter principle, though. Certain persons who formerly held instruments cannot improve their positions by later reacquiring the instruments from HDCs [UCC 3–203(b)]. If a holder participated in fraud or illegality affecting the instrument, or had notice of a claim or defense against an instrument, that holder is not allowed to improve her or his status by repurchasing the instrument from a later HDC.

Signature and Warranty Liability

Liability on negotiable instruments can arise either from a person's signature or from the warranties that are implied when the person presents the instrument for negotiation. Signature liability requires the transferor's signature, but no signature is required to impose warranty liability. We discuss signature liability (both primary and secondary) and warranty liability in the subsections that follow.

Signature Liability

LEARNING OBJECTIVE 3
What is the difference between signature liability and warranty liability?

The general rule is that every party, except a qualified indorser,[6] who signs a negotiable instrument is either primarily or secondarily liable for payment of that instrument when it comes due. Signature liability is contractual liability—no person will be held contractually liable for an instrument that he or she has not signed.

Primary Liability   A person who is primarily liable on a negotiable instrument is absolutely required to pay the instrument—unless, of course, he or she has a valid defense to payment [UCC 3–305]. Only *makers* and *acceptors* of instruments are primarily liable.

The maker of a promissory note unconditionally promises to pay the note. It is the maker's promise to pay that makes the note a negotiable instrument. If the instrument was incomplete when the maker signed it, the maker is obligated to pay it according to its stated terms or according to terms that were agreed on and later filled in to complete the instrument [UCC 3–115, 3–407(a), 3–412].

EXAMPLE 13.23   Tristan executes a preprinted promissory note to Sharon, without filling in the blank for a due date. If Sharon does not complete the form by adding the date, the note will be payable on demand. If Sharon subsequently fills in a due date that Tristan authorized, the note is payable on the stated due date. In either situation, Tristan (the maker) is obligated to pay the note. •

As mentioned earlier, an *acceptor* is a drawee that promises to pay an instrument, such as a *trade acceptance* or a *certified check* (to be discussed in Chapter 14), when it is presented for payment. Once a drawee indicates acceptance by signing the draft, the drawee becomes an acceptor and is obligated to pay the draft when it is presented for payment [UCC 3–409(a)]. Failure to pay an accepted draft when presented leads to primary signature liability.

Secondary Liability   *Drawers* and *indorsers* are secondarily liable. On a negotiable instrument, secondary liability is similar to the liability of a guarantor in a simple contract in the sense that it is *contingent liability*. In other words, a drawer or an indorser will be liable only if the party that is responsible for paying the instrument refuses to do so (dishonors the instrument). The drawer's secondary liability on drafts and checks does not arise until the drawee fails to pay or to accept the instrument, whichever is required [UCC 3–412, 3–415].

---

6. A qualified indorser—one who indorses "without recourse"—undertakes no contractual obligation to pay. A qualified indorser merely assumes warranty liability, which will be discussed later in this chapter.

Dishonor of an instrument thus triggers the liability of parties who are secondarily liable on the instrument—that is, the drawer and *unqualified* indorsers. **EXAMPLE 13.24** Nina Lee writes a check on her account at Universal Bank payable to the order of Stephen Miller. Universal Bank refuses to pay the check when Miller presents it for payment, thus dishonoring the check. In this situation, Lee will be liable to Miller on the basis of her secondary liability. ● Drawers are secondarily liable on drafts unless they disclaim their liability by drawing the instruments "without recourse" (if the draft is a check, however, a drawer cannot disclaim liability) [UCC 3–414(e)].

Parties are secondarily liable on a negotiable instrument only if the following events occur:[7]

1. The instrument is properly and timely presented.
2. The instrument is dishonored.
3. Timely notice of dishonor is given to the secondarily liable party.

Proper Presentment As previously explained, *presentment* occurs when a person presents an instrument either to the party liable on the instrument for payment or to a drawee for acceptance. The UCC requires that a holder present the instrument to the appropriate party, in a timely fashion, and give reasonable identification if requested [UCC 3–414(f), 3–415(e), 3–501].

The party to whom the instrument must be presented depends on the type of instrument involved. A note or CD must be presented to the maker for payment. A draft is presented to the drawee for acceptance, payment, or both. A check is presented to the drawee for payment [UCC 3–501(a), 3–502(b)].

Presentment can be made by any commercially reasonable means, including oral, written, or electronic communication [UCC 3–501(b)]. Ordinarily, it is effective when the demand for payment or acceptance is received (if presentment takes place after an established cutoff hour, it may be treated as occurring the next business day).

Timely Presentment Timeliness is important for proper presentment [UCC 3–414(f), 3–415(e), 3–501(b)(4)]. Failure to present an instrument on time is the most common reason for improper presentment and leads to unqualified indorsers being discharged from secondary liability.

The holder of a domestic check must present that check for payment or collection within thirty days of its *date* to hold the drawer secondarily liable, and within thirty days after its indorsement to hold the indorser secondarily liable. The time for proper presentment for different types of instruments is shown in Exhibit 13.11 on the facing page.

Dishonor As mentioned previously, an instrument is dishonored when the required acceptance or payment is refused or cannot be obtained within the prescribed time. An instrument is also dishonored when the required presentment is excused (as it would be, for example, if the maker had died) and the instrument is not properly accepted or paid [UCC 3–502(e), 3–504].

In certain situations, postponement of payment or refusal to pay an instrument will *not* dishonor the instrument. When presentment is made after an established cutoff hour (not earlier than 2:00 P.M.), for instance, a bank can postpone payment until the following business day without dishonoring the instrument. In addition, when the holder refuses to exhibit the instrument, provide reasonable identification (such as a thumbprint), or sign a receipt for the payment, a bank's refusal to pay does not dishonor the instrument.

---

7. These requirements are necessary for a secondarily liable party to have signature liability on a negotiable instrument, but they are not necessary for a secondarily liable party to have warranty liability (as discussed on pages 400–401).

Exhibit 13.11 Time for Proper Presentment

TYPE OF INSTRUMENT	FOR ACCEPTANCE	FOR PAYMENT
Time	On or before due date.	On due date.
Demand	Within a reasonable time (after date of issue or after secondary party becomes liable on the instrument).	Within a reasonable time.
Check	Not applicable.	Within thirty days of its date, to hold drawer secondarily liable. Within thirty days of indorsement, to hold indorser secondarily liable.

Proper Notice   Once an instrument has been dishonored, proper notice must be given to secondary parties (drawers and indorsers) for them to be held contractually liable. Notice may be given in any reasonable manner, including an oral, written, e-mail, or other electronic communication, as well as notice written or stamped on the instrument itself. A bank must give any necessary notice before its midnight deadline (midnight of the next banking day after receipt). Notice by any party other than a bank must be given within thirty days following the day of dishonor or the day on which the person who is secondarily liable receives notice of dishonor [UCC 3–503].

(Bluestocking/iStockphoto.com)

Who is responsible for validating the signature on a check?

Unauthorized Signatures

Unauthorized signatures arise in two situations—when a person forges another person's name on a negotiable instrument and when an *agent* (see Chapter 17) who lacks authority signs an instrument on behalf of a principal. The general rule is that an unauthorized signature is wholly inoperative and will not bind the person whose name is signed or forged.

EXAMPLE 13.25 Parker finds Dolby's checkbook lying in the street, writes out a check to himself, and forges Dolby's signature. Banks normally have a duty to determine whether a person's signature on a check is forged. If a bank fails to determine that Dolby's signature is not genuine and cashes the check for Parker, the bank will generally be liable to Dolby for the amount. • (The liability of banks for paying checks with forged signatures will be discussed further in Chapter 14.) Similarly, if an agent lacks the authority to sign the principal's name or has exceeded the authority given by the principal, the signature does not bind the principal but will bind the "unauthorized signer" [UCC 3–403(a)].

There are two exceptions to the general rule that an unauthorized signature will not bind the person whose name is signed:

1. When the person whose name is signed ratifies (affirms) the signature, he or she will be bound [UCC 3–403(a)].
2. When the negligence of the person whose name was forged substantially contributed to the forgery, a court may not allow the person to deny the effectiveness of an unauthorized signature [UCC 3–115, 3–406, 4–401(d)(2)].

Special Rules for Unauthorized Indorsements

Generally, when an instrument has a forged or unauthorized indorsement, the burden of loss falls on the first party to take the instrument. The reason for this general rule is that the first party to take an instrument is in the best position to prevent the loss.

EXAMPLE 13.26 Jen Nilson steals a check that is payable to Inga Leed and drawn on Universal Bank. Nilson indorses the check "Inga Leed" and presents the check to Universal

Bank for payment. The bank, without asking Nilson for identification, pays the check, and Nilson disappears. In this situation, Leed will not be liable on the check because her indorsement was forged. The bank will bear the loss, which it might have avoided if it had asked Nilson for identification. •

This general rule has two important exceptions that cause the loss to fall on the maker or drawer. These exceptions arise when an indorsement is made by an imposter or by a fictitious payee.

Imposter One who, by use of the mails, Internet, telephone, or personal appearance, induces a maker or drawer to issue an instrument in the name of an impersonated payee. Indorsements by imposters are treated as authorized indorsements under Article 3 of the UCC.

Imposter Rule   An **imposter** is someone who pretends to be someone else and, by appearing in person or using the mails, Internet, telephone, or other electronic communication, induces a maker or drawer to issue an instrument in the name of the impersonated payee. If the maker or drawer believes the imposter to be the named payee at the time of issue, the indorsement by the imposter is not treated as unauthorized when the instrument is transferred to an innocent party. This is because the maker or drawer *intended* the imposter to receive the instrument.

In these situations, the unauthorized indorsement of a payee's name can be as effective as if the real payee had signed. The *imposter rule* provides that an imposter's indorsement will be effective—that is, not a forgery—insofar as the drawer or maker is concerned [UCC 3–404(a)].

EXAMPLE 13.27   Carol impersonates Donna and induces Edward to write a check payable to the order of Donna. Carol, continuing to impersonate Donna, negotiates the check to First National Bank as payment on her loan there. As the drawer of the check, Edward is liable for its amount to First National. •

Fictitious Payee A payee on a negotiable instrument whom the maker or drawer did not intend to have an interest in the instrument. Indorsements by fictitious payees are treated as authorized indorsements under Article 3 of the UCC.

Fictitious Payee Rule   When a person causes an instrument to be issued to a payee who will have *no interest* in the instrument, the payee is referred to as a **fictitious payee**. A fictitious payee can be a person or firm that does not truly exist, or it may be an identifiable party that will not acquire any interest in the instrument. Under the UCC's *fictitious payee rule,* the payee's indorsement is not treated as a forgery, and an innocent holder can hold the maker or drawer liable on the instrument [UCC 3–404(b), 3–405].

Situations involving fictitious payees most often arise when (1) a dishonest employee deceives the employer into signing an instrument payable to a party with no right to receive payment on the instrument or (2) a dishonest employee or agent has the authority to issue an instrument on behalf of the employer. For example, an employee might open a bank account in the name of a fictitious company and then deceive her or his employer into signing checks payable to that company. Regardless of whether the dishonest employee actually signs the check or merely supplies the employer with names of fictitious creditors (or with true names of creditors having fictitious debts), the result is the same under the UCC.

> "Life is unfair."
>
> Milton Friedman, 1912–2006
> (American economist)

Warranty Liability

In addition to signature liability, transferors make certain implied warranties regarding the instruments that they are negotiating. Warranty liability arises even when a transferor does not indorse (sign) the instrument [UCC 3–416, 3–417].

Warranty liability is particularly important when a holder cannot hold a party liable on her or his signature, such as when a person delivers a bearer instrument. Unlike secondary signature liability, warranty liability is not subject to the conditions of proper presentment, dishonor, or notice of dishonor.

Warranties fall into two categories: those that arise on the *transfer* of a negotiable instrument and those that arise on *presentment*. Both transfer and presentment warranties attempt to shift liability back to a wrongdoer or to the person who dealt face to face with the wrongdoer and thus was in the best position to prevent the wrongdoing.

Transfer Warranties   A person who transfers an instrument *for consideration* makes certain warranties to the transferee and, if the transfer is by *indorsement*, to all subsequent transferees and holders who take the instrument in good faith. There are five **transfer warranties** [UCC 3–416]:[8]

Transfer Warranties Five implied warranties made by any person who transfers an instrument for consideration to the transferee and, if the transfer is by indorsement, to all subsequent transferees and holders who take the instrument in good faith.

1. The transferor is entitled to enforce the instrument.
2. All signatures are authentic and authorized.
3. The instrument has not been altered.
4. The instrument is not subject to a defense or claim of any party that can be asserted against the transferor.
5. The transferor has no knowledge of any insolvency (bankruptcy) proceedings against the maker, the acceptor, or the drawer of the instrument.

Presentment Warranties   Any person who presents an instrument for payment or acceptance makes the following **presentment warranties** to any other person who in good faith pays or accepts the instrument [UCC 3–417(a), 3–417(d)]:

Presentment Warranties Implied warranties, made by any person who presents an instrument for payment or acceptance, that (1) the person is entitled to enforce the instrument or is authorized to act on behalf of a person who is so entitled, (2) the instrument has not been altered, and (3) the person has no knowledge that the drawer's signature is unauthorized.

1. The person obtaining payment or acceptance is entitled to enforce the instrument or is authorized to obtain payment or acceptance on behalf of a person who is entitled to enforce the instrument. (This is, in effect, a warranty that there are no missing or unauthorized indorsements.)
2. The instrument has not been altered.
3. The person obtaining payment or acceptance has no knowledge that the signature of the issuer of the instrument is unauthorized.[9]

These warranties are referred to as presentment warranties because they protect the person to whom the instrument is presented. They often have the effect of shifting liability back to the party that was in the best position to prevent the wrongdoing.

The second and third presentment warranties do not apply to makers, acceptors, and drawers when the presenter is an HDC. It is assumed that a drawer or a maker will recognize his or her own signature and that a maker or an acceptor will recognize whether an instrument has been materially altered.

Defenses, Limitations, and Discharge

LEARNING OBJECTIVE 4
Certain defenses are valid against all holders, including HDCs. What are these defenses called? Name four defenses that fall within this category.

Defenses can bar collection from persons who would otherwise be primarily or secondarily liable on a negotiable instrument. There are two general categories of defenses—*universal defenses* and *personal defenses*.

Universal Defenses

Universal Defenses Defenses that are valid against all holders of a negotiable instrument, including holders in due course (HDCs) and holders with the rights of HDCs.

Universal defenses (also called *real defenses*) are valid against *all* holders, including HDCs and holders who take through an HDC. Universal defenses include those described here.

1. *Forgery of a signature on the instrument.* A forged signature cannot bind the person whose name is used unless that person ratifies (approves or validates) the signature or is barred from denying it (because the forgery was made possible by the maker's or drawer's negligence, for example) [UCC 3–403(a)]. Thus, when an instrument is forged, the person

---

8. A 2002 amendment to UCC 3–416(a) adds a sixth warranty: "with respect to a remotely created consumer item," such as an electronic check, drawn on a consumer account, which is not created by the payor bank and does not contain the drawer's handwritten signature. Under this amendment, a bank that accepts and pays the instrument warrants to the next bank in the collection chain that the consumer authorized the item in that amount.
9. As discussed in Footnote 8, amendments to Article 3 of the UCC provide additional protection for "remotely created" consumer items in the context of presentment also [see Amended UCC 3–417(a)(4)].

whose name is forged normally has no liability to pay any holder or any HDC the value of the instrument.

2. *Fraud in the execution.* If a person is deceived into signing a negotiable instrument, believing that she or he is signing something other than a negotiable instrument (such as a receipt), fraud in the execution is committed against the signer [UCC 3–305(a)(1)]. Fraud in the execution is a universal defense that can be asserted unless a reasonable inquiry would have revealed the nature and terms of the instrument.

3. *Material alteration.* An alteration is material if it changes the obligations of the parties in the instrument *in any way.* Material alterations include completing an instrument, adding words or numbers, or making any unauthorized changes that affect the obligation of a party [UCC 3–407(a)]. It is not a material alteration, however, to correct the maker's address or to change the figures on a check so that they agree with the written amount. Material alteration is a *complete defense* against an ordinary holder, but only a partial defense against an HDC.

4. *Discharge in bankruptcy.* Discharge in bankruptcy (see Chapter 15) is an absolute defense on any instrument, regardless of the status of the holder, because the purpose of bankruptcy is to settle finally all of the insolvent party's debts [UCC 3–305(a)(1)].

5. *Minority.* Minority, or infancy, is a universal defense only to the extent that state law recognizes it as a defense to a simple contract (see page 228 of Chapter 8) [UCC 3–305(a)(1)(i)].

6. *Illegality, mental incapacity, or extreme duress.* When the law declares an instrument to be void because it was issued in connection with illegal conduct, illegality is a universal defense. Similarly, if a person who signed the instrument has been declared by a court to be mentally incompetent or was a under an immediate threat of force or violence (such as at gunpoint), the defense is universal [UCC 3–305(a)(1)(ii)].

KNOW THIS

Words outweigh figures on a negotiable instrument if the written amount and the amount given in figures are different.

Personal Defense A defense that can be used to avoid payment to an ordinary holder of a negotiable instrument but not a holder in due course (HDC) or a holder with the rights of an HDC.

LEARNING OBJECTIVE 5
Certain defenses can be used against an ordinary holder but are not effective against an HDC. What are these defenses called? Name four defenses that fall within this category.

Personal Defenses

Personal defenses (sometimes called *limited defenses*), such as those described here, can be used to avoid payment to an ordinary holder of a negotiable instrument, but not to an HDC or a holder with the rights of an HDC.

1. *Breach of contract or breach of warranty.* When there is a breach of the underlying contract for which the negotiable instrument was issued, the maker of a note can refuse to pay it, or the drawer of a check can stop payment.

2. *Lack or failure of consideration.* The absence of consideration (value) may be a successful personal defense in some instances [UCC 3–303(b), 3–305(a)(2)]. **EXAMPLE 13.28** Tara gives Clem, as a gift, a note that states, "I promise to pay you $100,000." Clem accepts the note. Because there is no consideration for Tara's promise, a court will not enforce the promise. •

3. *Fraud in the inducement (ordinary fraud).* A person who issues a negotiable instrument based on false statements by the other party will be able to avoid payment on that instrument, unless the holder is an HDC.

4. *Illegality, mental incapacity, or ordinary duress.* If the law declares that an instrument is voidable because of illegality, mental incapacity, or ordinary duress, the defense is personal [UCC 3–305(a)(1)(ii)].

Federal Limitations on the Rights of HDCs

Under the HDC doctrine, a consumer who purchased a defective product (such as a defective automobile) would continue to be liable to HDCs even if the consumer returned the defective product to the retailer. To protect consumers, in 1976 the Federal Trade

Commission (FTC) issued a rule that effectively abolished the HDC doctrine in consumer transactions. How does this rule curb the rights of HDCs? See this chapter's *Landmark in the Law* feature below.

Discharge from Liability

Discharge from liability on an instrument can come from payment, cancellation, or material alteration. The liability of all parties is discharged when the party primarily liable on the instrument pays to the holder the full amount due [UCC 3–602, 3–603]. Payment by any other party discharges only the liability of that party and subsequent parties.

Intentional cancellation by the holder of an instrument discharges the liability of all parties [UCC 3–604]. Intentionally writing "Paid" across the face of an instrument cancels it, as does intentionally tearing it up. If a holder intentionally crosses out a party's signature, that party's liability and the liability of subsequent indorsers who have already indorsed the instrument are discharged. Materially altering an instrument may discharge the liability of any party affected by the alteration, as previously discussed [UCC 3–407(b)]. (An HDC may be able to enforce a materially altered instrument against its maker or drawer according to the instrument's original terms, however.)

LANDMARK IN THE LAW
Federal Trade Commission Rule 433

In 1976, the Federal Trade Commission (FTC) issued Rule 433,[a] which severely limited the rights of HDCs that purchase instruments arising out of *consumer credit* transactions. The rule, entitled "Preservation of Consumers' Claims and Defenses," applies to any seller or lessor of goods or services who takes or receives a consumer credit contract. The rule also applies to a seller or lessor who accepts as full or partial payment for a sale or lease the proceeds of any purchase-money loan[b] made in connection with any consumer credit contract.

Under the rule, these parties must include the following provision in the consumer credit contract:

NOTICE

ANY HOLDER OF THIS CONSUMER CREDIT CONTRACT IS SUBJECT TO ALL CLAIMS AND DEFENSES WHICH THE DEBTOR COULD ASSERT AGAINST THE SELLER OF GOODS OR SERVICES OBTAINED PURSUANT HERETO OR WITH THE PROCEEDS HEREOF. RECOVERY HEREUNDER BY THE DEBTOR SHALL NOT EXCEED AMOUNTS PAID BY THE DEBTOR HEREUNDER.

Thus, a consumer who is a party to a consumer credit transaction can bring any defense she or he has against the seller of a product against a subsequent holder as well. In essence, the FTC rule places an HDC of the negotiable instrument in the position of a contract assignee. The rule makes the buyer's duty to pay conditional on the seller's full performance of the contract. Finally, the rule clearly reduces the degree of transferability of negotiable instruments resulting from consumer credit contracts.

What if the seller does not include the notice in a promissory note and then sells the note to a third party, such as a bank? In this situation, the seller has violated the rule, but the bank has not. Because the FTC rule does not prohibit third parties from purchasing notes or credit contracts that do *not* contain the required provision, the third party does not become subject to the buyer's defenses against the seller. Thus, a few consumers remain unprotected by the FTC rule.

Application to Today's World *The FTC rule has been invoked in many cases involving automobiles that turned out to be "lemons," even when the consumer credit contract did not contain the FTC notice. In these and other actions to collect on notes issued to finance purchases, when the notice was not included in the accompanying documents, the courts have generally implied its existence as a contract term.*

---

a. 16 C.F.R. Section 433.2. The rule was enacted pursuant to the FTC's authority under the Federal Trade Commission Act, 15 U.S.C. Sections 41–58.

b. In a *purchase-money loan*, a seller or lessor advances funds to a buyer or lessee, through a credit contract, for the purchase or lease of goods.

Discharge of liability can also occur when a holder impairs another party's right of recourse (right to seek reimbursement) on the instrument [UCC 3–605]. This occurs when, for example, the holder releases, or agrees not to sue, a party against whom the indorser has a right of recourse.

Reviewing . . . Negotiable Instruments

Robert Durbin, a student, borrowed funds from a bank for his education and signed a promissory note for their repayment. The bank loaned the funds under a federal program designed to assist students at postsecondary institutions. Under this program, repayment ordinarily begins nine to twelve months after the student borrower fails to carry at least one-half of the normal full-time course load at his or her school. The federal government guarantees that the note will be fully paid. If the student defaults on the payments, the lender presents the current balance—principal, interest, and costs—to the government. When the government pays the balance, it becomes the lender, and the borrower owes the government directly. After Durbin defaulted on his note, the government paid the lender the balance due and took possession of the note. Durbin then refused to pay the government, claiming that the government was not the holder of the note. The government filed a suit in a federal district court against Durbin to collect the amount due. Using the information presented in the chapter, answer the following questions.

1. Using the categories discussed in the chapter, what type of negotiable instrument was the note that Durbin signed (an order to pay or a promise to pay)? Explain.
2. Suppose that the note did not state a specific interest rate but instead referred to a statute that established the maximum interest rate for government-guaranteed student loans. Would the note fail to meet the requirements for negotiability in that situation? Why or why not?
3. How does a party who is not named by a negotiable instrument (in this situation, the government) obtain a right to enforce the instrument?
4. Suppose that, in court, Durbin argues that because the school closed down before he could finish his education, there was a failure of consideration: he did not get something of value in exchange for his promise to pay. Assuming that the government is a holder of the promissory note, would this argument likely be successful against it? Why or why not?

DEBATE THIS We should eliminate the status of holder in due course for those who possess negotiable instruments.

BUSINESS APPLICATION

Pitfalls When Writing and Indorsing Checks*

As a businessperson (and as a consumer), you will certainly be writing and receiving checks. Both activities can involve pitfalls.

Checks Drawn in Blank

The danger in signing a blank check is clear. Anyone can write in an unauthorized amount and cash the check. Although you may be

able to assert lack of authorization against the person who filled in the check, subsequent holders of the properly indorsed check may be able to enforce the check as completed. While you are haggling with the person who inserted the unauthorized amount and who may not be able to repay it, you will also have to honor the check for the unauthorized amount to a subsequent holder in due course.

*This *Business Application* is not meant to substitute for the services of an attorney who is licensed to practice law in your state.

Checks Payable to "Cash"

It is equally dangerous to write out and sign a check payable to "cash" until you are actually at the bank. Remember that checks payable to "cash" are bearer instruments. This means that if you lose or misplace the check, anybody who finds it can present it (with proper identification) to the bank for payment.

Checks Indorsed in Blank

A negotiable instrument with a blank indorsement also has dangers. As a bearer instrument, it may be as easily transferred as cash. Therefore, when you make a bank deposit, you should sign (indorse) the back of the check in blank only in the presence of a teller. If you choose to indorse the check ahead of time, always insert the words "For deposit only" before you sign your name. As a precaution, you should consider obtaining an indorsement stamp from your bank. Then, when you receive a check payable to your business, you can indorse it immediately. The stamped indorsement will indicate that the check is for deposit only to your business account specified by the number.

Checklist for the Use of Negotiable Instruments

1. A good rule of thumb is never to sign a blank check.
2. Another good rule of thumb is never to write and sign a check payable to "cash" until you are actually at the bank. If you must write the check ahead of time, consider making the check payable to the bank rather than to "cash."
3. Be wary of indorsing a check in blank unless a bank teller is simultaneously giving you a receipt for your deposit.
4. Consider obtaining an indorsement stamp from your bank so that when you receive checks, you can immediately indorse them "for deposit only" to your account.

Key Terms

acceleration clause 386	draft 379	maker 381	qualified indorsement 391
acceptance 379	drawee 379	negotiable instrument 378	restrictive indorsement 392
acceptor 385	drawer 379	negotiation 389	shelter principle 396
bearer 387	extension clause 386	order instrument 386	special indorsement 390
bearer instrument 387	fictitious payee 400	payee 379	transfer warranties 401
blank indorsement 390	holder 386	personal defense 402	trust indorsement 392
certificate of deposit (CD) 381	holder in due course (HDC) 394	presentment 385	universal defenses 401
check 380	imposter 400	presentment warranties 401	
dishonor 396	indorsement 389	promissory note 381	

Chapter Summary: Negotiable Instruments

Types of Instruments (See pages 379–382.)	The UCC specifies four types of negotiable instruments: drafts, checks, promissory notes, and certificates of deposit (CDs). These instruments fall into two basic classifications: 1. *Demand instruments versus time instruments*—A demand instrument is payable on demand (when the holder presents it to the maker or drawer). A time instrument is payable at a future date. 2. *Orders to pay versus promises to pay*—Checks and drafts are *orders* to pay. Promissory notes and CDs are *promises* to pay.

Requirements for Negotiability
(See pages 382–387.)
	To be negotiable, an instrument must meet the requirements stated below.
	1. *Be in writing*—A writing can be on anything that is readily transferable and has a degree of permanence [UCC 3–103(a)(6), (9)].
	2. *Be signed by the maker or drawer*—The signature can be anywhere on the face of the instrument, can be in any form (including a rubber stamp), and can be made in a representative capacity [UCC 3–103(a)(3), 3–401(b)].
	3. *Be an unconditional promise or order to pay*—
	  a. A promise must be more than a mere acknowledgment of a debt [UCC 3–103(a)(6), (9)].
	  b. The words "I/We promise" or "Pay" meet this criterion.
	  c. Payment cannot be expressly conditioned on the occurrence of an event and cannot be made subject to or governed by another contract [UCC 3–106].

Continued

Chapter Summary: Negotiable Instruments—Continued

Requirements for Negotiability—Continued	4. *State a fixed amount of money*—
	  a. An amount is considered a fixed sum if it is ascertainable from the face of the instrument or (for the interest rate) readily determinable by a formula described in the instrument [UCC –104(a), 3–112(b)].
	  b. Any medium of exchange recognized as the currency of a government as money [UCC 3—201(24)].
	5. *Be payable on demand or at a definite time*—
	  a. Any instrument that is payable on sight, presentation, or issue, or that does not state any time for payment, is a demand instrument [UCC 3—104(a)(2)].
	  b. An instrument is still payable at a definite time, even if it is payable on or before a stated date or within a fixed period after sight or if the drawer or maker has an option to extend the time for a definite period [UCC 3–108(a), (b), (c)].
	  c. Acceleration clauses do not affect the negotiability of the instrument.
	6. *Be payable to order or bearer*—
	  a. An order instrument must identify the payee with certainty.
	  b. An instrument that indicates it is not payable to an identified person is payable to bearer [UCC 3–109(a)(3)].

Factors That Do Not Affect Negotiability (See page 388.)	Certain ambiguities or omissions will not affect an instrument's negotiability. See page 388 for a list of these factors.

Transfer of Instruments (See pages 388–393.)	1. *Transfer by assignment*—A transfer by assignment to an assignee gives the assignee only those rights that the assignor possessed. Any defenses against payment that can be raised against an assignor normally can be raised against the assignee.
	2. *Transfer by negotiation*—An order instrument is negotiated by indorsement and delivery. A bearer instrument is negotiated by delivery only.
	3. *Indorsements*—
	  a. *Blank indorsements* do not specify a particular indorsee and can consist of a mere signature (see Exhibit 13.5 on page 390).
	  b. *Special indorsements* contain the signature of the indorser and identify the indorsee (see Exhibit 13.6 on page 390).
	  c. *Qualified indorsements* contain language, such as the notation "without recourse," that indicates the indorser is not guaranteeing payment of the instrument (see Exhibit 13.7 on page 391).
	  d. *Restrictive indorsements*, such as "For deposit only," require the indorsee to comply with certain instructions regarding the funds involved, but do not prohibit further negotiation of the instrument.

Holder in Due Course (HDC) (See pages 393–397.)	1. *Holder*—A person in possession of an instrument drawn, issued, or indorsed to him or her, to his or her order, to bearer, or in blank. A holder obtains only those rights that the transferor had in the instrument.
	2. *Holder in due course (HDC)*—A holder who, by meeting certain acquisition requirements (summarized next), takes an instrument free of most defenses and claims to which the transferor was subject.
	3. *Requirements for HDC status*—To be an HDC, a holder must take the instrument:
	  a. For value—A holder must give value to become an HDC and can take an instrument for value in any of the five ways listed on page 394 [UCC 3–303].
	  b. In good faith—Good faith is defined as "honesty in fact and the observance of reasonable commercial standards of fair dealing" [UCC 3–103(a)(4)].
	  c. Without notice—To be an HDC, a holder must not be on notice that the instrument is defective because it is overdue, has been dishonored, is part of a series of which at least one instrument has a uncured defect, contains an unauthorized signature or has been altered, or is so irregular or incomplete as to call its authenticity into question.
	4. *Shelter principle*—A holder who cannot qualify as an HDC has the *rights* of an HDC if the holder derives her or his title through an HDC, unless the holder engaged in fraud or illegality affecting the instrument [UCC 3–203(b)].

Signature and Warranty Liability (See pages 397–401.)	Liability on negotiable instruments can arise either from a person's signature or from the (transfer and presentment) warranties that are implied when a person presents the instrument for negotiation. 1. *Signature liability*—Every party (except a qualified indorser) who signs a negotiable instrument is either primarily or secondarily liable for payment of the instrument when it comes due. a. Primary liability—Makers and acceptors are primarily liable (an *acceptor* is a drawee that promises in writing to pay an instrument when it is presented for payment at a later time) [UCC 3–115, 3–407, 3–409, 3–412].

Chapter Summary: Negotiable Instruments—Continued

Signature and Warranty Liability—Continued	b. Secondary liability—Drawers and indorsers are secondarily liable [UCC 3–412, 3–414, 3–415, 3–501, 3–502, 3–503]. Parties are secondarily liable on an instrument only if (1) presentment is proper and timely, (2) the instrument is dishonored, and (3) they received timely notice of dishonor.
	2. *Transfer warranties*—Any person who transfers an instrument for consideration makes five warranties to subsequent transferees and holders [UCC 3–416]. See the list on page 401.
	3. *Presentment warranties*—Any person who presents an instrument for payment or acceptance makes three warranties to any person who in good faith pays or accepts the instrument [UCC 3–417(a), 3–417(d)]. See the list on page 401.
Defenses, Limitations, and Discharge (See pages 401–404.)	1. *Universal (real) defenses*—The following defenses are valid against all holders, including HDCs and holders with the rights of HDCs [UCC 3–305, 3–403, 3–407]: a. Forgery. b. Fraud in the execution. c. Material alteration. d. Discharge in bankruptcy. e. Minority—if the contract is voidable under state law. f. Illegality, mental incapacity, or extreme duress—if the contract is void under state law.
	2. *Personal (limited) defenses*—The following defenses are valid against ordinary holders but not against HDCs or holders with the rights of HDCs [UCC 3–303, 3–305]: a. Breach of contract or breach of warranty. b. Lack or failure of consideration (value). c. Fraud in the inducement. d. Illegality and mental incapacity—if the contract is voidable. e. Ordinary duress or undue influence that renders the contract voidable.
	3. *Federal limitations on the rights of HDCs*—Rule 433 of the Federal Trade Commission limits the rights of HDCs who purchase instruments arising out of consumer credit transactions. The rule allows a consumer who is a party to a consumer credit transaction to bring any defense he or she has against the seller against a subsequent holder as well, even if the subsequent holder is an HDC.
	4. *Discharge from liability*—All parties to a negotiable instrument will be discharged when the party primarily liable on it pays to the holder the full amount due. Discharge can also occur in other circumstances (if the instrument has been canceled or materially altered, for example) [UCC 3–602 through 3–605].

ExamPrep

ISSUE SPOTTERS

1. Sabrina owes $600 to Yale, who asks Sabrina to sign an instrument for the debt. If included on that instrument, which of the following would prevent its negotiability—"I.O.U. $600," "I promise to pay $600," or an instruction to Sabrina's bank stating, "I wish you would pay $600 to Yale"? Why? **(See pages 383–384.)**

2. Rye signs corporate checks for Suchin Corporation. Rye writes a check payable to U-All Company, even though Suchin does not owe U-All anything. Rye signs the check, forges U-All's indorsement, and cashes the check at Viceroy Bank, the drawee. Does Suchin have any recourse against the bank for the payment? Why or why not? **(See pages 399–400.)**

–Check your answers to the Issue Spotters against the answers provided in Appendix E at the end of this text.

BEFORE THE TEST

Go to www.cengagebrain.com, enter the ISBN 9781133191353 and click on "Find" to locate this textbook's Web site. Then, click on "Access Now" under "Study Tools," and select Chapter 13 at the top. There, you will find a Practice Quiz that you can take to assess your mastery of the concepts in this chapter, as well as Flashcards, a Glossary of important terms, and Video Questions (when assigned).

For Review

Answers to the even-numbered questions in this For Review section can be found in Appendix F at the end of this text.

1. What requirements must an instrument meet to be negotiable?
2. What are the requirements for attaining the status of a holder in due course (HDC)?
3. What is the difference between signature liability and warranty liability?
4. Certain defenses are valid against all holders, including HDCs. What are these defenses called? Name four defenses that fall within this category.
5. Certain defenses can be used against an ordinary holder but are not effective against an HDC. What are these defenses called? Name four defenses that fall within this category.

Business Scenarios and Case Problems

13–1 Indorsements. A check drawn by David for $500 is made payable to the order of Matthew and issued to Matthew. Matthew owes his landlord $500 in rent and transfers the check to his landlord with the following indorsement: "For rent paid. [Signed] Matthew." Matthew's landlord has contracted to have Lambert do some landscaping on the property. When Lambert insists on immediate payment, the landlord transfers the check to Lambert without indorsement. Later, to pay for some palm trees purchased from Green's Nursery, Lambert transfers the check with the following indorsement: "Pay to Green's Nursery, without recourse. [Signed] Lambert." Green's Nursery sends the check to its bank indorsed "For deposit only. [Signed] Green's Nursery." **(See pages 389–393.)**

1. Classify each of these indorsements.
2. Was the transfer from Matthew's landlord to Lambert, without indorsement, an assignment or a negotiation? Explain.

13–2 ❓ **Question with Sample Answer—Negotiable Instruments.** Muriel Evans writes the following note on the back of an envelope: "I, Muriel Evans, promise to pay Karen Marvin or bearer $100 on demand." Is this a negotiable instrument? Discuss fully. **(See pages 382–383.)**

—**For a sample answer to Question 13–2, go to Appendix G at the end of this text.**

13–3 Signature Liability. Marion makes a promissory note payable to the order of Perry. Perry indorses the note by writing "without recourse, Perry" and transfers the note for value to Steven. Steven, in need of cash, negotiates the note to Harriet by indorsing it with the words "Pay to Harriet, [signed] Steven." On the due date, Harriet presents the note to Marion for payment, only to learn that Marion has filed for bankruptcy and will have all debts (including the note) discharged in bankruptcy. Discuss fully whether Harriet can hold Marion, Perry, or Steven liable on the note. **(See pages 397–400.)**

13–4 Holder. Germanie Fequiere signed a note payable to BNC Mortgage. As security for the note, Fequiere signed a mortgage on certain real property. BNC indorsed the note in blank. Later, Chase Home Finance, LLC, became a holder in due course of the note and the holder of the mortgage.

When Fequiere failed to make payments on the note, Chase sought to foreclose on the property. Fequiere argued that the mortgage had not been properly transferred to Chase. If that is true, can Chase obtain payment on the note? Why or why not? [*Chase Home Finance, LLC v. Fequiere,* 119 Conn.App. 570, 989 A.2d 606 (2010)] **(See pages 393–394.)**

13–5 Negotiability. Michael Scotto borrowed $2,970 from Cindy Vinueza. Both of their signatures appeared at the bottom of a note that stated, "I Michael Scotto owe Cindy Vinueza $2,970 (two thousand and nine-hundred & seventy dollars) & agree to pay her back in full. Signed on this 26th day of September 2009." More than a year later, Vinueza filed a suit against Scotto to recover on the note. Scotto admitted that he had borrowed the funds, but he contended—without proof—that he had paid Vinueza in full. Is this note negotiable? Which party is likely to prevail? Why? [*Vinueza v. Scotto,* 30 Misc.3d 1229, 924 N.Y.S.2d 312 (1 Dist. 2011)] **(See pages 382–388.)**

13–6 ⚖ **Case Problem with Sample Answer—Payable on Demand or at a Definite Time.** Abby Novel signed a handwritten note that read, "Glen Gallwitz 1-8-2002 loaned me $5,000 at 6 percent interest a total of $10,000.00." The note did not state a time for repayment. Novel used the funds to manufacture and market a patented jewelry display design. More than seven years after Novel signed the note, Gallwitz filed a suit to recover the stated amount. Novel claimed that she did not have to pay because the note was not negotiable—it was incomplete. Is she correct? Explain. [*Gallwitz v. Novel,* 2011-Ohio-297, (5 Dist. 2011)] **(See page 385.)**

—**For a sample answer to Problem 13–6, go to Appendix H at the end of this text.**

13–7 Defenses. Thomas Klutz obtained a franchise from Kahala Franchise Corp. to operate a Samurai Sam's restaurant. Under their agreement, Klutz could transfer the franchise only if he obtained Kahala's approval and paid a transfer fee. Without telling Kahala, Klutz sold the restaurant to William Thorbecke. Thorbecke signed a note for the price. When Kahala learned of the deal, the franchisor told Thorbecke to stop using the

Samurai Sam's name. Thorbecke stopped paying on the note, and Klutz filed a claim for the unpaid amount. In defense, Thorbecke asserted breach of contract and fraud. Are these defenses effective against Klutz? Explain. [*Kahala Franchise Corp. v. Hit Enterprises, LLC,* 159 Wash.App. 1013, (Div. 2 2011)] **(See page 402.)**

13–8 Defenses. Damion and Kiya Carmichael took out a loan from Ameriquest Mortgage Co. to refinance their mortgage. They signed a note to make monthly payments on the loan. Later, Deutsche Bank National Trust Co. acquired the note. The Carmichaels stopped making payments and filed for bankruptcy. Deutsche asked the court to foreclose on the mortgage. The Carmichaels asserted that they had been fraudulently induced to make the loan and sign the note. Was the bank free of this defense? Explain. [*In re Carmichael,* 443 Bankr. 698 (E.D.Pa. 2011)] **(See page 402.)**

13–9 ⬌ **A Question of Ethics—Promissory Notes.** Clarence Morgan, Jr., owned Easy Way Automotive, a car dealership in D'Lo, Mississippi. Easy Way sold a truck to Loyd Barnard, who signed a note for the amount of the price payable to Trustmark National Bank in six months. Before the note came due, Barnard returned the truck to Easy Way, which sold it to another buyer. Using some of the proceeds from the second sale, Easy Way sent a check to Trustmark to pay Barnard's

note. Meanwhile, Barnard obtained another truck from Easy Way financed through another six-month note payable to Trustmark. After eight of these deals, some of which involved more than one truck, an Easy Way check to Trustmark was dishonored. In a suit in a Mississippi state court, Trustmark sought to recover the amounts of two of the notes from Barnard. Trustmark had not secured titles to two of the trucks covered by the notes, however, and this complicated Barnard's efforts to reclaim the vehicles from the later buyers. [*Trustmark National Bank v. Barnard,* 930 So.2d 1281 (Miss.App. 2006)] **(See pages 381, 397–399.)**

1. On what basis might Barnard be liable on the Trustmark notes? Would he be primarily or secondarily liable? Could this liability be discharged on the theory that Barnard's right of recourse had been impaired when Trustmark did not secure titles to the trucks covered by the notes? Explain.

2. Easy Way's account had been subject to other recent overdrafts, and a week after the check to Trustmark was returned for insufficient funds, Morgan committed suicide. At the same time, Barnard was unable to obtain a mortgage because the unpaid notes affected his credit rating. How do the circumstances of this case underscore the importance of practicing business ethics?

Critical Thinking and Writing Assignments

13–10 💡 **Business Law Critical Thinking Group Assignment.** Peter Gowin was an employee of a granite countertop business owned by Joann Stathis. In November 2012, Gowin signed a promissory note agreeing to pay $12,500 in order to become a co-owner of the business. The note was dated January 15, 2012 (ten months before it was signed) and required him to make installment payments starting in February 2012. Stathis told Gowin not to worry about the note and never requested any payments. Gowin continued to work at the business until 2014 when he quit, claiming that he owned half of the business. Stathis argued that Gowin was not a co-owner because he had never paid the $12,500 into the business.

1. The first group will formulate an argument in favor of Stathis that Gowin did not own any interest in the business because he had never paid the $12,500.

2. The second group will evaluate the strength of Gowin's argument. Gowin claimed that because compliance with the stated dates was impossible, the note effectively did not state a date for its payment and therefore was a demand note under UCC 3–108(a). Because no demand for payment had been made, Gowin argued that his obligation to pay had not arisen and the termination of his ownership interest in the granite business was improper.

Checks and Banking in the Digital Age

(Paul Paladin/Shutterstock.com)

LEARNING OBJECTIVES

The five learning objectives below are designed to help improve your understanding of the chapter. After reading this chapter, you should be able to answer the following questions:

1 What type of check does a bank agree in advance to accept when the check is presented for payment?

2 When may a bank properly dishonor a customer's check without being liable to the customer?

3 What duties does the Uniform Commercial Code impose on a bank's customers with regard to forged and altered checks? What are the consequences if a customer is negligent in performing those duties?

4 What is electronic check presentment, and how does it differ from the traditional check-clearing process?

5 What are the four most common types of electronic fund transfers?

"Money is just what we use to keep tally."
—Henry Ford, 1863–1947 (American automobile manufacturer)

Checks are the most common type of negotiable instruments regulated by the Uniform Commercial Code (UCC). Checks are convenient to use because they serve as a substitute for cash. Thus, as Henry Ford said in the chapter-opening quotation, checks help us to "keep tally." To be sure, most students today tend to use debit cards rather than checks for many retail transactions. Not only do debit cards now account for more retail payments than checks, but payments are increasingly being made via smartphones, iPads, and other mobile devices, as we discuss later in this chapter. Nonetheless, commercial checks remain an integral part of the U.S. economic system.

Articles 3 and 4 of the UCC govern issues relating to checks. Article 4 of the UCC governs bank deposits and collections as well as bank-customer relationships. Article 4 also regulates the relationships of banks with one another as they process checks for payment, and it establishes a framework for deposit and checking agreements between a bank and its customers. A check therefore may fall within the scope of Article 3 and yet be subject to the provisions of Article 4 while in the course of collection. If a conflict between Article 3 and Article 4 arises, Article 4 controls [UCC 4–102(a)].

Checks

As explained in Chapter 13 on page 380, a *check* is a special type of draft that is drawn on a bank, ordering the bank to pay a fixed amount of funds on demand [UCC 3–104(f)]. Article 4 defines a *bank* as "a person engaged in the business of banking, including a savings bank, savings and loan association, credit union or trust company" [UCC 4–105(1)]. If any other institution (such as a brokerage firm) handles a check for payment or for collection, the check is not covered by Article 4.

Recall from the preceding chapter that a person who writes a check is called the *drawer*. The drawer is a depositor in the bank on which the check is drawn. The person to whom the check is payable is the *payee*. The bank or financial institution on which the check is drawn is the *drawee*. When Anita Cruzak writes a check from her checking account to pay her college tuition, she is the drawer, her bank is the drawee, and her college is the payee. We now look at some special types of checks.

Cashier's Checks

Cashier's Check A check drawn by a bank on itself.

Checks usually are three-party instruments, but on certain types of checks, the bank can serve as both the drawer and the drawee. For example, when a bank draws a check on itself, the check is called a **cashier's check** and is a negotiable instrument at the moment it is issued (see Exhibit 14.1 below) [UCC 3–104(g)]. Normally, a cashier's check indicates a specific payee. In effect, with a cashier's check, the bank assumes responsibility for paying the check, thus making the check more readily acceptable as a substitute for cash.

EXAMPLE 14.1 Kramer needs to pay a moving company $8,000 for moving his household goods to his new home in another state. The moving company requests payment in the form of a cashier's check. Kramer goes to a bank (he does not need to have an account at the bank) and purchases a cashier's check, payable to the moving company, in the amount of $8,000. Kramer has to pay the bank the $8,000 for the check, plus a small service fee. He then gives the check to the moving company. •

Exhibit 14.1 A Cashier's Check

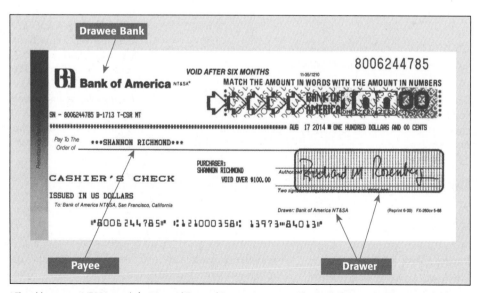

*The abbreviation *NT&SA* stands for National Trust and Savings Association. The Bank of America NT&SA is a subsidiary of Bank of America Corporation, which is engaged in financial services, insurance, investment management, and other businesses.

Cashier's checks are sometimes used in the business community as nearly the equivalent of cash. Except in very limited circumstances, the issuing bank must honor its cashier's checks when they are presented for payment. If a bank wrongfully dishonors a cashier's check, a holder can recover from the bank all expenses incurred, interest, and consequential damages [UCC 3–411]. This same rule applies if a bank wrongfully dishonors a certified check (to be discussed shortly).

Rather than being treated as the equivalent of cash, should a cashier's check be treated as a note with all of the applicable defenses? That was the question in the following case.

Case 14.1

MidAmerica Bank v. Charter One Bank

Illinois Supreme Court,
232 Ill.2d 560, 905 N.E.2d 839 (2009).

(John Quinn/Bloomberg via Getty Images)

A Charter One Bank branch.

FACTS Mary Christelle was the mother of David Hernandez, president of Essential Technologies of Illinois (ETI). Christelle bought a $50,000 cashier's check from Charter One Bank payable to ETI. ETI deposited the check into its account with MidAmerica Bank, FSB. Four days later, Christelle asked Charter One to *stop payment* (see the discussion on page 415). Charter One agreed and refused to honor the check. MidAmerica returned the check to ETI. Within two weeks, ETI's account had a negative balance of $52,000. MidAmerica closed the account and filed a suit in an Illinois state court against Charter One, alleging that the defendant wrongfully dishonored the cashier's check. Charter One argued that a cashier's check should be treated as a note subject to the defense of fraud. The court ruled in MidAmerica's favor, but a state intermediate appellate court reversed the ruling. MidAmerica appealed.

ISSUE Can a bank obtain payment on a cashier's check over the drawee bank's stop-payment order?

DECISION Yes. The Illinois Supreme Court reversed the lower court's decision, awarded MidAmerica the amount of the check, and remanded the case for a determination of interest and fees.

REASON A bank's refusal to pay a cashier's check based on its customer's request to stop payment is wrongful under UCC 3–411 because a customer has no right to stop payment on a cashier's check under UCC 4–403, which permits payment to be stopped only on items drawn "on the customer's account." A cashier's check is drawn on the issuing bank, not on the customer's account. Thus, Christelle had no right to stop payment after she gave the check to ETI. As for Charter One's argument that the check should be treated as a note, the court agreed that the drawer of a cashier's check has the same liability as the maker of a note "because a bank issuing a cashier's check is both the drawer and drawee of the check." But "the UCC provides that cashier's checks are drafts, not notes." Besides, the bank cannot assert fraud as a defense because it did not know of any fraud when it dishonored the check.

WHY IS THIS CASE IMPORTANT? *As noted earlier in the text, the UCC has been amended periodically since it was first published in 1952. In particular, Article 3 was significantly revised in 1990 when many sections were rewritten and renumbered. The reasoning in this case underscores that through all of the changes, the treatment of cashier's checks as "cash equivalents" in the world of commerce has never varied, and none of the amendments to Article 3 have been intended to alter that status.*

Traveler's Checks

Traveler's Check A check that is payable on demand, drawn on or payable through a financial institution, and designated as a traveler's check.

A **traveler's check** is an instrument that is payable on demand, drawn on or payable at or through a financial institution (such as a bank), and designated as a traveler's check. The issuing institution is directly obligated to accept and pay its traveler's check according to the check's terms.

Traveler's checks are designed to be a safe substitute for cash when a person is on vacation or traveling. They are issued for a fixed amount, such as $20, $50, or $100. The purchaser is required to sign the check at the time it is bought and again at the time it is used [UCC 3–104(i)]. Most major banks today do not issue their own traveler's checks but, instead, purchase and issue American Express traveler's checks for their customers (see Exhibit 14.2 below).

Certified Checks

Certified Check A check that has been accepted in writing by the bank on which it is drawn. By certifying (accepting) the check, the bank promises to pay the check at the time it is presented.

A **certified check** is a check that has been *accepted* in writing by the bank on which it is drawn [UCC 3–409(d)]. When a drawee bank *certifies* (accepts) a check, it immediately charges the drawer's account with the amount of the check and transfers those funds to its own certified check account. In effect, the bank is agreeing in advance to accept that check when it is presented for payment and to make payment from those funds reserved in the certified check account. Essentially, certification prevents the bank from denying liability. It is a promise that sufficient funds are on deposit *and have been set aside* to cover the check.

LEARNING OBJECTIVE 1
What type of check does a bank agree in advance to accept when the check is presented for payment?

To certify a check, the bank writes or stamps the word *certified* on the face of the check and typically writes the amount that it will pay.[1] Either the drawer or the holder (payee) of a check can request certification, but the drawee bank is not required to certify a check. (Note, though, that a bank's refusal to certify a check is not a dishonor of the check [UCC 3–409(d)].) Once a check is certified, the drawer and any prior indorsers are completely discharged from liability on the check [UCC 3–414(c), 3–415(d)]. Only the certifying bank is required to pay the instrument.

The Bank-Customer Relationship

The bank-customer relationship begins when the customer opens a checking account and deposits funds that the bank will use to pay for checks written by the customer. Essentially, three types of relationships come into being, as discussed next.

---

1. If the certification does not state an amount, and the amount is later increased and the instrument negotiated to a holder in due course (HDC), the obligation of the certifying bank is the amount of the instrument when it was taken by the HDC [UCC 3–413(b)].

Exhibit 14.2 A Traveler's Check

When you open a checking account with your local bank, you are establishing a contractual relationship.

(Goodluz/Shutterstock.com)

Creditor-Debtor Relationship

A creditor-debtor relationship is created between a customer and a bank when, for example, the customer makes cash deposits into a checking account. When a customer makes a deposit, the customer becomes a creditor, and the bank a debtor, for the amount deposited.

Agency Relationship

An agency relationship also arises between the customer and the bank when the customer writes a check on his or her account. In effect, the customer is ordering the bank to pay the amount specified on the check to the holder when the holder presents the check to the bank for payment. In this situation, the bank becomes the customer's agent and is obligated to honor the customer's request.

Similarly, if the customer deposits a check into his or her account, the bank, as the customer's agent, is obligated to collect payment on the check from the bank on which the check was drawn. To transfer checking account funds among different banks, each bank acts as the agent of collection for its customer [UCC 4–201(a)].

Contractual Relationship

Whenever a bank-customer relationship is established, certain contractual rights and duties arise. The specific rights and duties of the bank and its customer depend on the nature of the transaction. The respective rights and duties of banks and their customers are discussed in detail in the following pages. Another aspect of the bank-customer relationship—deposit insurance—is examined in the *Linking Business Law to Accounting and Finance* feature on pages 429–430.

Bank's Duty to Honor Checks

When a banking institution provides checking services, it agrees to honor the checks written by its customers, with the usual stipulation that the account must have sufficient funds available to pay each check [UCC 4–401(a)]. When a drawee bank *wrongfully* fails to honor a check, it is liable to its customer for damages resulting from its refusal to pay [UCC 4–402(b)]. The customer does not have to prove that the bank breached its contractual commitment or was negligent.

The customer's agreement with the bank includes a general obligation to keep sufficient funds on deposit to cover all checks written. The customer is liable to the payee or to the holder of a check in a civil suit if a check is dishonored for insufficient funds. If intent to defraud can be proved, the customer can also be subject to criminal prosecution for writing a bad check.

When the bank properly dishonors a check for insufficient funds, it has no liability to the customer. The bank may rightfully refuse payment on a customer's check in other circumstances as well. We look here at the rights and duties of both the bank and its customers in specific situations.

Overdrafts

Overdraft A check that is paid by the bank when the checking account on which the check is written contains insufficient funds to cover the check.

When the bank receives an item properly payable from its customer's checking account but the account contains insufficient funds to cover the amount of the check, the bank has two options. It can dishonor the item, or it can pay the item and charge the customer's account, thus creating an **overdraft.** The bank can subtract the amount of the overdraft (plus a service charge) from the customer's next deposit or other customer funds because a check carries with it an enforceable implied promise to reimburse the bank. With a joint account, however, the bank cannot hold any joint-account owner liable for payment of the overdraft unless that customer signed the check or benefited from its proceeds.

A bank can expressly agree with a customer to accept overdrafts through what is sometimes called an "overdraft protection agreement." If such an agreement is formed, any failure of the bank to honor a check because it would create an overdraft breaches this agreement and is treated as a wrongful dishonor [UCC 4–402(a)].

Postdated Checks

A bank may charge a postdated check against a customer's account, unless the customer notifies the bank, in a timely manner, not to pay the check until the stated date. The notice of postdating must be given in time to allow the bank to act on the notice before it pays the check. If the bank fails to act on the customer's notice and charges the customer's account before the date on the postdated check, the bank may be liable for any damages incurred by the customer [UCC 4–401(c)].[2]

Stale Checks

Stale Check A check, other than a certified check, that is presented for payment more than six months after its date.

Commercial banking practice regards a check that is presented for payment more than six months from its date as a **stale check.** A bank is not obligated to pay an uncertified check presented more than six months from its date [UCC 4–404]. When receiving a stale check for payment, the bank has the option of paying or not paying the check. The bank may consult the customer before paying the check. If a bank pays a stale check in good faith without consulting the customer, nonetheless, the bank has the right to charge the customer's account for the amount of the check.

Stop-Payment Orders

Stop-Payment Order An order by a bank customer to his or her bank not to pay or certify a certain check.

A **stop-payment order** is an order by a customer to his or her bank not to pay or certify a certain check. Only a customer (or a person authorized to draw on the account) can order the bank not to pay the check when it is presented for payment [UCC 4–403(a)].[3] A customer has no right to stop payment on a check that has been certified or accepted by a bank, however. In addition, the customer-drawer must have a *valid legal ground* for issuing such an order, or the holder can sue the customer-drawer for payment.

The customer must issue the stop-payment order within a reasonable time and in a reasonable manner to permit the bank to act on it [UCC 4–403(a)]. Most banks allow stop-payment orders to be submitted electronically via the bank's Web site. A written or electronic stop-payment order is effective for six months, at which time it must be renewed in writing [UCC 4–403(b)]. Although a stop-payment order can be given orally over the phone, it is binding on the bank for only fourteen calendar days unless confirmed in writing (or record).[4]

If the bank pays the check in spite of a stop-payment order, the bank will be obligated to recredit the customer's account. In addition, if the bank's payment over a stop-payment order causes subsequent checks written on the drawer's account to "bounce," the bank will be liable for the resultant costs the drawer incurs. The bank is liable only for the amount of actual damages suffered by the drawer, however [UCC 4–403(c)].

---

2. As noted in Chapter 13, postdating does not affect the negotiability of a check. A check is usually paid without respect to its date.

3. For a deceased customer, any person claiming a legitimate interest in the account may issue a stop-payment order [UCC 4–405].

4. Some states do not recognize oral stop-payment orders. They must be in writing.

Death or Incompetence of a Customer

Neither the death nor the incompetence of a customer revokes a bank's authority to pay an item until the bank is informed of the situation and has had a reasonable amount of time to act on the notice. Thus, if a bank is unaware that the customer who wrote a check has been declared incompetent or has died, the bank can pay the item without incurring liability [UCC 4–405]. Even when a bank knows of the death of its customer, for ten days after the *date of death,* it can pay or certify checks drawn on or before the date of death.

An exception to this rule is made if a person claiming an interest in that account, such as an heir, orders the bank to stop payment. Without this provision, banks would constantly be required to verify the continued life and competence of their drawers.

Checks Bearing Forged Drawers' Signatures

When a bank pays a check on which the drawer's signature is forged, generally the bank is liable. A bank may be able to recover at least some of the loss from the customer, however, if the customer's negligence contributed to the making of the forgery. A bank may also obtain partial recovery from the forger of the check (if he or she can be found) or from the holder who presented the check for payment (if the holder knew that the signature was forged).

> "Canceled checks will be to future historians and cultural anthropologists what the Dead Sea Scrolls and hieroglyphics are to us."
>
> Brent Staples, 1951–present (American journalist)

The General Rule

A forged signature on a check has no legal effect as the signature of a customer-drawer [UCC 3–403(a)]. For this reason, banks require a signature card from each customer who opens a checking account. Signature cards allow the bank to verify whether the signatures on its customers' checks are genuine.

The general rule is that the bank must recredit the customer's account when it pays a check with a forged signature. (Note that banks today normally verify signatures only on checks that exceed a certain threshold, such as $2,500 or some higher amount. Even though a bank sometimes incurs liability costs when it has paid forged checks, the costs of verifying every check's signature would be much higher.)

A bank may contractually shift to the customer the risk of forged checks created by the use of facsimile or other nonmanual signatures. For instance, the contract might stipulate that the customer is solely responsible for maintaining security over any device affixing a signature to the customer's checks.

Customer Negligence

When the customer's negligence substantially contributed to the forgery, the bank normally will not be obligated to recredit the customer's account for the amount of the check [UCC 3–406]. The customer's liability may be reduced, however, by the amount of loss caused by negligence on the part of the bank (or other "person") paying the instrument or taking it for value if the negligence substantially contributed to the loss [UCC 3–406(b)].

EXAMPLE 14.2 Gemco Corporation uses special check-writing equipment to write its payroll and business checks. Gemco discovers that an employee used the equipment to write himself a check for $10,000 and that the bank subsequently honored it. Gemco asks the bank to recredit $10,000 to its account for improperly paying the forged check. If the bank can show that Gemco failed to take reasonable care in controlling access to the check-writing equipment, the bank will not be required to recredit Gemco's account for the $10,000. If Gemco can show that negligence by the bank contributed substantially to the loss, however, then Gemco's liability may be reduced proportionately. •

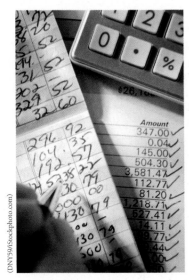

What are the duties of a bank customer with respect to the examination of monthly bank statements?

Timely Examination of Bank Statements Required Banks typically either mail customers monthly statements detailing activity in their checking accounts, or they make these statements available in some other way—for example, online. In the past, banks routinely included the canceled checks themselves (or copies of them) with the statement sent to the customer.

Today, most banks simply provide the customer with information (check number, amount, and date of payment) on the statement that will allow the customer to reasonably identify the checks that the bank has paid [UCC 4–406(a), (b)]. If the bank retains the canceled checks, it must keep the checks—or legible copies of the checks—for seven years [UCC 4–406(b)]. The customer can obtain a copy of a canceled check during this period of time.

The customer has a duty to promptly examine bank statements (and canceled checks or copies) with reasonable care and to report any alterations or forged signatures [UCC 4–406(c)]. This includes forged signatures of indorsers, if discovered (to be discussed shortly). If the customer fails to fulfill this duty and the bank suffers a loss as a result, the customer will be liable for the loss [UCC 4–406(d)].

Consequences of Failing to Detect Forgeries Sometimes, the same wrongdoer has forged the customer's signature on a series of checks. To recover for all the forged items, the customer must discover and report the *first* forged check to the bank within thirty calendar days of the receipt of the bank statement [UCC 4–406(d)(2)]. Failure to notify the bank within this period of time discharges the bank's liability for *all* of the forged checks that it pays prior to notification.

CASE EXAMPLE 14.3 Joseph Montanez, an employee at Espresso Roma Corporation, used stolen software and blank checks to generate company checks on his home computer. The series of forged checks spanned a period in excess of two years and totaled more than $330,000. When the bank statements containing the forged checks arrived in the mail, Montanez removed the checks so that the forgeries would go undetected. Eventually, Espresso Roma discovered the forgeries and asked the bank to recredit its account. The bank refused, and litigation ensued. The court held that the bank was not liable for the forged checks because Espresso Roma had failed to report the first forgeries within the UCC's time period of thirty days.[5] ●

When the Bank Is Also Negligent A bank customer can escape liability, at least in part, for failing to notify the bank of forged or altered checks within the required thirty-day period if the bank was also negligent—that is, failed to exercise ordinary care. In this situation, the loss will be allocated between the bank and the customer on the basis of *comparative negligence* (see page 121 in Chapter 4) [UCC 4–406(e)].

Ordinary Care The UCC defines *ordinary care* as the "observance of reasonable commercial standards, prevailing in . . . the business in which that person is engaged" [UCC 3–103]. As mentioned earlier, it is customary in the banking industry to manually examine signatures only on checks over a certain amount. Thus, if a bank fails to examine a signature on a particular check, the bank has not necessarily breached its duty to exercise ordinary care.

One-Year Time Limit Regardless of the degree of care exercised by the customer or the bank, the UCC places an absolute time limit on the liability of a bank for paying a check with a forged customer signature. A customer who fails to report a forged signature

---

5. *Espresso Roma Corp. v. Bank of America, N.A.*, 100 Cal.App.4th 525, 124 Cal.Rptr.2d 549 (2002).

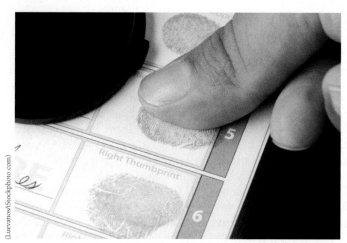

(Luevanos/iStockphoto.com)

Sometimes, when a person attempts to cash a check at a banking institution, the bank requests a thumbprint on the back of the check. Why?

within one year from the date that the statement was made available for inspection loses the legal right to have the bank recredit his or her account [UCC 4–406(f)]. The parties can also agree in their contract to a shorter time limit.

CASE EXAMPLE 14.4 Wanda Williamson, a clerk at Visiting Nurses Association (VNA), was responsible for making VNA bank deposits. Over a four-year period, Williamson embezzled more than $250,000 from VNA by forging its indorsement on checks and cashing them at the bank. Williamson was eventually arrested and convicted. VNA then filed a lawsuit against the bank, claiming that it had been negligent in allowing Williamson to cash the checks. The court found that the bank was not liable because VNA had failed to report the forged indorsements within the prescribed time period. Not only did UCC 4–406(f) preclude the action, but the bank's contract with VNA included a clause requiring customers to report a forgery within sixty days.[6] ●

PREVENTING LEGAL DISPUTES

Forgery of checks by employees and embezzlement of company funds are disturbingly common in today's business world. To avoid significant losses due to forgery or embezzlement, as well as litigation, use care in maintaining business bank accounts. Limit access to your business's bank accounts. Never leave company checkbooks or signature stamps in unsecured areas. Use passwords to limit access to computerized check-writing software. Examine bank statements in a timely fashion and be on the lookout for suspicious transactions. Remember that if a forgery is not reported within thirty days of the first statement in which the forged item appears, you, as the account holder, normally lose the right to hold the bank liable.

Checks Bearing Forged Indorsements

A bank that pays a customer's check bearing a forged indorsement must recredit the customer's account or be liable to the customer-drawer for breach of contract. **EXAMPLE 14.5** Simon issues a $500 check "to the order of Antonio." Juan steals the check, forges Antonio's indorsement, and cashes the check. When the check reaches Simon's bank, the bank pays it and debits Simon's account. The bank must recredit the $500 to Simon's account because it failed to carry out Simon's order to pay "to the order of Antonio" [UCC 4–401(a)]. Of course, Simon's bank can in turn recover—for breach of warranty (see pages 400–401 in Chapter 13)—from the bank that cashed the check when Juan presented it [UCC 4–207(a)(2)]. ●

Eventually, the loss usually falls on the first party to take the instrument bearing the forged indorsement because, as discussed in Chapter 13, a forged indorsement does not transfer title. Thus, whoever takes an instrument with a forged indorsement cannot become a holder.

In any event, the customer has a duty to report forged indorsements promptly. Failure to report forged indorsements within a three-year period after the forged items have been made available to the customer relieves the bank of liability [UCC 4–111].

In the following case, a bank's contract with its customer altered its statutory duties concerning forged indorsements. The court had to decide whether to follow the UCC or enforce the contract as written.

---

6. *Security State Bank v. Visiting Nurses Association of Telfair County, Inc.*, 568 S.E.2d 491 (Ga.App. 2002).

Case 14.2

Michigan Basic Property Insurance Association v. Washington

Court of Appeals of Michigan,
2012 WL 205753 (2012).
coa.courts.mi.gov[a]

Checks can be made out to more than one payee.

FACTS The Michigan Basic Property Insurance Association (MBP) issued a check for $69,559.06 from its account with Fifth Third Bank to Joyce Washington, Countrywide Home Loans, and T&C Federal Credit Union as co-payees. Washington indorsed the check herself by signing all three payees' names and did not distribute the proceeds to the co-payees. When the check reached Fifth Third Bank, it notified MBP of the payment through a daily account statement. MBP did not object, so Fifth Third Bank withdrew the funds from MBP's account. Fifth Third Bank also sent information about the check in a monthly account statement, and MBP still failed to object, even though the account agreement required it to provide prompt notice of any forgeries. MBP was forced to issue a second check to Countrywide, so it sued Fifth Third Bank and sought to have its account recredited. The trial court found that Fifth Third Bank was liable to MBP, and another party appealed on Fifth Third Bank's behalf.

ISSUE Was Fifth Third Bank liable to MBP for paying a check with forged indorsements?

DECISION No. The Michigan appellate court reversed the trial court's judgment.

REASON The court noted that, under the Uniform Commercial Code (UCC), the check was not properly payable because it had two forged indorsements. When a bank pays a check bearing a forged indorsement, the UCC ordinarily requires the bank to recredit the customer's account. Nevertheless, the court pointed out that the UCC allows parties to change their duties by contract. In this case, the account agreement obligated MBP to carefully review its checking account statements and to notify Fifth Third Bank of any problems within thirty days. In the absence of such notice, the contract provided that MBP, not Fifth Third Bank, was liable for any forged indorsements. Because MBP did not provide prompt notice of the forgeries, Fifth Third Bank was not required to recredit MBP's account.

CRITICAL THINKING—Legal Consideration As a practical matter, does it make sense for the customer to bear primary responsibility for discovering instances of fraud? Which party is in a better position to detect any irregularities? Explain.

a. Under "Resources," in the pull-down menu, select "Court Opinions/MSC Orders" and then "Search Options." On the next page, click on "Docket Number." When that page opens, select "Court of Appeals," type "299597" in the search box, and click on "Search." In the result, click on the case name to access the opinion.

Altered Checks

LEARNING OBJECTIVE 3
What duties does the Uniform Commercial Code impose on a bank's customers with regard to forged and altered checks? What are the consequences if a customer is negligent in performing those duties?

The customer's instruction to the bank is to pay the exact amount on the face of the check to the holder. The bank has a duty to examine each check before making final payment. If the bank fails to detect an alteration, it is liable to its customer for the loss because it did not pay as the customer ordered.

The bank's loss is the difference between the original amount of the check and the amount actually paid [UCC 4–401(d)(1)]. **EXAMPLE 14.6** A check written for $11 is altered to $111. The customer's account will be charged $11 (the amount the customer ordered the bank to pay). The bank normally will be responsible for the $100 difference. ●

Customer Negligence As in a situation involving a forged drawer's signature, a customer's negligence can shift the loss when payment is made on an altered check (unless the bank was also negligent). For example, a person may carelessly write a check leaving large gaps around the numbers and words where additional numbers and words can be inserted (see Exhibit 14.3 on the next page).

Exhibit 14.3 A Poorly Filled-Out Check

Similarly, a person who signs a check and leaves the dollar amount for someone else to fill in is barred from protesting when the bank unknowingly and in good faith pays whatever amount is shown [UCC 4–401(d)(2)]. Finally, if the bank can trace its loss on successive altered checks to the customer's failure to discover the initial alteration, the bank can reduce its liability for reimbursing the customer's account [UCC 4–406].

In every situation involving a forged drawer's signature or an alteration, a bank must observe reasonable commercial standards of care in paying on a customer's checks [UCC 4–406(e)]. The customer's negligence can be used as a defense only if the bank has exercised ordinary care.

Other Parties from Whom the Bank May Recover

The bank is entitled to recover the amount of loss from the transferor who, by presenting the check for payment, warrants that the check has not been materially altered (warranty liability was discussed in Chapter 13). This rule has two exceptions, though. If the bank is also the drawer (as it is on a cashier's check), it cannot recover from the presenting party if the party is a holder in due course (HDC) acting in good faith [UCC 3–417(a)(2), 4–208(a)(2)]. The reason is that an instrument's drawer is in a better position than an HDC to know whether the instrument has been altered.

Similarly, an HDC who presents a certified check for payment in good faith will not be held liable under warranty principles if the check was altered before the HDC acquired it [UCC 3–417(a)(2), 4–207(a)(2)]. **EXAMPLE 14.7**   Jordan draws a check for $500 payable to David. David alters the amount to $5,000. The drawee bank, First National, certifies the check for $5,000. David negotiates the check to Ethan, an HDC. The drawee bank pays Ethan $5,000. On discovering the mistake, the bank cannot recover from Ethan the $4,500 paid by mistake, even though the bank was not in a superior position to detect the alteration. This is in accord with the purpose of certification, which is to obtain the definite obligation of a bank to honor a definite instrument. •

Bank's Duty to Accept Deposits

A bank has a duty to its customer to accept the customer's deposits of cash and checks. When checks are deposited, the bank must make the funds represented by those checks available within certain time frames. A bank also has a duty to collect payment on any checks payable or indorsed to its customers and deposited by them into their accounts. Cash deposits made in U.S. currency are received into customers' accounts without being subject to further collection procedures.

Availability Schedule for Deposited Checks

The Expedited Funds Availability Act of 1987[7] and Regulation CC,[8] which was issued by the Federal Reserve Board of Governors (the *Federal Reserve System* will be discussed shortly) to implement the act, require that any local check deposited must be available for withdrawal by check or as cash within one business day from the date of deposit.

A check is classified as a local check if the first bank to receive the check for payment and the bank on which the check is drawn are located in the same check-processing region (check-processing regions are designated by the Federal Reserve Board of Governors). For nonlocal checks, the funds must be available for withdrawal within not more than five business days. Note that under the Check Clearing in the 21st Century Act (Check 21),[9] a bank has to credit a customer's account as soon as the bank receives the funds (Check 21 is discussed in this chapter's *Landmark in the Law* feature on the following page).

In addition, the Expedited Funds Availability Act requires the following:

1. That funds be available on the next business day for cash deposits and wire transfers, government checks, the first $100 of a day's check deposits, cashier's checks, certified checks, and checks for which the depositary and payor banks are branches of the same institution (*depositary* and *payor banks* will be discussed shortly).
2. That the first $100 of any deposit be available for cash withdrawal on the opening of the next business day after deposit. If a local check is deposited, the next $400 is to be available for withdrawal by no later than 5:00 p.m. the next business day. If, for example, you deposit a local check for $500 on Monday, you can withdraw $100 in cash at the opening of the business day on Tuesday, and an additional $400 must be available for withdrawal by no later than 5:00 P.M. on Wednesday.

A different availability schedule applies to deposits made at *nonproprietary* automated teller machines (ATMs). These are ATMs that are not owned or operated by the bank receiving the deposits. Basically, a five-day hold is permitted on all deposits, including cash deposits, made at nonproprietary ATMs.

The Traditional Collection Process

Usually, deposited checks involve parties that do business at different banks, but sometimes checks are written between customers of the same bank. Either situation brings into play the bank collection process as it operates within the statutory framework of Article 4 of the UCC. Note that the check-collection process described in the following subsections will be modified as the banking industry continues to implement Check 21.

Designations of Banks Involved in the Collection Process

The first bank to receive a check for payment is the **depositary bank**.[10] For example, when a person deposits a tax-refund check into a personal checking account at the local bank, that bank is the depositary bank. The bank on which a check is drawn (the drawee bank) is called the **payor bank**. Any bank except the payor bank that handles a check during some phase of the collection process is a **collecting bank**. Any bank except the payor bank or the depositary bank to which an item is transferred in the course of this collection process is called an **intermediary bank**.

(Yin Yang/iStockphoto.com)

If you deposit a check at your bank that is written on another bank, can you withdraw those funds in cash immediately? Why or why not?

Depositary Bank The first bank to receive a check for payment.

Payor Bank The bank on which a check is drawn (the drawee bank).

Collecting Bank Any bank handling an item for collection, except the payor bank.

Intermediary Bank Any bank to which an item is transferred in the course of collection, except the depositary or payor bank.

---

7. 12 U.S.C. Sections 4001–4010.
8. 12 C.F.R. Sections 229.1–229.42.
9. 12 U.S.C. Sections 5001–5018.
10. All definitions in this section are found in UCC 4–105. The terms *depositary* and *depository* have different meanings in the banking context. A depositary bank refers to a *physical place* (a bank or other institution) in which deposits or funds are held or stored.

LANDMARK IN THE LAW

Check Clearing in the 21st Century Act (Check 21)

In the traditional collection process, paper checks had to be physically transported before they could be cleared. To streamline this costly and time-consuming process and improve the overall efficiency of the nation's payment system, Congress passed the Check Clearing in the 21st Century Act (Check 21) in 2003.

Purpose of Check 21   Before the implementation of Check 21, banks generally had to present the original paper check for payment because there was no broad-based system of electronic presentment. Check 21 has changed this situation by creating a new negotiable instrument called a *substitute check*. Although the act does not require banks to change their check-collection practices, the creation of substitute checks facilitates the use of electronic check processing.

Substitute Checks   A substitute check is a paper reproduction of the front and back of an original check that contains all of the same information required on checks for automated processing. Banks create a substitute check from a digital image of an original check. Financial institutions that exchange digital images of checks do not have to send the original paper checks. They can simply transmit the information electronically and replace the original checks with the substitute checks. Banks that do not exchange checks electronically are required to accept substitute checks in the same way that they accept original checks.

By eliminating the original check after a substitute check is created, the financial system can prevent the check from being paid twice and reduce the expense of paper storage and retrieval. Nevertheless, at least for quite a while, not all checks will be converted to substitute checks. Thus, if a bank returns canceled checks to deposit holders at the end of each month, some of those returned checks may be substitute checks, and some may be original canceled paper checks.

Faster Access to Funds   The Expedited Funds Availability Act requires the Federal Reserve Board to revise the availability schedule for funds from deposited checks to correspond to reductions in check-processing time.[a] Therefore, as the speed of check processing increases under Check 21, the Federal Reserve Board will reduce the maximum time that a bank can hold funds from deposited checks before making them available to the depositor. Thus, account holders will have faster access to their deposited funds, but they will also have less *float time*—the time between when a check is written and when the amount is actually deducted from the account.

Application to Today's World   *As more financial institutions make agreements to transfer digital images of checks, the check-processing system will become more efficient and therefore less costly. Customers increasingly will be unable to rely on banking float when they are low on funds, so they should make sure that funds are available to cover checks when they are written. Customers cannot opt out of Check 21 and demand that their original canceled checks be returned with their monthly statements. Nor can they refuse to accept a substitute check as proof of payment.*

_____

a. 12 U.S.C. Sections 4001–4010.

During the collection process, any bank can take on one or more of the various roles of depositary, payor, collecting, and intermediary bank. **EXAMPLE 14.8**   A buyer in New York writes a check on her New York bank and sends it to a seller in San Francisco. The seller deposits the check in her San Francisco bank account. The seller's bank is both a *depositary bank* and a *collecting bank*. The buyer's bank in New York is the *payor bank*. As the check travels from San Francisco to New York, any collecting bank handling the item in the collection process (other than the depositary bank and the payor bank) is also called an *intermediary bank*. Exhibit 14.4 on the facing page illustrates how various banks function in the collection process in the context of this example. •

Check Collection between Customers of the Same Bank   An item that is payable by the depositary bank (also the payor bank) that receives it is called an "on-us item." Usually, the bank issues a "provisional credit" for on-us items within the same day. If the bank does not dishonor the check by the opening of the second banking day following its receipt, the check is considered paid [UCC 4–215(e)(2)].

Exhibit 14.4 The Check-Collection Process

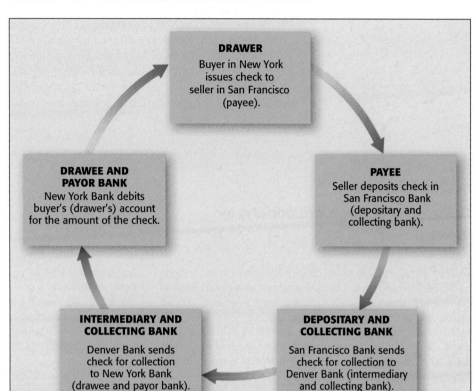

Check Collection between Customers of Different Banks   Once a depositary bank receives a check, it must arrange to present it either directly or through intermediary banks to the appropriate payor bank.

Deadline Is Midnight of the Next Banking Day   Each bank in the collection chain must pass the check on before midnight of the next banking day following its receipt [UCC 4–202(b)].[11] A "banking day" is any part of a day that the bank is open to carry on substantially all of its banking functions. Thus, if only a bank's drive-through facilities are open, a check deposited on Saturday will not trigger the bank's midnight deadline until the following Monday. When the check reaches the payor bank, that bank is liable for the face amount of the check, unless the payor bank dishonors the check or returns it by midnight on the next banking day following receipt [UCC 4–302].[12]

Deferred Posting after Cutoff Hour   Because of this deadline and because banks need to maintain an even workflow in the many items they handle daily, the UCC permits what is called *deferred posting*. According to UCC 4–108, "a bank may fix an afternoon hour of

---

11. A bank may take a "reasonably longer time" in certain circumstances, such as when the bank's computer system is down due to a power failure, but the bank must show that its action is still timely [UCC 4–202(b)].
12. Most checks are cleared by a computerized process, and communication and computer facilities may fail because of electrical outages, equipment malfunction, or other conditions. A bank may be "excused" from liability for failing to meet its midnight deadline if such conditions arise and the bank has exercised "such diligence as the circumstances require" [UCC 4–109(d)].

2:00 P.M. or later as a cutoff hour for the handling of money and items and the making of entries on its books." Any checks received after that hour "may be treated as being received at the opening of the next banking day." Thus, if a bank's "cutoff hour" is 3:00 P.M., a check received by a payor bank at 4:00 P.M. on Monday will be deferred for posting until Tuesday. In this situation, the payor bank's deadline will be midnight Wednesday.

The provisional credit mentioned on page 422 also applies to checks presented to one bank for collection from another. As the number of banks in the collection chain increases, so does the time before the credit becomes final and the check is considered paid, as illustrated in the following case.

Case 14.3

Cumis Mutual Insurance Society, Inc. v. Rosol

Superior Court of New Jersey, Appellate Division, 2011 WL 589397 (2011).

(sshepard/iStockphoto.com)

The Polish & Slavic Federal Credit Union.

FACTS Mizek Rosol received an e-mail message from someone he did not know, offering a fee if he would receive checks, deposit them, and transfer the funds to others. He agreed and opened an account at Polish & Slavic Federal Credit Union (PSFCU). He received and deposited a cashier's check for $9,800 issued by a credit union in Florida. Three days later, he deposited a check for $45,000 drawn on a Canadian bank. Within a week, PSFCU told him that payment on the first check had been stopped, but it did not disclose that the check was fraudulent. PSFCU issued a provisional credit for the amount of the Canadian check. After Rosol had transferred $36,240 to a party in Japan and $4,500 to a party in Great Britain, the Canadian check was dishonored. PSFCU demanded that Rosol repay the transferred funds. He refused. PSFCU filed a claim with its insurer, Cumis Mutual Insurance Society, Inc. Cumis paid the claim and filed a suit against Rosol to recover the amount. The court issued a summary judgment in Cumis's favor. Rosol appealed.

ISSUE Were the funds that Rosol deposited from the Canadian check provisional at the time he transferred them to the parties in Japan and Great Britain?

DECISION Yes. A state intermediate appellate court reversed the lower court's judgment and remanded the case because "there were genuine issues of material fact precluding summary

judgment." If PSFCU reasonably led Rosol to believe that the Canadian check had been finally credited to his account, the credit union could not rely on UCC 4–201(a) to recover the transferred funds.

REASON The appellate court explained that UCC 4–201(a) governed the relationship between PSFCU and Rosol. Under that provision, a credit to the account of "the owner" of a check is provisional until the final settlement of the check. The credit to Rosol's account for the checks was thus provisional between the time of their deposit and the time of their dishonor. During that period, PSFCU had a "right of recoupment" for the funds that Rosol had transferred. But Rosol contended that he would not have transferred those funds if PSFCU had told him that the first check was fraudulent—not just that it had been stopped. The court reasoned that "the state of his knowledge" about the first check could bear on the question of whether Rosol had acted reasonably in relying on what he was told about the second check.

CRITICAL THINKING—Ethical Consideration *In what ways was Rosol's apparent motive similar to the most common reason that ethical problems occur in business?*

ETHICAL ISSUE

Has the Expedited Funds Availability Act (EFAA) encouraged fraud? Since the EFAA was enacted in 1987, millions of people have fallen prey to a variety of check-fraud scams. The fraudsters contact a person—via e-mail, social media, telephone, or letter—and say that they will send that person a check for a certain amount if he or she agrees to wire some of the funds back to them, typically to cover "fees and taxes." The victim receives a check, deposits it into his or her account, and waits to see if the check "clears." A day or so later, when the law says the funds must be made available, the victim confirms that the funds are in his or her bank account and then wires the requested amount back to the fraudsters.

Unfortunately, by the time the bank discovers that the check is a fake and notifies the customer that the check has "bounced," the customer has already sent thousands of dollars to the fraudsters. Because the check was counterfeit, the bank has no liability on it, and the loss falls on the customer. The incidence of these scams is increasing, largely because the fraudsters know that the law requires U.S. banks to make the funds available almost immediately on deposited checks, even if those checks later prove to be counterfeit. Although the EFAA was intended to protect bank customers, it now appears to be having the opposite effect—making them a target for fraud.

Federal Reserve System A network of twelve district banks and related branches located around the country and headed by the Federal Reserve Board of Governors. Most banks in the United States have Federal Reserve accounts.

Clearinghouse A system or place where banks exchange checks and drafts drawn on each other and settle daily balances.

How the Federal Reserve System Clears Checks The **Federal Reserve System** is a network of twelve district banks, which are located around the country and headed by the Federal Reserve Board of Governors. Most banks in the United States have Federal Reserve accounts. The Federal Reserve System has greatly simplified the check-collection process by acting as a **clearinghouse**—a system or place where banks exchange checks and drafts drawn on each other and settle daily balances.

EXAMPLE 14.9 Pamela Moy of Philadelphia writes a check to Jeanne Sutton in San Francisco. When Sutton receives the check in the mail, she deposits it in her bank. Her bank then deposits the check in the Federal Reserve Bank of San Francisco, which transfers it to the Federal Reserve Bank of Philadelphia. That Federal Reserve bank then sends the check to Moy's bank, which deducts the amount of the check from Moy's account. •

LEARNING OBJECTIVE 4
What is electronic check presentment, and how does it differ from the traditional check-clearing process?

Electronic Check Presentment In the past, most checks were processed manually. The employees of each bank in the collection chain would physically handle each check that passed through the bank for collection or payment. Today, most checks are processed electronically—a practice that has been facilitated by Check 21, as described in the *Landmark in the Law* feature on page 422. Whereas manual check processing can take days, *electronic check presentment* can be done on the day of deposit. Items are encoded with information (such as the amount of the check) that is read and processed by other banks' computers. Sometimes, a check is retained at its place of deposit, and only its image or description is presented for payment under an electronic presentment agreement [UCC 4–110].[13]

A bank that encodes information on an item warrants to any subsequent bank or payor that the encoded information is correct [UCC 4–209]. This is also true for a bank that retains an item while transmitting its image or description as presentation for payment.

Regulation CC provides that a returned check must be encoded with the routing number of the depositary bank, the amount of the check, and other information and adds that this "does not affect a paying bank's responsibility to return a check within the deadlines required by the U.C.C." Under UCC 4–301(d)(2), an item is returned "when it is sent or delivered to the bank's customer or transferor or pursuant to his [or her] instructions."

Electronic Fund Transfers

By utilizing computer technology in the form of electronic fund transfer systems, banking institutions no longer have to move mountains of paperwork to process fund transfers. An **electronic fund transfer (EFT)** is a transfer of funds through the use of an electronic terminal, a telephone, a computer, a tablet device, or a smartphone.

Electronic Fund Transfer (EFT) A transfer of funds through the use of an electronic terminal, a telephone, a computer, or magnetic tape.

---

13. This section of the UCC assumes that no bank will participate in an electronic presentment program without an express agreement (which is no longer true since Check 21 went into effect). See Comment 2 to UCC 4–110.

LEARNING OBJECTIVE 5
What are the four most common types of electronic fund transfers?

Regulation E A set of rules issued by the Federal Reserve System's Board of Governors to protect users of electronic fund transfer systems.

The law governing EFTs depends on the type of transfer involved. Consumer fund transfers are governed by the Electronic Fund Transfer Act (EFTA).[14] Commercial fund transfers are governed by Article 4A of the UCC.

Although electronic banking offers numerous benefits, it also poses difficulties on occasion. It is difficult to issue stop-payment orders with electronic banking. Also, fewer records are available to prove or disprove that a transaction took place. The possibilities for tampering with a person's private banking information have also increased.

Types of EFT Systems

Most banks today offer EFT services to their customers. The following are the most common types of EFT systems used by bank customers:

1. *Automated teller machines* (ATMs)—The machines are connected online to the bank's computers. A customer inserts a plastic card (called an ATM or debit card) issued by the bank and keys in a *personal identification number* (PIN) to access her or his accounts and conduct banking transactions.
2. *Point-of-sale systems*—Online terminals allow consumers to transfer funds to merchants to pay for purchases using a debit card.
3. *Direct deposits and withdrawals*—Customers can authorize the bank to allow another party—such as the government or an employer—to make direct deposits into their accounts. Similarly, customers can request the bank to make automatic payments to a third party at regular, recurrent intervals from the customer's funds (insurance premiums or loan payments, for example).
4. *Internet payment systems*—Many financial institutions permit their customers to access the institution's computer system via the Internet and direct a transfer of funds between accounts or pay a particular bill.

Consumer Fund Transfers

The Electronic Fund Transfer Act (EFTA) provides a basic framework for the rights, liabilities, and responsibilities of users of EFT systems. Additionally, the act gave the Federal Reserve Board authority to issue rules and regulations to help implement the act's provisions. The Federal Reserve Board's implemental regulation is called **Regulation E.**

The EFTA governs financial institutions that offer electronic fund transfers involving consumer accounts. The types of accounts covered include checking accounts, savings accounts, and any other asset accounts established for personal, family, or household purposes. Telephone transfers are covered by the EFTA only if they are made in accordance with a prearranged plan under which periodic or recurring transfers are contemplated.

Disclosure Requirements The EFTA is essentially a disclosure law benefiting consumers. The act requires financial institutions to inform consumers of their rights and responsibilities, including those listed here, with respect to EFT systems.

1. If a customer's debit card is lost or stolen and used without his or her permission, the customer shall be required to pay no more than $50 if he or she notifies the bank of the loss or theft within two days of learning about it. Otherwise, the liability increases to $500.

    The customer may be liable for more than $500 if he or she fails to report the unauthorized use within sixty days after it appears on the customer's statement. (If a customer voluntarily gives her or his debit card to another, who then uses it improperly, the protections just mentioned do not apply.)

---

14. 15 U.S.C. Sections 1693–1693r. The EFTA amended Title IX of the Consumer Credit Protection Act.

2. The customer must discover any error on the monthly statement within sixty days and notify the bank. The bank then has ten days to investigate and must report its conclusions to the customer in writing. If the bank takes longer than ten days, it must return the disputed amount to the customer's account until it finds the error. If there is no error, the customer has to return the disputed funds to the bank.

3. The bank must provide a monthly statement for every month in which there is an electronic transfer of funds. The statement must show the amount and date of the transfer, the names of the retailers or other third parties involved, the location or identification of the terminal, and the fees.

Violations and Damages   Unauthorized access to an EFT system constitutes a federal felony, and those convicted may be fined up to $10,000 and sentenced to as long as ten years in prison. Banks must strictly comply with the terms of the EFTA and are liable for any failure to adhere to its provisions.

For a bank's violation of the EFTA, a consumer may recover both actual damages (including attorneys' fees and costs) and punitive damages of not less than $100 and not more than $1,000. Even when a customer has sustained no actual damage, the bank may be liable for legal costs and punitive damages if it fails to follow the proper procedures outlined by the EFTA in regard to error resolution.

Commercial Transfers

Funds are also transferred electronically "by wire" between commercial parties. In fact, the dollar volume of payments by wire transfer is more than $1 trillion a day—an amount that far exceeds the dollar volume of payments made by other means. The two major wire payment systems are the Federal Reserve's wire transfer network (Fedwire) and the New York Clearing House Interbank Payments System (CHIPS).

Commercial wire transfers are governed by Article 4A of the UCC, which has been adopted by most states.   **EXAMPLE 14.10**   Jellux, Inc., owes $5 million to Perot Corporation. Instead of sending Perot a check or some other instrument that would enable Perot to obtain payment, Jellux instructs its bank, East Bank, to credit $5 million to Perot's account in West Bank. East Bank debits Jellux's East Bank account and wires $5 million to Perot's West Bank account. In more complex transactions, additional banks would be involved. •

E-Money and Online Banking

New forms of electronic payments (e-payments) have the potential to replace *physical* cash—coins and paper currency—with *virtual* cash in the form of electronic impulses. This is the unique promise of **digital cash,** which consists of funds stored on microchips and on other computer devices. Online banking has also become commonplace in today's world.

In a few minutes, anybody with the proper software can access his or her account, transfer funds, write "checks," pay bills, monitor investments, and often even buy and sell stocks. (For a discussion of how smartphones are being used to make payments, see this chapter's *Adapting the Law to the Online Environment* feature on the following page.)

Forms of E-Money

Various forms of electronic money, or **e-money,** are emerging. The simplest kind of e-money system uses **stored-value cards.** These are plastic cards embossed with magnetic strips containing magnetically encoded data. In some applications, a stored-value card can be used only to purchase specific goods and services offered by the card issuer.

→ KNOW THIS ←

If any part of an electronic fund transfer is covered by the EFTA, the entire transfer is excluded from UCC Article 4A.

Digital Cash Funds contained on computer software, in the form of secure programs stored on microchips and on other computer devices.

E-Money Prepaid funds recorded on a computer or a card (such as a smart card or a stored-value card).

Stored-Value Card A card bearing a magnetic strip that holds magnetically encoded data, providing access to stored funds.

Smart Card A card containing a microprocessor that permits storage of funds via security programming, can communicate with other computers, and does not require online authorization for fund transfers.

Smart cards are plastic cards containing computer microchips that can hold more information than a magnetic strip can. A smart card carries and processes security programming. This capability gives smart cards a technical advantage over stored-value cards. The microprocessors on smart cards can also authenticate the validity of transactions. Retailers can program electronic cash registers to confirm the authenticity of a smart card by examining a unique digital signature stored on its microchip.

Online Banking Services

Most customers use three kinds of online banking services: bill consolidation and payment, transferring funds among accounts, and applying for loans. Customers typically have to appear in person to finalize the terms of a loan, however. Generally, customers are not yet able to deposit and withdraw funds online, although some mobile-banking applications allow checks up to a certain amount to be deposited when a user e-mails an image of the front and back of the check. Smart cards may also eventually be used for withdrawing and depositing funds.

Since the late 1990s, several banks have operated exclusively on the Internet. These "virtual banks" have no physical branch offices. Because few people are equipped to send funds to virtual banks via smart-card technology, the virtual banks accept deposits through physical delivery systems, such as the U.S. Postal Service or FedEx.

ADAPTING THE LAW TO THE ONLINE ENVIRONMENT

SMARTPHONE-BASED PAYMENT SYSTEMS

In 2009, customers at certain Starbucks locations in New York, San Francisco, and Seattle began downloading an iPhone app to pay for their cappuccinos. Once the app is downloaded, the customer pays by simply flashing a bar code that appears on the iPhone's screen. By 2012, more than seven thousand Starbucks locations were accepting payments from all types of smartphone-based operating systems.

The Competition Will Become Fierce

The promise of a "mobile or digital wallet" is becoming reality. Banks, credit-card issuers, and, of course, AT&T, T-Mobile, and Verizon Wireless want to be part of the smartphone payment system revolution. All wireless carriers have agreements with American Express, Discovery, MasterCard, and Visa. In fact, Visa has its own e-wallet service.

Mobile payments can take many forms. American Express's digital payment system, Serve, allows person-to-person payments over mobile phones. Some merchants that already accept American Express cards accept payments via mobile phones. In addition, Bank of America, JPMorgan Chase, and Wells Fargo have created ClearXchange, which also allows bank customers to make person-to-person payments using mobile phone numbers.

Linking Digital Wallets to Other Apps on a Smartphone

According to those in this burgeoning field, the Holy Grail is a link from a digital wallet to another app within a single smartphone. Google, for example, is combining its Google Wallet with its Google Offers (a discount-deal app). Presumably, when more app-enabled "stores" are linked to digital wallets within smartphones, mobile payment systems will grow rapidly. Today, mobile pay volume is only about $150 billion, but that is expected to explode as the mass market adopts these systems.

Critical Thinking

Does having a digital wallet in an iPhone, Android-based phone, or other smartphone entail more security risks than carrying a physical wallet? Explain.

Reviewing . . . Checks and Banking in the Digital Age

RPM Pizza, Inc., issued a check for $96,000 to Systems Marketing for an advertising campaign. A few days later, RPM decided not to go through with the deal and placed a written stop-payment order on the check. RPM and Systems had no further contact for many months. Three weeks after the stop-payment order expired, however, Toby Rierson, an employee at Systems, cashed the check. Bank One Cambridge, RPM's bank, paid the check with funds from RPM's account. Because the check was more than six months old, it was stale. Thus, according to standard banking procedures as well as Bank One's own policies, the signature on the check should have been specially verified, but it was not. RPM filed a suit in a federal district court against Bank One to recover the amount of the check. Using the information presented in the chapter, answer the following questions.

1. How long is a written stop-payment order effective? What else could RPM have done to prevent this check from being cashed?
2. What would happen if it turned out that RPM did not have a legitimate reason for stopping payment on the check?
3. What are a bank's obligations with respect to stale checks?
4. Would a court be likely to hold the bank liable for the amount of the check because it failed to verify the signature on the check? Why or why not?

DEBATE THIS   To reduce fraud, checks that utilize mechanical or electronic signature systems should not be honored.

LINKING BUSINESS LAW to Accounting and Finance

Banking in a Period of Crisis

In this chapter, you learned about the bank-customer relationship as well as a bank's duty to honor checks and accept deposits. In the macroeconomics courses that your business school offers, the focus on the banking sector is quite different. Among other things, the courses examine banking panics and bank runs and their effects on the economy.

Bank Runs during the Great Depression

A *bank run* occurs when depositors simultaneously rush to convert their bank deposits into currency because they believe that the assets of their bank are not sufficient to cover its liabilities—the customers' deposits. The largest number of bank runs in modern history occurred during the Great Depression in the 1930s, when nine thousand banks failed.

Enter Deposit Insurance

To prevent bank runs, the federal government set up a system of deposit insurance to assure depositors that their deposits would be safe. The Federal Deposit Insurance Corporation (FDIC) and

the Federal Savings and Loan Insurance Corporation (FSLIC) were created in the 1930s to insure deposits. In 1971, the National Credit Union Shares Insurance Fund (NCUSIF) was added to insure credit union deposits. Although the names and form of some of these organizations have changed over the years, the principle remains the same: to insure all accounts in these financial institutions against losses up to a specified limit. In 1933, each account was insured up to $2,500. During the recession that started in December 2007, the federal government wanted to make sure that no banking panics would occur. Therefore, in 2008 the insurance limit was raised to $250,000. Although federal insurance for bank deposits may seem like a good idea, some problems are associated with it.

Moral Hazard: An Unintended Consequence of Deposit Insurance

In your finance courses, you learn that the riskier a loan is, the higher the interest rate that a lending institution can charge the borrower. Bank managers must weigh the trade-off between risk and return

Continued

when deciding which loan applicants should receive funds. Loans to poor credit risks offer high profits, assuming that the borrowers actually pay off their debts. Good credit risks are more likely to pay their debts, but can obtain loans at lower rates.

Particularly since the fall of 2008, when the federal deposit insurance limit was increased to $250,000 per account, managers have had a greater incentive to make risky loans. By doing so, in the short run the banks make higher profits, and the managers receive higher salaries and bonuses. If some of these risky loans are not repaid, what is the likely outcome? A bank's losses are limited because the federal government—you, the taxpayer—will cover any shortfall between the bank's assets and its

liabilities. Consequently, federal deposit insurance means that banks get to enjoy all of the profits of risk taking without bearing all of the consequences of that risk taking.

Thus, an unintended consequence of federal deposit insurance is to encourage *moral hazard*. It creates an incentive for bank managers to take more risks in their lending policies than they would otherwise.

Critical Thinking

Imagine the United States without federal deposit insurance. What are some of the mechanisms that would arise to "punish" bank managers who acted irresponsibly?

Key Terms

cashier's check 411
certified check 413
clearinghouse 425
collecting bank 421
depositary bank 421

digital cash 427
electronic fund transfer (EFT) 425
e-money 427
Federal Reserve System 425
intermediary bank 421

overdraft 414
payor bank 421
Regulation E 426
smart card 428
stale check 415

stop-payment order 415
stored-value card 427
traveler's check 412

Chapter Summary: Checks and Banking in the Digital Age

Checks (See pages 411–413.)	1. *Cashier's check*—A check drawn by a bank on itself (the bank is both the drawer and the drawee) and purchased by a customer. In effect, the bank assumes responsibility for paying the check, thus making the check nearly the equivalent of cash. 2. *Traveler's check*—An instrument on which a financial institution is both the drawer and the drawee. The purchaser must provide his or her signature as a countersignature for a traveler's check to become a negotiable instrument. 3. *Certified check*—A check for which the drawee bank certifies in writing that it has set aside funds from the drawer's account to ensure payment of the check on presentation. On certification, the drawer and all prior indorsers are completely discharged from liability on the check.
The Bank-Customer Relationship (See pages 413–414.)	1. *Creditor-debtor relationship*—A customer and a bank have a creditor-debtor relationship (the bank is the debtor because it holds the customer's funds on deposit). 2. *Agency relationship*—Because a bank must act in accordance with the customer's orders in regard to the customer's deposited money, an agency relationship also arises—the bank is the agent for the customer, who is the principal. 3. *Contractual relationship*—The bank's relationship with its customer is also contractual. Both the bank and the customer assume certain contractual duties when a customer opens a bank account.
Bank's Duty to Honor Checks (See pages 414–420.)	Generally, a bank has a duty to honor its customers' checks, provided that the customers have sufficient funds on deposit to cover the checks [UCC 4–401(a)]. The bank is liable to its customers for actual damages proved to be due to wrongful dishonor [UCC 4–402]. 1. *Overdraft*—The bank has a right to charge a customer's account for any item properly payable, even if the charge results in an overdraft. [UCC 4–401] 2. *Postdated check*—The bank may charge a postdated check against a customer's account, unless the customer notifies the bank of the postdating in time to allow the bank to act on the customer's notice before paying on the check [UCC 4–401]. 3. *Stale check*—The bank is not obligated to pay an uncertified check presented more than six months after its date, but the bank may do so in good faith without liability [UCC 4–404].

Chapter Summary: Checks and Banking in the Digital Age— Continued

Bank's Duty to Honor Checks —Continued	4. *Stop-payment order*—The customer (or a person authorized to draw on the account) must make a stop-payment order in time for the bank to have a reasonable opportunity to act. Oral orders are binding for only fourteen days unless they are confirmed in writing. Written or electronic orders are effective for only six months unless renewed in writing [UCC 4–403]. The bank is liable for wrongful payment over a timely stop-payment order to the extent that the customer suffers a loss. 5. *Death or incompetence of a customer*—So long as the bank does not know of the death or incompetence of a customer, the bank can pay an item without liability. Even with knowledge of a customer's death, a bank can honor or certify checks (in the absence of a stop-payment order) for ten days after the date of the customer's death [UCC 4–405]. 6. *Forged signature or alteration*—The customer has a duty to examine account statements with reasonable care on receipt and to notify the bank promptly of any forged signatures or alterations. On a series of forged signatures or alterations by the same wrongdoer, examination and report must be made within thirty calendar days of receipt of the first statement containing a forged or altered item [UCC 4–406]. The customer's failure to comply with these rules releases the bank from liability unless the bank failed to exercise reasonable care, in which case liability may be apportioned according to a comparative negligence standard. Regardless of care or lack of care, the customer is barred from holding the bank liable after one year for forged customer signatures or alterations and after three years for forged indorsements.

Bank's Duty to Accept Deposits (See pages 420–425.)	A bank has a duty to accept deposits made by its customers into their accounts. Funds from deposited checks must be made available to customers according to a schedule mandated by the Expedited Funds Availability Act of 1987 and Regulation CC. A bank also has a duty to collect payment on any checks deposited by its customers. When checks deposited by customers are drawn on other banks, the check-collection process comes into play.
	1. *Definitions of banks*—UCC 4–105 provides the following definitions of banks involved in the collection process:
	  a. Depositary bank—The first bank to accept a check for payment.
	  b. Payor bank—The bank on which a check is drawn.
	  c. Collecting bank—Any bank except the payor bank that handles a check during the collection process.
	  d. Intermediary bank—Any bank except the payor bank or the depositary bank to which an item is transferred in the course of the collection process.
	2. *Check collection between customers of the same bank*—A check payable by the depositary bank that receives it is an "on-us item." If the bank does not dishonor the check by the opening of the second banking day following its receipt, the check is considered paid [UCC 4–215(e)(2)].
	3. *Check collection between customers of different banks*—Each bank in the collection process must pass the check on to the next appropriate bank before midnight of the next banking day following its receipt [UCC 4–108, 4–202(b), 4–302].
	4. *How the Federal Reserve System clears checks*—The Federal Reserve System facilitates the check-clearing process by serving as a clearinghouse for checks.
	5. *Electronic check presentment*—When checks are presented electronically, items are encoded with information (such as the amount of the check) that is read and processed by other banks' computers. Sometimes, a check is retained at its place of deposit, and only its image or description is presented for payment under a Federal Reserve agreement, clearinghouse rule, or other agreement [UCC 4–110].

Electronic Fund Transfers (See pages 425–427.)	1. *Types of EFT systems*—
	  a. Automated teller machines (ATMs).
	  b. Point-of-sale systems.
	  c. Direct deposits and withdrawals.
	  d. Internet payment systems.
	2. *Consumer fund transfers*—Consumer fund transfers are governed by the Electronic Fund Transfer Act (EFTA) of 1978. The EFTA is basically a disclosure law that sets forth the rights and duties of the bank and the customer with respect to EFT systems. Banks must comply strictly with EFTA requirements.
	3. *Commercial transfers*—Article 4A of the UCC, which has been adopted by almost all of the states, governs fund transfers not subject to the EFTA or other federal or state statutes.

E-Money and Online Banking (See pages 427–428.)	1. *New forms of e-payments*—These include stored-value cards and smart cards.
	2. *Current online banking services*—
	  a. Bill consolidation and payment.
	  b. Transferring funds among accounts.
	  c. Applying for loans.

ExamPrep

ISSUE SPOTTERS

1. Lyn writes a check for $900 to Mac, who indorses the check in blank and transfers it to Nan. She presents the check to Omega Bank, the drawee bank, for payment. Omega does not honor the check. Is Lyn liable to Nan? Could Lyn be subject to criminal prosecution? Why or why not? **(See page 414.)**

2. Roni writes a check for $700 to Sela. Sela indorses the check in blank and transfers it to Titus, who alters the check to read $7,000 and presents it to Union Bank, the drawee, for payment. The bank cashes it. Roni discovers the alteration and sues the bank. How much, if anything, can Roni recover? From whom can the bank recover this amount? **(See pages 419–420.)**

— Check your answers to the Issue Spotters against the answers provided in Appendix E at the end of this text.

BEFORE THE TEST

Go to www.cengagebrain.com, enter the ISBN 9781133191353, and click on "Find" to locate this textbook's Web site. Then, click on "Access Now" under "Study Tools," and select Chapter 14 at the top. There, you will find a Practice Quiz that you can take to assess your mastery of the concepts in this chapter, as well as Flashcards, a Glossary of important terms, and Video Questions (when assigned).

For Review

Answers to the even-numbered questions in this For Review section can be found in Appendix F at the end of this text.

1. What type of check does a bank agree in advance to accept when the check is presented for payment?
2. When may a bank properly dishonor a customer's check without being liable to the customer?
3. What duties does the Uniform Commercial Code impose on a bank's customers with regard to forged and altered checks? What are the consequences if a customer is negligent in performing those duties?
4. What is electronic check presentment, and how does it differ from the traditional check-clearing process?
5. What are the four most common types of electronic fund transfers?

Business Scenarios and Case Problems

14–1 Forged Checks. Roy Supply, Inc., and R. M. R. Drywall, Inc., had checking accounts at Wells Fargo Bank. Both accounts required all checks to carry two signatures—that of Edward Roy and that of Twila June Moore, both of whom were executive officers of both companies. Between January 2006 and March 2008, the bank honored hundreds of checks on which Roy's signature was forged by Moore. On January 31, 2009, Roy and the two corporations notified the bank of the forgeries and then filed a suit in a California state court against the bank, alleging negligence. Who is liable for the amounts of the forged checks? Why? **(See pages 416–418.)**

14–2 ❓ **Question with Sample Answer—Customer Negligence.** Gary goes grocery shopping and carelessly leaves his checkbook in his shopping cart. His checkbook, with two blank checks remaining, is stolen by Dolores. On May 5, Dolores forges Gary's name on a check for $100 and cashes the check at Gary's bank, Citizens Bank of Middletown. Gary has not reported the loss of his blank checks to his bank. On June 1, Gary receives his monthly bank statement from Citizens Bank that includes the forged check, but he does not

notice the item nor does he examine his bank statement. On June 20, Dolores forges Gary's last check. This check is for $1,000 and is cashed at Eastern City Bank, a bank with which Dolores has previously done business. Eastern City Bank puts the check through the collection process, and Citizens Bank honors it. On July 1, on receipt of his bank statement and canceled checks covering June transactions, Gary discovers both forgeries and immediately notifies Citizens Bank. Dolores cannot be found. Gary claims that Citizens Bank must recredit his account for both checks, as his signature was forged. Discuss fully Gary's claim. **(See pages 416–417.)**

—For a sample answer to Question 14–2, go to Appendix G at the end of this text.

14–3 🗂 **Spotlight on Embezzlement—Forged Drawers' Signatures.** In December 1999, Spacemakers of America, Inc., hired Jenny Triplett as a bookkeeper. Triplett was responsible for maintaining the company checkbook and reconciling it with the monthly statements from SunTrust Bank. She also handled invoices from vendors. Spacemakers' president, Dennis Rose, reviewed the invoices and signed the checks to pay them, but no other employee checked Triplett's work. By the end of her first full month of employment, Triplett had forged six checks totaling more than $22,000, all payable to Triple M Entertainment, which was not a Spacemakers vendor. By October 2000, Triplett had forged fifty-nine more checks, totaling more than $475,000. A SunTrust employee became suspicious of an item that required sight inspection under the bank's fraud detection standards, which exceeded those of other banks in the area. Triplett was arrested. Spacemakers sued SunTrust Bank, which filed a motion for summary judgment. On what basis could the bank avoid liability? In whose favor should the court rule, and why? [*Spacemakers of America, Inc. v. SunTrust Bank*, 271 Ga.App. 335, 609 S.E.2d 683 (2005)] **(See pages 416–418.)**

14–4 Bank's Duty of Care. When Arnett Gertrude was diagnosed with cancer, she added her nephew, Jack Scriber, as an authorized signatory to her checking account. Before Gertrude died, Scriber wrote checks on the account to transfer nearly all of the $600,000 in the account to his own account. After Gertrude's death, Bobbie Caudill, the administrator of her estate, discovered the withdrawals and filed a suit against the bank. What is the relationship between a bank and its customer? Is the bank liable in this case? Why or why not? [*Caudill v. Salyersville National Bank*, 2010 WL 45882 (Ky.App. 2010)] **(See page 416.)**

14–5 Forged Drawers' Signatures. Debbie Brooks and Martha Tingstrom lived together. Tingstrom handled their finances. For five years, Brooks did not look at any statements concerning her accounts. When she finally reviewed the statements, she discovered that Tingstrom had taken $85,500 from Brooks's checking account with Transamerica Financial Advisors. Tingstrom had forged Brooks's name on six checks paid between one and two years earlier. Another year passed before Brooks filed a suit against Transamerica. Who is most likely to suffer the loss for the checks paid with Brooks's forged signature? Why? [*Brooks v. Transamerica Financial Advisors*, 57 So.3d 1153 (La.App. 2 Cir. 2011)] **(See pages 416–418.)**

14–6 Case Problem with Sample Answer—Honoring Checks. Adley Abdulwahab (Wahab) opened an account on behalf of W Financial Group, LLC, with Wells Fargo Bank. Wahab was one of three authorized signers on the account. Five months later, Wahab withdrew $1,701,250 from W Financial's account to buy a cashier's check payable to Lubna Lateef. Wahab visited a different Wells Fargo branch and deposited the check into the account of CA Houston Investment Center, LLC. Wahab was the only authorized signer on this account. Lateef never received or indorsed the check. W Financial filed a suit to recover the amount. Applying the rules for payment on a forged indorsement, who is liable? [*Jones v. Wells Fargo Bank*, 666 F.3d 955 (5th Cir. 2012)] **(See page 418.)**

—For a sample answer to Problem 14–6, go to Appendix H at the end of this text.

14–7 ⬌ A Question of Ethics—Forged Signatures. From the 1960s, James Johnson served as Bradley Union's personal caretaker and assistant, and was authorized by Union to handle his banking transactions. Louise Johnson, James's wife, wrote checks on Union's checking account to pay his bills, normally signing the checks "Brad Union." Branch Banking & Trust Co. (BB&T) managed Union's account. In December 2000, on the basis of Union's deteriorating mental and physical condition, a North Carolina state court declared him incompetent. Douglas Maxwell was appointed as Union's guardian. Maxwell "froze" Union's checking account and asked BB&T for copies of the canceled checks, which were provided by July 2001. Maxwell believed that Union's signature on the checks had been forged. In August 2002, Maxwell contacted BB&T, which refused to recredit Union's account. Maxwell filed a suit on Union's behalf in a North Carolina state court against BB&T. [*Union v. Branch Banking & Trust Co.*, 176 N.C.App. 711, 627 S.E.2d 276 (2006)] **(See pages 416–418.)**

1. Before Maxwell's appointment, BB&T sent monthly statements and canceled checks to Union, and Johnson reviewed them, but no unauthorized signatures were ever reported. On whom can liability be imposed in the case of a forged drawer's signature on a check? What are the limits set by Section 4–406(f) of the Uniform Commercial Code? Should Johnson's position, Union's incompetence, or Maxwell's appointment affect the application of these principles? Explain.

2. Why was this suit brought against BB&T? Is BB&T liable? If not, who is? Why? Regardless of any violations of the law, did anyone act unethically in this case? If so, who and why?

Critical Thinking and Writing Assignments

14–8 Critical Legal Thinking. Since the 1990 revision of Article 4, a bank is no longer required to include the customer's canceled checks when it sends monthly statements to the customer. A bank may simply itemize the checks (by number, date, and amount). It may provide photocopies of the checks as well but is not required to do so. What implications do the revised rules have for bank customers in terms of liability for unauthorized signatures and indorsements? **(See pages 416–417.)**

14–9 Business Law Critical Thinking Group Assignment. On January 5, Brian drafts a check for $3,000 drawn on Southern Marine Bank and payable to his assistant,

Shanta. Brian puts last year's date on the check by mistake. On January 7, before Shanta has had a chance to go to the bank, Brian is killed in an automobile accident. Southern Marine Bank is aware of Brian's death. On January 10, Shanta presents the check to the bank, and the bank honors the check by payment to Shanta. Later, Brian's widow, Joyce, claims that because the bank knew of Brian's death and also because the check was by date over one year old, the bank acted wrongfully when it paid Shanta. Joyce, as executor of Brian's estate and sole heir by his will, demands that Southern Marine Bank recredit Brian's estate for the check paid to Shanta.

1. The first group will determine whether the bank acted wrongfully by honoring Brian's check and paying Shanta.
2. The second group will assess whether Joyce has a valid claim against Southern Marine Bank for the amount of the check paid to Shanta.
3. A third group will assume that the check Brian drafted was on his business account rather than on his personal bank account and that he had two partners in the business. Would a business partner be in a better position than his widow to force Southern Marine Bank to recredit Brian's account? Why or why not?

CHAPTER 15

Creditors' Rights and Bankruptcy

(Kameleon007/iStockphoto.com)

CHAPTER OUTLINE

- Laws Assisting Creditors
- Protection for Debtors
- Bankruptcy Proceedings
- Chapter 7—Liquidation
- Chapter 11—Reorganization
- Bankruptcy Relief under Chapter 12 and Chapter 13

LEARNING OBJECTIVES

The five learning objectives below are designed to help improve your understanding of the chapter. After reading this chapter, you should be able to answer the following questions:

1 What is a prejudgment attachment? What is a writ of execution? How does a creditor use these remedies?

2 What is garnishment? When might a creditor undertake a garnishment proceeding?

3 In a bankruptcy proceeding, what constitutes the debtor's estate in property? What property is exempt from the estate under federal bankruptcy law?

4 What is the difference between an exception to discharge and an objection to discharge?

5 In a Chapter 11 reorganization, what is the role of the debtor in possession?

"Capitalism without bankruptcy is like Christianity without hell."
—Frank Borman, 1928–present (U.S. astronaut and businessman)

Secured Transaction Any transaction in which the payment of a debt is guaranteed, or secured, by personal property owned by the debtor or in which the debtor has a legal interest.

Many people in today's economy are struggling to pay their monthly debts. Although in the old days, debtors were punished and sometimes even sent to jail for failing to pay their debts, people today rarely go to jail. They have many other options. In this chapter, we briefly look at **secured transactions,** which arise whenever payment of a debt is guaranteed, or secured, by personal property owned by a debtor. We also discuss some basic laws that assist the debtor and creditor in resolving disputes.

We then turn to the topic of bankruptcy—a last resort in resolving debtor-creditor problems. As implied by the chapter-opening quotation, bankruptcy may be a necessary evil in our capitalistic society. Hence, every businessperson should have some understanding of the bankruptcy process. Today, some bankruptcy courts are using social media to communicate with the public, as you will read about in the *Adapting the Law to the Online Environment* feature on page 447.

Laws Assisting Creditors

Article 9 of the Uniform Commercial Code (UCC) governs secured transactions, which we discuss first. In addition, both the common law and other statutory laws create various rights and remedies for creditors, which are examined on the following pages.

Secured Transactions

The concept of the secured transaction is as basic to modern business practice as the concept of credit. Logically, sellers and lenders want to get paid for their goods and services, so they usually will not sell goods or lend funds unless payment is somehow guaranteed. To insure that they will receive payment or performance, sellers and other creditors can take a *security interest* in the debtor's personal property as collateral for the debt. Personal property, as you will read in Chapter 23, can be *tangible* (physical, such as a building or a vehicle) or *intangible* (nonphysical, such as patents or stocks). The UCC sets forth the rules for creating and establishing security interests.

Default To fail to pay a debt when it is due.

Creating a Security Interest
A creditor has two main concerns if the debtor **defaults** (fails to pay the debt as promised): (1) Can the debt be satisfied through the possession and (usually) sale of the collateral? (2) Will the creditor have priority over any other creditors or buyers who may have rights in the same collateral? These two concerns are met through the creation and perfection of a security interest.

To become a secured party, the creditor must obtain a security interest in the collateral of the debtor. Three requirements must be met for a creditor to have an enforceable security interest:

1. Either the collateral must be in the possession of the secured party, or there must be a written security agreement. In most situations, a written security agreement is used. The agreement must be signed by the debtor and must contain a description that reasonably identifies the collateral.
2. The secured party must give something of value to the debtor. Normally, the value takes the form of a direct loan or a commitment to sell goods on credit.
3. The debtor must have "rights" in the collateral.

Once these requirements have been met, the creditor's rights are said to *attach* to the collateral. **EXAMPLE 15.1** Yuri applies for a credit card at an office supply store. The application contains a clause stating that the store will retain a security interest in the goods that he buys with the card until he has paid for the goods in full. This application would be considered a written security agreement, which is the first requirement for an enforceable security interest. The goods that Yuri buys with the card are the collateral (the second requirement), and his ownership interest in those goods is the right that he has in them (the third requirement). Thus, the requirements for an enforceable security interest are met. When Yuri buys something with the card, the store's rights attach to it. ●

Perfection The legal process by which secured parties protect themselves against the claims of third parties who may wish to have their debts satisfied out of the same collateral. It is usually accomplished by filing a financing statement with the appropriate government official.

Perfecting a Security Interest
Even though a security interest has attached, the secured party must take steps to protect its claim to the collateral in the event that the debtor *defaults* (fails to pay the debt as promised). **Perfection** is the legal process by which secured parties protect themselves against the claims of third parties who may wish to have their debts satisfied out of the same collateral. This sort of conflict may occur, for example, in bankruptcy proceedings, which we will discuss later in this chapter.

In most situations, a secured party perfects a claim by filing a uniform financing statement, or Form UCC-1, with the appropriate state or local government official. Filing the statement gives public notice to third parties of the secured party's security interest. Where or how a security interest is perfected sometimes depends on the type of collateral and whether it is tangible or intangible. In general, financing statements for timber to be cut, fixtures, or items to be extracted—such as oil, coal, gas, and minerals—are filed with the county clerk. Other kinds of collateral require filing with the secretary of state.

A financing statement is effective for five years from the date of filing. If a *continuation statement* is filed *within six months* before the expiration date, the effectiveness of the original statement is continued for another five years, starting with the expiration date of the first five-year period. The effectiveness of the statement can be continued in the same manner indefinitely.

The financing statement must contain the following:

1. The signature of the debtor.
2. The addresses of the debtor and the creditor.
3. A description of the collateral by type or item. (Note that the financing statement can have the same information and descriptions as the security agreement.)

Description of the Collateral   The UCC permits broad, general descriptions, such as "all assets" in the financing statement.   **CASE EXAMPLE 15.2**   Richard and Amanda Baker operated a dairy farm and bought fifty-eight cows from Jeanne Angell on credit. To perfect a claim in the cows (the collateral), Angell filed a financing statement that identified the cows by their names and ear-tag designations. She also gave the Bakers a certificate of registration for each cow that included the same information and a sketch showing distinctive markings.

Over the years, many of the cows' ear tags were lost or replaced with tags with different numbers. When a dispute arose between the parties, the cows' descriptions on the financing statement were questioned. A court held that the statement reasonably identified the cows. Both the statement and the certificates contained the names of the cows, and it is a common practice in the dairy farm industry to match cows to their certificates rather than rely on ear-tags.[1] •

Filing the Financing Statement   The state in which the financing statement must be filed depends on the debtor's location, not the location of the collateral. For individual debtors, the statement is filed in the state of the debtor's principal residence. Business entities and corporate debtors file the statement in the state in which they are incorporated or organized.

Improper filing of the financing statement can render the security interest unperfected and reduce the secured party's claim in bankruptcy proceedings to that of an unsecured creditor. For instance, if extra papers or lists are attached to the financing statement and not referred to in the form itself, that would most likely be considered misleading. Additionally, if the debtor's name on a financing statement is seriously misleading or if the collateral is not sufficiently described, the filing may not be effective.

Perfection without Filing   A few types of security interests can be perfected without filing a financing statement. When the collateral is transferred into the possession of the secured party (such as when a debtor gives a creditor a diamond necklace as collateral for a loan), perfection occurs without filing a financing statement. In addition, a limited number of security interests can be perfected on attachment (without a filing and without having to possess the goods).

Under the UCC, fourteen types of security interests are perfected automatically at the time they are created [UCC 9–309]. The most common of these is the **purchase-money security interest (PMSI)** in *consumer goods* (items bought primarily for personal, family, or household purposes). A PMSI in consumer goods is created when a person buys goods and the seller

Purchase-Money Security Interest (PMSI) A security interest that arises when a seller or lender extends credit for part or all of the purchase price of goods purchased by a buyer.

---

1. *In re Baker,* 456 Bankr. 359 (2012).

or lender agrees to extend credit for part or all of the purchase price of the goods. The entity that extends the credit and obtains the PMSI can be either the seller (a store, for example) or a financial institution that lends the buyer the funds with which to purchase the goods.

A PMSI in consumer goods is perfected automatically at the time of a credit sale—that is, at the time the PMSI is created. The seller in this situation does not need to do anything more to perfect her or his interest. **EXAMPLE 15.3** To purchase a 3D television from Fry's Electronics for $2,500, Jamie signs an agreement to pay $1,000 down and $100 per month until the balance plus interest is fully paid. Fry's is to retain a security interest in the television until full payment has been made. Because the security interest was created as part of the purchase agreement, it is a PMSI in consumer goods. Fry's does not need to do anything else to perfect its security interest. ●

General Rules of Priority

Rules of priority are important when more than one party claims an interest in the same collateral. The basic rule is that when more than one security interest has been perfected, the first security interest to be perfected (or filed) has priority over any security interests that are perfected later. If only one of the conflicting security interests has been perfected, then that security interest has priority. If none of the security interests have been perfected, then the first security interest that attaches has priority.

There are exceptions to these rules, of course. For instance, a person who buys "in the ordinary course of business" takes the goods free from any security interest created by the seller even if the security interest is perfected. Therefore, a person who buys a car from a dealership takes the car free and clear of any security interest the dealership had created to finance its inventory.

Basic Remedies

On the debtor's default, a secured party can repossess the collateral without the use of judicial process [UCC 9–609(b)]. This provision is often referred to as the "self-help" provision of Article 9. The secured party can then keep the collateral in full or partial satisfaction of the debt, or can sell, lease, or dispose of the property in any commercially reasonable manner. When the collateral no longer exists or has greatly declined in value, a secured party may choose to relinquish the security interest and use any judicial remedy available (such as obtaining a judgment on the underlying debt).

Liens

A *lien* is an encumbrance on (claim against) property to satisfy a debt or protect a claim for the payment of a debt. Creditors' liens may arise under the common law or under statutory law. Statutory liens include *mechanic's liens,* whereas *artisan's liens* were recognized by common law. *Judicial liens* arise when a creditor attempts to collect on a debt before or after a judgment is entered by a court.

Mechanic's and artisan's liens can be an important tool for creditors because these liens normally take priority over perfected security interests—unless a statute provides otherwise. Other types of liens can also be useful because a lien creditor generally has priority over an unperfected secured party. In other words, if a creditor obtains a lien *before* another party perfects a security interest in the same property, the lienholder has priority. If the lien is not obtained until *after* another's security interest in the property is perfected, the perfected security interest has priority.

Mechanic's Lien

Mechanic's Lien A statutory lien on the real property of another to ensure payment to a person who has performed work and furnished materials for the repair or improvement of that property.

If a person contracts for labor, services, or materials to be furnished for making improvements on real property (land and things attached to it, such as buildings and trees—see Chapter 24) and does not immediately pay for the improvements, the creditor can file a **mechanic's lien** on the property. This creates a special type of debtor-creditor relationship in which the real estate itself becomes security for the debt.

If the homeowner does not pay this painter, what can he do to recover payment?

Artisan's Lien A possessory lien on personal property of another person to ensure payment to a person who has made improvements on and added value to that property.

EXAMPLE 15.4 Jeff paints a house for Becky, a homeowner, for an agreed-on price to cover labor and materials. If Becky refuses to pay for the work or pays only a portion of the charges, a mechanic's lien against the property can be created. Jeff is the lienholder, and the real property is encumbered (burdened) with a mechanic's lien for the amount owed. If Becky does not pay the lien, the property can be sold to satisfy the debt. ●

State law governs the procedures that must be followed to create a mechanic's lien. Generally, the lienholder must file a written notice of lien within a specific time period (usually 60 to 120 days) from the last date labor or materials were provided. Notice of the foreclosure and sale must be given to the debtor in advance, however. (*Foreclosure* is the process by which the creditor deprives the debtor of the property.)

Artisan's Lien
When a debtor fails to pay for labor and materials furnished for the repair or improvement of personal property, a creditor can recover payment through an **artisan's lien.** In contrast to a mechanic's lien, an artisan's lien is *possessory.* The lienholder ordinarily must have retained possession of the property and have expressly or impliedly agreed to provide the services on a cash, not a credit, basis. The lien remains in existence as long as the lienholder maintains possession of the property, and the lien is terminated once possession is voluntarily surrendered—unless the surrender is only temporary.

EXAMPLE 15.5 Selena leaves her diamond ring at the jeweler's to be repaired and to have her initials engraved on the band. In the absence of an agreement, the jeweler can keep the ring until Selena pays for the services. Should Selena fail to pay, the jeweler has a lien on Selena's ring for the amount of the bill and normally can sell the ring in satisfaction of the lien. ●

Modern statutes permit the holder of an artisan's lien to foreclose and sell the property subject to the lien to satisfy payment of the debt. As with a mechanic's lien, the holder of an artisan's lien must give notice to the owner of the property prior to foreclosure and sale. The sale proceeds are used to pay the debt and the costs of the legal proceedings, and the surplus, if any, is paid to the former owner.

Judicial Liens
A creditor can bring a legal action against a debtor to collect a past-due debt. If the creditor is successful, the court awards the creditor a judgment against a debtor (usually for the amount of the debt plus any interest and legal costs incurred). Frequently, however, the creditor is unable to collect the awarded amount.

To ensure that a judgment will be collectible, the creditor can request that certain non-exempt property of the debtor be seized to satisfy the debt. (As will be discussed later in this chapter, under state or federal statutes, certain property is exempt from attachment by creditors.) A court's order to seize the debtor's property is known as a *writ of attachment* if it is issued before a judgment. If the court's order is issued after a judgment, it is referred to as a *writ of execution*.

Writ of Attachment
In the context of judicial liens, **attachment** is a court-ordered seizure of property before a judgment is secured for a past-due debt. Attachment rights are created by state statutes. Normally, attachment is a *prejudgment* remedy occurring either at the time a lawsuit is filed or immediately afterwards. The due process clause of the Fourteenth Amendment to the U.S. Constitution requires that the debtor be given notice and an opportunity to be heard (see Chapter 1).

To attach before judgment, a creditor must comply with the specific state's statutory requirements. The creditor must have an enforceable right to payment of the debt under law and must follow certain procedures or risk liability for wrongful attachment. Typically, the creditor must file an *affidavit*—that is, a written statement, made under oath—with the court and post a bond. The affidavit states that the debtor is in default and indicates the statutory grounds under which attachment is sought. The bond covers

LEARNING OBJECTIVE 1
What is a prejudgment attachment? What is a writ of execution? How does a creditor use these remedies?

Attachment The legal process of seizing another's property under a court order to secure satisfaction of a judgment yet to be rendered.

(dans_prat/iStockphoto.com)

Under what conditions could a creditor obtain a writ of attachment on this speed boat?

Writ of Attachment A writ used to enforce obedience to an order or judgment of the court.

Writ of Execution A writ that puts in force a court's decree or judgment.

Garnishment A legal process whereby a creditor appropriates a debtor's property or wages that are in the hands of a third party.

LEARNING OBJECTIVE 2
What is garnishment? When might a creditor undertake a garnishment proceeding?

at least the court costs, the value of the debtor's loss of use of the goods, and the value of the property attached.

When the court is satisfied that all of the requirements have been met, it issues a **writ of attachment**, which directs the sheriff or other public officer to seize nonexempt property. If the creditor prevails at trial, the seized property can be sold to satisfy the judgment.

Writ of Execution   If the creditor wins at trial and the debtor will not or cannot pay the judgment, the creditor is entitled to go back to the court and request a **writ of execution.** This writ is a court order directing the sheriff to seize (levy) and sell any of the debtor's nonexempt real or personal property that is within the court's geographic jurisdiction (usually the county in which the courthouse is located).

The proceeds of the sale are used to pay off the judgment, accrued interest, and the costs of the sale. Any excess is paid to the debtor. The debtor can pay the judgment and redeem the nonexempt property any time before the sale takes place. (Because of exemption laws and bankruptcy laws, however, many judgments are uncollectible.)

Garnishment

Garnishment occurs when a creditor is permitted to collect a debt by seizing property of the debtor (such as wages or funds in a bank account) that is being held by a third party. As a result of a garnishment proceeding, the debtor's employer may be ordered by the court to turn over a portion of the debtor's wages to pay the debt.

CASE EXAMPLE 15.6   Helen Griffin failed to pay a debt she owed to Indiana Surgical Specialists. When Indiana Surgical filed a lawsuit to collect, the court issued a garnishment order to withhold the appropriate amount from Griffin's earnings until her debt was paid even though Griffin was working as an independent contractor (see Chapter 17) rather than as an employee at the time. The court held that payments for the services of an independent contractor fall within the definition of earnings and can be garnished.[2] ●

State law governs garnishment, so the procedure varies. In some states, the creditor needs to obtain only one order of garnishment, which will then apply continuously to the debtor's wages until the entire debt is paid. In other states, the judgment creditor must go back to court for a separate order of garnishment for each pay period.

Both federal and state laws limit the amount that can be taken from a debtor's weekly take-home pay through garnishment proceedings.[3] Federal law provides a framework to protect debtors from suffering unduly when paying judgment debts.[4] State laws also provide dollar exemptions, and these amounts are often larger than those provided by federal law. Under federal law, an employer cannot dismiss an employee because his or her wages are being garnished.

Creditors' Composition Agreements

Creditors' Composition Agreement An agreement formed between a debtor and his or her creditors in which the creditors agree to accept a lesser sum than that owed by the debtor in full satisfaction of the debt.

Creditors may contract with the debtor for discharge of the debtor's liquidated debts (debts that are definite, or fixed, in amount) on payment of a sum less than that owed. These agreements are called **creditors' composition agreements,** or simply *composition agreements,* and usually are held to be enforceable.

---

2. *Indiana Surgical Specialists v. Griffin,* 867 N.E.2d 260 (Ind.App. 2007).

3. Some states (for example, Texas) do not permit garnishment of wages by private parties except under a child-support order.

4. For example, the federal Consumer Credit Protection Act of 1968, 15 U.S.C. Sections 1601–1693r, provides that a debtor can retain either 75 percent of disposable earnings per week or a sum equivalent to thirty hours of work paid at federal minimum-wage rates, whichever is greater.

Exhibit 15.1 Suretyship and Guaranty Parties

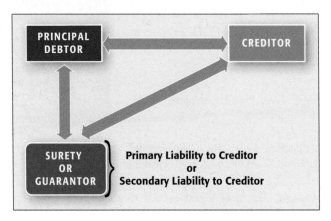

PRINCIPAL DEBTOR ⟷ CREDITOR

SURETY OR GUARANTOR

Primary Liability to Creditor
or
Secondary Liability to Creditor

Suretyship An express contract in which a third party (the surety) promises to be primarily responsible for a debtor's obligation to a creditor.

Surety A third party who agrees to be primarily responsible for the debt of another.

Guarantor A person who agrees to satisfy the debt of another (the debtor) only after the principal debtor defaults. Thus, a guarantor's liability is secondary.

How can a minor with little or no income convince a car dealer to sell him or her a car?

(Callietar/iStockphoto.com)

Suretyship and Guaranty

When a third person promises to pay a debt owed by another in the event the debtor does not pay, either a *suretyship* or a *guaranty* relationship is created. Exhibit 15.1 on the left illustrates these relationships. The third person's income and assets become the security for the debt owed.

Suretyship and guaranty provide creditors with the right to seek payment from the third party if the primary debtor defaults on her or his obligations. At common law, there were significant differences in the liability of a surety and a guarantor, as discussed in the following subsections. Today, however, the distinctions outlined here have been abolished in some states.

Surety A contract of strict **suretyship** is a promise made by a third person to be responsible for the debtor's obligation. It is an express contract between the **surety** (the third party) and the creditor. The surety in the strictest sense is primarily liable for the debt of the principal. The creditor need not exhaust all legal remedies against the principal debtor before holding the surety responsible for payment. The creditor can demand payment from the surety from the moment the debt is due.

EXAMPLE 15.7 Roberto Delmar wants to borrow from the bank to buy a used car. Because Roberto is still in college, the bank will not lend him the funds unless his father, José Delmar, who has dealt with the bank before, will cosign the note (add his signature to the note, thereby becoming a surety and thus jointly liable for payment of the debt). When José cosigns the note, he becomes primarily liable to the bank. On the note's due date, the bank can seek payment from either Roberto or José, or both jointly. •

Guaranty With a suretyship arrangement, the surety is *primarily* liable for the debtor's obligation. With a guaranty arrangement, the **guarantor**—the third person making the guaranty—is *secondarily* liable. The guarantor can be required to pay the obligation *only after the principal debtor defaults,* and default usually takes place only after the creditor has made an attempt to collect from the debtor.

EXAMPLE 15.8 BX Enterprises, a small corporation, needs to borrow funds to meet its payroll. The bank is skeptical about the creditworthiness of BX and requires Dawson, its president, who is a wealthy businessperson and the owner of 70 percent of BX Enterprises, to sign an agreement making himself personally liable for payment if BX does not pay off the loan. As a guarantor of the loan, Dawson cannot be held liable until BX Enterprises is in default. •

Under the Statute of Frauds, a guaranty contract between the guarantor and the creditor must be in writing to be enforceable unless the *main purpose rule* applies (see Chapter 8 on page 245).[5] Under common law, a suretyship agreement did not need to be in writing to be enforceable, and oral surety agreements were sufficient. Today, however, some states require a writing (record) to enforce a suretyship.

In the following *Spotlight Case,* the issue was whether a guaranty of a lease signed by the president of a corporation was enforceable against the officer personally, although he claimed to have signed the guaranty only as a representative of the corporation.

---

5. Briefly, the main purpose rule, or exception, provides that if the main purpose of the guaranty agreement is to benefit the guarantor, then the contract need not be in writing to be enforceable.

Spotlight on Personal Guaranties

Case 15.1
Wilson Court Limited Partnership v. Tony Maroni's, Inc.
Supreme Court of Washington, 134 Wash.2d 692, 952 P.2d 590 (1998).

(cristianl/iStockphoto.com)

Tony Maroni's pizza.

COMPANY PROFILE *Tony Riviera founded Tony Maroni's, Inc., to sell Tony Maroni's Famous Gourmet Pizza in Seattle, Washington, in the late 1980s. Tony Maroni's began by offering pizzas, salads, calzones, and lasagna for delivery only. By 1995, the firm had begun franchising its brand (franchising will be discussed in Chapter 19). Two years later, with eleven locations in the Seattle area, including six franchise outlets, and ten more stores in development, the company announced plans to open five hundred locations nationwide before 2002. Despite these plans, by the end of 1997, the firm had yet to turn a profit and was nearly $1 million in debt.*

FACTS Tony Maroni's, Inc., agreed to lease retail space owned by Wilson Court Limited Partnership. Tony Riviera, Tony Maroni's president, signed the lease for 1,676 square feet of space for a sixty-month term. When he signed the lease, Riviera also signed a guaranty agreement that was incorporated by reference in the lease.

On the signature line of the guaranty, Riviera wrote "President" after his name. The guaranty did not specifically identify who was bound, referring only to "the undersigned" or "Guarantor." Riviera also signed the lease in a representative capacity, but the lease clearly indicated that only Tony Maroni's was bound by its terms. When Tony Maroni's defaulted on the lease, Wilson filed a suit in a Washington state court against Tony Maroni's, Riviera, and others. Riviera asserted, in part, that he was not personally liable on the guaranty because he signed only in his capacity as a corporate officer. The court issued a summary judgment in favor of Wilson. Riviera appealed to the Washington Supreme Court.

ISSUE Was Riviera personally liable on the guaranty?

DECISION Yes. The Washington Supreme Court affirmed the judgment of the lower court.

REASON The state supreme court reasoned that if Riviera, the president, were not personally liable, the corporation would be the guarantor of its own lease. That conclusion would be commercially unreasonable because a party cannot be the guarantor of its own contract. The court pointed out that "any ambiguity in the Guaranty was created by Riviera" and "such ambiguity will be construed against Riviera as the party who drafted this language." The court noted that the "combination of circumstances" made the guaranty ambiguous. Nevertheless, by referring to three parties, including the "Guarantor," "the language of the Guaranty itself compels the view Riviera is personally liable." The court explained that "[i]f Riviera signed the Guaranty only in his representative capacity, Tony Maroni's would be both Tenant and Guarantor, rendering the Guaranty provisions absurd." Thus, "the very nature of a guaranty is such that Riviera created personal liability by his signature."

CRITICAL THINKING—Ethical Consideration *Are there any circumstances in which a collateral document signed by a corporate officer to secure a corporate debt might not create personal liability? Explain.*

Actions That Release the Surety and Guarantor   Basically, the same actions will release a surety or a guarantor from an obligation. In general, the same rules apply to both sureties and guarantors. So, for simplicity, this subsection and the following subsections will refer just to sureties.

If a material modification is made in the terms of the original contract between the principal debtor and the creditor—without the surety's consent—the surety's obligation will be discharged. (The extent to which the surety is discharged depends on whether he or she was compensated and the amount of the loss suffered a result of the modification.) Similarly, if a debt is secured by collateral and the creditor surrenders the collateral to the debtor or impairs the collateral without the surety's consent, these acts can reduce the surety's obligation.

Naturally, any payment of the principal obligation by the debtor or by another person on the debtor's behalf will discharge the surety from the obligation. Even if the creditor refused to accept payment of the principal debt when it was tendered, the surety's obligation can be discharged.

Defenses of the Surety and the Guarantor

Generally, the surety (or guarantor) can also assert any of the defenses available to a principal debtor to avoid liability on the obligation to the creditor. A few exceptions do exist, however. The surety cannot assert the principal debtor's incapacity or bankruptcy as a defense, nor can the surety assert the statute of limitations as a defense.

Obviously, a surety may also have her or his own defenses—for example, her or his own incapacity or bankruptcy. If the creditor fraudulently induced the surety to guarantee the debt of the debtor, the surety can assert fraud as a defense. In most states, the creditor has a legal duty to inform the surety, before the formation of the suretyship contract, of material facts known by the creditor that would substantially increase the surety's risk. Failure to so inform may constitute fraud and renders the suretyship obligation voidable.

Rights of the Surety and the Guarantor

Usually, when the surety (or guarantor) pays the debt owed to the creditor, the surety (or guarantor) is entitled to certain rights.

Right of Subrogation The right of a surety or guarantor to stand in the place of (be substituted for) the creditors, giving the surety or guarantor the same legal rights against the debtor that the creditor had.

The Right of Subrogation The surety has the legal **right of subrogation,** which means that any right the creditor had against the debtor now becomes the right of the surety. Included are creditor rights in bankruptcy, rights to collateral possessed by the creditor, and rights to judgments secured by the creditor. In short, the surety stands in the shoes of the creditor and may pursue any remedies that were available to the creditor against the debtor.

Right of Reimbursement The legal right of a person to be repaid or indemnified for costs, expenses, or losses incurred or expended on behalf of another.

The Right of Reimbursement The surety has a **right of reimbursement** from the debtor. Basically, the surety is entitled to receive from the debtor all outlays made on behalf of the suretyship arrangement. Such outlays can include expenses incurred as well as the actual amount of the debt paid to the creditor.

Co-Surety A person who assumes liability jointly with another surety for the payment of an obligation.

Right of Contribution The right of a co-surety who pays more than her or his proportionate share on a debtor's default to recover the excess paid from other co-sureties.

The Right of Contribution Two or more sureties are called **co-sureties.** When one co-surety pays more than her or his proportionate share on a debtor's default, she or he is entitled to recover from the other co-sureties the amount paid above that surety's obligation. This is the **right of contribution.** Generally, a co-surety's liability either is determined by agreement between the co-sureties or, in the absence of an agreement, is specified in the suretyship contract itself.

EXAMPLE 15.9 Two co-sureties—Yasser and Itzhak—are obligated under a suretyship contract to guarantee the debt of Jules. Itzhak's maximum liability is $15,000, and Yasser's is $10,000. Jules owes $10,000 and is in default. Itzhak pays the creditor the entire $10,000. In the absence of an agreement to the contrary, Itzhak can recover $4,000 from Yasser. The amount of the debt that Yasser agreed to cover is divided by the total amount that Itzhak and Yasser together agreed to cover. The result is multiplied by the amount of the default, yielding the amount that Yasser owes—($10,000 ÷ $25,000) × $10,000 = $4,000. •

PREVENTING LEGAL DISPUTES

Be careful when signing guaranty contracts. In particular, explicitly indicate if you are signing on behalf of a company rather than personally. If you are a corporate officer or director and you sign your name on a guaranty without indicating that you are signing as a representative of the corporation, you might be held personally liable. Although a guaranty contract may be preferable to a suretyship contract, in some states, because it creates secondary rather than primary liability, a guaranty still involves substantial risk. Depending on the wording used in a guaranty contract, the extent of the guarantor's liability may be unlimited or may continue over a series of transactions. Be absolutely clear about the potential liability before agreeing to serve as a guarantor, and contact an attorney for guidance.

Protection for Debtors

The law protects debtors as well as creditors. Certain property of the debtor, for example, is exempt from creditors' actions. Of course, bankruptcy laws, which will be discussed shortly, are designed specifically to assist debtors.

In most states, certain types of real and personal property are exempt from execution or attachment. State exemption statutes usually include both real and personal property.

Exempted Real Property

Homestead Exemption A law permitting a debtor to retain the family home, either in its entirety or up to a specified dollar amount, free from the claims of unsecured creditors or trustees in bankruptcy.

Probably the most familiar real property exemption is the **homestead exemption.** Each state permits the debtor to retain the family home, either in its entirety or up to a specified dollar amount, free from the claims of unsecured creditors or trustees in bankruptcy (discussed later in this chapter). The purpose of the homestead exemption is to ensure that the debtor will retain some form of shelter. (Note that federal bankruptcy law now places a cap on the amount that debtors can claim under a state's homestead exemption—see page 454.)

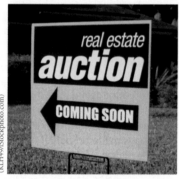

If a house is sold at auction to satisfy a debt, can the creditor always keep the full proceeds from that sale?

EXAMPLE 15.10   Van Cleave owes Acosta $40,000. The debt is the subject of a lawsuit, and the court awards Acosta a judgment of $40,000 against Van Cleave. Van Cleave's home is valued at $50,000, and the state exemption on homesteads is $25,000. There are no outstanding mortgages or other liens. To satisfy the judgment debt, Van Cleave's family home is sold at public auction for $45,000. The proceeds of the sale are distributed as follows:

1. Van Cleave is given $25,000 as his homestead exemption.
2. Acosta is paid $20,000 toward the judgment debt, leaving a $20,000 deficiency judgment that can be satisfied from any other nonexempt property (personal or real) that Van Cleave may have, if allowed by state law. •

In a few states, statutes allow the homestead exemption only if the judgment debtor has a family. If a judgment debtor does not have a family, a creditor may be entitled to collect the full amount realized from the sale of the debtor's home. In addition, the homestead exemption interacts with other areas of law and can sometimes operate to cancel out a portion of a lien on a debtor's real property.

CASE EXAMPLE 15.11   Antonio Stanley purchased a modular home from Yates Mobile Services Corporation. When Stanley failed to pay the purchase price of the home, Yates obtained a judicial lien against Stanley's property in the amount of $165,138.05. Stanley then filed for bankruptcy and asserted the homestead exemption. The court found that Stanley was entitled to avoid the lien to the extent that it impaired his exemption. Using a bankruptcy law formula, the court determined that the total impairment was $143,639.05 and that Stanley could avoid paying this amount to Yates. Thus, Yates was left with a judicial lien on Stanley's home in the amount of $21,499.[6] •

Exempted Personal Property

Personal property that is most often exempt under state law includes the following:

1. Household furniture up to a specified dollar amount.
2. Clothing and certain personal possessions, such as family pictures or a religious text.
3. A vehicle (or vehicles) for transportation (at least up to a specified dollar amount).
4. Certain classified animals, usually livestock but including pets.
5. Equipment that the debtor uses in a business or trade, such as tools or professional instruments, up to a specified dollar amount.

---

6. *In re Stanley,* 2010 WL 2103441 (M.D.N.C. 2010).

Bankruptcy Proceedings

Bankruptcy law in the United States has two goals—to protect a debtor by giving him or her a fresh start, free from creditors' claims, and to ensure equitable treatment to creditors who are competing for the debtor's assets. Bankruptcy law is federal law, but state laws on secured transactions, liens, judgments, and exemptions also play a role in federal bankruptcy proceedings.

Bankruptcy law before 2005 was based on the Bankruptcy Reform Act of 1978, as amended (called the Bankruptcy Code, or simply, the Code). In 2005, Congress enacted bankruptcy reform legislation that significantly overhauled certain provisions of the Bankruptcy Code for the first time in twenty-five years.[7] Because of its significance for creditors and debtors alike, we present the Bankruptcy Reform Act of 2005 as this chapter's *Landmark in the Law* feature below.

---

7. The full title of the act is the Bankruptcy Abuse Prevention and Consumer Protection Act of 2005, Pub. L. No. 109-8, 119 Stat. 23 (April 20, 2005).

LANDMARK IN THE LAW
The Bankruptcy Reform Act of 2005

When Congress enacted the Bankruptcy Reform Act of 1978, many claimed that the new act made it too easy for debtors to file for bankruptcy protection. The Bankruptcy Reform Act of 2005 was passed, in part, in response to businesses' concerns about the rise in personal bankruptcy filings. From 1978 to 2005, personal bankruptcy filings increased dramatically. Various business groups—including credit-card companies, retailers, and banks—claimed that the bankruptcy process was being abused and that reform was necessary.

More Repayment Plans, Fewer Liquidation Bankruptcies

One of the major goals of the Bankruptcy Reform Act of 2005 is to require consumers to pay as many of their debts as they possibly can instead of having those debts fully discharged in bankruptcy. Before the reforms, the vast majority of bankruptcies were filed under Chapter 7 of the Bankruptcy Code, which permits debtors, with some exceptions, to have *all* of their debts discharged in bankruptcy. Only about 20 percent of personal bankruptcies were filed under Chapter 13 of the Bankruptcy Code. As you will read later in this chapter, this part of the Bankruptcy Code requires the debtor to establish a repayment plan and pay off as many of his or her debts as possible over a maximum period of five years. Under the 2005 legislation, more debtors have to file for bankruptcy under Chapter 13.

Other Significant Provisions of the Act

Another important provision of the Bankruptcy Reform Act of 2005 involves the homestead exemption. Before the passage of the act, some states allowed debtors petitioning for bankruptcy to exempt all of the *equity* (the market value minus the outstanding mortgage owed) in their homes during bankruptcy proceedings. The 2005 act leaves these exemptions in place but puts some limits on their use. The 2005 act also included a number of other changes. For example, one provision gives child-support obligations priority over other debts and allows enforcement agencies to continue efforts to collect child-support payments.

Application to Today's World

Under the Bankruptcy Reform Act of 2005, fewer debtors are allowed to have their debts discharged in Chapter 7 liquidation proceedings. At the same time, the act makes it more difficult for debtors to obtain a "fresh start" financially—one of the major goals of bankruptcy law in the United States. Today, more debtors are forced to file under Chapter 13. Additionally, the bankruptcy process has become more time consuming and costly because it requires more extensive documentation and certification. These changes in the law, in conjunction with the global financial crisis that began in 2007, have left many Americans unable to obtain relief from their debts.

Bankruptcy Courts

Bankruptcy proceedings are held in federal bankruptcy courts, which are under the authority of U.S. district courts. Rulings by bankruptcy courts can be appealed to the district courts. The bankruptcy court holds proceedings dealing with the procedures required to administer the debtor's estate in bankruptcy (the debtor's assets, as will be discussed shortly). For a discussion of how bankruptcy courts are adapting to the use of social media, see this chapter's *Adapting the Law to the Online Environment* feature on the facing page.

Types of Bankruptcy Relief

The Bankruptcy Code is contained in Title 11 of the *United States Code* (U.S.C.) and has eight "chapters." Chapters 1, 3, and 5 of the Code include general definitional provisions and provisions governing case administration and procedures, creditors, the debtor, and the estate. These three chapters of the Code normally apply to all types of bankruptcies.

Four chapters of the Code set forth the most important types of relief that debtors can seek.

1. Chapter 7 provides for *liquidation* proceedings—that is, the selling of all nonexempt assets and the distribution of the proceeds to the debtor's creditors.
2. Chapter 11 governs reorganizations.
3. Chapter 12 (for family farmers and family fishermen) and Chapter 13 (for individuals) provide for adjustment of the debts of parties with regular income.[8]

Note that a debtor (except for a municipality) need not be insolvent[9] to file for bankruptcy relief under the Bankruptcy Code. Anyone obligated to a creditor can declare bankruptcy.

A **consumer-debtor** is a debtor whose debts result primarily from the purchase of goods for personal, family, or household use. The Bankruptcy Code requires that the clerk of the court give all consumer-debtors written notice of the general purpose, benefits, and costs of each chapter of bankruptcy under which they may proceed. In addition, the clerk must provide consumer-debtors with information on the types of services available from credit counseling agencies.

Consumer-Debtor A person whose debts result primarily from the purchases of goods for personal, family, or household use.

Chapter 7—Liquidation

Liquidation under Chapter 7 is the most familiar type of bankruptcy proceeding and is often referred to as an *ordinary*, or *straight*, *bankruptcy*. Put simply, a debtor in a liquidation bankruptcy turns all assets over to a trustee. The trustee sells the nonexempt assets and distributes the proceeds to creditors. With certain exceptions, the remaining debts are then **discharged** (extinguished), and the debtor is relieved of the obligation to pay the debts.

Any "person"—defined as including individuals, partnerships, and corporations—may be a debtor under Chapter 7. Railroads, insurance companies, banks, savings and loan associations, investment companies licensed by the U.S. Small Business Administration, and credit unions *cannot* be Chapter 7 debtors, however. Other chapters of the Code or other federal or state statutes apply to them. A husband and wife may file jointly for bankruptcy under a single petition.

Liquidation The sale of the nonexempt assets of a debtor and the distribution of the funds received to creditors.

Discharge The termination of a bankruptcy debtor's obligation to pay debts.

---

8. There are no Chapters 2, 4, 6, 8, or 10 in Title 11. Such "gaps" are not uncommon in the *United States Code*. They occur because, when a statute is enacted, chapter numbers (or other subdivisional unit numbers) are sometimes reserved for future use. (A gap may also appear if a law has been repealed.)

9. The inability to pay debts as they come due is known as *equitable* insolvency. A *balance-sheet* insolvency, which exists when a debtor's liabilities exceed assets, is not the test. Thus, it is possible for debtors to petition voluntarily for bankruptcy even though their assets far exceed their liabilities. This situation may occur when a debtor's cash-flow problems become severe.

ADAPTING THE LAW TO THE ONLINE ENVIRONMENT

LIVE CHATTING WITH YOUR STATE'S BANKRUPTCY COURT

Chatting on social media has become a way of life for most younger people in this country and elsewhere. Online chats preceded social media and are still used at retail Web sites. Today, some tech-savvy employees at bankruptcy courts are using the retail online chat model to answer questions about bankruptcy.

Arizona Was First to Use Live Chats

The U.S. Bankruptcy Court for the District of Arizona started live chatting several years ago. It added live chat to its Web site as part of a strategic initiative to educate the public about bankruptcy. Rather than leaving voice messages, people who access the court's Web site can send and receive text messages via an easy-to-use chat box. The court's goal is to respond to a live chat request within thirty seconds.

In 2011, New Mexico became the second state to add online chatting to its bankruptcy court's Web site. Nevada followed with its live chat in 2012.

The courts that have adopted online chatting average about ten chats a day. Most chats last less than ten minutes.

Who Uses Bankruptcy Court Chat Rooms?

At first, only individuals interested in filing for bankruptcy without an attorney used the live chat services. When paralegals learned that they could get quick answers to their questions online, they also began to use the services.

Then, during the real estate meltdown of the last few years, many real estate lawyers expanded into the area of bankruptcy law, often as a way to help their clients avoid foreclosure through bankruptcy filings. Many of these lawyers also have used live chat to expand their knowledge of bankruptcy law.

Critical Thinking

Are there any downsides to live chats with bankruptcy courts? If so, what are they?

Petition in Bankruptcy The document that is filed with a bankruptcy court to initiate bankruptcy proceedings.

A straight bankruptcy may be commenced by the filing of either a voluntary or an involuntary **petition in bankruptcy**—the document that is filed with a bankruptcy court to initiate bankruptcy proceedings. If a debtor files the petition, then it is a *voluntary bankruptcy*. If one or more creditors file a petition to force the debtor into bankruptcy, then it is called an *involuntary bankruptcy*. We discuss both voluntary and involuntary bankruptcy proceedings under Chapter 7 in the following subsections.

Voluntary Bankruptcy

To bring a voluntary petition in bankruptcy, the debtor files official forms designated for that purpose in the bankruptcy court. The law now requires that *before* debtors can file a petition, they must receive credit counseling from an approved nonprofit agency within the 180-day period preceding the date of filing. Debtors filing a Chapter 7 petition must include a certificate proving that they have received individual or group counseling from an approved agency within the last 180 days (roughly six months).

A consumer-debtor who is filing a liquidation bankruptcy must confirm the accuracy of the petition's contents. The debtor must also state in the petition, at the time of filing, that he or she understands the relief available under other chapters of the Code and has chosen to proceed under Chapter 7. Attorneys representing consumer-debtors must file an affidavit stating that they have informed the debtors of the relief available under each chapter of the Code. In addition, the attorneys must reasonably attempt to verify the accuracy of the consumer-debtors' petitions and schedules (described on the next page). Failure to do so is considered perjury.

Which creditors have claims on the proceeds from liquidation sales?

(WendellandCarolyn/iStockphoto.com)

Chapter 7 Schedules   The voluntary petition contains the following schedules:

1. A list of both secured and unsecured creditors, their addresses, and the amount of debt owed to each.
2. A statement of the financial affairs of the debtor.
3. A list of all property owned by the debtor, including property claimed by the debtor to be exempt.
4. A list of current income and expenses.
5. A certificate of credit counseling (as discussed previously).
6. Proof of payments received from employers within sixty days prior to the filing of the petition.
7. A statement of the amount of monthly income, itemized to show how the amount is calculated.
8. A copy of the debtor's federal income tax return for the most recent year ending immediately before the filing of the petition.

The official forms must be completed accurately, sworn to under oath, and signed by the debtor. To conceal assets or knowingly supply false information on these schedules is a crime under the bankruptcy laws.

With the exception of tax returns, failure to file the required schedules within forty-five days after the filing of the petition (unless an extension is granted) will result in an automatic dismissal of the petition. The debtor has up to seven days before the date of the first creditors' meeting to provide a copy of the most recent tax returns to the trustee.

Tax Returns during Bankruptcy   In addition, a debtor may be required to file a tax return at the end of each tax year while the case is pending and to provide a copy to the court. This may be done at the request of the court or of the **U.S. trustee**—a government official who performs administrative tasks that a bankruptcy judge would otherwise have to perform, including supervising the work of the bankruptcy trustee.

Any *party in interest* (a party, such as a creditor, who has a valid interest in the outcome of the proceedings) may make this request as well. Debtors may also be required to file tax returns during Chapter 11 and 13 bankruptcies.

Substantial Abuse and the Means Test   In the past, a bankruptcy court could dismiss a Chapter 7 petition for relief (discharge of debts) if the use of Chapter 7 would constitute a "substantial abuse" of bankruptcy law. Today, the law provides a *means test* to determine a debtor's eligibility for Chapter 7. The purpose of the test is to keep upper-income people from abusing the bankruptcy process by filing for Chapter 7, as was thought to have happened in the past. The test forces more people to file for Chapter 13 bankruptcy rather than have their debts discharged under Chapter 7.

A debtor wishing to file for bankruptcy must complete the means test to determine whether she or he qualifies for Chapter 7. The debtor's average monthly income in recent months is compared with the median income in the geographic area in which the person lives. (The U.S. Trustee Program provides these data at its Web site.) If the debtor's income is below the median income, the debtor usually is allowed to file for Chapter 7 bankruptcy, as there is no presumption of bankruptcy abuse.

Applying the Means Test to Future Disposable Income   If the debtor's income is above the median income, then further calculations must be made to determine whether the person will have sufficient disposable income in the future to repay at least some of his or her unsecured debts. *Disposable income* is calculated by subtracting living expenses and interest payments on secured debt, such as mortgage payments, from monthly income.

U.S. Trustee A government official who performs certain administrative tasks that a bankruptcy judge would otherwise have to perform.

In making this calculation, the debtor's recent monthly income is presumed to continue for the next sixty months. Living expenses are the amounts allowed under formulas used by the Internal Revenue Service (IRS). The IRS allowances include modest allocations for food, clothing, housing, utilities, transportation (including car payments), health care, and other necessities. (The U.S. Trustee Program's Web site also provides these amounts.) The allowances do not include expenditures for items such as cell phones and cable television service.

Can the Debtor Afford to Pay Unsecured Debts?   Once future disposable income has been estimated, that amount is used to determine whether the debtor will have income that could be applied to unsecured debts. The court may also consider the debtor's bad faith or other circumstances indicating abuse.

CASE EXAMPLE 15.12   At thirty-three years old, Lisa Hebbring owned a home and a car, but had $11,124 in credit-card debt. Hebbring was earning $49,000 per year when she filed for Chapter 7 bankruptcy. Her petition listed monthly net income of $2,813 and expenditures of $2,897, for a deficit of $84.

In calculating her income, Hebbring excluded a $313 monthly deduction for contributions to retirement plans. The U.S. trustee filed a motion to dismiss Hebbring's petition due to substantial abuse, claiming that the retirement contributions should be disallowed. The court agreed and dismissed the Chapter 7 petition. Because Hebbring's retirement contributions were not reasonably necessary based on her age and financial circumstances, the court found that she was capable of paying her unsecured debts.[10] •

Additional Grounds for Dismissal

As noted, a debtor's voluntary petition for Chapter 7 relief may be dismissed for substantial abuse or for failing to provide the necessary documents (such as schedules and tax returns) within the specified time.

In addition, a motion to dismiss a Chapter 7 filing may be granted in two other situations. First, if the debtor has been convicted of a violent crime or a drug-trafficking offense, the victim can file a motion to dismiss the voluntary petition.[11] Second, if the debtor fails to pay postpetition domestic-support obligations (which include child and spousal support), the court may dismiss the debtor's Chapter 7 petition.

Order for Relief

If the voluntary petition for bankruptcy is found to be proper, the filing of the petition will itself constitute an order for relief. (An **order for relief** is the court's grant of assistance to a debtor.) Once a consumer-debtor's voluntary petition has been filed, the clerk of the court (or other appointee) must give the trustee and creditors notice of the order for relief by mail not more than twenty days after the entry of the order.

Order for Relief A court's grant of assistance to a complainant. In bankruptcy proceedings, the order relieves the debtor of the immediate obligation to pay the debts listed in the bankruptcy petition.

Involuntary Bankruptcy

An involuntary bankruptcy occurs when the debtor's creditors force the debtor into bankruptcy proceedings. An involuntary case cannot be filed against a farmer[12] or a charitable institution. For an involuntary action to be filed against other debtors, the following requirements must be met: If the debtor has twelve or more creditors, three or more of those creditors having unsecured claims totaling at least $14,425 must join in the petition. If a debtor has fewer than twelve creditors, one or more creditors having a claim of $14,425 or more may file.

---

10. *Hebbring v. U.S. Trustee,* 463 F.3d 902 (9th Cir. 2006).
11. Note that the court may not dismiss a case on this ground if the debtor's bankruptcy is necessary to satisfy a claim for a domestic-support obligation.
12. The definition of *farmer* includes persons who receive more than 50 percent of their gross income from farming operations, such as tilling the soil; dairy farming; ranching; or the production or raising of crops, poultry, or livestock. Corporations and partnerships, as well as individuals, can be farmers.

If the debtor challenges the involuntary petition, a hearing will be held, and the debtor's challenge will fail if the bankruptcy court finds either of the following:

1. The debtor generally is not paying debts as they become due.
2. A general receiver, assignee, or custodian took possession of, or was appointed to take charge of, substantially all of the debtor's property within 120 days before the filing of the involuntary petition.

If the court allows the bankruptcy to proceed, the debtor will be required to supply the same information in the bankruptcy schedules as in a voluntary bankruptcy.

An involuntary petition should not be used as an everyday debt-collection device, and the Code provides penalties for the filing of frivolous (unjustified) petitions against debtors. If the court dismisses an involuntary petition, the petitioning creditors may be required to pay the costs and attorneys' fees incurred by the debtor in defending against the petition. If the petition was filed in bad faith, damages can be awarded for injury to the debtor's reputation. Punitive damages may also be awarded.

Automatic Stay

The moment a petition, either voluntary or involuntary, is filed, an **automatic stay,** or suspension, of almost all actions by creditors against the debtor or the debtor's property normally goes into effect. In other words, once a petition has been filed, creditors cannot contact the debtor by phone or mail or start any legal proceedings to recover debts or to repossess property.

If a creditor *knowingly* violates the automatic stay (a willful violation), any injured party, including the debtor, is entitled to recover actual damages, costs, and attorneys' fees and may be entitled to punitive damages as well.

Until the bankruptcy proceeding is closed or dismissed, the automatic stay prohibits a creditor from taking any act to collect, assess, or recover a claim against the debtor that arose before the filing of the petition.

CASE EXAMPLE 15.13   Stefanie Kuehn filed for bankruptcy. When she requested a transcript from the university at which she obtained her master's degree, the university refused because she owed more than $6,000 in tuition. Kuehn complained to the court. The court ruled that the university had violated the automatic stay when it refused to provide a transcript because it was attempting to collect an unpaid tuition debt.[13] ●

Exceptions to the Automatic Stay   The Code provides several exceptions to the automatic stay. Collection efforts can continue for domestic-support obligations, which include any debt owed to or recoverable by a spouse, former spouse, child of the debtor, a child's parent or guardian, or a governmental unit. In addition, proceedings against the debtor related to divorce, child custody or visitation, domestic violence, and support enforcement are not stayed. Also excepted are investigations by a securities regulatory agency (see Chapter 21) and certain statutory liens for property taxes.

Limitations on the Automatic Stay   A secured creditor or other party in interest can petition the bankruptcy court for relief from the automatic stay. If a creditor or other party requests relief from the stay, the stay will automatically terminate sixty days after the request, unless the court grants an extension[14] or the parties agree otherwise. Also, the automatic stay on secured debts normally will terminate thirty days after the petition is filed if the debtor had filed a bankruptcy petition that was dismissed within the prior year.

---

13. *In re Kuehn,* 563 F.3d 289 (7th Cir. 2009).
14. The court might grant an extension, for example, on a motion by the trustee that the property is of value to the estate.

If the debtor had two or more bankruptcy petitions dismissed during the prior year, the Code presumes bad faith, and the automatic stay does not go into effect until the court determines that the petition was filed in good faith. In addition, the automatic stay on secured property terminates forty-five days after the creditors' meeting (see page 454) unless the debtor redeems or reaffirms certain debts (*reaffirmation* will be discussed on page 456). In other words, the debtor cannot keep the secured property (such as a financed automobile), even if she or he continues to make payments on it, without reinstating the rights of the secured party to collect on the debt.

Estate in Bankruptcy

Estate in Property All of the property owned by a person, including real estate and personal property.

On the commencement of a liquidation proceeding under Chapter 7, an **estate in property** is created. The estate consists of all the debtor's interests in property currently held, wherever located, together with *community property* (property jointly owned by a husband and wife in certain states—see Chapter 24), property transferred in a transaction voidable by the trustee, proceeds and profits from the property of the estate, and certain after-acquired property.

Interests in certain property—such as gifts, inheritances, property settlements (from divorce), and life insurance death proceeds—to which the debtor becomes entitled *within 180 days after filing* may also become part of the estate. Withholdings for employee benefit plan contributions are excluded from the estate.

Generally, though, the filing of a bankruptcy petition fixes a dividing line: property acquired before the filing of the petition becomes property of the estate, and property acquired after the filing of the petition, except as just noted, remains the debtor's.

LEARNING OBJECTIVE 3
In a bankruptcy proceeding, what constitutes the debtor's estate in property? What property is exempt from the estate under federal bankruptcy law?

The Bankruptcy Trustee

Promptly after the order for relief has been entered, a bankruptcy trustee is appointed. The basic duty of the trustee is to collect the debtor's available estate and reduce it to cash for distribution, preserving the interests of both the debtor and the unsecured creditors. This requires that the trustee be accountable for administering the debtor's estate.

To enable the trustee to accomplish this duty, the Code gives the trustee certain powers, stated in both general and specific terms. These powers must be exercised within two years of the order for relief.

Duties for Means Testing
The trustee is required to review promptly all materials filed by the debtor to determine if there is substantial abuse. Within ten days after the first meeting of the creditors (discussed shortly), the trustee must file a statement as to whether the case is presumed to be an abuse under the means test. The trustee must provide all creditors with a copy of this statement.

When there is a presumption of abuse, the trustee must either file a motion to dismiss the petition (or convert it to a Chapter 13 case) or file a statement setting forth the reasons why the motion would not be appropriate.

Trustee's Powers
The trustee has the power to require persons holding the debtor's property at the time the petition is filed to deliver the property to the trustee.[15] To enable the trustee to implement this power, the Code provides that the trustee has rights *equivalent* to those of certain other parties, such as a creditor who has a judicial lien. This power of a trustee, which is equivalent to that of a lien creditor, is known as the *strong-arm power.*

---

15. Usually, though, the trustee takes constructive, rather than actual, possession of the debtor's property. For instance, a trustee might change the locks on the doors and hire a security guard to constructively take possession of a business's inventory.

In addition, the trustee also has specific *powers of avoidance*—that is, the trustee can set aside (avoid) a sale or other transfer of the debtor's property, taking it back as a part of the debtor's estate. These powers of avoidance extend to any voidable rights available to the debtor, preferences, and fraudulent transfers by the debtor (these will each be discussed next). A trustee can also avoid certain statutory liens (creditors' claims against the debtor's property).

The debtor shares most of the trustee's avoidance powers. Thus, if the trustee does not take action to enforce one of these rights, the debtor in a liquidation bankruptcy can enforce it.

Voidable Rights   A trustee steps into the shoes of the debtor. Thus, any reason that a debtor can use to obtain the return of his or her property can be used by the trustee as well. The grounds for recovery include fraud, duress, incapacity, and mutual mistake.

EXAMPLE 15.14   Blane sells his boat to Inga. Inga gives Blane a check, knowing that she has insufficient funds in her bank account to cover the check. Inga has committed fraud. Blane has the right to avoid that transfer and recover the boat from Inga. If Blane files for Chapter 7 bankruptcy, the trustee can exercise the same right to recover the boat from Inga, and the boat becomes part of the debtor's estate. •

Preferences   A debtor is not permitted to make a property transfer or a payment that favors—or gives a **preference** to—one creditor over others. The trustee is allowed to recover payments made both voluntarily and involuntarily to one creditor in preference over another.

To have made a preferential payment that can be recovered, an *insolvent* debtor generally must have transferred property, for a *preexisting* debt, during the *ninety days* before the filing of the petition in bankruptcy. The transfer must have given the creditor more than the creditor would have received as a result of the bankruptcy proceedings. The Code presumes that the debtor is insolvent during the ninety-day period before filing a petition.

If a **preferred creditor** (one who has received a preferential transfer from the debtor) has sold the property to an innocent third party, the trustee cannot recover the property from the innocent party. The trustee can generally force the preferred creditor to pay the value of the property, however.

Preferences to Insiders   Sometimes, the creditor receiving the preference is an *insider*. An insider is any individual, partner, partnership, or officer or director of a corporation (or a relative of one of these) who has a close relationship with the debtor. In this situation, the avoidance power of the trustee is extended to transfers made within *one year* before filing. (If the transfer was fraudulent, as will be discussed shortly, the trustee can avoid transfers made within *two years* before filing.)

Note, however, that if the transfer occurred before the ninety-day period, the trustee is required to prove that the debtor was insolvent at the time it occurred or that the transfer was made to or for the benefit of an insider.

Transfers That Do Not Constitute Preferences   Not all transfers are preferences. To be a preference, the transfer must be made in exchange for something other than current consideration.

Most courts do not consider a debtor's payment for services rendered within fifteen days prior to the payment to be a preference. If a creditor receives payment in the ordinary course of business, such as payment of last month's cell phone bill, the trustee in bankruptcy cannot recover the payment.

Preference In bankruptcy proceedings, a property transfer or payment made by the debtor that favors one creditor over others.

Preferred Creditor In the context of bankruptcy, a creditor who has received a preferential transfer from a debtor.

KNOW THIS Usually, when property is recovered as a preference, the trustee sells it and distributes the proceeds to the debtor's creditors.

When is the sale of gold jewelry considered a fraudulent transfer?

To be recoverable, a preference must be a transfer for an antecedent (preexisting) debt, such as a year-old landscaping bill. In addition, the Code permits a consumer-debtor to transfer any property to a creditor up to a total value of $5,850, without the transfer constituting a preference. Payments of domestic-support debts do not constitute a preference. Neither do payments required under a plan created by an approved credit-counseling agency.

Fraudulent Transfers A trustee can avoid (set aside, or cancel) fraudulent transfers or obligations if (1) they were made within two years of the filing of the petition or (2) they were made with actual intent to hinder, delay, or defraud a creditor. **EXAMPLE 15.15** April is planning to petition for bankruptcy, so she sells her gold jewelry, worth $10,000, to a friend for $500. The friend agrees that in the future he will "sell" the jewelry back to April for the same amount. This is a fraudulent transfer that the trustee can undo. ●

Exemptions

The trustee takes control over the debtor's property, but an individual debtor is entitled to exempt certain property from the bankruptcy. The Code exempts the following property:[16]

1. Up to $21,625 in equity in the debtor's residence and burial plot (the homestead exemption).
2. Interest in a motor vehicle up to $3,450.
3. Interest, up to $550 for a particular item, in household goods and furnishings, wearing apparel, appliances, books, animals, crops, and musical instruments (the aggregate total of all items is limited to $11,525).
4. Interest in jewelry up to $1,450.
5. Interest in any other property up to $1,150, plus any unused part of the $21,625 homestead exemption up to $10,825.
6. Interest in any tools of the debtor's trade up to $2,175.
7. A life insurance contract owned by the debtor (other than a credit life insurance contract).
8. Certain interests in accrued dividends and interest under life insurance contracts owned by the debtor, not to exceed $11,525.
9. Professionally prescribed health aids.
10. The right to receive Social Security and certain welfare benefits, alimony and support, certain retirement funds and pensions, and education savings accounts held for specific periods of time.
11. The right to receive certain personal-injury and other awards up to $21,625.

Individual states have the power to pass legislation precluding debtors from using the federal exemptions within the state. A majority of the states have done this, as mentioned earlier in this chapter. In those states, debtors may use only state, not federal, exemptions. In the rest of the states, an individual debtor (or a husband and wife filing jointly) may choose either the exemptions provided under state law or the federal exemptions.

---

16. The dollar amounts stated in the Bankruptcy Code are adjusted automatically every three years on April 1 based on changes in the Consumer Price Index. The adjusted amounts are rounded to the nearest $25. The amounts stated in this chapter are in accordance with those computed on April 1, 2010.

The Homestead Exemption

The Bankruptcy Code limits the amount that can be claimed under the homestead exemption in bankruptcy. In general, if the debtor acquired the home within three and one-half years preceding the date of filing, the maximum equity exempted is $146,450, even if state law would permit a higher amount.

In addition, the state homestead exemption is available only if the debtor has lived in the state for two years before filing the petition. Furthermore, a debtor who has violated securities law, been convicted of a felony, or engaged in certain other intentional misconduct may not be permitted to claim the homestead exemption at all.

Creditors' Meeting and Claims

Within a reasonable time after the order of relief has been granted (not more than forty days), the trustee must call a meeting of the creditors listed in the schedules filed by the debtor. The bankruptcy judge does not attend this meeting, but the debtor must attend and submit to an examination under oath. At the meeting, the trustee ensures that the debtor is aware of the potential consequences of bankruptcy and the possibility of filing under a different chapter of the Code.

To be entitled to receive a portion of the debtor's estate, each creditor normally files a *proof of claim* with the bankruptcy court clerk within ninety days of the creditors' meeting. The proof of claim lists the creditor's name and address, as well as the amount that the creditor asserts is owed to the creditor by the debtor.

In a bankruptcy case in which the debtor has no assets (called a "no-asset case"), creditors are notified of the debtor's petition for bankruptcy but are instructed not to file a claim. In no-asset cases, the unsecured creditors will receive no payment, and most, if not all, of these debts will be discharged.

Distribution of Property

The Code provides specific rules for the distribution of the debtor's property to secured and unsecured creditors. If any amount remains after the priority classes of creditors have been satisfied, it is turned over to the debtor. Exhibit 15.2 on the facing page illustrates the collection and distribution of property in most voluntary bankruptcies.

Distribution to Secured Creditors
The Code requires that consumer-debtors file a statement of intention with respect to the secured collateral. They can choose to pay off the debt and redeem the collateral, claim it is exempt, reaffirm the debt and continue making payments, or surrender the property to the secured party. If the collateral is surrendered to the secured party, the secured creditor can enforce the security interest either by accepting the property in full satisfaction of the debt or by selling the collateral and using the proceeds to pay off the debt.

Thus, the secured party has priority over unsecured parties as to the proceeds from the disposition of the collateral. Should the collateral be insufficient to cover the secured debt owed, the secured creditor becomes an unsecured creditor for the difference.

Distribution to Unsecured Creditors
Bankruptcy law establishes an order of priority for classes of debts owed to *unsecured* creditors, and they are paid in the order of their priority. Each class must be fully paid before the next class is entitled to any of the remaining proceeds.

If there are insufficient proceeds to pay the full amount to all the creditors in a class, the proceeds are distributed *proportionately* to the creditors in that class, and classes lower in

Exhibit 15.2 Collection and Distribution of Property in Most Voluntary Bankruptcies

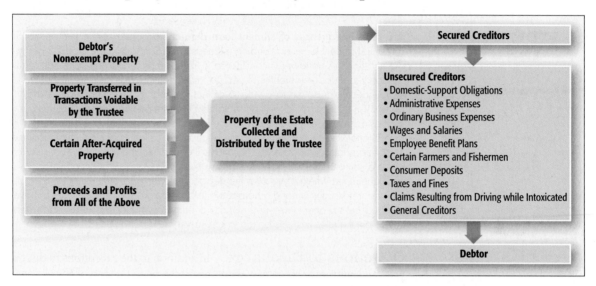

priority receive nothing. If there is any balance remaining after all the creditors are paid, it is returned to the debtor.

In almost all Chapter 7 bankruptcies, the funds will be insufficient to pay all creditors. Note that claims for domestic-support obligations, such as child support and alimony, have the highest priority among unsecured claims, so these debts must be paid first. If any amount remains after the priority classes of creditors have been satisfied, it is turned over to the debtor.

Discharge

From the debtor's point of view, the primary purpose of liquidation is to obtain a fresh start through the discharge of debts. A discharge voids, or sets aside, any judgment on a discharged debt and prevents any action to collect it. Certain debts, however, are not dischargeable in bankruptcy. Also, certain debtors may not qualify to have all debts discharged in bankruptcy. These situations are discussed next.

LEARNING OBJECTIVE 4
What is the difference between an exception to discharge and an objection to discharge?

Exceptions to Discharge   The most important claims that are not dischargeable under Chapter 7 include the following:

1. Claims for back taxes accruing within two years prior to bankruptcy.
2. Claims for amounts borrowed by the debtor to pay federal taxes or any nondischargeable taxes.
3. Claims against property or funds obtained by the debtor under false pretenses or by false misrepresentations.
4. Claims based on fraud or misuse of funds by the debtor or claims involving the debtor's *embezzlement* or *larceny* (see pages 168 and 165, respectively, in Chapter 6).
5. Domestic-support obligations and property settlements.
6. Claims for amounts due on a retirement loan account.
7. Claims based on willful or malicious conduct by the debtor toward another or the property of another.

8. Certain government fines and penalties.
9. Certain student loans, unless payment of the loans causes an undue hardship for the debtor and the debtor's dependents.

ETHICAL ISSUE

Are the consequences of student loan defaults too onerous? In the United States today, the amount of student loans outstanding exceeds $1 trillion, and more than 20 percent of these loans are in default. A borrower is considered in default if he or she has not made regular payments on a student loan for nine months. If you go into default on your student loans, the U.S. Department of Education can do the following to collect the debt: (1) keep your tax refund, if you have one, (2) garnish your paycheck without obtaining a court judgment, and (3) take your federal benefits, such as Social Security retirement payments or disability payments. In addition, in some states, any professional license that you have can be revoked. Last but not least, the Department of Education can bring a lawsuit against you. If it wins, it can collect the judgment from your bank accounts or place a lien on any real property that you own.

Furthermore, whether you owe the debt to the federal government or to a private lender, student loan debt generally is *not* dischargeable in bankruptcy. You may be able to have your payments deferred but for only three years. Under certain circumstances, student loan debts may be canceled, but the rules limit this option to only a very few borrowers.

Objections to Discharge

In addition to the exceptions to discharge previously listed, a bankruptcy court may deny the discharge to the debtor for reasons relating to the debtor's *conduct* and not to the debt. The situations in which a court can deny discharge include the following:

1. The debtor's concealment or destruction of property with the intent to hinder, delay, or defraud a creditor.
2. The debtor's fraudulent concealment or destruction of financial records.
3. The granting of a discharge to the debtor within eight years prior to the filing of the petition.
4. The debtor's failure to complete the required consumer education course (unless such a course was not available).
5. Proceedings in which the debtor could be found guilty of a felony. (Basically, a court may not discharge any debt until the completion of the felony proceedings against the debtor.)

When a discharge is denied under these circumstances, the debtor's assets are still distributed to the creditors. After the bankruptcy proceeding, however, the debtor remains liable for the unpaid portions of all claims.

A discharge may be revoked (taken back) within one year if it is discovered that the debtor acted fraudulently or dishonestly during the bankruptcy proceeding. If that occurs, a creditor whose claim was not satisfied in the distribution of the debtor's property can proceed with his or her claim against the debtor.

Reaffirmation of Debt

An agreement to pay a debt dischargeable in bankruptcy is called a **reaffirmation agreement**. A debtor may wish to pay a debt—for example, a debt owed to a family member, physician, bank, or some other creditor—even though the debt could be discharged in bankruptcy. Also, as noted previously, a debtor cannot retain secured property while continuing to pay without entering into a reaffirmation agreement.

To be enforceable, reaffirmation agreements must be made before the debtor is granted a discharge. The agreement must be signed and filed with the court (along with the original disclosure documents, as you will read shortly). Court approval is required unless the debtor is represented by an attorney. The court will approve the reaffirmation only if it finds that the agreement will not result in undue hardship to the debtor and that the reaffirmation is consistent with the debtor's best interests.

Reaffirmation Agreement An agreement between a debtor and a creditor in which the debtor voluntarily agrees to pay a debt dischargeable in bankruptcy.

To discourage creditors from engaging in abusive reaffirmation practices, the law provides specific language for disclosures that must be given to debtors entering reaffirmation agreements. Among other things, these disclosures explain that the debtor is not required to reaffirm any debt, but that liens on secured property, such as mortgages and cars, will remain in effect even if the debt is not reaffirmed. The original disclosure documents must be signed by the debtor, certified by the debtor's attorney, and filed with the court at the same time as the reaffirmation agreement.

Chapter 11—Reorganization

The type of bankruptcy proceeding used most commonly by corporate debtors is the Chapter 11 *reorganization*. In a reorganization, the creditors and the debtor formulate a plan under which the debtor pays a portion of its debts and the rest of the debts are discharged. The debtor is allowed to continue in business. Although this type of bankruptcy is generally a corporate reorganization, any debtors (including individuals but excluding stockbrokers and commodities brokers) who are eligible for Chapter 7 relief are eligible for relief under Chapter 11.

In 1994, Congress established a "fast-track" Chapter 11 procedure for small-business debtors whose liabilities do not exceed $2.19 million and who do not own or manage real estate. The fast track enables a debtor to avoid the appointment of a creditors' committee and also shortens the filing periods and relaxes certain other requirements. Because the process is shorter and simpler, it is less costly (see the *Linking Business Law to Corporate Management* feature on page 464 for suggestions on how small businesses can prepare for Chapter 11).

The same principles that govern the filing of a liquidation (Chapter 7) petition apply to reorganization (Chapter 11) proceedings. The case may be brought either voluntarily or involuntarily. The automatic-stay provision and its exceptions apply in reorganizations as well, as do the provisions regarding substantial abuse and additional grounds for dismissal (or conversion) of bankruptcy petitions.

Workouts

Workout An out-of-court agreement between a debtor and creditors that establishes a payment plan for discharging the debtor's debts.

In some instances, to avoid bankruptcy proceedings, creditors may prefer private, negotiated adjustments of creditor-debtor relations, also known as a **workout.** Often, these out-of-court workouts are much more flexible and thus conducive to a speedy settlement. Speed is critical because delay is one of the most costly elements in any bankruptcy proceeding. Another advantage of workouts is that they avoid the various administrative costs of bankruptcy proceedings.

Creditors' Best Interests

Once a petition for Chapter 11 has been filed, a bankruptcy court, after notice and a hearing, can dismiss or suspend all proceedings in a case at any time if dismissal or suspension would better serve the interests of the creditors. The Bankruptcy Code also allows a court, after notice and a hearing, to dismiss a case under reorganization "for cause." Cause includes the absence of a reasonable likelihood of rehabilitation, the inability to effect a plan, and an unreasonable delay by the debtor that is prejudicial to (may harm the interests of) creditors.[17]

---

17. See 11 U.S.C. Section 1112(b). A debtor whose petition is dismissed under this provision can file a new Chapter 11 petition (which may be granted unless it is filed in bad faith).

LEARNING OBJECTIVE 5
In a Chapter 11 reorganization, what is the role of the debtor in possession?

Debtor in Possession (DIP) In Chapter 11 bankruptcy proceedings, a debtor who is allowed to continue in possession of the estate in property (the business) and to continue business operations.

Debtor in Possession

On entry of the order for relief, the debtor in Chapter 11 generally continues to operate the business as a **debtor in possession (DIP)**. The court, however, may appoint a trustee (often referred to as a *receiver*) to operate the debtor's business if gross mismanagement of the business is shown or if appointing a trustee is in the best interests of the estate.

The DIP's role is similar to that of a trustee in a liquidation. The DIP is entitled to avoid preferential payments made to creditors and fraudulent transfers of assets. The DIP has the power to decide whether to cancel or assume prepetition *executory contracts* (those that are not yet performed—see Chapter 7 on page 199) or unexpired leases. Cancellation of executory contracts or unexpired leases can be a substantial benefit to a Chapter 11 debtor.

EXAMPLE 15.16   Five years ago, before a national recession, APT Corporation leased an office building for a twenty-year term. Now, APT can no longer pay the rent due under the lease and has filed for Chapter 11 reorganization. In this situation, the debtor in possession could cancel the lease so that APT will not be required to continue paying the substantial rent due for fifteen more years. •

Creditors' Committees

As soon as practicable after the entry of the order for relief, a committee of unsecured creditors is appointed. If the debtor has filed a plan accepted by the creditors, however, the trustee may decide not to call a meeting of the creditors. The committee may consult with the trustee or the debtor concerning the administration of the case or the formulation of the plan. Additional creditors' committees may be appointed to represent special interest creditors, and a court may order the trustee to change a committee's membership as needed to ensure adequate representation of the creditors.

Generally, no orders affecting the estate will be entered without the consent of the committee or a hearing in which the judge is informed of the position of the committee. As mentioned earlier, businesses with debts of less than $2.19 million that do not own or manage real estate can avoid creditors' committees. In these fast-track proceedings, orders can be entered without a committee's consent.

The Reorganization Plan

A reorganization plan is established to conserve and administer the debtor's assets in the hope of an eventual return to successful operation and solvency. The plan must be fair and equitable and must do the following:

1. Designate classes of claims and interests.
2. Specify the treatment to be afforded the classes. (The plan must provide the same treatment for all claims in a particular class.)
3. Provide an adequate means for execution. (Individual debtors must utilize postpetition assets as necessary to execute the plan.)
4. Provide for payment of tax claims over a five-year period.

Filing the Plan   Only the debtor may file a plan within the first 120 days after the date of the order for relief. This period may be extended up to eighteen months from the date of the order for relief. If the debtor does not meet the 120-day deadline or obtain an extension, or if the debtor fails to obtain the required creditor consent (discussed on the facing page) within 180 days, any party may propose a plan. If a small-business debtor chooses to avoid a creditors' committee, the time for the debtor's filing is 180 days.

Acceptance and Confirmation of the Plan Once the plan has been developed, it is submitted to each class of creditors for acceptance. Each class must accept the plan unless the class is adversely affected by it. The plan need not provide for full repayment to unsecured creditors. Instead, creditors receive a percentage of each dollar owed to them by the debtor.

A class has accepted the plan when a majority of the creditors, representing two-thirds of the amount of the total claim, vote to approve it. Confirmation is conditioned on the debtor's certifying that all postpetition domestic-support obligations have been paid in full. For small-business debtors, if the plan meets the listed requirements, the court must confirm the plan within forty-five days (unless this period is extended).

Even when all classes of creditors accept the plan, the court may refuse to confirm it if it is not "in the best interests of the creditors." The plan can also be modified upon the request of the debtor, DIP, trustee, U.S. trustee, or holder of an unsecured claim. If an unsecured creditor objects to the plan, specific rules apply to the value of property to be distributed under the plan. Tax claims must be paid over a five-year period.

Even if only one class of creditors has accepted the plan, the court may still confirm the plan under the Code's so-called **cram-down provision.** In other words, the court may confirm the plan over the objections of a class of creditors. Before the court can exercise this right of cram-down confirmation, it must be demonstrated that the plan is fair and equitable, and does not discriminate unfairly against any creditors.

Cram-Down Provision A provision of the Bankruptcy Code that allows a court to confirm a debtor's Chapter 11 reorganization plan even though only one class of creditors has accepted it.

Discharge The plan is binding on confirmation. The law provides, however, that confirmation of a plan does not discharge an individual debtor. *For individual debtors, the plan must be completed before discharge will be granted,* unless the court orders otherwise. For all other debtors, the court may order discharge at any time after the plan is confirmed. The debtor is given a reorganization discharge from all claims not protected under the plan. This discharge does not apply to any claims that would be denied discharge under liquidation.

Bankruptcy Relief under Chapter 12 and Chapter 13

In addition to bankruptcy relief through liquidation (Chapter 7) and reorganization (Chapter 11), the Code also provides for family-farmer and family-fisherman debt adjustments (Chapter 12) and individuals' repayment plans (Chapter 13).

Family Farmers and Fishermen—Chapter 12

In 1986, to help relieve economic pressure on small farmers, Congress created Chapter 12 of the Bankruptcy Code. In 2005, Congress extended this protection to family fishermen, modified its provisions somewhat, and made it a permanent chapter in the Bankruptcy Code (previously, it had to be periodically renewed by Congress).

For purposes of Chapter 12, a *family farmer* is one whose gross income is at least 50 percent farm dependent and whose debts are at least 50 percent farm related.[18] The total debt must not exceed $3,792,650. A partnership or a close corporation (see Chapters 19 and 20) that is at least 50 percent owned by the farm family can also qualify as a family farmer.[19]

---

18. Note that the Bankruptcy Code defines a *family farmer* and a *farmer* differently. To be a farmer, a person or business must receive 50 percent of gross income from a farming operation that the person or business owns or operates—see footnote 12.

19. Note that for a corporation or partnership to qualify under Chapter 12, at least 80 percent of the value of the firm's assets must consist of assets related to the farming operation.

A *family fisherman* is one whose gross income is at least 50 percent dependent on commercial fishing operations and whose debts are at least 80 percent related to commercial fishing. The total debt for a family fisherman must not exceed $1,757,475. As with family farmers, a partnership or close corporation can also qualify.

Filing the Petition   The procedure for filing a family-farmer or family-fisherman bankruptcy plan is similar to the procedure for filing a repayment plan under Chapter 13, which will be discussed shortly. The debtor must file a plan not later than ninety days after the order for relief. The filing of the petition acts as an automatic stay against creditors' and co-obligors' actions against the estate.

A farmer or fisherman who has already filed a reorganization or repayment plan may convert the plan to a Chapter 12 plan. The debtor may also convert a Chapter 12 plan to a liquidation plan.

Content and Confirmation of the Plan   The content of a plan under Chapter 12 is basically the same as that of a Chapter 13 repayment plan (described below). The plan can be modified by the debtor but, except for cause, must be confirmed or denied within forty-five days of the filing of the plan.

The plan must provide for payment of secured debts at the value of the collateral. If the secured debt exceeds the value of the collateral, the remaining debt is unsecured. For unsecured debtors, the plan must be confirmed if either the value of the property to be distributed under the plan equals the amount of the claim or the plan provides that all of the debtor's disposable income to be received in a three-year period (or longer, by court approval) will be applied to making payments. Completion of payments under the plan discharges all debts provided for by the plan.

Individuals' Repayment Plan—Chapter 13

Chapter 13 of the Bankruptcy Code provides for the "Adjustment of Debts of an Individual with Regular Income." Individuals (not partnerships or corporations) with regular income who owe fixed unsecured debts of less than $360,475 or fixed secured debts of less than $1,081,400 may take advantage of bankruptcy repayment plans.

Many small-business debtors have a choice of filing under either Chapter 11 or Chapter 13. Repayment plans offer some advantages because they are typically less expensive and less complicated than reorganization or liquidation proceedings.

Filing the Petition   A Chapter 13 repayment plan case can be initiated only by the filing of a voluntary petition by the debtor or by the conversion of a Chapter 7 petition (because of a finding of substantial abuse under the means test, for instance). Certain liquidation and reorganization cases may be converted to Chapter 13 with the consent of the debtor.[20] A trustee, who will make payments under the plan, must be appointed. On the filing of a repayment plan petition, the automatic stay previously discussed takes effect. Although the stay applies to all or part of the debtor's consumer debt, it does not apply to any business debt incurred by the debtor or to any domestic-support obligations.

Good Faith Requirement   The Bankruptcy Code imposes the requirement of good faith on a debtor in both the filing of the petition and the filing of the plan. The Code does not define good faith, but if the circumstances as a whole indicate bad faith, a court can dismiss a debtor's Chapter 13 petition.

20. A Chapter 13 repayment plan may be converted to a Chapter 7 liquidation either at the request of the debtor or, under certain circumstances, "for cause" by a creditor. A Chapter 13 case may be converted to a Chapter 11 case after a hearing.

CASE EXAMPLE 15.17 Roger and Pauline Buis formed an air show business called Otto Airshows that included a helicopter decorated as "Otto the Clown." After a competitor won a defamation lawsuit against the Buises and Otto Airshows, the Buises stopped doing business as Otto Airshows and formed a new firm, Prop and Rotor Aviation, Inc., to which they leased the Otto equipment. Within a month, they filed a bankruptcy petition under Chapter 13. The plan and the schedules did not mention the lawsuit, the equipment lease, and several other items. The court therefore dismissed the Buises' petition due to bad faith. The debtors had not included all of their assets and liabilities on their initial petition, and they had timed its filing to avoid payment on the defamation judgment.[21] •

The Repayment Plan   A plan of rehabilitation by repayment must provide for the following:

1. The turning over to the trustee of future earnings or income of the debtor as necessary for execution of the plan.
2. Full payment through deferred cash payments of all claims entitled to priority, such as taxes.[22]
3. Identical treatment of all claims within a particular class. (The Code permits the debtor to list co-debtors, such as guarantors or sureties, as a separate class.)

The repayment plan may provide for payment of all obligations in full or for payment of a lesser amount. The debtor must begin making payments under the proposed plan within thirty days after the plan has been filed and must continue to make "timely" payments from her or his disposable income. If the debtor fails to make timely payments or does not commence payments within the thirty-day period, the court can convert the case to a liquidation bankruptcy or dismiss the petition.

In putting together a repayment plan, a debtor must apply the means test to identify the amount of disposable income that will be available to repay creditors. The debtor is allowed to deduct certain expenses from monthly income to arrive at this amount. Can a debtor who owns a car outright claim the costs of car ownership as an expense? That was the issue in the following case.

---

21. *In re Buis*, 337 Bankr. 243 (N.D.Fla. 2006).
22. As with a Chapter 11 reorganization plan, full repayment of all claims is not always required.

Case 15.2

Ransom v. FIA Card Services, N.A.

Supreme Court of the United States,
__ U.S. __, 131 S.Ct. 716, 178 L.Ed.2d 603 (2011).
www.supremecourt.gov [a]

A debtor owns a Toyota Camry free and clear. Can he claim a car-ownership deduction on the repayment plan?

FACTS Jason Ransom filed a petition in a federal bankruptcy court to declare bankruptcy under Chapter 13. Among his assets, Ransom reported a Toyota Camry that he owned free of any debt. In listing monthly expenses for the means test, he claimed a deduction of $471 for car ownership and a separate deduction of $388 for car-operating costs. Based on his means-test calculations, Ransom proposed a five-year plan that would repay about 25 percent of his unsecured debt. He listed FIA Card Services, N.A., as an unsecured creditor. FIA objected to Ransom's plan, arguing that he should not have claimed the car-ownership allowance because he did not make payments on his car. The court agreed with FIA and issued a decision in

---

a. In the "Supreme Court Documents" column, in the "Opinions" pull-down menu, select "Bound Volumes." On the next page, in the "For Search Term:" box, type "Ransom" and click on "Search." In the result, click on the name of the case to access the opinion. The United States Supreme Court maintains this Web site.

Case 15.2—Continues next page ➡

Case 15.2—Continued

its favor. A Bankruptcy Appellate Panel and the U.S. Court of Appeals for the Ninth Circuit affirmed the decision. Ransom appealed to the United States Supreme Court.

ISSUE Can a debtor in bankruptcy claim the car-ownership deduction even though the debtor owns the car outright and does not make payments on it?

DECISION No. The United States Supreme Court affirmed the lower court's decision.

REASON The Supreme Court referred to tables of standardized expense amounts that a debtor could claim as reasonable living expenses and shield from creditors. The Bankruptcy Code limits a debtor's expense amounts to those that are "applicable," or appropriate. A deduction is appropriate only if the debtor will incur that expense during the life of the Chapter 13 plan. Because Ransom owned the car free and clear, the "Ownership Costs" category was not "applicable" to him, and he could not claim such an expense. The ultimate result was that confirmation of his repayment plan was denied. (Confirmation of repayment plans is discussed below.)

CRITICAL THINKING—Economic Consideration *Should debtors with older vehicles be allowed to take an additional deduction for operating expenses? Explain.*

The Length of the Plan The length of the payment plan can be three or five years, depending on the debtor's family income. If the debtor's family income is less than the median family income in the relevant geographic area under the means test, the term of the proposed plan must be three years.[23] The term may not exceed five years.

Confirmation of the Plan After the plan is filed, the court holds a confirmation hearing, at which interested parties (such as creditors) may object to the plan. The hearing must be held at least twenty days, but no more than forty-five days, after the meeting of the creditors. The debtor must have filed all prepetition tax returns and paid all postpetition domestic-support obligations before a court will confirm any plan. The court will confirm a plan with respect to each claim of a secured creditor under any of the following circumstances:

1. If the secured creditors have accepted the plan.
2. If the plan provides that secured creditors retain their liens until there is payment in full or until the debtor receives a discharge.
3. If the debtor surrenders the property securing the claims to the creditors.

Discharge After the completion of all payments, the court grants a discharge of all debts provided for by the repayment plan. Except for allowed claims not provided for by the plan, certain long-term debts provided for by the plan, certain tax claims, payments on retirement accounts, and claims for domestic-support obligations, all other debts are dischargeable. Under current law, debts related to injury or property damage caused while driving under the influence of alcohol or drugs are nondischargeable.

In the following case, a debtor had proposed to discharge some of his student loan debt in a Chapter 13 repayment plan. Certain student loan debts can be discharged under Chapter 13, but only if the court finds that payment of the debt would constitute an "undue hardship" for the debtor. Due to an oversight by the creditor and an error by the bankruptcy court, the plan was approved and subsequently confirmed without the required finding of "undue hardship." The United States Supreme Court had to decide whether these problems rendered the discharge of the debt void.

➤ KNOW THIS ◄

Courts, trustees, and creditors carefully monitor Chapter 13 debtors. If payments are not made, a court can require that the debtor explain why and may allow a creditor to take back the property.

---

23. See 11 U.S.C. Section 1322(d) for details.

Case 15.3

United Student Aid Funds, Inc. v. Espinosa

Supreme Court of the United States,
__ U.S. __, 130 S.Ct. 1367,
176 L.Ed.2d 158 (2010).
www.supremecourt.gov [a]

Can student loans be avoided?

FACTS Francisco Espinosa filed a petition for an individual repayment plan under Chapter 13 of the Bankruptcy Code. His plan proposed to pay only the principal on his student loan and to discharge the interest. United Student Aid Funds, Inc. (the creditor), had notice of the plan and did not object. Without finding that payment of the interest would cause undue hardship (as required under the Code), the court confirmed the plan. Years later, however, United filed a motion under Federal Rule of Civil Procedure 60(b)(4) asking the bankruptcy court to rule that its order confirming the plan was void because the order was issued in violation of the laws and rules governing bankruptcy. The court denied United's petition and ordered the creditor to cease its collection efforts. United appealed, and the case ultimately reached the United States Supreme Court.

ISSUE If a bankruptcy court committed a legal error by confirming a debtor's repayment plan to discharge student loan debt without the required finding of undue hardship, but the creditor did not object, is the court's judgment void?

DECISION No. The United States Supreme Court affirmed the decision of the lower court that the bankruptcy court's order

was not void and that the student loan debt was thus discharged.

REASON The Supreme Court pointed out that the bankruptcy court's order confirming Espinosa's proposed plan was a final judgment from which United did not appeal. Federal Rule of Civil Procedure 60(b)(4) authorizes a court to relieve a party from a final judgment if that judgment is void, but a judgment is not void simply because it is or may have been erroneous. Moreover, a motion under this rule is not a substitute for a timely appeal. "The Bankruptcy Court's failure to find undue hardship before confirming Espinosa's plan was a legal error. But the order remains enforceable and binding on United because United had notice of the error and failed to object or timely appeal."

CRITICAL THINKING—Ethical Consideration At one point, United argued that if the Court did not declare the bankruptcy court's order void, dishonest debtors would be encouraged to abuse the Chapter 13 process. How might such abuse occur, and should the possibility of such abuse affect the Court's decision? Discuss your answer.

a. In the "Supreme Court Documents" column, in the "Opinions" pull-down menu, select "Bound Volumes." On the next page, in the "For Search Term:" box, type "Espinosa" and click on "Search." In the result, click on the name of the case to access the opinion. The United States Supreme Court maintains this Web site.

Reviewing . . . Creditors' Rights and Bankruptcy

Three months ago, Janet Hart's husband of twenty years died of cancer. Although he had medical insurance, he left Janet with outstanding medical bills of more than $50,000. Janet has worked at the local library for the past ten years, earning $1,500 per month. Since her husband's death, Janet also has received $1,500 in Social Security benefits and $1,100 in life insurance proceeds every month, giving her a monthly income of $4,100. After she pays the mortgage payment of $1,500 and the amounts due on other debts each month, Janet barely has enough left over to buy groceries for her family (she has two teenage daughters at home). She decides to file for Chapter 7 bankruptcy, hoping for a fresh start. Using the information provided in the chapter, answer the following questions.

Continued

1. Under the Bankruptcy Code after the reform act, what must Janet do before filing a petition for relief under Chapter 7?
2. How much time does Janet have after filing the bankruptcy petition to submit the required schedules? What happens if Janet does not meet the deadline?
3. Assume that Janet files a petition under Chapter 7. Further assume that the median family income in the state in which Janet lives is $49,300. What steps would a court take to determine whether Janet's petition is presumed to be "substantial abuse" under the means test?
4. Suppose that the court determines that no presumption of substantial abuse applies in Janet's case. Nevertheless, the court finds that Janet does have the ability to pay at least a portion of the medical bills out of her disposable income. What would the court likely order in that situation?

DEBATE THIS Rather than being allowed to file Chapter 7 bankruptcy petitions, individuals and couples should always be forced to make an effort to pay off their debts through Chapter 13.

LINKING BUSINESS LAW to Corporate Management

What Can You Do to Prepare for a Chapter 11 Reorganization?

Chapter 11 of the Bankruptcy Code expresses the broad public policy of encouraging commerce. To this end, Chapter 11 allows a financially troubled business firm to petition for reorganization in bankruptcy while it is still solvent so that the firm's business can continue. Small businesses, however, do not fare very well under Chapter 11. Although a few corporations that enter into Chapter 11 emerge as functioning entities, only a small number of companies survive the process.

Plan Ahead

If you ever are a small-business owner contemplating Chapter 11 reorganization, you can improve your chances of being among the survivors by planning ahead. To ensure the greatest possibility of success, you should take action before, not after, entering bankruptcy proceedings. Discuss your financial troubles openly and cooperatively with creditors to see if you can agree on a workout or some other arrangement.

If you appear to have no choice but to file for a Chapter 11 protection, try to persuade a lender to loan you funds to see you through the bankruptcy. If your business is a small corporation,

you might try to negotiate a favorable deal with a major investor. For example, a small business could offer to transfer ownership of stock to the investor in return for a loan to pay the costs of the bankruptcy proceedings and an option to repurchase the stock when the firm becomes profitable again.

Consult with Creditors

Most important, you should form a Chapter 11 plan before entering bankruptcy proceedings. Consult with creditors in advance to see what kind of plan would be acceptable to them, and prepare your plan accordingly. Having an acceptable plan prepared before you file will expedite the proceedings and thus save substantially on costs.

Critical Thinking

More bankruptcy filings are under Chapter 11, which may increase the time needed to complete the proceedings. How might this affect the likelihood that a firm will be able to negotiate a workout agreement with its creditors?

Key Terms

artisan's lien 439	discharge 446	perfection 436	right of subrogation 443
attachment 439	estate in property 451	petition in bankruptcy 447	secured transactions 435
automatic stay 450	garnishment 440	preference 452	surety 441
consumer-debtor 446	guarantor 441	preferred creditor 452	suretyship 441
co-surety 443	homestead exemption 444	purchase-money security interest (PMSI) 437	U.S. trustee 448
cram-down provision 459	liquidation 446	reaffirmation agreement 456	workout 457
creditors' composition agreement 440	mechanic's lien 438	right of contribution 443	writ of attachment 440
debtor in possession (DIP) 458	order for relief 449	right of reimbursement 443	writ of execution 440
default 436			

Chapter Summary: Creditors' Rights and Bankruptcy

LAWS ASSISTING CREDITORS	
Secured Transactions (See pages 436–438.)	1. *Creating a security interest*—The following requirements must be met to create an enforceable security interest: a. The creditor must possess the collateral, or there must be a written security agreement signed by the debtor and reasonably identifying the collateral. b. The secured party must give value to the debtor. c. The debtor must have rights in the collateral. 2. *Perfecting a security interest*—The most common method of perfection is by filing a financing statement that contains the names and addresses of the secured party and the debtor, describes the collateral, and is signed by the debtor. A few types of security interests can be perfected without filing, including the purchase-money security interest in consumer goods, which is automatically perfected at the time of creation. 3. *Priority*—When more than one creditor claims rights in the same collateral, the first security interest to be perfected has priority. If only one of the conflicting security interests has been perfect, it has priority. When both security interests are perfected, the interest that was first to perfect generally has priority. A secured creditor does not prevail against a buyer in the ordinary course of business. 4. *Remedies*—On the debtor's default, a secured party can repossess the collateral and retain it in part or full satisfaction of the debt, or can sell or dispose of the collateral in any commercially reasonable manner. Alternatively, the secured party can choose any judicial remedy available, such as obtaining a judgment against the debtor.
Liens (See pages 438–440.)	1. *Mechanic's lien*—A nonpossessory, filed lien on an owner's real estate for labor, services, or materials furnished for making improvements on the realty. 2. *Artisan's lien*—A possessory lien on an owner's personal property for labor performed or value added. 3. *Judicial liens*— a. Writ of attachment—A court order to seize a debtor's nonexempt property prior to a court's final determination of the creditor's rights to the property. Attachment is available only if the creditor posts a bond and complies with the applicable state statutes. b. Writ of execution—A court order directing the sheriff to seize (levy) and sell a debtor's nonexempt real or personal property to satisfy a court's judgment in the creditor's favor.
Garnishment (See page 440.)	A collection remedy that allows a creditor to attach a debtor's funds (such as wages owed or bank accounts) and property that are held by a third person.
Creditors' Composition Agreements (See page 440.)	A contract between a debtor and his or her creditors by which the debtor's debts are discharged by payment of a sum less than the amount actually owed.
Suretyship and Guaranty (See pages 441–443.)	Under contract, a third person agrees to be primarily or secondarily liable for the debt owed by the principal debtor. A creditor can turn to this third person for satisfaction of the debt.

Continued

Chapter Summary: Creditors' Rights and Bankruptcy—Continued

PROTECTION FOR DEBTORS	
Exemptions (See page 444.)	Certain property of a debtor is exempt from creditors' actions under state laws. Each state permits a debtor to retain the family home, either in its entirety or up to a specified dollar amount, free from the claims of unsecured creditors or trustees in bankruptcy (homestead exemption).

BANKRUPTCY—A COMPARISON OF CHAPTERS 7, 11, 12, AND 13

Issue	Chapter 7	Chapter 11	Chapters 12 and 13
Who Can Petition	Debtor (voluntary) or creditors (involuntary).	Debtor (voluntary) or creditors (involuntary).	Debtor (voluntary) only.
Who Can Be a Debtor	Any "person" (including partnerships and corporations) except railroads, insurance companies, banks, savings and loan institutions, investment companies licensed by the U.S. Small Business Administration, and credit unions. Farmers and charitable institutions cannot be involuntarily petitioned.	Any debtor eligible for Chapter 7 relief; railroads are also eligible.	Chapter 12—Any family farmer (one whose gross income is at least 50 percent farm dependent and whose debts are at least 50 percent farm related) or family fisherman (one whose gross income is at least 50 percent dependent on and whose debts are at least 80 percent related to commercial fishing) or any partnership or close corporation at least 50 percent owned by a family farmer or fisherman, when total debt does not exceed $3,792,650 for a family farmer and $1,757,475 for a family fisherman. Chapter 13—Any individual (not partnerships or corporations) with regular income who owes fixed (liquidated) unsecured debts of less than $360,475 or fixed secured debts of less than $1,081,400.
Procedure Leading to Discharge	Nonexempt property is sold with proceeds to be distributed (in order) to priority groups. Dischargeable debts are terminated.	Plan is submitted. If it is approved and followed, debts are discharged.	Plan is submitted and must be approved if the value of the property to be distributed equals the amount of the claims or if the debtor turns over disposable income for a three-year or five-year period. If the plan is followed, debts are discharged.
Advantages	On liquidation and distribution, most debts are discharged, and the debtor has an opportunity for a fresh start.	Debtor continues in business. Creditors can either accept the plan or have it "crammed down" on them. The plan allows for the reorganization and liquidation of debts over the plan period.	Debtor continues in business or possession of assets. If the plan is approved, most debts are discharged after a three-year period.

ExamPrep

ISSUE SPOTTERS

1. Joe contracts with Larry of Midwest Roofing to fix Joe's roof. Joe pays half of the contract price in advance. Larry and Midwest complete the job, but Joe refuses to pay the rest of the price. What can Larry and Midwest do? **(See pages 438–439.)**
2. Ogden is a vice president of Plumbing Service, Inc. (PSI). On May 1, Ogden loans PSI $10,000. On June 1, the firm repays the loan. On July 1, PSI files for bankruptcy. Quentin is appointed trustee. Can Quentin recover the $10,000 paid to Ogden on June 1? Why or why not? **(See pages 452–453.)**

—Check your answers to the Issue Spotters against the answers provided in Appendix E at the end of this text.

BEFORE THE TEST

Go to www.cengagebrain.com, enter the ISBN 9781133191353, and click on "Find" to locate this textbook's Web site. Then, click on "Access Now" under "Study Tools," and select Chapter 15 at the top. There, you will find a Practice Quiz that you can take to assess your mastery of the concepts in this chapter, as well as Flashcards, a Glossary of important terms, and Video Questions (when assigned).

For Review

Answers to the even-numbered questions in this For Review section can be found in Appendix F at the end of this text.

1. What is a prejudgment attachment? What is a writ of execution? How does a creditor use these remedies?
2. What is garnishment? When might a creditor undertake a garnishment proceeding?
3. In a bankruptcy proceeding, what constitutes the debtor's estate in property? What property is exempt from the estate under federal bankruptcy law?
4. What is the difference between an exception to discharge and an objection to discharge?
5. In a Chapter 11 reorganization, what is the role of the debtor in possession?

Business Scenarios and Case Problems

15–1 Artisan's Lien. Air Ruidoso, Ltd., operated a commuter airline and air charter service between Ruidoso, New Mexico, and airports in Albuquerque and El Paso. Executive Aviation Center, Inc., provided services for airlines at the Albuquerque International Airport. When Air Ruidoso failed to pay more than $10,000 that it owed for fuel, oil, and oxygen, Executive Aviation took possession of Air Ruidoso's plane. Executive Aviation claimed that it had a lien on the plane and filed a suit in a New Mexico state court to foreclose. Do supplies such as fuel, oil, and oxygen qualify as "materials" for the purpose of creating an artisan's lien? Why or why not? **(See page 439.)**

15–2 Question with Sample Answer—Perfection. Marsh has a prize horse named Arabian Knight. In need of working capital, Marsh borrows $5,000 from Mendez, who takes possession of Arabian Knight as security for the loan. No written agreement is signed. Discuss whether, in the absence of a written agreement, Mendez has a security interest in Arabian Knight. If Mendez does have a security interest, is it a perfected security interest? Explain. **(See pages 436–438.)**

—For a sample answer to Question 15–2, go to Appendix G at the end of this text.

15–3 Discharge in Bankruptcy. Cathy Coleman took out loans to complete her college education. After graduation, Coleman worked as a teacher before she filed a Chapter 13 bankruptcy petition. The court confirmed a five-year plan that required Coleman to commit all of her disposable income to paying the student loans. Less than a year later, she was laid off. Still owing more than $100,000 in student loans, Coleman asked the court to discharge the debt on the ground that paying it would be an undue hardship for her. Under Chapter 13, are student loans dischargeable? Should the court grant her request? What argument could be made in support of Coleman's request? [*In re Coleman,* 560 F.3d 1000 (9th Cir. 2009)] **(See pages 446–449.)**

15–4 Discharge. Caroline McAfee loaned $400,000 to Carter Oaks Crossing. Joseph Harman, Carter's president, signed a personal guaranty for the loan. Later, Harman obtained a discharge in bankruptcy under Chapter 7 for his personal debts. His petition did not list the guaranty among the debts. When Carter defaulted on the loan, McAfee sought to collect the unpaid amount from Harman based on the guaranty.

Harman argued that the guaranty had been discharged in his bankruptcy. Is Harman correct? Why or why not? [*Harman v. McAfee,* 302 Ga.App. 698, 691 S.E.2d 586 (2010)] **(See pages 441–443.)**

15–5 Liens. Autolign Manufacturing Group, Inc., borrowed funds from Wamco 34, Ltd., to operate its auto parts business. The loan was secured by the molds that were used to form the parts. Autolign contracted with Delta Engineered Plastics, LLC, to make the parts and provided Delta with the molds. When Autolign defaulted on its obligations to Wamco and Delta, Delta asserted a "molder's lien" against the molds in its possession. A molder's lien is similar to an artisan's lien. Wamco argued that the molds were its property. Which claim had priority? Explain. [*Delta Engineered Plastics, LLC v. Autolign Manufacturing Group, Inc.,* 286 Mich.App. 115, 777 N.W.2d 502 (2010)] **(See page 439.)**

15–6 Guaranty. Majestic Group Korea, Ltd., borrowed $1.5 million from Overseas Private Investment Corp. (OPIC) to finance a Ruby Tuesday's restaurant. Nam Koo Kim, the sole owner of Majestic, and his spouse Hee Sun Kim signed personal guaranties for full payment of the loan. Majestic defaulted. OPIC filed a suit against the Kims to recover. Hee claimed that she did not understand the extent of her liability when she signed the guaranty. Was Hee liable for the debt? Explain. [*Overseas Private Investment Corp. v. Kim,* 69 A.D.3d 1185, 895 N.Y.S.2d 217 (2010)] **(See pages 441–443.)**

15–7 Protection for Debtors. Bill and Betty Ma owned half of a two-unit residential building. Betty lived in the unit, but Bill did not. To collect a judgment against the Mas, Mei-Fang Zhang obtained a writ of execution directing the sheriff to seize and sell the building. State law allowed a $100,000 homestead exemption if the debtor lived in the home and $175,000 if the debtor was also disabled and "unable to engage in gainful employment." Bill argued that he could not work because of "gout and dizziness." How much of an exemption were the Mas allowed? Why? [*Zhang v. Tse,* __ F.Supp.2d __ (N.D.Cal. 2011)] **(See page 444.)**

15–8 Case Problem with Sample Answer—Automatic Stay. Michelle Gholston leased a Chevy Impala from EZ Auto Van Rentals. In November 2011, Gholston filed for bankruptcy. Around November 21, the bankruptcy court notified EZ Auto of Gholston's bankruptcy and the imposition of an automatic stay. Nevertheless, because Gholston had fallen behind on her payments, EZ Auto repossessed the vehicle on November 28. Gholston's attorney then reminded EZ Auto about the automatic stay, but the company failed to return the car. As a result of the car's repossession, Gholston suffered damages that included emotional distress, lost wages, attorneys' fees, and car rental expenses. Can Gholston recover from EZ Auto? Why or why not? [*In re Gholston*, ___ Bankr. ___, 2012 WL 639288 (M.D.Fla. 2012)] **(See pages 450–451.)**

—For a sample answer to Problem 15–8, go to Appendix H at the end of this text.

15–9 ⬌ **A Question of Ethics—Guaranty Contracts.** 73-75 Main Avenue, LLC, agreed to lease commercial property to PP Door Enterprise, Inc., if its principal officers executed personal guaranties and provided credit information. Nan Zhang signed the lease as manager of PP Door. The principals of PP Door signed the lease and guaranty agreements. When PP Door failed to make monthly payments, the lessor sued PP Door and its owner, Ping Ying Li. Li testified that she was the sole owner of PP Door but denied that Zhang was its manager. She also denied signing the guaranty agreement. She claimed that she had signed the credit authorization form because Zhang had told her he was too young to have good credit. Li claimed to have no knowledge of the lease agreement. She did admit, however, that she had paid the rent because Zhang had been in a car accident and had asked her to help pay his bills, including the rent. [*73-75 Main Avenue, LLC v. PP Door Enterprise, Inc.*, 120 Conn.App. 150, 991 A.2d 650 (2010)]

1. Li argued that she was not liable on the lease agreement because Zhang was not authorized to bind her to the lease. Do the facts support Li? Why or why not? **(See page 443.)**

2. Li claimed that the guaranty for rent was not enforceable against her. Why might the court agree? **(See pages 441–443.)**

Critical Thinking and Writing Assignments

15–10 **Business Law Writing.** Write a few sentences describing the circumstances in which a creditor would resort to each of the following remedies when trying to collect on debt. **(See pages 439–440.)**
1. Mechanic's lien
2. Artisan's lien
3. Writ of attachment

15–11 💡 **Business Law Critical Thinking Group Assignment.** Grant owns an older home valued at $45,000. He contracts with Jane's Plumbing to replace the bathtubs and fixtures in both bathrooms. Jane replaces them, and on June 1 she submits her bill of $4,000 to Grant. Because of financial difficulties, Grant does not pay the bill. Grant's only asset is his home, but his state's homestead exemption is $40,000.

1. The first group will determine whether Jane's Plumbing can obtain a lien to pay for the renovations. What type of lien would it be, and how is it created?

2. A second group will determine what would happen if Grant filed for Chapter 7 bankruptcy before Jane took any legal action to collect on her claim. Would Jane be a secured or unsecured creditor? Would Jane's position be different if she had obtained a lien before Grant's petition for bankruptcy? Explain.

CHAPTER 16

Mortgages and Foreclosures after the Recession

(wavebreakmedia/Shutterstock.com)

CHAPTER OUTLINE

- Mortgages
- Real Estate Financing Law
- Foreclosures

LEARNING OBJECTIVES

The five learning objectives below are designed to help improve your understanding of the chapter. After reading this chapter, you should be able to answer the following questions:

1 What is a subprime mortgage? How does it differ from a standard fixed-rate mortgage? What is a home equity loan?

2 When is private mortgage insurance required? Which party does it protect?

3 Does the Truth-in-Lending Act (TILA) apply to all mortgages? How do the TILA provisions protect borrowers and curb abusive practices by mortgage lenders?

4 What is a short sale? What advantages over mortgage foreclosure might it offer borrowers? Does the lender receive the full balance due on the mortgage loan in a short sale?

5 In a mortgage foreclosure, what legal rights do mortgage holders have if the sale proceeds are insufficient to pay the underlying debt?

"These days America is looking like the Bernie Madoff of economies:
For many years it was held in respect, even awe, but it turns out to have been a fraud all along."
—Paul Krugman, 1953–present (U.S. columnist and winner of Nobel Prize in Economics)

During the first decade of the 2000s, the United States experienced one of the biggest real estate bubbles in its history as housing prices in many areas increased at unprecedented rates. The bubble started to shrink in 2006 and was still deflating in 2013. As a result of the collapse of the housing market and the financial crisis that accompanied it, the United States and much of the rest of the world suffered through what is now called the Great Recession.

Today, the real estate market is still in turmoil. Many people have lost their homes to foreclosure because they could not make the payments on their *mortgages*—the loans that borrowers obtain to purchase homes. Others can afford the payments but choose not to pay because they owe more on the properties than those properties are worth. The ongoing flood of foreclosures led the Obama administration in 2012 to propose an extension (for another few years) of the laws that were aimed at temporarily modifying mortgages.

It has become apparent that some of the mortgage process during the bubble years was fraught with fraud, as the chapter-opening quotation on the previous page suggests. Bank of America, for instance, paid nearly $20 billion in 2011 to settle claims involving mortgage-backed securities that it had designated as safe investments. In reality, many of the securities were based on mortgages granted to borrowers who could not afford to repay them. Other major mortgage companies, including Chase, Citigroup, JPMorgan and Wells Fargo, faced similar fraud claims. Furthermore, the U.S. Justice Department has accused some mortgage lenders of engaging in discriminatory practices—see this chapter's *Law, Diversity, and Business: Managerial Implications* feature below.

Mortgages

When individuals purchase real property, they typically borrow funds from a financial institution for part or all of the purchase price. A **mortgage** is a written instrument that gives a creditor (the **mortgagee**) an interest in, or lien on, the debtor's (the **mortgagor's**) real property as security for the payment of a debt. Here, we look first at the different types of mortgages, including some new varieties that helped to inflate the housing bubble. Then we consider some of the ways that creditors protect their interest in the property and examine some of the more important provisions in a typical mortgage document.

Mortgage A written document that gives a creditor (the mortgagee) an interest in, or lien on, the debtor's (mortgagor's) real property as security for a debt. If the debt is not paid, the property can be sold by the creditor and the proceeds used to pay the debt.

Mortgagee Under a mortgage agreement, the creditor who takes a security interest in the debtor's property.

Mortgagor Under a mortgage agreement, the debtor who gives the creditor a security interest in the debtor's property in return for a mortgage loan.

LAW, DIVERSITY, AND BUSINESS: MANAGERIAL IMPLICATIONS

REVERSE REDLINING IN THE MORTGAGE MARKET

In December 2011, Bank of America reached a settlement with the U.S. Department of Justice in which it agreed to pay $335 million to compensate 200,000 borrowers who allegedly were discriminated against by Countrywide Financial, a subsidiary that Bank of America had acquired in 2008 when Countrywide was collapsing under its burden of bad loans. The Justice Department alleged that Countrywide had engaged in reverse redlining.

First, There Was Redlining For decades, the mortgage lending industry was accused of *redlining*—that is, drawing a red line on a map around poorer neighborhoods and refusing to offer mortgages to borrowers, often members of minority groups, who wished to purchase homes in those areas. In 1977, Congress passed the Community Reinvestment Act to require lenders to make mortgages more readily obtainable in redlined areas. Nonetheless, in the mid-1990s African American and Hispanic applicants for mortgages were still being rejected at a rate 1.6 times higher than that of white applicants with similar credit histories. Under the Clinton administration, organizations in redlined areas increasingly pressured banks to make more loans available. The lenders responded with *reverse redlining*.

Then, Reverse Redlining Became Profitable *Reverse redlining* is the opposite of redlining—instead of denying mortgages to

members of minority groups, lenders targeted them. During the housing boom, lenders aggressively marketed their subprime mortgages in poorer areas. Wells Fargo, for instance, enlisted pastors in churches in African American communities to offer wealth-building seminars. The bank would make a donation to the church for every new mortgage application it received.

Why were lenders suddenly so interested in these borrowers? The answer is that subprime mortgages carry much higher interest rates than standard mortgages and are usually accompanied by higher up-front fees. In many instances, the Justice Department asserted, mortgage companies pushed African American and Hispanic borrowers into high-cost subprime mortgages even when they could qualify for standard mortgages. Other borrowers were given mortgages that they would not be able to pay—the lender pocketed the fees and sold the worthless mortgages to investors. As a result of such practices, minority groups have incurred a disproportionate percentage of foreclosures.

Business Implications *As a result of numerous charges of reverse redlining, banks and other financial institutions have increased their requirements for home loans. Bank managers have told their loan officers to make sure that all mortgage applicants can prove that they will be able to stay current on their mortgage payments.*

Types of Mortgages

Mortgage loans are contracts and, as such, come in a variety of forms. Lenders offer several types of mortgage loans to meet the needs of borrowers. In recent decades, the expansion of home ownership became a political goal, and lenders were encouraged to become more creative in devising new types of mortgages. In many instances, these new mortgages were aimed at borrowers who could not qualify for traditional mortgages and lacked the funds to make a **down payment** (the part of the purchase price that is paid up front).

In general, these mortgages, which include some adjustable-rate mortgages, interest-only mortgages, and balloon mortgages, feature a low initial interest rate. Often, the borrower hopes to refinance—pay off the original mortgage and obtain a new one with more favorable terms—within a few years. When the housing bubble burst and house prices began to decline, however, refinancing became more difficult than many borrowers had anticipated.

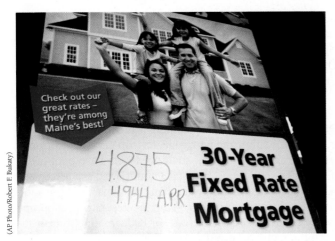

Why do many home buyers opt for thirty-year mortgages?

Down Payment The part of the purchase price of real property that is paid up front, reducing the amount of the loan or mortgage.

Fixed-Rate Mortgage A standard mortgage with a fixed, or unchanging, rate of interest. The loan payments remain the same for the duration of the loan, which ranges between fifteen and forty years.

Adjustable-Rate Mortgage (ARM) A mortgage with a rate of interest that changes periodically, often with reference to a predetermined government interest rate (the index).

"Mortgage:
a house with a
guilty conscience."

Anonymous

Fixed-Rate Mortgages   *Fixed-rate mortgages* are the simplest mortgage loans. A **fixed-rate mortgage** is a standard mortgage with a fixed, or unchanging, rate of interest. Payments on the loan remain the same for the duration of the mortgage, which ranges from fifteen to forty years.

Lenders determine the interest rate based on a variety of factors, including the borrower's credit history, credit score, income, and debts. Today, for a borrower to qualify for a standard fixed-rate mortgage loan, lenders typically require that the monthly mortgage payment (including principal, interest, taxes, and insurance) not exceed 28 percent of the person's gross income.

Adjustable-Rate Mortgages   With an **adjustable-rate mortgage (ARM),** the rate of interest paid by the borrower changes periodically. Typically, the interest rate is set at a relatively low fixed rate for a specified period, such as a year or three years. After that time, the interest rate adjusts annually or by some other period, such as biannually or monthly.

ARMs generally are described in terms of the initial fixed period and the adjustment period. For instance, if the interest rate is fixed for three years and then adjusts annually, the mortgage is called a 3/1 ARM, whereas if the rate adjusts annually after five years, the mortgage is a 5/1 ARM.

The interest rate adjustment is calculated by adding a certain number of percentage points (called the margin) to an index rate (one of various government interest rates). The margin and index rate are specified in the mortgage loan documents. **EXAMPLE 16.1**   Greta and Marcus obtain a 3/1 ARM to purchase a home. After three years, when the first adjustment is to be made, the index rate is 6 percent. If the margin specified in the loan documents is 3 percentage points, the fully indexed interest rate for the ARM would be 9 percent. ● Most ARMs, however, have lifetime interest rate caps that limit the amount that the rate can rise over the duration of the loan.

Some ARMs also have caps that stipulate the maximum increase that can occur in any particular adjustment period. **EXAMPLE 16.2**   In the Greta and Marcus example above, if the initial interest rate was 5 percent and the loan stipulated that the rate could rise no more than 3 percentage points in one adjustment period, the interest rate after three years would increase to 8 percent, not 9 percent, because of the cap. ● Note that the interest rate could be adjusted downward as well as upward. If the index rate was 1 percent, the adjusted rate would potentially fall to 4 percent, although some ARMs also limit the amount that the rate can fall.

Interest-Only (IO) Mortgage A mortgage that allows the borrower to pay only the interest portion of the monthly payment and forgo paying any principal for a specified period of time, such as five years.

LEARNING OBJECTIVE 1
What is a subprime mortgage? How does it differ from a standard fixed-rate mortgage? What is a home equity loan?

Subprime Mortgage A high-risk loan made to a borrower who does not qualify for a standard mortgage because of a poor credit rating or high debt-to-income ratio. Lenders typically charge a higher interest rate on subprime mortgages.

Balloon Mortgage A mortgage that allows the borrower to make small monthly payments for an initial period, such as eight years, but then requires the entire remaining balance of the mortgage loan to be paid at the end of that period.

ETHICAL ISSUE

Home Equity Loan A loan for which the borrower's home equity (the portion of the home's value that is paid off) is the collateral.

Interest-Only (IO) Mortgages

With an **interest-only (IO) mortgage**, the borrower can choose to pay only the interest portion of the monthly payments and forgo paying any of the principal for a specified period of time. (IO loans can be for fixed-rate or adjustable-rate mortgages.) This IO payment usually is available for three to ten years. After the IO payment option is exhausted, the borrower's payment increases to include payments on the principal.

Subprime Mortgages

During the late 1990s and the first decade of the 2000s, *subprime lending* increased significantly. A **subprime mortgage** is a loan made to a borrower who does not qualify for a standard mortgage. Often, such borrowers have poor credit scores or a high current *debt-to-income ratio*—that is, the total amount owed as a percentage of current after-tax income. Subprime mortgages are riskier than traditional mortgages and have a higher default rate. Consequently, lenders charge a higher interest rate for subprime loans. Subprime mortgages can be fixed-rate, adjustable-rate, or IO loans. Subprime lending allows many people who could not otherwise purchase real property to do so, but at a higher risk to the lender.

Balloon Mortgages

Like an ARM, a **balloon mortgage** starts with low payments for a specified period, usually seven to ten years. At the end of that period, a large balloon payment for the entire balance of the mortgage loan is due. Because the balloon payment is often very large, many borrowers refinance when it is due. A potential disadvantage is that the market interest rate may have risen by the time the loan is refinanced. As a result, the payments may be higher than they would have been if the buyer had initially obtained a fixed-rate mortgage instead of a balloon mortgage.

Who should benefit when a mortgage-participating bank fails? During the heyday of mortgage lending in the first decade of the 2000s, many banks wanted a "piece of the action." A bank could do this by becoming a *participating* bank when another bank contemplated making a multimillion-dollar mortgage and wanted to share the risk. In this way, Silverton Bank participated in half of a $4 million loan that Renasant Bank made to Eric and Tricia Ericson for the construction of a house in Tennessee.

By the time the construction was completed, however, the housing market had started to collapse, and ultimately the Ericsons defaulted on the $4 million loan. In the meantime, Silverton Bank, the participating bank, had failed and been taken over by the Federal Deposit Insurance Corporation. The principal lender, Renasant Bank, orally promised the Ericsons that if it could purchase Silverton's participating loan at a discount, it would credit the Ericsons with the full discount. When Renasant acquired the loan at a $475,000 discount, however, it refused to grant the Ericsons the credit.

Renasant argued that it did not have to apply the discount to the Ericsons' loan balance until they had repaid the entire balance, but the court ruled in favor of the Ericsons. Renasant had breached the oral agreement by refusing to give the Ericsons the $475,000 discount that it had obtained when it repurchased Silverton's participating loan.[1]

Home Equity Loans

Home equity refers to the portion of a home's value that is "paid off." **EXAMPLE 16.3** If Susanna has a home valued at $200,000 and owes the bank $120,000 on her mortgage, she has 40 percent equity in her house ($80,000/$200,000 = 40 percent). With a **home equity loan,** a bank accepts the borrower's equity as *collateral*, which can be seized if the loan is not repaid on time. If Susanna takes out a $30,000 home equity loan, the amount is added to the amount of her mortgage ($30,000 + $120,000 = $150,000), so she now has only $50,000 (25 percent) equity in her $200,000 home. ●

---

1. *Renasant Bank v. Ericson*, 2012 WL 640659 (M.D. Tenn. 2012).

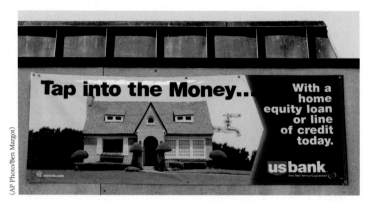

(AP Photo/Ben Margot)

Who can qualify for a home equity loan?

Borrowers often take out home equity loans to obtain funds to renovate the property itself. Others obtain home equity loans to pay off debt, such as credit-card debt, that carries a higher interest rate than they will pay on the home equity loan. This strategy can lead to problems, however, if the borrower cannot keep up the payments. Many Americans who lost their homes during the latest major recession were able to pay their original mortgage loans, but not their home equity loans.

From the lender's perspective, a home equity loan is riskier than a mortgage loan because home equity loans are *subordinated,* which means that they take a lower priority in any proceeding that occurs if the homeowner fails to make the payments on the primary mortgage.

Creditor Protection

When creditors grant mortgages, they are advancing a significant amount of funds for a number of years. Consequently, creditors take a number of steps to protect their interest.

One precaution is to require debtors to obtain private mortgage insurance if they do not make a down payment of at least 20 percent of the purchase price. If a borrower makes a down payment of only 5 percent of the purchase price, the creditor might require insurance covering 15 percent of the cost. Then, if the debtor defaults, the creditor repossesses the house and receives reimbursement from the insurer for the covered portion of the loan.

In addition, the creditor will record the mortgage with the appropriate office in the county where the property is located. Recording "perfects" the security interest (see page 436 of Chapter 15) and ensures that the creditor is officially on record as holding an interest in the property. A lender that fails to record a mortgage could find itself in the position of an unsecured creditor.

Mortgages normally are lengthy documents that include a number of provisions. Many of these provisions are aimed at protecting the creditors' investment.

Statute of Frauds
Because a mortgage involves a transfer of real property, it must be in writing to comply with the Statute of Frauds (see page 243 in Chapter 8). Most mortgages today are highly formal documents with similar formats, but a mortgage is not required to follow any particular form. Indeed, as long as the mortgage satisfies the Statute of Frauds, it generally will be effective.

Important Mortgage Provisions
Mortgage documents ordinarily contain all or most of the following terms:

1. *The terms of the underlying loan.* These include the loan amount, the interest rate, the period of repayment, and other important financial terms, such as the margin and index rate for an ARM. Many lenders include a **prepayment penalty clause,** which requires the borrower to pay a penalty if the mortgage is repaid in full within a certain period. A prepayment penalty helps to protect the lender should the borrower refinance within a short time after obtaining a mortgage.
2. *Provisions relating to the maintenance of the property.* Because the mortgage conveys an interest in the property to the lender, the lender will require the borrower to maintain the property in such a way that the lender's investment is protected.
3. *A statement obligating the borrower to maintain homeowners' insurance on the property.* **Homeowner's insurance** (also known as *hazard insurance*) protects the lender's interest in the event of a loss due to certain hazards, such as fire or storm damage.

Prepayment Penalty Clause A clause in a mortgage loan contract that requires the borrower to pay a penalty if the mortgage is repaid in full within a certain period.

Homeowners' Insurance Insurance that protects a homeowner's property against damage from storms, fire, and other hazards.

4. *A list of the nonloan financial obligations to be borne by the borrower.* For instance, the borrower typically is required to pay all property taxes, assessments, and other claims against the property.

5. *A provision requiring that the borrower pay certain obligations in a specific way.* For instance, a borrower may be required to pay some or all of the taxes, insurance, assessments, or other expenses associated with the property in advance or through the lender. In this way, the lender is assured that the funds for these expenses will be available when the bills come due.

Although a record number of homeowners have failed to keep up with their mortgage payments in recent years, courts have continued to enforce the terms of plainly written financing documents. Even in today's more protective environment, borrowers cannot avoid the clear meaning of terms in financing documents, although the effect may be harsh.

Real Estate Financing Law

During the real estate boom in the first years of the 2000s, some lenders were less than honest with borrowers about the loan terms that they were signing. As a result, many individuals failed to understand how much the monthly payments on ARMs, interest-only mortgages, and other exotic types of loans might increase. In addition, fees and penalties were not always properly disclosed.

In an effort to provide more protection for borrowers, Congress and the Federal Reserve Board have instituted a number of new requirements, mostly in the form of required disclosures. Here, we examine the most important statutes that provide protection for borrowers. First, though, we look at some of the practices that led to the enactment of these statutes.

Predatory Lending and Other Improper Practices

The general term *predatory lending* is often used to describe situations in which borrowers are the victims of loan terms or lending procedures that are excessive, deceptive, or not properly disclosed. Predatory lending typically occurs during the loan origination process. It includes a number of practices ranging from failure to disclose terms to providing misleading information to outright dishonesty.

Two specific types of improper practices are often at the core of a violation. *Steering and targeting* occurs when the lender manipulates a borrower into accepting a loan product that benefits the lender but is not the best loan for the borrower. For instance, a lender may steer a borrower toward an ARM, even though the buyer qualifies for a fixed-rate mortgage. *Loan flipping* occurs when a lender convinces a homeowner to refinance soon after obtaining a mortgage. Such early refinancing rarely benefits the homeowner and may, in fact, result in prepayment penalties.

The Truth-in-Lending Act (TILA)

LEARNING OBJECTIVE 3
Does the Truth-in-Lending Act (TILA) apply to all mortgages? How do the TILA provisions protect borrowers and curb abusive practices by mortgage lenders?

Annual Percentage Rate (APR) The cost of credit on a yearly basis, typically expressed as an annual percentage.

The Truth-in-Lending Act (TILA) of 1968[2] requires lenders to disclose the terms of a loan in clear, readily understandable language so that borrowers can make rational choices. (We discussed the TILA on pages 368–369 of Chapter 12 in the context of consumer law.) With respect to real estate transactions, the TILA applies only to residential loans.

Required Disclosures   The major terms that must be disclosed under the TILA include the loan principal, the interest rate at which the loan is made, the **annual percentage rate,** or **APR** (the actual cost of the loan on a yearly basis), and all fees and

---

2. 15 U.S.C. Sections 1601–1693r.

costs associated with the loan. The TILA requires that these disclosures be made on standardized forms and based on uniform calculation formulas.

Certain types of loans—including ARMs, open-ended home equity loans, and high-interest loans—have specially tailored disclosure requirements. The Mortgage Disclosure Improvement Act of 2008[3] amended the TILA to strengthen the disclosures required for ARMs, which, as mentioned earlier, played a leading role in the recent real estate meltdown.

Prohibitions and Requirements   The TILA prohibits certain lender abuses and creates certain borrower rights. Among the prohibited practices is the charging of prepayment penalties on most subprime mortgages and home equity loans.

The TILA also addresses other unfair, abusive, or deceptive home mortgage–lending practices. It provides that lenders may not coerce an **appraiser** (an individual who specializes in determining the value of specified real or personal property) into misstating the value of a property on which a loan is to be issued. Also, a loan cannot be advertised as a fixed-rate loan if, in fact, its rate or payment amounts will change.

Appraiser An individual who specializes in determining the value of specified real or personal property.

Right to Rescind   A mortgage cannot be finalized until at least seven days after a borrower has received the TILA paperwork. Even if all required disclosures are provided, the TILA gives the borrower the right to rescind (cancel) a mortgage *within three business days*. Sunday is the only day of the week that is not a business day. If the lender fails to provide material TILA disclosures, including the three-day right to rescind, the rescission period lasts up to three years.

Written Representations   The TILA requirements apply to the written materials the lender provides, not to any oral representations. If a lender provides the required TILA disclosures, a borrower who fails to read the relevant documents cannot claim fraud, even if the lender orally misrepresented the terms of the loan. **CASE EXAMPLE 16.4**   Patricia Ostolaza and José Diaz owned a home on which they had two mortgage loans provided by Bank of America. Anthony Falcone told them that he could refinance their mortgages in a manner that would reduce their monthly payments. Falcone said that he represented Bank of America when in fact he represented Countrywide Home Loans, Inc.

At the closing of the new loan, the homeowners were given all of the relevant documents, including the TILA disclosure statement. The documents accurately stated the monthly payment under the new loan, which was higher than the couple's original payments. The homeowners later sued Falcone and Countrywide Bank, alleging fraud, but the court dismissed the suit because the homeowners had been given the opportunity to read all of the relevant documents but had not done so.[4] ●

Protection for High-Cost Mortgage Loan Recipients

In the last twenty years, lenders have provided many high-cost and high-fee mortgage products to people who could not easily obtain credit under other loan programs. These loans are commonly known as HOEPA loans, named after the Home Ownership and Equity Protection Act (HOEPA) of 1994,[5] which amended the TILA to create this special category of loans.

A loan can qualify for protection under HOEPA either because it carries a high rate of interest or because it entails high fees for the borrower. HOEPA applies if the APR disclosed

---

3. This act was contained in Sections 2501 through 2503 of the Housing and Economic Recovery Act of 2008, Pub. L. No. 110-289, enacted on July 30, 2008. Congress then amended its provisions as part of the Emergency Economic Stabilization Act of 2008 (also known as the Bailout Bill), Pub. L. No. 110-343, enacted on October 3, 2008.

4. *Ostolaza-Diaz v. Countrywide Bank, N.A.*, 2010 WL 95145 (4th Cir. 2010).

5. 15 U.S.C. Sections 1637 and 1647.

Treasury Securities Government debt issued by the U.S. Department of the Treasury. The interest rate on Treasury securities is often used as a baseline for measuring the rate on loan products with higher interest rates.

for the loan exceeds the interest rates of **Treasury securities** (or bonds) of comparable maturity by more than 8 percentage points for a first mortgage and 10 percentage points for a second mortgage. HOEPA can also apply when the total fees paid by the consumer exceed 8 percent of the loan amount or a set dollar amount (based on changes in the Consumer Price Index), whichever is larger.

Special Consumer Protections

If a loan qualifies for HOEPA protection, the consumer must receive several disclosures in addition to those required by the TILA. The lender must disclose the APR, the regular payment amount, and any required balloon payments. For loans with a variable rate of interest, the lender must disclose that the rate and monthly payments may increase and state the potential maximum monthly payment. These disclosures must be provided at least three business days before the loan is finalized.

In addition, the lender must provide a written notice stating that the consumer is not required to complete the loan process simply because he or she received the disclosures or signed the loan application. Borrowers must also be informed that they could lose their home (and all funds invested in it) if they default on the loan.

HOEPA also prohibits lenders from engaging in certain practices, such as requiring balloon payments for loans with terms of five years or less. Loans that result in negative amortization are also prohibited. **Negative amortization** occurs when the monthly payments are insufficient to cover the interest due on the loan. The difference is then added to the principal, so the balance owed on the loan increases over time.

Negative Amortization The condition when the payment made by the borrower is less than the interest due on the loan and the difference is added to the principal, thereby increasing the balance owed on the loan over time.

Remedies and Liabilities

For HOEPA violations, consumers can obtain damages in an amount equal to all finance charges and fees paid if the lender's failure to disclose is deemed material. Any failure to comply with HOEPA provisions also extends the borrower's right to rescind the loan for up to three years.

Whether a particular loan is covered by HOEPA and thus is entitled to the statute's significant protections can have important ramifications because it can determine whether a borrower can recover on a lender's failure to comply with HOEPA's provisions and the amount of the recovery. In the following case, a consumer attempted to recover from a lender for alleged violations of the TILA and HOEPA.

Case 16.1

In re Kitts

United States Bankruptcy Court, District of Utah, Central Division, 447 Bankr. 330 (2011).

Many financial institutions offer home refinancing.

FACTS Facing the loss of his family's home in Park City, Utah, to creditors, Brian Kitts sought to refinance the debt. He entered into two mortgage loan agreements for $1.35 million and $39,603.47, respectively, with Winterfox, LLC. As part of the deal, Kitts paid $87,500 in "loan origination fees." Kitts defaulted on the loans and filed a petition to declare bankruptcy. He also filed a complaint against Winterfox to recover damages for alleged violations of the federal Truth-in-Lending Act (TILA). The bankruptcy court dismissed the action, but on appeal, a federal district court ruled that Winterfox had failed to make certain required disclosures. The district court remanded the case for "further fact finding concerning damages" for violation of the TILA, as well as for Kitts's request for attorneys' fees.

ISSUE Was Kitts entitled to recover damages and attorneys' fees because Winterfox charged him $87,500 in finance charges in violation of HOEPA and TILA provisions?

DECISION Yes. The court concluded that HOEPA covered the Winterfox loans because they were high-cost mortgages. Because Winterfox had not provided any disclosures, Kitts was awarded statutory TILA damages of $4,000, compensatory damages of $87,500 under HOEPA for the finance charges paid in connection with the loans, and $150,000 for attorneys' fees.

Case 16.1—Continued

REASON The parties did not dispute that Winterfox had charged $87,500 in fees. The dispute was whether those fees qualified as "finance charges paid by the consumer" under TILA even though the funds were paid from the loan proceeds rather than coming out of the debtor's pocket. The court reasoned that because Kitts was obligated to pay the fees, they qualified as finance charges paid by the debtor. Thus, Winterfox violated the TILA by failing to provide disclosures on these high-cost loans, and Kitts was entitled to the statutory damages under the TILA. The court further reasoned that Winterfox's failure to provide notice of the required disclosures (under TILA) constituted a material failure to comply with HOEPA. Under the HOEPA, the plaintiff is entitled to compensatory damages, so the court awarded damages in the amount of the fees paid ($87,500), plus reasonable attorneys' fees ($150,000, calculated as 750 hours at $200 per hour).

CRITICAL THINKING—Legal Consideration *The TILA, HOEPA, and other consumer protection laws exist to protect purchasers from "unscrupulous" lenders or sellers. As consumers become better informed about these issues, will these laws still be needed? Discuss.*

Protection for Higher-Priced Mortgage Loans

The Federal Reserve Board enacted a rule that created a second category of expensive loans, called Higher-Priced Mortgage Loans (HPMLs). Only mortgages secured by a consumer's principal home qualify to receive the HPML designation.

Requirements to Qualify   To be an HPML, a mortgage must have an APR that exceeds the *average prime offer rate* for a comparable transaction by 1.5 percentage points or more if the loan is a first lien on a dwelling. (The **average prime offer rate** is the rate offered to the best-qualified borrowers as established by a survey of lenders.) If the loan is secured by a subordinate lien on a home, then the APR must exceed the average prime offer rate by 3.5 percentage points or more in order for the loan to be considered an HPML.

> **Average Prime Offer Rate**   The mortgage rate offered to the best-qualified borrowers as established by a survey of lenders.

Mortgages excluded from coverage include those for the initial construction of a home, temporary or *bridge loans* that are one year or shorter in duration, and home equity lines of credit. (**Bridge loans** are short-term loans that allow a buyer to make a down payment on a new home before selling her or his current home.)

> **Bridge Loan**   A short-term loan that allows a buyer to make a down payment on a new home before selling the current home, which is used as collateral for the loan.

Special Protections for Consumers   As with a HOEPA loan, consumers receiving an HPML receive additional protections. First, lenders cannot make an HPML based on the value of the consumer's home without verifying the consumer's ability to repay the loan. This verification is typically accomplished through review of the consumer's financial records such as tax returns, bank account statements, and payroll records. The creditor must also verify the consumer's other credit obligations.

Second, prepayment penalties are severely restricted for HPMLs. Prepayment penalties are allowed only if they are limited to two years, and they will not apply if the source of the prepayment funds is a refinancing by the creditor or the creditor's affiliate. Additionally, lenders must establish *escrow accounts* for borrowers' payments for homeowners' insurance and property taxes for all first mortgages. (An escrow account holds funds to be paid to a third party.) Finally, lenders cannot structure a loan specifically to evade the HPML protections.

Foreclosures

> **Foreclosure**   A proceeding in which a mortgagee either takes title to or forces the sale of the mortgagor's property in satisfaction of the debt.

If a homeowner defaults, or fails to make mortgage payments, the lender has the right to foreclose on the mortgaged property. **Foreclosure** is a process that allows a lender to legally repossess and auction off the property that is securing a loan.

(Olivier Le Queinec/Shutterstock.com)

When banks foreclose, they often end up owning the property.

Forbearance An agreement between the lender and the borrower in which the lender agrees to temporarily cease requiring mortgage payments, to delay foreclosure, or to accept smaller payments than previously scheduled.

Workout Agreement A formal contract between a debtor and his or her creditors in which the parties agree to negotiate a payment plan for the amount due on the loan instead of proceeding to foreclosure.

Short Sale A sale of real property for an amount that is less than the balance owed on the mortgage loan. The lender must consent to the sale and receives the proceeds, and the borrower still owes the balance of the mortgage debt to the lender unless the lender agrees to forgive it.

LEARNING OBJECTIVE 4
What is a short sale? What advantages over mortgage foreclosure might it offer borrowers? Does the lender receive the full balance due on the mortgage loan in a short sale?

Foreclosure is expensive and time consuming, however, and generally benefits neither the borrower, who loses his or her home, nor the lender, which faces the prospect of a loss on its loans. Therefore, various methods to avoid foreclosure have been developed. We look first at some of these methods and then turn to the foreclosure process itself.

How to Avoid Foreclosure

In the past, especially during the Great Depression of the 1930s, a number of alternatives to foreclosure were developed. More recently, as foreclosures have become more common than at any time since the Great Depression, Congress has intervened to aid in the modification of mortgage loans.

Forbearance and Workout Agreements
The first preforeclosure option a borrower has is called forbearance. **Forbearance** is the postponement, for a limited time, of part or all of the payments on a loan in jeopardy of foreclosure. A lender grants forbearance when it expects that, during the forbearance period, the borrower can solve the problem by securing a new job, selling the property, or finding another acceptable solution.

When a borrower fails to make payments as required, the lender may attempt to negotiate a workout. As noted in Chapter 15, a *workout* is a voluntary process to cure the default in some fashion. The parties may even create a formal **workout agreement**—a written document that describes the rights and responsibilities of the parties as they try to resolve the default without proceeding to foreclosure. In such an agreement, the lender will likely agree to delay seeking foreclosure or other legal rights. In exchange, the borrower may agree to provide the lender with financial information on which a workout might be constructed.

Whether a workout is possible or preferable to foreclosure depends on many factors, including the value of the property, the amount of the unpaid principal, the market in which the property will be sold, the relationship of the lender and the borrower, and the financial condition of the borrower.

Housing and Urban Development Assistance
A lender may be able to work with the borrower to obtain an interest-free loan from the U.S. Department of Housing and Urban Development (HUD) to bring the mortgage current. HUD assistance may be available if the loan is at least four months (but not more than twelve months) delinquent, if the property is not in foreclosure, and if the borrower is able to make full mortgage payments. When the lender files a claim, HUD pays the lender the amount necessary to make the mortgage current. The borrower executes a note to HUD, and a lien for the second loan is placed on the property. The promissory note is interest free and comes due if the property is sold.

Short Sales
When a borrower is unable to make mortgage payments, the lender may agree to a **short sale**—that is, a sale of the property for less than the balance due on the mortgage loan. The borrower must obtain the lender's permission for the short sale and typically has to show some hardship, such as the loss of a job, a decline in the value of the home, a divorce, or a death in the household. The lender receives the proceeds of the sale, and the borrower still owes the balance of the debt to the lender, unless the lender specifically agrees to forgive the remaining debt.

A short sale can offer several advantages. Although the borrower's credit rating is affected, the negative impact is less than it would be with a foreclosure, which generally remains on the borrower's credit report for seven years. The short sale process also avoids the expense of foreclosure for the lender and the trauma of being evicted from the home for the homeowner. But because the lender often has approval rights in a short sale, the sale process can take much longer than a standard real estate transaction. In addition, although the parties' losses are mitigated, the borrower still loses her or his home.

(Andy Dean Photography/Shutterstock.com)

Why would mortgage holders agree to short sales?

"People are living longer than ever before, a phenomenon undoubtedly made necessary by the 30-year mortgage."

Doug Larson, 1926–present (U.S. columnist)

Reamortize To change the way mortgage payments are configured, extending the term over which payments will be made.

Deed in Lieu of Foreclosure An alternative to foreclosure in which the mortgagor voluntarily conveys the property to the lender in satisfaction of the mortgage.

Sale and Leaseback In some situations, the homeowner may be able to sell the property to an investor who is looking for an income property. The owner sells the property to the investor and then leases it back at an amount that is less than the monthly mortgage payment. The owner-seller uses the proceeds of the sale to pay off the mortgage and still has the use and possession of the property. In some circumstances, this strategy can also be used to raise capital when there is no risk of loss of the property.

Home Affordable Modification Program In 2009, the U.S. Treasury Department launched the Home Affordable Modification Program (HAMP) to encourage private lenders to modify mortgages so as to lower the monthly payments of borrowers who are in default. The purpose of HAMP is not to force lenders to forgive all high-risk mortgages, but rather to reduce monthly mortgage payments to a level that the homeowner can reasonably pay. The program may share in the costs of modifying the loan and provides incentives to lenders based on successful loan modification.

Qualifications HAMP modifications are not available for every mortgage. To qualify for a HAMP modification, all of the following must be true:

1. The loan must have originated on or before January 1, 2009.
2. The home must be occupied by the owner and must be the homeowner's primary residence.[6]
3. The unpaid balance may not exceed $729,750 for a single-unit property.[7]
4. The homeowner must be facing financial hardship and be either more than sixty days late on mortgage payments or at risk of imminent default. Homeowners are required to verify their hardship through appropriate documentation.

Restructuring the Mortgage The goal is to reduce the debtor's mortgage payment to 31 percent of his or her gross monthly income. The loan is restructured by adding any delinquencies (such as accrued interest, past-due taxes, or unpaid insurance premiums) to the principal amount. This increases the number of payments but eliminates the delinquencies by spreading them over the life of the loan.

Once the loan is restructured, lenders try to incrementally lower the mortgage interest rate to a level at which the payments are less than 31 percent of the debtor's income. If the lender cannot reach the 31 percent target by lowering the interest rate to 2 percent, then the lender can **reamortize** the loan (change the way the payments are configured), extending the schedule of payments for up to forty years.

The borrower then begins a ninety-day trial period to determine his or her ability to make three modified monthly payments. If the borrower succeeds, the lender offers permanent modifications.

Voluntary Conveyance Under some circumstances, the parties may benefit from a **deed in lieu of foreclosure**, by which the property is voluntarily conveyed (transferred) to the lender in satisfaction of the mortgage. A property that has a current market value close to the outstanding loan principal and on which no other loans have been taken might be the subject of such a conveyance.

Although the lender faces the risk that it may ultimately sell the property for less than the loan amount, the lender avoids the time, risk, and expense of foreclosure litigation. The borrower who gives the property to the lender without a fight also avoids the foreclosure process and may preserve a better credit rating than if he or she had been forced to give up the property involuntarily.

---

6. Investor-owned homes, vacant homes, and condemned properties are not eligible under the program.

7. Higher limits are allowed for properties with two to four units.

Friendly Foreclosure   Another way for the parties to avoid a contested foreclosure is to engage in a friendly foreclosure. In such a transaction, the borrower in default agrees to submit to the court's jurisdiction, to waive any defenses as well as the right to appeal, and to cooperate with the lender. This process takes longer than a voluntary conveyance, but all of the parties have greater certainty as to the finality of the transaction with respect to others who might have a financial interest in the property.

The Foreclosure Procedure

If all efforts to find another solution fail, the lender will proceed to foreclosure—a process that dates back to English law. A formal foreclosure is necessary to extinguish the borrower's equitable *right of redemption* (see page 482).

To bring a foreclosure action, a creditor must have *standing to sue* (see page 73 in Chapter 3). In the following *Spotlight Case,* the court had to decide whether a bank could foreclose on a mortgage even though it could not prove when it became the owner of the debtor's promissory note.

Spotlight on Foreclosures

Case 16.2
McLean v. JPMorgan Chase Bank, N.A.
District Court of Appeal of Florida, 79 So.3d 170 (2012).
caselaw.findlaw.com[a]

How can Chase Bank foreclose on delinquent mortgages?

FACTS On May 11, 2009, JPMorgan Chase Bank (Chase) filed a foreclosure action against Robert McLean. The complaint alleged that Chase was entitled to enforce the mortgage and promissory note on which McLean had defaulted. Nevertheless, the attached mortgage identified a different mortgagee and lender, and Chase claimed that the note had been "lost, stolen, or destroyed." When McLean filed a motion to dismiss, Chase produced a mortgage assignment dated May 14, 2009, which was three days after it had filed the lawsuit. Eventually, Chase also filed the original note. Although the indorsement to Chase was undated, Chase then filed a motion for summary judgment. The trial court granted Chase's motion even though the accompanying affidavit failed to show that Chase owned the mortgage or note when it had filed the complaint. McLean appealed.

ISSUE Did Chase prove that it had standing to bring a foreclosure action against McLean?

DECISION No. The Florida appellate court reversed the trial court's grant of summary judgment to Chase.

REASON A party seeking foreclosure must have standing to foreclose when it files its complaint. In this case, the mortgage was assigned after Chase had filed its complaint, so Chase argued that it had standing because the promissory note was indorsed in its name. The indorsement was undated, however, and Chase's affidavit also did not show that Chase owned the note when it filed its lawsuit. The court therefore reversed summary judgment and instructed the trial court to find for Chase only if it proved that it had owned the note at the time of the complaint. Otherwise, the case would have to be dismissed and Chase would need to file a new complaint.

CRITICAL THINKING—Legal Consideration *If Chase cannot prove that it owned the note at the time of its complaint, what will happen next? Will Chase prevail? Why or why not?*

---

a. Under "Popular State Resources," click on "Florida Caselaw." When the page opens, click on "District Court of Appeal of Florida." On the next page, type "McLean" in the "Party name:" box and click on "Search." In the result, click on the case name to access the opinion.

Types of Foreclosures

Judicial Foreclosure A court-supervised fore-closure proceeding in which the court determines the validity of the debt and, if the borrower is in default, issues a judgment for the lender.

Power of Sale Foreclosure A foreclosure procedure that is not court supervised and is available only in some states.

Types of Foreclosures   Generally, two types of foreclosure are used in the United States: **judicial foreclosure** and **power of sale foreclosure.** In a judicial fore-closure, which is available in all states, a court supervises the process. In a power of sale foreclosure, the lender is allowed to foreclose on and sell the property without judicial supervision.

Only a few states permit power of sale foreclosures because borrowers have less pro-tection when a court does not supervise the process. In these states, lenders must strictly comply with the terms of the state statute governing power of sale foreclosures. Failure to follow the statutory requirements can lead to the foreclosure being invalidated. **CASE EXAMPLE 16.5**   Antonio Ibanez obtained a home loan, as did Mark and Tammy LaRace. Each of the loans subsequently changed hands several times through various banks, as is common in the mortgage-lending industry. Both Ibanez and the LaRaces defaulted on their mortgages.

U.S. Bank, N.A., foreclosed on the Ibanez mortgage, and Wells Fargo foreclosed on the LaRace mortgage. Both banks published notices of the foreclosure sales in a newspaper, as required by statute, and then bought the homes at the foreclosure auctions. Both banks purchased the properties for significantly less than the purported market value. At the time of the foreclosures, each bank represented that it was the "owner and holder" of the mort-gage. When the banks later filed for a court declaration stating that they owned the proper-ties, however, the court ruled against them. The court found that the banks had failed to show that they were holders of the mortgages at the time of the foreclosures. Therefore, they did not have the authority to foreclose, and the foreclosure sales were invalid.[8] ●

Acceleration Clauses

Acceleration Clause In a mortgage loan contract, a clause that makes the entire loan bal-ance become due if the borrower misses or is late making the monthly payments.

Acceleration Clauses   In a strict foreclosure, the lender may seek only the amount of the missed payments, not the entire loan amount. Therefore, lenders often include an *acceleration clause* in their loan documents. An **acceleration clause** allows the lender to call the entire loan due—even if only one payment is late or missed. Thus, with an acceleration clause, the lender can foreclose only once on the entire amount of the loan rather than having to foreclose on smaller amounts over a period of time as each payment is missed.

Notice of Default and Notice of Sale

Notice of Default A formal notice to a borrower who is behind in making mortgage pay-ments that the borrower is in default and may face foreclosure. The notice is filed by the lender in the county where the property is located.

Notice of Sale A formal notice to a bor-rower who is in default on a mortgage that the mortgaged property will be sold in a foreclosure proceeding.

Notice of Default and Notice of Sale   To initiate a foreclosure, a lender must record a **notice of default** with the appropriate county office. The borrower is then on notice of a possible foreclosure and can take steps to pay the loan and cure the default. If the loan is not paid within a reasonable time (usually three months), the borrower will receive a **notice of sale.** In addition, the notice of sale usually is posted on the property, recorded with the county, and published in a newspaper.

The property is then sold in an auction on the courthouse steps at the time and loca-tion indicated in the notice of sale. The buyer generally has to pay cash within twenty-four hours for the property. If the procedures are not followed precisely, the parties may have to resort to litigation to establish clear ownership of the property. The following case illus-trates how the notice requirements work.

---

8. These two foreclosure cases were consolidated on appeal and ruled on jointly by the Massachusetts Supreme Court in *U.S. Bank, N.A. v. Ibanez,* 458 Mass. 637, 941 N.E.2d 40 (2011).

Case 16.3

Mitchell v. Valteau[a]

Court of Appeal of Louisiana, Fourth Circuit,
30 So.3d 1108 (2010).
www.la4th.org/Opinions.aspx[b]

A branch of Washington Mutual Bank.

(Jb Reed/Bloomberg via Getty Images)

FACTS Dr. Pamela Mitchell borrowed $143,724 to buy a house and lot. A mortgage on the property secured the loan and provided for the sale of the house on default. When Mitchell defaulted, the mortgage holder, Washington Mutual Bank, obtained a court order to seize and sell the property and notified Mitchell. The parties negotiated a new agreement that postponed the seizure and sale. After making two payments, Mitchell again defaulted, and the court issued an amended order of seizure. Despite several attempts, Mitchell was not notified of this order personally. The house was seized and sold. Several months later, Mitchell filed a petition to invalidate the judicial sale and request damages for wrongful seizure.

ISSUE Is a debtor (Mitchell), who received the notice of seizure and sale in a foreclosure proceeding and then entered into a repayment agreement with the lender entitled to receive a second notice of sale if she defaults again?

DECISION No. The Louisiana appellate court affirmed the lower court's decision in favor of the bank. Mitchell was not entitled to another notice of seizure and sale under Louisiana law.

REASON After examining Louisiana law and other cases, the reviewing court concluded that there was "no Louisiana authority for requiring a creditor to provide a debtor with notice of a rescheduled judicial sale." Further, it was clear from the repayment agreement that the seizure and sale proceedings would be placed on hold only during the time the repayment agreement was in place. "The agreement also provided for the resumption of the foreclosure in the event of a default in its terms, which Dr. Mitchell acknowledged occurred. There was no obligation to serve Dr. Mitchell with another notice of seizure."

CRITICAL THINKING—Ethical Consideration What is the underlying purpose for requiring lenders to serve a written notice of seizure of property? Was the court's holding fair to Mitchell? Why or why not?

---

a. Paul Valteau, in his capacity of civil sheriff, was named as one of the defendants.

b. From the search mode choices, select "Search Cases by Published Date." When that page opens, select "Click for Calendar." Using the arrow at the top of the calendar, go to January 2010, select "27," and then click on "Search." Scroll through the list at the bottom of the page to the case title and click on "Download" to access the opinion. The Louisiana court system maintains this Web site.

LEARNING OBJECTIVE 5

In a mortgage foreclosure, what legal rights do mortgage holders have if the sale proceeds are insufficient to pay the underlying debt?

Equitable Right of Redemption The right of a borrower who is in default on a mortgage loan to redeem or purchase the property before foreclosure.

Statutory Right of Redemption A right provided by statute in some states under which mortgagors can buy back their property after a judicial foreclosure for a limited period of time, such as one year.

Deficiency Judgments If any equity remains after the foreclosed property is sold, the borrower is often able to keep the difference between the sale price and the mortgage amount. If the sale amount is not enough to cover the loan amount, the lender (in the majority of states) can ask a court for a *deficiency judgment*. A deficiency judgment is a judgment against the borrower for the amount of debt remaining unpaid after the collateral is sold. A deficiency judgment requires the borrower to make up the difference to the lender over time. Note that some states do not allow deficiency judgments for mortgaged residential real estate.

Redemption Rights

Every state allows a homeowner to buy the property *after default and before the foreclosure sale* by paying the full amount of the debt, plus any interest and costs that have accrued. This **equitable right of redemption** allows a defaulting borrower to gain title and regain possession of a property, but it ends when the property is sold at a foreclosure auction.

The **statutory right of redemption**, in contrast, entitles the borrower to repurchase property even *after a judicial foreclosure*. In other words, in states that provide for statutory redemption, the homeowner has a right to buy the property back from a third party who bought it at a foreclosure sale. Generally, the borrower may exercise this right for up to one year from the time the house is sold at a foreclosure sale.[9]

The borrower[10] must pay the price at which the house was sold at the foreclosure sale (the redemption price), plus taxes, interest, and assessments, as opposed to the balance owed on the foreclosed loan. Some states allow the borrower to retain possession of the property after the foreclosure sale and up until the statutory redemption period ends. If the borrower does not exercise the right of redemption, the new buyer receives title to and possession of the property.

---

9. Some states do not allow a borrower to waive the statutory right of redemption. This means that a buyer at auction must wait one year to obtain title to, and possession of, a foreclosed property.

10. Some states also allow spouses of a defaulting borrower or creditors holding liens on the property to purchase the property under the statutory right of redemption.

Reviewing . . . Mortgages and Foreclosures after the Recession

Al and Betty Smith own their home, which is valued at $200,000, completely—they have 100 percent home equity. They lost most of their savings in the stock market during the Great Recession. Needing funds to start a new business, they decide to take out a home equity loan. They borrow $150,000 for ten years at an interest rate of 12 percent. On the date they take out the loan, a ten-year Treasury bond is yielding 3 percent. The Smiths pay a total of $10,000 in "points and fees" to Alpha Bank. The Smiths are not given any notices that they can lose their home if they do not meet their obligations under the loan. Two weeks after consummating the loan, the Smiths change their minds and want to rescind the loan. Using the information presented in the chapter, answer the following questions.

1. Is the Smiths' loan covered by the Truth-in-Lending Act as amended by the Home Ownership and Equity Protection Act? Why or why not?
2. Do the Smiths have a right to rescind the loan two weeks after the fact, or is it too late? Explain.
3. Assume now that Alpha Bank had given the Smiths all of the required notices before the loan was consummated. If all other facts remain the same, would the Smiths have a right to rescind? Why or why not?
4. Suppose now that the Smiths never rescind the loan and that they default four years later while still owing Alpha Bank $120,000. The bank forecloses and raises only $110,000 when the house is sold at auction. In the majority of states, what options does Alpha Bank have to recover the difference? Explain.

DEBATE THIS Federal legislation enacted in the past few years has unfairly benefited those who should not have bought such expensive houses and taken on so much debt.

Key Terms

acceleration clause 481
adjustable-rate mortgage (ARM) 471
annual percentage rate (APR) 474
appraiser 475
average prime offer rate 477

balloon mortgage 472
bridge loan 477
deed in lieu of foreclosure 479
down payment 471
equitable right of redemption 482

fixed-rate mortgage 471
forbearance 478
foreclosure 477
home equity loan 472
homeowners' insurance 473

interest-only (IO) mortgage 472
judicial foreclosure 481
mortgage 470
mortgagee 470
mortgagor 470

negative amortization 476	power of sale foreclosure 481
notice of default 481	prepayment penalty clause 473
notice of sale 481	reamortize 479

Chapter Summary: Mortgages and Foreclosures after the Recession

Mortgages
(See pages 470–474.)
	1. *Types of mortgages*—A mortgage loan is a contract between a creditor (mortgagee) and a borrower (mortgagor). A down payment is the part of the purchase price that is paid up front. There are many types of mortgages, including:
	   a. Fixed-rate mortgages, which are standard mortgages with a fixed rate of interest and payments that stay the same for the duration of the loan.
	   b. Adjustable-rate mortgages (ARMs), in which the interest rate changes periodically, usually starting low and increasing over time.
	   c. Interest-only mortgages, which allow borrowers to pay only the interest portion of the monthly payments for a limited time, after which the size of the payment increases.
	   d. Subprime mortgages, which carry higher rates of interest because they are made to borrowers who do not qualify for standard mortgages.
	2. *Creditor protection*—To protect its interests, a creditor may (a) require private mortgage insurance if the down payment is less than 20 percent of the purchase price, (b) perfect its security interest by recording the mortgage in the appropriate office, and (c) include a prepayment penalty clause and a clause requiring the borrower to maintain homeowners' insurance in the mortgage contract.

Real Estate Financing Law
(See pages 474–477.)
	1. *Predatory lending*—The practice of using loan terms or lending procedures that are excessive, deceptive, or not properly disclosed. Examples include steering and targeting, and loan flipping.
	2. *Truth-in-Lending Act (TILA)*—This federal statute requires mortgage lenders to disclose the terms of a loan in clear, readily understandable language on standardized forms.
	   a. Terms that must be disclosed include the loan principal, the interest rate at which the loan is made, the annual percentage rate, and all fees and costs.
	   b. The TILA prohibits certain unfair lender practices, such as charging prepayment penalties on most subprime mortgages and home equity loans and coercing an appraiser into misstating the value of property.
	   c. A borrower has the right to rescind a mortgage within three business days. If a lender does not provide the required disclosures, the rescission period runs for three years.
	3. *High-cost mortgages*—The Home Ownership and Equity Protection Act (HOEPA) of 1994 creates special rules for high-cost and high-fee mortgage products.
	   a. In addition to the TILA disclosures, HOEPA requires lenders to disclose the APR, the regular payment amount, and any balloon payments. Lenders must also disclose that the home may be lost if the borrower defaults, that the rate and payment amounts of variable-rate loans may increase, and what the maximum increase could be. HOEPA also prohibits short-term loans requiring balloon payments and loans that result in negative amortization.
	   b. On a lender's material failure to disclose, a consumer may receive damages equal to all finance charges and fees paid. If a lender fails to comply with HOEPA, the borrower's right to rescind is extended to three years.
	4. *Higher-priced mortgages*—Special protections apply to Higher-Priced Mortgage Loans (HPMLs). To qualify as an HPML, a mortgage must have an APR that exceeds the average prime offer rate by a certain amount for a comparable transaction.

Foreclosures
(See pages 477–483.)
	If the borrower defaults, the lender can foreclose on the mortgaged property. The foreclosure process allows a lender to repossess and auction the property.
	1. *Ways to avoid foreclosure proceedings*—Foreclosure can sometimes be avoided through a forbearance or a workout agreement, an interest-free loan from the U.S. Department of Housing and Urban Development, a short sale, a sale and leaseback, a modification under the Home Affordable Modification Program, a deed in lieu of foreclosure, or a friendly foreclosure.
	2. *Foreclosure procedures*—In a judicial foreclosure, which is available in all states, a court supervises the process. In a power of sale foreclosure, which is permitted in only a few states, the lender can foreclose on and sell the property without judicial supervision.
	   a. To initiate a foreclosure, the lender records a notice of default with the county. If the loan is not paid, the borrower receives a notice of sale, and the property is sold at auction.
	   b. In most states, if the sale proceeds do not cover the loan amount, the lender can obtain a deficiency judgment for the amount due.
	3. *Redemption rights*—
	   a. Equitable right of redemption—In all states, the borrower has the right to purchase the property after default by paying the full amount of the debt, plus interest and costs, before the foreclosure sale.
	   b. Statutory right of redemption—In some states, the borrower has the right to repurchase the property even after a judicial foreclosure.

ExamPrep

ISSUE SPOTTERS

1. Ruth Ann borrows $175,000 from Sunny Valley Bank to buy a home. What are the major terms of the mortgage that must be disclosed in the writing under the Truth-in-Lending Act? (**See pages 474–475.**)
2. Tanner borrows $150,000 from Southeast Credit Union to buy a home, which secures the loan. Two years into the term, Tanner stops making payments on the mortgage. After six months without payments, Southeast informs Tanner that he is in default and that it will proceed to foreclosure. What is foreclosure, and what is the usual procedure? (**See pages 477, 480–482.**)

—Check your answers to the Issue Spotters against the answers provided in Appendix E at the end of this text.

BEFORE THE TEST

Go to www.cengagebrain.com, enter the ISBN 9781133191353, and click on "Find" to locate this textbook's Web site. Then, click on "Access Now" under "Study Tools," and select Chapter 16 at the top. There, you will find a Practice Quiz that you can take to assess your mastery of the concepts in this chapter, as well as Flashcards, a Glossary of important terms, and Video Questions (when assigned).

For Review

Answers to the even-numbered questions in this For Review section can be found in Appendix F at the end of this text.

1. What is a subprime mortgage? How does it differ from a standard fixed-rate mortgage? What is a home equity loan?
2. When is private mortgage insurance required? Which party does it protect?
3. Does the Truth-in-Lending Act (TILA) apply to all mortgages? How do the TILA provisions protect borrowers and curb abusive practices by mortgage lenders?
4. What is a short sale? What advantages over mortgage foreclosure might it offer borrowers? Does the lender receive the full balance due on the mortgage loan in a short sale?
5. In a mortgage foreclosure, what legal rights do mortgage holders have if the sale proceeds are insufficient to pay the underlying debt?

Business Scenarios and Case Problems

16–1 Disclosure Requirements. Rancho Mortgage, Inc., wants to launch a new advertising campaign designed to attract home-buyers in a difficult economic environment. Rancho plans to promote its new loan product, which offers a fixed interest rate for the first five years and then switches to a variable interest rate. Rancho believes that Spanish-speaking home-buyers have been underserved in recent years, and it wants to advertise particularly to that market. What must Rancho say (and not say) in its advertising campaigns about the structure of the loan product? Why? (**See pages 474–475.**)

16–2 **Question with Sample Answer—Real Estate Financing.** Jane Lane refinanced her mortgage with Central Equity, Inc. Central Equity split the transaction into two separate loan documents with separate Truth-in-Lending disclosure statements and settlement statements. Two years later, Lane tried to exercise her right to rescission under the Home Ownership and Equity Protection Act (HOEPA), but Central Equity refused. Central Equity said that the loans were two separate loan transactions and because neither loan imposed sufficient fees and costs to trigger HOEPA, its protections did not apply. Lane claimed that the costs and fees combined into a single transaction (which Lane expected the loan to be) would surpass the HOEPA threshold and trigger its protections. Because Central Equity did not provide the necessary disclosures under HOEPA, Lane argues that she can properly rescind under its provisions. Is Lane correct? Does loan splitting allow the lender to count each loan transaction with a borrower separately for purposes of HOEPA? Why or why not? (**See page 476.**)

—For a sample answer to Question 16–2, go to Appendix G at the end of this text.

16–3 Lender's Options. In 2011, Frank relocates and purchases a five-year-old house for $450,000. He pays $90,000 as a down payment and finances the remaining $360,000 of the purchase price with a loan from Bank of Town. Frank signs mortgage paperwork, giving Bank of Town a mortgage interest in the home. Frank pays on the loan for three years. At that point, the housing market has declined significantly. Frank's home is now valued at $265,000. The balance due on his loan is $354,000. In addition, the economy has slowed, and the booming business that Frank started when he bought the home has seen a decrease in revenues. It seems inevitable that Frank will not be able to make his payments. Discuss Bank of Town's options in this situation. (**See pages 478–480.**)

16–4 Right of Rescission. George and Mona Antanuos obtained a mortgage loan secured with rental property from the First National Bank of Arizona. At the closing, First National provided the Antanuoses with a "Notice of Right to Cancel," informing them about their TILA three-day rescission period. The following day, according to the Antanuoses, they informed the bank via fax that they wished to exercise their right to rescind. When First National refused to rescind the agreement, the Antanuoses sued the bank. The Antanuoses did not dispute that a consumer's right to rescind under the TILA applies only to the consumer's original dwelling and that they used their commercial property as a security interest. Instead, the Antanuoses argued that the bank was prohibited from denying them the rescission right because they relied on the bank's disclosure, which would have been required under the TILA, to their detriment. Would the court be convinced? Explain. [*Antanuos v. First National Bank of Arizona,* 508 F.Supp.2d 466 (E.D.Va. 2007)] **(See page 475.)**

16–5 Mortgage Foreclosure. In January 2003, Gary Ryder and Washington Mutual Bank, F.A., executed a note in which Ryder promised to pay $2,450,000, plus interest at a rate that could vary from month to month. The amount of the first payment was $10,933. The note was to be paid in full by February 1, 2033. A mortgage on Ryder's real property at 345 Round Hill Road in Greenwich, Connecticut, in favor of the bank secured his obligations under the note. The note and mortgage required Ryder to pay the taxes on the property, which he did not do in 2004 and 2005. The bank notified him that he was in default and, when he failed to act, paid $50,095.92 in taxes, penalties, interest, and fees. Other disputes arose between the parties, and Ryder filed a suit against the bank, alleging, in part, breach of contract. He charged, among other things, that some of his timely payments were not processed and were subjected to incorrect late fees, forcing him to make excessive payments and ultimately resulting in "non-payment by Ryder." The bank filed a counterclaim, seeking to foreclose on the mortgage. What should a creditor be required to prove to foreclose on mortgaged property? What would be a debtor's most effective defense? Which party in this case is likely to prevail on the bank's counterclaim? Why? [*Ryder v. Washington Mutual Bank, F.A.,* 501 F.Supp.2d 311 (D.Conn. 2007)] **(See pages 477–482.)**

16–6 Foreclosures. Roderick and Linda Sharpe borrowed $51,300 secured by a mortgage on their home. About six years later, with more than $68,000 needed to pay off the mortgage, the Sharpes defaulted. The mortgage holder, Wells Fargo Home Mortgage, foreclosed on the property. Immediately before and after the foreclosure sale, Wells Fargo obtained two separate real estate brokers' opinions as to the property's fair market value. Each opinion was based on the prices of three comparable houses then on the market and three comparable houses that had sold within the previous six months. Both opinions set the value at $33,500. This was the price at the sale. The Sharpes objected, arguing that the value of the property was $65,000 based on an appraisal that they could not provide. Was the sale price fair? Explain. [*In re Sharpe,* 425 Bankr. 620 (N.D.Ala. 2010)] **(See pages 481–482.)**

16–7 Foreclosure on Mortgage and Liens. LaSalle Bank loaned $8 million to Cypress Creek 1, LP, to build an apartment complex. The loan was secured by a mortgage. Cypress Creek hired contractors to provide concrete work, plumbing, carpentry, and other construction services. Cypress Creek went bankrupt, owing LaSalle $3 million. The contractors recorded *mechanic's liens* (see page 438 in Chapter 15) when they did not get paid for their work. The property was sold to LaSalle at a sheriff's sale for $1.3 million. The contractors claimed that they should be paid the amounts they were owed out of the $1.3 million and that the mechanic's liens should be satisfied before any funds were distributed to LaSalle for its mortgage. The trial court distributed the $1.3 million primarily to LaSalle, with only a small fraction going to the contractors. Do the liens come before the mortgage in priority of payment? Discuss. [*LaSalle Bank National Association v. Cypress Creek 1, LP,* 242 Ill.2d 231, 950 N.E.2d 1109 (2011)] **(See pages 480–482.)**

16–8 Case Problem with Sample Answer—Deficiency Judgment. First Brownsville Co. executed a promissory note secured by a mortgage so that it could build and operate a mini-warehouse storage business. When First Brownsville defaulted on the loan, Beach Community Bank sought to foreclose on the property in Florida state court. The court determined that First Brownsville owed $1,224,475; entered judgment for Beach Community; and scheduled a foreclosure sale. Beach Community was the only interested bidder at the foreclosure sale, so it bought the property for a mere $1,300. Pursuant to Florida law, Beach Community then sought a deficiency judgment. At the hearing, expert testimony established that the property's fair market value had been $1,480,000 a year earlier, but that the property was worth only $770,000 at the time of the sale. What should be the amount of Beach Community's deficiency judgment? Why? [*Beach Community Bank v. First Brownsville Co.,* 85 So.3d 1119 (Fla.App. 1st Dist. 2012)] **(See page 482.)**

—For a sample answer to Problem 16–8, go to Appendix H at the end of this text.

16–9 A Question of Ethics—Predatory Lending. Peter Sutton's home was subject to two mortgages with payments of more than $1,400 per month, but his only source of income was $1,080 monthly from Social Security. Hoping to reduce the size of the payments, Sutton contacted Apex Mortgage Services. According to Sutton, the broker led him to believe that he could refinance with Countrywide Home Loans, Inc., for payments of $428 per month. In the end, the broker arranged an adjustable-rate loan from Countrywide with initial payments of about $1,000 per month subject to future increases. The loan included a prepayment penalty. Sutton paid the broker fee and signed the agreement, but later claimed that he did not understand the terms. The payments proved too much for Sutton to afford, and he defaulted on the loan. Sutton sued the broker and lender claiming violations of federal law. [*Sutton v. Countrywide Home Loans, Inc.*, ___ F.3d ___ (11th Cir. 2009)] **(See page 474.)**

1. Who is ethically responsible for Sutton's predicament? To what extent did Sutton have a duty to read and understand what he signed? Discuss.

2. Sutton argued that he should not have to pay the broker's fee because the broker did not provide any services that were of value. Do you agree? Why or why not?

3. Did Countrywide, the lender, have any ethical obligation to monitor the activities of the broker? Would the result have been different if Countrywide had intervened before the documents were signed? Explain.

Critical Thinking and Writing Assignments

16–10 **Business Law Critical Thinking Group Assignment.** Mr. and Mrs. Jones owned a home that went into foreclosure. During this time, they received a brochure from Rees-Max that read: "There are only a few months to go in your redemption period! Your options to save the equity in your home are fading. Call me immediately for a no-bull, no-obligation assessment of your situation. Even if you have been 'promised' by a mortgage broker or investor that they will help, CALL ME . . . ." The Joneses contacted Rees-Max, and they entered into an agreement. Rees-Max would buy the property from the Joneses, the Joneses would lease the property for a few months, and then the Joneses would purchase the property back from Rees-Max on a contract for deed. The agreement did not use the terms *debt*, *security*, or *mortgage*, and the documents stated that no security interest was granted. The Joneses property was appraised at $278,000 and purchased by Rees-Max for $214,000 with more than $30,000 in fees. When the Joneses complained about the fees, Rees-Max started eviction proceedings.

1. The first group will use the chapter materials to identify what type of transaction the Joneses entered into with Rees-Max.

2. The second group will determine whether this transaction constituted a mortgage that would receive TILA and HOEPA protection. Do the Joneses have any right to complain about the fees? Why or why not?

17 CHAPTER

Agency

(Goodluz/iStockphoto.com)

LEARNING OBJECTIVES

The five learning objectives below are designed to help improve your understanding of the chapter. After reading this chapter, you should be able to answer the following questions:

1 What is the difference between an employee and an independent contractor?

2 How do agency relationships arise?

3 What duties do agents and principals owe to each other?

4 When is a principal liable for the agent's actions with respect to third parties? When is the agent liable?

5 What are some of the ways in which an agency relationship can be terminated?

"[It] is a universal principle in the law of agency, that the powers of the agent are to be exercised for the benefit of the principal only, and not of the agent or of third parties."
—Joseph Story, 1779–1845 (Associate justice of the United States Supreme Court, 1811–1844)

Agency A relationship between two parties in which one party (the agent) agrees to represent or act for the other (the principal).

One of the most common, important, and pervasive legal relationships is that of **agency.** In an agency relationship between two parties, one of the parties, called the *agent,* agrees to represent or act for the other, called the *principal.* The principal has the right to control the agent's conduct in matters entrusted to the agent, and the agent must exercise his or her powers "for the benefit of the principal only," as Justice Joseph Story indicated in the chapter-opening quotation.

By using agents, a principal can conduct multiple business operations, such as entering contracts, at the same time in different locations. Using agents provides clear benefits to principals, but agents also create liability for their principals. For this reason, small businesses sometimes attempt to retain workers as independent contractors or "permalancers," but this strategy may lead to problems with federal and state tax authorities, as you will read later in this chapter.

Agency relationships are crucial to the business world. Indeed, the only way that some business entities—including corporations and limited liability companies—can function is through their agents. A familiar example of an agent is a corporate officer who serves in a representative capacity for the owners of the corporation. In this capacity, the officer has the authority to bind the principal (the corporation) to a contract.

Agency Relationships

Section 1(1) of the *Restatement (Third) of Agency*[1] defines agency as "the fiduciary relation which results from the manifestation of consent by one person to another that the other shall act in his [or her] behalf and subject to his [or her] control, and consent by the other so to act." In other words, in a principal-agent relationship, the parties have agreed that the agent will act *on behalf and instead of* the principal in negotiating and transacting business with third parties.

Fiduciary   As a noun, a person having a duty created by his or her undertaking to act primarily for another's benefit in matters connected with the undertaking. As an adjective, a relationship founded on trust and confidence.

The term **fiduciary** is at the heart of agency law. The term can be used both as a noun and as an adjective. When used as a noun, it refers to a person having a duty created by her or his undertaking to act primarily for another's benefit in matters connected with the undertaking. When used as an adjective, as in "fiduciary relationship," it means that the relationship involves trust and confidence.

Agency relationships commonly exist between employers and employees. Agency relationships may sometimes also exist between employers and independent contractors who are hired to perform special tasks or services.

Employer-Employee Relationships

Normally, all employees who deal with third parties are deemed to be agents. A salesperson in a department store, for instance, is an agent of the store's owner (the principal) and acts on the owner's behalf. Any sale of goods made by the salesperson to a customer is binding on the principal. Similarly, most representations of fact made by the salesperson with respect to the goods sold are binding on the principal.

(Lisegagne/iStockphoto.com)

Corporations could not operate without employing agents.

Because employees who deal with third parties are generally deemed to be agents of their employers, agency law and employment law overlap considerably. Agency relationships, however, can exist outside an employer-employee relationship, so agency law has a broader reach than employment law. Additionally, agency law is based on the common law, whereas much employment law is statutory law.

Employment laws (state and federal) apply only to the employer-employee relationship. Statutes governing Social Security, withholding taxes, workers' compensation, unemployment compensation, workplace safety, employment discrimination, and the like (see Chapter 18) are applicable only if employer-employee status exists. *These laws do not apply to an independent contractor.*

LEARNING OBJECTIVE 1
What is the difference between an employee and an independent contractor?

Employer–Independent Contractor Relationships

Independent contractors are not employees because, by definition, those who hire them have no control over the details of their physical performance. Section 2 of the *Restatement (Third) of Agency* defines an **independent contractor** as follows:

Independent Contractor   One who works for, and receives payment from, an employer but whose working conditions and methods are not controlled by the employer. An independent contractor is not an employee but may be an agent.

[An independent contractor is] a person who contracts with another to do something for him [or her] but who is not controlled by the other nor subject to the other's right to control with

---

1. The *Restatement (Third) of Agency* is an authoritative summary of the law of agency and is often referred to by judges and other legal professionals.

respect to his [or her] physical conduct in the performance of the undertaking. *He [or she] may or may not be an agent.* [Emphasis added.]

Building contractors and subcontractors are independent contractors. A property owner does not control the acts of either of these professionals. Truck drivers who own their equipment and hire themselves out on a per-job basis are independent contractors, but truck drivers who drive company trucks on a regular basis are usually employees.

The relationship between a person or firm and an independent contractor may or may not involve an agency relationship. To illustrate: An owner of real estate who hires a real estate broker to negotiate a sale of the property not only has contracted with an independent contractor (the broker) but also has established an agency relationship for the specific purpose of selling the property. Another example is an insurance agent, who is both an independent contractor and an agent of the insurance company for which she or he sells policies. (Note that an insurance *broker,* in contrast, normally is an agent of the person obtaining insurance and not of the insurance company.)

"I'd like to think of you as a person, David, but it's my job to think of you as personnel."

Determining Employee Status

The courts are frequently asked to determine whether a particular worker is an employee or an independent contractor. How a court decides this issue can have a significant effect on the rights and liabilities of the parties. Employers are required to pay certain taxes, such as Social Security and unemployment insurance taxes, for employees but not for independent contractors.

Criteria Used by the Courts In determining whether a worker has the status of an employee or an independent contractor, the courts often consider the following questions:

1. How much control can the employer exercise over the details of the work? (If an employer can exercise considerable control over the details of the work, this would indicate employee status. This is perhaps the most important factor weighed by the courts in determining employee status.)
2. Is the worker engaged in an occupation or business distinct from that of the employer? (If so, this points to independent-contractor status, not employee status.)
3. Is the work usually done under the employer's direction or by a specialist without supervision? (If the work is usually done under the employer's direction, this would indicate employee status.)
4. Does the employer supply the tools at the place of work? (If so, this would indicate employee status.)
5. For how long is the person employed? (If the person is employed for a long period of time, this would indicate employee status.)
6. What is the method of payment—by time period or at the completion of the job? (Payment by time period, such as once every two weeks or once a month, would indicate employee status.)
7. What degree of skill is required of the worker? (If little skill is required, this may indicate employee status.)

Disputes Involving Employment Law Sometimes, workers may benefit from having employee status—for tax purposes and to be protected under certain employment laws, for example. As mentioned earlier, federal statutes governing employment discrimination apply only when an employer-employee relationship exists. Protection under antidiscrimination statutes provides a significant incentive for workers to claim that they are employees rather than independent contractors.

CASE EXAMPLE 17.1 A Puerto Rican television station, WIPR, contracted with a woman to co-host a television show. The woman signed a new contract for each episode and was committed to work for WIPR only during the filming of the episodes. WIPR paid her a lump sum for each contract and did not withhold any taxes.

When the woman became pregnant, WIPR stopped contracting with her. She filed a lawsuit claiming that WIPR was discriminating against her in violation of federal antidiscrimination laws, but the court found in favor of WIPR. Because the parties had structured their relationship through repeated fixed-length contracts and had described the woman as an independent contractor on tax documents, she could not maintain an employment-discrimination suit.[2] ●

Disputes Involving Tort Liability Whether a worker is an employee or an independent contractor can also affect the employer's liability for the worker's actions. **CASE EXAMPLE 17.2** El Palmar Taxi, Inc., requires its drivers to supply their own cabs, which must display El Palmar's logo. The drivers pay gas, maintenance, and insurance costs, and a fee to El Palmar. They can work when they want for as long as they want. Mario Julaju drove a taxi under a contract with El Palmar that described him as an independent contractor.

El Palmar sent Julaju to pick up Maria Lopez and her children. During the ride, Julaju's cab collided with a truck. To recover for their injuries, the Lopezes sued El Palmar. The employer argued that it was not liable because Julaju was an independent contractor. The court held in favor of El Palmar. An employer normally is not responsible for the actions of an independent contractor with whom the employer contracts. Here, the employment contract had clearly specified that Julaju was an independent contractor, and there were no facts indicating that he was an employee (or that the employer controlled his activities).[3] ●

Criteria Used by the IRS

The Internal Revenue Service (IRS) has established its own criteria for determining whether a worker is an independent contractor or an employee. The most important factor in this determination is the degree of control the business exercises over the worker.

The IRS tends to closely scrutinize a firm's classification of its workers because, as mentioned, employers can avoid certain tax liabilities by hiring independent contractors instead of employees. Even when a firm classifies a worker as an independent contractor, the IRS may decide that the worker is actually an employee. In that situation, the employer will be responsible for paying any applicable Social Security, withholding, and unemployment taxes. Microsoft Corporation, for example, was once ordered to pay back payroll taxes for hundreds of workers that the IRS determined had been misclassified as independent contractors.[4] (The *Business Application* feature on page 510 offers suggestions on using independent contractors.)

ETHICAL ISSUE

Should small businesses be allowed to hire "permalancers"? Freelancers, of course, are independent contractors. Now small businesses across the country are turning increasingly to *permalancers*—freelancers who stay on a business's payroll for years. From the business's perspective, the advantages are obvious—the cost savings from using freelancers rather than employees can be as much as 30 percent because the business does not have to pay payroll and unemployment taxes or workers' compensation. Additionally, freelancers do not receive health-care and

2. *Alberty-Vélez v. Corporación de Puerto Rico para la Difusión Pública*, 361 F.3d 1 (1st Cir. 2004).
3. *Lopez v. El Palmar Taxi, Inc.*, 297 Ga.App. 121, 676 S.E.2d 460 (2009).
4. See *Vizcaino v. U.S. District Court for the Western District of Washington*, 173 F.3d 713 (9th Cir. 1999).

other benefits offered to employees. Finally, during an economic downturn, the business has more flexibility—it can let freelancers go quickly and usually without cost.

The IRS and state tax authorities, however, view permalancers differently. In early 2010, the IRS launched an ongoing program that will examine six thousand companies to make sure that permanent workers have not been misclassified as independent contractors. The Obama administration also revised some regulations to make it harder for businesses to classify workers as freelancers. The IRS is targeting small businesses not only because they hire lots of freelancers but also because, unlike larger companies, they usually do not have on-staff attorneys to defend them and thus are likely to acquiesce when the IRS clamps down.

But these efforts raise some ethical issues. Certainly, the tax authorities will gain some revenues but at the cost of reducing the flexibility of small businesses. If the businesses hire fewer workers as a result, are the taxes collected worth the possible increase in unemployment? Another trade-off to consider is between the advantages that a business obtains from hiring permalancers and the disadvantages to those workers of having no employee benefits.

Employee Status and "Works for Hire"   Under the Copyright Act of 1976, any copyrighted work created by an employee within the scope of her or his employment at the request of the employer is a "work for hire," and the *employer* owns the copyright to the work. When an employer hires an independent contractor—a freelance artist, writer, or computer programmer, for example—the independent contractor owns the copyright *unless* the parties agree in writing that the work is a "work for hire" and the work falls into one of nine specific categories, including audiovisual and other works.

CASE EXAMPLE 17.3   Artisan House, Inc., hired a professional photographer, Steven H. Lindner, owner of SHL Imaging, Inc., to take pictures of its products for the creation of color slides to be used by Artisan's sales force. Lindner controlled his own work and carefully chose the lighting and angles used in the photographs. When Artisan published the photographs in a catalogue without Lindner's permission, SHL filed a lawsuit for copyright infringement. Artisan claimed that its publication of the photographs was authorized because they were works for hire. The court, however, held that SHL was an independent contractor and owned the copyrights to the photographs. Because SHL had not given Artisan permission (a license) to reproduce the photographs in other publications, Artisan was liable for copyright infringement.[5] •

How Agency Relationships Are Formed

Agency relationships normally are consensual. They come about by voluntary consent and agreement between the parties. Generally, the agreement need not be in writing,[6] and consideration is not required.

A person must have contractual capacity to be a principal. Those who cannot legally enter into contracts directly should not be allowed to do so indirectly through an agent. Any person can be an agent, though, regardless of whether he or she has the capacity to enter a contract (including minors).

An agency relationship can be created for any legal purpose. An agency relationship that is created for an illegal purpose or that is contrary to public policy is unenforceable.

EXAMPLE 17.4   Sharp (as principal) contracts with McKenzie (as agent) to sell illegal narcotics. This agency relationship is unenforceable because selling illegal narcotics is a felony and is contrary to public policy. •   It is also illegal for physicians and other licensed professionals to employ unlicensed agents to perform professional actions.

---

5. *SHL Imaging, Inc. v. Artisan House, Inc.,* 117 F.Supp.2d 301 (S.D.N.Y. 2000).

6. The following are two main exceptions to the statement that agency agreements need not be in writing: (1) Whenever agency authority empowers the agent to enter into a contract that the Statute of Frauds requires to be in writing, the agent's authority from the principal must likewise be in writing (this is called the *equal dignity rule*—see page 498), and (2) a power of attorney, which confers authority to an agent, must be in writing.

LEARNING OBJECTIVE 2
How do agency relationships arise?

If a homeowner contracted with a landscaper to hire this gardener, who is the agent of whom?

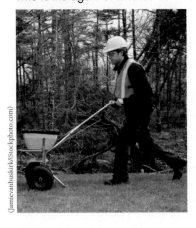

(Jamievanbuskirk/iStockphoto.com)

Generally, an agency relationship can arise in four ways: by agreement of the parties, by ratification, by estoppel, or by operation of law.

Agency by Agreement

Most agency relationships are based on an express or implied agreement that the agent will act for the principal and that the principal agrees to have the agent so act. An agency agreement can take the form of an express written contract or be created by an oral agreement. **EXAMPLE 17.5** Reese asks Cary, a gardener, to contract with others for the care of his lawn on a regular basis. Cary agrees. An agency relationship is established between Reese (the principal) and Cary (the agent) for the lawn care. •

An agency agreement can also be implied by conduct. **EXAMPLE 17.6** A hotel expressly allows only Boris Koontz to park cars, but Boris has no employment contract there. The hotel's manager tells Boris when to work, as well as where and how to park the cars. The hotel's conduct amounts to a manifestation of its willingness to have Boris park its customers' cars, and Boris can infer from the hotel's conduct that he has authority to act as a parking valet. It can be inferred that Boris is an agent-employee for the hotel, his purpose being to provide valet parking services for hotel guests. •

In the following case, the court had to decide whether an agency relationship arose when a man who was being hospitalized asked his wife to sign the admissions papers for him.

Case 17.1

Laurel Creek Health Care Center v. Bishop

Court of Appeals of Kentucky, 2010 WL 985299 (2010).

(Franck-Boston/iStockphoto.com)

Hospitals require patients to sign admissions papers.

FACTS Gilbert Bishop was admitted to Laurel Creek Health Care Center suffering from various physical ailments. During an examination, Bishop told Laurel Creek staff that he could not use his hands well enough to write or hold a pencil, but he was otherwise found to be mentally competent. Bishop's sister, Rachel Combs, testified that when she arrived at the facility she offered to sign the admissions forms, but Laurel Creek employees told her that it was their policy to have a patient's spouse sign the admissions papers if the patient was unable to do so. Combs also testified that Bishop asked her to get his wife, Anna, so that she could sign his admissions papers.

Combs then brought Anna to the hospital, and Anna signed the admissions paperwork, which contained a provision for mandatory arbitration. Subsequently, Bishop went into cardiopulmonary arrest and died. Following his death, Bishop's family filed a negligence lawsuit against Laurel Creek, which asked the court to compel arbitration in accordance with the provision in the admissions paperwork signed by Anna. The trial court denied the request on the ground that Anna was not Bishop's agent and had no legal authority to make decisions for him. Laurel Creek appealed.

ISSUE Did Anna Bishop become her husband's agent by agreeing to sign the hospital admission papers on his behalf?

DECISION Yes. The Kentucky Court of Appeals reversed the lower court's judgment and remanded the case. An actual agency relationship between Bishop and his wife, Anna, had been formed, and the trial court had erred when it found otherwise.

REASON The court reasoned that to establish an agency relationship, a principal must voluntarily consent to be affected by the agent's actions, and the agent's actions must express consent to act on the principal's behalf. The court noted that "according to his sister, Rachel, Gilbert [Bishop] specifically asked that his wife be brought to the nursing home so that she could sign the admissions documents for him, and [his wife] acted upon that delegation of authority and signed the admissions papers." Another requirement is that the agent's actions affect the principal's legal relations. Clearly here, the

Case 17.1—Continues next page ➡

Case 17.1—Continued

court concluded, Anna's actions "affected Gilbert's relations with Laurel Creek, a third party." Therefore, "Gilbert had created an agency relationship upon which Laurel Creek justifiably relied."

CRITICAL THINKING—Legal Consideration   *Laurel Creek argued that even if there was no actual agency relationship, an implied agency relationship existed. Is this argument valid? Why or why not?*

Agency by Ratification

Ratification A party's act of accepting or giving legal force to a contract or other obligation entered into by another that previously was not enforceable.

On occasion, a person who is in fact not an agent (or who is an agent acting outside the scope of her or his authority) may make a contract on behalf of another (a principal). If the principal affirms that contract by word or by action, an agency relationship is created by **ratification**. Ratification involves a question of intent, and intent can be expressed by either words or conduct. The basic requirements for ratification will be discussed later in this chapter.

Agency by Estoppel

When a principal causes a third person to believe that another person is his or her agent, and the third person deals with the supposed agent, the principal is "estopped to deny" the agency relationship. In such a situation, the principal's actions create the *appearance* of an agency that does not in fact exist. The third person must prove that she or he *reasonably* believed that an agency relationship existed, though.[7] Facts and circumstances must show that an ordinary, prudent person familiar with business practice and custom would have been justified in concluding that the agent had authority.

     CASE EXAMPLE 17.7   Marsha and Jerry Wiedmaier owned Wiedmaier, Inc., a corporation that operated a truck stop. Their son, Michael, did not own any interest in the corporation but had worked at the truck stop as a fuel operator. Michael decided to form his own business called Extreme Diecast, LLC. To obtain a line of credit with Motorsport Marketing, Inc., Michael asked his mother to sign the credit application form. After Marsha had signed as "Secretary-Owner" of Wiedmaier, Inc., Michael added his name to the list of corporate owners and faxed the form to Motorsport. Later, when Michael stopped making payments on merchandise he had ordered, Motorsport sued Wiedmaier for the unpaid balance. The court ruled that Michael was an apparent agent of Wiedmaier, Inc., because the credit application had caused Motorsport to reasonably believe that Michael was acting as Wiedmaier's agent in ordering merchandise.[8] •

     Note that the acts or declarations of a purported *agent* in and of themselves do not create an agency by estoppel. Rather, it is the deeds or statements *of the principal* that create an agency by estoppel. In other words, in *Case Example 17.7* above, if Marsha Wiedmaier had not signed the credit application on behalf of the principal-corporation, it would not have been reasonable for Motorsport to believe that Michael was Wiedmaier's agent.

Agency by Operation of Law

The courts may find an agency relationship in the absence of a formal agreement in other situations as well. This can occur in the family setting. When one spouse purchases certain necessaries and charges them to the other spouse's account, for example, the courts will

---

7. These concepts also apply when an agent undertakes an action that is beyond the scope of her or his authority, as will be discussed later in this chapter.

8. *Motorsport Marketing, Inc. v. Wiedmaier, Inc.*, 195 S.W.3d 492 (Mo.App. 2006).

often rule that the second spouse is liable to pay for the necessaries, either because of a social policy of promoting the general welfare of a spouse or because of a legal duty to supply necessaries to family members.

Agency by operation of law may also occur in emergency situations, when the agent's failure to act outside the scope of his or her authority would cause the principal substantial loss. If the agent is unable to contact the principal, the courts will often grant this emergency power. For instance, a railroad engineer may contract on behalf of her or his employer for medical care for an injured motorist hit by the train.

LEARNING OBJECTIVE 3
What duties do agents and principals owe to each other?

Duties of Agents and Principals

Once the principal-agent relationship has been created, both parties have duties that govern their conduct. As mentioned previously, an agency relationship is *fiduciary*—one of trust. In a fiduciary relationship, each party owes the other the duty to act with the utmost good faith.

In general, for every duty of the principal, the agent has a corresponding right, and vice versa. When one party to the agency relationship violates his or her duty to the other party, the remedies available to the nonbreaching party arise out of contract and tort law. These remedies include monetary damages, termination of the agency relationship, an injunction, and required accountings.

(sjlocke/iStockphoto.com)

What five duties does a real estate agent owe to his clients?

Agent's Duties to the Principal

Generally, the agent owes the principal five duties: (1) performance, (2) notification, (3) loyalty, (4) obedience, and (5) accounting.

Performance An implied condition in every agency contract is the agent's agreement to use reasonable diligence and skill in performing the work. When an agent fails entirely to perform her or his duties, liability for breach of contract normally will result. The degree of skill or care required of an agent is usually that expected of a reasonable person under similar circumstances. Generally, this is interpreted to mean ordinary care. If an agent has claimed to possess special skill, however, failure to exercise that degree of skill constitutes a breach of the agent's duty.

Not all agency relationships are based on contract. In some situations, an agent acts gratuitously—that is, not for monetary compensation. A gratuitous agent cannot be liable for breach of contract, as there is no contract, but he or she can be subject to tort liability. Once a gratuitous agent has begun to act in an agency capacity, he or she has the duty to continue to perform in that capacity in an acceptable manner and is subject to the same standards of care and duty to perform as other agents.

Notification An agent is required to notify the principal of all matters that come to her or his attention concerning the subject matter of the agency. This is the duty of notification, or the duty to inform. **EXAMPLE 17.8** Lang, an artist, is about to negotiate a contract to sell a series of paintings to Barber's Art Gallery for $25,000. Lang's agent learns that Barber is insolvent and will be unable to pay for the paintings. The agent has a duty to inform Lang of this fact because it is relevant to the subject matter of the agency—the sale of Lang's paintings. •

Generally, the law assumes that the principal knows of any information acquired by the agent that is relevant to the agency—regardless of whether the agent actually passes on this information to the principal. It is a basic tenet of agency law that notice to the agent is notice to the principal.

> "If God had an agent, the world wouldn't be built yet. It'd only be about Thursday."
>
> Jerry Reynolds, 1940–present (National Basketball Association executive)

Loyalty   Loyalty is one of the most fundamental duties in a fiduciary relationship. Basically, the agent has the duty to act *solely for the benefit of his or her principal* and not in the interest of the agent or a third party. For instance, an agent cannot represent two principals in the same transaction unless both know of the dual capacity and consent to it.

The duty of loyalty also means that any information or knowledge acquired through the agency relationship is considered confidential. It would be a breach of loyalty to disclose such information either during the agency relationship or after its termination. Typical examples of confidential information are trade secrets and customer lists that are compiled by the principal.

In short, the agent's loyalty must be undivided. The agent's actions must be strictly for the benefit of the principal and must not result in any secret profit for the agent. **CASE EXAMPLE 17.9**   Don Cousins contracts with Leo Hodgins, a real estate agent, to negotiate the purchase of an office building. While working for Cousins, Hodgins discovers that the property owner will sell the building only as a package deal with another parcel, so he buys the two properties, intending to resell the building to Cousins. Hodgins has breached his fiduciary duties. As a real estate agent, Hodgins has a duty to communicate all offers to his principal and not to purchase the property secretly and then resell it to his principal. Hodgins is required to act in Cousins's best interests and can become the purchaser in this situation only with Cousins's knowledge and approval.[9] •

Obedience   When acting on behalf of a principal, an agent has a duty to follow all lawful and clearly stated instructions of the principal. Any deviation from such instructions is a violation of this duty. During emergency situations, however, when the principal cannot be consulted, the agent may deviate from the instructions without violating this duty. Whenever instructions are not clearly stated, the agent can fulfill the duty of obedience by acting in good faith and in a manner reasonable under the circumstances.

Accounting   Unless an agent and a principal agree otherwise, the agent has the duty to keep and make available to the principal an account of all property and funds received and paid out on behalf of the principal. This includes gifts from third parties in connection with the agency. For example, a gift from a customer to a salesperson for prompt deliveries made by the salesperson's firm, in the absence of a company policy to the contrary, belongs to the firm. The agent has a duty to maintain separate accounts for the principal's funds and for the agent's personal funds, and the agent must not intermingle these accounts.

Principal's Duties to the Agent

The principal also owes certain duties to the agent. These duties relate to compensation, reimbursement and indemnification, cooperation, and safe working conditions.

Compensation   In general, when a principal requests services from an agent, the agent reasonably expects payment. The principal therefore has a duty to pay the agent for services rendered. For instance, when an accountant or an attorney is asked to act as an agent, an agreement to compensate the agent for service is implied. The principal also has a duty to pay that compensation in a timely manner. Except in a *gratuitous agency* relationship, in which an agent does not act for payment in return, the principal must pay the agreed-on value for an agent's services. If no amount has been expressly agreed on, the principal owes the agent the customary compensation for such services.

---

9. *Cousins v. Realty Ventures, Inc.*, 844 So.2d 860 (La.App. 5th Cir. 2003).

**PREVENTING
LEGAL DISPUTES**

Many disputes arise because the principal and agent did not specify how much the agent would be paid. To avoid such disputes, always state in advance, and in writing, the amount or rate of compensation that you will pay your agents. Even when dealing with salespersons, such as real estate agents, who customarily are paid a percentage of the value of the sale, it is best to explicitly state the rate of compensation.

Reimbursement and Indemnification Whenever an agent disburses funds at the request of the principal or to pay for necessary expenses in the reasonable performance of his or her agency duties, the principal has the duty to reimburse the agent for these payments. Agents cannot recover for expenses incurred through their own misconduct or negligence, though.

Subject to the terms of the agency agreement, the principal has the duty to compensate, or *indemnify*, an agent for liabilities incurred because of authorized and lawful acts and transactions. For instance, if the principal fails to perform a contract formed by the agent with a third party and the third party then sues the agent, the principal must compensate the agent for any costs incurred in defending against the lawsuit.

Additionally, the principal must indemnify (pay) the agent for the value of benefits that the agent confers on the principal. The amount of indemnification is usually specified in the agency contract. If it is not, the courts will look to the nature of the business and the type of loss to determine the amount. Note that this rule applies to acts by gratuitous agents (see page 496) as well. If the finder of a dog that becomes sick takes the dog to a veterinarian and pays the required fees for the veterinarian's services, the (gratuitous) agent is entitled to be reimbursed by the dog's owner for those fees.

Cooperation A principal has a duty to cooperate with the agent and to assist the agent in performing her or his duties. The principal must do nothing to prevent that performance.

When a principal grants an agent an exclusive territory, for instance, the principal creates an *exclusive agency* and cannot compete with the agent or appoint or allow another agent to so compete. If the principal does so, she or he may be liable for the agent's lost sales or profits. **EXAMPLE 17.10** A newspaper (the principal) grants Emir (the agent) the right to sell its newspapers at a busy downtown intersection to the exclusion of all other vendors. This creates an exclusive territory within which only Emir has the right to sell that newspaper. If the newspaper allows another vendor to sell its paper in that area, Emir can sue for lost profits. •

Safe Working Conditions A principal is required to provide safe working premises, equipment, and conditions for all agents and employees. The principal has a duty to inspect the working conditions and to warn agents and employees about any hazards. When the agent is an employee, the employer's liability is frequently covered by state workers' compensation insurance, and federal and state statutes often require the employer to meet certain safety standards (to be discussed in Chapter 18).

Agent's Authority

An agent's authority to act can be either *actual* (express or implied) or *apparent*. If an agent contracts outside the scope of his or her authority, the principal may still become liable by ratifying the contract.

Express Authority

Express authority is authority declared in clear, direct, and definite terms. Express authority can be given orally or in writing.

Equal Dignity Rule A rule requiring that an agent's authority be in writing if the contract to be made on behalf of the principal must be in writing.

Equal Dignity Rule   In most states, the **equal dignity rule** requires that if the contract being executed is or must be in writing, then the agent's authority must also be in writing. Failure to comply with the equal dignity rule can make a contract voidable *at the option of the principal.* The law regards the contract at that point as a mere offer. If the principal decides to accept the offer, the agent's authority must be ratified, or affirmed, in writing.

EXAMPLE 17.11   Lee (the principal) orally asks Parkinson (the agent) to sell a ranch that Lee owns. Parkinson finds a buyer and signs a sales contract (a contract for an interest in realty must be in writing) on behalf of Lee to sell the ranch. The buyer cannot enforce the contract unless Lee subsequently ratifies Parkinson's agency status *in writing.* Once Parkinson's agency status is ratified, either party can enforce rights under the contract. •

Modern business practice allows exceptions to the equal dignity rule. An executive officer of a corporation normally is not required to obtain written authority from the corporation to conduct *ordinary* business transactions. The equal dignity rule also does not apply when an agent acts in the presence of a principal or when the agent's act of signing is merely perfunctory (automatic). Thus, if the principal negotiates a contract but is called out of town the day it is to be signed and orally authorizes his or her agent to sign the contract, the oral authorization is sufficient.

Power of Attorney Authorization for another to act as one's agent or attorney in either specified circumstances (special) or in all situations (general).

Notary Public A public official authorized to attest to the authenticity of signatures.

Power of Attorney   Giving an agent a **power of attorney** confers express authority.[10] The power of attorney normally is a written document and is usually notarized. (A document is notarized when a **notary public**—a person authorized by the state to attest to the authenticity of signatures—signs and dates the document and imprints it with his or her seal of authority.) Most states have statutory provisions for creating a power of attorney.

A power of attorney can be special (permitting the agent to do specified acts only), or it can be general (permitting the agent to transact all business for the principal). Because a general power of attorney grants extensive authority to an agent to act on behalf of the principal in many ways, it should be used with great caution. Ordinarily, a power of attorney terminates on the incapacity or death of the person giving the power.[11]

(Lucky Business/Shutterstock.com)

What functions does a notary public perform?

Implied Authority

An agent has the *implied authority* to do what is reasonably necessary to carry out his or her express authority and accomplish the objectives of the agency. Authority can also be implied by custom or inferred from the position the agent occupies.

EXAMPLE 17.12   Mueller is employed by Al's Supermarket to manage one of its stores. Al's has not expressly stated that Mueller has authority to contract with third persons. In this situation, though, authority to manage a business implies authority to do what is reasonably required (as is customary or can be inferred from a manager's position) to operate the business. This includes forming contracts to hire employees, to buy merchandise and equipment, and to advertise the products sold in the store. •

---

10. An agent who holds the power of attorney is called an *attorney-in-fact* for the principal. The holder does not have to be an attorney-at-law (and often is not).

11. A *durable* power of attorney, however, continues to be effective despite the principal's incapacity. An elderly person, for example, might grant a durable power of attorney to provide for the handling of property and investments or specific health-care needs should she or he become incompetent.

If an employee-agent makes unauthorized use of his employer's computer data, has he committed a crime? See this chapter's *Adapting the Law to the Online Environment* feature below for a discussion of this issue.

Apparent Authority

Apparent Authority Authority that is only apparent, not real. An agent's apparent authority arises when the principal causes a third party to believe that the agent has authority, even though she or he does not.

Actual authority (express or implied) arises from what the principal manifests *to the agent*. An agent has **apparent authority** when the principal, by either words or actions, causes a *third party* reasonably to believe that an agent has authority to act, even though the agent has no express or implied authority. If the third party changes his or her position in reliance on the principal's representations, the principal may be *estopped* (prevented) from denying that the agent had authority.

ADAPTING THE LAW TO THE ONLINE ENVIRONMENT

WHAT HAPPENS WHEN AN AGENT BREACHES COMPANY POLICY ON THE USE OF ELECTRONIC DATA?

Suppose that an employee-agent who is authorized to access company trade secrets contained in computer files takes those secrets to a competitor for whom the employee is about to begin working. Clearly, the agent has violated the ethical—and legal—duty of loyalty to the principal. Does this breach of loyalty mean that the employee's act of accessing the trade secrets was unauthorized?

The question has significant implications for both parties. If the act was unauthorized, the employee will be subject to state and federal laws prohibiting unauthorized access to computer information and data, including the Computer Fraud and Abuse Act (CFAA, discussed on page 187 in Chapter 6). If the act was authorized, these laws will not apply.

Employees "Exceed Authorized Access" to Their Company's Database

David Nosal once worked for Korn/Ferry and had access to the company's confidential database. When he left, he encouraged several former colleagues who still worked there to join him in starting a competing firm. He asked them to access Korn/Ferry's database and download source lists, names, and client contact information before they quit. The employees had authority to access the database, but Korn/Ferry's policy forbade disclosure of confidential information.

The government filed charges against Nosal and his colleagues for violating the CFAA, among other things.

A Court Rules That Violating an Employer's Use Restrictions Is Not a Crime

The U.S. Court of Appeals for the Ninth Circuit refused to find that the defendants had violated the CFAA. The court ruled that the phrase "exceed authorized access" in the CFAA refers to restrictions on access, not restrictions on use. The court reasoned that Congress's intent in enacting the CFAA was to prohibit people from hacking into computers without authorization.

The court also stated that the CFAA should not be used to criminally prosecute persons who use data in an unauthorized or unethical way. The court pointed out that "adopting the government's interpretation would turn vast numbers of teens and preteens into juvenile delinquents—and their parents and teachers into delinquency contributors." Furthermore, "the effect this broad construction of the CFAA has on workplace conduct pales by comparison with its effect on everyone else who uses a computer, smart-phone, iPad, Kindle, Nook, X-box, Blu-Ray player or any other Internet-enabled device."[a]

Critical Thinking

If an employee accesses Facebook at work even though personal use of a workplace computer is against the employer's stated policies, can the employee be criminally prosecuted? Why or why not?

a. *United States. v. Nosal,* 676 F.3d 854 (9th Cir. 2012).

Apparent authority usually comes into existence through a principal's pattern of conduct over time. **EXAMPLE 17.13** Bailey is a traveling salesperson. She solicits orders for goods but does not carry them with her. She normally would not have the implied authority to collect payments from customers on behalf of the principal. Suppose that she does accept payments from Corgley Enterprises, however, and submits them to the principal's accounting department for processing. If the principal does nothing to stop Bailey from continuing this practice, a pattern develops over time, and the principal confers apparent authority on Bailey to accept payments from Corgley. ●

At issue in the following *Spotlight Case* was whether the manager of a horse breeding operation had the authority to bind the farm's owner in a contract guaranteeing breeding rights.

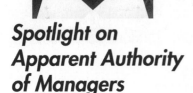

Spotlight on Apparent Authority of Managers

Case 17.2
Lundberg v. Church Farm, Inc.
Court of Appeals of Illinois, 502 N.E.2d 806, 151 Ill.App.3d 452 (1986).

Who can guarantee a minimum number of foals during a limited time period?

FACTS Gilbert Church owned a horse breeding farm in Illinois managed by Herb Bagley. Advertisements for the breeding rights to one of Church Farm's stallions, Imperial Guard, directed all inquiries to "Herb Bagley, Manager." Vern and Gail Lundberg bred Thoroughbred horses. The Lundbergs contacted Bagley and executed a preprinted contract giving them breeding rights to Imperial Guard "at Imperial Guard's location," subject to approval of the mares by Church. Bagley handwrote a statement on the contract that guaranteed the Lundbergs "six live foals in the first two years." He then signed it "Gilbert G. Church by H. Bagley."

The Lundbergs bred four mares, which resulted in one live foal. Church then moved Imperial Guard from Illinois to Oklahoma. The Lundbergs sued Church for breaching the contract by moving the horse. Church claimed that Bagley was not authorized to sign contracts for Church or to change or add terms, but only to present preprinted contracts to potential buyers. Church testified that although Bagley was his farm manager and the contact person for breeding rights, Bagley had never before modified the preprinted forms or signed Church's name on these contracts. The jury found in favor of the Lundbergs and awarded $147,000 in damages. Church appealed.

ISSUE Was Bagley authorized to sign and modify contracts on behalf of Church?

DECISION Yes. The state appellate court affirmed the lower court's award of $147,000 to the Lundbergs. Because Church allowed circumstances to lead the Lundbergs to believe Bagley had authority, Church was bound by Bagley's actions.

REASON A principal may be bound by the unauthorized acts of an agent if the principal leads a third party to believe, or allows a third party to believe, that the agent has authority to perform the act. In this case, Church approved the advertisement listing Bagley as Church Farm's manager and point of contact. Bagley generally was the only person available to visitors to the farm. Bagley answered the farm's phone, and the breeding contract had a preprinted signature line for him. Church was not engaged in the actual negotiation or signing of the contracts but left that business for Bagley to complete. Based on Church's actions, a reasonable third party would believe that Bagley had authority to sign and modify contracts.

CRITICAL THINKING—Legal Consideration *What duties to Church might Bagley have violated in this situation?*

Ratification

As already mentioned, ratification occurs when the principal affirms an agent's *unauthorized* act. When ratification occurs, the principal is bound to the agent's act, and the act is treated as if it had been authorized by the principal *from the outset*. Ratification can be either express or implied.

If the principal does not ratify the contract, the principal is not bound, and the third party's agreement with the agent is viewed as merely an unaccepted offer. Because the third party's agreement is an unaccepted offer, the third party can revoke the offer at any time, without liability, before the principal ratifies the contract.

The requirements for ratification can be summarized as follows:

1. The agent must have acted on behalf of an identified principal who subsequently ratifies the action.
2. The principal must know of all material facts involved in the transaction. If a principal ratifies a contract without knowing all of the facts, the principal can rescind (cancel) the contract.
3. The principal must affirm the agent's act in its entirety.
4. The principal must have the legal capacity to authorize the transaction at the time the agent engages in the act and at the time the principal ratifies. The third party must also have the legal capacity to engage in the transaction.
5. The principal's affirmation must occur before the third party withdraws from the transaction.
6. The principal must observe the same formalities when approving the act done by the agent as would have been required to authorize it initially.

Liability in Agency Relationships

LEARNING OBJECTIVE 4
When is a principal liable for the agent's actions with respect to third parties? When is the agent liable?

Frequently, a question arises as to which party, the principal or the agent, should be held liable for contracts formed by the agent or for torts or crimes committed by the agent. We look here at these aspects of agency law.

Liability for Contracts

Liability for contracts formed by an agent depends on how the principal is classified and on whether the actions of the agent were authorized or unauthorized. Principals are classified as disclosed, partially disclosed, or undisclosed.[12]

Disclosed Principal A principal whose identity is known to a third party at the time the agent makes a contract with the third party.

Partially Disclosed Principal A principal whose identity is unknown by a third party, but the third party knows that the agent is or may be acting for a principal at the time the agent and the third party form a contract.

Undisclosed Principal A principal whose identity is unknown by a third party, and that person has no knowledge that the agent is acting for a principal at the time the agent and the third party form a contract.

A **disclosed principal** is a principal whose identity is known by the third party at the time the contract is made by the agent. A **partially disclosed principal** is a principal whose identity is not known by the third party, but the third party knows that the agent is or may be acting for a principal at the time the contract is made. **EXAMPLE 17.14** Sarah has contracted with a real estate agent to sell certain property. She wishes to keep her identity a secret, but the agent makes it clear to potential buyers of the property that the agent is acting in an agency capacity. In this situation, Sarah is a partially disclosed principal. • An **undisclosed principal** is a principal whose identity is totally unknown by the third party, and the third party has no knowledge that the agent is acting in an agency capacity at the time the contract is made.

Authorized Acts

If an agent acts within the scope of her or his authority, normally the principal is obligated to perform the contract regardless of whether the principal was disclosed, partially disclosed, or undisclosed. Whether the agent may also be held liable under the contract, however, depends on the status of the principal.

---

12. *Restatement (Third) of Agency*, Section 1.04(2).

Disclosed or Partially Disclosed Principal   A disclosed or partially disclosed principal is liable to a third party for a contract made by an agent who is acting within the scope of her or his authority. If the principal is disclosed, an agent has no contractual liability for the nonperformance of the principal or the third party. If the principal is partially disclosed, in most states the agent is also treated as a party to the contract, and the third party can hold the agent liable for contractual nonperformance.[13]

CASE EXAMPLE 17.15   Walgreens leased commercial property to operate a drugstore at a mall owned by Kedzie Plaza Associates. A property management company, Taxman Corporation, signed the lease on behalf of the principal, Kedzie. The lease required the landlord to keep the sidewalks free of snow and ice, so Taxman, on behalf of Kedzie, contracted with another company to clear the sidewalks surrounding the Walgreens store. When a Walgreens employee slipped on ice outside the store and was injured, she sued Walgreens, Kedzie, and Taxman for negligence. Because the principal's identity (Kedzie) was fully disclosed in the snow-removal contract, the Illinois court ruled that the agent, Taxman, could not be held liable. Taxman did not assume a contractual obligation to remove the snow but merely retained a contractor to do so on behalf of the owner.[14] ●

Undisclosed Principal   When neither the fact of agency nor the identity of the principal is disclosed, the undisclosed principal is bound to perform just as if the principal had been fully disclosed at the time the contract was made. The agent is also liable as a party to the contract.

When a principal's identity is undisclosed and the agent is forced to pay the third party, the agent is entitled to be indemnified (compensated) by the principal. The principal had a duty to perform, even though his or her identity was undisclosed, and failure to do so will make the principal ultimately liable.

Once the undisclosed principal's identity is revealed, the third party generally can elect to hold either the principal or the agent liable on the contract. Conversely, the undisclosed principal can require the third party to fulfill the contract, *unless* (1) the undisclosed principal was expressly excluded as a party in the contract, (2) the contract is a negotiable instrument signed by the agent with no indication of signing in a representative capacity, or (3) the performance of the agent is personal to the contract, allowing the third party to refuse the principal's performance.

In the following case, three parties involved in an auto sales transaction were embroiled in a dispute over who was liable when the car's engine caught fire.

---

13. *Restatement (Third) of Agency*, Section 6.02.
14. *McBride v. Taxman Corp.*, 327 Ill.App.3d 992, 765 N.E.2d 51 (2002).

Case 17.3

Williams v. Pike

Court of Appeal of Louisiana, Second Circuit,
58 So.3d 525 (2011).
www.lacoa2.org[a]

FACTS   Bobby Williams bought a car for $3,000 at Sherman Henderson's auto repair business in Monroe, Louisiana. Although the car's owner was Joe Pike, the owner of Justice Wrecker Service, Henderson negotiated the sale, accepted Williams's payment, and gave him two receipts. Williams drove the car to Memphis, Tennessee, where his daughter

---

a. At the top, click on "Opinions." On the next page, in the "Search:" box, type "Williams v. Pike." In the result, click on the case number to access the opinion. The Court of Appeal of Louisiana for the Second Circuit maintains this Web site.

Case 17.3—Continued

was a student. Three days after the sale, the car began to emit smoke and flames from under the hood. Williams extinguished the blaze and contacted Henderson. The next day, Williams's daughter had the vehicle towed at her expense to her apartment's parking lot, from which it was soon stolen. Williams filed a suit in a Louisiana state court against Pike and Henderson. The court awarded Williams $2,000, plus the costs of the suit, adding that if Williams had returned the car, it would have awarded him the entire price. Pike and Henderson appealed.

ISSUE Can the buyer of a defective car (Williams), hold both the agent and the principal liable when the agent (Henderson) sold the car for an undisclosed principal (Pike)?

DECISION Yes. A state intermediate appellate court affirmed the ruling of the lower court, including its judgment and the assessment of costs against both defendants. The appellate court added the costs of the appeal to the amount. Both Pike and Henderson were liable to Williams.

REASON The court noted that a state permit to sell the car had been issued to Pike and it showed that he was the owner. The car was displayed for sale at Henderson's business, however, and he actually sold it. The court reasoned that this made Pike the principal and Henderson his agent. The fact that their agency relationship was not made clear to Williams made Pike an undisclosed principal. Williams could thus choose to hold either Pike or Henderson liable for the condition of the car, which constituted a breach of implied warranty because the car did not fulfill the purpose for which it was intended. The loss of the use of the car, the "inconvenience" caused by the defect, the price, and the cost of the tow were among the factors that supported the award.

WHAT IF THE FACTS WERE DIFFERENT? *Suppose that Henderson had fully disclosed the fact of his agency relationship and the identity of his principal. Would the result have been different? Why or why not?*

When ski patrollers help an injured skier, is there an agency involved?

(LifeJourneys/iStockphoto.com)

Unauthorized Acts If an agent has no authority but nevertheless contracts with a third party, the principal cannot be held liable on the contract. It does not matter whether the principal was disclosed, partially disclosed, or undisclosed. The *agent* is liable, however. **EXAMPLE 17.16** Scranton signs a contract for the purchase of a truck, purportedly acting as an agent under authority granted by Johnson. In fact, Johnson has not given Scranton any such authority. Johnson refuses to pay for the truck, claiming that Scranton had no authority to purchase it. The seller of the truck is entitled to hold Scranton liable for payment. •

If the principal is disclosed or partially disclosed, the agent is liable to the third party as long as the third party relied on the agency status. The agent's liability here is based on the breach of an *implied warranty of authority* (an agent impliedly warrants that he or she has the authority to enter a contract on behalf of the principal), not on breach of the contract itself.[15] If the third party knows at the time the contract is made that the agent does not have authority—or if the agent expresses to the third party *uncertainty* as to the extent of her or his authority—then the agent is not personally liable.

Liability for Torts and Crimes

Obviously, any person, including an agent, is liable for her or his own torts and crimes. Whether a principal can also be held liable for an agent's torts and crimes depends on several factors. In some situations, a principal may be held liable not only for the torts of an agent, but also for the torts committed by an independent contractor.

Principal's Tortious Conduct
A principal conducting an activity through an agent may be liable for harm resulting from the principal's own negligence or recklessness. Thus, a principal may be liable for giving improper instructions, authorizing the use

---

15. The agent is not liable on the contract because the agent was never intended personally to be a party to the contract.

of improper materials or tools, or establishing improper rules that resulted in the agent's committing a tort. **EXAMPLE 17.17** Jack knows that Suki is not qualified to drive large trucks but nevertheless tells her to use the company truck to deliver some equipment to a customer. If someone is injured as a result, Jack (the principal) will be liable for his own negligence in giving improper instructions to Suki. •

Principal's Authorization of Agent's Tortious Conduct

A principal who authorizes an agent to commit a tort may be liable to persons or property injured thereby, because the act is considered to be the principal's. **EXAMPLE 17.18** Selkow directs his agent, Warren, to cut the corn on specific acreage, which neither of them has the right to do. The harvest is therefore a trespass (a tort), and Selkow is liable to the owner of the corn. •

Note also that an agent acting at the principal's direction can be liable as a *tortfeasor* (one who commits a wrong, or tort), along with the principal, for committing the tortious act even if the agent was unaware of the wrongfulness of the act. Assume in the above example that Warren, the agent, did not know that Selkow had no right to harvest the corn. Warren can be held liable to the owner of the field for damages, along with Selkow, the principal.

Liability for Agent's Misrepresentation

A principal is exposed to tort liability whenever a third person sustains a loss due to the agent's misrepresentation. The principal's liability depends on whether the agent was actually or apparently authorized to make representations and whether the representations were made within the scope of the agency. The principal is always directly responsible for an agent's misrepresentation made within the scope of the agent's authority. **EXAMPLE 17.19** Bassett is a demonstrator for Moore's products. Moore sends Bassett to a home show to demonstrate the products and to answer questions from consumers. Moore has given Bassett authority to make statements about the products. If Bassett makes only true representations, all is fine, but if he makes false claims, Moore will be liable for any injuries or damages sustained by third parties in reliance on Bassett's false representations. •

Liability for Agent's Negligence

As mentioned, an agent is liable for his or her own torts. A principal may also be liable for harm an agent caused to a third party under the doctrine of **respondeat superior,**[16] a Latin term meaning "let the master respond."

This doctrine, which is discussed in this chapter's *Landmark in the Law* feature on the facing page, is similar to the theory of strict liability discussed in Chapters 4 and 12. It imposes **vicarious liability,** or indirect liability, on the employer—that is, liability without regard to the personal fault of the employer—for torts committed by an employee in the course or scope of employment.

When an agent commits a negligent act, both the agent and the principal are liable. **CASE EXAMPLE 17.20** Aegis Communications hired Southwest Desert Images (SDI) to provide landscaping services for its property. An herbicide sprayed by SDI employee David Hoggatt entered the Aegis building through the air-conditioning system and caused Catherine Warner, an Aegis employee, to suffer a heart attack. Warner sued SDI and Hoggatt for negligence, but the lower court dismissed the suit against Hoggatt. On appeal, the court found that Hoggatt was

Respondeat Superior A doctrine under which a principal or an employer is held liable for the wrongful acts committed by agents or employees while acting within the course and scope of their agency or employment.

Vicarious Liability Indirect liability imposed on a supervisory party (such as an employer) for the actions of a subordinate (such as an employee) because of the relationship between the two parties.

Under what circumstances can a school bus driver be charged individually with negligence?

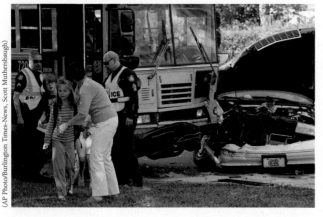

(AP Photo/Burlington Times-News, Scott Muthersbaugh)

---
16. Pronounced ree-*spahn*-dee-uht soo-*peer*-ee-your.

LANDMARK IN THE LAW
The Doctrine of *Respondeat Superior*

The idea that a master (employer) must respond to third persons for losses negligently caused by the master's servant (employee) first appeared in Lord Holt's opinion in *Jones v. Hart* (1698).[a] By the early nineteenth century, this maxim had been adopted by most courts and was referred to as the doctrine of *respondeat superior*.

Theories of Liability   The vicarious (indirect) liability of the master for the acts of the servant has been supported primarily by two theories. The first theory rests on the issue of *control*, or *fault*—the master has control over the acts of the servant and is thus responsible for injuries arising out of such service. The second theory is economic in nature—the master receives the benefits or profits of the servant's service and therefore should also suffer the losses. Moreover, the master is better able than the servant to absorb such losses.

The control theory is clearly recognized in the *Restatement (Third) of Agency*, which defines a master as "a principal who employs an agent to perform service in his [or her] affairs and who controls, or has the right to control, the physical conduct of the other in the performance of the service." Accordingly, a

servant is defined as "an agent employed by a master to perform service in his [or her] affairs whose physical conduct in his [or her] performance of the service is controlled, or is subject to control, by the master."

Limitations on the Employer's Liability   There are limitations on the master's liability for the acts of the servant, however. As discussed in the text, an employer (master) is responsible only for the wrongful conduct of an employee (servant) that occurs in "the scope of employment." Generally, the act must be of a kind that the servant was employed to do, it must have occurred within "authorized time and space limits," and it must have been "activated, at least in part, by a purpose to serve the master."

Application to Today's World   *The courts have accepted the doctrine of* respondeat superior *for some two centuries. This theory of vicarious liability has practical implications in all situations in which a principal-agent (master-servant, employer-employee) relationship exists. Today, the small-town grocer with one clerk and the multinational corporation with thousands of employees are equally subject to the doctrine.*

a. K.B. 642, 90 Eng.Rep. 1255 (1698).

also liable. An agent is not excused from responsibility for tortious conduct just because he is working for a principal.[17] ●

Determining the Scope of Employment   The key to determining whether a principal may be liable for the torts of an agent under the doctrine of *respondeat superior* is whether the torts are committed within the scope of the agency or employment. The factors that courts consider in determining whether a particular act occurred within the course and scope of employment are as follows:

1. Whether the employee's act was authorized by the employer.
2. The time, place, and purpose of the act.
3. Whether the act was one commonly performed by employees on behalf of their employers.
4. The extent to which the employer's interest was advanced by the act.
5. The extent to which the private interests of the employee were involved.
6. Whether the employer furnished the means or instrumentality (for example, a truck or a machine) by which the injury was inflicted.
7. Whether the employer had reason to know that the employee would do the act in question and whether the employee had ever done it before.
8. Whether the act involved the commission of a serious crime.

17. *Warner v. Southwest Desert Images, LLC,* 218 Ariz. 121, 180 P.3d 986 (2008).

The Distinction between a "Detour" and a "Frolic"   A useful insight into the "scope of employment" concept may be gained from the judge's classic distinction between a "detour" and a "frolic" in the case of *Joel v. Morison.*[18] In this case, the English court held that if a servant merely took a detour from his master's business, the master is responsible. If, however, the servant was on a "frolic of his own" and not in any way "on his master's business," the master is not liable.

EXAMPLE 17.21   While driving his employer's vehicle to call on a customer, Mandel decides to stop at the post office—which is one block off his route—to mail a personal letter. Mandel then negligently runs into a parked vehicle owned by Chan. In this situation, because Mandel's detour from the employer's business is not substantial, he is still acting within the scope of employment, and the employer is liable.

The result would be different if Mandel had decided to pick up a few friends for cocktails in another city and in the process had negligently run into Chan's vehicle. In that situation, the departure from the employer's business would be substantial, and the employer normally would not be liable to Chan for damages. Mandel would be considered to have been on a "frolic" of his own. ●

Employee Travel Time   An employee going to and from work or to and from meals is usually considered outside the scope of employment. If travel is part of a person's position, however, such as a traveling salesperson or a regional representative of a company, then travel time is normally considered within the scope of employment. Thus, the duration of the business trip, including the return trip home, is within the scope of employment unless there is a significant departure from the employer's business.

Notice of Dangerous Conditions   The employer is charged with knowledge of any dangerous conditions discovered by an employee and pertinent to the employment situation. **EXAMPLE 17.22**   Brad, a maintenance employee in Martin's apartment building, notices a lead pipe protruding from the ground in the building's courtyard. Brad neglects either to fix the pipe or to inform Martin of the danger. John trips on the pipe and is injured. The employer is charged with knowledge of the dangerous condition regardless of whether or not Brad actually informed him. That knowledge is imputed to the employer by virtue of the employment relationship. ●

Liability for Agent's Intentional Torts

Most intentional torts that employees commit have no relation to their employment. Thus, their employers will not be held liable. Nevertheless, under the doctrine of *respondeat superior,* the employer can be liable for an employee's intentional torts that are committed within the course and scope of employment, just as the employer is liable for negligence. For instance, an employer is liable when an employee (such as a "bouncer" at a nightclub or a security guard at a department store) commits the tort of assault and battery or false imprisonment while acting within the scope of employment.

In addition, an employer who knows or should know that an employee has a propensity for committing tortious acts is liable for the employee's acts even if they ordinarily would not be considered within the scope of employment. For instance, if the employer hires a bouncer knowing that he has a history of arrests for assault and battery, the employer may be liable if the employee viciously attacks a patron in the parking lot after hours.

An employer may also be liable for permitting an employee to engage in reckless actions that can injure others. **EXAMPLE 17.23**   The owner of Bates Trucking observes an employee smoking while filling containerized trucks with highly flammable liquids. Failure to stop the employee will cause the employer to be liable for any injuries that result if a truck

<hr>

18. 6 Car. & P. 501, 172 Eng.Rep. 1338 (1834).

explodes. ● (See this chapter's *Beyond Our Borders* feature below for a discussion of another approach to an employer's liability for an employee's acts.)

Liability for Independent Contractor's Torts

Generally, an employer is not liable for physical harm caused to a third person by the negligent act of an independent contractor in the performance of the contract. This is because the employer does not have *the right to control* the details of an independent contractor's performance.

Exceptions to this rule are made in certain situations, though, such as when unusually hazardous activities are involved. Typical examples of such activities include blasting operations, the transportation of highly volatile chemicals, or the use of poisonous gases. In these situations, an employer cannot be shielded from liability merely by using an independent contractor. Strict liability is imposed on the employer-principal as a matter of law. Also, in some states, strict liability may be imposed by statute.

Liability for Agent's Crimes

An agent is liable for his or her own crimes. A principal or employer is not liable for an agent's crime even if the crime was committed within the scope of authority or employment—unless the principal participated by conspiracy or other action. In some jurisdictions, under specific statutes, a principal may be liable for an agent's violation—in the course and scope of employment—of regulations, such as those governing sanitation, prices, weights, and the sale of liquor.

How Agency Relationships Are Terminated

Agency law is similar to contract law in that both an agency and a contract can be terminated *by an act of the parties* or *by operation of law.* Once the relationship between the principal and the agent has ended, the agent no longer has the right (*actual* authority) to bind the principal. For an agent's *apparent* authority to be terminated, though, third persons may also need to be notified that the agency has been terminated.

Termination by Act of the Parties

An agency may be terminated by act of the parties in any of the following ways:

1. *Lapse of time.* When an agency agreement specifies the time period during which the agency relationship will exist, the agency ends when that period expires. If no definite

BEYOND OUR BORDERS   Islamic Law and *Respondeat Superior*

The doctrine of *respondeat superior* is well established in the legal systems of the United States and most Western countries. As you have already read, under this doctrine employers can be held liable for the acts of their agents, including employees. The doctrine of *respondeat superior* is not universal, however. Most Middle Eastern countries, for example, do not follow this doctrine.

Islamic law, as codified in the *sharia*, holds to a strict belief that responsibility for human actions lies with the individual and cannot be vicariously extended to others. This belief and other concepts of Islamic law are based on the writings of Muhammad, the seventh-century prophet whose revelations form the basis of the Islamic religion and, by extension, the *sharia*. Muhammad's

prophecies are documented in the Koran (Qur'an), which is the principal source of the *sharia*.

Critical Thinking
How would U.S. society be affected if employers could not be held vicariously liable for their employees' torts?

time is stated, the agency continues for a reasonable time and can be terminated at will by either party. What constitutes a "reasonable time" depends, of course, on the circumstances and the nature of the agency relationship.

2. *Purpose achieved.* If an agent is employed to accomplish a particular objective, such as the purchase of breeding stock for a cattle rancher, the agency automatically ends after the cattle have been purchased. If more than one agent is employed to accomplish the same purpose, such as the sale of real estate, the first agent to complete the sale automatically terminates the agency relationship for all the others.

3. *Occurrence of a specific event.* When an agency relationship is to terminate on the happening of a certain event, the agency automatically ends when the event occurs. If Posner appoints Rubik to handle her business affairs while she is away, the agency terminates when Posner returns.

4. *Mutual agreement.* The parties to an agency can cancel (rescind) their contract by mutually agreeing to terminate the agency relationship, even if it is for a specific duration.

5. *Termination by one party.* As a general rule, either party can terminate the agency relationship (the act of termination is called *revocation* if done by the principal and *renunciation* if done by the agent). Although both parties have the *power* to terminate the agency, they may not possess the *right*.

LEARNING OBJECTIVE 5
What are some of the ways in which an agency relationship can be terminated?

Wrongful Termination Wrongful termination (see Chapter 18) can subject the canceling party to a suit for breach of contract. **EXAMPLE 17.24** Rawlins has a one-year employment contract with Munro to act as an agent in return for $65,000. Although Munro has the *power* to discharge Rawlins before the contract period expires, if he does so, he can be sued for breaching the contract because he had no *right* to terminate the agency. •

Notice of Termination When an agency has been terminated by act of the parties, it is the principal's duty to inform any third parties who know of the existence of the agency that it has been terminated (although notice of the termination may be given by others). Although an agent's actual authority ends when the agency is terminated, an agent's *apparent authority* continues until the third party receives notice (from any source) that such authority has been terminated. If the principal knows that a third party has dealt with the agent, the principal is expected to notify that person *directly*. For third parties who have heard about the agency but have not yet dealt with the agent, *constructive notice* is sufficient.[19]

No particular form is required for notice of agency termination to be effective. The principal can personally notify the agent, or the agent can learn of the termination through some other means. **EXAMPLE 17.25** Manning bids on a shipment of steel, and Stone is hired as an agent to arrange transportation of the shipment. When Stone learns that Manning has lost the bid, Stone's authority to make the transportation arrangement terminates. • If the agent's authority is written, however, it normally must be revoked in writing.

Termination by Operation of Law

Termination of an agency by operation of law occurs in the circumstances discussed here. Note that when an agency terminates by operation of law, there is no duty to notify third persons.

1. *Death or insanity.* The general rule is that the death or mental incompetence of either the principal or the agent automatically and immediately terminates an ordinary agency relationship. Knowledge of the death is not required. **EXAMPLE 17.26** Geer sends Tyron to China to purchase a rare painting. Before Tyron makes the purchase, Geer dies. Tyron's

---

19. *Constructive notice* is information or knowledge of a fact imputed by law to a person if he or she could have discovered the fact by proper diligence. Constructive notice is often accomplished by newspaper publication.

agent status is terminated at the moment of Geer's death, even though Tyron does not know that Geer has died. ● Some states, however, have enacted statutes changing this common law rule to make knowledge of the principal's death a requirement for agency termination.

2. *Impossibility.* When the specific subject matter of an agency is destroyed or lost, the agency terminates. **EXAMPLE 17.27**   Bullard employs Gonzalez to sell Bullard's house, but before any sale, the house is destroyed by fire. In this situation, Gonzalez's agency and authority to sell Bullard's house terminate. ● Similarly, when it is impossible for the agent to perform the agency lawfully because of a change in the law, the agency terminates.

3. *Changed circumstances.* When an event occurs that has such an unusual effect on the subject matter of the agency that the agent can reasonably infer that the principal will not want the agency to continue, the agency terminates. **EXAMPLE 17.28**   Roberts hires Mullen to sell a tract of land for $20,000. Subsequently, Mullen learns that there is oil under the land and that the land is worth $1 million. The agency and Mullen's authority to sell the land for $20,000 are terminated. ●

4. *Bankruptcy.* If either the principal or the agent petitions for bankruptcy, the agency is *usually* terminated. In certain circumstances, as when the agent's financial status is irrelevant to the purpose of the agency, the agency relationship may continue. Insolvency (defined as the inability to pay debts when they become due or when liabilities exceed assets), as distinguished from bankruptcy, does not necessarily terminate the relationship.

5. *War.* When the principal's country and the agent's country are at war with each other, the agency is terminated. In this situation, the agency is automatically suspended or terminated because there is no way to enforce the legal rights and obligations of the parties.

Reviewing . . . Agency

Lynne Meyer, on her way to a business meeting and in a hurry, stopped by a Buy-Mart store for a new pair of nylons to wear to the meeting. There was a long line at one of the checkout counters, but a cashier, Valerie Watts, opened another counter and began loading the cash drawer. Meyer told Watts that she was in a hurry and asked Watts to work faster. Watts, however, only slowed her pace. At this point, Meyer hit Watts. It is not clear from the record whether Meyer hit Watts intentionally or, in an attempt to retrieve the nylons, hit her inadvertently. In response, Watts grabbed Meyer by the hair and hit her repeatedly in the back of the head, while Meyer screamed for help. Management personnel separated the two women and questioned them about the incident. Watts was immediately fired for violating the store's no-fighting policy. Meyer subsequently sued Buy-Mart, alleging that the store was liable for the tort (assault and battery) committed by its employee. Using the information presented in the chapter, answer the following questions.

1. Under what doctrine discussed in this chapter might Buy-Mart be held liable for the tort committed by Watts?
2. What is the key factor in determining whether Buy-Mart is liable under this doctrine?
3. How is Buy-Mart's potential liability affected depending on whether Watts's behavior constituted an intentional tort or a tort of negligence?
4. Suppose that when Watts applied for the job at Buy-Mart, she disclosed in her application that she had previously been convicted of felony assault and battery. Nevertheless, Buy-Mart hired Watts as a cashier. How might this fact affect Buy-Mart's liability for Watts's actions?

DEBATE THIS The doctrine of *respondeat superior* should be modified to make agents solely liable for some of their tortious (wrongful) acts.

BUSINESS APPLICATION

How Can an Employer Use Independent Contractors?*

As an employer, you may at some time consider hiring an independent contractor. Hiring workers as independent contractors instead of as employees may help you reduce both your potential tort liability and your tax liability.

Minimizing Potential Tort Liability

One reason for using an independent contractor is that employers usually are not liable for torts that independent contractors commit against third parties. Nevertheless, there are exceptions. If an employer exercises significant control over the activities of the independent contractor, for example, the contractor may be considered an employee, and the employer can then be liable for the contractor's torts.

To minimize possible liability, you should check an independent contractor's qualifications before hiring him or her. How extensively you need to investigate depends, of course, on the nature of the work. Hiring an independent contractor to maintain the landscaping should require a relatively limited investigation. A more thorough investigation will be necessary when employing an independent contractor to install the electrical systems that you sell. Complete investigations should also be performed anytime the contractor's activities present a potential danger to the public (as in delivering explosives).

Generally, the independent contractor should assume, in a written contract, liability for harms caused to third parties by the contractor's negligence. You should also require that the independent contractor purchase liability insurance to cover these costs.

Reducing Tax Liability and Other Costs

Another reason for hiring an independent contractor is that you do not need to pay or withhold Social Security, income, or unemployment taxes on his or her behalf. The independent contractor is responsible for paying these taxes. Additionally, an independent contractor is not eligible for any retirement or medical plans you provide to your employees, and this is a cost saving to you. Make sure that your contract with an independent contractor spells out that the contractor is responsible for paying taxes and is not entitled to any employment benefits.

A word of caution, though: simply designating a person as an independent contractor does not make her or him one. The Internal Revenue Service (IRS) will reclassify individuals as employees if it determines that they are "in fact" employees, regardless of how you have designated them. Keep proper documentation of the independent contractor's business identification number, business cards, and letterhead so that you can show the IRS that the contractor works independently.

If you improperly designate an employee as an independent contractor, the penalty may be high. Usually, you will be liable for back Social Security and unemployment taxes, plus interest and penalties. When in doubt, seek professional assistance in such matters.

Checklist for the Employer

1. Check the qualifications of any independent contractor you plan to use to reduce the possibility that you might be legally liable for the contractor's negligence.
2. Require in any contract with an independent contractor that the contractor assume liability for harm to a third person caused by the contractor's negligence.
3. Require that independent contractors carry liability insurance. Examine the policy to make sure that it is current, particularly when the contractor will be undertaking actions that are more than normally hazardous to the public.
4. Do not do anything that would lead a third person to believe that an independent contractor is your employee, and do not allow independent contractors to represent themselves as your employees.
5. Regularly inspect the work of the independent contractor to make sure that it is being performed in accordance with contract specifications. Such supervision on your part will not change the worker's status as an independent contractor.

*This *Business Application* is not meant to substitute for the services of an attorney who is licensed to practice law in your state.

Key Terms

agency 488

apparent authority 499

disclosed principal 501

equal dignity rule 498

fiduciary 489

independent contractor 489

notary public 498

partially disclosed principal 501

power of attorney 498

ratification 494

respondeat superior 504

undisclosed principal 501

vicarious liability 504

Chapter Summary: Agency

Agency Relationships (See pages 489–492.)	In a *principal-agent* relationship, an agent acts on behalf of and instead of the principal in dealing with third parties. An employee who deals with third parties is normally an agent. An independent contractor is not an employee, and the employer has no control over the details of the person's physical performance. An independent contractor may or may not be an agent.
How Agency Relationships Are Formed (See pages 492–495.)	Agency relationships may be formed by the following methods: 1. *Agreement*—The agency relationship is formed through express consent (oral or written) or implied by conduct. 2. *Ratification*—The principal either by act or by agreement ratifies the conduct of a person who is not in fact an agent. 3. *Estoppel*—The principal causes a third person to believe that another person is the principal's agent, and the third person acts to his or her detriment in reasonable reliance on that belief. 4. *Operation of law*—The agency relationship is based on a social duty (such as the need to support family members) or formed in emergency situations when the agent is unable to contact the principal and failure to act outside the scope of the agent's authority would cause the principal substantial loss.

Duties of Agents and Principals
(See pages 495–497.)
	1. *Duties of the agent*—
	  a. Performance—The agent must use reasonable diligence and skill in performing her or his duties or use the special skills that the agent has claimed to possess.
	  b. Notification—The agent is required to notify the principal of all matters that come to his or her attention concerning the subject matter of the agency.
	  c. Loyalty—The agent has a duty to act solely for the benefit of the principal and not in the interest of the agent or a third party.
	  d. Obedience—The agent must follow all lawful and clearly stated instructions of the principal.
	  e. Accounting—The agent has a duty to make available to the principal records of all property and funds received and paid out on behalf of the principal.
	2. *Duties of the principal*—
	  a. Compensation—Except in a gratuitous agency relationship, the principal must pay the agreed-on value (or reasonable value) for the agent's services.
	  b. Reimbursement and indemnification—The principal must reimburse the agent for all funds disbursed at the request of the principal and for all funds that the agent disburses for necessary expenses in the reasonable performance of his or her agency duties.
	  c. Cooperation—A principal must cooperate with and assist an agent in performing her or his duties.
	  d. Safe working conditions—A principal must provide safe working conditions for agents and employees.

Agent's Authority (See pages 497–501.)	1. *Express authority*—Can be oral or in writing. Authorization must be in writing if the agent is to execute a contract that must be in writing. 2. *Implied authority*—Authority customarily associated with the position of the agent or authority that is deemed necessary for the agent to carry out expressly authorized tasks. 3. *Apparent authority*—Exists when the principal, by word or action, causes a third party reasonably to believe that an agent has authority to act, even though the agent has no express or implied authority. 4. *Ratification*—Affirmation by the principal of an agent's unauthorized action or promise. For the ratification to be effective, the principal must be aware of all material facts.

Liability in Agency Relationships
(See pages 501–507.)
	1. *Liability for contracts*—If the principal's identity is disclosed or partially disclosed at the time the agent forms a contract with a third party, the principal is liable to the third party under the contract if the agent acted within the scope of his or her authority. If the principal's identity is undisclosed at the time of contract formation, the agent is personally liable to the third party, but if the agent acted within the scope of his or her authority, the principal is also bound by the contract.
	2. *Liability for agent's negligence*—Under the doctrine of *respondeat superior*, the principal is liable for any harm caused to another through the agent's torts if the agent was acting within the scope of her or his employment at the time the harmful act occurred.
	3. *Liability for agent's intentional torts*—Usually, employers are not liable for the intentional torts that their agents commit, unless:
	  a. The acts are committed within the scope of employment, and thus the doctrine of *respondeat superior* applies.
	  b. The employer knows or should know that the employee has a propensity for committing tortious acts.
	  c. The employer allowed the employee to engage in reckless acts that caused injury to another.
	  d. The agent's misrepresentation causes a third party to sustain damage, and the agent had either actual or apparent authority to act.
	4. *Liability for independent contractor's torts*—A principal is not liable for harm caused by an independent contractor's negligence, unless hazardous activities are involved or other exceptions apply.
	5. *Liability for agent's crimes*—An agent is responsible for his or her own crimes, even if the crimes were committed while the agent was acting within the scope of authority or employment. A principal will be liable for an agent's crime only if the principal participated by conspiracy or other action or (in some jurisdictions) if the agent violated certain government regulations in the course of employment.

Continued

Chapter Summary: Agency—Continued

How Agency Relationships Are Terminated (See pages 507–509.)	1. *By act of the parties—* Notice to third parties is required when an agency is terminated by act of the parties. Direct notice is required for those who have previously dealt with the agency, but constructive notice will suffice for all other third parties. See pages 507–508 for a list of the ways that an agency may be terminated by act of the parties. 2. *By operation of law—* Notice to third parties is not required when an agency is terminated by operation of law. See pages 508–509 for a list of the ways that an agency can be terminated by operation of law.

ExamPrep

ISSUE SPOTTERS

1. Vivian, owner of Wonder Goods Company, employs Xena as an administrative assistant. In Vivian's absence, and without authority, Xena represents herself as Vivian and signs a promissory note in Vivian's name. In what circumstance is Vivian liable on the note? **(See page 501.)**
2. Davis contracts with Estee to buy a certain horse on her behalf. Estee asks Davis not to reveal her identity. Davis makes a deal with Farmland Stables, the owner of the horse, and makes a down payment. Estee does not pay the rest of the price. Farmland Stables sues Davis for breach of contract. Can Davis hold Estee liable for whatever damages he has to pay? Why or why not? **(See page 497.)**

—**Check your answers to the Issue Spotters against the answers provided in Appendix E at the end of this text.**

BEFORE THE TEST

Go to www.cengagebrain.com, enter the ISBN 9781133191353, and click on "Find" to locate this textbook's Web site. Then, click on "Access Now" under "Study Tools," and select Chapter 17 at the top. There, you will find a Practice Quiz that you can take to assess your mastery of the concepts in this chapter, as well as Flashcards, a Glossary of important terms, and Video Questions (when assigned).

For Review

Answers to the even-numbered questions in this For Review section can be found in Appendix F at the end of this text.

1. What is the difference between an employee and an independent contractor?
2. How do agency relationships arise?
3. What duties do agents and principals owe to each other?
4. When is a principal liable for the agent's actions with respect to third parties? When is the agent liable?
5. What are some of the ways in which an agency relationship can be terminated?

Business Scenarios and Case Problems

17–1 Employee versus Independent Contractor. Stephen Hemmerling was a driver for the Happy Cab Co. Hemmerling paid certain fixed expenses and abided by a variety of rules relating to the use of the cab, the hours that could be worked, and the solicitation of fares, among other things. Rates were set by the state. Happy Cab did not withhold taxes from Hemmerling's pay. While driving the cab, Hemmerling was injured in an accident and filed a claim against Happy Cab in a Nebraska state court for workers' compensation benefits. Such benefits are not available to independent contractors. On what basis might the court hold that Hemmerling is an employee? Explain. **(See pages 489–492.)**

17–2 **? Question with Sample Answer—Formation of an Agency.** Paul Gett is a well-known, wealthy financial expert living in the city of Torris. Adam Wade, Gett's friend, tells Timothy Brown that he is Gett's agent for the purchase of rare coins. Wade even shows Brown a local newspaper clipping mentioning Gett's interest in coin collecting.

Brown, knowing of Wade's friendship with Gett, contracts with Wade to sell a rare coin valued at $25,000 to Gett. Wade takes the coin and disappears with it. On the payment due date, Brown seeks to collect from Gett, claiming that Wade's agency made Gett liable. Gett does not deny that Wade was a friend, but he claims that Wade was never his agent. Discuss fully whether an agency was in existence at the time the contract for the rare coin was made. **(See pages 492–495.)**

—For a sample answer to Question 17–2, go to Appendix G at the end of this text.

17–3 **Spotlight on Agency—Independent Contractors.** Frank Frausto delivered newspapers for Phoenix Newspapers, Inc., under a renewable six-month contract called a "Delivery Agent Agreement." The agreement identified Frausto as an independent contractor. Phoenix collected payments from customers and took complaints about delivery. Frausto was assigned the route for his deliveries and was required to deliver the papers within a certain time period each day. Frausto used his own vehicle to deliver the papers and had to provide proof of insurance to Phoenix. Phoenix provided him with health and disability insurance but did not withhold taxes from his weekly income. One morning while delivering papers, Frausto collided with a motorcycle ridden by William Santiago. Santiago filed a negligence action against Frausto and Phoenix. Phoenix argued that it should not be liable because Frausto was an independent contractor. What factors should the court consider in making its ruling? [*Santiago v. Phoenix Newspapers, Inc.,* 794 P.2d 138 (Ariz. 1990)] **(See pages 489–492.)**

17–4 **Loyalty.** Taser International, Inc., develops and makes video and audio recording devices. Steve Ward was Taser's vice president of marketing when he began to explore the possibility of developing and marketing devices of his own design, including a clip-on camera. Ward talked to patent attorneys and a product development company and completed most of a business plan before he resigned from Taser. He then formed Vievu, LLC, to market the clip-on camera. Did Ward breach the duty of loyalty? Could he have taken any steps toward starting his own firm without breaching this duty? Discuss. [*Taser International, Inc. v. Ward,* 224 Ariz. 389, 231 P.3d 921 (App. Div. 1 2010)] **(See page 496.)**

17–5 **Employment Relationships.** William Moore owned Moore Enterprises, a wholesale tire business. William's son, Jonathan, worked as a Moore Enterprises employee while he was in high school. Later, Jonathan started his own business, called Morecedes Tire. Morecedes regrooved tires and sold them to businesses, including Moore Enterprises. A decade after Jonathan started Morecedes, William offered him work with Moore Enterprises. On the first day, William told Jonathan to load certain tires on a trailer but did not tell him how to do it. Was Jonathan an independent contractor?

Discuss. [*Moore v. Moore,* 152 Idaho 245, 269 P.3d 802 (2011)] **(See pages 489–492.)**

17–6 **Disclosed Principal.** To display desserts in restaurants, Mario Sclafani ordered refrigeration units from Felix Storch, Inc. Felix faxed a credit application to Sclafani. The application was faxed back with a signature that appeared to be Sclafani's. Felix delivered the units. When they were not paid for, Felix filed a suit against Sclafani to collect. Sclafani denied that he had seen the application or signed it. He testified that he referred all credit questions to "the girl in the office." Who was the principal? Who was the agent? Who is liable on the contract? Explain. [*Felix Storch, Inc. v. Martinucci Desserts USA, Inc.,* 30 Misc.2d 1217, 924 N.Y.S.2d 308 (Suffolk Co. 2011)] **(See page 502.)**

17–7 **Case Problem with Sample Answer—Liability for Contracts.** Thomas Huskin and his wife entered into a contract to have their home remodeled by House Medic Handyman Service. Todd Hall signed the contract as an authorized representative of House Medic. It turned out that House Medic was a fictitious name for Hall Hauling, Ltd. The contract did not indicate this, however, and Hall did not inform the Huskins about Hall Hauling. When a contract dispute later arose, the Huskins sued Todd Hall personally for breach of contract. Can Hall be held personally liable? Why or why not? [*Huskin v. Hall,* 2012 WL 553136 (Ohio Ct.App. 2012)] **(See pages 501–502.)**

—For a sample answer to Problem 17–7, go to Appendix H at the end of this text.

17–8 **A Question of Ethics—Agency.** Emergency One, Inc. (EO), makes fire and rescue vehicles. Western Fire Truck, Inc., contracted with EO to be its exclusive dealer in Colorado and Wyoming through December 2003. James Costello, a Western salesperson, was authorized to order EO vehicles for his customers. Without informing Western, Costello e-mailed EO about Western's financial difficulties, discussed the viability of Western's contract, and asked about the possibility of working for EO. On EO's request, and in disregard of Western's instructions, Costello sent some payments for EO vehicles directly to EO. In addition, Costello, with EO's help, sent a competing bid to a potential Western customer. EO's representative e-mailed Costello, "You have my permission to kick [Western's] ass." In April 2002, EO terminated its contract with Western, which, after reviewing Costello's e-mail, fired Costello. Western filed a lawsuit against Costello and EO, alleging that Costello breached his duty as an agent and that EO aided and abetted the breach. [*Western Fire Truck, Inc. v. Emergency One, Inc.,* 134 P.3d 570 (Colo.App. 2006)] **(See pages 492–496.)**

1. Was there an agency relationship between Western and Costello? Western required monthly reports from its sales staff, but Costello did not report regularly. Does this indicate that Costello was *not* Western's agent? In

determining whether an agency relationship exists, is the *right* to control or the *fact* of control more important? Explain.

2. Did Costello owe Western a duty? If so, what was the duty? Did Costello breach it? How?

3. A Colorado state statute allows a court to award punitive damages in "circumstances of fraud, malice, or willful and wanton conduct." Did any of these circumstances exist in this case? Should punitive damages be assessed against either defendant? Why or why not?

Critical Thinking and Writing Assignments

17–9   Critical Legal Thinking. What policy is served by the law that employers do not own the copyrights for works created by independent contractors (unless there is a written "work for hire" agreement)? **(See page 492.)**

17–10   Business Law Critical Thinking Group Assignment. Dean Brothers Corp. owns and operates a steel drum manufacturing plant. Lowell Wyden, the plant superintendent, hired Best Security Patrol, Inc. (BSP), a security company, to guard Dean property and "deter thieves and vandals." Some BSP security guards, as Wyden knew, carried firearms. Pete Sidell, a BSP security guard, was not certified as an armed guard but nevertheless took his gun to work. While working at the Dean plant on October 31, 2014, Sidell fired his gun at Tyrone Gaines, in the belief that Gaines was an intruder. The bullet struck and killed Gaines. Gaines's mother filed a lawsuit claiming that her son's death was the result of BSP's negligence, for which Dean was responsible.

1. The first group will determine what the plaintiff's best argument is to establish that Dean is responsible for BSP's actions.

2. The second group will discuss Dean's best defense and formulate arguments in support of it.

CHAPTER 18

Employment Law

(Andres/Shutterstock.com)

CHAPTER OUTLINE

- Employment at Will
- Wages, Hours, and Layoffs
- Family and Medical Leave
- Worker Health, Safety, and Income Security
- Employee Privacy Rights
- Immigration Law
- Employment Discrimination

LEARNING OBJECTIVES

The five learning objectives below are designed to help improve your understanding of the chapter. After reading this chapter, you should be able to answer the following questions:

1 What is the employment-at-will doctrine? When and why are exceptions to this doctrine made?

2 What federal statute governs working hours and wages?

3 Under the Family and Medical Leave Act, in what circumstances may an employee take family or medical leave?

4 What are the two most important federal statutes governing immigration and employment today?

5 What is the difference between disparate-treatment discrimination and disparate-impact discrimination?

"The employer generally gets the employees he deserves."
—Sir Walter Gilbey, 1831–1914 (English merchant)

Until the early 1900s, most employer-employee relationships were governed by the common law. Even today, as we will see, private employers have considerable freedom to hire and fire workers under the common law. (This is one reason that employers generally get the employees they deserve, as the chapter-opening quotation observed.)

In addition, however, numerous statutes and administrative agency regulations now govern the workplace. In this chapter, we look at the most significant laws regulating employment relationships and at how these laws are changing to adapt to new technologies and new problems, such as the influx of illegal immigrants. We also consider some current controversies, such as the degree to which employers can regulate their employees' use of social media and whether the states can enact their own laws to regulate immigration. Finally, we examine federal laws that prohibit employment discrimination.

Employment at Will

Employment at Will A common law doctrine under which either party may terminate an employment relationship at any time for any reason, unless a contract specifies otherwise.

Employment relationships have traditionally been governed by the common law doctrine of **employment at will,** which allows either the employer or the employee to end the relationship at any time and for any reason. Thus, employers can fire workers for any reason or for no reason, unless doing so violates an employee's statutory or contractual rights.

Today, the majority of U.S. workers continue to have the legal status of "employees at will." Indeed, only one state (Montana) does not apply this doctrine. Nonetheless, federal and state statutes prevent the doctrine from being applied in a number of circumstances, and the courts have also created several exceptions.

Exceptions to the Employment-at-Will Doctrine

LEARNING OBJECTIVE 1
What is the employment-at-will doctrine? When and why are exceptions to this doctrine made?

Because of the sometimes harsh effects of the employment-at-will doctrine for employees, the courts have carved out various exceptions to it. These exceptions are based on contract theory, tort theory, and public policy.

Exceptions Based on Contract Theory
Some courts have held that an *implied* employment contract exists between an employer and an employee. If an employee is fired outside the terms of the implied contract, he or she may succeed in an action for breach of contract even though no written employment contract exists. **EXAMPLE 18.1** BDI Enterprises' employment manual and personnel bulletin both state that, as a matter of policy, workers will be dismissed only for good cause. If an employee reasonably expects BDI to follow this policy, a court may find that there is an implied contract based on the terms stated in the manual and bulletin.[1] ● Generally, the employee's reasonable expectations are the key to whether an employment manual creates an implied contractual obligation.

An employer's oral promises to employees regarding discharge policy may also be considered part of an implied contract. If the employer fires a worker in a manner contrary to what was promised, a court may hold that the employer has violated the implied contract and is liable for damages. Most state courts will judge a claim of breach of an implied employment contract by traditional contract standards.

➤ KNOW THIS ➤
An implied contract may exist if a party furnishes a service expecting to be paid, and the other party, who knows (or should know) of this expectation, has a chance to reject the service and does not.

Exceptions Based on Tort Theory
In a few situations, the discharge of an employee may give rise to an action for wrongful discharge under tort theories. Abusive discharge procedures may result in a suit for intentional infliction of emotional distress or defamation.

In addition, some courts have permitted workers to sue their employers under the tort theory of fraud. **EXAMPLE 18.2** Goldfinch, Inc., induces a prospective employee to leave a lucrative job and move to another state by offering "a long-term job with a thriving business." In fact, Goldfinch is not only having significant financial problems but is also planning a merger that will result in the elimination of the position offered to the prospective employee. If the employee takes the job in reliance on Goldfinch's representations and is fired shortly thereafter, the employee may be able to bring an action against the employer for fraud. ●

Exceptions Based on Public Policy
The most common exception to the employment-at-will doctrine is made on the basis that the worker was fired for reasons that violate a fundamental public policy of the jurisdiction. Generally, the public policy involved must be expressed clearly in the jurisdiction's statutory law.

---

1. See, for example, *Ross v. May Co.,* 377 Ill.App.3d 387, 880 N.E.2d 210 (1 Dist. 2007).

Whistleblowing An employee's disclosure to government authorities, upper-level managers, or the media that the employer is engaged in unsafe or illegal activities.

The public-policy exception may apply to an employee who is discharged for **whistleblowing**—that is, telling government authorities, upper-level managers, or the media that her or his employer is engaged in some unsafe or illegal activity. Normally, whistleblowers seek protection from retaliatory discharge under federal and state statutory laws, such as the Whistleblower Protection Act of 1989.[2] Sometimes, however, other approaches are used.

CASE EXAMPLE 18.3 Boyce Thompson Institute for Plant Research, Inc., hired Donald Waddell as an employee, but he did not have an employment contract. Several months later, the institute implemented a whistleblower policy stating that employees would not be fired for making complaints. In May 2010, Waddell repeatedly told his supervisor, Sophia Darling, that she needed to file certain financial documents more promptly. In August 2010, Darling fired Waddell for disrespectful and insubordinate conduct.

Waddell sued, claiming that the institute had breached an implied contract based on its written whistleblower policy. The court found that because Waddell did not have an employment contract, he was employed at will. Furthermore, the institute's whistleblower policy was implemented after Waddell had accepted the job, so he had not relied on it as a term of his employment.[3] ●

Wrongful Discharge

Wrongful Discharge An employer's termination of an employee's employment in violation of the law or an employment contract.

Whenever an employer discharges an employee in violation of an employment contract or a statute protecting employees, the employee may bring an action for **wrongful discharge.** Even if an employer's actions do not violate any provisions in an employment contract or a statute, the employer may still be subject to liability under a common law doctrine, such as a tort theory or agency. Note that in today's business world, an employment contract may be established or modified via e-mail exchanges.[4]

Wages, Hours, and Layoffs

LEARNING OBJECTIVE 2
What federal statute governs working hours and wages?

In the 1930s, Congress enacted several laws regulating the wages and working hours of employees. In 1931, Congress passed the Davis-Bacon Act,[5] which requires contractors and subcontractors working on federal government construction projects to pay "prevailing wages" to their employees. In 1936, the Walsh-Healey Act[6] was passed. This act requires that a minimum wage, as well as overtime pay at 1.5 times regular pay rates, be paid to employees of manufacturers or suppliers that enter into contracts with agencies of the federal government.

"All I've ever wanted was an honest week's pay for an honest day's work."

Steve Martin, 1945–present
(American actor and comedian)

In 1938, Congress passed the Fair Labor Standards Act[7] (FLSA), which extended wage and hour requirements to cover all employers engaged in interstate commerce or in the production of goods for interstate commerce, plus certain other businesses. More than 130 million American workers are protected (or covered) by the FLSA, which is enforced by the Wage and Hour Division of the U.S. Department of Labor. Here, we examine the FLSA's provisions in regard to child labor, maximum hours, and minimum wages.

---

2. 5 U.S.C. Section 1201.
3. *Waddell v. Boyce Thompson Institute for Plant Research, Inc.*, 92 A.D.3d 1172, 940 N.Y.S.2d 331 (2012).
4. See, for example, *Moroni v. Medco Health Solutions, Inc.*, 2008 WL 3539476 (E.D.Mich. 2008).
5. 40 U.S.C. Sections 276a–276a-5.
6. 41 U.S.C. Sections 35–45.
7. 29 U.S.C. Sections 201–260.

Child Labor

The FLSA prohibits oppressive child labor. Children under fourteen years of age are allowed to do certain types of work, such as deliver newspapers or work for their parents. They may also work in the entertainment industry and (with some exceptions) in agriculture. Children who are fourteen or fifteen years of age are allowed to work, but not in hazardous occupations. There are also numerous restrictions on how many hours per day (particularly on school days) and per week they can work.

Working times and hours are not restricted for persons between the ages of sixteen and eighteen, but they cannot be employed in hazardous jobs or in jobs detrimental to their health and well-being. None of these restrictions apply to individuals over the age of eighteen.

Wages and Hours

Minimum Wage The lowest wage, either by government regulation or union contract, that an employer may pay an hourly worker.

The FLSA provides that a **minimum wage** (now $7.25 per hour) must be paid to employees in covered industries. Congress periodically revises this minimum wage. Additionally, many states have minimum wages. When the state minimum wage is higher than the federal minimum wage, the employee is entitled to the higher wage.

When an employee receives tips while on the job, the employer is required to pay only $2.13 an hour in direct wages—but only if that amount, plus the tips received, equals at least the federal minimum wage. If an employee's tips combined with the employer's direct wages do not equal the federal minimum wage, the employer must make up the difference. If employers pay at least the federal minimum wage, the FLSA allows them to take employee tips and make other arrangements for their distribution.

Overtime Exemptions

Under the FLSA, employees who work more than forty hours per week normally must be paid 1.5 times their regular pay for all hours over forty. Note that the FLSA overtime provisions apply only after an employee has worked more than forty hours per *week*. Thus, employees who work for ten hours a day, four days per week, are not entitled to overtime pay because they do not work more than forty hours per week.

Certain employees—usually executive, administrative, and professional employees, as well as outside salespersons and computer programmers—are exempt from the FLSA's overtime provisions. Employers are not required to pay overtime wages to exempt employees. Employers can voluntarily pay overtime to ineligible employees but cannot waive or reduce the overtime requirements of the FLSA. (Smartphones and other technology have raised new issues concerning overtime wages, as discussed in this chapter's *Beyond Our Borders* feature on the facing page.)

"By working faithfully eight hours a day, you may eventually get to be a boss and work twelve hours a day."

Robert Frost, 1875–1963
(American poet)

Administrative Employees   To qualify under the administrative employee exemption, the employee must be paid a salary, not hourly wages, and the employee's primary duty must be directly related to the management or general business operations of the employer. In addition, the employee's primary duty must include the exercise of discretion and independent judgment with respect to matters of significance.

CASE EXAMPLE 18.4   Patty Lee Smith was a pharmaceutical sales representative at Johnson and Johnson (J&J). She traveled to ten physicians' offices a day to promote the benefits of J&J's drug Concerta. Smith's work was unsupervised, she controlled her own schedule, and she received a salary of $66,000. When she filed a claim for overtime pay, the court held that she was an administrative employee and therefore exempt from the FLSA's overtime provisions.[8] ●

---

8. *Smith v. Johnson and Johnson*, 593 F.3d 280 (3d Cir. 2010).

BEYOND OUR BORDERS

Brazil Requires Employers to Pay Overtime for Use of Smartphones after Work Hours

Workers in the United States are increasingly arguing that they should receive overtime pay for the time they spend staying connected to work through their iPads, smartphones, or other electronic devices. Indeed, many employers require their employees to carry a mobile device (BlackBerry, iPhone, or other smartphone or tablet) to keep in contact.

Checking e-mail, responding to text messages, tweeting, and using LinkedIn or other employment-related apps can be considered work. So if employees who are not exempt under the overtime regulations are required to use mobile devices after office hours, do the workers have a valid claim to overtime wages? That question is still to be answered, because the FLSA is not clear about what constitutes work.

In Brazil, however, workers who answer work e-mails on their smartphones or other electronic devices after work are now entitled to receive overtime wages. Under legislation enacted in 2012, e-mail from an employer is considered the equivalent of orders given directly to an employee, so it constitutes work. A few other nations also require payment to workers for staying connected through smartphones and other devices after hours.

Critical Thinking
What are the pros and cons of paying overtime wages to workers who check e-mail and perform other work-related tasks electronically after hours?

Executive Employees An executive employee is one whose primary duty is management. An employee's primary duty is determined by what he or she does that is of principal value to the employer, not by how much time the employee spends doing particular tasks. An employer cannot deny overtime wages to an employee based only on the employee's job title, however, and must be able to show that the employee's primary duty qualifies her or him for an exemption.[9]

CASE EXAMPLE 18.5 Kevin Keevican, a manager at a Starbucks store, worked seventy hours a week for $650 to $800, a 10 to 20 percent bonus, and paid sick leave. Keevican (and other former managers) filed a claim against Starbucks for unpaid overtime, claiming that he had spent 70 to 80 percent of his time waiting on customers and thus was not an executive employee. The court, however, found that Keevican was "the single highest-ranking employee" in his particular store and was responsible on site for that store's day-to-day overall operations. Because his primary duty was managerial, Starbucks was not required to pay overtime.[10] ●

Layoffs

During the latest economic recession in the United States, hundreds of thousands of workers lost their jobs as many businesses disappeared. Other companies struggling to keep afloat reduced costs by restructuring their operations and downsizing their workforces, which meant layoffs. In this section, we discuss the laws pertaining to employee layoffs—an area that is increasingly the subject of litigation.

The federal Worker Adjustment and Retraining Notification Act,[11] or WARN Act, requires large employers to provide sixty days' notice before implementing a mass layoff or closing a plant that employs more than fifty full-time workers. The act applies to employers with at least one hundred full-time employees. A

"EARLY RETIREMENT? BUT, BOSS, I CAN'T AFFORD to RETIRE UNTIL I PAY OFF MY STUDENT LOANS."

(© 2012 Harley Schwadron)

---

9. See, for example, *Slusser v. Vantage Builders, Inc.*, 576 F.Supp.2d 1207 (D.N.M. 2008).
10. *Mims v. Starbucks Corp.*, 2007 WL 10369 (S.D.Tex. 2007).
11. 29 U.S.C. Sections 2101 *et seq.*

mass layoff means a layoff of at least one-third of the full-time employees at a particular job site.

The WARN Act is intended to give workers advance notice so that they can start looking for a new job while they are still employed and to alert state agencies so that they can provide training and other resources for displaced workers. Even companies that anticipate filing for bankruptcy normally must provide notice under the WARN Act before implementing a mass layoff.

Many states also have statutes requiring employers to provide notice before initiating mass layoffs, and these laws may have different and even stricter requirements than the WARN Act. In New York, for instance, companies with fifty or more employees must provide ninety days' notice before any layoff that affects twenty-five or more full-time employees.

Family and Medical Leave

LEARNING OBJECTIVE 3
Under the Family and Medical Leave Act, in what circumstances may an employee take family or medical leave?

The Family and Medical Leave Act (FMLA)[12] is a federal law that allows employees to take time off from work for family or medical reasons. A majority of the states have similar legislation, and many employers maintain private family-leave plans for their workers. Recently, additional categories of FMLA leave have been created for military caregivers and for qualifying exigencies (emergencies) that arise due to military service.

Coverage and Applicability

The FMLA requires employers who have fifty or more employees to provide employees with up to twelve weeks of unpaid family or medical leave during any twelve-month period. The FMLA expressly covers private and public (government) employees who have worked for their employers for at least a year. An employee may take *family leave* to care for a newborn baby or a child recently placed for adoption or foster care. An employee can take *medical leave* when the employee or the employee's spouse, child, or parent has a "serious health condition" requiring care.

A daughter helps her ailing father. Under what circumstances will she be protected by the Family and Medical Leave Act?

In addition, an employee caring for a family member with a serious injury or illness incurred as a result of military duty can take up to twenty-six weeks of *military caregiver leave* within a twelve-month period.[13] Also, an employee can take up to twelve weeks of *qualifying exigency leave* to handle specified nonmedical emergencies when a spouse, parent, or child is in, or called to, active military duty.[14] For instance, when a spouse is deployed to Afghanistan, an employee may take exigency leave to arrange for child care or to deal with financial or legal matters.

When an employee takes FMLA leave, the employer must continue the worker's healthcare coverage on the same terms as if the employee had continued to work. On returning from FMLA leave, most employees must be restored to their original position or to a comparable position (with nearly equivalent pay and benefits, for example). An important exception allows the employer to avoid reinstating a *key employee*—defined as an employee whose pay falls within the top 10 percent of the firm's workforce.

Violations

An employer that violates the FMLA can be required to provide various remedies, including the following:

1. Damages to compensate an employee for lost benefits, denied compensation, and actual monetary losses (such as the cost of providing for care of the family member) up to an amount equivalent to the employee's wages for twelve weeks (twenty-six weeks for military caregiver leave).

---

12. 29 U.S.C. Sections 2601, 2611–2619, 2651–2654.
13. 29 C.F.R. Section 825.200.
14. 29 C.F.R. Section 825.126.

2. Job reinstatement.

3. Promotion, if a promotion has been denied.

A successful plaintiff is entitled to court costs and attorneys' fees, and, in cases involving bad faith on the part of the employer, two times the amount of damages awarded by a judge or jury. Supervisors can also be held personally liable, as employers, for violations of the act.

Employers generally are required to notify employees when an absence will be counted against leave authorized under the act. If an employer fails to provide such notice, and the employee consequently suffers an injury because he or she did not receive notice, the employer may be sanctioned.

Worker Health, Safety, and Income Security

Under the common law, employees who were injured on the job had to file lawsuits against their employers to obtain recovery. Today, numerous state and federal statutes protect employees and their families from the risk of accidental injury, death, or disease resulting from employment and provide a right to compensation for on-the-job injuries. Laws also protect employees by requiring employers to pay into Social Security, Medicare, and unemployment insurance, and to follow specific requirements for pension plans and health insurance.

The Occupational Safety and Health Act

At the federal level, the primary legislation protecting employees' health and safety is the Occupational Safety and Health Act,[15] which is administered by the Occupational Safety and Health Administration (OSHA). The act imposes on employers a general duty to keep workplaces safe. In addition, the act prohibits employers from firing or discriminating against any employee who refuses to work when he or she believes a workplace is unsafe. OSHA has established specific safety standards for various industries. For instance, OSHA regulations require the use of safety guards on certain mechanical equipment and set maximum levels of exposure to substances in the workplace that may be harmful to a worker's health.

The act also requires that employers post certain notices in the workplace, perform prescribed record keeping, and submit specific reports. For instance, employers with eleven or more employees are required to keep occupational injury and illness records for each employee. Each record must be made available for inspection when requested by an OSHA compliance officer.

Whenever a work-related injury or disease occurs, employers must make reports directly to OSHA. If an employee dies or three or more employees are hospitalized because of a work-related incident, the employer must notify OSHA within eight hours. A company that fails to do so will be fined and may also be prosecuted under state law. Following the incident, a complete inspection of the premises is mandatory.

OSHA compliance officers may enter and inspect facilities of any establishment covered by the Occupational Safety and Health Act. Employees may also file complaints of violations and cannot be fired by their employers for doing so.

State Workers' Compensation Laws

Workers' Compensation Laws State statutes that establish an administrative process for compensating workers for injuries that arise in the course of their employment, regardless of fault.

State **workers' compensation laws** establish an administrative procedure for compensating workers injured on the job. Instead of suing, an injured worker files a claim with the administrative agency or board that administers local workers' compensation

---

15. 29 U.S.C. Sections 553, 651–678.

claims. An employee's acceptance of workers' compensation benefits bars the employee from suing for injuries caused by the employer's negligence. A worker may sue an employer who has *intentionally* injured the worker, however.

Most workers' compensation statutes are similar. No state covers all employees. Typically, domestic workers, agricultural workers, temporary employees, and employees of common carriers (companies that provide transportation services to the public) are excluded, but minors are covered. Usually, the statutes allow employers to purchase insurance from a private insurer or a state fund to pay workers' compensation benefits in the event of a claim. Most states also allow employers to be self-insured—that is, employers that show an ability to pay claims do not need to buy insurance.

In general, there are only two requirements for an employee to receive benefits under a state workers' compensation law:

1. The existence of an employment relationship.
2. An *accidental* injury that *occurred on the job or in the course of employment,* regardless of fault. (An injury that occurs while an employee is commuting to or from work usually is not considered to have occurred on the job or in the course of employment and hence is not covered.)

An injured employee must notify her or his employer promptly (usually within thirty days of the accident). Generally, an employee must also file a workers' compensation claim with the appropriate state agency or board within a certain period (sixty days to two years) from the time the injury is first noticed, rather than from the time of the accident.

Almost every aspect of Social Security programs is now online.

(www.ssa.gov)

Social Security

Federal and state governments participate in insurance programs designed to protect employees and their families by covering the financial impact of retirement, disability, death, hospitalization, and unemployment. The key federal law on this subject is the Social Security Act of 1935.[16]

The Social Security Act provides for old-age (retirement), survivors', and disability insurance. Hence, the act is often referred to as OASDI. Both employers and employees must "contribute" under the Federal Insurance Contributions Act (FICA)[17] to help pay for benefits that will partially make up for the employees' loss of income on retirement.

The basis for the employee's and the employer's contributions is the employee's annual wage base—the maximum amount of the employee's wages that are subject to the tax. The employer withholds the employee's FICA contribution from the employee's wages and ordinarily matches this contribution.

Retired workers are eligible to receive monthly payments from the Social Security Administration, which administers the Social Security Act. Social Security benefits are fixed by statute but increase automatically with increases in the cost of living.

Medicare

Medicare is a federal government health-insurance program that is administered by the Social Security Administration for people sixty-five years of age and older and for some under the age of sixty-five who are disabled. It originally had two parts, one pertaining

---

16. 42 U.S.C. Sections 301–1397e.
17. 26 U.S.C. Sections 3101–3125.

to hospital costs and the other to nonhospital medical costs, such as visits to physicians' offices, but now offers additional coverage options and a prescription-drug plan. People who have Medicare hospital insurance can also obtain additional federal medical insurance if they pay small monthly premiums, which increase as the cost of medical care increases.

As with Social Security contributions, both the employer and the employee "contribute" to Medicare, but unlike Social Security, there is no cap on the amount of wages subject to the Medicare tax. In 2012, both the employer and the employee were required to pay 1.45 percent of *all* wages and salaries to finance Medicare.[18]

Thus, for Social Security and Medicare together, typically the employer and the employee each pay 7.65 percent (6.2 percent for Social Security + 1.45 percent for Medicare) of the wage base, up to the maximum, for a combined total of 15.3 percent.[19] In addition, all wages and salaries above the maximum wage base are taxed at a combined (employer and employee) rate of 2.9 percent for Medicare.

Self-employed persons pay both the employer and the employee portions of the Social Security and Medicare taxes (13.3 percent of income up to $110,100 and 2.9 percent of income above that amount in 2012). In addition, starting in 2013, a Medicare tax of 3.8 percent is applied to all investment income for those making more than $200,000.

Private Pension Plans

The major federal act regulating employee retirement plans is the Employee Retirement Income Security Act (ERISA) of 1974.[20] This act empowers a branch of the U.S. Department of Labor to enforce its provisions governing employers that have private pension funds for their employees.

ERISA created the Pension Benefit Guaranty Corporation (PBGC), an independent federal agency, to provide timely and uninterrupted payment of voluntary private pension benefits. The pension plans pay annual insurance premiums (at set rates adjusted for inflation) to the PBGC, which then pays benefits to participants in the event that a plan is unable to do so.

ERISA does not require an employer to establish a pension plan. When a plan exists, however, ERISA specifies standards for its management, including investment of funds and record-keeping requirements. A key provision of ERISA concerns vesting. **Vesting** gives an employee a legal right to receive pension benefits at some future date when he or she stops working. ERISA establishes complex vesting rules. Generally, however, all employee contributions to pension plans vest immediately, and employee rights to employer contributions to a plan vest after five years of employment.

Vesting The creation of an absolute or unconditional right or power.

Unemployment Insurance

To ease the financial impact of unemployment, the United States has a system of unemployment insurance. The Federal Unemployment Tax Act (FUTA) of 1935[21] created a state-administered system that provides unemployment compensation to eligible individuals. Under this system, employers pay into a fund, and the proceeds are paid out to qualified unemployed workers. The FUTA and state laws require employers that fall under the provisions of the act to pay unemployment taxes at regular intervals.

KNOW THIS

If an employer does not pay unemployment taxes, a state government can place a lien (claim) on the business's property to secure the debt. (Liens were discussed in Chapter 15.)

---

18. As a result of the Health Care and Education Reconciliation Act of 2010, Medicare tax rates are expected to rise, and the applicable compensation base will expand to include more than just wage and salary income.

19. For 2012, the employee's contribution for Social Security was reduced to 4.2 percent, so the combined total was 13.3 percent. The maximum wage base in 2012 was $110,100.

20. 29 U.S.C. Sections 1001 *et seq.*

21. 26 U.S.C. Sections 3301–3310.

To be eligible for unemployment compensation, a worker must be willing and able to work. Workers who have been fired for misconduct or who have voluntarily left their jobs are not eligible for benefits. In the past, workers had to be actively seeking employment to continue receiving benefits. This rule was changed, however, in response to the high unemployment rates after the latest economic recession. President Barack Obama took measures that allow jobless persons to retain their unemployment benefits while pursuing additional education and training (rather than seeking employment).

COBRA

Federal law also enables workers to continue their health-care coverage after their jobs have been terminated and they are no longer eligible for their employers' group health-insurance plans. The Consolidated Omnibus Budget Reconciliation Act (COBRA)[22] prohibits an employer from eliminating a worker's medical, optical, or dental insurance on the voluntary or involuntary termination of the worker's employment. The former employee—not the employer—pays the premiums under COBRA.

Employers, with some exceptions, must inform an employee of COBRA's provisions when the employee faces termination or a reduction of hours that would affect his or her eligibility for coverage under the plan. Only workers fired for gross misconduct are excluded from protection. An employer that does not comply with COBRA risks substantial penalties, such as a tax of up to 10 percent of the annual cost of the group plan or $500,000, whichever is less.

Employer-Sponsored Group Health Plans

The Health Insurance Portability and Accountability Act (HIPAA),[23] which was mentioned in Chapter 1, contains provisions that affect employer-sponsored group health plans. HIPAA does not require employers to provide health insurance, but it does establish requirements for those that do. For instance, HIPAA strictly limits an employer's ability to exclude coverage for *preexisting conditions,* except pregnancy.

In addition, HIPAA restricts the manner in which covered employers collect, use, and disclose the health information of employees and their families. Employers must train employees, designate privacy officials, and distribute privacy notices to ensure that employees' health information is not disclosed to unauthorized parties. Failure to comply with HIPAA regulations can result in civil penalties of up to $100 per person per violation (with a cap of $25,000 per year). The employer is also subject to criminal prosecution for certain types of HIPAA violations and can face up to $250,000 in criminal fines and imprisonment for up to ten years if convicted.

Employee Privacy Rights

In the last thirty years, concerns about the privacy rights of employees have arisen in response to the sometimes invasive tactics used by employers to monitor and screen workers. Some types of monitoring used by employers in the past, such as lie-detector tests and genetic tests (to identify individuals predisposed to illness), are now prohibited, except in limited circumstances. Perhaps the greatest privacy concern in today's employment arena has to do with electronic performance monitoring.

---

22. 29 U.S.C. Sections 1161–1169.
23. 29 U.S.C.A. Sections 1181 *et seq.*

Electronic Monitoring in the Workplace

More than half of employers engage in some form of surveillance of their employees. Many employers review employees' e-mail, blogs, instant messages, tweets, social media, smartphone, and Internet use. Employers also make digital video recordings of employees to assess job performance and record and review telephone conversations, voice mail, and text messages.

Although employees of private (nongovernment) employers have some privacy protection under tort law (see Chapter 4), state constitutions, and a number of state and federal statutes, employers have considerable leeway to monitor employees in the workplace. When determining whether an employer should be held liable for violating an employee's privacy rights, the courts generally weigh the employer's interests against the employee's reasonable expectation of privacy.

Normally, if employees have been informed that their communications are being monitored, they cannot reasonably expect those interactions to be private. If employees are not informed that certain communications are being monitored, however, the employer may be held liable for invading their privacy.

Employers often use video surveillance to monitor employees. In addition, some employers monitor employee-generated e-mails.

In addition, private employers generally can use specially designed software to track employees' Internet use and block access to certain Web sites without violating the First Amendment's protection of free speech, which applies only to government employees. In other words, the First Amendment generally prevents only *government employers* from restraining speech by blocking Web sites.

The Electronic Communications Privacy Act Employers must comply with the Electronic Communications Privacy Act (ECPA) of 1986.[24] This act amended existing federal wiretapping law to cover electronic forms of communications, such as communications via smartphones or e-mail.

The ECPA prohibits the intentional interception of any wire, oral, or electronic communication and the intentional disclosure or use of the information obtained by the interception. Excluded from coverage, however, are any electronic communications through devices that are "furnished to the subscriber or user by a provider of wire or electronic communication service" and that are being used by the subscriber or user, or by the provider of the service, "in the ordinary course of its business." In other words, if a company provided the electronic device to the employee for ordinary business use, the company is not prohibited from intercepting business communications made on it.

This "business-extension exception" to the ECPA permits employers to monitor employees' electronic communications made in the ordinary course of business. It does not permit employers to monitor employees' personal communications. Under another exception to the ECPA, however, an employer may avoid liability under the act if the employees consent to having their electronic communications intercepted by the employer. Thus, an employer may be able to avoid liability by requiring employees to sign forms indicating that they consent to the monitoring of personal as well as business communications.

The Stored Communications Act Part of the ECPA is known as the Stored Communications Act (SCA).[25] The SCA prohibits intentional and unauthorized access to

24. 18 U.S.C. Sections 2510–2521.
25. 18 U.S.C. Sections 2701–2711.

stored electronic communications and sets forth criminal and civil sanctions for violators. The SCA also prevents "providers" of communication services (such as smartphone companies and social media networks) from divulging private communications to certain entities and individuals.

For a discussion of how some employers are creating their own social media networks, see this chapter's *Adapting the Law to the Online Environment* feature below.

Drug Testing

In the interests of public safety, many employers, including government employers, require their employees to submit to drug testing. Government (public) employers are constrained in drug testing by the Fourth Amendment to the U.S. Constitution, which prohibits unreasonable searches and seizures (see Chapter 6). Drug testing of public employees is allowed by statute for transportation workers and is normally upheld by the courts when drug use in a particular job may threaten public safety. Also, when there is a reasonable basis for suspecting government employees of using drugs, courts often find that drug testing does not violate the Fourth Amendment.

The Fourth Amendment does not apply to drug testing conducted by private employers. Hence, the privacy rights and drug testing of private-sector employees are governed by state law, which varies widely. Many states have statutes that allow drug testing by private employers but place restrictions on when and how the testing may be performed. A collective bargaining agreement may also provide protection against drug testing (or authorize drug testing under certain conditions).

ADAPTING THE LAW TO THE ONLINE ENVIRONMENT

SOCIAL MEDIA IN THE WORKPLACE COME OF AGE

What do corporate giant Dell, Inc., and relatively small Nikon Instruments have in common? They—and many other companies—have created internal social media networks using enterprise social networking software and systems, such as Salesforce.com, Chatter, Yammer, and Socialcast. A glance at the posts on these internal networks reveals that they are quite different from typical posts on Facebook, LinkedIn, and Twitter. The tone is more businesslike, and the posts deal with workplace concerns such as how a team is solving a problem or how to sell a new product.

Benefits and Pitfalls of Internal Social Media Networks

Internal social media networks offer businesses several advantages. Perhaps the most important is that employees can obtain real-time information about important issues such as production glitches. They can also exchange tips about how to deal with problems, such as difficult customers. News about the company's new products or those of a competitor is available immediately. Furthermore, employees spend much less time sorting through e-mail. Rather than wasting their fellow employees' time

by sending mass e-mailings, workers can post messages or collaborate on presentations via the company's internal network.

Of course, the downside is that these networks may become polluted with annoying "white noise." If employees start posting comments about what they ate for lunch, for example, the system will lose much of its utility. Companies can prevent this from happening by establishing explicit guidelines on what can be posted.

Keeping the Data Safe

Another concern is how to keep all those data and corporate secrets safe. When a company sets up a social media network, it usually decides which employees can see which files and which employees will belong to each specific "social" group within the company. Often, the data created through a social media network are kept on the company's own servers in secure "clouds."

Critical Thinking

What problems might arise if data from an internal social media system are stored on third party servers?

Whether a private employer's drug tests are permissible typically depends on whether the tests are reasonable. Random drug tests and even "zero-tolerance" policies (which deny a "second chance" to employees who test positive for drugs) have been held to be reasonable.

A related issue involves the inclusion of questions about drug use in background checks. Federal government employees have long been required to submit to background checks as a condition of employment. Many workers who work at U.S. government facilities are employees of private contractors, not of the government. They generally have not been subject to background checks. Recent standards, however, require background checks for all federal workers, including contract employees. In the following case, several contract workers asserted that their privacy rights had been violated.

Case 18.1

National Aeronautics and Space Administration v. Nelson

Supreme Court of the United States,
__ U.S. __, 131 S.Ct. 746, 178 L.Ed.2d 667 (2011).
www.supremecourt.gov[a]

FACTS The National Aeronautics and Space Administration (NASA) is an independent federal agency charged with planning and conducting "space activities." One of NASA's facilities is the Jet Propulsion Laboratory (JPL) in Pasadena, California, which is staffed exclusively by contract employees.

In 2007, under newly implemented standards, contract employees with long-term access to federal facilities were ordered to complete a standard background check—the National Agency Check with Inquiries (NACI). The NACI is designed to obtain information on such matters as counseling and treatment for illegal drug use, as well as mental and financial stability.

Robert Nelson and other JPL employees filed a lawsuit in a federal district court against NASA, claiming that the NACI violated their privacy rights. NASA argued that the employees' privacy rights were already protected by the Privacy Act of 1974, which allows the government to retain information only for "relevant and necessary" purposes and requires written consent before disclosure. The trial court ruled in favor of NASA, but the U.S. Court of Appeals for the Ninth Circuit reversed. NASA appealed to the United States Supreme Court.

ISSUE Does subjecting private employees who work at government facilities to a standard (NACI) background investigation violate their privacy rights?

DECISION No. The United States Supreme Court reversed the judgment of the federal appellate court and remanded the

case. The inquiries made by the NACI are reasonable and do not violate an individual's right to privacy. The Privacy Act protects against the disclosure of private information.

REASON The Court reasoned that the government can ask reasonable questions as part of an employment background check even if those questions may touch on an individual's constitutional right to privacy. The Privacy Act provides safeguards against the public disclosure of an individual's private information without the individual's consent. The government has conducted employment investigations of applicants for the federal civil service for more than fifty years, and it simply extended this requirement to contract employees with long-term access to federal facilities. "Reasonable investigations of applicants and employees aid the Government in ensuring the security of its facilities and in employing a competent, reliable workforce." The Court concluded that a government employer's reasonable questions as part of a background check do not violate the right to privacy.

CRITICAL THINKING—Social Consideration *Suppose that after the decision in this case, a JPL employee refused to cooperate in an NACI background check. What would be the most likely consequences?*

---

a. In the "Supreme Court Documents" column, in the "Opinions" pull-down menu, select "Bound Volumes." On the next page, in the "For Search Term:" box, type "NASA v. Nelson," and click on "Search." In the results, click on the name of the case to access the opinion. The United States Supreme Court maintains this Web site.

Immigration Law

The United States had no laws restricting immigration until the late nineteenth century. Today, the most important laws governing immigration and employment are the Immigration Reform and Control Act[26] (IRCA) and the Immigration Act.[27] Immigration law has become increasingly important in recent years. An estimated 12 million illegal immigrants now live in the United States, many of whom came to find jobs. Because U.S. employers face serious penalties if they hire illegal immigrants, it is necessary for businesspersons to have a thorough understanding of immigration laws.

Immigration Reform and Control Act (IRCA)

When the IRCA was enacted in 1986, it provided amnesty to certain groups of illegal aliens living in the United States at the time. It also established a system that sanctions employers who hire illegal immigrants lacking work authorization.

The IRCA makes it illegal to hire, recruit, or refer for a fee someone not authorized to work in this country. Through Immigration and Customs Enforcement officers, the federal government conducts random compliance audits and engages in enforcement actions against employers who hire illegal immigrants.

I-9 Employment Verification

To comply with the IRCA, an employer must perform **I-9 verifications** for new hires, including those hired as "contractors" or "day workers" if they work under the employer's direct supervision. Form I-9, Employment Eligibility Verification, must be completed *within three days* of a worker's commencement of employment. The three-day period allows the employer to check the form's accuracy and to review and verify documents establishing the prospective worker's identity and eligibility for employment in the United States. (The form is available from U.S. Citizenship and Immigration Services, a federal agency that is part of the U.S. Department of Homeland Security.)

The employer must declare, under penalty of perjury, that an employee produced documents establishing his or her identity and legal employability. Acceptable documents include a U.S. passport establishing the person's citizenship and a document authorizing a foreign citizen to work in the United States, such as a Permanent Resident Card or an Alien Registration Receipt (discussed on the next page).

Most legal actions for violations of I-9 rules are brought against employees who provide false information or documentation. If the employee enters false information on an I-9 form or presents false documentation, the employer can fire the worker, who then may be subject to deportation. Nevertheless, employers must be honest when verifying an employee's documentation: if an employer "should have known" that the worker was unauthorized, the employer has violated the rules.

Enforcement

U.S. Immigration and Customs Enforcement (ICE) is the largest investigative arm of the U.S. Department of Homeland Security. ICE has a general inspection program that conducts random compliance audits. The agency may also conduct an audit if it receives a written complaint alleging violations. Government inspections include a review of an employer's file of I-9 forms. The government does not need a subpoena or a warrant to conduct such an inspection.

If an investigation reveals a possible violation, ICE brings an administrative action and issues a Notice of Intent to Fine, which sets out the charges against the employer. The employer has a right to a hearing on the enforcement action if a request is filed within thirty

LEARNING OBJECTIVE 4
What are the two most important federal statutes governing immigration and employment today?

I-9 Verification The process of verifying the employment eligibility and identity of a new worker. It must be completed within three days after the worker commences employment.

Who is eligible for a permanent residence card?

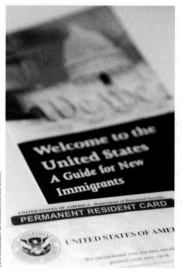

(Konstantin L/Shutterstock.com)

---

26. 29 U.S.C. Section 1802.
27. This act amended various provisions of the Immigration and Nationality Act of 1952, 8 U.S.C. Sections 1101 *et seq.*

days. This hearing is conducted before an *administrative law judge* (see page 5 of Chapter 1), and the employer has a right to counsel and to *discovery* (see pages 81–82 of Chapter 3). The typical defense in such actions is good faith or substantial compliance with the documentation provisions.

Penalties An employer who violates the law by hiring an unauthorized alien is subject to substantial penalties. The employer may be fined up to $2,200 for each unauthorized employee for a first offense, $5,000 per employee for a second offense, and up to $11,000 for subsequent offenses. Criminal penalties, including additional fines and imprisonment for up to ten years, apply to employers who have engaged in a "pattern or practice of violations." A company may also be barred from future government contracts for violations.

In determining the penalty, ICE considers the seriousness of the violation (such as intentional falsification of documents) and the employer's past compliance. ICE regulations also identify factors that will mitigate or aggravate the penalty under certain circumstances, such as whether the employer cooperated in the investigation or is a small business.

▸ KNOW THIS ◂

If an employer had any reason to suspect that a worker's documents were forged or inaccurate at the time of hiring, the employer can be fined for violating the IRCA.

The Immigration Act

U.S. immigration laws have long made provisions for businesses to hire specially qualified foreign workers when not enough qualified workers are available in the United States. The Immigration Act of 1990 placed caps on the number of visas (entry permits) that can be issued to immigrants each year.

Most temporary visas are set aside for workers who can be characterized as "persons of extraordinary ability," members of the professions holding advanced degrees, or other skilled workers and professionals. To hire such an individual, an employer must submit a petition to ICE, which determines whether the job candidate meets the legal standards. Each visa is for a specific job, and there are legal limits on the employee's ability to change jobs once in the United States.

I-551 Alien Registration Receipts

A company seeking to hire a noncitizen worker may do so if the worker is self-authorized. This means that the worker either is a lawful permanent resident or has a valid temporary Employment Authorization Document. A lawful permanent resident can prove his or her status to an employer by presenting an **I-551 Alien Registration Receipt**, known as a "green card," or a properly stamped foreign passport.

I-551 Alien Registration Receipt
A document, known as a "green card," that shows that a foreign-born individual can legally work in the United States.

Many immigrant workers are not already self-authorized, and employers may attempt to obtain labor certification, or green cards, for the immigrants they wish to hire. Approximately fifty thousand new green cards are issued each year. A green card can be obtained only for a person who is being hired for a permanent, full-time position. (A separate authorization system provides for the temporary entry and hiring of nonimmigrant visa workers.)

The employer must show that no U.S. worker is qualified, willing, and able to take the job. The government has detailed regulations governing the advertising of positions as well as the certification process. Any U.S. applicants who meet the stated job qualifications must be interviewed for the position. The employer must also be able to show that the qualifications required for the job are a business necessity.

"Immigration is the sincerest form of flattery."

Jack Paar, 1918–2004
(American entertainer)

The H-1B Visa Program

The most common and controversial visa program today is the H-1B visa system. To obtain an H-1B visa, the potential employee must be qualified in a "specialty occupation," meaning that the individual has highly specialized knowledge and has attained a bachelor's or higher degree or its equivalent. Individuals with H-1B visas can stay in the United States for three to six years and can work only for the sponsoring employer.

The recipients of these visas include many high-tech workers, such as computer programmers and electronics specialists. A maximum of sixty-five thousand H-1B visas are set aside each year for new immigrants. That limit is typically reached within the first few weeks of the year. Consequently, many businesses, such as Microsoft, continue to lobby Congress to expand the number of H-1B visas available to immigrants.

A common criticism of the H-1B visa system is that it depresses the wages of U.S. workers because H-1B workers may be willing to work for less. The law addresses this complaint by requiring employers to pay H-1B workers the prevailing wage. Before submitting an H-1B application, an employer must file a Labor Certification application on a form known as ETA 9035.

The employer must agree to provide a wage level at least equal to the wages offered to other individuals with similar experience and qualifications and attest that the hiring will not adversely affect other workers similarly employed. The employer must also inform U.S. workers of the intent to hire a foreign worker by posting the form. The U.S. Department of Labor reviews the applications and may reject them for omissions or inaccuracies.

H-2, O, L, and E Visas

Other specialty temporary visas are available for other categories of employees. H-2 visas provide for workers performing agricultural labor of a seasonal nature. O visas provide entry for persons who have "extraordinary ability in the sciences, arts, education, business or athletics which has been demonstrated by sustained national or international acclaim." L visas allow a company's foreign managers or executives to work inside the United States. E visas permit the entry of certain foreign investors and entrepreneurs.

ETHICAL ISSUE

Should Arizona and other states be allowed to engage in cooperative immigration law enforcement? As the unemployment rate has remained stubbornly high since the recession, public resentment toward illegal immigrants has grown. Some believe that illegal immigrants have taken jobs that otherwise would have gone to U.S. citizens. With state budgets under increasing pressure, there is also concern about the cost of providing education and other services for illegal immigrants.

Until recently, the laws governing immigration and the treatment of illegal immigrants have been federal. In 2010, however, Governor Jan Brewer of Arizona signed state legislation that required Arizona law enforcement officials to identify, charge, and possibly deport immigrants who were in the state illegally. Immigrants would have to carry their papers at all times, and police officers could verify individuals' immigration status during any law enforcement action and whenever they had a "reasonable suspicion" that someone was an illegal alien. In addition, Arizona citizens could sue police officers for not enforcing the law.

The federal government, however, insisted that federal immigration laws preempted state legislation. The United States Supreme Court ruled on the legality of the Arizona law in 2012—though not before several other states had passed similar legislation. In *Arizona v. United States*,[28] the Court upheld the controversial "show-me-your-papers" provision that requires police to check the immigration status of persons stopped for another violation. All the other provisions of Arizona's law were struck down as preempted by federal laws. States cannot pass laws that make it a crime for immigrants not to carry their registration documents or that make it a crime for those without work permits to seek employment. States also cannot authorize law enforcement to arrest people based solely on a reasonable suspicion that they are in the country illegally.

Employment Discrimination

Out of the civil rights movement of the 1960s grew a body of law protecting employees against discrimination in the workplace. Legislation, judicial decisions, and administrative agency actions restrict employers from discriminating against workers on the basis of race,

---

28. ___ U.S. ___, 132 S.Ct. 2492, 183 L.Ed.2d 351 (2012).

Protected Class A group of persons protected by specific laws because of the group's defining characteristics, including race, color, religion, national origin, gender, age, and disability.

Employment Discrimination Treating employees or job applicants unequally on the basis of race, color, national origin, religion, gender, age, or disability.

color, religion, national origin, gender, age, or disability. A class of persons defined by one or more of these criteria is known as a **protected class.**

Several federal statutes prohibit **employment discrimination** against members of protected classes. Although here we focus on federal statutes, many states have their own laws that protect employees against discrimination, and some provide more protection to employees than federal laws do.

EXAMPLE 18.6 Even though the recession that started in 2007 has officially ended, unemployment is still high. Now, people who have been unemployed long term are facing apparent discrimination when they apply for jobs. Because people in this group do not form a protected class, they cannot sue for discrimination under federal law. They may soon get help from the states, however. At least thirteen states are considering legislation to prohibit discrimination against unemployed persons in help-wanted ads. •

(Lyndon Baines Johnson Presidential Library and Museum)

President Lyndon B. Johnson signs the 1964 Civil Rights Act. This legislation represented the most far-reaching set of antidiscrimination laws in modern times. Which groups in our country benefited most from this act?

Title VII of the Civil Rights Act of 1964

The most important statute covering employment discrimination is Title VII of the Civil Rights Act of 1964.[29] Title VII prohibits discrimination against employees, applicants, and union members on the basis of race, color, national origin, religion, or gender at any stage of employment. It prohibits both intentional and unintentional discrimination. (Although federal law prohibits job discrimination only if it is based on these specific categories, some jurisdictions are expanding their laws to include other types of discrimination. See this chapter's *Law, Diversity, and Business: Managerial Implications* feature on the following page for a discussion of this issue.)

Title VII applies to employers with fifteen or more employees and labor unions with fifteen or more members. Title VII also applies to labor unions that operate hiring halls (to which members go regularly to be rationed jobs as they become available), employment agencies, and state and local governing units or agencies A special section of the act prohibits discrimination in most federal government employment.

The Equal Employment Opportunity Commission Compliance with Title VII is monitored by the Equal Employment Opportunity Commission (EEOC). A victim of alleged discrimination must file a claim with the EEOC before bringing a suit against the employer. The EEOC may investigate the dispute and attempt to arrange an out-of-court settlement. If a voluntary agreement cannot be reached, the EEOC may file a suit against the employer on the employee's behalf.

The EEOC does not investigate every claim of employment discrimination. Generally, it investigates only "priority cases," such as cases involving retaliatory discharge (firing an employee in retaliation for submitting a claim to the EEOC) and cases involving types of discrimination that are of particular concern to the EEOC.

If the EEOC decides not to investigate the claim, the victim may bring her or his own lawsuit against the employer. In 2011, however, the United States Supreme Court issued a decision that limits the rights of employees—as a group, or class—to bring discrimination

---

29. 42 U.S.C. Sections 2000e–2000e-17.

LAW, DIVERSITY, AND BUSINESS: MANAGERIAL IMPLICATIONS

COMBATING APPEARANCE-BASED DISCRIMINATION

Research has shown that short men make less income than tall men. Statistical research has also shown that compared with attractive individuals, less attractive people generally receive poorer performance reviews, lower salaries, and smaller damages awards if they win lawsuits. Should something be done about this?

Can "Lookism" Be Prohibited?

Although there is certainly evidence that appearance-based discrimination exists in the workplace and elsewhere, it is not so clear that it can be prohibited. In the 1970s, Michigan decided to do something about "lookism" and passed a law barring various kinds of appearance-based discrimination.[a] Whether because of the cost or the difficulty of proving this type of discrimination, however, only a few lawsuits based on the law have been filed each year. At least six cities have similar laws, but these laws also have not given rise to many lawsuits.

Federal and state laws prohibit discrimination against people who are clinically obese, but discrimination against those who are merely overweight is usually not illegal. Given that one study found that more than 40 percent of overweight women felt stigmatized by their employers, this remains a serious problem.

A Double Standard for Grooming

Women sometimes complain that they are held to different grooming standards in the workplace than are their male counterparts. A female bartender at a casino in Nevada brought a lawsuit after she was fired for not complying with rules that required her to wear makeup and teased hair while male bartenders were just told to "look neat." The court ruled, however, that these allegations were not enough to outweigh an at-will employment contract.[b]

At the same time, women in senior management positions find that they can look "too sexy." A few years ago, a Citibank employee made headlines when she claimed that she was fired for her excessive sexiness, which supposedly distracted her male co-workers.

Business Implications

The United States has fought racism, sexism, and homophobia, and it seems likely that businesses will see an effort to combat "lookism." Managers should make sure that the jurisdiction in which their business operates does not already have laws against appearance-based discrimination.

---

a. Michigan Compiled Laws Section 37.2202.

b. *Jespersen v. Harrah's Operating Co.*, 444 F.3d 1104 (9th Cir. 2006).

---

claims against their employer under some circumstances. **CASE EXAMPLE 18.7** A group of female employees sued Wal-Mart, the nation's largest private employer, alleging that store managers who had discretion over pay and promotions were biased against women and disproportionately favored men. Wal-Mart argued that the women should not be allowed to bring the suit as a *class action*—a lawsuit in which a small number of plaintiffs sue on behalf of a larger group.

The United States Supreme Court ruled in favor of Wal-Mart, effectively blocking the class action. The Court held that the women could not maintain a class action because they had failed to prove a company-wide policy of discrimination that had a common effect on all women covered by the class action.[30] ● This decision did not affect the rights of individual employees to sue under Title VII.

Intentional Discrimination Intentional discrimination by an employer against an employee is known as **disparate-treatment discrimination.** Because intent can be difficult to prove, courts have established certain procedures for resolving disparate-treatment cases. Suppose that a woman applies for employment with a construction firm and is rejected. If she sues on the basis of disparate-treatment discrimination in hiring, she must show that (1) she is a member of a protected class, (2) she applied and was qualified for the job in

Disparate-Treatment Discrimination
A form of employment discrimination that results when an employer intentionally discriminates against employees who are members of protected classes.

---

30. *Wal-Mart Stores, Inc. v. Dukes,* ___ U.S. ___, 131 S.Ct. 2541, 180 L.Ed.2d 374 (2011).

question, (3) she was rejected by the employer, and (4) the employer continued to seek applicants for the position or filled the position with a person not in a protected class.

If the woman can meet these relatively easy requirements, she has made out a ***prima facie case*** of illegal discrimination. *Prima facie* is Latin for "at first sight." Legally, it refers to a fact that is presumed to be true unless contradicted by evidence. Making out a *prima facie* case of discrimination means that the plaintiff has met her initial burden of proof and will win in the absence of a legally acceptable employer defense. (Defenses are discussed later in this chapter.)

The burden then shifts to the employer-defendant, who must articulate a legal reason for not hiring the plaintiff. To prevail, the plaintiff must then show that the employer's reason is a *pretext* (not the true reason) and that the employer's decision was actually motivated by discriminatory intent.

Unintentional Discrimination
Employers often use interviews and tests to choose from among a large number of applicants for job openings. Minimum educational requirements are also common. These practices and procedures may have an unintended discriminatory impact on a protected class.

Disparate-impact discrimination occurs when a protected group of people is adversely affected by an employer's practices, procedures, or tests, even though they do not appear to be discriminatory. In a disparate-impact discrimination case, the complaining party must first show statistically that the employer's practices, procedures, or tests are discriminatory in effect. Once the plaintiff has made out a *prima facie* case, the burden of proof shifts to the employer to show that the practices or procedures in question were justified. There are two ways of proving that disparate-impact discrimination exists, as discussed next.

Pool of Applicants A plaintiff can prove a disparate impact by comparing the employer's workforce to the pool of qualified individuals available in the local labor market. The plaintiff must show that (1) as a result of educational or other job requirements or hiring procedures, (2) the percentage of nonwhites, women, or members of other protected classes in the employer's workforce (3) does not reflect the percentage of that group in the pool of qualified applicants. If the plaintiff can show a connection between the practice and the disparity, he or she has made out a *prima facie* case and need not provide evidence of discriminatory intent.

Rate of Hiring A plaintiff can also prove disparate-impact discrimination by comparing the selection rates of members and nonmembers of a protected class. When a job requirement or hiring procedure excludes members of a protected class from an employer's workforce at a substantially higher rate than nonmembers, discrimination occurs.

The EEOC has devised a test, called the "four-fifths rule," to determine whether an employment selection procedure is discriminatory on its face. Under this rule, a selection rate for protected classes that is less than four-fifths, or 80 percent, of the rate for the group with the highest rate will generally be regarded as evidence of disparate impact. **EXAMPLE 18.8** One hundred white applicants take an employment test, and fifty pass the test and are hired. One hundred minority applicants take the test, and twenty pass the test and are hired. Because twenty is less than four-fifths (80 percent) of fifty, the test would be considered discriminatory under the EEOC guidelines. •

Discrimination Based on Race, Color, and National Origin
Title VII prohibits employers from discriminating against employees or job applicants on the basis of race, color, or national origin. If an employer's standards for selecting or promoting employees have a discriminatory effect on job applicants or employees in these

LEARNING OBJECTIVE 5
What is the difference between disparate-treatment discrimination and disparate-impact discrimination?

Disparate-Impact Discrimination Discrimination that results from certain employer practices or procedures that, although not discriminatory on their face, have a discriminatory effect.

***Prima Facie* Case** A case in which the plaintiff has produced sufficient evidence of his or her claim that the case will be decided for the plaintiff unless the defendant produces no evidence to rebut it.

protected classes, then a presumption of illegal discrimination arises. To avoid liability, the employer must then show that its standards have a substantial, demonstrable relationship to realistic qualifications for the job in question.

CASE EXAMPLE 18.9   Jiann Min Chang was an instructor at Alabama Agricultural and Mechanical University (AAMU). When AAMU terminated his employment, Chang filed a lawsuit claiming discrimination based on national origin. Chang established a *prima facie* case because he (1) was a member of a protected class, (2) was qualified for the job, (3) suffered an adverse employment action, and (4) was replaced by someone outside his protected class (a non-Asian instructor). AAMU, however, showed that Chang had argued with a university vice president and refused to comply with her instructions. The court ruled that the university had not renewed Chang's contract for a legitimate reason— insubordination—and therefore was not liable for unlawful discrimination.[31] ●

Note that discrimination based on race can also take the form of *reverse discrimination,* or discrimination against "majority" individuals, such as white males. **CASE EXAMPLE 18.10**   An African American woman fired four white men from their management positions at a school district. The men filed a lawsuit for racial discrimination, alleging that the woman was trying to eliminate white males from the department. The woman claimed that the terminations were part of a reorganization plan to cut costs. The jury sided with the men and awarded them damages.[32] ●

Victims of racial or ethnic discrimination may also have a cause of action under 42 U.S.C. Section 1981 which prohibits discrimination on the basis of race or ethnicity in the formation or enforcement of contracts.

Discrimination Based on Religion

Title VII also prohibits government employers, private employers, and unions from discriminating against persons because of their religion. Employers cannot treat their employees more or less favorably based on their religious beliefs or practices and cannot require employees to participate in any religious activity (or forbid them from participating in one).

An employer must also "reasonably accommodate" the religious practices of its employees, unless to do so would cause undue hardship to the employer's business. This is true even if an employee's religious beliefs are not based on the doctrines of a traditionally recognized religion or denomination. The only requirement is that the beliefs be sincerely held by the employee. If an employee's religion prohibits him or her from working on a certain day of the week or at a certain type of job, for instance, the employer must make a reasonable attempt to accommodate these religious requirements.

A reasonable attempt to accommodate does not necessarily require the employer to give an employee the requested day off permanently, if to do so would cause the employer undue hardship. **CASE EXAMPLE 18.11**   Miguel Sánchez–Rodríguez sold cell phones in shopping malls for AT&T. After six years, Sánchez informed his supervisors that he had become a Seventh Day Adventist and could no longer work on Saturdays for religious reasons. AT&T responded that his inability to work on Saturdays would cause it hardship.

As a reasonable accommodation, the company suggested that Sánchez swap schedules with others and offered him two other positions that did not require work on Saturdays. Sánchez could not find workers to swap shifts with him, however, and he declined the other jobs because the pay was lower. He began missing work on Saturdays. After he was disciplined by AT&T, Sánchez resigned and filed a religious discrimination lawsuit against the company. The court found in favor of AT&T, and a federal appellate court affirmed. The

Under Title VII, can employers prohibit employees from participating in religious activities such as reciting prayers? Why or why not?

(Juanmonino/iStockphoto.com)

---

31. *Jiann Min Chang v. Alabama Agricultural and Mechanical University,* 2009 WL 3403180 (11th Cir. 2009).
32. *Johnston v. School District of Philadelphia,* 2006 WL 999966 (E.D.Pa. 2006).

company had made adequate efforts to accommodate by allowing Sánchez to swap shifts and offering him other positions that did not require work on Saturdays.[33] ●

"A sign that says 'men only' looks very different on a bathroom door than a courthouse door."

Thurgood Marshall, 1908–1993 (Associate justice of the United States Supreme Court, 1967–1991)

President Obama signed the Lilly Ledbetter Fair Pay Act in 2009.

(AP Photo/Pablo Martinez Monsivais)

Constructive Discharge A termination of employment brought about by making the employee's working conditions so intolerable that the employee reasonably feels compelled to leave.

Discrimination Based on Gender

Under Title VII, as well as other federal acts, employers are forbidden from discriminating against employees on the basis of gender. Employers are prohibited from classifying jobs as male or female and from advertising positions as male or female unless the employer can prove that the gender of the applicant is essential to the job. In addition, employers cannot have separate male and female seniority lists or refuse to promote employees based on gender. In 1978, the definition of *gender discrimination* was expanded to include discrimination based on pregnancy.

Generally, to succeed in a suit for gender discrimination, a plaintiff must demonstrate that gender was a determining factor in the employer's decision to fire or refuse to hire or promote her or him. Typically, this involves looking at all of the surrounding circumstances.

CASE EXAMPLE 18.12 Wanda Collier worked for Turner Industries Group, LLC, in the maintenance department. She complained to her supervisor that Jack Daniell, the head of the department, treated her unfairly. Her supervisor told her that Daniell had a problem with her gender and was harder on women. The supervisor talked to Daniell but did not take any disciplinary action. A month later, Daniell confronted Collier, pushing her up against a wall and berating her. After this incident, Collier filed a formal complaint and kept a male co-worker with her at all times. A month later, she was fired. She subsequently filed a lawsuit alleging gender discrimination. The court concluded that there was enough evidence that gender was a determining factor in Daniell's conduct to allow Collier's claims to go to a jury.[34] ●

Several laws prohibit employers from gender-based wage discrimination. The Equal Pay Act requires equal pay for male and female employees doing similar work at the same establishment (a barber and a hair stylist, for example). To determine whether the Equal Pay Act has been violated, a court will look to the primary duties of the two jobs—the job content rather than the job description controls. If the wage differential is due to "any factor other than gender," such as a seniority or merit system, then it does not violate the Equal Pay Act.

The continuing disparity between the wages of men and women prompted Congress to pass two additional laws in 2009 to address wage discrimination. The Paycheck Fairness Act prohibited the use of gender-based differentials in assessing an employee's education, training, or experience and provided additional remedies for wage discrimination. The Lilly Ledbetter Fair Pay Act strengthened women's ability to file wage discrimination complaints by removing time restrictions on when a complaint could be filed.[35]

Constructive Discharge

Most Title VII complaints involve unlawful discrimination in decisions to hire or fire employees. In some situations, however, employees who leave their jobs voluntarily can claim that they were "constructively discharged" by the employer. **Constructive discharge** occurs when the employer causes the employee's working conditions to be so intolerable that a reasonable person in the employee's position would feel compelled to quit.

To prove constructive discharge, the plaintiff must present objective proof of intolerable working conditions. The employer must have known or had reason to know about these conditions yet failed to correct them within a reasonable time period. Courts generally also require the employee to show causation—that the employer's unlawful discrimination caused the working conditions to be intolerable.

---

33. *Sánchez-Rodríquez v. AT&T Mobility Puerto Rico, Inc.,* 673 F.3d 1 (1st Cir. 2012).
34. *Collier v. Turner Industries Group, LLC,* 797 F.Supp.2d 1029 (D. Idaho 2011).
35. Pub. L. No. 111-2, 123 Stat. 5 (January 5, 2009), amending 42 U.S.C. Section 2000e-5[e].

Employee demotion is one of the most frequently cited reasons for a finding of constructive discharge, particularly when the employee was subjected to humiliation. **EXAMPLE 18.13** Khalil's employer humiliates him in front of his co-workers by informing him that he is being demoted to an inferior position. Khalil's co-workers then continually insult and harass him about his national origin (he is from Iran). The employer is aware of this discriminatory treatment but does nothing to remedy the situation, despite repeated complaints from Khalil. After several months, Khalil quits his job and files a Title VII claim. In this situation, Khalil would likely have sufficient evidence to maintain an action for constructive discharge in violation of Title VII. •

Plaintiffs can use constructive discharge to establish any type of discrimination claims under Title VII, including race, color, national origin, religion, gender, and sexual harassment. Constructive discharge has also been successfully used in situations involving discrimination based on age or disability (discussed later in this chapter). Constructive discharge is most commonly asserted in cases involving sexual harassment, however.

When constructive discharge is claimed, the employee can pursue damages for loss of income, including back pay. These damages ordinarily are not available to an employee who left a job voluntarily.

Sexual Harassment The demanding of sexual favors in return for job promotions or other benefits, or language or conduct that is so sexually offensive that it creates a hostile working environment.

Sexual Harassment

Title VII also protects employees against **sexual harassment** in the workplace. Sexual harassment can take two forms: *quid pro quo* harassment and hostile-environment harassment. *Quid pro quo* is a Latin phrase that is often translated to mean "something in exchange for something else." *Quid pro quo* harassment occurs when sexual favors are demanded in return for job opportunities, promotions, salary increases, and the like. Hostile-environment harassment occurs when "the workplace is permeated with discriminatory intimidation, ridicule, and insult, that is sufficiently severe or pervasive to alter the conditions of the victim's employment and create an abusive working environment."[36]

The courts determine whether sexually offensive conduct was sufficiently severe or pervasive to create a hostile environment on a case-by-case basis. Typically, a single incident is not enough to create a hostile environment (although there have been exceptions when the conduct was particularly objectionable). Note also that if the employee who is alleging sexual harassment has signed an employment contract with an arbitration clause (see Chapter 3), she or he will most likely be required to arbitrate the claim.

PREVENTING LEGAL DISPUTES

To avoid sexual-harassment complaints, be proactive in preventing sexual harassment in the workplace. Establish written policies, distribute them to employees, and review them annually. Make it clear that the policies prohibiting harassment and discrimination apply to everyone at all levels of your organization. Provide training. Assure employees that no one will be punished for making a complaint. If you receive complaints, always take them seriously and investigate—no matter how trivial they might seem.

Prompt remedial action is key, but it must not include any adverse action against the complainant (such as immediate termination). Also, never discourage employees from seeking the assistance of government agencies (such as the EEOC) or threaten or punish them for doing so. It is generally best to obtain the advice of counsel when you receive a sexual-harassment complaint.

---

36. *Harris v. Forklift Systems,* 510 U.S. 17, 114 S.Ct. 367, 126 L.Ed.2d 295 (1993). See also *Billings v. Town of Grafton,* 515 F.3d 39 (1st Cir. 2008).

Harassment by Supervisors For an employer to be held liable for a supervisor's sexual harassment, the supervisor normally must have taken a *tangible employment action* against the employee. A **tangible employment action** is a significant change in employment status or benefits, such as when an employee is fired, refused a promotion, demoted, or reassigned to a position with significantly different responsibilities. Only a supervisor, or another person acting with the authority of the employer, can cause this sort of injury. A constructive discharge also qualifies as a tangible employment action.

Tangible Employment Action A significant change in employment status or benefits, such as occurs when an employee is fired, refused a promotion, or reassigned to a lesser position.

The United States Supreme Court has issued several important rulings that have had a lasting impact on cases alleging sexual harassment by supervisors.[37] The Court held that an employer (a city) was liable for a supervisor's harassment of employees even though the employer was unaware of the behavior. Although the city had a written policy against sexual harassment, it had not distributed the policy to its employees and had not established any complaint procedures for employees who felt that they had been sexually harassed. In another case, the Court held that an employer can be liable for a supervisor's sexual harassment even though the employee does not suffer adverse job consequences.

A presumed victim of sexual harassment attends a press conference with her attorney. What hurdles will she face in such litigation?

(AP Photo/Bay Area News Group, Oakland Tribune, Laura A. Oda)

The Court's decisions in these cases established what has become known as the *"Ellerth/Faragher* affirmative defense" to charges of sexual harassment. The defense has two elements:

1. The employer has taken reasonable care to prevent and promptly correct any sexually harassing behavior (by establishing effective antiharassment policies and complaint procedures, for example).
2. The plaintiff-employee unreasonably failed to take advantage of any preventive or corrective opportunities provided by the employer to avoid harm.

An employer that can prove both elements will not be liable for a supervisor's harassment.

Retaliation by Employers Employers sometimes retaliate against employees who complain about sexual harassment or other Title VII violations. An employer might demote or fire the person, for instance, or otherwise change the terms, conditions, and benefits of employment. Title VII prohibits retaliation, and employees can sue their employers. In a *retaliation claim,* an individual asserts that she or he has suffered a harm as a result of making a charge, testifying, or participating in a Title VII investigation or proceeding.

> "Sexual harassment at work: Is it a problem for the self-employed?"
>
> Victoria Wood, 1953–present (English comedian and actor)

To prove retaliation, plaintiffs must show that the challenged action was one that would likely have dissuaded a reasonable worker from making or supporting a charge of discrimination. Title VII's retaliation protection extends to an employee who speaks out about discrimination against another employee during an employer's internal investigation. A court also held that it protected an employee who was fired after his fiancée filed a gender discrimination claim against their employer.[38]

In the following case, a female law professor lost her job after she complained about comments made by her dean and colleagues. The court had to decide whether she had been retaliated against for engaging in protected conduct.

---

37. *Burlington Industries, Inc. v. Ellerth,* 524 U.S. 742, 118 S.Ct. 2257, 141 L.Ed.2d 633 (1998); and *Faragher v. City of Boca Raton,* 524 U.S. 775, 118 S.Ct. 2275, 141 L.Ed.2d 662 (1998).

38. See *Thompson v. North American Stainless, LP,* ___ U.S. ___, 131 S.Ct. 863, 178 L.Ed.2d 694 (2011).

Case 18.2

Morales-Cruz v. University of Puerto Rico

United States Court of Appeals, First Circuit,
676 F.3d 220 (2012).
www.ca1.uscourts.gov [a]

(Diego Cervo/Shutterstock.com)

FACTS In 2003, Myrta Morales-Cruz began a tenure-track teaching position at the University of Puerto Rico School of Law. During her probationary period, one of her colleagues in a law school clinic had an affair with a student that resulted in a pregnancy. In 2008, Morales-Cruz asked the university's administrative committee to approve a one-year extension for her tenure review. The law school's dean criticized Morales-Cruz for failing to report her colleague's affair. He later recommended granting the extension but called Morales-Cruz "insecure," "immature," and "fragile." Similarly, a law school committee recommended granting the extension, but a dissenting professor commented that Morales-Cruz had shown poor judgment, had "personality flaws," and had trouble with "complex and sensitive" situations.

Morales-Cruz soon learned about the negative comments and complained in writing to the university's chancellor. The dean then recommended denying the one-year extension, and the administrative committee ultimately did so. When her employment was terminated, Morales-Cruz sued the university under Title VII. Among other things, she asserted that the dean had retaliated against her for complaining to the chancellor. A federal district court found that Morales-Cruz had not stated a proper retaliation claim under Title VII, and she appealed.

ISSUE Can Morales-Cruz bring a retaliation claim under Title VII based on her assertion that the law school's dean had retaliated against her for complaining to the university's chancellor?

DECISION No. The appellate court affirmed the district court's judgment for the University of Puerto Rico.

REASON Under Title VII, an employer may not retaliate against an employee because he or she has opposed a practice prohibited by Title VII. In this case, Morales-Cruz argued that the dean recommended against the one-year extension because she had complained about "discriminatory" comments. The court found that Morales-Cruz did not allege any facts that could be construed as gender-based discrimination. While the comments were hardly flattering, they were entirely gender-neutral. After all, the dean and dissenting professor said only that Morales-Cruz had shown poor judgment, had personality flaws, and was fragile, insecure, and immature. Thus, even if the dean retaliated against Morales-Cruz, it was not for engaging in conduct protected by Title VII.

CRITICAL THINKING—Ethical Consideration *Could the dean have had legitimate reasons for changing his mind about the one-year extension? If so, what might they have been?*

---

a. In the right-hand column, click on "Opinions." On the next page, in the "Short Title *contains*" box, type "Morales-Cruz," and click on "Submit Search." In the result, click on the link to access the opinion.

Harassment by Co-Workers and Nonemployees When the harassment of co-workers, rather than supervisors, creates a hostile working environment, an employee may still have a cause of action against the employer. Normally, though, the employer will be held liable only if the employer knew, or should have known, about the harassment and failed to take immediate remedial action.

Same-Gender Harassment In *Oncale v. Sundowner Offshore Services, Inc.,*[39] the United States Supreme Court held that Title VII protection extends to individuals who are sexually harassed by members of the same gender. Proving that the harassment in same-gender cases is "based on sex" can be difficult, though. When the victim is homosexual, some courts have found that the harasser's conduct does not qualify as sexual harassment under Title VII because it was based on the employee's sexual orientation, not on his or her "sex."

Although federal law (Title VII) does not prohibit discrimination or harassment based on sexual orientation, a growing number of states have enacted laws that prohibit such

---

39. 523 U.S. 75, 118 S.Ct. 998, 140 L.Ed.2d 207 (1998).

discrimination in private employment. Some states, such as Michigan, explicitly prohibit discrimination based on a person's gender identity or expression. Also, many companies have voluntarily established nondiscrimination policies that include sexual orientation.

Online Harassment   Employees' online activities can create a hostile working environment in many ways. Racial jokes, ethnic slurs, or other comments contained in e-mail, text or instant messages, and social media or blog posts can become the basis for a claim of hostile-environment harassment or other forms of discrimination. A worker who regularly sees sexually explicit and offensive images on a co-worker's computer screen or tablet device may claim that they create a hostile working environment.

Employers may be able to avoid liability for online harassment if they take prompt remedial action.   **EXAMPLE 18.14**   While working at TriCom, Shonda Dean receives racially harassing e-mail from another employee. Shortly afterward, the company issues a warning to the offending employee about the proper use of the e-mail system and holds two meetings to discuss company policy on the use of the system. If Dean sues TriCom for racial discrimination, a court may find that because the employer took prompt remedial action, TriCom should not be held liable for its employee's racially harassing e-mails. •

Remedies under Title VII   Employer liability under Title VII may be extensive. If the plaintiff proves that unlawful discrimination occurred, he or she may be awarded reinstatement, back pay, retroactive promotions, and damages. Compensatory damages are available only in cases of intentional discrimination. Punitive damages may be recovered against a private employer only if the employer acted with malice or reckless indifference to an individual's rights. The total amount of compensatory and punitive damages that the plaintiff can recover depends on the size of the employer. The cap ranges from $50,000 for employers with one hundred or fewer employees to $300,000 for employers with more than five hundred employees.

Discrimination Based on Age

Age discrimination is potentially the most widespread form of discrimination, because anyone—regardless of race, color, national origin, or gender—could eventually be a victim. The Age Discrimination in Employment Act (ADEA)[40] prohibits employment discrimination on the basis of age against individuals forty years of age or older. The act also prohibits mandatory retirement for nonmanagerial workers. For the act to apply, an employer must have twenty or more employees, and the employer's business activities must affect interstate commerce. The EEOC administers the ADEA, but the act also permits private causes of action against employers for age discrimination.

Procedures under the ADEA   The burden-shifting procedure under the ADEA differs from the procedure under Title VII as a result of a 2009 United States Supreme Court decision that dramatically changed the burden of proof in age discrimination cases.[41] As explained earlier, if the plaintiff in a Title VII case can show that the employer was motivated, at least in part, by unlawful discrimination, the burden of proof shifts to the employer. Thus, in cases in which the employer has a "mixed motive" for discharging an employee, the employer has the burden of proving its reason was legitimate.

Under the ADEA, in contrast, a plaintiff must show that the unlawful discrimination was not just a reason but *the* reason for the adverse employment action. Thus, to establish a *prima facie* case, the plaintiff must show that he or she (1) was a member of the protected

---

40. 29 U.S.C. Sections 621–634.
41. *Gross v. FBL Financial Services,* 557 U.S. 167, 129 S.Ct. 2343, 174 L.Ed.2d 119 (2009).

age group, (2) was qualified for the position, and (3) was discharged or rejected because of age discrimination. Then the burden shifts to the employer. If the employer offers a legitimate reason for its action, then the plaintiff must show that the stated reason is only a pretext and that the plaintiff's age was the real reason for the employer's decision. The following case illustrates this procedure.

Case 18.3

Mora v. Jackson Memorial Foundation, Inc.

United States Court of Appeals, Eleventh Circuit,
597 F.3d 1201 (2010).
www.ca11.uscourts.gov/opinions/search.php[a]

When is firing an older worker considered age discrimination?

FACTS Josephine Mora, a fund-raiser for Jackson Memorial Foundation, Inc., was sixty-two years old when the foundation's chief executive officer (CEO) fired her, citing errors and issues with professionalism. Mora filed a suit against the foundation, alleging age discrimination. She asserted that when she was fired, the CEO told her, "I need someone younger I can pay less." She had a witness who had heard that statement as well as another in which the CEO said that Mora was "too old to be working here anyway." The foundation moved for summary judgment, arguing that Mora was fired chiefly because she was incompetent. The district court granted the motion, and Mora appealed.

ISSUE Did Mora present sufficient evidence that the employer's stated reason for firing her was only a pretext?

DECISION Yes. The U.S. Court of Appeals for the Eleventh Circuit set aside the decision of the trial court and remanded the case for a trial.

REASON Because there was a "disputed question of material fact" as to whether the plaintiff had been fired because of her age, the defendant was not entitled to summary judgment. The district court should *not* have examined the question of whether Mora would have been fired no matter what her age was simply because she had become incompetent. "The resolution of this case depends on whose account of the pertinent conversations a jury would credit. A reasonable juror could accept that [the CEO] made the discriminatory-sounding remarks and that the remarks are sufficient evidence of a discriminatory motive." A reasonable juror could conclude that that the CEO fired Mora because of her age.

CRITICAL THINKING—Ethical Consideration *Is the court's decision fair to employers? Why or why not?*

a. In the "Search by Keyword:" box, type "Jackson Memorial," and click on "Search." When that page opens, click on the link to access the opinion.

"Growing old is like being increasingly penalized for a crime you have not committed."

Anthony Powell, 1905–2000
(English novelist)

State Employees Not Covered by the ADEA   Generally, the states are immune from lawsuits brought by private individuals in federal court. This immunity stems from the United States Supreme Court's interpretation of the Eleventh Amendment (included in Appendix B of this text). In some situations, such as when fundamental rights are at stake, Congress has the power to override state immunity to private suits through legislation. As a general rule, though, the Court has found that state employers are immune from private suits brought by employees under the ADEA (for age discrimination), the Americans with Disabilities Act (for disability discrimination), and the Fair Labor Standards Act (which relates to wages and hours). States are not immune from the requirements of the Family and Medical Leave Act, however.

Discrimination Based on Disability

The Americans with Disabilities Act (ADA)[42] prohibits disability-based discrimination in workplaces with fifteen or more workers (with the exception of state government employers, who are generally immune under the Eleventh Amendment, as just discussed). Basically, the ADA requires that employers reasonably accommodate the needs of persons with disabilities unless to do so would cause the employer to suffer an undue hardship. In 2008, Congress amended and broadened the coverage of the ADA's protections.

Procedures under the ADA

To prevail on a claim under the ADA, a plaintiff must show that he or she (1) has a disability, (2) is otherwise qualified for the employment in question, and (3) was excluded from the employment solely because of the disability. As in Title VII cases, a plaintiff must pursue her or his claim through the EEOC before filing an action in court for a violation of the ADA.

The EEOC may decide to investigate and perhaps even sue the employer on behalf of the employee. If the EEOC decides not to sue, then the employee is entitled to sue in court. According to the United States Supreme Court, the EEOC can bring a suit against an employer for disability-based discrimination even though the employee previously agreed to submit any job-related disputes to arbitration (see Chapter 3).[43]

Plaintiffs in lawsuits brought under the ADA may obtain many of the same remedies available under Title VII. These include reinstatement, back pay, a limited amount of compensatory and punitive damages (for intentional discrimination), and certain other forms of relief. Repeat violators may be ordered to pay fines of up to $100,000.

What Is a Disability?

The ADA is broadly drafted to cover persons with a wide range of disabilities. Specifically, the ADA defines *disability* to include any of the following:

1. A physical or mental impairment that substantially limits one or more of an individual's major life activities.
2. A record of such impairment.
3. Being regarded as having such an impairment.

Health conditions that have been considered disabilities under the federal law include blindness, alcoholism, heart disease, cancer, muscular dystrophy, cerebral palsy, paraplegia, diabetes, acquired immune deficiency syndrome (AIDS), testing positive for the human immunodeficiency virus (HIV), and morbid obesity (defined as existing when an individual's weight is two times the normal weight for his or her height).

Reasonable Accommodation and Undue Hardship

The ADA does not require that employers accommodate the needs of job applicants or employees with disabilities who are not otherwise qualified for the work. If a job applicant or an employee with a disability can perform essential job functions with a reasonable accommodation, however, the employer must make the accommodation.

Required modifications may include installing ramps for a wheelchair, establishing more flexible working hours, creating or modifying job assignments, and creating or improving training materials and procedures. Generally, employers should give primary consideration to employees' preferences in deciding what accommodations should be made.

> "Jobs are physically easier, but the worker now takes home worries instead of an aching back."
>
> Homer Bigart, 1907–1991
> (American journalist)

42. 42 U.S.C. Sections 12102–12118.
43. *EEOC v. Waffle House, Inc.,* 534 U.S. 279, 122 S.Ct. 754, 151 L.Ed.2d 755 (2002).

Employers who do not accommodate the needs of persons with disabilities must demonstrate that the accommodations will cause "undue hardship" in terms of being significantly difficult or expensive for the employer. Usually, the courts decide whether an accommodation constitutes an undue hardship on a case-by-case basis by looking at the employer's resources in relation to the specific accommodation.

Job Applications and Preemployment Physical Exams Employers must modify their job-application process so that those with disabilities can compete for jobs with those who do not have disabilities. For instance, a job announcement might be modified to allow job applicants to respond by e-mail or letter, as well as by telephone, so that it does not discriminate against potential applicants with hearing impairments.

Employers are restricted in the kinds of questions they may ask on job-application forms and during preemployment interviews. Furthermore, they cannot require persons with disabilities to submit to preemployment physicals unless such exams are required of all other applicants. Employers can condition an offer of employment on the applicant's successfully passing a medical examination, but can disqualify the applicant only if the medical problems they discover would render the applicant unable to perform the job.

CASE EXAMPLE 18.15 When filling the position of delivery truck driver, a company cannot automatically screen out all applicants who are unable to meet the U.S. Department of Transportation's hearing standard. The company would first have to prove that drivers who are deaf are not qualified to perform the essential job function of driving safely and pose a higher risk of accidents than drivers who are not deaf.[44] ●

Substance Abusers Drug addiction is a disability under the ADA because drug addiction is a substantially limiting impairment. Those who are actually using illegal drugs are not protected by the act, however. The ADA protects only persons with *former* drug addictions—those who have completed or are now in a supervised drug-rehabilitation program. Individuals who have used drugs casually in the past are not protected under the act. They are not considered addicts and therefore do not have a disability (addiction).

People suffering from alcoholism are protected by the ADA. Of course, employers have the right to prohibit the use of alcohol in the workplace and can require that employees not be under the influence of alcohol while working. Employers can also fire or refuse to hire a person who is an alcoholic if he or she poses a substantial risk of harm either to himself or herself or to others and the risk cannot be reduced by reasonable accommodation.

Health-Insurance Plans Workers with disabilities must be given equal access to any health insurance provided to other employees. Under 2010 health-care reforms, employers cannot exclude preexisting health conditions from coverage. An employer can put a limit, or cap, on health-care payments under its group health policy as long as such caps are "applied equally to all insured employees" and do not "discriminate on the basis of disability."

Defenses to Employment Discrimination

The first line of defense for an employer charged with employment discrimination is, of course, to assert that the plaintiff has failed to meet his or her initial burden of proving that discrimination occurred. Once a plaintiff succeeds in proving discrimination, the burden shifts to the employer to justify the discriminatory practice. In some situations, as noted

---

44. *Bates v. United Parcel Service, Inc.,* 465 F.3d 1069 (9th Cir. 2006).

earlier, an effective antiharassment policy and prompt remedial action when harassment occurs may shield employers from liability for sexual harassment under Title VII. Other possible defenses are discussed next.

Business Necessity A defense to an allegation of employment discrimination in which the employer demonstrates that an employment practice that discriminates against members of a protected class is related to job performance.

Business Necessity

An employer may defend against a claim of disparate-impact (unintentional) discrimination by asserting that a practice that has a discriminatory effect is a **business necessity**. **EXAMPLE 18.16** If requiring a high school diploma is shown to have a discriminatory effect, an employer might argue that a high school education is necessary for workers to perform the job at a required level of competence. If the employer can demonstrate a definite connection between a high school education and job performance, the employer normally will succeed in this business necessity defense. ●

Bona Fide Occupational Qualification (BFOQ) Identifiable characteristics reasonably necessary to the normal operation of a particular business. These characteristics can include gender, national origin, and religion, but not race.

Bona Fide Occupational Qualification

Another defense applies when discrimination against a protected class is essential to a job—that is, when a particular trait is a **bona fide occupational qualification (BFOQ)**. **EXAMPLE 18.17** A women's clothing store might legitimately hire only female sales attendants if part of an attendant's job involves assisting clients in the store's dressing rooms. Similarly, the Federal Aviation Administration can legitimately impose age limits for airline pilots. In contrast, an airline cannot impose weight limits only on female flight attendants. ●

Note that race can never be a BFOQ. Generally, courts have restricted the BFOQ defense to instances in which the employee's gender is essential to the job.

Seniority System A system in which those who have worked longest for an employer are first in line for promotions, salary increases, and other benefits, and are last to be laid off if the workforce must be reduced.

Seniority Systems

An employer with a history of discrimination might have no members of protected classes in upper-level positions. Even if the employer now seeks to be unbiased, some employees may bring a lawsuit asking a court to order that minorities be promoted ahead of schedule to compensate for past discrimination. If no present intent to discriminate is shown, however, and if promotions or other job benefits are distributed according to a fair **seniority system**, the employer normally has a good defense against the suit.

CASE EXAMPLE 18.18 A baggage handler who had injured his back asked to be reassigned to a mailroom at U.S. Airways, Inc. The airline refused to give the employee the position because another employee had seniority. The Court sided with U.S. Airways. If an employee with a disability requests an accommodation that conflicts with an employer's seniority system, the accommodation generally will not be considered "reasonable" under the act.[45] ●

After-Acquired Evidence of Employee Misconduct

In some situations, employers have attempted to avoid liability for employment discrimination on the basis of "after-acquired evidence" of an employee's misconduct. **EXAMPLE 18.19** An employer fires a worker who then sues the employer for employment discrimination. During pretrial investigation, the employer learns that the employee made material misrepresentations on his employment application—misrepresentations that, had the employer known about them, would have served as grounds to fire the individual. ●

After-acquired evidence of wrongdoing cannot shield an employer entirely from liability for employment discrimination. It may, however, be used to limit the amount of damages for which the employer is liable.

---

45. *U.S. Airways, Inc. v. Barnett,* 535 U.S. 391, 122 S.Ct. 1516, 152 L.Ed.2d 589 (2002).

Reviewing . . . Employment Law

Amaani Lyle, an African American woman, took a job as a scriptwriters' assistant at Warner Brothers Television Productions. She worked for the writers of *Friends,* a popular, adult-oriented television series. One of her essential job duties was to type detailed notes for the scriptwriters during brainstorming sessions in which they discussed jokes, dialogue, and story lines. The writers then combed through Lyle's notes after the meetings for script material. During these meetings, the three male scriptwriters told lewd and vulgar jokes and made sexually explicit comments and gestures. They often talked about their personal sexual experiences and fantasies, and some of these conversations were then used in episodes of *Friends.*

During the meetings, Lyle never complained that she found the writers' conduct offensive. After four months, she was fired because she could not type fast enough to keep up with the writers' conversations during the meetings. She filed a suit against Warner Brothers alleging sexual harassment and claiming that her termination was based on racial discrimination. Using the information presented in the chapter, answer the following questions.

1. Would Lyle's claim of racial discrimination be for intentional (disparate-treatment) or unintentional (disparate-impact) discrimination? Explain.
2. Can Lyle establish a *prima facie* case of racial discrimination? Why or why not?
3. When she was hired, Lyle was told that typing speed was extremely important to her position. At the time, she maintained that she could type eighty words per minute, so she was not given a typing test. It later turned out that Lyle could type only fifty words per minute. What impact might typing speed have on Lyle's lawsuit?
4. Lyle's sexual-harassment claim is based on the hostile work environment created by the writers' sexually offensive conduct at meetings that she was required to attend. The writers, however, argue that their behavior was essential to the "creative process" of writing *Friends,* a show that routinely contained sexual innuendos and adult humor. Which defense discussed in the chapter might Warner Brothers assert using this argument?

DEBATE THIS: Members of minority groups and women have made enough economic progress in the last several decades that they no longer need special legislation to protect them.

BUSINESS APPLICATION

How to Develop a Policy on Employee Use of the Internet and Social Media*

Employers that make the Internet, e-mail, smartphones, and social networking sites available to their employees face some obvious risks. The employer could be liable if an employee harasses another employee via e-mail or a social networking site such as Facebook. Similarly, the employer could be liable if an employee uses the Internet to violate copyright and other intellectual property laws. Another risk is that an outside party might intercept confidential information or trade secrets contained in communications transmitted via the Internet.

But if the employer monitors employees' use of the Internet and social media in an attempt to avoid these problems, the employer risks being held liable for violating employees' privacy. Remember that a small company can be bankrupted by just one successful lawsuit against it. Even if the company wins the suit, it will likely have incurred substantial legal fees. Therefore, if you are an employer

*This *Business Application* is not meant to substitute for the services of an attorney who is licensed to practice law in your state.

and find it necessary to monitor your employees' use of the Internet and social media, you should take care when creating your policy.

Inform Employees of the Monitoring and Obtain Their Consent

First, notify your employees that you will be monitoring their online communications and specify what will be monitored (e-mail, smartphones, text messages, posts on Facebook and other social media, and the like). Also state clearly whether you will monitor all work-related communications, even those sent via the employees' own devices, or whether you will monitor only communications sent via devices furnished by the company. Second, ask all employees to consent, in writing, to this monitoring.

Spell Out Permissible and Impermissible Uses

To ensure that employees understand what they may and may not do, develop comprehensive guidelines for Internet and social media use. Include specific examples of prohibited activities.

Policies for Social Media

Be careful when creating policies on social media use. Employees have free speech and privacy rights, so make sure that you have a legitimate business reason for any restrictions you impose. Do not attempt to interfere with employees' discussions of wages and working conditions on social media sites—these are protected under federal labor law.

An employer can encourage employees to use discretion in posts on social media and can discourage them from making negative comments about co-workers. You probably can prohibit employees from disclosing confidential or personal information about customers, clients, co-workers, and possibly suppliers. You might also be able to restrict employees from making negative statements about the firm or its products and services.

Checklist for the Employer

1. *Inform employees that their Internet and social media communications will be monitored, and indicate which communications and which devices will be monitored.*
2. *Obtain employees' written consent to having their electronic communications monitored.*
3. *Develop a comprehensive policy statement that explains how the Internet and social media should and should not be used.*
4. *Designate a person at the company that employees can go to if they have questions or concerns about the firm's policies on Internet or social media use.*

Key Terms

bona fide occupational qualification (BFOQ) 543	disparate-treatment discrimination 532	minimum wage 518	tangible employment action 537
business necessity 543	employment at will 516	*prima facie* case 533	vesting 523
constructive discharge 535	employment discrimination 531	protected class 531	whistleblowing 517
disparate-impact discrimination 533	I-9 verification 528	seniority system 543	workers' compensation laws 521
	I-551 Alien Registration Receipt 529	sexual harassment 536	wrongful discharge 517

Chapter Summary: Employment Law

Employment at Will (See pages 516–517.)	1. *Employment-at-will doctrine*—Under this common law doctrine, either party may terminate the employment relationship at any time and for any reason ("at will").
	2. *Exceptions to the employment-at-will doctrine*—Courts have made exceptions to the doctrine on the basis of contract theory, tort theory, and public policy. Whistleblowers have occasionally received protection under the common law for reasons of public policy.
	3. *Wrongful discharge*—Whenever an employer discharges an employee in violation of an employment contract or statutory law protecting employees, the employee may bring a suit for wrongful discharge.
Wages, Hours, and Layoffs (See pages 517–520.)	1. *Davis-Bacon Act (1931)*—Requires contractors and subcontractors working on federal government construction projects to pay their employees "prevailing wages."
	2. *Walsh-Healey Act (1936)*—Requires firms that contract with federal agencies to pay their employees a minimum wage and overtime pay.
	3. *Fair Labor Standards Act (1938)*—Extended wage and hour requirements to cover all employers whose activities affect interstate commerce plus certain other businesses. The act has specific requirements in regard to child labor, maximum hours, and minimum wages.
	4. *The Worker Adjustment and Retraining Notification (WARN) Act*—Applies to employers with at least one hundred full-time employees and requires that sixty days' advance notice of mass layoffs be given to affected employees.
	5. *State layoff notice requirements*—May be different from and even stricter than the WARN Act's requirements.

Continued

Chapter Summary: Employment Law—Continued

Family and Medical Leave (See pages 520–521.)	The Family and Medical Leave Act (FMLA) requires employers with fifty or more employees to provide employees with up to twelve weeks of unpaid leave (twenty-six weeks for military caregiver leave) during any twelve-month period. 1. *Family leave*—May be taken to care for a newborn baby, a newly adopted child, or a new foster child. 2. *Medical leave*—May be taken when the employee or the employee's spouse, child, or parent has a serious health condition requiring care. 3. *Military caregiver leave*—May be taken to care for a family member with a serious injury or illness incurred as a result of military duty. 4. *Qualifying exigency leave*—May be taken to handle specified nonmedical emergencies when a spouse, parent, or child is in, or called to, active military duty.
Worker Health, Safety, and Income Security (See pages 521–524.)	1. *Occupational Safety and Health Act*—Requires employers to meet specific safety and health standards that are established and enforced by the Occupational Safety and Health Administration (OSHA). 2. *State workers' compensation laws*—Establish an administrative procedure for compensating workers who are injured in accidents that occur on the job, regardless of fault. 3. *Social Security and Medicare*—The Social Security Act of 1935 provides for old-age (retirement), survivors', and disability insurance. Both employers and employees must make contributions under the Federal Insurance Contributions Act (FICA). The Social Security Administration also administers Medicare, a health-insurance program for older or disabled persons. 4. *Private pension plans*—The federal Employee Retirement Income Security Act (ERISA) of 1974 establishes standards for the management of employer-provided pension plans. 5. *Unemployment insurance*—The Federal Unemployment Tax Act (FUTA) of 1935 created a system that provides unemployment compensation to eligible individuals. Employers are taxed to cover the costs. 6. *COBRA*—The Consolidated Omnibus Budget Reconciliation Act (COBRA) of 1985 requires employers to give employees, on termination of employment, the option of continuing their medical, optical, or dental insurance coverage for a certain period. 7. *HIPAA*—The Health Insurance Portability and Accountability Act (HIPAA) establishes requirements for employer-sponsored group health plans. The plans must also comply with various safeguards to ensure the privacy of employees' health information.
Employee Privacy Rights (See pages 524–527.)	In addition to the U.S. Constitution, tort law, state constitutions, and federal and state statutes may provide some protection for employees' privacy rights. Employer practices that are often challenged by employees as invasive of their privacy rights include electronic performance monitoring and drug testing.
Immigration Law (See pages 528–530.)	1. *Immigration Reform and Control Act (1986)*—Prohibits employers from hiring illegal immigrants. The act is administered by U.S. Citizenship and Immigration Services. Compliance audits and enforcement actions are conducted by U.S. Immigration and Customs Enforcement. 2. *Immigration Act (1990)*—Limits the number of legal immigrants entering the United States by capping the number of visas (entry permits) that are issued each year.
Employment Discrimination (See pages 530–543.)	1. *Title VII of the Civil Rights Act of 1964*—Title VII prohibits both intentional (disparate-treatment) and unintentional (disparate-impact) discrimination. Disparate-impact discrimination occurs when an employer's practice, such as requiring a certain level of education, has the effect of discriminating against a protected class. Remedies include reinstatement, back pay, and retroactive promotions. Damages (both compensatory and punitive) may be awarded for intentional discrimination. 2. *Discrimination Based on Age*—The Age Discrimination in Employment Act (ADEA) prohibits employment discrimination on the basis of age against individuals forty years of age or older. Procedures for bringing a case under the ADEA are similar to those for bringing a case under Title VII, but under the ADEA, a plaintiff must show that age was the *only* reason for the adverse employment action. 3. *Discrimination Based on Disability*—The Americans with Disabilities Act (ADA) prohibits employment discrimination against persons with disabilities who are otherwise qualified to perform the essential functions of the jobs for which they apply. To prevail on a claim, the plaintiff must show that she or he has a disability, is otherwise qualified for the employment in question, and was excluded from it solely because of the disability. Procedures and remedies under the ADA are similar to those in Title VII cases. Employers are required to reasonably accommodate the needs of persons with disabilities through such measures as modifying the physical work environment and permitting more flexible work schedules. Employers are not required to accommodate the needs of workers with disabilities who pose a definite threat to health and safety in the workplace or who are not otherwise qualified for their jobs. 4. *Defenses to Employment Discrimination*—As defenses to claims of employment discrimination, employers may assert that the discrimination was required for reasons of business necessity, to meet a bona fide occupational qualification, or to maintain a legitimate seniority system. Evidence of prior employee misconduct acquired after the employee has filed a suit is not a defense to discrimination.

ExamPrep

ISSUE SPOTTERS

1. Erin, an employee of Fine Print Shop, is injured on the job. For Erin to obtain workers' compensation, does her injury have to have been caused by Fine Print's negligence? Does it matter whether the action causing the injury was intentional? Explain. **(See pages 521–522.)**
2. Ruth is a supervisor for a Subs & Suds restaurant. Tim is a Subs & Suds employee. The owner announces that some employees will be discharged. Ruth tells Tim that if he has sex with her, he can keep his job. Is this sexual harassment? Why or why not? **(See pages 536–537.)**

—**Check your answers to the Issue Spotters against the answers provided in Appendix E at the end of this text.**

BEFORE THE TEST

Go to www.cengagebrain.com, enter the ISBN 9781133191353, and click on "Find" to locate this textbook's Web site. Then, click on "Access Now" under "Study Tools," and select Chapter 18 at the top. There, you will find a Practice Quiz that you can take to assess your mastery of the concepts in this chapter, as well as Flashcards, a Glossary of important terms, and Video Questions (when assigned).

For Review

Answers to the even-numbered questions in this For Review section can be found in Appendix F at the end of this text.

1. What is the employment-at-will doctrine? When and why are exceptions to this doctrine made?
2. What federal statute governs working hours and wages?
3. Under the Family and Medical Leave Act, in what circumstances may an employee take family or medical leave?
4. What are the two most important federal statutes governing immigration and employment today?
5. What is the difference between disparate-treatment discrimination and disparate-impact discrimination?

Business Scenarios and Case Problems

18–1 Wrongful Discharge. Denton and Carlo worked at an appliance plant. Their job required them to do occasional maintenance work while standing on a wire mesh twenty feet above the plant floor. Other employees had fallen through the mesh, and one was killed by the fall. When Denton and Carlo were asked by their supervisor to do work that would likely require them to walk on the mesh, they refused due to their fear of bodily harm or death. Because of their refusal to do the requested work, the two employees were fired from their jobs. Was their discharge wrongful? If so, under what federal employment law? What federal agency or department could assist them? **(See pages 517–521.)**

18–2 Question with Sample Answer—Disparate-Impact Discrimination. Chinawa, a major cheese processor, employs one hundred workers at its main plant. The plant is located in Heartland Corners, which has a population that is 50 percent white and 25 percent African American, with the balance Hispanic American, Asian American, and others. Chinawa requires a high school diploma as a condition of employment for its cleaning crew. Three-fourths of the white population complete high school, compared with only one-fourth of those in the minority groups. Chinawa has an all-white cleaning crew. Has Chinawa violated Title VII of the Civil Rights Act of 1964? Explain. **(See pages 533 and 543.)**

—**For a sample answer to Question 18–2, go to Appendix G at the end of this text.**

18–3 Spotlight on the Civil Rights Act—Discrimination Based on Gender. Burlington Coat Factory Warehouse, Inc., had a dress code that required male salesclerks to wear business attire consisting of slacks, a shirt, and a necktie. Female salesclerks, by contrast, were required to wear a smock so that customers could readily identify them. Karen O'Donnell and other female employees refused to wear the smock. Instead, they reported to work in business attire and were suspended. After numerous suspensions, the female employees were fired for violating Burlington's dress code. All other conditions of employment, including salary, hours, and benefits, were the same for female and male employees. Was the dress code policy discriminatory? Why or why not? [*O'Donnell v. Burlington Coat Factory Warehouse, Inc.,* 656 F.Supp. 263 (S.D. Ohio 1987)] **(See page 535.)**

18–4 **Workers' Compensation.** As a safety measure, Dynea USA, Inc., required an employee, Tony Fairbanks, to wear steel-toed boots. One of the boots caused a sore on Fairbanks's leg. The skin over the sore broke, and within a week, Fairbanks was hospitalized with a serious infection. He filed a workers' compensation claim. Dynea argued that the bacteria that caused the infection had been on Fairbanks's skin before he came to work. What are the requirements to recover workers' compensation benefits? Does this claim qualify? Explain. [*Dynea USA, Inc. v. Fairbanks,* 241 Or.App. 311, 250 P.3d 389 (2011)] **(See pages 521–522.)**

18–5 **Case Problem with Sample Answer— Retaliation by Employers.** Entek International hired Shane Dawson, a male homosexual. Some of Dawson's co-workers, including his supervisor, made derogatory comments about his sexual orientation. Dawson's work deteriorated. He filed a complaint with Entek's human resources department. Two days later, he was fired. State law made it unlawful for an employer to discriminate against an individual based on sexual orientation. Could Dawson establish a claim for retaliation? Explain. [*Dawson v. Entek International,* 630 F.3d 928 (9th Cir. 2011)] **(See page 537.)**

—**For a sample answer to Problem 18–5, go to Appendix H at the end of this text.**

18–6 **Sexual Harassment by Co-Worker.** Billie Bradford worked for the Kentucky Department of Community Based Services (DCBS). One of Bradford's co-workers, Lisa Stander, routinely engaged in extreme sexual behavior (such as touching herself and making crude comments) in Bradford's presence. Bradford and others regularly complained about Stander's conduct to their supervisor, Angie Taylor. Rather than resolve the problem, Taylor nonchalantly told Stander to stop, encouraged Bradford to talk to Stander, and suggested that Stander was just having fun. Assuming that Bradford was subjected to a hostile work environment, could DCBS be liable? Why or why not? [*Bradford v. Department of Community Based Services,* 2012 WL 360032 (E.D.Ky. 2012)] **(See page 537.)**

18–7 **Exceptions to the Employment-at-Will Doctrine.** Li Li worked for Packard Bioscience, and Mark Schmeizl was her supervisor. In March 2000, Schmeizl asked Li to call Packard's competitors, pretend to be a potential customer,

and request "pricing information and literature." Li refused. She told Schmeizl that she thought the work was illegal and recommended that he contact Packard's legal department. Although a lawyer recommended against the practice, Schmeizl insisted that Li perform the calls. He then wrote negative performance reviews because she was unable to get the requested information when she called competitors and identified herself as a Packard employee. Li was terminated on Schmeizl's recommendation. Can Li bring a claim for wrongful discharge? Why or why not? [*Li v. Canberra Industries,* 134 Conn.App. 448, 39 A.3d 789 (2012)] **(See pages 516–517.)**

18–8 **A Question of Ethics—Discrimination Based on Disability.** Titan Distribution, Inc., employed Quintak, Inc., to run its tire mounting and distribution operation. Robert Chalfant worked for Quintak as a second-shift supervisor at Titan. He suffered a heart attack in 1992 and underwent heart bypass surgery in 1997. He also had arthritis. In July 2002, Titan decided to terminate its relationship with Quintak. Chalfant applied to work at Titan. On his application, he described himself as having a disibility. After a physical exam, Titan's doctor concluded that Chalfant could work in his current capacity, and he was notified that he would be hired. Nevertheless, a Titan employee, wrote "not pass px" at the top of Chalfant's application, and he was not hired. He took a job with another company that involved walking up to five miles a day and lifting more weight than he had at Titan. In September, Titan eliminated its second shift. Chalfant filed a suit against Titan under the Americans with Disabilities Act (ADA). Titan argued that its failure to hire Chalfant was not based on the impression that he had not passed the physical, but could not explain why "not pass px" was written on his application. Later, Titan claimed that Chalfant was not hired because the entire second shift was going to be eliminated. [*Chalfant v. Titan Distribution, Inc.,* 475 F.3d 982 (8th Cir. 2007)] **(See pages 541–542.)**

1. What must Chalfant establish to make his case under the ADA? Can he meet these requirements? Explain.
2. Punitive damages can be appropriate when an employer acts with malice or reckless indifference to an employee's protected rights. Would punitive damages be appropriate in this case? Discuss.

Critical Thinking and Writing Assignments

18–9 **Business Law Critical Thinking Group Assignment.** Nicole Tipton and Sadik Seferi owned and operated a restaurant in Iowa. Acting on a tip from the local police, agents of Immigration and Customs Enforcement executed search warrants at the restaurant and at an apartment where some restaurant workers lived. The agents discovered six undocumented aliens working at the restaurant and living together. When the I-9 forms for the restaurant's employees were reviewed, none were found for the six aliens. They

were paid in cash, while other employees were paid by check. Tipton and Seferi were charged with hiring and harboring illegal aliens.

1. The first group will develop an argument that Tipton and Seferi were guilty of hiring and harboring illegal aliens.
2. The second group will assess whether Tipton and Seferi can assert a defense by claiming that they did not know that the workers were unauthorized aliens.

CHAPTER 19

The Entrepreneur's Options

CHAPTER OUTLINE

- Major Business Forms
- Special Business Forms
- Franchises

LEARNING OBJECTIVES

The five learning objectives below are designed to help improve your understanding of the chapter. After reading this chapter, you should be able to answer the following questions:

1 What are some of the major forms of business organization in the United States?

2 What advantages and disadvantages are associated with the sole proprietorship?

3 What advantages do limited liability companies offer to businesspersons that are not offered by sole proprietorships or partnerships?

4 What are the two options for managing limited liability companies?

5 What is a franchise?

(track5/iStockphoto.com)

"Why not go out on a limb? Isn't that where the fruit is?"
Frank Scully, 1892–1964 (American author)

M any Americans would agree, that to succeed in business one must "go out on a limb," as Frank Scully commented in the chapter-opening quotation. Certainly, an entrepreneur's primary motive for undertaking a business enterprise is to make profits. An **entrepreneur** is one who initiates and assumes the financial risks of a new enterprise and undertakes to provide or control its management.

A question faced by anyone who wishes to start a business is what form of business organization to use. In making this determination, the entrepreneur needs to consider a number of important factors, including (1) ease of creation, (2) liability of the owners, (3) tax considerations, and (4) the need for capital. In studying this chapter and the next one, keep these factors in mind as you read about the various organizational forms available to entrepreneurs.

Entrepreneur One who initiates and assumes the financial risk of a new business enterprise and undertakes to provide or control its management.

LEARNING OBJECTIVE 1
What are some of the major forms of business organization in the United States?

Major Business Forms

Traditionally, entrepreneurs have used three major forms to structure their business enterprises—the sole proprietorship, the partnership, and the corporation. In the last twenty years, the limited liability company and the limited liability partnership have become popular alternative forms of doing business. We examine each of these business forms in this section.

Sole Proprietorships

Sole Proprietorship The simplest form of business organization, in which the owner is the business. The owner reports business income on his or her personal income tax return and is legally responsible for all debts and obligations incurred by the business.

The simplest form of business organization is a **sole proprietorship.** In this form, the owner is the business. Thus, anyone who does business without creating a separate business organization has a sole proprietorship. More than two-thirds of all U.S. businesses are sole proprietorships. They are usually small enterprises—about 99 percent of the sole proprietorships in the United States have revenues of less than $1 million per year. A sole proprietorship can be any type of business, ranging from an informal, home-office or Internet undertaking to a large restaurant or construction firm. (See this chapter's *Adapting Law to the Online Environment* feature below for a discussion of a sole proprietor who tried to change his name to match his business's Web site.)

LEARNING OBJECTIVE 2
What advantages and disadvantages are associated with the sole proprietorship?

Advantages of the Sole Proprietorship A major advantage of the sole proprietorship is that the proprietor owns the entire business and has a right to receive all of the profits (because he or she assumes all of the risk). In addition, it is often easier and

ADAPTING THE LAW TO THE ONLINE ENVIRONMENT

CAN A SOLE PROPRIETOR CHANGE HIS NAME TO MATCH HIS DOMAIN NAME?

Because of the ease of formation and inherent flexibility, many online businesses start out as sole proprietorships. Often, a Web site's domain name can contribute substantially to the business's success. One sole proprietor took that idea a step further. He asked the courts to allow him to change his name to match his domain name.

Introducing Mr. NJweedman.com . . .

Robert Edward Forchion, Jr., has devoted his life to promoting the legalization of marijuana. While living in New Jersey, he became popularly known as NJweedman, after his Web site *NJweedman. com*, which discusses his efforts to legalize marijuana.

In 2009, claiming that he was being persecuted in New Jersey, Forchion moved to California, where he has managed a Rastafarian temple and a medical marijuana dispensary. (California is one of nearly twenty states that allow the legal distribution of medical marijuana.)

Petitioning the Courts for a Name Change

In 2001, while still living in New Jersey, Forchion tried to change his name legally to "NJweedman.com." When his petition was

denied, he appealed, but the New Jersey Superior Court agreed with the lower court "that 'in his zeal to legalize marijuana . . . [Forchion seeks] to glamorize, persuade others to use marijuana, and to violate the law.'"[a]

After Forchion moved to California, he tried again to change his name legally to "NJweedman.com." Again, his petition was denied, and the appellate court upheld the denial. The court pointed out that the change could lead to confusion if Forchion ever lost control of the domain or if the name was similar to another domain name or a trademark. Finally, the court said that granting Forchion a personal name that is the same as the name of a Web site that advocates violating the law was not permissible, even in California, where medical marijuana is legal.[b]

Critical Thinking

If a sole proprietor's Web site did not advocate any illegal action, would the courts be likely to allow the proprietor to change his or her name to match the site's domain name? Why or why not?

---

a. *State v. Forchion,* 182 N.J. 150, 862 A.2d 58 (2004).
b. *In re Forchion,* 198 Cal.App.4th 1284, 130 Cal.Rptr.3d 690 (2011).

> "Always tell yourself:
> The difference
> between running a
> business and ruining
> a business is *I*."
>
> Anonymous

This sole proprietor enjoys full flexibility in how she runs her business. What are the downsides of this form of business organization?

(YinYang/iStockphoto)

less costly to start a sole proprietorship than to start any other kind of business, as few legal formalities are involved.[1] No documents need to be filed with the government to start a sole proprietorship (though a state business license may be required to operate certain types of businesses).

A sole proprietorship also offers more flexibility than does a partnership or a corporation. The sole proprietor is free to make any decision she or he wishes concerning the business—including whom to hire, when to take a vacation, and what kind of business to pursue. In addition, the proprietor can sell or transfer all or part of the business to another party at any time without seeking approval from anyone else. In contrast, approval is typically required from partners in a partnership and from shareholders in a corporation.

A sole proprietor pays only personal income taxes (including Social Security and Medicare taxes) on the business's profits, which are reported as personal income on the proprietor's personal income tax return. Sole proprietors are also allowed to establish retirement accounts that are tax-exempt until the funds are withdrawn.

Disadvantages of the Sole Proprietorship The major disadvantage of the sole proprietorship is that the proprietor alone bears the burden of any losses or liabilities incurred by the business enterprise. In other words, the sole proprietor has unlimited liability, or legal responsibility, for all obligations incurred in doing business. Any lawsuit against the business or its employees can lead to unlimited personal liability for the owner of a sole proprietorship.

The sole proprietorship also has the disadvantage of lacking continuity on the death of the proprietor. When the owner dies, so does the business—it is automatically dissolved. Another disadvantage is that in raising capital, the proprietor is limited to his or her personal funds and any personal loans that he or she can obtain.

The personal liability of a sole proprietorship's owner was at issue in the following *Spotlight Case*. The case involved the federal Cable Communications Act, which prohibits a commercial establishment from broadcasting television programs to its patrons without authorization. The court had to decide whether the owner of the sole proprietorship that had installed a satellite television system was personally liable for violating this act.

---

1. Although starting a sole proprietorship involves relatively few legal formalities compared with other business organizational forms, even small sole proprietorships may need to comply with certain zoning requirements, obtain appropriate licenses, and the like.

Spotlight on
Sole Proprietorship
Personal Liability

Case 19.1
Garden City Boxing Club, Inc. v. Dominguez
United States District Court, Northern District of Illinois,
Eastern Division, 2006 WL 1517775 (2006).

(AP Photo/Laura Rauch)

Who is liable for paying the fee for closed-circuit broadcast rights to a prizefight?

FACTS Garden City Boxing Club, Inc. (GCB), owned the exclusive right to broadcast several prizefights via closed-circuit television, including a match between Oscar De La Hoya and Fernando Vargas on September 14, 2002. GCB sold the right to receive the broadcasts to bars and other commercial venues. The fee was $20 multiplied by an establishment's maximum fire code occupancy. Antenas Enterprises in Chicago, Illinois,

sells and installs satellite television systems under a contract with DISH Network. After installing a system, Antenas sends the buyer's address and other identifying information to DISH.

In January 2002, Luis Garcia, an Antenas employee, identified a new customer as José Melendez at 220 Hawthorn Commons in Vernon Hills. The address was a restaurant—Mundelein Burrito—but Garcia designated the account as residential.

Spotlight Case 19.1—Continues next page ➡

Mundelein's patrons watched the De La Hoya–Vargas match, as well as three other fights on other dates, for which the restaurant paid only the residential rate to DISH and nothing to GCB. GCB filed a suit in a federal district court against Luis Dominguez, the sole proprietor of Antenas, to collect the fee.

ISSUE   Was Dominguez personally liable for the restaurant's commercial fee to GCB?

DECISION   Yes. The court issued a summary judgment in GCB's favor, holding that the plaintiff was entitled to the amount of the fee, plus damages and attorneys' fees.

REASON   The court found that Mundelein Burrito was clearly a commercial establishment. "The structure of the building, an exterior identification sign, and its location in a strip mall made this obvious." Under the Cable Communications Act, "an

authorized intermediary of a communication violates the Act when it divulges communication through an electronic channel to one other than the addressee."

Antenas's improper designation of Mundelein Burrito as residential allowed the unauthorized broadcast of four prizefights to the restaurant. Antenas is a sole proprietorship, and a sole proprietorship has no legal identity apart from that of the individual who owns it. A sole proprietor is personally responsible for the acts that his or her employees commit within the scope of their employment. Dominguez owns Antenas, and Garcia is Dominguez's employee. "Accordingly, Dominguez is personally liable for the damages caused by the violation of . . . the [Cable Communications] Act."

WHAT IF THE FACTS WERE DIFFERENT?   *If Mundelein Burrito had identified itself as a residence when ordering the satellite system, how might the result have been different?*

Partnerships

Partnership An agreement by two or more persons to carry on, as co-owners, a business for profit.

Articles of Partnership A written agreement that sets forth each partner's rights and obligations with respect to the partnership.

A **partnership** arises from an agreement, express or implied, between two or more persons to carry on a business for profit. Partners are co-owners of a business and have joint control over its operation and the right to share in its profits. No particular form of partnership agreement is necessary for the creation of a general partnership, but for practical reasons, the agreement should be in writing. Basically, in a partnership agreement, called **articles of partnership,** the partners may agree to almost any terms so long as they are not illegal or contrary to public policy.

The Uniform Partnership Act (UPA) governs the operation of partnerships *in the absence of express agreement* and has done much to reduce controversies in the law relating to partnerships. The UPA defines a *partnership* as "an association of two or more persons to carry on as co-owners a business for profit" [UPA 101(6)]. The *intent* to associate is a key element of a partnership, and a person cannot join a partnership unless all other partners consent [UPA 401(i)]. In determining whether a partnership exists, courts usually look for the following three essential elements, which are implicit in the UPA's definition of the term:

1. A sharing of profits *and* losses (sharing only profits is not usually sufficient).
2. A joint ownership of the business.
3. An equal right in the management of the business.

Rights and Duties of Partners   Under the UPA, all partners have equal rights in managing the partnership [UPA 401(f)]. Each partner in an ordinary partnership has one vote in management matters *regardless of the proportional size of his or her interest in the firm.* Each partner is entitled to the proportion of business profits and losses designated in the partnership agreement. If the agreement does not apportion profits or losses, the UPA provides that *profits shall be shared equally and losses shall be shared in the same ratio as profits* [UPA 401(b)]. Each partner, however, can be held fully liable for all debts of the partnership. Each partner has a right to inspect the partnership books and records, as well as to request an accounting to determine the value of each partner's share in the partnership.

The duties and liabilities of partners are basically derived from agency law. Each partner is an agent of every other partner and acts as both a principal and an agent in any business transaction within the scope of the partnership agreement. A partner owes to the partnership and to the other partners fiduciary duties, including the *duty of care* and the *duty of loyalty* [UPA 404(a)]. Under the UPA, a partner's duty of care involves refraining from "grossly negligent or reckless conduct, intentional misconduct, or a knowing violation of law" [UPA 404(c)]. A partner is not liable to the partnership for simple negligence or honest errors in judgment in conducting partnership business, though.

The duty of loyalty requires a partner to account to the partnership for "any property, profit, or benefit" derived by the partner from the partnership's business or the use of its property [UPA 404(b)]. A partner must also refrain from competing with the partnership in business or dealing with the firm as an adverse party.

The duty of loyalty can be breached by self-dealing, misusing partnership property, disclosing trade secrets, or usurping a partnership business opportunity, as the following *Classic Case* illustrates.

Classic Case 19.2

Meinhard v. Salmon

Court of Appeals of New York,
249 N.Y. 458, 164 N.E. 545 (1928).
www.nycourts.gov/reporter/Index.htm[a]

(olaser/iStockphoto)

What fiduciary duties does a partner have with respect to renewing a hotel lease?

FACTS Walter Salmon negotiated a twenty-year lease for the Hotel Bristol in New York City. To pay for the conversion of the building into shops and offices, Salmon entered into an agreement with Morton Meinhard to assume half of the cost. They agreed to share the profits and losses from the joint venture. (A *joint venture* is similar to a partnership but typically is created for a single project, whereas a partnership usually involves an ongoing business.) Salmon was to have the sole power to manage the building, however. Less than four months before the end of the lease term, the building's owner approached Salmon about a project to raze the converted structure and construct a new building. Salmon agreed and signed a new lease in the name of his own business, Midpoint Realty Company, without telling Meinhard. When Meinhard learned of the deal, he filed a suit against Salmon. The court ruled in Meinhard's favor. Salmon appealed.

ISSUE Did Salmon breach his fiduciary duty of loyalty to Meinhard?

DECISION Yes. The Court of Appeals of New York held that Salmon had breached his fiduciary duty by failing to inform Meinhard of the business opportunity and secretly taking advantage of it for himself. The court therefore granted Meinhard an interest "measured by the value of half of the entire lease."

REASON The court stated, "Joint adventurers, like copartners, owe to one another, while the enterprise continues, the duty of the finest loyalty." Salmon's conduct excluded Meinhard from any chance to compete and from any chance to enjoy the opportunity for benefit. As a partner, Salmon was bound by his "obligation to his copartners in such dealings not to separate his interest from theirs, but, if he acquires any benefit, to communicate it to them." Salmon was also the managing co-adventurer, and thus the court found that "for him and for those like him the rule of undivided loyalty is relentless and supreme."

WHAT IF THE FACTS WERE DIFFERENT? *Suppose that Salmon had disclosed the proposed deal to Meinhard, who had said that he was not interested. Would the result in this case have been different? Explain.*

IMPACT OF THIS CASE ON TODAY'S LAW *This landmark case involved a joint venture, not a partnership. At the time, a member of a joint venture had only the duty to refrain from actively subverting the rights of the other members. The decision in this case imposed the highest standard of loyalty on joint-venture members. The duty is now the same in both joint ventures and partnerships. The eloquent language in this case that describes the standard of loyalty is frequently quoted approvingly by courts in cases involving partnerships.*

---

a. In the links at the bottom of the page, click on "Archives." In the result, scroll to the name of the case and click on it to access the opinion. The New York State Law Reporting Bureau maintains this Web site.

Advantages and Disadvantages of Partnerships   As with a sole proprietorship, one of the advantages of a partnership is that it can be organized fairly easily and inexpensively. Additionally, the partnership form of business offers important tax advantages. The partnership itself files only an informational tax return with the Internal Revenue Service. In other words, the firm itself pays no taxes. Rather, a partner's profit from the partnership (whether distributed or not) is "passed through" and taxed as individual income to the partner.

A partnership may also allow for greater capital contributions to the business than is possible in a sole proprietorship. Two or more persons can invest in the business, and lenders may be more willing to make loans to a partnership than to a sole proprietorship.

The main disadvantage of the partnership form of business is that the partners are subject to personal liability for partnership obligations. In the majority of states, under UPA 306(a), partners are jointly and severally (separately, or individually) liable for all partnership obligations, including contracts, torts, and breaches of trust. **Joint and several liability** means that a third party may sue all of the partners together (jointly) or one or more of the partners separately (severally) at his or her option. This is true even if the partner did not participate in, ratify, or know about whatever it was that gave rise to the cause of action.

Limited Liability Partnerships

The **limited liability partnership (LLP)** is a hybrid form of business designed mostly for professionals who normally do business as partners in a partnership. The major advantage of the LLP is that it allows a partnership to continue as a pass-through entity for tax purposes but limits the personal liability of the partners. In most states, it is relatively easy to convert a traditional partnership into an LLP because the firm's basic organizational structure remains the same. The appropriate form must be filed with a central state agency, usually the secretary of state's office, and the business's name must include either "Limited Liability Partnership" or "LLP" [UPA 1001, 1002].

The LLP is especially attractive for two categories of businesses: professional service firms and family businesses. In fact, the largest international accountancy and professional services firms are organized as LLPs, including Ernst & Young, LLP, and PricewaterhouseCoopers, LLP.

An LLP allows professionals, such as attorneys and accountants, to avoid personal liability for the malpractice of other partners. Although LLP statutes vary from state to state, generally each state statute limits the liability of partners in some way. A partner in an LLP is still liable for her or his own wrongful acts, such as negligence, however. Also liable is the partner who supervised the individual who committed a wrongful act.

Limited Partnerships

The **limited partnership (LP)** is a business organizational form that limits the liability of *some* of its owners. A limited partnership consists of at least one **general partner** and one or more **limited partners.**

The general partner assumes management responsibility for the partnership and has full responsibility for the partnership and for all of its debts. General partners are personally liable to the partnership's creditors.

Limited partners contribute cash or other property and own an interest in the firm but do not undertake any management responsibilities and are not personally liable for partnership debts beyond the amount of their investment. A limited partner can forfeit limited liability by taking part in the management of the business, however.

In contrast to the informal, private, and voluntary agreement that usually suffices for a general partnership, the formation of a limited partnership is a public and formal

---

Joint and Several Liability In partnership law, a doctrine under which a plaintiff may sue, and collect a judgment from, all of the partners together (jointly) or one or more of the partners separately (severally, or individually).

Limited Liability Partnership (LLP) A hybrid form of business organization that is used mainly by professionals who normally do business in a partnership. An LLP is a pass-through entity for tax purposes, but a partner's personal liability for the malpractice of other partners is limited.

➤ KNOW THIS ◄

A limited partner is liable only to the extent of any contribution that she or he made to the partnership, but can lose this limited liability by participating in management.

Limited Partnership (LP) A partnership consisting of one or more general partners and one or more limited partners.

General Partner In a limited partnership, a partner who assumes responsibility for the management of the partnership and has full liability for all partnership debts.

Limited Partner In a limited partnership, a partner who contributes capital to the partnership but has no right to participate in its management and no liability for partnership debts beyond the amount of her or his investment.

Certificate of Limited Partnership The document that must be filed with a designated state official to form a limited partnership.

proceeding that must follow statutory requirements. The partners must sign a **certificate of limited partnership.** This certificate must include certain information required by statute, such as the name, mailing address, and capital contribution of each general and limited partner. The certificate must be filed with the designated state official—usually the secretary of state.

Corporations

Corporation A legal entity formed in compliance with statutory requirements that is distinct from its shareholder-owners.

A widely used type of business organizational form is the **corporation** (discussed in detail in Chapter 20). The corporation, like the limited partnership, is a creature of statute. The corporation's existence as a legal entity, which can be perpetual, generally depends on state law.

Corporations are owned by *shareholders*—those who have purchased ownership shares in the business. A *board of directors,* elected by the shareholders, manages the business. The board of directors normally employs *officers* to oversee day-to-day operations.

One of the key advantages of the corporate form of business is that the liability of its owners (shareholders) is limited to their investments. The shareholders usually are not personally liable for the obligations of the corporation. A disadvantage of the corporate form is that profits are taxed twice (double taxation). First, the corporation as an entity pays income taxes on corporate profits, and second, the shareholders pay income taxes on those profits that are distributed to them.

Limited Liability Company (LLC) A hybrid form of business enterprise that offers the limited liability of a corporation and the tax advantages of a partnership.

Limited Liability Companies

Articles of Organization The document filed with a designated state official by which a limited liability company is formed.

A **limited liability company (LLC)** is a hybrid that combines the limited liability aspects of a corporation and the tax advantages of a partnership, which makes it the ideal form of business for many entrepreneurs and investors. LLCs are governed by state LLC statutes, which vary, of course, from state to state. Although the National Conference of Commissioners on Uniform State Laws (NCCUSL) issued the Uniform Limited Liability Company Act (ULLCA) in an attempt to create more uniformity among the states, less than one-fifth of the states have adopted it. Thus, the law governing LLCs remains far from uniform. We discuss the origin and evolution of the LLC in this chapter's *Landmark in the Law* feature on the following page.

Some well-known companies, including Chrysler, SUBWAY, and DISH Network, are limited liability companies.

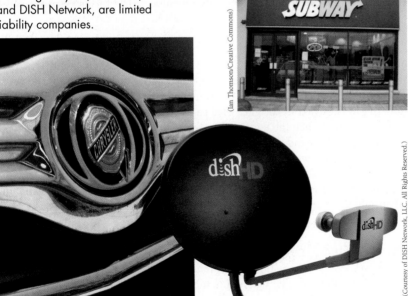

(Ian Thomson/Creative Commons)

(Photo by Bill Stryker)

(Courtesy of DISH Network, LLC. All Rights Reserved.)

To form an LLC, **articles of organization** must be filed with a central state agency—usually the secretary of state's office [ULLCA 202].[2] Typically, the articles must include such information as the name of the business, its principal address, the name and address of a registered agent, the names of the members, and information on how the LLC will be managed [ULLCA 203]. Although a majority of the states permit

2. In addition to requiring the filing of articles of organization, a few states require that a notice of the intention to form an LLC be published in a local newspaper.

LANDMARK IN THE LAW

Limited Liability Company (LLC) Statutes

In 1977, Wyoming became the first state to pass legislation authorizing the creation of a limited liability company (LLC). Although LLCs did not emerge in the United States until the late 1970s, they have been used for more than a century in various foreign jurisdictions, including several European and South American nations.

Taxation of LLCs   In the United States, after Wyoming's adoption of an LLC statute, it still was unclear how the Internal Revenue Service (IRS) would treat LLCs for tax purposes. In 1988, however, the IRS ruled that Wyoming LLCs would be taxed as partnerships instead of corporations, providing that certain requirements were met. Before this ruling, only one other state—Florida, in 1982—had authorized LLCs. The 1988 ruling encouraged additional states to enact LLC statutes, and in less than a decade, all states had done so.

Other IRS rules also encouraged more widespread use of LLCs in the business world. Under these rules, any unincorporated business with more than one owner is automatically taxed as a partnership unless it indicates otherwise on the tax form or fits

into one of the exceptions. The exceptions involve publicly traded companies, companies formed under a state incorporation statute, and certain foreign-owned companies. If a business chooses to be taxed as a corporation, it can indicate this preference by checking a box on the IRS form.

Foreign Entities May Be LLC Members   Part of the impetus behind the creation of LLCs in this country is that foreign investors are allowed to become LLC members. In an era increasingly characterized by global business efforts and investments, the LLC often offers U.S. firms and potential investors from other countries greater flexibility and opportunities than are available through partnerships or corporations.

Application to Today's World   *Once it became clear that LLCs could be taxed as partnerships, the LLC form of business organization was widely adopted. Members could avoid the personal liability associated with the partnership form of business as well as the double taxation of the corporate form of business (see Chapter 20). Today, LLCs are a common form of business organization.*

---

one-member LLCs, some states require at least two members. The business's name must include the words *Limited Liability Company* or the initials *LLC* [ULLCA 105(a)].

Member A person who has an ownership interest in a limited liability company.

Limited Liability
Like shareholders in a corporation, owners of an LLC, who are called **members,** enjoy limited liability [ULLCA 303]. Members are shielded from personal liability in many situations, sometimes even when sued by employees of the firm. **CASE EXAMPLE 19.1** Penny McFarland was the activities director at a retirement community in Virginia that was owned by an LLC. Her supervisor told her to take the residents outside for a walk on a day when the temperature was 95 degrees. McFarland complained to the state health department and was fired from her job. She sued a number of managers and members of the LLC for wrongful discharge. The court held that under Virginia law, members, managers, and agents of an LLC are not responsible for its liabilities "solely" by virtue of their status. The court dismissed the action against all but one defendant, concluding that only those who "have played a key role in contributing to the company's tortious conduct" can be part of a wrongful discharge claim.[3] •

Jurisdictional Requirements
A significant difference between LLCs and corporations involves federal jurisdictional requirements. Under federal law, a corporation is deemed to be a citizen of the state where it is incorporated and maintains its principal place of business.[4] The statute does not mention the citizenship of partnerships, LLCs, and

---

3. *McFarland v. Virginia Retirement Services of Chesterfield, LLC,* 477 F.Supp.2d 727 (D.Va. 2007).
4. 28 U.S.C. Section 1332.

other unincorporated associations, but the courts have tended to regard these entities as citizens of every state of which their members are citizens.

The state citizenship of LLCs may come into play when a party sues an LLC based on diversity of citizenship. Remember from Chapter 3 that when parties to a lawsuit are from different states, a federal court can exercise diversity jurisdiction if the amount in controversy exceeds $75,000. *Total* diversity of citizenship must exist, however.

EXAMPLE 19.2 Jen Fong, a citizen of New York, wishes to bring a lawsuit against Skycel, an LLC formed under the laws of Connecticut. One of Skycel's members also lives in New York. Fong will not be able to bring the action against Skycel in federal court on the basis of diversity jurisdiction because the defendant LLC is also considered a citizen of New York. •

LEARNING OBJECTIVE 3
What advantages do limited liability companies offer to businesspersons that are not offered by sole proprietorships or partnerships?

Stan Ovshinsky, founder of Ovonic Hydrogen Systems, LLC. What are some of the advantages of doing business as an LLC instead of a corporation? Are there any disadvantages?

(Photo Courtesy of ECD Ovonics)

Operating Agreement An agreement in which the members of a limited liability company set forth the details of how the business will be managed and operated.

Advantages of the LLC A key advantage of the LLC is that the liability of members is limited to the amount of their investments. Although the LLC as an entity can be held liable for any loss or injury caused by the wrongful acts or omissions of its members, the members themselves generally are not personally liable. (See the *Business Application* feature on page 568 for a discussion of choosing between an LLC and an LLP form of business.)

Another advantage is the flexibility of the LLC in regard to taxation. An LLC that has *two or more members* can choose to be taxed either as a partnership or as a corporation. As mentioned earlier, a corporate entity must pay income taxes on its profits, and the shareholders then pay personal income taxes on profits distributed as dividends. An LLC that wants to distribute profits to its members may prefer to be taxed as a partnership to avoid the "double taxation" that is characteristic of the corporate entity.

Unless an LLC indicates that it wishes to be taxed as a corporation, the IRS automatically taxes it as a partnership. This means that the LLC as an entity pays no taxes. Rather, as in a partnership, profits are "passed through" the LLC to the members, who then personally pay taxes on the profits. If an LLC's members want to reinvest the profits in the business, however, rather than distribute the profits to members, they may prefer that the LLC be taxed as a corporation. Corporate income tax rates may be lower than personal tax rates.

Still another advantage of the LLC for businesspersons is the flexibility it offers in terms of business operations and management—as will be discussed shortly. Finally, because foreign investors can participate in an LLC, the LLC form of business is attractive as a way to encourage investment. For a discussion of business organizations in other nations that are similar to the LLC, see this chapter's *Beyond Our Borders* feature on the following page.

Disadvantages of the LLC The main disadvantage of the LLC is that state LLC statutes are not uniform. Therefore, businesses that operate in more than one state may be treated differently in different states. Generally, most states apply to a foreign LLC (an LLC formed in another state) the law of the state where the LLC was formed. Difficulties can arise, though, when one state's court must interpret and apply another state's laws.

LLC Operation The members of an LLC can decide how to operate the various aspects of the business by forming an **operating agreement** [ULLCA 103(a)]. Operating agreements typically contain provisions relating to management, decision-making procedures, how profits will be divided, the transfer of membership interests, whether the LLC will be dissolved on the death or departure of a member, and other important issues.

In many states, an operating agreement is not required for an LLC to exist, and if there is one, it need not be in writing. Generally, though, LLC members should protect their interests by creating a written operating agreement. As in any business, disputes may arise over any number of issues. When an issue is not covered by an operating agreement or by

BEYOND OUR BORDERS

Limited Liability Companies in Other Nations

Limited liability companies are not unique to the United States. Many nations have business forms that provide limited liability, although these organizations may differ significantly from our domestic limited liability companies (LLCs). In Germany, the *GmbH*, or *Gesellschaft mit beschränkter Haftung* (which means "company with limited liability") is a type of business entity that resembles the LLC. The GmbH is now the most widely used business form in Germany. A GmbH, however, is owned by shareholders and thus resembles a U.S. corporation in

certain respects. German laws also impose numerous restrictions on the operations and business transactions of GmbHs, whereas LLCs in the United States are not even required to have an operating agreement.

Business forms that limit the liability of owners can also be found in various other countries. Limited liability companies known as *limitadas* are common in many Latin American nations. In France, a *société à responsabilité limitée* (meaning "society with limited liability") provides business owners with limited liability. Although laws

in the United Kingdom and Ireland use the term *limited liability partnership*, the entities are similar to our domestic LLCs. Japan has created a new type of business organization called the *godo kaisha (GK)*, which is also quite similar to an LLC in the United States.

Critical Thinking

Clearly, limited liability is an important aspect of doing business globally. Why might a nation limit the number of member-owners in a limited liability entity?

---

an LLC statute, the courts often apply principles of partnership law. These principles can give the members of an LLC broad authority to bind the LLC unless the operating agreement provides otherwise.

CASE EXAMPLE 19.3   Clifford Kuhn, Jr., and Joseph Tumminelli formed a limousine service as an LLC. They did not create a written operating agreement but orally agreed that Kuhn would provide the financial backing and procure customers, and that Tumminelli would manage the day-to-day operations. Tumminelli embezzled $283,000 from the company after cashing customers' checks at Quick Cash, Inc., a local check-cashing service. Kuhn filed a lawsuit against Tumminelli, the banks, and Quick Cash to recover the embezzled funds. He argued that Quick Cash and the banks were liable because Tumminelli did not have the authority to cash the company's checks. The court, however, held that in the absence of a written operating agreement to the contrary, a member of an LLC, like a partner in a partnership, does have the authority to cash the firm's checks.[5] ●

LEARNING OBJECTIVE 4
What are the two options for managing limited liability companies?

LLC Management   Basically, the members of an LLC have two options for managing the firm. It can be either a "member-managed" LLC or a "manager-managed" LLC. Most LLC statutes and the ULLCA provide that unless the articles of organization specify otherwise, an LLC is assumed to be member managed [ULLCA 203(a)(6)].

In a *member-managed* LLC, all of the members participate in management, and decisions are made by majority vote [ULLCA 404(a)]. In a *manager-managed* LLC, the members designate a group of persons to manage the firm. The management group may consist of only members, both members and nonmembers, or only nonmembers. Managers in a manager-managed LLC owe fiduciary duties (the duty of loyalty and the duty of care) to the LLC and to its members. Procedures for choosing and removing managers may be included in the operating agreement.

Managers of LLCs need to be cognizant of the firm's potential liability under the employment-discrimination laws discussed in Chapter 18. Those laws may also extend to individuals who are not members of a protected class, as discussed in this chapter's *Law, Diversity, and Business: Managerial Implications* feature on the facing page.

---

5. *Kuhn v. Tumminelli*, 366 N.J.Super. 431, 841 A.2d 496 (2004).

LAW, DIVERSITY, AND BUSINESS: MANAGERIAL IMPLICATIONS

CAN A PERSON WHO IS NOT A MEMBER OF A PROTECTED CLASS SUE FOR DISCRIMINATION?

Under federal law and the laws of most states, discrimination in employment based on race, color, religion, national origin, gender, age, or disability is prohibited. Persons who are members of these protected classes can sue if they are subjected to discrimination. But can a person subjected to discrimination bring a lawsuit if he is not a member of a protected class, even though managers and other employees think that he is? This somewhat unusual situation occurred in New Jersey.

A Hostile Work Environment   Myron Cowher worked at Carson & Roberts Site Construction & Engineering, Inc. For more than a year, at least two of his supervisors directed an almost daily barrage of anti-Semitic remarks at him. They believed that he was Jewish, although his actual background was German-Irish and Lutheran.

Cowher brought a suit against the supervisors and the construction company, claiming a hostile work environment. The trial court, however, ruled that he did not have *standing to sue* (see page 73 in Chapter 3) under New Jersey law because he was

not Jewish and, thus, was not a member of a protected class. Cowher appealed.

Anti-Semitic Slurs Are Actionable—Even When Mistaken
The appellate court disagreed. The court ruled that if Cowher can prove that the discrimination "would not have occurred but for the perception that he was Jewish," his claim is covered by New Jersey's antidiscrimination law.[a] The case was remanded for trial. Thus, in the appellate court's view, the nature of the discriminatory remarks, and not the actual characteristics of the plaintiff (Cowher), determines whether the remarks are actionable.

Business Implications   *The New Jersey appellate court's ruling clearly indicates that even misdirected personal slurs in the workplace are unacceptable. What might have been considered playful banter in the past may be actionable today under various states' antidiscrimination laws.*

a. *Cowher v. Carson & Roberts Site Construction & Engineering, Inc.*, 425 N.J.Super 285, 40 A.3d 1171 (2012).

Dissociation   The severance of the relationship between an individual and a business firm when the individual ceases to be associated with the carrying on of the firm's business.

Dissociation from an LLC   Dissociation occurs when a partner in a partnership or a member of an LLC ceases to be associated with the carrying on of the firm's business. In either case, the individual has the *power* to dissociate, or withdraw, but may not have the *right* to dissociate. Events that trigger a member's dissociation from an LLC include voluntary withdrawal, expulsion by other members or by court order, bankruptcy, incompetence, and death. Generally, if a member dies or otherwise dissociates from an LLC, the other members may continue to carry on the LLC's business, unless the operating agreement provides otherwise.

When a member dissociates from an LLC, he or she loses the right to participate in management and the right to act as an agent for the LLC. The member's duty of loyalty to the LLC also terminates, and the duty of care continues only with respect to events that occurred before dissociation. Generally, the dissociated member also has a right to have his or her interest in the LLC bought out by the other members. The LLC's operating agreement may contain provisions establishing a buyout price, but if it does not, the member's interest is usually purchased at a fair value.

If the member's dissociation violates the LLC's operating agreement, it is considered legally wrongful, and the dissociated member can be held liable for damages caused by the dissociation. **EXAMPLE 19.4**   Chadwick and Barrel are members of an LLC. Chadwick manages the accounts, and Barrel, who has many connections in the community and is a skilled investor, brings in the business. If Barrel wrongfully dissociates from the LLC, the LLC's business will suffer, and Chadwick can hold Barrel liable for the loss of business resulting from her withdrawal. ●

ETHICAL ISSUE

When LLC members transfer personal real property to their LLC, can they later claim a homestead exemption for the property when filing for bankruptcy? James and Susan Kane deeded their home to their two-member LLC and recorded ownership of the property in the LLC's name. The Kanes subsequently filed for personal bankruptcy and claimed a *homestead exemption* (see page 444 in Chapter 15) for the property on the basis that the LLC had been administratively dissolved and that since they were its only members, the property had reverted to them.

When one of the couple's debtors objected to the exemption, the court discovered that the LLC still maintained a bank account in its name and had taken out a mortgage on the property. Hence, the court said that the LLC still existed and that the property belonged to the LLC because no deed had been executed transferring the property back to the Kanes. The Kanes' membership interests in the LLC were personal property and thus the property of their bankruptcy estate. Therefore, they could not claim the homestead exemption.[6]

Dissolution   A member's dissociation does not necessarily result in dissolution of the LLC. Rather, the remaining members can opt to either continue or dissolve the business. Members can also stipulate in their operating agreement that certain events will cause dissolution, or they can agree that they have the power to dissolve the LLC by vote. A court can order an LLC to be dissolved in certain circumstances, such as when the members have engaged in illegal or oppressive conduct, or when it is no longer feasible to carry on the business. When an LLC is dissolved, its members must collect, liquidate, and distribute the LLC's assets.

In the following case, three members formed an LLC to develop real estate. The court had to decide whether the LLC could be dissolved because continuing the business was impracticable.

---

6. *In re Kane,* 2011 WL 2119015 (Bank.D.Mass. 2011).

Case 19.3

Venture Sales, LLC v. Perkins

Supreme Court of Mississippi,
86 So. 3d 910 (2012).

An undeveloped subdivision.

FACTS   Walter Perkins, Gary Fordham, and David Thompson formed Venture Sales, LLC, to develop a subdivision in Petal, Mississippi. All three men contributed land and funds to Venture Sales, resulting in total holdings of 466 acres of land and about $158,000 in cash.

Perkins, an assistant coach for the Cleveland Browns, trusted Fordham and Thompson to develop the property. More than a decade later, however, Fordham and Thompson still had not done anything with the property, although they had developed at least two other subdivisions in the area. Fordham and Thompson suggested selling the property, but Perkins disagreed with the proposed listing price of $3.5 million. Perkins then sought a judicial dissolution of Venture Sales. Fordham and Thompson told the court that they did not know when they could develop the property and that they had been unable to get the additional funds that they needed to proceed. The trial court ordered the company dissolved. Fordham, Thompson, and Venture Sales appealed.

ISSUE   Can Venture Sales be judicially dissolved?

DECISION   Yes. The Mississippi Supreme Court affirmed the judgment of the trial court.

REASON   Under Mississippi law, an LLC may be judicially dissolved if, among other reasons, "it is not reasonably practicable to carry on the business in conformity with . . . the limited liability company agreement." The statute does not explain when continuing an LLC is "not reasonably practicable." The court therefore followed decisions from other jurisdictions recognizing that dissolution is appropriate when an LLC "is not meeting the economic purpose for which it was established."

According to Venture Sales' operating agreement, the company's purpose was "to initially acquire, develop and [sell] commercial and residential properties near Petal, Forrest County, Mississippi."

Case 19.3—Continued

Nevertheless, more than a decade later, the LLC's property remained undeveloped. Fordham and Thompson pointed to a number of reasons, including the financial crisis and Hurricane Katrina. But regardless of the reasons, Fordham and Thompson lacked the funds needed to proceed and did not know when they could develop the property as planned. It was immaterial that Perkins had not agreed to other business opportunities, such as selling the property for $3.5 million. After all, Venture Sales was formed to develop a subdivision. Because the LLC was not meeting that purpose, dissolution was warranted.

CRITICAL THINKING—Legal Consideration *Would dissolution be appropriate if the parties had formed a partnership rather than an LLC? Explain your answer.*

PREVENTING LEGAL DISPUTES

When forming an LLC, carefully draft the operating agreement. Stipulate the events that will cause dissociation and how the fair-value buyout price will be calculated. Set a time limit within which the LLC must compensate the dissociated member (or her or his estate) in the event of withdrawal, disability, or death. Include provisions that clearly limit the authority of dissociated members to act on behalf of the LLC and provide a right to seek damages from members who exceed the agreed-on parameters.

Major Business Forms Compared

"Business opportunities are like buses, there's always another one coming."

Richard Branson, 1950–present (British entrepreneur)

As mentioned at the outset of this chapter, when deciding which form of business organization would be most appropriate, businesspersons normally take into account several factors, including ease of creation, the liability of the owners, tax considerations, and the need for capital. Each major form of business organization offers distinct advantages and disadvantages with respect to these and other factors. Exhibit 19.1 on the following two pages summarizes the essential advantages and disadvantages of each of the forms of business organization discussed in this chapter and Chapter 20.

Special Business Forms

Besides the business forms already discussed, several other forms can be used to organize a business. For the most part, these special business forms are hybrid organizations—that is, they have characteristics similar to those of partnerships or corporations or combine features of both.

Joint Ventures

Joint Venture A joint undertaking for a specific commercial enterprise by two or more persons or business entities. A joint venture is treated like a partnership for federal income tax purposes.

A **joint venture**, sometimes referred to as a *joint adventure*, is a relationship in which two or more persons or business entities combine their efforts or their property for a single transaction or project or for a related series of transactions or projects. Unless otherwise agreed, joint venturers share profits and losses equally. For instance, when several contractors combine their resources to build and sell houses in a single development, their relationship is a joint venture.

The joint venture resembles a partnership and is taxed like a partnership. For this reason, most courts apply the same principles to joint ventures as they apply to partnerships. Joint venturers owe to each other the same fiduciary duties, including the duty of loyalty, that partners owe each other.

Because the activities of a joint venture are more limited than the business of a partnership, the members of a joint venture are presumed to have less power to bind their

Exhibit 19.1 Major Forms of Business Compared

CHARACTERISTIC	SOLE PROPRIETORSHIP	PARTNERSHIP	CORPORATION
Method of Creation	Created at will by owner.	Created by agreement of the parties.	Authorized by the state under the state's corporation law.
Legal Position	Not a separate entity; owner is the business.	A traditional partnership is a separate legal entity in most states.	Always a legal entity separate and distinct from its owners—a legal fiction for the purposes of owning property and being a party to litigation.
Liability	Unlimited liability.	Unlimited liability.	Limited liability of shareholders—shareholders are not liable for the debts of the corporation.
Duration	Determined by owner; automatically dissolved on owner's death.	Terminated by agreement of the partners, but can continue to do business even when a partner dissociates from the partnership.	Can have perpetual existence.
Transferability of Interest	Interest can be transferred, but individual's proprietorship then ends.	Although partnership interest can be assigned, assignee does not have full rights of a partner.	Shares of stock can be transferred.
Management	Completely at owner's discretion.	Each partner has a direct and equal voice in management unless expressly agreed otherwise in the partnership agreement.	Shareholders elect directors, who set policy and appoint officers.
Taxation	Owner pays personal taxes on business income.	Each partner pays pro rata share of income taxes on net profits, whether or not they are distributed.	Double taxation—corporation pays income tax on net profits, with no deduction for dividends, and shareholders pay income tax on disbursed dividends they receive.
Organizational Fees, Annual License Fees, and Annual Reports	None or minimal.	None or minimal.	All required.
Transaction of Business in Other States	Generally no limitation.	Generally no limitation.ª	Normally must qualify to do business and obtain certificate of authority.

a. A few states have enacted statutes requiring that foreign partnerships qualify to do business there.

co-adventurers. Nevertheless, when engaged in the joint venture's business, joint venturers have authority as agents to enter into contracts that will bind the joint venture. **CASE EXAMPLE 19.5** Murdo Cameron developed components for replicas of vintage P-51 Mustang planes. Cameron and Douglas Anderson agreed in writing to collaborate on the design and manufacture of two P-51s, one for each of them.

Without Cameron's knowledge, Anderson borrowed funds from SPW Associates, LLP, to finance the construction, using the first plane as security for the loan. After Anderson built one plane, he defaulted on the loan. SPW filed a lawsuit to obtain possession of the aircraft. The court ruled that Anderson and Cameron had entered into a joint venture and that the plane was the venture's property. Anderson had the authority to grant SPW a security interest in the plane, and SPW was entitled to take possession of the plane.[7] ●

Syndicates

A group of individuals or firms that join together to finance a particular project, such as the building of a shopping center or the purchase of a professional basketball franchise, is called a **syndicate** or an *investment group*. The form of such groups varies considerably. A syndicate may exist as a corporation or as a general or limited partnership. In some instances, the members do not have a legally recognized business arrangement but merely purchase and own property jointly.

> ➤ **KNOW THIS** ➤
> A partnership involves a continuing relationship of the partners. A joint venture is often a one-time association.

Syndicate A group of individuals or firms that join together to finance a project. A syndicate is also called an *investment group*.

---

7. *SPW Associates, LLP v. Anderson*, 2006 ND 159, 718 N.W.2d 580 (N.D.Sup.Ct. 2006).

Exhibit 19.1 Major Forms of Business Compared—Continued

CHARACTERISTIC	LIMITED PARTNERSHIP	LIMITED LIABILITY COMPANY	LIMITED LIABILITY PARTNERSHIP
Method of Creation	Created by agreement to carry on a business for profit. At least one party must be a general partner and the other(s) limited partner(s). Certificate of limited partnership is filed. Charter must be issued by the state.	Created by an agreement of the member-owners of the company. Articles of organization are filed. Charter must be issued by the state.	Created by agreement of the partners. A statement of qualification for the limited liability partnership is filed.
Legal Position	Treated as a legal entity.	Treated as a legal entity.	Generally, treated same as a traditional partnership.
Liability	Unlimited liability of all general partners. Limited partners are liable only to the extent of capital contributions.	Member-owners' liability is limited to the amount of capital contributions or investments.	Varies, but under the Uniform Partnership Act, liability of a partner for acts committed by other partners is limited.
Duration	By agreement in certificate, or by termination of the last general partner (retirement, death, and the like) or last limited partner.	Unless a single-member LLC, can have perpetual existence (same as a corporation).	Remains in existence until cancellation or revocation.
Transferability of Interest	Interest can be assigned (same as a traditional partnership), but if assignee becomes a member with consent of other partners, certificate must be amended.	Member interests are freely transferable.	Interest can be assigned same as in a traditional partnership.
Management	General partners have equal voice or by agreement. Limited partners may not retain limited liability if they actively participate in management.	Member-owners can fully participate in management or can designate a group of persons to manage on behalf of the members.	Same as a traditional partnership.
Taxation	Generally taxed as a partnership.	LLC is not taxed, and members are taxed personally on profits "passed through" the LLC.	Same as a traditional partnership.
Organizational Fees, Annual License Fees, and Annual Reports	Organizational fee required; usually not others.	Organizational fee required. Others vary with states.	Fees are set by each state for filing statements of qualification, statements of foreign qualification, and annual reports.
Transaction of Business in Other States	Generally no limitations.	Generally no limitations, but may vary depending on state.	Must file a statement of foreign qualification before doing business in another state.

Joint Stock Companies

Joint Stock Company A hybrid form of business organization that combines characteristics of a corporation and a partnership. Usually, a joint stock company is regarded as a partnership for tax and other legal purposes.

A **joint stock company** is a true hybrid of a partnership and a corporation. It has many characteristics of a corporation: its ownership is represented by transferable shares of stock, it is usually managed by directors and officers of the company or association, and it can have a perpetual existence. Most of its other features, however, are more characteristic of a partnership, and it is usually treated like a partnership.

As with a partnership, a joint stock company is formed by agreement (not statute), property is usually held in the names of the members, shareholders have personal liability, and the company generally is not treated as a legal entity for purposes of a lawsuit. In a joint stock company, however, shareholders are not considered to be agents of one another, as they are in a partnership.

Business Trusts

Business Trust A form of business organization, created by a written trust agreement, that resembles a corporation. Legal ownership and management of the trust's property stay with the trustees, and the profits are distributed to the beneficiaries, who have limited liability.

A **business trust** is created by a written trust agreement that sets forth the interests of the beneficiaries and the obligations and powers of the trustees. With a business trust, legal ownership and management of the property of the business stay with one or more of the trustees, and the profits are distributed to the beneficiaries. A business trust resembles a corporation in many respects. Beneficiaries of the trust, for example, are not personally responsible for

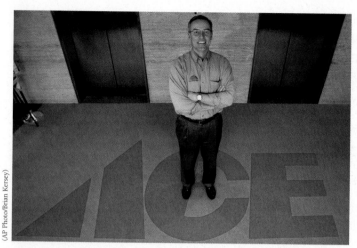

(AP Photo/Brian Kersey)

Most people believe that cooperatives are small enterprises, but not all are. Ace Hardware is a nationwide "co-op" that has been in operation for more than eighty years. Above, Ray Griffith, its chief executive officer, stands in the company's headquarters in Illinois.

Cooperative An association, which may or may not be incorporated, that is organized to provide an economic service to its members. Unincorporated cooperatives are often treated like partnerships for tax and other legal purposes.

Franchise Any arrangement in which the owner of a trademark, trade name, or copyright licenses another to use that trademark, trade name, or copyright in the selling of goods or services.

Franchisee One receiving a license to use another's (the franchisor's) trademark, trade name, or copyright in the sale of goods and services.

Franchisor One licensing another (the franchisee) to use the owner's trademark, trade name, or copyright in the selling of goods or services.

the debts or obligations of the business trust. In fact, in a number of states, business trusts must pay corporate taxes.

Cooperatives

A **cooperative** is an association that is organized to provide an economic service to its members. It may or may not be incorporated. Most cooperatives are organized under state statutes for cooperatives, general business corporations, or LLCs. Generally, an incorporated cooperative will distribute dividends, or profits, to its owners on the basis of their transactions with the cooperative rather than on the basis of the amount of capital they contributed.

Members of incorporated cooperatives have limited liability, as do shareholders of corporations and members of LLCs. Cooperatives that are unincorporated are often treated like partnerships. The members have joint liability for the cooperative's acts.

This form of business generally is adopted by groups of individuals who wish to pool their resources to gain some advantage in the marketplace. Consumer purchasing co-ops are formed to obtain lower prices through quantity discounts. Seller marketing co-ops are formed to control the market and thereby enable members to sell their goods at higher prices. Co-ops range in size from small, local, consumer cooperatives to national businesses such as Ace Hardware and Land O' Lakes, a well-known producer of dairy products.

Franchises

Instead of setting up a business to market their own products or services, many entrepreneurs opt to purchase a franchise. A **franchise** is defined as any arrangement in which the owner of a trademark, a trade name, or a copyright licenses others to use the trademark, trade name, or copyright in the selling of goods or services.

A **franchisee** (a purchaser of a franchise) is generally legally independent of the **franchisor** (the seller of the franchise). At the same time, the franchisee is economically dependent on the franchisor's integrated business system. In other words, a franchisee can operate as an independent businessperson but still obtain the advantages of a regional or national organization.

Today, franchising companies and their franchisees account for a significant portion of all retail sales in this country. Well-known franchises include McDonald's, 7-Eleven, and Holiday Inn. Franchising has also become a popular way for businesses to expand their operations internationally.

Types of Franchises

Many types of franchises are available. Generally, though, franchises fall into one of three classifications: distributorships, chain-style business operations, and manufacturing or processing-plant arrangements.

In a *distributorship,* a manufacturer (the franchisor) licenses a dealer (the franchisee) to sell its product. Often, a distributorship covers an exclusive territory. Automobile dealerships and beer distributorships are examples of this type of franchise.

In a *chain-style business operation,* a franchise operates under a franchisor's trade name and is identified as a member of a select group of dealers that engage in the franchisor's

(Imaginechina via AP Images)

Many franchises operate worldwide. McDonald's is what type of franchise?

business. The franchisee is generally required to follow standardized or prescribed methods of operation. Often, the franchisor requires that the franchisee maintain certain standards of performance. In addition, the franchisee may be required to obtain materials and supplies exclusively from the franchisor. Fast-food chains and real estate brokerage firms such as Century 21 are examples of this type of franchise.

In a *manufacturing or processing-plant arrangement*, the franchisor transmits to the franchisee the essential ingredients or formula to make a particular product. The franchisee then markets the product either at wholesale or at retail in accordance with the franchisor's standards. Examples of this type of franchise are Pepsi-Cola and other soft-drink bottling companies.

Laws Governing Franchising

Because a franchise relationship is primarily a contractual relationship, it is governed by contract law. If the franchise exists primarily for the sale of products manufactured by the franchisor, the law governing sales contracts as expressed in Article 2 of the Uniform Commercial Code applies (see Chapters 10 and 11).

Additionally, the federal government and most states have enacted laws governing certain aspects of franchising. Generally, these laws are designed to protect prospective franchisees from dishonest franchisors and to prohibit franchisors from terminating franchises without good cause.

Federal Regulation of Franchising
The federal government regulates franchising in part through the Franchise Rule, which requires franchisors to disclose certain material facts that a prospective franchisee needs to make an informed decision concerning the purchase of a franchise.[8] The rule was designed to enable potential franchisees to weigh the risks and benefits of an investment. It requires the franchisor to make numerous written disclosures to prospective franchisees.

All representations made to a prospective franchisee must have a reasonable basis. For instance, if a franchisor provides projected earnings figures, the franchisor must indicate whether the figures are based on actual data or hypothetical examples. Franchisors are also required to explain termination, cancellation, and renewal provisions of the franchise contract to potential franchisees before the agreement is signed.

The Franchise Rule has been amended to apply to franchise opportunities advertised on Web sites and communications sent electronically by franchisors. Prospective franchisees must be able to download or save all electronic disclosure documents. Additional disclosures are required about lawsuits that the franchisor has filed and any past settlement agreements.

State Regulation of Franchising
State legislation often is aimed at protecting franchisees from unfair practices and bad faith terminations by franchisors. A number of states have laws similar to the federal rules requiring franchisors to provide presale disclosures to prospective franchisees.[9]

---

8. 16 C.F.R. Part 436.
9. These states include California, Florida, Hawaii, Illinois, Indiana, Maryland, Michigan, Minnesota, New York, North Dakota, Oregon, Rhode Island, South Dakota, Texas, Utah, Virginia, Washington, and Wisconsin.

*"You have written more than a book, Ms. McBean—
you have written a franchise."*

Many state laws require that a disclosure document (known as the Franchise Disclosure Document, or FDD) be registered or filed with a state official. State laws also may require that the franchisor's advertising be submitted to the state for review or approval. To prevent arbitrary or bad faith terminations, state law may prohibit termination without "good cause" or require that certain procedures be followed in terminating a franchising relationship.

The Franchise Contract

The franchise relationship is defined by a contract between the franchisor and the franchisee. The franchise contract specifies the terms and conditions of the franchise and spells out the rights and duties of the franchisor and the franchisee. If either party fails to perform the contractual duties, that party may be subject to a lawsuit for breach of contract. Generally, statutes and case law governing franchising tend to emphasize the importance of good faith and fair dealing in franchise relationships.

The franchise contract typically covers a number of issues, including fees to be paid by the franchisee and other economic aspects of the franchise relationship. The contract may specify details about the business premises and equipment. An important consideration is the territory to be served. Some franchise contracts give the franchisee exclusive rights, or "territorial rights," to a certain geographic area. Other franchise contracts, though they define the territory allotted to a particular franchise, either specifically state that the franchise is nonexclusive or are silent on the issue of territorial rights.

Although the daily operation of the franchise is normally left to the franchisee, the franchise agreement may specify that the franchisor will provide some amount of supervision and control. When the franchisee prepares a product, such as food, or provides a service, such as a motel, the contract often provides that the franchisor will establish certain standards. Typically, the contract states that the franchisor is permitted to make periodic inspections to ensure that the standards are being maintained. As a general rule, the validity of a provision permitting the franchisor to establish and enforce certain quality standards is unquestioned. The courts reason that the franchisor has a legitimate interest in maintaining the quality of the product or service to protect its name and reputation.

➤ **KNOW THIS** ◄

Under the doctrine of *respondeat superior,* an employer may be liable for the torts of employees if they occur within the scope of employment, without regard to the personal fault of the employer.

Termination of the Franchise

The duration of the franchise is a matter to be determined between the parties. Sometimes, a franchise will start out for a short period, such as a year, so that the franchisor can determine whether it wants to stay in business with the franchisee. Other times, the duration of the franchise contract correlates with the term of the lease for the business premises, and both are renewable at the end of that period.

Usually, the franchise agreement specifies that termination must be "for cause," such as death or disability of the franchisee, insolvency of the franchisee, breach of the franchise agreement, or failure to meet specified sales quotas. Most franchise contracts provide that notice of termination must be given. If no set time for termination is specified, then a reasonable time, with notice, is implied. A franchisee must be given reasonable time to wind up the business—that is, to do the accounting and return any property of the franchisor, including confidential proprietary information and trade secrets.

Because a franchisor's termination of a franchise often has adverse consequences for the franchisee, much franchise litigation involves claims of wrongful termination. In determining whether a franchisor has acted in good faith when terminating a franchise agreement, the courts generally try to balance the rights of both parties. If a court perceives that a franchisor has arbitrarily or unfairly terminated a franchise, the franchisee will be provided with a remedy for wrongful termination. If a franchisor's decision to terminate a franchise was made in the normal course of the franchisor's business operations, however, and reasonable notice of termination was given to the franchisee, generally a court will not consider termination wrongful.

Reviewing . . . The Entrepreneur's Options

In Papagos, Arizona, a deteriorating bridge on a prominent public roadway needed repair. The city posted notices seeking proposals for an artistic bridge design and reconstruction. Davidson Masonry, LLC—owned and managed by Carl Davidson and his wife, Marilyn Rowe—decided to submit a bid for a decorative concrete project that incorporated artistic metalwork. They contacted Shana Lafayette, a local sculptor who specialized in large-scale metal creations, to help them design the bridge. The city selected their bridge design and awarded them the contract for a commission of $184,000.

Davidson Masonry and Lafayette then entered into an agreement to work together on the bridge project. Davidson Masonry agreed to install and pay for concrete and structural work, and Lafayette agreed to install the metalwork at her expense. They agreed that overall profits would be split, with 25 percent going to Lafayette and 75 percent going to Davidson Masonry. Lafayette designed numerous metal sculptures that were incorporated into colorful decorative concrete forms designed by Rowe, while Davidson performed the structural engineering. The group worked together successfully until the completion of the project. Using the information presented in the chapter, answer the following questions.

1. Would Davidson Masonry automatically be taxed as a partnership or a corporation? Why?
2. Is Davidson Masonry member managed or manager managed?
3. When Davidson Masonry and Lafayette entered into an agreement to work together, what kind of special business form was created? Explain.
4. Suppose that during construction, Lafayette entered into an agreement to rent space in a warehouse that was close to the bridge so that she could work on her sculptures near the location where they would be installed. She entered into the contract without the knowledge or consent of Davidson Masonry. In this situation, would a court be likely to hold that Davidson Masonry was bound by the contract that Lafayette entered? Why or why not?

DEBATE THIS Because LLCs are essentially just partnerships with limited liability for members, all partnership laws should apply.

BUSINESS APPLICATION

How Do You Choose between an LLC and an LLP?*

Selecting a business form is one of the most important decisions that an entrepreneur makes. To make the best decision, a business-person needs to consider all the legal, tax, licensing, and business consequences.

New forms of business organizations, including limited liability partnerships (LLPs) and limited liability companies (LLCs), provide additional options. An initial consideration in choosing between these forms is the number of participants. An LLP must have two or more partners, but in many states, an LLC can have a single member (owner).

Liability Considerations

The members of an LLC are not liable for the obligations of the organization. Members' liability is limited to the amount of their property (investment) interest. The liability of the partners in an LLP varies from state to state. About half of the states exempt the partners from liability for any obligation of the firm. In some states, the partners are individually liable for the contractual obligations of the firm but are not liable for obligations arising from the torts of others. In either situation, a partner who is sued for malpractice may be on his or her own with respect to liability unless the other partners agree to help.

Distributions from the Firm

Members and partners generally are paid by allowing them to withdraw funds from the firm against their share of the profits. In many states, a member of an LLC must repay so-called wrongful distributions even if she or he did not know that the distributions were wrongful (wrongful distributions include those made when the LLC is insolvent). Under most LLP statutes, by contrast, the partners must repay only distributions that were fraudulent.

Management Structure

Both LLPs and LLCs can set up whatever management structure the participants desire. Also, all unincorporated business organizations, including LLPs and LLCs with two or more members, are treated as partnerships for federal income tax purposes (unless an LLC elects to be treated as a corporation[a]).

This means that the firms are not taxed at the entity level. Their income is passed through to the partners or members, who report it on their individual income tax returns. Some states impose additional taxes on LLCs.

Financial and Personal Relationships

Although the legal consequences of choosing a business form are certainly important, they are often secondary to the financial and personal relationships among the participants. Work effort, motivation, ability, and other personal attributes can be significant factors, as can fundamental business concerns such as the expenses and debts of the firm—and the extent of personal liability for these obligations.

Another practical factor to consider is the willingness of others to do business with an LLP or an LLC. A supplier, for example, may not be willing to extend credit to a firm whose partners or members will not accept personal liability for the debt.

Checklist for Choosing a Limited Liability Business Form

1. Determine the number of participants a state requires, the forms it allows, and the limits on liability the state provides for the participants.
2. Evaluate the tax considerations.
3. Weigh such practical concerns as the financial and personal relationships among the participants and the willingness of others to do business with a particular organizational form.

---

a. The chief benefits of electing corporate status for tax purposes are that the members generally are not subject to self-employment taxes and that fringe benefits may be provided to employee-members on a tax-reduced basis. The tax laws are complicated, however, and a professional should be consulted about the details.

---

*This *Business Application* is not meant to substitute for the services of an attorney who is licensed to practice law in your state.

Key Terms

Chapter Summary: The Entrepreneur's Options

Major Business Forms
(See pages 550–561.)
	1. *Sole proprietorships*—The simplest form of business; used by anyone who does business without creating an organization. The owner is the business. The owner pays personal income taxes on all profits and is personally liable for all business debts.
	2. *Partnerships*—Created by agreement of the parties; not treated as an entity except for limited purposes. Partners have unlimited liability for partnership debts, and each partner normally has an equal voice in management. Income is "passed through" the partnership to the individual partners, who pay personal taxes on the income.
	3. *Limited liability partnerships (LLPs)*—Typically, an LLP is formed by professionals who work together as partners in a partnership. Under most state LLP statutes, it is relatively easy to convert a traditional partnership into an LLP. LLP statutes generally allow professionals to avoid personal liability for the malpractice of other partners.
	4. *Limited partnerships*—Must be formed in compliance with statutory requirements. A limited partnership consists of one or more general partners, who have unlimited liability for partnership losses, and one or more limited partners, who are liable only to the extent of their contributions. Only general partners can participate in management.
	5. *Corporations*—A corporation is formed in compliance with statutory requirements, is a legal entity separate and distinct from its owners, and can have perpetual existence. The shareholder-owners elect directors, who set policy and hire officers to run the day-to-day business of the corporation. Shareholders normally are not personally liable for the debts of the corporation. The corporation pays income tax on net profits; shareholders pay income tax on disbursed dividends.
	6. *Limited liability companies (LLCs)*—The LLC is a hybrid form of business organization that offers the limited liability feature of corporations and the tax benefits of partnerships. LLC members participate in management. Members of LLCs may be corporations or partnerships, are not restricted in number, and may be residents of other countries.
	   a. *LLC operation*—When an LLC is formed, the members decide, in an operating agreement, how the business will be managed and what rules will apply to the organization.
	   b. *Management*—An LLC may be managed by members only, by some members and some nonmembers, or by nonmembers only.
	   c. *Dissociation and dissolution*—Members of an LLC have the power to dissociate from the LLC at any time, but they may not have the right to dissociate. Dissociation does not always result in the dissolution of an LLC. The remaining members can choose to continue the business. If the LLC is dissolved, the business must be wound up and the assets sold.

Special Business Forms (See pages 561–564.)	1. *Joint venture*—An organization created by two or more persons or business entities in contemplation of a limited activity or a single transaction. Otherwise, similar to a partnership. 2. *Syndicate*—An investment group that undertakes to finance a particular project. A syndicate may exist as a corporation or as a general or limited partnership. 3. *Joint stock company*—A business form similar to a corporation in some respects (transferable shares of stock, management by directors and officers, perpetual existence) but otherwise resembling a partnership. 4. *Business trust*—Created by a written trust agreement that sets forth the interests of the beneficiaries and obligations and powers of the trustee(s). Similar to a corporation in many respects. Beneficiaries are not personally liable for the debts or obligations of the business trust. 5. *Cooperative*—An association organized to provide an economic service to its members. May be incorporated or unincorporated.

Franchises
(See pages 564–567.)
	1. *Types of franchises*—
	   a. Distributorship (for example, automobile dealerships).
	   b. Chain-style operation (for example, fast-food chains).
	   c. Manufacturing/processing-plant arrangement (for example, soft-drink bottling companies, such as Pepsi-Cola).
	2. *Laws governing franchising*—
	   a. Franchises are governed by contract law.
	   b. Franchises are also governed by federal and state statutory laws and agency regulations, such as the Franchise Rule.
	3. *The franchise contract*—The franchise relationship is defined by a contract between the franchisor and the franchisee. The contract normally spells out the terms and conditions of the franchise and the rights and duties of the franchisor and franchisee. Usually, the franchisor specifies the territory to be served. The franchisor may require the franchisee to abide by certain standards of quality relating to the product or service offered.
	4. *Termination of the franchise*—Usually, the contract provides for the date and/or conditions of termination of the franchise arrangement. Both federal and state statutes attempt to protect franchisees from franchisors who unfairly or arbitrarily terminate franchises.

ExamPrep

ISSUE SPOTTERS

1. Gomer, Harry, and Ida are members of Jeweled Watches, LLC. What are their options with respect to the management of their firm? **(See page 558.)**
2. Thirsty Bottling Company and U.S. Beverages, Inc. (USB), enter into a franchise agreement that states that the franchise may be terminated at any time "for cause." Thirsty fails to meet USB's specified sales quota. Does this constitute "cause" for termination? Why or why not? **(See pages 566–567.)**

—**Check your answers to the Issue Spotters against the answers provided in Appendix E at the end of this text.**

BEFORE THE TEST

Go to www.cengagebrain.com, enter the ISBN 9781133191353, and click on "Find" to locate this textbook's Web site. Then, click on "Access Now" under "Study Tools," and select Chapter 19 at the top. There, you will find a Practice Quiz that you can take to assess your mastery of the concepts in this chapter, as well as Flashcards, a Glossary of important terms, and Video Questions (when assigned).

For Review

Answers to the even-numbered questions in this For Review section can be found in Appendix F at the end of this text.

1. What are some of the major forms of business organization in the United States?
2. What advantages and disadvantages are associated with the sole proprietorship?
3. What advantages do limited liability companies offer to businesspersons that are not offered by sole proprietorships or partnerships?
4. What are two options for managing limited liability companies?
5. What is a franchise?

Business Scenarios and Case Problems

19–1 **Jurisdiction.** Joe, a resident of New Jersey, wants to open a restaurant. He asks his friend Kay, who is an experienced attorney and a New Yorker, for her business and legal advice in exchange for a 20 percent ownership interest in the restaurant. Kay helps Joe negotiate a lease for the restaurant premises and advises Joe to organize the business as a limited liability company (LLC). Joe forms Café Olé, LLC, and, with Kay's help, obtains financing. Then, the night before the restaurant opens, Joe tells Kay that he is "cutting her out of the deal." The restaurant proves to be a success. Kay wants to file a suit in a federal district court against Joe and the LLC. Can a federal court exercise jurisdiction over the parties based on diversity of citizenship? Explain. **(See pages 566–567.)**

19–2 ![?] **Question with Sample Answer—Special Business Forms.** Faraway Corp. is considering entering into two contracts, one with a joint stock company that distributes home products east of the Mississippi River and the other with a business trust formed by a number of sole proprietors who are sellers of home products on the West Coast. Both contracts involve large capital outlays for

Faraway, which will supply each business with soft-drink dispensers. In both business organizations, at least two shareholders or beneficiaries are personally wealthy, but each organization has limited financial resources. The owner-managers of Faraway are not familiar with either form of business organization. Because each form resembles a corporation, they are concerned about whether they will be able to collect payments from the wealthy members of the business organizations in the event that either organization breaches the contract by failing to make the payments. Discuss fully Faraway's concern. **(See pages 563–564.)**

—**For a sample answer to Question 19–2, go to Appendix G at the end of this text.**

19–3 ![icon] **Spotlight on McDonald's—Franchise Termination.** C.B. Management, Inc., had a franchise agreement with McDonald's Corp to operate McDonald's restaurants in Cleveland, Ohio. The agreement required C.B. to make monthly payments of certain percentages of the gross sales to McDonald's. If any payment was more than thirty days late, McDonald's had the right to terminate the franchise. The agreement also stated that even if McDonald's accepted a late payment, that would not "constitute a waiver of any subsequent breach." McDonald's sometimes accepted C.B.'s late payments, but when C.B. defaulted on the payments in July 2010, McDonald's gave notice of thirty days to comply or surrender possession of the restaurants. C.B. missed the deadline. McDonald's demanded that C.B. vacate the restaurants, but C.B. refused. McDonald's alleged that C.B. had violated the franchise agreement. C.B. claimed that McDonald's had breached the implied covenant of good faith and fair dealing. Which party should prevail and why? [*McDonald's Corp. v. C.B. Management Co.,* 13 F.Supp.2d 705 (N.D.Ill. 1998)] **(See pages 566–567.)**

19–4 **Joint Ventures.** Holiday Isle Resort & Marina, Inc., operated four restaurants, five bars, and various food kiosks at its resort in Islamorada, Florida. Holiday entered into a "joint venture agreement" with Rip Tosun to operate a fifth restaurant called Rip's—A Place for Ribs. The agreement gave Tosun authority over the employees and "full authority as to the conduct of the business." It also prohibited Tosun from competing with Rip's without Holiday's approval but did not prevent Holiday from competing. Later, Tosun sold half of his interest in Rip's to Thomas Hallock. Soon, Tosun and Holiday opened the Olde Florida Steakhouse next to Rip's. Holiday stopped serving breakfast at Rip's and diverted employees and equipment from Rip's to the steakhouse, which then started offering breakfast. Hallock filed a suit in a Florida state court against Holiday. Did Holiday breach the joint-venture agreement? Did it breach the duties that joint venturers owe each other? Explain. [*Hallock v. Holiday Isle Resort & Marina, Inc.,* 4 So.3d 17 (Fla.App. 3 Dist. 2009)] **(See pages 561–562.)**

19–5 **LLC Operation.** After Hurricane Katrina, James Williford, Patricia Mosser, Marquetta Smith, and Michael Floyd formed Bluewater Logistics, LLC, to bid on construction contracts. Under Mississippi law, every member of a member-managed LLC is entitled to participate in managing the business. The operating agreement provided for a "super majority" 75 percent vote to remove a member "under any other circumstances that would jeopardize the company status" as a contractor. After Bluewater had completed more than $5 million in contracts, Smith told Williford that she, Mosser, and Floyd were exercising their "super majority" vote to fire him. No reason was provided. Williford sued Bluewater and the other members. Did Smith, Mosser, and Floyd breach the state LLC statute, their fiduciary duties, or the Bluewater operating agreements? Discuss. [*Bluewater Logistics, LLC v. Williford,* 55 So.3d 148 (Miss. 2011)] **(See pages 557–558.)**

19–6 **Fiduciary Duties of Partners.** Karl Horvath, Hein Rüsen, and Carl Thomas formed a partnership, HRT Enterprises, to buy a manufacturing plant. Rüsen and Thomas leased the plant to their own company, Merkur Steel. Merkur

then sublet the premises to other companies owned by Rüsen and Thomas. The rent that these companies paid to Merkur was higher than the rent from the arrangement. Rüsen and Thomas did not tell Horvath about the subleases. Did Rüsen and Thomas breach their fiduciary duties to HRT and Horvath? Discuss. [*Horvath v. HRT Enterprises,* 489 Mich.App. 992, 800 N.W.2d 595 (2011)] **(See pages 552–553.)**

19–7 **Wrongful Termination of Franchise.** George Oshana and GTO Investments, Inc., operated a Mobil gas station franchise in Itasca, Illinois. In 2010, Oshana and GTO became involved in a rental dispute with Buchanan Energy, to which Mobil had assigned the lease. In November 2011, Buchanan terminated the franchise because Oshana and GTO had failed to pay the rent. Oshana and GTO, however, alleged that they were "ready, willing, and able to pay the rent" but that Buchanan failed to accept their electronic funds transfer. Have Oshana and GTO stated a claim for wrongful termination of their franchise? Why or why not? [*Oshana v. Buchanan Energy,* 2012 WL 426921 (N.D.Ill. 2012)] **(See pages 566–567.)**

19–8 ⚖ **Case Problem with Sample Answer—Jurisdictional Requirements.** Fadal Machining Centers, LLC, and MAG Industrial Automation Centers, LLC, sued a New Jersey–based corporation, Mid-Atlantic CNC, Inc., in federal district court. Ten percent of MAG was owned by SP MAG Holdings, a Delaware LLC. SP MAG had six members, including a Delaware limited partnership called Silver Point Capital Fund and a Delaware LLC called SPCP Group III. In turn, Silver Point and SPCP Group had a common member, Robert O'Shea, who was a New Jersey citizen. Assuming that the amount in controversy exceeds $75,000, does the district court have diversity jurisdiction? Why or why not? [*Fadal Machining Centers, LLC v. Mid-Atlantic CNC, Inc.,* 2012 WL 8669 (9th Cir. 2012)] **(See pages 556–557.)**

—**For a sample answer to Problem 19–8, go to Appendix H at the end of this text.**

19–9 ◆▶ **A Question of Ethics—LLC Operation.** Blushing Brides, LLC, a publisher of wedding planning magazines in Columbus, Ohio, opened an account with Gray Printing Co. in July 2000. On behalf of Blushing Brides, Louis Zacks, the firm's member-manager, signed a credit agreement that identified the firm as the "purchaser" and required payment within thirty days. Despite the agreement, Blushing Brides typically took up to six months to pay the full amount for its orders. Gray printed and shipped 10,000 copies of a fall/winter 2001 issue for Blushing Brides but had not been paid when the firm ordered 15,000 copies of a spring/summer 2002 issue. Gray refused to print the new order without an assurance of payment. Zacks signed a promissory note for $14,778, plus interest at 6 percent per year, payable to Gray on June 22. Gray printed the new order but by October had been paid only $7,500. Gray filed a suit in an Ohio state court against Blushing Brides and Zacks to collect the balance. [*Gray Printing Co. v. Blushing Brides, LLC* 2006 WL 832587 (Ohio App. 2006)] **(See pages 557–558.)**

1. Under what circumstances is a member of an LLC liable for the firm's debts? In this case, is Zacks personally liable under the credit agreement for the unpaid amount on Blushing Brides' account? Did Zacks's promissory note affect the parties' liability on the account? Explain.

2. Does a member of an LLC have an ethical responsibility to meet the obligations of the firm? Discuss.

3. Gray shipped only 10,000 copies of the spring/summer 2002 issue of Blushing Brides' magazine, waiting for the publisher to identify a destination for the other 5,000 copies. The magazine had a retail price of $4.50 per copy. Did Gray have a legal or ethical duty to "mitigate the damages" by attempting to sell or otherwise distribute these copies itself? Why or why not?

Critical Thinking and Writing Assignments

19–10   **Business Law Critical Thinking Group Assignment.** Walid Elkhatib, an Arab American, bought a Dunkin' Donuts franchise in Illinois. Ten years later, Dunkin' Donuts began offering breakfast sandwiches with bacon, ham, or sausage through its franchises. Elkhatib refused to sell these items at his store on the ground that his religion forbade the handling of pork. Elkhatib then opened a second franchise, at which he also refused to sell pork products. The next year, at both locations, Elkhatib began selling meatless sandwiches. He also opened a third franchise. When he proposed to relocate this franchise, Dunkin' Donuts refused to approve the new location and informed him that it would not renew any of his franchise agreements because he did not carry the full sandwich line. Elkhatib filed a lawsuit against Dunkin' Donuts.

1. The first group will argue on behalf of Elkhatib that Dunkin' Donuts wrongfully terminated his franchises.

2. The second group will take the side of Dunkin' Donuts and justify its decision to terminate the franchises.

3. The third group will assess whether Dunkin' Donuts acted in good faith in its relationship with Elkhatib. Also, consider whether Dunkin' Donuts should be required to accommodate Elkhatib's religious beliefs and allow him not to serve pork in these three locations.

CHAPTER 20

Corporations

(pixhook/iStockphoto.com)

CHAPTER OUTLINE

- Nature and Classification
- Formation and Powers
- Corporate Financing
- Directors, Officers, and Shareholders
- Mergers and Acquisitions
- Corporate Termination

LEARNING OBJECTIVES

The five learning objectives below are designed to help improve your understanding of the chapter. After reading this chapter, you should be able to answer the following questions:

1 What is a close corporation?

2 In what circumstances might a court disregard the corporate entity ("pierce the corporate veil") and hold the shareholders personally liable?

3 What are the duties of corporate directors and officers?

4 What is a voting proxy?

5 What are the basic differences between a merger, a consolidation, and a share exchange?

"A corporation is an artificial being, invisible, intangible, and existing only in contemplation of law."

—John Marshall, 1755–1835 (Chief Justice of the United States Supreme Court, 1801–1835)

The corporation is a creature of statute. As John Marshall indicated in the chapter-opening quotation, a corporation is an artificial being, existing only in law and neither tangible nor visible. Its existence generally depends on state law. This chapter examines many aspects of corporations—how they are formed, owned, controlled, financed, combined, and terminated. You will also read about a new method of financing corporations through crowdfunding Web sites in a feature on page 584.

Each state has its own body of corporate law, and these laws are not entirely uniform. The Model Business Corporation Act (MBCA) is a codification of modern corporation law that has been influential in the drafting and revision of state corporation statutes. Today, the majority of state statutes are guided by the revised version of the MBCA, which is often referred to as the Revised Model Business Corporation Act (RMBCA). Even statutes based on the MBCA or RMBCA vary from state to state, however, so it is important to consult the laws of the individual states.

Musicians celebrate Wal-Mart at its shareholders' meeting in Fayetteville, Arkansas.

Corporation A legal entity formed in compliance with statutory requirements that is distinct from its shareholder-owners.

Dividend A distribution of corporate profits to the corporation's shareholders in proportion to the number of shares held.

Retained Earnings The portion of a corporation's profits that has not been paid out as dividends to shareholders.

Who hires corporate personnel?

Nature and Classification

A **corporation** is a legal entity created and recognized by state law. It can consist of one or more *natural persons* (as opposed to the artificial *legal person* of the corporation) identified under a common name. A corporation can be owned by a single person, or it can have hundreds, thousands, or even millions of owners (shareholders). The corporation substitutes itself for its shareholders in conducting corporate business and in incurring liability, yet its authority to act and the liability for its actions are separate from the individuals who own it.

A corporation is recognized as a "person," and it enjoys many of the same rights and privileges under state and federal law that natural persons enjoy. For instance, corporations possess the same right of access to the courts as natural persons and can sue or be sued. The constitutional guarantees of due process, free speech, and freedom from unreasonable searches and seizures also apply to corporations. In addition, corporations have a right under the First Amendment to fund political broadcasts—a topic discussed in this chapter's *Landmark in Law* feature on the facing page.

Corporate Personnel

In a corporation, the responsibility for the overall management of the firm is entrusted to a *board of directors,* whose members are elected by the shareholders. The board of directors hires *corporate officers* and other employees to run the corporation's daily business operations of the corporation. The rights and duties of directors and officers will be examined later in this chapter, as will the rights and duties of shareholders.

The Limited Liability of Shareholders

One of the key advantages of the corporate form is the limited liability of its shareholders. Corporate shareholders normally are not personally liable for the obligations of the corporation beyond the extent of their investments. In certain limited situations, however, a court can *pierce the corporate veil* (see pages 582 and 583) and impose liability on shareholders for the corporation's obligations. Additionally, to enable the firm to obtain credit, shareholders in small companies sometimes voluntarily assume personal liability, as guarantors, for corporate obligations.

Corporate Earnings and Taxation

When a corporation earns profits, it can either pass them on to its shareholders in the form of **dividends** or retain them as profits. These **retained earnings,** if invested properly, will yield higher corporate profits in the future and thus cause the price of the company's stock to rise. Individual shareholders can then reap the benefits of these retained earnings in the capital gains that they receive when they sell their stock.

Whether a corporation retains its profits or passes them on to the shareholders as dividends, those profits are subject to income tax by various levels of government. As you will read later in this chapter, failure

LANDMARK IN THE LAW

Citizens United v. Federal Election Commission (2010)

In *Citizens United v. Federal Election Commission,*[a] the United States Supreme Court held that the First Amendment prevents limits from being placed on corporate funding of independent political broadcasts. The case involved broadcasts of political material by Citizens United, a nonprofit corporation that has a *political action committee* (an organization that is registered with the government and campaigns for political candidates).

Background   In 2002, in an effort to reform campaign financing, Congress enacted the Bipartisan Campaign Reform Act (BCRA), also known as the McCain-Feingold Act. One provision of the BCRA prohibited corporations and labor unions from using their general treasury funds to make independent expenditures for speech that is an "electioneering communication" or for speech that expressly advocates the election or defeat of a candidate.[b] The act defined an electioneering communication as "any broadcast, cable, or satellite communication" that "refers to a clearly identified candidate for Federal office" and is made within thirty days of a primary election.

In 2008, Citizens United produced a film called *Hillary: The Movie* that was critical of Hillary Clinton, who at the time was a candidate for the Democratic presidential nomination. As part of its distribution plans for *Hillary,* Citizens United wanted to make the film available on television through video-on-demand systems within thirty days of primary elections, but it was concerned about potential civil and criminal penalties for violating the BCRA.

Citizens United filed an action in federal court against the Federal Election Commission (FEC) seeking a declaratory judgment that the BCRA was unconstitutional as applied to *Hillary.* The court, however, ruled in favor of the FEC, finding that the film had no purpose except to discredit Clinton's candidacy. Citizens United appealed.

A Surprising Decision   To the surprise of many commentators, the United States Supreme Court explicitly overruled two of its earlier decisions on campaign financing.[c] In a five-to-four decision, the Court struck down the provision of the BCRA that prohibited both for-profit and nonprofit corporations, as well as labor unions, from broadcasting "electioneering communications." Other provisions of the BCRA were upheld, however, including the provision that requires disclosures that identify the person or entity responsible for the content of electioneering communications.

Justice Anthony Kennedy, writing for the majority, said, "All speakers, including individuals and the media, use money amassed from the economic marketplace to fund their speech. The First Amendment protects the resulting speech, even if it was enabled by economic transactions with persons or entities who disagree with the speaker's ideas."

In dissent, Justice John Paul Stevens argued that the Court's ruling "threatens to undermine the integrity of elected institutions across the Nation. The path it has taken to reach its outcome will, I fear, do damage to this institution."

Application to Today's World   *Many critics of the decision argued that it opens the door for corporations, including foreign-owned corporations, to spend without limit to influence our elections. Although federal law still prohibits corporations and unions from giving funds directly to political campaigns, these entities can fund advertising and other actions that seek to persuade the voting public.*

---

a. ___ U.S. ___, 130 S.Ct. 876, 175 L.Ed.2d 753 (2010).
b. 2 U.S.C. Section 441b.

c. *Austin v. Michigan Chamber of Commerce,* 494 U.S. 652, 110 S.Ct. 1391, 108 L.Ed.2d 652 (1990); and *McConnell v. Federal Election Commission,* 540 U.S. 93, 124 S.Ct. 619, 157 L.Ed.2d 491 (2003).

---

to pay taxes can lead to severe consequences. The state can suspend the entity's corporate status until the taxes are paid or even dissolve the corporation.

Another important aspect of corporate taxation is that corporate profits can be subject to double taxation. The company pays tax on its profits, and then if the profits are passed on to the shareholders as dividends, the shareholders must also pay income tax on them. The corporation normally does not receive a tax deduction for dividends it distributes to shareholders. This double-taxation feature is one of the major disadvantages of the corporate business form.

Holding Company A company whose
business activity is holding shares in another
company.

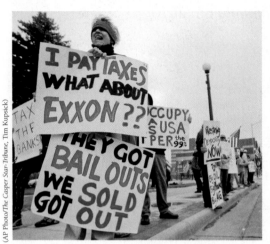

(AP Photo/The Casper Star-Tribune, Tim Kupsick)

What are some of the reasons that these
demonstrators believe that large corporations are
not paying enough taxes?

Some U.S. corporations use holding companies to reduce—or at least defer—their U.S. income taxes. At its simplest, a **holding company** (sometimes referred to as a *parent company*) is a company whose business activity consists of holding shares in another company. Typically, the holding company is established in a low-tax or no-tax offshore jurisdiction. Among the best known are the Cayman Islands, Dubai, Hong Kong, Luxembourg, Monaco, and Panama. In general, any profits received by the holding company on investments are taxed at the rate of the offshore jurisdiction where the company is registered, not the rates applicable to the parent company or its shareholders in their country of residence. Once the profits are brought "onshore," though, they are taxed at the federal corporate income tax rate, and any payments received by the shareholders are also taxable at the full U.S. rates.

Torts and Criminal Acts

A corporation is liable for the torts committed by its agents or officers within the course and scope of their employment. This principle applies to a corporation exactly as it applies to the ordinary agency relationships discussed in Chapter 17. It follows the doctrine of *respondeat superior.*

Recall from Chapter 6 that under modern criminal law, a corporation may be held liable for the criminal acts of its agents and employees. Although corporations cannot be imprisoned, they can be fined. (Of course, corporate directors and officers can be imprisoned, and many have been in recent years.) In addition, under sentencing guidelines for crimes committed by corporate employees (white-collar crimes), corporations can face fines amounting to hundreds of millions of dollars.[1]

CASE EXAMPLE 20.1   Brian Gauthier drove a dump truck for Angelo Todesca Corporation. The truck was missing its back-up alarm, but Angelo allowed Gauthier to continue driving it. At a worksite, Gauthier backed up the truck and struck and killed a police officer who was directing traffic. The state charged Angelo and Gauthier with the crime of vehicular homicide. Angelo argued that a "corporation" could not be guilty of vehicular homicide because it cannot "operate" a vehicle. The court ruled that if an employee commits a crime "while engaged in corporate business that the employee has been authorized to conduct," a corporation can be held liable for the crime. Hence, Angelo was liable for Gauthier's negligent operation of its truck, which resulted in a person's death.[2] ●

Classification of Corporations

Corporations can be classified in several ways. The classification of a corporation normally depends on its location, purpose, and ownership characteristics, as described in the following subsections.

Domestic, Foreign, and Alien Corporations   A corporation is referred to as a **domestic corporation** by its home state (the state in which it incorporates). A corporation formed in one state but doing business in another is referred to in the second state as a **foreign corporation.** A corporation formed in another country (say, Mexico) but doing business in the United States is referred to in the United States as an **alien corporation.**

A corporation does not have an automatic right to do business in a state other than its state of incorporation. In some instances, it must obtain a *certificate of authority* in any

Domestic Corporation In a given state,
a corporation that is organized under the law of
that state.

Foreign Corporation In a given state, a
corporation that does business in that state but
is not incorporated there.

Alien Corporation A corporation formed in
another country but doing business in the United
States.

---

1. Note that the Sarbanes-Oxley Act, discussed in Chapter 2, stiffened the penalties for certain types of corporate crime and ordered the U.S. Sentencing Commission to revise the sentencing guidelines accordingly.
2. *Commonwealth v. Angelo Todesca Corp.*, 446 Mass. 128, 842 N.E.2d 930 (2006).

(EdStock/iStockphoto.com)

Is AMTRAK a public or a publicly held corporation?

state in which it plans to do business. Once the certificate has been issued, the corporation generally can exercise in that state all of the powers conferred on it by its home state. If a foreign corporation does business in a state without obtaining a certificate of authority, the state can impose fines and sanctions on the corporation, and sometimes on its officers, directors, or agents.

Note that most state statutes specify that engaging in certain activities, such as soliciting orders via the Internet, is not considered doing business within the state. Thus, a foreign corporation normally does not need a certificate of authority to sell goods or services via the Internet or by mail.

Public and Private Corporations

A *public corporation* is one formed by the government to meet some political or governmental purpose. Cities and towns that incorporate are common examples. In addition, many federal government organizations—such as the U.S. Postal Service, the Tennessee Valley Authority, and AMTRAK—are public corporations. Note that a public corporation is not the same as a *publicly held corporation* (often called a *public company*). A publicly held corporation is any corporation whose shares are publicly traded in securities markets, such as the New York Stock Exchange or the over-the-counter market.

A *private corporation* is created either wholly or in part for private benefit. Most corporations are private. Although they may serve a public purpose, as a public electric or gas utility does, they are owned by private persons rather than by the government.

> **KNOW THIS**
>
> A private corporation is a voluntary association, but a public corporation is not.

Nonprofit Corporations

Corporations formed for purposes other than making a profit are called *nonprofit* or *not-for-profit* corporations. Private hospitals, educational institutions, charities, and religious organizations, for example, are frequently organized as nonprofit corporations. The nonprofit corporation is a convenient form of organization that allows various groups to own property and to form contracts without exposing the individual members to personal liability.

Close Corporations

Most corporate enterprises in the United States fall into the category of close corporations. A **close corporation** is one whose shares are held by members of a family or by relatively few persons. Close corporations are also referred to as *closely held, family,* or *privately held* corporations. Usually, the members of the small group constituting a close corporation are personally known to one another. Because the number of shareholders is so small, there is no trading market for the shares.

Close Corporation A corporation whose shareholders are limited to a small group of persons, often family members.

In practice, a close corporation is often operated like a partnership. Some states have enacted special statutory provisions that permit close corporations to depart significantly from certain formalities required by traditional corporation law.[3]

Additionally, the RMBCA gives close corporations considerable flexibility in determining their operating rules [RMBCA 7.32]. If all of a corporation's shareholders agree in writing, the corporation can operate without directors, bylaws, annual or special shareholders' or directors' meetings, stock certificates, or formal records of shareholders' or directors' decisions.[4]

LEARNING OBJECTIVE 1
What is a close corporation?

Transfer of Shares in Close Corporations

By definition, a close corporation has a small number of shareholders. Thus, the transfer of one shareholder's shares to someone else can cause serious management problems. The other shareholders may find themselves required to share control with someone they do not know or like.

---

3. For example, in some states (such as Maryland), a close corporation need not have a board of directors.

4. Shareholders cannot agree, however, to eliminate certain rights of shareholders, such as the right to inspect corporate books and records or the right to bring *derivative actions* (lawsuits on behalf of the corporation, discussed on pages 596–597 of this chapter).

To avoid this situation, the corporation can restrict the transferability of shares to outside persons. Shareholders can be required to offer their shares to the corporation or the other shareholders before selling them to an outside purchaser. In fact, a few states have statutes that prohibit the transfer of close corporation shares unless certain persons—including shareholders, family members, and the corporation—are first given the opportunity to purchase the shares for the same price.

Control of a close corporation can also be stabilized through the use of a *shareholder agreement*. A shareholder agreement can provide that when one of the original shareholders dies, her or his shares of stock in the corporation will be divided in such a way that the proportionate holdings of the survivors, and thus their proportionate control, will be maintained. Courts are generally reluctant to interfere with private agreements, including shareholder agreements.

Misappropriation of Close Corporation Funds   Sometimes, a majority shareholder in a close corporation takes advantage of his or her position and misappropriates company funds. In such situations, the normal remedy for the injured minority shareholders is to have their shares appraised and to be paid the fair market value for them.

CASE EXAMPLE 20.2   John Murray, Stephen Hopkins, and Paul Ryan were the controlling shareholders of Olympic Adhesives, Inc. They were also officers, directors, and employees and received salaries from Olympic. Twice a year, the three men paid themselves a large percentage of Olympic's net profits allocated according to their stock ownership. The percentage increased over the years to 98 percent. Merek Rubin, a minority shareholder, sued, claiming that Murray, Hopkins, and Ryan had paid themselves excessive compensation and deprived him of his share of Olympic's profits. The court agreed. Murray, Hopkins, and Ryan, as majority shareholders, had breached their fiduciary duty to Rubin as a minority shareholder by paying themselves an unreasonable amount of the company's net profits. The court ordered the defendants to repay Olympic nearly $6 million to be distributed among its shareholders.[5] ●

S Corporations

S Corporation A close corporation that has most corporate attributes, including limited liability, but qualifies under the Internal Revenue Code to be taxed as a partnership.

A close corporation that meets the qualifying requirements specified in Subchapter S of the Internal Revenue Code can operate as an **S corporation**. If a corporation has S corporation status, it can avoid the imposition of income taxes at the corporate level while retaining many of the advantages of a corporation, particularly limited liability. Among the numerous requirements for S corporation status, the following are the most important:

1. The corporation must be a domestic corporation.
2. The corporation must not be a member of an affiliated group of corporations.
3. The shareholders of the corporation must be individuals, estates, or certain trusts. Partnerships and nonqualifying trusts cannot be shareholders. Corporations can be shareholders under certain circumstances.
4. The corporation must have no more than one hundred shareholders.
5. The corporation must have only one class of stock, although all shareholders do not have to have the same voting rights. (Stock classes are discussed later in this chapter.)
6. No shareholder of the corporation may be a nonresident alien.

As mentioned, an S corporation is treated differently from a regular corporation for tax purposes. An S corporation is taxed like a partnership, so the corporate income passes through to the shareholders, who pay personal income tax on it. This treatment enables the S corporation to avoid the double taxation that is imposed on regular corporations.

---

5. *Rubin v. Murray,* 79 Mass.App.Ct 64, 943 N.E.2d 949 (2011).

Because the limited liability company and the limited liability partnership (see Chapter 19) offer similar tax advantages and greater flexibility, the S corporation has lost much of its significance in recent years.

Formation and Powers

Incorporating a business is much simpler today than it was twenty years ago, and many states allow businesses to incorporate via the Internet. In the past, preliminary steps were taken to organize and promote the business prior to incorporating. Contracts were made with investors and others on behalf of the future corporation. Today, due to the relative ease of forming a corporation in most states, persons incorporating their business rarely, if ever, engage in preliminary promotional activities.

Nevertheless, it is important for businesspersons to understand that they are personally liable for all preincorporation contracts made with investors, accountants, or others on behalf of the future corporation. This personal liability continues until the corporation assumes the preincorporation contracts by *novation* (discussed on page 266 in Chapter 9).

EXAMPLE 20.3   Jade Sorrel contracts with an accountant, Ray Cooper, to provide tax advice for a proposed corporation, Blackstone, Inc. Cooper provides the services to Sorrel, knowing that the corporation has not yet been formed. Once Blackstone, Inc., is formed, Cooper sends an invoice to the corporation and to Sorrel personally, but the bill is not paid. Because Sorrel is personally liable for the preincorporation contract, Cooper can file a lawsuit against Sorrel for breaching the contract. Cooper cannot hold Blackstone, Inc., liable unless he has entered into a novation contract with the corporation. •

Incorporation Procedures

Exact procedures for incorporation differ among states, but the basic steps are as follows: (1) select a state of incorporation, (2) secure the corporate name by confirming its availability, (3) prepare the articles of incorporation, and (4) file the articles of incorporation with the secretary of state and pay the specified fees. These steps are discussed in more detail in the following subsections.

Select the State of Incorporation   The first step in the incorporation process is to select a state in which to incorporate. Because state corporation laws differ, individuals may look for the states that offer the most advantageous tax or other provisions. Another consideration is the fee that a particular state charges to incorporate, as well as the annual fees and the fees for specific transactions (such as stock transfers).

Delaware has historically had the least restrictive laws and provisions that favor corporate management. Consequently, many corporations, including a number of the largest, have incorporated there. Close corporations generally incorporate in the state where their principal shareholders live and work. For reasons of convenience and cost, businesses often choose to incorporate in the state in which the corporation's business will primarily be conducted.

Secure the Corporate Name   The choice of a corporate name is subject to state approval to ensure against duplication or deception. State statutes usually require that the secretary of state (or sometimes the incorporators themselves) run a check on the proposed name in the state of incorporation. All corporate statutes require the corporation name to include the word *Corporation, Incorporated, Company,* or *Limited,* or abbreviations of these terms.

(www.sba.gov/content/how-name-business)

What important requirement for naming new companies is not mentioned in the above list from the SBA.gov Web site?

First Check Available Domain Names   Most corporations need to have an online presence to compete effectively in today's business climate. The corporate name should be one that can be used as the business's Internet domain name. Therefore, it is advisable to check what domain names are available *before* securing a corporate name with the state. Incorporators can do this by going to one of the many companies that issue domain names, such as Network Solutions, and finding out if the preferred name is available. If another business is using that name, incorporators will have to select an alternative name that can be used as the business's URL, and then they should seek approval from the state.

Trade Name Disputes   A new corporation's name cannot be the same as (or deceptively similar to) the name of an existing corporation doing business within the state. **EXAMPLE 20.4** If an existing corporation is named Digital Synergy, Inc., you cannot choose the name Digital Synergy Company, because that name is deceptively similar to the first. The state will be unlikely to allow you to use the name because it could transfer a part of the goodwill established by the first corporate user to your company. In addition, you would not want the name because you might be unable to acquire an Internet domain name using even part of it. ●

If those incorporating a firm contemplate doing business in other states—or over the Internet—they also need to check existing corporate names in those states. Otherwise, if the firm does business under a name that is the same as or deceptively similar to an existing company's name, it may be liable for trade name infringement.

PREVENTING LEGAL DISPUTES

Be cautious when choosing a corporate name. Always check the availability of a particular domain name before selecting a corporate name and clearing it with the state. Recognize that even if a particular state does not require the incorporator to run a name check, doing so can help prevent future disputes. Trade name disputes may also arise if your business's name is deceptively similar to the name of a partnership or limited liability company. Disputes are even more likely to arise among online firms. It is often worth incurring the additional cost of hiring a professional to conduct a name search.

Articles of Incorporation A document containing basic information that is filed with the appropriate state official, usually the secretary of state, when a business is incorporated.

Prepare the Articles of Incorporation   The primary document needed to incorporate a business is the **articles of incorporation**. The articles include basic information about the corporation and serve as a primary source of authority for its future organization and business functions. The person or persons who execute (sign) the articles are called *incorporators*. Generally, the articles of incorporation *must* include the following information [RMBCA 2.02]:

1. The name of the corporation.
2. The number of shares the corporation is authorized to issue.
3. The name and address of the corporation's initial *registered agent*. The registered agent is a person who can receive legal documents on behalf of the corporation.
4. The name and address of each incorporator.

In addition, the articles *may* include other information, such as the names and addresses of the initial directors, the duration and purpose of the corporation, the par value of the corporation's shares, and other information pertinent to the rights and duties of the corporation's shareholders and directors. Articles of incorporation vary widely depending on the size and type of corporation and the jurisdiction.

The articles may describe the internal structure of the corporation. This information, however, is usually included in the **bylaws,** which are the internal rules of management adopted by the corporation at its first organizational meeting. The articles of incorporation commence the corporation, whereas the bylaws are formed after commencement by the board of directors.

Bylaws The internal rules of management adopted by a corporation at its first organizational meeting.

> ►**KNOW THIS**◄
>
> Unlike the articles of incorporation, bylaws do not need to be filed with a state official.

File the Articles with the State   Once the articles of incorporation have been prepared, signed, and authenticated by the incorporators, they are sent to the appropriate state official, usually the secretary of state, along with the required filing fee. In most states, the secretary of state then stamps the articles as "Filed" and returns a copy of the articles to the incorporators. Once this occurs, the corporation officially exists.

Improper Incorporation   The procedures for incorporation are very specific. If they are not followed precisely, others may be able to challenge the existence of the corporation. If a corporation has substantially complied with all the statutory requirements, the corporation is said to have *de jure* (rightful and lawful) existence. If the defect in formation is substantial, however, such as a corporation's failure to hold an organizational meeting to adopt bylaws, the outcome will vary depending on the court.

Corporation by Estoppel   Sometimes, a business association holds itself out to others as being a corporation when it has made no attempt to incorporate. In those situations, the firm normally will be estopped (prevented) from denying corporate status in a lawsuit by a third party. When justice requires, the courts treat an alleged corporation as if it were an actual corporation for the purpose of determining its rights and liabilities in a particular circumstance.

CASE EXAMPLE 20.5   W. P. Media, Inc., and Alabama MBA, Inc., agreed to form a wireless Internet services company. W. P. Media was to create a wireless network, and Alabama MBA was to contribute the capital. Hugh Brown signed the parties' contract on behalf of Alabama MBA as the chair of its board. At the time, however, Alabama MBA's articles of incorporation had not yet been filed. Brown filed the articles of incorporation the following year. Later, Brown and Alabama MBA filed a suit alleging that W. P. Media had breached their contract by not building the wireless network. The Supreme Court of Alabama held that because W. P. Media had treated Alabama MBA as a corporation, W. P. Media was estopped from denying Alabama MBA's corporate existence.[6] ●

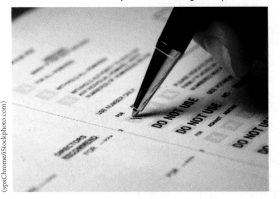

What are the routine aspects of forming a corporation?

(spxChrome/iStockphoto.com)

Corporate Powers

When a corporation is created, the express and implied powers necessary to achieve its purpose also come into existence. The express powers of a corporation are found in its articles of incorporation, in the law of the state of incorporation, and in the state and federal constitutions.

Corporate bylaws also establish express powers. Because state corporation statutes frequently provide default rules that apply if the company's bylaws are silent on an issue, it is important that the bylaws set forth the specific operating rules of the corporation. In addition, after the bylaws are adopted, the corporation's board of directors will pass resolutions that

---

6. *Brown v. W. P. Media, Inc.,* 17 So.3d 1167 (2009).

grant or restrict corporate powers. The following order of priority is used when conflicts arise among these various documents:

1. The U.S. Constitution.
2. State constitutions.
3. State statutes.
4. The articles of incorporation.
5. Bylaws.
6. Resolutions of the board of directors.

Barring express constitutional, statutory, or other prohibitions, the corporation has the implied power to perform all acts reasonably appropriate and necessary to accomplish its corporate purposes. For this reason, a corporation has the implied power to borrow funds within certain limits, to lend funds, and to extend credit to those with whom it has a legal or contractual relationship.

Piercing the Corporate Veil

Piercing the Corporate Veil The action of a court to disregard the corporate entity and hold the shareholders personally liable for corporate debts and obligations.

LEARNING OBJECTIVE 2

In what circumstances might a court disregard the corporate entity ("pierce the corporate veil") and hold the shareholders personally liable?

Commingle To put funds or goods together into one mass to such a degree that they no longer have separate identities, as when personal and corporate interests are mixed to the extent that the corporation has no separate identity.

We noted earlier that a corporation's owners—its shareholders—are not personally liable for the obligations of the corporation. Occasionally, however, the owners use a corporate entity to perpetrate a fraud, circumvent the law, or in some other way accomplish an illegitimate objective. In these situations, the court will ignore the corporate structure by **piercing the corporate veil** and exposing the shareholders to personal liability.

Generally, courts pierce the veil when the corporate privilege is abused for personal benefit or when the corporate business is treated so carelessly that the corporation and the controlling shareholders are no longer separate entities. The shareholders are then required to assume personal liability to creditors for the corporation's debts. The following are some of the factors that frequently cause the courts to pierce the corporate veil:

1. A party is tricked or misled into dealing with the corporation rather than the individual.
2. The corporation is set up never to make a profit or always to be insolvent, or it is too "thinly" capitalized—that is, it has insufficient capital at the time of formation to meet its prospective debts or other potential liabilities.
3. Statutory corporate formalities, such as holding required corporation meetings, are not followed.
4. Personal and corporate interests are **commingled** to such an extent that the corporation has no separate identity.

The potential for corporate assets to be used for personal benefit is especially great in a *close corporation* (see page 577). In such a situation, the separate status of the corporate entity and the shareholders must be carefully preserved. In the following case, when a close corporation failed to pay its legal fees, its attorneys sought to hold the family-member shareholders personally liable. Could the attorneys pierce the corporate veil?

Case 20.1

Brennan's, Inc. v. Colbert

Court of Appeal of Louisiana, 85 So.3d 787 (2012).

FACTS Three brothers—Pip, Jimmy, and Theodore Brennan— are shareholders of Brennan's, Inc., which owns and operates New Orleans' famous Brennan's Restaurant. The Brennan brothers retained attorney Edward Colbert and his firm, Kenyon & Kenyon, LLP,

(hatman12/iStockphoto.com)

Can the shareholders of a close corporation be sued individually?

Case 20.1—Continued

to represent Brennan's, Inc., in a dispute. All invoices were sent to Brennan's, Inc., and the Brennan brothers' payments came from the corporation's checking accounts.

As a close corporation, Brennan's, Inc., did not hold formal corporate meetings with agendas and minutes. Nevertheless, it did maintain corporate books, hold corporate bank accounts, and file corporate tax returns. In 2005, Brennan's, Inc., sued Colbert and Kenyon & Kenyon for legal malpractice. In its answer, Kenyon & Kenyon demanded unpaid legal fees both from Brennan's, Inc., and from the Brennan brothers personally. The court found that the Brennan brothers could not be held personally liable. On appeal, Kenyon & Kenyon argued that it should be allowed to pierce the corporate veil because Brennan's, Inc., did not observe corporate formalities and because the Brennan brothers did not honor their promises to pay their legal bills.

ISSUE Should the court pierce the corporate veil and allow Kenyon & Kenyon to hold the Brennan brothers personally liable?

DECISION No. The Louisiana appellate court affirmed the trial court's judgment for the Brennan brothers.

REASON Corporate shareholders generally may not be held personally liable, but a court may pierce the corporate veil if the shareholders fail to observe corporate formalities or use the corporation to perpetrate a fraud. In this case, the Brennan brothers never agreed to personally pay Kenyon & Kenyon's legal fees. Instead, they simply spoke as shareholders for the firm's real client, Brennan's, Inc. Moreover, Kenyon & Kenyon knew that Brennan's, Inc., was a close corporation that operated somewhat informally. Although the corporation did not hold formal corporate meetings, it maintained corporate books, held corporate bank accounts, filed corporate tax returns, and even paid Kenyon & Kenyon with its own checks. Finally, the Brennan brothers did not defraud Kenyon & Kenyon by failing to pay their legal fees. "[I]f a broken promise to pay was sufficient to establish fraud," the court reasoned, "then every lawsuit against a corporation for a debt would automatically allow for the piercing of the corporate veil."

CRITICAL THINKING—Ethical Consideration *Should the Brennan brothers be held personally liable because they misled their attorneys? Why or why not?*

Corporate Financing

Part of the process of corporate formation involves corporate financing. Corporations normally are financed by the issuance and sale of corporate securities. **Securities** (stocks and bonds) evidence the right to participate in earnings and the distribution of corporate property or the obligation to pay funds. (See the *Adapting the Law to the Online Environment* feature on the following page for a discussion of how start-ups can seek financing online.)

Stocks, or *equity securities*, represent the purchase of ownership in the business firm. **Bonds** (debentures), or *debt securities*, represent the borrowing of funds by firms (and governments). Of course, not all debt is in the form of debt securities. For instance, some debt is in the form of accounts payable and notes payable, which typically are short-term debts. Bonds are simply a way for the corporation to split up its long-term debt so that it can be more easily marketed. (See this chapter's *Linking Business Law to Accounting and Finance* feature on page 603 for further discussion of corporate financing.)

Bonds

Bonds are issued by business firms and by governments at all levels as evidence of the funds they are borrowing from investors. Bonds normally have a designated *maturity date*—the date when the principal, or face, amount of the bond is returned to the investor. They are sometimes referred to as *fixed-income securities* because their owners (that is, the creditors) receive fixed-dollar interest payments, usually semiannually, during the period of time before maturity.

Because debt financing represents a legal obligation on the part of the corporation, various features and terms of a particular bond issue are specified in a lending agreement called a **bond indenture.** A corporate trustee, often a commercial bank trust department, acts on behalf of all bondholders in ensuring that the corporation meets the terms of the

---

Securities Generally, stocks, bonds, or other items that represent an ownership interest in a corporation or a promise of repayment of debt by a corporation.

Stock An ownership (equity) interest in a corporation, measured in units of shares.

Bond A security that evidences a corporate (or government) debt.

"Gentlemen prefer bonds."

Andrew Mellon, 1855–1937 (American banker)

Bond Indenture The agreement between the issuer of a bond and the bondholder that sets out the terms and features of the bond issue.

ADAPTING THE LAW TO THE ONLINE ENVIRONMENT

THE NEW ERA OF CROWDFUNDING

Every new company needs funds to grow, but banks are generally unwilling to finance a company with prospects but no profits as of yet. Venture capitalists (see page 586) do finance young companies, but there are not enough of them to fund all the companies looking for help. Now, start-ups that are unable to attract venture capitalists have a new way to obtain funding—crowdfunding.

What Is Crowdfunding?

Crowdfunding is a cooperative activity in which people network and pool funds and other resources via the Internet to assist a cause or invest in a venture. Sometimes, crowdfunding is used to raise funds for charitable purposes, such as disaster relief, but increasingly it is being used to finance budding entrepreneurs. Several rock bands have financed tours in this way, and now ventures of all kinds are trying to raise funds through crowdfunding.

Crowdfunding Becomes More Specialized

Over a very short time, crowdfunding Web sites have proliferated. They offer partial ownership of start-ups in exchange for cash investments. At first, there were mostly generalized sites, such as Profounder.com and Startup Addict, but today the sites have become specialized. If you are interested only in new mobile apps, for example, you can go to the Apps Funder

(www.appsfunder.com). As you might imagine, many of the apps are games, but this site also has a more serious side. For instance, one new app that was funded involves sharing music scores. NewJelly (www.newjelly.com) raises funds for "dream" projects for artists and filmmakers.

Less Regulation Increases Crowdfunding's Appeal

Crowdfunding has taken off in many other countries, including France and Germany. Other countries' investor protection laws and regulations are often less stringent than U.S. laws, so we can expect to see more crowdfunding sites based abroad.

In 2012, President Barack Obama signed the JOBS Act (the acronym stands for "Jump-Start Our Business Start-Ups"), which relieved some of the regulatory burdens that you will read about in Chapter 21. Before this legislation, start-ups could look for financing only from investors who were "accredited," meaning that they had investment experience and a high net worth. If companies sought investment funds from the general public, they had to meet expensive and lengthy disclosure requirements. Under the new legislation, investing in start-ups will be more accessible to so-called nonaccredited investors.

Critical Thinking

What risks might be involved in crowdfunding investments?

---

bond issue. The bond indenture specifies the maturity date of the bond and the pattern of interest payments until maturity.

Stocks

Issuing stocks is another way that corporations can obtain financing. The ways in which stocks differ from bonds are summarized in Exhibit 20.1 on the facing page. Basically, as mentioned, stocks represent ownership in a business firm, whereas bonds represent borrowing by the firm.

Exhibit 20.2 on the bottom of page 585 summarizes the types of stocks issued by corporations. We look now at the two major types of stock—*common stock* and *preferred stock*.

Common Stock Shares of ownership in a corporation that give the owner of the stock a proportionate interest in the corporation with regard to control, earnings, and net assets. Common stock is lowest in priority with respect to payment of dividends and distribution of the corporation's assets on dissolution.

Common Stock   The true ownership of a corporation is represented by **common stock.** Common stock provides a proportionate interest in the corporation with regard to (1) control, (2) earnings, and (3) net assets. A shareholder's interest is generally in proportion to the number of shares he or she owns out of the total number of shares issued.

Voting Rights   Voting rights in a corporation apply to the election of the firm's board of directors and to proposed changes in the ownership structure of the firm. For example, a holder of common stock generally has the right to vote in a decision on a proposed merger,

Exhibit 20.1 How Do Stocks and Bonds Differ?

STOCKS	BONDS
1. Stocks represent ownership.	1. Bonds represent debt.
2. Stocks (common) do not have a fixed dividend rate.	2. Interest on bonds must always be paid, whether or not any profit is earned.
3. Stockholders can elect the board of directors, which controls the corporation.	3. Bondholders usually have no voice in, or control over, management of the corporation.
4. Stocks do not have a maturity date. The corporation usually does not repay the stockholder.	4. Bonds have a maturity date, when the corporation is to repay the bondholder the face value of the bond.
5. All corporations issue or offer to sell stocks. This is the usual definition of a corporation.	5. Corporations do not necessarily issue bonds.
6. Stockholders have a claim against the property and income of a corporation after all creditors' claims have been met.	6. Bondholders have a claim against the property and income of a corporation that must be met *before* the claims of stockholders.

as mergers can change the proportion of ownership. State corporation law specifies the types of actions for which shareholder approval must be obtained.

Earnings Holders of common stock are investors who assume a *residual* position in the overall financial structure of a business. In terms of receiving payment for their investments, they are last in line. They are entitled to the earnings that are left after preferred stockholders, bondholders, suppliers, employees, and other groups have been paid. Once those groups are paid, however, the owners of common stock may be entitled to *all* the remaining earnings as dividends. (The board of directors normally is not under any duty to declare the remaining earnings as dividends, however.)

Preferred Stock Stock that has priority over common stock as to payment of dividends and distribution of assets on the corporation's dissolution.

Preferred Stock

Preferred stock is stock with *preferences*. Usually, this means that holders of preferred stock have priority over holders of common stock as to dividends and payment on dissolution of the corporation. Holders of preferred stock may or may not have the right to vote.

Preferred stock is not included among the corporation's liabilities because it is equity. Like other equity securities, preferred shares have no fixed maturity date on which the firm must pay them off. Although firms occasionally buy back preferred stock, they are not legally obligated to do so.

Holders of preferred stock are investors who have assumed a rather cautious position in their relationship to the corporation. They have a stronger position than common shareholders with respect to dividends and claims on assets, but they will not share in the full

Exhibit 20.2 Types of Stocks

TYPE OF STOCK	DEFINITION
Common stock	Voting shares that represent ownership interest in a corporation. Common stock has the lowest priority with respect to payment of dividends and distribution of assets on the corporation's dissolution.
Preferred stock	Shares of stock that have priority over common-stock shares as to payment of dividends and distribution of assets on dissolution. Dividend payments are usually a fixed percentage of the face value of the share.
Cumulative preferred stock	Preferred shares on which required dividends not paid in a given year must be paid in a subsequent year before any common-stock dividends are paid.
Participating preferred stock	Preferred shares entitling the owner to receive the preferred-stock dividend and additional dividends if the corporation has paid dividends on common stock.
Convertible preferred stock	Preferred shares that, under certain conditions, can be converted into a specified number of common shares either in the issuing corporation or, sometimes, in another corporation.
Redeemable, or callable, preferred stock	Preferred shares issued with the express condition that the issuing corporation has the right to repurchase the shares as specified.

prosperity of the firm if it grows successfully over time. Preferred stockholders do receive fixed dividends periodically, however, and they may benefit to some extent from changes in the market price of the shares.

Venture Capital and Private Equity Capital

As discussed, corporations traditionally obtain financing through issuing and selling securities (stocks and bonds) in the capital market. In reality, however, many investors do not want to purchase stock in a business that lacks a track record, and banks are generally reluctant to extend loans to high-risk enterprises. Numerous corporations fail because they are undercapitalized. Therefore, to obtain sufficient financing, many entrepreneurs seek alternative financing.

Venture Capital   Start-up businesses and high-risk enterprises often obtain venture capital financing. **Venture capital** is capital provided to new business ventures by professional outside investors (*venture capitalists,* usually groups of wealthy investors and securities firms). Venture capital investments are high risk—the investors must be willing to lose all of their invested funds—but offer the potential for well-above-average returns at some point in the future.

> **Venture Capital** Financing provided by professional, outside investors (venture capitalists) to new business ventures.

To obtain venture capital financing, the start-up business typically gives up a share of its ownership to the venture capitalists. In addition to funding, venture capitalists may provide managerial and technical expertise, and they nearly always are given some control over the new company's decisions. Many Internet-based companies, such as Google, were initially financed by venture capital.

Private Equity Capital   Private equity firms obtain their capital from wealthy investors in private markets. The firms use their **private equity capital** to invest in existing—often, publicly traded—corporations. Usually, they buy an entire corporation and then reorganize it. Sometimes, divisions of the purchased company are sold off to pay down debt. Ultimately, the private equity firm may sell shares in the reorganized (and perhaps more profitable) company to the public in an *initial public offering* (usually called an IPO—see Chapter 21). In this way, the private equity firm can make profits by selling its shares in the company to the public.

> **Private Equity Capital** Funds invested in an existing corporation by a private equity firm, usually to purchase and reorganize the corporation.

Directors, Officers, and Shareholders

Corporate directors, officers, and shareholders all play different roles within the corporate entity. No one individual shareholder or director bears sole responsibility for the corporation and its actions. Rather, a corporation joins the efforts and resources of a large number of individuals for the purpose of producing greater returns than those persons could have obtained individually. Sometimes, though, actions that benefit the corporation as a whole do not coincide with the separate interests of the individuals making up the corporation. In such situations, it is important to know the rights and duties of all participants in the corporate enterprise.

Directors

The board of directors is the ultimate authority in every corporation. Directors have responsibility for all policymaking decisions necessary to the management of corporate affairs. The board selects and removes the corporate officers, determines the capital structure of the corporation, and declares dividends. Each director has one vote, and customarily the majority rules.

Are directors of a corporation normally compensated?

Inside Director A person on the board of directors who is also an officer of the corporation.

Outside Director A person on the board of directors who does not hold a management position in the corporation.

Quorum The minimum number of members of a decision-making body that must be present before business may be transacted.

➤ KNOW THIS ➤
The articles of incorporation may provide that a director can be removed only for cause.

Normally, the incorporators appoint the first board of directors at the time the corporation is created. The initial board serves until the first annual shareholders' meeting. Subsequent directors are elected by a majority vote of the shareholders.

A director usually serves for a term of one year—from annual meeting to annual meeting. Most state statutes permit longer and staggered terms. A common practice is to elect one-third of the board members each year for a three-year term. In this way, there is greater management continuity.

A director can be removed *for cause*—that is, for failing to perform a required duty—either as specified in the articles or bylaws or by shareholder action. If a director is removed, dies, or resigns, or if a new position is created through amendment of the articles or bylaws, either the shareholders or the board itself can fill the vacant position, depending on state law or the provisions of the bylaws.

Compensation of Directors In the past, corporate directors rarely were compensated, but today they are often paid at least nominal sums and may receive more substantial compensation in large corporations. Most states permit the corporate articles or bylaws to authorize compensation for directors. In fact, the Revised Model Business Corporation Act (RMBCA) states that unless the articles or bylaws provide otherwise, the board of directors itself may set directors' compensation [RMBCA 8.11]. Directors also gain through indirect benefits, such as business contacts and prestige, and other rewards, such as stock options.

In many corporations, directors are also chief corporate officers (president or chief executive officer, for example) and receive compensation in their managerial positions. A director who is also an officer of the corporation is referred to as an **inside director**, whereas a director who does not hold a management position is an **outside director**. Typically, a corporation's board of directors includes both inside and outside directors.

Board of Directors' Meetings The board of directors conducts business by holding formal meetings with recorded minutes. Today, most states allow directors to participate in board meetings from remote locations via telephone, Web conferencing, or Skype, provided that all the directors can simultaneously hear each other during the meeting [RMBCA 8.20].

Unless the articles of incorporation or bylaws specify a greater number, a majority of the board of directors normally constitutes a quorum [RMBCA 8.24]. (A **quorum** is the minimum number of members of a body of officials or other group that must be present in order for business to be validly transacted.) Some state statutes specifically allow corporations to set a quorum at less than a majority but not less than one-third of the directors.[7]

Once a quorum is present, the directors transact business and vote on issues affecting the corporation. Each director present at the meeting has one vote.[8] Ordinary matters generally require a simple majority vote, but certain extraordinary issues may require a greater-than-majority vote.

Rights of Directors A corporate director must have certain rights to function properly in that position and make informed policy decisions for the company. The *right to participation* means that directors are entitled to participate in all board of directors' meetings and to be notified of these meetings. Because the dates of regular board meetings are usually specified in the bylaws, no notice of these meetings is required. If special meetings are called, however, notice is required unless waived by the director.

---

7. See, for example, Delaware Code Annotated Title 8, Section 141(b); and New York Business Corporation Law Section 707.

8. Except in Louisiana, which allows a director to authorize another person to cast a vote in his or her place under certain circumstances.

A director also has the *right of inspection,* which means that each director can access the corporation's books and records, facilities, and premises. Inspection rights are essential for directors to make informed decisions and to exercise the necessary supervision over corporate officers and employees. This right of inspection is almost absolute and cannot be restricted (by the articles, bylaws, or any act of the board).

When a director becomes involved in litigation by virtue of her or his position or actions, the director may also have a right to indemnification (reimbursement) for legal costs, fees, and damages incurred. Most states allow corporations to indemnify and purchase liability insurance for corporate directors [RMBCA 8.51].

Corporate Officers and Executives

Corporate officers and other executive employees are hired by the board of directors. At a minimum, most corporations have a president, one or more vice presidents, a secretary, and a treasurer. In most states, an individual can hold more than one office, such as president and secretary, and can be both an officer and a director of the corporation. In addition to carrying out the duties articulated in the bylaws, corporate and managerial officers act as agents of the corporation, and the ordinary rules of agency (discussed in Chapter 17) normally apply to their employment.

Corporate officers and other high-level managers are employees of the company, so their rights are defined by employment contracts. The board of directors, though, normally can remove corporate officers at any time with or without cause and regardless of the terms of the employment contracts—although in so doing, the corporation may be liable for breach of contract.

> **KNOW THIS**
> Shareholders own the corporation and directors make policy decisions, but the officers who run the corporation's daily business often have significant decision-making power.

Duties and Liabilities of Directors and Officers

LEARNING OBJECTIVE 3
What are the duties of corporate directors and officers?

The duties of directors and corporate officers are the same. Directors and officers are deemed fiduciaries of the corporation because their relationship with the corporation and its shareholders is one of trust and confidence. As fiduciaries, directors and officers owe ethical—and legal—duties to the corporation and to the shareholders as a whole. These fiduciary duties include the duty of care and the duty of loyalty.

Duty of Care   Directors and officers must exercise due care in performing their duties. The standard of *due care* has been variously described in judicial decisions and codified in many state corporation codes. Generally, a director or officer is expected to act in good faith, to exercise the care that an ordinarily prudent person would exercise in similar circumstances, and to act in what he or she considers to be the best interests of the corporation [RMBCA 8.30]. Directors and officers whose failure to exercise due care results in harm to the corporation or its shareholders can be held liable for negligence (unless the *business judgment rule* applies, as will be discussed shortly).

Directors and officers are expected to be informed on corporate matters and to conduct a reasonable investigation of a situation before making a decision. This means that they must do what is necessary to keep adequately informed: attend meetings and presentations, ask for information from those who have it, read reports, and review other written materials. In other words, directors and officers must investigate, study, and discuss matters and evaluate alternatives before making a decision.

Although directors and officers are expected to act in accordance with their own knowledge and training, they are also normally entitled to rely on information given to them by certain other persons. Most states and Section 8.30(b) of the RMBCA allow a director to make decisions in reliance on information furnished by competent officers or employees, professionals such as attorneys and accountants, and committees of the board of directors (on which the director does not serve). The reliance must be in good faith, of course, to insulate a director from liability if the information later proves to be inaccurate or unreliable. Directors are also expected to exercise a reasonable amount of supervision when they delegate work to corporate officers and employees.

Business Judgment Rule A rule that immunizes corporate directors and officers from liability for decisions that result in corporate losses or damages as long as the decision makers took reasonable steps to become informed, had a rational basis for their decisions, and did not have a conflict of interest with the corporation.

The Business Judgment Rule

Directors and officers are expected to exercise due care and to use their best judgment in guiding corporate management, but they are not insurers of business success. Under the **business judgment rule**, a corporate director or officer will not be liable to the corporation or to its shareholders for honest mistakes of judgment and bad business decisions.

Courts give significant deference to the decisions of corporate directors and officers. The business judgment rule will apply as long as the director or officer did the following:

1. Took reasonable steps to become informed about the matter.
2. Had a rational basis for his or her decision.
3. Did not have a conflict between his or her personal interest and that of the corporation.

In fact, unless there is evidence of bad faith, fraud, or a clear breach of fiduciary duties, most courts will apply the rule and protect directors and officers who make bad business decisions from liability for those choices. **CASE EXAMPLE 20.6** After a foreign firm announced its intention to acquire Lyondell Chemical Company, Lyondell's directors did nothing to prepare for a possible merger. They failed to research Lyondell's market value and made no attempt to seek out other potential buyers. The $13 billion cash merger was negotiated and finalized in less than a week—and the directors met for only seven hours to discuss it. Shareholders sued, claiming that the directors had breached their fiduciary duties by failing to maximize the sale price of the corporation. The Delaware Supreme Court, however, ruled that the directors were protected by the business judgment rule.[9] •

Duty of Loyalty

Loyalty can be defined as faithfulness to one's obligations and duties. In the corporate context, the duty of loyalty requires directors and officers to subordinate their personal interests to the welfare of the corporation. Directors cannot use corporate funds or confidential corporate information for personal advantage and must refrain from self-dealing. For instance, a director should not oppose a tender offer (see page 601) that is in the corporation's best interest simply because its acceptance may cost the director her or his position.

Cases dealing with the duty of loyalty typically involve one or more of the following:

1. Competing with the corporation.
2. Usurping (taking personal advantage of) a corporate opportunity.
3. Having an interest that conflicts with the interest of the corporation.
4. Engaging in insider trading (using information that is not public to make a profit trading securities, as will be discussed in Chapter 21).
5. Authorizing a corporate transaction that is detrimental to minority shareholders.
6. Selling control over the corporation.

The *Classic Case* on the following page illustrates the conflict that can arise between a corporate official's personal interest and his or her duty of loyalty.

9. *Lyondell Chemical Co. v. Ryan,* 970 A.2d 235 (Del.Sup. 2009).

Classic Case 20.2

Guth v. Loft, Inc.

Supreme Court of Delaware,
23 Del.Ch. 255, 5 A.2d 503 (1939).

Pepsi-Cola got its start when the head of Loft Candy Company usurped a corporate opportunity.

(Dalton Rowe/Creative Commons)

HISTORICAL SETTING   In the 1920s, Loft Candy Company (Loft, Inc.), based in Long Island City, New York, was a publicly held company with a $13 million candy-and-restaurant chain. The company manufactured its own candies, syrups, and beverages and sold its products in its more than one hundred retail locations throughout the Northeast. The retail stores featured old-fashioned soda fountains and were very popular. In 1930, Charles Guth became Loft's president after a contentious stockholders' meeting. His position there set the stage for the rise of the soft drink Pepsi-Cola.

FACTS   At the time Charles Guth became Loft's president, Guth and his family owned Grace Company, which made syrups for soft drinks in a plant in Baltimore, Maryland. Coca-Cola Company supplied Loft with cola syrup. Unhappy with what he felt was Coca-Cola's high price, Guth entered into an agreement with Roy Megargel to acquire the trademark and formula for Pepsi-Cola and form Pepsi-Cola Corporation. Neither Guth nor Megargel could finance the new venture, however, and Grace Company was insolvent. Without the knowledge of Loft's board of directors, Guth used Loft's capital, credit, facilities, and employees to further the Pepsi enterprise. At Guth's direction, a Loft employee made the concentrate for the syrup, which was sent to Grace Company to add sugar and water. Loft charged Grace Company for the concentrate but allowed forty months' credit. Grace charged Pepsi for the syrup but also granted substantial credit. Grace sold the syrup to Pepsi's customers, including Loft, which paid on delivery or within thirty days. Loft also paid for Pepsi's advertising.

Finally, losing profits at its stores as a result of switching from Coca-Cola, Loft filed a suit in a Delaware state court against Guth, Grace, and Pepsi, seeking their Pepsi stock and an accounting. The court entered a judgment in the plaintiff's favor. The defendants appealed to the Delaware Supreme Court.

ISSUE   Did Guth violate his duty of loyalty to Loft, Inc., by acquiring the Pepsi-Cola trademark and formula for himself without the knowledge of Loft's board of directors?

DECISION   Yes. The Delaware Supreme Court upheld the judgment of the lower court. The state supreme court was "convinced that the opportunity to acquire the Pepsi-Cola trademark and formula, goodwill and business belonged to [Loft], and that Guth, as its president, had no right to appropriate the opportunity to himself."

REASON   The court pointed out that the officers and directors of a corporation stand in a fiduciary relationship to that corporation and to its shareholders. Corporate officers and directors must protect the corporation's interest at all times. They must also "refrain from doing anything that works injury to the corporation." In other words, corporate officers and directors must provide undivided and unselfish loyalty to the corporation, and "there should be no conflict between duty and self-interest." Whenever an opportunity is presented to the corporation, officers and directors with knowledge of that opportunity cannot seize it for themselves. "The corporation may elect to claim all of the benefits of the transaction for itself, and the law will impress a trust in favor of the corporation upon the property, interest, and profits required."

Guth clearly created a conflict between his self-interest and his duty to Loft—the corporation of which he was president and director. Guth illegally appropriated the Pepsi-Cola opportunity for himself and thereby placed himself in the position of competing with the company for which he worked.

WHAT IF THE FACTS WERE DIFFERENT?   Suppose that Loft's board of directors had approved Pepsi-Cola's use of its personnel and equipment. Would the court's decision have been different? Discuss.

IMPACT OF THIS CASE ON TODAY'S LAW   This early Delaware decision was one of the first to set forth a test for determining when a corporate officer or director has breached the duty of loyalty. The test has two basic parts—whether the opportunity was reasonably related to the corporation's line of business and whether the corporation was financially able to undertake the opportunity. The court also considered whether the corporation had an interest or expectancy in the opportunity and recognized that when the corporation had "no interest or expectancy, the officer or director is entitled to treat the opportunity as his own."

Disclosure of Conflicts of Interest   Corporate directors often have many business affiliations, and a director may sit on the board of more than one corporation. Of course, directors are precluded from entering into or supporting businesses that operate in direct competition with corporations on whose boards they serve. Their fiduciary duty requires them to make a full disclosure of any potential conflicts of interest that might arise in any corporate transaction [RMBCA 8.60].

Sometimes, for example, a corporation enters into a contract or engages in a transaction in which an officer or director has a personal interest. The director or officer must make a full disclosure of that interest and must abstain from voting on the proposed transaction.

EXAMPLE 20.7 Southwood Corporation needs office space. Lambert Alden, one of its five directors, owns the building adjoining the corporation's main office building. He negotiates a lease with Southwood for the space, making a full disclosure to Southwood and the other four directors. The lease arrangement is fair and reasonable, and it is unanimously approved by the other four directors. In this situation, Alden has not breached his duty of loyalty to the corporation, and thus the contract is valid. If it were otherwise, directors would be prevented from ever transacting business with the corporations they serve. ●

Liability of Directors and Officers   Directors and officers are exposed to liability on many fronts. They may be held liable for crimes and torts committed by themselves or by corporate employees under their supervision, as discussed in Chapter 6 and Chapter 17, respectively.

Additionally, if shareholders perceive that the corporate directors are not acting in the best interests of the corporation, they may sue the directors, in what is called a *shareholder's derivative suit,* on behalf of the corporation. (This type of action will be discussed later in this chapter.) Directors and officers can also be held personally liable under a number of statutes, such as those enacted to protect consumers (see Chapter 12), or the environment (see Chapter 24).

Shareholders

The acquisition of a share of stock makes a person an owner and shareholder in a corporation. Shareholders thus own the corporation. Although they have no legal title to corporate property, such as buildings and equipment, they do have an equitable (ownership) interest in the firm.

KNOW THIS

Shareholders normally are not agents of the corporation.

As a general rule, shareholders have no responsibility for the daily management of the corporation, even if they are ultimately responsible for choosing the board of directors, which does have such control. Ordinarily, corporate officers and directors owe no duty to individual shareholders unless some contract or special relationship exists between them in addition to the corporate relationship. The duty of the officers and directors is to act in the best interests of the corporation and its shareholder-owners as a whole. Normally, there is no legal relationship between shareholders and creditors of the corporation.

Can shareholders vote at a shareholders' meeting?

(AP Photo/Sue Ogrocki)

Shareholders' Powers   Shareholders must approve fundamental changes affecting the corporation before the changes can be implemented. Hence, shareholders are empowered to amend the articles of incorporation and bylaws, approve a merger or the dissolution of the corporation, and approve the sale of all or substantially all of the corporation's assets. Some of these powers are subject to prior board approval.

Members of the board of directors are elected and removed by a vote of the shareholders. As mentioned earlier, the incorporators choose the first directors, who serve until the first shareholders' meeting. From that time on, the selection and retention of directors are exclusively shareholder functions.

Directors usually serve their full terms. If the shareholders judge them unsatisfactory, they are simply not reelected. Shareholders have the inherent power, however, to remove a director from office for cause (such as for

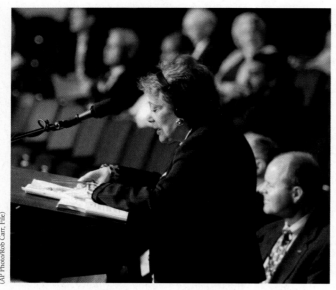

Who has the right to speak at a shareholders' meeting?

Proxy In corporate law, a written or electronically transmitted form in which a stockholder authorizes another party to vote the stockholder's shares in a certain manner.

LEARNING OBJECTIVE 4
What is a voting proxy?

breach of duty or misconduct) by a majority vote.[10] Some state statutes (and some corporate articles) permit removal of directors without cause by the vote of a majority of the holders of outstanding shares entitled to vote.

Shareholders' Meetings Shareholders' meetings must occur at least annually. In addition, special meetings can be called to deal with urgent matters. A corporation must notify its shareholders of the date, time, and place of an annual or special shareholders' meeting at least ten days, but not more than sixty days, before the meeting date [RMBCA 7.05].[11] Notice of a special meeting must include a statement of the purpose of the meeting, and business transacted at the meeting is limited to that purpose. In some states, obtaining the unanimous written consent of shareholders is a permissible alternative to holding a shareholders' meeting [RMBCA 7.25].

Proxies It is usually not practical for owners of only a few shares of stock of publicly traded corporations to attend shareholders' meetings. Therefore, the law allows stockholders to either vote in person or appoint another person as their agent to vote their shares at the meeting. The signed appointment form or electronic transmission authorizing an agent to vote the shares is called a **proxy** (from the Latin *procurare,* meaning "to manage, take care of"). Management often solicits proxies, but any person can solicit proxies to concentrate voting power. Proxies normally are revocable (that is, they can be withdrawn), unless they are specifically designated as irrevocable.

Proxy materials may be accompanied by shareholder proposals. When shareholders want to change a company policy, they can put their idea up for a shareholder vote. They can do this by submitting a shareholder proposal to the board of directors and asking the board to include the proposal in the proxy materials that are sent to all shareholders before meetings.

The Securities and Exchange Commission (SEC), which regulates the purchase and sale of securities (see Chapter 21), has special provisions relating to proxies and shareholder proposals. SEC Rule 14a-8 provides that all shareholders who own stock worth at least $1,000 are eligible to submit proposals for inclusion in corporate proxy materials. The corporation is required to include information on whatever proposals will be considered at the shareholders' meeting along with proxy materials. Only proposals that relate to significant policy considerations rather than ordinary business operations must be included.

Electronic Proxy Materials In the past, corporations had to send large packets of paper documents to shareholders, but today, the SEC requires all publicly held companies to distribute electronic proxy (e-proxy) materials. Although companies must post their proxy materials on the Internet, they may still choose among several options—including paper documents sent by mail—for actually delivering the materials to shareholders.[12]

If a company wishes to distribute proxy materials only via the Internet, it can choose the notice-and-access delivery option. Under this model, the corporation posts the proxy

---

10. A director can often demand court review of removal for cause.

11. A shareholder can waive the requirement of written notice by signing a waiver form. In some states, a shareholder who does not receive written notice, but who learns of the meeting and attends without protesting the lack of notice, is said to have waived notice by such conduct. State statutes and corporate bylaws typically set forth the time within which notice must be sent, what methods can be used, and what the notice must contain.

12. 17 C.F.R. Parts 240, 249, and 274.

materials on a Web site and notifies the shareholders that the proxy materials are available online. If a shareholder requests paper proxy materials, the company must send them within three business days. Shareholders can permanently elect to receive all future proxy materials on paper or by e-mail.

Should interest groups have free access to proxy materials in order to nominate their own candidates for corporate boards? During many years of lobbying, unions, pension funds, and other institutional investors sought a rule that would allow them access to corporate proxy materials without cost. The SEC ultimately passed a rule that required companies' proxy materials to include information about shareholder-nominated candidates for boards of directors. In the past, investor groups that wanted to replace directors had to mail separate ballots to all shareholders and then conduct a costly campaign. Before the new SEC rule went into effect, however, the U.S. Chamber of Commerce and the Business Roundtable challenged it in court. The U.S. Court of Appeals for the District of Columbia Circuit struck down the rule, holding that the SEC "acted arbitrarily and capriciously for having failed . . . adequately to assess economic effects of a new rule."[13]

Ann Yerger, head of the Council of Institutional Investors, said, "We think the court got it wrong. We will continue to advocate for proxy access." Other shareholder advocates agreed. Shareholder groups believe that the proxy access rule would make boards of directors more accountable and would allow shareholders to have more say in corporations' strategic and financial decisions.

Shareholder Voting

Shareholders exercise ownership control through the power of their votes. Corporate business matters are presented in the form of *resolutions,* which shareholders vote to approve or disapprove. Each common shareholder is entitled to one vote per share, although the voting techniques to be discussed shortly enhance the power of the shareholder's vote. The articles of incorporation can exclude or limit voting rights, particularly for certain classes of shares. For example, owners of preferred shares are usually denied the right to vote [RMBCA 7.21]. If a state statute requires specific voting procedures, the corporation's articles or bylaws must be consistent with the statute.

Quorum Requirements

For shareholders to conduct business at a meeting, a quorum must be present. Generally, a quorum exists when shareholders holding more than 50 percent of the outstanding shares are present. Once a quorum is present, voting can proceed.

A majority vote of the shares represented at the meeting usually is required to pass resolutions. At times, more than a simple majority vote will be required either by a state statute or by the corporate articles. Extraordinary corporate matters, such as a merger, consolidation, or dissolution of the corporation (discussed later in this chapter), require a higher percentage of corporate shares entitled to vote [RMBCA 7.27].

Cumulative Voting

Most states permit, and some require, shareholders to elect directors by *cumulative voting,* which is a voting method designed to allow minority shareholders to be represented on the board of directors.[14] With cumulative voting, each shareholder is entitled to a total number of votes equal to the number of board members to be elected multiplied by the number of voting shares a shareholder owns. The shareholder can cast all of these votes for one candidate or split them among several nominees for director. All nominees stand for election at the same time.

EXAMPLE 20.8 A corporation has 10,000 shares issued and outstanding. The minority shareholders hold 3,000 shares, and the majority shareholders hold the other 7,000 shares. Three members of the board are to be elected. The majority shareholders' nominees are Acevedo, Barkley, and Craycik. The minority shareholders' nominee is Drake. Can Drake be elected by the minority shareholders?

---

13. *Business Roundtable v. SEC,* 647 F.3d 1144 (2011).
14. See, for example, California Corporations Code Section 708. Under RMBCA 7.28, however, no cumulative voting rights exist unless the articles of incorporation provide for them.

If cumulative voting is allowed, the answer is yes. Together, the minority shareholders have 9,000 votes (the number of directors to be elected times the number of shares held by the minority shareholders equals 3 times 3,000, which equals 9,000 votes). All of these votes can be cast to elect Drake. The majority shareholders have 21,000 votes (3 times 7,000 equals 21,000 votes), but these votes have to be distributed among their three nominees. The principle of cumulative voting is that no matter how the majority shareholders cast their 21,000 votes, they will not be able to elect all three directors if the minority shareholders cast all of their 9,000 votes for Drake, as illustrated in Exhibit 20.3 below. ●

Other Voting Techniques   When cumulative voting is not required either by statute or under the articles, the entire board can be elected by a simple majority of shares at a shareholders' meeting. In addition, before a shareholders' meeting, a group of shareholders can agree in writing to vote their shares together in a specified manner. Such agreements, called *shareholder voting agreements,* usually are held to be valid and enforceable. A shareholder can also appoint a voting agent and vote by proxy.

CASE EXAMPLE 20.9   Several shareholders of Cryo-Cell International, Inc., mounted a proxy contest in an effort to replace the board of directors. Another stockholder, Andrew Filipowski, entered into a shareholder voting agreement to support management in exchange for being included in management's slate of directors. The company's chief executive officer, Mercedes Walton, secretly promised Filipowski that if management's slate won, the board of directors would add another board seat to be filled by a Filipowski designee.

After management won the election, Walton prepared to add Filipowski's designee to the board. Dissident shareholders challenged the election's results. The court held that although the voting agreement to include Filipowski on the management slate was legal, the board's actions and Walton's secret agreement constituted serious breaches of fiduciary duty that had tainted the election. The court therefore ordered a new election to be held.[15] ●

Rights of Shareholders

Shareholders possess numerous rights. A significant right—the right to vote their shares—has already been discussed. We now look at some additional rights of shareholders.

Stock Certificate A certificate issued by a corporation evidencing the ownership of a specified number of shares in the corporation.

Stock Certificates   In the past, corporations typically issued a **stock certificate** that evidenced ownership of a specified number of shares in the corporation. Only a few jurisdictions still require physical stock certificates, and shareholders there have the right to demand that the corporation issue certificates (or replace those that were lost or destroyed).

In most states and under RMBCA 6.26, boards of directors may provide that shares of stock will be uncertificated, or "paperless"—that is, no actual, physical stock certificates will be issued. When shares are uncertificated, the corporation may be required to send each shareholder a letter or some other form of notice that contains the same information that traditionally appeared on stock certificates.

---

15. *Portnoy v. Cryo-Cell International, Inc.*, 940 A.2d 43 (Del.Ch. 2008).

Exhibit 20.3   Results of Cumulative Voting

BALLOT	MAJORITY SHAREHOLDERS' VOTES			MINORITY SHAREHOLDERS' VOTES	DIRECTORS ELECTED
	Acevedo	Barkley	Craycik	Drake	
1	10,000	10,000	1,000	9,000	Acevedo/Barkley/Drake
2	9,001	9,000	2,999	9,000	Acevedo/Barkley/Drake
3	6,000	7,000	8,000	9,000	Barkley/Craycik/Drake

(PhotoDisc)

Stock certificates. To be a shareholder, is it necessary to have physical possession of a certificate? Why or why not?

Preemptive Rights Rights that entitle shareholders to purchase newly issued shares of a corporation's stock, equal in percentage to shares already held, before the stock is offered to outside buyers. Preemptive rights enable shareholders to maintain their proportionate ownership and voice in the corporation.

In any event, stock is intangible personal property, and the ownership right exists independently of the certificate itself. Notice of shareholders' meetings, dividends, and operational and financial reports are all distributed according to the recorded ownership listed in the corporation's books, not on the basis of possession of a stock certificate.

Preemptive Rights   Sometimes, the articles of incorporation grant preemptive rights to shareholders [RMBCA 6.30]. With **preemptive rights,** a shareholder receives a preference over all other purchasers to subscribe to or purchase a prorated share of a new issue of stock.

Generally, preemptive rights apply only to additional, newly issued stock sold for cash, and the preemptive rights must be exercised within a specified time period, usually thirty days. A shareholder with preemptive rights can purchase a percentage of the new shares that is equal to his or her current percentage of ownership in the company. This allows each shareholder to maintain her or his proportionate control, voting power, or financial interest in the corporation. Preemptive rights are most important in close corporations because each shareholder owns a relatively small number of shares but controls a substantial interest in the corporation.

Dividends   As mentioned on page 574, a *dividend* is a distribution of corporate profits or income *ordered by the directors* and paid to the shareholders in proportion to their respective shares in the corporation. Dividends can be paid in cash, property, stock of the corporation that is paying the dividends, or stock of other corporations.

State laws vary, but each state determines the general circumstances and legal requirements under which dividends are paid. State laws also control the sources of revenue to be used. Only certain funds are legally available for paying dividends. Depending on state law, dividends may be paid from the following sources:

1. *Retained earnings.* All states allow dividends to be paid from the undistributed net profits earned by the corporation, including capital gains from the sale of fixed assets. The undistributed net profits are called *retained earnings.*
2. *Net profits.* A few states allow dividends to be issued from current net profits without regard to deficits in prior years.
3. *Surplus.* A number of states allow dividends to be paid out of any kind of surplus.

Illegal Dividends   Sometimes, dividends are improperly paid from an unauthorized account, or their payment causes the corporation to become insolvent. Generally, shareholders must return illegal dividends only if they knew that the dividends were illegal when the payment was received (or if the dividends were paid when the corporation was insolvent). Whenever dividends are illegal or improper, the board of directors can be held personally liable for the amount of the payment.

Directors' Failure to Declare a Dividend   When directors fail to declare a dividend, shareholders can ask a court to compel the directors to meet and to declare a dividend. To succeed, the shareholders must show that the directors have acted so unreasonably in withholding the dividend that their conduct is an abuse of their discretion.

Often, a corporation accumulates large cash reserves for a legitimate corporate purpose, such as expansion or research. The mere fact that the firm has sufficient earnings or surplus available to pay a dividend is not enough to compel directors to distribute funds that, in the board's opinion, should not be distributed. The courts are reluctant to interfere with corporate operations and will not compel directors to declare dividends unless abuse of discretion is clearly shown.

Inspection Rights

Shareholders in a corporation enjoy both common law and statutory inspection rights. The RMBCA provides that every shareholder is entitled to examine specified corporate records. The shareholder's right of inspection is limited, however, to the inspection and copying of corporate books and records for a *proper purpose.* Furthermore, the request must be made in advance. The shareholder can inspect in person, or an attorney, accountant, or other authorized assistant can do so as the shareholder's agent.

The power of inspection is fraught with potential abuses, and the corporation is allowed to protect itself from them. For instance, a corporation can properly deny a shareholder access to corporate records to prevent harassment or to protect trade secrets or other confidential corporate information. In some states, a shareholder must have held his or her shares for a minimum time immediately preceding the demand to inspect or must hold a minimum number of shares. A shareholder who is denied the right of inspection can seek a court order to compel the inspection.

Transfer of Shares

Corporate stock represents an ownership right in intangible personal property. The law generally recognizes the right to transfer property to another person unless there are valid restrictions on its transferability. Transfer of stock in closely held corporations usually is restricted, for instance. When shares are transferred, a new entry is made in the corporate stock book to indicate the new owner. Until the corporation is notified and the entry is complete, all rights—including voting rights, the right to notice of shareholders' meetings, and the right to dividend distributions—remain with the current record owner.

The Shareholder's Derivative Suit

Shareholder's Derivative Suit A suit brought by a shareholder to enforce a corporate cause of action against a third person.

When the corporation is harmed by the actions of a third party, the directors can bring a lawsuit in the name of the corporation against that party. If the corporate directors fail to bring a lawsuit, shareholders can do so "derivatively" in what is known as a **shareholder's derivative suit.** (Derivative actions are less common in other countries than in the United States, as this chapter's *Beyond Our Borders* feature below explains.)

A shareholder cannot bring a derivative suit until ninety days after making a written demand on the corporation (the board of directors) to take suitable action [RMBCA 7.40]. Only if the directors refuse to take appropriate action can the derivative suit go forward.

BEYOND OUR BORDERS   Derivative Actions in Other Nations

Today, shareholders' derivative suits account for most of the claims brought against directors and officers in the United States. Other nations, however, put more restrictions on the use of such suits. German law, for example, does not provide for derivative litigation, and a corporation's duty to its employees is just as significant as its duty to its shareholder-owners. The United Kingdom has no statute authorizing derivative actions and only permits them in very limited circumstances. Japan authorizes derivative actions but also permits a company to sue the plaintiff-shareholder for damages if the action is unsuccessful.

Critical Thinking

Do corporations benefit from shareholders' derivative suits? If so, how?

The right of shareholders to bring a derivative action is especially important when the wrong suffered by the corporation results from the actions of corporate directors or officers. This is because the directors and officers would probably be unwilling to take any action against themselves. Nevertheless, a court will dismiss a derivative suit if the majority of directors or an independent panel determines in good faith that the lawsuit is not in the best interests of the corporation [RMBCA 7.44].

When shareholders bring a derivative suit, they are not pursuing rights or benefits for themselves personally but are acting as guardians of the corporate entity. Therefore, if the suit is successful, any damages recovered normally go into the corporation's treasury, not to the shareholders personally.[16]

In the following case, the plaintiff was a minority shareholder who alleged that the directors of the corporation had denied him the benefits of his ownership interest in breach of their fiduciary duties. The trial court determined that the plaintiff's lawsuit had to be brought as a derivative action, which would mean that any damages obtained would go to the corporation. The state's highest court had to decide whether the shareholder could bring an individual claim rather than a derivative suit.

---

16. The shareholders may be entitled to reimbursement for reasonable expenses involved in the derivative suit, however, including attorneys' fees.

Case 20.3

McCann v. McCann

Supreme Court of Idaho,
152 Idaho 809, 275 P.3d 824 (2012).

The McCann Ranch and Livestock Company.

FACTS In the 1970s, William McCann gave each of his sons, Bill and Ron, 36.7 percent of the shares of his close corporation, McCann Ranch and Livestock Company. The remaining shares went to William's wife, Gertrude. When William died, Bill became the corporation's president and chief executive officer. The corporation paid Gertrude's personal expenses in an amount that represented about 75 percent of the net corporate income. Bill received regular salary increases. The corporation did not issue a dividend. In 2008, Ron filed a lawsuit alleging that the corporation's directors had breached the fiduciary duty they owed him as a minority shareholder. According to the complaint, the directors had subjected Ron to a "squeeze-out" designed to deprive him of the benefits of being a shareholder.

Ron alleged that the directors had refused to give him a corporate job or board membership, failed to pay him dividends, and deprived him of other income through a series of business decisions that benefited only Bill and Gertrude. The court granted judgment for the defendants, finding that Ron had essentially filed a derivative suit without making a written demand on the corporation. Ron appealed.

ISSUE Can Ron sue Bill and Gertrude directly for breach of fiduciary duty rather than bringing a derivative action?

DECISION Yes. The Idaho Supreme Court reversed the trial court's decision and held that Ron could proceed with his suit for breach of fiduciary duty.

REASON Ordinarily, a shareholder must bring a derivative suit for claims arising from harm to a corporation. Nevertheless, a minority shareholder of a close corporation may bring an individual suit "if the shareholder alleges harm to himself distinct from that suffered by other shareholders." In this case, McCann Ranch's payments to Gertrude hurt the corporation as a whole. Nevertheless, Ron could sue individually under the theory that he had been subjected to a squeeze-out. Unlike Bill and Gertrude, who were the only other shareholders, Ron did not benefit from any of the decisions at issue. Thus, Ron could bring an individual suit for breach of fiduciary duty because he could show that he had been uniquely harmed.

CRITICAL THINKING—Legal Consideration *If this case proceeds to trial, how might the directors try to defend their decisions? What rule concerning director liability might protect them? Explain your answer.*

Duties and Liabilities of Shareholders

One of the hallmarks of the corporate form of business organization is that shareholders are not personally liable for the debts of the corporation. If the corporation fails, shareholders can lose their investments, but generally that is the limit of their liability. As discussed earlier, in certain instances a court will pierce the corporate veil and hold the shareholders individually liable. These situations are the exception, however, not the rule.

Another situation in which a shareholder may incur personal liability occurs when a majority shareholder engages in oppressive conduct or attempts to exclude minority shareholders from receiving certain benefits. If a majority shareholder breaches her or his fiduciary duty to a minority shareholder, the minority shareholder can sue for damages. A breach of fiduciary duties by those who control a close corporation normally constitutes what is known as *oppressive conduct*. A common example of a breach of fiduciary duty occurs when the majority shareholders "freeze out" the minority shareholders and exclude them from certain benefits of participating in the firm.

CASE EXAMPLE 20.10   Brodie, Jordan, and Barbuto formed a close corporation to operate a machine shop. Each owned one-third of the shares in the company, and all three were directors. Brodie served as the corporate president for twelve years but thereafter met with the other shareholders only a few times a year. After disagreements arose, Brodie asked the company to purchase his shares, but his requests were refused. A few years later, Brodie died, and his wife inherited his shares in the company. Jordan and Barbuto refused to perform a valuation of the company, denied her access to the corporate information she requested, did not declare any dividends, and refused to elect her as a director. In this situation, a court found that the majority shareholders had violated their fiduciary duty to Brodie's wife.[17] ●

Mergers and Acquisitions

Merger The legal combination of two or more corporations in such a way that only one corporation (the surviving corporation) continues to exist, having acquired all of the assets and liabilities of the other corporation.

A corporation typically extends its operations by combining with another corporation through a merger, a consolidation, a share exchange, a purchase of assets, or a purchase of a controlling interest in the other corporation. The terms *merger* and *consolidation* traditionally referred to two legally distinct proceedings. Some people today use the term *consolidation* to refer to all types of combinations, including mergers and acquisitions. Whether a combination is a merger, a consolidation, or a share exchange, the rights and liabilities of shareholders, the corporation, and the corporation's creditors are the same.

Facebook acquired Instagram. Did Instagram cease to exist?

(sd619/iStockphoto.com)

Merger

A **merger** involves the legal combination of two or more corporations in such a way that only one of the corporations continues to exist. Suppose that Corporation A and Corporation B decide to merge. They agree that A will absorb B. Therefore, on merging, B ceases to exist as a separate entity, and A continues as the *surviving corporation*. Exhibit 20.4 on the next page graphically illustrates this process.

After the merger, Corporation A is recognized as a single corporation, possessing all the rights, privileges, and powers of itself and Corporation B. It automatically acquires all of B's property and assets

---

17. *Brodie v. Jordan,* 447 Mass. 866, 857 N.E.2d 1076 (2006).

Exhibit 20.4 Merger

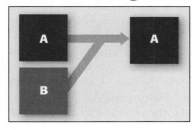

Consolidation The legal combination of two or more corporations in such a way that the original corporations cease to exist and a new corporation emerges with all their assets and liabilities.

Exhibit 20.5 Consolidation

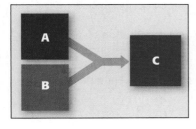

Share Exchange A transaction in which some or all of the shares of one corporation are exchanged for some or all of the shares of another corporation, but both corporations continue to exist.

LEARNING OBJECTIVE 5
What are the basic differences between a merger, a consolidation, and a share exchange?

without the necessity of a formal transfer. Additionally, A becomes liable for all of B's debts and obligations. Finally, A's articles of incorporation are deemed amended to include any changes that are stated in the *articles of merger* (a document setting forth the terms and conditions of the merger that is filed with the secretary of state).

In a merger, the surviving corporation also inherits the disappearing corporation's pre-existing legal rights and obligations. If the disappearing corporation had a right of action against a third party under tort or property law, for example, the surviving corporation can bring a suit after the merger to recover the disappearing corporation's damages.

Consolidation

In a **consolidation,** two or more corporations combine in such a way that each corporation ceases to exist and a new one emerges. For example, Corporation A and Corporation B consolidate to form an entirely new organization, Corporation C. In the process, A and B both terminate, and C comes into existence as an entirely new entity. Exhibit 20.5 on the lower left graphically illustrates this process.

The results of a consolidation are similar to the results of a merger—only one corporation remains. Here, however, Corporation C is recognized as a new corporation, while A and B cease to exist. Corporation C inherits all of the rights, privileges, and powers previously held by A and B. Title to any property and assets owned by A and B passes to C without a formal transfer. Corporation C assumes liability for all of the debts and obligations owed by A and B. The *articles of consolidation,* which state the terms of the consolidation, take the place of A's and B's original corporate articles and are thereafter regarded as C's corporate articles.

When a merger or consolidation takes place, the surviving corporation or newly formed corporation will issue shares or pay some fair consideration to the shareholders of the corporation or corporations that cease to exist. True consolidations have become less common among for-profit corporations because it is often advantageous for one of the firms to survive. In contrast, nonprofit corporations and associations may prefer consolidation because it suggests a new beginning in which neither of the two initial entities is dominant.

Share Exchange

In a **share exchange,** some or all of the shares of one corporation are exchanged for some or all of the shares of another corporation, but both companies continue to exist. Share exchanges are often used to create holding companies (discussed earlier in this chapter). For example, UAL Corporation is a large holding company that owns United Airlines. If one corporation owns *all* of the shares of another corporation, it is referred to as the *parent corporation,* and the wholly owned company is the *subsidiary corporation.*

Merger, Consolidation, or Share Exchange Procedures

All states have statutes authorizing mergers, consolidations, and share exchanges for domestic (in-state) and foreign (out-of-state) corporations. The procedures vary somewhat among jurisdictions. In some states, a consolidation resulting in an entirely new corporation simply follows the initial incorporation procedures discussed earlier in this chapter, whereas other business combinations must follow the procedures outlined below.

The RMBCA sets forth the following basic requirements [RMBCA 11.01–11.07]:

1. The board of directors of *each* corporation involved must approve the merger or consolidation plan.

2. The plan must specify any terms and conditions of the merger. It also must state how the value of the shares of each merging corporation will be determined and how they will be converted into shares or other securities, cash, property, or other interests in another corporation.

3. The majority of the shareholders of *each* corporation must vote to approve the plan at a shareholders' meeting. If any class of stock is entitled to vote as a separate group, the majority of each separate voting group must approve the plan. Although RMBCA 11.04(e) requires only a simple majority of the shareholders entitled to vote once a quorum is present, frequently a corporation's articles of incorporation or bylaws require approval by more than a simple majority. In addition, some state statutes require the approval of two-thirds of the outstanding shares of voting stock, and others require a four-fifths vote.

4. Once the plan is approved by the directors and the shareholders of both corporations, the surviving corporation files the plan (articles of merger, consolidation, or share exchange) with the appropriate official, usually the secretary of state.

5. When state formalities are satisfied, the state issues a certificate of merger to the surviving corporation or a certificate of consolidation to the newly consolidated corporation.

Short-Form Mergers

RMBCA 11.04 provides a simplified procedure for the merger of a substantially owned subsidiary corporation into its parent corporation. Under these provisions, a *short-form merger*—also referred to as a *parent-subsidiary merger*—can be accomplished *without* the approval of the shareholders of either corporation.

The short-form merger can be used only when the parent corporation owns at least 90 percent of the outstanding shares of each class of stock of the subsidiary corporation. Once the board of directors of the parent corporation approves the plan, it is filed with the state, and copies are sent to each shareholder of record in the subsidiary corporation.

Purchase of Assets

When a corporation acquires all or substantially all of the assets of another corporation by direct purchase, the purchasing, or *acquiring,* corporation simply extends its ownership and control over more physical assets. Because no change in the legal entity occurs, the acquiring corporation normally is not required to obtain shareholder approval for the purchase.

Note that the corporation that is *selling* all of its assets is substantially changing its business position and perhaps its ability to carry out its corporate purposes. For that reason, the corporation whose assets are being sold must obtain the approval of both the board of directors and the shareholders.

Successor Liability in Purchases of Assets

Generally, a corporation that purchases the assets of another corporation is not responsible for the liabilities of the selling corporation. Exceptions to this rule are made in certain circumstances, however. In any of the following situations, the acquiring corporation will be held to have assumed *both* the assets and the liabilities of the selling corporation.

1. When the purchasing corporation impliedly or expressly assumes the seller's liabilities.
2. When the sale transaction is actually a merger or consolidation of the two companies.
3. When the purchaser continues the seller's business and retains the same personnel (same shareholders, directors, and officers).
4. When the sale is fraudulently executed to escape liability.

KNOW THIS

In a merger or consolidation, the surviving corporation inherits the disappearing corporation's rights and obligations.

CASE EXAMPLE 20.11 American Standard, Inc., sold the assets and liabilities of its Kewanee Boiler division to OakFabco, Inc. The boilers manufactured by Kewanee were insulated with asbestos, and as a result, many tort claims arose in the years after the sale took place. American Standard filed a suit to establish that OakFabco was liable for these claims. OakFabco argued that it was only responsible for the liabilities that were existing and outstanding as of the closing date of the sale. The court held that the transaction was a purchase and sale of substantially all of the assets of the Kewanee Boiler business, subject to all its debts, liabilities, and obligations. Therefore, the liabilities assumed by OakFabco included claims bought by tort claimants injured after the closing date by boilers installed before that date.[18] •

Purchase of Stock and Tender Offers

An alternative to the purchase of another corporation's assets is the purchase of a substantial number of the voting shares of its stock. This enables the acquiring corporation to control the **target corporation** (the corporation being acquired). The process of acquiring control over a corporation in this way is commonly referred to as a corporate **takeover.**

> **Target Corporation** The corporation to be acquired in a corporate takeover.

> **Takeover** The acquisition of control over a corporation through the purchase of a substantial number of the voting shares of the corporation.

> **Tender Offer** An offer made by one company directly to the shareholders of another (target) company to purchase their shares of stock.

The acquiring corporation deals directly with the target company's shareholders in seeking to purchase the shares they hold. It does this by making a **tender offer** to all of the shareholders of the target corporation. The acquiring corporation generally offers a price higher than the market price of the target corporation's stock prior to the announcement of the tender offer to induce shareholders to accept the offer.

EXAMPLE 20.12 In a merger of two Fortune 500 pharmaceutical companies, Pfizer, Inc., paid $68 billion to acquire its rival Wyeth. Wyeth shareholders reportedly received approximately $50.19 per share (part in cash and part in Pfizer stock), which amounted to a 15 percent premium over the market price of the stock. • Federal securities laws strictly control the terms, duration, and circumstances under which most tender offers are made. In addition, many states have passed antitakeover statutes.

Responses to Tender Offers

A firm may respond to a tender offer in numerous ways. Sometimes, a target firm's board of directors will see a tender offer as favorable and will recommend to the shareholders that they accept it. In contrast, to resist a takeover, a target company can make a *self-tender,* which is an offer to acquire stock from its own shareholders and thereby retain corporate control.

Alternatively, a target corporation might resort to one of several other defensive tactics to resist a takeover. In one commonly used tactic, known as a "poison pill," a target company gives its shareholders rights to purchase additional shares at low prices when there is a takeover attempt. This tactic makes the takeover more expensive for the acquiring firm by increasing the number of shares it must buy.

> "In the takeover business, if you want a friend, you buy a dog."
>
> Carl Icahn, 1936–present
> (American financier)

Corporate Termination

> **Dissolution** The formal disbanding of a corporation, which can take place by (1) an act of the state, (2) an agreement of the shareholders and the board of directors, (3) the expiration of a time period stated in the certificate of incorporation, or (4) a court order.

The termination of a corporation's existence has two phases—dissolution and winding up. **Dissolution** is the legal death of the artificial "person" of the corporation. *Winding up* is the process by which corporate assets are liquidated, or converted into cash and distributed among creditors and shareholders.[19]

---

18. *American Standard, Inc. v. OakFabco, Inc.,* 14 N.Y.3d 399, 901 N.Y.S.2d 572 (2010).

19. Some prefer to call this phase *liquidation,* but we use the term *winding up* to mean all acts needed to bring the legal and financial affairs of the business to an end, including liquidating the assets and distributing them among creditors and shareholders. See RMBCA 14.05.

Voluntary Dissolution

Dissolution can be brought about voluntarily by the directors and the shareholders. State corporation statutes establish the procedures required to voluntarily dissolve a corporation. Basically, there are two possible methods: (1) by the shareholders' unanimous vote to initiate dissolution proceedings (in some states) or (2) by a proposal of the board of directors that is submitted to the shareholders at a shareholders' meeting.

When a corporation is dissolved voluntarily, the corporation must file *articles of dissolution* with the state and notify its creditors of the dissolution. The corporation must also establish a date (at least 120 days after the date of dissolution) by which all claims against the corporation must be received [RMBCA 14.06].

Involuntary Dissolution

Because corporations are creatures of statute, the state can also dissolve a corporation in certain circumstances. The secretary of state or the state attorney general can bring an action to dissolve a corporation that has failed to pay its annual taxes or to submit required annual reports, for example. A state court can also dissolve a corporation that has engaged in acts that exceed its express or implied powers or that has committed fraud or misrepresentation to the state during incorporation.

Sometimes, a shareholder or a group of shareholders petitions a court for corporate dissolution. A court may dissolve a corporation if the controlling shareholders or directors have engaged in fraudulent, illegal, or oppressive conduct. Shareholders may also petition a court for dissolution when the board of directors is deadlocked and the affairs of the corporation can no longer be conducted because of the deadlock.

Winding Up

When dissolution takes place by voluntary action, the members of the board of directors act as trustees of the corporate assets. As trustees, they are responsible for winding up the affairs of the corporation for the benefit of corporate creditors and shareholders. This makes the board members personally liable for any breach of their fiduciary trustee duties.

Receiver In a corporate dissolution, a court-appointed person who winds up corporate affairs and liquidates corporate assets.

When the dissolution is involuntary—or if board members do not wish to act as trustees of the assets—the court will appoint a **receiver** to wind up the corporate affairs and liquidate corporate assets. Courts may also appoint a receiver when shareholders or creditors can show that the board of directors should not be permitted to act as trustees of the corporate assets.

Reviewing . . . Corporations

David Brock is on the board of directors of Firm Body Fitness, Inc., which owns a string of fitness clubs in New Mexico. Brock owns 15 percent of the Firm Body stock, and he is also employed as a tanning technician at one of the fitness clubs. After the January financial report showed that Firm Body's tanning division was operating at a substantial net loss, the board of directors, led by Marty Levinson, discussed terminating the tanning operations. Brock successfully convinced a majority of the board that the tanning division was necessary to market the club's overall fitness package. By April, the tanning division's financial losses had risen. The board hired a business analyst, who conducted surveys and determined that the tanning operations did not significantly increase membership. A shareholder, Diego Peñada, discovered that Brock owned stock in Sunglow, Inc., the company from which Firm Body purchased its tanning equipment. Peñada notified Levinson, who privately reprimanded Brock. Shortly thereafter, Brock and Mandy Vail, who owned 37 percent of the Firm Body stock and also held shares of Sunglow, voted to replace Levinson on the board of directors. Using the information presented in the chapter, answer the following questions.

1. What duties did Brock, as a director, owe to Firm Body?
2. Does the fact that Brock owned shares in Sunglow establish a conflict of interest? Why or why not?
3. Suppose that Firm Body brought an action against Brock claiming that he had breached the duty of loyalty by not disclosing his interest in Sunglow to the other directors. What theory might Brock use in his defense?
4. Now suppose that Firm Body did not bring an action against Brock. What type of lawsuit might Peñada be able to bring based on these facts?

DEBATE THIS Because most shareholders never bother to vote for directors, shareholders have no real control over corporations.

LINKING BUSINESS LAW to Accounting and Finance
Sources of Funds

Your career may take you from business intern or management trainee through other corporate positions to finance manager. A finance manager helps corporate directors and officers determine the sources of funds for ongoing corporate expenses and, hopefully, continued business expansion and growth.

Stocks and Bonds

Corporate finance managers have a variety of sources for funds. They include issuing shares of stock (equity) and selling corporate debt. A finance manager must weigh the advantages and disadvantages of each of these alternatives.

For instance, an issue of common stock does not create an obligation to make fixed interest payments to investors every year, as a sale of bonds would, but the additional shares dilute the holdings of current stockholders. In the case of preferred stock, a sale of shares creates additional preferences, as holders of preferred stock have priority over holders of common stock with respect to dividends and to payment on the dissolution of the corporation.

Lines of Credit

Another option for a source of corporate funds is to borrow the funds. Commercial banks loan funds to all types of businesses.

A bank typically provides a successful corporation with a line of credit that can be drawn on at any time and can be repaid when the business's cash flow warrants it. A commercial bank's line of credit, however, normally costs more in terms of interest than an issuance of corporate bonds.

Self-Financing

Finance managers sometimes decide that the best type of financing is self-financing. To accomplish this type of financing, a corporation retains its earnings on sales and uses those earnings for additional investments. The use of retained earnings is not without cost—there is an *opportunity cost* involved. That opportunity cost is the value that could have been earned if the retained earnings had been used for other investments, such as U.S. Treasury bonds. Retained earnings might also otherwise have been used to pay dividends to shareholders.

Critical Thinking

What is the benefit of paying dividends to shareholders rather than using retained earnings to expand?

Key Terms

Chapter Summary: Corporations

Nature and Classification (See pages 574–579.)	A corporation is a legal entity distinct from its owners. Formal statutory requirements, which vary somewhat from state to state, must be followed in forming a corporation. 1. *Corporate personnel*—The shareholders elect a board of directors to govern the corporation. The board of directors hires corporate officers and other employees to run the firm's daily business. 2. *Corporate taxation*—The corporation pays income tax on net profits, and shareholders pay income tax on the disbursed dividends that they receive from the corporation (double-taxation feature). 3. *Torts and criminal acts*—The corporation is liable for the torts committed by its agents or officers within the course and scope of their employment (under the doctrine of *respondeat superior*). A corporation can be held liable (and be fined) for the criminal acts of its agents and employees. 4. *Domestic, foreign, and alien corporations*—A corporation is referred to as a *domestic corporation* within its home state (the state in which it incorporates), as a *foreign corporation* by any state that is not its home state, and as an *alien corporation* if it originates in another country but does business in the United States. 5. *Public and private corporations*—A public corporation is formed by a government. A private corporation is formed wholly or in part for private benefit. Most corporations are private corporations. 6. *Nonprofit corporations*—Corporations formed without a profit-making purpose. 7. *Close corporations*—Corporations owned by a family or a relatively small number of individuals. Transfer of shares is usually restricted. 8. *S corporations*—Small domestic corporations that, under Subchapter S of the Internal Revenue Code, are taxed like partnerships, thereby allowing shareholders to enjoy limited liability while avoiding double taxation.
Formation and Powers (See pages 579–583.)	1. *Incorporation procedures*—Procedures vary among the states, but the basic steps are as follows: (a) select a state of incorporation, (b) secure the corporate name, (c) prepare the articles of incorporation, and (d) file the articles with the secretary of state. 2. *Articles of incorporation*—The articles must include the corporate name, the number of shares of stock the corporation is authorized to issue, the registered office and agent, and the names and addresses of the incorporators. The state's filing of the articles authorizes the corporation to conduct business. 3. *Corporation by estoppel*—If a firm is not incorporated but represents itself to be a corporation and is sued as such by a third party, it may be held to be a corporation by estoppel. 4. *Corporate powers*—Express powers are granted by the (listed in order of priority): federal constitution, state constitutions, state statutes, articles of incorporation, bylaws, and resolutions of the board of directors. The corporation also has the implied power to do all acts reasonably appropriate and necessary to accomplish its corporate purposes. 5. *Piercing the corporate veil*—To avoid injustice, courts may "pierce the corporate veil" and hold shareholders personally liable. This usually occurs only when the corporation was established to circumvent the law, when the corporate form is used for an illegitimate or fraudulent purpose, or when the controlling shareholder commingles his or her own interests with those of the corporation to such an extent that the corporation no longer has a separate identity.
Corporate Financing (See pages 583–586.)	1. *Bonds*—Securities representing *corporate debt,* which are funds borrowed by a corporation. 2. *Stocks*—Equity securities issued by a corporation that represent the purchase of ownership in the firm. Exhibit 20.1 on page 585 describes how stocks differ from bonds, and Exhibit 20.2 on page 585 describes the types of stocks issued by corporations.

Chapter Summary: Corporations—Continued

Directors, Officers, and Shareholders (See pages 586–598.)	1. *Directors*—Directors are responsible for all policymaking decisions necessary to the management of corporate affairs, including hiring officers. The first board of directors is usually appointed by the incorporators. After that, directors are elected by the shareholders. Directors usually serve a one-year term, although their terms can be longer or staggered. Compensation is usually specified in the corporate articles or bylaws.
	   a. *Board of directors' meetings*—The board of directors holds formal meetings with recorded minutes. The date of regular meetings is usually established in the corporate articles or bylaws. Special meetings can be called, with notice sent to all directors. Quorum requirements vary from state to state. Usually, a quorum is a majority of the directors. Voting usually must be done in person, and in ordinary matters only a majority vote is required.
	   b. *Rights of directors*—Directors' rights include the rights of participation, inspection, and indemnification.
	2. *Corporate officers and executives*—Corporate officers and other executive employees are normally hired by the board of directors and have the rights defined by their employment contracts.
	3. *Duties and liabilities of directors and officers*—
	   a. *Duty of care*—Directors and officers are obligated to act in good faith, to use prudent business judgment in the conduct of corporate affairs, and to act in the corporation's best interests. If a director fails to exercise this duty of care, she or he can be answerable to the corporation and to the shareholders for breaching the duty.
	   b. *The business judgment rule*—This rule immunizes directors and officers from liability when they acted in good faith, acted in the best interests of the corporation, and exercised due care. For the rule to apply, the directors and officers must have made an informed, reasonable, and loyal decision.
	   c. *Duty of loyalty*—Directors and officers have a fiduciary duty to subordinate their own interests to those of the corporation in matters relating to the corporation.
	   d. *Conflicts of interest*—To fulfill their duty of loyalty, directors and officers must make a full disclosure of any potential conflicts between their personal interests and those of the corporation.
	   e. *Liability of directors and officers*—Corporate directors and officers are personally liable for their own torts and crimes. Additionally, they may be held personally liable for the torts and crimes committed by corporate personnel under their supervision (see Chapters 6 and 17).
	4. *Shareholders*—
	   a. *Shareholders' powers*—Shareholders' powers include the approval of all fundamental changes affecting the corporation and the election of the board of directors.
	   b. *Shareholders' meetings*—Shareholders' meetings must occur at least annually, and special meetings can be called when necessary. Notice of the date, time, and place of the meeting (and its purpose, if it is specially called) must be sent to shareholders. Shareholders may vote by proxy (authorizing someone else to vote their shares) and may submit proposals to be included in the company's proxy materials sent to shareholders before meetings.
	   c. *Shareholder voting*—A minimum number of shareholders (a quorum—generally, shareholders holding more than 50 percent of the outstanding shares) must be present at a meeting for business to be conducted. Resolutions are passed (usually) by a simple majority vote. Cumulative voting may or may not be required or permitted. Cumulative voting gives minority shareholders a better chance to be represented on the board of directors. Shareholder voting agreements are usually held to be valid and enforceable.
	5. *Rights of shareholders*—In addition to voting rights, shareholder rights may include the right to a stock certificate, preemptive rights, the right to obtain a dividend, the right to inspect the corporate records, the right to transfer shares, and the right to sue on behalf of the corporation (bring a shareholder's derivative suit) when the directors fail to do so.
	6. *Duties and liabilities of shareholders*—In certain situations, majority shareholders may be regarded as having a fiduciary duty to minority shareholders and will be liable if that duty is breached.

Mergers and Acquisitions (See pages 598–601.)	1. *Merger*—The legal combination of two or more corporations, with the result that the surviving corporation acquires all the assets and obligations of the other corporation, which then ceases to exist. 2. *Consolidation*—The legal combination of two or more corporations, with the result that each corporation ceases to exist and a new one emerges. The new corporation assumes all the assets and obligations of the former corporations. 3. *Share exchange*—Some or all of the shares of one corporation are exchanged for some or all of the shares of another corporation, but both corporations continue to exist. 4. *Procedures*—Determined by state statutes. The basic requirements are listed on pages 599–600. 5. *Short-form (parent-subsidiary) merger*—Possible when the parent corporation owns at least 90 percent of the outstanding shares of each class of stock of the subsidiary corporation. Shareholder approval is not required. The merger need be approved only by the board of directors of the parent corporation.

Continued

Chapter Summary: Corporations—Continued

Mergers and Acquisitions—Continued	6. *Purchase of assets*—When one corporation acquires all or substantially all of the assets of another corporation, the acquiring (purchasing) corporation is not required to obtain shareholder approval, but the selling corporation must obtain the approval of both its directors and its shareholders for the asset sale. 7. *Purchase of stock and tender offers*—One corporation may acquire a substantial number of the voting shares of the stock of another (target) corporation through a tender offer, which is a public offer to all shareholders of the target corporation to purchase its stock. The price offered generally is higher than the market price. Responses to takeover bids include self-tender (the target firm's offer to acquire its own shareholders' stock) and defensive strategies such as a poison pill tactic.
Corporate Termination (See pages 601–602.)	The termination of a corporation involves the following two phases: 1. *Dissolution*—The legal death of the artificial "person" of the corporation. Dissolution can be brought about voluntarily by the directors and shareholders or involuntarily by the state or through a court order. 2. *Winding up (liquidation)*—The process by which corporate assets are converted into cash and distributed to creditors and shareholders. May be supervised by members of the board of directors (when dissolution is voluntary) or by a receiver appointed by the court.

ExamPrep

ISSUE SPOTTERS

1. Name Brand, Inc., is a small business. Twelve members of a single family own all of its stock. Ordinarily, corporate income is taxed at the corporate and shareholder levels. How can Name Brand avoid this double taxation of income? **(See page 578.)**
2. Nico is Omega Corporation's majority shareholder. He owns enough stock in Omega that if he were to sell it, the sale would be a transfer of control of the firm. Discuss whether Nico owes a duty to Omega or the minority shareholders in selling his shares. **(See page 598.)**

—**Check your answers to the Issue Spotters against the answers provided in Appendix E at the end of this text.**

BEFORE THE TEST

Go to www.cengagebrain.com, enter the ISBN 9781133191353, and click on "Find" to locate this textbook's Web site. Then, click on "Access Now" under "Study Tools," and select Chapter 20 at the top. There, you will find a Practice Quiz that you can take to assess your mastery of the concepts in this chapter, as well as Flashcards, a Glossary of important terms, and Video Questions (when assigned).

For Review

Answers to the even-numbered questions in this For Review section can be found in Appendix F at the end of this text.

1. What is a close corporation?
2. In what circumstances might a court disregard the corporate entity ("pierce the corporate veil") and hold the shareholders personally liable?
3. What are the duties of corporate directors and officers?
4. What is a voting proxy?
5. What are the basic differences between a merger, a consolidation, and a share exchange?

Business Scenarios and Case Problems

20–1 Rights of Shareholders. Lucia has acquired one share of common stock of a multimillion-dollar corporation with more than 500,000 shareholders. Lucia's ownership is so small that she is wondering what her rights are as a shareholder. For example, she wants to know whether owning this one share entitles her to (1) attend and vote at shareholders' meetings, (2) inspect the corporate books, and (3) receive yearly dividends. Discuss Lucia's rights in these three matters. **(See pages 594–597.)**

20–2 **Question with Sample Answer—Mergers and Acquisitions.** Jolson is the chair of the board of directors of Artel, Inc., and Douglas is the chair of the board of directors of Fox Express, Inc. Artel is a manufacturing corporation, and Fox Express is a transportation corporation. Jolson and Douglas meet to consider the possibility of combining their corporations and activities into a single corporate entity. They consider two alternative courses of action: Artel could acquire all of the stock and assets of Fox Express, or the corporations could combine to form a new corporation, called A&F Enterprises, Inc. Both Jolson and Douglas are concerned about the necessity of a formal transfer of property, liability for existing debts, and the need to amend the articles of incorporation. Discuss what the two proposed combinations are called and the legal effect each has on the transfer of property, the liabilities of the combined corporations, and the need to amend the articles of incorporation. **(See pages 598–601.)**

—**For a sample answer to Question 20–2, go to Appendix G at the end of this text.**

20–3 **Spotlight on Smart Inventions—Piercing the Corporate Veil.** Thomas Persson and Jon Nokes founded Smart Inventions, Inc., to market household consumer products. The success of their first product, the Smart Mop, continued with later products, which were sold through infomercials. Persson and Nokes were the firm's officers and equal shareholders, with Persson responsible for product development and Nokes in charge of day-to-day activities. By 1998, they had become dissatisfied with each other's efforts. Nokes represented the firm as financially "dying," "in a grim state, . . . worse than ever," and offered to buy all of Persson's shares for $1.6 million. Persson accepted. On the day that they signed the agreement to transfer the shares, Smart Inventions began marketing a new product—the Tap Light. It was an instant success, generating millions of dollars in revenues. In negotiating with Persson, Nokes had intentionally kept the Tap Light a secret. Persson sued Smart Inventions, asserting fraud and other claims. Under what principle might Smart Inventions be liable for Nokes's fraud? Is Smart Inventions liable in this case? Explain. [*Persson v. Smart Inventions, Inc.,* 125 Cal.App.4th 1141, 23 Cal.Rptr.3d 335 (2 Dist. 2005)] **(See pages 582–583.)**

20–4 **Close Corporations.** Mark Burnett and Kamran Pourgol were the only shareholders in a corporation that built and sold a house. When the buyers discovered that the house exceeded the amount of square footage allowed by the building permit, Pourgol agreed to renovate the house to conform to the permit. No work was done, however, and Burnett filed a suit against Pourgol. Burnett claimed that without his knowledge, Pourgol had submitted incorrect plans to obtain the building permit, misrepresented the

extent of the renovation, and failed to fix the house. Was Pourgol guilty of misconduct? If so, how might it have been avoided? Discuss. [*Burnett v. Pourgol,* 83 A.D.3d 756, 921 N.Y.S.2d 280 (2 Dept. 2011)] **(See pages 577–578.)**

20–5 **Purchase of Stock.** Air Products & Chemicals, Inc., made a tender offer of $70 per share to the shareholders of Airgas, Inc. The Airgas board rejected the offer as inadequate and took defensive measures to block the bid. Some Airgas shareholders filed a suit against Airgas, seeking an order to compel the board to allow the shareholders to decide whether to accept Air Products' offer. Who should have the power to accept or reject a tender offer? Why? How can directors best fulfill their duty to act in the interest of their shareholders? [*Air Products & Chemicals, Inc. v. Airgas, Inc.,* 16 A.3d 48 (Del.Ch. 2011)] **(See page 601.)**

20–6 **Case Problem with Sample Answer—Rights of Shareholders.** Stanka Woods is the sole member of Hair Ventures, LLC. Hair Ventures owns 3 million shares of stock in Biolustré, Inc. For several years, Woods and other Biolustré shareholders did not receive notice of shareholders' meetings or financial reports. When Woods learned that Biolustré planned to issue more stock, Woods, through Hair Ventures, demanded to see Biolustré's books and records. Biolustré asserted that the request was not for a proper purpose. Does Woods have a right to inspect Biolustré's books and records? If so, what are the limits? Do any of those limits apply in this case? Explain. [*Biolustré, Inc. v. Hair Ventures, LLC,* __ S.W.3d __ (Tex.App.—San Antonio 2011)] **(See page 596.)**

—**For a sample answer to Problem 20–6, go to Appendix H at the end of this text.**

20–7 **Duty of Loyalty.** Kids International Corp. produced children's wear for Wal-Mart and other retailers. Gila Dweck was a Kids director and its chief executive officer. Because she felt that she was not paid enough for the company's success, she started another firm, Success Apparel, to compete with Kids. Success operated out of Kids' premises, used its employees, borrowed on its credit, took advantage of its business opportunities, and capitalized on its customer relationships. As an "administrative fee," Dweck paid Kids 1 percent of Success's total sales. Did Dweck breach any fiduciary duties? Explain. [*Dweck v. Nasser,* 2012 WL 3194069 (Del.Ch. 2012)] **(See pages 588–591.)**

20–8 **Piercing the Corporate Veil.** In 1997, Leon Greenblatt, Andrew Jahelka, and Richard Nichols incorporated Loop Corp. with only $1,000 of capital. Three years later, Banco Panamericano, Inc., which was run entirely by Greenblatt and owned by a Greenblatt family trust, extended a large line of credit to Loop. Loop's subsidiaries used the credit to acquire a security interest in Loop. Loop then opened an account with Wachovia Securities, LLC, to buy stock shares using credit provided by Wachovia. When the stock values plummeted, Loop owed Wachovia $1.89 million. Loop also defaulted on its loan from Banco, but Banco agreed to lend Loop millions of dollars more. Rather than repay Wachovia with the influx of funds, Loop gave the funds to closely related entities and "compensated" Nichols and Jahelka without issuing any W-2 forms (forms reporting compensation to the Internal Revenue Service). Loop made loans to other related entities and shared office space, equipment, and telephone and fax numbers with related entities. Loop also moved employees among related entities, failed to file its tax returns on time (or, sometimes, at all), and failed to follow its own bylaws. In a lawsuit brought by Wachovia, can the court hold Greenblatt, Jahelka, and Nichols personally liable by piercing the corporate veil? Why or why not? [*Wachovia Securities, LLC v. Banco Panamericano, Inc.,* 674 F.3d 743 (9th Cir. 2012)] **(See pages 582–583.)**

20–9   ◆➤ **A Question of Ethics—Duties of Directors and Officers.** New Orleans Paddlewheels, Inc. (NOP), is a Louisiana corporation formed in 1982. At that time, James Smith, Sr., and Warren Reuther were its only shareholders, with each holding 50 percent of the stock. NOP was part of a sprawling enterprise of tourism and hospitality companies in New Orleans. The positions on the board of each company were split equally between the Smith and Reuther families. At Smith's request, his son James Smith, Jr. (JES), became involved in the businesses. In 1999, NOP's board elected JES as president, in charge of day-to-day operations, and Reuther as chief executive officer (CEO), in charge of

marketing and development. Over the next few years, animosity developed between Reuther and JES. In October 2001, JES terminated Reuther as CEO and denied him access to the offices and books of NOP and the other companies, literally changing the locks on the doors. At the next meetings of the boards of NOP and the overall enterprise, deadlock ensued, with the directors voting along family lines on every issue. Complaining that the meetings were a "waste of time," JES began to run the entire enterprise by taking advantage of an unequal balance of power on the companies' executive committees. In NOP's subsequent bankruptcy proceeding, Reuther filed a motion for the appointment of a trustee to formulate a plan for the firm's reorganization, alleging, among other things, misconduct by NOP's management. [*In re New Orleans Paddlewheels, Inc.,* 350 Bankr. 667 (E.D.La. 2006)] **(See pages 588–591.)**

1. Was Reuther legally entitled to have access to the books and records of NOP and the other companies? JES maintained, among other things, that NOP's books were "a mess." Was JES's denial of that access unethical? Explain.

2. How would you describe JES's attempt to gain control of NOP and the other companies? Were his actions deceptive and self-serving in the pursuit of personal gain or legitimate and reasonable in the pursuit of a business goal? Discuss.

Critical Thinking and Writing Assignments

20–10   💡 **Business Law Critical Thinking Group Assignment.** Milena Weintraub and Larry Griffith were shareholders in Grand Casino, Inc., which operated a casino in South Dakota. Griffith owned 51 percent of the stock and Weintraub 49 percent. Weintraub managed the casino, which Griffith typically visited once a week. At the end of 2012, an accounting audit showed that the cash on hand was less than the amount posted in the casino's books. Later, more shortfalls were discovered. In October 2014, Griffith did a complete audit. Weintraub was unable to account for $200,500 in missing cash. After that, Griffith kept all of the casino's most recent profits, including Weintraub's $90,447.20 share, and, without telling Weintraub, sold the

casino for $400,000 and kept all of the proceeds. Weintraub filed a suit against Griffith, asserting a breach of fiduciary duty. Griffith countered with evidence of Weintraub's misappropriation of corporate cash.

1. The first group will discuss the duties that these parties owed to each other and determine whether Weintraub, Griffith, or both breached those duties.

2. The second group will decide how this dispute should be resolved and who should pay what to whom to reconcile the finances.

3. A third group will discuss whether Weintraub or Griffin violated any ethical duties to each other or to the corporation.

CHAPTER 21

Investor Protection, Insider Trading, and Corporate Governance

(TommL/iStockphoto.com)

CHAPTER OUTLINE	LEARNING OBJECTIVES
• Securities Act of 1933 • Securities Exchange Act of 1934 • State Securities Laws • Corporate Governance • Online Securities Fraud	*The five learning objectives below are designed to help improve your understanding of the chapter. After reading this chapter, you should be able to answer the following questions:* 1 What is meant by the term *securities?* 2 What are the two major statutes regulating the securities industry? 3 What is insider trading? Why is it prohibited? 4 What are some of the features of state securities laws? 5 What certification requirements does the Sarbanes-Oxley Act impose on corporate executives?

"You are remembered for the rules you break."
—General Douglas MacArthur, 1880–1964 (U.S. Army general)

Security Generally, a stock, bond, note, debenture, warrant, or other instrument representing an ownership interest in a corporation or a promise of repayment of debt by a corporation.

After the stock market crash of 1929, Congress enacted legislation to regulate securities markets. **Securities** generally are defined as any instruments representing corporate ownership (stock) or debts (bonds). The goal of regulation was to provide investors with more information to help them make buying and selling decisions about securities and to prohibit deceptive, unfair, and manipulative practices.

Today, the sale and transfer of securities are heavily regulated by federal and state statutes and by government agencies. Moreover, the Securities and Exchange Commission (SEC) has implemented new regulations since Congress passed the Dodd-Frank Wall Street Reform and Consumer Protection Act,[1] in reaction to the economic recession. We discuss the role of the SEC in the regulation of securities laws in this chapter's *Landmark in the Law* feature on the next page.

Despite all efforts to regulate the securities markets, people continue to break the rules and are often remembered for it, as observed in the chapter-opening quotation above. Violations are not always clear, though. Consider what happened when Facebook went

---

1. Pub. L. No. 111-203, July 21, 2010, 124 Stat. 1376; 12 U.S.C. Sections 5301 *et seq.*

LANDMARK IN THE LAW
The Securities and Exchange Commission

In 1931, in the wake of the stock market crash of 1929, the U.S. Senate passed a resolution calling for an extensive investigation of securities trading. The investigation led, ultimately, to the enactment of the Securities Act of 1933, which is also known as the *truth-in-securities* bill. In the following year, Congress passed the Securities Exchange Act. This 1934 act created the Securities and Exchange Commission (SEC).

Major Responsibilities of the SEC The SEC was created as an independent regulatory agency with the function of administering the 1933 and 1934 acts. Its major responsibilities in this respect are as follows:

1. Interprets federal securities laws and investigates securities law violations.
2. Issues new rules and amends existing rules.
3. Oversees the inspection of securities firms, brokers, investment advisers, and ratings agencies.
4. Oversees private regulatory organizations in the securities, accounting, and auditing fields.
5. Coordinates U.S. securities regulation with federal, state, and foreign authorities.

The SEC's Expanding Regulatory Powers Since its creation, the SEC's regulatory functions have gradually been increased by legislation granting it authority in different areas. For example, to curb further securities fraud, the Securities Enforcement Remedies and Penny Stock Reform Act of 1990[a] was enacted to expand the SEC's enforcement options and allow SEC administrative law judges to hear cases involving more types of alleged securities

a. 15 U.S.C. Section 77g.

law violations. In addition, the act provides that courts can prevent persons who have engaged in securities fraud from serving as officers and directors of publicly held corporations. The Securities Acts Amendments of 1990 authorized the SEC to seek sanctions against those who violate foreign securities laws.[b]

The National Securities Markets Improvement Act of 1996 expanded the power of the SEC to exempt persons, securities, and transactions from the requirements of the securities laws.[c] (This part of the act is also known as the Capital Markets Efficiency Act.) The act also limited the authority of the states to regulate certain securities transactions and particular investment advisory firms.[d] The Sarbanes-Oxley Act of 2002,[e] which you will read about later in this chapter, further expanded the authority of the SEC by directing the agency to issue new rules relating to corporate disclosure requirements and by creating an oversight board to regulate public accounting firms.

Application to Today's World *The SEC is working to make the regulatory process more efficient and more relevant to today's securities trading practices. To this end, the SEC has embraced modern technology and communications methods, especially the Internet, more completely than many other federal agencies have. For example, the agency now requires—not just allows—companies to file certain information electronically so that it can be posted on the SEC's EDGAR (Electronic Data Gathering, Analysis, and Retrieval) database.*

b. 15 U.S.C. Section 78a.
c. 15 U.S.C. Sections 77z-3, 78mm.
d. 15 U.S.C. Section 80b-3a.
e. 15 U.S.C. Sections 7201 *et seq.*

public and issued stock in 2012. Facebook and its underwriters at Morgan Stanley determined that there was enough interest by investors to justify an opening price of $38 per share. Within a few weeks, however, the value of a share was $25.75—30 percent below the original price. A rash of lawsuits were filed, and government regulators began an investigation. Many suspected that Facebook had provided information only to underwriters and certain (institutional) investors rather than making it available to all investors. Such an action is a violation of the securities laws, as you will read in this chapter.

Securities Act of 1933

The Securities Act of 1933[2] governs initial sales of stock by businesses. The act was designed to prohibit various forms of fraud and to stabilize the securities industry by requiring that all essential information concerning the issuance of securities be made available to the investing public. Basically, the purpose of this act is to require disclosure. The 1933 act provides that

2. 15 U.S.C. Sections 77–77aa.

(National Archives)

During the stock market crash of 1929, hordes of investors crowded Wall Street to find out the latest news. How did the "crash" affect stock trading in the years thereafter?

Investment Contract In securities law, a transaction in which a person invests in a common enterprise reasonably expecting profits that are derived primarily from the efforts of others.

LEARNING OBJECTIVE 1
What is meant by the term *securities*?

all securities transactions must be registered with the SEC or be exempt from registration requirements.

What Is a Security?

Section 2(1) of the Securities Act of 1933 contains a broad definition of securities, which generally include the following:[3]

1. Instruments and interests commonly known as securities, such as preferred and common stocks, treasury stocks, bonds, debentures, and stock warrants.
2. Any interests, such as stock options, puts, calls, or other types of privilege on a security or on the right to purchase a security or a group of securities in a national security exchange.
3. Notes, instruments, or other evidence of indebtedness, including certificates of interest in a profit-sharing agreement and certificates of deposit.
4. Any fractional undivided interest in oil, gas, or other mineral rights.
5. Investment contracts, which include interests in limited partnerships and other investment schemes.

The *Howey* Test   In interpreting the act, the United States Supreme Court has held that an **investment contract** is any transaction in which a person (1) invests (2) in a common enterprise (3) reasonably expecting profits (4) derived *primarily* or *substantially* from others' managerial or entrepreneurial efforts. Known as the *Howey* test, this definition continues to guide the determination of what types of contracts can be considered securities.[4]

CASE EXAMPLE 21.1   Alpha Telcom sold, installed, and maintained pay-phone systems. As part of its pay-phone program, Alpha guaranteed buyers a 14 percent return on their investment. Alpha was operating at a net loss, however, and continually borrowed funds to pay investors the fixed rate of return it had promised. Eventually, the company filed for bankruptcy, and the SEC brought an action alleging that Alpha had violated the Securities Act of 1933. A federal court concluded that Alpha's pay-phone program was a security because it involved an investment contract.[5] •

Many Types of Securities   For our purposes, it is probably convenient to think of securities in their most common forms—stocks and bonds issued by corporations. Bear in mind, though, that securities can take many forms, including interests in whiskey, cosmetics, worms, beavers, boats, vacuum cleaners, muskrats, and cemetery lots. Almost any stake in the ownership or debt of a company can be considered a security. Investment contracts in condominiums, franchises, limited partnerships in real estate, and oil or gas or other mineral rights have qualified as securities.

....
**PREVENTING
LEGAL DISPUTES**

Securities are not limited to stocks and bonds but can encompass a wide variety of legal claims. The analysis hinges on the nature of the transaction rather than on the particular instrument or rights involved. Because Congress enacted securities laws to regulate investments, in whatever form and by whatever name they are called, almost any type of security that might be sold as an investment can be subject to securities laws. When in doubt about whether an investment transaction involves securities, seek the advice of a specialized attorney.

---

3. 15 U.S.C. Section 77b(1). Amendments in 1982 added stock options.
4. *SEC v. W. J. Howey Co.,* 328 U.S. 293, 66 S.Ct. 1100, 90 L.Ed. 1244 (1946).
5. *SEC v. Alpha Telcom, Inc.,* 187 F.Supp.2d 1250 (2002). See also *SEC v. Edwards,* 540 U.S. 389, 124 S.Ct. 892, 157 L.Ed.2d 813 (2004), in which the United States Supreme Court held that an investment scheme offering contractual entitlement to a fixed rate of return can be an investment contract and therefore can be considered a security under federal law.

Registration Statement

Section 5 of the Securities Act of 1933 broadly provides that a security must be *registered* before being offered to the public unless it qualifies for an exemption. The issuing corporation must file a *registration statement* with the SEC and must provide all investors with a *prospectus*.

A **prospectus** is a written disclosure document that describes the security being sold, the financial operations of the issuing corporation, and the investment or risk attaching to the security. The prospectus also serves as a selling tool for the issuing corporation. The SEC now allows an issuer to deliver its prospectus to investors electronically via the Internet.[6]

In principle, the registration statement and the prospectus supply sufficient information to enable unsophisticated investors to evaluate the financial risk involved.

Contents of the Registration Statement The registration statement must be written in plain English and fully describe the following:

1. The securities being offered for sale, including their relationship to the issuer's other capital securities.
2. The corporation's properties and business (including a financial statement certified by an independent public accounting firm).
3. The management of the corporation, including managerial compensation, stock options, pensions, and other benefits. Any interests of directors or officers in any material transactions with the corporation must be disclosed.
4. How the corporation intends to use the proceeds of the sale.
5. Any pending lawsuits or special risk factors.

All companies, both domestic and foreign, must file their registration statements electronically so that they can be posted on the SEC's EDGAR (Electronic Data Gathering, Analysis, and Retrieval) database. The EDGAR database includes material on initial public offerings, proxy statements, corporations' annual reports, registration statements, and other documents that have been filed with the SEC. Investors can access the database via the Internet (**www.sec.gov/edgar.shtml**) to obtain information that can be used to make investment decisions.

Registration Process The registration statement does not become effective until after it has been reviewed and approved by the SEC (unless it is filed by a *well-known seasoned issuer,* as will be discussed shortly). The 1933 act restricted the types of activities that an issuer can engage in at each stage in the registration process.

Prefiling Period During the *prefiling period* (before filing the registration statement), the issuer normally cannot sell or offer to sell the securities. Once the registration statement has been filed, a waiting period begins while the SEC reviews the registration statement for completeness.[7]

Prospectus A written document required by securities laws when a security is being sold. The prospectus describes the security, the financial operations of the issuing corporation, and the risk attaching to the security so that investors will have sufficient information to evaluate the risk involved in purchasing the security.

► KNOW THIS ◄

The purpose of the Securities Act of 1933 is disclosure. The SEC does not consider whether a security is worth the investment price.

What act requires securities to be registered?

(PictureLake/iStockphoto.com)

---

6. Basically, an electronic prospectus must meet the same requirements as a printed prospectus. The SEC has special rules that address situations in which the graphics, images, or audio files in a printed prospectus cannot be reproduced in an electronic form. 17 C.F.R. Section 232.304.
7. The waiting period must last at least twenty days but always extends much longer because the SEC invariably requires numerous changes and additions to the registration statement.

Waiting Period During the *waiting period,* the securities can be offered for sale but cannot be sold by the issuing corporation. Only certain types of offers are allowed. All issuers can distribute a *preliminary prospectus,* which contains most of the information that will be included in the final prospectus but often does not include a price.

Most issuers can also use a *free-writing prospectus* during this period (although some inexperienced issuers will need to file a preliminary prospectus first).[8] A **free-writing prospectus** is any type of written, electronic, or graphic offer that describes the issuer or its securities and includes a legend indicating that the investor may obtain the prospectus at the SEC's Web site.

Free-Writing Prospectus A written, electronic, or graphic offer that is used during the waiting period and describes securities that are being offered for sale, or describes the issuing corporation and includes a legend indicating that the investor may obtain the prospectus at the Securities and Exchange Commission's Web site.

Posteffective Period Once the SEC has reviewed and approved the registration statement and the waiting period is over, the registration is effective, and the *posteffective period* begins. The issuer can now offer and sell the securities without restrictions. If the company issued a preliminary or free-writing prospectus to investors, it must provide those investors with a final prospectus either before or at the time they purchase the securities. The issuer can require investors to download the final prospectus from a Web site if it notifies them of the appropriate Internet address.

Well-Known Seasoned Issuers

In 2005, the SEC revised the registration process and loosened some of the restrictions on large, experienced issuers.[9] The rules created new categories of issuers depending on their size and presence in the market and provided a simplified registration process for these issuers. The large, well-known securities firms that issue most securities have the greatest flexibility.

A firm that has issued at least $1 billion in securities in the previous three years or has at least $700 million of value of outstanding stock in the hands of the public is considered a *well-known seasoned issuer* (WKSI). WKSIs can file registration statements the day they announce a new offering and are not required to wait for SEC review and approval. They can also use a free-writing prospectus at any time, even during the prefiling period.

Exempt Securities and Transactions

Certain types of securities are exempt from the registration requirements of the Securities Act of 1933. These securities—which generally can also be resold without being registered—are summarized in Exhibit 21.1 on the next page under the "Exempt Securities" heading.[10] The exhibit also lists and describes certain transactions that are exempt from registration requirements under various SEC regulations.

The transaction exemptions are the most important because they are very broad and can enable an issuer to avoid the high cost and complicated procedures associated with registration. Because the coverage of the exemptions overlaps somewhat, an offering may qualify for more than one. Therefore, many sales of securities occur without registration. Even when a transaction is exempt from the registration requirements, the offering is still subject to the antifraud provisions of the 1933 act (as well as those of the 1934 act, to be discussed later in this chapter).

► KNOW THIS ◄
The issuer of an exempt security does not have to disclose the same information as other issuers.

Regulation A Offerings

Securities issued by an issuer that has offered less than $5 million in securities during any twelve-month period are exempt from registration.[11] Under Regulation A,[12] the issuer must file with the SEC a notice of the issue and an offering

---

8. See SEC Rules 164 and 433.
9. *Securities Offering Reform,* codified at 17 C.F.R. Sections 200, 228, 229, 230, 239, 240, 243, 249, and 274.
10. 15 U.S.C. Section 77c.
11. 15 U.S.C. Section 77c(b).
12. 17 C.F.R. Sections 230.251–230.263.

Exhibit 21.1 Exemptions for Securities Offerings under the 1933 Securities Act

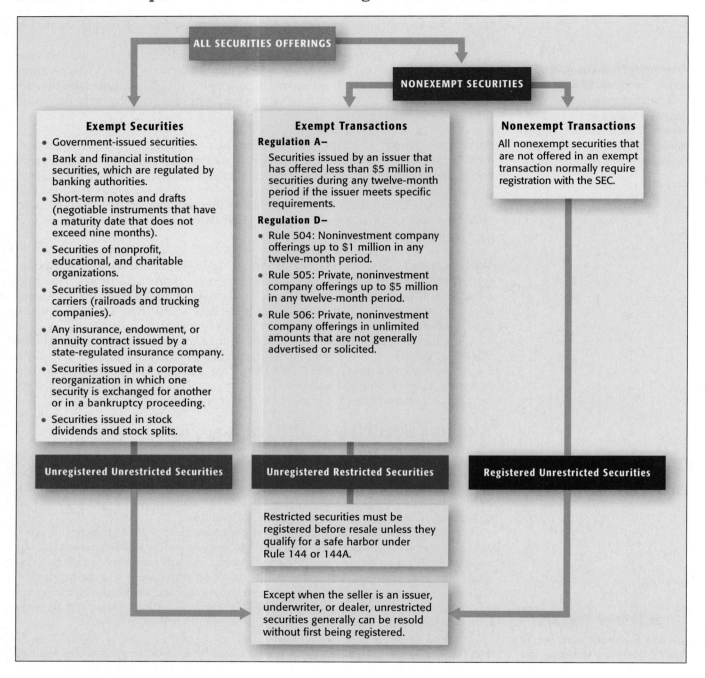

circular, which must also be provided to investors before the sale. This is a much simpler and less expensive process than the procedures associated with full registration.

Testing the Waters Companies are allowed to "test the waters" for potential interest before preparing the offering circular. To *test the waters* means to determine potential interest without actually selling any securities or requiring any commitment on the part of those who express interest. Small-business issuers (companies with annual revenues of less than $25 million) can use an integrated registration and reporting system that uses simpler forms than the full registration system.

Using the Internet Some companies have sold their securities via the Internet using Regulation A. **EXAMPLE 21.2** The Spring Street Brewing Company became the first company to sell securities via an online initial public offering (IPO). Spring Street raised about $1.6 million—without having to pay any commissions to brokers or underwriters. • Such online IPOs are particularly attractive to small companies and start-up ventures that may find it difficult to raise capital from institutional investors or through underwriters.

Small Offerings—Regulation D
The SEC's Regulation D contains several exemptions from registration requirements (Rules 504, 504a, 505, and 506) for offers that either involve a small dollar amount or are made in a limited manner.

Rule 504 Rule 504 is the exemption used by most small businesses. It provides that non-investment company offerings up to $1 million in any twelve-month period are exempt. Noninvestment companies are firms that are not engaged primarily in the business of investing or trading in securities. (In contrast, an **investment company** is a firm that buys a large portfolio of securities and professionally manages it on behalf of many smaller shareholders-owners. A **mutual fund** is a type of investment company.)

EXAMPLE 21.3 Zeta Enterprises is a limited partnership that develops commercial property. Zeta intends to offer $600,000 of its limited partnership interests for sale between June 1 and next May 31. Because an interest in a limited partnership meets the definition of a security (discussed earlier in this chapter), this offering would be subject to the registration and prospectus requirements of the Securities Act of 1933. Under Rule 504, however, the sales of Zeta's interests are exempt from these requirements because Zeta is a noninvestment company making an offering of less than $1 million in a twelve-month period. Therefore, Zeta can sell its limited partnership interests without filing a registration statement with the SEC or issuing a prospectus to any investor. •

Rule 505 Another exemption is available under Rule 505 for private, noninvestment company offerings up to $5 million in any twelve-month period. The offer may be made to an unlimited number of *accredited investors* and up to thirty-five unaccredited investors. **Accredited investors** include banks, insurance companies, investment companies, employee benefit plans, the issuer's executive officers and directors, and persons whose income or net worth exceeds a certain threshold.

The SEC must be notified of the sales, and precautions must be taken because these restricted securities may be resold only by registration or in an exempt transaction. No general solicitation or advertising is allowed. The issuer must provide any unaccredited investors with disclosure documents that generally are the same as those used in registered offerings.

Rule 506—Private Placement Exemption Rule 506 exempts private, noninvestment company offerings in unlimited amounts that are not generally solicited or advertised. This exemption is often referred to as the *private placement* exemption because it exempts "transactions not involving any public offering."[13] To qualify for the exemption, the issuer must believe that each unaccredited investor has sufficient knowledge or experience in financial matters to be capable of evaluating the investment's merits and risks.[14]

---

13. 15 U.S.C. Section 77d(2).
14. 17 C.F.R. Section 230.506.

Investment Company A company that acts on the behalf of many smaller shareholders-owners by buying a large portfolio of securities and professionally managing that portfolio.

Mutual Fund A specific type of investment company that continually buys or sells to investors shares of ownership in a portfolio.

Accredited Investor In the context of securities offerings, "sophisticated" investors, such as banks, insurance companies, investment companies, the issuer's executive officers and directors, and persons whose income or net worth exceeds certain limits.

➤ KNOW THIS ◄

An investor can be "sophisticated" by virtue of his or her education and experience or by investing through a knowledgeable, experienced representative.

The private placement exemption is perhaps most important to firms that want to raise funds through the sale of securities without registering them. **EXAMPLE 21.4** Citco Corporation needs to raise capital to expand its operations. Citco decides to make a private $10 million offering of its common stock directly to two hundred accredited investors and thirty highly sophisticated, but unaccredited, investors. Citco provides all of these investors with a prospectus and material information about the firm, including its most recent financial statements.

As long as Citco notifies the SEC of the sale, this offering will likely qualify for the private placement exemption. The offering is nonpublic and not generally advertised. There are fewer than thirty-five unaccredited investors, and each of them possesses sufficient knowledge and experience to evaluate the risks involved. The issuer has provided all purchasers with the material information. Thus, Citco will *not* be required to comply with the registration requirements of the Securities Act of 1933. •

Resales and Safe Harbor Rules Most securities can be resold without registration. The Securities Act of 1933 provides exemptions for resales by most persons other than issuers or underwriters. The average investor who sells shares of stock does not have to file a registration statement with the SEC.

Resales of restricted securities, however, trigger the registration requirements unless the party selling them complies with Rule 144 or Rule 144A. These rules are sometimes referred to as "safe harbors."

Rule 144 Rule 144 exempts restricted securities from registration on resale if all of the following conditions are met:

1. There is adequate current public information about the issuer. ("Adequate current public information" refers to the reports that certain companies are required to file under the Securities Exchange Act of 1934.)
2. The person selling the securities has owned them for at least six months if the issuer is subject to the reporting requirements of the 1934 act.[15] If the issuer is not subject to the 1934 act's reporting requirements, the seller must have owned the securities for at least one year.
3. The securities are sold in certain limited amounts in unsolicited brokers' transactions.
4. The SEC is notified of the resale.[16]

⟩ KNOW THIS ⟨

Securities do not have to be held for a specific period (six months or one year) to be exempt from registration on a resale under Rule 144A, as they do under Rule 144.

Rule 144A Securities that at the time of issue are not of the same class as securities listed on a national securities exchange or quoted in a U.S. automated interdealer quotation system may be resold under Rule 144A.[17] They may be sold only to a qualified institutional buyer (an institution, such as an insurance company or a bank that owns and invests at least $100 million in securities). The seller must take reasonable steps to ensure that the buyer knows that the seller is relying on the exemption under Rule 144A.

Violations of the 1933 Act

It is a violation of the Securities Act of 1933 to intentionally defraud investors by misrepresenting or omitting facts in a registration statement or prospectus. Liability is also imposed on those who are negligent for not discovering the fraud. Selling securities before the

---

15. Before 2008, when amendments to Rule 144 became effective, the holding period was one year if the issuer was subject to the reporting requirements of the 1934 act. See the revised SEC Rules and Regulations at 72 Federal Rules 71546-01, 2007 WL 4368599, Release No. 33-8869. This reduced holding period allows nonpublic issuers to raise capital electronically from private and overseas sources more quickly.
16. 17 C.F.R. Section 230.144.
17. 17 C.F.R. Section 230.144A.

effective date of the registration statement or under an exemption for which the securities do not qualify also results in liability.

Remedies   Criminal violations are prosecuted by the U.S. Department of Justice. Violators may be fined up to $10,000, imprisoned for up to five years, or both.

The SEC is authorized to seek civil sanctions against those who willfully violate the 1933 act. It can request an injunction to prevent further sales of the securities involved or ask the court to grant other relief, such as an order to a violator to refund profits. Parties who purchase securities and suffer harm as a result of false or omitted statements may also bring suits in a federal court to recover their losses and other damages.

Defenses   There are three basic defenses to charges of violations under the 1933 act. A defendant can avoid liability by proving that (1) the statement or omission was not material, (2) the plaintiff knew about the misrepresentation at the time of purchasing the stock, or (3) the defendant exercised *due diligence* in preparing the registration and reasonably believed at the time that the statements were true.

The due diligence defense is the most important because it can be asserted by any defendant, except the issuer of the stock. The defendant must prove that she or he reasonably believed, at the time the registration statement became effective, that the statements in it were true and there were no omissions of material facts.

The following case involved allegations of omissions of material information from an issuing company's registration statement. The defendants contended that the omissions were not material.

Case 21.1

Litwin v. Blackstone Group, LP

United States Court of Appeals, Second Circuit, 634 F.3d 706 (2011). www.ca2.uscourts.gov[a]

(AP Photo/Mary Altaffer)

FACTS   Blackstone Group, LP, manages investments. Its Corporate Private Equity Division accounts for nearly 40 percent of the assets under the company's management. In preparation for an initial public offering (IPO), Blackstone filed a registration statement with the Securities and Exchange Commission (SEC). At the time, Blackstone's investments included FGIC Corporation—a company that insured investments in subprime mortgages—and Freescale Semiconductor, Inc., which made wireless 3G chipsets for cell phones.

Before the IPO, FGIC's mortgage insurance experienced problems, and Freescale lost an exclusive contract with Motorola, Inc. (its largest customer). Consequently, both FGIC and Freescale began to generate substantial losses for Blackstone. Blackstone's registration statement did not mention the impact on its revenue of the investments in FGIC and Freescale. Martin Litwin and others

who invested in the IPO filed a suit against Blackstone and its officers, alleging material omissions from the statement. Blackstone filed a motion to dismiss, which the court granted. The plaintiffs appealed.

ISSUE   Was the fact that Blackstone had recently suffered substantial losses on two of its investments sufficient proof of material information that should have been disclosed in its registration statement?

DECISION   Yes. The federal appellate court vacated the lower court's dismissal and remanded the case. The plaintiffs had provided sufficient allegations that Blackstone had omitted material information that it was required to disclose under securities law for the case to go to trial.

---

a. In the left column, click on "Decisions." On the next page, in the "Enter Docket #, Date, Party Name or find decisions that contain:" box, type "09-4426" and click on "Search." In the result, click on the docket number to access the opinion (the case name is shown as *Landmen Partners, Inc. v. Blackstone Group, LP*). The U.S. Court of Appeals for the Second Circuit maintains this Web site.

Case 21.1—Continues next page ➡

Case 21.1—Continued

REASON Information is material if a reasonable investor would consider it significant in making an investment decision. A complaint can be dismissed on the ground that an omission is not material only if it would be "so obviously unimportant to a reasonable investor that reasonable minds could not differ on the question." In this case, the information concerned the extent to which known events and trends could reasonably be expected to affect Blackstone's investments and revenue. The plaintiffs alleged that Blackstone should have disclosed this information. In particular, a reasonable investor would want to know the expected effect on the corporate private equity sector's future revenue. Thus "the alleged . . . omissions relating to FGIC and Freescale were plausibly material."

CRITICAL THINKING—Legal Consideration *Litwin alleged that Blackstone had negligently omitted material information from the registration statement. What will he and the others have to show to prove their case?*

Securities Exchange Act of 1934

LEARNING OBJECTIVE 2
What are the two major statutes regulating the securities industry?

The Securities Exchange Act of 1934 provides for the regulation and registration of securities exchanges, brokers, dealers, and national securities associations, such as the National Association of Securities Dealers (NASD). Unlike the 1933 act, which is a one-time disclosure law, the 1934 act provides for continuous periodic disclosures by publicly held corporations to enable the SEC to regulate subsequent trading.

The Securities Exchange Act of 1934 applies to companies that have assets in excess of $10 million and five hundred or more shareholders. These corporations are referred to as Section 12 companies because they are required to register their securities under Section 12 of the 1934 act. Section 12 companies must file reports with the SEC annually and quarterly, and sometimes even monthly if specified events occur (such as a merger). Other provisions in the 1934 act require all securities brokers and dealers to be registered, to keep detailed records of their activities, and to file annual reports with the SEC.

The act also authorizes the SEC to engage in market surveillance to deter undesirable market practices such as fraud, market manipulation (attempts at illegally influencing stock prices), and misrepresentation. In addition, the act provides for the SEC's regulation of proxy solicitations for voting (discussed in Chapter 20).

Section 10(b), SEC Rule 10b-5, and Insider Trading

SEC Rule 10b-5 A rule of the Securities and Exchange Commission that prohibits the commission of fraud in connection with the purchase or sale of any security. It is unlawful to make any untrue statement of a material fact or to omit a material fact if doing so causes the statement to be misleading.

Section 10(b) is one of the more important sections of the Securities Exchange Act of 1934. This section proscribes the use of any manipulative or deceptive mechanism in violation of SEC rules and regulations. Among the rules that the SEC has promulgated pursuant to the 1934 act is **SEC Rule 10b-5**, which prohibits the commission of fraud in connection with the purchase or sale of any security.

SEC Rule 10b-5 applies to almost all cases concerning the trading of securities, whether on organized exchanges, in over-the-counter markets, or in private transactions. Generally, the rule covers just about any form of security, and the securities need not be registered under the 1933 act for the 1934 act to apply.

Private parties can sue for securities fraud under the 1934 act and SEC rules. The basic elements of a securities fraud action are as follows:

KNOW THIS

A required element in any fraud claim is reliance. The innocent party must justifiably have relied on the misrepresentation.

1. A *material misrepresentation* (or omission) in connection with the purchase and sale of securities.
2. *Scienter* (a wrongful state of mind).
3. *Reliance* by the plaintiff on the material misrepresentation.
4. An *economic loss*.
5. *Causation*, meaning that there is a causal connection between the misrepresentation and the loss.

Insider Trading The purchase or sale of securities on the basis of information that has not been made available to the public.

LEARNING OBJECTIVE 3
What is insider trading?
Why is it prohibited?

Insider Trading   One of the major goals of Section 10(b) and SEC Rule 10b-5 is to prevent so-called **insider trading,** which occurs when persons buy or sell securities on the basis of information that is not available to the public. Corporate directors, officers, and others such as majority shareholders, for instance, often have advance inside information that can affect the future market value of the corporate stock. Obviously, if they act on this information, their positions give them a trading advantage over the general public and other shareholders.

The 1934 Securities Exchange Act defines inside information and extends liability to those who take advantage of such information in their personal transactions when they know that the information is unavailable to those with whom they are dealing. Section 10(b) of the 1934 act and SEC Rule 10b-5 apply to anyone who has access to or receives information of a nonpublic nature on which trading is based—not just to corporate "insiders."

A government official outlines what he believes was an insider trading scandal that involved computer company Dell, Inc.

(AP Photo/Mary Altaffer)

Disclosure under SEC Rule 10b-5   Any material omission or misrepresentation of material facts in connection with the purchase or sale of a security may violate not only the Securities Act of 1933 but also the antifraud provisions of Section 10(b) of the 1934 act and SEC Rule 10b-5. The key to liability (which can be civil or criminal) under Section 10(b) and SEC Rule 10b-5 is whether the insider's information is *material*.

The following are some examples of material facts calling for disclosure under SEC Rule 10b-5:

1. Fraudulent trading in the company's stock by a broker-dealer.
2. A dividend change (whether up or down).
3. A contract for the sale of corporate assets.
4. A new discovery, a new process, or a new product.
5. A significant change in the firm's financial condition.
6. Potential litigation against the company.

Note that any one of these facts, by itself, is not *automatically* considered a material fact. Rather, it will be regarded as a material fact if it is significant enough that it would likely affect an investor's decision as to whether to purchase or sell the company's securities. **EXAMPLE 21.5**   Sheen, Inc., is the defendant in a class-action product liability suit that its attorney, Paula Frasier, believes that the company will lose. Frasier has advised Sheen's directors, officers, and accountants that the company will likely have to pay a substantial damages award. Sheen plans to make a $5 million offering of newly issued stock before the date when the trial is expected to end. Sheen's potential liability and the financial consequences to the firm are material facts that must be disclosed because they are significant enough to affect an investor's decision as to whether to purchase the stock. •

The following is one of the *Classic Cases* interpreting materiality under SEC Rule 10b-5.

✳ Classic Case 21.2

Securities and Exchange Commission v. Texas Gulf Sulphur Co.

United States Court of Appeals, Second Circuit,
401 F.2d 833 (1968).

(©Dmitri Melnik, 2009. Used under license from Shutterstock.com)

After sample drilling revealed potential mineral deposits, company executives made substantial stock purchases. Did they violate insider-trading laws?

HISTORICAL AND ENVIRONMENTAL SETTING *In 1957, the Texas Gulf Sulphur Company began exploring for minerals in eastern Canada. In March 1959, aerial geophysical surveys were conducted over more than fifteen thousand square miles of the area. The operations revealed numerous variations in the conductivity of the rock, which indicated a remarkable* *concentration of commercially exploitable minerals. One site of such variations was near Timmins, Ontario. On October 29 and 30, 1963, a ground survey of the site near Timmins indicated a need to drill for further evaluation.*

Classic Case 21.2—Continues next page ➡

Classic Case 21.2—Continued

FACTS On November 12, 1963, the Texas Gulf Sulphur Company (TGS) drilled a hole that appeared to yield a core with an exceedingly high mineral content, although further drilling would be necessary to establish whether there was enough ore to be mined commercially. TGS kept secret the results of the core sample. After learning of the ore discovery, officers and employees of the company made substantial purchases of TGS's stock or accepted stock options (rights to purchase stock). On April 11, 1964, an unauthorized report of the mineral find appeared in the newspapers. On the following day, April 12, TGS issued a press release that played down the discovery and stated that it was too early to tell whether the ore find would be significant.

Later on, TGS announced a strike of at least 25 million tons of ore. The news led to a substantial increase in the price of TGS stock. The Securities and Exchange Commission (SEC) brought a suit in a federal district court against the officers and employees of TGS for violating the insider-trading prohibition of SEC Rule 10b-5. The officers and employees argued that the prohibition did not apply. They reasoned that the information on which they had traded was not material, as the find had not been commercially proved. The trial court held that most of the defendants had not violated SEC Rule 10b-5, and the SEC appealed.

ISSUE Did the officers and employees of TGS violate SEC Rule 10b-5 by buying the stock, even though they did not know the full extent and profit potential of the ore discovery at the time of their purchases?

DECISION Yes. The U.S. Court of Appeals for the Second Circuit reversed the lower court's decision and remanded the case for further proceedings, holding that the employees and officers had violated SEC Rule 10b-5's prohibition against insider trading.

REASON For SEC Rule 10b-5 purposes, the test of materiality is whether the information would affect the judgment of reasonable investors. Reasonable investors include speculative as well as conservative investors. "A major factor in determining whether the . . . discovery [of the ore] was a material fact is the importance attached to the drilling results by those who knew about it. . . . The timing by those who knew of it of their stock purchases and their purchases of short-term calls [rights to buy shares at a specified price within a specified time period]—purchases in some cases by individuals who had never before purchased calls or even TGS stock—virtually compels the inference that the insiders were influenced by the drilling results. . . . We hold, therefore, that all transactions in TGS stock or calls by individuals apprised of the drilling results . . . were made in violation of Rule 10b-5."

IMPACT OF THIS CASE ON TODAY'S LAW *This landmark case affirmed the principle that the test of whether information is "material," for SEC Rule 10b-5 purposes, is whether it would affect the judgment of reasonable investors. The corporate insiders' purchases of stock and stock options indicated that they were influenced by the results and that the information about the drilling results was material. The courts continue to cite this case when applying SEC Rule 10b-5 to other cases of alleged insider trading.*

Outsiders and SEC Rule 10b-5 The traditional insider-trading case involves true insiders—corporate officers, directors, and majority shareholders who have access to (and trade on) inside information. Increasingly, liability under Section 10(b) of the 1934 act and SEC Rule 10b-5 is being extended to certain "outsiders"—those persons who trade on inside information acquired indirectly. Two theories have been developed under which outsiders may be held liable for insider trading: the *tipper/tippee theory* and the *misappropriation theory.*

Tippee A person who receives inside information.

Tipper/Tippee Theory Anyone who acquires inside information as a result of a corporate insider's breach of his or her fiduciary duty can be liable under SEC Rule 10b-5. This liability extends to **tippees** (those who receive "tips" from insiders) and even remote tippees (tippees of tippees).

The key to liability under this theory is that the inside information must be obtained as a result of someone's breach of a fiduciary duty to the corporation whose shares are involved in the trading. The tippee is liable under this theory only if (1) there is a breach of a duty not to disclose inside information, (2) the disclosure is in exchange for personal benefit, and (3) the tippee knows (or should know) of this breach and benefits from it.[18]

---

18. See, for example, *Chiarella v. United States,* 445 U.S. 222, 100 S.Ct. 1108, 63 L.Ed.2d 348 (1980); and *Dirks v. SEC,* 463 U.S. 646, 103 S.Ct. 3255, 77 L.Ed.2d 911 (1983).

Short-Swing Profits Profits earned by a purchase and sale, or sale and purchase, of the same security within a six-month period. Under Section 16(b) of the 1934 Securities Exchange Act, the profits must be returned to the corporation if earned by company insiders from transactions in the company's stock.

Misappropriation Theory Liability for insider trading may also be established under the misappropriation theory. This theory holds that an individual who wrongfully obtains (misappropriates) inside information and trades on it for her or his personal gain should be held liable because, in essence, she or he stole information rightfully belonging to another.

The misappropriation theory has been controversial because it significantly extends the reach of SEC Rule 10b-5 to outsiders who ordinarily would *not* be deemed fiduciaries of the corporations in whose stock they trade. The United States Supreme Court, however, has held that liability under SEC Rule 10b-5 can be based on the misappropriation theory.[19]

It is not always wrong to disclose material, nonpublic information about a company to another person. Nevertheless, a person who obtains the information and trades securities on it can be liable.

Insider Reporting and Trading—Section 16(b)

Section 16(b) of the 1934 act provides for the recapture by the corporation of all profits realized by an insider on any purchase and sale or sale and purchase of the corporation's stock within any six-month period.[20] It is irrelevant whether the insider actually uses inside information—*all such* **short-swing profits** *must be returned to the corporation.*

In this context, *insiders* means officers, directors, and large stockholders of Section 12 corporations (those owning at least 10 percent of the class of equity securities registered under Section 12 of the 1934 act). To discourage such insiders from using nonpublic information about their companies for their personal benefit in the stock market, the SEC requires them to file reports with the SEC concerning their ownership and trading of the corporation's securities.

Section 16(b) applies not only to stock but also to options (see page 626), and securities convertible into stock. In addition, the courts have fashioned complex rules for determining profits. Note that the SEC exempts a number of transactions under Rule 16b-3.[21] For all of these reasons, corporate insiders are wise to seek specialized counsel before trading in the corporation's stock. Exhibit 21.2 below compares the effects of SEC Rule 10b-5 and Section 16(b).

---

19. *United States v. O'Hagan,* 521 U.S. 642, 117 S.Ct. 2199, 138 L.Ed.2d 724 (1997).
20. A person who expects the price of a particular stock to decline can realize profits by "selling short"—selling at a high price and repurchasing later at a lower price to cover the "short sale."
21. 17 C.F.R. Section 240.16b-3.

Exhibit 21.2 Comparison of Coverage, Application, and Liability under SEC Rule 10b-5 and Section 16(b)

AREA OF COMPARISON	SEC RULE 10b-5	SECTION 16(b)
What is the subject matter of the transaction?	Any security (does not have to be registered).	Any security (does not have to be registered).
What transactions are covered?	Purchase or sale.	Short-swing purchase and sale or short-swing sale and purchase.
Who is subject to liability?	Almost anyone with inside information under a duty to disclose—including officers, directors, controlling shareholders, and tippees.	Officers, directors, and certain shareholders who earn 10 percent or more.
Is omission or misrepresentation necessary for liability?	Yes.	No.
Are there any exempt transactions?	No.	Yes, there are a number of exemptions.
Who may bring an action?	A person transacting with an insider, the SEC, or a purchaser or seller damaged by a wrongful act.	A corporation or a shareholder by derivative action.

The Private Securities Litigation Reform Act of 1995 The disclosure requirements of SEC Rule 10b-5 had the unintended effect of deterring the disclosure of forward-looking information. To understand why, consider an example. **EXAMPLE 21.6** QT Company announces that its projected earnings in a future time period will be a certain amount, but the forecast turns out to be wrong. The earnings are in fact much lower, and the price of QT's stock is affected—negatively. The shareholders then file suit against the company, alleging that the directors violated SEC Rule 10b-5 by disclosing misleading financial information. •

In an attempt to rectify this problem and promote disclosure, Congress passed the Private Securities Litigation Reform Act of 1995.

Safe Harbor Provisions The Private Securities Litigation Reform Act provides a "safe harbor" for publicly held companies that make forward-looking statements, such as financial forecasts. Those who make such statements are protected against liability for securities fraud as long as the statements are accompanied by "meaningful cautionary statements identifying important factors that could cause actual results to differ materially from those in the forward-looking statement."[22]

Pleading Requirements The Private Securities Litigation Reform Act also affected the level of detail required in securities fraud complaints. Plaintiffs must specify each misleading statement and say how it led them to a mistaken belief. A plaintiff must also state facts that give "rise to a strong inference that the defendant acted with the required state of mind," and indicate how the defendant's misrepresentations "caused the loss for which the plaintiff seeks to recover."[23]

In the following *Spotlight Case*, the plaintiffs claimed that the company's misrepresentations about a new product had artificially inflated the price of the stock that the plaintiffs had purchased. The issue was whether the allegations in the complaint were sufficient to show that the defendant's misrepresentations had caused the plaintiffs' economic loss.

---

22. 15 U.S.C. Sections 77z-2, 78u-5.
23. 15 U.S.C. Section 78u-4(b)(1).

Spotlight on Proving Securities Fraud

Case 21.3
Dura Pharmaceuticals, Inc. v. Broudo
Supreme Court of the United States, 544 U.S. 336, 125 S.Ct. 1627, 161 L.Ed.2d 577 (2005).

(pagadesign/iStockphoto.com)

How can the FDA affect a drug company's stock price?

FACTS Michael Broudo and other investors purchased stock in Dura Pharmaceuticals, Inc. The company represented that its drug sales were profitable and that the U.S. Food and Drug Administration (FDA) would soon approve the sale of its new asthmatic spray device. Both statements turned out to be untrue. Dura's stock price fell by almost half after the company announced lower earnings due to slow drug sales. When Dura announced that the FDA would not approve its spray device, the price fell again, although it soon rebounded close to its previous level. The investors sued Dura under Section 10(b).

The investors argued that Dura's statements had inflated the price of the stock, causing them to suffer a greater loss when the bad news was disclosed. The investors provided no other evidence about the connection between the statements and the loss. The trial court dismissed the case, in part, because the investors failed to sufficiently prove that their loss was caused by Dura's statements. The appellate court reversed, and the case was appealed to the United States Supreme Court.

Spotlight Case 21.3—Continued

ISSUE Can the investors prove that Dura's misstatements caused the loss simply by establishing that the price on the date of purchase was inflated because of the misrepresentations?

DECISION No. The fact that the stock price dropped after the firm's disclosure of bad news, without other evidence, is not sufficient to prove that the misrepresentations caused the economic loss under Section 10(b) of the 1934 act.

REASON Although an inflated share price can cause a later economic loss, that causation cannot be assumed in every situation. When a purchaser resells shares at a lower price, that

price might reflect other factors besides the earlier misrepresentation. Changed economic circumstances, industry-specific challenges, and investor expectations can all affect the price of a stock. The longer the time between the purchase and the sale, the more likely it is that other factors besides the misrepresentation caused the loss. Investors must show not only that had they known the truth about the stock they would not have purchased it, but also that they suffered an actual economic loss.

CRITICAL THINKING—Financial Consideration *How does the decision in this case make it more difficult for plaintiffs to prove fraud?*

Limitations on Class Actions

Limitations on Class Actions After the Private Securities Litigation Reform Act was passed, a number of securities class-action suits were filed in state courts to skirt its requirements. In response to this problem, Congress passed the Securities Litigation Uniform Standards Act of 1998 (SLUSA).[24] The act placed stringent limits on the ability of plaintiffs to bring class-action suits in state courts against firms whose securities are traded on national stock exchanges. SLUSA not only prevents the purchasers and sellers of securities from bringing class-action fraud claims under state securities laws, but also applies to investors who are fraudulently induced to hold on to their securities.[25]

Regulation of Proxy Statements

Section 14(a) of the Securities Exchange Act of 1934 regulates the solicitation of proxies (see Chapter 20) from shareholders of Section 12 companies. The SEC regulates the content of proxy statements. Whoever solicits a proxy must fully and accurately disclose in the proxy statement all of the facts that are pertinent to the matter on which the shareholders are to vote. SEC Rule 14a-9 is similar to the antifraud provisions of SEC Rule 10b-5. Remedies for violations are extensive, ranging from injunctions to prevent a vote from being taken to monetary damages.

Violations of the 1934 Act

As mentioned earlier, violations of Section 10(b) of the Securities Exchange Act of 1934 and SEC Rule 10b-5, including insider trading, may be subject to criminal or civil liability.

Scienter Requirement

Scienter **Requirement** For either criminal or civil sanctions to be imposed, *scienter* must exist—that is, the violator must have had an intent to defraud or knowledge of her or his misconduct (see page 242 of Chapter 8). *Scienter* can be proved by showing that the defendant made false statements or wrongfully failed to disclose material facts. In some situations, *scienter* can even be proved by showing that the defendant was consciously reckless as to the truth or falsity of his or her statements.

---

24. Pub. L. No. 105-353. This act amended many sections of Title 15 of the *United States Code.*
25. *Merrill Lynch, Pierce, Fenner & Smith, Inc. v. Dabit,* 547 U.S. 71, 126 S.Ct. 1503, 164 L.Ed.2d 179 (2006).

CASE EXAMPLE 21.7   Alvin Gebhart and Jack Archer started a business venture purchasing mobile home parks (MHPs) from owners and converting them to resident ownership. They formed MHP Conversions, LP, to facilitate the conversion process and issue promissory notes that were sold to investors to raise funds for the purchases. Archer ran the MHP program, and Gebhart sold the promissory notes. Gebhart sold nearly $2.4 million in MHP promissory notes to clients, who bought notes based on the Gebhart's positive statements about the investment.

During the time Gebhart was selling the notes, however, he never actually looked into the finances of the MHP program. He relied entirely on information that Archer gave him, some of which was not true. When Gebhart was later sued for securities fraud, a federal appellate court concluded that there was sufficient evidence of *scienter*. Gebhart knew that he had no knowledge of the financial affairs of MHP, and he had been consciously reckless as to the truth or falsity of his statements about investing in MHP.[26] •

Scienter Not Required for Section 16(b) Violations
Violations of Section 16(b) include the sale by insiders of stock acquired less than six months before the sale (or less than six months after the sale if selling short). These violations are subject to civil sanctions. Liability under Section 16(b) is strict liability. Neither *scienter* nor negligence is required.

Criminal Penalties
For violations of Section 10(b) and Rule 10b-5, an individual may be fined up to $5 million, imprisoned for up to twenty years, or both. A partnership or a corporation may be fined up to $25 million. Section 807 of the Sarbanes-Oxley Act provides that for a *willful* violation of the 1934 act, the violator may be imprisoned for up to twenty-five years in addition to being fined.

For a defendant to be convicted in a criminal prosecution under the securities laws, there can be no reasonable doubt that the defendant knew he or she was acting wrongfully. A jury is not allowed merely to speculate that the defendant may have acted willfully.

CASE EXAMPLE 21.8   Martha Stewart, founder of a well-known media and homemaking empire, was charged with intentionally deceiving investors based on public statements she made. In 2001, Stewart's stockbroker allegedly had informed Stewart that the head of ImClone Systems, Inc., was selling his shares in that company. Stewart then sold her ImClone shares. The next day, ImClone announced that the U.S. Food and Drug Administration had not approved Erbitux, the company's greatly anticipated medication.

After the government began investigating Stewart's ImClone trades, she publicly stated that she had previously instructed her stockbroker to sell her ImClone stock if the price fell to $60 per share. The government prosecutor claimed that Stewart's statement showed she had the intent to deceive investors. The court, however, acquitted Stewart on this charge because "to find the essential element of criminal intent beyond a reasonable doubt, a rational juror would have to speculate."[27] •

Civil Sanctions
The SEC can also bring suit in a federal district court against anyone violating or aiding in a violation of the 1934 act or SEC rules by purchasing or selling a security while in the possession of material nonpublic information.[28] The violation must occur on or through the facilities of a national securities exchange or from or through a broker or dealer.

---

26. *Gebhart v. SEC*, 595 F.3d 1034 (9th Cir. 2010).

27. *United States v. Stewart*, 305 F.Supp.2d 368 (S.D.N.Y. 2004). Stewart was later convicted on other charges relating to her ImClone trading that did not require proof of intent.

28. The Insider Trading Sanctions Act of 1984, 15 U.S.C. Section 78u(d)(2)(A).

A court may assess a penalty for as much as triple the profits gained or the loss avoided by the guilty party.[29] The Insider Trading and Securities Fraud Enforcement Act of 1988 increased the number of persons who may be subject to civil liability for insider trading and gave the SEC authority to pay monetary rewards to informants.[30]

Private parties may also sue violators of Section 10(b) and Rule 10b-5. A private party may obtain rescission (cancellation) of a contract to buy securities or damages to the extent of the violator's illegal profits. Those found liable have a right to seek contribution from those who share responsibility for the violations, including accountants, attorneys, and corporations. For violations of Section 16(b), a corporation can bring an action to recover the short-swing profits.

State Securities Laws

LEARNING OBJECTIVE 4
What are some of the features of state securities laws?

Today, every state has its own corporate securities laws, or "blue sky laws," that regulate the offer and sale of securities within its borders. The phrase *blue sky laws* dates to a 1917 decision by the United States Supreme Court in which the Court declared that the purpose of such laws was to prevent "speculative schemes which have no more basis than so many feet of 'blue sky.'"[31] Article 8 of the Uniform Commercial Code, which has been adopted by all of the states, also imposes various requirements relating to the purchase and sale of securities.

Requirements under State Securities Laws

Typically, state laws have disclosure requirements and antifraud provisions, many of which are patterned after Section 10(b) of the Securities Exchange Act of 1934 and SEC Rule 10b-5. State laws also provide for the registration of securities offered or issued for sale within the state and impose disclosure requirements.

Methods of registration, required disclosures, and exemptions from registration vary among states. Unless an exemption from registration is applicable, issuers must register or qualify their stock with the appropriate state official, often called a *corporations commissioner.* Additionally, most state securities laws regulate securities brokers and dealers.

Concurrent Regulation

State securities laws apply mainly to intrastate transactions. Since the adoption of the 1933 and 1934 federal securities acts, the state and federal governments have regulated securities concurrently. Issuers must comply with both federal and state securities laws, and exemptions from federal law are not exemptions from state laws.

The dual federal and state system has not always worked well, particularly during the early 1990s, when the securities markets underwent considerable expansion. Today, most of the duplicate regulations have been eliminated, and the SEC has exclusive power to regulate most national securities activities. The National Conference of Commissioners on Uniform State Laws also substantially revised the Uniform Securities Act in 2002 to coordinate state and federal securities regulation and enforcement efforts. Seventeen states have adopted the most recent version of the Uniform Securities Act.[32]

> ⮞ **KNOW THIS** ⮜
>
> Federal securities laws do not take priority over state securities laws.

---

29. Profit or loss is defined as "the difference between the purchase or sale price of the security and the value of that security as measured by the trading price of the security at a reasonable period of time after public dissemination of the nonpublic information." 15 U.S.C. Section 78u(d)(2)(C).

30. 15 U.S.C. Section 78u-1.

31. *Hall v. Geiger-Jones Co.*, 242 U.S. 539, 37 S.Ct. 217, 61 L.Ed. 480 (1917).

32. At the time this book went to press, the Uniform Securities Act had been adopted in Georgia, Hawaii, Idaho, Indiana, Iowa, Kansas, Maine, Michigan, Minnesota, Mississippi, Missouri, New Mexico, Oklahoma, South Carolina, South Dakota, Vermont, and Wisconsin, as well as in the U.S. Virgin Islands. You can find current information on state adoptions at www.uniformlaws.org.

Corporate Governance

Corporate Governance A set of policies specifying the rights and responsibilities of the various participants in a corporation and spelling out the rules and procedures for making corporate decisions.

Corporate governance can be narrowly defined as the relationship between a corporation and its shareholders. Some argue for a broader definition—that corporate governance specifies the rights and responsibilities among different participants in the corporation, such as the board of directors, managers, shareholders, and other stakeholders, and spells out the rules and procedures for making decisions on corporate affairs. Regardless of the way it is defined, effective corporate governance requires more than just compliance with laws and regulations. (For a discussion of corporate governance in other nations, see this chapter's *Beyond Our Borders* feature below.)

Effective corporate governance is essential in large corporations because corporate ownership (by shareholders) is separated from corporate control (by officers and managers). Under these circumstances, officers and managers may attempt to advance their own interests at the expense of the shareholders. The well-publicized corporate scandals in the first decade of the 2000s clearly illustrate the reasons for concern about managerial opportunism.

Attempts at Aligning the Interests of Officers with Those of Shareholders

Stock Option A right to buy a given number of shares of stock at a set price, usually within a specified time period.

Some corporations have sought to align the financial interests of their officers with those of the company's shareholders by providing the officers with **stock options**, which enable them to purchase shares of the corporation's stock at a set price. When the market price rises above that level, the officers can sell their shares for a profit. Because a stock's market price generally increases as the corporation prospers, the options give the officers a financial stake in the corporation's well-being and supposedly encourage them to work hard for the benefit of the shareholders.

Options have turned out to be an imperfect device for providing effective governance, however. Executives in some companies have been tempted to "cook" the company's books in order to keep share prices higher so that they could sell their stock for a profit. Executives in other corporations have experienced no losses when share prices dropped because their options were "repriced" so that they did not suffer from the share price decline. Thus, although stock options theoretically can motivate officers to protect shareholder interests, stock option plans have sometimes become a way for officers to take advantage of shareholders.

With stock options generally failing to work as planned, there has been an outcry for more "outside" directors (those with no formal employment affiliation with the company). The theory is that independent directors will more closely monitor the actions of corporate

BEYOND OUR BORDERS   Corporate Governance in Other Nations

Corporate governance has become an issue of concern not only for U.S. corporations, but also for corporate entities around the world. With the globalization of business, a corporation's bad acts (or lack of control systems) can have far-reaching consequences.

Different models of corporate governance exist, often depending on the degree of capitalism in the particular nation. In the United States, corporate governance tends to give priority to shareholders' interests. This approach encourages significant innovation and cost and quality competition.

In contrast, the coordinated model of governance that prevails in continental Europe and Japan gives priority to the interests of so-called stakeholders—employees, managers, suppliers, customers, and the community. The coordinated model still encourages innovation and cost and quality competition, but not to the same extent as the U.S. model.

Critical Thinking

Why does the presence of a capitalist system affect a nation's perspective on corporate governance?

officers. Hence, today we see more boards with outside directors. Note, though, that outside directors may not be truly independent of corporate officers. They may be friends or business associates of the leading officers.

ETHICAL ISSUE

Should shareholders have more control over corporate officers' compensation? Over the last several years, executive compensation has become a hotly debated issue. Many critics argue that the chief executive officers (CEOs) of public companies are paid too much, especially in comparison with the wages earned by the average worker.

The Dodd-Frank Wall Street Reform and Consumer Protection Act includes a "say-on-pay" provision that gives shareholders the right to vote on executive compensation for senior executives at every public U.S. company. In 2009, shareholders defeated a pay package for a CEO for the first time, voting against proposed compensation of more than $50 million for Ray Irani, the head of Occidental Petroleum. Two years later, shareholders voted to reject executive pay arrangements at thirty-five U.S. firms.

These votes on executive pay are nonbinding, however—the board of directors does not have to abide by them. Furthermore, more than 90 percent of shareholder votes on executive pay have been in favor of the proposed compensation plans. Despite the "say on pay" provision, the average compensation for a CEO in 2011 was almost $10 million, up 6 percent from the previous year. The average U.S. employee would have to work almost 250 years to match that salary.

The Goal Is to Promote Accountability

Effective corporate governance standards are designed to address problems (such as those just discussed) and to motivate officers to make decisions that promote the financial interests of the company's shareholders. Generally, corporate governance entails corporate decision-making structures that monitor employees (particularly officers) to ensure that they are acting for the benefit of the shareholders. Thus, corporate governance involves, at a minimum:

1. The audited reporting of financial progress at the corporation, so that managers can be evaluated.
2. Legal protections for shareholders, so that violators of the law, who attempt to take advantage of shareholders, can be punished for misbehavior and victims may recover damages for any associated losses.

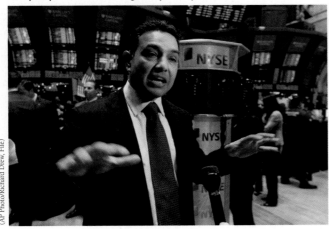

Stock options are valuable when the market price of a company's shares rises greatly. Why?

(AP Photo/Richard Drew, File)

The Company Benefits   Effective corporate governance may have considerable practical significance. Firms that are more accountable to shareholders typically report higher profits, higher sales growth, higher firm value, and other economic advantages. Thus, a corporation that provides better corporate governance in the form of greater accountability to investors may also have a higher valuation than a corporation that is less concerned about governance.

Corporations that promote diversity in the workplace, and especially in management, may also experience increased profits, growth, and value. Nevertheless, one aspect of corporations around the world still is not very diverse—see this chapter's *Law, Diversity, and Business: Managerial Implications* feature on the following page.

Governance and Corporation Law   State corporation statutes set up the legal framework for corporate governance. Under the corporate law of Delaware, where most major companies incorporate, all corporations must have certain

LAW, DIVERSITY, AND BUSINESS: MANAGERIAL IMPLICATIONS

THE WORLDWIDE LACK OF WOMEN ON BOARDS OF DIRECTORS

Certainly, the saying "It's a man's world" applies to corporate boardrooms around the world. In France, Germany, Great Britain, and the United States, women account for only 10 to 15 percent of the directors of publicly traded companies. The average for the twenty-seven members of the European Union (EU) is slightly above 10 percent. In Europe, Norway and Sweden stand out with more than 30 percent and 25 percent, respectively. Elsewhere, boards of directors in Brazil, China, India, and Russia average only about 5 percent female members.

More Female Board Members Lead to Higher Profits The absence of women from corporate boards is somewhat surprising because there is evidence that suggests companies may benefit when they have more female board members. The consulting firm McKinsey & Company looked at almost one hundred public companies in Europe that had a high proportion of women in senior management positions. Comparing the financial performance of those firms with the average for firms in the same industry, McKinsey concluded that firms with more women in "high places" had a higher rate of return on investment, higher operating profits, and higher share prices for their stock.

Are Mandatory Quotas the Way to Go? One way to increase the number of women on corporate boards is to mandate that companies add more women. Some countries are doing exactly that. France recently passed a law that requires public companies to reserve 40 percent of board seats for women by 2017. Norway and Spain already have similar legislation, and Germany is considering such a law. The European Parliament recently passed a resolution calling for all nations in the EU to enact legislation that would require major public companies to have a minimum of 40 percent female board members by 2020.

Those in favor of such quotas believe that they are long overdue. They argue that women bring a different perspective to board meetings and that the current dearth of women in boardrooms is due to subtle gender discrimination.

Others point out that quotas might harm some companies. If companies cannot find sufficient well-trained women to fill their quotas, they may have to appoint inexperienced women to their boards. In Norway, for example, women accounted for only 9 percent of directors in 2003. When Norwegian companies were required to increase this percentage to 40 percent within five years, many firms had to promote women who were less experienced than the directors they were replacing. Some of those companies subsequently suffered a drop in their market capitalization.

Business Implications *In the United States today, women earn the majority of master's degrees and hold more than half of the entry-level jobs in major U.S. companies. Corporate managers need to develop more flexible schedules and career paths for women who want to balance work and family. In the process, the "fast track" to upper management positions could be modified to enable more women to eventually become board members.*

structures of corporate governance in place. The most important structure, of course, is the board of directors because the board makes the major decisions about the future of the corporation.

The Board of Directors Under corporate law, a corporation must have a board of directors elected by the shareholders. Almost anyone can become a director, though some organizations, such as the New York Stock Exchange, require certain standards of service for directors of their listed corporations.

Directors are responsible for ensuring that the corporation's officers are operating wisely and in the exclusive interest of shareholders. The directors receive reports from the officers and give them managerial directions. In reality, though, corporate directors devote a relatively small amount of time to monitoring officers.

Ideally, shareholders would monitor the directors' supervision of the officers. In practice, however, it can be difficult for shareholders to monitor directors and hold them responsible for corporate failings. Although the directors can be sued for failing to do their jobs effectively, directors are rarely held personally liable.

The Audit Committee   A crucial committee of the board of directors is the *audit committee,* which oversees the corporation's accounting and financial reporting processes, including both internal and outside auditors. Unless the committee members have sufficient expertise and are willing to spend the time to carefully examine the corporation's bookkeeping methods, however, the audit committee may be ineffective.

The audit committee also oversees the corporation's "internal controls," which are the measures taken to ensure that reported results are accurate. As an example, these controls—carried out largely by the company's internal auditing staff—help to determine whether a corporation's debts are collectible. If the debts are not collectible, it is up to the audit committee to make sure that the corporation's financial officers do not simply pretend that payment will eventually be made.

The Compensation Committee   Another important committee of the board of directors is the *compensation committee.* This committee monitors and determines the compensation the company's officers are paid. As part of this process, it is responsible for assessing the officers' performance and for designing a compensation system that will better align the officers' interests with those of the shareholders.

The Sarbanes-Oxley Act

In 2002, following a series of corporate scandals, Congress passed the Sarbanes-Oxley Act (see Chapter 2). The act separately addresses certain issues relating to corporate governance. Generally, the act attempts to increase corporate accountability by imposing strict disclosure requirements and harsh penalties for violations of securities laws. Among other things, the act requires chief corporate executives to take responsibility for the accuracy of financial statements and reports that are filed with the SEC.

Additionally, the act requires that certain financial and stock-transaction reports be filed with the SEC earlier than was required under the previous rules. The act also created a new entity, called the Public Company Accounting Oversight Board, which regulates and oversees public accounting firms. Other provisions of the act established private civil actions and expanded the SEC's remedies in administrative and civil actions.

Because of the importance of this act for corporate leaders and for those dealing with securities transactions, we present excerpts and explanatory comments in Appendix D at the end of this text. We also highlight some of its key provisions relating to corporate accountability in Exhibit 21.3 on the next page.

Michael Oxley is a former member of the U.S. House of Representatives and vice president of NASDAQ, the over-the-counter stock exchange. When in Congress, he cosponsored legislation that imposed large compliance costs on publicly held companies. What is the name of that legislation?

(Fred Prouser/Reuters/Landov)

More Internal Controls and Accountability   The
Sarbanes-Oxley Act also introduced direct *federal* corporate governance requirements for public companies (companies whose shares are traded in the public securities markets). The law addressed many of the corporate governance procedures just discussed and created new requirements in an attempt to make the system work more effectively. The requirements deal with independent monitoring of company officers by both the board of directors and auditors.

Sections 302 and 404 of Sarbanes-Oxley require high-level managers (the most senior officers) to establish and maintain an effective system of internal controls, including "disclosure controls and procedures" to ensure that company financial reports are accurate and timely and to document financial results prior to reporting. Moreover, senior management must reassess the system's effectiveness annually. Some companies

Exhibit 21.3 Some Key Provisions of the Sarbanes-Oxley Act Relating to Corporate Accountability

Certification Requirements — Under Section 906 of the Sarbanes-Oxley Act, the chief executive officers (CEOs) and chief financial officers (CFOs) of most major companies listed on public stock exchanges must certify financial statements that are filed with the SEC. CEOs and CFOs have to certify that filed financial reports "fully comply" with SEC requirements and that all of the information reported "fairly represents in all material respects, the financial conditions and results of operations of the issuer."

Under Section 302 of the act, CEOs and CFOs of reporting companies are required to certify that a signing officer reviewed each quarterly and annual filing with the SEC and that it contains no untrue statements of material fact. Also, the signing officer or officers must certify that they have established an internal control system to identify all material information and that any deficiencies in the system were disclosed to the auditors.

Effectiveness of Internal Controls on Financial Reporting — Under Section 404(a), all public companies are required to assess the effectiveness of their internal control over financial reporting. Section 404(b) requires independent auditors to report on management's assessment of internal controls, but companies with a public float of less than $75 million are exempted from this requirement.

Loans to Directors and Officers — Section 402 prohibits any reporting company, as well as any private company that is filing an initial public offering, from making personal loans to directors and executive officers (with a few limited exceptions, such as for certain consumer and housing loans).

Protection for Whistleblowers — Section 806 protects "whistleblowers" — employees who report ("blow the whistle" on) securities violations by their employers — from being fired or in any way discriminated against by their employers.

Blackout Periods — Section 306 prohibits certain types of securities transactions during "blackout periods" — periods during which the issuer's ability to purchase, sell, or otherwise transfer funds in individual account plans (such as pension funds) is suspended.

Enhanced Penalties for —

- *Violations of Section 906 Certification Requirements* — A CEO or CFO who certifies a financial report or statement filed with the SEC knowing that the report or statement does not fulfill all of the requirements of Section 906 will be subject to criminal penalties of up to $1 million in fines, ten years in prison, or both. *Willful* violators of the certification requirements may be subject to $5 million in fines, twenty years in prison, or both.

- *Violations of the Securities Exchange Act of 1934* — Penalties for securities fraud under the 1934 act were also increased (as discussed earlier in this chapter). Individual violators may be fined up to $5 million, imprisoned for up to twenty years, or both. *Willful* violators may be imprisoned for up to twenty-five years in addition to being fined.

- *Destruction or Alteration of Documents* — Anyone who alters, destroys, or conceals documents or otherwise obstructs any official proceeding will be subject to fines, imprisonment for up to twenty years, or both.

- *Other Forms of White-Collar Crime* — The act stiffened the penalties for certain criminal violations, such as federal mail and wire fraud, and ordered the U.S. Sentencing Commission to revise the sentencing guidelines for white-collar crimes (see Chapter 6).

Statute of Limitations for Securities Fraud — Section 804 provides that a private right of action for securities fraud may be brought no later than two years after the discovery of the violation or five years after the violation, whichever is earlier.

had to take expensive steps to bring their internal controls up to the new federal standard. After the act was passed, hundreds of companies reported that they had identified and corrected shortcomings in their internal control systems.

Exemptions for Smaller Companies The Sarbanes-Oxley Act initially required all public companies to have an independent auditor file a report with the SEC on management's assessment of internal controls. In 2010, however, Congress enacted an exemption for smaller companies in an effort to reduce compliance costs. Public companies with a market capitalization, or public float (price times total shares publicly owned), of less than $75 million no longer need to have an auditor report on management's assessment of internal controls.

LEARNING OBJECTIVE 5

What certification requirements does the Sarbanes-Oxley Act impose on corporate executives?

Certification and Monitoring Requirements Section 906 requires that chief executive officers (CEOs) and chief financial officers (CFOs) certify that the information in the corporate financial statements "fairly represents in all material respects, the financial conditions and results of operations of the issuer." These corporate officers are subject to both civil and criminal penalties for violation of this section. This requirement makes officers directly accountable for the accuracy of their financial reporting and avoids any "ignorance defense" if shortcomings are later discovered.

Sarbanes-Oxley also includes requirements to improve directors' monitoring of officers' activities. All members of the corporate audit committee for public companies must be outside directors. The New York Stock Exchange has a similar rule that also extends to the board's compensation committee. The audit committee must have a written charter that sets out its duties and provides for performance appraisal. At least one "financial expert" must serve on the audit committee, which must hold executive meetings without company officers being present. The audit committee must establish procedures to encourage "whistleblowers" to report violations. In addition to reviewing the internal controls, the committee also monitors the actions of the outside auditor.

Online Securities Fraud

A major problem facing the SEC today is how to enforce the antifraud provisions of the securities laws in the online environment. In 1999, in the first cases involving illegal online securities offerings, the SEC filed suit against three individuals for illegally offering securities on an Internet auction site.[33] In essence, all three indicated that their companies would go public soon and attempted to sell unregistered securities via the Web auction site. Since then, the SEC has brought a variety of Internet-related fraud cases and regularly issues interpretive releases to explain how securities laws apply in the online environment.

Online Investment Scams

"Make money your God and it will plague you like the devil."

Henry Fielding, 1707–1754
(English author)

An ongoing problem is how to curb online investment scams. As discussed in Chapter 6, the Internet has created a new vehicle for criminals to use to commit fraud and has provided them with new ways of targeting innocent investors. The criminally inclined can use spam, online newsletters and bulletin boards, chat rooms, blogs, social media, and tweets to spread false information and perpetrate fraud. For a relatively small cost, criminals can even build sophisticated Web pages to facilitate their investment scams.

Fraudulent E-Mails

There are countless variations of investment scams, most of which promise spectacular returns for small investments. A person might receive spam e-mail that falsely claims the earnings potential of a home business can "turn $5 into $60,000 in just three to six weeks." A few years ago, an investment scam claimed "your stimulus package has arrived" and promised recipients that they could make $100,000 a year using their home computers.

Although most people are dubious of the bogus claims made in spam messages, such offers can be more attractive during times of economic recession. Often, investment scams are simply the electronic version of pyramid schemes in which the participants attempt to profit solely by recruiting new participants.

Online Investment Newsletters and Forums

Hundreds of online investment newsletters provide free information on stocks. Legitimate online newsletters can help investors gather valuable information, but some of these newsletters are used for fraud. The law allows companies to pay people who write these newsletters to tout their securities, but the newsletters are required to disclose who paid for the advertising.

---

33. *In re Davis*, SEC Administrative File No. 3-10080 (October 20, 1999); *In re Haas*, SEC Administrative File No. 3-10081 (October 20, 1999); and *In re Sitaras*, SEC Administrative File No. 3-10082 (October 20, 1999).

Many fraudsters either fail to disclose or lie about who paid them. Thus, an investor reading an online newsletter may believe that the information is unbiased, when in fact the fraudsters will directly profit by convincing investors to buy or sell particular stocks.

The same deceptive tactics can be used on online bulletin boards (such as newsgroups and usenet groups), blogs, and social networking sites, including Twitter and Facebook. While hiding their true identity, fraudsters may falsely pump up a company or reveal some "inside" information about a new product or lucrative contract to convince people to invest. By using multiple aliases on an online forum, a single person can easily create the illusion of widespread interest in a small stock.

Ponzi Schemes

Although securities fraud is increasingly occurring online, schemes conducted primarily offline have not disappeared. In recent years, the SEC has filed an increasing number of enforcement actions against perpetrators of *Ponzi schemes* (discussed on page 44 of Chapter 2).

Since 2010, the SEC has brought more than a hundred enforcement actions against nearly two hundred individuals and two hundred and fifty entities for carrying out Ponzi schemes. It has also barred more than sixty-five persons from working in the securities industry.

Bernard Madoff (right) perpetuated the largest fraudulent Ponzi scheme in modern history.

Offshore Fraud   Ponzi schemes sometimes target U.S. residents and convince them to invest in offshore companies or banks. **CASE EXAMPLE 21.9** In 2012, Texas billionaire R. Allen Stanford, of the Stanford Financial Group, was convicted for orchestrating a $7 billion scheme to defraud more than five thousand investors. Stanford had advised clients to buy certificates of deposit with improbably high interest rates from his Antigua-based Stanford International Bank. Although some early investors were paid returns from the funds provided by later investors, Stanford used $1.6 billion of the funds for personal purchases. He also falsified financial statements that were filed with the SEC and reportedly paid more than $100,000 in bribes to an Antigua official to ensure that the bank would not be audited.[34] ●

"Risk-Free" Fraud   Another type of fraud scheme offers risk-free or low-risk investments to lure investors. **EXAMPLE 21.10** Debi Mitchom used her firm, Mitchom & Company, to fraudulently obtain at least $10 million from dozens of investors by selling securities in her special investment fund. Mitchom told investors that she had a proven track record of successful securities trading and showed them false account statements that showed artificially high balances.

In reality, Mitchom was not a registered investment adviser, had not traded any securities for several years, and had suffered substantial losses on investments she did make. Mitchom promised investors returns averaging 20 percent with minimal risk to their principal and claimed to be using an investment strategy based on short-term price trends. She used less than half of the funds entrusted to her for trading purposes and spent at least $5 million for her personal expenses. The SEC filed a complaint alleging that Mitchom and her company had engaged in a multimillion-dollar Ponzi scheme. Mitchom agreed to settle the case and return more than $7 million (plus interest) of the wrongfully acquired funds. ●

---

34. *United States v. Stanford*, 2012 WL 1699459 (S.D.Tex. 2012).

Reviewing . . . Investor Protection, Insider Trading, and Corporate Governance

Dale Emerson served as the chief financial officer for Reliant Electric Company, a distributor of electricity serving portions of Montana and North Dakota. Reliant was in the final stages of planning a takeover of Dakota Gasworks, Inc., a natural gas distributor that operated solely within North Dakota. Emerson went on a weekend fishing trip with his uncle, Ernest Wallace. Emerson mentioned to Wallace that he had been putting in a lot of extra hours at the office planning a takeover of Dakota Gasworks. When he returned from the fishing trip, Wallace purchased $20,000 worth of Reliant stock. Three weeks later, Reliant made a tender offer to Dakota Gasworks stockholders and purchased 57 percent of Dakota Gasworks stock. Over the next two weeks, the price of Reliant stock rose 72 percent before leveling out. Wallace then sold his Reliant stock for a gross profit of $14,400. Using the information presented in the chapter, answer the following questions.

1. Would registration with the SEC be required for Dakota Gasworks securities? Why or why not?
2. Did Emerson violate Section 10(b) of the Securities Exchange Act of 1934 and SEC Rule 10b-5? Why or why not?
3. What theory or theories might a court use to hold Wallace liable for insider trading?
4. Under the Sarbanes-Oxley Act, who would be required to certify the accuracy of financial statements filed with the SEC?

DEBATE THIS Insider trading should be legalized.

Key Terms

accredited investor 615
corporate governance 626
free-writing prospectus 613
insider trading 619

investment company 615
investment contract 611
mutual fund 615

prospectus 612
SEC Rule 10b-5 618
security 609

short-swing profits 621
stock option 626
tippee 620

Chapter Summary: Investor Protection, Insider Trading, and Corporate Governance

Securities Act of 1933 (See pages 610–618.)	Prohibits fraud and stabilizes the securities industry by requiring disclosure of all essential information relating to the issuance of securities to the investing public. 1. *Registration requirements*—Securities, unless exempt, must be registered with the SEC before being offered to the public. The *registration statement* must include detailed financial information about the issuing corporation; the intended use of the proceeds of the securities being issued; and certain disclosures, such as interests of directors or officers and pending lawsuits. 2. *Prospectus*—The issuer must provide investors with a *prospectus* that describes the security being sold, the issuing corporation, and the risk attaching to the security. 3. *Exemptions*—The SEC has exempted certain offerings from the requirements of the Securities Act of 1933. Exemptions may be determined on the basis of the size of the issue, whether the offering is private or public, and whether advertising is involved. Exemptions are summarized in Exhibit 21.1 on page 614.
Securities Exchange Act of 1934 (See pages 618–625.)	Provides for the regulation and registration of securities exchanges, brokers, dealers, and national securities associations (such as the NASD). Maintains a continuous disclosure system for all corporations with securities on the securities exchanges and for those companies that have assets in excess of $10 million and five hundred or more shareholders (Section 12 companies).

Continued

Chapter Summary: Investor Protection, Insider Trading, and Corporate Governance—Continued

Securities Exchange Act of 1934—Continued	1. *SEC Rule 10b-5 (under Section 10(b) of the 1934 act)*—
	    a. Applies to almost all trading of securities—a firm's securities do not have to be registered under the 1933 act for the 1934 act to apply.
	    b. Applies to insider trading by corporate officers, directors, majority shareholders, and any persons receiving inside information (information not available to the public) who base their trading on this information.
	    c. Liability for insider trading may be based on the tipper/tippee or the misappropriation theory.
	    d. May be violated by failing to disclose "material facts" that must be disclosed under this rule.
	    e. Liability for violations can be civil or criminal.
	2. *Insider trading (under Section 16(b) of the 1934 act)*—To prevent corporate insiders from taking advantage of inside information, the 1934 act requires officers, directors, and shareholders owning 10 percent or more of the issued stock of a corporation to turn over to the corporation all short-term profits (called *short-swing profits*) realized from the purchase and sale or sale and purchase of corporate stock within any six-month period.
	3. *Regulation of proxies*—The SEC regulates the content of proxy statements sent to shareholders of Section 12 companies. Section 14(a) is essentially a disclosure law, with provisions similar to the antifraud provisions of SEC Rule 10b-5.

State Securities Laws (See page 625.)	All states have corporate securities laws (*blue sky laws*) that regulate the offer and sale of securities within state borders. These laws are designed to prevent "speculative schemes which have no more basis than so many feet of 'blue sky.'" States regulate securities concurrently with the federal government. The Uniform Securities Act of 2002, which has been adopted by seventeen states and is being considered by several others, is designed to promote coordination and reduce duplication between state and federal securities regulation.
Corporate Governance (See pages 626–631.)	1. *Definition*—Corporate governance involves a set of policies specifying the rights and responsibilities of the various participants in a corporation and spelling out the rules and procedures for making decisions on corporate affairs. 2. *The need for corporate governance*—Corporate governance is necessary in large corporations because corporate ownership (by the shareholders) is separated from corporate control (by officers and managers). This separation of corporate ownership and control can often result in conflicting interests. Corporate governance standards address such issues. 3. *Sarbanes-Oxley Act*—This act attempts to increase corporate accountability by imposing strict disclosure requirements and harsh penalties for violations of securities laws.
Online Securities Fraud (See pages 631–632.)	A major problem facing the SEC today is how to enforce the antifraud provisions of the securities laws in the online environment. Internet-related forms of securities fraud include many types of investment scams. The SEC has brought numerous enforcement actions against perpetrators of Ponzi schemes, both online and offline.

ExamPrep

ISSUE SPOTTERS

1. When a corporation wishes to issue certain securities, it must provide sufficient information for an unsophisticated investor to evaluate the financial risk involved. Specifically, the law imposes liability for making a false statement or omission that is "material." What sort of information would an investor consider material? **(See page 612.)**
2. Lee is an officer of Magma Oil, Inc. Lee knows that a Magma geologist has just discovered a new deposit of oil. Can Lee take advantage of this information to buy and sell Magma stock? Why or why not? **(See page 619.)**

—Check your answers to the Issue Spotters against the answers provided in Appendix E at the end of this text.

BEFORE THE TEST

Go to www.cengagebrain.com, enter the ISBN 9781133191353, and click on "Find" to locate this textbook's Web site. Then, click on "Access Now" under "Study Tools," and select Chapter 21 at the top. There, you will find a Practice Quiz that you can take to assess your mastery of the concepts in this chapter, as well as Flashcards, a Glossary of important terms, and Video Questions (when assigned).

For Review

Answers to the even-numbered questions in this For Review section can be found in Appendix F at the end of this text.

1. What is meant by the term *securities*?
2. What are the two major statutes regulating the securities industry?
3. What is insider trading? Why is it prohibited?
4. What are some of the features of state securities laws?
5. What certification requirements does the Sarbanes-Oxley Act impose on corporate executives?

Business Scenarios and Case Problems

21–1 Registration Requirements. Langley Brothers, Inc., a corporation incorporated and doing business in Kansas, decides to sell common stock worth $1 million to the public. The stock will be sold only within the state of Kansas. Joseph Langley, the chair of the board, says the offering need not be registered with the Securities and Exchange Commission. His brother, Harry, disagrees. Who is right? Explain. **(See page 615.)**

21–2 ❓ Question with Sample Answer—Registration of Stock. Huron Corp. has 300,000 common shares outstanding. The owners of these outstanding shares live in several different states. Huron has decided to split the 300,000 shares two for one. Will Huron Corp. have to file a registration statement and prospectus on the 300,000 new shares to be issued as a result of the split? Explain. **(See pages 613–616.)**

—For a sample answer to Question 21–2, go to Appendix G at the end of this text.

21–3 Violations of the 1934 Act. To comply with accounting principles, a company that engages in software development must either "expense" the cost (record it immediately on the company's financial statement) or "capitalize" it (record it as a cost incurred in increments over time). If the project is in the pre- or post-development stage, the cost must be expensed. Otherwise it may be capitalized. Capitalizing a cost makes a company look more profitable in the short term. Digimarc Corp. announced that it had improperly capitalized software development costs over at least the previous eighteen months. The errors resulted in $2.7 million in overstated earnings, requiring a restatement of prior financial statements. Zucco Partners, LLC, which had bought Digimarc stock within the relevant period, filed a suit in a federal district court against the firm. Zucco claimed that it could show that there had been disagreements within Digimarc over its accounting. Is this sufficient to establish a violation of SEC Rule 10b-5? Why or why not? [*Zucco Partners, LLC v. Digimarc Corp.,* 552 F.3d 981 (9th Cir. 2009)] **(See pages 623–625.)**

21–4 Insider Trading. Jabil Circuit, Inc., is a publicly traded electronics and technology company. A group of shareholders who owned Jabil stock from 2001 to 2007 sued the company and its auditors, directors, and officers for insider trading. Stock options were a part of Jabil's compensation for executives.

Sometimes, stock options were backdated to a point in time when the stock price was lower, so the options would be worth more to certain company executives. Backdating is not illegal so long as it is reported, but Jabil did not report the fact that backdating had occurred. Thus, expenses were underreported, and net income was overstated by millions of dollars. The shareholders claimed that by rigging the stock price by backdating, the executives had engaged in insider trading and could pick favorable purchase prices and that there was a general practice of selling stock before unfavorable news about the company was reported to the public. The shareholders, however, had no specific information about these stock trades or when (or even if) a particular executive was aware of any accounting errors during the time of any backdating purchases. Were the shareholders' allegations sufficient to assert that insider trading had occurred under Rule 10b-5? Why or why not? [*Edward J. Goodman Life Income Trust v. Jabil Circuit, Inc.,* 594 F.3d 783 (11th Cir. 2010)] **(See pages 618–620.)**

21–5 Case Problem with Sample Answer—Violations of the 1934 Act. Matrixx Initiatives, Inc., makes and sells over-the-counter pharmaceutical products. Its core brand is Zicam, which accounts for 70 percent of its sales. Matrixx received reports that some consumers had lost their sense of smell (a condition called *anosmia*) after using Zicam Cold Remedy. Four product liability suits were filed against Matrixx, seeking damages for anosmia. In public statements relating to revenues and product safety, however, Matrixx did not reveal this information. James Siracusano and other Matrixx investors filed a suit in a federal district court against the company and its executives under Section 10(b) of the Securities Exchange Act of 1934 and SEC Rule 10b-5, claiming that the statements were misleading because they did not disclose the information about the product liability suits. Matrixx argued that to be material, information must consist of a statistically significant number of adverse events that require disclosure. Because Siracusano's claim did not allege that Matrixx knew of a statistically significant number of adverse events, the company contended that the claim should be dismissed. What is the standard for materiality in this context? Should Siracusano's claim be dismissed? Explain. [*Matrixx Initiatives, Inc. v. Siracusano,* __ U.S. __, 131 S.Ct. 1309, 179 L.Ed.2d 398 (2011)] **(See pages 623–625.)**

—For a sample answer to Problem 21–5, go to Appendix H at the end of this text.

21–6 Disclosure under SEC Rule 10b-5. Dodona I, LLC, invested $4 million in two securities offerings from Goldman, Sachs & Co. The investments were in collateralized debt obligations (CDOs). Their value depended on residential mortgage-backed securities (RMBS), whose value in turn depended on the performance of subprime residential mortgages. Before marketing the CDOs, Goldman had noticed several "red flags" relating to investments in the subprime market, in which it had invested heavily. To limit its risk, Goldman began betting against subprime mortgages, RMBS, and CDOs, including the CDOs it had sold to Dodona. In an internal e-mail, one Goldman official commented that the company had managed to "make some lemonade from some big old lemons." Nevertheless, Goldman's marketing materials provided only boilerplate statements about the risks of investing in the securities. The CDOs were later downgraded to junk status, and Dodona suffered a major loss while Goldman profited. Assuming that Goldman did not affirmatively misrepresent any facts about the CDOs, can Dodona still recover under SEC Rule 10b-5? If so, how? [*Dodona I, LLC v. Goldman, Sachs & Co.,* 847 F.Supp.2d 624 (S.D.N.Y. 2012)] **(See pages 618–621.)**

21–7 ◄► **A Question of Ethics—Violations of the 1934 Act.** Melvin Lyttle told John Montana and Paul Knight about a "Trading Program" that purportedly would buy and sell securities in deals that were fully insured, as well as monitored and controlled by the Federal Reserve Board. Without checking the details or even verifying whether the program existed, Montana and Knight, with Lyttle's help, began to sell interests in the program to investors. For a minimum investment of $1 million, the investors were promised extraordinary rates of return—from 10 percent to as much as 100 percent per week—without risk. They were also told that the Program would "utilize banks that can ensure full bank integrity of The Transaction whose undertaking[s] are in complete harmony with international banking rules and protocol and who [sic] guarantee maximum security of a Funder's Capital Placement Amount." Nothing was required but the investors' funds and their silence—the program was to be kept secret. Over a four-month period, Montana raised nearly $23 million from twenty-two investors. The promised gains did not accrue, however. Instead, Montana, Lyttle, and Knight depleted the investors' funds in high-risk trades or spent the funds on themselves. [*SEC v. Montana,* 464 F.Supp.2d 772 (S.D.Ind. 2006)] **(See pages 623–625.)**

1. The Securities and Exchange Commission (SEC) filed a suit against Montana alleging violations of Section 10(b) and SEC Rule 10b-5. What is required to establish a violation of these laws? Explain how and why the facts in this case meet, or fail to meet, these requirements.

2. Ultimately, about half of the investors recouped the amount they had invested. Should the others be considered at least partly responsible for their own losses? Discuss.

Critical Thinking and Writing Assignments

21–8 💡 Business Law Critical Thinking Group Assignment. Karel Svoboda, a credit officer for Rogue Bank, evaluated and approved his employer's extensions of credit to clients. These responsibilities gave Svoboda access to nonpublic information about the clients' earnings, performance, acquisitions, and business plans from confidential memos, e-mail, and other sources. Svoboda devised a scheme with Alena Robles, an independent accountant, to use this information to trade securities. Pursuant to their scheme, Robles traded in the securities of more than twenty different companies and profited by more than $2 million. Svoboda also executed trades for his own profit of more than $800,000, despite their agreement that Robles would do all of the trading. Aware that their scheme violated Rogue Bank's policy, they attempted to conduct their trades to avoid suspicion. When the bank questioned Svoboda about his actions, he lied, refused to cooperate, and was fired.

1. The first group will determine whether Svoboda or Robles committed any crimes.

2. The second group will decide whether Svoboda or Robles are subject to civil liability. If so, who could file a suit and on what ground? What are the possible sanctions?

3. A third group will identify any defenses that Svoboda or Robles could raise, and determine their likelihood of success.

CHAPTER 22

Antitrust Law and Promoting Competition

(J-Elgaard/iStockphoto.com)

CHAPTER OUTLINE

- The Sherman Antitrust Act
- Section 1 of the Sherman Act
- Section 2 of the Sherman Act
- The Clayton Act
- Enforcement and Exemptions
- U.S. Antitrust Laws in the Global Context

LEARNING OBJECTIVES

The five learning objectives below are designed to help improve your understanding of the chapter. After reading this chapter, you should be able to answer the following questions:

1 What is a monopoly? What is market power? How do these concepts relate to each other?

2 What anticompetitive activities are prohibited by Section 1 of the Sherman Act?

3 What type of activity is prohibited by Section 2 of the Sherman Act?

4 What are the four major provisions of the Clayton Act, and what types of activities do these provisions prohibit?

5 What agencies of the federal government enforce the federal antitrust laws?

"Competition is not only the basis of protection to the consumer but is the incentive to progress."

—Herbert Hoover, 1874–1964 (Thirty-first president of the United States, 1929–1933)

Antitrust Law Laws protecting commerce from unlawful restraints and anticompetitive practices.

The laws regulating economic competition in the United States are referred to as **antitrust laws.** They include the Sherman Antitrust Act of 1890[1] and the Clayton Act[2] and the Federal Trade Commission Act,[3] passed by Congress in 1914 to further curb anticompetitive or unfair business practices. Congress later amended the 1914 acts to broaden and strengthen their coverage. We examine these major federal antitrust statutes in this chapter.

The basis of antitrust legislation is the desire to foster competition. Antitrust legislation was initially created—and continues to be enforced—because of our society's belief that competition leads to lower prices and generates more product information. As President Herbert Hoover indicated in the chapter-opening quotation, competition not only protects the consumer, but also provides "the incentive to progress."

---

1. 15 U.S.C. Sections 1–7.
2. 15 U.S.C. Sections 12–27.
3. 15 U.S.C. Sections 41–58.

Consumers and society as a whole benefit when producers strive to develop better products that they can sell at lower prices to beat the competition. This is still true today, which is why the government is concerned about the pricing of e-books, as you will read later in this chapter.

The Sherman Antitrust Act

Today's antitrust laws are the direct descendants of common law actions intended to limit *restraints of trade* (agreements between or among firms that have the effect of reducing competition in the marketplace). Such actions date to the fifteenth century in England.

In the United States, concern over monopolistic practices arose after the Civil War with the growth of large corporate enterprises and their attempts to reduce competition. To thwart competition, they legally tied themselves together in business trusts. As discussed in Chapter 19 on page 563, a business trust is a form of business organization in which trustees hold title to property for the benefit of others. The most powerful of these trusts, the Standard Oil trust, is examined in this chapter's *Landmark in the Law* feature on the facing page.

In 1890, Congress passed "An Act to Protect Trade and Commerce against Unlawful Restraints and Monopolies"—commonly known as the Sherman Antitrust Act or, more simply, as the Sherman Act. The Sherman Act became (and still is) one of the government's most powerful weapons in the effort to maintain a competitive economy.

Major Provisions of the Sherman Act

Sections 1 and 2 contain the main provisions of the Sherman Act:

1. Every contract, combination in the form of trust or otherwise, or conspiracy, in restraint of trade or commerce among the several States, or with foreign nations, is hereby declared to be illegal [and is a felony punishable by a fine and/or imprisonment].
2. Every person who shall monopolize, or attempt to monopolize, or combine or conspire with any other person or persons, to monopolize any part of the trade or commerce among the several States, or with foreign nations, shall be deemed guilty of a felony [and is similarly punishable].

Differences Between Section 1 and Section 2

These two sections of the Sherman Act are quite different. Violation of Section 1 requires two or more persons, as a person cannot contract or combine or conspire alone. Thus, the essence of the illegal activity is *the act of joining together.* Section 2, though, can apply either to one person or to two or more persons because it refers to "every person." Thus, unilateral conduct can result in a violation of Section 2.

The cases brought under Section 1 of the Sherman Act differ from those brought under Section 2. Section 1 cases are often concerned with finding an agreement (written or oral)

One of Standard Oil's refineries in Richmond, California, around 1900.

LANDMARK IN THE LAW
The Sherman Antitrust Act of 1890

The author of the Sherman Antitrust Act of 1890, Senator John Sherman, was the brother of the famous Civil War general William Tecumseh Sherman and a recognized financial authority. Sherman had been concerned for years about diminishing competition in U.S. industry and the emergence of monopolies, such as the Standard Oil trust.

The Standard Oil Trust By 1890, the Standard Oil trust had become the foremost petroleum refining and marketing combination in the United States. Streamlined, integrated, and centrally controlled, Standard Oil maintained an indisputable monopoly over the industry. The trust controlled 90 percent of the U.S. market for refined petroleum products, making it impossible for small producers to compete with such a leviathan.

The increasing consolidation in U.S. industry, and particularly the Standard Oil trust, came to the attention of the public in March 1881. Henry Demarest Lloyd, a young journalist from Chicago, published an article in the *Atlantic Monthly* entitled "The Story of a Great Monopoly." The article argued that the U.S. petroleum industry was dominated by one firm—Standard Oil. Lloyd's article was so popular that the issue was reprinted six times. It marked the beginning of the U.S. public's growing concern over monopolies.

The Passage of the Sherman Antitrust Act The common law regarding trade regulation was not always consistent.

Certainly, it was not very familiar to the members of Congress. The public concern over large business integrations and trusts was familiar, however. In 1888, 1889, and again in 1890, Senator Sherman introduced in Congress bills designed to destroy the large combinations of capital that, he felt, were creating an imbalance within the nation's economy.

Sherman told Congress that the Sherman Act "does not announce a new principle of law, but applies old and well-recognized principles of the common law."[a] In 1890, the Fifty-First Congress enacted the bill into law. Generally, the act prohibits business combinations and conspiracies that restrain trade and commerce, as well as certain monopolistic practices.

Application to Today's World *The Sherman Antitrust Act remains very relevant to today's world. Since the widely publicized monopolization case against Microsoft Corporation in 2001,[b] the U.S. Department of Justice and state attorneys general have brought numerous Sherman Act cases against other corporations, including eBay, Intel, and Philip Morris.[c]*

---

a. 21 *Congressional Record* 2456 (1890).
b. *United States v. Microsoft Corp.*, 253 F.3d 34 (D.C.Cir. 2001). This case will be discussed in *Case Example 22.7* on page 647.
c. See, for example, *United States v. Philip Morris USA, Inc.*, 566 F.3d 1095 (D.C.Cir. 2009); *In re eBay Seller Antitrust Litigation*, 545 F.Supp.2d 1027 (N.D.Cal. 2008); and *In re Intel Corp. Microprocessor Antitrust Litigation*, 2007 WL 137152 (D.Del. 2007).

LEARNING OBJECTIVE 1
What is a monopoly? What is market power? How do these concepts relate to each other?

Monopoly A market in which there is a single seller or a very limited number of sellers.

Monopoly Power The ability of a monopoly to dictate what takes place in a given market.

Market Power The power of a firm to control the market price of its product. A monopoly has the greatest degree of market power.

that leads to a restraint of trade. Section 2 cases deal with the structure of a monopoly that already exists in the marketplace. The term **monopoly** generally is used to describe a market in which there is a single seller or a very limited number of sellers. Whereas Section 1 focuses on agreements that are restrictive—that is, agreements that have a wrongful purpose—Section 2 addresses the misuse of **monopoly power** in the marketplace.

Monopoly power exists when a firm has an extreme amount of **market power**—the power to affect the market price of its product. Both Section 1 and Section 2 seek to curtail market practices that result in undesired monopoly pricing and output behavior. For a case to be brought under Section 2, however, the "threshold" or "necessary" amount of monopoly power must already exist. We will return to a discussion of these two sections of the Sherman Act after we look at the act's jurisdictional requirements.

Jurisdictional Requirements

The Sherman Act applies only to restraints that have a substantial impact on interstate commerce. Generally, any activity that substantially affects interstate commerce falls within the scope of the Sherman Act. As will be discussed later in this chapter, the Sherman Act also extends to U.S. nationals abroad who are engaged in activities that have an effect on U.S. foreign commerce. Federal courts have exclusive jurisdiction over antitrust cases brought under the Sherman Act. State laws regulate local restraints on competition, and state courts decide claims brought under those laws.

Section 1 of the Sherman Act

LEARNING OBJECTIVE 2
What anticompetitive activities are prohibited by Section 1 of the Sherman Act?

The underlying assumption of Section 1 of the Sherman Act is that society's welfare is harmed if rival firms are permitted to join in an agreement that consolidates their market power or otherwise restrains competition. The types of trade restraints that Section 1 of the Sherman Act prohibits generally fall into two broad categories: *horizontal restraints* and *vertical restraints,* both of which will be discussed shortly. First, though, we look at the rules that the courts may apply when assessing the anticompetitive impact of alleged restraints on trade.

Per Se Violations versus the Rule of Reason

Per Se Violation A restraint of trade that is so anticompetitive that it is deemed inherently (*per se*) illegal.

Some restraints are so blatantly and substantially anticompetitive that they are deemed ***per se*** violations—illegal *per se* (on their face, or inherently)—under Section 1. Other agreements, however, even though they result in enhanced market power, do not *unreasonably* restrain trade. Using what is called the **rule of reason,** the courts analyze anticompetitive agreements that allegedly violate Section 1 of the Sherman Act to determine whether they actually constitute reasonable restraints on trade.

Rule of Reason A test used to determine whether an anticompetitive agreement constitutes a reasonable restraint on trade. Courts consider such factors as the purpose of the agreement, its effect on competition, and whether less restrictive means could have been used.

Why the Rule of Reason Was Developed   The need for a rule-of-reason analysis of some agreements in restraint of trade is obvious—if the rule of reason had not been developed, almost any business agreement could conceivably be held to violate the Sherman Act. Justice Louis Brandeis effectively phrased this sentiment in *Chicago Board of Trade v. United States,* a case decided in 1918:

> Every agreement concerning trade, every regulation of trade, restrains. To bind, to restrain, is of their very essence. The true test of legality is whether the restraint imposed is such as merely regulates and perhaps thereby promotes competition or whether it is such as may suppress or even destroy competition.[4]

Factors Courts Consider under the Rule of Reason   When analyzing an alleged Section 1 violation under the rule of reason, a court will consider several factors. These factors include the purpose of the agreement, the parties' market ability to implement the agreement to achieve that purpose, and the effect or potential effect of the agreement on competition. Another factor that a court might consider is whether the parties could have relied on less restrictive means to achieve their purpose.

> "I don't know what a monopoly is until somebody tells me."
>
> Steve Ballmer, 1956–present (Chief executive officer of Microsoft Corporation)

CASE EXAMPLE 22.1   The National Football League (NFL) includes thirty-two separately owned professional football teams. Each team has its own name, colors, and logo, and owns related intellectual property that it markets through National Football League Properties (NFLP). Until 2000, the NFLP granted nonexclusive licenses to a number of vendors, permitting them to manufacture and sell apparel bearing NFL team insignias. American Needle, Inc., was one of those licensees.

In late 2000, the teams authorized the NFLP to grant exclusive licenses, and the NFLP granted Reebok International, Ltd., an exclusive ten-year license to manufacture and sell trademarked headwear for all thirty-two teams. It then declined to renew American Needle's

---

4. 246 U.S. 231, 38 S.Ct. 242, 62 L.Ed. 683 (1918).

nonexclusive license. American Needle sued, claiming that the NFL teams, the NFLP, and Reebok had violated Section 1 of the Sherman Act. The United States Supreme Court agreed. The Court concluded that the agreement among the NFL teams to license their intellectual property exclusively through the NFLP to Reebok constituted concerted activity.[5] ●

ETHICAL ISSUE

Should TV programmers and distributors be held in violation of the Sherman Act? When consumers want cable or satellite television programming, they can choose among various cable and satellite providers, or distributors, but each distributor will offer multichannel packages. In other words, a consumer cannot order just the channels that she or he watches regularly. All of the multichannel packages include some very popular channels and some other channels that have very low viewership. Thus, consumers are forced to pay for some unwanted channels in order to get the ones they do want.

A group of consumers sued NBC Universal, the Walt Disney Company, and other programmers, as well as cable and satellite distributors. The consumers claimed that the defendants, because of their full or partial ownership of broadcast channels and their ownership or control of multiple cable or satellite channels, had a higher degree of market power vis-à-vis all distributors. They also claimed that the programmers had exploited this power by requiring the "bundling" of numerous channels in each multichannel package offered to consumers.

The U.S. Court of Appeals for the Ninth Circuit disagreed. The court pointed out that the Sherman Act applies to actions that diminish competition and, in this instance, there was still competition among programmers and distributors.[6]

Horizontal Restraints

Horizontal Restraint Any agreement that restrains competition between rival firms competing in the same market.

The term **horizontal restraint** is encountered frequently in antitrust law. A horizontal restraint is any agreement that in some way restrains competition between rival firms competing in the same market.

Price-Fixing Agreement An agreement among competitors to fix the prices of products or services at a certain level.

Price Fixing   Any **price-fixing agreement**—an agreement among competitors to fix prices—constitutes a *per se* violation of Section 1. The agreement on price need not be explicit: as long as it restricts output or artificially fixes price, it violates the law. The U.S. government is concerned that price fixing is occurring in the e-book industry. See this chapter's *Adapting the Law to the Online Environment* feature on the following page.

Price Fixing Is Never Reasonable   Perhaps the definitive case involving price-fixing agreements is still the 1940 case of *United States v. Socony-Vacuum Oil Co.*[7] In that case, a group of independent oil producers in Texas and Louisiana were caught between falling demand due to the Great Depression of the 1930s and increasing supply from newly discovered oil fields in the region. In response to these conditions, a group of major refining companies agreed to buy "distress" gasoline (excess supplies) from the independents so as to dispose of it in an "orderly manner." Although there was no explicit agreement as to price, it was clear that the purpose of the agreement was to limit the supply of gasoline on the market and thereby raise prices.

The United States Supreme Court recognized the effects that such an agreement could have on open and free competition. The Court held that the reasonableness of a price-fixing agreement is never a defense. Any agreement that restricts output or artificially fixes price is a *per se* violation of Section 1. The rationale of the *per se* rule was best stated in what is now the most famous portion of the Court's opinion—footnote 59. In that footnote, Justice William O. Douglas compared a freely functioning price system to a body's central nervous

---

5. *American Needle, Inc. v. National Football League,* ___ U.S. ___, 130 S.Ct. 2201, 176 L.Ed.2d 947 (2010).
6. *Brantley v. NBC Universal, Inc.,* 675 F.3d 1192 (9th Cir. 2012).
7. 310 U.S. 150, 60 S.Ct. 811, 84 L.Ed. 1129 (1940).

ADAPTING THE LAW TO THE ONLINE ENVIRONMENT

THE JUSTICE DEPARTMENT GOES AFTER E-BOOK PRICING

In 2012, the U.S. Justice Department filed a lawsuit against five major book publishers and Apple, Inc., charging that they had conspired to fix the prices of e-books. According to the thirty-six-page complaint, publishing executives met "in private rooms for dinner in upscale Manhattan restaurants" to discuss ways to limit e-book price competition. As a result, claims the Justice Department, consumers paid "tens of millions of dollars more for e-books than they otherwise would have paid."

The E-Book Market Explodes

E-books were only a niche product until a few years ago when Amazon.com released its first Kindle e-book reader. To sell more Kindles, Amazon offered thousands of popular books for downloading at $9.99 per e-book. Amazon kept 50 percent and gave 50 percent to the publishers, who had to agree to Amazon's pricing. Although Amazon lost on its e-book sales, it made up the losses by selling more Kindles.

Enter Apple's iPad

When the iPad entered the scene, Apple and the book publishers agreed to use Apple's "agency" model, which allowed the publishers to set their own prices while Apple kept 30 percent as a commission. Apple was already using this model for games and apps for its iPhones and iPads.

The Justice Department, however, decided that because the publishers chose prices that were relatively similar, price fixing was evident. Nowhere in the Justice Department's complaint did it acknowledge that the agency model is the standard approach for many types of sales. Indeed, the Justice Department claimed that the agency model is *per se* illegal and "would not have

occurred without the conspiracy among the defendants." Yet the model is used in many industries and has been upheld by federal courts for years.

Amazon Still Leads but Not by Much

(Photo by Bill Stryker)

When the Kindle was king, Amazon had 90 percent of the e-book market. Since the advent of the the iPad, Barnes & Noble's Nook, and other e-book readers, Kindle's market share has fallen to 60 percent because of increased competition. E-books now cost anywhere from zero to $14.99.

It's *Gone with the Wind* All Over Again

During the Great Depression, the federal government brought a similar antitrust lawsuit. At the time, Macy's, the department store chain, sold books at a steep discount. It was selling *Gone with the Wind* for the equivalent of $15 in today's dollars, whereas smaller stores charged double or triple that price. Publishers and booksellers lobbied for protection from what they called predatory pricing. Ultimately, the federal government did not prevail, but for a while, retail book prices remained high.

Critical Thinking

The publishing business is in dire straits today with retail bookstores going bankrupt and publishers laying off hundreds of employees. Why do you think the declining book business was worthy of so much attention from the Justice Department?

What major company tried to fix LCD prices?

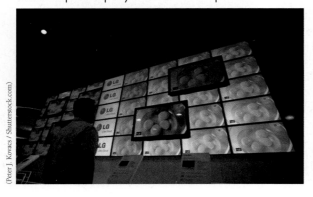

(Peter J. Kovacs / Shutterstock.com)

system, condemning price-fixing agreements as threats to "the central nervous system of the economy."

Price Fixing Today Price-fixing cartels (groups) are still commonplace in today's business world, particularly among global companies (see pages 654–655 for a discussion of the extraterritorial application of the Sherman Act). For instance, in 2011, Samsung Electronics, Sharp Corporation, and five other makers of liquid crystal displays (LCDs) for notebooks and other devices agreed to pay more than $553 million to settle price-fixing claims against them. Price-fixing accusations are also frequently made against drug manufacturers.

CASE EXAMPLE 22.2 The manufacturer of the prescription drug Cardizem CD, which can help prevent heart attacks, was about to lose its patent on the drug. Another company developed a generic version in anticipation of the patent expiring. After the two firms became involved in litigation over the patent, the first company agreed to pay the second company $40 million per year not to market the generic version until their dispute was resolved. This agreement was held to be a *per se* violation of the Sherman Act because it restrained competition between rival firms and delayed the entry of generic versions of Cardizem into the market.[8] •

Group Boycott An agreement by two or more sellers to refuse to deal with a particular person or firm.

Group Boycotts   A **group boycott** is an agreement by two or more sellers to refuse to deal with (boycott) a particular person or firm. Such group boycotts have been held to constitute *per se* violations of Section 1 of the Sherman Act. Section 1 has been violated if it can be demonstrated that the boycott or joint refusal to deal was undertaken with the intention of eliminating competition or preventing entry into a given market. Some boycotts, such as group boycotts against a supplier for political reasons, may be protected under the First Amendment right to freedom of expression, however.

Horizontal Market Division   It is a *per se* violation of Section 1 of the Sherman Act for competitors to divide up territories or customers. **EXAMPLE 22.3**   Alred Office Supply, Belmont Business, and Carlson's, Inc., compete against each other in the states of Kansas, Nebraska, and Oklahoma. The three firms agree that Alred will sell products only in Kansas, Belmont will sell only in Nebraska, and Carlson's will sell only in Oklahoma. This concerted action reduces marketing costs and allows all three (assuming there is no other competition) to raise the price of the goods sold in their respective states.

The same violation would take place if the three firms agreed to divide up their customers by having Alred sell only to institutional purchasers (such as governments and schools) in all three states, Belmont only to wholesalers, and Carlson only to retailers. •

Trade Associations   Businesses in the same general industry or profession frequently organize trade associations to pursue common interests. A trade association may engage in various joint activities such as exchanging information, representing the members' business interests before governmental bodies, conducting advertising campaigns, and setting regulatory standards to govern the industry or profession.

Generally, the rule of reason is applied to many of these horizontal actions. If a court finds that a trade association practice or agreement that restrains trade is sufficiently beneficial both to the association and to the public, it may deem the restraint reasonable.

Concentrated Industry An industry in which a single firm or a small number of firms control a large percentage of market sales.

In concentrated industries, however, trade associations can be, and have been, used as a means to facilitate anticompetitive actions, such as fixing prices or allocating markets. A **concentrated industry** is one in which either a single firm or a small number of firms control a large percentage of market sales. When trade association agreements have substantially anticompetitive effects, a court will consider them to be in violation of Section 1 of the Sherman Act.

Vertical Restraints

Vertical Restraint A restraint of trade created by an agreement between firms at different levels in the manufacturing and distribution process.

Vertically Integrated Firm A firm that carries out two or more functional phases (manufacturing, distribution, and retailing, for example) of the chain of production.

A **vertical restraint** of trade results from an agreement between firms at different levels in the manufacturing and distribution process. In contrast to horizontal relationships, which occur at the same level of operation, vertical relationships encompass the entire chain of production. The chain of production normally includes the purchase of inventory, basic manufacturing, distribution to wholesalers, and eventual sale of a product at the retail level. When a single firm carries out two or more of the separate functional phases, it is considered to be a **vertically integrated firm.**

---

8. *In re Cardizem CD Antitrust Litigation*, 332 F.3d 896 (6th Cir. 2003).

Even though firms operating at different functional levels are not in direct competition with one another, they are in competition with other firms. Thus, agreements between firms standing in a vertical relationship may affect competition. Some vertical restraints are *per se* violations of Section 1. Others are judged under the rule of reason.

Territorial or Customer Restrictions   In arranging for the distribution of its products, a manufacturing firm often wishes to insulate dealers from direct competition with other dealers selling the product. To do so, it may institute territorial restrictions or attempt to prohibit wholesalers or retailers from reselling the product to certain classes of buyers, such as competing retailers.

Territorial and customer restrictions were once considered *per se* violations of Section 1, but in 1977, the United States Supreme Court held that they should be judged under the rule of reason.   **CASE EXAMPLE 22.4**   GTE Sylvania, Inc., limited the number of retail franchises that it granted in any given geographic area and required them to sell only Sylvania products. Sylvania retained sole discretion to increase the number of retailers in an area. When Sylvania decided to open a new franchise, it terminated the franchise of Continental T.V., Inc. Continental sued, claiming that Sylvania's vertically restrictive franchise system violated Section 1. The Supreme Court found that "vertical restrictions promote interbrand competition by allowing the manufacturer to achieve certain efficiencies in the distribution of his products." Therefore, Sylvania's vertical system, which was not price restrictive, did not constitute a *per se* violation of Section 1 of the Sherman Act.[9] ●

The decision in the *Continental* case marked a definite shift from rigid characterization of these kinds of vertical restraints to a more flexible, economic analysis of the restraints under the rule of reason. A firm may have legitimate reasons for imposing territorial or customer restrictions, and not all such restrictions harm competition.

Resale Price Maintenance Agreements   An agreement between a manufacturer and a distributor or retailer in which the manufacturer specifies what the retail prices of its products must be is referred to as a **resale price maintenance agreement.** Such agreements were also once considered to be *per se* violations of Section 1, but the United States Supreme Court ruled in 1997 that *maximum* resale price maintenance agreements should be judged under the rule of reason.[10]

The setting of a maximum price that retailers and distributors can charge for a manufacturer's products may sometimes increase competition and benefit consumers. In 2007, the Supreme Court held that *minimum* resale price maintenance agreements should also be judged under the rule of reason.[11]

Section 2 of the Sherman Act

Section 1 of the Sherman Act prohibits certain concerted, or joint, activities that restrain trade. In contrast, Section 2 condemns "every person who shall monopolize, or attempt to monopolize." Thus, two distinct types of behavior are subject to sanction under Section 2: *monopolization* and *attempts to monopolize.*

One tactic that may be involved in either offense is **predatory pricing.** Predatory pricing involves an attempt by one firm to drive its competitors from the market by selling its product at prices substantially *below* the normal costs of production. Once the competitors are eliminated, the firm will presumably attempt to recapture its losses and go on to earn higher profits by driving prices up far above their competitive levels.

Resale Price Maintenance Agreement An agreement between a manufacturer and a retailer in which the manufacturer specifies what the retail prices of its products must be.

LEARNING OBJECTIVE 3
What type of activity is prohibited by Section 2 of the Sherman Act?

Predatory Pricing The pricing of a product below cost with the intent to drive competitors out of the market.

---

9. *Continental T.V., Inc. v. GTE Sylvania, Inc.,* 433 U.S. 36, 97 S.Ct. 2549, 53 L.Ed.2d 568 (1977).
10. *State Oil Co. v. Khan,* 522 U.S. 3, 118 S.Ct. 275, 139 L.Ed.2d 199 (1997).
11. *Leegin Creative Leather Products, Inc. v. PSKS, Inc.,* 551 U.S. 877, 127 S.Ct. 2705, 168 L.Ed.2d 623 (2007).

Monopolization

Monopolization The possession of monopoly power in the relevant market and the willful acquisition or maintenance of that power, as distinguished from growth or development as a consequence of a superior product, business acumen, or historic accident.

The United States Supreme Court has defined the offense of **monopolization** as involving two elements: "(1) the possession of monopoly power in the relevant market and (2) the willful acquisition or maintenance of [that] power as distinguished from growth or development as a consequence of a superior product, business acumen, or historic accident."[12] A violation of Section 2 requires that both these elements—monopoly power and an intent to monopolize—be established.

Monopoly Power   The Sherman Act does not define *monopoly*. In economic theory, monopoly refers to control of a single market by a single entity. It is well established in antitrust law, however, that a firm may be deemed a monopolist even though it is not the sole seller in a market. Additionally, size alone does not determine whether a firm is a monopoly.

EXAMPLE 22.5   A "mom and pop" grocery located in the isolated town of Happy Camp, Idaho, is a monopolist if it is the only grocery serving that particular market. Size in relation to the market is what matters because monopoly involves the power to affect prices. ●

Monopoly power may be proved by direct evidence that the firm used its power to control prices and restrict output.[13] Usually, however, there is not enough evidence to show that the firm was intentionally controlling prices, so the plaintiff has to offer indirect, or circumstantial, evidence of monopoly power. To prove monopoly power indirectly, the plaintiff must show that the firm has a dominant share of the relevant market and that there are significant barriers for new competitors entering that market.

In the following case, the court had to decide whether there was sufficient evidence to show that the company possessed monopoly power in the relevant market.

---

12. *United States v. Grinnell Corp.*, 384 U.S. 563, 86 S.Ct. 1698, 16 L.Ed.2d 778 (1966).
13. See, for example, *Broadcom Corp. v. Qualcomm, Inc.*, 501 F.3d 297 (3d Cir. 2007).

Case 22.1

E. I. du Pont de Nemours and Co. v. Kolon Industries, Inc.

United States Court of Appeals, Fourth Circuit, 637 F.3d 435 (2011).

COMPANY PROFILE   *DuPont, founded in 1802, started as a gunpowder manufacturer. Today, it operates in ninety countries in the fields of agriculture, apparel, communications, electronics, home construction, nutrition, and transportation. Its latest major investment was in a biodegradable ingredient used in cosmetics, liquid detergents, and antifreeze.*

FACTS   DuPont manufactures and sells para-aramid fiber, which is a complex synthetic fiber used to make body armor, fiber-optic cables, and tires, among other things. Only three producers of this fiber—DuPont (based in the United States), Teijin (based in the Netherlands), and Kolon Industries, Inc.

(based in South Korea)—sell it in the U.S. market. DuPont is the industry leader, accounting for more than 70 percent of all para-aramid fibers purchased in the United States. In 2009, DuPont brought a lawsuit against Kolon for misappropriation of trade secrets. Kolon counterclaimed that DuPont had monopolized and attempted to monopolize the para-aramid market in violation of Section 2 of the Sherman Act.

Kolon claimed that DuPont illegally used multiyear supply agreements requiring its high-volume para-aramid fiber customers to purchase from 80 to 100 percent of their needs from DuPont. Kolon alleged that these agreements limited the other producers' ability to compete. DuPont moved to dismiss

Case 22.1—Continues next page ➡

Case 22.1—Continued

the counterclaim, arguing, in part, that Kolon's allegations of unlawful exclusionary conduct were insufficient. A federal district court agreed and dismissed Kolon's counterclaim. Kolon appealed. The U.S. Court of Appeals for the Fourth Circuit examined the trial court's reasoning.

ISSUE Did Kolon present sufficient evidence that DuPont possessed monopoly power in the para-aramid market to maintain a claim for monopolization and attempted monopolization?

DECISION Yes. The U.S. Court of Appeals for the Fourth Circuit reversed the district court's decision, finding that Kolon had alleged sufficient facts to show that DuPont's behavior violated Section 2 of the Sherman Act.

REASON The federal appellate court reasoned that DuPont's control of more than 70 percent of the U.S. para-aramid fiber market showed its monopoly power. "A monopolist is not free to take certain actions that a company in a competitive . . . market may take because there is no market constraint on a monopolist's behavior." The multiyear contracts that DuPont imposed on its highest-volume purchasers severely limited Kolon from competing for the most important customers. "DuPont's conduct has had a direct, substantial, and adverse effect on competition . . . [and] has constrained the only potential entrant [Kolon] to the United States in decades from effectively entering the market." Because DuPont's conduct reduced or eliminated additional competition, and preserved DuPont's monopoly position, the court concluded that it violated Section 2.

WHAT IF THE FACTS WERE DIFFERENT? *Assume that DuPont had 45 percent of the market and Kolon, along with numerous other competitors, had the remaining 65 percent. Would the appellate court have ruled the same? Why or why not?*

Relevant Market Before a court can determine whether a firm has a dominant market share, it must define the relevant market. The relevant market consists of two elements: a relevant product market and a relevant geographic market.

Relevant Product Market The relevant product market includes all products that, although produced by different firms, have identical attributes, such as sugar. It also includes products that are reasonably interchangeable for the purpose for which they are produced. Products will be considered reasonably interchangeable if consumers treat them as acceptable substitutes.[14]

Establishing the relevant product market is often a key issue in monopolization cases because the way the market is defined may determine whether a firm has monopoly power. By defining the product market narrowly, the degree of a firm's market power is enhanced.

CASE EXAMPLE 22.6 Whole Foods Market, Inc., wished to acquire Wild Oats Markets, Inc., its main competitor in nationwide high-end organic food supermarkets. The Federal Trade Commission (FTC) filed a Section 2 claim against Whole Foods to prevent the merger. The FTC argued that the relevant product market consisted of only "premium natural and organic supermarkets" rather than all supermarkets, as Whole Foods maintained. An appellate court accepted the FTC's narrow definition of the relevant market and remanded the case to the lower court to decide what remedies were appropriate, as the merger had already taken place. Whole Foods and the FTC later entered into a settlement that required Whole Foods to divest (sell or give up control over) thirteen stores, most of which were formerly Wild Oats outlets.[15] ●

Relevant Geographic Market The second component of the relevant market is the geographic extent of the market. For products that are sold nationwide, the geographic market encompasses the entire United States. If transportation costs are significant or a producer and its competitors sell in only a limited area (one in which customers have no access to

---

14. See, for example, *HDC Medical, Inc. v. Minntech Corp.,* 474 F.3d 543 (8th Cir. 2007).
15. *FTC v. Whole Foods Market, Inc.,* 548 F.3d 1028 (D.C.Cir. 2008); and 592 F.Supp.2d 107 (D.D.C. 2009).

other sources of the product), the geographic market is limited to that area. A national firm may thus compete in several distinct areas and have monopoly power in one area but not in another.

Generally, the geographic market is that section of the country within which a firm can increase its price a bit without attracting new sellers or without losing many customers to alternative suppliers outside that area. Of course, the Internet and e-commerce are changing the notion of the size and limits of a geographic market. It may become difficult to perceive any geographic market as local, except for products that are not easily transported, such as concrete. The reality is that we live in a global world, including one for commerce.

The Intent Requirement Monopoly power, in and of itself, does not constitute the offense of monopolization under Section 2 of the Sherman Act. The offense also requires an *intent* to monopolize.

Why Intent Is Required A dominant market share may be the result of business acumen or the development of a superior product. It may simply be the result of a historic accident. In these situations, the acquisition of monopoly power is not an antitrust violation. Indeed, it would be contrary to society's interest to condemn every firm that acquired a position of power because it was well managed and efficient and marketed a product desired by consumers.

Why did Netscape sue Microsoft?

(AP Photo)

Inferred from Anticompetitive Conduct If a firm possesses market power as a result of carrying out some purposeful act to acquire or maintain that power through anticompetitive means, then it is in violation of Section 2. In most monopolization cases, intent may be inferred from evidence that the firm had monopoly power and engaged in anticompetitive behavior.

CASE EXAMPLE 22.7 When Navigator, the first popular graphical Internet browser by Netscape Communications Corporation, was introduced, Microsoft perceived a threat to its dominance of the operating-system market. Microsoft, Inc., developed a competing browser, Internet Explorer, and then began to require computer makers that wanted to install the Windows operating system to also install Explorer and exclude Navigator. Microsoft included codes in Windows that would cripple the operating system if Explorer was deleted, and paid Internet service providers to distribute Explorer and exclude Navigator. Because of this pattern of exclusionary conduct, a court found Microsoft guilty of monopolization. Microsoft's pattern of conduct could be rational only if the firm knew that it possessed monopoly power.[16] ●

PREVENTING LEGAL DISPUTES

Because exclusionary conduct can have legitimate efficiency-enhancing effects, it can be difficult to determine when conduct will be viewed as anticompetitive and a violation of Section 2 of the Sherman Act. Thus, a business that possesses monopoly power must be careful that its actions cannot be inferred to be evidence of intent to monopolize. Even if your business does not have a dominant market share, you would be wise to take precautions.

Make sure that you can articulate clear, legitimate reasons for the particular conduct or contract and that you do not provide any direct evidence (damaging e-mails, for example) of an intent to exclude competitors. A court will be less likely to infer the intent to monopolize if the specific conduct was aimed at increasing output and lowering per-unit costs, improving product quality, or protecting a patented technology or innovation.

---

16. *United States v. Microsoft Corp.,* 253 F.3d 34 (D.C.Cir. 2001). Microsoft has faced numerous antitrust claims and has settled a number of lawsuits in which it was accused of antitrust violations and anticompetitive tactics.

Why did the smallest Aspen ski resort sue Aspen Skiing Company?

Unilateral Refusals to Deal   Group boycotts, discussed earlier, are also joint refusals to deal—sellers acting as a group jointly refuse to deal with another business or individual. These group refusals are subject to close scrutiny under Section 1 of the Sherman Act. A single manufacturer acting unilaterally, though, normally is free to deal, or not to deal, with whomever it wishes.[17]

Nevertheless, in limited circumstances, a unilateral refusal to deal will violate antitrust laws. These instances involve offenses proscribed under Section 2 of the Sherman Act and occur only if (1) the firm refusing to deal has—or is likely to acquire—monopoly power and (2) the refusal is likely to have an anticompetitive effect on a particular market.

CASE EXAMPLE 22.8   Aspen Skiing Company, the owner of three of the four major downhill ski areas in Aspen, Colorado, refused to continue participating in a jointly offered six-day "all Aspen" lift ticket. The Supreme Court ruled that Aspen Skiing's refusal to cooperate with its smaller competitor was a violation of Section 2 of the Sherman Act. Because the company owned three-fourths of the local ski areas, it had monopoly power, and thus its unilateral refusal had an anticompetitive effect on the market.[18] ●

Attempts to Monopolize

Attempted Monopolization   An action by a firm that involves anticompetitive conduct, the intent to gain monopoly power, and a "dangerous probability" of success in achieving monopoly power.

Section 2 also prohibits **attempted monopolization** of a market, which requires proof of the following three elements:

1. Anticompetitive conduct.
2. The specific intent to exclude competitors and garner monopoly power.
3. A "dangerous probability" of success in achieving monopoly power. The probability cannot be dangerous unless the alleged offender possesses some degree of market power. Only *serious* threats of monopolization are condemned as violations.

As mentioned earlier, predatory pricing is a form of anticompetitive conduct that, in theory, could be used by firms that are attempting to monopolize. (Predatory pricing may also lead to claims of price discrimination, to be discussed shortly.) Predatory bidding involves the acquisition and use of *monopsony power,* which is market power on the *buy* side of a market. This may occur when a buyer bids up the price of an input too high for its competitors to pay, causing them to leave the market. The predatory bidder may then attempt to drive down input prices to reap above-competitive profits and recoup any losses it suffered in bidding up the prices.

The question in the following *Spotlight Case* was whether a claim of predatory bidding was sufficiently similar to a claim of predatory pricing so that the same antitrust test should apply to both.

---

17. See, for example, *Pacific Bell Telephone Co. v. Linkline Communications, Inc.,* 555 U.S. 438, 129 S.Ct. 1109, 172 L.Ed.2d 836 (2009).

18. *Aspen Skiing Co. v. Aspen Highlands Skiing Corp.,* 472 U.S. 585, 105 S.Ct. 2847, 86 L.Ed.2d 467 (1985).

Spotlight on Weyerhaeuser Co.

Case 22.2
**Weyerhaeuser Co.
v. Ross-Simmons Hardwood Lumber Co.**
Supreme Court of the United States, 549 U.S. 312, 127 S.Ct. 1069, 166 L.Ed.2d 911 (2007).
www.findlaw.com/casecode/supreme.html[a]

Was predatory bidding on the price of alder logs tantamount to predatory pricing and therefore illegal?

FACTS   Weyerhaeuser Company entered the Pacific Northwest's hardwood lumber market in 1980. By 2000, Weyerhaeuser owned six mills processing 65 percent of the red alder logs in the region. Meanwhile, Ross-Simmons Hardwood Lumber Company operated a single

---

a. In the "Browse Supreme Court Opinions" section, click on "2007." On that page, scroll to the name of the case and click on it to access the opinion.

Spotlight Case 22.2—Continued

competing mill. When the prices of the logs rose and those for the lumber fell, Ross-Simmons suffered heavy losses. Several million dollars in debt, the mill closed in 2001. Ross-Simmons filed a suit in a federal district court against Weyerhaeuser, alleging attempted monopolization under Section 2 of the Sherman Act. Ross-Simmons claimed that Weyerhaeuser used its dominant position in the market to bid up the prices of logs and prevent its competitors from being profitable. Weyerhaeuser argued that the antitrust test for predatory pricing applies to a claim of predatory bidding and that Ross-Simmons had not met this standard. The district court ruled in favor of the plaintiff, the U.S. Court of Appeals for the Ninth Circuit affirmed, and Weyerhaeuser appealed to the United States Supreme Court.

ISSUE Does the antitrust test that applies to a claim of predatory pricing also apply to a claim of predatory bidding?

DECISION Yes. Because Ross-Simmons conceded that it had not met this standard, the Supreme Court vacated the lower court's judgment and remanded the case.

REASON Both predatory pricing and predatory bidding involve a company's intentional use of pricing for an anticompetitive pur-

pose. Both actions require a company to incur a short-term loss on the possibility of later making a "supracompetitive" profit. Because a "rational" firm is unlikely to "make this sacrifice," both schemes are "rarely tried and even more rarely successful." A failed scheme of either type can benefit consumers. Thus, the two-part predatory-pricing test should apply to predatory-bidding claims. A plaintiff alleging predatory bidding must then prove that the defendant's "bidding on the buy side caused the cost of the relevant output to rise above the revenues generated in the sale of those outputs." The plaintiff must also prove that "the defendant has a dangerous probability of recouping the losses incurred in bidding up input prices through the exercise of monopsony power."

WHY IS THIS CASE IMPORTANT? *Predatory-bidding schemes of the type that Ross-Simmons alleged Weyerhaeuser had committed are rare. Under the standard that the Court imposed in this case, a plaintiff's successful claim will likely be even more rare. But this may not be a negative development, at least for consumers. A predatory-bidding scheme can actually benefit consumers—a predator's high bidding can cause it to acquire more inputs, which can lead to the manufacture of more outputs, and increases in output generally result in lower prices to consumers.*

The Clayton Act

In 1914, Congress attempted to strengthen federal antitrust laws by enacting the Clayton Act. The Clayton Act was aimed at specific anticompetitive or monopolistic practices that the Sherman Act did not cover. The substantive provisions of the act deal with four distinct forms of business behavior, which are declared illegal but not criminal. In each instance, the act states that the behavior is illegal only if it tends to substantially lessen competition or to create monopoly power.

The major offenses under the Clayton Act are set out in Sections 2, 3, 7, and 8 of the act.

LEARNING OBJECTIVE 4
What are the four major provisions of the Clayton Act, and what types of activities do these provisions prohibit?

Section 2 (The Robinson-Patman Act)— Price Discrimination

Section 2 of the Clayton Act prohibits **price discrimination**, which occurs when a seller charges different prices to competing buyers for identical goods or services. Congress strengthened this section by amending it with the passage of the Robinson-Patman Act in 1936.

As amended, Section 2 prohibits price discrimination that cannot be justified by differences in production costs, transportation costs, or cost differences due to other reasons. In short, a seller is prohibited from charging a lower price to one buyer than is charged to that buyer's competitor.

Price Discrimination A seller's act of charging competing buyers different prices for identical products or services.

Requirements To violate Section 2, the seller must be engaged in interstate commerce, the goods must be of like grade and quality, and goods must have been sold to two or more purchasers. In addition, the effect of the price discrimination must be to substantially lessen competition, tend to create a monopoly, or otherwise injure competition. Without proof of an actual injury resulting from the price discrimination, the plaintiff cannot recover damages.

Note that price discrimination claims can arise from discounts, offsets, rebates, or allowances given to one buyer over another. Giving favorable credit terms, delivery, or freight charges to only some buyers can also lead to allegations of price discrimination. For instance, offering goods to different customers at the same price but including free delivery for certain buyers may violate Section 2 in some circumstances.

Defenses   There are several statutory defenses to liability for price discrimination.

1. *Cost justification.* If the seller can justify the price reduction by demonstrating that a particular buyer's purchases saved the seller costs in producing and selling the goods, the seller will not be liable for price discrimination.
2. *Meeting competitor's prices.* If the seller charged the lower price in a good faith attempt to meet an equally low price of a competitor, the seller will not be liable for price discrimination. **CASE EXAMPLE 22.9**   Water Craft was a retail dealership of Mercury Marine outboard motors in Baton Rouge, Louisiana. Mercury Marine also sold its motors to other dealers in the Baton Rouge area. When Water Craft discovered that Mercury was selling its outboard motors at a substantial discount to Water Craft's largest competitor, it filed a price discrimination lawsuit against Mercury. The court ruled in favor of Mercury Marine, however, because it was able to show that the discounts given to Water Craft's competitor were made in good faith to meet the low price charged by another manufacturer of marine motors.[19] ●
3. *Changing market conditions.* A seller may lower its price on an item in response to changing conditions affecting the market for or the marketability of the goods concerned. Thus, if an advance in technology makes a particular product less marketable than it was previously, a seller can lower the product's price.

Section 3—Exclusionary Practices

Under Section 3 of the Clayton Act, sellers or lessors cannot condition the sale or lease of goods on the buyer's or lessee's promise not to use or deal in the goods of the seller's competitor. In effect, this section prohibits two types of vertical agreements involving exclusionary practices—*exclusive-dealing contracts* and *tying arrangements*.

Exclusive-Dealing Contracts   A contract under which a seller forbids a buyer to purchase products from the seller's competitors is called an **exclusive-dealing contract.** A seller is prohibited from making an exclusive-dealing contract under Section 3 if the effect of the contract is "to substantially lessen competition or tend to create a monopoly."

CASE EXAMPLE 22.10   In a classic case decided by the United States Supreme Court in 1949, Standard Oil Company, the largest gasoline seller in the nation at that time, made exclusive-dealing contracts with independent stations in seven western states. The contracts involved 16 percent of all retail outlets, with sales amounting to approximately 7 percent of all retail sales in that market. The market was substantially concentrated because the seven largest gasoline suppliers all used exclusive-dealing contracts with their independent retailers. Together, these suppliers controlled 65 percent of the market. The Court looked at market conditions after the arrangements were instituted and found that market shares were extremely stable and entry into the market was apparently restricted. Because

Exclusive-Dealing Contract An agreement under which a seller forbids a buyer to purchase products from the seller's competitors.

---

19. *Water Craft Management, LLC v. Mercury Marine,* 457 F.3d 484 (5th Cir. 2006).

competition was "foreclosed in a substantial share" of the relevant market, the Court held that Section 3 of the Clayton Act had been violated.[20] ● Note that since the Supreme Court's 1949 decision, a number of subsequent decisions have called the holding in this case into doubt.[21]

Today, it is clear that to violate antitrust law, an exclusive-dealing agreement (or *tying arrangement,* discussed next) must qualitatively and substantially harm competition. To prevail, a plaintiff must present affirmative evidence that the performance of the agreement will foreclose competition and harm consumers.

Tying Arrangement A seller's act of conditioning the sale of a product or service on the buyer's agreement to purchase another product or service from the seller.

Tying Arrangements When a seller conditions the sale of a product (the tying product) on the buyer's agreement to purchase another product (the tied product) produced or distributed by the same seller, a **tying arrangement** results. The legality of a tying arrangement (or *tie-in sales agreement*) depends on many factors, particularly the purpose of the agreement and its likely effect on competition in the relevant markets (the market for the tying product and the market for the tied product).

> **EXAMPLE 22.11** Morshigi Precision, Inc., manufactures laptop hardware and provides repair service for the hardware. Morshigi also makes and markets software, but the company will provide support for buyers of the software only if they also buy its hardware service. This is a tying arrangement. Depending on the purpose of the agreement and the effect of the agreement on competition in the market for the two products, the agreement may be illegal. ●

Section 3 of the Clayton Act has been held to apply only to commodities, not to services. Some tying arrangements, however, can also be considered agreements that restrain trade in violation of Section 1 of the Sherman Act. Thus, cases involving tying arrangements of services have been brought under Section 1 of the Sherman Act. Although earlier cases condemned tying arrangements as illegal *per se,* courts now evaluate tying agreements under the rule of reason.[22]

Section 7—Mergers

Under Section 7 of the Clayton Act, a person or business organization cannot hold stock and/or assets in another entity "where the effect . . . may be to substantially lessen competition." Section 7 is the statutory authority for preventing mergers or acquisitions (discussed in Chapter 20 on page 598) that could result in monopoly power or a substantial lessening of competition in the marketplace.

Market Concentration The degree to which a small number of firms control a large percentage of a relevant market.

A crucial consideration in most merger cases is the **market concentration** of a product or business. Determining market concentration involves allocating percentage market shares among the various companies in the relevant market. When a small number of companies control a large share of the market, the market is concentrated. **EXAMPLE 22.12** If the four largest grocery stores in Chicago accounted for 80 percent of all retail food sales, the market clearly would be concentrated in those four firms. If one of these stores absorbed the assets and liabilities of another so that the other ceased to exist, the result would be a merger that would further concentrate the market and thereby possibly diminish competition. ●

Competition, however, is not necessarily diminished solely as a result of market concentration, and courts will consider other factors in determining whether a merger will violate Section 7. One factor of particular importance in evaluating the effects of a merger is whether the merger will make it more difficult for *potential* competitors to enter the relevant market.

---

20. *Standard Oil Co. of California v. United States,* 337 U.S. 293, 69 S.Ct. 1051, 93 L.Ed. 1371 (1949).

21. See, for example, *Illinois Tool Works, Inc. v. Independent Ink, Inc.,* 547 U.S. 28, 126 S.Ct. 1281, 164 L.Ed.2d 26 (2006); and *Stop & Shop Supermarket Co. v. Blue Cross & Blue Shield of Rhode Island,* 373 F.3d 57 (1st Cir. 2004).

22. See, for example, *Illinois Tool Works, Inc. v. Independent Ink, Inc.,* cited in footnote 21.

Horizontal Merger A merger between two firms that are competing in the same market.

Horizontal Mergers

Mergers between firms that compete with each other in the same market are called **horizontal mergers.** If a horizontal merger creates an entity with a significant market share, the merger will be presumed illegal because it increases market concentration.

When analyzing the legality of a horizontal merger, the courts also consider three other factors: the overall concentration of the relevant product market, the relevant market's history of tending toward concentration, and whether the apparent design of the merger is to establish market power or to restrict competition.

Vertical Merger The acquisition by a company at one stage of production of a company at a higher or lower stage of production (such as a company merging with one of its suppliers or retailers).

Vertical Mergers

A **vertical merger** occurs when a company at one stage of production acquires a company at a higher or lower stage of production. An example of a vertical merger is a company merging with one of its suppliers or retailers. Whether a vertical merger is illegal generally depends on several factors, such as whether the merger would produce a firm controlling an undue percentage share of the relevant market.

The courts also analyze whether the merger would result in a significant increase in the concentration of firms in that market, the barriers to entry into the market, and the apparent intent of the merging parties. Mergers that do not prevent competitors of either merging firm from competing in a segment of the market are legal.

Section 8—Interlocking Directorates

Section 8 of the Clayton Act deals with *interlocking directorates*—that is, the practice of having individuals serve as directors on the boards of two or more competing companies simultaneously. Specifically, no person may be a director in two or more competing corporations at the same time if either of the corporations has capital, surplus, or undivided profits aggregating more than $27,784,000 or competitive sales of $2,778,100 or more. The FTC adjusts the threshold amounts each year. (The amounts given here are those announced by the FTC in 2012.)

The reasoning behind the FTC's prohibition of interlocking directorates is that if two competing businesses share the same officers and directors, the firms are unlikely to compete with one another, or to compete aggressively. If directors or officers do not comply with this prohibition, they may be liable under the Clayton Act.

LEARNING OBJECTIVE 5
What agencies of the federal government enforce the federal antitrust laws?

Enforcement and Exemptions

The federal agencies that enforce the federal antitrust laws are the U.S. Department of Justice (DOJ) and the Federal Trade Commission (FTC). The FTC was established in 1914 by the Federal Trade Commission Act. Section 5 of that act condemns all forms of anticompetitive behavior that are not covered under other federal antitrust laws.

KNOW THIS

Section 5 of the Federal Trade Commission Act is broader than the other antitrust laws. It covers nearly all anticompetitive behavior, including conduct that does not violate either the Sherman Act or the Clayton Act.

Enforcement by Federal Agencies

Only the DOJ can prosecute violations of the Sherman Act, which can be either criminal or civil offenses. Violations of the Clayton Act are not crimes, but the act can be enforced by either the DOJ or the FTC through civil proceedings.

Divestiture A company's sale of one or more of its operating functions under court order as part of the enforcement of the antitrust laws.

The DOJ or the FTC may ask the courts to impose various remedies, including **divestiture** (making a company give up one or more of its operating functions) and dissolution. A meatpacking firm, for instance, might be forced to divest itself of control or ownership of butcher shops. (To find out how you can avoid antitrust problems, see the *Business Application* feature on page 656.)

The FTC has the sole authority to enforce violations of Section 5 of the Federal Trade Commission Act. FTC actions are effected through administrative orders, but if a firm violates an FTC order, the FTC can seek court sanctions for the violation.

Enforcement by Private Parties

Treble Damages Damages that, by statute, are three times the amount of actual damages suffered.

A private party who has been injured as a result of a violation of the Sherman Act or the Clayton Act can sue for **treble damages** (three times the actual damages suffered) and attorneys' fees. In some instances, private parties may also seek injunctive relief to prevent antitrust violations. A party wishing to sue under the Sherman Act must prove the following:

1. The antitrust violation either caused or was a substantial factor in causing the injury that was suffered.
2. The unlawful actions of the accused party affected business activities of the plaintiff that were protected by the antitrust laws.

Exemptions from Antitrust Laws

There are many legislative and constitutional limitations on antitrust enforcement. Most of the statutory or judicially created exemptions to antitrust laws apply in such areas as labor, insurance, and foreign trade, and are listed in Exhibit 22.1 below.

Exhibit 22.1 Exemptions to Antitrust Enforcement

EXEMPTION	SOURCE AND SCOPE
Labor	Clayton Act—Permits unions to organize and bargain without violating antitrust laws and specifies that strikes and other labor activities normally do not violate any federal law.
Agricultural associations	Clayton Act and Capper-Volstead Act of 1922—Allow agricultural cooperatives to set prices.
Fisheries	Fisheries Cooperative Marketing Act of 1976—Allows the fishing industry to set prices.
Insurance companies	McCarran-Ferguson Act of 1945—Exempts the insurance business in states in which the industry is regulated.
Exporters	Webb-Pomerene Act of 1918—Allows U.S. exporters to engage in cooperative activity to compete with similar foreign associations. Export Trading Company Act of 1982—Permits the U.S. Department of Justice to exempt certain exporters.
Professional baseball	The United States Supreme Court has held that professional baseball is exempt because it is not "interstate commerce."[a]
Oil marketing	Interstate Oil Compact of 1935—Allows states to set quotas on oil to be marketed in interstate commerce.
Defense activities	Defense Production Act of 1950—Allows the president to approve, and thereby exempt, certain activities to further the military defense of the United States.
Small businesses' cooperative research	Small Business Administration Act of 1958—Allows small firms to undertake cooperative research.
State actions	The United States Supreme Court has held that actions by a state are exempt if the state clearly articulates and actively supervises the policy behind its action.[b]
Regulated industries	Industries (such as airlines) are exempt when a federal administrative agency (such as the Federal Aviation Administration) has primary regulatory authority.
Businesspersons' joint efforts to seek government action	Cooperative efforts by businesspersons to obtain legislative, judicial, or executive action are exempt unless it is clear that an effort is "objectively baseless" and is an attempt to make anticompetitive use of government processes.[c]

a. *Federal Baseball Club of Baltimore, Inc. v. National League of Professional Baseball Clubs*, 259 U.S. 200, 42 S.Ct. 465, 66 L.Ed. 898 (1922). A federal district court has held that this exemption applies only to the game's reserve system. (Under the reserve system, teams hold players' contracts for the players' entire careers. The reserve system generally is being replaced by the free agency system.) See *Piazza v. Major League Baseball*, 831 F.Supp. 420 (E.D.Pa. 1993).

b. See *Parker v. Brown*, 317 U.S. 341, 63 S.Ct. 307, 87 L.Ed. 315 (1943).

c. *Eastern Railroad Presidents Conference v. Noerr Motor Freight, Inc.*, 365 U.S. 127, 81 S.Ct. 523, 5 L.Ed.2d 464 (1961); and *United Mine Workers of America v. Pennington*, 381 U.S. 657, 89 S.Ct. 1585, 14 L.Ed.2d 626 (1965). These two cases established the exception often referred to as the *Noerr-Pennington* doctrine.

One of the most significant of these exemptions covers joint efforts by businesspersons to obtain legislative, judicial, or executive action. Under this exemption, Blu-ray producers can jointly lobby Congress to change the copyright laws without being held liable for attempting to restrain trade. Another exemption covers professional baseball teams.

U.S. Antitrust Laws in the Global Context

U.S. antitrust laws have a broad application. Not only may persons in foreign nations be subject to their provisions, but the laws may also be applied to protect foreign consumers and competitors from violations committed by U.S. business firms. Consequently, *foreign persons,* a term that by definition includes foreign governments, may sue under U.S. antitrust laws in U.S. courts.

The Extraterritorial Application of U.S. Antitrust Laws

Section 1 of the Sherman Act provides for the extraterritorial effect of the U.S. antitrust laws. The United States is a major proponent of free competition in the global economy, and thus any conspiracy that has a *substantial effect* on U.S. commerce is within the reach of the Sherman Act. The violation may even occur outside the United States, and foreign persons including governments can be sued for violation of U.S. antitrust laws. Before U.S. courts will exercise jurisdiction and apply antitrust laws, it must be shown that the alleged violation had a substantial effect on U.S. commerce. U.S. jurisdiction is automatically invoked, however, when a *per se* violation occurs.

If a domestic firm, for example, joins a foreign cartel to control the production, price, or distribution of goods, and this cartel has a *substantial effect* on U.S. commerce, a *per se* violation may exist. Hence, both the domestic firm and the foreign cartel could be sued for violation of the U.S. antitrust laws. Likewise, if a foreign firm doing business in the United States enters into a price-fixing or other anticompetitive agreement to control a portion of U.S. markets, a *per se* violation may exist.

In the following case, the court had to decide whether an alleged anticompetitive conspiracy had a substantial effect on U.S. commerce.

Case 22.3

Carrier Corp. v. Outokumpu Oyj

United States Court of Appeals, Sixth Circuit, 673 F.3d 430 (2012). www.ca6.uscourts.gov[a]

(thabasade/iStockphoto.com)

Why did Carrier sue Outokumpu Oyj?

FACTS Carrier Corporation is a U.S. firm that manufactures air-conditioning and refrigeration (ACR) equipment. To make these products, Carrier uses ACR copper tubing bought from Outokumpu Oyj, a Finnish company. Carrier is one of the world's largest purchasers of ACR copper tubing. The Commission of the European Communities (EC) found that Outokumpu had conspired with other companies to fix ACR tubing prices in Europe. Carrier then filed a suit in a U.S. court, alleging that the cartel (group) had also conspired to fix prices in the United States by agreeing that only Outokumpu would sell ACR tubing in the U.S. market. The district court dismissed Carrier's claim for lack of jurisdiction. Carrier appealed.

ISSUE Did the Finnish company's anticompetitive actions have a sufficient effect on U.S. commerce to enable a U.S. court to exercise jurisdiction over it under the Sherman Act?

---

a. In the left-hand column, under "Opinions," click on "Opinions Search." When that page opens, type "Outokumpu Oyj" in the "Short Title *contains*" box, and click on "Submit Query." In the result, click on the opinion number to access the opinion. The U.S. Court of Appeals for the Sixth Circuit maintains this Web site.

Case 22.3—Continued

DECISION   Yes. The federal appellate court reversed the district court's judgment for the defendant.

REASON   Carrier's complaint sufficiently alleged that Outokumpu's conspiracy had a substantial effect on U.S. commerce. Carrier alleged that Outokumpu had conspired to divide up U.S. customers, which caused higher prices for ACR copper tubing. The complaint also alleged specific details about the conspiracy by drawing from the EC's decisions. It did not matter that the EC did not identify a conspiracy aimed

at the United States because that was beyond the scope of its decision. Carrier had some evidence that the conspiracy reached the United States because Outokumpu's competitors solicited its business only after the conspiracy ended. Therefore, the district court had jurisdiction over Carrier's Sherman Act claims.

CRITICAL THINKING—Legal Consideration   *When this case proceeds, should the district court apply the rule of reason? Why or why not?*

The Application of Foreign Antitrust Laws

Large U.S. companies increasingly need to worry about the application of foreign antitrust laws as well. The European Union, in particular, has stepped up its enforcement actions against antitrust violators, as discussed in this chapter's *Beyond Our Borders* feature below.

Many other nations also have laws that promote competition and prohibit trade restraints. For instance, Japanese antitrust laws forbid unfair trade practices, monopolization, and restrictions that unreasonably restrain trade. China's antitrust rules restrict monopolization and price fixing (although China has claimed that the government may set prices on exported goods without violating these rules). Indonesia, Malaysia, South Korea, and Vietnam all have statutes protecting competition. Argentina, Brazil, Chile, Peru, and several other Latin American countries have adopted modern antitrust laws as well.

Most of these antitrust laws apply extraterritorially, as U.S. antitrust laws do. This means that a U.S. company may be subject to another nation's antitrust laws if the company's conduct has a substantial effect on that nation's commerce. For instance, South Korea fined Intel, Inc., the world's largest semiconductor chip maker, $25 million for antitrust violations in 2008. Japan settled an antitrust case against Intel in 2005.

BEYOND OUR BORDERS

The European Union's Expanding Role in Antitrust Litigation

The European Union (EU) has laws promoting competition that are stricter in many respects than those of the United States. Although the EU's laws provide only for civil, rather than criminal, penalties, the rules define more conduct as anticompetitive than U.S. laws do.

The EU actively pursues antitrust violators, especially individual companies and cartels that engage in alleged monopolistic conduct. For example, in 2009, the EU fined chip-making giant Intel, Inc., $1.44 billion in an antitrust case. According to European regulators, Intel offered computer manufacturers and retailers price discounts and marketing subsidies if they agreed to buy

Intel's chips rather than the chips produced by Intel's main competitor in Europe. The EU has also fined Microsoft Corporation more than $2 billion in the last twelve years for anticompetitive conduct.

The EU is investigating Google, Inc., for potentially violating European antitrust laws by thwarting competition in Internet search engines. Ironically, in 2011, Microsoft—which has paid substantial fines to the EU for anticompetitive conduct—filed its own complaint with the EU against Google. Among other things, Microsoft claims that Google has unlawfully restricted competing search engines from accessing YouTube, content from book publishers, advertiser data,

and more. (A similar case brought against Google in the United States, for monopolizing or attempting to monopolize Internet search engines, was dismissed in 2011.[a])

Critical Thinking

Some commentators argue that EU regulators are too focused on reining in powerful U.S. technology companies, such as Microsoft and Intel. How might the large fines imposed by the EU on successful U.S. technology firms affect competition in the United States?

---

a. See *TradeComet.com, LLC v. Google, Inc.,* 647 F.3d 472 (2d Cir. 2011).

Reviewing . . . Antitrust Law and Promoting Competition

The Internet Corporation for Assigned Names and Numbers (ICANN) is a nonprofit entity that organizes Internet domain names. It is governed by a board of directors elected by various groups with commercial interests in the Internet. One of ICANN's functions is to authorize an entity to serve as a registrar for certain "top level domains" (TLDs). ICANN entered into an agreement with VeriSign to provide registry services for the ".com" TLD in accordance with ICANN's specifications. VeriSign complained that ICANN was restricting the services that it could make available as a registrar and was blocking new services, imposing unnecessary conditions on those services, and setting prices at which the services were offered. VeriSign claimed that ICANN's control of the registry services for domain names violated Section 1 of the Sherman Act. Using the information presented in the chapter, answer the following questions.

1. Should ICANN's actions be judged under the rule of reason or be deemed a *per se* violation of Section 1 of the Sherman Act? Explain.
2. Should ICANN's actions be viewed as a horizontal or a vertical restraint of trade? Explain.
3. Does it matter that ICANN's directors are chosen by groups with a commercial interest in the Internet? Why or why not?
4. If the dispute is judged under the rule of reason, what might be ICANN's defense for having a standardized set of registry services that must be used?

DEBATE THIS   The Internet and the rise of e-commerce have rendered our antitrust concepts and laws obsolete.

BUSINESS APPLICATION

How Can You Avoid Antitrust Problems?*

Business managers need to be aware of how antitrust legislation may affect their activities. In addition to the federal antitrust laws covered in this chapter, the states also have antitrust and unfair competition laws. Moreover, state authorities have the power to bring civil lawsuits to enforce federal antitrust laws. Additionally, antitrust law is subject to various interpretations by the courts. Unless a businessperson exercises caution, a court may decide that his or her actions are in violation of a federal or state statute.

Pricing Issues

Almost all businesses have competitors and want to outsell those competitors. The pricing of a business's goods or services is extremely important not only for its volume of sales, but also for its bottom-line profit. When setting or changing prices, businesses

frequently hire a cost accountant to perform an analysis. This is only a start because a firm must also consider the prices of a competitor's similar or identical products. Most businesses do not want a "price war" with rapidly declining prices.

Thus, it is not uncommon for a business to charge basically the same price as its competitors. A problem arises when there is an agreement (express or implied) to fix the price. This is a *per se* violation of Section 1 of the Sherman Act and can result in criminal or civil actions (including treble damages).

Knowing the price a competitor charges—and meeting that price—is not a violation in and of itself. Frequently, the legality depends on how the information was obtained. Violations occur when there is a communication (regardless of purpose) between a business owner (or employee) and a direct competitor. If concerned that a communication may cause antitrust pricing problems, businesspersons should consult with an attorney who can explain what is legal when dealing with competitors.

---

*This *Business Application* is not meant to substitute for the services of an attorney who is licensed to practice law in your state.

Implications of Foreign Law

Antitrust issues are not limited to domestic firms doing business in the United States. In today's global economy, many companies conduct business in other nations and with foreign businesses. Antitrust laws in other countries differ from U.S. law and can apply to a U.S. firm that has dealings with businesses located in a foreign nation even though the firm does not have a physical presence there. Always be aware of the antitrust laws of any country in which you are doing business. Generally, any businessperson who is considering doing business overseas should seek counsel from a competent attorney concerning potential antitrust violations.

Checklist for Avoiding Antitrust Problems

1. *Exercise caution when communicating and dealing with competitors.*
2. *Seek the advice of an attorney specializing in antitrust law to ensure that your business practices and agreements do not violate antitrust laws.*
3. *If you conduct business in other nations, obtain the advice of an attorney who is familiar with the antitrust laws of those nations.*

Key Terms

antitrust law 637
attempted monopolization 648
concentrated industry 643
divestiture 652
exclusive-dealing contract 650
group boycott 643

horizontal merger 652
horizontal restraint 641
market concentration 651
market power 639
monopolization 645
monopoly 639

monopoly power 639
per se violation 640
predatory pricing 644
price discrimination 649
price-fixing agreement 641
resale price maintenance agreement 644

rule of reason 640
treble damages 653
tying arrangement 651
vertical merger 652
vertical restraint 643
vertically integrated firm 643

Chapter Summary: Antitrust Law and Promoting Competition

The Sherman Antitrust Act (1890) (See pages 638–649.)	1. *Major provisions—*
	a. Section 1—Prohibits contracts, combinations, and conspiracies in restraint of trade.
	  (1) Horizontal restraints subject to Section 1 include price-fixing agreements, group boycotts (joint refusals to deal), horizontal market divisions, and trade association agreements.
	  (2) Vertical restraints subject to Section 1 include territorial or customer restrictions, resale price maintenance agreements, and refusals to deal.
	b. Section 2—Prohibits monopolies and attempts to monopolize.
	2. *Jurisdictional requirements*—The Sherman Act applies only to activities that have a significant impact on interstate commerce.
	3. *Interpretive rules—*
	a. *Per se* rule—Applied to restraints on trade that are so inherently anticompetitive that they cannot be justified and are deemed illegal as a matter of law.
	b. Rule of reason—Applied when an anticompetitive agreement may be justified by legitimate benefits. Under the rule of reason, the lawfulness of a trade restraint will be determined by the purpose and effects of the restraint.

The Clayton Act (1914) (See pages 649–652.)	The major provisions are as follows: 1. *Section 2*—As amended in 1936 by the Robinson-Patman Act, prohibits a seller engaged in interstate commerce from price discrimination that substantially lessens competition. 2. *Section 3*—Prohibits exclusionary practices, such as exclusive-dealing contracts and tying arrangements, when the effect may be to substantially lessen competition. 3. *Section 7*—Prohibits mergers when the effect may be to substantially lessen competition or to tend to create a monopoly. a. A horizontal merger will be presumed unlawful if the entity created by the merger will have a significant market share. b. A vertical merger will be unlawful if the merger prevents competitors of either merging firm from competing in a segment of the market that otherwise would be open to them, resulting in a substantial lessening of competition. 4. *Section 8*—Prohibits interlocking directorates.

Continued

Chapter Summary: Antitrust Law and Promoting Competition— Continued

Enforcement and Exemptions (See pages 652–654.)	1. *Enforcement*—The U.S. Department of Justice and the Federal Trade Commission enforce the federal antitrust laws. Private parties who have been injured as a result of violations of the Sherman Act or Clayton Act may bring civil suits, and, if successful, they may be awarded treble damages and attorneys' fees. 2. *Exemptions*—Numerous exemptions from the antitrust laws have been created. See Exhibit 22.1 on page 653 for a list of significant exemptions.
U.S. Antitrust Laws in the Global Context (See pages 654–655.)	1. *Application of U.S. laws*—U.S. antitrust laws can be applied in foreign nations to protect foreign consumers and competitors. Foreign governments and persons can also bring actions under U.S. antitrust laws. Section 1 of the Sherman Act applies to any conspiracy that has a substantial effect on U.S. commerce. 2. *Application of foreign laws*—Many other nations also have laws that promote competition and prohibit trade restraints, and some are more restrictive than U.S. laws. These foreign antitrust laws are increasingly being applied to U.S. firms.

ExamPrep

ISSUE SPOTTERS

1. Under what circumstances would Pop's Market, a small store in a small, isolated town, be considered a monopolist? If Pop's is a monopolist, is it in violation of Section 2 of the Sherman Act? Why or why not? **(See page 645.)**
2. Maple Corporation conditions the sale of its syrup on the buyer's agreement to buy Maple's pancake mix. What factors would a court consider to decide whether this arrangement violates the Clayton Act? **(See page 651.)**

—**Check your answers to the Issue Spotters against the answers provided in Appendix E at the end of this text.**

BEFORE THE TEST

Go to www.cengagebrain.com, enter the ISBN 9781133191353, and click on "Find" to locate this textbook's Web site. Then, click on "Access Now" under "Study Tools," and select Chapter 22 at the top. There, you will find a Practice Quiz that you can take to assess your mastery of the concepts in this chapter, as well as Flashcards, a Glossary of important terms, and Video Questions (when assigned).

For Review

Answers to the even-numbered questions in this For Review section can be found in Appendix F at the end of this text.

1. What is a monopoly? What is market power? How do these concepts relate to each other?
2. What anticompetitive activities are prohibited by Section 1 of the Sherman Act?
3. What type of activity is prohibited by Section 2 of the Sherman Act?
4. What are the four major provisions of the Clayton Act, and what types of activities do these provisions prohibit?
5. What agencies of the federal government enforce the federal antitrust laws?

Business Scenarios and Case Problems

22–1 **Sherman Act.** An agreement that is blatantly and substantially anticompetitive is deemed a *per se* violation of Section 1 of the Sherman Act. Under what rule is an agreement analyzed if it appears to be anticompetitive but is not a *per se* violation? In making this analysis, what factors will a court consider? **(See pages 640–641.)**

22–2 ❓ **Question with Sample Answer—Antitrust Laws.** Allitron, Inc., and Donovan, Ltd., are interstate competitors selling similar appliances, principally in the states of Illinois, Indiana, Kentucky, and Ohio. Allitron and Donovan agree that Allitron will no longer sell in Indiana and Ohio and that Donovan will no longer sell in Illinois and Kentucky. Have Allitron and Donovan violated any antitrust laws? If so, which law? Explain. **(See page 643.)**

—**For a sample answer to Question 22–2, go to Appendix G at the end of this text.]**

22–3 **Tying Arrangement.** John Sheridan owned a Marathon gas station franchise. He sued Marathon Petroleum Co. under Section 1 of the Sherman Act and Section 3 of the Clayton Act, charging it with illegally tying the processing of credit-card sales to the gas station. As a condition of obtaining a Marathon dealership, dealers had to agree to let the franchisor process credit cards. They could not shop around to see if credit-card processing could be obtained at a lower price from another source. The district court dismissed the case for failure to state a claim. Sheridan appealed. Is there a tying arrangement? If so, does it violate the law? [*Sheridan v. Marathon Petroleum Co.,* 530 F.3d 590 (7th Cir. 2008)] **(See page 651.)**

22–4 **Case Problem with Sample Answer—Section 2 of the Sherman Act.** When Deer Valley Resort Co. (DVRC) was developing its ski resort in the Wasatch Mountains near Park City, Utah, it sold parcels of land in the resort village to third parties. Each sales contract reserved the right of approval over the conduct of certain businesses on the property, including ski rentals. For fifteen years, DVRC permitted Christy Sports, LLC, to rent skis in competition with DVRC's ski rental outlet. When DVRC opened a new midmountain ski rental outlet, it revoked Christy's permission to rent skis. This meant that most skiers who flew into Salt Lake City and shuttled to Deer Valley had few choices: they could carry their ski equipment onto their flights, take a shuttle into Park City and look for cheaper ski rentals there, or rent from DVRC. Christy filed a suit against DVRC. Was DVRC's action an attempt to monopolize in violation of Section 2 of the Sherman Act? Why or why not? [*Christy Sports, LLC v. Deer Valley Resort Co.,* 555 F.3d 1188 (10th Cir. 2009)] **(See pages 648–649.)**

—**For a sample answer to Problem 22–4, go to Appendix H at the end of this text.**

22–5 **The Sherman Act.** Together, EMI, Sony BMG Music Entertainment, Universal Music Group Recordings, Inc., and Warner Music Group Corp. produced, licensed, and distributed 80 percent of the digital music sold in the United States. The companies formed MusicNet to sell music to online services that sold the songs to consumers. MusicNet required all of the services to sell the songs at the same price and subject to the same restrictions. Digitization of music became cheaper, but MusicNet did not change its prices. Did MusicNet violate the antitrust laws? Explain. [*Starr v. Sony BMG Music Entertainment,* 592 F.3d 314 (2d Cir. 2010)] **(See pages 641–643.)**

22–6 **Price Discrimination.** Dayton Superior Corp. sells its products in interstate commerce to several companies, including Spa Steel Products, Inc. The purchasers often compete directly with each other for customers. From 2005 to 2007, one of Spa Steel's customers purchased Dayton Superior's products from two of Spa Steel's competitors. According to the customer, Spa Steel's prices were always 10 to 15 percent higher even though they were for the same products. As a result, Spa Steel lost sales to at least that customer and perhaps others. Spa Steel wants to sue Dayton Superior for price discrimination. Which requirements for such a claim under Section 2 of the Clayton Act does Spa Steel satisfy? What additional facts will it need to prove? [*Dayton Superior Corp. v. Spa Steel Products, Inc.,* 2012 WL 113663 (N.D.N.Y. 2012)] **(See pages 649–650.)**

22–7 ◆▶ **A Question of Ethics—Section 1 of the Sherman Act.** In the 1990s, DuCoa, LP, made choline chloride, a B-complex vitamin essential for the growth and development of animals. The U.S. market for choline chloride was divided into thirds among DuCoa, Bioproducts, Inc., and Chinook Group, Ltd. To stabilize the market and keep the price of the vitamin higher than it would otherwise be, the companies agreed to fix the price and allocate market share by deciding which of them would offer the lowest price to each customer. At times, however, the companies disregarded the agreement. During an increase in competitive activity in 1997, Daniel Rose became president of DuCoa and found out about the conspiracy. In 1998, Rose implemented a strategy to persuade DuCoa's competitors to rejoin the conspiracy. By April, the three companies had reallocated their market shares and increased their prices. In June, the U.S. Department of Justice began to investigate allegations of price fixing in the vitamin market. Ultimately, Rose was convicted of conspiracy to violate Section 1 of the Sherman Act. [*United States v. Rose,* 449 F.3d 627 (5th Cir. 2006)] **(See pages 640–644.)**

1. The court "enhanced" Rose's sentence to thirty months' imprisonment, one year of supervised release, and a $20,000 fine because of his role as "a manager or supervisor" in the conspiracy. Rose appealed this enhancement. Was it fair to increase Rose's sentence on this ground? Why or why not?

2. Was Rose's participation in the conspiracy unethical? If so, how might Rose have behaved ethically instead? Explain.

Critical Thinking and Writing Assignments

22–8 **Business Law Writing.** Write two paragraphs explaining some ways that antitrust laws might place too great of a burden on commerce in the global marketplace.

22–9 💡 **Business Law Critical Thinking Group Assignment.** Residents of the city of Madison, Wisconsin, became concerned about overconsumption of liquor near the campus of the University of Wisconsin. The city initiated a new policy, imposing conditions on area bars to discourage reduced-price "specials" that were believed to encourage high-volume and dangerous drinking. In 2012, the city began to draft an ordinance to ban all drink specials. Bar owners responded by announcing that they had "voluntarily" agreed to discontinue drink specials on Friday and Saturday nights after 8:00 P.M. The city put its ordinance on hold. Several UW students filed a lawsuit against the local bar owners' association alleging violations of antitrust law.

1. The first group will identify the grounds on which the plaintiffs might base their claim for relief and formulate an argument on behalf of the plaintiffs.

2. The second group will determine whether the defendants are exempt from the antitrust laws.

3. The third group will decide how the court should rule in this dispute and provide reasons for its answer.

23 CHAPTER

Personal Property, Bailments, and Insurance

(Iakov Filimonov/Shutterstock.com)

LEARNING OBJECTIVES

The five learning objectives below are designed to help improve your understanding of the chapter. After reading this chapter, you should be able to answer the following questions:

1 What is the difference between a joint tenancy and a tenancy in common?

2 What are the three necessary elements for an effective gift?

3 What are the three elements of a bailment?

4 Is an insurance broker the agent of the insurance applicant or the agent of the insurer?

5 What is an insurable interest? When must an insurable interest exist — at the time the insurance policy is obtained, at the time the loss occurs, or both?

"The great . . . end . . . of men united into commonwealths, and putting themselves under government, is the preservation of their property."
—John Locke, 1632–1704 (English political philosopher)

Property Legally protected rights and interests in anything with an ascertainable value that is subject to ownership.

Real Property Land and everything attached to it, such as trees and buildings.

Personal Property Any property that is not real property.

Chattel All forms of personal property.

Property consists of the legally protected rights and interests a person has in anything with an ascertainable value that is subject to ownership. For instance, virtual property has become quite valuable in today's world, as discussed in a feature on page 663. Property would have little value, however, if the law did not define the owner's rights to use her or his property, to sell or dispose of it, and to prevent others from using or taking it. Indeed, John Locke, as indicated in the chapter-opening quotation above, considered the preservation of property to be the primary reason for the establishment of government.

Property is divided into real property and personal property. **Real property** (sometimes called *realty* or *real estate*—see Chapter 24) consists of land and everything permanently attached to it. Everything else is **personal property,** or *personalty*. Attorneys sometimes refer to personal property as **chattel,** a term used under the common law to denote all forms of personal property. Personal property can be tangible or intangible. *Tangible* personal property, such as a television set or a car, has physical substance. *Intangible* personal property represents some set of rights and interests but has no real physical existence. Stocks and bonds, patents, and copyrights are examples of intangible personal property.

Property Ownership

Ownership of property—both real and personal property—can be viewed as a bundle of rights, including the right to possess the property and to dispose of it by sale, gift, lease, or other means. As explained on page 307 in Chapter 10, the right of ownership in property is often referred to as *title*.

Fee Simple

Fee Simple An absolute form of property ownership entitling the property owner to use, possess, or dispose of the property as he or she chooses during his or her lifetime. On death, the interest in the property descends to the owner's heirs.

A person who holds the entire bundle of rights to property is said to be an owner in **fee simple.** An owner in fee simple is entitled to use, possess, or dispose of the property as he or she chooses during his or her lifetime, and on this owner's death, the interests in the property descend to his or her heirs. We will return to this form of property ownership in Chapter 24, in the context of ownership rights in real property.

Concurrent Ownership

Concurrent Ownership Shared ownership rights.

Persons who share ownership rights simultaneously in a particular piece of property are said to be *concurrent* owners. There are two principal types of **concurrent ownership:** *tenancy in common* and *joint tenancy*. Additionally, in some states, married persons can hold property together as *community property*.

Tenancy in Common Co-ownership of property in which each party owns an undivided interest that passes to her or his heirs at death.

Tenancy in Common   A **tenancy in common** is a form of co-ownership in which each of two or more persons owns an *undivided* interest in the property. The interest is undivided because each tenant has rights in the *whole* property. On the death of a tenant in common, that tenant's interest in the property passes to her or his heirs.

EXAMPLE 23.1   Sofia and Greg own a rare baseball card collection together as tenants in common. This means that Sofia and Greg each have rights in the *entire* collection. (If Sofia owned some of the cards and Greg owned others, then the interest would be *divided*.) If Sofia dies before Greg, a one-half interest in the baseball card collection will become the property of Sofia's heirs. If Sofia sells her interest to Jorge before she dies, Jorge and Greg will be co-owners as tenants in common. If Jorge dies, his interest in the personal property will pass to his heirs, and they in turn will own the property with Greg as tenants in common. •

LEARNING OBJECTIVE 1
What is the difference between a joint tenancy and a tenancy in common?

Joint Tenancy Co-ownership of property in which each party owns an undivided portion of the property. On the death of a joint tenant, his or her interest automatically passes to the surviving joint tenant(s).

Joint Tenancy   In a **joint tenancy,** each of two or more persons owns an undivided interest in the property, but a deceased joint tenant's interest passes to the surviving joint tenant or tenants.[1] The rights of a surviving joint tenant to inherit a deceased joint tenant's ownership interest—referred to as *survivorship rights*—distinguish the joint tenancy from the tenancy in common. A joint tenancy can be terminated before a tenant's death by gift or by sale. In this situation, the person who receives the property as a gift or who purchases the property becomes a tenant in common, not a joint tenant.

EXAMPLE 23.2   In *Example 23.1,* suppose that Sofia and Greg hold their baseball card collection in a joint tenancy. In this situation, if Sofia dies before Greg, the entire collection will become the property of Greg. Sofia's heirs will receive no interest in the collection. If Sofia, while living, sells her interest to Jorge, however, the sale will terminate the joint tenancy, and Jorge and Greg will become co-owners as tenants in common. •

---

1. See, for example, *In re Estate of Grote,* 766 N.W.2d 82 (Minn.App. 2009).

Will this couple necessarily share equally in all income earned during their marriage?

In most states, it is presumed that a co-tenancy is a tenancy in common unless there is a clear intention to establish a joint tenancy. In those states, specific language is necessary to create a joint tenancy.

Community Property   A married couple is allowed to own property as **community property** in a limited number of states.[2] If property is held as community property, each spouse technically owns an undivided one-half interest in property acquired during the marriage. Generally, community property does *not* include property acquired before the marriage or property acquired by gift or inheritance as separate property during the marriage. After a divorce, community property is divided equally in some states and according to the discretion of the court in other states.

Community Property A form of concurrent ownership of property in which each spouse owns an undivided one-half interest in property acquired during the marriage.

Acquiring Ownership of Personal Property

The most common way of acquiring personal property is by purchasing it. (Even virtual property can be purchased—see this chapter's *Adapting the Law to the Online Environment* feature on the following page for a discussion.)

We have already discussed the purchase and sale of personal property (goods) in Chapters 10 and 11. Often, property is acquired by will or inheritance. Here, we look at additional ways in which ownership of personal property can be acquired, including acquisition by possession, production, gifts, accession, and confusion.

Possession

Sometimes, a person can become the owner of personal property merely by possessing it. An example is the capture of wild animals. Wild animals belong to no one in their natural state, and the first person to take possession of a wild animal normally owns it. A hunter who kills a deer, for instance, has assumed ownership of it (unless he or she acted in violation of the law). Those who find lost or abandoned property can also acquire ownership rights through mere possession of the property, such as *adverse possession*—see Chapter 24.

Gift A voluntary transfer of property made without consideration, past or present.

How does a person acquire ownership of wild animals?

Production

Production—the fruits of labor—is another means of acquiring ownership of personal property. For instance, writers, inventors, and manufacturers all produce personal property and thereby acquire title to it. (In some situations, though, as when a researcher is hired to invent a new product or technique, the researcher-producer may not own what is produced—see Chapter 17.)

Gifts

A **gift** is another fairly common means of acquiring and transferring ownership of real and personal property. A gift is essentially a *voluntary* transfer of property ownership for which no consideration is given. As discussed in Chapter 7, the presence of consideration is what distinguishes a contract from a gift.

---

2. These states include Alaska, Arizona, California, Idaho, Louisiana, Nevada, New Mexico, Texas, Washington, and Wisconsin. Puerto Rico allows property to be owned as community property as well.

ADAPTING THE LAW TO THE ONLINE ENVIRONMENT

THE EXPLODING WORLD OF VIRTUAL AND DIGITAL PROPERTY

Jon Jacobs took out a real mortgage on his real house so that he could pay $100,000 in real dollars for a virtual asteroid near the virtual Planet Calypso in the virtual world Entropia Universe. A few years later, he sold Club Neverdie, the virtual space resort he had constructed on the virtual asteroid, for more than $600,000. At the time, Jacobs was making $200,000 per year from players' purchases of virtual goods at the resort.

If the prospect of paying real funds for virtual property seems disconcerting, remember that property does not have to be tangible. Property consists of a bundle of rights in anything that has an ascertainable value and is subject to ownership—a definition that encompasses virtual property, including all the intangible objects used in virtual worlds like Entropia Universe and Second Life.

Digital Goods Have Value, Too

Digital goods include virtual goods, but more important, they include digital books, music libraries, and movie downloads. Like virtual property, digital property has real value. Some digital music libraries, for example, cost thousands of dollars.

Who Gets to Keep the Digital Goods?

Domain names, expensively created Web sites, digital music, and virtual real estate all create property interests. The growing value of virtual and digital goods raises some legal questions.

For example, what are the respective rights of the creator/owner of a virtual world Web site and the players at that site? And what happens when a husband and wife decide to divorce after they have purchased virtual real estate or digital goods with real-world dollars? The couple—or a court—will have to figure out a way to divide the goods, particularly in a community property state. Property and divorce laws will have to adapt to take this changing world into account.

Critical Thinking

How might a couple who enjoy purchasing virtual and digital goods together avoid property division issues in the event of a divorce?

LEARNING OBJECTIVE 2
What are the three necessary elements for an effective gift?

For a gift to be effective, three requirements must be met: (1) donative intent on the part of the *donor* (the one giving the gift), (2) delivery, and (3) acceptance by the *donee* (the one receiving the gift). We examine each of these requirements here, as well as the requirements of a gift made in contemplation of imminent death. Until these three requirements are met, no effective gift has been made. **EXAMPLE 23.3**   Your aunt tells you that she *intends* to give you a new Mercedes-Benz for your next birthday. This is simply a promise to make a gift. It is not considered a gift until the Mercedes-Benz is delivered and accepted. ●

ETHICAL ISSUE

Can a woman keep her engagement ring if the wedding is cancelled?

(jmalov/iStockphoto.com)

Who owns the engagement ring? Traditionally, when a man and a woman decide to marry, the man gives the woman an engagement ring. What if the engagement is called off? Etiquette authorities routinely counsel that if the woman breaks the engagement, she should return the ring, but if the man calls the wedding off, the woman is entitled to keep the ring. When the party who gave the ring (the donor) sues for its return after a breakup, the courts are split.

Courts in a majority of states, including Kansas, Michigan, New York, and Ohio, hold that an engagement ring is not a real gift. Rather, it is a "conditional gift" that becomes final only if the marriage occurs. If the marriage does not take place, the ring is returned to the donor regardless of who broke the engagement. This position is similar to the law of ancient Rome, which mandated that when an engagement was broken, the woman had to return the ring, as a penalty, regardless of who was at fault. Some judges, however, disagree with the conditional-gift theory and contend that an engagement ring is a gift and, as such, it belongs to the donee, even if the engagement is broken.

Donative Intent
When a gift is challenged in court, the court will determine whether donative intent exists by looking at the language of the donor and the surrounding circumstances. A court may look at the relationship between the parties and the size of

the gift in relation to the donor's other assets. When a person has given away a large portion of her or his assets, the court will scrutinize the transaction closely to determine the donor's mental capacity and look for indications of fraud or duress.

In the following case, the court examined the intent and capacity of a woman who gave more than $50,000 to her dogs' veterinarian.

Case 23.1

Goodman v. Atwood

Appeals Court of Massachusetts,
78 Mass.App.Ct. 655, 940 N.E.2d 514 (2011).

(joanek/iStockphoto.com)

FACTS Jean Knowles Goodman, who was eighty-five years old, gave Dr. Steven Atwood several checks over a period of three months that totaled $56,100. Atwood was a veterinarian who had cared for Goodman's dogs for nearly twenty years. Atwood and Goodman had become friends, and he had regularly visited her house to care for her dogs and socialize with her. Shortly after writing the last check, Goodman was hospitalized and diagnosed with dementia (loss of brain function) and alcohol dependency. A guardian was appointed for Goodman. The guardian filed a lawsuit against Atwood to invalidate the gifts, claiming that Goodman had lacked mental capacity and donative intent. At trial, a psychiatrist who had examined Goodman testified on behalf of Atwood that while Goodman lacked the capacity to care for herself, she would have understood that she was giving away her funds. The trial judge ruled that Goodman had the capacity and intent to make the gifts to Atwood. The guardian appealed.

ISSUE Was there sufficient proof that Goodman had donative intent to make the gifts to Atwood even though she was later found to be mentally incompetent?

DECISION Yes. The state appellate court affirmed the lower court's judgment in favor of Atwood.

REASON In a civil action, the plaintiff has the burden of proving the essential elements of a claim—in this case, the lack of capacity and intent. The court found that the trial judge had used the proper standard of evidence and had kept the burden of proof on the plaintiff (the guardian). There was sufficient evidence of the donor's capacity and intent to support the trial judge's findings. "The plaintiff's own witness conceded the possibility that the donor experienced periods of mental awareness in addition to her lucidity [clarity] regarding financial affairs." The appellate court acknowledged "that a reasonable and conscientious finder of fact could have reached a different conclusion." Nonetheless, it is not the task of an appellate court "to substitute our judgment for that of the fact finder, and on this record we do not conclude that a mistake has clearly been made."

WHAT IF THE FACTS WERE DIFFERENT? If there had been a jury trial, and the jury had concluded that Goodman lacked mental capacity and intent at the time she made the gifts to Atwood, would the appellate court still have affirmed the decision? Why or why not?

Delivery   The gift must be delivered to the donee. Delivery may be accomplished by means of a third person who is the agent of either the donor or the donee. Naturally, no delivery is necessary if the gift is already in the hands of the donee. Delivery is obvious in most cases, but some objects cannot be relinquished physically. Then the question of delivery depends on the surrounding circumstances.

Constructive Delivery   When the object itself cannot be physically delivered, a symbolic, or constructive, delivery will be sufficient. **Constructive delivery** confers the right to take possession of the object in question, but not the actual possession. **EXAMPLE 23.4** Angela wants to make a gift of various rare coins that she has stored in a safe-deposit box. She obviously cannot deliver the box itself to the donee and does not want to take the coins out of the bank. Angela can simply deliver the key to the box to the donee and authorize the donee's access to the box and its contents. This action constitutes a constructive delivery of the contents of the box. •

Constructive Delivery A symbolic delivery of property that cannot be physically delivered. Constructive delivery confers the right to possession of the property, but not the actual possession.

Constructive delivery is always necessary for gifts of intangible property, such as stocks, bonds, insurance policies, and contracts. What will be delivered are documents that represent rights and are not, in themselves, the true property.

Dominion Ownership rights in property, including the right to possess and control the property.

Relinquishing Dominion and Control An effective delivery also requires giving up complete control and **dominion** (ownership rights) over the subject matter of the gift. The outcome of disputes often turns on whether control has actually been relinquished. The Internal Revenue Service scrutinizes transactions between relatives, especially when one claims to have given income-producing property to another who is in a lower marginal tax bracket. Unless complete control over the property has been relinquished, the "donor"—not the family member who received the "gift"—will have to pay taxes on the income from that property.

In the following *Classic Case*, the court focused on the requirement that a donor must relinquish complete control and dominion over property given to the donee before a gift can be effectively delivered.

Classic Case 23.2

In re Estate of Piper

Missouri Court of Appeals,
676 S.W.2d 897 (1984).

(©Ingvar Bjork, 2009. Used under license from Shutterstock.com)

How can two diamond rings have been gifted if they remain in the owner's purse after her death?

FACTS Gladys Piper died intestate (without a will) in 1982. At her death, she owned miscellaneous personal property worth $5,000 and had in her purse $200 in cash and two diamond rings. Wanda Brown, Piper's niece, took the contents of the purse, allegedly to preserve the items for the estate. Clara Kaufmann, a friend of Piper's, filed a claim against the estate for $4,800. From October 1974 until Piper's death, Kaufmann had taken Piper to the doctor, beauty shop, and grocery store. Kaufmann had also written Piper's checks to pay her bills and had helped her care for her home. Kaufmann maintained that Piper had promised to pay her for these services and had given her the diamond rings as a gift. A Missouri state trial court denied her request for payment. The court found that her services had been voluntary. Kaufmann then filed a petition for delivery of personal property—the rings—which was granted by the trial court. Brown, other heirs, and the administrator of Piper's estate appealed.

ISSUE Had Gladys Piper made an effective gift of the rings to Clara Kaufmann?

DECISION No. The state appellate court reversed the judgment of the trial court on the ground that Piper had never delivered the rings to Kaufmann.

REASON Kaufmann claimed that the rings belonged to her by reason of a "consummated gift long prior to the death of Gladys Piper." Two witnesses testified at the trial that Piper had told them that she was going to wear the rings until she died but that the rings belonged to Kaufmann. The appellate court, however, found "no evidence of any actual delivery." The court pointed out that the essentials of a gift are (1) a present intention to make a gift on the part of the donor, (2) a delivery of the property by the donor to the donee, and (3) an acceptance by the donee. Here, the evidence showed only an intent to make a gift. Because there was no delivery—either actual or constructive—no valid gift was made.

WHAT IF THE FACTS WERE DIFFERENT? *Suppose that Gladys Piper had told Clara Kaufmann that she was giving the rings to Clara but wished to keep them in her possession for a few more days. Would this have affected the court's decision in this case? Explain.*

IMPACT OF THIS CASE ON TODAY'S LAW *This case clearly illustrates the delivery requirement when making a gift. Assuming that Piper did, indeed, intend for Kaufmann to have the rings, it was unfortunate that Kaufmann had no right to receive them after Piper's death. Yet the alternative could lead to perhaps even more unfairness. The policy behind the delivery requirement is to protect property owners and their heirs from fraudulent claims based solely on parol evidence. If not for this policy, a person could easily claim that a gift had been made when, in fact, it had not.*

Acceptance   The final requirement of a valid gift is acceptance by the donee. This rarely presents any problem, as most donees readily accept their gifts. The courts generally assume acceptance unless the circumstances indicate otherwise.

Gifts *Inter Vivos* and Gifts *Causa Mortis*

Gift *Inter Vivos* A gift made during lifetime and not in contemplation of imminent death, in contrast to a gift *causa mortis*.

Gift *Causa Mortis* A gift made in contemplation of imminent death. The gift is revoked if the donor does not die as contemplated.

Gifts *Inter Vivos* and Gifts *Causa Mortis*   A gift made during one's lifetime is termed a **gift *inter vivos*. Gifts *causa mortis*** (so-called *deathbed gifts*) are made in contemplation of imminent death. To be effective, a gift *causa mortis* must meet the three requirements discussed earlier—donative intent, delivery, and acceptance by the donee—and is also subject to some special rules.

A gift *causa mortis* does not become absolute until the donor dies from the contemplated event, and it is automatically revoked if the donor survives. **EXAMPLE 23.5** Yang, who is about to undergo surgery to remove a cancerous tumor, delivers an envelope to Chao, a close business associate. The envelope contains a letter saying, "I want to give you this check for $1 million in the event of my death from this operation." Chao cashes the check. The surgeon performs the operation and removes the tumor. Yang recovers fully. Several months later, Yang dies from a heart attack that is totally unrelated to the operation.

If Yang's estate tries to recover the $1 million, it will normally succeed. The gift *causa mortis* to Chao is automatically revoked if Yang recovers. The *specific event* that was contemplated in making the gift was death from a particular operation. Because Yang's death was not the result of this event, the gift is revoked, and the $1 million passes to Yang's estate. ●

A gift *causa mortis* is also revoked if the prospective donee dies before the donor. Therefore, even if Yang in *Example 23.5* had died during the operation, the gift would have been revoked if Chao had died a few minutes earlier. In that event, the $1 million would have passed to Yang's estate, and not to Chao's heirs.

Accession

Accession The addition of value to personal property by the use of labor or materials. In some situations, a person may acquire ownership rights in another's property through accession.

Accession means "something added." Accession occurs when someone adds value to an item of personal property by the use of either labor or materials. Generally, there is no dispute about who owns the property after the accession occurs, especially when the accession is accomplished with the owner's consent. **EXAMPLE 23.6** Hoshi buys all the materials necessary to customize his Corvette. He hires Zach, a customizing specialist, to come to his house to perform the work. Hoshi pays Zach for the value of the labor, obviously retaining title to the property. ●

If an improvement is made wrongfully—without the permission of the owner—the owner retains title to the property and normally does not have to pay for the improvement. This is true even if the accession increased the value of the property substantially. **EXAMPLE 23.7** Patti steals a car and puts expensive new tires on it. If the rightful owner later recovers the car, he obviously will not be required to compensate Patti, a car thief, for the value of the new tires. ●

In contrast, if an accession is performed in good faith—and the improvement was made due to an honest mistake of judgment—the owner normally still retains title to the property but usually must pay for the improvement. In rare instances, when the improvement greatly increases the value of the property or changes its identity, the court may rule that ownership has passed to the improver. In those rare situations, the improver must compensate the original owner for the value of the property before the accession occurred.

Confusion

Confusion The mixing together of goods belonging to two or more owners to such an extent that the separately owned goods cannot be identified.

Confusion is the commingling (mixing together) of goods to such an extent that one person's personal property cannot be distinguished from another's. Confusion frequently occurs with *fungible goods,* such as grain or oil, which consist of identical units.

If confusion occurs as a result of agreement, an honest mistake, or the act of some third party, the owners share ownership as tenants in common and will share any loss in proportion to their ownership interests in the property. **EXAMPLE 23.8** Five farmers in a small Iowa community enter into a cooperative arrangement. Each fall, the farmers harvest the same amount of number 2–grade yellow corn and store it in silos that are held by the cooperative. Each farmer thus owns one-fifth of the total corn in the silos. If a fire burns down one of the silos, each farmer will bear one-fifth of the loss. • When goods are confused due to an intentional wrongful act, then the innocent party ordinarily acquires title to the whole.

Mislaid, Lost, and Abandoned Property

As already mentioned, one of the methods of acquiring ownership of property is to possess it. Simply finding something and holding on to it, however, does not necessarily give the finder any legal rights in the property. Different rules apply, depending on whether the property was mislaid, lost, or abandoned.

Mislaid Property

Mislaid Property Property that the owner has voluntarily parted with and then has inadvertently forgotten.

Property that has voluntarily been placed somewhere by the owner and then inadvertently forgotten is **mislaid property.** A person who finds mislaid property does not obtain title to it. Instead, the owner of the place where the property was mislaid becomes the caretaker of the property because it is highly likely that the true owner will return.[3] **EXAMPLE 23.9** You go to a movie theater. While paying for popcorn at the concessions stand, you set your iPhone on the counter and then leave it there. The iPhone is mislaid property, and the theater owner is entrusted with the duty of reasonable care for it. •

Lost Property

Lost Property Property that the owner has involuntarily parted with and then cannot find or recover.

Property that is *involuntarily* left is **lost property.** A finder of the property can claim title to the property against the whole world—*except the true owner.*[4] The adage "Finders keepers, losers weepers" is actually written into law—provided that the loser (the rightful owner) cannot be found. If the true owner is identified and demands that the lost property be returned, the finder must return it. In contrast, if a third party attempts to take possession of the lost property, the finder will have a better title than the third party.

EXAMPLE 23.10 Khalia works in a large library at night. As she crosses the courtyard on her way home, she finds a gold bracelet set with what seem to be precious stones. She takes the bracelet to a jeweler to have it appraised. While pretending to weigh the bracelet, the jeweler's employee removes several of the stones. If Khalia brings an action to recover the stones from the jeweler, she normally will win because she found lost property and holds title against everyone *except the true owner.* •

Conversion of Lost Property When a finder of lost property knows the true owner and fails to return the property to that person, the finder has committed the tort of *conversion* (the wrongful taking of another's property—see Chapter 4). **EXAMPLE 23.11** In *Example 23.10* above, suppose that Khalia knows that the gold bracelet she found belongs to Geneva. If Khalia does not return the bracelet, she can be held liable for conversion. • Many states require the finder to make a reasonably diligent search to locate the true owner of lost property.

KNOW THIS
A finder who appropriates the personal property of another, knowing who the true owner is, can be guilty of conversion.

---
3. The finder of mislaid property is an involuntary bailee (see pages 669–670 of this chapter).
4. For a classic English case establishing this principle, see *Armory v. Delamirie,* 93 Eng.Rep. 664 (K.B. [King's Bench] 1722).

Estray Statute A statute defining finders' rights in property when the true owners are unknown.

Estray Statutes   Many states have **estray statutes,** which encourage and facilitate the return of property to its true owner and then reward the finder for honesty if the property remains unclaimed. These laws provide an incentive for finders to report their discoveries by making it possible for them, after a specified period of time, to acquire legal title to the property they have found. Generally, the item must be lost property, not merely mislaid property, for estray statutes to apply. Estray statutes usually require the finder or the county clerk to advertise the property in an attempt to help the owner recover it.

CASE EXAMPLE 23.12   Drug smugglers often enter the United States illegally from Canada via a frozen river that flows through Van Buren, Maine. When two railroad employees walking near the railroad tracks in Van Buren found a duffel bag that contained $165,580 in cash, they reported their find to U.S. Customs agents, who took custody of the bag and cash. A drug-sniffing dog gave a positive alert on the bag for the scent of drugs. The federal government filed a lawsuit claiming title to the property under forfeiture laws, which provide that cash and property involved in illegal drug transactions are forfeited to the government.

The two employees argued that they were entitled to the $165,580 under Maine's estray statute. The statute required finders to (1) provide written notice to the town clerk within seven days after finding the property, (2) post a public notice in the town, and (3) advertise in the town's newspaper for one month. The employees had not fulfilled these requirements, and so the court ruled that they had not acquired title to the property. Thus, the federal government had a right to seize the cash.[5] ●

Abandoned Property

Abandoned Property Property that has been discarded by the owner, who has no intention of reclaiming it.

Abandoned property has been discarded by the true owner, who has no intention of reclaiming title to it. Someone who finds abandoned property acquires title to it that is good against the whole world, *including the original owner.* If a person finds abandoned property while trespassing on the property of another, however, the owner of the land, not the finder, will acquire title to the property.

An owner of lost property who eventually gives up any further attempt to find it is frequently held to have abandoned the property. **EXAMPLE 23.13**   As Aleka is driving on the freeway, her valuable designer-label scarf blows out the window. She retraces her route and searches for the scarf but cannot find it. She finally gives up her search and proceeds to her destination five hundred miles away. When Frye later finds the scarf, he acquires title to it that is good even against Aleka. By completely giving up her search, Aleka abandoned the scarf just as effectively as if she had intentionally discarded it. ●

Bailment A situation in which the personal property of one person (a bailor) is entrusted to another (a bailee), who is obligated to return the bailed property to the bailor or dispose of it as directed.

Bailor One who entrusts goods to a bailee.

Bailee One to whom goods are entrusted by a bailor.

Bailments

Many routine personal and business transactions involve bailments. A **bailment** is formed by the delivery of personal property, without transfer of title, by one person, called a **bailor,** to another, called a **bailee.** Usually, a bailment is formed for a particular purpose—for example, to loan, lease, store, repair, or transport the property. What distinguishes a bailment from a sale or a gift is that there is no passage of title and no intent to transfer title. On completion of the purpose, the bailee is obligated to return the bailed property in the same or better condition to the bailor or a third person or to dispose of it as directed.

Bailments usually are created by agreement, but not necessarily by contract, because in many bailments not all of the elements of a contract (such as mutual assent and consideration) are present. **EXAMPLE 23.14**   If Amy lends her bicycle to a friend, a bailment is created, but not by contract, because there is no consideration. Many commercial bailments, such as the delivery of clothing to the cleaners for dry cleaning, are based on contract, though. ●

Is the bailment relationship between your dry cleaner and you based on a contract?

(sturti/iStockphoto.com)

---

5. *United States v. One Hundred Sixty-Five Thousand Five Hundred Eighty Dollars ($165,580) in U.S. Currency,* 502 F.Supp.2d 114 (D.Me. 2007).

....

PREVENTING LEGAL DISPUTES

The law of bailments applies to many routine personal and business transactions. When a transaction involves a bailment, whether you realize it or not, you are subject to the obligations and duties that arise from the bailment relationship. Consequently, knowing how bailment relationships are created, and what rights, duties, and liabilities flow from ordinary bailments, is critical in avoiding legal disputes. Also important is understanding that bailees can limit the dollar amount of their liability by contract.

Elements of a Bailment

LEARNING OBJECTIVE 3
What are the three elements of a bailment?

Not all transactions involving the delivery of property from one person to another create a bailment. For such a transfer to become a bailment, the following three elements must be present:

1. Personal property.
2. Delivery of possession (without title).
3. Agreement that the property will be returned to the bailor or otherwise disposed of according to its owner's directions.

Personal Property Requirement Only personal property, not real property or persons, can be the subject of a bailment. Although bailments commonly involve *tangible* items—jewelry, cattle, automobiles, and the like—*intangible* personal property, such as promissory notes and shares of corporate stock, may also be bailed.

Delivery of Possession *Delivery of possession* means the transfer of possession of the property to the bailee. For delivery to occur, the bailee must be given exclusive possession and control over the property, and the bailee must *knowingly* accept the personal property.[6] In other words, the bailee must *intend* to exercise control over it.

If either delivery of possession or knowing acceptance is lacking, there is no bailment relationship. **EXAMPLE 23.15** Olga goes to a five-star restaurant and checks her coat at the door. In the pocket of the coat is a diamond necklace worth $20,000. In accepting the coat, the bailee does not *knowingly* also accept the necklace. Thus, a bailment of the coat exists—because the restaurant has exclusive possession and control over the coat and knowingly accepted it—but not a bailment of the necklace. ●

Physical versus Constructive Delivery Either *physical* or *constructive* delivery will result in the bailee's exclusive possession of and control over the property. As discussed earlier in the context of gifts, constructive delivery is a substitute, or symbolic, delivery. What is delivered to the bailee is not the actual property bailed (such as a car) but something so related to the property (such as the car keys) that the requirement of delivery is satisfied.

Involuntary Bailments In certain situations, a bailment is found despite the apparent lack of the requisite elements of control and knowledge. One instance occurs when the bailee acquires the property accidentally or by mistake—as in finding someone else's lost or mislaid property. A bailment is created even though the bailor did not voluntarily deliver the property to the bailee. Such bailments are called *constructive* or *involuntary* bailments. **EXAMPLE 23.16** Several corporate managers attend an urgent meeting at the law firm of Jacobs & Matheson. One of the corporate officers, Kyle Gustafson, inadvertently leaves his briefcase at the firm at the conclusion of the meeting. In this situation, a court could find that an involuntary bailment was created, even though Gustafson did not voluntarily

---

6. We are dealing here with *voluntary bailments.* This does not apply to *involuntary bailments.*

deliver the briefcase and the law firm did not intentionally accept it. If an involuntary bailment existed, the firm would be responsible for taking care of the briefcase and returning it to Gustafson. •

Bailment Agreement   A bailment agreement can be express or implied. Although a written contract is not required for bailments of less than one year (that is, the Statute of Frauds does not apply—see Chapter 8), it is a good idea to have one, especially when valuable property is involved.

The bailment agreement expressly or impliedly provides for the return of the bailed property to the bailor or to a third person, or for the disposal of the property by the bailee. The agreement presupposes that the bailee will return the identical goods originally given by the bailor. In certain types of bailments, though, such as bailments of fungible goods, the property returned need only be equivalent property.

EXAMPLE 23.17   A bailment is created when Holman stores his grain (fungible goods) in Joe's Warehouse. At the end of the storage period, however, the warehouse is not obligated to return to Holman exactly the same grain that he stored. As long as the warehouse returns grain of the same *type, grade,* and *quantity,* the warehouse—the bailee—has performed its obligation. •

Ordinary Bailments

Bailments are either *ordinary* or *special (extraordinary)*. There are three types of ordinary bailments. They are distinguished according to *which party receives a benefit from the bailment.* This factor will dictate the rights and liabilities of the parties, and the courts use it to determine the standard of care required of the bailee in possession of the personal property. The three types of ordinary bailments are as follows:

1. *Bailment for the sole benefit of the bailor.* This is a gratuitous bailment (a bailment without consideration) for the convenience and benefit of the bailor. Basically, the bailee is caring for the bailor's property as a favor. **EXAMPLE 23.18**   Allen asks Sumi, his friend, to store his car in her garage while he is away. If Sumi agrees to do so, this is a gratuitous bailment because the bailment of the car is for the sole benefit of the bailor (Allen). •

2. *Bailment for the sole benefit of the bailee.* This type of bailment typically occurs when one person lends an item to another person (the bailee) solely for the bailee's convenience and benefit. **EXAMPLE 23.19**   Allen asks to borrow Sumi's boat so that he can go sailing over the weekend. The bailment of the boat is for Allen's (the bailee's) sole benefit. •

3. *Bailment for the mutual benefit of the bailee and the bailor.* This is the most common kind of bailment and involves some form of compensation for storing items or holding property while it is being serviced. It is a contractual bailment and may be referred to as a *bailment for hire* or a *commercial bailment.* **EXAMPLE 23.20**   Allen leaves his car at a service station for an oil change. Because the service station will be paid to change Allen's oil, this is a mutual-benefit bailment. •

Rights of the Bailee   Certain rights are implicit in the bailment agreement. Generally, the bailee has the right to take possession of the property, to utilize the property for accomplishing the purpose of the bailment, to receive some form of compensation, and to limit her or his liability for the bailed goods. These rights are present (with some limitations) in varying degrees in all bailment transactions.

Right of Possession A hallmark of the bailment agreement is that the bailee acquires the *right to control and possess the property temporarily.* The bailee's right of possession permits the bailee to recover damages from any third person for damage or loss of the property. **EXAMPLE 23.21** No-Spot Dry Cleaners sends all suede leather garments to Cleanall Company for special processing. If Cleanall loses or damages any leather goods, No-Spot has the right to recover against Cleanall. • If the bailed property is stolen, the bailee has a legal right to regain possession of it.

Right to Use Bailed Property Depending on the type of bailment and the terms of the bailment agreement, a bailee may also have a right to use the bailed property. When no provision is made, the extent of use depends on how necessary it is for the goods to be at the bailee's disposal for the ordinary purpose of the bailment to be carried out. **EXAMPLE 23.22** If you borrow a friend's car to drive to the airport, you, as the bailee, would obviously be expected to use the car. In a bailment involving the long-term storage of a car, however, the bailee is not expected to use the car because the ordinary purpose of a storage bailment does not include use of the property. •

Right of Compensation Except in a gratuitous bailment, a bailee has a right to be compensated as provided for in the bailment agreement. The bailee also has a right to be reimbursed for costs incurred and services rendered in the keeping of the bailed property—even in a gratuitous bailment.

To enforce the right of compensation, the bailee has a right to place a *possessory lien* on the bailed property until he or she has been fully compensated. A lien on bailed property is referred to as a **bailee's lien,** or *artisan's lien* (see page 439 in Chapter 15). If the bailor refuses to pay or cannot pay the charges (compensation), in most states the bailee is entitled to foreclose on the lien and sell the property to recover the amount owed.

Bailee's Lien A possessory (artisan's) lien that a bailee entitled to compensation can place on the bailed property to ensure that he or she will be paid for the services provided.

Right to Limit Liability In ordinary bailments, bailees have the right to limit their liability, provided that the limitations are called to the attention of the bailor and are not against public policy. It is essential that the bailor be informed of the limitation in some way.

Even when the bailor knows of the limitation, courts consider certain types of disclaimers of liability to be against public policy and therefore illegal. The courts carefully scrutinize *exculpatory clauses,* which limit a person's liability for her or his own wrongful acts, and in bailments they are often held to be illegal. This is particularly true in bailments for the mutual benefit of the bailor and the bailee. **EXAMPLE 23.23** A receipt from a parking garage expressly disclaims liability for any damage to parked cars, regardless of the cause. Because the bailee has attempted to exclude liability for the bailee's own negligence, including the parking attendant's negligence, the clause will likely be deemed unenforceable because it is against public policy. •

Can a valet parking service disclaim all liability for any actions of its parking attendants?

(AdShooter/iStockphoto.com)

Duties of the Bailee The bailee has two basic responsibilities: (1) to take appropriate care of the property and (2) to surrender the property to the bailor or dispose of it in accordance with the bailor's instructions at the end of the bailment.

The Duty of Care The bailee must exercise reasonable care in preserving the bailed property. What constitutes reasonable care in a bailment situation normally depends on the nature and specific circumstances of the bailment.

The courts determine the appropriate standard of care on the basis of the type of bailment involved. In a bailment for the sole benefit of the bailor, the bailee need exercise only a slight degree of care. In a bailment for the sole benefit of the bailee, however, the bailee must exercise great care. In a mutual-benefit bailment, courts normally impose a reasonable standard of care—that is, the bailee must exercise the degree of care that a reasonable and prudent person would exercise in the same circumstances. Exhibit 23.1 on the facing page illustrates these concepts. A bailee's failure to exercise appropriate care in handling the bailor's property results in tort liability.

In the following case, a bailee lost computer data while he was replacing a hard drive. The court had to decide whether the bailee was negligent.

Case 23.3

Bridge Tower Dental, P.A. v. Meridian Computer Center, Inc.

Supreme Court of Idaho,
152 Idaho 569, 272 P.3d 541 (2012).
www.isc.idaho.gov[a]

(Lorado/iStockphoto.com)

FACTS Bridge Tower Dental, P.A., contracted with Meridian Computer Center, Inc., to develop a computer system for its dental practice. Bridge Tower then paid a computer consultant, Al Colson, to install the system and provide maintenance and support. In 2004, Colson noticed that one of the server's two hard drives had stopped working and that the system was backing up data only on the mirrored hard drive. After telling Bridge Tower about the problem, Colson took the server to Meridian Computer to be repaired. The owner of Meridian Computer, Jason Patten, agreed to replace the failing hard drive under the warranty.

In attempting to copy data from the mirrored hard drive, however, Patten accidentally erased all the data. Following the industry standard, Patten had not backed up the mirrored drive because he was not asked to do so. As a result, Bridge Tower lost all of its patients' records and contact information. Bridge Tower sued Meridian Computer for negligence, and the jury found for Meridian Computer. Bridge Tower appealed.

ISSUE Did Meridian Computer breach its duty of care?

DECISION Yes. The Idaho Supreme Court reversed the judgment for Meridian Computer and held that Bridge Tower was entitled to recover.

REASON The parties agreed that a bailment existed because Colson acted as Bridge Tower's agent when he entrusted the server to Meridian Computer. The court found that the bailment included both the machine and its contents, including the data that Meridian Computer lost. The court presumed that Meridian Computer was negligent because it damaged the property by erasing all the data on the mirrored hard drive. That presumption was especially appropriate here because Patten admitted that he erased the data by mistake.

Meridian Computer argued that it had complied with the industry standard in not backing up the data, but the court found that, regardless of the industry standard, Meridian Computer owed "a duty to protect and safeguard bailed property in order to return it in the same condition as it was delivered." Because Meridian Computer could not overcome the presumption of negligence, Bridge Tower was entitled to judgment as a matter of law.

CRITICAL THINKING—Legal Consideration *Based on the facts presented here, what kind of bailment existed? Explain your answer.*

---

a. Under "Supreme Court Appeals," select "Opinions" and then "Supreme Court Civil Opinions." When the page opens, scroll down to March 5, 2012, and click on the case name to access the opinion. The Supreme Court of Idaho maintains this Web site.

Duty to Return Bailed Property At the end of the bailment, the bailee normally must hand over the original property to the bailor or to someone the bailor designates, or must otherwise dispose of it as directed. This is usually a *contractual* duty arising from the bailment agreement (contract). Failure to give up possession at the time the bailment ends is a breach of contract and could result in the tort of conversion or an action based on bailee negligence. A bailee may also be liable for conversion if the goods being held are delivered to the wrong person. Hence, the bailee should verify that the person (other than the bailor) to whom the goods are given is authorized to take possession.

Exhibit 23.1 Degree of Care Required of a Bailee

Bailment for the Sole Benefit of the Bailor	Mutual-Benefit Bailment	Bailment for the Sole Benefit of the Bailee
DEGREE OF CARE →		
SLIGHT	REASONABLE	GREAT

Lost or Damaged Property   If the bailed property has been lost or is returned damaged, a court will presume that the bailee was negligent. The bailee's obligation is excused, however, if the property was destroyed, lost, or stolen through no fault of the bailee (or claimed by a third party with a superior claim). In other words, the bailee can rebut the presumption of negligence by showing that he or she exercised due care.

CASE EXAMPLE 23.24   Michael LaPlace boarded a horse at Pierre Briere's stable, where Charlene Bridgwood also boarded a horse. LaPlace had previously boarded horses at the farm owned by Bridgwood's husband, and Bridgwood had often exercised LaPlace's horses there. One day, Bridgwood helped exercise the horses at Briere's stable. During the exercise, LaPlace's horse suddenly collapsed and died. LaPlace sued Briere for negligence. The court found that there was a presumption of negligence because the horse died in Briere's care during its bailment. Nevertheless, Briere successfully rebutted that presumption by showing that Bridgwood was an experienced handler and exercised the horse in an ordinary manner. Thus, Briere was not liable for the horse's death.[7] ●

Duties of the Bailor
The duties of a bailor are essentially the same as the rights of a bailee. A bailor has a duty to compensate the bailee either as agreed or as reimbursement for costs incurred by the bailee in keeping the bailed property. A bailor also has an all-encompassing duty to provide the bailee with goods or chattels that are free from known defects that could cause injury to the bailee.

Bailor's Duty to Reveal Defects   The bailor's duty to reveal defects to the bailee translates into two rules:

1. In a *mutual-benefit bailment,* the bailor must notify the bailee of all known defects and any hidden defects that the bailor knows of or could have discovered with reasonable diligence and proper inspection.
2. In a *bailment for the sole benefit of the bailee,* the bailor must notify the bailee of any known defects.

The bailor's duty to reveal defects is based on a negligence theory of tort law. A bailor who fails to give the appropriate notice is liable to the bailee and to any other person who might reasonably be expected to come into contact with the defective article.

EXAMPLE 23.25   Rentco (the bailor) rents a tractor to Hal Iverson. Unknown to Rentco, the brake mechanism on the tractor is defective at the time the bailment is made. Rentco could have discovered the defect on reasonable inspection. Iverson uses the defective tractor and is injured, along with two other field workers, when the tractor rolls downhill out of control after failing to stop. In this situation, Rentco is liable for the injuries sustained by Iverson and the other workers because it negligently failed to discover the defect and notify Iverson. ●

---

7. *LaPlace v. Briere,* 404 N.J.Super. 585, 962 A.2d 1139 (2009).

Warranty Liability for Defective Goods   A bailor can also incur *warranty liability* based on contract law (see Chapter 12) for injuries resulting from the bailment of defective articles. Property leased by a bailor must be *fit for the intended purpose of the bailment*. Warranties of fitness arise by law in sales contracts and leases, and judges have extended these warranties to situations in which the bailees are compensated for the bailment (such as when one leaves a car with a parking attendant). Article 2A of the Uniform Commercial Code (UCC) extends the implied warranties of merchantability and fitness for a particular purpose to bailments whenever the bailments include rights to use the bailed goods.[8]

Special Types of Bailments

In certain special types of bailment transactions, the bailee's duty of care is *extraordinary,* and the bailee's liability for loss or damage to the property is absolute. These special situations usually involve bailments made by common carriers and hotel operators. Warehouse companies have the same duty of care as ordinary bailees, but, like carriers, they are subject to extensive regulation under federal and state laws, including Article 7 of the UCC.

Common Carriers   *Common carriers* are publicly licensed to transport goods or passengers on regular routes at set rates. They provide transportation services to the general public, in contrast to private carriers, which operate transportation facilities for a select clientele.

Common carriers are legally bound to carry all passengers or freight as long as there is enough space, the fee is paid, and there are no reasonable grounds to refuse to do so. A private carrier is not required to provide service to every person or company making a request.

Strict Liability Applies   The delivery of goods to a common carrier creates a bailment relationship between the shipper (bailor) and the common carrier (bailee). Unlike ordinary bailees, the common carrier is held to a standard of care based on *strict liability,* rather than reasonable care, in protecting the bailed personal property. This means that the common carrier is absolutely liable, regardless of due care, for all loss or damage to goods except in limited circumstances, such as when damage was caused by a natural disaster or war.

Limitations on Liability   Common carriers cannot contract away their liability for damaged goods. Subject to government regulations, however, they are permitted to limit their dollar liability to an amount stated on the shipment contract or rate filing.[9]   **CASE EXAMPLE 23.26**   A jewelry store used UPS to ship a diamond ring worth $105,000. The owner of the jewelry store arranged for the shipment on UPS's Web site, which required him to click on two on-screen boxes to agree to "My UPS Terms and Conditions." Among these terms, UPS and its insurer limited their liability and the amount of insurance coverage on packages to $50,000 and refused to ship items worth more than $50,000. Both UPS and its insurer disclaimed liability *entirely* for such items.

When the ring was lost, the jewelry store filed suit against UPS to recover $50,000 under the insurance policy. The court held that UPS's disclaimer of liability was enforceable. It also found that the jewelry store had breached the contract by indicating that the shipment was worth less than $50,000 when the ring was worth a lot more.[10] •

---

8. UCC 2A–212, 2A–213.
9. Federal laws require common carriers to offer shippers the opportunity to obtain higher dollar limits for loss by paying a higher fee for the transport.
10. *Treiber & Straub, Inc. v. United Parcel Service, Inc.,* 474 F.3d 379 (7th Cir. 2007).

Warehouse Companies *Warehousing* is the business of storing property for compensation.[11] Like ordinary bailees, warehouse companies are liable for loss or damage to property resulting from *negligence*. A warehouse company, though, is a professional bailee and is therefore expected to exercise a high degree of care to protect and preserve the goods. A warehouse company can limit the dollar amount of its liability, but the bailor must be given the option of paying an increased storage rate for an increase in the liability limit.

Unlike ordinary bailees, a warehouse company can issue *documents of title*—in particular, *warehouse receipts*—and is subject to extensive government regulation, including Article 7 of the UCC.[12] A warehouse receipt describes the bailed property and the terms of the bailment contract. It can be negotiable or nonnegotiable, depending on how it is written. It is negotiable if its terms provide that the warehouse company will deliver the goods "to the bearer" of the receipt or "to the order of" a person named on the receipt.[13] The warehouse receipt represents the goods (that is, it indicates title) and hence has value and utility in financing commercial transactions.

EXAMPLE 23.27 Ossip delivers 6,500 cases of canned corn to Chaney, the owner of a warehouse. Chaney issues a negotiable warehouse receipt payable "to bearer" and gives it to Ossip. Ossip sells and delivers the warehouse receipt to Better Foods, Inc. Better Foods is now the owner of the corn and has the right to obtain the cases by simply presenting the warehouse receipt to Chaney. •

Hotel Operators At common law, hotel owners were strictly liable for the loss of any cash or property that guests brought into their rooms. Today, state statutes continue to apply strict liability to hotel operators for any loss or damage to their guests' personal property.

In many states, hotel operators can avoid strict liability for loss of guests' cash and valuables by (1) providing a safe in which to keep them and (2) notifying guests that a safe is available. In addition, statutes often limit the liability of hotels with regard to articles that are not kept in the safe and may limit the availability of damages in the absence of negligence. Most statutes require that the hotel post these limitations on the doors of the rooms or otherwise notify the guest. The failure of the hotel to follow the state statutory requirements can lead to liability.

EXAMPLE 23.28 A guest at the Four Seasons hotel in Washington, D.C., was traveling with jewelry valued at $1.2 million. She put the jewelry in the safe in her room, but someone came into the room and removed the jewelry from the safe without the use of force. The woman sued the hotel, which asserted that it was not liable under the state statute. A court ruled that the Four Seasons had not complied with the state statute, which required it to post the law in the guest rooms and public rooms. Therefore, the hotel could not assert the statute's limitation on liability. •

Insurance

One important aspect of personal property ownership is protecting property against loss. Most people, and most businesses, protect their property by purchasing insurance. Of course, insurance is used to protect against many other kinds of loss as well, as you will read in this section.

---

11. UCC 7–102(h) refers to the person engaged in the storing of goods for hire as a "warehouseman."

12. A *document of title* is defined in UCC 1–201(15) as any "document which in the regular course of business or financing is treated as adequately evidencing that the person in possession of it is entitled to receive, hold, and dispose of the document and the goods it covers." A *warehouse receipt* is a document of title issued by a person engaged for hire in the business of storing goods for hire.

13. UCC 7–104.

Insurance A contract in which, for a stipulated consideration, one party agrees to compensate the other for loss on a specific subject by a specified peril.

Risk A prediction concerning potential loss based on known and unknown factors.

Risk Management In the context of insurance, the transfer of certain risks from the insured to the insurance company by contractual agreement.

LEARNING OBJECTIVE 4
Is an insurance broker the agent of the insurance applicant or the agent of the insurer?

Policy In insurance law, the contract between the insurer and the insured.

Premium In insurance law, the price paid by the insured for insurance protection for a specified period of time.

Underwriter In insurance law, the insurer, or the one assuming a risk in return for the payment of a premium.

Insurable Interest An interest that exists when a person benefits from the preservation of the health or life of the insured or the property to be insured.

LEARNING OBJECTIVE 5
What is an insurable interest? When must an insurable interest exist—at the time the insurance policy is obtained, at the time the loss occurs, or both?

Insurance is a contract by which the insurance company (the insurer) promises to pay an amount or to give something of value to another (either the insured or the beneficiary) in the event that the insured is injured, dies, or sustains damage to property as a result of particular, stated contingencies. Basically, insurance is an arrangement for *transferring and allocating risk.* In many instances, **risk** can be described as a prediction concerning potential loss based on known and unknown factors. Insurance, however, involves much more than a game of chance.

Risk management normally involves the transfer of certain risks from the individual to the insurance company by a contractual agreement. The insurance contract and its provisions will be examined shortly. First, however, we look at the different types of insurance that can be obtained, insurance terminology, and the concept of insurable interest.

Classifications of Insurance

Insurance is classified according to the nature of the risk involved. For instance, fire insurance, casualty insurance, life insurance, and title insurance apply to different types of risk. Exhibit 23.2 on the facing page presents a list of selected insurance classifications. (For a discussion of insurance policies designed to cover the special kinds of risks faced by online businesses, see the *Business Application* feature on page 682.)

Insurance Terminology

An insurance contract is called a **policy,** the consideration paid to the insurer is called a **premium,** and the insurance company is sometimes called an **underwriter.** The parties to an insurance policy are the *insurer* (the insurance company) and the *insured* (the person covered by its provisions or the holder of the policy).

Insurance contracts are often obtained through an *agent,* who ordinarily works for the insurance company, or through a *broker,* who is ordinarily an *independent contractor.* When a broker deals with an applicant for insurance, the broker is, in effect, the applicant's agent and not an agent of the insurance company. In contrast, an insurance agent is an agent of the insurance company, not of the applicant. Thus, the agent owes fiduciary duties to the insurer (the insurance company), but not to the person who is applying for insurance.

As a general rule, the insurance company is bound by the acts of its insurance agents when they act within the agency relationship (discussed in Chapter 17). In most situations, state law determines the status of all parties writing or obtaining insurance.

Insurable Interest

A person can insure anything in which she or he has an **insurable interest.** In regard to real and personal property, an insurable interest exists when the insured derives a monetary benefit from the preservation and continued existence of the property. Put another way, a person has an insurable interest in property when she or he would sustain a financial loss from its destruction. Without an insurable interest, there is no enforceable contract, and a transaction to purchase insurance coverage would have to be treated as a wager.

Life Insurance   In regard to life insurance, a person must have a reasonable expectation of benefit from the continued life of another in order to have an insurable interest in that person's life. The insurable interest must exist *at the time the policy is obtained.* The benefit may be monetary (as with so-called *key-person insurance,* which insures the lives of important employees), or it may be founded on the relationship between the parties (by blood or other close relationship).

Exhibit 23.2 Selected Insurance Classifications

TYPE OF INSURANCE	COVERAGE
Accident	Covers expenses, losses, and suffering incurred by the insured because of accidents causing physical injury and any consequent disability; sometimes includes a specified payment to heirs of the insured if death results from an accident.
All-risk	Covers all losses that the insured may incur except those that are specifically excluded. Typical exclusions are war, pollution, earthquakes, and floods.
Automobile	May cover damage to automobiles resulting from specified hazards or occurrences (such as fire, vandalism, theft, or collision); normally provides protection against liability for personal injuries and property damage resulting from the operation of the vehicle.
Casualty	Protects against losses incurred by the insured as a result of being held liable for personal injuries or property damage sustained by others.
Decreasing-term life	Provides life insurance; requires uniform payments over the life (term) of the policy, but with a decreasing face value (amount of coverage).
Disability	Replaces a portion of the insured's monthly income from employment in the event that illness or injury causes a short- or long-term disability. Some states require employers to provide short-term disability insurance. Benefits typically last a set period of time.
Employer's liability	Insures an employer against liability for injuries or losses sustained by employees during the course of their employment; covers claims not covered under workers' compensation insurance.
Fidelity or guaranty	Provides indemnity against losses in trade or losses caused by the dishonesty of employees, the insolvency of debtors, or breaches of contract.
Fire	Covers losses incurred by the insured as a result of fire.
Floater	Covers movable property, as long as the property is within the territorial boundaries specified in the contract.
Homeowners'	Protects homeowners against some or all risks of loss to their residences and the residences' contents or liability arising from the use of the property.
Key-person	Protects a business in the event of the death or disability of a key employee.
Liability	Protects against liability imposed on the insured as a result of injuries to the person or property of another.
Life	Covers the death of the policyholder. On the death of the insured, the insurer pays the amount specified in the policy to the insured's beneficiary.
Major medical	Protects the insured against major hospital, medical, or surgical expenses.
Malpractice	Protects professionals (physicians, lawyers, and others) against malpractice claims brought against them by their patients or clients; a form of liability insurance.
Term life	Provides life insurance for a specified period of time (term) with no cash surrender value; usually renewable.

Property Insurance For property insurance, the insurable interest must exist at the time the loss occurs but need not exist when the policy is purchased. The existence of an insurable interest is a primary concern in determining liability under an insurance policy.

CASE EXAMPLE 23.29 ABM Industries, Inc., leased office and storage space in the World Trade Center (WTC) in New York City in 2001. ABM also ran the building's heating, ventilation, and air-conditioning systems, and maintained all of the WTC's common areas. At the time, ABM employed more than eight hundred workers at the WTC. Zurich American Insurance Company insured ABM against losses resulting from "business interruption" caused by direct physical loss or damage "to property owned, controlled, used, leased or intended for use" by ABM.

After the terrorist attacks on September 11, 2001, ABM filed a claim with Zurich to recover for the loss of all income derived from ABM's WTC operations. Zurich argued that ABM's recovery should be limited to the income lost as a result of the destruction of ABM's office and storage space and supplies. A court, however, ruled that ABM was entitled to compensation for the loss of all of its WTC operations. The court reasoned that the "policy's scope expressly includes real or personal property that the insured 'used,' 'controlled,' or 'intended for use.'" Because ABM's income depended on "the common areas and leased premises in the WTC complex," it had an insurable interest in that property at the time of the loss.[14] ●

---

14. *Zurich American Insurance Co. v. ABM Industries, Inc.*, 397 F.3d 158 (2d Cir. 2005).

The Insurance Contract

An insurance contract is governed by the general principles of contract law, although the insurance industry is heavily regulated by each state. Here, we discuss the application for insurance, the date when the contract takes effect, and some of the important provisions typically found in insurance contracts. We also discuss the cancellation of an insurance policy and defenses that insurance companies can raise against payment on a policy.

Application   The filled-in application form for insurance is usually attached to the policy and made a part of the insurance contract. Thus, an insurance applicant is bound by any false statements that appear in the application (subject to certain exceptions). Because the insurance company evaluates the risk factors based on the information included in the insurance application, misstatements or misrepresentations can void a policy, especially if the insurance company can show that it would not have extended insurance if it had known the true facts.

Effective Date   The effective date of an insurance contract—that is, the date on which the insurance coverage begins—is important. In some situations, the insurance applicant is not protected until a formal written policy is issued. For instance, if the parties agree that the policy will be issued and delivered at a later time, the contract is not effective until the policy is issued and delivered. Thus, any loss sustained between the time of application and the delivery of the policy is not covered.

Binder   In other situations, the applicant is protected between the time the application is received and the time the insurance company either accepts or rejects it. A person who seeks insurance from an insurance company's agent is usually protected from the moment the application is made, provided—for life insurance—that some form of premium has been paid. Usually, the agent will write a memorandum, or **binder**, indicating that a policy is pending and stating its essential terms.

Binder A written, temporary insurance policy.

Life Insurance   Parties may agree that a life insurance policy will be binding at the time the insured pays the first premium, or the policy may be expressly contingent on the applicant's passing a physical examination. If the applicant pays the premium but dies before having the physical examination, then in order to collect, the applicant's estate normally must show that the applicant *would have passed* the examination had he or she not died.

Coinsurance Clauses   Often, when taking out fire insurance policies, property owners insure their property for less than full value because most fires do not result in a total loss. To encourage owners to insure their property for an amount as close to full value as possible, fire insurance policies commonly include a coinsurance clause.

Typically, a *coinsurance clause* provides that if the owner insures the property up to a specified percentage—usually 80 percent—of its value, she or he will recover any loss up to the face amount of the policy. If the insurance is for less than the fixed percentage, the owner is responsible for a proportionate share of the loss.

Coinsurance applies only in instances of partial loss. The amount of the recovery is calculated by using the following formula:

$$\text{Loss} \times \left(\frac{\text{Amount of Insurance Coverage}}{\text{Coinsurance Percentage} \times \text{Property Value}} \right) = \text{Amount of Recovery}$$

EXAMPLE 23.30 Madison, who owns property valued at $200,000, takes out a policy in the amount of $100,000. If Madison then suffers a loss of $80,000, her recovery will be $50,000. Madison will be responsible for (coinsure) the balance of the loss, or $30,000, which is the amount of loss ($80,000) minus the amount of recovery ($50,000).

$$\$80,000 \times \left(\frac{\$100,000}{0.8 \times \$200,000} \right) = \$50,000$$

If Madison had taken out a policy in the amount of 80 percent of the value of the property, or $160,000, then according to the same formula, she would have recovered the full amount of the loss (the face amount of the policy). ●

Incontestability Clause A clause in a policy for life or health insurance stating that after the policy has been in force for a specified length of time (usually two or three years), the insurer cannot contest statements made in the policyholder's application.

Incontestability Clauses
Statutes commonly require that a policy for life or health insurance include an **incontestability clause.** Under this clause, after the policy has been in force for a specified length of time—often two or three years—the insurer cannot contest statements made in the application. Once a policy becomes incontestable, the insurer cannot later avoid a claim on the basis of, for instance, fraud on the part of the insured, unless the clause provides an exception for that circumstance.

Some important provisions and clauses contained in insurance contracts are defined in Exhibit 23.3 below.

Interpreting the Insurance Contract
The courts are aware that most people do not have the special training necessary to understand the intricate terminology used in insurance policies. Therefore, when disputes arise, the courts will interpret the words used in an insurance contract according to their ordinary meanings in light of the nature of the coverage involved.

When there is an ambiguity in the policy, the provision generally is interpreted *against* the insurance company. Also, when it is unclear whether an insurance contract actually exists because the written policy has not been delivered, the uncertainty normally is resolved against the insurance company. The court presumes that the policy is in effect unless the company can show otherwise. Similarly, an insurer must notify the insured of any change in coverage under an existing policy.

Exhibit 23.3 Insurance Contract Provisions and Clauses

TYPE OF CLAUSE	DESCRIPTION
Antilapse clause	An antilapse clause provides that the policy will not automatically lapse if no payment is made on the date due. Ordinarily, under such a provision, the insured has a *grace period* of thirty or thirty-one days within which to pay an overdue premium before the policy is canceled.
Appraisal clause	Insurance policies frequently provide that if the parties cannot agree on the amount of a loss covered under the policy or the value of the property lost, an appraisal, or estimate, by an impartial and qualified third party can be demanded.
Arbitration clause	Many insurance policies include clauses that call for arbitration of any disputes that arise between the insurer and the insured concerning the settlement of claims.
Incontestability clause	An incontestability clause provides that after a policy has been in force for a specified length of time—usually two or three years—the insurer cannot contest statements made in the application.
Multiple insurance	Many insurance policies include a clause providing that if the insured has multiple insurance policies that cover the same property and the amount of coverage exceeds the loss, the loss will be shared proportionately by the insurance companies.

Cancellation

The insured can cancel a policy at any time, and the insurer can cancel under certain circumstances. When an insurance company can cancel its insurance contract, the policy or a state statute usually requires that the insurer give advance written notice of the cancellation to the insured. The same requirement applies when only part of a policy is canceled. Any premium paid in advance may be refundable on the policy's cancellation. The insured may also be entitled to a life insurance policy's cash surrender value.

The insurer may cancel an insurance policy for various reasons, depending on the type of insurance. For instance, automobile insurance can be canceled for nonpayment of premiums or suspension of the insured's driver's license. Property insurance can be canceled for nonpayment of premiums, for the insured's fraud or misrepresentation, and for certain other reasons that would increase the risk assumed by the insurer.

Life and health policies can be canceled because of false statements made by the insured in the application, but the cancellation must take place before the effective date of an incontestability clause. An insurer cannot cancel—or refuse to renew—a policy for discriminatory reasons or other reasons that violate public policy, or because the insured has appeared as a witness in a case against the company.

Duties and Obligations

Both parties to an insurance contract are responsible for the obligations they assume under the contract. In addition, both the insured and the insurer have an implied duty to act in good faith.

Duties of the Insured

Good faith requires the party who is applying for insurance to disclose all material facts, including all facts that an insurer would consider in determining whether to charge a higher premium or to refuse to issue a policy altogether. Many insurance companies today require that an applicant give the company permission to access other information, such as private medical records and credit ratings, for the purpose of evaluating the risk.

Once the insurance policy is issued, the insured has three basic duties under the contract: (1) to pay the premiums as stated in the contract, (2) to notify the insurer within a reasonable time if an event occurs that gives rise to a claim, and (3) to cooperate with the insurer during any investigation or litigation.

Duties of the Insurer

Once the insurer has accepted the risk and some event occurs that gives rise to a claim, the insurer has a *duty to investigate* to determine the facts. When a policy provides insurance against third party claims, the insurer is obligated to make reasonable efforts to settle such a claim. If a settlement cannot be reached, then regardless of the claim's merit, the insurer has a *duty to defend* any suit against the insured. Usually, a policy provides that in this situation the insured must cooperate in the defense and attend hearings and trials, if necessary. The insurer also owes a *duty to pay* legitimate claims.

An insurer has a duty to provide or pay an attorney to defend its insured when a complaint alleges facts that could, if proved, impose liability on the insured within the policy's coverage. **CASE EXAMPLE 23.31** Dentist Robert Woo installed implants for one of his employees, Tina Alberts, whose family raised potbellied pigs. As a joke, while Alberts was anesthetized, Woo installed a set of "flippers" (temporary partial bridges) shaped like boar tusks and took photos. A month later, Woo's staff showed the photos to Alberts at a party. Alberts refused to return to work. She filed a suit against Woo for battery. Woo's insurance company refused to defend him in the suit, and he ended up paying Alberts $250,000 to settle her claim. Woo then sued the insurance company and won. The court held that the insurance company had a duty to defend Woo under the professional liability provision of his policy because Woo's practical joke took place during a routine dental procedure.[15] ●

---

15. *Woo v. Fireman's Fund Insurance Co.*, 161 Wash.2d 43, 164 P.3d 454 (2007).

Bad Faith Actions   Although the law of insurance generally follows contract law, most states now recognize a "bad faith" tort action against insurers. Thus, if an insurer in bad faith denies coverage of a claim, the insured may recover in tort in an amount exceeding the policy's coverage limits and may also recover punitive damages. Some courts have held insurers liable for bad faith refusals to settle claims for reasonable amounts within the policy limits.

Defenses against Payment

An insurance company can raise any of the defenses that would be valid in an ordinary action on a contract, as well as some defenses that do not apply in ordinary contract actions.

1. *Fraud or misrepresentation.* If the insurance company can show that the policy was procured by fraud or misrepresentation, it may have a valid defense for not paying on a claim. (The insurance company may also have the right to disaffirm or rescind the insurance contract.)
2. *Lack of an insurable interest.* An absolute defense exists if the insurer can show that the insured lacked an insurable interest—thus rendering the policy void from the beginning.
3. *Illegal actions of the insured.* Improper actions, such as those that are against public policy or that are otherwise illegal, can also give the insurance company a defense against the payment of a claim or allow it to rescind the contract.

An insurance company can be prevented, or estopped, from asserting some defenses that are usually available, however. For instance, an insurance company normally cannot escape payment on the death of an insured on the ground that the person's age was stated incorrectly on the application. Also, incontestability clauses prevent the insurer from asserting certain defenses.

Reviewing . . . Personal Property, Bailments, and Insurance

Vanessa Denai owned forty acres of land in rural Louisiana with a 1,600-square-foot house on it and a metal barn near the house. Denai met Lance Finney, who had been seeking a small plot of rural property to rent. After several meetings, Denai invited Finney to live on a corner of her land in exchange for Finney's assistance in cutting wood and tending her property. Denai agreed to store Finney's sailboat in her barn. With Denai's consent, Finney constructed a concrete and oak foundation on Denai's property and purchased a 190-square-foot dome from Dome Baja for $3,395. The dome was shipped by Doty Express, a transportation company licensed to serve the public. When it arrived, Finney installed the dome frame and fabric exterior so that the dome was detachable from the foundation. A year after Finney installed the dome, Denai wrote Finney a note stating, "I've decided to give you four acres of land surrounding your dome as drawn on this map." This gift violated no local land-use restrictions. Using the information presented in the chapter, answer the following questions.

1. Is the dome real property or personal property? Explain.
2. Is Denai's gift of land to Finney a testamentary gift, a gift *causa mortis,* or a gift *inter vivos?*
3. What type of bailment relationship was created when Denai agreed to store Finney's boat? What degree of care was Denai required to exercise in storing the boat?
4. What standard of care applied to the shipment of the dome by Doty Express?

DEBATE THIS: Common carriers should not be able to limit their liability.

BUSINESS APPLICATION

How Can You Manage Risk in Cyberspace?*

Companies doing business online face many risks that are not covered by traditional types of insurance. Not surprisingly, a growing number of companies are now offering policies designed to cover Web-related risks.

Insurance Coverage for Web-Related Risks

Insurance to cover Web-related incidents is frequently referred to as *network intrusion insurance*. Such insurance protects companies from losses stemming from hacking and computer viruses, programming errors, and network and Web site disruptions. It also protects against losses from theft of electronic data and assets, including intellectual property, and losses arising from claims of Web-related defamation, copyright infringement, false advertising, and violations of users' privacy rights.

InsureTrust.com, an insurer affiliated with three leading insurance companies—American International Group, Lloyd's of London, and Reliance National—is a leading provider of network intrusion insurance. Other insurers, such as Hartford Insurance and the Chubb Group of Insurance Companies, have also added insurance for Web-related perils to their offerings. Clearly, the market for such insurance is evolving rapidly, and new policies will continue to appear.

Customized Policies

Unlike traditional insurance policies, which are generally drafted by insurance companies and presented to insurance applicants on a take-it-or-leave-it basis, network intrusion policies are usually customized to protect against specific risks faced by a particular type of business. For example, an Internet service provider faces different

risks than an online merchant, and a banking institution faces different risks than a law firm. The specific business-related risks are taken into consideration when determining the policy premium.

Qualifying Criteria

Many companies that offer network intrusion insurance require applicants to meet high security standards. In other words, to qualify for a policy under an insurance company's risk management processes, a business must have Web-related security measures in place. Several companies assess the applicant's security system before underwriting a policy. For example, an insurer might assess the applicant's security measures and refuse to provide coverage unless the business scores higher than 60 percent. If the business does not score that high, it can contract with the company to improve its Web-related security.

Checklist for the Businessperson

1. Determine the types of risks that your business is exposed to on the Web and try to obtain an insurance policy that protects you against those specific risks.
2. As when procuring any type of insurance, read the policy carefully, including any exclusions contained in the fine print, before committing to it.
3. Do not be "penny wise and pound foolish" when it comes to insurance protection. Though insurance coverage may seem expensive, it may be much less costly than the loss of intellectual property or the cost of defending against a lawsuit. Opting for a higher deductible can reduce the amount you pay in premiums.
4. Find out what the company's underwriting standards are and determine whether your Web security measures meet its standards.

*This *Business Application* is not meant to substitute for the services of an attorney who is licensed to practice law in your state.

Key Terms

abandoned property 668
accession 666
bailee 668
bailee's lien 671
bailment 668
bailor 668
binder 678
chattel 660
community property 662

concurrent ownership 661
confusion 666
constructive delivery 664
dominion 665
estray statute 668
fee simple 661
gift 662
gift *causa mortis* 666

gift *inter vivos* 666
incontestability clause 679
insurable interest 676
insurance 676
joint tenancy 661
lost property 667
mislaid property 667
personal property 660

policy 676
premium 676
property 660
real property 660
trisk 676
risk management 676
tenancy in common 661
underwriter 676

Chapter Summary: Personal Property, Bailments, and Insurance

PERSONAL PROPERTY	
Definition of Personal Property (See pages 660–661.)	Personal property (personalty or chattel) includes all property not classified as real property (realty). Personal property can be tangible (such as a TV or a car) or intangible (such as stocks or bonds).
Property Ownership (See pages 661–662.)	1. *Fee simple*—The fullest ownership rights in property. Owners can use, possess, or dispose of the property as they choose during their lifetimes and pass on the property to their heirs at death. 2. *Tenancy in common*—Co-ownership in which two or more persons own an undivided interest in property. On a tenant's death, that tenant's property interest passes to his or her heirs. 3. *Joint tenancy*—Co-ownership in which two or more persons own an undivided interest in property. On the death of a joint tenant, that tenant's property interest transfers to the remaining tenant(s), *not* to the heirs of the deceased. 4. *Community property*—A form of co-ownership between a husband and wife in which each spouse technically owns an undivided one-half interest in property acquired during the marriage. This type of ownership exists only in certain states.

Acquiring Ownership of Personal Property (See pages 662–667.)	The most common way of acquiring ownership in personal property is by purchasing it. The following are additional methods of acquiring personal property:
	1. *Possession*—Property may be acquired by possession if no other person has title to it (for example, capturing wild animals or finding abandoned property).
	2. *Production*—Any product or item produced by an individual (with minor exceptions) becomes the property of that individual.
	3. *Gifts*—A gift is effective when the following conditions exist:
	  a. There is evidence of *intent* to make a gift of the property in question.
	  b. The gift is *delivered* (physically or constructively) to the donee or the donee's agent.
	  c. The gift is *accepted* by the donee.
	4. *Accession*—When value is added to personal property by the use of labor or materials, the added value generally becomes the property of the owner of the original property (although the owner sometimes must pay for good faith accessions). In rare situations, good faith accessions that substantially increase the value of the property or change its identity may cause title to pass to the improver.
	5. *Confusion*—If a person wrongfully and willfully commingles fungible goods with those of another in order to render them indistinguishable, the innocent party acquires title to the whole. Otherwise, the owners become tenants in common of the commingled goods.

Mislaid, Lost, and Abandoned Property (See pages 667–668.)	The finder of property acquires different rights depending on whether the property was mislaid, lost, or abandoned. 1. *Mislaid property*—Property that is placed somewhere voluntarily by the owner and then inadvertently forgotten. The finder does not acquire title. 2. *Lost property*—Property that is involuntarily left and forgotten. The finder can claim title to the property against the whole world *except the true owner*. 3. *Abandoned property*—Property that is discarded by the owner, who has no intention of claiming it in the future. The finder can claim title to the property against the whole world *including the original owner*.
BAILMENTS	
Elements of a Bailment (See pages 669–670.)	1. *Personal property*—Bailments involve only personal property. 2. *Delivery of possession*—For an effective bailment to exist, the bailee (the one receiving the property) must be given exclusive possession and control over the property, and in a voluntary bailment, the bailee must knowingly accept the personal property. 3. *The bailment agreement*—Expressly or impliedly provides for the return of the bailed property to the bailor or a third party, or for the disposal of the bailed property by the bailee.

Ordinary Bailments (See pages 670–674.)	1. *Types of bailments*—
	  a. Bailment for the sole benefit of the bailor—A gratuitous bailment undertaken for the sole benefit of the bailor (for example, as a favor to the bailor).
	  b. Bailment for the sole benefit of the bailee—A gratuitous loan of an article to a person (the bailee) solely for the bailee's benefit.
	  c. Mutual-benefit (contractual) bailment—The most common kind of bailment. It involves compensation between the bailee and bailor for the service provided.

Continued

Chapter Summary: Personal Property, Bailments, and Insurance—Continued

Ordinary Bailments—Continued	2. *Rights of a bailee (duties of a bailor)*—
	  a. The right of possession—Allows a bailee to sue any third persons who damage, lose, or convert the bailed property.
	  b. The right to be compensated and reimbursed for expenses—In the event of nonpayment, the bailee has the right to place a possessory (bailee's) lien on the bailed property.
	  c. The right to limit liability—An ordinary bailee can limit his or her liability for loss or damage, provided proper notice is given and the limitation is not against public policy. In special bailments, limitations on liability for negligence or on types of losses usually are not allowed, but limitations on the monetary amount of liability are permitted.
	3. *Duties of a bailee (rights of a bailor)*—
	  a. A bailee must exercise appropriate care over property entrusted to her or him. What constitutes appropriate care normally depends on the nature and circumstances of the bailment. See Exhibit 23.1 on page 673.
	  b. Bailed goods in a bailee's possession must be either returned to the bailor or disposed of according to the bailor's directions. A bailee's failure to return the bailed property creates a presumption of negligence and constitutes a breach of contract or the tort of conversion of goods.

Special Types of Bailments (See pages 674–675.)	1. *Common carriers*—Carriers that are publicly licensed to provide transportation services to the general public. A common carrier is held to a standard of care based on *strict liability*. 2. *Warehouse companies*—Warehouse operators differ from ordinary bailees in that they (a) can issue documents of title (warehouse receipts) and (b) are subject to state and federal statutes, including Article 7 of the UCC (as are common carriers). They must exercise a high degree of care over the bailed property and are liable for loss of or damage to property if they fail to do so. 3. *Hotel operators*—Operators of hotels are subject to strict liability for any loss or damage to their guests' personal property. State statutes may limit liability if the hotel provides a safe and properly notifies its guests.
INSURANCE	
Classifications (See page 676.)	See Exhibit 23.2 on page 677.
Terminology (See page 676.)	1. *Policy*—The insurance contract. 2. *Premium*—The consideration paid to the insurer for a policy. 3. *Underwriter*—The insurance company. 4. *Parties*—Include the insurer (the insurance company), the insured (the person covered by insurance), an agent (a representative of the insurance company) or a broker (ordinarily an independent contractor), and a beneficiary (a person to receive proceeds under the policy).
Insurable Interest (See pages 676–677.)	An insurable interest exists whenever an individual or entity benefits from the preservation of the health or life of the insured or the property to be insured. For life insurance, an insurable interest must exist at the time the policy is issued. For property insurance, an insurable interest must exist at the time of the loss.
The Insurance Contract (See pages 678–681.)	1. *Laws governing*—The general principles of contract law are applied. The insurance industry is also heavily regulated by the states. 2. *Application*—An insurance applicant is bound by any false statements that appear in the application (subject to certain exceptions), which is part of the insurance contract. Misstatements or misrepresentations may be grounds for voiding the policy. 3. *Effective date*—Coverage on an insurance policy can begin when a *binder* (a written memorandum indicating that a formal policy is pending and stating its essential terms) is written, when the policy is issued, at the time of contract formation, or depending on the terms of the contract, when certain conditions are met. 4. *Provisions and clauses*—See Exhibit 23.3 on page 679. Words will be given their ordinary meanings, and any ambiguity in the policy will be interpreted against the insurance company. When the written policy has not been delivered and it is unclear whether an insurance contract actually exists, the uncertainty will be resolved against the insurance company. The court will presume that the policy is in effect unless the company can show otherwise. 5. *Defenses against payment to the insured*—Defenses include misrepresentation or fraud by the applicant.

ExamPrep

ISSUE SPOTTERS

1. Quintana Corporation sends important documents to Regal Nursery, Inc., via Speedy Messenger Service. While the documents are in Speedy's care, a third party causes an accident to Speedy's delivery vehicle that results in the loss of the documents. Does Speedy have a right to recover from the third party for the loss of the documents? Why or why not? (**See page 670.**)
2. Rosa de la Mar Corporation ships a load of goods via Southeast Delivery Company. The load of goods is lost in a hurricane in Florida. Who suffers the loss? Explain your answer. (**See page 674.**)

—**Check your answers to the Issue Spotters against the answers provided in Appendix E at the end of this text.**

BEFORE THE TEST

Go to www.cengagebrain.com, enter the ISBN 9781133191353, and click on "Find" to locate this textbook's Web site. Then, click on "Access Now" under "Study Tools," and select Chapter 23 at the top. There, you will find a Practice Quiz that you can take to assess your mastery of the concepts in this chapter, as well as Flashcards, a Glossary of important terms, and Video Questions (when assigned).

For Review

Answers to the even-numbered questions in this For Review section can be found in Appendix F at the end of this text.

1. What is the difference between a joint tenancy and a tenancy in common?
2. What are the three necessary elements for an effective gift?
3. What are the three elements of a bailment?
4. Is an insurance broker the agent of the insurance applicant or the agent of the insurer?
5. What is an insurable interest? When must an insurable interest exist—at the time the insurance policy is obtained, at the time the loss occurs, or both?

Business Scenarios and Case Problems

23–1 Duties of the Bailee. Alicia owns a valuable speedboat. She is going on vacation and asks her neighbor, Maureen, to store the boat in one stall of Maureen's double garage. Maureen consents, and the boat is moved into the garage. Maureen needs some grocery items for dinner and drives to the store. She leaves the garage door open while she is gone, as is her custom, and the speedboat is stolen during that time. Discuss the standard of care traditionally required of the bailee, and determine whether Maureen breached that duty. (**See pages 671–672.**)

23–2 Question with Sample Answer—Bailments. Curtis is an executive on a business trip to the West Coast. He has driven his car on this trip and checks into the Hotel Ritz. The hotel has a guarded underground parking lot. Curtis gives his car keys to the parking lot attendant but fails to notify the attendant that his wife's $10,000 fur coat is in a box in the trunk. The next day, on checking out, he discovers that his car has been stolen. Curtis wants to hold the hotel liable for both the car and the coat. Discuss the probable success of his claim. (**See page 699.**)

—**For a sample answer to Question 23–2, go to Appendix G at the end of this text.**

23–3 Timing of Insurance Coverage. On October 10, Joleen Vora applied for a $50,000 life insurance policy with Magnum Life Insurance Co. She named her husband, Jay, as the beneficiary. Joleen paid the insurance company the first year's premium on making the application. Two days later, before she had a chance to take the physical examination required by the insurance company and before the policy was issued, Joleen was killed in an automobile accident. Jay submitted a claim to the insurance company for the $50,000. Can Jay collect? Explain. (**See page 678.**)

23–4 Spotlight on Joint Tenancy—Property Ownership. Vincent Slavin was a partner at Cantor Fitzgerald Securities in the World Trade Center (WTC) in New York City. In 1998, Slavin and Anna Baez became engaged and began living together. They placed both of their names on three accounts at Chase Manhattan Bank according to the bank's terms, which provided that "accounts with multiple owners are joint, payable to either owner or the survivor." Slavin arranged for the direct deposit of his salary and commissions into one of the accounts. On September 11, 2001, Slavin died when two planes piloted by terrorists crashed into the WTC towers, causing their collapse. At the time, the balance in the three accounts was $656,944.36. On September 14, Cantor Fitzgerald deposited an additional $58,264.73 into the direct-deposit account. Baez soon withdrew the entire amount from all of the accounts. Mary Jelnek, Slavin's mother, filed a suit against Baez to determine the ownership of the funds that had been in the accounts. In what form of ownership were the accounts held? Who is entitled to which of the funds and why? [*In re Jelnek*, 3 Misc.3d 725, 777 N.Y.S.2d 871 (2004)] **(See pages 661–662.)**

23–5   ⚖ **Case Problem with Sample Answer—Bailment Obligation.** Bob Moreland left his plane at Don Gray's aircraft repair shop to be painted. When Moreland picked up the airplane, he was disappointed in the quality of the work and pointed out numerous defects. Moreland refused to pay Gray and flew the plane to another shop to have the work redone. Gray sued to collect, contending that Moreland had no right to take the plane to another shop without giving Gray a chance to fix any defects. Gray further argued that by taking the plane, Moreland had accepted Gray's work. Moreland counterclaimed for his expenses. Which party should be awarded damages and why? [*Gray v. Moreland*, 2010 Ark.App. 207 (2010)] **(See pages 671–674.)**

—For a sample answer to Question 23–5, go to Appendix H at the end of this text.

23–6   **Bad Faith Actions.** Leo and Mary Deters owned Deters Tower Service, Inc., in Iowa. Deters Tower serviced television and radio towers and antennas in a multistate area. The firm obtained a commercial general liability policy issued by USF Insurance Co. to provide coverage for its officers, including Leo. One afternoon, Leo and two Deters Tower employees were working on a TV tower in Council Bluffs when they fell from the tower to their deaths. The workers' families filed a negligence suit against the Deters estate. USF refused to defend the Deters estate against the suit and pay any resulting claim and did not provide a reason for this response. Is USF liable to the Deters estate for this refusal? If so, on what basis might the estate recover, and how much? [*Deters v. USF Insurance Co.*, 797 N.W.2d 621 (Iowa App. 2011)] **(See page 681.)**

23–7   **Insurance Provisions and Clauses.** Darling's Rent-a-Car carried property insurance on its cars under a policy issued by Philadelphia Indemnity Insurance Co. The policy listed Darling's as the "insured." Darling's rented a car to Joshuah Farrington. In the rental contract, Farrington agreed to be responsible for any damage to the car and declined the optional insurance. Later, Farrington collided with a moose. Philadelphia paid Darling's for the damage to the car and sought to collect this amount from Farrington. Farrington argued that he was an "insured" under Darling's policy. How should "insured" be interpreted in this case? Why? [*Philadelphia Indemnity Insurance Co. v. Farrington*, 37 A.3d 305 (Me. 2012) **(See pages 677–681.)**

23–8   ⬌ **A Question of Ethics—Gifts.** Marcella Lashmett was engaged in farming in Illinois. Her daughter Christine Montgomery was also a farmer. Christine often borrowed Marcella's farm equipment. More than once, Christine used the equipment as a trade-in on the purchase of new equipment titled in Christine's name alone. After each transaction, Christine paid Marcella an agreed-to amount, and Marcella filed a gift tax return. Marcella died on December 19, 1999. Her heirs included Christine and Marcella's other daughter, Cheryl Thomas. Marcella's will gave whatever farm equipment remained on her death to Christine. If Christine chose to sell or trade any of the items, however, the proceeds were to be split equally with Cheryl. The will named Christine to handle the disposition of the estate, but she did nothing. Eventually, Cheryl filed a petition with an Illinois state court, which appointed her to administer the will. Cheryl then filed a suit against her sister to discover what assets their mother had owned. [*In re Estate of Lashmett*, 369 Ill.App.3d 1013, 874 N.E.2d 65 (4 Dist. 2007)] **(See pages 662–666.)**

1. Cheryl learned that three months before Marcella's death Christine had used Marcella's tractor as a trade-in on the purchase of a new tractor. The trade-in credit had been $55,296.28. Marcella had been paid nothing, and no gift tax return had been filed. Christine claimed, among other things, that the old tractor had been a gift. What is a "gift"? What are the elements of a gift? What do the facts suggest on this claim? Discuss.

2. Christine also claimed that she had tried to pay Marcella $20,000 on the trade-in of the tractor but that her mother had refused to accept it. Christine showed a check made out to Marcella for that amount and marked "void." Would you rule in Christine's favor on this claim? Why or why not?

Critical Thinking and Writing Assignments

23–9   💡 **Business Law Critical Thinking Group Assignment.** On learning that Sébastien planned to travel abroad, Roslyn asked him to deliver $25,000 in cash to her family in Mexico. During a customs inspection at the border, Sébastien told the customs inspector that he carried less than $10,000. The officer discovered the actual amount of cash that Sébastien was carrying, seized it, and arrested Sébastien. Roslyn asked the government to return what she claimed were her funds, arguing that the arrangement with Sébastien was a bailment and that she still held title to the cash.

1. The first group will argue that Roslyn is entitled to the cash.
2. The second group will take the position of the government and develop an argument that Roslyn's agreement with Sébastien does not qualify as a bailment.

CHAPTER 24

Real Property and Environmental Law

CHAPTER OUTLINE

- The Nature of Real Property
- Ownership Interests in Real Property
- Transfer of Ownership
- Landlord-Tenant Law
- Environmental Law

LEARNING OBJECTIVES

The five learning objectives below are designed to help improve your understanding of the chapter. After reading this chapter, you should be able to answer the following questions:

1 What is a fixture, and how does it relate to real property rights?

2 What is an easement? Describe three ways that easements are created.

3 What are the requirements for acquiring property by adverse possession?

4 What types of tenancies can be created when real property is leased?

5 What is contained in an environmental impact statement, and who must file one?

(Marje/iStockphoto.com)

"The right of property is the most sacred of all the rights of citizenship."
—Jean-Jacques Rousseau, 1712–1778 (French writer and philosopher)

From earliest times, property has provided a means for survival. Primitive peoples lived off the fruits of the land, eating the vegetation and wildlife. Later, as the vegetation was cultivated and the wildlife domesticated, property provided farmland and pasture.

Throughout history, property has continued to be an indicator of family wealth and social position. Indeed, an individual's right to his or her property has become, in the words of Jean-Jacques Rousseau, one of the "most sacred of all the rights of citizenship."

In this chapter, we examine the nature of real property and the ways in which it can be owned and transferred. We even consider the sale of a haunted house in this chapter's *Spotlight Case*. We also discuss leased property and landlord-tenant relationships. We conclude the chapter with a discussion of the major statutes that help to protect our environment.

The Nature of Real Property

Real property consists of land and the buildings, plants, and trees that are on it. Real property also includes subsurface and airspace rights, as well as personal property that has become permanently attached to real property. Whereas personal property is movable, real property—also called *real estate* or *realty*—is immovable.

Land

Land includes the soil on the surface of the earth and the natural or artificial structures that are attached to it. It further includes all the waters contained on or under the surface and much, but not necessarily all, of the airspace above it. The exterior boundaries of land extend down to the center of the earth and up to the farthest reaches of the atmosphere (subject to certain qualifications).

(Steve Mann/Shutterstock.com)

Who owns the airspace above residential land?

Airspace and Subsurface Rights

The owner of real property has rights to the airspace above the land, as well as to the soil and minerals underneath it. Limitations on either airspace rights or subsurface rights normally must be indicated on the document that transfers title at the time of purchase. When no such limitations, or *encumbrances,* are noted, a purchaser generally can expect to have an unlimited right to possession of the property.

Airspace Rights Disputes concerning airspace rights may involve the right of commercial and private planes to fly over property and the right of individuals and governments to seed clouds and produce rain artificially. Flights over private land normally do not violate property rights unless the flights are so low and so frequent that they directly interfere with the owner's enjoyment and use of the land.[1] Leaning walls or buildings and projecting eave spouts or roofs may also violate the airspace rights of an adjoining property owner.

Subsurface Rights In many states, land ownership can be separated, in that the surface of a piece of land and the subsurface may have different owners. Subsurface rights can be extremely valuable, as these rights include the ownership of minerals, oil, and natural gas. Subsurface rights would be of little value, however, if the owner could not use the surface to exercise those rights. Hence, a subsurface owner has a right (called a *profit,* to be discussed later in this chapter) to go onto the surface of the land to, for example, discover and mine minerals.

When ownership is separated into surface and subsurface rights, each owner can pass title to what she or he owns without the consent of the other owner. Of course, conflicts can arise between the surface owner's use of the property and the subsurface owner's need to extract minerals, oil, or natural gas. In that situation, one party's interest may become subservient (secondary) to the other party's interest either by statute or by case law. If the owners of the subsurface rights excavate (dig), they are absolutely liable if their excavation causes the surface to collapse. Many states have statutes that also make the excavators liable for any damage to structures on the land. Typically, these statutes provide precise requirements for excavations of various depths.

Plant Life and Vegetation

Plant life, both natural and cultivated, is also considered to be real property. In many instances, the natural vegetation, such as trees, adds greatly to the value of the realty. When

"The meek shall inherit the earth, but not the mineral rights."

J. Paul Getty, 1892–1976 (American entrepreneur and industrialist)

---

1. *United States v. Causby,* 328 U.S. 256, 66 S.Ct. 1062, 90 L.Ed. 1206 (1946).

a parcel of land is sold and the land has growing crops on it, the sale includes the crops, unless otherwise specified in the sales contract. When crops are sold by themselves, however, they are considered to be personal property or goods. Consequently, the sale of crops is a sale of goods and thus is governed by the Uniform Commercial Code (UCC) rather than by real property law.[2]

LEARNING OBJECTIVE 1

What is a fixture, and how does it relate to real property rights?

Fixture An item of personal property that has become so closely associated with real property that it is legally regarded as part of that real property.

Fixtures

Certain personal property can become so closely associated with the real property to which it is attached that the law views it as real property. Such property is known as a **fixture**— a thing affixed to realty. A thing is affixed to realty when it is attached to the realty by roots, embedded in it, or permanently attached by means of cement, plaster, bolts, nails, or screws. The fixture can be physically attached to real property or attached to another fixture. It can even be an item, such as a statue, that is not physically attached to the land, as long as the owner *intends* the property to be a fixture.

Fixtures are included in the sale of land if the sales contract does not provide otherwise. The sale of a house includes the land and the house and the garage on the land, as well as the cabinets, plumbing, and windows. Because these are permanently affixed to the property, they are considered to be a part of it. Certain items, such as drapes and window-unit air conditioners, are difficult to classify. Thus, a contract for the sale of a house or commercial realty should indicate which items of this sort are included in the sale.

Under what circumstances is an industry-quality irrigation system considered a fixture?

(Songbird839/iStockphoto.com)

CASE EXAMPLE 24.1   Sand & Sage Farm had an eight-tower center-pivot irrigation system bolted to a cement slab and connected to an underground well. The bank held a mortgage note on the farm secured by "all buildings, improvements, and fixtures." The farm's owners had also used the property as security for other loans, but the contracts for those loans did not specifically mention fixtures or the irrigation system. Later, when Sand & Sage filed for bankruptcy, a dispute arose between the bank and another creditor over the irrigation system. The court held that the irrigation system was a fixture because it was firmly attached to the land and integral to the operation of the farm. Therefore, the bank's security interest had priority over the other creditor's interest.[3] ●

PREVENTING LEGAL DISPUTES

When real property is being sold, transferred, or subjected to a security interest, make sure that any contract specifically lists which fixtures are to be included. Without such a list, the parties may have very different ideas as to what is being transferred with the real property (or included as collateral for a loan). It is much simpler and less expensive to itemize fixtures in a contract than to engage in litigation.

"Few . . . men own their property. The property owns them."

Robert G. Ingersoll, 1833–1899 (American politician and lecturer)

Ownership Interests in Real Property

Ownership of property is an abstract concept that cannot exist independently of the legal system. No one can actually possess or *hold* a piece of land, the airspace above it, the earth below it, and all the water contained on it. The legal system therefore recognizes certain rights and duties that constitute ownership interests in real property.

---

2. See UCC 2–107(2), discussed in Chapters 10 and 11.
3. *In re Sand & Sage Farm & Ranch, Inc.*, 266 Bankr. 507 (D.Kans. 2001).

Recall from Chapter 23 that property ownership is often viewed as a bundle of rights. One who possesses the entire bundle of rights is said to hold the property in *fee simple*, which is the most complete form of ownership. When only some of the rights in the bundle are transferred to another person, the effect is to limit the ownership rights of both the transferor of the rights and the recipient.

Ownership in Fee Simple

Fee Simple Absolute An ownership interest in land in which the owner has the greatest possible aggregation of rights, privileges, and power.

In a **fee simple absolute,** the owner has the greatest aggregation of rights, privileges, and power possible. The owner can give the property away or dispose of the property by *deed* (the instrument used to transfer property, as discussed later in this chapter) or by will. When there is no will, the fee simple ownership interest passes to the owner's legal heirs on her or his death. A fee simple is potentially infinite in duration and is assigned forever to a person and her or his heirs without limitation or condition. The owner has the rights of *exclusive* possession and use of the property.

The rights that accompany a fee simple include the right to use the land for whatever purpose the owner sees fit. Of course, other laws, including applicable zoning, noise, and environmental laws, may limit the owner's ability to use the property in certain ways. A person who uses his or her property in a manner that unreasonably interferes with others' right to use or enjoy their own property can be liable for the tort of **nuisance.**

Nuisance A common law doctrine under which persons may be held liable for using their property in a manner that unreasonably interferes with others' rights to use or enjoy their own property.

CASE EXAMPLE 24.2 Nancy and James Biglane owned and lived in a building in Natchez, Mississippi. Next door to the Biglanes' property was a popular bar, the Under the Hill Saloon, that featured live music. During the summer, the Saloon, which had no air-conditioning, opened its windows and doors, and live music echoed up and down the street. Although the Biglanes installed extra insulation, thicker windows, and air-conditioning units in their building, the noise from the Saloon kept them awake at night. Eventually, the Biglanes sued the owners of the Saloon for nuisance. The court held that the noise from the bar unreasonably interfered with the Biglanes' right to enjoy their property and enjoined (prohibited) the Saloon from opening its windows and doors while playing music.[4] ●

Life Estates

Life Estate An interest in land that exists only for the duration of the life of a specified individual, usually the holder of the estate.

Conveyance The transfer of title to real property from one person to another by deed or other document.

A **life estate** is an estate that lasts for the life of some specified individual. A **conveyance,** or transfer of real property, "to A for his life" creates a life estate. In a life estate, the life tenant's ownership rights cease to exist on the life tenant's death. The life tenant has the right to use the land, provided that he or she commits no waste (injury to the land). In other words, the life tenant cannot use the land in a manner that would adversely affect its value.

The life tenant is entitled to any rents generated by the land and can harvest crops from the land. If mines and oil wells are already on the land, the life tenant can extract minerals and oil and is entitled to the royalties, but he or she cannot exploit the land by creating new wells or mines.

The life tenant can create liens, *easements* (discussed next), and leases, but none can extend beyond the life of the tenant. In addition, with few exceptions, the owner of a life estate has an exclusive right to possession during her or his life.

Along with these rights, the life tenant also has some duties—to keep the property in repair and to pay property taxes. In short, the owner of the life estate has the same rights as a fee simple owner except that the life tenant must maintain the value of the property during her or his tenancy.

---

4. *Biglane v. Under the Hill Corp.*, 949 So.2d 9 (Miss.Sup.Ct. 2007).

Nonpossessory Interests

In contrast to the types of property interests just described, some interests in land do not include any rights to possess the property. These interests are therefore known as **nonpossessory interests.** They include easements, profits, and licenses.

An **easement** is the right of a person to make limited use of another person's real property without taking anything from the property. An easement, for instance, can be the right to walk or drive across another's property. In contrast, a **profit**[5] is the right to go onto land owned by another and take away some part of the land itself or some product of the land. **EXAMPLE 24.3**   Akmed owns The Dunes. Akmed gives Carmen the right to go there to remove all the sand and gravel that she needs for her cement business. Carmen has a profit. ●

Creation of an Easement or Profit
Most easements and profits are created by an express grant in a contract, deed, or will. This allows the parties to include terms defining the extent and length of time of use. In some situations, an easement or profit can also be created without an express agreement.

An easement or profit may arise by *implication* when the circumstances surrounding the division of a parcel of property imply its existence. **EXAMPLE 24.4**   Barrow divides a parcel of land that has only one well for drinking water. If Barrow conveys the half without a well to Jarad, a profit by implication arises because Jarad needs drinking water. ●

An easement may also be created by *necessity.* An easement by necessity does not require a division of property for its existence. A person who rents an apartment, for example, has an easement by necessity in the private road leading up to the apartment building.

An easement arises by *prescription* when one person exercises an easement, such as a right-of-way, on another person's land without the landowner's consent, and the use is apparent and continues for the length of time required by the applicable statute of limitations. (In much the same way, title to property may be obtained by *adverse possession,* as will be discussed on page 695.)

Termination of an Easement or Profit
An easement or profit can be terminated or extinguished in several ways. The simplest way is to deed it back to the owner of the land that is burdened by it. Another way is to abandon it and create evidence of intent to relinquish the right to use it. Mere nonuse will not extinguish an easement or profit *unless the nonuse is accompanied by an overt act showing the intent to abandon.* Also, if the owner of an easement or profit becomes the owner of the property burdened by it, then it is merged into the property.

License
In the context of real property, a **license** is the revocable right to enter onto another person's land. It is a personal privilege that arises from the consent of the owner of the land and can be revoked by the owner. A ticket to attend a movie at a theater or a concert is an example of a license.

In essence, a license grants a person the authority to enter the land of another and perform a specified act or series of acts without obtaining any permanent interest in the land. When a person with a license exceeds the authority granted and undertakes an action that is not permitted, the property owner can sue that person for trespass (discussed in Chapter 4).

Nonpossessory Interest In the context of real property, an interest that involves the right to use land but not the right to possess it.

Easement A nonpossessory right, established by express or implied agreement, to make limited use of another's property without removing anything from the property.

Profit In real property law, the right to enter onto another's property and remove something of value from that property.

LEARNING OBJECTIVE 2
What is an easement? Describe three ways that easements are created.

License In the context of real property, a revocable right or privilege to enter onto another person's land.

---

5. As used here, the term *profit* does not refer to the profits made by a business firm. Rather, it means a gain or an advantage.

CASE EXAMPLE 24.5 A Catholic church granted Prince Realty Management, LLC, a three-month license to use a three-foot strip of its property adjacent to Prince's property. The license authorized Prince to "put up plywood panels," creating a temporary fence to protect Prince's property during the construction of a new building. During the license's term, Prince installed steel piles and beams on the licensed property. When Prince ignored the church's demands that these structures be removed, the church sued Prince for trespass. The court held that because the license allowed only temporary structures and Prince had exceeded its authority by installing steel piles and beams, the church was entitled to damages.[6] •

Transfer of Ownership

Ownership interests in real property are frequently transferred (conveyed) by sale, and the terms of the transfer are specified in a real estate sales contract. Often, real estate brokers or agents who are licensed by the state assist the buyers and sellers during the sales transaction. Real property ownership can also be transferred by gift, by will or inheritance, by possession, or by *eminent domain*. When ownership rights in real property are transferred, the type of interest being transferred and the conditions of the transfer normally are set forth in a *deed*.

Real Estate Sales Contracts

A contract for a sale of real property includes such terms as the purchase price, the type of deed the buyer will receive, the condition of the premises, and any items that will be included. Unless the buyer pays cash for the property, he or she must obtain financing through a mortgage loan (see pages 469–472 in Chapter 16). Real estate sales contracts are often contingent on the buyer's ability to obtain financing at or below a specified rate of interest. The contract may also be contingent on other events, such as the completion of a survey of the property and its passing one or more inspections. Normally, the buyer is responsible for having the premises inspected for physical or mechanical defects and for insect infestation.

Implied Warranty of Habitability

An implied promise by a seller of a new house that the house is fit for human habitation. Also, the implied promise by a landlord that rented residential premises are habitable.

Implied Warranties in the Sale of New Homes   Most states recognize a warranty—the **implied warranty of habitability**—in the sale of new homes. The seller of a new house warrants that it will be fit for human habitation even if the deed or contract of sale does not include such a warranty.

Essentially, the seller is warranting that the house is in reasonable working order and is of reasonably sound construction. Thus, under this warranty, the seller of a new home is in effect a guarantor of its fitness. In some states, the warranty protects not only the first purchaser but any subsequent purchaser as well.

Seller's Duty to Disclose Hidden Defects   In most jurisdictions, courts impose on sellers a duty to disclose any known defect that materially affects the value of the property and that the buyer could not reasonably discover. Failure to disclose such a material defect gives the buyer the right to rescind the contract and to sue for damages based on fraud or misrepresentation. There is usually a limit to the time within which the buyer can bring a suit against the seller based on the defect, however.

---

6. *Roman Catholic Church of Our Lady of Sorrows v. Prince Realty Management, LLC,* 47 A.D.3d 909, 850 N.Y.S.2d 569 (2008).

CASE EXAMPLE 24.6 Matthew Humphrey partially renovated a house in Louisiana and sold it to Terry and Tabitha Whitehead for $67,000. A few months after the Whiteheads moved in, they discovered rotten wood behind the tile in the bathroom and experienced problems with the fireplace and the plumbing. Two years later, the Whiteheads filed a suit against Humphrey seeking to rescind the sale. They argued that the plumbing problems were a latent defect that the seller had failed to disclose. Evidence revealed that prior to the sale, the parties were made aware of issues regarding the sewer system and corrective actions were taken. At the time of the sale, neither side realized that the defects had not been resolved. The court ruled that rescission was not warranted because the Whiteheads had waited too long after their discovery to file a claim against Humphrey.[7] ●

In the following *Spotlight Case*, the court had to decide whether a buyer—who was not told that the house he had purchased was allegedly haunted—had the right to rescind the sales contract.

---

7. *Whitehead v. Humphrey*, 954 So.2d 859 (La.App. 2007).

Spotlight on Sales of Haunted Houses

Case 24.1
Stambovsky v. Ackley
Supreme Court, Appellate Division, New York, 572 N.Y.S.2d 672, 169 A.D.2d 254 (1991).

FACTS Jeffrey Stambovsky signed a contract to buy Helen Ackley's house in Nyack, New York. After the contract was signed, Stambovsky discovered that the house was widely reputed to be haunted. The Ackley family claimed to have seen poltergeists on numerous occasions over the previous nine years. The Ackleys had been interviewed about the house in both a national publication (*Reader's Digest*) and the local newspaper. The house was included on a walking tour of Nyack, New York, as "a riverfront Victorian (with ghost)." When Stambovsky learned of the house's reputation, he sued to rescind the contract, alleging that Ackley and her real estate agent had made material misrepresentations when they failed to disclose Ackley's belief that the home was haunted.

ISSUE Was the omission of the alleged haunted nature of the house a material misrepresentation that would allow Stambovsky to rescind the contract?

DECISION Yes. The court allowed Stambovsky to rescind the contract.

REASON Ackley and her family had created the house's reputation as haunted and profited from that reputation over a number of years. That reputation harmed the resale value of the home, however. Because the Ackleys had created the impairment and knew that it was not likely to be discovered by a purchaser from out of town, they had an obligation to disclose it. They should have brought the impairment to the attention of all prospective buyers, including Stambovsky. Even though the Ackleys did not actively mislead Stambovsky, they allowed him to sign the contract knowing that he was unaware of the home's haunted reputation. Because they unfairly took advantage of his ignorance, they could not enforce the contract.

CRITICAL THINKING—Ethical Consideration *Assuming that Ackley's behavior was unethical, was it unethical because she failed to tell Stambovsky something about the house that he did not know, or was it unethical because of the nature of the information she omitted? What if Ackley had failed to mention that the roof leaked or that the well was dry—conditions that a buyer would normally investigate? Explain your answer.*

Deeds

Possession and title to land are passed from person to person by means of a **deed**—the instrument of conveyance of real property. Unlike a contract, a deed does not have to be supported by legally sufficient consideration. To be valid, a deed must include the following:

1. The names of the buyer (*grantee*) and the seller (*grantor*).
2. Words indicating an intent to convey the property (for example, "I hereby bargain, sell, grant, or give").
3. A legally sufficient description of the land.
4. The grantor's (and usually her or his spouse's) signature.
5. Delivery of the deed.

Warranty Deeds
Different types of deeds provide different degrees of protection against defects of title. A **warranty deed** makes the greatest number of *covenants*, or promises, from the grantor to the grantee and thus provides the greatest protection against defects of title. In most states, special language is required to create a general warranty deed.

Warranty deeds commonly include the following:

1. A covenant that the grantor has the title to, and the power to convey, the property.
2. A covenant of quiet enjoyment (a warranty that the buyer will not be disturbed in her or his possession of the land).
3. A covenant that transfer of the property is made without knowledge of adverse claims of third parties.

Generally, the warranty deed makes the grantor liable for all defects of title during the time that the property was held by the grantor and previous titleholders. **EXAMPLE 24.7** Julio sells a two-acre lot and office building by warranty deed to Daniel. Subsequently, a third person shows up who has better title than Julio had and forces Daniel off the property. Here, the covenant of quiet enjoyment has been breached. Daniel can sue Julio to recover the purchase price of the land, plus any other damages incurred as a result. •

Special Warranty Deeds
In contrast to a warranty deed, a **special warranty deed,** which is also referred to as a *limited warranty deed,* warrants only that the grantor or seller held good title during his or her ownership of the property. In other words, the grantor is not warranting that there were no defects of title when the property was held by previous owners. If the special warranty deed discloses all liens or other encumbrances, the seller will not be liable to the buyer if a third person subsequently interferes with the buyer's ownership.

Quitclaim Deeds
A **quitclaim deed** offers the least amount of protection against defects of title. Basically, a quitclaim deed conveys to the grantee whatever interest the grantor had. Therefore, if the grantor had no interest, then the grantee receives no interest.

Quitclaim deeds are often used when the seller, or grantor, is uncertain as to the extent of his or her rights in the property. They may also be used to release a party's interest in a particular parcel of property, such as in divorce settlements or business dissolutions when the grantors are dividing up their interests in real property.

Recording Statutes
Every jurisdiction has **recording statutes,** which allow deeds to be recorded for a fee. Deeds are recorded in the county where the property is located. Recording a deed gives notice to the public that a certain person is now the owner of a particular parcel of real estate. Thus, prospective buyers can check the public records

---

Deed A document by which title to real property is conveyed.

> ► **KNOW THIS** ◄
> Gifts of real property are common, and they require deeds even though there is no consideration for the gift.

Warranty Deed A deed that provides the greatest amount of protection for the grantee, in that the grantor promises that she or he has title to the property conveyed in the deed, that there are no undisclosed encumbrances on the property, and that the grantee will enjoy quiet possession of the property.

Special Warranty Deed A deed that warrants only that the grantor held good title during his or her ownership of the property and does not warrant that there were no defects of title when the property was held by previous owners.

Quitclaim Deed A deed that conveys only whatever interest the grantor had in the property and therefore offers the least amount of protection against defects of title.

Recording Statutes Statutes that allow deeds, mortgages, and other real property transactions to be recorded so as to provide notice to future purchasers or creditors of an existing claim on the property.

to see whether there have been earlier transactions creating interests or rights in specific parcels of real property.

Will or Inheritance

Property that is transferred on an owner's death is passed either by will or by state inheritance laws. If the owner of land dies with a will, the land passes in accordance with the terms of the will. If the owner dies without a will, state inheritance statutes prescribe how and to whom the property will pass.

Adverse Possession

Adverse Possession The acquisition of title to real property by occupying it openly, without the consent of the owner, for a period of time specified by a state statute. The occupation must be actual, exclusive, open, continuous, and in opposition to all others, including the owner.

LEARNING OBJECTIVE 3
What are the requirements for acquiring property by adverse possession?

Adverse possession is a means of obtaining title to land without delivery of a deed. Essentially, when one person possesses the property of another for a certain statutory period of time (three to thirty years, with ten years being most common), that person, called the *adverse possessor,* acquires title to the land and cannot be removed from it by the original owner. The adverse possessor may ultimately obtain a perfect title just as if there had been a conveyance by deed.

Requirements for Adverse Possession   For property to be held adversely, four elements must be satisfied:

1. Possession must be *actual and exclusive*—that is, the possessor must take sole physical occupancy of the property.
2. The possession must be *open, visible, and notorious,* not secret or clandestine. The possessor must occupy the land for all the world to see.
3. Possession must be *continuous and peaceable for the required period of time.* This requirement means that the possessor must not be interrupted in the occupancy by the true owner or by the courts.
4. Possession must be *hostile and adverse.* In other words, the possessor must claim the property as against the whole world. He or she cannot be living on the property with the permission of the owner.

Purpose of the Doctrine   There are a number of public-policy reasons for the adverse possession doctrine. These include society's interest in resolving boundary disputes, determining title when title to property is in question, and ensuring that real property remains in the stream of commerce. More fundamentally, policies behind the doctrine include rewarding possessors for putting land to productive use and punishing owners who sit on their rights too long and do not take action when they see adverse possession.

CASE EXAMPLE 24.8   Charles Scarborough and Mildred Rollins were adjoining landowners, sharing one common boundary. Based on Rollins's survey of the property, Rollins believed that she owned a portion of a gravel road located to the south of the apartment buildings she owned. In contrast, Scarborough believed that the gravel road was located totally on his property and that he owned some property north of the gravel road toward Rollins's apartment buildings. Scarborough filed a complaint seeking to quiet title to the property and prove he was the sole owner. The court ruled that Rollins owned a portion of the gravel road by adverse possession. She had used it openly for more than thirty-five years, it was generally thought to be part of her apartment complex, and she had paid taxes on it.[8] •

---

8. *Scarborough v. Rollins,* 44 So.3d 381 (Miss.App. 2010).

Eminent Domain

Eminent Domain The power of a government to take land from private citizens for public use on the payment of just compensation.

Even ownership in fee simple absolute is limited by a superior ownership. The U.S. government has an ultimate ownership right in all land. This right, known as **eminent domain,** is sometimes referred to as the *condemnation power* of government to take land for public use. It gives the government the right to acquire possession of real property in the manner directed by the U.S. Constitution and the laws of the state whenever the public interest requires it. Property may be taken only for public use, not for private benefit.

When a new public highway is to be built, for instance, the government must decide where to build it and how much land to condemn. After the government determines that a particular parcel of land is necessary for public use, it first offers to buy the property. If the owner refuses the offer, the government brings a judicial **condemnation** proceeding to obtain title to the land. Then, in another proceeding, the court determines the *fair value* of the land, which usually is approximately equal to its market value.

Condemnation The process of taking private property for public use through the government's power of eminent domain.

Taking The taking of private property by the government for public use through the power of eminent domain.

When the government uses its power of eminent domain to acquire land owned by a private party, a **taking** occurs. Under the *takings clause* of the Fifth Amendment to the U.S. Constitution, the government must pay "just compensation" to the property owner. State constitutions contain similar provisions.

The following case involved condemnation actions brought by a town to acquire rights-of-way for a natural gas pipeline to be constructed through the town. The issue was whether the pipeline was for public use, even though it was not built to furnish natural gas to the residents of that town.

Case 24.2

Town of Midland v. Morris

Court of Appeals of North Carolina,
704 S.E.2d 329 (2011).

(Lingbeek/iStockphoto.com)

FACTS The Transcontinental Pipeline transports and distributes natural gas from the Gulf of Mexico to the northeastern United States. The city of Monroe, North Carolina, decided to supply its citizens and the surrounding area with natural gas by constructing a direct connection between its natural gas distribution system and the Transcontinental Pipeline. To construct the connecting pipeline, Monroe needed to acquire the rights to property along a forty-two-mile route. To do this, Monroe entered into an agreement with the town of Midland under which Midland would acquire the property (either by voluntary transfer or by eminent domain) and grant an easement to Monroe. In exchange, Midland would have the right to install a tap on the pipeline and receive discounted natural gas services.

In 2008, Midland began the process of acquiring the property necessary for construction of the pipeline. When negotiations for voluntary acquisitions of the rights-of-way failed, Midland exercised its eminent domain authority to condemn the needed property. Midland filed fifteen condemnation actions, which the property owners (including Harry Morris) challenged. The trial court ruled in favor of Midland, and the property owners appealed. The property owners claimed, among other things, that Midland had not condemned the property for public use or benefit because Midland had no

concrete plans to furnish natural gas services from the pipeline to the city and its citizens.

ISSUE Was Midland's condemnation of property to construct a natural gas pipeline a taking for public use even though the city had no immediate plan to furnish gas to its residents?

DECISION Yes. The appellate court affirmed the lower court's decision that Midland had lawfully exercised its eminent domain power.

REASON The court chose to interpret the relevant state statutes broadly rather than narrowly. A narrow interpretation would have limited the city's power to establish a public utility to situations in which the city had a concrete plan to furnish services. Under the court's broader interpretation, it was enough that the city had a plan to develop the infrastructure and capability even if it had no immediate plan to actually furnish the services. The agreement with Monroe gave Midland control over a tap on the pipeline and the right to receive a specific amount of natural gas per day at a discounted cost.

Even though Midland might never tap into the pipeline, the court found that the condemnation satisfied the public use test

Case 24.2—Continued

because it gave the citizens of Midland a right to a definite use of the condemned property. Furthermore, the court reasoned that the availability of natural gas benefited the public by contributing to the general welfare and prosperity of the public at large. "Midland's tap on the Pipeline, and its potential to provide natural gas service, likely will spur growth, as well as provide Midland with an advantage in industrial recruitment. These opportunities

must be seen as public benefits accruing to the citizens of Midland, such that Midland's condemnations are for the public benefit."

CRITICAL THINKING—Ethical Consideration *Is it fair that a city can exercise its eminent domain power to take property even though the property will not be used immediately to benefit the city's residents? Why or why not?*

ETHICAL ISSUE

Should eminent domain be used to promote private development? Issues of fairness often arise when the government takes private property for public use. One issue is whether it is fair for a government to take property by eminent domain and then convey it to private developers. For example, suppose that a city government decides that it is in the public interest to have a larger parking lot for a local, privately owned sports stadium or to have a manufacturing plant locate in the city to create more jobs. The government may condemn certain tracts of existing housing or business property and then convey the land to the privately owned stadium or manufacturing plant. Such actions may attract private developers and businesses that provide jobs and increase tax revenues, thus revitalizing communities. But is the land really being taken for "public use," as required by the Fifth Amendment to the U.S. Constitution?

Although the United States Supreme Court has approved this type of taking, the Court also recognized that individual states have the right to pass laws that prohibit takings for economic development.[9] Thirty-five states have done exactly that, limiting the government's ability to take private property and give it to private developers. At least eight states have amended their state constitutions, and a number of other states have passed ballot measures. Thus, the debate over whether it is fair for a government to take its citizens' property for economic redevelopment continues.

Landlord-Tenant Law

Lease A contract by which the owner of real or personal property (the landlord or lessor) grants someone else (the tenant or lessee) an exclusive right to use and possess the property, usually for a specified period of time, in return for rent or some other form of payment.

A sizable amount of real property is used by people who do not own it. A **lease** is a contract by which the owner of real property (the landlord) grants someone else (the tenant) an exclusive right to use and possess the property, usually for a specified period of time, in return for rent or some other form of payment. When this occurs, a **leasehold estate** is created.

In a leasehold estate, the tenant has a *qualified* right to exclusive possession—it is qualified because the landlord has a right to enter on the premises to ensure that waste is not being committed. The *temporary* nature of possession under a lease is what distinguishes a tenant from a purchaser, who acquires title to the property. The tenant can use the land—for example, by harvesting crops—but cannot injure it by such activities as cutting down timber for sale or extracting oil.

Leasehold Estate An interest in real property that gives a tenant a qualified right to possess and/or use the property for a limited time under a lease.

Types of Tenancies

Several types of leasehold estates, or tenancies, can be created when property is leased.

Fixed-Term Tenancy A type of tenancy under which property is leased for a specified period of time, such as a month, a year, or a period of years.

Fixed-Term Tenancy

A **fixed-term tenancy,** also called a *tenancy for years,* is created by an express contract by which property is leased for a specified period of time, such as a day, a month, a year, or a period of years. Signing a one-year lease to occupy an apartment, for instance, creates a fixed-term tenancy.

---

9. See *Kelo v. City of New London, Connecticut,* 545 U.S. 469, 125 S.Ct. 2655, 162 L.Ed.2d 439 (2005).

Note that the term need not be specified by date and can be conditioned on the occurrence of an event, such as leasing a cabin for the summer or an apartment during Mardi Gras. At the end of the period specified in the lease, the lease ends (without notice), and possession of the property returns to the lessor. If the tenant dies during the period of the lease, the lease interest passes to the tenant's heirs as personal property. Often, leases include renewal or extension provisions.

Periodic Tenancy A type of tenancy created by lease for an indefinite period with payment of rent at fixed intervals, such as week to week, month to month, or year to year.

Periodic Tenancy

A **periodic tenancy** is created by a lease that does not specify how long it is to last but does specify that rent is to be paid at certain intervals. This type of tenancy is automatically renewed for another rental period unless properly terminated.

EXAMPLE 24.9 Kayla enters into a lease with Capital Properties. The lease states, "Rent is due on the tenth day of every month." This provision creates a periodic tenancy from month to month. • This type of tenancy can also extend from week to week or from year to year.

Under the common law, to terminate a periodic tenancy, the landlord or tenant must give at least one period's notice to the other party. If the tenancy extends from month to month, for example, one month's notice must be given prior to the last month's rent payment. Today, however, many state's statutes require a different period for notice of termination in a periodic tenancy.

Tenancy at Will A type of tenancy that either the landlord or the tenant can terminate without notice.

Tenancy at Will

With a **tenancy at will**, either party can terminate the tenancy without notice. This type of tenancy can arise if a landlord allows a person to live on the premises without paying rent or rents property to a tenant "for as long as both agree." Tenancies at will are rare today because most state statutes require a landlord to provide some period of notice to terminate a tenancy. States may also require a landowner to have sufficient cause to end a residential tenancy.

Tenancy at Sufferance A type of tenancy under which a tenant continues wrongfully to occupy leased property after the lease has terminated.

Tenancy at Sufferance

The mere possession of land without right is called a **tenancy at sufferance.** A tenancy at sufferance is not a true tenancy because it is created when a tenant *wrongfully* retains possession of property. Whenever a tenancy for years or a periodic tenancy ends and the tenant continues to retain possession of the premises without the owner's permission, a tenancy at sufferance is created.

When a commercial or residential tenant wrongfully retains possession, the landlord is entitled to damages. Typically, the damages are based on the fair market rental value of the premises after the expiration of the lease.

The Lease Agreement

A landlord-tenant relationship is established by a lease contract. In most states, statutes require leases for terms exceeding one year to be in writing. The lease should describe the property and indicate the length of the term, the amount of the rent, and how and when it is to be paid.

State or local law often dictates permissible lease terms. For example, a statute or ordinance might prohibit the leasing of a structure that is in a certain physical condition or is not in compliance with local building codes. As in other areas of law, the National Conference of Commissioners on Uniform State Laws has issued an act to create more uniformity in the laws governing landlord-tenant relationships. Twenty-one states have adopted variations of the Uniform Residential Landlord and Tenant Act (URLTA).

The rights and duties of landlords and tenants generally pertain to four broad areas of concern—the possession, use, maintenance, and, of course, rent of leased property.

Possession

A landlord is obligated to give a tenant possession of the property that the tenant has agreed to lease. After obtaining possession, the tenant retains the property exclusively until the lease expires, unless the lease states otherwise.

Eviction A landlord's act of depriving a tenant of possession of the leased premises.

Constructive Eviction A form of eviction that occurs when a landlord fails to perform adequately any of the duties required by the lease, thereby making the tenant's further use and enjoyment of the property exceedingly difficult or impossible.

The covenant of quiet enjoyment mentioned previously also applies to leased premises. Under this covenant, the landlord promises that during the lease term, neither the landlord nor anyone having a superior title to the property will disturb the tenant's use and enjoyment of the property. This covenant forms the essence of the landlord-tenant relationship, and if it is breached, the tenant can terminate the lease and sue for damages.

If the landlord deprives the tenant of possession of the leased property or interferes with the tenant's use or enjoyment of it, an eviction occurs. An **eviction** arises, for instance, when the landlord changes the lock and refuses to give the tenant a new key. A **constructive eviction** occurs when the landlord wrongfully performs or fails to perform any of the duties the lease requires, thereby making the tenant's further use and enjoyment of the property exceedingly difficult or impossible. Examples of constructive eviction include a landlord's failure to provide heat in the winter, electricity, or other essential utilities.

Use and Maintenance of the Premises   The tenant normally may make any use of the leased property, provided the use is legal and does not injure the landlord's interest. The parties are free to limit by agreement the uses to which the property may be put.

The tenant is responsible for any damage to the premises that he or she causes, intentionally or negligently, and may be held liable for the cost of returning the property to the physical condition it was in at the lease's inception. The tenant is not responsible for ordinary wear and tear and the property's consequent depreciation in value. Also, the tenant is not entitled to create a *nuisance* by substantially interfering with others' quiet enjoyment of their property rights (nuisance was defined on page 690 and illustrated in *Case Example 24.2*).

In some jurisdictions, landlords of residential property are required by statute to maintain the premises in good repair. Landlords must also comply with any applicable state statutes and city ordinances regarding maintenance and repair of buildings.

The *implied warranty of habitability* (see page 692) also applies to *residential* leases. It requires a landlord who leases residential property to ensure that the premises are habitable—that is, a safe and suitable place for people to live. Generally, this warranty applies to major, or *substantial,* physical defects that the landlord knows or should know about and has had a reasonable time to repair—for example, a large hole in the roof.

Rent   *Rent* is the tenant's payment to the landlord for the tenant's occupancy or use of the landlord's real property. Usually, the tenant must pay the rent even if she or he refuses to occupy the property or moves out, as long as the refusal or the move is unjustified and the lease is in force. Under the common law, if the leased premises were destroyed by fire or flood, the tenant still had to pay rent. Today, however, if an apartment building burns down, most state's laws do not require tenants to continue to pay rent.

In some situations, such as when a landlord breaches the implied warranty of habitability, a tenant may be allowed to withhold rent as a remedy. When rent withholding is authorized under a statute, the tenant must usually put the amount withheld into an *escrow account.* The funds are held in the name of the tenant and are returned to the tenant if the landlord fails to make the premises habitable.

KNOW THIS

Options that may be available to a tenant on a landlord's breach of the implied warranty of habitability include repairing the defect and deducting the cost from the rent, canceling the lease, and suing for damages.

Transferring Rights to Leased Property

Either the landlord or the tenant may wish to transfer her or his rights to the leased property during the term of the lease. If a landlord transfers complete title to the leased property to another, the tenant becomes the tenant of the new owner. The new owner may collect subsequent rent but must abide by the terms of the existing lease.

Assignment   The tenant's transfer of his or her entire interest in the leased property to a third person is an *assignment* of the lease. Many leases require the landlord's written consent for an assignment to be valid. An assignment made without such consent can be avoided (nullified). State statutes may prohibit the landlord from unreasonably withholding consent, though. In addition, a landlord who knowingly accepts rent from the assignee may be held to have waived the consent requirement.

When an assignment is valid, the assignee acquires all of the tenant's rights under the lease. Nevertheless, an assignment does not release the original tenant (the assignor) from the obligation to pay rent should the assignee default. Also, if the assignee exercises an option under the original lease to extend the term, the assigning tenant remains liable for the rent during the extension, unless the landlord agrees otherwise.

Sublease A tenant's transfer of all or part of the leased premises to a third person for a period shorter than the lease term.

Subleases The tenant's transfer of all or part of the premises for a period shorter than the lease term is a **sublease.** Many leases also require the landlord's written consent for a sublease. If the landlord's consent is required, a sublease without such permission is ineffective. Like an assignment, a sublease does not release the tenant from her or his obligations under the lease.

EXAMPLE 24.10 Derek, a student, leases an apartment for a two-year period. Although Derek had planned on attending summer school, he decides to accept a job offer in Europe for the summer months instead. Derek therefore obtains his landlord's consent to sublease the apartment to Ava. Ava is bound by the same terms of the lease as Derek, and the landlord can hold Derek liable if Ava violates the lease terms. ●

Environmental Law

We now turn to a discussion of the various ways in which businesses are regulated by the government in the interest of attempting to protect the environment. Environmental protection is not without a price. For many businesses, the costs of complying with environmental regulations are high, and for some, they may seem too high.

Common Law Actions

Common law remedies against environmental pollution originated centuries ago in England. Those responsible for operations that created dirt, smoke, noxious odors, noise, or toxic substances were sometimes held liable under common law theories of nuisance or negligence. Today, injured individuals continue to rely on the common law to obtain damages and injunctions against business polluters.

Nuisance Under the common law doctrine of nuisance, as mentioned earlier, persons may be held liable if they use their property in a manner that unreasonably interferes with others' rights to use or enjoy their own property. In applying this doctrine to polluters, the courts commonly balance the harm caused by the pollution against the costs of stopping it.

Courts have often denied injunctive relief on the ground that the hardships that would be imposed on the polluter and on the community are relatively greater than the hardships suffered by the plaintiff. **EXAMPLE 24.11** Hewitt's Factory causes neighboring landowners to suffer from smoke, soot, and vibrations. The factory, however, may be left in operation if it is the core of the local economy. The injured parties may be awarded only monetary damages, which may include compensation for the decrease in the value of their property caused by Hewitt's operation. ●

To obtain relief from pollution under the nuisance doctrine, a property owner may have to identify a distinct harm separate from that affecting the general public. This harm is referred to as a "private" nuisance. Under the common law, individuals were denied standing (access to the courts) unless they suffered a harm distinct from the harm suffered by the public at large. Some states still require this. A public authority (such as a state's attorney general) can sue to abate a "public" nuisance, though.

Toxic Tort A civil wrong arising from exposure to a toxic substance, such as asbestos, radiation, or hazardous waste.

Negligence and Strict Liability   An injured party may sue a business polluter in tort under the negligence and strict liability theories discussed in Chapter 4. The basis for a negligence action is a business's failure to use reasonable care toward a party whose injury was foreseeable and was caused by the lack of reasonable care. For instance, employees might sue an employer whose failure to use proper pollution controls contaminated the air and caused the employees to suffer respiratory illnesses. Lawsuits for personal injuries caused by exposure to a toxic substance, such as asbestos, radiation, or hazardous waste, have given rise to a growing body of tort law known as **toxic torts.**

Businesses that engage in ultrahazardous activities—such as the transportation of radioactive materials—are strictly liable for any injuries the activities cause. In a strict liability action, the injured party does not need to prove that the business failed to exercise reasonable care.

Federal Regulation

Congress has enacted a number of statutes to control the impact of human activities on the environment. Some of these laws have been passed in an attempt to improve the quality of air and water. Other laws specifically regulate toxic chemicals, including pesticides, herbicides, and hazardous wastes.

Environmental Regulatory Agencies   The primary agency regulating environmental law is the Environmental Protection Agency (EPA). Other federal agencies with authority to regulate specific environmental matters include the Department of the Interior, the Department of Defense, the Department of Labor, the Food and Drug Administration, and the Nuclear Regulatory Commission. All agencies of the federal government must take environmental factors into consideration when making significant decisions. In addition, state and local agencies also play an important role in enforcing federal environmental legislation.

Most federal environmental laws provide that private parties can sue to enforce environmental regulations if government agencies fail to do so. Typically, a threshold hurdle in such suits is meeting the requirements for standing to sue.

LEARNING OBJECTIVE 5
What is contained in an environmental impact statement, and who must file one?

Environmental Impact Statement (EIS)
A formal analysis required for any major federal action that will significantly affect the quality of the environment to determine the action's impact and explore alternatives.

Environmental Impact Statements   The National Environmental Policy Act (NEPA)[10] requires that an **environmental impact statement (EIS)** be prepared for every major federal action that significantly affects the quality of the environment. An EIS must analyze the following:

1. The impact on the environment that the action will have.
2. Any adverse effects on the environment and alternative actions that might be taken.
3. Irreversible effects the action might generate.

An action qualifies as "major" if it involves a substantial commitment of resources (monetary or otherwise). An action is "federal" if a federal agency has the power to control it. Construction by a private developer of a ski resort on federal land, for example, may require an EIS. Building or operating a nuclear plant, which requires a federal permit, requires an EIS. If an agency decides that an EIS is unnecessary, it must issue a statement supporting this conclusion. Private individuals, consumer interest groups, businesses, and others who believe that a federal agency's actions threaten the environment often use EISs as a means of challenging those actions.

---

10. 42 U.S.C. Sections 4321–4370d.

(AP Photo/David J. Phillip)

Why are stationary sources of air pollution regulated differently than mobile sources?

Air Pollution

The Clean Air Act[11] provides the basis for issuing regulations to control multistate air pollution coming from mobile sources (such as automobiles and other vehicles) and stationary sources (such as electric utilities and industrial plants).

Mobile Sources of Air Pollution   Regulations governing air pollution from automobiles and other mobile sources specify pollution standards and establish time schedules for meeting the standards. The EPA periodically updates the pollution standards to reduce the amount of emissions allowed in light of new developments and data.

The Obama administration announced a long-term goal of reducing emissions of nitrogen oxide and other pollutants, including those from automobiles, by 80 percent by 2050. In 2010, the administration ordered the EPA to develop national standards regulating fuel economy and emissions for medium- and heavy-duty trucks, starting with 2014 models.

Stationary Sources of Air Pollution   The Clean Air Act authorizes the EPA to establish air-quality standards for stationary sources (such as manufacturing plants) but recognizes that the primary responsibility for preventing and controlling air pollution rests with state and local governments.

The EPA sets primary and secondary levels of ambient standards—that is, the maximum permissible levels of certain pollutants—and the states formulate plans to achieve those standards. Different standards apply depending on whether the sources of pollution are located in clean areas or polluted areas and whether they are existing sources or major new sources.

The EPA standards are aimed at controlling *hazardous air pollutants*—those likely to cause death or serious irreversible or incapacitating illness such as cancer or neurological and reproductive damage. The Clean Air Act requires the EPA to list all regulated hazardous air pollutants on a prioritized schedule. In all, nearly two hundred substances, including asbestos, benzene, beryllium, cadmium, and vinyl chloride, have been classified as hazardous. They are emitted from stationary sources by a variety of business activities, including smelting (melting ore to produce metal), dry cleaning, house painting, and commercial baking.

Instead of establishing specific emissions standards for each hazardous air pollutant, the Clean Air Act requires major sources of pollutants to use pollution-control equipment that represents the *maximum achievable control technology,* or MACT, to reduce emissions. The EPA issues guidelines as to what equipment meets this standard.[12]

Greenhouse Gases   A growing concern has been that greenhouse gases, such as carbon dioxide (CO_2), may contribute to global warming. The Clean Air Act, as amended, does not specifically mention CO_2 emissions, however. Therefore, until 2009, the EPA did not regulate CO_2 emissions.

> "There's so much pollution in the air now that if it weren't for our lungs, there'd be no place to put it all."
>
> Robert Orben, 1927–present
> (American comedian)

---

11. 42 U.S.C. Sections 7401 *et seq.*

12. The EPA has also issued rules to regulate hazardous air pollutants emitted by landfills. See 40 C.F.R. Sections 60.750–60.759.

CASE EXAMPLE 24.12   Environmental groups and several states sued the EPA in an effort to force the agency to regulate CO_2 emissions. When the case reached the United States Supreme Court, the EPA argued that the plaintiffs lacked *standing to sue* (see page 73 of Chapter 3). The agency claimed that because global warming has widespread effects, an individual plaintiff could not show the particularized harm required for standing. The agency also maintained that it did not have authority under the Clean Air Act to address global climate change and regulate CO_2.

The Court, however, ruled that Massachusetts had standing because its coastline, including state-owned lands, faced a threat from rising sea levels potentially caused by global warming. The Court also held that the Clean Air Act's broad definition of *air pollutant* gives the EPA authority to regulate CO_2 and requires the EPA to regulate any air pollutants that might "endanger public health or welfare." Accordingly, the Court ordered the EPA to determine whether CO_2 was a pollutant that endangered the public health.[13] The EPA later concluded that greenhouse gases, including CO_2 emissions, do constitute a public danger. •

Violations of the Clean Air Act   For violations of emission limits under the Clean Air Act, the EPA can assess civil penalties of up to $25,000 per day. Additional fines of up to $5,000 per day can be assessed for other violations, such as failing to maintain the required records. To penalize those who find it more cost-effective to violate the act than to comply with it, the EPA is authorized to obtain a penalty equal to the violator's economic benefits from noncompliance. Persons who provide information about violators may be paid up to $10,000. Private individuals can also sue violators.

Those who knowingly violate the act may be subject to criminal penalties, including fines of up to $1 million and imprisonment for up to two years (for false statements or failures to report violations). Corporate officers are among those who may be subject to these penalties.

Water Pollution

Water pollution stems mostly from industrial, municipal, and agricultural sources. Pollutants entering streams, lakes, and oceans include organic wastes, heated water, sediments from soil runoff, nutrients (including fertilizers and human and animal wastes), and toxic chemicals and other hazardous substances.

The Clean Water Act   In 1972, Congress enacted the Clean Water Act (CWA) with the following goals: (1) to make waters safe for swimming, (2) to protect fish and wildlife, and (3) to eliminate the discharge of pollutants into the water. The act set specific time schedules, which were extended by amendment and by the Water Quality Act.[14] Under these schedules, the EPA limits the discharge of various types of pollutants based on the technology available for controlling them.

The CWA established a permit system, called the *National Pollutant Discharge Elimination System (NPDES)*, for regulating discharges from "point sources" of pollution. Point sources include industrial facilities, municipal facilities (such as sewer pipes and sewage treatment plants), and agricultural facilities.[15] Under this system, industrial, municipal, and agricultural polluters must apply for permits before discharging wastes into surface waters.

NPDES permits can be issued by the EPA and authorized state agencies and Indian tribes, but only if the discharge will not violate federal or state water-quality standards. Special requirements must be met to discharge toxic chemicals and residue from oil spills. NPDES permits must be renewed every five years. Although initially the NPDES system focused mainly on industrial wastewater, it was later expanded to cover storm water discharges.

---

13. *Massachusetts v. EPA*, 549 U.S. 497, 127 S.Ct. 1438, 167 L.Ed.2d 248 (2007).
14. See 33 U.S.C. Section 1251.
15. 33 U.S.C. Section 1342.

When water from rainstorms flows over streets, parking lots, commercial sites, and other developed areas, the water collects sediments, trash, used motor oil, raw sewage, pesticides, and other toxic contaminants. This polluted runoff flows into urban storm sewers, which often empty into rivers or oceans. In the following case, the plaintiffs claimed that Los Angeles County, California, was responsible for heavily polluted storm water runoff flowing into navigable rivers in the surrounding area.

Case 24.3

Natural Resources Defense Council, Inc. v. County of Los Angeles

United States Court of Appeals, Ninth Circuit, 673 F.3d 880 (2011).

Which entities can be sued for discharge of urban storm water into navigable waters?

FACTS Two environmental organizations—the Natural Resources Defense Council (NRDC) and the Santa Monica Baykeeper—brought a lawsuit against the county of Los Angeles and the Los Angeles County Flood Control District, which includes eighty-four cities and some unincorporated areas. The NRDC and Santa Monica alleged that the county and the district were discharging urban storm water runoff into navigable waters in violation of the Clean Water Act. The levels of pollutants detected in four rivers—the Santa Clara River, the Los Angeles River, the San Gabriel River, and Malibu Creek—exceeded the limits allowed in the National Pollutant Discharge Elimination System (NPDES) permit that governs municipal storm water discharges in Los Angeles County.

All parties agreed that the rivers did not meet water-quality standards. The issue was whether the NRDC and Santa Monica had proved that the county and the district were responsible. The defendants claimed that there was no evidence establishing their responsibility for discharging storm water carrying pollutants into the rivers. The federal district court held in favor of the defendants (the county and district agencies), and the NRDC and Santa Monica appealed.

ISSUE Were Los Angeles County and its Flood Control District responsible for discharging pollutants into navigable rivers?

DECISION Yes. The federal appellate court held that the agencies were liable for discharging polluted storm water into two of the four waterways. The court reversed the district court's decision regarding the Los Angeles River and the San Gabriel River

and affirmed it with regard to the other two waterways.

REASON The court noted that in Los Angeles County, storm water runoff is collected by thousands of storm drains and channeled to a main storm-sewer system, or MS4. The Los Angeles River and San Gabriel River Monitoring Stations are located in a channelized portion of the MS4 that is owned and operated by the district. Storm water known to contain standards-exceeding pollutants passes through these monitoring stations and is discharged into the two rivers. Because the monitoring makes the district aware of the pollution levels in the water, the court found that there was sufficient evidence to establish liability. The district (along with the county) was responsible for exceeding the amount of pollutants it was permitted to discharge from the storm-sewer systems into the Los Angeles River and the San Gabriel River. Evidence did not establish that the district was responsible for excess pollution in the Santa Clara River and Malibu Creek, because those monitoring stations were not located within the channelized portion of the MS4, and thus they were not under the district's control.

WHAT IF THE FACTS WERE DIFFERENT? *Suppose that Los Angeles County had moved all of its monitoring stations outside the "channelized portion of the MS4." If none of the stations that monitored pollution in the four waterways was located within the district's MS4 system, how might the outcome have been changed?*

Regulations generally specify that the *best available control technology,* or BACT, be installed to prevent water pollution. New sources must install BACT equipment before beginning operations. Existing sources are subject to timetables for the installation of BACT equipment and must immediately install equipment that utilizes the *best practical control technology,* or BPCT. The EPA issues guidelines as to what equipment meets the BACT and BPCT standards.

Wetlands Water-saturated, protected areas of land that support wildlife.

Wetlands

The CWA prohibits the filling or dredging of **wetlands** unless a permit is obtained from the Army Corps of Engineers. The EPA defines *wetlands* as "those areas that are inundated or saturated by surface or ground water at a frequency and duration sufficient to support . . . vegetation typically adapted for life in saturated soil conditions."

Wetlands are thought to be vital to the ecosystem because they filter streams and rivers and provide habitat for wildlife. In the past, the EPA's broad interpretation of what constitutes a wetland generated substantial controversy, but the courts have considerably scaled back the CWA's protection of wetlands in recent years.[16]

Violations of the Clean Water Act

Under the CWA, violators are subject to a variety of civil and criminal penalties. Depending on the violation, civil penalties range from $10,000 per day to $25,000 per day, but not more than $25,000 per violation. Criminal penalties, which apply only if a violation was intentional, range from a fine of $2,500 per day and imprisonment for up to one year to a fine of $1 million and fifteen years' imprisonment. Injunctive relief and damages can also be imposed. The polluting party can be required to clean up the pollution or pay for the cost of doing so.

Drinking Water

The Safe Drinking Water Act[17] requires the EPA to set maximum levels for pollutants in public water systems. These systems must come as close as possible to meeting the EPA's standards by using the best available technology that is economically and technologically feasible. Each year, every supplier of drinking water is required to send every household that it supplies with water a statement describing the source of its water. Suppliers must also disclose the level of any contaminants contained in the water and any possible health concerns associated with the contaminants.

The EPA is particularly concerned about contamination from underground sources, such as pesticides and wastes leaked from landfills or disposed of in underground injection wells. Many of these substances are associated with cancer and may cause damage to the central nervous system, liver, and kidneys. Although some evidence suggests that trace amounts of pharmaceuticals may be entering the nation's drinking water, the law does not yet require suppliers to test for or report these substances. The drugs come from prescription medications taken by humans and antibiotics and other medications given to livestock.

Oil Pollution

When more than 10 million gallons of oil leaked into Alaska's Prince William Sound from the *Exxon Valdez* supertanker in 1989, Congress responded by passing the Oil Pollution Act.[18] (At that time, the *Exxon Valdez* disaster was the worst oil spill in U.S. history, but the British Petroleum oil spill in the Gulf of Mexico in 2010 surpassed it.) Under this act, any onshore or offshore oil facility, oil shipper, vessel owner, or vessel operator that discharges oil into navigable waters or onto an adjoining shore can be liable for clean-up costs and damages.

Toxic Chemicals

Today, the control of toxic chemicals used in agriculture and in industry has become increasingly important.

Pesticides and Herbicides

Under the Federal Insecticide, Fungicide, and Rodenticide Act (FIFRA),[19] pesticides and herbicides must be (1) registered before they can

---

16. See, for example, *Rapanos v. United States*, 547 U.S. 715, 126 S.Ct. 2208, 165 L.Ed.2d 159 (2006).
17. 42 U.S.C. Sections 300f to 300j-25.
18. 33 U.S.C. Sections 2701–2761.
19. 7 U.S.C. Sections 135–136y.

be sold, (2) certified and used only for approved applications, and (3) used in limited quantities when applied to food crops. The EPA can cancel or suspend registration of substances that are identified as harmful and may also inspect factories where the chemicals are made. A substance is deemed harmful if people face a risk of more than a one in a million of developing cancer from any kind of exposure to the substance, including eating food that contains pesticide residues.

It is a violation of FIFRA to sell a pesticide or herbicide that is unregistered or has had its registration canceled or suspended. It is also a violation to sell a pesticide or herbicide with a false or misleading label or to destroy or deface any labeling required under the act. Penalties for commercial dealers include imprisonment for up to one year and a fine of up to $25,000. Farmers and other private users of pesticides or herbicides who violate the act are subject to a $1,000 fine and incarceration for up to thirty days.

Note that a state can also regulate the sale and use of federally registered pesticides. **CASE EXAMPLE 24.13**   The EPA conditionally registered Strongarm, a weed-killing pesticide, in 2000. Dow Agrosciences, LLC, immediately sold Strongarm to Texas peanut farmers. When the farmers applied it, however, Strongarm damaged their crops while failing to control the growth of weeds. The farmers sued Dow, but the lower courts ruled that FIFRA preempted their claims. The farmers appealed to the United States Supreme Court. The Supreme Court held that under a specific provision of FIFRA, a state can regulate the sale and use of federally registered pesticides so long as the regulation does not permit anything that FIFRA prohibits.[20] •

Toxic Substances   The Toxic Substances Control Act[21] was passed to regulate chemicals and chemical compounds that are known to be toxic and to institute investigation of any possible harmful effects from new chemical compounds. The act applies to compounds such as asbestos and polychlorinated biphenyls, popularly known as PCBs.

The regulations authorize the EPA to require that manufacturers, processors, and other organizations planning to use chemicals first determine their effects on human health and the environment. The EPA can regulate substances that potentially pose an imminent hazard or an unreasonable risk of injury to health or the environment. The EPA may require special labeling, limit the use of a substance, set production quotas, or prohibit the use of a substance altogether.

Hazardous Waste Disposal

Some industrial, agricultural, and household wastes pose more serious threats than others. If not properly disposed of, these toxic chemicals may present a substantial danger to human health and the environment. If released into the environment, they may contaminate public drinking water resources.

Resource Conservation and Recovery Act   The Resource Conservation and Recovery Act (RCRA)[22] addresses the effects of hazardous waste materials on the environment. The RCRA requires the EPA to determine which forms of solid waste should be considered hazardous and to establish regulations to monitor and control hazardous waste disposal. The act also requires all producers of hazardous waste materials to label and package properly any hazardous waste to be transported.

Under the RCRA, a company may be assessed a civil penalty of up to $25,000 for each violation. Penalties are based on the seriousness of the violation, the probability of harm, and the extent to which the violation deviates from RCRA requirements. Criminal penalties

---

20. *Bates v. Dow Agrosciences, LLC,* 544 U.S. 431, 125 S.Ct. 1788, 161 L.Ed.2d 687 (2005).
21. 15 U.S.C. Sections 2601–2692.
22. 42 U.S.C. Sections 6901 *et seq.*

include fines of up to $50,000 for each day of violation, imprisonment for up to two years (in most instances), or both. Criminal fines and the period of imprisonment can be doubled for certain repeat offenders.

Superfund

In 1980, Congress passed the Comprehensive Environmental Response, Compensation, and Liability Act (CERCLA),[23] commonly known as Superfund, to regulate the clean-up of disposal sites that are leaking hazardous waste into the environment. A special federal fund was created for that purpose.

CERCLA, as amended, has four primary elements:

1. It established an information-gathering and analysis system that enables the government to identify chemical dump sites and determine the appropriate action.
2. It authorized the EPA to respond to hazardous substance emergencies and to arrange for the clean-up of a leaking site directly if the persons responsible for the problem fail to clean up the site.
3. It created a Hazardous Substance Response Trust Fund (also called Superfund) to pay for the clean-up of hazardous sites using funds obtained through taxes on certain businesses.
4. It allowed the government to recover the cost of clean-up from the persons who were (even remotely) responsible for hazardous substance releases.

Potentially Responsible Parties under Superfund   Superfund provides that when a release or a threatened release of hazardous chemicals from a site occurs, the EPA can clean up the site and recover the cost of the clean-up from the following persons: (1) the person who generated the wastes disposed of at the site, (2) the person who transported the wastes to the site, (3) the person who owned or operated the site at the time of the disposal, or (4) the current owner or operator.

A person falling within one of these categories is referred to as a **potentially responsible party (PRP)**. If the PRPs do not clean up the site, the EPA can clean up the site and recover the clean-up costs from the PRPs.

Joint and Several Liability under Superfund   Liability under Superfund is usually joint and several—that is, a person who generated *only a fraction of the hazardous waste* disposed of at the site may nevertheless be liable for *all* of the clean-up costs. CERCLA authorizes a party who has incurred clean-up costs to bring a "contribution action" against any other person who is liable or potentially liable for a percentage of the costs.

Potentially Responsible Party (PRP)
A party liable for the costs of cleaning up a waste-disposal site under the Comprehensive Environmental Response, Compensation, and Liability Act. Any person who generated the waste, transported, owned or operated the site at the time of disposal, or owns or operates the site at the present time may be responsible for some or all of the clean-up costs.

---

23. 42 U.S.C. Sections 9601–9675.

Reviewing . . . Real Property and Environmental Law

Vern Shoepke bought a two-story home in Roche, Maine. The warranty deed did not specify what covenants would be included in the conveyance. The property was adjacent to a public park that included a popular Frisbee golf course. (Frisbee golf is a sport similar to golf but using Frisbees.) Wayakichi Creek ran along the north end of the park and along Shoepke's property. The deed allowed Roche citizens the right to walk across a five-foot-wide section of the lot beside Wayakichi Creek as part of a two-mile public trail system.

Teenagers regularly threw Frisbee golf discs from the walking path behind Shoepke's property over his yard to the adjacent park. Shoepke habitually shouted and cursed at the teenagers, demanding that they not throw the discs over his yard.

Continued

Two months after moving into his Roche home, Shoepke leased the second floor to Lauren Slater for nine months. (The lease agreement did not specify that Shoepke's consent would be required to sublease the second floor.) After three months of tenancy, Slater sublet the second floor to a local artist, Javier Indalecio. Over the remaining six months, Indalecio's use of oil paints damaged the carpeting in Shoepke's home. Using the information presented in the chapter, answer the following questions.

1. What is the term for the right of Roche citizens to walk across Shoepke's land on the trail?
2. What covenants would most courts infer were included in the warranty deed that Shoepke received when he bought his house?
3. Can Shoepke hold Slater financially responsible for the damage to the carpeting caused by Indalecio? Explain.
4. Suppose that Slater—to offset her liability for the carpet damage caused by Indalecio—files a counterclaim against Shoepke for breach of the covenant of quiet enjoyment. Could the fact that teenagers continually throw Frisbees over Shoepke's yard outside the second-floor windows arguably be a breach of the covenant of quiet enjoyment? Why or why not?

DEBATE THIS Under no circumstances should a local government be able to condemn property in order to sell it later to real estate developers for private use.

Key Terms

adverse possession 695	eviction 699	life estate 690	special warranty deed 694
condemnation 696	fee simple absolute 690	nonpossessory interest 691	sublease 700
constructive eviction 699	fixed-term tenancy 697	nuisance 690	taking 696
conveyance 690	fixture 689	periodic tenancy 698	tenancy at sufferance 698
deed 694	implied warranty of habitability 692	potentially responsible party (PRP) 707	tenancy at will 698
easement 691	lease 697	profit 691	toxic tort 701
eminent domain 696	leasehold estate 697	quitclaim deed 694	warranty deed 694
environmental impact statement (EIS) 701	license 691	recording statutes 694	wetlands 705

Chapter Summary: Real Property and Environmental Law

The Nature of Real Property (See pages 687–689.)	Real property (also called real estate or realty) is immovable. It includes land, subsurface and airspace rights, plant life and vegetation, and fixtures.
Ownership Interests in Real Property (See pages 689–692.)	1. *Fee simple absolute*—The most complete form of ownership. 2. *Life estate*—An estate that lasts for the life of a specified individual, during which time the individual is entitled to possess, use, and benefit from the estate. The life tenant's ownership rights cease to exist on her or his death. 3. *Nonpossessory interest*—An interest that involves the right to use real property but not to possess it. Easements, profits, and licenses are nonpossessory interests.
Transfer of Ownership (See pages 692–697.)	1. *By deed*—When real property is sold or transferred as a gift, title to the property is conveyed by means of a deed. A deed must meet specific legal requirements. A *warranty deed* provides the most extensive protection against defects of title. A *quitclaim deed* conveys to the grantee only whatever interest the grantor had in the property. A deed may be recorded in the manner prescribed by *recording statutes* in the appropriate jurisdiction to give third parties notice of the owner's interest. 2. *By will or inheritance*—If the owner dies after having made a valid will, the land passes as specified in the will. If the owner dies without having made a will, the heirs inherit according to state inheritance statutes. 3. *By adverse possession*—When a person possesses the property of another for a statutory period of time (ten years is the most common), that person acquires title to the property, provided the possession is actual and exclusive, open and visible, continuous and peaceable, and hostile and adverse (without the permission of the owner). 4. *By eminent domain*—The government can take land for public use, with just compensation, when the public interest requires the taking.

Chapter Summary: Real Property and Environmental Law— Continued

Landlord-Tenant Law
(See pages 697–700.)
	1. *Types of tenancies*—A tenancy, or leasehold estate, is an interest in real property that is held for only a limited period of time, as specified in the lease agreement. Types of tenancies include the following:
	   a. *Fixed-term tenancy*—Tenancy for a period of time stated by express contract.
	   b. *Periodic tenancy*—Tenancy for a period determined by the frequency of rent payments and automatically renewed unless proper notice is given.
	   c. *Tenancy at will*—Tenancy for as long as both parties agree. No notice of termination is required.
	   d. *Tenancy at sufferance*—Possession of land without legal right.
	2. *Lease agreement*—The landlord-tenant relationship is created by a lease agreement. State or local laws may dictate whether the lease must be in writing and what lease terms are permissible. The rights and duties that arise under a lease agreement generally pertain to the following areas:
	   a. Possession—The tenant has an exclusive right to possess the leased premises. Under the covenant of quiet enjoyment, the landlord promises that during the lease term, neither the landlord nor anyone having superior title to the property will disturb the tenant's use and enjoyment of the property.
	   b. Use and maintenance of the premises—Unless the parties agree otherwise, the tenant may make any legal use of the property. The tenant is responsible for any damage that he or she causes. The landlord must comply with laws that set specific standards for the maintenance of real property. The implied warranty of habitability requires that the landlord provide and maintain residential premises in a habitable condition (that is, in a condition safe and suitable for human life).
	   c. Rent—The tenant must pay the rent as long as the lease is in force, unless the tenant justifiably refuses to occupy the property or withholds the rent because of the landlord's failure to maintain the premises properly.
	3. *Transferring rights to leased property*—
	   a. If the landlord transfers complete title to the leased property, the tenant becomes the tenant of the new owner. The new owner may then collect the rent but must abide by the existing lease.
	   b. Generally, in the absence of an agreement to the contrary, tenants may assign their rights (but not their duties) under a lease contract to a third person. Tenants may also sublease leased property to a third person, but the original tenant is not relieved of any obligations to the landlord under the lease. In either situation, the landlord's consent may be required, but statutes may prohibit the landlord from unreasonably withholding consent.

Environmental Law
(See pages 700–707.)
	1. *Common law actions*—Persons may be held liable for the tort of nuisance if their use of their property unreasonably interferes with others' rights to use their own property. In addition, persons may recover damages for injuries sustained as a result of a firm's pollution-causing activities if they can demonstrate that the harm was a foreseeable result of the firm's failure to exercise reasonable care (negligence). Businesses engaging in ultrahazardous activities are liable for whatever injuries the activities cause, regardless of whether the firms exercise reasonable care.
	2. *Federal regulations*—The primary agency regulating environmental law is the federal Environmental Protection Agency (EPA), which administers most federal environmental policies and statutes.
	   a. The National Environmental Policy Act requires the preparation of an environmental impact statement (EIS) for every major federal action. An EIS must analyze the action's impact on the environment, its adverse effects and possible alternatives, and its irreversible effects on environmental quality.
	   b. Air pollution—Regulated under the authority of the Clean Air Act and its amendments.
	   c. Water pollution—Regulated under the authority of the Clean Water Act.
	   d. Toxic chemicals and hazardous waste—Pesticides and herbicides, toxic substances, and hazardous waste are regulated under the authority of the Federal Insecticide, Fungicide, and Rodenticide Act, the Toxic Substances Control Act, and the Resource Conservation and Recovery Act, respectively. The Comprehensive Environmental Response, Compensation, and Liability Act (CERCLA), as amended, regulates the clean-up of disposal sites where hazardous waste is leaking into the environment.

ExamPrep

ISSUE SPOTTERS

1. Bernie sells his house to Consuela under a warranty deed. Later, Delmira appears, holding a better title to the house than Consuela has. Delmira wants Consuela off the property. What can Consuela do? **(See page 694.)**
2. Resource Refining Company's plant emits smoke and fumes. Resource's operation includes a short railway system, and trucks enter and exit the grounds continuously. Constant vibrations from the trains and trucks rattle nearby residential

neighborhoods. The residents sue Resource. Are there any reasons that the court might refuse to shut down or limit Resource's operation? Explain. (**See pages 700–701.**)

—Check your answers to the Issue Spotters against the answers provided in Appendix E at the end of this text.

BEFORE THE TEST

Go to www.cengagebrain.com, enter the ISBN 9781133191353, and click on "Find" to locate this textbook's Web site. Then, click on "Access Now" under "Study Tools," and select Chapter 24 at the top. There, you will find a Practice Quiz that you can take to assess your mastery of the concepts in this chapter, as well as Flashcards, a Glossary of important terms, and Video Questions (when assigned).

For Review

Answers to the even-numbered questions in this For Review *section can be found in Appendix F at the end of this text.*

1. What is a fixture, and how does it relate to real property rights?
2. What is an easement? Describe three ways that easements are created.
3. What are the requirements for acquiring property by adverse possession?
4. What types of tenancies can be created when real property is leased?
5. What is contained in an environmental impact statement, and who must file one?

Business Scenarios and Case Problems

24–1   Property Ownership. Twenty-two years ago, Lorenz was a wanderer. At that time, he decided to settle down on an unoccupied, three-acre parcel of land that he did not own. People in the area told him that they had no idea who owned the property. Lorenz built a house on the land, got married, and raised three children while living there. He fenced in the land, installed a gate with a sign above it that read "Lorenz's Homestead," and removed trespassers. Lorenz is now confronted by Joe Reese, who has a deed in his name as owner of the property. Reese, claiming ownership of the land, orders Lorenz and his family off the property. Discuss who has the better "title" to the property. (**See page 695.**)

24–2   ? Question with Sample Answer—Deeds. Wiley and Gemma are neighbors. Wiley's lot is extremely large, and his present and future use of it will not involve the entire area. Gemma wants to build a single-car garage and driveway along the present lot boundary. Because the placement of her existing structures makes it impossible for her to comply with an ordinance requiring buildings to be set back fifteen feet from an adjoining property line, Gemma cannot build the garage. Gemma contracts to purchase ten feet of Wiley's property along their boundary line for $3,000. Wiley is willing to sell but will give Gemma only a quitclaim deed, whereas Gemma wants a warranty deed. Discuss the differences between these deeds as they would affect the rights of the parties if the title to this ten feet of land later proves to be defective. (**See page 694.**)

—For a sample answer to Question 24–2, go to Appendix G at the end of this text.

24–3   Environmental Laws. Fruitade, Inc., is a processor of a soft drink called Freshen Up. Fruitade uses returnable bottles, which it cleans with a special acid to allow for further beverage processing. The acid is diluted with water and then allowed to pass into a navigable stream. Fruitade crushes its broken bottles and throws the crushed glass into the stream. Discuss fully any environmental laws that Fruitade has violated. (**See pages 703–705.**)

24–4   Eviction. James owns a three-story building. He leases the ground floor to Juan's Mexican restaurant. The lease is to run for a five-year period and contains an express covenant of quiet enjoyment. One year later, James leases the top two stories to the Upbeat Club, which features live music. The club's hours run from 7:00 P.M. to 1:00 A.M. The noise from the Upbeat Club is so loud that it is driving customers away from Juan's restaurant. Juan has notified James of the interference and has called the police on a number of occasions. James refuses to talk to the owners of the Upbeat Club or to do anything to remedy the situation. Juan abandons the premises. James files a suit for breach of the lease agreement and for the rental payments still due under the lease. Juan claims that he was constructively evicted and files a countersuit for damages. Discuss who will be held liable. (**See page 699.**)

24–5   Ownership in Fee Simple. Thomas and Teresa Cline built a house on 76 acres next to Roy Berg's home in Virginia. The homes were about 1,800 feet apart but in view of each other. After several disagreements between the parties, Berg equipped an 11-foot tripod with motion sensors and floodlights that intermittently illuminated the Clines' home. Berg also installed surveillance cameras that tracked some of the movement on the Clines' property. The cameras transmitted on an open frequency, which could be received by any television within range. The Clines asked Berg to turn off, or at least redirect, the lights. When he refused, they erected a fence for 200 feet along the parties' common property line. The 32-foot-high fence consisted of 20 utility poles spaced 10 feet apart with plastic wrap stretched between the poles. This effectively blocked the lights and cameras. Berg filed a suit against the Clines in a Virginia state court, complaining that the fence interfered unreasonably with his use and enjoyment of his property. He asked the court to order the Clines to take the fence down. What are the limits on an owner's use of property? How should the court rule in this case? Why? [*Cline v. Berg*, 273 Va. 142, 639 S.E.2d 231 (2007)] **(See page 690.)**

24–6 Environmental Impact Statement. The U.S. National Park Service (NPS) manages the Grand Canyon National Park in Arizona under a management plan that is subject to periodic review. In 2006, after nine years of background work and the completion of a comprehensive environmental impact statement, the NPS issued a new management plan for the park. One part of the plan allowed for the continued use of rafts on the Colorado River, which runs through the Grand Canyon. The number of the rafts was limited, however. Several environmental groups criticized the plan because they felt that it still allowed too many rafts on the river. The groups asked a federal appellate court to overturn the plan, claiming that it violated the wilderness status of the national park. When can a federal court overturn a determination by an agency such as the NPS? Explain. [*River Runners for Wilderness v. Martin*, 593 F.3d 1064 (9th Cir. 2010)] **(See page 701.)**

24–7 Case Problem with Sample Answer—Adverse Possession. The McKeag family operated a marina on their lakefront property in Bolton, New York. For more than forty years, the McKeags used a section of property belonging to their neighbors, the Finleys, as a beach for the marina's customers. The McKeags also stored a large float on the beach during the winter months, built their own retaining wall, and planted bushes and flowers there. The McKeags prevented others from using the property, including the Finleys. Nevertheless, the families always had a friendly relationship, and one of the Finleys gave the McKeags permission to continue using the beach in 1992. He also reminded them of his ownership several times, to which they said nothing. The McKeags also asked for permission to mow grass on the property and once apologized for leaving a jet ski there. Can the McKeags establish adverse possession over the statutory period of ten years? Why or why not? [*McKeag v. Finley*, 939 N.Y.S.2d 644 (N.Y.App.Div. 2012)] **(See page 695.)**

—**For a sample answer to Problem 24–7, go to Appendix H at the end of this text.**

24–8 A Question of Ethics—Adverse Possession. Alana Mansell built a garage on her property that encroached on the property of her neighbor, Betty Hunter, by fourteen feet. Hunter knew of the encroachment and informally agreed to it, but she did not transfer ownership of the property to Mansell. A survey twenty-eight years later confirmed the encroachment, and Hunter sought the removal of the garage. Mansell asked a court to declare that she was the owner of the property by adverse possession. [*Hunter v. Mansell*, 240 P.3d 469 (Colo.App. 2010)] **(See page 695.)**

1. Did Mansell obtain title by adverse possession? Would the open occupation of the property for nearly thirty years be in Mansell's favor? Why or why not?
2. Was her conduct in any way unethical? Discuss.

Critical Thinking and Writing Assignments

24–9 Business Law Critical Thinking Group Assignment. The Wallen family owned a cabin on Lummi Island in the state of Washington. A driveway ran from the cabin across their property to South Nugent Road. Floyd Massey bought the adjacent lot and built a cabin on it in 1980. To gain access to his property, Massey used a bulldozer to extend the driveway, without the Wallens' permission but also without their objection. In 2005, the Wallens sold their property to Wright Fish Co. Massey continued to use and maintain the driveway without permission or objection. In 2010, Massey sold his property to Robert Drake. Drake and his employees continued to use and maintain the driveway without permission or objection, although Drake knew it was located largely on Wright's property. In 2012, Wright sold its lot to Robert Smersh. The next year, Smersh told Drake to stop using the driveway. Drake filed a suit against Smersh, claiming an easement by prescription (which is created by meeting the same requirements as adverse possession).

1. The first group will decide whether Drake's use of the driveway meets all of the requirements for adverse possession (easement by prescription).
2. The second group will determine how the court should rule in this case and why. Does it matter that Drake knew the driveway was located largely on Wright's (and then Smersh's) property? Should it matter?
3. A third group will evaluate the underlying policy and fairness of adverse possession laws. Should the law reward persons who take possession of someone else's land for their own use? Does it make sense to punish owners who allow someone else to use their land without complaint?

International Law in a Global Economy

(AP Photo/Shuji Kajiyama)

CHAPTER OUTLINE

- International Law— Sources and Principles
- Doing Business Internationally
- Regulation of Specific Business Activities
- Commercial Contracts in an International Setting
- Payment Methods for International Transactions
- U.S. Laws in a Global Context

LEARNING OBJECTIVES

The five learning objectives below are designed to help improve your understanding of the chapter. After reading this chapter, you should be able to answer the following questions:

1 What is the principle of comity, and why do courts deciding disputes involving a foreign law or judicial decree apply this principle?

2 What is the act of state doctrine? In what circumstances is this doctrine applied?

3 Under the Foreign Sovereign Immunities Act, in what situations is a foreign state subject to the jurisdiction of U.S. courts?

4 What are three clauses commonly included in international business contracts?

5 What federal law allows U.S. citizens, as well as citizens of foreign nations, to file civil actions in U.S. courts for torts that were committed overseas?

"The merchant has no country."
—Thomas Jefferson, 1743–1826 (Third president of the United States, 1801–1809)

International business transactions are not unique to the modern world. Indeed, commerce has always crossed national borders, as President Thomas Jefferson noted in the chapter-opening quotation. What is new in our day is the dramatic growth in world trade and the emergence of a global business community. Because exchanges of goods, services, and intellectual property on a global level are now routine, students of business law and the legal environment should be familiar with the laws pertaining to international business transactions.

Laws affecting the international legal environment of business include both international law and national law. As discussed on page 9 of Chapter 1, *international law* is defined as a body of law—formed as a result of international customs, treaties, and organizations—that governs relations among or between nations. International law may be public, creating standards for the nations themselves. It may also be private, establishing international standards for private transactions that cross national borders. *National law,* as pointed out in Chapter 1 on page 18, is the law of a particular nation, such as Brazil, Germany, Japan, or the United States.

Because there is so much uncertainty with one of our largest trading partners, the European Union (EU), issues in international law are going to be in the news for years to come. When we trade with many EU countries, we buy their goods in euros, their common currency. What will happen if some countries leave the euro zone and go back to their former domestic currencies? We can't pretend to know the answer, but you will learn enough in this chapter to be able to follow the arguments.

International Law—
Sources and Principles

The major difference between international law and national law is that government authorities can enforce national law. What government, however, can enforce international law? By definition, a *nation* is a sovereign entity—meaning that there is no higher authority to which that nation must submit. If a nation violates an international law and persuasive tactics fail, other countries or international organizations have no recourse except to take coercive actions—from severance of diplomatic relations and boycotts to, as a last resort, war—against the violating nation.

In essence, international law attempts to reconcile the need of each country to be the final authority over its own affairs with the desire of nations to benefit economically from trade and harmonious relations with one another. Sovereign nations can, and do, voluntarily agree to be governed in certain respects by international law for the purpose of facilitating international trade and commerce, as well as civilized discourse. As a result, a body of international law has evolved.

Sources of International Law

Basically, there are three sources of international law: international customs, treaties and international agreements, and international organizations and conferences. We look at each of these sources here.

International Customs   One important source of international law consists of the international customs that have evolved among nations in their relations with one another. Article 38(1) of the Statute of the International Court of Justice refers to an international custom as "evidence of a general practice accepted as law." The legal principles and doctrines that you will read about shortly are rooted in international customs and traditions that have evolved over time in the international arena.

Treaties and International Agreements   Treaties and other explicit agreements between or among foreign nations provide another important source of international law. A **treaty** is an agreement or contract between two or more nations that must be authorized and ratified by the supreme power of each nation. Under Article II, Section 2, of the U.S. Constitution, the president has the power "by and with the Advice and Consent of the Senate, to make Treaties, provided two-thirds of the Senators present concur."

A *bilateral* agreement, as the term implies, is an agreement formed by two nations to govern their commercial exchanges or other relations with one another. A *multilateral* agreement is formed by several nations. For example, regional trade associations such as the Andean Common Market (ANCOM), the Association of Southeast Asian Nations (ASEAN), and the European Union (EU) are the result of multilateral trade agreements.

International Organizations   In international law, the term **international organization** generally refers to an organization that is composed mainly of member nations

Treaty A formal international agreement negotiated between two nations or among several nations. In the United States, all treaties must be approved by the Senate.

International Organization An organization that is composed mainly of member nations and usually established by treaty—for example, the United Nations. More broadly, the term also includes nongovernmental organizations (NGOs) such as the Red Cross.

General-Secretary of the United Nations (UN) Ban Ki-moon shakes hands with U.S. Secretary of State Hillary Clinton. Why do governments support the UN?

and usually established by treaty. The United States is a member of more than one hundred bilateral and multilateral organizations, including at least twenty through the United Nations. These organizations adopt resolutions, declarations, and other types of standards that often require nations to behave in a particular manner. The General Assembly of the United Nations, for example, has adopted numerous nonbinding resolutions and declarations that embody principles of international law.

Disputes involving these resolutions and declarations may be brought before the International Court of Justice. That court, however, normally has authority to settle legal disputes only when nations voluntarily submit to its jurisdiction.

The United Nations Commission on International Trade Law has made considerable progress in establishing uniformity in international law as it relates to trade. One of the commission's most significant creations to date is the 1980 Convention on Contracts for the International Sale of Goods (CISG—see pages 314 and 315 in Chapter 10). The CISG, which is similar to Article 2 of the Uniform Commercial Code, governs only sales contracts between trading partners in nations that have ratified the CISG.

International Principles and Doctrines

Over time, a number of legal principles and doctrines have evolved and have been employed by the courts of various nations to resolve or reduce conflicts that involve a foreign element. The three important legal principles discussed next are based primarily on courtesy and respect, and are applied in the interests of maintaining harmonious relations among nations.

Comity The principle by which one nation defers to and gives effect to the laws and judicial decrees of another nation. This recognition is based primarily on respect.

LEARNING OBJECTIVE 1
What is the principle of comity, and why do courts deciding disputes involving a foreign law or judicial decree apply this principle?

The Principle of Comity   Under the principle of **comity**, one nation will defer to and give effect to the laws and judicial decrees of another country, as long as they are consistent with the law and public policy of the accommodating nation.

CASE EXAMPLE 25.1   Karen Goldberg's husband was killed in a terrorist bombing in Israel. She filed a lawsuit in a federal court in New York against UBS AG, a Switzerland-based global financial services company with many offices in the United States. Goldberg claimed that UBS was liable under the U.S. Anti-Terrorism Act for aiding and abetting the murder of her husband because it provided financial services to the international terrorist organizations responsible for his murder. UBS argued that the case should be transferred to a court in Israel, which would offer a remedy "substantially the same" as the one available in the United States. The court refused to transfer the case, however, because that would require an Israeli court to take evidence and judge the emotional damage suffered by Goldberg, "raising distinct concerns of comity and enforceability." U.S. courts hesitate to impose U.S. law on foreign courts when such law is "an unwarranted intrusion" on the policies governing a foreign nation's judicial system.[1] •

One way to understand the principle of comity (and the *act of state doctrine,* which will be discussed shortly) is to consider the relationships among the states in our federal form of government. Each state honors (gives "full faith and credit" to) the contracts, property deeds, wills, and other legal obligations formed in other states, as well as judicial decisions

---
1. *Goldberg v. UBS AG,* 690 F.Supp.2d 92 (E.D.N.Y. 2010).

with respect to such obligations. On a worldwide basis, nations similarly attempt to honor judgments rendered in other countries when it is feasible to do so. Of course, in the United States the states are constitutionally required to honor other states' actions, whereas internationally, nations are not *required* to honor the actions of other nations.

Act of State Doctrine A doctrine providing that the judicial branch of one country will not examine the validity of public acts committed by a recognized foreign government within its own territory.

The Act of State Doctrine

The **act of state doctrine** provides that the judicial branch of one country will not examine the validity of public acts committed by a recognized foreign government within its own territory.

A government controls the natural resources, such as oil reserves, within its territory. It can decide to utilize the resources or preserve them, or to establish a balance between utilization and preservation. Does the act of state doctrine apply to such decisions even though they may affect market prices in other countries? That was the question in the following case.

Case 25.1

Spectrum Stores, Inc. v. Citgo Petroleum Corp.

United States Court of Appeals, Fifth District, 632 F.3d 938 (2011).
www.ca5.uscourts.gov[a]

Citgo is a Venezuelan state-owned oil company.

FACTS Spectrum Stores, Inc., and other U.S. gasoline retailers (the plaintiffs) filed a suit against Citgo Petroleum Corporation and other oil production companies in a federal district court. The plaintiffs alleged that the defendants had conspired to fix the prices of crude oil and refined petroleum products in the United States, primarily by limiting the production of crude oil. Citgo is owned by the national oil company of Venezuela, and most of the other defendants are owned entirely or in part by Venezuela or Saudi Arabia. Both nations are members of the Organization of Petroleum Exporting Countries (OPEC), which was formed by several oil-rich nations "to ensure the stabilization of oil markets in order to secure an efficient, economic and regular supply of petroleum." Spectrum sought damages, an injunction, and other relief. The court dismissed the suit, and Spectrum appealed.

ISSUE Does the act of state doctrine prevent a federal court from considering claims that companies owned by foreign governments illegally conspired to fix oil prices in the United States?

DECISION Yes. The U.S. Court of Appeals for the Fifth Circuit affirmed the lower court's dismissal. The act of state doctrine

bars consideration of Spectrum's claims.

REASON The court reasoned that under the act of state doctrine, a U.S. court will not rule on the validity of a foreign government's acts within its own territory. It is the sovereign right of each nation to decide how to exploit its own resources. Granting relief to Spectrum would effectively have ordered foreign governments to dismantle their chosen means of exploiting the resources within their own territories. Such a decision would also have had the effect of "embarrassing" the diplomacy carried out by the executive and legislative branches of the U.S. government. In other words, a ruling in this case would have interfered with the political branches' policy of engaging with the OPEC nations through diplomacy rather than litigation to affect the global supply of oil.

CRITICAL THINKING—Legal Consideration   *If the judicial branch does not have the authority to rule on matters of foreign policy, which branch of government does? Explain.*

---

a. In the left column, in the "Opinions" section, click on "Opinions Page." On the next page, in the "Search for opinions where:" section, in the "and/or Docket number is:" box, type "09-20084" and click on "Search." Then click on the docket number to access this case opinion. (The title listed is *In re: Refined Petro, et al.*) The U.S. Court of Appeals for the Fifth Circuit maintains this Web site.

Expropriation A government's seizure of a privately owned business or personal property for a proper public purpose and with just compensation.

Confiscation A government's taking of a privately owned business or personal property without a proper public purpose or an award of just compensation.

LEARNING OBJECTIVE 2

What is the act of state doctrine? In what circumstances is this doctrine applied?

Sovereign Immunity A doctrine that immunizes foreign nations from the jurisdiction of U.S. courts when certain conditions are satisfied.

When a Foreign Government Takes Private Property The act of state doctrine can have important consequences for individuals and firms doing business with, and investing in, other countries. This doctrine is frequently employed in situations involving expropriation or confiscation.

Expropriation occurs when a government seizes a privately owned business or privately owned goods for a proper public purpose and awards just compensation. When a government seizes private property for an illegal purpose or without just compensation, the taking is referred to as a **confiscation.** The line between these two forms of taking is sometimes blurred because of differing interpretations of what is illegal and what constitutes just compensation.

> **EXAMPLE 25.2** Flaherty, Inc., a U.S. company, owns a mine in Argentina. The government of Argentina seizes the mine for public use and claims that the profits that Flaherty realized from the mine in preceding years constitute just compensation. Flaherty disagrees, but the act of state doctrine may prevent the company's recovery in a U.S. court. • Note that in a case alleging that a foreign government has wrongfully taken the plaintiff's property, the defendant government has the burden of proving that the taking was an expropriation, not a confiscation.

Doctrine May Immunize a Foreign Government's Actions When applicable, both the act of state doctrine and the doctrine of *sovereign immunity* (to be discussed next) tend to immunize (protect) foreign governments from the jurisdiction of U.S. courts. This means that firms or individuals who own property overseas often have diminished legal protection against government actions in the countries in which they operate.

The Doctrine of Sovereign Immunity When certain conditions are satisfied, the doctrine of **sovereign immunity** immunizes foreign nations from the jurisdiction of U.S. courts. In 1976, Congress codified this rule in the Foreign Sovereign Immunities Act (FSIA).[2] The FSIA exclusively governs the circumstances in which an action may be brought in the United States against a foreign nation, including attempts to attach a foreign

---

2. 28 U.S.C. Sections 1602–1611.

These are employees of Owens Illinois, a glass company. The president of Venezuela expropriated this firm. What is the difference between expropriation and confiscation?

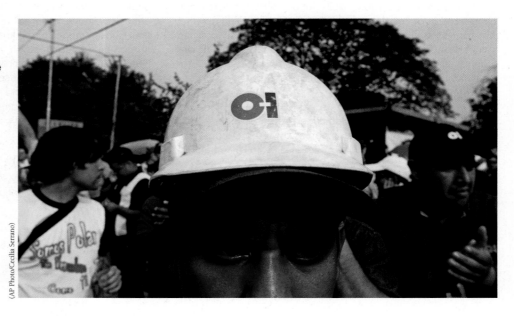

(AP Photo/Cecilia Serrano)

nation's property. Because the law is jurisdictional in nature, a plaintiff has the burden of showing that a defendant is not entitled to sovereign immunity.

Section 1605 of the FSIA sets forth the major exceptions to the jurisdictional immunity of a foreign state. A foreign state is not immune from the jurisdiction of U.S. courts in the following situations:

LEARNING OBJECTIVE 3
Under the Foreign Sovereign Immunities Act, in what situations is a foreign state subject to the jurisdiction of U.S. courts?

1. When the foreign state has waived its immunity either explicitly or by implication.
2. When the foreign state has engaged in commercial activity within the United States or in commercial activity outside the United States that has "a direct effect in the United States."[3]
3. When the foreign state has committed a tort in the United States or has violated certain international laws.

In applying the FSIA, questions frequently arise as to whether an entity is a "foreign state" and what constitutes a "commercial activity." Under Section 1603 of the FSIA, a *foreign state* includes both a political subdivision of a foreign state and an instrumentality of a foreign state. Section 1603 broadly defines a *commercial activity* as a commercial activity that is carried out by a foreign state within the United States, but it does not describe the particulars of what constitutes a commercial activity. Thus, the courts are left to decide whether a particular activity is governmental or commercial in nature.

Doing Business Internationally

Export The sale of goods and services by domestic firms to buyers located in other countries.

A U.S. domestic firm can engage in international business transactions in a number of ways. The simplest way is for U.S. firms to **export** their goods and services to markets abroad. Alternatively, a U.S. firm can establish foreign production facilities so as to be closer to the foreign market or markets in which its products are sold. The advantages may include lower labor costs, fewer government regulations, and lower taxes and trade barriers. A domestic firm may engage in manufacturing abroad by licensing its technology to an existing foreign company or by establishing overseas subsidiaries or joint ventures.

Exporting

"Commerce is the great civilizer. We exchange ideas when we exchange fabrics."

Robert G. Ingersoll, 1833–1899 (American politician and orator)

Exporting can take two forms: direct exporting and indirect exporting. In *direct exporting,* a U.S. company signs a sales contract with a foreign purchaser that provides for the conditions of shipment and payment for the goods. (How payments are made in international transactions will be discussed later in this chapter.) If sufficient business develops in a foreign country, a U.S. corporation may set up a specialized marketing organization in that foreign market by appointing a foreign agent or distributor. This is called *indirect exporting.*

When a U.S. firm desires to limit its involvement in an international market, it will typically establish an *agency relationship* with a foreign firm. (*Agency* was discussed in Chapter 17.) The foreign firm then acts as the U.S. firm's agent and can enter into contracts in the foreign location on behalf of the principal (the U.S. company).

Distribution Agreement A contract between a seller and a distributor of the seller's products setting out the terms and conditions of the distributorship.

Distributorships
When a foreign country represents a substantial market, a U.S. firm may wish to appoint a distributor located in that country. The U.S. firm and the distributor enter into a **distribution agreement,** which is a contract between the seller and the distributor setting out the terms and conditions of the distributorship. These terms and conditions—for example, price, currency of payment, availability of supplies, and method of payment—primarily involve contract law. Disputes concerning distribution agreements

---

3. See, for example, *O'Bryan v. Holy See,* 556 F.3d 361 (6th Cir. 2009).

(AP Photo)

Chinese workers assemble cars at a Ford plant in Chongqing, China. Why would Ford build a plant outside the United States?

may involve jurisdictional or other issues, as well as contract law, which will be discussed later in this chapter.

The National Export Initiative   Although the United States is one of the world's major exporters, exports make up a much smaller share of annual output in the United States than they do in our most important trading partners. In the past, the United States has not promoted exports as actively as many other nations have.

In an effort to increase U.S. exports, in 2010 the Obama administration created the National Export Initiative (NEI) with a goal of doubling U.S. exports by 2015. Some commentators believe that another goal of the NEI is to reduce outsourcing—the practice of having manufacturing or other activities performed in lower-wage countries such as China and India.

Export Promotion   An important component of the NEI is the Export Promotion Cabinet, which includes officials from sixteen government agencies and departments. All cabinet members must submit detailed plans to the president, outlining the steps that they will take to increase U.S. exports.

The U.S. Commerce Department plays a leading role in the NEI, and hundreds of its trade experts serve as advocates to help some twenty thousand U.S. companies increase their export sales. In addition, the Commerce Department and other cabinet members work to promote U.S. exports in the high-growth developing markets of Brazil, China, and India. The members also identify market opportunities in fast-growing sectors, such as environmental goods and services, biotechnology, and renewable energy.

Increased Export Financing   Under the NEI, the Export-Import Bank of the United States increased the financing that it makes available to small and medium-sized businesses by 50 percent. In the initial phase, the bank added hundreds of new small-business clients that sell a wide variety of products, from sophisticated polymers to date palm trees and nanotechnology-based cosmetics.

PREVENTING LEGAL DISPUTES

In light of the National Export Initiative, managers in companies that are now outsourcing or thinking of doing so may wish to reconsider. Increasingly, the federal government is taking a stance against outsourcing. As long as unemployment remains high in the United States, the emphasis will be on the creation of jobs at home. These efforts will often be backed by subsidies and access to federally supported borrowing initiatives.

Manufacturing Abroad

An alternative to direct or indirect exporting is the establishment of foreign manufacturing facilities. Typically, U.S. firms establish manufacturing plants abroad if they believe that doing so will reduce their costs—particularly for labor, shipping, and raw materials—and enable them to compete more effectively in foreign markets. Foreign firms have done the same in the United States. Sony, Nissan, and other Japanese manufacturers have established U.S. plants to avoid import duties that the U.S. Congress may impose on Japanese products entering this country.

(Imaginechina via AP Images)

What type of legal agreement do the distributors of Coca-Cola in China have with the Coca-Cola Company?

Licensing   A U.S. firm may license a foreign manufacturing company to use its copyrighted, patented, or trademarked intellectual property or trade secrets. Like any other licensing agreement (see Chapters 5 and 7), a licensing agreement with a foreign-based firm calls for a payment of royalties on some basis—such as so many cents per unit produced or a certain percentage of profits from units sold in a particular geographic territory.

EXAMPLE 25.3   The Coca-Cola Bottling Company licenses firms worldwide to use (and keep confidential) its secret formula for the syrup used in its soft drink. In return, the foreign firms licensed to make the syrup pay Coca-Cola a percentage of the income earned from the sale of the soft drink. ● Once a firm's trademark is known worldwide, the firm may experience increased demand for other products it manufactures or sells. As we discussed in Chapter 19, franchising is a well-known form of licensing.

Subsidiaries   A U.S. firm can also expand into a foreign market by establishing a wholly owned subsidiary firm in a foreign country. When a wholly owned subsidiary is established, the parent company, which remains in the United States, retains complete ownership of all the facilities in the foreign country, as well as complete authority and control over all phases of the operation. A U.S. firm can also expand into international markets through a joint venture. In a joint venture, the U.S. company owns only part of the operation. The rest is owned either by local owners in the foreign country or by another foreign entity. All of the firms involved in a joint venture (see Chapter 19) share responsibilities, as well as profits and liabilities.

Regulation of Specific Business Activities

Doing business abroad can affect the economies, foreign policies, domestic policies, and other national interests of the countries involved. For this reason, nations impose laws to restrict or facilitate international business. Controls may also be imposed by international agreements. Here, we discuss how different types of international activities are regulated.

Investment Protections

Firms that invest in foreign nations face the risk that the foreign government may take possession of the investment property. Expropriation, as already mentioned, occurs when property is taken and the owner is paid just compensation for what is taken. Expropriation does not violate generally observed principles of international law. Such principles are normally violated, however, when a government confiscates property without compensation (or without adequate compensation). Few remedies are available for confiscation of property by a foreign government. Claims are often resolved by lump-sum settlements after negotiations between the United States and the taking nation.

To counter the deterrent effect that the possibility of confiscation may have on potential investors, many countries guarantee that foreign investors will be compensated if their property is taken. A guaranty can take the form of statutory laws or provisions in international treaties. As further protection for foreign investments, some countries provide insurance for their citizens' investments abroad.

Export Controls

The U.S. Constitution provides in Article I, Section 9, that "No Tax or Duty shall be laid on Articles exported from any State." Thus, Congress cannot impose any export taxes. Congress can, however, use a variety of other devices to control exports. Congress may set export quotas

> "The notion dies hard that in some sort of way exports are patriotic but imports are immoral."
>
> Lord Harlech, 1918–1985
> (British writer)

on various items, such as grain being sold abroad. Under the Export Administration Act of 1979,[4] the flow of technologically advanced products and technical data can be restricted.

While restricting certain exports, the United States (and other nations) also uses devices such as export incentives and subsidies to stimulate other exports and thereby aid domestic businesses. Under the Export Trading Company Act of 1982,[5] U.S. banks are encouraged to invest in export trading companies, which are formed when exporting firms join together to export a line of goods. The Export-Import Bank of the United States provides financial assistance, consisting primarily of credit guaranties given to commercial banks that in turn lend funds to U.S. exporting companies.

Import Controls

Import restrictions include strict prohibitions, quotas, and tariffs. Under the Trading with the Enemy Act of 1917,[6] for instance, no goods may be imported from nations that have been designated enemies of the United States.

Other laws prohibit the importation of illegal drugs and agricultural products that pose dangers to domestic crops or animals. The import of goods that infringe U.S. patents is also prohibited. The International Trade Commission investigates allegations that imported goods infringe U.S. patents and imposes penalties if necessary.

Quotas and Tariffs

Quota A set limit on the amount of goods that can be imported.

Tariff A tax on imported goods.

Limits on the amounts of goods that can be imported are known as **quotas.** At one time, the United States had legal quotas on the number of automobiles that could be imported from Japan. Today, Japan "voluntarily" restricts the number of automobiles exported to the United States (but it builds most cars in U.S. factories).

Tariffs are taxes on imports. A tariff usually is a percentage of the value of the import, but it can be a flat rate per unit (for example, per barrel of oil). Tariffs raise the prices of goods, causing some consumers to purchase more domestically manufactured goods and fewer imported goods.

Political Factors

Sometimes, countries impose tariffs on goods from a particular nation in retaliation for political acts. **EXAMPLE 25.4** A few years ago, Mexico imposed tariffs of 10 to 20 percent on ninety products exported from the United States in retaliation for the Obama administration's cancellation of a cross-border trucking program. The program had been instituted to comply with a provision in the North American Free Trade Agreement (to be discussed shortly) intended to eventually grant Mexican trucks full access to U.S. highways.

U.S truck drivers opposed the program, however, and consumer protection groups claimed that the Mexican trucks posed safety issues. Because the Mexican tariffs were imposed annually on $2.4 billion of U.S. goods, in 2011 President Barack Obama negotiated a deal that allowed Mexican truckers to enter the United States. In exchange, Mexico agreed to suspend half of the tariffs immediately and the remainder when the first Mexican hauler complied with the new U.S. requirements. ●

Antidumping Duties

Dumping The sale of goods in a foreign country at a price below the price charged for the same goods in the domestic market.

The United States has specific laws directed at what it sees as unfair international trade practices. **Dumping,** for instance, is the sale of imported goods at "less than fair value." "Fair value" is usually determined by the price of those goods in the exporting country. Foreign firms that engage in dumping in the United States hope to undersell U.S. businesses to obtain a larger share of the U.S. market. To prevent this, an extra tariff—known as an *antidumping duty*—may be assessed on the imports.

---

4. 50 U.S.C. Sections 2401–2420.
5. 15 U.S.C. Sections 4001, 4003.
6. 12 U.S.C. Section 95a.

Minimizing Trade Barriers

Restrictions on imports are also known as *trade barriers*. The elimination of trade barriers is sometimes seen as essential to the world's economic well-being. Most of the world's leading trading nations are members of the World Trade Organization (WTO), which was established in 1995.

To minimize trade barriers among nations, each member country of the WTO is required to grant **normal trade relations (NTR) status** to other member countries. This means each member is obligated to treat other members at least as well as it treats the country that receives its most favorable treatment with regard to imports or exports. Various regional trade agreements and associations also help to minimize trade barriers between nations.

Normal Trade Relations (NTR) Status
A legal trade status granted to member countries of the World Trade Organization.

The European Union (EU)   The European Union (EU) arose out the 1957 Treaty of Rome, which created the Common Market, a free trade zone comprising the nations of Belgium, France, Italy, Luxembourg, the Netherlands, and West Germany. Today, the EU is a single integrated trading unit made up of twenty-seven European nations.

The EU has gone a long way toward creating a new body of law to govern all of the member nations—although some of its efforts to create uniform laws have been confounded by nationalism. The EU's council and commission issue regulations, or directives, that define EU law in various areas, such as environmental law, product liability, anticompetitive practices, and corporations. The directives normally are binding on all member countries.

The North American Free Trade Agreement (NAFTA)   The North American Free Trade Agreement (NAFTA) created a regional trading unit consisting of Canada, Mexico, and the United States. The goal of NAFTA is to eliminate tariffs among these three countries on substantially all goods by reducing the tariffs incrementally over a period of time. NAFTA gives the three countries a competitive advantage by retaining tariffs on goods imported from countries outside the NAFTA trading unit.

Additionally, NAFTA provides for the elimination of barriers that traditionally have prevented the cross-border movement of services, such as financial and transportation services. NAFTA also attempts to eliminate citizenship requirements for the licensing of accountants, attorneys, physicians, and other professionals.

The Central America–Dominican Republic–United States Free Trade Agreement (CAFTA-DR)   The Central America–Dominican Republic–United States Free Trade Agreement (CAFTA-DR) was formed by Costa Rica, the Dominican

A commercial truck crosses the border between Mexico and the United States. What treaty made this possible?

(AP Photo/*The Laredo Morning Times*, Ricardo Santos)

Flags from European countries fly in front of the European Parliament in Strasbourg, France.

Republic, El Salvador, Guatemala, Honduras, Nicaragua, and the United States. Its purpose is to reduce tariffs and improve market access among all of the signatory nations, including the United States. Legislatures in all seven countries have approved the CAFTA-DR, despite significant opposition in certain nations.

The Republic of Korea–United States Free Trade Agreement (KORUS FTA)   In 2011, the United States ratified its first free trade agreement with South Korea—the Republic of Korea–United States Free Trade Agreement (KORUS FTA). The treaty's provisions will eliminate 95 percent of each nation's tariffs on industrial and consumer exports within five years. KORUS is the largest free trade agreement the United States has entered since NAFTA and may boost U.S. exports by more than $10 billion a year. It will benefit U.S. automakers, farmers, ranchers, and manufacturers by enabling them to compete in new markets.

Also in 2011, Congress ratified free trade agreements with Colombia and Panama. The Colombian trade agreement included a provision requiring an exchange of tax information, and the Panama bill incorporated labor rights assurances. The Obama administration spent years negotiating these treaties in an effort to boost U.S. exports, reduce prices for U.S. consumers, and help our sluggish economy recover. The administration also hoped that the agreements will provide an impetus for continuing the negotiation of the trans-Pacific trade initiative, aimed at increasing exports to Japan and other Asian nations.

Bribing Foreign Officials

Giving cash or in-kind benefits to foreign government officials to obtain business contracts and other favors is often considered normal practice. To reduce such bribery by representatives of U.S. corporations, Congress enacted the Foreign Corrupt Practices Act in 1977.[7] This act and its implications for American businesspersons engaged in international business transactions were discussed in Chapter 2 on pages 58 and 59.

Commercial Contracts in an International Setting

Like all commercial contracts, an international contract should be in writing. For an example of an actual international sales contract from Starbucks Coffee Company, refer to the foldout exhibit in Chapter 10.

Contract Clauses

Language and legal differences among nations can create special problems for parties to international contracts when disputes arise. To avoid these problems, parties should include special provisions in the contract that designate the language of the contract, the jurisdiction where any disputes will be resolved, and the substantive law that will be applied in settling any disputes. Parties to international contracts should also indicate in their contracts what acts or events will excuse the parties from performance under the contract and whether disputes under the contract will be arbitrated or litigated.

Choice-of-Language Clause   A deal struck between a U.S. company and a company in another country normally involves two languages. Typically, many phrases in one language are not readily translatable into another. Consequently, the complex contractual terms involved may not be understood by one party in the other party's language. To

---

7. 15 U.S.C. Sections 78m–78ff.

Choice-of-Language Clause A clause in a contract designating the official language by which the contract will be interpreted in the event of a disagreement over the contract's terms.

make sure that no disputes arise out of this language problem, an international sales contract should have a **choice-of-language clause** designating the official language by which the contract will be interpreted in the event of disagreement.

Note also that some nations have mandatory language requirements. In France, for instance, certain legal documents, such as the prospectuses used in securities offerings (see Chapter 21), must be written in French. In addition, contracts with any departmental or local authority in France, instruction manuals, and warranties for goods and services offered for sale in France must also be written in French.

Forum-Selection Clause

Forum-Selection Clause A provision in a contract designating the court, jurisdiction, or tribunal that will decide any disputes arising under the contract.

When a dispute arises, litigation may be pursued in courts of different nations. There are no universally accepted rules as to which court has jurisdiction over a particular subject matter or parties to a dispute. Consequently, parties to an international transaction should always include in the contract a **forum-selection clause** indicating what court, jurisdiction, or tribunal will decide any disputes arising under the contract. It is especially important to indicate the specific court that will have jurisdiction. The forum does not necessarily have to be within the geographic boundaries of the home nation of either party.

CASE EXAMPLE 25.5 Garware Polyester, Ltd., based in Mumbai, India, made plastics and high-tech polyester film. Intermax Trading Corporation, based in New York, acted as Garware's North American sales agent and sold its products on a commission basis. Garware and Intermax had executed a series of agency agreements with provisions stating that the courts of Mumbai, India, would have exclusive jurisdiction over any disputes relating to the agreements. When Intermax fell behind in its payments to Garware, Garware filed a lawsuit in a U.S. court to collect the balance due, claiming that the forum-selection clause did not apply to sales of warehoused goods. The court, however, sided with Intermax. Because the forum-selection clause was valid and enforceable, Garware had to bring its complaints against Intermax in a court in India.[8] •

Choice-of-Law Clause

Choice-of-Law Clause A clause in a contract designating the law (such as the law of a particular state or nation) that will govern the contract.

A contractual provision designating the applicable law—such as the law of Germany or the United Kingdom or California—is called a **choice-of-law clause.** Every international contract typically includes a choice-of-law clause. At common law (and in European civil law systems), parties are allowed to choose the law that will govern their contractual relationship, provided that the law chosen is the law of a jurisdiction that has a substantial relationship to the parties and to the international business transaction.

Under Section 1–105 of the Uniform Commercial Code, parties may choose the law that will govern the contract as long as the choice is "reasonable." Article 6 of the United Nations Convention on Contracts for the International Sale of Goods (discussed in Chapter 10), however, imposes no limitation on the parties' choice. Similarly, the 1986 Hague Convention on the Law Applicable to Contracts for the International Sale of Goods—often referred to as the Choice-of-Law Convention—allows unlimited autonomy in the choice of law. The Hague Convention indicates that whenever a contract does not specify a choice of law, the governing law is that of the country in which the *seller's* place of business is located.

Force Majeure Clause

Force Majeure Clause A provision in a contract stipulating that certain unforeseen events—such as war, political upheavals, or acts of God—will excuse a party from liability for nonperformance of contractual obligations.

Every contract, particularly those involving international transactions, should have a ***force majeure* clause.** *Force majeure* is a French term meaning "impossible or irresistible force"—sometimes loosely identified as "an act of God." In international business contracts, *force majeure* clauses commonly stipulate that in addition to acts of God, a number of other eventualities (such as government orders or embargoes, for example) may excuse a party from liability for nonperformance.

---

8. *Garware Polyester, Ltd. v. Intermax Trading Corp.,* 2001 WL 1035134 (S.D.N.Y. 2001). See also *Laasko v. Xerox Corp.,* 566 F.Supp.2d 1018 (C.D.Cal. 2008).

Civil Dispute Resolution

International contracts frequently include arbitration clauses. By means of such clauses, the parties agree in advance to be bound by the decision of a specified third party in the event of a dispute, as discussed in Chapter 3. (For an example of an arbitration clause in an international contract, refer to the foldout exhibit in Chapter 10.) The United Nations Convention on the Recognition and Enforcement of Foreign Arbitral Awards (often referred to as the New York Convention) assists in the enforcement of arbitration clauses, as do provisions in specific treaties among nations. The New York Convention has been implemented in nearly one hundred countries, including the United States.

If a sales contract does not include an arbitration clause, litigation may occur. If the contract contains forum-selection and choice-of-law clauses, the lawsuit will be heard by a court in the specified forum and decided according to that forum's law. If no forum and choice of law have been specified, however, proceedings will be more complex and legally uncertain. For instance, litigation may take place in two or more countries, with each country applying its own choice-of-law rules to determine the substantive law that will be applied to the particular transactions. Even if a plaintiff wins a favorable judgment in the plaintiff's country, there is no way to predict whether courts in the defendant's country will enforce the judgment. (For further discussion of this issue, see this chapter's *Beyond Our Borders* feature on page 726.)

In the following case, the court had to decide whether an agreement was enforceable even though one party was a U.S. citizen and the other may have had its principal place of business in the United States.

Case 25.2

S&T Oil Equipment & Machinery, Ltd. v. Juridica Investments, Ltd.

United States Court of Appeals, Fifth Circuit, 2012 WL 28242 (2012).
www.ca5.uscourts.gov[a]

Oil-pumping equipment built by S&T Oil.

FACTS Juridica Investments, Ltd. (JIL), entered into a financing contract with S&T Oil Equipment & Machinery, Ltd., a U.S. company. The contract included an arbitration provision stating that any disputes would be arbitrated in Guernsey, which is one in a group of British islands in the English Channel. The contract also stated that it was executed in Guernsey and that it would be fully performed there. When a dispute arose between the parties, JIL initiated arbitration in Guernsey. Nevertheless, S&T filed a suit in federal district court in the United States. When JIL filed a motion to dismiss in favor of arbitration, the court granted the motion and compelled arbitration under the Convention on the Recognition and Enforcement of Foreign Arbitral Awards—an international agreement also known as the New York Convention. S&T appealed.

ISSUE Was arbitration required under the New York Convention?

DECISION Yes. The U.S. Court of Appeals for the Fifth Circuit affirmed the district court's judgment compelling arbitration.

REASON The court explained that the New York Convention requires arbitration if "(1) there is a written agreement to arbitrate the matter; (2) the agreement provides for arbitration in a Convention signatory nation; (3) the agreement arises out of a commercial legal relationship; and (4) a party to the agreement is not an American citizen." Here, the first three requirements were clearly satisfied, but there was some question about whether JIL was an American citizen based on its principal place of business. Nevertheless, under the statute implementing the Convention, an arbitration agreement between U.S. citizens is enforceable if it "involves property abroad, envisages performance or

---

a. In the left-hand column, click on "Opinions Page." Then, in the "and/or Docket number is:" box, type "11-20400" and click on "Search." In the result, click on the docket number to access the opinion.

Case 25.2—Continued

enforcement abroad, or has some other reasonable relation with one or more foreign states." In this case, JIL and S&T executed their contract in Guernsey and agreed that it would be fully performed there. Thus, the parties had a reasonable relation with a foreign state beyond the arbitration agreement itself. Arbitration was therefore required under the Convention.

CRITICAL THINKING—Global Consideration   *What would happen if Congress did not require a reasonable relationship with a foreign state for arbitration agreements between U.S. citizens? Would there be more or fewer agreements to arbitrate disputes abroad?*

(Ralf Siemieniec/Shutterstock.com)

How do businesses pay foreign firms?

Foreign Exchange Market A worldwide system in which foreign currencies are bought and sold.

Correspondent Bank A bank in which another bank has an account (and vice versa) for the purpose of facilitating fund transfers.

Letter of Credit A written document in which the issuer (usually a bank) promises to honor drafts or other demands for payment by third persons in accordance with the terms of the instrument.

Payment Methods for International Transactions

Currency differences between nations and the geographic distance between parties to international sales contracts add a degree of complexity to international sales that does not exist in the domestic market. Because international contracts involve greater financial risks, special care should be taken in drafting these contracts to specify both the currency in which payment is to be made and the method of payment.

Monetary Systems

Although our national currency, the U.S. dollar, is one of the primary forms of international currency, any U.S. firm undertaking business transactions abroad must be prepared to deal with one or more other currencies. After all, a Japanese firm may want to be paid in Japanese yen for goods and services sold outside Japan. Both firms therefore must rely on the convertibility of currencies.

Currencies are convertible when they can be freely exchanged one for the other at some specified market rate in a **foreign exchange market.** Foreign exchange markets make up a worldwide system for the buying and selling of foreign currencies. The foreign exchange rate is simply the price of a unit of one country's currency in terms of another country's currency. For instance, if today's exchange rate is eighty Japanese yen for one dollar, that means that anybody with eighty yen can obtain one dollar, and vice versa. Like other prices, the exchange rate is set by the forces of supply and demand.

Frequently, a U.S. company can rely on its domestic bank to take care of all international transfers of funds. Commercial banks often transfer funds internationally through their **correspondent banks** in other countries.   **EXAMPLE 25.6**   A customer of Citibank wishes to pay a bill in euros to a company in Paris. Citibank can draw a bank check payable in euros on its account in Crédit Agricole, a Paris correspondent bank, and then send the check to the French company to which its customer owes the funds. Alternatively, Citibank's customer can request a wire transfer of the funds to the French company. Citibank instructs Crédit Agricole by wire to pay the necessary amount in euros. •

Letters of Credit

Because buyers and sellers engaged in international business transactions are frequently separated by thousands of miles, special precautions are often taken to ensure performance under the contract. Sellers want to avoid delivering goods for which they might not be paid. Buyers desire the assurance that sellers will not be paid until there is evidence that the goods have been shipped. Thus, **letters of credit** are frequently used to facilitate international business transactions.

BEYOND OUR BORDERS   Arbitration versus Litigation

Businesspersons often find it advantageous to include arbitration clauses in their international contracts because arbitration awards are usually easier to enforce than court judgments. A problem in collecting court judgments is that the application of the principle of comity varies from one nation to another. Many nations have not signed bilateral agreements with the United States agreeing to enforce judgments rendered in U.S. courts.

When Constitutional Rights Are Involved

Even when the United States has an agreement with another nation, a judgment by a court in that nation may not be enforced in the United States if it conflicts with U.S. laws or policies, especially if the case involves important constitutional rights such as freedom of the press or freedom of religion.

For instance, a U.S. federal appellate court refused to enforce a French default judgment against a U.S. firm, Viewfinder, Inc., on constitutional grounds. Viewfinder operated a Web site that posted photographs from fashion shows and information

about the fashion industry. Several French clothing designers filed an action in a French court alleging that the Web site showed photos of their clothing designs. Because Viewfinder defaulted and did not appear in the French court to contest the allegations, the French court awarded the designers the equivalent of more than $175,000.

When the designers came to the United States to enforce the judgment, Viewfinder asserted a number of arguments as to why the U.S. court should not enforce the French judgment. Ultimately, Viewfinder convinced the U.S. court that its conduct on the Web site was protected expression under the First Amendment.[a]

Arbitration Can Also Prevent Enforcement of a Judgment

Sometimes, arbitration can also be used to prevent a judgment from being collected. Consider a dispute between Chevron Corporation and Ecuador. After years of litigation (that Chevron inherited when it

merged with Texaco), a group of thirty thousand Amazon Indians and farmers won an $18.2 billion verdict in an Ecuadoran court against Chevron for dumping toxic waste into the rivers and rain forests of Ecuador.

But Chevron did not own any property in Ecuador that the government could seize to collect the debt. Chevron filed an action in a New York federal court and convinced the judge that the Ecuadoran trial was tainted by fraud and corruption. Meanwhile, Chevron also took its case to an arbitration panel for the United Nations Commission on International Trade Law (UNCITRAL), which blocked the plaintiffs from collecting on the Ecuadoran judgment. UNCITRAL issued an order that bans enforcement of the Ecuadoran judgment in the United States or anywhere else in the world.[b]

Critical Thinking

What might be some advantages of arbitrating disputes involving international transactions? Are there any disadvantages?

a. *Sarl Louis Feraud International v. Viewfinder, Inc.,* 489 F.3d 474 (2d Cir. 2007).

b. *In re Chevron Corp.,* 650 F.3d 276 (3d Cir. 2011).

Parties to a Letter of Credit   In a simple letter-of-credit transaction, the *issuer* (a bank) agrees to issue a letter of credit and to ascertain whether the *beneficiary* (seller) performs certain acts. In return, the *account party* (buyer) promises to reimburse the issuer for the amount paid to the beneficiary. The transaction may also involve an *advising bank* that transmits information and a *paying bank* that expedites payment under the letter of credit. See Exhibit 25.1 on the facing page for an illustration of a letter-of-credit transaction.

Under a letter of credit, the issuer is bound to pay the beneficiary (seller) when the beneficiary has complied with the terms and conditions of the letter of credit. The beneficiary looks to the issuer, not to the account party (buyer), when it presents the documents required by the letter of credit.

Typically, the letter of credit will require that the beneficiary deliver a *bill of lading* to the issuing bank to prove that shipment has been made. A letter of credit assures the beneficiary (seller) of payment and at the same time assures the account party (buyer) that payment will not be made until the beneficiary has complied with the terms and conditions of the letter of credit.

> **KNOW THIS**
>
> A letter of credit is independent of the underlying contract between the buyer and the seller.

The Value of a Letter of Credit   The basic principle behind letters of credit is that payment is made against the documents presented by the beneficiary and not against the facts that the documents purport to reflect. Thus, in a letter-of-credit transaction, the issuer does not police the underlying contract. A letter of credit is independent of the underlying contract between the buyer and the seller. Eliminating the need for banks (issuers) to inquire

Exhibit 25.1 A Letter-of-Credit Transaction

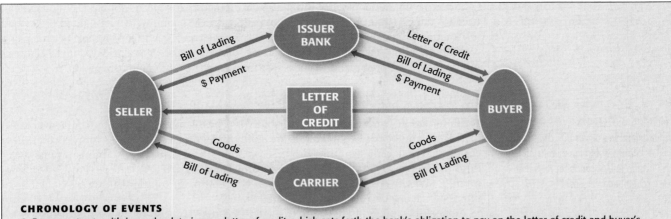

CHRONOLOGY OF EVENTS

1. Buyer contracts with issuer bank to issue a letter of credit, which sets forth the bank's obligation to pay on the letter of credit and buyer's obligation to pay the bank.
2. Letter of credit is sent to seller informing seller that on compliance with the terms of the letter of credit (such as presentment of necessary documents—in this example, a bill of lading), the bank willl issue payment for the goods.
3. Seller delivers goods to carrier and receives a bill of lading.
4. Seller delivers the bill of lading to issuer bank and, if the document is proper, receives payment.
5. Issuer bank delivers the bill of lading to buyer.
6. Buyer delivers the bill of lading to carrier.
7. Carrier delivers the goods to the buyer.
8. Buyer settles with issuer bank.

into whether actual contractual conditions have been satisfied greatly reduces the costs of letters of credit. Moreover, the use of a letter of credit protects both buyers and sellers.

U.S. Laws in a Global Context

The internationalization of business raises questions about the extraterritorial application of a nation's laws—that is, the effect of the country's laws outside its boundaries. To what extent do U.S. domestic laws apply to other nations' businesses? To what extent do U.S. domestic laws apply to U.S. firms doing business abroad? Here, we discuss the extraterritorial application of certain U.S. laws, including antitrust laws, tort laws, and laws prohibiting employment discrimination. (Because these issues can be quite complex, consulting an attorney may be advisable—see the *Business Application* feature on page 730.)

U.S. Antitrust Laws

U.S. antitrust laws (discussed in Chapter 22) have a wide application. They may *subject* firms in foreign nations to their provisions, as well as *protect* foreign consumers and competitors from violations committed by U.S. citizens. Section 1 of the Sherman Act—the most important U.S. antitrust law—provides for the extraterritorial effect of the U.S. antitrust laws.

The United States is a major proponent of free competition in the global economy. Thus, any conspiracy that has a *substantial effect* on U.S. commerce is within the reach of the Sherman Act. The law applies even if the violation occurs outside the United States, and foreign governments as well as businesses can be sued for violations.

EXAMPLE 25.7 An investigation by the U.S. government revealed that a Tokyo-based auto parts supplier, Furukawa Electric Company, and its executives conspired with competitors in an international price-fixing agreement (an agreement to set prices—see Chapter 22). The agreement lasted more than ten years and resulted in automobile manufacturers paying noncompetitive and higher prices for parts in cars sold to U.S. consumers. Because the conspiracy had a substantial effect on U.S. commerce, the United States had jurisdiction to prosecute the case. In 2011, Furukawa agreed to plead guilty and pay a $200 million fine. The Furukawa executives from Japan also agreed to serve up to eighteen months in a U.S. prison and to cooperate fully with the ongoing investigation. •

International Tort Claims

LEARNING OBJECTIVE 5
What federal law allows U.S. citizens, as well as citizens of foreign nations, to file civil actions in U.S. courts for torts that were committed overseas?

The international application of tort liability is growing in significance and controversy. An increasing number of U.S. plaintiffs are suing foreign (or U.S.) entities for torts that these entities have allegedly committed overseas. Often, these cases involve human rights violations by foreign governments. The Alien Tort Claims Act (ATCA),[9] adopted in 1789, allows even foreign citizens to bring civil suits in U.S. courts for injuries caused by violations of international law or a treaty of the United States.

Since 1980, plaintiffs have increasingly used the ATCA to bring actions against companies operating in other countries. ATCA actions have been brought against companies doing business in various nations including Colombia, Ecuador, Egypt, Guatemala, India, Indonesia, Nigeria, and Saudi Arabia. Some of these cases have involved alleged environmental destruction. In addition, mineral companies in Southeast Asia have been sued for collaborating with oppressive government regimes.

The following *Spotlight Case* involved claims against hundreds of corporations that allegedly "aided and abetted" the government of South Africa in maintaining its apartheid (racially discriminatory) regime.

---

9. 28 U.S.C. Section 1350.

Spotlight on International Torts Claims

Case 25.3
Khulumani v. Barclay National Bank, Ltd.
United States Court of Appeals, Second Circuit, 504 F.3d 254 (2007).[a]

(Tim Ireland/PA Wire/Press Association via AP Images)

FACTS A group of plaintiffs (the Khulumani plaintiffs), along with other plaintiff groups, filed class-action claims on behalf of victims of apartheid-related atrocities, human rights violations, crimes against humanity, and unfair and discriminatory forced-labor practices. The plaintiffs brought this action in federal district court under the Alien Tort Claims Act (ATCA) against a number of corporations, including Bank of America, Barclay National Bank, Citigroup, Credit Suisse Group, General Electric, and IBM. The district court dismissed the plaintiffs' complaints in their entirety. The court held that the plaintiffs had failed to establish subject-matter jurisdiction under the ATCA. The plaintiffs appealed to the U.S. Court of Appeals for the Second Circuit.

ISSUE Can the plaintiffs bring a claim against U.S. and foreign companies under the ATCA for "aiding and abetting" human rights violations?

DECISION Yes. The U.S. Court of Appeals for the Second Circuit vacated the district court's dismissal of the plaintiffs' claims and remanded the case for further proceedings. According to the reviewing court, a plaintiff may plead a theory of aiding and abetting liability under the ATCA.

REASON The court stated that the district court "erred in holding that aiding and abetting violations of a customary international law cannot provide a basis for ATCA jurisdiction."

---

a. See also 509 F.3d 148 (2d Cir. 2007), in which the court denied the defendants' motion for a stay; and *American Isuzu Motors, Inc. v. Ntsebeza*, 553 U.S. 1028, 128 S.Ct. 2424, 171 L.Ed.2d 225 (2008), in which the United States Supreme Court had to affirm the Second Circuit's decision in this case because it was unable to hear the appeal in the following term.

Spotlight Case 25.3—Continued

The court reasoned that the United States Supreme Court has instructed courts in this nation to exercise caution and carefully evaluate international norms and potential adverse foreign policy consequences in deciding whether to hear ATCA claims. Thus, "the determination whether a norm is sufficiently definite to support a cause of action should (indeed, inevitably must) involve an element of judgment about the practical consequences of making that cause available to litigants in the federal courts." The court rejected the defendants' argument that

an adjudication of the case by the U.S. court "would offend amicable working relationships with a foreign country."

CRITICAL THINKING—Ethical Consideration *Should the companies cited as defendants in this case have refused all business dealings with South Africa during the era of apartheid when the country's white government severely limited the rights of the majority black African population? Why or why not?*

ETHICAL ISSUE

Should U.S. courts allow "forum-shopping" plaintiffs to sue companies for aiding and abetting global terrorism? Some plaintiffs are bringing actions in U.S. courts alleging that certain banks and other companies in foreign countries have aided and abetted terrorist activities. Foreign plaintiffs may assert claims for aiding and abetting under the ATCA, while U.S. nationals may also bring claims under the Anti-Terrorism Act (ATA).[10]

In 2009, some 1,600 plaintiffs, including both U.S. and foreign nationals, brought claims against Arab Bank, PLC, alleging that the bank knowingly provided financial services to terrorist organizations that attacked Israel. A U.S. district court held that it had jurisdiction to hear the claims.[11] Similarly, in 2010, a federal court held that it had jurisdiction to hear a case brought by a U.S. citizen against a Switzerland-based financial institution for helping fund the terrorists that killed her husband, a Canadian citizen, in Israel.[12]

Although punishing those who aid terrorists is certainly desirable, some have suggested that such rulings may encourage international "forum shopping." Victims of global terrorism may bring lawsuits in U.S. courts against foreign defendants that have little or no contact with the United States because of the potential for large damages awards—and treble damages if the victims are U.S. nationals.

Antidiscrimination Laws

As discussed in Chapter 18, laws in the United States prohibit discrimination in employment on the basis of race, color, national origin, religion, gender, age, and disability. These laws, as they affect employment relationships, generally apply extraterritorially. U.S. employees working abroad for U.S. employers are protected under the Age Discrimination in Employment Act of 1967. The Americans with Disabilities Act of 1990, which requires employers to accommodate the needs of workers with disabilities, also applies to U.S. nationals working abroad for U.S. firms.

In addition, the major law regulating employment discrimination—Title VII of the Civil Rights Act of 1964—also applies extraterritorially to all U.S. employees working for U.S. employers abroad. U.S. employers must abide by U.S. discrimination laws unless to do so would violate the laws of the country where their workplaces are located. This "foreign laws exception" prevents employers from being subjected to conflicting laws.

10. 18 U.S.C. Sections 2331 *et seq.*
11. *Almog v. Arab Bank, PLC,* 471 F.Supp.2d 257 (E.D.N.Y. 2007). See also *Litle v. Arab Bank, PLC,* 611 F.Supp.2d 233 (E.D.N.Y. 2009).
12. *Goldberg v. UBS AG,* 690 F.Supp.2d 92 (E.D.N.Y. 2010). See *Case Example 25.1* on page 714 for further discussion of this case.

Reviewing . . . International Law in a Global Economy

Robco, Inc., was a Florida arms dealer. The armed forces of Honduras contracted to purchase weapons from Robco over a six-year period. After the government was replaced and a democracy installed, the Honduran government sought to reduce the size of its military, and its relationship with Robco deteriorated. Honduras refused to honor the contract by purchasing the inventory of arms, which Robco could sell only at a much lower price. Robco filed a suit in a federal district court in the United States to recover damages for this breach of contract by the government of Honduras. Using the information provided in the chapter, answer the following questions.

1. Should the Foreign Sovereign Immunities Act preclude this lawsuit? Why or why not?
2. Does the act of state doctrine bar Robco from seeking to enforce the contract? Explain.
3. Suppose that prior to this lawsuit, the new government of Honduras had enacted a law making it illegal to purchase weapons from foreign arms dealers. What doctrine might lead a U.S. court to dismiss Robco's case in that situation?
4. Now suppose that the U.S. court hears the case and awards damages to Robco, but the government of Honduras has no assets in the United States that can be used to satisfy the judgment. Under which doctrine might Robco be able to collect the damages by asking another nation's court to enforce the U.S. judgment?

DEBATE THIS The U.S. federal courts are accepting too many lawsuits initiated by foreigners that concern matters not relevant to this country.

BUSINESS APPLICATION

How to Choose and Use a Lawyer*

Most people in today's business world will sooner or later need to obtain legal advice from an attorney. Indeed, it is almost impossible for nonexperts to keep up with the myriad rules and regulations that govern business in the United States and around the globe. The application of laws in an international context, in particular, involves complex legal principles, treaties, jurisdictional issues, conflicts of law, political events, and customary rules and practices. Making informed business decisions in light of these factors may be difficult without the assistance of an attorney.

Weighing Costs and Benefits

Although lawyers may seem expensive—anywhere from $100 to $500 or more per hour—cautious businesspersons will make sure that they are not "penny wise and pound foolish." The consultation fee paid to an attorney can be insignificant compared with the potential liability facing a business. It is increasingly possible for businesspersons to incur penalties for violating laws or regulations of which they are totally unaware. Consider, for instance, the

*This *Business Application* is not meant to substitute for the services of an attorney who is licensed to practice law in your state.

federal criminal laws discussed in Chapter 6 or the international tort claims explained in this chapter.

Obtaining competent legal advice *before* a dispute arises may enable a businessperson to avoid potentially costly mistakes. It may also enable the business to keep a beneficial relationship with a trade partner or customer regardless of a dispute. Keep in mind that sometimes higher-priced attorneys from larger firms may be worth the extra expense. They may have more expertise in the field that is relevant to your business concern, such as international or patent law. Higher-priced attorneys may also have better relationships with firms in a particular industry, more contacts, or more clout in the legal community to wield on your behalf.

Selecting an Attorney

In selecting an attorney, you can ask friends, relatives, or business associates to recommend someone. Alternatively, you can call the local or state bar association to obtain the names of several lawyers or check the Yellow Pages in your local telephone directory for listings. FindLaw has an online database containing biographies of attorneys throughout the country, listed by area of specialty and by state. You can find attorneys in your area by accessing the FindLaw

Lawyer Directory online at <u>lawyers.findlaw.com</u>. You might also investigate legal clinics and prepaid legal service plans.

For your initial meeting with an attorney you are considering hiring, prepare a written list of your questions and a brief summary of the problem for which you need legal advice. Also, bring copies of any relevant documents that the lawyer might need to see. While at the meeting, ask about legal fees, discuss the legal problem you are facing (or anticipate facing), and clarify the scope of what you want the lawyer to do for you. Remember that almost everything you say at this meeting is protected by the attorney-client privilege of confidentiality.

Evaluating Your Attorney

Before hiring the attorney, ask yourself the following questions after your first meeting: Did the attorney seem knowledgeable about what is needed to address your concerns? Did she or he seem willing to investigate the law and the facts further to ensure an accurate understanding of your legal situation? Did the attorney have insight into how to approach the problem, and who to contact first on your behalf? Did you communicate well with each other? Did the attorney perceive which issues were of foremost concern to you and address those issues to your satisfaction? Did the attorney

"speak your language" when explaining the legal implications of those issues?

Checklist for Choosing and Using a Lawyer

1. *If you ever think that you need legal advice, you probably do.*
2. *When choosing an attorney, try to get recommendations from friends, relatives, or business associates who have had long-standing relationships with their attorneys. If that fails, check with your local or state bar association, FindLaw's online directory, or the Yellow Pages.*
3. *When you initially consult with an attorney, bring a written list of questions to which you want answers, perhaps a summary of your problem, and copies of relevant documents.*
4. *Do not hesitate to ask about the legal fees that your attorney will charge, and be sure to clarify the scope of the work to be undertaken by the attorney. Ask any and all questions that you feel are necessary to ensure that you understand your legal options.*
5. *Even after you hire the attorney, continue to evaluate the relationship over time. For many businesspersons, relationships with attorneys last for decades, so it pays to make sure that the relationship is a fruitful one.*

Key Terms

act of state doctrine 715	correspondent bank 725	*force majeure* clause 723	normal trade relations (NTR) status 721
choice-of-language clause 723	distribution agreement 717	foreign exchange market 725	quota 720
choice-of-law clause 723	dumping 720	forum-selection clause 723	sovereign immunity 716
comity 714	export 717	international organization 713	tariff 720
confiscation 716	expropriation 716	letter of credit 725	treaty 713

Chapter Summary: International Law in a Global Economy

International Law— Sources and Principles (See pages 713–717.)	1. *Principle of comity*—Under this principle, nations give effect to the laws and judicial decrees of other nations for reasons of courtesy and international harmony. 2. *Act of state doctrine*—Under this doctrine, U.S. courts avoid passing judgment on the validity of public acts committed by a recognized foreign government within its own territory. 3. *Doctrine of sovereign immunity*—When certain conditions are satisfied, foreign nations are immune from U.S. jurisdiction under the Foreign Sovereign Immunities Act. Exceptions are made when a foreign state (a) has waived its immunity either explicitly or by implication, (b) has engaged in commercial activity within the United States, or (c) has committed a tort within the United States.
Doing Business Internationally (See pages 717–719.)	U.S. domestic firms may engage in international business transactions in several ways, including (1) exporting, which may involve foreign agents or distributors, and (2) manufacturing abroad through licensing arrangements, franchising operations, wholly owned subsidiaries, or joint ventures.
Regulation of Specific Business Activities (See pages 719–722.)	In the interests of their economies, foreign policies, domestic policies, or other national priorities, nations impose laws that restrict or facilitate international business. Such laws regulate foreign investments, exporting, and importing. The World Trade Organization attempts to minimize trade barriers among nations, as do regional trade agreements and associations, including the European Union and the North American Free Trade Agreement.

Continued

Chapter Summary: International Law in a Global Economy— Continued

Commercial Contracts in an International Setting (See pages 722–725.)	International business contracts often include choice-of-language, forum-selection, and choice-of-law clauses to reduce the uncertainties associated with interpreting the language of the agreement and dealing with legal differences. Most domestic and international contracts include *force majeure* clauses. They commonly stipulate that acts of God and certain other events may excuse a party from liability for nonperformance of the contract. Arbitration clauses are also frequently found in international contracts.
Payment Methods for International Transactions (See pages 725–727.)	1. *Currency conversion*—Because nations have different monetary systems, payment on international contracts requires currency conversion at a rate specified in a foreign exchange market. 2. *Correspondent banking*—Correspondent banks facilitate the transfer of funds from a buyer in one country to a seller in another. 3. *Letters of credit*—Letters of credit facilitate international transactions by ensuring payment to sellers and assuring buyers that payment will not be made until the sellers have complied with the terms of the letters of credit. Typically, compliance occurs when a bill of lading is delivered to the issuing bank.
U.S. Laws in a Global Context (See pages 727–729.)	1. *Antitrust laws*—U.S. antitrust laws may be applied beyond the borders of the United States. Any conspiracy that has a substantial effect on commerce within the United States may be subject to the Sherman Act, even if the violation occurs outside the United States. 2. *Tort laws*—U.S. tort laws may be applied to wrongful acts that take place in foreign jurisdictions under the Alien Tort Claims Act. This act allows even foreign citizens to bring civil suits in U.S. Courts for injuries caused by violations of international law or a treaty of the United States. 3. *Antidiscrimination laws*—The major U.S. laws prohibiting employment discrimination, including Title VII of the Civil Rights Act of 1964, the Age Discrimination in Employment Act of 1967, and the Americans with Disabilities Act of 1990, cover U.S. employees working abroad for U.S. firms—*unless* to apply the U.S. laws would violate the laws of the host country.

ExamPrep

ISSUE SPOTTERS

1. Café Rojo, Ltd., an Ecuadoran firm, agrees to sell coffee beans to Dark Roast Coffee Company, a U.S. firm. Dark Roast accepts the beans but refuses to pay. Café Rojo sues Dark Roast in an Ecuadoran court and is awarded damages, but Dark Roast's assets are in the United States. Under what circumstances would a U.S. court enforce the judgment of the Ecuadoran court? **(See pages 714–715.)**
2. Gems International, Ltd., is a foreign firm that has a 12 percent share of the U.S. market for diamonds. To capture a larger share, Gems offers its products at a below-cost discount to U.S. buyers (and inflates the prices in its own country to make up the difference). How can this attempt to undersell U.S. businesses be defeated? **(See page 720.)**

—Check your answers to the Issue Spotters against the answers provided in Appendix E at the end of this text.

BEFORE THE TEST

Go to www.cengagebrain.com, enter the ISBN 9781133191353, and click on "Find" to locate this textbook's Web site. Then, click on "Access Now" under "Study Tools," and select Chapter 25 at the top. There, you will find a Practice Quiz that you can take to assess your mastery of the concepts in this chapter, as well as Flashcards, a Glossary of important terms, and Video Questions (when assigned).

For Review

Answers to the even-numbered questions in this For Review section can be found in Appendix F at the end of this text.

1. What is the principle of comity, and why do courts deciding disputes involving a foreign law or judicial decree apply this principle?
2. What is the act of state doctrine? In what circumstances is this doctrine applied?
3. Under the Foreign Sovereign Immunities Act, in what situations is a foreign state subject to the jurisdiction of U.S. courts?
4. What are three clauses commonly included in international business contracts?
5. What federal law allows U.S. citizens, as well as citizens of foreign nations, to file civil actions in U.S. courts for torts that were committed overseas?

Business Scenarios and Case Problems

25–1 **Letters of Credit.** Antex Industries, a Japanese firm, agreed to purchase 92,000 electronic integrated circuits from Electronic Arrays. The Swiss Credit Bank issued a letter of credit to cover the transaction. The letter of credit specified that the chips would be transported to Tokyo by ship. Electronic Arrays shipped the circuits by air. Payment on the letter of credit was dishonored because the shipment by air did not fulfill the precise terms of the letter of credit. Should a court compel payment? Explain. **(See pages 725–727.)**

25–2 **Question with Sample Answer—Dumping.** U.S. pineapple producers alleged that producers of canned pineapple from the Philippines were selling their canned pineapple in the United States for less than its fair market value (dumping). The Philippine producers also exported other products, such as pineapple juice and juice concentrate, which used separate parts of the same fresh pineapple, so they shared raw material costs, according to the producers' own financial records. To determine fair value and anti-dumping duties, the plaintiffs argued that a court should calculate the Philippine producers' cost of production and allocate a portion of the shared fruit costs to the canned fruit. The result of this allocation showed that more than 90 percent of the canned fruit sales were below the cost of production. Is this a reasonable approach to determining the production costs and fair market value of canned pineapple in the United States? Why or why not? **(See page 720.)**

—**For a sample answer to Question 25–2, go to Appendix G at the end of this text.**

25–3 **Case Problem with Sample Answer—Comity.** Jan Voda, M.D., a resident of Oklahoma City, Oklahoma, owns three U.S. patents related to guiding catheters for use in interventional cardiology, as well as corresponding foreign patents issued by the European Patent Office, Canada, France, Germany, and Great Britain. Voda filed a suit in a federal district court against Cordis Corp., a U.S. firm, alleging infringement of the U.S. patents under U.S. patent law and of the corresponding foreign patents under the patent law of the various foreign countries. Cordis admitted, "[T]he XB catheters have been sold domestically and internationally since 1994. The XB catheters were manufactured in Miami Lakes, Florida, from 1993 to 2001 and have been manufactured in Juarez, Mexico, since 2001." Cordis argued, however, that Voda could not assert infringement claims under foreign patent law because the court did not have jurisdiction over such claims. Which of the important international legal principles discussed in this chapter would be most likely to apply in this case? How should the court apply it? Explain. [*Voda v. Cordis Corp.,* 476 F.3d 887 (Fed.Cir. 2007)] **(See pages 714–715.)**

—**For a sample answer to Problem 25–3, go to Appendix H at the end of this text.**

25–4 **Sovereign Immunity.** When Ferdinand Marcos was president of the Republic of the Philippines, he put assets into

a company called Arelma. Its holdings are in New York. A group of plaintiffs, referred to as the Pimentel class, brought a class-action suit in a U.S. district court for human rights violations by Marcos. They won a judgment of $2 billion and sought to attach Arelma's assets to help pay the judgment. At the same time, the Republic of the Philippines established a commission to recover property wrongfully taken by Marcos. A court in the Philippines was determining whether Marcos's property, including Arelma, should be forfeited to the Republic or to other parties. The Philippine government, in opposition to the Pimentel judgment, moved to dismiss the U.S. court proceedings. The district court refused, and the U.S. Court of Appeals for the Ninth Circuit agreed that the Pimentel class should take the assets. The Republic of the Philippines appealed. What are the key international legal issues? [*Republic of the Philippines v. Pimentel,* 553 U.S. 851, 128 S.Ct. 2180, 171 L.Ed.2d 131 (2008)] **(See pages 716–717.)**

25–5 **Dumping.** The fuel for nuclear power plants is low enriched uranium (LEU). LEU consists of feed uranium enriched by energy to a certain assay—its percentage of the isotope necessary for a nuclear reaction. The amount of energy is described by an industry standard as a "separative work unit" (SWU). A nuclear utility may buy LEU from an enricher, or the utility may provide an enricher with feed uranium and pay for the SWUs necessary to produce LEU. Under an SWU contract, the LEU returned to the utility may not be exactly the particular uranium the utility provided. This is because feed uranium is fungible and trades like a commodity (such as wheat or corn), and profitable enrichment requires the constant processing of undifferentiated stock. LEU imported from foreign enrichers, including Eurodif, S.A., was purportedly being sold in the United States for "less than fair value." Does this constitute dumping? Explain. If so, what could be done to prevent it? [*United States v. Eurodif, S.A.,* 555 U.S. 305, 129 S.Ct. 878, 172 L.Ed.2d 679 (2009)] **(See page 720.)**

25–6 **International Agreements and Jurisdiction.** U.S. citizens who were descendants of victims of the Holocaust (the mass murder of 6 million Jews by the Nazis during World War II) in Europe filed a claim for breach of contract in the United States against an Italian insurance company, Assicurazioni Generali, S.P.A. (Generali). Before the Holocaust, the plaintiffs' ancestors had purchased insurance policies from Generali, but Generali refused to pay them benefits under the policies. Due to certain agreements among nations after World War II, such lawsuits could not be filed for many years. In 2000, however, the United States agreed that Germany could establish a foundation—the International Commission on Holocaust-Era Insurance Claims, or ICHEIC—that would compensate victims who had suffered losses at the hands of the Germans during the war. Whenever a German company was sued in a U.S. court based on a Holocaust-era claim, the U.S. government would inform the court that the matter should be referred to the

ICHEIC as the exclusive forum and remedy for the resolution. There was no such agreement with Italy, however, so the federal district court dismissed the suit. The plaintiffs appealed. Did the plaintiffs have to take their claim to the ICHEIC rather than sue in a U.S. court? Why or why not? [*In re Assicurazioni Generali, S.P.A.,* 592 F.3d 113 (2d Cir. 2010)] **(See page 724.)**

25–7 **Sovereign Immunity.** Bell Helicopter Textron, Inc., designs, makes, and sells helicopters with distinctive and famous trade dress that identifies them as Bell aircraft. Bell also owns the helicopters' design patents. Bell's Model 206 Series includes the Jet Ranger. Thirty-six years after Bell developed the Jet Ranger, the Islamic Republic of Iran began to make and sell counterfeit Model 206 Series helicopters and parts. Iran's counterfeit versions—the Shahed 278 and the Shahed 285—used Bell's *trade dress* (see Chapter 5). The Shahed aircraft was promoted at an international air show in Iran to aircraft customers. Bell filed a suit in a U.S. district court against Iran, alleging violations of trademark and patent laws. Is Iran—a foreign nation—exempt in these circumstances from the jurisdiction of U.S. courts? Explain. [*Bell Helicopter Textron, Inc. v. Islamic Republic of Iran,* 764 F.Supp.2d 122 (D.D.C. 2011)] **(See pages 716–717.)**

25–8 **Commercial Activity Exception.** Technology Incubation and Entrepreneurship Training Society (TIETS) entered into a joint-venture agreement with Mandana Farhang and M.A. Mobile to develop and market certain technology for commercial purposes. Farhang and M.A. Mobile filed a suit in a federal district court in California, where they both were based, alleging claims under the joint-venture agreement and a related nondisclosure agreement. The parties agreed that TIETS was a "foreign state" covered by the Foreign Sovereign Immunities Act because it was a part of the Indian government. Nevertheless, Farhang and M.A. Mobile argued that TIETS did not enjoy sovereign immunity because it had engaged in a commercial activity that had a direct effect in the United States. Could TIETS still be subject to the jurisdiction of U.S. courts under the commercial activity exception even though the joint venture was to take place outside the United States? If so, how? [*Farhang*

v. Indian Institute of Technology, 2012 WL 113739 (N.D.Cal. 2012)] **(See page 717.)**

25–9 ⬌ **A Question of Ethics—Terrorism.** On December 21, 1988, Pan Am Flight 103 exploded 31,000 feet in the air over Lockerbie, Scotland, killing all 259 passengers and crew on board and 11 people on the ground. Among those killed was Roger Hurst, a U.S. citizen. An investigation determined that a portable radio-cassette player packed in a brown Samsonite suitcase smuggled onto the plane was the source of the explosion. The explosive device was constructed with a digital timer specially made for, and bought by, Libya. Abdel Basset Ali Al-Megrahi, a Libyan government official and an employee of the Libyan Arab Airline (LAA), was convicted by the Scottish High Court of Justiciary on criminal charges that he planned and executed the bombing in association with members of the Jamahiriya Security Organization (JSO)—an agency of the former Libyan government that performed security and intelligence functions—or the Libyan military. Members of the victims' families filed a suit in a U.S. federal district court against the JSO, the LAA, Al-Megrahi, and others. The plaintiffs claimed violations of U.S. federal law, including the Anti-Terrorism Act, and state law, including the intentional infliction of emotional distress. [*Hurst v. Socialist People's Libyan Arab Jamahiriya,* 474 F.Supp.2d 19 (D.D.C. 2007)] **(See pages 728–729.)**

1. Under what doctrine, codified in which federal statute, might the defendants have claimed to be immune from the jurisdiction of a U.S. court? Should this law include an exception for "state-sponsored terrorism"? Why or why not?

2. The defendants agreed to pay $2.7 billion, or $10 million per victim, to settle all claims for "compensatory death damages." The families of eleven victims, including Hurst, were excluded from the settlement because they were "not wrongful death beneficiaries under applicable state law." These plaintiffs continued the suit. The defendants filed a motion to dismiss. Should the motion have been granted on the ground that the settlement barred the plaintiffs' claims? Explain.

Critical Thinking and Writing Assignments

25–10 💡 **Business Law Critical Thinking Group Assignment.** Assume that you are manufacturing iPad accessories and that your business is becoming more successful. You are now considering expanding operations into another country.

1. One group will explore the costs and benefits of advertising on the Internet.

2. Another group will examine whether to take in a partner from a foreign nation and explain the benefits and risks of taking in a partner.

3. A third group will discuss what problems will arise if you want to manufacture in a foreign location.

How to Brief Cases and Analyze Case Problems

How to Brief Cases

To fully understand the law with respect to business, you need to be able to read and understand court decisions. To make this task easier, you can use a method of case analysis that is called *briefing*. There is a fairly standard procedure that you can follow when you "brief" any court case. You must first read the case opinion carefully. When you feel you understand the case, you can prepare a brief of it.

Although the format of the brief may vary, typically it will present the essentials of the case under headings such as those listed below.

1. **Citation.** Give the full citation for the case, including the name of the case, the date it was decided, and the court that decided it.
2. **Facts.** Briefly indicate (a) the reasons for the lawsuit; (b) the identity and arguments of the plaintiff(s) and defendant(s), respectively; and (c) the lower court's decision—if appropriate.
3. **Issue.** Concisely phrase, in the form of a question, the essential issue before the court. (If more than one issue is involved, you may have two—or even more—questions here.)
4. **Decision.** Indicate here—with a "yes" or "no," if possible—the court's answer to the question (or questions) in the Issue section above.
5. **Reason.** Summarize as briefly as possible the reasons given by the court for its decision (or decisions) and the case or statutory law relied on by the court in arriving at its decision.

For a case-specific example of what should be included under each of the above headings when briefing a case, see the review of the sample court case presented in the appendix to Chapter 1 of this text on pages 42 and 43.

Analyzing Case Problems

In addition to learning how to brief cases, students of business law and the legal environment also find it helpful to know how to analyze case problems. Part of the study of business law and the legal environment usually involves analyzing case problems, such as those included in this text at the end of each chapter.

For each case problem in this book, we provide the relevant background and facts of the lawsuit and the issue before the court. When you are assigned one of these problems, your job will be to determine how the court should decide the issue, and why. In other words, you will need to engage in legal analysis and rea-

soning. Here, we offer some suggestions on how to make this task less daunting. We begin by presenting a sample case problem:

> While Janet Lawson, a famous pianist, was shopping in Quality Market, she slipped and fell on a wet floor in one of the aisles. The floor had recently been mopped by one of the store's employees, but there were no signs warning customers that the floor in that area was wet. As a result of the fall, Lawson injured her right arm and was unable to perform piano concerts for the next six months. Had she been able to perform the scheduled concerts, she would have earned approximately $60,000 over that period of time. Lawson sued Quality Market for this amount, plus another $10,000 in medical expenses. She claimed that the store's failure to warn customers of the wet floor constituted negligence and therefore the market was liable for her injuries. Will the court agree with Lawson? Discuss.

Understand the Facts

This may sound obvious, but before you can analyze or apply the relevant law to a specific set of facts, you must clearly understand those facts. In other words, you should read through the case problem carefully—more than once, if necessary—to make sure you understand the identity of the plaintiff(s) and defendant(s) in the case and the progression of events that led to the lawsuit.

In the sample case problem just given, the identity of the parties is fairly obvious. Janet Lawson is the one bringing the suit; therefore, she is the plaintiff. Lawson is bringing the suit against Quality Market, so it is the defendant. Some of the case problems you may work on have multiple plaintiffs or defendants. Often, it is helpful to use abbreviations for the parties. To indicate a reference to a plaintiff, for example, the *pi* symbol—π—is often used, and a defendant is denoted by a *delta*—Δ—a triangle.

The events leading to the lawsuit are also fairly straightforward. Lawson slipped and fell on a wet floor, and she contends that Quality Market should be liable for her injuries because it was negligent in not posting a sign warning customers of the wet floor.

When you are working on case problems, realize that the facts should be accepted as they are given. For instance, in our sample problem, it should be accepted that the floor was wet and that there was no sign. In other words, avoid making conjectures, such as "Maybe the floor wasn't too wet," or "Maybe an employee was getting a sign to put up," or "Maybe someone stole the sign." Questioning the facts as they are presented only adds confusion to your analysis.

Legal Analysis and Reasoning

Once you understand the facts given in the case problem, you can begin to analyze the case. Recall from Chapter 1 that the **IRAC method** is a helpful tool to use in the legal analysis and reasoning process. IRAC is an acronym for **I**ssue, **R**ule, **A**pplication, **C**onclusion. Applying this method to our sample problem would involve the following steps:

1. First, you need to decide what legal **issue** is involved in the case. In our sample case, the basic issue is whether Quality Market's failure to warn customers of the wet floor constituted negligence. As discussed in Chapter 4, negligence is a *tort*—a civil wrong. In a tort lawsuit, the plaintiff seeks to be compensated for another's wrongful act. A defendant will be deemed negligent if he or she breached a duty of care owed to the plaintiff and the breach of that duty caused the plaintiff to suffer harm.

2. Once you have identified the issue, the next step is to determine what **rule of law** applies to the issue. To make this determination, you will want to carefully review the text discussion relating to the issue involved in the problem. Our sample case problem involves the tort of negligence, which is covered in Chapter 4. The applicable rule of law is the tort law principle that business owners owe a duty to exercise reasonable care to protect their customers *(business invitees)*. Reasonable care, in this context, includes either removing—or warning customers of—*foreseeable* risks about which the owner *knew* or *should have known*. Business owners need not warn customers of "open and obvious" risks, however. If a business owner breaches this duty of care (fails to exercise the appropriate degree of care toward customers), and the breach of duty causes

a customer to be injured, the business owner will be liable to the customer for the customer's injuries.

3. The next—and usually the most difficult—step in analyzing case problems is the **application** of the relevant rule of law to the specific facts of the case you are studying. In our sample problem, applying the tort law principle just discussed presents few difficulties. An employee of the store had mopped the floor in the aisle where Lawson slipped and fell, but no sign was present indicating that the floor was wet. That a customer might fall on a wet floor is clearly a foreseeable risk. Therefore, the failure to warn customers about the wet floor was a breach of the duty of care owed by the business owner to the store's customers.

4. Once you have completed Step 3 in the IRAC method, you should be ready to draw your **conclusion.** In our sample problem, Quality Market is liable to Lawson for her injuries because the market's breach of its duty of care caused Lawson's injuries.

The fact patterns in the case problems presented in this text are not always as simple as those presented in our sample problem. Often, a case has more than one plaintiff or defendant. A case may also involve more than one issue and have more than one applicable rule of law. Furthermore, in some case problems the facts may indicate that the general rule of law should not apply. Suppose that a store employee told Lawson about the wet floor and advised her not to walk in that aisle, but Lawson decided to walk there anyway. This fact could alter the outcome of the case because the store could then raise the defense of *assumption of risk* (see Chapter 4).

Nonetheless, a careful review of the chapter should always provide you with the knowledge you need to analyze the problem thoroughly and arrive at accurate conclusions.

The Constitution of the United States

Preamble

We the People of the United States, in Order to form a more perfect Union, establish Justice, insure domestic Tranquility, provide for the common defence, promote the general Welfare, and secure the Blessings of Liberty to ourselves and our Posterity, do ordain and establish this Constitution for the United States of America.

Article I

Section 1. All legislative Powers herein granted shall be vested in a Congress of the United States, which shall consist of a Senate and House of Representatives.

Section 2. The House of Representatives shall be composed of Members chosen every second Year by the People of the several States, and the Electors in each State shall have the Qualifications requisite for Electors of the most numerous Branch of the State Legislature.

No Person shall be a Representative who shall not have attained to the Age of twenty five Years, and been seven Years a Citizen of the United States, and who shall not, when elected, be an Inhabitant of that State in which he shall be chosen.

Representatives and direct Taxes shall be apportioned among the several States which may be included within this Union, according to their respective Numbers, which shall be determined by adding to the whole Number of free Persons, including those bound to Service for a Term of Years, and excluding Indians not taxed, three fifths of all other Persons. The actual Enumeration shall be made within three Years after the first Meeting of the Congress of the United States, and within every subsequent Term of ten Years, in such Manner as they shall by Law direct. The Number of Representatives shall not exceed one for every thirty Thousand, but each State shall have at Least one Representative; and until such enumeration shall be made, the State of New Hampshire shall be entitled to chuse three, Massachusetts eight, Rhode Island and Providence Plantations one, Connecticut five, New York six, New Jersey four, Pennsylvania eight, Delaware one, Maryland six, Virginia ten, North Carolina five, South Carolina five, and Georgia three.

When vacancies happen in the Representation from any State, the Executive Authority thereof shall issue Writs of Election to fill such Vacancies.

The House of Representatives shall chuse their Speaker and other Officers; and shall have the sole Power of Impeachment.

Section 3. The Senate of the United States shall be composed of two Senators from each State, chosen by the Legislature thereof, for six Years; and each Senator shall have one Vote.

Immediately after they shall be assembled in Consequence of the first Election, they shall be divided as equally as may be into three Classes. The Seats of the Senators of the first Class shall be vacated at the Expiration of the second Year, of the second Class at the Expiration of the fourth Year, and of the third Class at the Expiration of the sixth Year, so that one third may be chosen every second Year; and if Vacancies happen by Resignation, or otherwise, during the Recess of the Legislature of any State, the Executive thereof may make temporary Appointments until the next Meeting of the Legislature, which shall then fill such Vacancies.

No Person shall be a Senator who shall not have attained to the Age of thirty Years, and been nine Years a Citizen of the United States, and who shall not, when elected, be an Inhabitant of that State for which he shall be chosen.

The Vice President of the United States shall be President of the Senate, but shall have no Vote, unless they be equally divided.

The Senate shall chuse their other Officers, and also a President pro tempore, in the Absence of the Vice President, or when he shall exercise the Office of President of the United States.

The Senate shall have the sole Power to try all Impeachments. When sitting for that Purpose, they shall be on Oath or Affirmation. When the President of the United States is tried, the Chief Justice shall preside: And no Person shall be convicted without the Concurrence of two thirds of the Members present.

Judgment in Cases of Impeachment shall not extend further than to removal from Office, and disqualification to hold and enjoy any Office of honor, Trust, or Profit under the United States: but the Party convicted shall nevertheless be liable and subject to Indictment, Trial, Judgment, and Punishment, according to Law.

Section 4. The Times, Places and Manner of holding Elections for Senators and Representatives, shall be prescribed in each State by the Legislature thereof; but the Congress may at any time by Law make or alter such Regulations, except as to the Places of chusing Senators.

The Congress shall assemble at least once in every Year, and such Meeting shall be on the first Monday in December, unless they shall by Law appoint a different Day.

Section 5. Each House shall be the Judge of the Elections, Returns, and Qualifications of its own Members, and a Majority of each shall constitute a Quorum to do Business; but a smaller Number may adjourn from day to day, and may be authorized to compel the Attendance of absent Members, in such Manner, and under such Penalties as each House may provide.

Each House may determine the Rules of its Proceedings, punish its Members for disorderly Behavior, and, with the Concurrence of two thirds, expel a Member.

Each House shall keep a Journal of its Proceedings, and from time to time publish the same, excepting such Parts as may in their Judgment require Secrecy; and the Yeas and Nays of the Members of either House on any question shall, at the Desire of one fifth of those Present, be entered on the Journal.

Neither House, during the Session of Congress, shall, without the Consent of the other, adjourn for more than three days, nor to any other Place than that in which the two Houses shall be sitting.

Section 6. The Senators and Representatives shall receive a Compensation for their Services, to be ascertained by Law, and paid out of the Treasury of the United States. They shall in all Cases, except Treason, Felony and Breach of the Peace, be privileged from Arrest during their Attendance at the Session of their respective Houses, and in going to and returning from the same; and for any Speech or Debate in either House, they shall not be questioned in any other Place.

No Senator or Representative shall, during the Time for which he was elected, be appointed to any civil Office under the Authority of the United States, which shall have been created, or the Emoluments whereof shall have been increased during such time; and no Person holding any Office under the United States, shall be a Member of either House during his Continuance in Office.

Section 7. All Bills for raising Revenue shall originate in the House of Representatives; but the Senate may propose or concur with Amendments as on other Bills.

Every Bill which shall have passed the House of Representatives and the Senate, shall, before it become a Law, be presented to the President of the United States; If he approve he shall sign it, but if not he shall return it, with his Objections to the House in which it shall have originated, who shall enter the Objections at large on their Journal, and proceed to reconsider it. If after such Reconsideration two thirds of that House shall agree to pass the Bill, it shall be sent together with the Objections, to the other House, by which it shall likewise be reconsidered, and if approved by two thirds of that House, it shall become a Law. But in all such Cases the Votes of both Houses shall be determined by Yeas and Nays, and the Names of the Persons voting for and against the Bill shall be entered on the Journal of each House respectively. If any Bill shall not be returned by the President within ten Days (Sundays excepted) after it shall have been presented to him, the Same shall be a Law, in like Manner as if he had signed it, unless the Congress by their Adjournment prevent its Return in which Case it shall not be a Law.

Every Order, Resolution, or Vote, to which the Concurrence of the Senate and House of Representatives may be necessary (except on a question of Adjournment) shall be presented to the President of the United States; and before the Same shall take Effect, shall be approved by him, or being disapproved by him, shall be repassed by two thirds of the Senate and House of Representatives, according to the Rules and Limitations prescribed in the Case of a Bill.

Section 8. The Congress shall have Power To lay and collect Taxes, Duties, Imposts and Excises, to pay the Debts and provide for the common Defence and general Welfare of the United States; but all Duties, Imposts and Excises shall be uniform throughout the United States;

To borrow Money on the credit of the United States;

To regulate Commerce with foreign Nations, and among the several States, and with the Indian Tribes;

To establish an uniform Rule of Naturalization, and uniform Laws on the subject of Bankruptcies throughout the United States;

To coin Money, regulate the Value thereof, and of foreign Coin, and fix the Standard of Weights and Measures;

To provide for the Punishment of counterfeiting the Securities and current Coin of the United States;

To establish Post Offices and post Roads;

To promote the Progress of Science and useful Arts, by securing for limited Times to Authors and Inventors the exclusive Right to their respective Writings and Discoveries;

To constitute Tribunals inferior to the supreme Court;

To define and punish Piracies and Felonies committed on the high Seas, and Offenses against the Law of Nations;

To declare War, grant Letters of Marque and Reprisal, and make Rules concerning Captures on Land and Water;

To raise and support Armies, but no Appropriation of Money to that Use shall be for a longer Term than two Years;

To provide and maintain a Navy;

To make Rules for the Government and Regulation of the land and naval Forces;

To provide for calling forth the Militia to execute the Laws of the Union, suppress Insurrections and repel Invasions;

To provide for organizing, arming, and disciplining, the Militia, and for governing such Part of them as may be employed in the Service of the United States, reserving to the States respectively, the Appointment of the Officers, and the Authority of training the Militia according to the discipline prescribed by Congress;

To exercise exclusive Legislation in all Cases whatsoever, over such District (not exceeding ten Miles square) as may, by Cession of particular States, and the Acceptance of Congress, become the Seat of the Government of the United States, and to exercise like Authority over all Places purchased by the Consent of the Legislature of the State in which the Same shall be, for the Erection of Forts, Magazines, Arsenals, dock-Yards, and other needful Buildings;—And

To make all Laws which shall be necessary and proper for carrying into Execution the foregoing Powers, and all other Powers vested by this Constitution in the Government of the United States, or in any Department or Officer thereof.

Section 9. The Migration or Importation of such Persons as any of the States now existing shall think proper to admit, shall not be prohibited by the Congress prior to the Year one thousand eight hundred and eight, but a Tax or duty may be imposed on such Importation, not exceeding ten dollars for each Person.

The privilege of the Writ of Habeas Corpus shall not be suspended, unless when in Cases of Rebellion or Invasion the public Safety may require it.

No Bill of Attainder or ex post facto Law shall be passed.

No Capitation, or other direct, Tax shall be laid, unless in Proportion to the Census or Enumeration herein before directed to be taken.

No Tax or Duty shall be laid on Articles exported from any State.

No Preference shall be given by any Regulation of Commerce or Revenue to the Ports of one State over those of another: nor shall Vessels bound to, or from, one State be obliged to enter, clear, or pay Duties in another.

No Money shall be drawn from the Treasury, but in Consequence of Appropriations made by Law; and a regular Statement and Account of the Receipts and Expenditures of all public Money shall be published from time to time.

No Title of Nobility shall be granted by the United States: And no Person holding any Office of Profit or Trust under them, shall, without the Consent of the Congress, accept of any present, Emolument, Office, or Title, of any kind whatever, from any King, Prince, or foreign State.

Section 10. No State shall enter into any Treaty, Alliance, or Confederation; grant Letters of Marque and Reprisal; coin Money; emit Bills of Credit; make any Thing but gold and silver Coin a Tender in Payment of Debts; pass any Bill of Attainder, ex post facto Law, or Law impairing the Obligation of Contracts, or grant any Title of Nobility.

No State shall, without the Consent of the Congress, lay any Imposts or Duties on Imports or Exports, except what may be absolutely necessary for executing its inspection Laws: and the net Produce of all Duties and Imposts, laid by any State on Imports or Exports, shall be for the Use of the Treasury of the United States; and all such Laws shall be subject to the Revision and Controul of the Congress.

No State shall, without the Consent of Congress, lay any Duty of Tonnage, keep Troops, or Ships of War in time of Peace, enter into any Agreement or Compact with another State, or with a foreign Power, or engage in War, unless actually invaded, or in such imminent Danger as will not admit of delay.

Article II

Section 1. The executive Power shall be vested in a President of the United States of America. He shall hold his Office during the Term of four Years, and, together with the Vice President, chosen for the same Term, be elected, as follows:

Each State shall appoint, in such Manner as the Legislature thereof may direct, a Number of Electors, equal to the whole Number of Senators and Representatives to which the State may be entitled in the Congress; but no Senator or Representative, or Person holding an Office of Trust or Profit under the United States, shall be appointed an Elector.

The Electors shall meet in their respective States, and vote by Ballot for two Persons, of whom one at least shall not be an Inhabitant of the same State with themselves. And they shall make a List of all the Persons voted for, and of the Number of Votes for each; which List they shall sign and certify, and transmit sealed to the Seat of the Government of the United States, directed to the President of the Senate. The President of the Senate shall, in the Presence of the Senate and House of Representatives, open all the Certificates, and the Votes shall then be counted. The Person having the greatest Number of Votes shall be the President, if such Number be a Majority of the whole Number of Electors appointed; and if there be more than one who have such Majority, and have an equal Number of Votes, then the House of Representatives shall immediately chuse by Ballot one of them for President; and if no Person have a Majority, then from the five highest on the List the said House

shall in like Manner chuse the President. But in chusing the President, the Votes shall be taken by States, the Representation from each State having one Vote; A quorum for this Purpose shall consist of a Member or Members from two thirds of the States, and a Majority of all the States shall be necessary to a Choice. In every Case, after the Choice of the President, the Person having the greater Number of Votes of the Electors shall be the Vice President. But if there should remain two or more who have equal Votes, the Senate shall chuse from them by Ballot the Vice President.

The Congress may determine the Time of chusing the Electors, and the Day on which they shall give their Votes; which Day shall be the same throughout the United States.

No person except a natural born Citizen, or a Citizen of the United States, at the time of the Adoption of this Constitution, shall be eligible to the Office of President; neither shall any Person be eligible to that Office who shall not have attained to the Age of thirty five Years, and been fourteen Years a Resident within the United States.

In Case of the Removal of the President from Office, or of his Death, Resignation or Inability to discharge the Powers and Duties of the said Office, the same shall devolve on the Vice President, and the Congress may by Law provide for the Case of Removal, Death, Resignation or Inability, both of the President and Vice President, declaring what Officer shall then act as President, and such Officer shall act accordingly, until the Disability be removed, or a President shall be elected.

The President shall, at stated Times, receive for his Services, a Compensation, which shall neither be increased nor diminished during the Period for which he shall have been elected, and he shall not receive within that Period any other Emolument from the United States, or any of them.

Before he enter on the Execution of his Office, he shall take the following Oath or Affirmation: "I do solemnly swear (or affirm) that I will faithfully execute the Office of President of the United States, and will to the best of my Ability, preserve, protect and defend the Constitution of the United States."

Section 2. The President shall be Commander in Chief of the Army and Navy of the United States, and of the Militia of the several States, when called into the actual Service of the United States; he may require the Opinion, in writing, of the principal Officer in each of the executive Departments, upon any Subject relating to the Duties of their respective Offices, and he shall have Power to grant Reprieves and Pardons for Offenses against the United States, except in Cases of Impeachment.

He shall have Power, by and with the Advice and Consent of the Senate to make Treaties, provided two thirds of the Senators present concur; and he shall nominate, and by and with the Advice and Consent of the Senate, shall appoint Ambassadors, other public Ministers and Consuls, Judges of the supreme Court, and all other Officers of the United States, whose Appointments are not herein otherwise provided for, and which shall be established by Law; but the Congress may by Law vest the Appointment of such inferior Officers, as they think proper, in the President alone, in the Courts of Law, or in the Heads of Departments.

The President shall have Power to fill up all Vacancies that may happen during the Recess of the Senate, by granting Commissions which shall expire at the End of their next Session.

Section 3. He shall from time to time give to the Congress Information of the State of the Union, and recommend to their Consideration such Measures as he shall judge necessary and expedient; he may, on extraordinary Occasions, convene both Houses, or either of them, and in Case of Disagreement between them, with Respect to the Time of Adjournment, he may adjourn them to such Time as he shall think proper; he shall receive Ambassadors and other public Ministers; he shall take Care that the Laws be faithfully executed, and shall Commission all the Officers of the United States.

Section 4. The President, Vice President and all civil Officers of the United States, shall be removed from Office on Impeachment for, and Conviction of, Treason, Bribery, or other high Crimes and Misdemeanors.

Article III

Section 1. The judicial Power of the United States, shall be vested in one supreme Court, and in such inferior Courts as the Congress may from time to time ordain and establish. The Judges, both of the supreme and inferior Courts, shall hold their Offices during good Behaviour, and shall, at stated Times, receive for their Services a Compensation, which shall not be diminished during their Continuance in Office.

Section 2. The judicial Power shall extend to all Cases, in Law and Equity, arising under this Constitution, the Laws of the United States, and Treaties made, or which shall be made, under their Authority;—to all Cases affecting Ambassadors, other public Ministers and Consuls;—to all Cases of admiralty and maritime Jurisdiction;—to Controversies to which the United States shall be a Party;—to Controversies between two or more States;—between a State and Citizens of another State;—between Citizens of different States;—between Citizens of the same State claiming Lands under Grants of different States, and between a State, or the Citizens thereof, and foreign States, Citizens or Subjects.

In all Cases affecting Ambassadors, other public Ministers and Consuls, and those in which a State shall be a Party, the supreme Court shall have original Jurisdiction. In all the other Cases before mentioned, the supreme Court shall have appellate Jurisdiction, both as to Law and Fact, with such Exceptions, and under such Regulations as the Congress shall make.

The Trial of all Crimes, except in Cases of Impeachment, shall be by Jury; and such Trial shall be held in the State where the said Crimes shall have been committed; but when not committed within any State, the Trial shall be at such Place or Places as the Congress may by Law have directed.

Section 3. Treason against the United States, shall consist only in levying War against them, or, in adhering to their Enemies, giving them Aid and Comfort. No Person shall be convicted of Treason unless on the Testimony of two Witnesses to the same overt Act, or on Confession in open Court.

The Congress shall have Power to declare the Punishment of Treason, but no Attainder of Treason shall work Corruption of Blood, or Forfeiture except during the Life of the Person attainted.

Article IV

Section 1. Full Faith and Credit shall be given in each State to the public Acts, Records, and judicial Proceedings of every other State. And the Congress may by general Laws prescribe the Manner in which such Acts, Records and Proceedings shall be proved, and the Effect thereof.

Section 2. The Citizens of each State shall be entitled to all Privileges and Immunities of Citizens in the several States.

A Person charged in any State with Treason, Felony, or other Crime, who shall flee from Justice, and be found in another State, shall on Demand of the executive Authority of the State from which he fled, be delivered up, to be removed to the State having Jurisdiction of the Crime.

No Person held to Service or Labour in one State, under the Laws thereof, escaping into another, shall, in Consequence of any Law or Regulation therein, be discharged from such Service or Labour, but shall be delivered up on Claim of the Party to whom such Service or Labour may be due.

Section 3. New States may be admitted by the Congress into this Union; but no new State shall be formed or erected within the Jurisdiction of any other State; nor any State be formed by the Junction of two or more States, or Parts of States, without the Consent of the Legislatures of the States concerned as well as of the Congress.

The Congress shall have Power to dispose of and make all needful Rules and Regulations respecting the Territory or other Property belonging to the United States; and nothing in this Constitution shall be so construed as to Prejudice any Claims of the United States, or of any particular State.

Section 4. The United States shall guarantee to every State in this Union a Republican Form of Government, and shall protect each of them against Invasion; and on Application of the Legislature, or of the Executive (when the Legislature cannot be convened) against domestic Violence.

Article V

The Congress, whenever two thirds of both Houses shall deem it necessary, shall propose Amendments to this Constitution, or, on the Application of the Legislatures of two thirds of the several States, shall call a Convention for proposing Amendments, which, in either Case, shall be valid to all Intents and Purposes, as part of this Constitution, when ratified by the Legislatures of three fourths of the several States, or by Conventions in three fourths thereof, as the one or the other Mode of Ratification may be proposed by the Congress; Provided that no Amendment which may be made prior to the Year One thousand eight hundred and eight shall in any Manner affect the first and fourth Clauses in the Ninth Section of the first Article; and that no State, without its Consent, shall be deprived of its equal Suffrage in the Senate.

Article VI

All Debts contracted and Engagements entered into, before the Adoption of this Constitution shall be as valid against the United States under this Constitution, as under the Confederation.

This Constitution, and the Laws of the United States which shall be made in Pursuance thereof; and all Treaties made, or which shall be made, under the Authority of the United States, shall be the supreme Law of the Land; and the Judges in every State shall be bound thereby, any Thing in the Constitution or Laws of any State to the Contrary notwithstanding.

The Senators and Representatives before mentioned, and the Members of the several State Legislatures, and all executive and judicial Officers, both of the United States and of the several States, shall be bound by Oath or Affirmation, to support this Constitution; but no religious Test shall ever be required as a Qualification to any Office or public Trust under the United States.

Article VII

The Ratification of the Conventions of nine States shall be sufficient for the Establishment of this Constitution between the States so ratifying the Same.

Amendment I [1791]

Congress shall make no law respecting an establishment of religion, or prohibiting the free exercise thereof; or abridging the freedom of speech, or of the press; or the right of the people peaceably to assembly, and to petition the Government for a redress of grievances.

Amendment II [1791]

A well regulated Militia, being necessary to the security of a free State, the right of the people to keep and bear Arms, shall not be infringed.

Amendment III [1791]

No Soldier shall, in time of peace be quartered in any house, without the consent of the Owner, nor in time of war, but in a manner to be prescribed by law.

Amendment IV [1791]

The right of the people to be secure in their persons, houses, papers, and effects, against unreasonable searches and seizures, shall not be violated, and no Warrants shall issue, but upon probable cause, supported by Oath or affirmation, and particularly describing the place to be searched, and the persons or things to be seized.

Amendment V [1791]

No person shall be held to answer for a capital, or otherwise infamous crime, unless on a presentment or indictment of a Grand Jury, except in cases arising in the land or naval forces, or in the Militia, when in actual service in time of War or public danger; nor shall any person be subject for the same offence to be twice put in jeopardy of life or limb; nor shall be compelled in any criminal case to be a witness against himself, nor be deprived of life, liberty, or property, without due process of law; nor shall private property be taken for public use, without just compensation.

Amendment VI [1791]

In all criminal prosecutions, the accused shall enjoy the right to a speedy and public trial, by an impartial jury of the State and district wherein the crime shall have been committed, which district shall have been previously ascertained by law, and to be informed of the nature and cause of the accusation; to be confronted with the witnesses against him; to have compulsory process for obtaining witnesses in his favor, and to have the Assistance of Counsel for his defence.

Amendment VII [1791]

In Suits at common law, where the value in controversy shall exceed twenty dollars, the right of trial by jury shall be preserved, and no fact tried by jury, shall be otherwise re-examined in any Court of the United States, than according to the rules of the common law.

Amendment VIII [1791]

Excessive bail shall not be required, nor excessive fines imposed, nor cruel and unusual punishments inflicted.

Amendment IX [1791]

The enumeration in the Constitution, of certain rights, shall not be construed to deny or disparage others retained by the people.

Amendment X [1791]

The powers not delegated to the United States by the Constitution, nor prohibited by it to the States, are reserved to the States respectively, or to the people.

Amendment XI [1798]

The Judicial power of the United States shall not be construed to extend to any suit in law or equity, commenced or prosecuted against one of the United States by Citizens of another State, or by Citizens or Subjects of any Foreign State.

Amendment XII [1804]

The Electors shall meet in their respective states, and vote by ballot for President and Vice-President, one of whom, at least, shall not be an inhabitant of the same state with themselves; they shall name in their ballots the person voted for as President, and in distinct ballots the person voted for as Vice-President, and they shall make distinct lists of all persons voted for as President, and of all persons voted for as Vice-President, and of the number of votes for each, which lists they shall sign and certify, and transmit sealed to the seat of the government of the United States, directed to the President of the Senate;—The President of the Senate shall, in the presence of the Senate and House of Representatives, open all the certificates and the votes shall then be counted;—The person having the greatest number of votes for President, shall be the President, if such number be a majority of the whole number of Electors appointed; and if no person have such majority, then from the persons having the highest numbers not exceeding three on the list of those voted for as President, the House of Representatives shall choose immediately, by ballot, the President. But in choosing the President, the votes shall be taken by states, the representation from each state having one vote; a quorum for this purpose shall consist of a member or members from two-thirds of the states, and a majority of all states shall be necessary to a choice. And if the House of Representatives shall not choose a President whenever the right of choice shall devolve upon them, before the fourth day of March next following, then the Vice-President shall act as President, as in the case of the death or other constitutional disability of the President.—The person having the greatest number of votes as Vice-President, shall be the Vice-President, if such number be a majority of the whole number of Electors appointed, and if no person have a majority, then from the two highest numbers on the list, the Senate shall choose the Vice-President; a quorum for the purpose shall consist of two-thirds of the whole number of Senators, and a majority of the whole number shall be necessary to a choice. But no person constitutionally ineligible to the office of President shall be eligible to that of Vice-President of the United States.

Amendment XIII [1865]

Section 1. Neither slavery nor involuntary servitude, except as a punishment for crime whereof the party shall have been duly convicted, shall exist within the United States, or any place subject to their jurisdiction.

Section 2. Congress shall have power to enforce this article by appropriate legislation.

Amendment XIV [1868]

Section 1. All persons born or naturalized in the United States, and subject to the jurisdiction thereof, are citizens of the United States and of the State wherein they reside. No State shall make or enforce any law which shall abridge the privileges or immunities of citizens of the United States; nor shall any State deprive any person of life, liberty, or property, without due process of law; nor deny to any person within its jurisdiction the equal protection of the laws.

Section 2. Representatives shall be apportioned among the several States according to their respective numbers, counting the whole number of persons in each State, excluding Indians not taxed. But when the right to vote at any election for the choice of electors for President and Vice President of the United States, Representatives in Congress, the Executive and Judicial officers of a State, or the members of the Legislature thereof, is denied to any of the male inhabitants of such State, being twenty-one years of age, and citizens of the United States, or in any way abridged, except for participation in rebellion, or other crime, the basis of representation therein shall be reduced in the proportion which the number of such male citizens shall bear to the whole number of male citizens twenty-one years of age in such State.

Section 3. No person shall be a Senator or Representative in Congress, or elector of President and Vice President, or hold any office, civil or military, under the United States, or under any State, who having previously taken an oath, as a member of Congress, or as an officer of the United States, or as a member of any State legislature, or as an executive or judicial officer of any State, to support the Constitution of the United States, shall have engaged in insurrection or rebellion against the same, or given aid or comfort to the enemies thereof. But Congress may by a vote of two-thirds of each House, remove such disability.

Section 4. The validity of the public debt of the United States, authorized by law, including debts incurred for payment of pensions and bounties for services in suppressing insurrection or rebellion, shall not be questioned. But neither the United States nor any State shall assume or pay any debt or obligation incurred in aid of insurrection or rebellion against the United States, or any claim for the loss or emancipation of any slave; but all such debts, obligations and claims shall be held illegal and void.

Section 5. The Congress shall have power to enforce, by appropriate legislation, the provisions of this article.

Amendment XV [1870]

Section 1. The right of citizens of the United States to vote shall not be denied or abridged by the United States or by any State on account of race, color, or previous condition of servitude.

Section 2. The Congress shall have power to enforce this article by appropriate legislation.

Amendment XVI [1913]

The Congress shall have power to lay and collect taxes on incomes, from whatever source derived, without apportionment among the several States, and without regard to any census or enumeration.

Amendment XVII [1913]

Section 1. The Senate of the United States shall be composed of two Senators from each State, elected by the people thereof, for six years; and each Senator shall have one vote. The electors in each State shall have the qualifications requisite for electors of the most numerous branch of the State legislatures.

Section 2. When vacancies happen in the representation of any State in the Senate, the executive authority of such State shall issue writs of election to fill such vacancies: *Provided,* That the legislature of any State may empower the executive thereof to make temporary appointments until the people fill the vacancies by election as the legislature may direct.

Section 3. This amendment shall not be so construed as to affect the election or term of any Senator chosen before it becomes valid as part of the Constitution.

Amendment XVIII [1919]

Section 1. After one year from the ratification of this article the manufacture, sale, or transportation of intoxicating liquors within, the importation thereof into, or the exportation thereof from the United States and all territory subject to the jurisdiction thereof for beverage purposes is hereby prohibited.

Section 2. The Congress and the several States shall have concurrent power to enforce this article by appropriate legislation.

Section 3. This article shall be inoperative unless it shall have been ratified as an amendment to the Constitution by the legislatures of the several States, as provided in the Constitution, within seven years from the date of the submission hereof to the States by the Congress.

Amendment XIX [1920]

Section 1. The right of citizens of the United States to vote shall not be denied or abridged by the United States or by any State on account of sex.

Section 2. Congress shall have power to enforce this article by appropriate legislation.

Amendment XX [1933]

Section 1. The terms of the President and Vice President shall end at noon on the 20th day of January, and the terms of Senators and Representatives at noon on the 3d day of January, of the years in which such terms would have ended if this article had not been ratified; and the terms of their successors shall then begin.

Section 2. The Congress shall assemble at least once in every year, and such meeting shall begin at noon on the 3d day of January, unless they shall by law appoint a different day.

Section 3. If, at the time fixed for the beginning of the term of the President, the President elect shall have died, the Vice President elect shall become President. If the President shall not have been chosen before the time fixed for the beginning of his term, or if the President elect shall have failed to qualify, then the Vice President elect shall act as President until a President shall have qualified; and the Congress may by law provide for the case wherein neither a President elect nor a Vice President elect shall have qualified, declaring who shall then act as President, or the manner in which one who is to act shall be selected, and such person shall act accordingly until a President or Vice President shall have qualified.

Section 4. The Congress may by law provide for the case of the death of any of the persons from whom the House of Representatives may choose a President whenever the right of choice shall have devolved upon them, and for the case of the death of any of the persons from whom the Senate may choose a Vice President whenever the right of choice shall have devolved upon them.

Section 5. Sections 1 and 2 shall take effect on the 15th day of October following the ratification of this article.

Section 6. This article shall be inoperative unless it shall have been ratified as an amendment to the Constitution by the legislatures of three-fourths of the several States within seven years from the date of its submission.

Amendment XXI [1933]

Section 1. The eighteenth article of amendment to the Constitution of the United States is hereby repealed.

Section 2. The transportation or importation into any State, Territory, or possession of the United States for delivery or use therein of intoxicating liquors, in violation of the laws thereof, is hereby prohibited.

Section 3. This article shall be inoperative unless it shall have been ratified as an amendment to the Constitution by conventions in the several States, as provided in the Constitution, within seven years from the date of the submission hereof to the States by the Congress.

Amendment XXII [1951]

Section 1. No person shall be elected to the office of the President more than twice, and no person who has held the office of President, or acted as President, for more than two years of a term to which some other person was elected President shall be elected to the office of President more than once. But this Article shall not apply to any person holding the office of President when this Article was proposed by the Congress, and shall not prevent any person who may be holding the office of President, or acting as President, during the term

within which this Article becomes operative from holding the office of President or acting as President during the remainder of such term.

Section 2. This article shall be inoperative unless it shall have been ratified as an amendment to the Constitution by the legislatures of three-fourths of the several States within seven years from the date of its submission to the States by the Congress.

Amendment XXIII [1961]

Section 1. The District constituting the seat of Government of the United States shall appoint in such manner as the Congress may direct:

A number of electors of President and Vice President equal to the whole number of Senators and Representatives in Congress to which the District would be entitled if it were a State, but in no event more than the least populous state; they shall be in addition to those appointed by the states, but they shall be considered, for the purposes of the election of President and Vice President, to be electors appointed by a state; and they shall meet in the District and perform such duties as provided by the twelfth article of amendment.

Section 2. The Congress shall have power to enforce this article by appropriate legislation.

Amendment XXIV [1964]

Section 1. The right of citizens of the United States to vote in any primary or other election for President or Vice President, for electors for President or Vice President, or for Senator or Representative in Congress, shall not be denied or abridged by the United States, or any State by reason of failure to pay any poll tax or other tax.

Section 2. The Congress shall have power to enforce this article by appropriate legislation.

Amendment XXV [1967]

Section 1. In case of the removal of the President from office or of his death or resignation, the Vice President shall become President.

Section 2. Whenever there is a vacancy in the office of the Vice President, the President shall nominate a Vice President who shall take office upon confirmation by a majority vote of both Houses of Congress.

Section 3. Whenever the President transmits to the President pro tempore of the Senate and the Speaker of the House of Representatives his written declaration that he is unable to discharge the powers and duties of his office, and until he transmits to them a written declaration to the contrary, such powers and duties shall be discharged by the Vice President as Acting President.

Section 4. Whenever the Vice President and a majority of either the principal officers of the executive departments or of such other body as Congress may by law provide, transmit to the President pro tempore of the Senate and the Speaker of the House of Representatives their written declaration that the President is unable to discharge the powers and duties of his office, the Vice President shall immediately assume the powers and duties of the office as Acting President.

Thereafter, when the President transmits to the President pro tempore of the Senate and the Speaker of the House of Representatives his written declaration that no inability exists, he shall resume the powers and duties of his office unless the Vice President and a majority of either the principal officers of the executive department or of such other body as Congress may by law provide, transmit within four days to the President pro tempore of the Senate and the Speaker of the House of Representatives their written declaration that the President is unable to discharge the powers and duties of his office. Thereupon Congress shall decide the issue, assembling within forty-eight hours for that purpose if not in session. If the Congress, within twenty-one days after receipt of the latter written declaration, or, if Congress is not in session, within twenty-one days after Congress is required to assemble, determines by two-thirds vote of both Houses that the President is unable to discharge the powers and duties of his office, the Vice President shall continue to discharge the same as Acting President; otherwise, the President shall resume the powers and duties of his office.

Amendment XXVI [1971]

Section 1. The right of citizens of the United States, who are eighteen years of age or older, to vote shall not be denied or abridged by the United States or by any State on account of age.

Section 2. The Congress shall have power to enforce this article by appropriate legislation.

Amendment XXVII [1992]

No law, varying the compensation for the services of the Senators and Representatives, shall take effect, until an election of Representatives shall have intervened.

Articles 2 and 2A of the Uniform Commercial Code

Article 2
SALES

Part 1 Short Title, General Construction and Subject Matter

§ 2–101. Short Title.

This Article shall be known and may be cited as Uniform Commercial Code—Sales.

§ 2–102. Scope; Certain Security and Other Transactions Excluded From This Article.

Unless the context otherwise requires, this Article applies to transactions in goods; it does not apply to any transaction which although in the form of an unconditional contract to sell or present sale is intended to operate only as a security transaction nor does this Article impair or repeal any statute regulating sales to consumers, farmers or other specified classes of buyers.

§ 2–103. Definitions and Index of Definitions.

(1) In this Article unless the context otherwise requires

    (a) "Buyer" means a person who buys or contracts to buy goods.

    (b) "Good faith" in the case of a merchant means honesty in fact and the observance of reasonable commercial standards of fair dealing in the trade.

    (c) "Receipt" of goods means taking physical possession of them.

    (d) "Seller" means a person who sells or contracts to sell goods.

(2) Other definitions applying to this Article or to specified Parts thereof, and the sections in which they appear are:

"Acceptance". Section 2–606.
"Banker's credit". Section 2–325.
"Between merchants". Section 2–104.
"Cancellation". Section 2–106(4).
"Commercial unit". Section 2–105.
"Confirmed credit". Section 2–325.
"Conforming to contract". Section 2–106.
"Contract for sale". Section 2–106.
"Cover". Section 2–712.
"Entrusting". Section 2–403.
"Financing agency". Section 2–104.
"Future goods". Section 2–105.

"Goods". Section 2–105.
"Identification". Section 2–501.
"Installment contract". Section 2–612.
"Letter of Credit". Section 2–325.
"Lot". Section 2–105.
"Merchant". Section 2–104.
"Overseas". Section 2–323.
"Person in position of seller". Section 2–707.
"Present sale". Section 2–106.
"Sale". Section 2–106.
"Sale on approval". Section 2–326.
"Sale or return". Section 2–326.
"Termination". Section 2–106.

(3) The following definitions in other Articles apply to this Article:
"Check". Section 3–104.
"Consignee". Section 7–102.
"Consignor". Section 7–102.
"Consumer goods". Section 9–109.
"Dishonor". Section 3–507.
"Draft". Section 3–104.

(4) In addition Article 1 contains general definitions and principles of construction and interpretation applicable throughout this Article.
As amended in 1994 and 1999.

§ 2–104. Definitions: "Merchant"; "Between Merchants"; "Financing Agency".

(1) "Merchant" means a person who deals in goods of the kind or otherwise by his occupation holds himself out as having knowledge or skill peculiar to the practices or goods involved in the transaction or to whom such knowledge or skill may be attributed by his employment of an agent or broker or other intermediary who by his occupation holds himself out as having such knowledge or skill.

(2) "Financing agency" means a bank, finance company or other person who in the ordinary course of business makes advances against goods or documents of title or who by arrangement with either the seller or the buyer intervenes in ordinary course to make or collect payment due or claimed under the contract for sale, as by purchasing or paying the seller's draft or making advances against it or by merely taking it for collection whether or not documents of title accompany the draft. "Financing agency" includes also a bank or other person who similarly intervenes between persons who are in the position of seller and buyer in respect to the goods (Section 2–707).

(3) "Between merchants" means in any transaction with respect to which both parties are chargeable with the knowledge or skill of merchants.

§ 2–105. Definitions: Transferability; "Goods"; "Future" Goods; "Lot"; "Commercial Unit".

(1) "Goods" means all things (including specially manufactured goods) which are movable at the time of identification to the contract for sale other than the money in which the price is to be paid, investment securities (Article 8) and things in action. "Goods" also includes the unborn young of animals and growing crops and other identified things attached to realty as described in the section on goods to be severed from realty (Section 2–107).

(2) Goods must be both existing and identified before any interest in them can pass. Goods which are not both existing and identified are "future" goods. A purported present sale of future goods or of any interest therein operates as a contract to sell.

(3) There may be a sale of a part interest in existing identified goods.

(4) An undivided share in an identified bulk of fungible goods is sufficiently identified to be sold although the quantity of the bulk is not determined. Any agreed proportion of such a bulk or any quantity thereof agreed upon by number, weight or other measure may to the extent of the seller's interest in the bulk be sold to the buyer who then becomes an owner in common.

(5) "Lot" means a parcel or a single article which is the subject matter of a separate sale or delivery, whether or not it is sufficient to perform the contract.

(6) "Commercial unit" means such a unit of goods as by commercial usage is a single whole for purposes of sale and division of which materially impairs its character or value on the market or in use. A commercial unit may be a single article (as a machine) or a set of articles (as a suite of furniture or an assortment of sizes) or a quantity (as a bale, gross, or carload) or any other unit treated in use or in the relevant market as a single whole.

§ 2–106. Definitions: "Contract"; "Agreement"; "Contract for Sale"; "Sale"; "Present Sale"; "Conforming" to Contract; "Termination"; "Cancellation".

(1) In this Article unless the context otherwise requires "contract" and "agreement" are limited to those relating to the present or future sale of goods. "Contract for sale" includes both a present sale of goods and a contract to sell goods at a future time. A "sale" consists in the passing of title from the seller to the buyer for a price (Section 2–401). A "present sale" means a sale which is accomplished by the making of the contract.

(2) Goods or conduct including any part of a performance are "conforming" or conform to the contract when they are in accordance with the obligations under the contract.

(3) "Termination" occurs when either party pursuant to a power created by agreement or law puts an end to the contract otherwise than for its breach. On "termination" all obligations which are still executory on both sides are discharged but any right based on prior breach or performance survives.

(4) "Cancellation" occurs when either party puts an end to the contract for breach by the other and its effect is the same as that of "termination" except that the cancelling party also retains any remedy for breach of the whole contract or any unperformed balance.

§ 2–107. Goods to Be Severed From Realty: Recording.

(1) A contract for the sale of minerals or the like (including oil and gas) or a structure or its materials to be removed from realty is a contract for the sale of goods within this Article if they are to be severed by the seller but until severance a purported present sale thereof which is not effective as a transfer of an interest in land is effective only as a contract to sell.

(2) A contract for the sale apart from the land of growing crops or other things attached to realty and capable of severance without material harm thereto but not described in subsection (1) or of timber to be cut is a contract for the sale of goods within this Article whether the subject matter is to be severed by the buyer or by the seller even though it forms part of the realty at the time of contracting, and the parties can by identification effect a present sale before severance.

(3) The provisions of this section are subject to any third party rights provided by the law relating to realty records, and the contract for sale may be executed and recorded as a document transferring an interest in land and shall then constitute notice to third parties of the buyer's rights under the contract for sale.

As amended in 1972.

Part 2 Form, Formation and Readjustment of Contract
§ 2–201. Formal Requirements; Statute of Frauds.

(1) Except as otherwise provided in this section a contract for the sale of goods for the price of $500 or more is not enforceable by way of action or defense unless there is some writing sufficient to indicate that a contract for sale has been made between the parties and signed by the party against whom enforcement is sought or by his authorized agent or broker. A writing is not insufficient because it omits or incorrectly states a term agreed upon but the contract is not enforceable under this paragraph beyond the quantity of goods shown in such writing.

(2) Between merchants if within a reasonable time a writing in confirmation of the contract and sufficient against the sender is received and the party receiving it has reason to know its contents, its satisfies the requirements of subsection (1) against such party unless written notice of objection to its contents is given within ten days after it is received.

(3) A contract which does not satisfy the requirements of subsection (1) but which is valid in other respects is enforceable

  (a) if the goods are to be specially manufactured for the buyer and are not suitable for sale to others in the ordinary course of the seller's business and the seller, before notice of repudiation is received and under circumstances which reasonably indicate that the goods are for the buyer, has made either a substantial beginning of their manufacture or commitments for their procurement; or

  (b) if the party against whom enforcement is sought admits in his pleading, testimony or otherwise in court that a contract for sale was made, but the contract is not enforceable under this provision beyond the quantity of goods admitted; or

(c) with respect to goods for which payment has been made and accepted or which have been received and accepted (Sec. 2–606).

§ 2–202. Final Written Expression: Parol or Extrinsic Evidence.

Terms with respect to which the confirmatory memoranda of the parties agree or which are otherwise set forth in a writing intended by the parties as a final expression of their agreement with respect to such terms as are included therein may not be contradicted by evidence of any prior agreement or of a contemporaneous oral agreement but may be explained or supplemented

(a) by course of dealing or usage of trade (Section 1–205) or by course of performance (Section 2–208); and

(b) by evidence of consistent additional terms unless the court finds the writing to have been intended also as a complete and exclusive statement of the terms of the agreement.

§ 2–203. Seals Inoperative.

The affixing of a seal to a writing evidencing a contract for sale or an offer to buy or sell goods does not constitute the writing a sealed instrument and the law with respect to sealed instruments does not apply to such a contract or offer.

§ 2–204. Formation in General.

(1) A contract for sale of goods may be made in any manner sufficient to show agreement, including conduct by both parties which recognizes the existence of such a contract.

(2) An agreement sufficient to constitute a contract for sale may be found even though the moment of its making is undetermined.

(3) Even though one or more terms are left open a contract for sale does not fail for indefiniteness if the parties have intended to make a contract and there is a reasonably certain basis for giving an appropriate remedy.

§ 2–205. Firm Offers.

An offer by a merchant to buy or sell goods in a signed writing which by its terms gives assurance that it will be held open is not revocable, for lack of consideration, during the time stated or if no time is stated for a reasonable time, but in no event may such period of irrevocability exceed three months; but any such term of assurance on a form supplied by the offeree must be separately signed by the offeror.

§ 2–206. Offer and Acceptance in Formation of Contract.

(1) Unless other unambiguously indicated by the language or circumstances

(a) an offer to make a contract shall be construed as inviting acceptance in any manner and by any medium reasonable in the circumstances;

(b) an order or other offer to buy goods for prompt or current shipment shall be construed as inviting acceptance either by a prompt promise to ship or by the prompt or current shipment of conforming or nonconforming goods, but such a shipment of non-conforming goods does not constitute an acceptance if the seller seasonably notifies the buyer that the shipment is offered only as an accommodation to the buyer.

(2) Where the beginning of a requested performance is a reasonable mode of acceptance an offeror who is not notified of acceptance within a reasonable time may treat the offer as having lapsed before acceptance.

§ 2–207. Additional Terms in Acceptance or Confirmation.

(1) A definite and seasonable expression of acceptance or a written confirmation which is sent within a reasonable time operates as an acceptance even though it states terms additional to or different from those offered or agreed upon, unless acceptance is expressly made conditional on assent to the additional or different terms.

(2) The additional terms are to be construed as proposals for addition to the contract. Between merchants such terms become part of the contract unless:

(a) the offer expressly limits acceptance to the terms of the offer;

(b) they materially alter it; or

(c) notification of objection to them has already been given or is given within a reasonable time after notice of them is received.

(3) Conduct by both parties which recognizes the existence of a contract is sufficient to establish a contract for sale although the writings of the parties do not otherwise establish a contract. In such case the terms of the particular contract consist of those terms on which the writings of the parties agree, together with any supplementary terms incorporated under any other provisions of this Act.

§ 2–208. Course of Performance or Practical Construction.

(1) Where the contract for sale involves repeated occasions for performance by either party with knowledge of the nature of the performance and opportunity for objection to it by the other, any course of performance accepted or acquiesced in without objection shall be relevant to determine the meaning of the agreement.

(2) The express terms of the agreement and any such course of performance, as well as any course of dealing and usage of trade, shall be construed whenever reasonable as consistent with each other; but when such construction is unreasonable, express terms shall control course of performance and course of performance shall control both course of dealing and usage of trade (Section 1–205).

(3) Subject to the provisions of the next section on modification and waiver, such course of performance shall be relevant to show a waiver or modification of any term inconsistent with such course of performance.

§ 2–209. Modification, Rescission and Waiver.

(1) An agreement modifying a contract within this Article needs no consideration to be binding.

(2) A signed agreement which excludes modification or rescission except by a signed writing cannot be otherwise modified or rescinded, but except as between merchants such a requirement on a form supplied by the merchant must be separately signed by the other party.

(3) The requirements of the statute of frauds section of this Article (Section 2–201) must be satisfied if the contract as modified is within its provisions.

(4) Although an attempt at modification or rescission does not satisfy the requirements of subsection (2) or (3) it can operate as a waiver.

(5) A party who has made a waiver affecting an executory portion of the contract may retract the waiver by reasonable notification received by the other party that strict performance will be required of any term waived, unless the retraction would be unjust in view of a material change of position in reliance on the waiver.

§ 2–210.   Delegation of Performance; Assignment of Rights.

(1) A party may perform his duty through a delegate unless otherwise agreed or unless the other party has a substantial interest in having his original promisor perform or control the acts required by the contract. No delegation of performance relieves the party delegating of any duty to perform or any liability for breach.

(2) Except as otherwise provided in Section 9–406, unless otherwise agreed, all rights of either seller or buyer can be assigned except where the assignment would materially change the duty of the other party, or increase materially the burden or risk imposed on him by his contract, or impair materially his chance of obtaining return performance. A right to damages for breach of the whole contract or a right arising out of the assignor's due performance of his entire obligation can be assigned despite agreement otherwise.

(3) The creation, attachment, perfection, or enforcement of a security interest in the seller's interest under a contract is not a transfer that materially changes the duty of or increases materially the burden or risk imposed on the buyer or impairs materially the buyer's chance of obtaining return performance within the purview of subsection (2) unless, and then only to the extent that, enforcement actually results in a delegation of material performance of the seller. Even in that event, the creation, attachment, perfection, and enforcement of the security interest remain effective, but (i) the seller is liable to the buyer for damages caused by the delegation to the extent that the damages could not reasonably by prevented by the buyer, and (ii) a court having jurisdiction may grant other appropriate relief, including cancellation of the contract for sale or an injunction against enforcement of the security interest or consummation of the enforcement.

(4) Unless the circumstances indicate the contrary a prohibition of assignment of "the contract" is to be construed as barring only the delegation to the assignee of the assignor's performance.

(5) An assignment of "the contract" or of "all my rights under the contract" or an assignment in similar general terms is an assignment of rights and unless the language or the circumstances (as in an assignment for security) indicate the contrary, it is a delegation of performance of the duties of the assignor and its acceptance by the assignee constitutes a promise by him to perform those duties. This promise is enforceable by either the assignor or the other party to the original contract.

(6) The other party may treat any assignment which delegates performance as creating reasonable grounds for insecurity and

may without prejudice to his rights against the assignor demand assurances from the assignee (Section 2–609).

As amended in 1999.

Part 3   General Obligation and Construction of Contract

§ 2–301.   General Obligations of Parties.

The obligation of the seller is to transfer and deliver and that of the buyer is to accept and pay in accordance with the contract.

§ 2–302.   Unconscionable Contract or Clause.

(1) If the court as a matter of law finds the contract or any clause of the contract to have been unconscionable at the time it was made the court may refuse to enforce the contract, or it may enforce the remainder of the contract without the unconscionable clause, or it may so limit the application of any unconscionable clause as to avoid any unconscionable result.

(2) When it is claimed or appears to the court that the contract or any clause thereof may be unconscionable the parties shall be afforded a reasonable opportunity to present evidence as to its commercial setting, purpose and effect to aid the court in making the determination.

§ 2–303.   Allocations or Division of Risks.

Where this Article allocates a risk or a burden as between the parties "unless otherwise agreed", the agreement may not only shift the allocation but may also divide the risk or burden.

§ 2–304.   Price Payable in Money, Goods, Realty, or Otherwise.

(1) The price can be made payable in money or otherwise. If it is payable in whole or in part in goods each party is a seller of the goods which he is to transfer.

(2) Even though all or part of the price is payable in an interest in realty the transfer of the goods and the seller's obligations with reference to them are subject to this Article, but not the transfer of the interest in realty or the transferor's obligations in connection therewith.

§ 2–305.   Open Price Term.

(1) The parties if they so intend can conclude a contract for sale even though the price is not settled. In such a case the price is a reasonable price at the time for delivery if

   (a) nothing is said as to price; or

   (b) the price is left to be agreed by the parties and they fail to agree; or

   (c) the price is to be fixed in terms of some agreed market or other standard as set or recorded by a third person or agency and it is not so set or recorded.

(2) A price to be fixed by the seller or by the buyer means a price for him to fix in good faith.

(3) When a price left to be fixed otherwise than by agreement of the parties fails to be fixed through fault of one party the other may at his option treat the contract as cancelled or himself fix a reasonable price.

(4) Where, however, the parties intend not to be bound unless the price be fixed or agreed and it is not fixed or agreed there is no contract. In such a case the buyer must return any goods already received or if unable so to do must pay their reasonable value at

the time of delivery and the seller must return any portion of the price paid on account.

§ 2–306.   Output, Requirements and Exclusive Dealings.

(1) A term which measures the quantity by the output of the seller or the requirements of the buyer means such actual output or requirements as may occur in good faith, except that no quantity unreasonably disproportionate to any stated estimate or in the absence of a stated estimate to any normal or otherwise comparable prior output or requirements may be tendered or demanded.

(2) A lawful agreement by either the seller or the buyer for exclusive dealing in the kind of goods concerned imposes unless otherwise agreed an obligation by the seller to use best efforts to supply the goods and by the buyer to use best efforts to promote their sale.

§ 2–307.   Delivery in Single Lot or Several Lots.

Unless otherwise agreed all goods called for by a contract for sale must be tendered in a single delivery and payment is due only on such tender but where the circumstances give either party the right to make or demand delivery in lots the price if it can be apportioned may be demanded for each lot.

§ 2–308.   Absence of Specified Place for Delivery.

Unless otherwise agreed

(a) the place for delivery of goods is the seller's place of business or if he has none his residence; but

(b) in a contract for sale of identified goods which to the knowledge of the parties at the time of contracting are in some other place, that place is the place for their delivery; and

(c) documents of title may be delivered through customary banking channels.

§ 2–309.   Absence of Specific Time Provisions; Notice of Termination.

(1) The time for shipment or delivery or any other action under a contract if not provided in this Article or agreed upon shall be a reasonable time.

(2) Where the contract provides for successive performances but is indefinite in duration it is valid for a reasonable time but unless otherwise agreed may be terminated at any time by either party.

(3) Termination of a contract by one party except on the happening of an agreed event requires that reasonable notification be received by the other party and an agreement dispensing with notification is invalid if its operation would be unconscionable.

§ 2–310.   Open Time for Payment or Running of Credit; Authority to Ship Under Reservation.

Unless otherwise agreed

(a) payment is due at the time and place at which the buyer is to receive the goods even though the place of shipment is the place of delivery; and

(b) if the seller is authorized to send the goods he may ship them under reservation, and may tender the documents of title, but the buyer may inspect the goods after their arrival before payment is due unless such inspection is inconsistent with the terms of the contract (Section 2–513); and

(c) if delivery is authorized and made by way of documents of

title otherwise than by subsection (b) then payment is due at the time and place at which the buyer is to receive the documents regardless of where the goods are to be received; and

(d) where the seller is required or authorized to ship the goods on credit the credit period runs from the time of shipment but post-dating the invoice or delaying its dispatch will correspondingly delay the starting of the credit period.

§ 2–311.   Options and Cooperation Respecting Performance.

(1) An agreement for sale which is otherwise sufficiently definite (subsection (3) of Section 2–204) to be a contract is not made invalid by the fact that it leaves particulars of performance to be specified by one of the parties. Any such specification must be made in good faith and within limits set by commercial reasonableness.

(2) Unless otherwise agreed specifications relating to assortment of the goods are at the buyer's option and except as otherwise provided in subsections (1)(c) and (3) of Section 2–319 specifications or arrangements relating to shipment are at the seller's option.

(3) Where such specification would materially affect the other party's performance but is not seasonably made or where one party's cooperation is necessary to the agreed performance of the other but is not seasonably forthcoming, the other party in addition to all other remedies

(a) is excused for any resulting delay in his own performance; and

(b) may also either proceed to perform in any reasonable manner or after the time for a material part of his own performance treat the failure to specify or to cooperate as a breach by failure to deliver or accept the goods.

§ 2–312.   Warranty of Title and Against Infringement; Buyer's Obligation Against Infringement.

(1) Subject to subsection (2) there is in a contract for sale a warranty by the seller that

(a) the title conveyed shall be good, and its transfer rightful; and

(b) the goods shall be delivered free from any security interest or other lien or encumbrance of which the buyer at the time of contracting has no knowledge.

(2) A warranty under subsection (1) will be excluded or modified only by specific language or by circumstances which give the buyer reason to know that the person selling does not claim title in himself or that he is purporting to sell only such right or title as he or a third person may have.

(3) Unless otherwise agreed a seller who is a merchant regularly dealing in goods of the kind warrants that the goods shall be delivered free of the rightful claim of any third person by way of infringement or the like but a buyer who furnishes specifications to the seller must hold the seller harmless against any such claim which arises out of compliance with the specifications.

§ 2–313.   Express Warranties by Affirmation, Promise, Description, Sample.

(1) Express warranties by the seller are created as follows:

(a) Any affirmation of fact or promise made by the seller to the buyer which relates to the goods and becomes part of the basis of the bargain creates an express warranty that the goods shall conform to the affirmation or promise.

(b) Any description of the goods which is made part of the basis of the bargain creates an express warranty that the goods shall conform to the description.

(c) Any sample or model which is made part of the basis of the bargain creates an express warranty that the whole of the goods shall conform to the sample or model.

(2) It is not necessary to the creation of an express warranty that the seller use formal words such as "warrant" or "guarantee" or that he have a specific intention to make a warranty, but an affirmation merely of the value of the goods or a statement purporting to be merely the seller's opinion or commendation of the goods does not create a warranty.

§ 2–314.   Implied Warranty: Merchantability; Usage of Trade.

(1) Unless excluded or modified (Section 2–316), a warranty that the goods shall be merchantable is implied in a contract for their sale if the seller is a merchant with respect to goods of that kind. Under this section the serving for value of food or drink to be consumed either on the premises or elsewhere is a sale.

(2) Goods to be merchantable must be at least such as

(a) pass without objection in the trade under the contract description; and

(b) in the case of fungible goods, are of fair average quality within the description; and

(c) are fit for the ordinary purposes for which such goods are used; and

(d) run, within the variations permitted by the agreement, of even kind, quality and quantity within each unit and among all units involved; and

(e) are adequately contained, packaged, and labeled as the agreement may require; and

(f) conform to the promises or affirmations of fact made on the container or label if any.

(3) Unless excluded or modified (Section 2–316) other implied warranties may arise from course of dealing or usage of trade.

§ 2–315.   Implied Warranty: Fitness for Particular Purpose.

Where the seller at the time of contracting has reason to know any particular purpose for which the goods are required and that the buyer is relying on the seller's skill or judgment to select or furnish suitable goods, there is unless excluded or modified under the next section an implied warranty that the goods shall be fit for such purpose.

§ 2–316.   Exclusion or Modification of Warranties.

(1) Words or conduct relevant to the creation of an express warranty and words or conduct tending to negate or limit warranty shall be construed wherever reasonable as consistent with each other; but subject to the provisions of this Article on parol or extrinsic evidence (Section 2–202) negation or limitation is inoperative to the extent that such construction is unreasonable.

(2) Subject to subsection (3), to exclude or modify the implied warranty of merchantability or any part of it the language must mention merchantability and in case of a writing must be conspicuous, and to exclude or modify any implied warranty of fitness the exclusion must be by a writing and conspicuous. Language to exclude all implied warranties of fitness is sufficient if it states, for example, that "There are no warranties which extend beyond the description on the face hereof."

(3) Notwithstanding subsection (2)

(a) unless the circumstances indicate otherwise, all implied warranties are excluded by expressions like "as is", "with all faults" or other language which in common understanding calls the buyer's attention to the exclusion of warranties and makes plain that there is no implied warranty; and

(b) when the buyer before entering into the contract has examined the goods or the sample or model as fully as he desired or has refused to examine the goods there is no implied warranty with regard to defects which an examination ought in the circumstances to have revealed to him; and

(c) an implied warranty can also be excluded or modified by course of dealing or course of performance or usage of trade.

(4) Remedies for breach of warranty can be limited in accordance with the provisions of this Article on liquidation or limitation of damages and on contractual modification of remedy (Sections 2–718 and 2–719).

§ 2–317.   Cumulation and Conflict of Warranties Express or Implied.

Warranties whether express or implied shall be construed as consistent with each other and as cumulative, but if such construction is unreasonable the intention of the parties shall determine which warranty is dominant. In ascertaining that intention the following rules apply:

(a) Exact or technical specifications displace an inconsistent sample or model or general language of description.

(b) A sample from an existing bulk displaces inconsistent general language of description.

(c) Express warranties displace inconsistent implied warranties other than an implied warranty of fitness for a particular purpose.

§ 2–318.   Third Party Beneficiaries of Warranties Express or Implied.

Note: If this Act is introduced in the Congress of the United States this section should be omitted. (States to select one alternative.)

Alternative A

A seller's warranty whether express or implied extends to any natural person who is in the family or household of his buyer or who is a guest in his home if it is reasonable to expect that such person may use, consume or be affected by the goods and who is injured in person by breach of the warranty. A seller may not exclude or limit the operation of this section.

Alternative B

A seller's warranty whether express or implied extends to any natural person who may reasonably be expected to use, consume or be affected by the goods and who is injured in person by breach of the warranty. A seller may not exclude or limit the operation of this section.

Alternative C

A seller's warranty whether express or implied extends to any person who may reasonably be expected to use, consume or be affected by the goods and who is injured by breach of the warranty. A seller may not exclude or limit the operation of this section with respect to injury to the person of an individual to whom the warranty extends.

As amended 1966.

§ 2–319. F.O.B. and F.A.S. Terms.

(1) Unless otherwise agreed the term F.O.B. (which means "free on board") at a named place, even though used only in connection with the stated price, is a delivery term under which

(a) when the term is F.O.B. the place of shipment, the seller must at that place ship the goods in the manner provided in this Article (Section 2–504) and bear the expense and risk of putting them into the possession of the carrier; or

(b) when the term is F.O.B. the place of destination, the seller must at his own expense and risk transport the goods to that place and there tender delivery of them in the manner provided in this Article (Section 2–503);

(c) when under either (a) or (b) the term is also F.O.B. vessel, car or other vehicle, the seller must in addition at his own expense and risk load the goods on board. If the term is F.O.B. vessel the buyer must name the vessel and in an appropriate case the seller must comply with the provisions of this Article on the form of bill of lading (Section 2–323).

(2) Unless otherwise agreed the term F.A.S. vessel (which means "free alongside") at a named port, even though used only in connection with the stated price, is a delivery term under which the seller must

(a) at his own expense and risk deliver the goods alongside the vessel in the manner usual in that port or on a dock designated and provided by the buyer; and

(b) obtain and tender a receipt for the goods in exchange for which the carrier is under a duty to issue a bill of lading.

(3) Unless otherwise agreed in any case falling within subsection (1)(a) or (c) or subsection (2) the buyer must seasonably give any needed instructions for making delivery, including when the term is F.A.S. or F.O.B. the loading berth of the vessel and in an appropriate case its name and sailing date. The seller may treat the failure of needed instructions as a failure of cooperation under this Article (Section 2–311). He may also at his option move the goods in any reasonable manner preparatory to delivery or shipment.

(4) Under the term F.O.B. vessel or F.A.S. unless otherwise agreed the buyer must make payment against tender of the required documents and the seller may not tender nor the buyer demand delivery of the goods in substitution for the documents.

§ 2–320. C.I.F. and C. & F. Terms.

(1) The term C.I.F. means that the price includes in a lump sum the cost of the goods and the insurance and freight to the named destination. The term C. & F. or C.F. means that the price so includes cost and freight to the named destination.

(2) Unless otherwise agreed and even though used only in connection with the stated price and destination, the term C.I.F. destination or its equivalent requires the seller at his own expense and risk to

(a) put the goods into the possession of a carrier at the port for shipment and obtain a negotiable bill or bills of lading covering the entire transportation to the named destination; and

(b) load the goods and obtain a receipt from the carrier (which may be contained in the bill of lading) showing that the freight has been paid or provided for; and

(c) obtain a policy or certificate of insurance, including any war risk insurance, of a kind and on terms then current at the port of shipment in the usual amount, in the currency of the contract, shown to cover the same goods covered by the bill of lading and providing for payment of loss to the order of the buyer or for the account of whom it may concern; but the seller may add to the price the amount of the premium for any such war risk insurance; and

(d) prepare an invoice of the goods and procure any other documents required to effect shipment or to comply with the contract; and

(e) forward and tender with commercial promptness all the documents in due form and with any indorsement necessary to perfect the buyer's rights.

(3) Unless otherwise agreed the term C. & F. or its equivalent has the same effect and imposes upon the seller the same obligations and risks as a C.I.F. term except the obligation as to insurance.

(4) Under the term C.I.F. or C. & F. unless otherwise agreed the buyer must make payment against tender of the required documents and the seller may not tender nor the buyer demand delivery of the goods in substitution for the documents.

§ 2–321. C.I.F. or C. & F.: "Net Landed Weights"; "Payment on Arrival"; Warranty of Condition on Arrival.

Under a contract containing a term C.I.F. or C. & F.

(1) Where the price is based on or is to be adjusted according to "net landed weights", "delivered weights", "out turn" quantity or quality or the like, unless otherwise agreed the seller must reasonably estimate the price. The payment due on tender of the documents called for by the contract is the amount so estimated, but after final adjustment of the price a settlement must be made with commercial promptness.

(2) An agreement described in subsection (1) or any warranty of quality or condition of the goods on arrival places upon the seller the risk of ordinary deterioration, shrinkage and the like in transportation but has no effect on the place or time of identification to the contract for sale or delivery or on the passing of the risk of loss.

(3) Unless otherwise agreed where the contract provides for payment on or after arrival of the goods the seller must before payment allow such preliminary inspection as is feasible; but if the goods are lost delivery of the documents and payment are due when the goods should have arrived.

§ 2–322.   Delivery "Ex-Ship".

(1) Unless otherwise agreed a term for delivery of goods "ex-ship" (which means from the carrying vessel) or in equivalent language is not restricted to a particular ship and requires delivery from a ship which has reached a place at the named port of destination where goods of the kind are usually discharged.

(2) Under such a term unless otherwise agreed

(a) the seller must discharge all liens arising out of the carriage and furnish the buyer with a direction which puts the carrier under a duty to deliver the goods; and

(b) the risk of loss does not pass to the buyer until the goods leave the ship's tackle or are otherwise properly unloaded.

§ 2–323.   Form of Bill of Lading Required in Overseas Shipment; "Overseas".

(1) Where the contract contemplates overseas shipment and contains a term C.I.F. or C. & F. or F.O.B. vessel, the seller unless otherwise agreed must obtain a negotiable bill of lading stating that the goods have been loaded on board or, in the case of a term C.I.F. or C. & F., received for shipment.

(2) Where in a case within subsection (1) a bill of lading has been issued in a set of parts, unless otherwise agreed if the documents are not to be sent from abroad the buyer may demand tender of the full set; otherwise only one part of the bill of lading need be tendered. Even if the agreement expressly requires a full set

(a) due tender of a single part is acceptable within the provisions of this Article on cure of improper delivery (subsection (1) of Section 2–508); and

(b) even though the full set is demanded, if the documents are sent from abroad the person tendering an incomplete set may nevertheless require payment upon furnishing an indemnity which the buyer in good faith deems adequate.

(3) A shipment by water or by air or a contract contemplating such shipment is "overseas" insofar as by usage of trade or agreement it is subject to the commercial, financing or shipping practices characteristic of international deep water commerce.

§ 2–324.   "No Arrival, No Sale" Term.

Under a term "no arrival, no sale" or terms of like meaning, unless otherwise agreed,

(a) the seller must properly ship conforming goods and if they arrive by any means he must tender them on arrival but he assumes no obligation that the goods will arrive unless he has caused the non-arrival; and

(b) where without fault of the seller the goods are in part lost or have so deteriorated as no longer to conform to the contract or arrive after the contract time, the buyer may proceed as if there had been casualty to identified goods (Section 2–613).

§ 2–325.   "Letter of Credit" Term; "Confirmed Credit".

(1) Failure of the buyer seasonably to furnish an agreed letter of credit is a breach of the contract for sale.

(2) The delivery to seller of a proper letter of credit suspends the buyer's obligation to pay. If the letter of credit is dishonored, the seller may on seasonable notification to the buyer require payment directly from him.

(3) Unless otherwise agreed the term "letter of credit" or "banker's credit" in a contract for sale means an irrevocable credit issued by a financing agency of good repute and, where the shipment is overseas, of good international repute. The term "confirmed credit" means that the credit must also carry the direct obligation of such an agency which does business in the seller's financial market.

§ 2–326.   Sale on Approval and Sale or Return; Rights of Creditors.

(1) Unless otherwise agreed, if delivered goods may be returned by the buyer even though they conform to the contract, the transaction is

(a) a "sale on approval" if the goods are delivered primarily for use, and

(b) a "sale or return" if the goods are delivered primarily for resale.

(2) Goods held on approval are not subject to the claims of the buyer's creditors until acceptance; goods held on sale or return are subject to such claims while in the buyer's possession.

(3) Any "or return" term of a contract for sale is to be treated as a separate contract for sale within the statute of frauds section of this Article (Section 2–201) and as contradicting the sale aspect of the contract within the provisions of this Article or on parol or extrinsic evidence (Section 2–202).

As amended in 1999.

§ 2–327.   Special Incidents of Sale on Approval and Sale or Return.

(1) Under a sale on approval unless otherwise agreed

(a) although the goods are identified to the contract the risk of loss and the title do not pass to the buyer until acceptance; and

(b) use of the goods consistent with the purpose of trial is not acceptance but failure seasonably to notify the seller of election to return the goods is acceptance, and if the goods conform to the contract acceptance of any part is acceptance of the whole; and

(c) after due notification of election to return, the return is at the seller's risk and expense but a merchant buyer must follow any reasonable instructions.

(2) Under a sale or return unless otherwise agreed

(a) the option to return extends to the whole or any commercial unit of the goods while in substantially their original condition, but must be exercised seasonably; and

(b) the return is at the buyer's risk and expense.

§ 2–328.   Sale by Auction.

(1) In a sale by auction if goods are put up in lots each lot is the subject of a separate sale.

(2) A sale by auction is complete when the auctioneer so announces by the fall of the hammer or in other customary manner. Where a bid is made while the hammer is falling in acceptance of a prior bid the auctioneer may in his discretion reopen the bidding or declare the goods sold under the bid on which the hammer was falling.

(3) Such a sale is with reserve unless the goods are in explicit terms put up without reserve. In an auction with reserve the auctioneer may withdraw the goods at any time until he announces completion of the sale. In an auction without reserve, after the auctioneer calls for bids on an article or lot, that article or lot cannot be withdrawn unless no bid is made within a reasonable time. In either case a bidder may retract his bid until the auctioneer's announcement of completion of the sale, but a bidder's retraction does not revive any previous bid.

(4) If the auctioneer knowingly receives a bid on the seller's behalf or the seller makes or procures such as bid, and notice has not been given that liberty for such bidding is reserved, the buyer may at his option avoid the sale or take the goods at the price of the last good faith bid prior to the completion of the sale. This subsection shall not apply to any bid at a forced sale.

Part 4   Title, Creditors and Good Faith Purchasers

§ 2–401.   Passing of Title; Reservation for Security; Limited Application of This Section.

Each provision of this Article with regard to the rights, obligations and remedies of the seller, the buyer, purchasers or other third parties applies irrespective of title to the goods except where the provision refers to such title. Insofar as situations are not covered by the other provisions of this Article and matters concerning title became material the following rules apply:

(1) Title to goods cannot pass under a contract for sale prior to their identification to the contract (Section 2–501), and unless otherwise explicitly agreed the buyer acquires by their identification a special property as limited by this Act. Any retention or reservation by the seller of the title (property) in goods shipped or delivered to the buyer is limited in effect to a reservation of a security interest. Subject to these provisions and to the provisions of the Article on Secured Transactions (Article 9), title to goods passes from the seller to the buyer in any manner and on any conditions explicitly agreed on by the parties.

(2) Unless otherwise explicitly agreed title passes to the buyer at the time and place at which the seller completes his performance with reference to the physical delivery of the goods, despite any reservation of a security interest and even though a document of title is to be delivered at a different time or place; and in particular and despite any reservation of a security interest by the bill of lading

(a) if the contract requires or authorizes the seller to send the goods to the buyer but does not require him to deliver them at destination, title passes to the buyer at the time and place of shipment; but

(b) if the contract requires delivery at destination, title passes on tender there.

(3) Unless otherwise explicitly agreed where delivery is to be made without moving the goods,

(a) if the seller is to deliver a document of title, title passes at the time when and the place where he delivers such documents; or

(b) if the goods are at the time of contracting already identified and no documents are to be delivered, title passes at the time and place of contracting.

(4) A rejection or other refusal by the buyer to receive or retain the goods, whether or not justified, or a justified revocation of acceptance revests title to the goods in the seller. Such revesting occurs by operation of law and is not a "sale".

§ 2–402.   Rights of Seller's Creditors Against Sold Goods.

(1) Except as provided in subsections (2) and (3), rights of unsecured creditors of the seller with respect to goods which have been identified to a contract for sale are subject to the buyer's rights to recover the goods under this Article (Sections 2–502 and 2–716).

(2) A creditor of the seller may treat a sale or an identification of goods to a contract for sale as void if as against him a retention of possession by the seller is fraudulent under any rule of law of the state where the goods are situated, except that retention of possession in good faith and current course of trade by a merchant-seller for a commercially reasonable time after a sale or identification is not fraudulent.

(3) Nothing in this Article shall be deemed to impair the rights of creditors of the seller

(a) under the provisions of the Article on Secured Transactions (Article 9); or

(b) where identification to the contract or delivery is made not in current course of trade but in satisfaction of or as security for a pre-existing claim for money, security or the like and is made under circumstances which under any rule of law of the state where the goods are situated would apart from this Article constitute the transaction a fraudulent transfer or voidable preference.

§ 2–403.   Power to Transfer; Good Faith Purchase of Goods; "Entrusting".

(1) A purchaser of goods acquires all title which his transferor had or had power to transfer except that a purchaser of a limited interest acquires rights only to the extent of the interest purchased. A person with voidable title has power to transfer a good title to a good faith purchaser for value. When goods have been delivered under a transaction of purchase the purchaser has such power even though

(a) the transferor was deceived as to the identity of the purchaser, or

(b) the delivery was in exchange for a check which is later dishonored, or

(c) it was agreed that the transaction was to be a "cash sale", or

(d) the delivery was procured through fraud punishable as larcenous under the criminal law.

(2) Any entrusting of possession of goods to a merchant who deals in goods of that kind gives him power to transfer all rights of the entruster to a buyer in ordinary course of business.

(3) "Entrusting" includes any delivery and any acquiescence in retention of possession regardless of any condition expressed between the parties to the delivery or acquiescence and regardless of whether the procurement of the entrusting or the possessor's disposition of the goods have been such as to be larcenous under the criminal law.

(4) The rights of other purchasers of goods and of lien creditors are governed by the Articles on Secured Transactions (Article 9), Bulk Transfers (Article 6) and Documents of Title (Article 7).

As amended in 1988.

Part 5   Performance

§ 2–501.   Insurable Interest in Goods; Manner of Identification of Goods.

(1) The buyer obtains a special property and an insurable interest in goods by identification of existing goods as goods to which the contract refers even though the goods so identified are nonconforming and he has an option to return or reject them. Such identification can be made at any time and in any manner explicitly agreed to by the parties. In the absence of explicit agreement identification occurs

(a) when the contract is made if it is for the sale of goods already existing and identified;

(b) if the contract is for the sale of future goods other than those described in paragraph (c), when goods are shipped, marked or otherwise designated by the seller as goods to which the contract refers;

(c) when the crops are planted or otherwise become growing crops or the young are conceived if the contract is for the sale of unborn young to be born within twelve months after contracting or for the sale of crops to be harvested within twelve months or the next normal harvest season after contracting whichever is longer.

(2) The seller retains an insurable interest in goods so long as title to or any security interest in the goods remains in him and where the identification is by the seller alone he may until default or insolvency or notification to the buyer that the identification is final substitute other goods for those identified.

(3) Nothing in this section impairs any insurable interest recognized under any other statute or rule of law.

§ 2–502.   Buyer's Right to Goods on Seller's Insolvency.

(1) Subject to subsections (2) and (3) and even though the goods have not been shipped a buyer who has paid a part or all of the price of goods in which he has a special property under the provisions of the immediately preceding section may on making and keeping good a tender of any unpaid portion of their price recover them from the seller if:

(a) in the case of goods bought for personal, family, or household purposes, the seller repudiates or fails to deliver as required by the contract; or

(b) in all cases, the seller becomes insolvent within ten days after receipt of the first installment on their price.

(2) The buyer's right to recover the goods under subsection (1)(a) vests upon acquisition of a special property, even if the seller had not then repudiated or failed to deliver.

(3) If the identification creating his special property has been made by the buyer he acquires the right to recover the goods only if they conform to the contract for sale.

As amended in 1999.

§ 2–503.   Manner of Seller's Tender of Delivery.

(1) Tender of delivery requires that the seller put and hold conforming goods at the buyer's disposition and give the buyer any notification reasonably necessary to enable him to take delivery. The manner, time and place for tender are determined by the agreement and this Article, and in particular

(a) tender must be at a reasonable hour, and if it is of goods they must be kept available for the period reasonably necessary to enable the buyer to take possession; but

(b) unless otherwise agreed the buyer must furnish facilities reasonably suited to the receipt of the goods.

(2) Where the case is within the next section respecting shipment tender requires that the seller comply with its provisions.

(3) Where the seller is required to deliver at a particular destination tender requires that he comply with subsection (1) and also in any appropriate case tender documents as described in subsections (4) and (5) of this section.

(4) Where goods are in the possession of a bailee and are to be delivered without being moved

(a) tender requires that the seller either tender a negotiable document of title covering such goods or procure acknowledgment by the bailee of the buyer's right to possession of the goods; but

(b) tender to the buyer of a non-negotiable document of title or of a written direction to the bailee to deliver is sufficient tender unless the buyer seasonably objects, and receipt by the bailee of notification of the buyer's rights fixes those rights as against the bailee and all third persons; but risk of loss of the goods and of any failure by the bailee to honor the non-negotiable document of title or to obey the direction remains on the seller until the buyer has had a reasonable time to present the document or direction, and a refusal by the bailee to honor the document or to obey the direction defeats the tender.

(5) Where the contract requires the seller to deliver documents

(a) he must tender all such documents in correct form, except as provided in this Article with respect to bills of lading in a set (subsection (2) of Section 2–323); and

(b) tender through customary banking channels is sufficient and dishonor of a draft accompanying the documents constitutes non-acceptance or rejection.

§ 2–504.   Shipment by Seller.

Where the seller is required or authorized to send the goods to the buyer and the contract does not require him to deliver them at a particular destination, then unless otherwise agreed he must

(a) put the goods in the possession of such a carrier and make such a contract for their transportation as may be reasonable having regard to the nature of the goods and other circumstances of the case; and

(b) obtain and promptly deliver or tender in due form any document necessary to enable the buyer to obtain possession of the goods or otherwise required by the agreement or by usage of trade; and

(c) promptly notify the buyer of the shipment.

Failure to notify the buyer under paragraph (c) or to make a proper contract under paragraph (a) is a ground for rejection only if material delay or loss ensues.

§ 2–505. Seller's Shipment under Reservation.

(1) Where the seller has identified goods to the contract by or before shipment:

(a) his procurement of a negotiable bill of lading to his own order or otherwise reserves in him a security interest in the goods. His procurement of the bill to the order of a financing agency or of the buyer indicates in addition only the seller's expectation of transferring that interest to the person named.

(b) a non-negotiable bill of lading to himself or his nominee reserves possession of the goods as security but except in a case of conditional delivery (subsection (2) of Section 2–507) a non-negotiable bill of lading naming the buyer as consignee reserves no security interest even though the seller retains possession of the bill of lading.

(2) When shipment by the seller with reservation of a security interest is in violation of the contract for sale it constitutes an improper contract for transportation within the preceding section but impairs neither the rights given to the buyer by shipment and identification of the goods to the contract nor the seller's powers as a holder of a negotiable document.

§ 2–506. Rights of Financing Agency.

(1) A financing agency by paying or purchasing for value a draft which relates to a shipment of goods acquires to the extent of the payment or purchase and in addition to its own rights under the draft and any document of title securing it any rights of the shipper in the goods including the right to stop delivery and the shipper's right to have the draft honored by the buyer.

(2) The right to reimbursement of a financing agency which has in good faith honored or purchased the draft under commitment to or authority from the buyer is not impaired by subsequent discovery of defects with reference to any relevant document which was apparently regular on its face.

§ 2–507. Effect of Seller's Tender; Delivery on Condition.

(1) Tender of delivery is a condition to the buyer's duty to accept the goods and, unless otherwise agreed, to his duty to pay for them. Tender entitles the seller to acceptance of the goods and to payment according to the contract.

(2) Where payment is due and demanded on the delivery to the buyer of goods or documents of title, his right as against the seller to retain or dispose of them is conditional upon his making the payment due.

§ 2–508. Cure by Seller of Improper Tender or Delivery; Replacement.

(1) Where any tender or delivery by the seller is rejected because non-conforming and the time for performance has not yet expired, the seller may seasonably notify the buyer of his intention to cure and may then within the contract time make a conforming delivery.

(2) Where the buyer rejects a non-conforming tender which the seller had reasonable grounds to believe would be acceptable with or without money allowance the seller may if he seasonably notifies the buyer have a further reasonable time to substitute a conforming tender.

§ 2–509. Risk of Loss in the Absence of Breach.

(1) Where the contract requires or authorizes the seller to ship the goods by carrier

(a) if it does not require him to deliver them at a particular destination, the risk of loss passes to the buyer when the goods are duly delivered to the carrier even though the shipment is under reservation (Section 2–505); but

(b) if it does require him to deliver them at a particular destination and the goods are there duly tendered while in the possession of the carrier, the risk of loss passes to the buyer when the goods are there duly so tendered as to enable the buyer to take delivery.

(2) Where the goods are held by a bailee to be delivered without being moved, the risk of loss passes to the buyer

(a) on his receipt of a negotiable document of title covering the goods; or

(b) on acknowledgment by the bailee of the buyer's right to possession of the goods; or

(c) after his receipt of a non-negotiable document of title or other written direction to deliver, as provided in subsection (4) (b) of Section 2–503.

(3) In any case not within subsection (1) or (2), the risk of loss passes to the buyer on his receipt of the goods if the seller is a merchant; otherwise the risk passes to the buyer on tender of delivery.

(4) The provisions of this section are subject to contrary agreement of the parties and to the provisions of this Article on sale on approval (Section 2–327) and on effect of breach on risk of loss (Section 2–510).

§ 2–510. Effect of Breach on Risk of Loss.

(1) Where a tender or delivery of goods so fails to conform to the contract as to give a right of rejection the risk of their loss remains on the seller until cure or acceptance.

(2) Where the buyer rightfully revokes acceptance he may to the extent of any deficiency in his effective insurance coverage treat the risk of loss as having rested on the seller from the beginning.

(3) Where the buyer as to conforming goods already identified to the contract for sale repudiates or is otherwise in breach before risk of their loss has passed to him, the seller may to the extent of any deficiency in his effective insurance coverage treat the risk of loss as resting on the buyer for a commercially reasonable time.

§ 2–511.   Tender of Payment by Buyer; Payment by Check.

(1) Unless otherwise agreed tender of payment is a condition to the seller's duty to tender and complete any delivery.

(2) Tender of payment is sufficient when made by any means or in any manner current in the ordinary course of business unless the seller demands payment in legal tender and gives any extension of time reasonably necessary to procure it.

(3) Subject to the provisions of this Act on the effect of an instrument on an obligation (Section 3–310), payment by check is conditional and is defeated as between the parties by dishonor of the check on due presentment.

As amended in 1994.

§ 2–512.   Payment by Buyer Before Inspection.

(1) Where the contract requires payment before inspection non-conformity of the goods does not excuse the buyer from so making payment unless

(a) the non-conformity appears without inspection; or

(b) despite tender of the required documents the circumstances would justify injunction against honor under this Act (Section 5–109(b)).

(2) Payment pursuant to subsection (1) does not constitute an acceptance of goods or impair the buyer's right to inspect or any of his remedies.

As amended in 1995.

§ 2–513.   Buyer's Right to Inspection of Goods.

(1) Unless otherwise agreed and subject to subsection (3), where goods are tendered or delivered or identified to the contract for sale, the buyer has a right before payment or acceptance to inspect them at any reasonable place and time and in any reasonable manner. When the seller is required or authorized to send the goods to the buyer, the inspection may be after their arrival.

(2) Expenses of inspection must be borne by the buyer but may be recovered from the seller if the goods do not conform and are rejected.

(3) Unless otherwise agreed and subject to the provisions of this Article on C.I.F. contracts (subsection (3) of Section 2–321), the buyer is not entitled to inspect the goods before payment of the price when the contract provides

(a) for delivery "C.O.D." or on other like terms; or

(b) for payment against documents of title, except where such payment is due only after the goods are to become available for inspection.

(4) A place or method of inspection fixed by the parties is presumed to be exclusive but unless otherwise expressly agreed it does not postpone identification or shift the place for delivery or for passing the risk of loss. If compliance becomes impossible, inspection shall be as provided in this section unless the place or method fixed was clearly intended as an indispensable condition failure of which avoids the contract.

§ 2–514.   When Documents Deliverable on Acceptance; When on Payment.

Unless otherwise agreed documents against which a draft is drawn are to be delivered to the drawee on acceptance of the draft if it is payable more than three days after presentment; otherwise, only on payment.

§ 2–515.   Preserving Evidence of Goods in Dispute.

In furtherance of the adjustment of any claim or dispute

(a) either party on reasonable notification to the other and for the purpose of ascertaining the facts and preserving evidence has the right to inspect, test and sample the goods including such of them as may be in the possession or control of the other; and

(b) the parties may agree to a third party inspection or survey to determine the conformity or condition of the goods and may agree that the findings shall be binding upon them in any subsequent litigation or adjustment.

Part 6   Breach, Repudiation and Excuse

§ 2–601.   Buyer's Rights on Improper Delivery.

Subject to the provisions of this Article on breach in installment contracts (Section 2–612) and unless otherwise agreed under the sections on contractual limitations of remedy (Sections 2–718 and 2–719), if the goods or the tender of delivery fail in any respect to conform to the contract, the buyer may

(a) reject the whole; or

(b) accept the whole; or

(c) accept any commercial unit or units and reject the rest.

§ 2–602.   Manner and Effect of Rightful Rejection.

(1) Rejection of goods must be within a reasonable time after their delivery or tender. It is ineffective unless the buyer seasonably notifies the seller.

(2) Subject to the provisions of the two following sections on rejected goods (Sections 2–603 and 2–604),

(a) after rejection any exercise of ownership by the buyer with respect to any commercial unit is wrongful as against the seller; and

(b) if the buyer has before rejection taken physical possession of goods in which he does not have a security interest under the provisions of this Article (subsection (3) of Section 2–711), he is under a duty after rejection to hold them with reasonable care at the seller's disposition for a time sufficient to permit the seller to remove them; but

(c) the buyer has no further obligations with regard to goods rightfully rejected.

(3) The seller's rights with respect to goods wrongfully rejected are governed by the provisions of this Article on Seller's remedies in general (Section 2–703).

§ 2–603.   Merchant Buyer's Duties as to Rightfully Rejected Goods.

(1) Subject to any security interest in the buyer (subsection (3) of Section 2–711), when the seller has no agent or place of business at the market of rejection a merchant buyer is under a duty after rejection of goods in his possession or control to follow any reasonable instructions received from the seller with respect to the goods and in the absence of such instructions to make reasonable efforts to sell them for the seller's account if they are perishable or threaten to decline in value speedily. Instructions are not reasonable if on demand indemnity for expenses is not forthcoming.

(2) When the buyer sells goods under subsection (1), he is entitled to reimbursement from the seller or out of the proceeds for reasonable expenses of caring for and selling them, and if the expenses include no selling commission then to such commission as is usual in the trade or if there is none to a reasonable sum not exceeding ten per cent on the gross proceeds.

(3) In complying with this section the buyer is held only to good faith and good faith conduct hereunder is neither acceptance nor conversion nor the basis of an action for damages.

§ 2–604.   Buyer's Options as to Salvage of Rightfully Rejected Goods.

Subject to the provisions of the immediately preceding section on perishables if the seller gives no instructions within a reasonable time after notification of rejection the buyer may store the rejected goods for the seller's account or reship them to him or resell them for the seller's account with reimbursement as provided in the preceding section. Such action is not acceptance or conversion.

§ 2–605.   Waiver of Buyer's Objections by Failure to Particularize.

(1) The buyer's failure to state in connection with rejection a particular defect which is ascertainable by reasonable inspection precludes him from relying on the unstated defect to justify rejection or to establish breach

(a) where the seller could have cured it if stated seasonably; or

(b) between merchants when the seller has after rejection made a request in writing for a full and final written statement of all defects on which the buyer proposes to rely.

(2) Payment against documents made without reservation of rights precludes recovery of the payment for defects apparent on the face of the documents.

§ 2–606.   What Constitutes Acceptance of Goods.

(1) Acceptance of goods occurs when the buyer

(a) after a reasonable opportunity to inspect the goods signifies to the seller that the goods are conforming or that he will take or retain them in spite of their nonconformity; or

(b) fails to make an effective rejection (subsection (1) of Section 2–602), but such acceptance does not occur until the buyer has had a reasonable opportunity to inspect them; or

(c) does any act inconsistent with the seller's ownership; but if such act is wrongful as against the seller it is an acceptance only if ratified by him.

(2) Acceptance of a part of any commercial unit is acceptance of that entire unit.

§ 2–607.   Effect of Acceptance; Notice of Breach; Burden of Establishing Breach After Acceptance; Notice of Claim or Litigation to Person Answerable Over.

(1) The buyer must pay at the contract rate for any goods accepted.

(2) Acceptance of goods by the buyer precludes rejection of the goods accepted and if made with knowledge of a non-conformity cannot be revoked because of it unless the acceptance was on the reasonable assumption that the non-conformity would be seasonably cured but acceptance does not of itself impair any other remedy provided by this Article for non-conformity.

(3) Where a tender has been accepted

(a) the buyer must within a reasonable time after he discovers or should have discovered any breach notify the seller of breach or be barred from any remedy; and

(b) if the claim is one for infringement or the like (subsection (3) of Section 2–312) and the buyer is sued as a result of such a breach he must so notify the seller within a reasonable time after he receives notice of the litigation or be barred from any remedy over for liability established by the litigation.

(4) The burden is on the buyer to establish any breach with respect to the goods accepted.

(5) Where the buyer is sued for breach of a warranty or other obligation for which his seller is answerable over

(a) he may give his seller written notice of the litigation. If the notice states that the seller may come in and defend and that if the seller does not do so he will be bound in any action against him by his buyer by any determination of fact common to the two litigations, then unless the seller after seasonable receipt of the notice does come in and defend he is so bound.

(b) if the claim is one for infringement or the like (subsection (3) of Section 2–312) the original seller may demand in writing that his buyer turn over to him control of the litigation including settlement or else be barred from any remedy over and if he also agrees to bear all expense and to satisfy any adverse judgment, then unless the buyer after seasonable receipt of the demand does turn over control the buyer is so barred.

(6) The provisions of subsections (3), (4) and (5) apply to any obligation of a buyer to hold the seller harmless against infringement or the like (subsection (3) of Section 2–312).

§ 2–608.   Revocation of Acceptance in Whole or in Part.

(1) The buyer may revoke his acceptance of a lot or commercial unit whose non-conformity substantially impairs its value to him if he has accepted it

(a) on the reasonable assumption that its nonconformity would be cured and it has not been seasonably cured; or

(b) without discovery of such non-conformity if his acceptance was reasonably induced either by the difficulty of discovery before acceptance or by the seller's assurances.

(2) Revocation of acceptance must occur within a reasonable time after the buyer discovers or should have discovered the ground for it and before any substantial change in condition of the goods which is not caused by their own defects. It is not effective until the buyer notifies the seller of it.

(3) A buyer who so revokes has the same rights and duties with regard to the goods involved as if he had rejected them.

§ 2–609.   Right to Adequate Assurance of Performance.

(1) A contract for sale imposes an obligation on each party that the other's expectation of receiving due performance will not be impaired. When reasonable grounds for insecurity arise with respect to the performance of either party the other may in writing demand adequate assurance of due performance and until he receives such assurance may if commercially reasonable suspend any performance for which he has not already received the agreed return.

(2) Between merchants the reasonableness of grounds for insecurity and the adequacy of any assurance offered shall be determined according to commercial standards.

(3) Acceptance of any improper delivery or payment does not prejudice the party's right to demand adequate assurance of future performance.

(4) After receipt of a justified demand failure to provide within a reasonable time not exceeding thirty days such assurance of due performance as is adequate under the circumstances of the particular case is a repudiation of the contract.

§ 2–610.   Anticipatory Repudiation.

When either party repudiates the contract with respect to a performance not yet due the loss of which will substantially impair the value of the contract to the other, the aggrieved party may

(a) for a commercially reasonable time await performance by the repudiating party; or

(b) resort to any remedy for breach (Section 2–703 or Section 2–711), even though he has notified the repudiating party that he would await the latter's performance and has urged retraction; and

(c) in either case suspend his own performance or proceed in accordance with the provisions of this Article on the seller's right to identify goods to the contract notwithstanding breach or to salvage unfinished goods (Section 2–704).

§ 2–611.   Retraction of Anticipatory Repudiation.

(1) Until the repudiating party's next performance is due he can retract his repudiation unless the aggrieved party has since the repudiation cancelled or materially changed his position or otherwise indicated that he considers the repudiation final.

(2) Retraction may be by any method which clearly indicates to the aggrieved party that the repudiating party intends to perform, but must include any assurance justifiably demanded under the provisions of this Article (Section 2–609).

(3) Retraction reinstates the repudiating party's rights under the contract with due excuse and allowance to the aggrieved party for any delay occasioned by the repudiation.

§ 2–612.   "Installment Contract"; Breach.

(1) An "installment contract" is one which requires or authorizes the delivery of goods in separate lots to be separately accepted, even though the contract contains a clause "each delivery is a separate contract" or its equivalent.

(2) The buyer may reject any installment which is non-conforming if the non-conformity substantially impairs the value of that installment and cannot be cured or if the non-conformity is a defect in the required documents; but if the non-conformity does not fall within subsection (3) and the seller gives adequate assurance of its cure the buyer must accept that installment.

(3) Whenever non-conformity or default with respect to one or more installments substantially impairs the value of the whole contract there is a breach of the whole. But the aggrieved party reinstates the contract if he accepts a non-conforming installment without seasonably notifying of cancellation or if he brings an action with respect only to past installments or demands performance as to future installments.

§ 2–613.   Casualty to Identified Goods.

Where the contract requires for its performance goods identified when the contract is made, and the goods suffer casualty without fault of either party before the risk of loss passes to the buyer, or in a proper case under a "no arrival, no sale" term (Section 2–324) then

(a) if the loss is total the contract is avoided; and

(b) if the loss is partial or the goods have so deteriorated as no longer to conform to the contract the buyer may nevertheless demand inspection and at his option either treat the contract as voided or accept the goods with due allowance from the contract price for the deterioration or the deficiency in quantity but without further right against the seller.

§ 2–614.   Substituted Performance.

(1) Where without fault of either party the agreed berthing, loading, or unloading facilities fail or an agreed type of carrier becomes unavailable or the agreed manner of delivery otherwise becomes commercially impracticable but a commercially reasonable substitute is available, such substitute performance must be tendered and accepted.

(2) If the agreed means or manner of payment fails because of domestic or foreign governmental regulation, the seller may withhold or stop delivery unless the buyer provides a means or manner of payment which is commercially a substantial equivalent. If delivery has already been taken, payment by the means or in the manner provided by the regulation discharges the buyer's obligation unless the regulation is discriminatory, oppressive or predatory.

§ 2–615.   Excuse by Failure of Presupposed Conditions.

Except so far as a seller may have assumed a greater obligation and subject to the preceding section on substituted performance:

(a) Delay in delivery or non-delivery in whole or in part by a seller who complies with paragraphs (b) and (c) is not a breach of his duty under a contract for sale if performance as agreed has been made impracticable by the occurrence of a contingency the nonoccurrence of which was a basic assumption on which the contract was made or by compliance in good faith with any applicable foreign or domestic governmental regulation or order whether or not it later proves to be invalid.

(b) Where the causes mentioned in paragraph (a) affect only a part of the seller's capacity to perform, he must allocate production and deliveries among his customers but may at his option include regular customers not then under contract as well as his own requirements for further manufacture. He may so allocate in any manner which is fair and reasonable.

(c) The seller must notify the buyer seasonably that there will be delay or non-delivery and, when allocation is required under paragraph (b), of the estimated quota thus made available for the buyer.

§ 2–616.   Procedure on Notice Claiming Excuse.

(1) Where the buyer receives notification of a material or indefinite delay or an allocation justified under the preceding section he may by written notification to the seller as to any delivery concerned, and where the prospective deficiency substantially impairs the value of the whole contract under the provisions of this Article relating to

breach of installment contracts (Section 2–612), then also as to the whole,

(a) terminate and thereby discharge any unexecuted portion of the contract; or

(b) modify the contract by agreeing to take his available quota in substitution.

(2) If after receipt of such notification from the seller the buyer fails so to modify the contract within a reasonable time not exceeding thirty days the contract lapses with respect to any deliveries affected.

(3) The provisions of this section may not be negated by agreement except in so far as the seller has assumed a greater obligation under the preceding section.

Part 7   Remedies

§ 2–701.   Remedies for Breach of Collateral Contracts Not Impaired.

Remedies for breach of any obligation or promise collateral or ancillary to a contract for sale are not impaired by the provisions of this Article.

§ 2–702.   Seller's Remedies on Discovery of Buyer's Insolvency.

(1) Where the seller discovers the buyer to be insolvent he may refuse delivery except for cash including payment for all goods theretofore delivered under the contract, and stop delivery under this Article (Section 2–705).

(2) Where the seller discovers that the buyer has received goods on credit while insolvent he may reclaim the goods upon demand made within ten days after the receipt, but if misrepresentation of solvency has been made to the particular seller in writing within three months before delivery the ten day limitation does not apply. Except as provided in this subsection the seller may not base a right to reclaim goods on the buyer's fraudulent or innocent misrepresentation of solvency or of intent to pay.

(3) The seller's right to reclaim under subsection (2) is subject to the rights of a buyer in ordinary course or other good faith purchaser under this Article (Section 2–403). Successful reclamation of goods excludes all other remedies with respect to them.

§ 2–703.   Seller's Remedies in General.

Where the buyer wrongfully rejects or revokes acceptance of goods or fails to make a payment due on or before delivery or repudiates with respect to a part or the whole, then with respect to any goods directly affected and, if the breach is of the whole contract (Section 2–612), then also with respect to the whole undelivered balance, the aggrieved seller may

(a) withhold delivery of such goods;

(b) stop delivery by any bailee as hereafter provided (Section 2–705);

(c) proceed under the next section respecting goods still unidentified to the contract;

(d) resell and recover damages as hereafter provided (Section 2–706);

(e) recover damages for non-acceptance (Section 2–708) or in a proper case the price (Section 2–709);

(f) cancel.

§ 2–704.   Seller's Right to Identify Goods to the Contract Notwithstanding Breach or to Salvage Unfinished Goods.

(1) An aggrieved seller under the preceding section may

(a) identify to the contract conforming goods not already identified if at the time he learned of the breach they are in his possession or control;

(b) treat as the subject of resale goods which have demonstrably been intended for the particular contract even though those goods are unfinished.

(2) Where the goods are unfinished an aggrieved seller may in the exercise of reasonable commercial judgment for the purposes of avoiding loss and of effective realization either complete the manufacture and wholly identify the goods to the contract or cease manufacture and resell for scrap or salvage value or proceed in any other reasonable manner.

§ 2–705.   Seller's Stoppage of Delivery in Transit or Otherwise.

(1) The seller may stop delivery of goods in the possession of a carrier or other bailee when he discovers the buyer to be insolvent (Section 2–702) and may stop delivery of carload, truckload, planeload or larger shipments of express or freight when the buyer repudiates or fails to make a payment due before delivery or if for any other reason the seller has a right to withhold or reclaim the goods.

(2) As against such buyer the seller may stop delivery until

(a) receipt of the goods by the buyer; or

(b) acknowledgment to the buyer by any bailee of the goods except a carrier that the bailee holds the goods for the buyer; or

(c) such acknowledgment to the buyer by a carrier by reshipment or as warehouseman; or

(d) negotiation to the buyer of any negotiable document of title covering the goods.

(3) (a) To stop delivery the seller must so notify as to enable the bailee by reasonable diligence to prevent delivery of the goods.

(b) After such notification the bailee must hold and deliver the goods according to the directions of the seller but the seller is liable to the bailee for any ensuing charges or damages.

(c) If a negotiable document of title has been issued for goods the bailee is not obliged to obey a notification to stop until surrender of the document.

(d) A carrier who has issued a non-negotiable bill of lading is not obliged to obey a notification to stop received from a person other than the consignor.

§ 2–706.   Seller's Resale Including Contract for Resale.

(1) Under the conditions stated in Section 2–703 on seller's remedies, the seller may resell the goods concerned or the undelivered balance thereof. Where the resale is made in good faith and in a commercially reasonable manner the seller may recover the difference between the resale price and the contract price together with any incidental damages allowed under the provisions of this

Article (Section 2–710), but less expenses saved in consequence of the buyer's breach.

(2) Except as otherwise provided in subsection (3) or unless otherwise agreed resale may be at public or private sale including sale by way of one or more contracts to sell or of identification to an existing contract of the seller. Sale may be as a unit or in parcels and at any time and place and on any terms but every aspect of the sale including the method, manner, time, place and terms must be commercially reasonable. The resale must be reasonably identified as referring to the broken contract, but it is not necessary that the goods be in existence or that any or all of them have been identified to the contract before the breach.

(3) Where the resale is at private sale the seller must give the buyer reasonable notification of his intention to resell.

(4) Where the resale is at public sale

    (a) only identified goods can be sold except where there is a recognized market for a public sale of futures in goods of the kind; and

    (b) it must be made at a usual place or market for public sale if one is reasonably available and except in the case of goods which are perishable or threaten to decline in value speedily the seller must give the buyer reasonable notice of the time and place of the resale; and

    (c) if the goods are not to be within the view of those attending the sale the notification of sale must state the place where the goods are located and provide for their reasonable inspection by prospective bidders; and

    (d) the seller may buy.

(5) A purchaser who buys in good faith at a resale takes the goods free of any rights of the original buyer even though the seller fails to comply with one or more of the requirements of this section.

(6) The seller is not accountable to the buyer for any profit made on any resale. A person in the position of a seller (Section 2–707) or a buyer who has rightfully rejected or justifiably revoked acceptance must account for any excess over the amount of his security interest, as hereinafter defined (subsection (3) of Section 2–711).

§ 2–707.   "Person in the Position of a Seller".

(1) A "person in the position of a seller" includes as against a principal an agent who has paid or become responsible for the price of goods on behalf of his principal or anyone who otherwise holds a security interest or other right in goods similar to that of a seller.

(2) A person in the position of a seller may as provided in this Article withhold or stop delivery (Section 2–705) and resell (Section 2–706) and recover incidental damages (Section 2–710).

§ 2–708.   Seller's Damages for Non-Acceptance or Repudiation.

(1) Subject to subsection (2) and to the provisions of this Article with respect to proof of market price (Section 2–723), the measure of damages for non-acceptance or repudiation by the buyer is the difference between the market price at the time and place for tender and the unpaid contract price together with any incidental damages provided in this Article (Section 2–710), but less expenses saved in consequence of the buyer's breach.

(2) If the measure of damages provided in subsection (1) is inadequate to put the seller in as good a position as performance would have done then the measure of damages is the profit (including reasonable overhead) which the seller would have made from full performance by the buyer, together with any incidental damages provided in this Article (Section 2–710), due allowance for costs reasonably incurred and due credit for payments or proceeds of resale.

§ 2–709.   Action for the Price.

(1) When the buyer fails to pay the price as it becomes due the seller may recover, together with any incidental damages under the next section, the price

    (a) of goods accepted or of conforming goods lost or damaged within a commercially reasonable time after risk of their loss has passed to the buyer; and

    (b) of goods identified to the contract if the seller is unable after reasonable effort to resell them at a reasonable price or the circumstances reasonably indicate that such effort will be unavailing.

(2) Where the seller sues for the price he must hold for the buyer any goods which have been identified to the contract and are still in his control except that if resale becomes possible he may resell them at any time prior to the collection of the judgment. The net proceeds of any such resale must be credited to the buyer and payment of the judgment entitles him to any goods not resold.

(3) After the buyer has wrongfully rejected or revoked acceptance of the goods or has failed to make a payment due or has repudiated (Section 2–610), a seller who is held not entitled to the price under this section shall nevertheless be awarded damages for non-acceptance under the preceding section.

§ 2–710.   Seller's Incidental Damages.

Incidental damages to an aggrieved seller include any commercially reasonable charges, expenses or commissions incurred in stopping delivery, in the transportation, care and custody of goods after the buyer's breach, in connection with return or resale of the goods or otherwise resulting from the breach.

§ 2–711.   Buyer's Remedies in General; Buyer's Security Interest in Rejected Goods.

(1) Where the seller fails to make delivery or repudiates or the buyer rightfully rejects or justifiably revokes acceptance then with respect to any goods involved, and with respect to the whole if the breach goes to the whole contract (Section 2–612), the buyer may cancel and whether or not he has done so may in addition to recovering so much of the price as has been paid

    (a) "cover" and have damages under the next section as to all the goods affected whether or not they have been identified to the contract; or

    (b) recover damages for non-delivery as provided in this Article (Section 2–713).

(2) Where the seller fails to deliver or repudiates the buyer may also

    (a) if the goods have been identified recover them as provided in this Article (Section 2–502); or

    (b) in a proper case obtain specific performance or replevy the goods as provided in this Article (Section 2–716).

(3) On rightful rejection or justifiable revocation of acceptance a buyer has a security interest in goods in his possession or control for any payments made on their price and any expenses reasonably incurred in their inspection, receipt, transportation, care and custody and may hold such goods and resell them in like manner as an aggrieved seller (Section 2–706).

§ 2–712.   "Cover"; Buyer's Procurement of Substitute Goods.

(1) After a breach within the preceding section the buyer may "cover" by making in good faith and without unreasonable delay any reasonable purchase of or contract to purchase goods in substitution for those due from the seller.

(2) The buyer may recover from the seller as damages the difference between the cost of cover and the contract price together with any incidental or consequential damages as hereinafter defined (Section 2–715), but less expenses saved in consequence of the seller's breach.

(3) Failure of the buyer to effect cover within this section does not bar him from any other remedy.

§ 2–713.   Buyer's Damages for Non-Delivery or Repudiation.

(1) Subject to the provisions of this Article with respect to proof of market price (Section 2–723), the measure of damages for non-delivery or repudiation by the seller is the difference between the market price at the time when the buyer learned of the breach and the contract price together with any incidental and consequential damages provided in this Article (Section 2–715), but less expenses saved in consequence of the seller's breach.

(2) Market price is to be determined as of the place for tender or, in cases of rejection after arrival or revocation of acceptance, as of the place of arrival.

§ 2–714.   Buyer's Damages for Breach in Regard to Accepted Goods.

(1) Where the buyer has accepted goods and given notification (subsection (3) of Section 2–607) he may recover as damages for any non-conformity of tender the loss resulting in the ordinary course of events from the seller's breach as determined in any manner which is reasonable.

(2) The measure of damages for breach of warranty is the difference at the time and place of acceptance between the value of the goods accepted and the value they would have had if they had been as warranted, unless special circumstances show proximate damages of a different amount.

(3) In a proper case any incidental and consequential damages under the next section may also be recovered.

§ 2–715.   Buyer's Incidental and Consequential Damages.

(1) Incidental damages resulting from the seller's breach include expenses reasonably incurred in inspection, receipt, transportation and care and custody of goods rightfully rejected, any commercially reasonable charges, expenses or commissions in connection with effecting cover and any other reasonable expense incident to the delay or other breach.

(2) Consequential damages resulting from the seller's breach include

(a) any loss resulting from general or particular requirements and needs of which the seller at the time of contracting had

reason to know and which could not reasonably be prevented by cover or otherwise; and

(b) injury to person or property proximately resulting from any breach of warranty.

§ 2–716.   Buyer's Right to Specific Performance or Replevin.

(1) Specific performance may be decreed where the goods are unique or in other proper circumstances.

(2) The decree for specific performance may include such terms and conditions as to payment of the price, damages, or other relief as the court may deem just.

(3) The buyer has a right of replevin for goods identified to the contract if after reasonable effort he is unable to effect cover for such goods or the circumstances reasonably indicate that such effort will be unavailing or if the goods have been shipped under reservation and satisfaction of the security interest in them has been made or tendered. In the case of goods bought for personal, family, or household purposes, the buyer's right of replevin vests upon acquisition of a special property, even if the seller had not then repudiated or failed to deliver.

As amended in 1999.

§ 2–717.   Deduction of Damages From the Price.

The buyer on notifying the seller of his intention to do so may deduct all or any part of the damages resulting from any breach of the contract from any part of the price still due under the same contract.

§ 2–718.   Liquidation or Limitation of Damages; Deposits.

(1) Damages for breach by either party may be liquidated in the agreement but only at an amount which is reasonable in the light of the anticipated or actual harm caused by the breach, the difficulties of proof of loss, and the inconvenience or nonfeasibility of otherwise obtaining an adequate remedy. A term fixing unreasonably large liquidated damages is void as a penalty.

(2) Where the seller justifiably withholds delivery of goods because of the buyer's breach, the buyer is entitled to restitution of any amount by which the sum of his payments exceeds

(a) the amount to which the seller is entitled by virtue of terms liquidating the seller's damages in accordance with subsection (1), or

(b) in the absence of such terms, twenty per cent of the value of the total performance for which the buyer is obligated under the contract or $500, whichever is smaller.

(3) The buyer's right to restitution under subsection (2) is subject to offset to the extent that the seller establishes

(a) a right to recover damages under the provisions of this Article other than subsection (1), and

(b) the amount or value of any benefits received by the buyer directly or indirectly by reason of the contract.

(4) Where a seller has received payment in goods their reasonable value or the proceeds of their resale shall be treated as payments for the purposes of subsection (2); but if the seller has notice of the buyer's breach before reselling goods received in part performance, his resale is subject to the conditions laid down in this Article on resale by an aggrieved seller (Section 2–706).

§ 2–719.   Contractual Modification or Limitation of Remedy.

(1) Subject to the provisions of subsections (2) and (3) of this section and of the preceding section on liquidation and limitation of damages,

(a) the agreement may provide for remedies in addition to or in substitution for those provided in this Article and may limit or alter the measure of damages recoverable under this Article, as by limiting the buyer's remedies to return of the goods and repayment of the price or to repair and replacement of nonconforming goods or parts; and

(b) resort to a remedy as provided is optional unless the remedy is expressly agreed to be exclusive, in which case it is the sole remedy.

(2) Where circumstances cause an exclusive or limited remedy to fail of its essential purpose, remedy may be had as provided in this Act.

(3) Consequential damages may be limited or excluded unless the limitation or exclusion is unconscionable. Limitation of consequential damages for injury to the person in the case of consumer goods is prima facie unconscionable but limitation of damages where the loss is commercial is not.

§ 2–720.   Effect of "Cancellation" or "Rescission" on Claims for Antecedent Breach.

Unless the contrary intention clearly appears, expressions of "cancellation" or "rescission" of the contract or the like shall not be construed as a renunciation or discharge of any claim in damages for an antecedent breach.

§ 2–721.   Remedies for Fraud.

Remedies for material misrepresentation or fraud include all remedies available under this Article for non-fraudulent breach. Neither rescission or a claim for rescission of the contract for sale nor rejection or return of the goods shall bar or be deemed inconsistent with a claim for damages or other remedy.

§ 2–722.   Who Can Sue Third Parties for Injury to Goods.

Where a third party so deals with goods which have been identified to a contract for sale as to cause actionable injury to a party to that contract

(a) a right of action against the third party is in either party to the contract for sale who has title to or a security interest or a special property or an insurable interest in the goods; and if the goods have been destroyed or converted a right of action is also in the party who either bore the risk of loss under the contract for sale or has since the injury assumed that risk as against the other;

(b) if at the time of the injury the party plaintiff did not bear the risk of loss as against the other party to the contract for sale and there is no arrangement between them for disposition of the recovery, his suit or settlement is, subject to his own interest, as a fiduciary for the other party to the contract;

(c) either party may with the consent of the other sue for the benefit of whom it may concern.

§ 2–723.   Proof of Market Price: Time and Place.

(1) If an action based on anticipatory repudiation comes to trial before the time for performance with respect to some or all of the goods, any damages based on market price (Section 2–708 or Section 2–713) shall be determined according to the price of such goods prevailing at the time when the aggrieved party learned of the repudiation.

(2) If evidence of a price prevailing at the times or places described in this Article is not readily available the price prevailing within any reasonable time before or after the time described or at any other place which in commercial judgment or under usage of trade would serve as a reasonable substitute for the one described may be used, making any proper allowance for the cost of transporting the goods to or from such other place.

(3) Evidence of a relevant price prevailing at a time or place other than the one described in this Article offered by one party is not admissible unless and until he has given the other party such notice as the court finds sufficient to prevent unfair surprise.

§ 2–724.   Admissibility of Market Quotations.

Whenever the prevailing price or value of any goods regularly bought and sold in any established commodity market is in issue, reports in official publications or trade journals or in newspapers or periodicals of general circulation published as the reports of such market shall be admissible in evidence. The circumstances of the preparation of such a report may be shown to affect its weight but not its admissibility.

§ 2–725.   Statute of Limitations in Contracts for Sale.

(1) An action for breach of any contract for sale must be commenced within four years after the cause of action has accrued. By the original agreement the parties may reduce the period of limitation to not less than one year but may not extend it.

(2) A cause of action accrues when the breach occurs, regardless of the aggrieved party's lack of knowledge of the breach. A breach of warranty occurs when tender of delivery is made, except that where a warranty explicitly extends to future performance of the goods and discovery of the breach must await the time of such performance the cause of action accrues when the breach is or should have been discovered.

(3) Where an action commenced within the time limited by subsection (1) is so terminated as to leave available a remedy by another action for the same breach such other action may be commenced after the expiration of the time limited and within six months after the termination of the first action unless the termination resulted from voluntary discontinuance or from dismissal for failure or neglect to prosecute.

(4) This section does not alter the law on tolling of the statute of limitations nor does it apply to causes of action which have accrued before this Act becomes effective.

Article 2A
LEASES

Part 1   General Provisions

§ 2A–101.   Short Title.

This Article shall be known and may be cited as the Uniform Commercial Code—Leases.

§ 2A–102.   Scope.

This Article applies to any transaction, regardless of form, that creates a lease.

§ 2A–103.   Definitions and Index of Definitions.

(1) In this Article unless the context otherwise requires:

(a) "Buyer in ordinary course of business" means a person who in good faith and without knowledge that the sale to him [or her] is in violation of the ownership rights or security interest or leasehold interest of a third party in the goods buys in ordinary course from a person in the business of selling goods of that kind but does not include a pawnbroker. "Buying" may be for cash or by exchange of other property or on secured or unsecured credit and includes receiving goods or documents of title under a pre-existing contract for sale but does not include a transfer in bulk or as security for or in total or partial satisfaction of a money debt.

(b) "Cancellation" occurs when either party puts an end to the lease contract for default by the other party.

(c) "Commercial unit" means such a unit of goods as by commercial usage is a single whole for purposes of lease and division of which materially impairs its character or value on the market or in use. A commercial unit may be a single article, as a machine, or a set of articles, as a suite of furniture or a line of machinery, or a quantity, as a gross or carload, or any other unit treated in use or in the relevant market as a single whole.

(d) "Conforming" goods or performance under a lease contract means goods or performance that are in accordance with the obligations under the lease contract.

(e) "Consumer lease" means a lease that a lessor regularly engaged in the business of leasing or selling makes to a lessee who is an individual and who takes under the lease primarily for a personal, family, or household purpose [, if the total payments to be made under the lease contract, excluding payments for options to renew or buy, do not exceed $_____].

(f) "Fault" means wrongful act, omission, breach, or default.

(g) "Finance lease" means a lease with respect to which:

(i) the lessor does not select, manufacture or supply the goods;

(ii) the lessor acquires the goods or the right to possession and use of the goods in connection with the lease; and

(iii) one of the following occurs:

(A) the lessee receives a copy of the contract by which the lessor acquired the goods or the right to possession and use of the goods before signing the lease contract;

(B) the lessee's approval of the contract by which the lessor acquired the goods or the right to possession and use of the goods is a condition to effectiveness of the lease contract;

(C) the lessee, before signing the lease contract, receives an accurate and complete statement designating the promises and warranties, and any disclaimers of warranties, limitations or modifications of remedies, or liquidated damages, including those of a third party, such as the manufacturer of the goods, provided to the lessor by the person supplying the goods in connection with or as part of the contract by which the lessor acquired the goods or the right to possession and use of the goods; or

(D) if the lease is not a consumer lease, the lessor, before the lessee signs the lease contract, informs the lessee in writing (a) of the identity of the person supplying the goods to the lessor, unless the lessee has selected that person and directed the lessor to acquire the goods or the right to possession and use of the goods from that person, (b) that the lessee is entitled under this Article to any promises and warranties, including those of any third party, provided to the lessor by the person supplying the goods in connection with or as part of the contract by which the lessor acquired the goods or the right to possession and use of the goods, and (c) that the lessee may communicate with the person supplying the goods to the lessor and receive an accurate and complete statement of those promises and warranties, including any disclaimers and limitations of them or of remedies.

(h) "Goods" means all things that are movable at the time of identification to the lease contract, or are fixtures (Section 2A–309), but the term does not include money, documents, instruments, accounts, chattel paper, general intangibles, or minerals or the like, including oil and gas, before extraction. The term also includes the unborn young of animals.

(i) "Installment lease contract" means a lease contract that authorizes or requires the delivery of goods in separate lots to be separately accepted, even though the lease contract contains a clause "each delivery is a separate lease" or its equivalent.

(j) "Lease" means a transfer of the right to possession and use of goods for a term in return for consideration, but a sale, including a sale on approval or a sale or return, or retention or creation of a security interest is not a lease. Unless the context clearly indicates otherwise, the term includes a sublease.

(k) "Lease agreement" means the bargain, with respect to the lease, of the lessor and the lessee in fact as found in their language or by implication from other circumstances including course of dealing or usage of trade or course of performance as provided in this Article. Unless the context clearly indicates otherwise, the term includes a sublease agreement.

(l) "Lease contract" means the total legal obligation that results from the lease agreement as affected by this Article and any other applicable rules of law. Unless the context clearly indicates otherwise, the term includes a sublease contract.

(m) "Leasehold interest" means the interest of the lessor or the lessee under a lease contract.

(n) "Lessee" means a person who acquires the right to possession and use of goods under a lease. Unless the context clearly indicates otherwise, the term includes a sublessee.

(o) "Lessee in ordinary course of business" means a person who in good faith and without knowledge that the lease to him [or her] is in violation of the ownership rights or security interest or leasehold interest of a third party in the goods, leases in ordinary course from a person in the business of selling or leasing goods of that kind but does not include a pawnbroker. "Leasing" may be for cash or by exchange of other property or on secured or unsecured credit and includes receiving goods or documents of title under a pre-existing lease contract but does not include a transfer in bulk or as security for or in total or partial satisfaction of a money debt.

(p) "Lessor" means a person who transfers the right to possession and use of goods under a lease. Unless the context clearly indicates otherwise, the term includes a sublessor.

(q) "Lessor's residual interest" means the lessor's interest in the goods after expiration, termination, or cancellation of the lease contract.

(r) "Lien" means a charge against or interest in goods to secure payment of a debt or performance of an obligation, but the term does not include a security interest.

(s) "Lot" means a parcel or a single article that is the subject matter of a separate lease or delivery, whether or not it is sufficient to perform the lease contract.

(t) "Merchant lessee" means a lessee that is a merchant with respect to goods of the kind subject to the lease.

(u) "Present value" means the amount as of a date certain of one or more sums payable in the future, discounted to the date certain. The discount is determined by the interest rate specified by the parties if the rate was not manifestly unreasonable at the time the transaction was entered into; otherwise, the discount is determined by a commercially reasonable rate that takes into account the facts and circumstances of each case at the time the transaction was entered into.

(v) "Purchase" includes taking by sale, lease, mortgage, security interest, pledge, gift, or any other voluntary transaction creating an interest in goods.

(w) "Sublease" means a lease of goods the right to possession and use of which was acquired by the lessor as a lessee under an existing lease.

(x) "Supplier" means a person from whom a lessor buys or leases goods to be leased under a finance lease.

(y) "Supply contract" means a contract under which a lessor buys or leases goods to be leased.

(z) "Termination" occurs when either party pursuant to a power created by agreement or law puts an end to the lease contract otherwise than for default.

(2) Other definitions applying to this Article and the sections in which they appear are:

"Accessions". Section 2A–310(1).

"Construction mortgage". Section 2A–309(1)(d).

"Encumbrance". Section 2A–309(1)(e).

"Fixtures". Section 2A–309(1)(a).

"Fixture filing". Section 2A–309(1)(b).

"Purchase money lease". Section 2A–309(1)(c).

(3) The following definitions in other Articles apply to this Article:

"Accounts". Section 9–106.

"Between merchants". Section 2–104(3).

"Buyer". Section 2–103(1)(a).

"Chattel paper". Section 9–105(1)(b).

"Consumer goods". Section 9–109(1).

"Document". Section 9–105(1)(f).

"Entrusting". Section 2–403(3).

"General intangibles". Section 9–106.

"Good faith". Section 2–103(1)(b).

"Instrument". Section 9–105(1)(i).

"Merchant". Section 2–104(1).

"Mortgage". Section 9–105(1)(j).

"Pursuant to commitment". Section 9–105(1)(k).

"Receipt". Section 2–103(1)(c).

"Sale". Section 2–106(1).

"Sale on approval". Section 2–326.

"Sale or return". Section 2–326.

"Seller". Section 2–103(1)(d).

(4) In addition Article 1 contains general definitions and principles of construction and interpretation applicable throughout this Article.
As amended in 1990 and 1999.

§ 2A–104.   Leases Subject to Other Law.

(1) A lease, although subject to this Article, is also subject to any applicable:

(a) certificate of title statute of this State: (list any certificate of title statutes covering automobiles, trailers, mobile homes, boats, farm tractors, and the like);

(b) certificate of title statute of another jurisdiction (Section 2A–105); or

(c) consumer protection statute of this State, or final consumer protection decision of a court of this State existing on the effective date of this Article.

(2) In case of conflict between this Article, other than Sections 2A–105, 2A–304(3), and 2A–305(3), and a statute or decision referred to in subsection (1), the statute or decision controls.

(3) Failure to comply with an applicable law has only the effect specified therein.

As amended in 1990.

§ 2A–105.   Territorial Application of Article to Goods Covered by Certificate of Title.

Subject to the provisions of Sections 2A–304(3) and 2A–305(3), with respect to goods covered by a certificate of title issued under a statute of this State or of another jurisdiction, compliance and the effect of compliance or noncompliance with a certificate of title statute are governed by the law (including the conflict of laws rules) of the jurisdiction issuing the certificate until the earlier of (a) surrender of the certificate, or (b) four months after the goods are removed from that jurisdiction and thereafter until a new certificate of title is issued by another jurisdiction.

§ 2A–106.   Limitation on Power of Parties to Consumer Lease to Choose Applicable Law and Judicial Forum.

(1) If the law chosen by the parties to a consumer lease is that of a jurisdiction other than a jurisdiction in which the lessee resides at the time the lease agreement becomes enforceable or within

30 days thereafter or in which the goods are to be used, the choice is not enforceable.

(2) If the judicial forum chosen by the parties to a consumer lease is a forum that would not otherwise have jurisdiction over the lessee, the choice is not enforceable.

§ 2A–107.   Waiver or Renunciation of Claim or Right After Default.

Any claim or right arising out of an alleged default or breach of warranty may be discharged in whole or in part without consideration by a written waiver or renunciation signed and delivered by the aggrieved party.

§ 2A–108.   Unconscionability.

(1) If the court as a matter of law finds a lease contract or any clause of a lease contract to have been unconscionable at the time it was made the court may refuse to enforce the lease contract, or it may enforce the remainder of the lease contract without the unconscionable clause, or it may so limit the application of any unconscionable clause as to avoid any unconscionable result.

(2) With respect to a consumer lease, if the court as a matter of law finds that a lease contract or any clause of a lease contract has been induced by unconscionable conduct or that unconscionable conduct has occurred in the collection of a claim arising from a lease contract, the court may grant appropriate relief.

(3) Before making a finding of unconscionability under subsection (1) or (2), the court, on its own motion or that of a party, shall afford the parties a reasonable opportunity to present evidence as to the setting, purpose, and effect of the lease contract or clause thereof, or of the conduct.

(4) In an action in which the lessee claims unconscionability with respect to a consumer lease:

   (a) If the court finds unconscionability under subsection (1) or (2), the court shall award reasonable attorney's fees to the lessee.

   (b) If the court does not find unconscionability and the lessee claiming unconscionability has brought or maintained an action he [or she] knew to be groundless, the court shall award reasonable attorney's fees to the party against whom the claim is made.

   (c) In determining attorney's fees, the amount of the recovery on behalf of the claimant under subsections (1) and (2) is not controlling.

§ 2A–109.   Option to Accelerate at Will.

(1) A term providing that one party or his [or her] successor in interest may accelerate payment or performance or require collateral or additional collateral "at will" or "when he [or she] deems himself [or herself] insecure" or in words of similar import must be construed to mean that he [or she] has power to do so only if he [or she] in good faith believes that the prospect of payment or performance is impaired.

(2) With respect to a consumer lease, the burden of establishing good faith under subsection (1) is on the party who exercised the power; otherwise the burden of establishing lack of good faith is on the party against whom the power has been exercised.

Part 2   Formation and Construction of Lease Contract
§ 2A–201.   Statute of Frauds.

(1) A lease contract is not enforceable by way of action or defense unless:

   (a) the total payments to be made under the lease contract, excluding payments for options to renew or buy, are less than $1,000; or

   (b) there is a writing, signed by the party against whom enforcement is sought or by that party's authorized agent, sufficient to indicate that a lease contract has been made between the parties and to describe the goods leased and the lease term.

(2) Any description of leased goods or of the lease term is sufficient and satisfies subsection (1)(b), whether or not it is specific, if it reasonably identifies what is described.

(3) A writing is not insufficient because it omits or incorrectly states a term agreed upon, but the lease contract is not enforceable under subsection (1)(b) beyond the lease term and the quantity of goods shown in the writing.

(4) A lease contract that does not satisfy the requirements of subsection (1), but which is valid in other respects, is enforceable:

   (a) if the goods are to be specially manufactured or obtained for the lessee and are not suitable for lease or sale to others in the ordinary course of the lessor's business, and the lessor, before notice of repudiation is received and under circumstances that reasonably indicate that the goods are for the lessee, has made either a substantial beginning of their manufacture or commitments for their procurement;

   (b) if the party against whom enforcement is sought admits in that party's pleading, testimony or otherwise in court that a lease contract was made, but the lease contract is not enforceable under this provision beyond the quantity of goods admitted; or

   (c) with respect to goods that have been received and accepted by the lessee.

(5) The lease term under a lease contract referred to in subsection (4) is:

   (a) if there is a writing signed by the party against whom enforcement is sought or by that party's authorized agent specifying the lease term, the term so specified;

   (b) if the party against whom enforcement is sought admits in that party's pleading, testimony, or otherwise in court a lease term, the term so admitted; or

   (c) a reasonable lease term.

§ 2A–202.   Final Written Expression: Parol or Extrinsic Evidence.

Terms with respect to which the confirmatory memoranda of the parties agree or which are otherwise set forth in a writing intended by the parties as a final expression of their agreement with respect to such terms as are included therein may not be contradicted by evidence of any prior agreement or of a contemporaneous oral agreement but may be explained or supplemented:

(a) by course of dealing or usage of trade or by course of performance; and

(b) by evidence of consistent additional terms unless the court finds the writing to have been intended also as a complete and exclusive statement of the terms of the agreement.

§ 2A–203.   Seals Inoperative.

The affixing of a seal to a writing evidencing a lease contract or an offer to enter into a lease contract does not render the writing a sealed instrument and the law with respect to sealed instruments does not apply to the lease contract or offer.

§ 2A–204.   Formation in General.

(1) A lease contract may be made in any manner sufficient to show agreement, including conduct by both parties which recognizes the existence of a lease contract.

(2) An agreement sufficient to constitute a lease contract may be found although the moment of its making is undetermined.

(3) Although one or more terms are left open, a lease contract does not fail for indefiniteness if the parties have intended to make a lease contract and there is a reasonably certain basis for giving an appropriate remedy.

§ 2A–205.   Firm Offers.

An offer by a merchant to lease goods to or from another person in a signed writing that by its terms gives assurance it will be held open is not revocable, for lack of consideration, during the time stated or, if no time is stated, for a reasonable time, but in no event may the period of irrevocability exceed 3 months. Any such term of assurance on a form supplied by the offeree must be separately signed by the offeror.

§ 2A–206.   Offer and Acceptance in Formation of Lease Contract.

(1) Unless otherwise unambiguously indicated by the language or circumstances, an offer to make a lease contract must be construed as inviting acceptance in any manner and by any medium reasonable in the circumstances.

(2) If the beginning of a requested performance is a reasonable mode of acceptance, an offeror who is not notified of acceptance within a reasonable time may treat the offer as having lapsed before acceptance.

§ 2A–207.   Course of Performance or Practical Construction.

(1) If a lease contract involves repeated occasions for performance by either party with knowledge of the nature of the performance and opportunity for objection to it by the other, any course of performance accepted or acquiesced in without objection is relevant to determine the meaning of the lease agreement.

(2) The express terms of a lease agreement and any course of performance, as well as any course of dealing and usage of trade, must be construed whenever reasonable as consistent with each other; but if that construction is unreasonable, express terms control course of performance, course of performance controls both course of dealing and usage of trade, and course of dealing controls usage of trade.

(3) Subject to the provisions of Section 2A–208 on modification and waiver, course of performance is relevant to show a waiver or modification of any term inconsistent with the course of performance.

§ 2A–208.   Modification, Rescission and Waiver.

(1) An agreement modifying a lease contract needs no consideration to be binding.

(2) A signed lease agreement that excludes modification or rescission except by a signed writing may not be otherwise modified or rescinded, but, except as between merchants, such a requirement on a form supplied by a merchant must be separately signed by the other party.

(3) Although an attempt at modification or rescission does not satisfy the requirements of subsection (2), it may operate as a waiver.

(4) A party who has made a waiver affecting an executory portion of a lease contract may retract the waiver by reasonable notification received by the other party that strict performance will be required of any term waived, unless the retraction would be unjust in view of a material change of position in reliance on the waiver.

§ 2A–209.   Lessee under Finance Lease as Beneficiary of Supply Contract.

(1) The benefit of the supplier's promises to the lessor under the supply contract and of all warranties, whether express or implied, including those of any third party provided in connection with or as part of the supply contract, extends to the lessee to the extent of the lessee's leasehold interest under a finance lease related to the supply contract, but is subject to the terms warranty and of the supply contract and all defenses or claims arising therefrom.

(2) The extension of the benefit of supplier's promises and of warranties to the lessee (Section 2A–209(1)) does not: (i) modify the rights and obligations of the parties to the supply contract, whether arising therefrom or otherwise, or (ii) impose any duty or liability under the supply contract on the lessee.

(3) Any modification or rescission of the supply contract by the supplier and the lessor is effective between the supplier and the lessee unless, before the modification or rescission, the supplier has received notice that the lessee has entered into a finance lease related to the supply contract. If the modification or rescission is effective between the supplier and the lessee, the lessor is deemed to have assumed, in addition to the obligations of the lessor to the lessee under the lease contract, promises of the supplier to the lessor and warranties that were so modified or rescinded as they existed and were available to the lessee before modification or rescission.

(4) In addition to the extension of the benefit of the supplier's promises and of warranties to the lessee under subsection (1), the lessee retains all rights that the lessee may have against the supplier which arise from an agreement between the lessee and the supplier or under other law.

As amended in 1990.

§ 2A-210. Express Warranties.

(1) Express warranties by the lessor are created as follows:

(a) Any affirmation of fact or promise made by the lessor to the lessee which relates to the goods and becomes part of the basis of the bargain creates an express warranty that the goods will conform to the affirmation or promise.

(b) Any description of the goods which is made part of the basis of the bargain creates an express warranty that the goods will conform to the description.

(c) Any sample or model that is made part of the basis of the bargain creates an express warranty that the whole of the goods will conform to the sample or model.

(2) It is not necessary to the creation of an express warranty that the lessor use formal words, such as "warrant" or "guarantee," or that the lessor have a specific intention to make a warranty, but an affirmation merely of the value of the goods or a statement purporting to be merely the lessor's opinion or commendation of the goods does not create a warranty.

§ 2A-211. Warranties Against Interference and Against Infringement; Lessee's Obligation Against Infringement.

(1) There is in a lease contract a warranty that for the lease term no person holds a claim to or interest in the goods that arose from an act or omission of the lessor, other than a claim by way of infringement or the like, which will interfere with the lessee's enjoyment of its leasehold interest.

(2) Except in a finance lease there is in a lease contract by a lessor who is a merchant regularly dealing in goods of the kind a warranty that the goods are delivered free of the rightful claim of any person by way of infringement or the like.

(3) A lessee who furnishes specifications to a lessor or a supplier shall hold the lessor and the supplier harmless against any claim by way of infringement or the like that arises out of compliance with the specifications.

§ 2A-212. Implied Warranty of Merchantability.

(1) Except in a finance lease, a warranty that the goods will be merchantable is implied in a lease contract if the lessor is a merchant with respect to goods of that kind.

(2) Goods to be merchantable must be at least such as

(a) pass without objection in the trade under the description in the lease agreement;

(b) in the case of fungible goods, are of fair average quality within the description;

(c) are fit for the ordinary purposes for which goods of that type are used;

(d) run, within the variation permitted by the lease agreement, of even kind, quality, and quantity within each unit and among all units involved;

(e) are adequately contained, packaged, and labeled as the lease agreement may require; and

(f) conform to any promises or affirmations of fact made on the container or label.

(3) Other implied warranties may arise from course of dealing or usage of trade.

§ 2A-213. Implied Warranty of Fitness for Particular Purpose.

Except in a finance of lease, if the lessor at the time the lease contract is made has reason to know of any particular purpose for which the goods are required and that the lessee is relying on the lessor's skill or judgment to select or furnish suitable goods, there is in the lease contract an implied warranty that the goods will be fit for that purpose.

§ 2A-214. Exclusion or Modification of Warranties.

(1) Words or conduct relevant to the creation of an express warranty and words or conduct tending to negate or limit a warranty must be construed wherever reasonable as consistent with each other; but, subject to the provisions of Section 2A-202 on parol or extrinsic evidence, negation or limitation is inoperative to the extent that the construction is unreasonable.

(2) Subject to subsection (3), to exclude or modify the implied warranty of merchantability or any part of it the language must mention "merchantability", be by a writing, and be conspicuous. Subject to subsection (3), to exclude or modify any implied warranty of fitness the exclusion must be by a writing and be conspicuous. Language to exclude all implied warranties of fitness is sufficient if it is in writing, is conspicuous and states, for example, "There is no warranty that the goods will be fit for a particular purpose".

(3) Notwithstanding subsection (2), but subject to subsection (4),

(a) unless the circumstances indicate otherwise, all implied warranties are excluded by expressions like "as is" or "with all faults" or by other language that in common understanding calls the lessee's attention to the exclusion of warranties and makes plain that there is no implied warranty, if in writing and conspicuous;

(b) if the lessee before entering into the lease contract has examined the goods or the sample or model as fully as desired or has refused to examine the goods, there is no implied warranty with regard to defects that an examination ought in the circumstances to have revealed; and

(c) an implied warranty may also be excluded or modified by course of dealing, course of performance, or usage of trade.

(4) To exclude or modify a warranty against interference or against infringement (Section 2A-211) or any part of it, the language must be specific, be by a writing, and be conspicuous, unless the circumstances, including course of performance, course of dealing, or usage of trade, give the lessee reason to know that the goods are being leased subject to a claim or interest of any person.

§ 2A-215. Cumulation and Conflict of Warranties Express or Implied.

Warranties, whether express or implied, must be construed as consistent with each other and as cumulative, but if that construction is unreasonable, the intention of the parties determines which warranty is dominant. In ascertaining that intention the following rules apply:

(a) Exact or technical specifications displace an inconsistent sample or model or general language of description.

(b) A sample from an existing bulk displaces inconsistent general language of description.

(c) Express warranties displace inconsistent implied warranties other than an implied warranty of fitness for a particular purpose.

§ 2A–216.   Third-Party Beneficiaries of Express and Implied Warranties.

Alternative A

A warranty to or for the benefit of a lessee under this Article, whether express or implied, extends to any natural person who is in the family or household of the lessee or who is a guest in the lessee's home if it is reasonable to expect that such person may use, consume, or be affected by the goods and who is injured in person by breach of the warranty. This section does not displace principles of law and equity that extend a warranty to or for the benefit of a lessee to other persons. The operation of this section may not be excluded, modified, or limited, but an exclusion, modification, or limitation of the warranty, including any with respect to rights and remedies, effective against the lessee is also effective against any beneficiary designated under this section.

Alternative B

A warranty to or for the benefit of a lessee under this Article, whether express or implied, extends to any natural person who may reasonably be expected to use, consume, or be affected by the goods and who is injured in person by breach of the warranty. This section does not displace principles of law and equity that extend a warranty to or for the benefit of a lessee to other persons. The operation of this section may not be excluded, modified, or limited, but an exclusion, modification, or limitation of the warranty, including any with respect to rights and remedies, effective against the lessee is also effective against the beneficiary designated under this section.

Alternative C

A warranty to or for the benefit of a lessee under this Article, whether express or implied, extends to any person who may reasonably be expected to use, consume, or be affected by the goods and who is injured by breach of the warranty. The operation of this section may not be excluded, modified, or limited with respect to injury to the person of an individual to whom the warranty extends, but an exclusion, modification, or limitation of the warranty, including any with respect to rights and remedies, effective against the lessee is also effective against the beneficiary designated under this section.

§ 2A–217.   Identification.

Identification of goods as goods to which a lease contract refers may be made at any time and in any manner explicitly agreed to by the parties. In the absence of explicit agreement, identification occurs:

(a) when the lease contract is made if the lease contract is for a lease of goods that are existing and identified;

(b) when the goods are shipped, marked, or otherwise designated by the lessor as goods to which the lease contract refers, if the lease contract is for a lease of goods that are not existing and identified; or

(c) when the young are conceived, if the lease contract is for a lease of unborn young of animals.

§ 2A–218.   Insurance and Proceeds.

(1) A lessee obtains an insurable interest when existing goods are identified to the lease contract even though the goods identified are nonconforming and the lessee has an option to reject them.

(2) If a lessee has an insurable interest only by reason of the lessor's identification of the goods, the lessor, until default or insolvency or notification to the lessee that identification is final, may substitute other goods for those identified.

(3) Notwithstanding a lessee's insurable interest under subsections (1) and (2), the lessor retains an insurable interest until an option to buy has been exercised by the lessee and risk of loss has passed to the lessee.

(4) Nothing in this section impairs any insurable interest recognized under any other statute or rule of law.

(5) The parties by agreement may determine that one or more parties have an obligation to obtain and pay for insurance covering the goods and by agreement may determine the beneficiary of the proceeds of the insurance.

§ 2A–219.   Risk of Loss.

(1) Except in the case of a finance lease, risk of loss is retained by the lessor and does not pass to the lessee. In the case of a finance lease, risk of loss passes to the lessee.

(2) Subject to the provisions of this Article on the effect of default on risk of loss (Section 2A–220), if risk of loss is to pass to the lessee and the time of passage is not stated, the following rules apply:

(a) If the lease contract requires or authorizes the goods to be shipped by carrier

(i) and it does not require delivery at a particular destination, the risk of loss passes to the lessee when the goods are duly delivered to the carrier; but

(ii) if it does require delivery at a particular destination and the goods are there duly tendered while in the possession of the carrier, the risk of loss passes to the lessee when the goods are there duly so tendered as to enable the lessee to take delivery.

(b) If the goods are held by a bailee to be delivered without being moved, the risk of loss passes to the lessee on acknowledgment by the bailee of the lessee's right to possession of the goods.

(c) In any case not within subsection (a) or (b), the risk of loss passes to the lessee on the lessee's receipt of the goods if the lessor, or, in the case of a finance lease, the supplier, is a merchant; otherwise the risk passes to the lessee on tender of delivery.

§ 2A–220.   Effect of Default on Risk of Loss.

(1) Where risk of loss is to pass to the lessee and the time of passage is not stated:

(a) If a tender or delivery of goods so fails to conform to the lease contract as to give a right of rejection, the risk of their loss remains with the lessor, or, in the case of a finance lease, the supplier, until cure or acceptance.

(b) If the lessee rightfully revokes acceptance, he [or she], to the extent of any deficiency in his [or her] effective insurance coverage, may treat the risk of loss as having remained with the lessor from the beginning.

(2) Whether or not risk of loss is to pass to the lessee, if the lessee as to conforming goods already identified to a lease contract repudiates or is otherwise in default under the lease contract, the lessor, or, in the case of a finance lease, the supplier, to the extent of any deficiency in his [or her] effective insurance coverage may treat the risk of loss as resting on the lessee for a commercially reasonable time.

§ 2A–221.   Casualty to Identified Goods.

If a lease contract requires goods identified when the lease contract is made, and the goods suffer casualty without fault of the lessee, the lessor or the supplier before delivery, or the goods suffer casualty before risk of loss passes to the lessee pursuant to the lease agreement or Section 2A–219, then:

(a) if the loss is total, the lease contract is avoided; and

(b) if the loss is partial or the goods have so deteriorated as to no longer conform to the lease contract, the lessee may nevertheless demand inspection and at his [or her] option either treat the lease contract as avoided or, except in a finance lease that is not a consumer lease, accept the goods with due allowance from the rent payable for the balance of the lease term for the deterioration or the deficiency in quantity but without further right against the lessor.

Part 3   Effect of Lease Contract

§ 2A–301.   Enforceability of Lease Contract.

Except as otherwise provided in this Article, a lease contract is effective and enforceable according to its terms between the parties, against purchasers of the goods and against creditors of the parties.

§ 2A–302.   Title to and Possession of Goods.

Except as otherwise provided in this Article, each provision of this Article applies whether the lessor or a third party has title to the goods, and whether the lessor, the lessee, or a third party has possession of the goods, notwithstanding any statute or rule of law that possession or the absence of possession is fraudulent.

§ 2A–303.   Alienability of Party's Interest Under Lease Contract or of Lessor's Residual Interest in Goods; Delegation of Performance; Transfer of Rights.

(1) As used in this section, "creation of a security interest" includes the sale of a lease contract that is subject to Article 9, Secured Transactions, by reason of Section 9–109(a)(3).

(2) Except as provided in subsections (3) and Section 9–407, a provision in a lease agreement which (i) prohibits the voluntary or involuntary transfer, including a transfer by sale, sublease, creation or enforcement of a security interest, or attachment, levy, or other judicial process, of an interest of a party under the lease contract or of the lessor's residual interest in the goods, or (ii) makes such a transfer an event of default, gives rise to the rights and remedies provided in subsection (4), but a transfer that is prohibited or is an event of default under the lease agreement is otherwise effective.

(3) A provision in a lease agreement which (i) prohibits a transfer of a right to damages for default with respect to the whole lease contract or of a right to payment arising out of the transferor's due performance of the transferor's entire obligation, or (ii) makes such a transfer an event of default, is not enforceable, and such a transfer is not a transfer that materially impairs the propsect of obtaining return performance by, materially changes the duty of, or materially increases the burden or risk imposed on, the other party to the lease contract within the purview of subsection (4).

(4) Subject to subsection (3) and Section 9–407:

(a) if a transfer is made which is made an event of default under a lease agreement, the party to the lease contract not making the transfer, unless that party waives the default or otherwise agrees, has the rights and remedies described in Section 2A–501(2);

(b) if paragraph (a) is not applicable and if a transfer is made that (i) is prohibited under a lease agreement or (ii) materially impairs the prospect of obtaining return performance by, materially changes the duty of, or materially increases the burden or risk imposed on, the other party to the lease contract, unless the party not making the transfer agrees at any time to the transfer in the lease contract or otherwise, then, except as limited by contract, (i) the transferor is liable to the party not making the transfer for damages caused by the transfer to the extent that the damages could not reasonably be prevented by the party not making the transfer and (ii) a court having jurisdiction may grant other appropriate relief, including cancellation of the lease contract or an injunction against the transfer.

(5) A transfer of "the lease" or of "all my rights under the lease", or a transfer in similar general terms, is a transfer of rights and, unless the language or the circumstances, as in a transfer for security, indicate the contrary, the transfer is a delegation of duties by the transferor to the transferee. Acceptance by the transferee constitutes a promise by the transferee to perform those duties. The promise is enforceable by either the transferor or the other party to the lease contract.

(6) Unless otherwise agreed by the lessor and the lessee, a delegation of performance does not relieve the transferor as against the other party of any duty to perform or of any liability for default.

(7) In a consumer lease, to prohibit the transfer of an interest of a party under the lease contract or to make a transfer an event of default, the language must be specific, by a writing, and conspicuous.

As amended in 1990 and 1999.

§ 2A–304.   Subsequent Lease of Goods by Lessor.

(1) Subject to Section 2A–303, a subsequent lessee from a lessor of goods under an existing lease contract obtains, to the extent of the leasehold interest transferred, the leasehold interest in the goods that the lessor had or had power to transfer, and except as provided in subsection (2) and Section 2A–527(4), takes subject to the existing lease contract. A lessor with voidable title has power to transfer a good leasehold interest to a good faith subsequent lessee for value, but only to the extent set forth in the preceding

sentence. If goods have been delivered under a transaction of purchase the lessor has that power even though:

(a) the lessor's transferor was deceived as to the identity of the lessor;

(b) the delivery was in exchange for a check which is later dishonored;

(c) it was agreed that the transaction was to be a "cash sale"; or

(d) the delivery was procured through fraud punishable as larcenous under the criminal law.

(2) A subsequent lessee in the ordinary course of business from a lessor who is a merchant dealing in goods of that kind to whom the goods were entrusted by the existing lessee of that lessor before the interest of the subsequent lessee became enforceable against that lessor obtains, to the extent of the leasehold interest transferred, all of that lessor's and the existing lessee's rights to the goods, and takes free of the existing lease contract.

(3) A subsequent lessee from the lessor of goods that are subject to an existing lease contract and are covered by a certificate of title issued under a statute of this State or of another jurisdiction takes no greater rights than those provided both by this section and by the certificate of title statute.

As amended in 1990.

§ 2A–305.   Sale or Sublease of Goods by Lessee.

(1) Subject to the provisions of Section 2A–303, a buyer or sublessee from the lessee of goods under an existing lease contract obtains, to the extent of the interest transferred, the leasehold interest in the goods that the lessee had or had power to transfer, and except as provided in subsection (2) and Section 2A–511(4), takes subject to the existing lease contract. A lessee with a voidable leasehold interest has power to transfer a good leasehold interest to a good faith buyer for value or a good faith sublessee for value, but only to the extent set forth in the preceding sentence. When goods have been delivered under a transaction of lease the lessee has that power even though:

(a) the lessor was deceived as to the identity of the lessee;

(b) the delivery was in exchange for a check which is later dishonored; or

(c) the delivery was procured through fraud punishable as larcenous under the criminal law.

(2) A buyer in the ordinary course of business or a sublessee in the ordinary course of business from a lessee who is a merchant dealing in goods of that kind to whom the goods were entrusted by the lessor obtains, to the extent of the interest transferred, all of the lessor's and lessee's rights to the goods, and takes free of the existing lease contract.

(3) A buyer or sublessee from the lessee of goods that are subject to an existing lease contract and are covered by a certificate of title issued under a statute of this State or of another jurisdiction takes no greater rights than those provided both by this section and by the certificate of title statute.

§ 2A–306.   Priority of Certain Liens Arising by Operation of Law.

If a person in the ordinary course of his [or her] business furnishes services or materials with respect to goods subject to a lease contract, a lien upon those goods in the possession of that person given by statute or rule of law for those materials or services takes priority over any interest of the lessor or lessee under the lease contract or this Article unless the lien is created by statute and the statute provides otherwise or unless the lien is created by rule of law and the rule of law provides otherwise.

§ 2A–307.   Priority of Liens Arising by Attachment or Levy on, Security Interests in, and Other Claims to Goods.

(1) Except as otherwise provided in Section 2A–306, a creditor of a lessee takes subject to the lease contract.

(2) Except as otherwise provided in subsection (3) and in Sections 2A–306 and 2A–308, a creditor of a lessor takes subject to the lease contract unless the creditor holds a lien that attached to the goods before the lease contract became enforceable.

(3) Except as otherwise provided in Sections 9–317, 9–321, and 9–323, a lessee takes a leasehold interest subject to a security interest held by a creditor of the lessor.

As amended in 1990 and 1999.

§ 2A–308.   Special Rights of Creditors.

(1) A creditor of a lessor in possession of goods subject to a lease contract may treat the lease contract as void if as against the creditor retention of possession by the lessor is fraudulent under any statute or rule of law, but retention of possession in good faith and current course of trade by the lessor for a commercially reasonable time after the lease contract becomes enforceable is not fraudulent.

(2) Nothing in this Article impairs the rights of creditors of a lessor if the lease contract (a) becomes enforceable, not in current course of trade but in satisfaction of or as security for a pre-existing claim for money, security, or the like, and (b) is made under circumstances which under any statute or rule of law apart from this Article would constitute the transaction a fraudulent transfer or voidable preference.

(3) A creditor of a seller may treat a sale or an identification of goods to a contract for sale as void if as against the creditor retention of possession by the seller is fraudulent under any statute or rule of law, but retention of possession of the goods pursuant to a lease contract entered into by the seller as lessee and the buyer as lessor in connection with the sale or identification of the goods is not fraudulent if the buyer bought for value and in good faith.

§ 2A–309.   Lessor's and Lessee's Rights When Goods Become Fixtures.

(1) In this section:

(a) goods are "fixtures" when they become so related to particular real estate that an interest in them arises under real estate law;

(b) a "fixture filing" is the filing, in the office where a mortgage on the real estate would be filed or recorded, of a financing statement covering goods that are or are to become fixtures and conforming to the requirements of Section 9–502(a) and (b);

(c) a lease is a "purchase money lease" unless the lessee has possession or use of the goods or the right to possession or use of the goods before the lease agreement is enforceable;

(d) a mortgage is a "construction mortgage" to the extent it secures an obligation incurred for the construction of an improvement on land including the acquisition cost of the land, if the recorded writing so indicates; and

(e) "encumbrance" includes real estate mortgages and other liens on real estate and all other rights in real estate that are not ownership interests.

(2) Under this Article a lease may be of goods that are fixtures or may continue in goods that become fixtures, but no lease exists under this Article of ordinary building materials incorporated into an improvement on land.

(3) This Article does not prevent creation of a lease of fixtures pursuant to real estate law.

(4) The perfected interest of a lessor of fixtures has priority over a conflicting interest of an encumbrancer or owner of the real estate if:

(a) the lease is a purchase money lease, the conflicting interest of the encumbrancer or owner arises before the goods become fixtures, the interest of the lessor is perfected by a fixture filing before the goods become fixtures or within ten days thereafter, and the lessee has an interest of record in the real estate or is in possession of the real estate; or

(b) the interest of the lessor is perfected by a fixture filing before the interest of the encumbrancer or owner is of record, the lessor's interest has priority over any conflicting interest of a predecessor in title of the encumbrancer or owner, and the lessee has an interest of record in the real estate or is in possession of the real estate.

(5) The interest of a lessor of fixtures, whether or not perfected, has priority over the conflicting interest of an encumbrancer or owner of the real estate if:

(a) the fixtures are readily removable factory or office machines, readily removable equipment that is not primarily used or leased for use in the operation of the real estate, or readily removable replacements of domestic appliances that are goods subject to a consumer lease, and before the goods become fixtures the lease contract is enforceable; or

(b) the conflicting interest is a lien on the real estate obtained by legal or equitable proceedings after the lease contract is enforceable; or

(c) the encumbrancer or owner has consented in writing to the lease or has disclaimed an interest in the goods as fixtures; or

(d) the lessee has a right to remove the goods as against the encumbrancer or owner. If the lessee's right to remove terminates, the priority of the interest of the lessor continues for a reasonable time.

(6) Notwithstanding paragraph (4)(a) but otherwise subject to subsections (4) and (5), the interest of a lessor of fixtures, including the lessor's residual interest, is subordinate to the conflicting interest of an encumbrancer of the real estate under a construction mortgage recorded before the goods become fixtures if the goods become fixtures before the completion of the construction. To the extent given to refinance a construction mortgage, the conflicting interest of an encumbrancer of the real estate under a mortgage has this priority to the same extent as the encumbrancer of the real estate under the construction mortgage.

(7) In cases not within the preceding subsections, priority between the interest of a lessor of fixtures, including the lessor's residual interest, and the conflicting interest of an encumbrancer or owner of the real estate who is not the lessee is determined by the priority rules governing conflicting interests in real estate.

(8) If the interest of a lessor of fixtures, including the lessor's residual interest, has priority over all conflicting interests of all owners and encumbrancers of the real estate, the lessor or the lessee may (i) on default, expiration, termination, or cancellation of the lease agreement but subject to the agreement and this Article, or (ii) if necessary to enforce other rights and remedies of the lessor or lessee under this Article, remove the goods from the real estate, free and clear of all conflicting interests of all owners and encumbrancers of the real estate, but the lessor or lessee must reimburse any encumbrancer or owner of the real estate who is not the lessee and who has not otherwise agreed for the cost of repair of any physical injury, but not for any diminution in value of the real estate caused by the absence of the goods removed or by any necessity of replacing them. A person entitled to reimbursement may refuse permission to remove until the party seeking removal gives adequate security for the performance of this obligation.

(9) Even though the lease agreement does not create a security interest, the interest of a lessor of fixtures, including the lessor's residual interest, is perfected by filing a financing statement as a fixture filing for leased goods that are or are to become fixtures in accordance with the relevant provisions of the Article on Secured Transactions (Article 9).

As amended in 1990 and 1999.

§ 2A–310.   Lessor's and Lessee's Rights When Goods Become Accessions.

(1) Goods are "accessions" when they are installed in or affixed to other goods.

(2) The interest of a lessor or a lessee under a lease contract entered into before the goods became accessions is superior to all interests in the whole except as stated in subsection (4).

(3) The interest of a lessor or a lessee under a lease contract entered into at the time or after the goods became accessions is superior to all subsequently acquired interests in the whole except as stated in subsection (4) but is subordinate to interests in the whole existing at the time the lease contract was made unless the holders of such interests in the whole have in writing consented to the lease or disclaimed an interest in the goods as part of the whole.

(4) The interest of a lessor or a lessee under a lease contract described in subsection (2) or (3) is subordinate to the interest of

(a) a buyer in the ordinary course of business or a lessee in the ordinary course of business of any interest in the whole acquired after the goods became accessions; or

(b) a creditor with a security interest in the whole perfected before the lease contract was made to the extent that the creditor makes subsequent advances without knowledge of the lease contract.

(5) When under subsections (2) or (3) and (4) a lessor or a lessee of accessions holds an interest that is superior to all interests in the whole, the lessor or the lessee may (a) on default, expiration, termination, or cancellation of the lease contract by the other party but subject to the provisions of the lease contract and this Article, or (b) if necessary to enforce his [or her] other rights and remedies under this Article, remove the goods from the whole, free and clear of all interests in the whole, but he [or she] must reimburse any holder of an interest in the whole who is not the lessee and who has not otherwise agreed for the cost of repair of any physical injury but not for any diminution in value of the whole caused by the absence of the goods removed or by any necessity for replacing them. A person entitled to reimbursement may refuse permission to remove until the party seeking removal gives adequate security for the performance of this obligation.

§ 2A-311.   Priority Subject to Subordination.

Nothing in this Article prevents subordination by agreement by any person entitled to priority.

As added in 1990.

Part 4   Performance of Lease Contract: Repudiated, Substituted and Excused

§ 2A-401.   Insecurity: Adequate Assurance of Performance.

(1) A lease contract imposes an obligation on each party that the other's expectation of receiving due performance will not be impaired.

(2) If reasonable grounds for insecurity arise with respect to the performance of either party, the insecure party may demand in writing adequate assurance of due performance. Until the insecure party receives that assurance, if commercially reasonable the insecure party may suspend any performance for which he [or she] has not already received the agreed return.

(3) A repudiation of the lease contract occurs if assurance of due performance adequate under the circumstances of the particular case is not provided to the insecure party within a reasonable time, not to exceed 30 days after receipt of a demand by the other party.

(4) Between merchants, the reasonableness of grounds for insecurity and the adequacy of any assurance offered must be determined according to commercial standards.

(5) Acceptance of any nonconforming delivery or payment does not prejudice the aggrieved party's right to demand adequate assurance of future performance.

§ 2A-402.   Anticipatory Repudiation.

If either party repudiates a lease contract with respect to a performance not yet due under the lease contract, the loss of which performance will substantially impair the value of the lease contract to the other, the aggrieved party may:

(a) for a commercially reasonable time, await retraction of repudiation and performance by the repudiating party;

(b) make demand pursuant to Section 2A-401 and await assurance of future performance adequate under the circumstances of the particular case; or

(c) resort to any right or remedy upon default under the lease contract or this Article, even though the aggrieved party has notified the repudiating party that the aggrieved party would await the repudiating party's performance and assurance and has urged retraction. In addition, whether or not the aggrieved party is pursuing one of the foregoing remedies, the aggrieved party may suspend performance or, if the aggrieved party is the lessor, proceed in accordance with the provisions of this Article on the lessor's right to identify goods to the lease contract notwithstanding default or to salvage unfinished goods (Section 2A-524).

§ 2A-403.   Retraction of Anticipatory Repudiation.

(1) Until the repudiating party's next performance is due, the repudiating party can retract the repudiation unless, since the repudiation, the aggrieved party has cancelled the lease contract or materially changed the aggrieved party's position or otherwise indicated that the aggrieved party considers the repudiation final.

(2) Retraction may be by any method that clearly indicates to the aggrieved party that the repudiating party intends to perform under the lease contract and includes any assurance demanded under Section 2A-401.

(3) Retraction reinstates a repudiating party's rights under a lease contract with due excuse and allowance to the aggrieved party for any delay occasioned by the repudiation.

§ 2A-404.   Substituted Performance.

(1) If without fault of the lessee, the lessor and the supplier, the agreed berthing, loading, or unloading facilities fail or the agreed type of carrier becomes unavailable or the agreed manner of delivery otherwise becomes commercially impracticable, but a commercially reasonable substitute is available, the substitute performance must be tendered and accepted.

(2) If the agreed means or manner of payment fails because of domestic or foreign governmental regulation:

(a) the lessor may withhold or stop delivery or cause the supplier to withhold or stop delivery unless the lessee provides a means or manner of payment that is commercially a substantial equivalent; and

(b) if delivery has already been taken, payment by the means or in the manner provided by the regulation discharges the lessee's obligation unless the regulation is discriminatory, oppressive, or predatory.

§ 2A-405.   Excused Performance.

Subject to Section 2A-404 on substituted performance, the following rules apply:

(a) Delay in delivery or nondelivery in whole or in part by a lessor or a supplier who complies with paragraphs (b) and (c) is not a default under the lease contract if performance as agreed has been made impracticable by the occurrence of a contingency the nonoccurrence of which was a basic assumption on which the lease contract was made or by compliance in good faith with any applicable foreign or domestic governmental regulation or order, whether or not the regulation or order later proves to be invalid.

(b) If the causes mentioned in paragraph (a) affect only part of the lessor's or the supplier's capacity to perform, he [or she] shall allocate production and deliveries among his [or her] customers but at his [or her] option may include regular customers not then under contract for sale or lease as well as his [or her] own requirements for further manufacture. He [or she] may so allocate in any manner that is fair and reasonable.

(c) The lessor seasonably shall notify the lessee and in the case of a finance lease the supplier seasonably shall notify the lessor and the lessee, if known, that there will be delay or nondelivery and, if allocation is required under paragraph (b), of the estimated quota thus made available for the lessee.

§ 2A–406.   Procedure on Excused Performance.

(1) If the lessee receives notification of a material or indefinite delay or an allocation justified under Section 2A–405, the lessee may by written notification to the lessor as to any goods involved, and with respect to all of the goods if under an installment lease contract the value of the whole lease contract is substantially impaired (Section 2A–510):

   (a) terminate the lease contract (Section 2A–505(2)); or

   (b) except in a finance lease that is not a consumer lease, modify the lease contract by accepting the available quota in substitution, with due allowance from the rent payable for the balance of the lease term for the deficiency but without further right against the lessor.

(2) If, after receipt of a notification from the lessor under Section 2A–405, the lessee fails so to modify the lease agreement within a reasonable time not exceeding 30 days, the lease contract lapses with respect to any deliveries affected.

§ 2A–407.   Irrevocable Promises: Finance Leases.

(1) In the case of a finance lease that is not a consumer lease the lessee's promises under the lease contract become irrevocable and independent upon the lessee's acceptance of the goods.

(2) A promise that has become irrevocable and independent under subsection (1):

   (a) is effective and enforceable between the parties, and by or against third parties including assignees of the parties, and

   (b) is not subject to cancellation, termination, modification, repudiation, excuse, or substitution without the consent of the party to whom the promise runs.

(3) This section does not affect the validity under any other law of a covenant in any lease contract making the lessee's promises irrevocable and independent upon the lessee's acceptance of the goods.

As amended in 1990.

Part 5   Default

A. In General

§ 2A–501.   Default: Procedure.

(1) Whether the lessor or the lessee is in default under a lease contract is determined by the lease agreement and this Article.

(2) If the lessor or the lessee is in default under the lease contract, the party seeking enforcement has rights and remedies as provided in this Article and, except as limited by this Article, as provided in the lease agreement.

(3) If the lessor or the lessee is in default under the lease contract, the party seeking enforcement may reduce the party's claim to judgment, or otherwise enforce the lease contract by self-help or any available judicial procedure or nonjudicial procedure, including administrative proceeding, arbitration, or the like, in accordance with this Article.

(4) Except as otherwise provided in Section 1–106(1) or this Article or the lease agreement, the rights and remedies referred to in subsections (2) and (3) are cumulative.

(5) If the lease agreement covers both real property and goods, the party seeking enforcement may proceed under this Part as to the goods, or under other applicable law as to both the real property and the goods in accordance with that party's rights and remedies in respect of the real property, in which case this Part does not apply.

As amended in 1990.

§ 2A–502.   Notice After Default.

Except as otherwise provided in this Article or the lease agreement, the lessor or lessee in default under the lease contract is not entitled to notice of default or notice of enforcement from the other party to the lease agreement.

§ 2A–503.   Modification or Impairment of Rights and Remedies.

(1) Except as otherwise provided in this Article, the lease agreement may include rights and remedies for default in addition to or in substitution for those provided in this Article and may limit or alter the measure of damages recoverable under this Article.

(2) Resort to a remedy provided under this Article or in the lease agreement is optional unless the remedy is expressly agreed to be exclusive. If circumstances cause an exclusive or limited remedy to fail of its essential purpose, or provision for an exclusive remedy is unconscionable, remedy may be had as provided in this Article.

(3) Consequential damages may be liquidated under Section 2A–504, or may otherwise be limited, altered, or excluded unless the limitation, alteration, or exclusion is unconscionable. Limitation, alteration, or exclusion of consequential damages for injury to the person in the case of consumer goods is prima facie unconscionable but limitation, alteration, or exclusion of damages where the loss is commercial is not prima facie unconscionable.

(4) Rights and remedies on default by the lessor or the lessee with respect to any obligation or promise collateral or ancillary to the lease contract are not impaired by this Article.

As amended in 1990.

§ 2A–504.   Liquidation of Damages.

(1) Damages payable by either party for default, or any other act or omission, including indemnity for loss or diminution of anticipated tax benefits or loss or damage to lessor's residual interest, may be liquidated in the lease agreement but only at an amount or by a formula that is reasonable in light of the then anticipated harm caused by the default or other act or omission.

(2) If the lease agreement provides for liquidation of damages, and such provision does not comply with subsection (1), or such provision is an exclusive or limited remedy that circumstances cause to fail of its essential purpose, remedy may be had as provided in this Article.

(3) If the lessor justifiably withholds or stops delivery of goods because of the lessee's default or insolvency (Section 2A-525 or 2A-526), the lessee is entitled to restitution of any amount by which the sum of his [or her] payments exceeds:

(a) the amount to which the lessor is entitled by virtue of terms liquidating the lessor's damages in accordance with subsection (1); or

(b) in the absence of those terms, 20 percent of the then present value of the total rent the lessee was obligated to pay for the balance of the lease term, or, in the case of a consumer lease, the lesser of such amount or $500.

(4) A lessee's right to restitution under subsection (3) is subject to offset to the extent the lessor establishes:

(a) a right to recover damages under the provisions of this Article other than subsection (1); and

(b) the amount or value of any benefits received by the lessee directly or indirectly by reason of the lease contract.

§ 2A-505.   Cancellation and Termination and Effect of Cancellation, Termination, Rescission, or Fraud on Rights and Remedies.

(1) On cancellation of the lease contract, all obligations that are still executory on both sides are discharged, but any right based on prior default or performance survives, and the cancelling party also retains any remedy for default of the whole lease contract or any unperformed balance.

(2) On termination of the lease contract, all obligations that are still executory on both sides are discharged but any right based on prior default or performance survives.

(3) Unless the contrary intention clearly appears, expressions of "cancellation," "rescission," or the like of the lease contract may not be construed as a renunciation or discharge of any claim in damages for an antecedent default.

(4) Rights and remedies for material misrepresentation or fraud include all rights and remedies available under this Article for default.

(5) Neither rescission nor a claim for rescission of the lease contract nor rejection or return of the goods may bar or be deemed inconsistent with a claim for damages or other right or remedy.

§ 2A-506.   Statute of Limitations.

(1) An action for default under a lease contract, including breach of warranty or indemnity, must be commenced within 4 years after the cause of action accrued. By the original lease contract the parties may reduce the period of limitation to not less than one year.

(2) A cause of action for default accrues when the act or omission on which the default or breach of warranty is based is or should have been discovered by the aggrieved party, or when the default occurs, whichever is later. A cause of action for indemnity accrues when the act or omission on which the claim for indemnity is based is or should have been discovered by the indemnified party, whichever is later.

(3) If an action commenced within the time limited by subsection (1) is so terminated as to leave available a remedy by another action for the same default or breach of warranty or indemnity, the other action may be commenced after the expiration of the time limited and within 6 months after the termination of the first action unless the termination resulted from voluntary discontinuance or from dismissal for failure or neglect to prosecute.

(4) This section does not alter the law on tolling of the statute of limitations nor does it apply to causes of action that have accrued before this Article becomes effective.

§ 2A-507.   Proof of Market Rent: Time and Place.

(1) Damages based on market rent (Section 2A-519 or 2A-528) are determined according to the rent for the use of the goods concerned for a lease term identical to the remaining lease term of the original lease agreement and prevailing at the times specified in Sections 2A-519 and 2A-528.

(2) If evidence of rent for the use of the goods concerned for a lease term identical to the remaining lease term of the original lease agreement and prevailing at the times or places described in this Article is not readily available, the rent prevailing within any reasonable time before or after the time described or at any other place or for a different lease term which in commercial judgment or under usage of trade would serve as a reasonable substitute for the one described may be used, making any proper allowance for the difference, including the cost of transporting the goods to or from the other place.

(3) Evidence of a relevant rent prevailing at a time or place or for a lease term other than the one described in this Article offered by one party is not admissible unless and until he [or she] has given the other party notice the court finds sufficient to prevent unfair surprise.

(4) If the prevailing rent or value of any goods regularly leased in any established market is in issue, reports in official publications or trade journals or in newspapers or periodicals of general circulation published as the reports of that market are admissible in evidence. The circumstances of the preparation of the report may be shown to affect its weight but not its admissibility.

As amended in 1990.

B. Default by Lessor

§ 2A-508.   Lessee's Remedies.

(1) If a lessor fails to deliver the goods in conformity to the lease contract (Section 2A-509) or repudiates the lease contract (Section 2A-402), or a lessee rightfully rejects the goods (Section 2A-509) or justifiably revokes acceptance of the goods (Section 2A-517), then with respect to any goods involved, and with respect to all of the goods if under an installment lease contract the value of the whole lease contract is substantially impaired (Section 2A-510), the lessor is in default under the lease contract and the lessee may:

(a) cancel the lease contract (Section 2A-505(1));

(b) recover so much of the rent and security as has been paid and is just under the circumstances;

(c) cover and recover damages as to all goods affected whether or not they have been identified to the lease contract

(Sections 2A–518 and 2A–520), or recover damages for non-delivery (Sections 2A–519 and 2A–520);

(d) exercise any other rights or pursue any other remedies provided in the lease contract.

(2) If a lessor fails to deliver the goods in conformity to the lease contract or repudiates the lease contract, the lessee may also:

(a) if the goods have been identified, recover them (Section 2A–522); or

(b) in a proper case, obtain specific performance or replevy the goods (Section 2A–521).

(3) If a lessor is otherwise in default under a lease contract, the lessee may exercise the rights and pursue the remedies provided in the lease contract, which may include a right to cancel the lease, and in Section 2A–519(3).

(4) If a lessor has breached a warranty, whether express or implied, the lessee may recover damages (Section 2A–519(4)).

(5) On rightful rejection or justifiable revocation of acceptance, a lessee has a security interest in goods in the lessee's possession or control for any rent and security that has been paid and any expenses reasonably incurred in their inspection, receipt, transportation, and care and custody and may hold those goods and dispose of them in good faith and in a commercially reasonable manner, subject to Section 2A–527(5).

(6) Subject to the provisions of Section 2A–407, a lessee, on notifying the lessor of the lessee's intention to do so, may deduct all or any part of the damages resulting from any default under the lease contract from any part of the rent still due under the same lease contract.

As amended in 1990.

§ 2A–509.   Lessee's Rights on Improper Delivery; Rightful Rejection.

(1) Subject to the provisions of Section 2A–510 on default in installment lease contracts, if the goods or the tender or delivery fail in any respect to conform to the lease contract, the lessee may reject or accept the goods or accept any commercial unit or units and reject the rest of the goods.

(2) Rejection of goods is ineffective unless it is within a reasonable time after tender or delivery of the goods and the lessee seasonably notifies the lessor.

§ 2A–510.   Installment Lease Contracts: Rejection and Default.

(1) Under an installment lease contract a lessee may reject any delivery that is nonconforming if the nonconformity substantially impairs the value of that delivery and cannot be cured or the nonconformity is a defect in the required documents; but if the nonconformity does not fall within subsection (2) and the lessor or the supplier gives adequate assurance of its cure, the lessee must accept that delivery.

(2) Whenever nonconformity or default with respect to one or more deliveries substantially impairs the value of the installment lease contract as a whole there is a default with respect to the whole. But, the aggrieved party reinstates the installment lease contract as a whole if the aggrieved party accepts a nonconforming delivery without seasonably notifying of cancellation or brings an action with respect only to past deliveries or demands performance as to future deliveries.

§ 2A–511.   Merchant Lessee's Duties as to Rightfully Rejected Goods.

(1) Subject to any security interest of a lessee (Section 2A–508(5)), if a lessor or a supplier has no agent or place of business at the market of rejection, a merchant lessee, after rejection of goods in his [or her] possession or control, shall follow any reasonable instructions received from the lessor or the supplier with respect to the goods. In the absence of those instructions, a merchant lessee shall make reasonable efforts to sell, lease, or otherwise dispose of the goods for the lessor's account if they threaten to decline in value speedily. Instructions are not reasonable if on demand indemnity for expenses is not forthcoming.

(2) If a merchant lessee (subsection (1)) or any other lessee (Section 2A–512) disposes of goods, he [or she] is entitled to reimbursement either from the lessor or the supplier or out of the proceeds for reasonable expenses of caring for and disposing of the goods and, if the expenses include no disposition commission, to such commission as is usual in the trade, or if there is none, to a reasonable sum not exceeding 10 percent of the gross proceeds.

(3) In complying with this section or Section 2A–512, the lessee is held only to good faith. Good faith conduct hereunder is neither acceptance or conversion nor the basis of an action for damages.

(4) A purchaser who purchases in good faith from a lessee pursuant to this section or Section 2A–512 takes the goods free of any rights of the lessor and the supplier even though the lessee fails to comply with one or more of the requirements of this Article.

§ 2A–512.   Lessee's Duties as to Rightfully Rejected Goods.

(1) Except as otherwise provided with respect to goods that threaten to decline in value speedily (Section 2A–511) and subject to any security interest of a lessee (Section 2A–508(5)):

(a) the lessee, after rejection of goods in the lessee's possession, shall hold them with reasonable care at the lessor's or the supplier's disposition for a reasonable time after the lessee's seasonable notification of rejection;

(b) if the lessor or the supplier gives no instructions within a reasonable time after notification of rejection, the lessee may store the rejected goods for the lessor's or the supplier's account or ship them to the lessor or the supplier or dispose of them for the lessor's or the supplier's account with reimbursement in the manner provided in Section 2A–511; but

(c) the lessee has no further obligations with regard to goods rightfully rejected.

(2) Action by the lessee pursuant to subsection (1) is not acceptance or conversion.

§ 2A–513.   Cure by Lessor of Improper Tender or Delivery; Replacement.

(1) If any tender or delivery by the lessor or the supplier is rejected because nonconforming and the time for performance has not yet

expired, the lessor or the supplier may seasonably notify the lessee of the lessor's or the supplier's intention to cure and may then make a conforming delivery within the time provided in the lease contract.

(2) If the lessee rejects a nonconforming tender that the lessor or the supplier had reasonable grounds to believe would be acceptable with or without money allowance, the lessor or the supplier may have a further reasonable time to substitute a conforming tender if he [or she] seasonably notifies the lessee.

§ 2A–514.   Waiver of Lessee's Objections.

(1) In rejecting goods, a lessee's failure to state a particular defect that is ascertainable by reasonable inspection precludes the lessee from relying on the defect to justify rejection or to establish default:

(a) if, stated seasonably, the lessor or the supplier could have cured it (Section 2A–513); or

(b) between merchants if the lessor or the supplier after rejection has made a request in writing for a full and final written statement of all defects on which the lessee proposes to rely.

(2) A lessee's failure to reserve rights when paying rent or other consideration against documents precludes recovery of the payment for defects apparent on the face of the documents.

§ 2A–515.   Acceptance of Goods.

(1) Acceptance of goods occurs after the lessee has had a reasonable opportunity to inspect the goods and

(a) the lessee signifies or acts with respect to the goods in a manner that signifies to the lessor or the supplier that the goods are conforming or that the lessee will take or retain them in spite of their nonconformity; or

(b) the lessee fails to make an effective rejection of the goods (Section 2A–509(2)).

(2) Acceptance of a part of any commercial unit is acceptance of that entire unit.

§ 2A–516.   Effect of Acceptance of Goods; Notice of Default; Burden of Establishing Default after Acceptance; Notice of Claim or Litigation to Person Answerable Over.

(1) A lessee must pay rent for any goods accepted in accordance with the lease contract, with due allowance for goods rightfully rejected or not delivered.

(2) A lessee's acceptance of goods precludes rejection of the goods accepted. In the case of a finance lease, if made with knowledge of a nonconformity, acceptance cannot be revoked because of it. In any other case, if made with knowledge of a nonconformity, acceptance cannot be revoked because of it unless the acceptance was on the reasonable assumption that the nonconformity would be seasonably cured. Acceptance does not of itself impair any other remedy provided by this Article or the lease agreement for nonconformity.

(3) If a tender has been accepted:

(a) within a reasonable time after the lessee discovers or should have discovered any default, the lessee shall notify the lessor

and the supplier, if any, or be barred from any remedy against the party notified;

(b) except in the case of a consumer lease, within a reasonable time after the lessee receives notice of litigation for infringement or the like (Section 2A–211) the lessee shall notify the lessor or be barred from any remedy over for liability established by the litigation; and

(c) the burden is on the lessee to establish any default.

(4) If a lessee is sued for breach of a warranty or other obligation for which a lessor or a supplier is answerable over the following apply:

(a) The lessee may give the lessor or the supplier, or both, written notice of the litigation. If the notice states that the person notified may come in and defend and that if the person notified does not do so that person will be bound in any action against that person by the lessee by any determination of fact common to the two litigations, then unless the person notified after seasonable receipt of the notice does come in and defend that person is so bound.

(b) The lessor or the supplier may demand in writing that the lessee turn over control of the litigation including settlement if the claim is one for infringement or the like (Section 2A–211) or else be barred from any remedy over. If the demand states that the lessor or the supplier agrees to bear all expense and to satisfy any adverse judgment, then unless the lessee after seasonable receipt of the demand does turn over control the lessee is so barred.

(5) Subsections (3) and (4) apply to any obligation of a lessee to hold the lessor or the supplier harmless against infringement or the like (Section 2A–211).

As amended in 1990.

§ 2A–517.   Revocation of Acceptance of Goods.

(1) A lessee may revoke acceptance of a lot or commercial unit whose nonconformity substantially impairs its value to the lessee if the lessee has accepted it:

(a) except in the case of a finance lease, on the reasonable assumption that its nonconformity would be cured and it has not been seasonably cured; or

(b) without discovery of the nonconformity if the lessee's acceptance was reasonably induced either by the lessor's assurances or, except in the case of a finance lease, by the difficulty of discovery before acceptance.

(2) Except in the case of a finance lease that is not a consumer lease, a lessee may revoke acceptance of a lot or commercial unit if the lessor defaults under the lease contract and the default substantially impairs the value of that lot or commercial unit to the lessee.

(3) If the lease agreement so provides, the lessee may revoke acceptance of a lot or commercial unit because of other defaults by the lessor.

(4) Revocation of acceptance must occur within a reasonable time after the lessee discovers or should have discovered the ground for it and before any substantial change in condition of the goods

which is not caused by the nonconformity. Revocation is not effective until the lessee notifies the lessor.

(5) A lessee who so revokes has the same rights and duties with regard to the goods involved as if the lessee had rejected them.

As amended in 1990.

§ 2A–518. Cover; Substitute Goods.

(1) After a default by a lessor under the lease contract of the type described in Section 2A–508(1), or, if agreed, after other default by the lessor, the lessee may cover by making any purchase or lease of or contract to purchase or lease goods in substitution for those due from the lessor.

(2) Except as otherwise provided with respect to damages liquidated in the lease agreement (Section 2A–504) or otherwise determined pursuant to agreement of the parties (Sections 1–102(3) and 2A–503), if a lessee's cover is by lease agreement substantially similar to the original lease agreement and the new lease agreement is made in good faith and in a commercially reasonable manner, the lessee may recover from the lessor as damages (i) the present value, as of the date of the commencement of the term of the new lease agreement, of the rent under the new lease agreement applicable to that period of the new lease term which is comparable to the then remaining term of the original lease agreement minus the present value as of the same date of the total rent for the then remaining lease term of the original lease agreement, and (ii) any incidental or consequential damages, less expenses saved in consequence of the lessor's default.

(3) If a lessee's cover is by lease agreement that for any reason does not qualify for treatment under subsection (2), or is by purchase or otherwise, the lessee may recover from the lessor as if the lessee had elected not to cover and Section 2A–519 governs.

As amended in 1990.

§ 2A–519. Lessee's Damages for Non-Delivery, Repudiation, Default, and Breach of Warranty in Regard to Accepted Goods.

(1) Except as otherwise provided with respect to damages liquidated in the lease agreement (Section 2A–504) or otherwise determined pursuant to agreement of the parties (Sections 1–102(3) and 2A–503), if a lessee elects not to cover or a lessee elects to cover and the cover is by lease agreement that for any reason does not qualify for treatment under Section 2A–518(2), or is by purchase or otherwise, the measure of damages for non-delivery or repudiation by the lessor or for rejection or revocation of acceptance by the lessee is the present value, as of the date of the default, of the then market rent minus the present value as of the same date of the original rent, computed for the remaining lease term of the original lease agreement, together with incidental and consequential damages, less expenses saved in consequence of the lessor's default.

(2) Market rent is to be determined as of the place for tender or, in cases of rejection after arrival or revocation of acceptance, as of the place of arrival.

(3) Except as otherwise agreed, if the lessee has accepted goods and given notification (Section 2A–516(3)), the measure of dam-

ages for non-conforming tender or delivery or other default by a lessor is the loss resulting in the ordinary course of events from the lessor's default as determined in any manner that is reasonable together with incidental and consequential damages, less expenses saved in consequence of the lessor's default.

(4) Except as otherwise agreed, the measure of damages for breach of warranty is the present value at the time and place of acceptance of the difference between the value of the use of the goods accepted and the value if they had been as warranted for the lease term, unless special circumstances show proximate damages of a different amount, together with incidental and consequential damages, less expenses saved in consequence of the lessor's default or breach of warranty.

As amended in 1990.

§ 2A–520. Lessee's Incidental and Consequential Damages.

(1) Incidental damages resulting from a lessor's default include expenses reasonably incurred in inspection, receipt, transportation, and care and custody of goods rightfully rejected or goods the acceptance of which is justifiably revoked, any commercially reasonable charges, expenses or commissions in connection with effecting cover, and any other reasonable expense incident to the default.

(2) Consequential damages resulting from a lessor's default include:

(a) any loss resulting from general or particular requirements and needs of which the lessor at the time of contracting had reason to know and which could not reasonably be prevented by cover or otherwise; and

(b) injury to person or property proximately resulting from any breach of warranty.

§ 2A–521. Lessee's Right to Specific Performance or Replevin.

(1) Specific performance may be decreed if the goods are unique or in other proper circumstances.

(2) A decree for specific performance may include any terms and conditions as to payment of the rent, damages, or other relief that the court deems just.

(3) A lessee has a right of replevin, detinue, sequestration, claim and delivery, or the like for goods identified to the lease contract if after reasonable effort the lessee is unable to effect cover for those goods or the circumstances reasonably indicate that the effort will be unavailing.

§ 2A–522. Lessee's Right to Goods on Lessor's Insolvency.

(1) Subject to subsection (2) and even though the goods have not been shipped, a lessee who has paid a part or all of the rent and security for goods identified to a lease contract (Section 2A–217) on making and keeping good a tender of any unpaid portion of the rent and security due under the lease contract may recover the goods identified from the lessor if the lessor becomes insolvent within 10 days after receipt of the first installment of rent and security.

(2) A lessee acquires the right to recover goods identified to a lease contract only if they conform to the lease contract.

C. Default by Lessee

§ 2A–523.   Lessor's Remedies.

(1) If a lessee wrongfully rejects or revokes acceptance of goods or fails to make a payment when due or repudiates with respect to a part or the whole, then, with respect to any goods involved, and with respect to all of the goods if under an installment lease contract the value of the whole lease contract is substantially impaired (Section 2A–510), the lessee is in default under the lease contract and the lessor may:

(a) cancel the lease contract (Section 2A–505(1));

(b) proceed respecting goods not identified to the lease contract (Section 2A–524);

(c) withhold delivery of the goods and take possession of goods previously delivered (Section 2A–525);

(d) stop delivery of the goods by any bailee (Section 2A–526);

(e) dispose of the goods and recover damages (Section 2A–527), or retain the goods and recover damages (Section 2A–528), or in a proper case recover rent (Section 2A–529)

(f) exercise any other rights or pursue any other remedies provided in the lease contract.

(2) If a lessor does not fully exercise a right or obtain a remedy to which the lessor is entitled under subsection (1), the lessor may recover the loss resulting in the ordinary course of events from the lessee's default as determined in any reasonable manner, together with incidental damages, less expenses saved in consequence of the lessee's default.

(3) If a lessee is otherwise in default under a lease contract, the lessor may exercise the rights and pursue the remedies provided in the lease contract, which may include a right to cancel the lease. In addition, unless otherwise provided in the lease contract:

(a) if the default substantially impairs the value of the lease contract to the lessor, the lessor may exercise the rights and pursue the remedies provided in subsections (1) or (2); or

(b) if the default does not substantially impair the value of the lease contract to the lessor, the lessor may recover as provided in subsection (2).

As amended in 1990.

§ 2A–524.   Lessor's Right to Identify Goods to Lease Contract.

(1) After default by the lessee under the lease contract of the type described in Section 2A–523(1) or 2A–523(3)(a) or, if agreed, after other default by the lessee, the lessor may:

(a) identify to the lease contract conforming goods not already identified if at the time the lessor learned of the default they were in the lessor's or the supplier's possession or control; and

(b) dispose of goods (Section 2A–527(1)) that demonstrably have been intended for the particular lease contract even though those goods are unfinished.

(2) If the goods are unfinished, in the exercise of reasonable commercial judgment for the purposes of avoiding loss and of effective realization, an aggrieved lessor or the supplier may either complete manufacture and wholly identify the goods to the lease contract or cease manufacture and lease, sell, or otherwise dispose of the goods for scrap or salvage value or proceed in any other reasonable manner.

As amended in 1990.

§ 2A–525.   Lessor's Right to Possession of Goods.

(1) If a lessor discovers the lessee to be insolvent, the lessor may refuse to deliver the goods.

(2) After a default by the lessee under the lease contract of the type described in Section 2A–523(1) or 2A–523(3)(a) or, if agreed, after other default by the lessee, the lessor has the right to take possession of the goods. If the lease contract so provides, the lessor may require the lessee to assemble the goods and make them available to the lessor at a place to be designated by the lessor which is reasonably convenient to both parties. Without removal, the lessor may render unusable any goods employed in trade or business, and may dispose of goods on the lessee's premises (Section 2A–527).

(3) The lessor may proceed under subsection (2) without judicial process if that can be done without breach of the peace or the lessor may proceed by action.

As amended in 1990.

§ 2A–526.   Lessor's Stoppage of Delivery in Transit or Otherwise.

(1) A lessor may stop delivery of goods in the possession of a carrier or other bailee if the lessor discovers the lessee to be insolvent and may stop delivery of carload, truckload, planeload, or larger shipments of express or freight if the lessee repudiates or fails to make a payment due before delivery, whether for rent, security or otherwise under the lease contract, or for any other reason the lessor has a right to withhold or take possession of the goods.

(2) In pursuing its remedies under subsection (1), the lessor may stop delivery until

(a) receipt of the goods by the lessee;

(b) acknowledgment to the lessee by any bailee of the goods, except a carrier, that the bailee holds the goods for the lessee; or

(c) such an acknowledgment to the lessee by a carrier via reshipment or as warehouseman.

(3) (a) To stop delivery, a lessor shall so notify as to enable the bailee by reasonable diligence to prevent delivery of the goods.

(b) After notification, the bailee shall hold and deliver the goods according to the directions of the lessor, but the lessor is liable to the bailee for any ensuing charges or damages.

(c) A carrier who has issued a nonnegotiable bill of lading is not obliged to obey a notification to stop received from a person other than the consignor.

§ 2A–527.   Lessor's Rights to Dispose of Goods.

(1) After a default by a lessee under the lease contract of the type described in Section 2A–523(1) or 2A–523(3)(a) or after the lessor refuses to deliver or takes possession of goods (Section

2A–525 or 2A–526), or, if agreed, after other default by a lessee, the lessor may dispose of the goods concerned or the undelivered balance thereof by lease, sale, or otherwise.

(2) Except as otherwise provided with respect to damages liquidated in the lease agreement (Section 2A–504) or otherwise determined pursuant to agreement of the parties (Sections 1–102(3) and 2A–503), if the disposition is by lease agreement substantially similar to the original lease agreement and the new lease agreement is made in good faith and in a commercially reasonable manner, the lessor may recover from the lessee as damages (i) accrued and unpaid rent as of the date of the commencement of the term of the new lease agreement, (ii) the present value, as of the same date, of the total rent for the then remaining lease term of the original lease agreement minus the present value, as of the same date, of the rent under the new lease agreement applicable to that period of the new lease term which is comparable to the then remaining term of the original lease agreement, and (iii) any incidental damages allowed under Section 2A–530, less expenses saved in consequence of the lessee's default.

(3) If the lessor's disposition is by lease agreement that for any reason does not qualify for treatment under subsection (2), or is by sale or otherwise, the lessor may recover from the lessee as if the lessor had elected not to dispose of the goods and Section 2A–528 governs.

(4) A subsequent buyer or lessee who buys or leases from the lessor in good faith for value as a result of a disposition under this section takes the goods free of the original lease contract and any rights of the original lessee even though the lessor fails to comply with one or more of the requirements of this Article.

(5) The lessor is not accountable to the lessee for any profit made on any disposition. A lessee who has rightfully rejected or justifiably revoked acceptance shall account to the lessor for any excess over the amount of the lessee's security interest (Section 2A–508(5)).
As amended in 1990.

§ 2A–528.   Lessor's Damages for Non-acceptance, Failure to Pay, Repudiation, or Other Default.

(1) Except as otherwise provided with respect to damages liquidated in the lease agreement (Section 2A–504) or otherwise determined pursuant to agreement of the parties (Section 1–102(3) and 2A–503), if a lessor elects to retain the goods or a lessor elects to dispose of the goods and the disposition is by lease agreement that for any reason does not qualify for treatment under Section 2A–527(2), or is by sale or otherwise, the lessor may recover from the lessee as damages for a default of the type described in Section 2A–523(1) or 2A–523(3)(a), or if agreed, for other default of the lessee, (i) accrued and unpaid rent as of the date of the default if the lessee has never taken possession of the goods, or, if the lessee has taken possession of the goods, as of the date the lessor repossesses the goods or an earlier date on which the lessee makes a tender of the goods to the lessor, (ii) the present value as of the date determined under clause (i) of the total rent for the then remaining lease term of the original lease agreement minus the

present value as of the same date of the market rent as the place where the goods are located computed for the same lease term, and (iii) any incidental damages allowed under Section 2A–530, less expenses saved in consequence of the lessee's default.

(2) If the measure of damages provided in subsection (1) is inadequate to put a lessor in as good a position as performance would have, the measure of damages is the present value of the profit, including reasonable overhead, the lessor would have made from full performance by the lessee, together with any incidental damages allowed under Section 2A–530, due allowance for costs reasonably incurred and due credit for payments or proceeds of disposition.
As amended in 1990.

§ 2A–529.   Lessor's Action for the Rent.

(1) After default by the lessee under the lease contract of the type described in Section 2A–523(1) or 2A–523(3)(a) or, if agreed, after other default by the lessee, if the lessor complies with subsection (2), the lessor may recover from the lessee as damages:

> (a) for goods accepted by the lessee and not repossessed by or tendered to the lessor, and for conforming goods lost or damaged within a commercially reasonable time after risk of loss passes to the lessee (Section 2A–219), (i) accrued and unpaid rent as of the date of entry of judgment in favor of the lessor (ii) the present value as of the same date of the rent for the then remaining lease term of the lease agreement, and (iii) any incidental damages allowed under Section 2A–530, less expenses saved in consequence of the lessee's default; and

> (b) for goods identified to the lease contract if the lessor is unable after reasonable effort to dispose of them at a reasonable price or the circumstances reasonably indicate that effort will be unavailing, (i) accrued and unpaid rent as of the date of entry of judgment in favor of the lessor, (ii) the present value as of the same date of the rent for the then remaining lease term of the lease agreement, and (iii) any incidental damages allowed under Section 2A–530, less expenses saved in consequence of the lessee's default.

(2) Except as provided in subsection (3), the lessor shall hold for the lessee for the remaining lease term of the lease agreement any goods that have been identified to the lease contract and are in the lessor's control.

(3) The lessor may dispose of the goods at any time before collection of the judgment for damages obtained pursuant to subsection (1). If the disposition is before the end of the remaining lease term of the lease agreement, the lessor's recovery against the lessee for damages is governed by Section 2A–527 or Section 2A–528, and the lessor will cause an appropriate credit to be provided against a judgment for damages to the extent that the amount of the judgment exceeds the recovery available pursuant to Section 2A–527 or 2A–528.

(4) Payment of the judgment for damages obtained pursuant to subsection (1) entitles the lessee to the use and possession of the goods not then disposed of for the remaining lease term of and in accordance with the lease agreement.

(5) After default by the lessee under the lease contract of the type described in Section 2A–523(1) or Section 2A–523(3)(a) or, if agreed, after other default by the lessee, a lessor who is held not entitled to rent under this section must nevertheless be awarded damages for non-acceptance under Sections 2A–527 and 2A–528.

As amended in 1990.

§ 2A–530.   Lessor's Incidental Damages.

Incidental damages to an aggrieved lessor include any commercially reasonable charges, expenses, or commissions incurred in stopping delivery, in the transportation, care and custody of goods after the lessee's default, in connection with return or disposition of the goods, or otherwise resulting from the default.

§ 2A–531.   Standing to Sue Third Parties for Injury to Goods.

(1) If a third party so deals with goods that have been identified to a lease contract as to cause actionable injury to a party to the lease contract (a) the lessor has a right of action against the third party, and (b) the lessee also has a right of action against the third party if the lessee:

(i) has a security interest in the goods;

(ii) has an insurable interest in the goods; or

(iii) bears the risk of loss under the lease contract or has since the injury assumed that risk as against the lessor and the goods have been converted or destroyed.

(2) If at the time of the injury the party plaintiff did not bear the risk of loss as against the other party to the lease contract and there is no arrangement between them for disposition of the recovery, his [or her] suit or settlement, subject to his [or her] own interest, is as a fiduciary for the other party to the lease contract.

(3) Either party with the consent of the other may sue for the benefit of whom it may concern.

§ 2A–532.   Lessor's Rights to Residual Interest.

In addition to any other recovery permitted by this Article or other law, the lessor may recover from the lessee an amount that will fully compensate the lessor for any loss of or damage to the lessor's residual interest in the goods caused by the default of the lessee.

As added in 1990.

The Sarbanes-Oxley Act (Excerpts and Explanatory Comments)

Note: The author's explanatory comments appear in italics following the excerpt from each section.

Section 302
Corporate responsibility for financial reports[1]

(a) Regulations required

The Commission shall, by rule, require, for each company filing periodic reports under section 13(a) or 15(d) of the Securities Exchange Act of 1934 (15 U.S.C. 78m, 78o(d)), that the principal executive officer or officers and the principal financial officer or officers, or persons performing similar functions, certify in each annual or quarterly report filed or submitted under either such section of such Act that—

(1) the signing officer has reviewed the report;

(2) based on the officer's knowledge, the report does not contain any untrue statement of a material fact or omit to state a material fact necessary in order to make the statements made, in light of the circumstances under which such statements were made, not misleading;

(3) based on such officer's knowledge, the financial statements, and other financial information included in the report, fairly present in all material respects the financial condition and results of operations of the issuer as of, and for, the periods presented in the report;

(4) the signing officers—

(A) are responsible for establishing and maintaining internal controls;

(B) have designed such internal controls to ensure that material information relating to the issuer and its consolidated subsidiaries is made known to such officers by others within those entities, particularly during the period in which the periodic reports are being prepared;

(C) have evaluated the effectiveness of the issuer's internal controls as of a date within 90 days prior to the report; and

(D) have presented in the report their conclusions about the effectiveness of their internal controls based on their evaluation as of that date;

(5) the signing officers have disclosed to the issuer's auditors and the audit committee of the board of directors (or persons fulfilling the equivalent function)—

(A) all significant deficiencies in the design or operation of internal controls which could adversely affect the issuer's ability to record, process, summarize, and report financial data and have identified for the issuer's auditors any material weaknesses in internal controls; and

(B) any fraud, whether or not material, that involves management or other employees who have a significant role in the issuer's internal controls; and

(6) the signing officers have indicated in the report whether or not there were significant changes in internal controls or in other factors that could significantly affect internal controls subsequent to the date of their evaluation, including any corrective actions with regard to significant deficiencies and material weaknesses.

(b) Foreign reincorporations have no effect

Nothing in this section shall be interpreted or applied in any way to allow any issuer to lessen the legal force of the statement required under this section, by an issuer having reincorporated or having engaged in any other transaction that resulted in the transfer of the corporate domicile or offices of the issuer from inside the United States to outside of the United States.

(c) Deadline

The rules required by subsection (a) of this section shall be effective not later than 30 days after July 30, 2002.

*   *   *   *

Explanatory Comments:

Section 302 requires the chief executive officer (CEO) and chief financial officer (CFO) of each public company to certify that they have reviewed the company's quarterly and annual reports to be filed with the Securities and Exchange Commission (SEC). The CEO and CFO must certify that, based on their knowledge, the reports do not contain any untrue statement of a material fact or any half-truth that would make the report misleading, and that the information contained in the reports fairly presents the company's financial condition.

In addition, this section also requires the CEO and CFO to certify that they have created and designed an internal control system for their company and have recently evaluated that system to ensure that it is effectively providing them with relevant and accurate financial information. If the signing officers have found any significant deficiencies or weaknesses in the company's system or have discovered any evidence of fraud, they must have reported the situation, and any corrective actions they have taken, to the auditors and the audit committee.

---

[1]. This section of the Sarbanes-Oxley Act is codified at 15 U.S.C. Section 7241.

Section 306
Insider trades during pension fund blackout periods[2]

(a) Prohibition of insider trading during pension fund blackout periods

(1) In general

Except to the extent otherwise provided by rule of the Commission pursuant to paragraph (3), it shall be unlawful for any director or executive officer of an issuer of any equity security (other than an exempted security), directly or indirectly, to purchase, sell, or otherwise acquire or transfer any equity security of the issuer (other than an exempted security) during any blackout period with respect to such equity security if such director or officer acquires such equity security in connection with his or her service or employment as a director or executive officer.

(2) Remedy

(A) In general

Any profit realized by a director or executive officer referred to in paragraph (1) from any purchase, sale, or other acquisition or transfer in violation of this subsection shall inure to and be recoverable by the issuer, irrespective of any intention on the part of such director or executive officer in entering into the transaction.

(B) Actions to recover profits

An action to recover profits in accordance with this subsection may be instituted at law or in equity in any court of competent jurisdiction by the issuer, or by the owner of any security of the issuer in the name and in behalf of the issuer if the issuer fails or refuses to bring such action within 60 days after the date of request, or fails diligently to prosecute the action thereafter, except that no such suit shall be brought more than 2 years after the date on which such profit was realized.

(3) Rulemaking authorized

The Commission shall, in consultation with the Secretary of Labor, issue rules to clarify the application of this subsection and to prevent evasion thereof. Such rules shall provide for the application of the requirements of paragraph (1) with respect to entities treated as a single employer with respect to an issuer under section 414(b), (c), (m), or (o) of Title 26 to the extent necessary to clarify the application of such requirements and to prevent evasion thereof. Such rules may also provide for appropriate exceptions from the requirements of this subsection, including exceptions for purchases pursuant to an automatic dividend reinvestment program or purchases or sales made pursuant to an advance election.

(4) Blackout period

For purposes of this subsection, the term "blackout period", with respect to the equity securities of any issuer—

(A) means any period of more than 3 consecutive business days during which the ability of not fewer than 50 percent of the participants or beneficiaries under all individual account plans maintained by the issuer to purchase, sell, or other-

wise acquire or transfer an interest in any equity of such issuer held in such an individual account plan is temporarily suspended by the issuer or by a fiduciary of the plan; and

(B) does not include, under regulations which shall be prescribed by the Commission—

(i) a regularly scheduled period in which the participants and beneficiaries may not purchase, sell, or otherwise acquire or transfer an interest in any equity of such issuer, if such period is—

(I) incorporated into the individual account plan; and

(II) timely disclosed to employees before becoming participants under the individual account plan or as a subsequent amendment to the plan; or

(ii) any suspension described in subparagraph (A) that is imposed solely in connection with persons becoming participants or beneficiaries, or ceasing to be participants or beneficiaries, in an individual account plan by reason of a corporate merger, acquisition, divestiture, or similar transaction involving the plan or plan sponsor.

(5) Individual account plan

For purposes of this subsection, the term "individual account plan" has the meaning provided in section 1002(34) of Title 29, except that such term shall not include a one-participant retirement plan (within the meaning of section 1021(i)(8)(B) of Title 29).

(6) Notice to directors, executive officers, and the Commission

In any case in which a director or executive officer is subject to the requirements of this subsection in connection with a blackout period (as defined in paragraph (4)) with respect to any equity securities, the issuer of such equity securities shall timely notify such director or officer and the Securities and Exchange Commission of such blackout period.

*   *   *   *

Explanatory Comments:

Corporate pension funds typically prohibit employees from trading shares of the corporation during periods when the pension fund is undergoing significant change. Before 2002, however, these blackout periods did not affect the corporation's executives, who frequently received shares of the corporate stock as part of their compensation. Section 306 was Congress's solution to the basic unfairness of this situation. This section of the act required the SEC to issue rules that prohibit any director or executive officer from trading during pension fund blackout periods. (The SEC later issued these rules, entitled Regulation Blackout Trading Restriction, or Reg BTR.)

Section 306 also provided shareholders with a right to file a shareholder's derivative suit against officers and directors who have profited from trading during these blackout periods (provided that the corporation has failed to bring a suit). The officer or director can be forced to return to the corporation any profits received, regardless of whether the director or officer acted with bad intent.

---

2. Codified at 15 U.S.C. Section 7244.

Section 402
Periodical and other reports[3]

*   *   *   *

(i) Accuracy of financial reports

Each financial report that contains financial statements, and that is required to be prepared in accordance with (or reconciled to) generally accepted accounting principles under this chapter and filed with the Commission shall reflect all material correcting adjustments that have been identified by a registered public accounting firm in accordance with generally accepted accounting principles and the rules and regulations of the Commission.

(j) Off-balance sheet transactions

Not later than 180 days after July 30, 2002, the Commission shall issue final rules providing that each annual and quarterly financial report required to be filed with the Commission shall disclose all material off-balance sheet transactions, arrangements, obligations (including contingent obligations), and other relationships of the issuer with unconsolidated entities or other persons, that may have a material current or future effect on financial condition, changes in financial condition, results of operations, liquidity, capital expenditures, capital resources, or significant components of revenues or expenses.

(k) Prohibition on personal loans to executives

(1) In general

It shall be unlawful for any issuer (as defined in section 7201 of this title), directly or indirectly, including through any subsidiary, to extend or maintain credit, to arrange for the extension of credit, or to renew an extension of credit, in the form of a personal loan to or for any director or executive officer (or equivalent thereof) of that issuer. An extension of credit maintained by the issuer on July 30, 2002, shall not be subject to the provisions of this subsection, provided that there is no material modification to any term of any such extension of credit or any renewal of any such extension of credit on or after July 30, 2002.

(2) Limitation

Paragraph (1) does not preclude any home improvement and manufactured home loans (as that term is defined in section 1464 of Title 12), consumer credit (as defined in section 1602 of this title), or any extension of credit under an open end credit plan (as defined in section 1602 of this title), or a charge card (as defined in section 1637(c)(4)(e) of this title), or any extension of credit by a broker or dealer registered under section 78o of this title to an employee of that broker or dealer to buy, trade, or carry securities, that is permitted under rules or regulations of the Board of Governors of the Federal Reserve System pursuant to section 78g of this title (other than an extension of credit that would be used to purchase the stock of that issuer), that is—

(A) made or provided in the ordinary course of the consumer credit business of such issuer;

(B) of a type that is generally made available by such issuer to the public; and

(C) made by such issuer on market terms, or terms that are no more favorable than those offered by the issuer to the general public for such extensions of credit.

(3) Rule of construction for certain loans

Paragraph (1) does not apply to any loan made or maintained by an insured depository institution (as defined in section 1813 of Title 12), if the loan is subject to the insider lending restrictions of section 375b of Title 12.

(l) Real time issuer disclosures

Each issuer reporting under subsection (a) of this section or section 78o(d) of this title shall disclose to the public on a rapid and current basis such additional information concerning material changes in the financial condition or operations of the issuer, in plain English, which may include trend and qualitative information and graphic presentations, as the Commission determines, by rule, is necessary or useful for the protection of investors and in the public interest.

Explanatory Comments:

Before this act, many corporate executives typically received extremely large salaries, significant bonuses, and abundant stock options, even when the companies for which they worked were suffering. Executives were also routinely given personal loans from corporate funds, many of which were never paid back. The average large company during that period loaned almost $1 million a year to top executives, and some companies loaned hundreds of millions of dollars to their executives every year. Section 402 amended the 1934 Securities Exchange Act to prohibit public companies from making personal loans to executive officers and directors.

There are a few exceptions to this prohibition, such as home-improvement loans made in the ordinary course of business. Note also that while loans are forbidden, outright gifts are not. A corporation is free to give gifts to its executives, including cash, provided that these gifts are disclosed on its financial reports. The idea is that corporate directors will be deterred from making substantial gifts to their executives by the disclosure requirement—particularly if the corporation's financial condition is questionable—because making such gifts could be perceived as abusing their authority.

Section 403
Directors, officers, and principal stockholders[4]

(a) Disclosures required

(1) Directors, officers, and principal stockholders required to file

Every person who is directly or indirectly the beneficial owner of more than 10 percent of any class of any equity security (other than an exempted security) which is registered pursuant to section 78l of this title, or who is a director or an officer

---

3. This section of the Sarbanes-Oxley Act amended some of the provisions of the 1934 Securities Exchange Act and added the paragraphs reproduced here at 15 U.S.C. Section 78m.

4. This section of the Sarbanes-Oxley Act amended the disclosure provisions of the 1934 Securities Exchange Act, at 15 U.S.C. Section 78p.

of the issuer of such security, shall file the statements required by this subsection with the Commission (and, if such security is registered on a national securities exchange, also with the exchange).

(2) Time of filing

The statements required by this subsection shall be filed—

    (A) at the time of the registration of such security on a national securities exchange or by the effective date of a registration statement filed pursuant to section 78l(g) of this title;

    (B) within 10 days after he or she becomes such beneficial owner, director, or officer;

    (C) if there has been a change in such ownership, or if such person shall have purchased or sold a security-based swap agreement (as defined in section 206(b) of the Gramm-Leach-Bliley Act (15 U.S.C. 78c note)) involving such equity security, before the end of the second business day following the day on which the subject transaction has been executed, or at such other time as the Commission shall establish, by rule, in any case in which the Commission determines that such 2-day period is not feasible.

(3) Contents of statements

A statement filed—

    (A) under subparagraph (A) or (B) of paragraph (2) shall contain a statement of the amount of all equity securities of such issuer of which the filing person is the beneficial owner; and

    (B) under subparagraph (C) of such paragraph shall indicate ownership by the filing person at the date of filing, any such changes in such ownership, and such purchases and sales of the security-based swap agreements as have occurred since the most recent such filing under such subparagraph.

(4) Electronic filing and availability

Beginning not later than 1 year after July 30, 2002—

    (A) a statement filed under subparagraph (C) of paragraph (2) shall be filed electronically;

    (B) the Commission shall provide each such statement on a publicly accessible Internet site not later than the end of the business day following that filing; and

    (C) the issuer (if the issuer maintains a corporate website) shall provide that statement on that corporate website, not later than the end of the business day following that filing.

*   *   *   *

Explanatory Comments:

This section dramatically shortens the time period provided in the Securities Exchange Act of 1934 for disclosing transactions by insiders. The prior law stated that most transactions had to be reported within ten days of the beginning of the following month, although certain transactions did not have to be reported until the following fiscal year (within the first forty-five days).

In several instances, some insider trading was not disclosed (and was therefore not discovered) until long after the transactions. So Congress added this section to reduce the time period for making disclosures. Under Section 403, most transactions by

insiders must be electronically filed with the SEC within two business days.

Also, any company that maintains a Web site must post these SEC filings on its site by the end of the next business day. Congress enacted this section in the belief that if insiders are required to file reports of their transactions promptly with the SEC, companies will do more to police themselves and prevent insider trading.

Section 404
Management assessment of internal controls[5]

(a) Rules required

The Commission shall prescribe rules requiring each annual report required by section 78m(a) or 78o(d) of this title to contain an internal control report, which shall—

    (1) state the responsibility of management for establishing and maintaining an adequate internal control structure and procedures for financial reporting; and

    (2) contain an assessment, as of the end of the most recent fiscal year of the issuer, of the effectiveness of the internal control structure and procedures of the issuer for financial reporting.

(b) Internal control evaluation and reporting

With respect to the internal control assessment required by subsection (a) of this section, each registered public accounting firm that prepares or issues the audit report for the issuer shall attest to, and report on, the assessment made by the management of the issuer. An attestation made under this subsection shall be made in accordance with standards for attestation engagements issued or adopted by the Board. Any such attestation shall not be the subject of a separate engagement.

*   *   *   *

Explanatory Comments:

This section was enacted to prevent corporate executives from claiming they were ignorant of significant errors in their companies' financial reports. For instance, several CEOs testified before Congress that they simply had no idea that the corporations' financial statements were off by billions of dollars. Congress therefore passed Section 404, which requires each annual report to contain a description and assessment of the company's internal control structure and financial reporting procedures. The section also requires that an audit be conducted of the internal control assessment, as well as the financial statements contained in the report. This section goes hand in hand with Section 302 (which, as discussed previously, requires various certifications attesting to the accuracy of the information in financial reports).

Section 404 has been one of the more controversial and expensive provisions in the Sarbanes-Oxley Act because it requires companies to assess their own internal financial controls to make sure that their financial statements are reliable and accurate. A corporation might need to set up a disclosure committee and a coordinator, establish codes of conduct for accounting and financial personnel, create documentation procedures, provide train-

---

5. Codified at 15 U.S.C. Section 7262.

ing, and outline the individuals who are responsible for performing each of the procedures. Companies that were already well managed have not experienced substantial difficulty complying with this section. Other companies, however, have spent millions of dollars setting up, documenting, and evaluating their internal financial control systems. Although initially creating the internal financial control system is a one-time-only expense, the costs of maintaining and evaluating it are ongoing. Some corporations that spent considerable sums complying with Section 404 have been able to offset these costs by discovering and correcting inefficiencies or frauds within their systems. Nevertheless, it is unlikely that any corporation will find compliance with this section to be inexpensive.

Section 802(a)
Destruction, alteration, or falsification of records in Federal investigations and bankruptcy[6]

Whoever knowingly alters, destroys, mutilates, conceals, covers up, falsifies, or makes a false entry in any record, document, or tangible object with the intent to impede, obstruct, or influence the investigation or proper administration of any matter within the jurisdiction of any department or agency of the United States or any case filed under title 11, or in relation to or contemplation of any such matter or case, shall be fined under this title, imprisoned not more than 20 years, or both.

Destruction of corporate audit records[7]

(a) (1) Any accountant who conducts an audit of an issuer of securities to which section 10A(a) of the Securities Exchange Act of 1934 (15 U.S.C. 78j-1(a)) applies, shall maintain all audit or review workpapers for a period of 5 years from the end of the fiscal period in which the audit or review was concluded.

(2) The Securities and Exchange Commission shall promulgate, within 180 days, after adequate notice and an opportunity for comment, such rules and regulations, as are reasonably necessary, relating to the retention of relevant records such as workpapers, documents that form the basis of an audit or review, memoranda, correspondence, communications, other documents, and records (including electronic records) which are created, sent, or received in connection with an audit or review and contain conclusions, opinions, analyses, or financial data relating to such an audit or review, which is conducted by any accountant who conducts an audit of an issuer of securities to which section 10A(a) of the Securities Exchange Act of 1934 (15 U.S.C. 78j-1(a)) applies. The Commission may, from time to time, amend or supplement the rules and regulations that it is required to promulgate under this section, after adequate notice and an opportunity for comment, in order to ensure that such rules and regulations adequately comport with the purposes of this section.

(b) Whoever knowingly and willfully violates subsection (a)(1), or any rule or regulation promulgated by the Securities and Exchange Commission under subsection (a)(2), shall be fined under this title, imprisoned not more than 10 years, or both.

(c) Nothing in this section shall be deemed to diminish or relieve any person of any other duty or obligation imposed by Federal or State law or regulation to maintain, or refrain from destroying, any document.

*   *   *   *

Explanatory Comments:

Section 802(a) enacted two new statutes that punish those who alter or destroy documents. The first statute is not specifically limited to securities fraud cases. It provides that anyone who alters, destroys, or falsifies records in federal investigations or bankruptcy may be criminally prosecuted and sentenced to a fine or to up to twenty years in prison, or both. The second statute requires auditors of public companies to keep all audit or review working papers for five years but expressly allows the SEC to amend or supplement these requirements as it sees fit. The SEC has, in fact, amended this section by issuing a rule that requires auditors who audit reporting companies to retain working papers for seven years from the conclusion of the review. Section 802(a) further provides that anyone who knowingly and willfully violates this statute is subject to criminal prosecution and can be sentenced to a fine, imprisoned for up to ten years, or both if convicted.

This portion of the Sarbanes-Oxley Act implicitly recognizes that persons who are under investigation often are tempted to respond by destroying or falsifying documents that might prove their complicity in wrongdoing. The severity of the punishment should provide a strong incentive for these individuals to resist the temptation.

Section 804
Time limitations on the commencement of civil actions arising under Acts of Congress[8]

(a) Except as otherwise provided by law, a civil action arising under an Act of Congress enacted after the date of the enactment of this section may not be commenced later than 4 years after the cause of action accrues.

(b) Notwithstanding subsection (a), a private right of action that involves a claim of fraud, deceit, manipulation, or contrivance in contravention of a regulatory requirement concerning the securities laws, as defined in section 3(a)(47) of the Securities Exchange Act of 1934 (15 U.S.C. 78c(a)(47)), may be brought not later than the earlier of—

(1) 2 years after the discovery of the facts constituting the violation; or

(2) 5 years after such violation.

*   *   *   *

Explanatory Comments:

Before the enactment of this section, Section 10(b) of the Securities Exchange Act of 1934 had no express statute of limitations. The courts generally required plaintiffs to have filed suit within one year from the date that they should (using due diligence) have discovered that a fraud had been committed but no later than three years

---

6. Codified at 15 U.S.C. Section 1519.
7. Codified at 15 U.S.C. Section 1520.

8. Codified at 28 U.S.C. Section 1658.

after the fraud occurred. Section 804 extends this period by specifying that plaintiffs must file a lawsuit within two years after they discover (or should have discovered) a fraud but no later than five years after the fraud's occurrence. This provision has prevented the courts from dismissing numerous securities fraud lawsuits.

Section 806
Civil action to protect against retaliation in fraud cases[9]

(a) Whistleblower protection for employees of publicly traded companies.—

No company with a class of securities registered under section 12 of the Securities Exchange Act of 1934 (15 U.S.C. 78l), or that is required to file reports under section 15(d) of the Securities Exchange Act of 1934 (15 U.S.C. 78o(d)), or any officer, employee, contractor, subcontractor, or agent of such company, may discharge, demote, suspend, threaten, harass, or in any other manner discriminate against an employee in the terms and conditions of employment because of any lawful act done by the employee—

(1) to provide information, cause information to be provided, or otherwise assist in an investigation regarding any conduct which the employee reasonably believes constitutes a violation of section 1341, 1343, 1344, or 1348, any rule or regulation of the Securities and Exchange Commission, or any provision of Federal law relating to fraud against shareholders, when the information or assistance is provided to or the investigation is conducted by—

(A) a Federal regulatory or law enforcement agency;

(B) any Member of Congress or any committee of Congress; or

(C) a person with supervisory authority over the employee (or such other person working for the employer who has the authority to investigate, discover, or terminate misconduct); or

(2) to file, cause to be filed, testify, participate in, or otherwise assist in a proceeding filed or about to be filed (with any knowledge of the employer) relating to an alleged violation of section 1341, 1343, 1344, or 1348, any rule or regulation of the Securities and Exchange Commission, or any provision of Federal law relating to fraud against shareholders.

(b) Enforcement action.—

(1) In general.—A person who alleges discharge or other discrimination by any person in violation of subsection (a) may seek relief under subsection (c), by—

(A) filing a complaint with the Secretary of Labor; or

(B) if the Secretary has not issued a final decision within 180 days of the filing of the complaint and there is no showing that such delay is due to the bad faith of the claimant, bringing an action at law or equity for de novo review in the appropriate district court of the United States, which shall have jurisdiction over such an action without regard to the amount in controversy.

(2) Procedure.—

(A) In general.—An action under paragraph (1)(A) shall be governed under the rules and procedures set forth in section 42121(b) of title 49, United States Code.

(B) Exception.—Notification made under section 42121(b) (1) of title 49, United States Code, shall be made to the person named in the complaint and to the employer.

(C) Burdens of proof.—An action brought under paragraph (1)(B) shall be governed by the legal burdens of proof set forth in section 42121(b) of title 49, United States Code.

(D) Statute of limitations.—An action under paragraph (1) shall be commenced not later than 90 days after the date on which the violation occurs.

(c) Remedies.—

(1) In general.—An employee prevailing in any action under subsection (b)(1) shall be entitled to all relief necessary to make the employee whole.

(2) Compensatory damages.—Relief for any action under paragraph (1) shall include—

(A) reinstatement with the same seniority status that the employee would have had, but for the discrimination;

(B) the amount of back pay, with interest; and

(C) compensation for any special damages sustained as a result of the discrimination, including litigation costs, expert witness fees, and reasonable attorney fees.

(d) Rights retained by employee.—Nothing in this section shall be deemed to diminish the rights, privileges, or remedies of any employee under any Federal or State law, or under any collective bargaining agreement.

Explanatory Comments:

Section 806 is one of several provisions that were included in the Sarbanes-Oxley Act to encourage and protect whistleblowers—that is, employees who report their employer's alleged violations of securities law to the authorities. This section applies to employees, agents, and independent contractors who work for publicly traded companies or testify about such a company during an investigation. It sets up an administrative procedure at the U.S. Department of Labor for individuals who claim that their employer retaliated against them (fired or demoted them, for example) for blowing the whistle on the employer's wrongful conduct. It also allows the award of civil damages—including back pay, reinstatement, special damages, attorneys' fees, and court costs—to employees who prove that they suffered retaliation. Since this provision was enacted, whistleblowers have filed numerous complaints with the U.S. Department of Labor under this section.

Section 807
Securities fraud[10]

Whoever knowingly executes, or attempts to execute, a scheme or artifice—

---

9. Codified at 18 U.S.C. Section 1514A.

10. Codified at 18 U.S.C. Section 1348.

(1) to defraud any person in connection with any security of an issuer with a class of securities registered under section 12 of the Securities Exchange Act of 1934 (15 U.S.C. 78l) or that is required to file reports under section 15(d) of the Securities Exchange Act of 1934 (15 U.S.C. 78o(d)); or

(2) to obtain, by means of false or fraudulent pretenses, representations, or promises, any money or property in connection with the purchase or sale of any security of an issuer with a class of securities registered under section 12 of the Securities Exchange Act of 1934 (15 U.S.C. 78l) or that is required to file reports under section 15(d) of the Securities Exchange Act of 1934 (15 U.S.C. 78o(d)); shall be fined under this title, or imprisoned not more than 25 years, or both.

*   *   *   *

Explanatory Comments:

Section 807 adds a new provision to the federal criminal code that addresses securities fraud. Before 2002, federal securities law had already made it a crime—under Section 10(b) of the Securities Exchange Act of 1934 and SEC Rule 10b-5, both of which were discussed in Chapter 21—to intentionally defraud someone in connection with a purchase or sale of securities, but the offense was not listed in the federal criminal code.

Also, paragraph 2 of Section 807 goes beyond what is prohibited under securities law by making it a crime to obtain by means of false or fraudulent pretenses any money or property from the purchase or sale of securities. This new provision allows violators to be punished by up to twenty-five years in prison, a fine, or both.

Section 906
Failure of corporate officers to certify financial reports[11]

(a) Certification of periodic financial reports.—Each periodic report containing financial statements filed by an issuer with the Securities Exchange Commission pursuant to section 13(a) or

---

11. Codified at 18 U.S.C. Section 1350.

15(d) of the Securities Exchange Act of 1934 (15 U.S.C. 78m(a) or 78o(d)) shall be accompanied by a written statement by the chief executive officer and chief financial officer (or equivalent thereof) of the issuer.

(b) Content.—The statement required under subsection (a) shall certify that the periodic report containing the financial statements fully complies with the requirements of section 13(a) or 15(d) of the Securities Exchange Act of 1934 (15 U.S.C. 78m or 78o(d)) and that information contained in the periodic report fairly presents, in all material respects, the financial condition and results of operations of the issuer.

(c) Criminal penalties.—Whoever—

(1) certifies any statement as set forth in subsections (a) and (b) of this section knowing that the periodic report accompanying the statement does not comport with all the requirements set forth in this section shall be fined not more than $1,000,000 or imprisoned not more than 10 years, or both; or

(2) willfully certifies any statement as set forth in subsections (a) and (b) of this section knowing that the periodic report accompanying the statement does not comport with all the requirements set forth in this section shall be fined not more than $5,000,000, or imprisoned not more than 20 years, or both.

Explanatory Comments:

As previously discussed, under Section 302 a corporation's CEO and CFO are required to certify that they believe the quarterly and annual reports their company files with the SEC are accurate and fairly present the company's financial condition. Section 906 adds "teeth" to these requirements by authorizing criminal penalties for those officers who intentionally certify inaccurate SEC filings.

Knowing violations of the requirements are punishable by a fine of up to $1 million, ten years' imprisonment, or both. Willful violators may be fined up to $5 million, sentenced to up to twenty years' imprisonment, or both. Although the difference between a knowing and a willful violation is not entirely clear, the section is obviously intended to remind corporate officers of the serious consequences of certifying inaccurate reports to the SEC.

Answers to *Issue Spotters*

Chapter 1

1A: Yes. Administrative rulemaking starts with the publication of a notice of the rulemaking in the *Federal Register*. Among other details, this notice states where and when the proceedings, such as a public hearing, will be held. Proponents and opponents can offer their comments and concerns regarding the pending rule. After reviewing all the comments from the proceedings, the agency's decision makers consider what was presented and draft the final rule.

2A: No. Even if commercial speech is not related to illegal activities or misleading, it may be restricted if a state has a substantial government interest that cannot be achieved by less restrictive means. In this case, the interest in energy conservation is substantial, but it could be achieved by less restrictive means. That would be the utilities' defense against the enforcement of this state law.

Chapter 2

1A: Maybe. On the one hand, it is not the company's "fault" when a product is misused. Also, keeping the product on the market is not a violation of the law, and stopping sales would hurt profits. On the other hand, suspending sales could reduce suffering and could prevent negative publicity that might occur if sales continued.

2A: When a corporation decides to respond to what it sees as a moral obligation to correct for past discrimination by adjusting pay differences among its employees, an ethical conflict is raised between the firm and its employees and between the firm and its shareholders. This dilemma arises directly out of the effect such a decision has on the firm's profits. If satisfying this obligation increases profitability, then the dilemma is easily resolved in favor of "doing the right thing."

Chapter 3

1A: Yes. Submission of the dispute to mediation or nonbinding arbitration is mandatory, but compliance with the decision of the mediator or arbitrator is voluntary.

2A: Tom could file a motion for a directed verdict. This motion asks the judge to direct a verdict for Tom on the ground that Sue presented no evidence that would justify granting her relief. The judge grants the motion if there is insufficient evidence to raise an issue of fact.

Chapter 4

1A: Probably. To recover on the basis of negligence, the injured party as a plaintiff must show that the truck's owner owed the plaintiff a duty of care, that the owner breached that duty, that the plaintiff was injured, and that the breach caused the injury. In this problem, the owner's actions breached the duty of reasonable care. The billboard falling on the plaintiff was the direct cause of the injury, not the plaintiff's own negligence. Thus, liability turns on whether the plaintiff can connect the breach of duty to the injury. This involves the test of proximate cause—the question of foreseeability. The consequences to the injured party must have been a foreseeable result of the owner's carelessness.

2A: The company might defend against this electrician's claim by asserting that the electrician should have known of the risk and, therefore, the company had no duty to warn. According to the problem, the danger is common knowledge in the electrician's field and should have been apparent to this electrician, given his years of training and experience. In other words, the company most likely had no need to warn the electrician of the risk.

The firm could also raise comparative negligence. Both parties' negligence, if any, could be weighed and the liability distributed proportionately. The defendant could furthermore assert assumption of risk, claiming that the electrician voluntarily entered into a dangerous situation, knowing the risk involved.

Chapter 5

1A: This is patent infringement. A software maker in this situation might best protect its product, save litigation costs, and profit from its patent by the use of a license. In the context of this problem, a license would grant permission to sell a patented item. (A license can be limited to certain purposes and to the licensee only.)

2A: Yes. This may be an instance of trademark dilution. Dilution occurs when a trademark is used, without permission, in a way that diminishes the distinctive quality of the mark. Dilution does not require proof that consumers are likely to be confused by the use of the unauthorized mark. The products involved do not have to be similar. Dilution does require, however, that a mark be famous when the dilution occurs.

Chapter 6

1A: Yes. With respect to the gas station, Daisy has obtained goods by false pretenses. She might also be charged with the crimes of larceny and forgery, and most states have special statutes covering illegal use of credit cards.

2A: Yes. The Counterfeit Access Device and Computer Fraud and Abuse Act of 1984 provides that a person who accesses a computer online, without permission, to obtain classified data—such as consumer credit files in a credit agency's database—is subject to criminal prosecution. The crime has two elements: accessing the computer without permission and taking data. It is a felony if done for private financial gain. Penalties include fines and imprisonment for up to twenty years. The victim of the theft can also bring a civil suit against the criminal to obtain damages and other relief.

Chapter 7

1A: No. Revocation of an offer may be implied by conduct inconsistent with the offer. When Fidelity Corporation rehired Monica, and Ron learned of the hiring, the offer was revoked. His acceptance was too late.

2A: Yes. The original contract was executory—that is, not yet performed by both parties. The parties rescinded the original contract and agreed to a new contract.

Chapter 8

1A: No. Generally, an exculpatory clause (a clause attempting to absolve parties of negligence or other wrongs) is not enforced if the party seeking its enforcement is involved in a business that is important to the public as a matter of practical necessity, such as an airline. Because of the essential nature of such services, the parties have an advantage in bargaining strength and could insist that anyone contracting for its services agree not to hold it liable.

2A: No. The memo would be a sufficient writing to enforce the contract against My-T if that party chose not to complete the deal, however. Letterhead stationery can constitute a signature. If the memo names the parties, the subject matter, the consideration, and the quantity involved in the transaction, it may be sufficient to be enforced against the party whose letterhead appears on it.

Chapter 9

1A: Yes. Generally, if a contract clearly states that a right is not assignable, no assignment will be effective, but there are exceptions. Assignment of the right to receive monetary payment cannot be prohibited.

2A: A nonbreaching party is entitled to her or his benefit of the bargain under the contract. Here, the innocent party is entitled to be put in the position she would have been in if the contract had been fully performed. The measure of the benefit is the cost to complete the work ($500). These are compensatory damages.

Chapter 10

1A: A shipment of nonconforming goods constitutes an acceptance and a breach, unless the seller seasonably notifies the buyer that the nonconforming shipment does not constitute an acceptance and is offered only as an accommodation. Thus, since there was no notification in this problem, the shipment was both an acceptance and a breach.

2A: Yes. In a transaction between merchants, the requirement of a writing is satisfied if one of them sends to the other a signed written confirmation that indicates the terms of the agreement, and the merchant receiving it has reason to know of its contents. If the merchant who receives the confirmation does not object in writing within ten days after receipt, the writing will be enforceable against him or her even though he or she has not signed anything.

Chapter 11

1A: Yes. A seller is obligated to deliver goods in conformity with a contract in every detail. This is the perfect tender rule. The exception of the seller's right to cure does not apply here because the seller delivered too little too late to take advantage of this exception.

2A: Yes. When anticipatory repudiation occurs, a buyer (or lessee) can resort to any remedy for breach even if the buyer tells the seller (the repudiating party in this problem) that the buyer will wait for the seller's performance.

Chapter 12

1A: Yes. The manufacturer is liable for the injuries to the user of the product. A manufacturer is liable for its failure to exercise due care to any person who sustains an injury proximately caused by a negligently made (defective) product. In this problem, the failure to inspect is a failure to use due care. Of course, the maker of the component part may also be liable.

2A: Yes. Under the doctrine of strict liability, persons may be liable for the results of their acts regardless of their intentions or their exercise of reasonable care (that is, regardless of fault).

Chapter 13

1A: A statement that "I.O.U." money (or anything else) or an instruction to a bank stating, "I wish you would pay," would render any instrument nonnegotiable. To be negotiable, an instrument must contain an express promise to pay. An I.O.U. is only an acknowledgment of indebtedness. An order stating, "I wish you would pay," is not sufficiently precise.

2A: No. When a drawer's employee provides the drawer with the name of a fictitious payee (a payee whom the drawer does not actually intend to have any interest in an instrument), a forgery of the payee's name is effective to pass good title to subsequent transferees.

Chapter 14

1A: Yes, to both questions. In a civil suit, a drawer (Lyn) is liable to a payee (Nan) or to a holder of a check that is not honored.

If intent to defraud can be proved, the drawer (Lyn) can also be subject to criminal prosecution for writing a bad check.

2A: The drawer is entitled to $6,300—the amount to which the check was altered ($7,000) less the amount that the drawer ordered the bank to pay ($700). The bank may recover this amount from the party who presented the altered check for payment.

Chapter 15

1A: Each of the parties can place a mechanic's lien on the debtor's property. If the debtor does not pay what is owed, the property can be sold to satisfy the debt. The only requirements are that the lien be filed within a specific time from the time of the work, depending on the state statute, and that notice of the foreclosure and sale be given to the debtor in advance.

2A: Yes. A debtor's payment to a creditor made for a preexisting debt, within ninety days (one year in the case of an insider or fraud) of a bankruptcy filing, can be recovered if it gives the creditor more than he or she would have received in the bankruptcy proceedings. A trustee can recover this preference using her or his specific avoidance powers.

Chapter 16

1A: The major terms that must be disclosed under the Truth-in-Lending Act include the loan principal, the interest rate at which the loan is made, the annual percentage rate or APR (the actual cost of the loan on a yearly basis), and all fees and costs associated with the loan. These disclosures must be made on standardized forms and based on uniform formulas of calculation. Certain types of loans have special disclosure requirements.

2A: Foreclosure is the process that allows a lender to repossess and auction off property that is securing a loan. The two most common types of foreclosure are judicial foreclosure and power of sale foreclosure. In the former—available in all states—a court supervises the process. This is the more common method of foreclosure. In the latter—available in only a few states—a lender forecloses on and sells the property without court supervision.

    If the sale proceeds cover the mortgage debt and foreclosure costs, the debtor receives any surplus. If the proceeds do not cover the debt and costs, the mortgagee can seek to recover the difference through a deficiency judgment, which is obtained in a separate action. A deficiency judgment entitles the creditor to recover this difference from a sale of the debtor's other nonexempt property. Before a foreclosure sale, a mortgagor can redeem the property by paying the debt, plus any interest and costs. This is called the equitable right of redemption.

Chapter 17

1A: When a person enters into a contract on another's behalf without the authority to do so, the other may be liable on the contract if he or she approves or affirms that contract. In other words, the employer-principal (Wonder Goods Company) would be liable for the note on ratifying it. Whether the employer-principal ratifies the note or not, the unauthorized agent (Xena) is most likely also liable for it.

2A: Yes. A principal has a duty to indemnify (reimburse) an agent for liabilities incurred because of authorized and lawful acts and transactions and for losses suffered because of the principal's failure to perform his or her duties.

Chapter 18

1A: Workers' compensation laws establish a procedure for compensating workers who are injured on the job. Instead of suing to collect benefits, an injured worker notifies the employer of the injury and files a claim with the appropriate state agency. The right to recover is normally determined without regard to negligence or fault, but intentionally inflicted injuries are not covered. Unlike the potential for recovery in a lawsuit based on negligence or fault, recovery under a workers' compensation statute is limited to the specific amount designated in the statute for the employee's injury.

2A: Yes. One type of sexual harassment occurs when a request for sexual favors is a condition of employment, and the person making the request is a supervisor or acts with the authority of the employer. A tangible employment action, such as continued employment, may also lead to the employer's liability for the supervisor's conduct. That the injured employee is a male and the supervisor a female, instead of the other way around, would not affect the outcome. Same-gender harassment is also actionable.

Chapter 19

1A: The members of a limited liability company (LLC) may designate a group to run their firm. In that situation, the firm would be a manager-managed LLC. The group may include only members, only nonmembers, or members and nonmembers. If, instead, all members participate in management, the firm would be a member-managed LLC. In fact, unless the members agree otherwise, all members are considered to participate in the management of the firm.

2A: Yes. Failing to meet a specified sales quota can constitute a breach of a franchise agreement. If the franchisor is acting in good faith, "cause" may also include the death or disability of the franchisee, the insolvency of the franchisee, and a breach of another term of the franchise agreement.

Chapter 20

1A: Yes. Small businesses that meet certain requirements can qualify as S corporations, created specifically to permit small businesses to avoid double taxation. The six requirements of an S corporation are (1) the firm must be a domestic corporation; (2) the firm must not be a member of an affiliated group of corporations; (3) the firm must have fewer than a certain number of shareholders; (4) the shareholders must be individuals, estates, or qualified trusts (or corporations in some cases); (5) there can be only one class of stock; and (6) no shareholder can be a nonresident alien.

2A: Yes. A single shareholder—or a few shareholders acting together—who owns enough stock to exercise *de facto* control over a corporation owes the corporation and the minority shareholders a fiduciary duty when transferring those shares.

Chapter 21

1A: The average investor is not concerned with minor inaccuracies but with facts that if disclosed would tend to deter him or her from buying the securities. These would include material facts that have an important bearing on the condition of the issuer and its business—such as liabilities, loans to officers and directors, customer delinquencies, and pending lawsuits.

2A: No. The Securities Exchange Act of 1934 extends liability to officers and directors in their personal transactions for taking advantage of inside information when they know it is unavailable to the persons with whom they are dealing.

Chapter 22

1A: Size alone does not determine whether a firm is a monopoly—size in relation to the market is what matters. A small store in a small, isolated town is a monopolist if it is the only store serving that market. Monopoly involves the power to affect prices and output. If a firm has sufficient market power to control prices and exclude competition, that firm has monopoly power. Monopoly power in itself is not a violation of Section 2 of the Sherman Act. The offense also requires an intent to acquire or maintain that power through anticompetitive means.

2A: This agreement is a tying arrangement. The legality of a tying arrangement depends on the purpose of the agreement, the agreement's likely effect on competition in the relevant markets (the market for the tying product and the market for the tied product), and other factors. Tying arrangements for commodities are subject to Section 3 of the Clayton Act. Tying arrangements for services can be agreements in restraint of trade in violation of Section 1 of the Sherman Act.

Chapter 23

1A: Yes. A bailee's right of possession, even though temporary, permits the bailee to recover damages from any third persons for damage or loss to the property.

2A: Rosa de la Mar Corporation, the shipper, suffers the loss. A common carrier is liable for damage caused by the willful acts of third persons or by an accident. Other losses must be borne by the shipper (or the recipient, depending on the terms of their contract). In this situation, this shipment was lost due to an act of God.

Chapter 24

1A: This is a breach of the warranty deed's covenant of quiet enjoyment. Consuela can sue Bernie and recover the purchase price of the house, plus any damages.

2A: Yes. On the ground that the hardships to be imposed on the polluter and on the community are greater than the hardships suffered by the residents, the court might deny an injunction—if the plant is the core of the local economy, for instance, the residents may only be awarded damages.

Chapter 25

1A: Under the principle of comity, a U.S court would defer and give effect to foreign laws and judicial decrees that are consistent with U.S. law and public policy.

2A: The practice described in this problem is known as dumping, which is regarded as an unfair international trade practice. Dumping is the sale of imported goods at "less than fair value." Based on the price of those goods in the exporting country, an extra tariff—known as an antidumping duty—can be imposed on the imports.

Answers to Even-Numbered *For Review* Questions

Chapter 1

2. **What is a precedent? When might a court depart from precedent?**

Judges attempt to be consistent, and when possible, they base their decisions on the principles suggested by earlier cases. They seek to decide similar cases in a similar way and consider new cases with care, because they know that their conflicting decisions make new law. Each interpretation becomes part of the law on the subject and serves as a legal precedent—a decision that furnishes an example or authority for deciding subsequent cases involving similar legal principles or facts.

A court will depart from the rule of a precedent when it decides that the rule should no longer be followed. If a court decides that a precedent is simply incorrect or that technological or social changes have rendered the precedent inapplicable, the court might rule contrary to the precedent.

4. **What constitutional clause gives the federal government the power to regulate commercial activities among the various states?**

To prevent states from establishing laws and regulations that would interfere with trade and commerce among the states, the Constitution expressly delegated to the national government the power to regulate interstate commerce. The commerce clause—Article I, Section 8, of the U.S. Constitution—expressly permits Congress "to regulate Commerce with foreign Nations, and among the several States, and with the Indian Tribes."

Chapter 2

2. **How can business leaders encourage their companies to act ethically?**

Ethical leadership is important to create and maintain an ethical workplace. Managers can set standards and then apply those standards to themselves and their firm's employees.

4. **What are six guidelines that an employee can use to evaluate whether his or her actions are ethical?**

Guidelines for evaluating whether behavior is ethical can be found (1) in the law, (2) business rules and procedures, (3) social values, (4) an individual's conscience, (5) an individual's promises and obligations to others, and (6) personal or societal heroes.

An action is most likely ethical if it is consistent with the law, or at least the "spirit" of the law, as well as company policies, and if it can survive the scrutiny of one's conscience and the regard of one's heroes without betraying commitments to others.

Chapter 3

2. **Before a court can hear a case, it must have jurisdiction. Over what must it have jurisdiction? How are the courts applying traditional jurisdictional concepts to cases involving Internet transactions?**

To hear a case, a court must have jurisdiction over the person against whom the suit is brought or over the property involved in the suit. The court must also have jurisdiction over the subject matter. Generally, courts apply a "sliding-scale" standard to determine when it is proper to exercise jurisdiction over a defendant whose only connection with the jurisdiction is the Internet.

4. **What is discovery, and how does electronic discovery differ from traditional discovery?**

Discovery is the process of obtaining information and evidence about a case from the other party or third parties. Discovery entails gaining access to witnesses, documents, records, and other types of evidence. Electronic discovery differs in its subject—that is, e-media, such as e-mail or text messages, rather than traditional sources of information, such as paper documents.

Chapter 4

2. **What are two basic categories of torts?**

Generally, the purpose of tort law is to provide remedies for the invasion of legally recognized and protected interests, such as personal safety, freedom of movement, property, and some intangibles, including privacy and reputation. The two broad categories of torts are intentional and unintentional.

4. **Identify the four elements of negligence.**

The four elements of negligence are as follows:

1. A duty of care owed by the defendant to the plaintiff.
2. The defendant's breach of that duty.
3. The plaintiff's suffering a legally recognizable injury.
4. The in-fact and proximate cause of that injury by the defendant's breach.

Chapter 5

2. **Why is the protection of trademarks important?**

Article I, Section 8, of the U.S. Constitution authorizes Congress "to promote the Progress of Science and useful Arts, by securing for limited Times to Authors and Inventors the exclusive Right to their respective Writings and Discoveries." Laws protecting trademarks—and patents and copyrights as well—are designed to protect and reward inventive and artistic creativity.

4. What laws protect authors' rights in the works they create?

Copyright law protects the rights of the authors of certain literary or artistic productions. The Copyright Act of 1976, as amended, covers these rights.

Chapter 6

2. What are five broad categories of crimes? What is white-collar crime?

Traditionally, crimes have been grouped into the following categories: violent crime (crimes against persons), property crime, public order crime, white-collar crime, and organized crime.

White-collar crime is an illegal act or series of acts committed by an individual or business entity using some nonviolent means, usually in the course of a legitimate occupation.

4. What constitutional safeguards exist to protect persons accused of crimes?

Under the Fourth Amendment, before searching or seizing private property, law enforcement officers must obtain a search warrant, which requires probable cause.

Under the Fifth Amendment, no one can be deprived of "life, liberty, or property without due process of law." The Fifth Amendment also protects persons against double jeopardy and self-incrimination.

The Sixth Amendment guarantees the right to a speedy trial, the right to a jury trial, the right to a public trial, the right to confront witnesses, and the right to counsel. Individuals who are arrested must be informed of certain constitutional rights, including their Fifth Amendment right to remain silent and their Sixth Amendment right to counsel. All evidence obtained in violation of the Fourth, Fifth, and Sixth Amendments, as well as all evidence derived from the illegally obtained evidence, must be excluded from the trial.

The Eighth Amendment prohibits excessive bail and fines, and cruel and unusual punishment.

Chapter 7

2. What are the four basic elements necessary to the formation of a valid contract?

The basic elements for the formation of a valid contract are an agreement, consideration, contractual capacity, and legality.

4. How do shrink-wrap and click-on agreements differ from other contracts? How have traditional laws been applied to these agreements?

With a shrink-wrap agreement, the terms are expressed inside the box in which the goods are packaged. A click-on agreement arises when a buyer, completing a transaction on a computer, is required to indicate assent to the terms by clicking on a button that says, for example, "I agree."

Generally, courts have enforced the terms of these agreements the same as the terms of other contracts, applying the traditional common law of contracts. Article 2 of the Uniform Commercial Code provides that acceptance can be made by conduct. The *Restatement (Second) of Contracts* has a similar provision. Under these provisions, a binding contract can be created by conduct, including conduct accepting the terms in a shrink-wrap or click-on agreement.

Chapter 8

2. Under what circumstances will a covenant not to compete be enforced? When will such covenants not be enforced?

A covenant not to compete can be enforced:

1. If it is ancillary (secondary) to an agreement to sell an ongoing business, thus enabling the seller to sell, and the purchaser to buy, the goodwill and reputation of the business.
2. If it is contained in an employment contract and is reasonable in terms of time and geographic area.

A covenant not to compete will be unenforceable if it does not protect a legitimate business interest or is broader than necessary to protect a legitimate interest. This is because such a covenant would unreasonably restrain trade and be contrary to public policy.

4. What is the difference between a mistake of value or quality and a mistake of fact?

A mistake as to the value of a deal is an ordinary risk of business for which a court normally will not provide relief. A mistake concerning a fact important to the subject matter of a contract, however, may provide a basis for relief.

Chapter 9

2. How are most contracts discharged?

The most common way to discharge, or terminate, a contract is by the performance of contractual duties.

4. Under what circumstances is the remedy of rescission and restitution available?

When fraud, mistake, duress, or failure of consideration is present, rescission is available. The failure of one party to perform under a contract entitles the other party to rescind the contract.

Chapter 10

2. In a sales contract, if an offeree includes additional or different terms in an acceptance, will a contract result? If so, what happens to these terms?

Under the Uniform Commercial Code, a contract can be formed, even if the offeree's acceptance includes additional or different terms. If one of the parties is a nonmerchant, the contract does not include the additional terms. If both parties are merchants, the additional terms automatically become part of the contract unless one of the following occurs:

1. The original offer expressly limits acceptance to the terms of the offer.
2. The new or changed terms materially alter the contract.
3. The offeror objects to the new or changed terms within a reasonable period of time.

(If the additional terms expressly require the offeror's assent, the offeree's response is not an acceptance, but a counteroffer.) Under some circumstances, a court might strike the additional terms.

4. Risk of loss does not necessarily pass with title. If the parties to a contract do not expressly agree when risk passes and the goods are to be delivered without movement by the seller, when does risk pass?

If the seller holds the goods and is a merchant, the risk of loss passes to the buyer when the buyer takes physical possession of the goods. If the seller holds the goods and is not a merchant, the risk of loss passes to the buyer on tender of delivery. When a bailee is holding the goods, the risk of loss passes to the buyer when (1) the buyer receives a negotiable document of title for the goods, (2) the bailee acknowledges the buyer's right to possess the goods, or (3) the buyer receives a nonnegotiable document of title and has had a reasonable time to present the document to the bailee and demand the goods.

Chapter 11

2. What is the perfect tender rule? What are some important exceptions to this rule that apply to sales and lease contracts?

Under the perfect tender rule, the seller or lessor has an obligation to ship or tender conforming goods. If the goods or tender of delivery fails in any respect, the buyer or lessee has the right to accept the goods, reject the entire shipment, or accept part and reject part. Exceptions to the rule may be established by agreement.

When goods are rejected because they are nonconforming and the time for performance has not expired, the seller or lessor can notify the buyer or lessee promptly of the intention to cure and then do so within the contract time for performance. If the time for performance has expired, the seller or lessor can still cure within a reasonable time if, at the time of delivery, he or she had reasonable grounds to believe that the nonconforming tender would be acceptable. When an agreed-on manner of delivery becomes impracticable or unavailable through no fault of either party, a seller may choose a commercially reasonable substitute.

4. What remedies are available to a seller or lessor when the buyer or lessee breaches the contract? What remedies are available to a buyer or lessee if the seller or lessor breaches the contract?

Depending on the circumstances at the time of a buyer's or lessee's breach, a seller or lessor may have the right to cancel the contract, withhold delivery, resell or dispose of the goods subject to the contract, recover the purchase price (or lease payments), recover damages, stop delivery in transit, or reclaim the goods.

Similarly, on a seller's or lessor's breach, a buyer or lessee may have the right to cancel the contract, recover the goods, obtain specific performance, obtain cover, replevy the goods, recover damages, reject the goods, withhold delivery, resell or dispose of the goods, stop delivery, or revoke acceptance.

Chapter 12

2. Can a manufacturer be held liable to any person who suffers an injury proximately caused by the manufacturer's negligently made product?

Privity of contract is not required for recovery by an injured plaintiff on the ground of negligence in a product liability action. In other words, a manufacturer is liable for its failure to exercise due care to *any* person who sustains an injury proximately caused by a negligently made product, regardless of whether the injured person is in privity with the manufacturer.

4. What defenses to liability can be raised in a product liability lawsuit?

Defenses to product liability include plaintiff's assumption of risk, product misuse, and comparative negligence, as well as the attribution of injuries to commonly known dangers. Also, as in any suit, a defendant can avoid liability by showing that the elements of the cause of action have not been properly pleaded or proved.

Chapter 13

2. What are the requirements for attaining the status of a holder in due course (HDC)?

A holder of a negotiable instrument becomes an HDC if he or she takes the instrument (1) for value; (2) in good faith; and (3) without notice that the instrument is overdue, that it has been dishonored, that any person has a defense against it or a claim to it, or that it contains unauthorized signatures or alterations, or is so irregular or incomplete as to call into question its authenticity.

4. Certain defenses are valid against all holders, including HDCs. What are these defenses called? Name four defenses that fall within this category.

Universal, or real, defenses are good against the claims of all holders, including HDCs. These defenses include forgery of a maker's or drawer's signature, fraud in the execution of an instrument, material alteration of an instrument, discharge in bankruptcy, minority to the extent recognized by state law, illegality to the extent that state law makes a transaction void, mental incapacity if a person has been so adjudged in a state proceeding, and extreme duress.

Chapter 14

2. When may a bank properly dishonor a customer's check without being liable to the customer?

A bank may dishonor a customer's check without liability to the customer when the customer's account contains insufficient funds to pay the check, providing the bank did not agree to cover overdrafts. A bank may also properly dishonor a stale check, a timely check subject to a valid stop-payment order, a check drawn after the customer's death, and forged or altered checks.

4. What is electronic check presentment, and how does it differ from the traditional check-clearing process?

With electronic check presentment, items are encoded with information (such as the amount of the check) that is read and processed by other banks' computers. A check may sometimes be retained at its place of deposit, and then only its image or description is presented for payment. A bank that encodes information on an item warrants to any subsequent bank or payor that the encoded information is correct.

This differs from the traditional check-clearing process because employees of each bank in the collection chain no longer have to physically handle each check that passes through the bank for collection or payment. Therefore, obtaining payment is much quicker. Whereas manual check processing can take days, electronic check presentment can be done on the day of deposit.

Chapter 15

2. What is garnishment? When might a creditor undertake a garnishment proceeding?

Garnishment occurs when a creditor is permitted to collect a debt by seizing property of the debtor that is being held by a third party (such as a paycheck held by an employer or a checking account held by a bank). A creditor might use garnishment in a situation in which a debt has not been paid, but the process is closely regulated.

4. What is the difference between an exception to discharge and an objection to discharge?

An exception to discharge is a claim that is not dischargeable in bankruptcy, such as a government claim for unpaid taxes. An objection to discharge is a circumstance that causes a discharge to be denied, such as concealing assets.

Chapter 16

2. When is private mortgage insurance required? Which party does it protect?

A creditor may require private mortgage insurance if a mortgagor does not make a down payment of at least 20 percent of the purchase price for residential real property.

The creditor is protected if the borrower defaults because in that event the insurer reimburses the creditor for a portion of the loan.

4. What is a short sale? What advantages over mortgage foreclosure might it offer borrowers? Does the lender receive the full balance due on the mortgage loan in a short sale?

A short sale is a sale of real property for an amount that is less than the balance owed on the mortgage loan. Unlike a mortgage foreclosure, both the lender and the borrower must consent to a short sale. A short sale can be advantageous for a borrower because it has a less negative effect on the homeowner's credit than a foreclosure does and because the homeowner is not evicted from her or his home.

Following a short sale, and after the sale proceeds are applied, the borrower still owes the balance of the mortgage debt to the lender unless the lender agrees to forgive the remaining debt.

Chapter 17

2. How do agency relationships arise?

Agency relationships normally are consensual—that is, they arise by voluntary consent and agreement between the parties.

4. When is a principal liable for the agent's actions with respect to third parties? When is the agent liable?

A disclosed or partially disclosed principal is liable to a third party for a contract made by an agent who was acting within the scope of her or his authority. If the agent exceeds the scope of authority and the principal fails to ratify the contract, the agent may be liable (and the principal may not).

When neither the fact of agency nor the identity of the principal is disclosed, the agent is liable, and if the agent has acted within the scope of his or her authority, the undisclosed principal is also liable. Each party is liable for his or her own torts and crimes. A principal may also be liable for an agent's torts committed within the course or scope of employment. A principal is liable for an agent's crime if the principal participated by conspiracy or other action.

Chapter 18

2. What federal statute governs working hours and wages?

The Fair Labor Standards Act is the most significant federal statute governing working hours and wages.

4. What are the two most important federal statutes governing immigration and employment today?

The most important federal statutes governing immigration and the employment of noncitizens are the Immigration Reform and Control Act (IRCA) of 1986 and the Immigration Act of 1990.

Chapter 19

2. What advantages and disadvantages are associated with the sole proprietorship?

A major advantage of the sole proprietorship is that the proprietor receives all of the profits. Also, it is often easier and less costly to start a sole proprietorship than to start any other kind of business. This type of business organization entails more flexibility than does a partnership or a corporation. A sole proprietor pays only personal income taxes on profits. Sole proprietors can establish tax-exempt retirement accounts in the form of Keogh plans.

The major disadvantage is that the proprietor bears the burden of any losses or liabilities incurred by the enterprise. The sole proprietorship also lacks continuity on the death of the proprietor. Another disadvantage is that the opportunity to raise capital is limited to personal funds and the funds of those who are willing to make loans.

4. What are two options for managing limited liability companies?

An LLC may be member-managed or manager-managed. If the articles of organization do not specify otherwise, an LLC is considered to be member-managed, with all members participating in management. In a manager-managed LLC, the members designate a group of persons, who may or may not be members, to manage the firm.

Chapter 20

2. In what circumstances might a court disregard the corporate entity ("pierce the corporate veil") and hold the shareholders personally liable?

Generally, when the corporate privilege is abused for personal benefit or when the corporate business is treated in such a careless manner that the corporation and the shareholder in control are no longer separate entities, a court will require an owner to assume personal liability. Commingled assets, fraud, noncompliance with corporate formalities, and thin capitalization are among the circumstances that may justify piercing the corporate veil.

4. What is a voting proxy?

A proxy is written authorization given by a shareholder to a third party to vote the shareholder's shares at a shareholders' meeting.

Chapter 21

2. What are the two major statutes regulating the securities industry?

The major statutes regulating the securities industry are the Securities Act of 1933 and the Securities Exchange Act of 1934, which created the Securities and Exchange Commission.

4. What are some of the features of state securities laws?

Typically, state laws have disclosure requirements and antifraud provisions patterned after Section 10(b) of the Securities Exchange Act of 1934 and SEC Rule 10b-5. State laws provide for the registration or qualification of securities offered or issued for sale within the state with the appropriate state official. Also, most state securities laws regulate securities brokers and dealers.

Chapter 22

2. What anticompetitive activities are prohibited by Section 1 of the Sherman Act?

Section 1 prohibits agreements that are anticompetitively restrictive—that is, agreements that have the wrongful purpose of restraining competition, such as price fixing.

4. What agencies of the federal government enforce the federal antitrust laws?

The federal agencies that enforce the antitrust laws are the U.S. Department of Justice and the Federal Trade Commission.

Chapter 23

2. What are the three necessary elements for an effective gift?

To make an effective gift, the donor must intend to make the gift, the gift must be delivered to the donee, and the donee must accept the gift.

4. Is an insurance broker the agent of the insurance applicant or the agent of the insurer?

A broker is the agent of an insurance applicant.

Chapter 24

2. What is an easement? Describe three ways that easements are created.

An easement is the right of a person to make limited use of another person's real property without taking anything from the property, such as a right-of-way to cross another's property. Most easements are created by express grant in a contract.

An easement may also be created by the following:

1. *Implication* when surrounding circumstances imply its existence.
2. *Necessity* when an easement is required to access one's own property.
3. *Prescription* when authorized by a statute. Prescription occurs when someone utilizes an easement on property without the owner's permission and the use is apparent and continues for the length of time required by the applicable statute of limitations.

4. What types of tenancies can be created when real property is leased?

A lease of real property can create a fixed-term tenancy, periodic tenancy, tenancy at will, or tenancy at sufferance.

Chapter 25

2. What is the act of state doctrine? In what circumstances is this doctrine applied?

The act of state doctrine is a judicially created doctrine that provides that the judicial branch of one country will not examine the validity of public acts committed by a recognized foreign government within its own territory. This doctrine is often employed in cases involving expropriation or confiscation.

4. What are three clauses commonly included in international business contracts?

Choice-of-language, forum-selection, and choice-of-law clauses are commonly used in international business contracts.

APPENDIX G

Sample Answers for *Questions with Sample Answer*

1–2A. Question with Sample Answer

The U.S. Constitution is the supreme law of the land. A law in violation of the Constitution, no matter what its source, will be declared unconstitutional and will not be enforced. In this problem, the court determined that a Massachusetts state statute was in conflict with the U.S. Constitution. The Constitution takes priority, so the statute will not be enforced.

In the actual case on which this problem is based, the trial court held that the statute violated the Constitution, and the U.S. Court of Appeals for the First Circuit affirmed this holding. Under the statute's definitions of large and small wineries, most of the small wineries were in state, and all of the large wineries were out of state. The court found that the purpose of the statute was to "ensure that Massachusetts' wineries obtained an advantage over their out-of-state counterparts."

2–2A. Question with Sample Answer

Factors for the firm to consider in making its decision include the appropriate ethical standard. Under the utilitarian standard, an action is correct, or "right," when, among the people it affects, it produces the greatest amount of good for the greatest number of people. When an action affects the majority adversely, it is morally wrong.

Applying the utilitarian standard requires three steps: (1) determine which individuals will be affected by the action in question; (2) perform an assessment, or cost-benefit analysis, of the negative and positive effects of alternative actions on these individuals; and (3) choose the alternative that will produce the maximum societal utility.

Ethical standards may also be based on a concept of duty, which suggests that the end can never justify the means and that human beings should not be treated as mere means to an end. But ethical decision making in a business context is not always simple. It is particularly difficult when an action will have different effects on different groups of people—shareholders, employees, society, and other stakeholders, such as the local community. Thus, another factor to consider is to whom the firm believes it owes a duty.

3–2A. Question with Sample Answer

Marya can bring suit in all three courts. The trucking firm did business in Florida, and the accident occurred there. Thus, the state of Florida would have jurisdiction over the defendant. Because the firm was headquartered in Georgia and had its principal place of business in that state, Marya could also sue in a Georgia court. Finally, because the amount in controversy exceeds $75,000, the suit could be brought in federal court on the basis of diversity of citizenship.

4–2A. Question with Sample Answer

Yes. The *Restatement (Second) of Torts* defines *negligence* as "conduct that falls below the standard established by law for the protection of others against unreasonable risk of harm." The standard established by law is that of a reasonable person acting with due care in the circumstances. Shannon was well aware that the medication she took would make her drowsy, and her failure to observe due care—that is, refrain from driving—under the circumstances was negligent.

5–2A. Question with Sample Answer

1. Making a photocopy of an article in a scholarly journal "for purposes such as . . . scholarship, or research, is not an infringement of copyright" under Section 107 of the Copyright Act.
2. This is an example of trademark infringement. When a trademark is copied to a substantial degree or used in its entirety by one who is not entitled to use it, the trademark has been infringed.
3. This is the most likely example of copyright infringement. Generally, the determination of whether the reproduction of copyrighted material constitutes copyright infringement is made on a case-by-case basis under the "fair use" doctrine, as expressed in Section 107 of the Copyright Act. Courts consider such factors as the "purpose and character" of the use, such as whether it is "of a commercial nature"; "the amount and substantiality of the portion used in relation to the copyrighted work as a whole"; and "the effect of the use on the potential market" for the copied work. Here, the DVD storeowner is copying copyrighted works in their entirety for commercial purposes, thereby affecting the market for the works.

6–2A. Question with Sample Answer

Kayla has committed fraud in her e-mail. The elements of the tort of fraud are as follows:

1. The misrepresentation of material facts or conditions was made with knowledge that they were false or with reckless disregard for the truth.
2. There was an intent to induce another to rely on the misrepresentation.
3. There was justifiable reliance on the misrepresentation by the deceived party.

4. Damages were suffered as a result of the reliance.
5. There was a causal connection between the misrepresentation and the injury.

If any of Kayla's recipients reply to her false plea with cash, it is likely that all of these requirements for fraud will have been met.

7–2A. Question with Sample Answer

Past consideration is no consideration. Therefore, a promise to pay for an event that has already taken place is not enforceable. There is nothing to bargain for in this situation. Also, there is no consideration if the promise is based on a moral duty (obligation) to pay. Because Daniel is presumed to be an adult responsible for his own care, Fred has no legal duty of care to Daniel. Because Fred had at best only a moral obligation to reimburse the elderly couple for the care rendered, and because the promise to pay was for an event already performed, Fred's promise cannot be enforced.

Because of the harshness of this rule, a few states have passed statutes enforcing such agreements (usually only up to the value of care received), or a court will enforce such a promise if the promisor received a substantial benefit (such as being saved from physical harm or financial disaster). In this situation, though, it is unlikely that the court would hold for the elderly couple, as the recipient of the benefit was Daniel, and not the promisor, Fred.

8–2A. Question with Sample Answer

In this situation, Gemma becomes a guarantor on the loan. That is, she guarantees the hardware store that she will pay for the mower if her brother fails to do so. This kind of collateral promise, in which the guarantor states that he or she will become responsible only if the primary party does not perform, must be in writing to be enforceable.

There is an exception, however. If the main purpose in accepting secondary liability is to secure a personal benefit—for example, if Gemma's brother bought the mower for her—the contract need not be in writing. The court will determine from the circumstances of the case whether the main purpose was to secure a personal benefit and thus, in effect, to answer for the guarantor's own debt.

9–2A. Question with Sample Answer

The question of whether a party has properly mitigated damages is a question of fact. Here, there is evidence to support a finding that Barton attempted to mitigate her damages—she apparently made reasonable efforts to find, and did find, employment. Because the position paid a significantly lower salary, it was not unreasonable for her to refuse it. Thus, under the circumstances, it was not unreasonable for her to choose to move to London.

A court should therefore award Barton $72,000 for the one year's salary she would have been paid if VanHorn had not repudiated their contract and the costs to move to London.

10–2A. Question with Sample Answer

Yes. Under UCC 2–205, a merchant offeror, who in a signed writing gives assurance that an offer will remain open, creates an irrevocable offer (without payment of consideration) for the time period stated in the assurance up to a period of three months. As a merchant, Jennings was obliged to hold the offer (which had been made in a signed writing—the letter) open until October 9. Wheeler's acceptance of the offer before October 9 created a valid contract, which Jennings breached when he sold the Thunderbird to a third party.

11–2A. Question with Sample Answer

Hammer is correct. Moore's refusal to deliver the car to Hammer on Friday, when Hammer tendered the $8,500 to Moore, constituted a breach of their contract. Moore could have canceled the contract on Hammer's anticipatory repudiation but did not do so and did not change her position in any way as a result of Hammer's anticipatory breach. Hammer could retract his repudiation of the contract at any time prior to the time performance was due.

Because Hammer did retract his repudiation and decided to buy the car at the time performance was due (and not later), Moore was obligated to abide by the terms of the contract

12–2A. Question with Sample Answer

Yes. To disclaim the implied warranty of fitness for a particular purpose, the disclaimer must be in writing and be conspicuous. Although the implied warranty of merchantability can be disclaimed orally, if the disclaimer is in writing, it must be conspicuously written. This means that through different color or size of type or some other technique, the disclaimer must stand out from the context in which it is printed so as to alert the reader of the document to the disclaimer.

In this case, the disclaimer was printed in the same size and color of type as the rest of the contract and was not conspicuous. If this was the only warranty disclaimer, it is not effective and Tandy can recover.

13–2A. Question with Sample Answer

For an instrument to be negotiable, it must meet the following requirements:

1. Be in writing.
2. Be signed by the maker or the drawer.
3. Be an unconditional promise or order to pay.
4. State a fixed amount of money.
5. Be payable on demand or at a definite time.
6. Be payable to order or to bearer, unless it is a check.

The instrument in this case meets the writing requirement because it is handwritten on something with a degree of permanence that is transferable. The instrument meets the requirement of being signed by the maker, as Muriel Evans's signature (her name in her handwriting) appears in the body of the instrument. The instrument's payment is not conditional and contains Muriel Evans's definite promise to pay.

In addition, the sum of $100 is both a fixed amount and payable in money (U.S. currency). Because the instrument is payable on demand and to bearer (Karen Marvin or any holder), the instrument is negotiable.

14–2A. Question with Sample Answer

Gary goes grocery shopping and carelessly leaves his checkbook in his shopping cart. His checkbook, with two blank checks remaining, is stolen by Dolores. On May 5, Dolores forges Gary's name on a check for $100 and cashes the check at Gary's bank, Citizens Bank of Middletown. Gary has not reported the loss of his blank checks to his bank.

On June 1, Gary receives his monthly bank statement from Citizens Bank that includes the forged check, but he does not notice the item nor does he examine his bank statement.

On June 20, Dolores forges Gary's last check. This check is for $1,000 and is cashed at Eastern City Bank, a bank with which Dolores has previously done business. Eastern City Bank puts the check through the collection process, and Citizens Bank honors it.

On July 1, on receipt of his bank statement and canceled checks covering June transactions, Gary discovers both forgeries and immediately notifies Citizens Bank. Dolores cannot be found. Gary claims that Citizens Bank must recredit his account for both checks, as his signature was forged. Discuss fully Gary's claim.

15–2A. Question with Sample Answer

Yes. Mendez has both a security interest in Arabian Knight and is a perfected secured party. He has met all the necessary criteria listed under UCC 9–203 to be a secured creditor. Mendez has given value of $5,000 and has taken possession of the collateral, Arabian Knight, owned by Marsh (who has rights in the collateral). Thus, Mendez has a security interest even though Marsh did not sign a security agreement. Once a security interest attaches, a transfer of possession of the collateral to the secured party can perfect the party's security interest without a filing [UCC 9–310(b)(6), 9–313]. Thus, a security interest was created and perfected at the time Marsh transferred Arabian Knight to Mendez as security for the loan.

16–2A. Question with Sample Answer

The answer is likely no. If the loan was split without the consumer's consent, prior court cases have found that such practices violate the requirement of the Truth-in-Lending Act (TILA) that all disclosures for a single transaction must be grouped into a single writing.

Even if the plaintiff acquiesced to splitting the loan, the practice appears to circumvent the purpose of the Home Ownership and Equity Protection Act through an artificial restructuring of the loan transaction. If consumer protections could be circumvented by splitting loans, lenders would have a strong incentive to divide loans as necessary to keep individual loan costs as low as possible.

17–2A. Question with Sample Answer

Agency is usually a consensual relationship in that the principal and agent agree that the agent will have the authority to act for the principal, binding the principal to any contract with a third party. If no agency in fact exists, the purported agent's contracts with third parties are not binding on the principal. In this case, no agency by agreement was created.

Brown may claim that an agency by estoppel was created, but this argument will fail. Agency by estoppel is applicable only when a principal causes a third person to believe that another person is the principal's agent. In that situation, the principal's words or actions lead the third party to reasonably believe that the agent has authority. Hence, the principal is estopped (prevented) from claiming that no agency actually existed. Acts and declarations of the agent, however, do not in and of themselves create an agency by estoppel, because such actions should not reasonably lead a third person to believe that the purported agent has authority.

In this case, Wade's declarations and allegations alone led Brown to believe that Wade was an agent. Gett's actions were not involved. It is not reasonable to believe that someone is an agent solely because he or she is a friend of the principal. Therefore, Brown cannot hold Gett liable unless Gett ratifies Wade's contract—which is unlikely, as Wade has disappeared with the rare coin.

18–2A. Question with Sample Answer

Educational requirements can be legally imposed as long as the requirement is directly related to, and necessary for, performance of the job. The requirement of a high school diploma is not a direct, job-related requirement in this case. Chinawa obviously comes under the 1964 Civil Rights Act, Title VII, as amended, and the educational requirement under the circumstances is definitely discriminatory against minorities.

19–2A. Question with Sample Answer

Although a joint stock company has characteristics of a corporation, it is usually treated as a partnership. Therefore, although the joint stock company issues transferable shares of stock and is managed by directors and officers, the shareholders have personal liability. Unless the shareholders transfer their stock and ownership to a third party, not only are the joint stock company's assets available for damages caused by a breach, but the individual shareholders' assets are also subject to such liability.

A business trust resembles and is treated like a corporation in many respects. One is the limited liability of the beneficiaries. Unless state law treats the beneficiaries as partners, making them liable to the business trust's creditors, Faraway Corp. can look to only the business trust's assets in the event of a breach.

20–2A. Question with Sample Answer

If Artel acquires the stocks and assets of Fox Express, a *merger* will take place. Artel will be the surviving corporation, and Fox Express will disappear as a corporation. If Artel and Fox Express combine so that both corporations cease to exist and a new corporation, A&F Enterprises, is formed, a *consolidation* will take place.

In either situation, title to the property of the corporation that ceases to exist will pass automatically to the surviving or new corporation without a formal transfer being necessary. In addition, in a merger, the debt liabilities of Fox Express become the liabilities of Artel. Artel's articles of incorporation are deemed to be amended to include the terms stated in the articles of merger.

If a consolidation takes place, A&F Enterprises will automatically acquire title to the properties of both Artel and Fox Express without a formal transfer being necessary. A&F Enterprises also will assume liability for the debts and obligations of Artel and Fox Express. The articles of consolidation take the place of the articles of incorporation of Artel and Fox Express, and they will be regarded thereafter as the articles of incorporation of A&F Enterprises.

21–2A. Question with Sample Answer

No. Under federal securities law, a stock split is exempt from registration requirements because no stock is being sold. The existing shares are merely being split, and the corporation does not receive any consideration for the additional shares created.

22–2A. Question with Sample Answer

Yes. The major antitrust law being violated is the Sherman Act, Section 1. Allitron and Donovan are engaged in interstate commerce, and the agreement to divide marketing territories between them is a contract in restraint of trade. The U.S. Department of Justice could seek fines of up to $1 million from each corporation, and the officers or directors responsible could be imprisoned for up to three years.

23–2A. Question with Sample Answer

For Curtis to recover against the hotel, he must first prove that a bailment relationship was created between himself and the hotel as to the car or the fur coat, or both. For a bailment to exist, there must be a delivery of personal property that gives the bailee exclusive possession of the property, and the bailee must knowingly accept the bailed property. If either element is lacking, there is no bailment relationship and no liability on the part of the bailee hotel.

The facts clearly indicate that the bailee hotel took exclusive possession and control of Curtis's car. The hotel knowingly accepted the car when the attendant took the car from Curtis and parked it in the underground garage, retaining the keys. Thus, a bailment was created as to the car. Since this was a mutual-benefit bailment, the hotel owed Curtis the duty to exercise reasonable care over the car and to return it at the end of the bailment.

Failure to return the car creates a presumption of negligence (lack of reasonable care). Unless the hotel can rebut this presumption, the hotel is liable to Curtis for the loss of the car. As to the fur coat, the hotel neither knew nor expected that the trunk contained an expensive fur coat. Thus, although the hotel knowingly took exclusive possession of the car, the hotel did not do so with the fur coat. (But for a regular coat and other items likely to be in a car, the hotel would be liable.) Because no bailment of the expensive fur coat was created, the hotel has no liability for its loss.

24–2A. Question with Sample Answer

Wiley understandably wants a general warranty deed, as this type of deed will give him the most extensive protection against any defects of title claimed against the property transferred. The general warranty deed would have Gemma warranting the following:

1. That she has the title to, and the power to convey, the property.
2. A covenant of quiet enjoyment (a warranty that the buyer will not be disturbed in his possession of the land).
3. That transfer of the property is made without knowledge of adverse claims of third parties.

Gemma, however, is conveying only ten feet along a property line that may not even be accurately surveyed. Therefore, she does not wish to make these warranties.

Consequently, Gemma is offering a quitclaim deed, which does not convey any warranties but conveys only whatever interest, if any, the grantor owns. Although title is passed by a quitclaim deed, the quality of the title is not warranted. Because Wiley really needs the property, it appears that he has three choices. He can accept the quitclaim deed, he can increase his offer price to obtain the general warranty deed he wants, or he can offer to have a title search made, which should satisfy both parties.

25–2A. Question with Sample Answer

Yes, it is reasonable to rely on the producers' financial records, which are reasonably reflective of their costs because their normal allocation methods were used for a number of years. These records are historically relied on to present important financial information to shareholders, lenders, tax authorities, auditors, and other third parties. Provided that the producers' records and books comply with generally accepted accounting principles and were verified by independent auditors, it is reasonable to use them to determine the production costs and fair market value of canned pineapple in the United States.

Sample Answers for *Case Problems with Sample Answer*

1–5A. Case Problem with Sample Answer

The establishment clause prohibits the government from passing laws or taking actions that promote religion or show a preference for one religion over another. In assessing a government action, the courts look at the predominant purpose for the action and ask whether the action has the effect of endorsing religion.

Although DeWeese claimed to have a nonreligious purpose for displaying the poster of the Ten Commandments in a courtroom, his own statements showed a religious purpose. These statements reflected his views about "warring" legal philosophies and his belief that "our legal system is based on moral absolutes from divine law handed down by God through the Ten Commandments." This plainly constitutes a religious purpose that violates the establishment clause because it has the effect of endorsing Judaism or Christianity over other religions. In the case on which this problem is based, the court ruled in favor of the American Civil Liberties Union.

2–4A. Case Problem with Sample Answer

The law does not codify all ethical requirements. A firm may have acted unethically but still not be legally accountable unless the party that was wronged can establish some basis for liability. Rules of law are designed to require plaintiffs to prove certain elements that establish a defendant's liability in order to recover for injuries or loss. Ethical codes and internal guidelines may have significance in evaluating a company's conduct, but they are not rules of law—a violation of a company policy is not a basis for liability.

In this case, Havensure had the burden of proving liability. Prudential's violation of its own company guideline was clearly wrongful—and might be a matter of concern for insurance regulators—but this misconduct did not create an obligation to Havensure. Havensure cannot establish a cause of action against Prudential for violating its own policy. In the actual case on which this problem is based, the court ruled in Prudential's favor.

3–4A. Case Problem with Sample Answer

Based on a recent holding by the Washington state supreme court, the federal appeals court held that the arbitration provision was *unconscionable* (see page 235 in Chapter 8) and therefore invalid. Because it was invalid, the restriction on class-action suits was also invalid. The state court reasoned that by offering a contract that restricted class actions and required arbitration, the company had improperly stripped consumers of rights they would normally have to attack certain industry practices. Class-action suits are often brought in cases of deceptive or unfair industry practices when the losses suffered by an individual consumer are too small to warrant a consumer suing.

In this case, the alleged added cell phone fees are so small that no one consumer would be likely to litigate or arbitrate the matter due to the expenses involved. Because the arbitration agreement eliminates the possibility of class actions, it violates public policy and is void and unenforceable.

4–4A. Case Problem with Sample Answer

Defamation involves wrongfully hurting a person's good reputation. Doing so in writing is the tort of libel. The basis of the tort of defamation is the publication of a statement that holds an individual up to contempt, ridicule, or hatred. Publication means that the statement is communicated to someone other than the defamed party. A person who republishes defamatory statements is liable. The publication of information that places a person in a false light, such as a story that she did something she did not actually do, could also constitute an invasion of privacy. Truth normally is an absolute defense to a charge of defamation.

In this problem, the police communicated to the *Herald* that Eubanks was charged with a crime, and the paper published the information. Its publication might hold Eubanks up to contempt, ridicule, or hatred. The information was not correct, placing Eubanks in a false light. Yet the *Herald*'s publication of the information was an accurate, truthful summary of a police report. No information was changed. There is no indication that the paper was aware of the second e-mail before it published its summary of the first. Thus, truth is most likely an absolute defense to Eubanks's charges. In the actual case on which this problem is based, the court issued a judgment in favor of the newspaper.

5–5A. Case Problem with Sample Answer

Some business information that cannot be protected by trademark, patent, or copyright law is protected against appropriation by competitors as trade secrets. Trade secrets consist of anything that makes a company unique and that would have value to a competitor—customer lists, plans, research and development, pricing information, marketing techniques, and production techniques, for example. Theft of trade secrets is a federal crime.

In this problem, the documents in the boxes in the car could constitute trade secrets. But a number of factors suggest that a finding of theft and imposition of liability would not be appropriate.

The boxes were not marked in any way that would indicate they contained confidential information. The boxes were stored in an employee's car. The alleged thief was the employee's spouse, not a CPR competitor, and she apparently had no idea what was in the boxes. Leaving trade secrets so accessible does not show an effort to protect the information. In the case on which this problem is based, the court dismissed Jones's claim, in part, on the reasoning stated above.

6–5A. Case Problem with Sample Answer

Under the Fourth Amendment, a police officer must obtain a search warrant to search private property. In a traffic stop, however, it seems unreasonable to require an officer to obtain a warrant to search one of the vehicle's occupants. But it seems reasonable to apply some standard to prevent police misconduct. An officer might be held to a standard of probable cause, which consists of reasonable grounds to believe that a person should be searched.

In some situations, however, an officer may have a reasonable suspicion short of probable cause to believe that a person poses a risk of violence. In a traffic-stop setting, for example, the normal reaction of a person stopped for a driving infraction would not pose this risk, but it might arise if the person feared that evidence of a more serious crime might be discovered. A criminal's motivation to use violence to prevent the discovery could be great, and because the vehicle is already stopped, the additional intrusion is minimal. Under these circumstances, a limited search of the person for weapons would protect the officer, the individual, and the public. Thus, an officer who conducts a routine traffic stop could perform a pat-down search of a passenger on a reasonable suspicion that the person may be armed and dangerous.

7–5A. Case Problem with Sample Answer

Gutkowski does not have a valid claim for payment, nor should he recover on the basis of a quasi contract. Quasi contracts are imposed by courts on parties in the interest of fairness and justice. Usually, a quasi contract is imposed to avoid the unjust enrichment of one party at the expense of another. Gutkowski was compensated as a consultant. For him to establish a claim that he is due more compensation based on unjust enrichment, he must have proof. As it is, he has only his claim that there were discussions about him being a part owner of YES. Discussions and negotiations are not a basis for recovery on a quasi contract. In the actual case on which this problem is based, the court dismissed Gutkowski's claim for payment.

8–5A. Case Problem with Sample Answer

In this case, the agreement that restricted the buyer's options for resolution of a dispute to arbitration and limited the amount of damages was both procedurally and substantively unconscionable. Procedural unconscionability concerns the manner in which the parties enter into a contract. Substantive unconscionability can occur when a contract leaves one party to the agreement without a remedy for the nonperformance of the other.

Here, GeoEx told customers that the arbitration terms in its release form were nonnegotiable and that climbers would encounter the same requirements with any other travel company. This amounted to procedural unconscionability, underscoring the customers' lack of bargaining power. The imbalance resulted in oppressive terms, with no real negotiation and an absence of meaningful choice. Furthermore, the restriction on forum (San Francisco) and the limitation on damages (the cost of the trip)—with no limitation on GeoEx's damages—amounted to substantive unconscionability. In the actual case on which this problem is based, the court ruled that the agreement was unconscionable.

9–7A. Case Problem with Sample Answer

Simard is liable only for the losses and expenses related to the first resale. Simard could reasonably anticipate that his breach would require another sale and that the sales price might be less than what he agreed to pay. Therefore, he should be liable for the difference between his sales price and the first resale price ($29,000), plus any expenses arising from the first resale.

Simard is not liable, however, for any expenses and losses related to the second resale. After all, Simard did not cause the second purchaser's default, and he could not reasonably foresee that default as a probable result of his breach.

10–4A. Case Problem with Sample Answer

Altieri held title to the car that she was driving at the time of the accident in which Godfrey was injured. Once goods exist and are identified, title can be determined. Under the UCC, any explicit understanding between the buyer and the seller determines when title passes. If there is no such agreement, title passes to the buyer at the time and place that the seller physically delivers the goods.

In lease contracts, title to the goods is retained by the lessor-owner of the goods. The UCC's provisions relating to passage to title do not apply to leased goods. Here, Altieri originally leased the car from G.E. Capital Auto Lease, Inc., but by the time of the accident she had bought it. Even though she had not fully paid for the car or completed the transfer-of-title paperwork, she owned it. Title to the car passed to Altieri when she bought it and took delivery of it. Thus, Altieri, not G.E., was the owner of the car at the time of the accident. In the actual case on which this problem is based, the court concluded that G.E. was not the owner of the vehicle when Godfrey was injured.

11–7A. Case Problem with Sample Answer

Padma notified Universal Exports about its breach, so Padma has two ways to recover even though it accepted the goods. Padma's first option is to argue that it revoked its acceptance, giving it the right to reject the goods. To revoke acceptance, Padma would have to show that:

1. The nonconformity substantially impaired the value of the shipment.
2. It predicated its acceptance on a reasonable assumption that Universal Exports would cure the nonconformity.

3. Universal Exports did not cure the nonconformity within a reasonable time.

Padma's second option is to keep the goods and recover for the damages caused by Universal Exports' breach. Under this option, Padma could recover at least the difference between the value of the goods as promised and their value as accepted.

12–6A. Case Problem with Sample Answer

No. Dobrovolny's claim is not likely to succeed. The majority of states recognize strict product liability. The purpose of strict product liability is to ensure that the costs of injuries resulting from defective products are borne by the manufacturers rather than by the injured persons. The law imposes this liability as a matter of public policy. Some state courts limit the application of the tort theory of strict product liability to situations involving personal injuries rather than property damage.

In this problem, Nebraska recognizes strict product liability, but the state's courts limit its application. The issue is whether these limits apply when a product self-destructs without causing damage to persons or other property. When a product injures only itself, the reasons for imposing liability in tort lose their significance. The consumer has not been injured, and the loss concerns the consumer's benefit of the bargain from the contract with the seller of the product.

Although a consumer with only a damaged product may not recover in tort, the consumer is not without other remedies. Recovery can be sought on a contract theory for breach of warranty. Product value and quality are the purposes of warranties. Thus, even though the court is likely to deny Dobrovolny's strict product liability claim, he might seek to recover for breach of warranty on contract principles for the loss of his truck. If there were no express warranties that the truck would not spontaneously combust, relief may be possible for breach of the implied warranty of merchantability or fitness for a particular purpose. In the actual case on which this problem is based, the court issued a decision in Ford's favor.

13–6A. Case Problem with Sample Answer

No. Novel is not correct. The instrument is a note and Novel is bound to pay it. For an instrument to be negotiable under UCC 3–104, it must meet the following requirements: (1) be in writing, (2) be signed by the maker or the drawer, (3) be an unconditional promise or order to pay, (4) state a fixed amount of money, (5) be payable on demand or at a definite time, and (6) be payable to order or to bearer unless it is a check. When no time for payment is stated on an instrument, the instrument is payable on demand.

Applying these principles to the facts in this problem, all of the requirements to establish the instrument as negotiable are met:

1. The instrument is in writing.
2. It is signed by Novel.
3. There are no conditions or promises other than the unconditional promise to pay.
4. The instrument states a fixed amount—$10,000.

5. The instrument does not include a definite repayment date, which means that it is payable on demand.
6. The instrument is payable to Gallwitz.

In the actual case on which this problem is based, the court ruled in favor of Gallwitz for payment of the note.

14–6A. Case Problem with Sample Answer

Wells Fargo is liable to W Financial for the amount of the check. A bank that pays a customer's check bearing a forged indorsement must recredit the customer's account or be liable to the customer-drawer for breach of contract. The bank must recredit the account because it failed to carry out the drawer's order to pay to the order of the named party. Eventually, the loss falls on the first party to take the instrument bearing the forged indorsement because a forged indorsement does not transfer title. Thus, whoever takes an instrument with a forged indorsement cannot become a holder.

Under these rules, Wells Fargo is liable to W Financial for the amount of the check. The bank had an obligation to ensure that the check was properly indorsed. The bank did not pay the check to the order of Lateef, the named payee, but accepted the check for deposit into the account of CA Houston without Lateef's indorsement. The bank did not obtain title to the instrument and could not become a holder, nor was it entitled to enforce the instrument on behalf of any other party who was entitled to enforce it. In the actual case on which this problem is based, the court held the bank liable to pay the amount of the check to W Financial.

15–8A. Case Problem with Sample Answer

Gholston can recover damages because EZ Auto willfully violated the automatic stay. EZ Auto repossessed the car even though it received notice of the automatic stay from the bankruptcy court. Moreover, EZ Auto retained the car even after it was reminded of the stay by Gholston's attorney. Thus, EZ Auto knew about the automatic stay and violated it intentionally. Because Gholston suffered direct damages as a result, she can recover from EZ Auto.

16–8A. Case Problem with Sample Answer

Ordinarily, a deficiency judgment will be for the difference between the borrower's outstanding debt and the final sales price at the foreclosure sale. Courts will not apply the sales price, however, if the property sells for far less than its fair market value. That happened here, so Beach Community Bank is entitled to the difference between First Brownsville's outstanding debt and the property's fair market value at the time of the foreclosure sale. Based on the court's foreclosure judgment and the expert testimony at the deficiency judgment hearing, First Brownsville owes $454,475.

17–7A. Case Problem with Sample Answer

Hall may be held personally liable. Hall could not be an agent for House Medic because it was a fictitious name and not a real entity. Moreover, when the contract was formed, Hall did not disclose his true principal, which was Hall Hauling, Ltd. Thus, Hall may be held personally liable as a party to the contract.

18–5A. Case Problem with Sample Answer

Yes. Dawson could establish a claim for retaliation. Title VII prohibits retaliation. In a retaliation claim, an individual asserts that he or she suffered harm as a result of making a charge, testifying, or participating in a Title VII investigation or proceeding. To prove retaliation, a plaintiff must show that the challenged action was one that would likely have dissuaded a reasonable worker from making or supporting a charge of discrimination.

In this problem, under applicable state law, it was unlawful for an employer to discriminate against an individual based on sexual orientation. Dawson was subjected to derision on the part of co-workers, including his supervisor, based on his sexual orientation. He filed a complaint with his employer's human resources department. Two days later, he was fired. The proximity in time and the other circumstances, especially the supervisor's conduct, would support a retaliation claim. Also, the discharge would likely have dissuaded Dawson, or any reasonable worker, from making a claim of discrimination. In the actual case on which this problem is based, the court held that Dawson offered enough evidence that "a reasonable trier of fact could find in favor of Dawson on his retaliation claim."

19–8A. Case Problem with Sample Answer

The district court does not have diversity jurisdiction. For diversity jurisdiction to exist, there must be complete diversity of citizenship, meaning that all of the plaintiffs must be from different states than all of the defendants.

In this case, Mid-Atlantic is not diverse from MAG. Mid-Atlantic is a New Jersey citizen because it is a New Jersey corporation. MAG is also a New Jersey citizen because LLCs and partnerships are citizens of every state of which their members are citizens. In this instance, Robert O'Shea is a New Jersey citizen. Because O'Shea is a member of Silver Point and SPCP, they are also New Jersey citizens, and so are SP MAG and MAG itself.

20–6A. Case Problem with Sample Answer

Yes. Woods has a right to inspect Biolustré's books and records. Every shareholder is entitled to examine corporate records. A shareholder can inspect the books in person or through an agent such as an attorney, accountant, or other authorized assistant.

The right of inspection is limited to the inspection and copying of corporate books and records for a proper purpose. This is because the power of inspection is fraught with potential for abuse—for example, it can involve the disclosure of trade secrets and other confidential information. Thus, a corporation is allowed to protect itself.

Here, Woods, through Hair Ventures, has the right to inspect Biolustré's books and records. She has a proper purpose for the inspection—to obtain information about Biolustré's financial situation. She, and other shareholders, had not received notice of shareholders' meetings or corporate financial reports for years, or notice of Biolustré's plan to issue additional stock. Hair Ventures had a substantial investment in the company. In the actual case

on which this problem is based, the court ordered Biolustré to produce its books and records for Hair Ventures' inspection.

21–5A. Case Problem with Sample Answer

An omission or misrepresentation of a material fact in connection with the purchase or sale of a security may violate Section 10(b) of the Securities Exchange Act of 1934 and SEC Rule 10b-5. The key question is whether the omitted or misrepresented information is material. A fact, by itself, is not automatically material. A fact will be regarded as material only if it is significant enough that it would likely affect an investor's decision as to whether to buy or sell the company's securities. For example, a company's potential liability in a product liability suit and the financial consequences to the firm are material facts that must be disclosed because they are significant enough to affect an investor's decision as to whether to buy stock in the company.

In this case, the plaintiffs' claim should not be dismissed. To prevail on their claim that the defendants made material omissions in violation of Section 10(b) and SEC Rule 10-5, the plaintiffs must prove that the omission was material. Their complaint alleged the omission of information linking Zicam and anosmia (a loss of the sense of smell) and plausibly suggested that reasonable investors would have viewed this information as material. Zicam products account for 70 percent of Matrixx's sales. Matrixx received reports of consumers who suffered anosia after using Zicam Cold Remedy.

In public statements discussing revenues and product safety, Matrixx did not disclose this information. But the information was significant enough to likely affect a consumer's decision to use the product, and this would affect revenue and ultimately the commercial viability of the product. The information was therefore significant enough to likely affect an investor's decision whether to buy or sell Matrixx's stock, and this would affect the stock price. Thus, the plaintiffs' allegations were sufficient. Contrary to the defendants' assertion, statistical sampling is not required to show materiality—reasonable investors could view reports of adverse events as material even if the reports did not provide statistically significant evidence.

22–4A. Case Problem with Sample Answer

No. DVRC's action does not represent an attempt to monopolize in violation of the Sherman Act. DVRC merely returned to a position that it had a right to have from the beginning. In their contract DVRC had expressly informed Christy that their relationship could change at any time. Thus, Christy knew from the beginning that its ski rental business could operate only with DVRC's permission, subject to DVRC's business judgment.

If DVRC had terminated a profitable relationship without any economic justification, it might have shown a willingness to forgo short-term profits to achieve an anticompetitive end. But there is no indication that DVRC terminated a profitable business relationship or that DVRC was motivated by anything other than a desire to increase profits. Rather than forgoing short-term profits, DVRC can expect to increase its short-term profits by operating its own ski rental facility. The court in the case on which this problem is based dismissed Christy's suit, a decision that the U.S. Court of Appeals for the Tenth Circuit affirmed.

23–5A. Case Problem with Sample Answer

Moreland should be awarded damages, and Gray should take nothing. The bailee must exercise reasonable care in preserving the bailed property. What constitutes reasonable care in a bailment situation normally depends on the nature and specific circumstances of the bailment. If the bailed property has been lost or is returned damaged, a court will presume that the bailee was negligent.

In the circumstances of this problem, when the bailor (Moreland, the owner of the aircraft) entrusted the plane to the bailee's (Gray's) repair shop for painting, the work was not properly performed. This violated the bailee's duty to exercise reasonable care and breached the bailment contract. Because the plane was returned damaged, this may also constitute negligence. In the event of a breach, the bailor may sue for damages. The measure of damages is the difference between the value of the bailed property in its present condition and what it would have been worth if the work had been properly performed.

Thus, Gray is liable to Moreland for failing to properly paint the plane. In the actual case on which this problem is based, the court upheld a jury award to Moreland of damages and attorneys' fees.

24–7A. Case Problem with Sample Answer

The McKeags satisfied the first three requirements for adverse possession:

1. Their possession was actual and exclusive because they used the beach and prevented others from doing so, including the Finleys.
2. Their possession was open, visible, and notorious because they made improvements to the beach and regularly kept their belongings there.
3. Their possession was continuous and peaceable for the required ten years. They possessed the property for more than four decades, and they even kept a large float there during the winter months.

Nevertheless, the McKeags' possession was *not* hostile and adverse, which is the fourth requirement. The Finleys had substantial evidence that they gave the McKeags permission to use the beach. Rather than reject the Finleys' permission as unnecessary, the McKeags sometimes said nothing and other times seemingly affirmed that the property belonged to the Finleys. Thus, because the McKeags did not satisfy all four requirements, they cannot establish adverse possession.

25–3A. Case Problem with Sample Answer

The court ruled that it had jurisdiction over Voda's foreign patent infringement claims. Cordis appealed to a federal appellate court, which concluded that the lower court did not have jurisdiction. The appellate court found that "considerations of comity" "constitute compelling reasons to decline jurisdiction" in this case.

The court explained, "Comity, in the legal sense, is neither a matter of absolute obligation, on the one hand, nor of mere courtesy and good will, upon the other. But it is the recognition which one nation allows within its territory to the legislative, executive or judicial acts of another nation, having due regard both to international duty and convenience, and to the rights of its own citizens or of other persons who are under the protection of its laws.

Courts must also bear in mind that whatever laws are carried into execution, within the limits of any government, are considered as having the same effect everywhere, so far as they do not occasion a prejudice to the rights of the other governments, or their citizens."

Here, Voda did not identify any international duty that required the U.S. judicial system to adjudicate foreign patent infringement claims, and the court found none. Voda also did not show that it would be more convenient for U.S. courts to assume jurisdiction or that foreign courts would inadequately protect his foreign patent rights. Therefore, the court saw "no reason why American courts should supplant British, Canadian, French, or German courts in interpreting and enforcing British, Canadian, European, French, or German patents. . . . Because the purpose underlying comity is not furthered and potentially hindered in this case, adjudication of Voda's foreign patent infringement claims should be left to the sovereigns that create the property rights in the first instance."

Glossary

A

Abandoned Property Property that has been discarded by the owner, who has no intention of reclaiming it.

Acceleration Clause A clause that allows a payee or other holder of a time instrument to demand payment of the entire amount due, with interest, if a certain event occurs, such as a default in the payment of an installment when due. In a mortgage loan contract, a clause that makes the entire loan balance become due if the borrower misses or is late making the monthly payments.

Acceptance The act of voluntarily agreeing, through words or conduct, to the terms of an offer, thereby creating a contract. In negotiable instruments law, a drawee's signed agreement to pay a draft when it is presented.

Acceptor A drawee that accepts, or promises to pay, an instrument when it is presented later for payment.

Accession The addition of value to personal property by the use of labor or materials. In some situations, a person may acquire ownership rights in another's property through accession.

Accord and Satisfaction A common means of settling a disputed claim, whereby a debtor offers to pay a lesser amount than the creditor purports to be owed.

Accredited Investor In the context of securities offerings, "sophisticated" investors, such as banks, insurance companies, investment companies, the issuer's executive officers and directors, and persons whose income or net worth exceeds certain limits.

Actionable Capable of serving as the basis of a lawsuit. An actionable claim can be pursued in a lawsuit or other court action.

Act of State Doctrine A doctrine providing that the judicial branch of one country will not examine the validity of public acts committed by a recognized foreign government within its own territory.

Actual Malice The deliberate intent to cause harm that exists when a person makes a statement with either knowledge of its falsity or reckless disregard of the truth. Actual malice is required to establish defamation against public figures.

Actus reus A guilty (prohibited) act. The commission of a prohibited act is one of the two essential elements required for criminal liability, the other element being the intent to commit a crime.

Adhesion Contract A standard-form contract in which the stronger party dictates the terms.

Adjudicate To render a judicial decision. Adjudication is the trial-like proceeding in which an administrative law judge hears and resolves disputes involving an administrative agency's regulations.

Adjustable-Rate Mortgage (ARM) A mortgage with a rate of interest that changes periodically, often with reference to a predetermined government interest rate (the index).

Administrative Agency A federal, state, or local government agency created by the legislature to perform a specific function, such as to make and enforce rules pertaining to the environment.

Administrative Law The body of law created by administrative agencies in order to carry out their duties and responsibilities.

Administrative Law Judge (ALJ) One who presides over an administrative agency hearing and has the power to administer oaths, take testimony, rule on questions of evidence, and make determinations of fact.

Administrative Process The procedure used by administrative agencies in administering the law.

Adverse Possession The acquisition of title to real property by occupying it openly, without the consent of the owner, for a period of time specified by a state statute. The occupation must be actual, exclusive, open, continuous, and in opposition to all others, including the owner.

Agency A relationship between two parties in which one party (the agent) agrees to represent or act for the other (the principal).

Agreement A mutual understanding or meeting of the minds between two or more individuals regarding the terms of a contract.

Alienation The voluntary transfer of land out of one's possession (thus "alienating" the land from oneself).

Alien Corporation A corporation formed in another country but doing business in the United States.

Alternative Dispute Resolution (ADR) The resolution of disputes in ways other than those involved in the traditional judicial process, such as negotiation, mediation, and arbitration.

Annual Percentage Rate (APR) The cost of credit on a yearly basis, typically expressed as an annual percentage.

Answer Procedurally, a defendant's response to the plaintiff's complaint.

Anticipatory Repudiation An assertion or action by a party indicating that he or she will not perform a contractual obligation.

Antitrust Law Laws protecting commerce from unlawful restraints and anticompetitive practices.

Appraiser An individual who specializes in determining the value of specified real or personal property.

Appropriation In tort law, the use by one person of another person's name, likeness, or other identifying characteristic without permission and for the benefit of the user.

Arbitration The settling of a dispute by submitting it to a disinterested third party (other than a court), who renders a decision.

Arbitration Clause A clause in a contract that provides that, in the event of a dispute, the parties will submit the dispute to arbitration rather than litigate the dispute in court.

Arson The intentional burning of a building.

Articles of Incorporation A document containing basic information that is filed with the appropriate state official, usually the secretary of state, when a business is incorporated.

Articles of Organization The document filed with a designated state official by which a limited liability company is formed.

Articles of Partnership A written agreement that sets forth each partner's rights and obligations with respect to the partnership.

Artisan's Lien A possessory lien on personal property of another person to ensure payment to a person who has made improvements on and added value to that property.

Assault Any word or action intended to make another person fearful of immediate physical harm—a reasonably believable threat.

Assignee A party to whom the rights under a contract are transferred, or assigned.

Assignment The transfer to another of all or part of one's rights under a contract.

Assignor A party who transfers (assigns) his or her rights under a contract to another party.

Assumption of Risk A defense to negligence. A plaintiff may not recover for injuries or damage suffered from risks he or she knows of and has voluntarily assumed.

Attachment The legal process of seizing another's property under a court order to secure satisfaction of a judgment yet to be rendered.

Attempted Monopolization An action by a firm that involves anticompetitive conduct, the intent to gain monopoly power, and a "dangerous probability" of success in achieving monopoly power.

Automatic Stay In bankruptcy proceedings, the suspension of almost all litigation and other action by creditors against the debtor or the debtor's property. The stay is effective the moment the debtor files a petition in bankruptcy.

Average Prime Offer Rate The mortgage rate offered to the best-qualified borrowers as established by a survey of lenders.

Award The monetary compensation given to a party at the end of a trial or other proceeding.

B

Bailee Under the UCC, a party who, by a bill of lading, warehouse receipt, or other document of title, acknowledges possession of goods and/or contracts to deliver them.

Bailee's Lien A possessory (artisan's) lien that a bailee entitled to compensation can place on the bailed property to ensure that he or she will be paid for the services provided.

Bailment A situation in which the personal property of one person (a bailor) is entrusted to another (a bailee), who is obligated to return the bailed property to the bailor or dispose of it as directed.

Bailor One who entrusts goods to a bailee.

Bait-and-Switch Advertising Advertising a product at an attractive price and then telling the consumer that the advertised product is not available or is of poor quality and encouraging her or him to purchase a more expensive item.

Balloon Mortgage A mortgage that allows the borrower to make small monthly payments for an initial period, such as eight years, but then requires the entire remaining balance of the mortgage loan to be paid at the end of that period.

Bankruptcy Court A federal court of limited jurisdiction that handles only bankruptcy proceedings, which are governed by federal bankruptcy law.

Battery Unexcused, harmful or offensive, physical contact with another that is intentionally performed.

Bearer A person in possession of an instrument payable to bearer or indorsed in blank.

Bearer Instrument Any instrument that is not payable to a specific person, including instruments payable to the bearer or to "cash."

Beyond a Reasonable Doubt The standard of proof used in criminal cases.

Bilateral Contract A type of contract that arises when a promise is given in exchange for a return promise.

Bill of Rights The first ten amendments to the U.S. Constitution.

Binder A written, temporary insurance policy.

Binding Authority Any source of law that a court *must* follow when deciding a case.

Blank Indorsement An indorsement that specifies no particular indorsee and can consist of a mere signature. An order instrument that is indorsed in blank becomes a bearer instrument.

Bona Fide Occupational Qualification (BFOQ) Identifiable characteristics reasonably necessary to the normal operation of a particular business. These characteristics can include gender, national origin, and religion, but not race.

Bond A security that evidences a corporate (or government) debt.

Bond Indenture The agreement between the issuer of a bond and the bondholder that sets out the terms and features of the bond issue.

Botnet A network of compromised computers connected to the Internet that can be used to generate spam, relay viruses, or cause servers to fail.

Breach of Contract Failure, without legal excuse, of a promisor to perform the obligations of a contract.

Bridge Loan A short-term loan that allows a buyer to make a down payment on a new home before selling the current home, which is used as collateral for the loan.

Brief A written summary or statement prepared by one side in a lawsuit to explain its case to the judge.

Browse-Wrap Term A term or condition of use that is presented when an online buyer downloads a product but that the buyer does not have to agree to before installing or using the product.

Burglary The unlawful entry or breaking into a building with the intent to commit a felony.

Business Ethics What constitutes right or wrong behavior and the application of moral principles in a business context.

Business Invitee A person, such as a customer or a client, who is invited onto business premises by the owner of those premises for business purposes.

Business Judgment Rule A rule that immunizes corporate directors and officers from liability for decisions that result in corporate losses or damages as long as the decision makers took reasonable steps to become informed, had a rational basis for their decisions, and did not have a conflict of interest with the corporation.

Business Necessity A defense to an allegation of employment discrimination in which the employer demonstrates that an employment practice that discriminates against members of a protected class is related to job performance.

Business Tort Wrongful interference with another's business rights and relationships.

Business Trust A form of business organization, created by a written trust agreement, that resembles a corporation. Legal ownership and management of the trust's property stay with the trustees, and the profits are distributed to the beneficiaries, who have limited liability.

Bylaws The internal rules of management adopted by a corporation at its first organizational meeting.

C

Case Law The rules of law announced in court decisions. Case law interprets statutes, regulations, constitutional provisions, and other case law.

Cashier's Check A check drawn by a bank on itself.

Categorical Imperative An ethical guideline developed by Immanuel Kant under which an action is evaluated in terms of what would happen if everybody else in the same situation, or category, acted the same way.

Causation in Fact An act or omission without which an event would not have occurred.

Cease-and-Desist Order An administrative or judicial order prohibiting a person or business firm from conducting activities that an agency or court has deemed illegal.

Certificate of Deposit (CD) A note issued by a bank in which the bank acknowledges the receipt of funds from a party and promises to repay that amount, with interest, to the party on a certain date.

Certificate of Limited Partnership The document that must be filed with a designated state official to form a limited partnership.

Certification Mark A mark used by one or more persons, other than the owner, to certify the region, materials, mode of manufacture, quality, or other characteristic of specific goods or services.

Certified Check A check that has been accepted in writing by the bank on which it is drawn. By certifying (accepting) the check, the bank promises to pay the check at the time it is presented.

Chattel All forms of personal property.

Check A draft drawn by a drawer ordering the drawee bank or financial institution to pay a certain amount of funds to the payee on demand.

Checks and Balances The principle under which the powers of the national government are divided among three separate branches—the executive, legislative, and judicial branches—each of which exercises a check on the actions of the others.

Choice-of-Language Clause A clause in a contract designating the official language by which the contract will be interpreted in the event of a disagreement over the contract's terms.

Choice-of-Law Clause A clause in a contract designating the law (such as the law of a particular state or nation) that will govern the contract.

Citation A reference to a publication in which a legal authority—such as a statute or a court decision—or other source can be found.

Civil Law The branch of law dealing with the definition and enforcement of all private or public rights, as opposed to criminal matters.

Civil Law System A system of law derived from Roman law that is based on codified laws (rather than on case precedents).

Clearinghouse A system or place where banks exchange checks and drafts drawn on each other and settle daily balances.

Click-On Agreement An agreement that arises when an online buyer clicks on "I agree" or otherwise indicates her or his assent to be bound by the terms of an offer.

Close Corporation A corporation whose shareholders are limited to a small group of persons, often family members.

Cloud Computing A Web-based service that extends a computer's software or storage capabilities by allowing users to remotely access excess storage and computing capacity as needed.

Collateral Promise A secondary promise to a primary transaction, such as a promise made by one person to pay the debts of another if the latter fails to perform. A collateral promise normally must be in writing to be enforceable.

Collecting Bank Any bank handling an item for collection, except the payor bank.

Collective Mark A mark used by members of a cooperative, association, union, or other organization to certify the region, materials, mode of manufacture, quality, or other characteristic of specific goods or services.

Comity The principle by which one nation defers to and gives effect to the laws and judicial decrees of another nation. This recognition is based primarily on respect.

Commerce Clause The provision in Article I, Section 8, of the U.S. Constitution that gives Congress the power to regulate interstate commerce.

Commercial Impracticability A doctrine that may excuse the duty to perform a contract when performance becomes much more difficult or costly due to forces that neither party could have controlled or contemplated at the time the contract was formed.

Commingle To put funds or goods together into one mass to such a degree that they no longer have separate identities, as when personal and corporate interests are mixed to the extent that the corporation has no separate identity.

Common Law The body of law developed from custom or judicial decisions in English and U.S. courts, not attributable to a legislature.

Common Stock Shares of ownership in a corporation that give the owner of the stock a proportionate interest in the corporation with regard to control, earnings, and net assets.

Common stock is lowest in priority with respect to payment of dividends and distribution of the corporation's assets on dissolution.

Community Property A form of concurrent ownership of property in which each spouse owns an undivided one-half interest in property acquired during the marriage.

Comparative Negligence A rule in tort law, used in the majority of states, that reduces the plaintiff's recovery in proportion to the plaintiff's degree of fault, rather than barring recovery completely.

Compelling Government Interest A test of constitutionality that requires the government to have convincing reasons for passing any law that restricts fundamental rights, such as free speech, or distinguishes between people based on a suspect trait.

Compensatory Damages A monetary award equivalent to the actual value of injuries or damage sustained by the aggrieved party.

Complaint The pleading made by a plaintiff alleging wrongdoing on the part of the defendant. When filed with a court, the complaint initiates a lawsuit.

Computer Crime The unlawful use of a computer or network to take or alter data, or to gain the use of computers or services without authorization.

Concentrated Industry An industry in which a single firm or a small number of firms control a large percentage of market sales.

Concurrent Conditions Conditions that must occur or be performed at the same time—they are mutually dependent. No obligations arise until these conditions are simultaneously performed.

Concurrent Jurisdiction Jurisdiction that exists when two different courts have the power to hear a case.

Concurrent Ownership Shared ownership rights.

Concurring Opinion A court opinion by one or more judges or justices who agree with the majority but want to make or emphasize a point that was not made or emphasized in the majority's opinion.

Condemnation The process of taking private property for public use through the government's power of eminent domain.

Condition A qualification, provision, or clause in a contractual agreement, the occurrence or nonoccurrence of which creates, suspends, or terminates the obligations of the contracting parties.

Condition Precedent A condition in a contract that must be met before a party's promise becomes absolute.

Condition Subsequent A condition in a contract that, if it occurs, operates to terminate a party's absolute promise to perform.

Confiscation A government's taking of a privately owned business or personal property without a proper public purpose or an award of just compensation.

Conforming Goods Goods that conform to contract specifications.

Confusion The mixing together of goods belonging to two or more owners to such an extent that the separately owned goods cannot be identified.

Consequential Damages Foreseeable damages that result from a party's breach of contract but are caused by special circumstances beyond the contract itself.

Consideration The value given in return for a promise or performance in a contractual agreement.

Consolidation The legal combination of two or more corporations in such a way that the original corporations cease to exist and a new corporation emerges with all their assets and liabilities.

Constitutional Law The body of law derived from the U.S. Constitution and the constitutions of the various states.

Constructive Delivery A symbolic delivery of property that cannot be physically delivered. Constructive delivery confers the right to possession of the property, but not the actual possession.

Constructive Discharge A termination of employment brought about by making the employee's working conditions so intolerable that the employee reasonably feels compelled to leave.

Constructive Eviction A form of eviction that occurs when a landlord fails to perform adequately any of the duties required by the lease, thereby making the tenant's further use and enjoyment of the property exceedingly difficult or impossible.

Consumer-Debtor A person whose debts result primarily from the purchases of goods for personal, family, or household use.

Contract A set of promises constituting an agreement between parties, giving each a legal duty to the other and also the right to seek a remedy for the breach of the promises or duties.

Contractual Capacity The capacity required by the law for a party who enters into a contract to be bound by that contract.

Contributory Negligence A rule in tort law, used in only a few states, that completely bars the plaintiff from recovering any damages if the damage suffered is partly the plaintiff's own fault.

Conversion Wrongfully taking or retaining possession of an individual's personal property and placing it in the service of another.

Conveyance The transfer of title to real property from one person to another by deed or other document.

"Cooling-Off" Laws Laws that allow buyers to cancel door-to-door sales contracts within a certain period of time, such as three business days.

Cooperative An association, which may or may not be incorporated, that is organized to provide an economic service to its members. Unincorporated cooperatives are often treated like partnerships for tax and other legal purposes.

Copyright The exclusive right of an author or originator of a literary or artistic production to publish, print, sell, or otherwise use that production for a statutory period of time.

Corporate Governance A set of policies specifying the rights and responsibilities of the various participants in a corporation and spelling out the rules and procedures for making corporate decisions.

Corporate Social Responsibility The idea that corporations can and should act ethically and be accountable to society for their actions.

Corporation A legal entity formed in compliance with statutory requirements that is distinct from its shareholder-owners.

Correspondent Bank A bank in which another bank has an account (and vice versa) for the purpose of facilitating fund transfers.

Cost-Benefit Analysis A decision-making technique that involves weighing the costs of a given action against the benefits of that action.

Co-Surety A person who assumes liability jointly with another surety for the payment of an obligation.

Counteradvertising New advertising that is undertaken to correct earlier false claims made about a product.

Counterclaim A claim made by a defendant in a civil lawsuit against the plaintiff. In effect, the defendant is suing the plaintiff.

Counteroffer An offeree's response to an offer in which the offeree rejects the original offer and at the same time makes a new offer.

Course of Dealing Prior conduct between the parties to a contract that establishes a common basis for their understanding.

Course of Performance The conduct that occurs under the terms of a particular agreement, which indicates what the parties to that agreement intended it to mean.

Covenant Not to Compete A contractual promise of one party to refrain from con-

ducting business similar to that of another party for a certain period of time and within a specified geographical area.

Covenant Not to Sue An agreement to substitute a contractual obligation for some other type of legal action based on a valid claim.

Cover A remedy that allows the buyer or lessee, on the seller's or lessor's breach, to obtain substitute goods from another seller or lessor.

Cram-Down Provision A provision of the Bankruptcy Code that allows a court to confirm a debtor's Chapter 11 reorganization plan even though only one class of creditors has accepted it.

Creditors' Composition Agreement An agreement formed between a debtor and his or her creditors in which the creditors agree to accept a lesser sum than that owed by the debtor in full satisfaction of the debt.

Crime A wrong against society proclaimed in a statute and, if committed, punishable by society through fines, imprisonment, or death.

Criminal Law The branch of law that defines and punishes wrongful actions committed against the public.

Cure The rights of a party who tenders nonconforming performance to correct his or her performance within the contract period.

Cyber Crime A crime that occurs in the online environment rather than in the physical world.

Cyber Fraud Any misrepresentation knowingly made over the Internet with the intention of deceiving another for the purpose of obtaining property or funds.

Cyberlaw An informal term used to refer to all laws governing electronic communications and transactions, particularly those conducted via the Internet.

Cyber Mark A trademark in cyberspace.

Cybersquatting The act of registering a domain name that is the same as, or confusingly similar to, the trademark of another and then offering to sell that domain name back to the trademark owner.

Cyber Tort A tort committed in cyberspace.

D

Damages A monetary award sought as a remedy for a breach of contract or a tortious action.

Debtor in Possession (DIP) In Chapter 11 bankruptcy proceedings, a debtor who is allowed to continue in possession of the estate in property (the business) and to continue business operations.

Deceptive Advertising Advertising that misleads consumers, either by making unjustified claims about a product's performance or by omitting a material fact concerning the product's composition or performance.

Deed A document by which title to real property is conveyed.

Deed in Lieu of Foreclosure An alternative to foreclosure in which the mortgagor voluntarily conveys the property to the lender in satisfaction of the mortgage.

Defamation Anything published or publicly spoken that causes injury to another's good name, reputation, or character.

Default To fail to pay a debt when it is due.

Default Judgment A judgment entered by a court against a defendant who has failed to appear in court to answer or defend against the plaintiff's claim.

Defendant One against whom a lawsuit is brought, or the accused person in a criminal proceeding.

Defense A reason offered and alleged by a defendant in an action or lawsuit as to why the plaintiff should not recover or establish what she or he seeks.

Delegatee A party to whom contractual obligations are transferred, or delegated.

Delegation of Duties The transfer to another of all or part of one's duties under a contract.

Delegator A party who transfers (delegates) her or his obligations under a contract to another party.

Depositary Bank The first bank to receive a check for payment.

Deposition The testimony of a party to a lawsuit or a witness taken under oath before a trial.

Destination Contract A contract for the sale of goods in which the seller is required or authorized to ship the goods by carrier and tender delivery of the goods at a particular destination. The seller assumes liability for any losses or damage to the goods until they are tendered at the destination specified in the contract.

Digital Cash Funds contained on computer software, in the form of secure programs stored on microchips and on other computer devices.

Disaffirmance The legal avoidance, or setting aside, of a contractual obligation.

Discharge The termination of an obligation, such as occurs when the parties to a contract have fully performed their contractual obligations. In bankruptcy law, the termination of a debtor's obligation to pay debts.

Disclosed Principal A principal whose identity is known to a third party at the time the agent makes a contract with the third party.

Discovery A method by which the opposing parties obtain information from each other to prepare for trial.

Dishonor To refuse to pay or accept a negotiable instrument, whichever is required, even though the instrument is presented in a timely and proper manner.

Disparagement of Property An economically injurious falsehood about another's product or property.

Disparate-Impact Discrimination Discrimination that results from certain employer practices or procedures that, although not discriminatory on their face, have a discriminatory effect.

Disparate-Treatment Discrimination A form of employment discrimination that results when an employer intentionally discriminates against employees who are members of protected classes.

Dissenting Opinion A court opinion that presents the views of one or more judges or justices who disagree with the majority's decision.

Dissociation The severance of the relationship between an individual and a business firm when the individual ceases to be associated with the carrying on of the firm's business.

Dissolution The formal disbanding of a corporation, which can take place by (1) an act of the state, (2) an agreement of the shareholders and the board of directors, (3) the expiration of a time period stated in the certificate of incorporation, or (4) a court order.

Distributed Network A network used by persons located (distributed) in different places to share computer files.

Distribution Agreement A contract between a seller and a distributor of the seller's products setting out the terms and conditions of the distributorship.

Diversity of Citizenship A basis for federal court jurisdiction over a lawsuit between citizens of different states and countries.

Divestiture A company's sale of one or more of its operating functions under court order as part of the enforcement of the antitrust laws.

Dividend A distribution of corporate profits to the corporation's shareholders in proportion to the number of shares held.

Docket The list of cases entered on a court's calendar and thus scheduled to be heard by the court.

Document of Title A paper exchanged in the regular course of business that evidences the right to possession of goods (for example, a bill of lading or a warehouse receipt).

Domain Name Part of an Internet address, such as "cengage.com." The part to the right of the period is the top level domain and indicates the type of entity that operates the site, and the part to the left of the period, called the second level domain, is chosen by the entity.

Domestic Corporation In a given state, a corporation that is organized under the law of that state.

Dominion Ownership rights in property, including the right to possess and control the property.

Double Jeopardy The Fifth Amendment requirement that prohibits a person from being tried twice for the same criminal offense.

Down Payment The part of the purchase price of real property that is paid up front, reducing the amount of the loan or mortgage.

Draft Any instrument drawn on a drawee that orders the drawee to pay a certain amount of funds, usually to a third party (the payee), on demand or at a definite future time.

Dram Shop Act A state statute that imposes liability on the owners of bars and taverns, as well as those who serve alcoholic drinks to the public, for injuries resulting from accidents caused by intoxicated persons when the sellers or servers of alcoholic drinks contributed to the intoxication.

Drawee The party that is ordered to pay a draft or check. With a check, a bank or a financial institution is always the drawee.

Drawer The party that initiates a draft (such as a check), thereby ordering the drawee to pay.

Due Process Clause The provisions in the Fifth and Fourteenth Amendments that guarantee that no person shall be deprived of life, liberty, or property without due process of law. State constitutions often include similar clauses.

Dumping The sale of goods in a foreign country at a price below the price charged for the same goods in the domestic market.

Duress Unlawful pressure brought to bear on a person, causing the person to perform an act that she or he would not otherwise perform.

Duty of Care The duty of all persons, as established by tort law, to exercise a reasonable amount of care in their dealings with others. Failure to exercise due care, which is normally determined by the reasonable person standard, constitutes the tort of negligence.

E

Easement A nonpossessory right, established by express or implied agreement, to make limited use of another's property without removing anything from the property.

E-Contract A contract that is formed electronically.

E-Evidence A type of evidence that consists of all computer-generated or electronically recorded information.

Electronic Fund Transfer (EFT) A transfer of funds through the use of an electronic terminal, a telephone, a computer, or magnetic tape.

Emancipation In regard to minors, the act of being freed from parental control.

Embezzlement The fraudulent appropriation of funds or other property by a person who was entrusted with the funds or property.

Eminent Domain The power of a government to take land from private citizens for public use on the payment of just compensation.

E-Money Prepaid funds recorded on a computer or a card (such as a smart card or a stored-value card).

Employment at Will A common law doctrine under which either party may terminate an employment relationship at any time for any reason, unless a contract specifies otherwise.

Employment Contract A contract between an employer and an employee in which the terms and conditions of employment are stated.

Employment Discrimination Treating employees or job applicants unequally on the basis of race, color, national origin, religion, gender, age, or disability.

Enabling Legislation A statute enacted by Congress that authorizes the creation of an administrative agency and specifies the name, composition, purpose, and powers of the agency being created.

Entrapment A defense in which a defendant claims that he or she was induced by a public official to commit a crime that he or she would otherwise not have committed.

Entrepreneur One who initiates and assumes the financial risk of a new business enterprise and undertakes to provide or control its management.

Entrustment Rule The rule that entrusting goods to a merchant who deals in goods of that kind gives that merchant the power to transfer those goods and all rights to them to a buyer in the ordinary course of business.

Environmental Impact Statement (EIS) A formal analysis required for any major federal action that will significantly affect the quality of the environment to determine the action's impact and explore alternatives.

Equal Dignity Rule A rule requiring that an agent's authority be in writing if the contract to be made on behalf of the principal must be in writing.

Equal Protection Clause The provision in the Fourteenth Amendment that requires state governments to treat similarly situated individuals in a similar manner.

Equitable Right of Redemption The right of a borrower who is in default on a mortgage loan to redeem or purchase the property before foreclosure.

E-Signature An electronic sound, symbol, or process attached to or logically associated with a record and adopted by a person with the intent to sign the record.

Establishment Clause The provision in the First Amendment that prohibits the government from establishing any state-sponsored religion or enacting any law that promotes religion or favors one religion over another.

Estate in Property All of the property owned by a person, including real estate and personal property.

Estopped Barred, impeded, or precluded.

Estray Statute A statute defining finders' rights in property when the true owners are unknown.

Ethical Reasoning A reasoning process in which an individual links his or her moral convictions or ethical standards to the particular situation at hand.

Ethics Moral principles and values applied to social behavior.

Eviction A landlord's act of depriving a tenant of possession of the leased premises.

Exclusionary Rule A rule that prevents evidence that is obtained illegally or without a proper search warrant—and any evidence derived from illegally obtained evidence—from being admissible in court.

Exclusive-Dealing Contract An agreement under which a seller forbids a buyer to purchase products from the seller's competitors.

Exclusive Jurisdiction Jurisdiction that exists when a case can be heard only in a particular court or type of court.

Exculpatory Clause A clause that releases a contractual party from liability in the event of monetary or physical injury, no matter who is at fault.

Executed Contract A contract that has been fully performed by both parties.

Executory Contract A contract that has not yet been fully performed.

Export The sale of goods and services by domestic firms to buyers located in other countries.

Express Contract A contract in which the terms of the agreement are stated in words, oral or written.

Express Warranty A contractual promise concerning the quality, condition, description, or performance of the goods being sold or leased.

Expropriation A government's seizure of a privately owned business or personal property for a proper public purpose and with just compensation.

Extension Clause A clause in a time instrument that allows the instrument's date of maturity to be extended into the future.

F

Federal Form of Government A system of government in which the states form a union and the sovereign power is divided between the central government and the member states.

Federal Question A question that pertains to the U.S. Constitution, an act of Congress, or a treaty and provides a basis for federal jurisdiction in a case.

Federal Reserve System A network of twelve district banks and related branches located around the country and headed by the Federal Reserve Board of Governors. Most banks in the United States have Federal Reserve accounts.

Fee Simple An absolute form of property ownership entitling the property owner to use, possess, or dispose of the property as he or she chooses during his or her lifetime. On death, the interest in the property descends to the owner's heirs.

Fee Simple Absolute An ownership interest in land in which the owner has the greatest possible aggregation of rights, privileges, and power.

Felony A crime—such as arson, murder, rape, or robbery—that carries the most severe sanctions, ranging from more than one year in a state or federal prison to the death penalty.

Fictitious Payee A payee on a negotiable instrument whom the maker or drawer did not intend to have an interest in the instrument. Indorsements by fictitious payees are treated as authorized indorsements under Article 3 of the UCC.

Fiduciary As a noun, a person having a duty created by his or her undertaking to act primarily for another's benefit in matters connected with the undertaking. As an adjective, a relationship founded on trust and confidence.

Filtering Software A computer program that is designed to block access to certain Web sites, based on their content. The software blocks the retrieval of a site whose URL or key words are on a list within the program.

Firm Offer An offer (by a merchant) that is irrevocable without the necessity of consideration for a stated period of time or, if no definite period is stated, for a reasonable time (neither period to exceed three months).

Fixed-Rate Mortgage A standard mortgage with a fixed, or unchanging, rate of interest. The loan payments remain the same for the duration of the loan, which ranges between fifteen and forty years.

Fixed-Term Tenancy A type of tenancy under which property is leased for a specified period of time, such as a month, a year, or a period of years.

Fixture An item of personal property that has become so closely associated with real property that it is legally regarded as part of that real property.

Forbearance An agreement between the lender and the borrower in which the lender agrees to temporarily cease requiring mortgage payments, to delay foreclosure, or to accept smaller payments than previously scheduled.

Forbearance The act of refraining from an action that one has a legal right to undertake.

Force Majeure Clause A provision in a contract stipulating that certain unforeseen events—such as war, political upheavals, or acts of God—will excuse a party from liability for nonperformance of contractual obligations.

Foreclosure A proceeding in which a mortgagee either takes title to or forces the sale of the mortgagor's property in satisfaction of the debt.

Foreign Corporation In a given state, a corporation that does business in that state but is not incorporated there.

Foreign Exchange Market A worldwide system in which foreign currencies are bought and sold.

Forgery The fraudulent making or altering of any writing in a way that changes the legal rights and liabilities of another.

Formal Contract An agreement that by law requires a specific form for its validity.

Forum-Selection Clause A provision in a contract designating the court, jurisdiction, or tribunal that will decide any disputes arising under the contract.

Franchise Any arrangement in which the owner of a trademark, trade name, or copyright licenses another to use that trademark, trade name, or copyright in the selling of goods or services.

Franchisee One receiving a license to use another's (the franchisor's) trademark, trade name, or copyright in the sale of goods and services.

Franchisor One licensing another (the franchisee) to use the owner's trademark, trade name, or copyright in the selling of goods or services.

Fraudulent Misrepresentation Any misrepresentation, either by misstatement or by omission of a material fact, knowingly made with the intention of deceiving another and on which a reasonable person would and does rely to his or her detriment.

Free Exercise Clause The provision in the First Amendment that prohibits the government from interfering with people's religious practices or forms of worship.

Free-Writing Prospectus A written, electronic, or graphic offer that is used during the waiting period and describes securities that are being offered for sale, or describes the issuing corporation and includes a legend indicating that the investor may obtain the prospectus at the Securities and Exchange Commission's Web site.

Frustration of Purpose A court-created doctrine under which a party to a contract will be relieved of her or his duty to perform when the objective purpose for performance no longer exists (due to reasons beyond that party's control).

Fungible Goods Goods that are alike by physical nature, agreement, or trade usage.

G

Garnishment A legal process whereby a creditor appropriates a debtor's property or wages that are in the hands of a third party.

General Partner In a limited partnership, a partner who assumes responsibility for the management of the partnership and has full liability for all partnership debts.

Gift A voluntary transfer of property made without consideration, past or present.

Gift Causa Mortis A gift made in contemplation of imminent death. The gift is revoked if the donor does not die as contemplated.

Gift Inter Vivos A gift made during lifetime and not in contemplation of imminent death, in contrast to a gift causa mortis.

Good Faith Purchaser A purchaser who buys without notice of any circumstance that would cause a person of ordinary prudence to inquire as to whether the seller has valid title to the goods being sold.

Good Samaritan Statute A state statute stipulating that persons who provide emergency services to, or rescue, someone in peril cannot be sued for negligence unless they act recklessly, thereby causing further harm.

Grand Jury A group of citizens who decide, after hearing the state's evidence, whether a reasonable basis (probable cause) exists for believing that a crime has been committed and that a trial ought to be held.

Group Boycott An agreement by two or more sellers to refuse to deal with a particular person or firm.

Guarantor A person who agrees to satisfy the debt of another (the debtor) only after the principal debtor defaults. Thus, a guarantor's liability is secondary.

H

Hacker A person who uses computers to gain unauthorized access to data.

Holder Any person in possession of an instrument drawn, issued, or indorsed to him or her, to his or her order, to bearer, or in blank.

Holder in Due Course (HDC) A holder who acquires a negotiable instrument for value, in good faith, and without notice that the instrument is defective (such as that it is overdue, has been dishonored, is subject to a defense against it or a claim to it, contains unauthorized signatures, has been altered, or is so irregular or incomplete as to call its authenticity into question).

Holding Company A company whose business activity is holding shares in another company.

Home Equity Loan A loan for which the borrower's home equity (the portion of the home's value that is paid off) is the collateral.

Homeowners' Insurance Insurance that protects a homeowner's property against damage from storms, fire, and other hazards.

Homestead Exemption A law permitting a debtor to retain the family home, either in its entirety or up to a specified dollar amount, free from the claims of unsecured creditors or trustees in bankruptcy.

Horizontal Merger A merger between two firms that are competing in the same market.

Horizontal Restraint Any agreement that restrains competition between rival firms competing in the same market.

I

I-9 Verification The process of verifying the employment eligibility and identity of a new worker. It must be completed within three days after the worker commences employment.

I-551 Alien Registration Receipt A document, known as a "green card," that shows that a foreign-born individual can legally work in the United States.

Identification In a sale of goods, the express designation of the goods provided for in the contract.

Identity Theft The illegal use of someone else's personal information to access the victim's financial resources.

Implied Contract A contract formed in whole or in part from the conduct of the parties.

Implied Warranty A warranty that arises by law because of the circumstances of a sale rather than by the seller's express promise.

Implied Warranty of Fitness for a Particular Purpose A warranty that goods sold or leased are fit for the particular purpose for which the buyer or lessee will use the goods.

Implied Warranty of Habitability An implied promise by a seller of a new house that the house is fit for human habitation. Also, the implied promise by a landlord that rented residential premises are habitable.

Implied Warranty of Merchantability A warranty that goods being sold or leased are reasonably fit for the general purpose for which they are sold or leased, are properly packaged and labeled, and are of proper quality.

Impossibility of Performance A doctrine under which a party to a contract is relieved of his or her duty to perform when performance becomes objectively impossible.

Imposter One who, by use of the mails, Internet, telephone, or personal appearance, induces a maker or drawer to issue an instrument in the name of an imperson-

ated payee. Indorsements by imposters are treated as authorized indorsements under Article 3 of the UCC.

Incidental Beneficiary A third party who benefits from a contract even though the contract was not formed for that purpose. An incidental beneficiary has no rights in the contract and cannot sue to have it enforced.

Incidental Damages All costs resulting from a breach of contract, including all reasonable expenses incurred because of the breach.

Incontestability Clause A clause in a policy for life or health insurance stating that after the policy has been in force for a specified length of time (usually two or three years), the insurer cannot contest statements made in the policyholder's application.

Independent Contractor One who works for, and receives payment from, an employer but whose working conditions and methods are not controlled by the employer. An independent contractor is not an employee but may be an agent.

Indictment A formal charge by a grand jury that there is probable cause to believe that a named person has committed a crime.

Indorsement A signature placed on an instrument for the purpose of transferring one's ownership rights in the instrument.

Informal Contract A contract that does not require a specific form or method of creation to be valid.

Information A formal accusation or complaint (without an indictment) issued in certain types of actions (usually criminal actions involving lesser crimes) by a government prosecutor.

Inside Director A person on the board of directors who is also an officer of the corporation.

Insider Trading The purchase or sale of securities on the basis of information that has not been made available to the public.

Insolvent A condition in which a person cannot pay his or her debts as they become due or ceases to pay debts in the ordinary course of business.

Installment Contract A contract that requires or authorizes delivery in two or more separate lots to be accepted and paid for separately.

Insurable Interest An interest that exists when a person benefits from the preservation of the health or life of the insured or the property to be insured. A property interest in goods being sold or leased that is sufficiently substantial to permit a party to insure against damage to the goods.

Insurance A contract in which, for a stipulated consideration, one party agrees to compensate the other for loss on a specific subject by a specified peril.

Intangible Property Property that cannot be seen or touched but exists only conceptually, such as corporate stocks. Such property is not governed by Article 2 of the UCC.

Intellectual Property Property resulting from intellectual and creative processes.

Intended Beneficiary A third party for whose benefit a contract is formed. An intended beneficiary can sue the promisor if the contract is breached.

Intentional Tort A wrongful act knowingly committed.

Interest-Only (IO) Mortgage A mortgage that allows the borrower to pay only the interest portion of the monthly payment and forgo paying any principal for a specified period of time, such as five years.

Intermediary Bank Any bank to which an item is transferred in the course of collection, except the depositary or payor bank.

International Law The law that governs relations among nations.

International Organization An organization that is composed mainly of member nations and usually established by treaty—for example, the United Nations. More broadly, the term also includes nongovernmental organizations (NGOs) such as the Red Cross.

Interpretive Rule A nonbinding rule or policy statement issued by an administrative agency that explains how it interprets and intends to apply the statutes it enforces.

Interrogatories A series of written questions for which written answers are prepared by a party to a lawsuit, usually with the assistance of the party's attorney, and then signed under oath.

Investment Company A company that acts on the behalf of many smaller shareholders-owners by buying a large portfolio of securities and professionally managing that portfolio.

Investment Contract In securities law, a transaction in which a person invests in a common enterprise reasonably expecting profits that are derived primarily from the efforts of others.

J

Joint and Several Liability In partnership law, a doctrine under which a plaintiff may sue, and collect a judgment from, all of the partners together (jointly) or one or more of the partners separately (severally, or individually).

Joint Stock Company A hybrid form of business organization that combines characteristics of a corporation and a partnership. Usually, a joint stock company is regarded as a partnership for tax and other legal purposes.

Joint Tenancy Co-ownership of property in which each party owns an undivided portion of the property. On the death of a joint tenant, his or her interest automatically passes to the surviving joint tenant(s).

Joint Venture A joint undertaking for a specific commercial enterprise by two or more persons or business entities. A joint venture is treated like a partnership for federal income tax purposes.

Judicial Foreclosure A court-supervised foreclosure proceeding in which the court determines the validity of the debt and, if the borrower is in default, issues a judgment for the lender.

Judicial Review The process by which a court decides on the constitutionality of legislative enactments and actions of the executive branch.

Jurisdiction The authority of a court to hear and decide a specific case.

Justiciable Controversy A controversy that is not hypothetical or academic but real and substantial; a requirement that must be satisfied before a court will hear a case.

L

Larceny The wrongful taking and carrying away of another person's personal property with the intent to permanently deprive the owner of the property.

Law A body of enforceable rules governing relationships among individuals and between individuals and their society.

Lease A contract by which the owner of real or personal property (the landlord or lessor) grants someone else (the tenant or lessee) an exclusive right to use and possess the property, usually for a specified period of time, in return for rent or some other form of payment.

Lease Agreement An agreement in which one person (the lessor) agrees to transfer the right to the possession and use of property to another person (the lessee) in exchange for rental payments.

Leasehold Estate An interest in real property that gives a tenant a qualified right to pos-

sess and/or use the property for a limited time under a lease.

Legislative Rule An administrative agency's rule that carries the same weight as a congressionally enacted statute.

Lessee A person who acquires the right to the possession and use of another's goods in exchange for rental payments.

Lessor A person who transfers the right to the possession and use of goods to another in exchange for rental payments.

Letter of Credit A written document in which the issuer (usually a bank) promises to honor drafts or other demands for payment by third persons in accordance with the terms of the instrument.

Libel Defamation in writing or another form having the quality of permanence (such as a digital recording).

License An agreement by the owner of intellectual property to permit another to use a trademark, copyright, patent, or trade secret for certain limited purposes. In the context of real property, a revocable right or privilege to enter onto another person's land.

Lien An encumbrance on a property to satisfy a debt or protect a claim for payment of a debt.

Life Estate An interest in land that exists only for the duration of the life of a specified individual, usually the holder of the estate.

Limited Liability Company (LLC) A hybrid form of business enterprise that offers the limited liability of a corporation and the tax advantages of a partnership.

Limited Liability Partnership (LLP) A hybrid form of business organization that is used mainly by professionals who normally do business in a partnership. An LLP is a pass-through entity for tax purposes, but a partner's personal liability for the malpractice of other partners is limited.

Limited Partner In a limited partnership, a partner who contributes capital to the partnership but has no right to participate in its management and no liability for partnership debts beyond the amount of her or his investment.

Limited Partnership (LP) A partnership consisting of one or more general partners and one or more limited partners.

Liquidated Damages An amount, stipulated in a contract, that the parties to the contract believe to be a reasonable estimation of the damages that will occur in the event of a breach.

Liquidated Debt A debt whose amount has been ascertained, fixed, agreed on, settled, or exactly determined.

Liquidation The sale of the nonexempt assets of a debtor and the distribution of the funds received to creditors.

Litigation The process of resolving a dispute through the court system.

Long Arm Statute A state statute that permits a state to exercise jurisdiction over nonresident defendants.

Lost Property Property that the owner has involuntarily parted with and then cannot find or recover.

M

Mailbox Rule A common law rule that acceptance takes effect, and thus completes formation of the contract, at the time the offeree sends or delivers the acceptance via the communication mode expressly or impliedly authorized by the offeror.

Majority Opinion A court opinion that represents the views of the majority (more than half) of the judges or justices deciding the case.

Maker One who promises to pay a fixed amount of funds to the holder of a promissory note or a certificate of deposit (CD).

Malpractice Professional misconduct or the lack of the requisite degree of skill as a professional (negligence).

Malware Malicious software programs, such as viruses and worms, that are designed to cause harm to a computer, network, or other device.

Market Concentration The degree to which a small number of firms control a large percentage of a relevant market.

Market Power The power of a firm to control the market price of its product. A monopoly has the greatest degree of market power.

Mechanic's Lien A statutory lien on the real property of another to ensure payment to a person who has performed work and furnished materials for the repair or improvement of that property.

Mediation A method of settling disputes outside the courts by using the services of a neutral third party, who acts as a communicating agent between the parties and assists them in negotiating a settlement.

Member A person who has an ownership interest in a limited liability company.

Mens rea The wrongful mental state ("guilty mind"), or intent, that is one of the key requirements to establish criminal liability for an act.

Merchant Under the UCC, a person who deals in goods of the kind involved in the sales contract or who holds herself or himself out as having skill or knowledge peculiar to the practices or goods being purchased or sold.

Merger The legal combination of two or more corporations in such a way that only one corporation (the surviving corporation) continues to exist, having acquired all of the assets and liabilities of the other corporation.

Meta Tag A key word in a document that can serve as an index reference to the document. On the Web, search engines return results based, in part, on the tags in Web documents.

Minimum Wage The lowest wage, either by government regulation or union contract, that an employer may pay an hourly worker.

Mirror Image Rule A common law rule that requires that the terms of the offeree's acceptance adhere exactly to the terms of the offeror's offer for a valid contract to be formed.

Misdemeanor A lesser crime than a felony, punishable by a fine or incarceration in jail for up to one year.

Mislaid Property Property that the owner has voluntarily parted with and then has inadvertently forgotten.

Mitigation of Damages The requirement that a plaintiff do whatever is reasonable to minimize the damages caused by the defendant.

Money Laundering Engaging in financial transactions to conceal the identity, source, or destination of illegally gained funds.

Monopolization The possession of monopoly power in the relevant market and the willful acquisition or maintenance of that power, as distinguished from growth or development as a consequence of a superior product, business acumen, or historic accident.

Monopoly A market in which there is a single seller or a very limited number of sellers.

Monopoly Power The ability of a monopoly to dictate what takes place in a given market.

Moral Minimum The minimum degree of ethical behavior expected of a businessperson, which is usually defined as compliance with the law.

Mortgage A written document that gives a creditor (the mortgagee) an interest in, or lien on, the debtor's (mortgagor's) real property as security for a debt. If the debt is not paid, the property can be sold by the creditor and the proceeds used to pay the debt.

Mortgagee Under a mortgage agreement, the creditor who takes a security interest in the debtor's property.

Mortgagor Under a mortgage agreement, the debtor who gives the creditor a security interest in the debtor's property in return for a mortgage loan.

Motion for a Directed Verdict A motion for the judge to take the decision out of the hands of the jury and to direct a verdict for the party making the motion on the ground that the other party has not produced sufficient evidence to support her or his claim.

Motion for a New Trial A motion asserting that the trial was so fundamentally flawed (because of error, newly discovered evidence, prejudice, or another reason) that a new trial is necessary to prevent a miscarriage of justice.

Motion for Judgment n.o.v. A motion requesting the court to grant judgment in favor of the party making the motion on the ground that the jury's verdict against him or her was unreasonable and erroneous.

Motion for Judgment on the Pleadings A motion by either party to a lawsuit at the close of the pleadings requesting the court to decide the issue solely on the pleadings without proceeding to trial. The motion will be granted only if no facts are in dispute.

Motion for Summary Judgment A motion requesting the court to enter a judgment without proceeding to trial. The motion can be based on evidence outside the pleadings and will be granted only if no facts are in dispute.

Motion to Dismiss A pleading in which a defendant admits the facts as alleged by the plaintiff but asserts that the plaintiff's claim to state a cause of action has no basis in law.

Mutual Fund A specific type of investment company that continually buys or sells to investors shares of ownership in a portfolio.

N

National Law Law that pertains to a particular nation (as opposed to international law).

Necessaries Necessities required for life, such as food, shelter, clothing, and medical attention.

Negative Amortization The condition when the payment made by the borrower is less than the interest due on the loan and the difference is added to the principal, thereby increasing the balance owed on the loan over time.

Negligence The failure to exercise the standard of care that a reasonable person would exercise in similar circumstances.

Negligence *Per Se* An action or failure to act in violation of a statutory requirement.

Negotiable Instrument A signed writing (record) that contains an unconditional promise or order to pay an exact sum on demand or at a specified future time to a specific person or order, or to bearer.

Negotiation A process in which parties attempt to settle their dispute informally, with or without attorneys to represent them. In the context of negotiable instruments law, the transfer of an instrument in such form that the transferee—the person to whom the instrument is transferred—becomes a holder.

Nominal Damages A small monetary award (often one dollar) granted to a plaintiff when no actual damage was suffered.

Nonpossessory Interest In the context of real property, an interest that involves the right to use land but not the right to possess it.

Normal Trade Relations (NTR) Status A legal trade status granted to member countries of the World Trade Organization.

Notary Public A public official authorized to attest to the authenticity of signatures.

Notice of Default A formal notice to a borrower who is behind in making mortgage payments that the borrower is in default and may face foreclosure. The notice is filed by the lender in the county where the property is located.

Notice of Sale A formal notice to a borrower who is in default on a mortgage that the mortgaged property will be sold in a foreclosure proceeding.

Novation The substitution, by agreement, of a new contract for an old one, with the rights under the old one being terminated.

Nuisance A common law doctrine under which persons may be held liable for using their property in a manner that unreasonably interferes with others' rights to use or enjoy their own property.

O

Objective Theory of Contracts The view that contracting parties are bound only by terms that can be objectively inferred from promises made.

Obligee One to whom an obligation is owed.

Obligor One who owes an obligation to another.

Offer A promise or commitment to perform or refrain from performing some specified act in the future.

Offeree A person to whom an offer is made.

Offeror A person who makes an offer.

Online Dispute Resolution (ODR) The resolution of disputes with the assistance of organizations that offer dispute-resolution services via the Internet.

Operating Agreement An agreement in which the members of a limited liability company set forth the details of how the business will be managed and operated.

Option Contract A contract under which the offeror cannot revoke the offer for a stipulated time period (because the offeree has given consideration for the offer to remain open).

Order for Relief A court's grant of assistance to a complainant. In bankruptcy proceedings, the order relieves the debtor of the immediate obligation to pay the debts listed in the bankruptcy petition.

Order Instrument A negotiable instrument that is payable "to the order of an identified person" or "to an identified person or order."

Ordinance A regulation enacted by a city or county legislative body that becomes part of that state's statutory law.

Output Contract An agreement in which a seller agrees to sell and a buyer agrees to buy all or up to a stated amount of what the seller produces.

Outside Director A person on the board of directors who does not hold a management position in the corporation.

Overdraft A check that is paid by the bank when the checking account on which the check is written contains insufficient funds to cover the check.

P

Parol Evidence Rule A rule of contracts under which a court will not receive into evidence oral statements that contradict a written agreement.

Partially Disclosed Principal A principal whose identity is unknown by a third party, but the third party knows that the agent is or may be acting for a principal at the time the agent and the third party form a contract.

Partnership An agreement by two or more persons to carry on, as co-owners, a business for profit.

Past Consideration An act that took place in the past and that ordinarily, by itself, cannot be consideration for a later promise to pay for the act.

Patent A property right granted by the federal government that gives an inventor an exclusive right to make, use, sell, or offer to sell an invention in the United States for a limited time.

Payee The party to whom an instrument is made payable.

Payor Bank The bank on which a check is drawn (the drawee bank).

Peer-to-Peer (P2P) Networking The sharing of resources (such as files, hard drives, and processing styles) among multiple computers.

Penalty A contract clause that specifies a certain amount to be paid in the event of a default or breach of contract but that is designed to punish the breaching party rather than to provide a reasonable estimate of damages.

***Per Curiam* Opinion** A court opinion that does not indicate which judge or justice authored the opinion.

Perfection The legal process by which secured parties protect themselves against the claims of third parties who may wish to have their debts satisfied out of the same collateral. It is usually accomplished by filing a financing statement with the appropriate government official.

Performance The fulfillment of one's duties under a contract—the normal way of discharging one's contractual obligations.

Periodic Tenancy A type of tenancy created by lease for an indefinite period with payment of rent at fixed intervals, such as week to week, month to month, or year to year.

***Per Se* Violation** A restraint of trade that is so anticompetitive that it is deemed inherently (*per se*) illegal.

Personal Defense A defense that can be used to avoid payment to an ordinary holder of a negotiable instrument but not a holder in due course (HDC) or a holder with the rights of an HDC.

Personal Property Any property that is not real property.

Persuasive Authority Any legal authority or source of law that a court may look to for guidance but need not follow when making its decision.

Petition in Bankruptcy The document that is filed with a bankruptcy court to initiate bankruptcy proceedings.

Petty Offense The least serious kind of criminal offense, such as a traffic or building-code violation.

Phishing An e-mail fraud scam in which the messages purport to be from legitimate busi-

nesses to induce individuals into revealing their personal financial data, passwords, or other information.

Piercing the Corporate Veil The action of a court to disregard the corporate entity and hold the shareholders personally liable for corporate debts and obligations.

Plaintiff One who initiates a lawsuit.

Plea Bargaining The process by which a criminal defendant and the prosecutor work out an agreement to dispose of the criminal case, subject to court approval.

Pleadings Statements by the plaintiff and the defendant that detail the facts, charges, and defenses of a case.

Plurality Opinion A court opinion that is supported by the largest number of the judges or justices hearing the case, but less than half of the total number.

Police Powers Powers possessed by the states to protect or promote the public order, health, safety, morals, and general welfare.

Policy In insurance law, the contract between the insurer and the insured.

Potentially Responsible Party (PRP) A party liable for the costs of cleaning up a waste-disposal site under the Comprehensive Environmental Response, Compensation, and Liability Act. Any person who generated the waste, transported, owned or operated the site at the time of disposal, or owns or operates the site at the present time may be responsible for some or all of the clean-up costs.

Power of Attorney Authorization for another to act as one's agent or attorney in either specified circumstances (special) or in all situations (general).

Power of Sale Foreclosure A foreclosure procedure that is not court supervised and is available only in some states.

Precedent A court decision that furnishes an example or authority for deciding subsequent cases involving identical or similar facts.

Predatory Pricing The pricing of a product below cost with the intent to drive competitors out of the market.

Predominant-Factor Test A test courts use to determine whether a contract is primarily for the sale of goods or for the sale of services.

Preemption A doctrine under which certain federal laws preempt, or take precedence over, conflicting state or local laws.

Preemptive Rights Rights that entitle shareholders to purchase newly issued shares of a corporation's stock, equal in percentage to shares already held, before the stock is offered to outside buyers. Preemptive rights enable shareholders to maintain their proportionate ownership and voice in the corporation.

Preference In bankruptcy proceedings, a property transfer or payment made by the debtor that favors one creditor over others.

Preferred Creditor In the context of bankruptcy, a creditor who has received a preferential transfer from a debtor.

Preferred Stock Stock that has priority over common stock as to payment of dividends and distribution of assets on the corporation's dissolution.

Premium In insurance law, the price paid by the insured for insurance protection for a specified period of time.

Prenuptial Agreement An agreement made before marriage that defines each partner's ownership rights in the other partner's property. Prenuptial agreements must be in writing to be enforceable.

Prepayment Penalty Clause A clause in a mortgage loan contract that requires the borrower to pay a penalty if the mortgage is repaid in full within a certain period.

Presentment The act of presenting an instrument to the party liable on the instrument in order to collect payment. Presentment also occurs when a person presents an instrument to a drawee for a required acceptance.

Presentment Warranties Implied warranties, made by any person who presents an instrument for payment or acceptance, that (1) the person is entitled to enforce the instrument or is authorized to act on behalf of a person who is so entitled, (2) the instrument has not been altered, and (3) the person has no knowledge that the drawer's signature is unauthorized.

Price Discrimination A seller's act of charging competing buyers different prices for identical products or services.

Price-Fixing Agreement An agreement among competitors to fix the prices of products or services at a certain level.

Prima Facie Case A case in which the plaintiff has produced sufficient evidence of his or her claim that the case will be decided for the plaintiff unless the defendant produces no evidence to rebut it.

Primary Source of Law A statement that establishes the law on a particular issue, such as a constitution, a statute, an administrative rule, or a court decision.

Principle of Rights The belief that human beings have certain fundamental rights. Whether a business action or decision is ethical depends on how it affects the rights of various groups, such as owners, employees, consumers, suppliers, the community, and society.

Private Equity Capital Funds invested in an existing corporation by a private equity firm, usually to purchase and reorganize the corporation.

Privilege In tort law, immunity from liability for an action that would otherwise be a tort.

Privity of Contract The relationship that exists between the promisor and the promisee of a contract.

Probable Cause Reasonable grounds for believing that a search should be conducted or that a person should be arrested.

Probate Court A state court of limited jurisdiction that conducts proceedings relating to the settlement of a deceased person's estate.

Procedural Law Law that establishes the methods of enforcing the rights established by substantive law.

Product Liability The legal liability of manufacturers, sellers, and lessors of goods for injuries or damage caused by the goods to consumers, users, or bystanders.

Profit In real property law, the right to enter onto another's property and remove something of value from that property.

Promise A declaration that binds the person who makes it (the promisor) to do or not to do a certain act.

Promisee A person to whom a promise is made.

Promisor A person who makes a promise.

Promissory Estoppel A doctrine that can be used to enforce a promise when the promisee has justifiably relied on it and when justice will be better served by enforcing the promise.

Promissory Note A written promise made by one person (the maker) to pay a fixed amount of funds to another person (the payee or a subsequent holder) on demand or on a specified date.

Property Legally protected rights and interests in anything with an ascertainable value that is subject to ownership.

Prospectus A written document required by securities laws when a security is being sold. The prospectus describes the security, the financial operations of the issuing corporation, and the risk attaching to the security so that investors will have sufficient information to evaluate the risk involved in purchasing the security.

Protected Class A group of persons protected by specific laws because of the group's defining characteristics, including race, color, religion, national origin, gender, age, and disability.

Proximate Cause Legal cause. It exists when the connection between an act and an injury is strong enough to justify imposing liability.

Proxy In corporate law, a written or electronically transmitted form in which a stockholder authorizes another party to vote the stockholder's shares in a certain manner.

Puffery A salesperson's often exaggerated claims concerning the quality of property offered for sale. Such claims involve opinions rather than facts and are not legally binding promises or warranties.

Punitive Damages Monetary damages that may be awarded to a plaintiff to punish the defendant and deter similar conduct in the future.

Purchase-Money Security Interest (PMSI) A security interest that arises when a seller or lender extends credit for part or all of the purchase price of goods purchased by a buyer.

Q

Qualified Indorsement An indorsement on a negotiable instrument in which the indorser disclaims any contract liability on the instrument. The notation "without recourse" is commonly used to create a qualified indorsement.

Quasi Contract An obligation or contract imposed by law (a court), in the absence of an agreement, to prevent the unjust enrichment of one party.

Question of Fact In a lawsuit, an issue that involves only disputed facts, and not what the law is on a given point.

Question of Law In a lawsuit, an issue involving the application or interpretation of a law.

Quitclaim Deed A deed that conveys only whatever interest the grantor had in the property and therefore offers the least amount of protection against defects of title.

Quorum The minimum number of members of a decision-making body that must be present before business may be transacted.

Quota A set limit on the amount of goods that can be imported.

R

Ratification A party's act of accepting or giving legal force to a contract or other obligation entered into by another that previously was not enforceable.

Reaffirmation Agreement An agreement between a debtor and a creditor in which the debtor voluntarily agrees to pay a debt dischargeable in bankruptcy.

Real Property Land and everything attached to it, such as trees and buildings.

Reamortize To change the way mortgage payments are configured, extending the term over which payments will be made.

Reasonable Person Standard The standard of behavior expected of a hypothetical "reasonable person." It is the standard against which negligence is measured and that must be observed to avoid liability for negligence.

Receiver In a corporate dissolution, a court-appointed person who winds up corporate affairs and liquidates corporate assets.

Record Information that is either inscribed on a tangible medium or stored in an electronic or other medium and is retrievable.

Recording Statutes Statutes that allow deeds, mortgages, and other real property transactions to be recorded so as to provide notice to future purchasers or creditors of an existing claim on the property.

Reformation A court-ordered correction of a written contract so that it reflects the true intentions of the parties.

Regulation E A set of rules issued by the Federal Reserve System's Board of Governors to protect users of electronic fund transfer systems.

Regulation Z A set of rules issued by the Federal Reserve Board of Governors to implement the provisions of the Truth-in-Lending Act.

Release An agreement in which one party gives up the right to pursue a legal claim against another party.

Remedy The relief given to an innocent party to enforce a right or compensate for the violation of a right.

Replevin An action that can be used by a buyer or lessee to recover identified goods from a third party, such as a bailee, who is wrongfully withholding them.

Reply Procedurally, a plaintiff's response to a defendant's answer.

Requirements Contract An agreement in which a buyer agrees to purchase and the seller agrees to sell all or up to a stated amount of what the buyer needs or requires.

Resale Price Maintenance Agreement An agreement between a manufacturer and a retailer in which the manufacturer specifies what the retail prices of its products must be.

Rescission A remedy whereby a contract is canceled and the parties are returned to the positions they occupied before the contract was made.

Res Ipsa Loquitur A doctrine under which negligence may be inferred simply because an event occurred, if it is the type of event that would not occur in the absence of negligence. Literally, the term means "the facts speak for themselves."

Respondeat Superior A doctrine under which a principal or an employer is held liable for the wrongful acts committed by agents or employees while acting within the course and scope of their agency or employment.

Restitution An equitable remedy under which a person is restored to his or her original position prior to loss or injury, or placed in the position he or she would have been in had the breach not occurred.

Restrictive Indorsement Any indorsement on a negotiable instrument that requires the indorsee to comply with certain instructions regarding the funds involved. A restrictive indorsement does not prohibit the further negotiation of the instrument.

Retained Earnings The portion of a corporation's profits that has not been paid out as dividends to shareholders.

Revocation The withdrawal of a contract offer by the offeror. Unless an offer is irrevocable, it can be revoked at any time prior to acceptance without liability.

Right of Contribution The right of a co-surety who pays more than her or his proportionate share on a debtor's default to recover the excess paid from other co-sureties.

Right of Reimbursement The legal right of a person to be repaid or indemnified for costs, expenses, or losses incurred or expended on behalf of another.

Right of Subrogation The right of a surety or guarantor to stand in the place of (be substituted for) the creditors, giving the surety or guarantor the same legal rights against the debtor that the creditor had.

Risk A prediction concerning potential loss based on known and unknown factors.

Risk Management In the context of insurance, the transfer of certain risks from the insured to the insurance company by contractual agreement.

Robbery The act of forcefully and unlawfully taking personal property of any value from another.

Rulemaking The process by which an administrative agency formally adopts a new regulation or amends an old one.

Rule of Four A rule of the United States Supreme Court under which the Court will not issue a writ of *certiorari* unless at least four justices approve of the decision to issue the writ.

Rule of Reason A test used to determine whether an anticompetitive agreement constitutes a reasonable restraint on trade. Courts consider such factors as the purpose of the agreement, its effect on competition, and whether less restrictive means could have been used.

S

Sale The passing of title to property from the seller to the buyer for a price.

Sales Contract A contract for the sale of goods.

Scienter Knowledge by a misrepresenting party that material facts have been falsely represented or omitted with an intent to deceive.

S Corporation A close corporation that has most corporate attributes, including limited liability, but qualifies under the Internal Revenue Code to be taxed as a partnership.

Search Warrant An order granted by a public authority, such as a judge, that authorizes law enforcement personnel to search particular premises or property.

Seasonably Within a specified time period or, if no period is specified, within a reasonable time.

Secondary Source of Law A publication that summarizes or interprets the law, such as a legal encyclopedia, a legal treatise, or an article in a law review.

SEC Rule 10b-5 A rule of the Securities and Exchange Commission that prohibits the commission of fraud in connection with the purchase or sale of any security. It is unlawful to make any untrue statement of a material fact or to omit a material fact if doing so causes the statement to be misleading.

Secured Transaction Any transaction in which the payment of a debt is guaranteed, or secured, by personal property owned by the debtor or in which the debtor has a legal interest.

Securities Generally, stocks, bonds, or other items that represent an ownership interest in a corporation or a promise of repayment of debt by a corporation.

Self-Defense The legally recognized privilege to do what is reasonably necessary to protect oneself, one's property, or someone else against injury by another.

Self-Incrimination Giving testimony in a trial or other legal proceeding that could expose the person testifying to criminal prosecution.

Seniority System A system in which those who have worked longest for an employer are first in line for promotions, salary increases, and other benefits, and are last to be laid off if the workforce must be reduced.

Service Mark A trademark that is used to distinguish the services (rather than the products) of one person or company from those of another.

Sexual Harassment The demanding of sexual favors in return for job promotions or other benefits, or language or conduct that is so sexually offensive that it creates a hostile working environment.

Share Exchange A transaction in which some or all of the shares of one corporation are exchanged for some or all of the shares of another corporation, but both corporations continue to exist.

Shareholder's Derivative Suit A suit brought by a shareholder to enforce a corporate cause of action against a third person.

Shelter Principle The principle that the holder of a negotiable instrument who cannot qualify as a holder in due course (HDC), but who derives his or her title through an HDC, acquires the rights of an HDC.

Shipment Contract A contract for the sale of goods in which the seller is required or authorized to ship the goods by carrier. The seller assumes liability for any losses or damage to the goods until they are delivered to the carrier.

Short Sale A sale of real property for an amount that is less than the balance owed on the mortgage loan. The lender must consent to the sale and receives the proceeds, and the borrower still owes the balance of the mortgage debt to the lender unless the lender agrees to forgive it.

Short-Swing Profits Profits earned by a purchase and sale, or sale and purchase, of the same security within a six-month period. Under Section 16(b) of the 1934 Securities Exchange Act, the profits must be returned to the corporation if earned by company insiders from transactions in the company's stock.

Shrink-Wrap Agreement An agreement whose terms are expressed in a document located inside a box in which goods (usually software) are packaged.

Slander Defamation in oral form.

Slander of Quality (Trade Libel) The publication of false information about another's product, alleging that it is not what its seller claims.

Slander of Title The publication of a statement that denies or casts doubt on another's legal ownership of any property, causing financial loss to that property's owner.

Small Claims Court A special court in which parties can litigate small claims without an attorney.

Smart Card A card containing a microprocessor that permits storage of funds via security programming, can communicate with other computers, and does not require online authorization for fund transfers.

Sole Proprietorship The simplest form of business organization, in which the owner is the business. The owner reports business income on his or her personal income tax return and is legally responsible for all debts and obligations incurred by the business.

Sovereign Immunity A doctrine that immunizes foreign nations from the jurisdiction of U.S. courts when certain conditions are satisfied.

Special Indorsement An indorsement on an instrument that identifies the specific person to whom the indorser intends to make the instrument payable. Thus, it names the indorsee.

Special Warranty Deed A deed that warrants only that the grantor held good title during his or her ownership of the property and does not warrant that there were no defects of title when the property was held by previous owners.

Specific Performance An equitable remedy in which a court orders the parties to perform as promised in the contract. This remedy normally is granted only when the legal remedy (monetary damages) is inadequate.

Stale Check A check, other than a certified check, that is presented for payment more than six months after its date.

Standing to Sue The legal requirement that an individual must have a sufficient stake in a controversy before he or she can bring a lawsuit.

Stare Decisis A common law doctrine under which judges are obligated to follow the precedents established in prior decisions.

Statute of Frauds A state statute that requires certain types of contracts to be in writing to be enforceable.

Statutory Law The body of law enacted by legislative bodies (as opposed to constitutional law, administrative law, or case law).

Statutory Right of Redemption A right provided by statute in some states under which mortgagors can buy back their property after a judicial foreclosure for a limited period of time, such as one year.

Stock An ownership (equity) interest in a corporation, measured in units of shares.

Stock Buyback The purchase of shares of a company's own stock by that company on the open market.

Stock Certificate A certificate issued by a corporation evidencing the ownership of a specified number of shares in the corporation.

Stock Option A right to buy a given number of shares of stock at a set price, usually within a specified time period.

Stop-Payment Order An order by a bank customer to his or her bank not to pay or certify a certain check.

Stored-Value Card A card bearing a magnetic strip that holds magnetically encoded data, providing access to stored funds.

Strict Liability Liability regardless of fault, which is imposed on those engaged in abnormally dangerous activities, on persons who keep dangerous animals, and on manufacturers or sellers that introduce into commerce defective and unreasonably dangerous goods.

Sublease A tenant's transfer of all or part of the leased premises to a third person for a period shorter than the lease term.

Subprime Mortgage A high-risk loan made to a borrower who does not qualify for a standard mortgage because of a poor credit rating or high debt-to-income ratio. Lenders typically charge a higher interest rate on subprime mortgages.

Substantive Law Law that defines, describes, regulates, and creates legal rights and obligations.

Summary Jury Trial (SJT) A method of settling disputes by holding a trial in which the jury's verdict is not binding but instead guides the parties toward reaching an agreement during the mandatory negotiations that immediately follow.

Summons A document informing a defendant that a legal action has been commenced against her or him and that the defendant must appear in court on a certain date to answer the plaintiff's complaint.

Supremacy Clause The requirement in Article VI of the U.S. Constitution that provides that the Constitution, laws, and treaties of the United States are "the supreme Law of the Land."

Surety A third party who agrees to be primarily responsible for the debt of another.

Suretyship An express contract in which a third party (the surety) promises to be primarily responsible for a debtor's obligation to a creditor.

Symbolic Speech Nonverbal expressions of beliefs. Symbolic speech, which includes gestures, movements, and articles of clothing, is given substantial protection by the courts.

Syndicate A group of individuals or firms that join together to finance a project. A syndicate is also called an *investment group*.

T

Takeover The acquisition of control over a corporation through the purchase of a substantial number of the voting shares of the corporation.

Taking The taking of private property by the government for public use through the power of eminent domain.

Tangible Employment Action A significant change in employment status or benefits, such as occurs when an employee is fired, refused a promotion, or reassigned to a lesser position.

Tangible Property Property that has physical existence and can be distinguished by the senses of touch and sight.

Target Corporation The corporation to be acquired in a corporate takeover.

Tariff A tax on imported goods.

Tenancy at Sufferance A type of tenancy under which a tenant continues wrongfully to occupy leased property after the lease has terminated.

Tenancy at Will A type of tenancy that either the landlord or the tenant can terminate without notice.

Tenancy in Common Co-ownership of property in which each party owns an undivided interest that passes to her or his heirs at death.

Tender An unconditional offer to perform an obligation by a person who is ready, willing, and able to do so.

Tender of Delivery A seller's or lessor's act of placing conforming goods at the disposal of the buyer or lessee and providing whatever notification is reasonably necessary to enable the buyer or lessee to take delivery.

Tender Offer An offer made by one company directly to the shareholders of another (target) company to purchase their shares of stock.

Third Party Beneficiary One for whose benefit a promise is made in a contract but who is not a party to the contract.

Tippee A person who receives inside information.

Tort A wrongful act (other than a breach of contract) that results in harm or injury to another and leads to civil liability.

Tortfeasor One who commits a tort.

Toxic Tort A civil wrong arising from exposure to a toxic substance, such as asbestos, radiation, or hazardous waste.

Trade Dress The image and overall appearance ("look and feel") of a product that is protected by trademark law.

Trademark A distinctive word, symbol, or design that identifies the manufacturer as the source of particular goods and distinguishes its products from those made or sold by others.

Trade Name A name that a business uses to identify itself and its brand. A trade name is directly related to a business's reputation and goodwill and is protected under trademark law.

Trade Secret A formula, device, idea, process, or other information used in a business that gives the owner a competitive advantage in the marketplace.

Transfer Warranties Five implied warranties made by any person who transfers an instrument for consideration to the transferee and, if the transfer is by indorsement, to all subsequent transferees and holders who take the instrument in good faith.

Traveler's Check A check that is payable on demand, drawn on or payable through a financial institution, and designated as a traveler's check.

Treasury Securities Government debt issued by the U.S. Department of the Treasury. The interest rate on Treasury securities is often used as a baseline for measuring the rate on loan products with higher interest rates.

Treaty A formal international agreement negotiated between two nations or among several nations. In the United States, all treaties must be approved by the Senate.

Treble Damages Damages that, by statute, are three times the amount of actual damages suffered.

Trespass to Land Entry onto, above, or below the surface of land owned by another without the owner's permission or legal authorization.

Trespass to Personal Property Wrongfully taking or harming the personal property of another or otherwise interfering with the lawful owner's possession of personal property.

Trust Indorsement An indorsement to a person who is to hold or use funds for the benefit of the indorser or a third person. It is also known as an *agency indorsement*.

Tying Arrangement A seller's act of conditioning the sale of a product or service on the buyer's agreement to purchase another product or service from the seller.

U

Unconscionable Unscrupulous or grossly unfair.

Underwriter In insurance law, the insurer, or the one assuming a risk in return for the payment of a premium.

Undisclosed Principal A principal whose identity is unknown by a third party, and that person has no knowledge that the agent is acting for a principal at the time the agent and the third party form a contract.

Unenforceable Contract A valid contract rendered unenforceable by some statute or law.

Uniform Law A model law developed by the National Conference of Commissioners on Uniform State Laws for the states to consider enacting into statute.

Unilateral Contract A contract that results when an offer can be accepted only by the offeree's performance.

Universal Defenses Defenses that are valid against all holders of a negotiable instrument, including holders in due course (HDCs) and holders with the rights of HDCs.

Unreasonably Dangerous Product A product that is so defective that it is dangerous beyond the expectation of an ordinary consumer or a product for which a less dangerous alternative was feasible but the manufacturer failed to produce it.

Usage of Trade Any practice or method of dealing that is so regularly observed in a place, vocation, or trade that parties justifiably expect it will be observed in their transaction.

U.S. Trustee A government official who performs certain administrative tasks that a bankruptcy judge would otherwise have to perform.

Usury Charging an illegal rate of interest.

Utilitarianism An approach to ethical reasoning in which an action is evaluated in terms of its consequences for those whom it will affect. A "good" action is one that results in the greatest good for the greatest number of people.

V

Valid Contract A contract that results when the elements necessary for contract formation (agreement, consideration, legal purpose, and contractual capacity) are present.

Venture Capital Financing provided by professional, outside investors (venture capitalists) to new business ventures.

Venue The geographic district in which a legal action is tried and from which the jury is selected.

Vertically Integrated Firm A firm that carries out two or more functional phases (manufacturing, distribution, and retailing, for example) of the chain of production.

Vertical Merger The acquisition by a company at one stage of production of a company at a higher or lower stage of production (such as a company merging with one of its suppliers or retailers).

Vertical Restraint A restraint of trade created by an agreement between firms at different levels in the manufacturing and distribution process.

Vesting The creation of an absolute or unconditional right or power.

Vicarious Liability Indirect liability imposed on a supervisory party (such as an employer) for the actions of a subordinate (such as an employee) because of the relationship between the two parties.

Virus A software program that can replicate itself over a network and spread from one device to another, altering files and interfering with normal operations.

Voidable Contract A contract that may be legally avoided at the option of one or both of the parties.

Void Contract A contract having no legal force or binding effect.

Voir Dire An important part of the jury selection process in which the attorneys question prospective jurors about their backgrounds, attitudes, and biases to ascertain whether they can be impartial jurors.

W

Warranty Deed A deed that provides the greatest amount of protection for the grantee, in that the grantor promises that she or he has title to the property conveyed in the deed, that there are no undisclosed encumbrances on the property, and that the grantee will enjoy quiet possession of the property.

Wetlands Water-saturated, protected areas of land that support wildlife.

Whistleblowing An employee's disclosure to government authorities, upper-level managers, or the media that the employer is engaged in unsafe or illegal activities.

White-Collar Crime Nonviolent crime committed by individuals or corporations to obtain a personal or business advantage.

Workers' Compensation Laws State statutes that establish an administrative process for compensating workers for injuries that arise in the course of their employment, regardless of fault.

Workout An out-of-court agreement between a debtor and creditors that establishes a payment plan for discharging the debtor's debts.

Workout Agreement A formal contract between a debtor and his or her creditors in which the parties agree to negotiate a payment plan for the amount due on the loan instead of proceeding to foreclosure.

Worm A software program that automatically replicates itself over a network but does not alter files and is usually invisible to the user until it has consumed system resources.

Writ of Attachment A writ used to enforce obedience to an order or judgment of the court.

Writ of Certiorari A writ from a higher court asking a lower court for the record of a case.

Writ of Execution A writ that puts in force a court's decree or judgment.

Wrongful Discharge An employer's termination of an employee's employment in violation of the law or an employment contract.

Table of Cases

For your convenience and reference, here is a list of all the cases mentioned in this text, including those within the footnotes, features, and case problems. The summarized cases in the chapters of this text are given special emphasis by having their titles appear in **boldface.**

Index

D

Q

Questions of law/fact, 76
Quitclaim deeds, 694
Quotas, 720

R

Racketeering Influenced and Corrupt Organizations Act (RICO), 171
Ratification, 229, 494, 501
"Rational basis" test, 24
"Rationality" test, 23
Reaffirmation agreement, 451, 456–457
Real estate, 469
  financing law for, 474–475, 692
  sales contracts for, 692–693
Real property, 660, 687–700
  of debtors, 444
  deeds to, 694–695
  eminent domain and, 696–697
  fixtures as, 689
  homestead exemption and, 444, 560
  landlord-tenant law and, 697–700
  ownership of, 689–697
  state inheritance laws and, 695
  transfer of, 692–697
  wills and, 695
Reamortization, 479
Reasonable accommodation, 541–542
Reasonable person standard, 115–116
  objective theory of contracts and, 195, 202, 203
  and performance to satisfaction, 264–265
Recession, 44, 469, 609
Record (defined), 215
Redemption, 480, 482–483
Regulation A, 613–615, 614
Regulation CC, 421, 425
Regulation D, 614, 615–616
Regulation E, 426–427
Regulation Z, 368
Regulations, international, 719–722
Regulatory agencies. *See* Administrative law/agencies
Reimbursement, 443
Release (contract), 219
Relevant market, 646–647, 651, 652
Reliance (in securities law), 618
Religion
  discrimination based on, 534–535
  ethics and, 52
  freedom of, 20–22

global companies and, 56
  Islamic, 10, 75, 76, 507
Remedies
  in contract law, 340–341
    of buyer/lessee, 334–335
    contract provisions limiting, 277–279
    equitable, 274–277
    exclusive, 339
    limitation of, 339–341
    of seller/lessor, 331–333
  at law *vs.* in equity, 7–8
  prejudgment, 439
  in securities law, 617, 623
  under Title VII, 539
  in tort law, 100
Rent, 699
Repayment, 445, 460–463
Replevin, 335
Reply, 80
Republic of Korea–United States Free Trade Agreement (KORUS FTA), 722
Res ipsa loquitur, 121
Resale price maintenance agreement, 644
Rescission (of contract), 7, 218, 274, 625
Resource Conservation and Recovery Act (RCRA), 706–707
Respondeat superior, 504, 505, 506, 507
  corporations and, 576
  franchises and, 566
Restatement (Third) of Agency, 489, 505
Restatement (Second) of Contracts, 247
Restatement of Torts, 150
Restatement (Second) of Torts, 354
Restatement (Third) of Torts, 355, 356
Restraint of trade, 233–235, 643
  horizontal, 640, 641–643
  Sherman Act and, 638, 639
  vertical, 640, 643–644
Reverse discrimination, 534
Revised Model Business Corporation Act (RMBCA), 573
Right(s)
  of contribution, 443
  principle of, 53
  to privacy (*See* Privacy rights)
  of publicity, 109 (*See also* Appropriation)
  of redemption, 480, 482–483
  of surety and guarantor, 443
  to trial by jury, 82
Right to Financial Privacy Act, 27
Rights theory, 53
Risk
  assumption of, 119, 120, 360